THE
THEATRE
HANDBOOK

and Digest of Plays

Edited by

BERNARD SOBEL

Preface by George Freedley

CROWN PUBLISHERS

NEW YORK   1940

PN2035
S67

PRINTED IN THE UNITED STATES OF AMERICA
BY J. J. LITTLE AND IVES COMPANY, NEW YORK

FOR

JEAN TENNYSON

BEAUTIFUL, WISE
AND EXACTING.

ACKNOWLEDGMENTS

The editor offers his thanks for help in the preparation of this volume:

First to George Freedley who has given his scholarship and continuous cooperation.

To Kenyon Nicholson, who went over the first script.

To Silas Seadler, who sat in on the original plan.

To Barrett H. Clark, whose experience and advice were of immeasurable value.

To John Mason Brown, the first to discuss the contents.

To John Adams Reeves for his tireless industry and patience.

To S. Frank Plasmati and Younghill Kang for the sections on the Oriental theatre.

To W. C. Zellars for the entries on the Spanish theatre.

To Albert J. McCusker, E. Lawrence Goodman, John Sellman, Leighton Brill, James E. Phillips, Jr., John Hastings, to the staffs of the Theatre Collection and the Fifty-Eighth Street Branch of the New York Public Library, and to all the many others who have assisted.

CONTENTS

All articles are to be found in alphabetical order.
The attention of the reader is directed to
the following major articles.

PREFACE

This book is intended for the serious student of the theatre, and at the same time it is the intention of editor and publisher that no lover of the theatre escape. Theatre is several parts glamor, drama is several parts literature and the make up of the handbook must establish a nice balance between the two. A book filled with the fascinating apocrypha of the theatre would undoubtedly be attractive, at the same time that the more austere book of facts might be considered an unlikely candidate for the best seller list. It is our hope that we have combined the two to make this volume a book to keep on your desk against that emergency question we all know will come. At the same time Bernard Sobel and I trust that it is a volume that those lovers of the theatre in our country can *read,* quietly with pleasure and profit.

Despite the alphabetical arrangement of the text, a table of contents has been provided to indicate the most important articles for the seeker after information; many of the theatre experts of the country have assembled their knowledge in readable form for those who may have temporary need of it.

We have included a few topics that are unusual and are proud to point out that no more extensive grouping of plays by subject exists. We make haste to assure you that the list is incomplete, experimental, taken from a working list in an existing library and is not intended to be in any way exhaustive. If the list becomes useful, ways and means of extending it and amplifying the classifications will be found.

A special effort has been made to cover the Oriental Theatre because no easily accessible book deals briefly, yet authoritatively, with the subject. Certain volumes have been included in the bibliography and the compiler wishes to acknowledge his indebtedness for that section to the gracious and able Rosamond Gilder, who showed the way in *A Theatre Library.*

The cinema has been for the most part ignored (despite the fact that the film is a part of theatre in its broadest sense) because it is felt that many directories of motion pictures exist. Radio is not included except for the drama which has been ably covered by Mr. Arch Oboler, and a play is always part of the theatre. Television terms *have* been included because many people feel that television will be an important factor in the future; in fact there are those who say it will be *the* Theatre of the future. We are not so lugubrious as that. We believe that so long as there are people in the world who can enjoy the emotional and intellectual contact with the voice of their poets and dramatists through the medium of fine actors in a building set aside for that purpose, that no mechanical medium can take the place of the stage.

GEORGE FREEDLEY

CURTAIN! CURTAIN!

Welcome to the Theatre Handbook, brightly expectant guest. You have arrived in good time. The show will start soon. The orchestra is already tuning up in the pit. The ushers are shouting "Curtain."

As you walk to your seat in the first row, center, First Nighters greet you on all sides. Beautiful ladies flash jewels and decolletage. Orchids intensify ermine white. The air crackles with opening-night excitement. Everyone, self-conscious yet curious, is busy seeing and being seen. Then suddenly in the midst of sibilant conversation, laughter and commotion, the curtain rises and the show is on.

The chorus surges forth in rainbow colors. The dancers make a trek across the boards, pass woodland back-drop and verdant wings, only to give way eventually for the laughing entrance of the comedian. He— the gay favorite—is all agog, with his large white goggles, toy baby cart and meandering geese. But he spots you speedily across the footlights and throws you a friendly smile of recognition so that all the audience feels that you're important.

And this impression is confirmed when, just before the final curtain, an usher hurries down the aisle and hands you a note. Eagerly, you open it to discover that the prima donna invites you to visit her in her dressing room. The usher points out the way; and you follow him, behind the parquet box seats to a concealed door which leads to the forbidden land —backstage.

To the right is the star's dressing-room and there you take in, at a glance, autographed pictures on the walls, pictures of Jane Cowl, Chester Morris, Cedric Hardwicke, Guthrie McClintic, Rosalind Russell. Congratulatory telegrams line the tall mirror. Cut flowers, perfumes and cosmetics decorate the dressing table.

The prima donna is now wearing a wondrous, flimsy negligée. She is in repose now and happy. As she talks with you, she removes her entire stage make-up; then paints and powders all over again, for the street. Meanwhile, the maid brings you a highball, and the author steps in long enough to tell you how he happened to write the big scene. Five minutes later the newspapermen and photographers arrive for interviews. Friends crowd the room and corridor. It is time now to go. Reluctantly you leave by the stage door, pass the crowd of autograph hunters waiting in the rain, grab a taxicab, stop a moment at "21" and just as morning breaks, reach home.

Then, if you're like me, you'll drop off blissfully to sleep, dreaming of footlights, grease paint and the free masonry of backstage life. For the theatre to me has always been a land of enchantment. The more I see of it, the more I want to see. In my effort to learn the mystery of writing plays, producing, acting and direction, I talk to stars, ushers, doormen, managers, hangers-on and chorus girls. The stage is a great leveller. Everyone and everything has a contributory force from the director who governs the performance to the black cat which slinks across the stage and revives a superstition.

Above all, the audience exerts a reciprocal influence. It helps create the illusion, builds up or destroys. The dandies who sat on the Elizabethan stage sometimes spoiled a performance. The fanatics who caused the Astor Place riot of 1840, would have murdered the star had he not managed to escape, with the help of his friends. Soviet audiences, in contrast, were orderly participants in the action of post-war propaganda plays. Today, however, according to rumor, the jitterbugs who form the early morning audiences at New York stage shows, insure their disorganized part in the performance by dancing in the aisles. These examples are exceptional, but they are indicative of audience potentialities.

But the human element is only one of innumerable factors which go into the making of a play. Abstract theories have their direct effect, theories about architecture, history, stage history, criticism, mechanics, histrionics, dramaturgy, lighting, direction, temperament, production, advertising and costs.

Furthermore, from the first moment that the play is announced until the final first-night curtain, Chance becomes the co-producer. No matter who the star or the author, no matter how perfect the production, no prediction can be certain. The unexpected always happens. An unknown player makes a hit. A veteran goes up in his lines. A piece of scenery falls. The conductor forgets his cue. A new dancer stops the show. A critic gets the wrong seas. Heat stifles the audience.

And it must have been like this from the first days of the theatre. The weather must have played the dickens with outdoor performances of Euripides. Drunken carpenters' apperntices must have ruined many a morality show. The mistress of an "angel" or a king has regularly given the drama a serious setback. Examples pyramid.

When Victor Herbert, after a quarrel with Emma Trentini, refused to write the score for *Naughty Marietta,* Arthur Hammerstein, producer, started search for another composer, and after listening to dozens of compositions, found him in a book of piano lessons for beginners, Rudolf Friml, then the obscure accompanist for Kubelik.

When Will Rogers came before the curtain to make his début in the second act of a musical at the George M. Cohan Theatre, he confronted an empty house, because the audience had discovered during the intermission, by way of the electric sign on the Times building, that the *Titanic* had been sunk. More recently, Sidney Kingsley's highly realistic play, *Dead End,* almost died at the premiere because the villain broke the illusion by jumping up from his death scene just a second before the curtain fell.

The play, nevertheless, must go on, and has gone on thus, through the ages, a combination of genius, physical endowment and circumstance.

And this Handbook, I hope, opens a vicarious experience in the theatre, whereby the stage may exert its continuous influence. All matters great and small I have striven to touch upon, because they are one and inseparable; the historicity of Seneca; the mystery of Shakespeare's genius: was he great because he willed it, or because he couldn't help being so? The right make-up technique for an ingenue. The popularity of the pratt fall. The efficacy of the baby spotlight. The structure of the Center Theatre. The disappearance of the stage door Johnny.

One time-old thought, above all things, I hope, to reaffirm: the theatre is the meeting place of the human heart, the heart which beats through the ages, through suspense, pain, joy and understanding, through progress and disintegration, through World War and threatening war. It is Humanity's escape from bitter experience. It is the land of appeased realization through recognition, and the perpetual domain of wish fulfillment. Here, surely, the arts unite for the enjoyment of the soul.

BERNARD SOBEL

THE THEATRE HANDBOOK

AND DIGEST OF PLAYS

Abarbanell, Lina (1880-   ). German musical comedy star. Born in Berlin. She played many engagements abroad, and made her American debut in 1905 at the Irving Place Theatre. Her best known roles were those of Gretel in Humperdinck's opera, *Hansel and Gretel,* Yvonne in *Madame Sherry,* Sonia in *The Merry Widow.* Today she is a member of the directorial staff of Dwight Deere Wiman, the producer.

Abe Lincoln in Illinois. Robert E. Sherwood (American). Drama. 2 acts. 1938.

Twelve episodes in Lincoln's life, from the time he studied Blackstone in a New Salem log cabin, to his farewell speech at Springfield when he entrained for Washington as President of the United States. He is seen as an Illinois postmaster, agreeing to run for the State Senate, at a time when his prowess as a wrestler was winning him the admiration of the townsfolk. His romance with Ann Rutledge and his disheartenment at her death are followed by Mary Todd's pursuit and capture of him, after Lincoln has once run out on their wedding. His famous anti-slavery debate with Douglas is dramatically represented.

Throughout, the play gains eloquence and authenticity by using Lincoln's own words whenever feasible. Moving, and filled with a high patriotism, it was awarded the Pulitzer Prize in 1939.

Abbey Theatre. A famous organization founded in Dublin in 1904 by Miss E. F. Horniman of the Irish National Theatre Society, called by Fay and Carswell in their book *The Fays of the Abbey Theatre* "first and foremost a theatrical, not a literary movement." It was the discoverer of Synge, performing his *Riders to the Sea, The Playboy of the Western World* and others. Plays were chosen to suit the theatre so that an individual mode of its own was established. Famous dramatists associated with the theatre were W. B. Yeats, AE, Lady Gregory, Lennox Robinson, Sean O'Casey and Paul Vincent Carroll. Among the famous actors who have appeared here are Dudley Digges, Sara Allgood, Maire O'Neill and Arthur Sinclair. Players of this theatre have had several American tours, in the seasons 1911-12, 1932-33, 1934-35, 1937-38.

Abbott, George (1887-   ). American playwright. A modern Molière, George Abbott is perhaps equally well known as actor, director, playwright and play doctor. Swift-paced farce is his forte, and to the enlightened theatre-goer "a George Abbott production," meaning a rapid-fire, craftily staged comedy in which each laugh is made to count, is self-descriptive.

He was born in Forestville, New York, and received his A.B. from the University of Rochester. After that he studied under Harvard's famous Professor Baker. His first Broadway appearance as an actor was at the Fulton Theatre in 1913 in *A Misleading Lady*. Other plays in which he has had roles have been *Dulcy, Hell-Bent fer Heaven* and *Processional*. His productions include *Chicago,* 1926; *Twentieth Century,* 1932; *Boy Meets Girl,* 1935; *Room Service,* 1936; and *See My Lawyer,* 1939. Among the plays which he has written, wholly or in part, are *The Fall Guy* (with James Gleason), 1925; *Broadway* (with Philip Dunning), 1926; *Love 'em and Leave 'em* (with John V. A. Weaver), 1926; *Coquette* (with Ann Bridgers), 1927; *Ladies' Money,* 1934; and *Three Men on a Horse* (with John Cecil Holm), 1935.

Abie's Irish Rose. Anne Nichols (American). Comedy. 3 acts. 1922.
Abie marries an Irish girl, Rosemary Murphy, and starts a family feud. The bride and groom are married three times, first by a Methodist minister, then by a Rabbi, and finally by a Catholic priest.

The two families are appeased, however, when Rosemary has twins, Rebecca and Patrick Joseph. The play ends on a Christmas Eve celebration with Abraham Levy and Patrick Murphy admiring their grandchildren.

This play is notable largely for its long run (2,327 performances).

Abington, Frances Barton (1737-1815). English actress. Flower-seller, street singer and reciter in taverns, and servant to a French milliner in London. She made her stage debut at the Haymarket as Miranda in Mrs. Centlivre's comedy, *The Busybody,* 1755, and in 1759 married her music master Abington. After five years in Dublin, she was invited by David Garrick to Drury Lane, where she remained for eighteen years, playing the great ladies of comedy, Shakespearean heroines, romps and even chambermaids, and creating the part of Lady Teazle in the original production of *The School for Scandal,* 1777. Acclaimed the greatest comedy actress of her time, she went to Covent Garden in 1782. She made her last stage appearance as Lady Racket in *Three Weeks after Marriage,* April 12, 1799.

Abraham and Isaac. See *Mystery of Abraham and Isaac.*

Abraham Lincoln. John Drinkwater (English). Poetic chronicle play. 6 scenes. 1919.
The play covers Lincoln's life during the War years. In successive scenes he accepts the presidential nomination in Springfield; ten months later, orders the relief of Fort Sumter; two years afterward, heart-sick at the prolonged war, still sees no way of stopping it without being disloyal to the cause of Justice; at the

close of the struggle, reads the Emancipation Proclamation and tenders his resignation; witnesses Lee's surrender to Grant at Appomattox and warns the one against reprisals as he pleads with the other to be merciful; is assassinated by Booth in Ford's Theatre in Washington.

Lord Charnwood's biography of Lincoln is Drinkwater's chief source book. Lincoln's British chronicler makes no attempt to stress his hero's Americanism which he is little qualified to judge, but emphasizes the universal quality of his humanity.

Abuelo, El (The Grandfather). Benito Perez Galdos (Spanish). Drama. 3 acts. 1904.

A drama in which a ruined nobleman, who adores his two granddaughters, at last finds perfect love in the offspring of the infidelity of a daughter-in-law, instead of in the affection of the legitimate grandchild.

Academy, The French (L'Académie française). Established by order of the king in 1635. Its object was the "purification of the French language." The number of members was fixed at forty. On the death of a member, his successor was to be elected by the members themselves.

It ceased during the Revolution, then was re-established and now consists of 5 classes of which the language and literature class is foremost. It is non-political and non-profit making. It awards prizes and though influential, the extent of its influence is debatable. Many of the foremost men of letters were never elected—Alphonse Daudet, the de Goncourts, etc. The members are known as "The Immortals."

Academy of Actors. German organization founded by Konrad Ekhof in 1753 within the Schoeneman acting company; the members of the academy discussed parts, read plays, talked and debated about dramatic art. Helped to raise the standard of German acting and the status of German actors.

Accent on Youth. Samson Raphaelson (American). Comedy. 3 acts. 1935.

Stephen Gaye, a middle-aged playwright, and his young secretary, Linda Brown, work together harmoniously. Gaye has written a play "Old Love" which concerns itself with an older man who leaves his wife for a girl and does not return. The actors who are to play it rebel but Linda stands up for Stephen's idea. Stephen decides to go abroad. This brings out his realization of Linda's love. Dickie Wells, young actor, is also in love with her. Stephen throws them together but Linda's love survives and she returns to work for and to marry Stephen.

Acharnians, The. Aristophanes (Greek). Comedy. 425 B.C.

A satire on war and peace, characterized by alternate passages of rapier-like wit and Rabelaisian gusto. The author produced it in the name of Callistratus at the age of nineteen.

The protagonist, Dicaeopholis, a good-natured countryman, has been driven from his home and forced to take shelter in the city by the Peloponnesian invasion. His wish for a speedy peace is thwarted by the Assembly, who refuse the offer of a demi-god from Heaven to serve as mediator. Instead waste time listening to the ridiculous tales of two envoys sent to Persia. In disgust Dicaeopholis sends his own envoy to conclude a separate peace for himself and his family. The messenger returns from Sparta with samples of truces, which consist of the wines in which the ratification of each is drunk. The countryman samples them all and then hastens back to his native village to observe the feast of Bacchus.

Acorn-Planter, The. Jack London (American). A play with music in prologue, epilogue and 2 acts. 1916.

A dramatization in idealistic terms of a plea for better understanding between Indians and White Men. Not a drama of importance but it shows the novelist's relation to the theatre.

Acoubar; ou La Loyaute trahie. By Jacques du Hamel, who died about 1611. Republished with introduction by Margaret Adams White, New York, 1931.

The earliest French play about America. It deals with the Aboriginal Indians of North America.

Acoustics. The proper handling of the Sound and Hearing elements is one of the prime essentials in the performed drama. Clear and proper enunciation by the performers is, of course, vital. This need for clarity applies to all other sound production. But the sound must reach the audience and all the audience correctly. In order to achieve this, the nature and behavior of sound must be understood.

Sound travels rapidly in spherical waves. When it reaches a surface, it is absorbed or reflected in greater or less degree, in accordance with the nature of the surface. When a sound is made it will travel in all directions and be reflected from every surface in every direction so that it will be completely spread throughout the room. But since so much depends upon the reflection from the walls, floors, curtains, ceilings, etc., unevennesses and faults in the transmission of sound are bound to occur.

The chief faults are inaudibility, super-audibility (loudness, outside sounds, noises), distortion, echoes, reverberation. Stated positively, in an auditorium the performance must be heard by all (but not too loudly), accurately as to intonation and pitch and without the interference of other sounds echoes or reverberations. To achieve this the following points must be borne in mind.

Audibility. Audience should have uninterrupted view of performers. Therefore, stage should be raised and rows of seats should slope gradually upward from the stage.

Low ceilings and closer walls will increase sound. Curtains, drapes, and carpets will reduce sound by absorbing it. Thus, undesired sounds may be kept out by curtains. But, on the other hand, a fabric drape instead of a solid surface will deaden sound instead of reflecting it and thus reduce the desired audibility.

A solid surface behind the stage will project sound forward, and sound may be directed by the inclination of reflectors (solid surfaces). In any problem of audibility the chief surfaces that are reflecting the sound must be considered and changed, eliminated or enhanced as may be necessary.

Echoes and Distortion, Vibration, Reverberation. These faults are chiefly due to sound that is reflected instead of absorbed. In the case of alcoves, boxes, high ceilings, etc., the sound waves may bound back and forth, thus producing echoes or reverberation. This condition may be eliminated by reducing the area of the enclosure by lowering the ceiling, by false walls, glass or fabric curtains, etc., or by placing absorbent surfaces on the too solid surfaces. Such absorbent surfaces should be porous. There are various fibrous boards, asbestos jute and felt tiles available.

Finally, whatever the acoustic fault or need, knowledge of the nature of reflection of sound and of the sound-reflecting materials will provide the key to the solution.

Materials will absorb or reflect sound in accordance with their porosity. The more porous, the more absorbent.

Act. A natural division of a play, consisting of one or more scenes. It was effected originally by the chorus in Greek dramas, and then came to be a definite division with a unity and climax of its own. Among the Greeks, five acts was the standard length, and this standard continued through the Elizabethan and Restoration periods. Gradually, with the elaboration of stage settings, the impatience of audiences with overlong productions, and the growth of the feeling for simplified form and continuity, there was a reduction. Now the 3-act form is rather definitely established.

The first act is devoted to laying the groundwork, preparing the situation and arousing interest. The second act is the meat of the play wherein the conflict is definitely fought. The third act is the resolution, the result of the drama. Of course, plays may vary from this form.

ACTING

BY RAYMOND MASSEY

I look on the actor as an interpreter, not as a creator. In the modern theatre, which has outgrown the old idea of the vehicle play, the creative force is supplied by the author.

This is not to minimize the actor. He is an all-important factor in the theatre, for after all people want to *see* plays, not read them. But it may help to explain why there is no basis, in my opinion, on which to compare actors and acting. Every job— every part—is a new problem. The minute one generalizes, one finds every rule promptly refuted. In the theatre everything, from playwriting to set-design, has to be tackled free of convention or precedent.

As to whether an actor "feels the part" or merely simulates feeling, it seems to me that every actor has his own method. I can speak only of mine. In the period of gestation of a performance, the actor must immerse himself, not in the "feelings" of the character he is portraying, but in an understanding of the character. In this process he does actually lose some of his emotional identity—but only temporarily. It must be clear that in the course of *the run of a play,* it is quite impossible for any actor so to lose his identity; if he allows his emotion to dominate the performance, he will lose all unity, all power of reproducing the character. And it must be remembered that performances are given under any and all circumstances.

Personally, I have not "felt the part" before an audience in twenty years. Acting, to me, is always a case of "outside looking in." Without that detachment it is impossible for me to maintain the control necessary to keep the performance at proper pitch.

Naturally an actor, like anyone else, is much moved by a play. He reads it, reacts to it, works into it—gets fond of it—feels that he understands it. But once that reaction to a piece of writing has "jelled" and become part of his experience, it is the actor's job to get that understanding over to an audience according to the author's intention. It is quite possible for an actor to be impressed and moved, or depressed and disturbed, by his own performance. But unless he detaches himself from these personal feelings, he can never acquire the discipline which gives tempo, rhythm and balance to the production as a whole.

In the case of a long part—as that of Lincoln in "Abe Lincoln in Illinois"—it is necessary for an actor, as the run progresses, to obtain an almost mechanical grasp of the character, precisely in order not to seem mechanical from out front. By a "mechanical grasp" I mean having the character so thoroughly in hand that it can be played with the actor's mind at rest, detached, and therefore able to avoid "mechanical acting." The part of Lincoln being very long, I have found it necessary to let it run in its stride, for stretches; then, every few performances, to take it apart and put it together again—in order to avoid stagnation.

This method is particularly applicable to emotional or romantic parts. In comedy, it is more a question of timing and so-called technique. The actor must be even more flexible, because audiences and their reactions to comedy are more variable. But in all acting, the actor's one aim must be to convey the illusion of complete spontaneity—except in certain poetic or declamatory parts where a certain studied quality may be of value.

Again and again I am asked the question: how much research should an actor do in preparing his part? While getting ready for Robert Sherwood's "Abe Lincoln in Illinois," which I have played on both stage and screen, I deliberately avoided more than a cursory research. The deep study of Lincoln which Mr. Sherwood had made supplied me with a wealth of relevant material which an author of his genius and theatrical knowledge considered sufficient—and *not more than sufficient*—for developing the character. Over-embellishment—a satiety of detail—might have seriously jeopardized in performance a figure which the author had conceived in superb economy and sincerity. I think an actor should always assume that the author has purposely cut off the ragged edges of a character.

Of the person of Lincoln in "Abe Lincoln in Illinois," the movement, control of hands, body and expression are mine, not the author's. And my face is my own except for a little nose putty. As to the voice—here is an example of the dangers of research:

In the months preceding and during rehearsals of "Abe Lincoln in Illinois," I talked to several people who had known Mr. Lincoln, and I read in the Herndon letters and other sources about Mr. Lincoln's mannerisms and physical characteristics not covered by the author's specific stage directions. I found that his voice was shrill, raucous, high-pitched. I also found that his voice was deep and resonant. I found that he spoke with a slow drawl—and also with a staccato nervousness. That he moved with the panther grace of an Indian—and also with quick steps. All of which information I eventually threw aside in favor of a physical delineation which I considered most theatrically effective to project Mr. Sherwood's Lincoln across the footlights.

To sum up, it seems to me essential in the theatre—where projection and enlargement are the core of acting, and where everything must be slightly larger than life to survive the trip across the footlights—that technical control and detachment govern the performance completely. At least, that is the only way I have found to accomplish anything. I am convinced that abandonment of this control to the vagaries of the artist's own emotions may blur and distort the author's intention which, after all, is what we are trying to deliver, clear-cut, to the audience.

I should like to be able to close with an analysis of "types of acting," giving examples from the work of many fine people of the stage; but I cannot do it. After twenty-one years of experience in the theatre I do not believe there is such a thing as a type of acting. I am still unable to analyze someone else's performance. I do not know what problems presented themselves during preparation or how they were overcome. I still believe that every actor is an individual who does not belong to a "school" or subscribe to a "system" or conform to a "type."

Good actors, like good plays, are made of flesh and blood, not bundles of tricks.

Acting area. The space on stage on which the action of the play takes place.

Acting, Chinese. Acting is symbolical and highly conventional in the Chinese theatre. A tasseled wand serves as a riding whip; when held in the left hand it represents the actor dismounting from a horse or mule; if the whip is in the right hand, he is mounting, and a walk around the stage is a journey. The distance between characters is recognized by their actions; and doors, windows and walls exist only because the actors designate their presence—and the audience sees them vividly! The actor is scenery, singer, dancer, acrobat and mime as well as Thespian in the Western sense. Every gesture of the head, hand or foot has some special meaning and each actor must guard against forgetting to lift his foot when stepping over the imaginary threshold of a door or face the displeasure of his discriminating audience. A fan held up along the side of the face represents the player as walking bareheaded in the sun; the fan may be exchanged for an umbrella to signify a rainstorm; walking with arms extended and feeling to the right and left represents the actor to be walking in the dark; pieces of white paper shaken out of red umbrella indicate a snowstorm. A player standing stiffly up against a pillar shows he is hiding. Bringing the hands together at arms length closes an invisible door. A boat is represented by an old man with a pole and a girl with an oar standing or walking at a fixed distance from each other, the girl sculling in the stern. Passing one long sleeve in front of tearless eyes indicates that the character is weeping.

Painting the face in establishing a type is common. Each player paints his own face in his own characteristic and grotesque manner. Through these false faces, which are a survival of the ancient masks, the actors escape themselves and become imaginary individuals. During the time of the Three Kingdoms (A.D. 221-280), Lan Lin-wang, famous actor, is said to have introduced the custom of wearing face masks in Military plays. Later the masks were worn as well by actors representing various deities. The Chinese stage masks resemble very closely the ceremonial masks and painted faces of totem-pole figures found among the Indians of Alaska and British Columbia.

In painting the face, several colors are often used in a single makeup. The colors have a meaning: red for sacred, courageous, loyal or virtuous; black to denote the fierce, the coarse or the uncouth; and blue to denote cruelty. Purple indicates loyalty to a lesser degree than red. Devils have green faces; gods and goddesses have gold or yellow faces. A white face represents a treacherous, cunning, but dignified person. Women characters appear without painted faces except for simple cosmetics.

An actor with black splashes on his face is an enemy officer; a dab of color at the corner of the eyes means a sick person or a villain. A ghost or dead person is represented by an actor wearing a black hood, or a slip of white paper stuck on the cheek, or a streamer of white paper suspended from the head and falling down over the breast.

When a person is killed, there are fireworks. Fireworks are also used whenever a demon appears. A death is also indicated by a red cloth thrown over the face. A dead man—recently slain—gravely gets up and walks away, often doing so with a characteristic stoop which serves to indicate that he is being carried off by four men.

A barbarian wears a piece of fur around his neck; a beggar wears a silk coat with a design of large gaudy-colored patches. An emperor wears a yellow robe embroidered with coiled dragons. High officials have yellow robes with flying dragons looking downward.

The art of juggling and tumbling in the Chinese military plays is carried to such superlative virtuosity that it would bring blushes to the cheeks of the most talented Western vaudeville acrobats. Another interesting feature of the Chinese theatre is the property man who moves about the stage deliciously indifferent to whatever is taking place among the actors and the audience. The property man slips stools under actors, arranges pillows under a swooning official, and hands out the riding whips and swords.

A play is not limited by time and space. In one play there are 830,000 soldiers on stage, and they are all represented by only thirty men. The Chinese believe that drama is nothing but pretence, so why have characters on stage act realistically? Nature is not imitated but observed and contemplated. The Chinese esthetic is essentially that the elements and some of the combinations found in nature are legitimate raw material for the artist, but the way in which the artist reorganizes them may depart from natural patterns in any degree that his purpose may dictate. The result is a higher standard of finish than anything thus far seen in the Western theatre.

Most actors are members of traveling troupes who set up outdoor theatres of bamboo platforms and poles or even plain bamboo mats. A number of troupes stage their performances on canal boats like the American steamboat performers of Show Boat fame. Still another type of actor, the most despised of the profession, is the wandering story-teller who recites, sings and acts out history and adventure on the streets of every village and city. There is one great story-teller in China today named Liu Pao-chuan, aged seventy-one, who performs before vast audiences in the greatest theatres. His diction is taken as standard for Mandarin dialect; he has a remarkable singing voice, and tickets for his performances are priced as high as ten dollars. The *Geisha* or Sing-song Girl is also of the theatre; for despite her low social position the *Geisha* is successful in her profession insofar as she has charm, beauty, a talent for music and dancing, and some knowledge of the classics.

An elaborate system of precedence is current among the actors based upon the importance of the parts they play. The system refers to the choice of seats in the make-up or *greenroom,* sleeping quarters and the group or society in which the actors are allowed to move. Actors who impersonate emperors are the favored ones. Impersonating a living emperor or member of the royal family has always been prohibited by law, but in most cases, Chinese custom looked the other way and the actor kept playing the emperor, notwithstanding.

An actor's standing in society may be very low, but sometimes he is able to surmount this obstacle and gain the respect and admiration of vast audiences and his fame may become considerable if he is fortunate enough to belong to one of the permanent theatres in a large city. Mei Lan-fang is an example. He is regarded as the greatest living actor and has won his coveted position because of his outstanding impersonations of women and for his remarkable proficiency in the dance, song, diction and pantomime of the traditional drama. Other great actors are: Cheng Yen-chiü, Shang Hsiao-yün, Ma Lien-liang. Mei Lan-fang's every gesture and pose is beautiful. His company only recently completed a very successful tour of the United States.

See also *Drama, Chinese; Staging, Chinese.*

Acting families. Among famous acting families are the Barrymores, Booths, Boucicaults, Cohans, Coopers, Davenports, Drews, Foys, Irvings, Kembles, Rooneys, Trees and Wallacks. For a more complete list see *Who's Who in the Theatre,* edited by John Parker.

Acting, Japanese. In *Nō* Dramas the actors use masks, not make-up. These are of great variety and classified as follows: (1) old man; (2) old woman; (3) middle-aged man; (4) middle-aged woman; (5) young man; (6) young woman; (7) child; (8) blind man; (9) gentle god; (10) powerful god; (11) formidable god; (12) fairy; (13) supernatural being; (14) monster; (15) wild animal.

In *Nō* dramas, after the entrance of the musicians and chorus the Second Actor or Deuteragonist (*Waki*) usually enters first . . . but sometimes the First Actor or Protagonist (*Shite*) enters first; both are accompanied by one or more companions (*Tsure*) or the clown (*Kyōgen*).

After the musicians have made their entrance, the Chorus enters through the

Hurry-door and sits on the verandah. The men in the front row, after having repeated the opening song of the actor who comes first, sit quiet till the chorus singing begins when those in the back row join them. In the middle of the back row sits the chorus leader (*Ji-gashira*). The chorus intones either alone or with performers.

The entrance of the actors is accompanied by music. The Second Actor enters and his music is called *Shidai*. To this he recites his opening song. He never wears a mask for he represents the audience; declares his name and reason for his appearance, called the Declaration or *Nanori*. When he is supposed to be travelling he recites the Travelling song (*Mich-yuki*) and reaches his destination at the end of the song.

The entrance of the First Actor is represented by the Traditional music called *Issei,* which indicates the subject of the play in the middle of which he enters on the Bridge behind the First Pine Tree, and recites his opening song accompanied by a musical instrument. The *Shite* tells his story as he performs, or he merely dances without any intonation.

In *Nō* dramas the Actor indicates the end of his performance by tapping the floor with his foot; sometimes he disappears into the curtain still dancing and the Second Actor then draws near the First Actor's Pillar and taps the floor with his foot. The First Actor exits first followed by the Second Actor and the companions; the chorus exits through the Hurry-door, musicians exit last through the Bridge in the same order of their entrance.

Elocution is distinct but artificial; the voice never strikes a natural note but is pitched very high or low to avoid the continual background music of the samisen; the traditional stage-gait was copied from puppets by which many 17th century plays were performed; the Japanese actor however has dignity of pose and great facial control, never fidgets but goes from one studied pose to another with artistic and effective design.

During some dances the outer gown is slipped off and a handsomer one revealed underneath. The movements appear graceful in these flowing garments and the actor makes good use of the long sleeves, which sometimes hang nearly to the floor; but without this drapery the dancing would appear stiff and unnatural.

In the *Kabuki* plays, the climax of a piece of acting is accentuated by an impressive pose in which the actor becomes statue-like with his eyes wide open; *Mie* is the name for this pose which heightens esthetic appeal. A *Mie* is emphasized by the striking of wooden clappers against a thick board by an assistant stage manager; this clapping is called *tuke* and serves to call attention to the posing of the actor.

The musicians consist ordinarily of a player each on the transverse flute, the *tsuzumi* (small drum struck with the fingertips over the shoulder), the *okawa* (a slightly larger drum struck on the knee also with the fingertips), and the drum beaten with two sticks.

A fan is much in evidence in the dance, the studied use of which is very effective with the manipulation of big sleeves. The costumes used are marvels of textile fabric and design, refined taste is evident in the bold patterns and colors. Above all, the mask to be worn by the principal character (*Shite*) and the assistant (*Shite-tsure*) is a very important part of the *Nō* performance. There have been great masters among the carvers of *Nō* masks whose works still remain in a large number. *Nō* masks were carved out of wood and were, with portrait sculpture, the only kinds of sculpture which made any progress in the Muromachi period (1334-1573). The masks are still preserved by the head of each school as family treasures. Wigs worn by male actors to impersonate females are called *Katsura.*

The most gorgeous textile fabrics worn by the *Nō* actors, were produced mostly in Yedo and *Kyōtō.* There were four different kinds: *Kara-ori,* a kind of rich brocade; *Atsu-ita,* a kind of silk fabric; *Nuy-haku,* a fabric having a design in embroidery as well as in gold leaf; and *Suri-haku,* a fabric with a pattern of gold leaf only. The taste for richly costumed drama had been introduced by the great military statesman and patron of all the arts, Toyotomi Hideyoshi in the *Momoyama* period (1574-1614).

Hideyoshi's taste for the gorgeous and flowery was also carried on in the *Yedo* period. The particularly interesting feature of the *Nō* costume is the variety of warm hues, such as gold, red, and yellow, which appear in the slow dance rhythm, punctuated by symbolic gestures of the *Nō* actors.

Since *Nō* plays do not aim at realism but at a special world of beauty, the costumes are adapted to promote this conception.

Women do not appear on the stage. Their parts are taken by men trained for that purpose. Action in *Nō* dramas is symbolical; a tap on the knee with one hand indicates excitement; a few steps forward indicates the end of a journey.

The property-men are dressed in black and busy themselves with handing out props and bearing away those discarded by the actors. But they are perfect little artists in their own right—and the audience doesn't notice them.

The characters in a *Nō* play are always few in number and usually include a ghost or two who often relate a story of love that never reached its earthly close.

In the puppet theatre (*Ayatsuri*), the puppets are finely carved and richly clothed dolls three or more feet in height. They are not controlled from above by wires as are the marionettes familiar to Westerners, but are carried on stage each by four puppeteers, one of whom holds the puppet while the others manipulate the head, arms and feet. The play is read and enacted on the side by a reader who uses several voices in the performance. The puppeteers are never noticed by the audience; they are clad from head to toe in black, and even their hands are camouflaged in black gloves.

See also *Drama, Japanese; Kabuki drama; Nō drama; Staging, Japanese.*

Action. (1) The physical course of plot in a play; (2) the physical motions of actors on stage or screen; (3) a single specific movement.

Actor. The actor originated when the Greek religious dances evolved into the Greek drama. At first all the people took part in these dramatic dances but later the most capable were chosen to play the outstanding roles—to be chosen one of the best *actors* was a great distinction and acting became therefore a distinguished and highly respected profession.

But in Roman times actors were in disrepute and disgrace. In fact, most were slaves. Kings and churches have employed them and cast them out. They have been alternately honored and condemned.

During the Elizabethan period, strolling players were little higher in the social scale than public beggars. The English Statute Law on Vagabonds and Players stated "all persons calling themselves Schollers going abroad begging . . .; all Fencers, Bearwards, common players of Interludes and Minstrels wandering abroad (other than players of Interludes belonging to any Baron of this realm, or any honourable personage of greater degree to be auctorised to play under the hand and seale of Arms. . . .); all Juglers, Tinkers, Pedlars, and Petty Chapmen wandering abroad . . . shall be taken, adjudged, and deemed Rogues, Vagabonds, and Sturdy Beggars, and shall sustain such payne and punishment. . . ." (See *Obiter Dicta,* New York, Charles Scribner's Sons, 1886.) In Molière's time actors were said to rank with "sword-swallowers, peddlers and rat-catchers."

"That situation," says Brooks Atkinson in *Enter the Actor* (The *New York Times,* Sept. 10, 1939), "no longer prevails. The prestige of Henry Irving changed the conception of the actor. . . . It would be misleading to imply that the theatre is even yet as respectable as the library. . . . All we can say is that actors now are culturally acceptable, although, like artists in general, they are still somewhat suspect by middle class moralists. . . ."

John Anderson, in the *New York Journal-American* says: "The Truth is that every time the theatre strays away from the Drama Page, it hurts itself. . . . Every time the glamour girls and boys begin calling names, shouting into the radio, and mussing their hair and mascara, the amusement industry takes a setback. It takes a dozen or so nicely retouched studio portraits to make up for one snarling off-guard picture in a news photo. It doesn't do a boxoffice beauty much good to get caught on a picture page with the fangs showing. One look and the public can't be coaxed into a dreamy mood again by a dozen press agents. It isn't that the public lacks sympathy, but the amusement business is based on illusion."

Actor, protean. Variety actor of the Nineties who made quick changes from one costume and make-up to another almost before the eyes of the audience, changing the song or monologue with each change. This was a development of the protean drama of the early 19th century. Albert Chevalier is one of the foremost players of this type.

Actors' Equity Association. An affiliate of the American Federation of Labor; theatrical union, founded December 22nd, 1912. By-laws and constitution were adopted May 26th, 1913. Original members of the committee were Albert Bruning, Charles D. Coburn, Frank Gillmore, William Harcourt, Milton Sills and Grant Stewart.

It is the bargaining agency of the theatre. Almost without exception no one may appear in a professional production of a play, without membership in this organization.

English equivalent: British Actors' Equity Association, patterned after the American organization.

Actors, medieval. In England, the guilds dominated the drama and the actors were guild members. In France, there were *confréries pieuses,* troupes expressly organized for the performances of mystery plays; also the *confreries des fous,* deriving from the notorious Feast of Fools, who played interlude and scandalous farce, making fun of the absent to the present. These "fools," belonging really to the mime tradition, had tremendous effect on later drama and theatre, their influence being manifest in much of Shakespeare. In England the performers were all men; in France there were some women.

Actors, types. (1) Amateurs—performers for love, not for financial gain or prestige; (2) professional—those who perform as a vocation, to make a living and also, if possible, a reputation; (3) boy actors—originally the performers of all women's parts in the Elizabethan era when there were no women on the stage; today they act their age with other child actors; (4) child actors—in many cities children under a certain age are forbidden on the stage; in New York City the ruling is liberal (see also *children as actors*); (5) women—first began to come on the stage in the 16th century on the Continent, the 17th in England. See also *character actors, extra, heavy, juvenile, lead, star, super, walkon.*

Actress. There were no female performers in the earliest dramas. The profession of actress really did not exist until the 16th century on the continent, the 17th century in England.

Among the earliest actresses identifiable by name are: the 10th century German nun, Hrotsvitha; Isabella Andreini who played with the Italian company, the *Gelosi;* the two 17th century French actresses in Molière's plays, Madeleine and Armande Béjart; the English Mrs. Charles Coleman, Margaret Hughes, Mary Saunderson (Mrs. Thomas Betterton), Nell Gwynn and the two Marshall sisters, Anne and Rebecca; the German pioneer actress-manager, Carolina Neuber; and La Montansier, 18th century French actress. In Rosamond Gilder's *Enter the Actress,* 1931, these actresses and others are considered in detail.

THE STAGE AS A CAREER

BY TALLULAH BANKHEAD

Almost every day that passes I receive letters from people asking me for advice about going on the stage. To reply helpfully is difficult, for everyone at the outset has a different problem—matters which he must solve for himself. But aside from this, I would say that one of the first things one must have for a stage career is confidence in oneself. I don't mean conceit; the greatest people are the most modest. But you must believe in yourself, or you have no business trying for a stage career. Self-confidence should be a kind of obsession.

Next in importance is the matter of health. You've got to have a great deal of reserve. After all, you're in someone else's investment, and for this alone you should keep yourself well. People say to me, "Tallulah, you must take care of yourself." But I am not built in the same way as most people. It is abnormal for me to lead a normal life. I sleep like a child. I go to bed late, so I feel I am entitled to go out when my work is done. After all, a business man doesn't go to sleep the moment he gets home from work. He goes out for several hours afterwards, plays bridge, attends club meetings, sees a show. And it's that way with me. I go out after my work is done, about 11:30 or 12:00, and get home quite late. But then, again, I don't have to get up early. I can sleep until three or four the next day. My working hours aren't really demanding; it's the attendant fuss, rather, that makes them long: going to the photographers, hairdresser, fittings, interviews, keeping appointments of all kinds—accumulation of all these things.

The next thing that most people must consider in taking up a stage career is the financial question, the obligations they have, the people who are dependent on them.

Once resolved to go on the stage, my advice is usually to go out and find a professional job for yourself and act. I don't mean in a dramatic school but in a real honest-to-goodness professional job where you actually do something, whether it is a "bit" part, work in the chorus or understudy. The important thing is that it's a job. And when you have to prove you are worth what you are doing, you are on the road to accomplishment.

Don't think because you have personal beauty that your success is certain. I think beauty without personality is just as dull and dead as it can be. I have seen people with homely features who had more individuality and attraction than others supposedly beautiful. Take Nazimova and Elizabeth Bergner—you can't call them beautiful. On the other hand, you can be beautiful, and your beauty will not project on the stage; whereas, you can have the proper bone structure which will make you look beautiful. After all, the most important thing in any acting career is originality; then personality,—originality first. Talent—I'm taking for granted. People may call it mannerism, but it's these mannerisms peculiar to the person having them which makes him stand out to the public. You may not even know that you have these mannerisms. You never even know what your voice sounds like until you hear it on a "playback," and even then you don't get it altogether, because it is mechanical.

I used to have a habit of throwing back my head because my hair was shingled and so very thick and heavy. When I had to bend over, I immediately shook back my head without realizing I was doing it. To do it occasionally was all right, but to do it often was not so good, so I had to guard against the habit.

When I was in England, certain critics remarked about my slouch walk, the way I held my shoulders, the toss of my head. But even though I antagonized them, they gave me good advice. "Hold up your shoulders," one of them told me, "and breathe deeply."

Mannerisms mean something, though. I remember what Ethel Barrymore told me. She was playing in Boston many years ago in a play whose name I don't remember. Sir Henry Irving was playing in "Richard III" at the time, and after her own performance was over, Ethel would go to Sir Henry's theatre and stand in the wings and watch the last scene. There she would stand alone and remain for a few minutes after the curtain was down. One day, Sir Henry saw Ethel standing there, looking very sad, so he went over to her and asked her what was the matter. "I am depressed," she answered. "No matter what role I do, people say I am still Ethel Barrymore." "Well," said Sir Henry, "see that they say nothing else." And without knowing of this circumstance, I had the same experience in London, while playing in "The

Dancers," with Gerald DuMaurier. I complained similarly and Gerald made the same response.

The trouble with some actors I believe, is that they read lines without any reality. You don't get the impression that they say these lines for the first time but that they are reading them out of a book. Personally, I believe you must be natural even when playing the classics. I don't mean that you should neglect the rhythm and the beauty and certain technical points that are peculiar to them; but when you read the lines you should give the impression of believing what you say. Again, when you play in a modern piece, you must be yourself. What else can you pattern yourself on? Even though you play a character part, you are still Tallulah Bankhead. You can be old, or put on glasses, or do anything else. But you can't disassociate yourself from your personality. When people say, "Do you feel your part?", I think they are so stupid that I could slap them.

If you get lost in a play, you won't remember what city you are in. I remember a story about one of those stock companies that changes its play two or three times a week. In the midst of a performance, the leading woman cried, "My God! What's the line?" Whereupon the other actor cried, "What's the play?"

Direction is all important. A very fine actor can get bad direction. I think direction is the most valuable thing in the theatre, apart from good play or type casting. The more talent you have, the more discipline you need.

An actor is the servant of the public. He has certain duties and responsibilities to fill, including good manners, particularly on and off the stage. Never offend an audience. Good manners are inexpensive. You must put yourself out a lot for other people. I don't mean, of course, that you should be a damn fool and let people take advantage of you. Autograph hunters, for instance, I loathe; the professional ones who don't even go to the theatre but just hold up the performance so that you can oblige them. I do say, however, that it is a discourtesy not to sign a programme or card when someone has seen your play and has waited patiently outside for your signature. That is a real compliment.

Adam. Author unknown. (Norman-French, probably written in England.) Miracle play. 5 acts. 12th century.

This is probably the first dramatic work in medieval French. A miracle or mystery play, it deals with Adam and Eve, Cain and Abel, the fall of man, and the promise of salvation. It seems to have been considerably popular in its time. It is also known as *Representatio Adae* and *Le Mystère d'Adam*. It was performed on a platform in front of a church with the audience in the public square.

Adam the Creator. Karel and Josef Capek (Czechoslovak). Revue. 7 scenes. Translated by Dora Round. 1927.

Adam destroys the world in order to rebuild it according to his dreams, only to find his own shortcomings are very apparent in his creation.

Adams, Maude (1872-   ). American actress. Born in Salt Lake City where her mother was a leading woman in a stock company. Her father, James Adams, was also an actor. She made her first stage appearance when but a baby and later appeared in child parts at the same time she attended school. Made a big success as Little Schneider in *Fritz* in 1877. At the age of 16 she joined E. H. Sothern's company in New York, playing an ingenue role in *A Midnight Bell*. She became a member of Charles Frohman's company and supported John Drew. Her most famous roles include Lady Babbie in *The Little Minister*, Juliet, the title role in *Peter Pan*, Maggie Wylie in *What Every Woman Knows*, and the principal parts in *Men and Women*, *Quality Street*, and *A Kiss for Cinderella*. After an absence of thirteen years from the stage (1918-1931) she emerged from retirement to play the part of Portia in *The Merchant of Venice*, in which she toured during the season of 1931-32. She toured the summer theatres as Maria in *Twelfth Night* in 1937.

Adaptation. The rearrangement of a story, poem, novel or play implying changes in form, language, locale or period. A translation is merely the conversion from one language to another. But an adaptation implies reshaping and rewording the original while retaining its essence.

Adaptations. A list of plays adapted for the radio and motion pictures may be found in annual volumes of *Film Daily Yearbook*, under "Original Titles," and *Variety Radio Directory*.

Adding Machine, The. Elmer Rice (American). Expressionistic fantasy-tragedy. 7 scenes. 1923.

A satire on the modern mechanized world. After working for twenty-five years as bookkeeper without either raise or promotion, Mr. Zero is fired, being replaced by adding machines. Mr. Zero, enraged at this injustice, stabs his boss, for which he is tried for murder and executed. After travels through graveyards and the Elysian Fields, he reaches Heaven where he is employed on a gigantic adding machine. The keeper of the place, however, finds that Mr. Zero's soul needs further seasoning and sends him, still a failure, back to earth.

Addison, Joseph (1672-1719). English author. Famed for his wit, style, and writings in *The Spectator*.

The eldest son of an English clergyman. While at the Charterhouse as a private pupil, his friendship with Richard Steele began. He went to Oxford, and in 1698 became a fellow of Magdalen College, where he was a scholar of note. He was dissuaded by Charles Montague (Lord Halifax) from taking orders and, supplied with a state pension, he traveled much on the Continent in order to qualify for political service. Upon his return to England, he was in straitened circumstances, but through Halifax, he was commissioned to write a poem in celebration of the victory of Blenheim. This poem, *The Campaign*, 1704, secured for him the succession to John Locke as a commissioner of excise and an under-secretaryship of state. In 1709 he was elected for Malmesbury, a seat he held for the rest of his life.

His literary fame mainly depends on his essays, and especially his portrait of Sir Roger de Coverley. His *Cato: a Tragedy*, proved for political reasons to be a great success in 1713. It is not a great play, but with it Addison closed a particular cycle of drama in blank verse—writing it in heroic couplets without the rhymes. At a time of

Tory triumph, he cleverly managed to avoid giving offense to either the Tories or his own party. Pope, a well-known Tory, wrote the prologue, the zealous Steele suitably packed the house, and the performance was received with rapture on the first night by Whig and Tory alike. His contribution to dramatic theory is best found in five or six of his *Spectator* essays.

Ade, George (1866-1938). American author. Well-known humorist, noted for his modern fables.

Born at Kentland, Indiana. From 1890 to 1900 he was engaged in newspaper work and in 1917 he was a member of the Indiana Council of State Defence. He wrote plays of contemporary life and the American scene. Among his plays are: *The College Widow; Father and the Boys; The County Chairman; Just Out of College; Marse Covington; The Mayor and the Manicure; Nettie; Speaking to Father.*

Adelphi. Terrence (Roman). Comedy. 160 B.C.

The play is probably derived from the Greek of Diphilus and Menander.

Aeschimus, the son of Demea, lives with Micio, his uncle, in the city. He has betrayed an Athenian girl and promised to marry her. When his brother, Ctesipho, brought up on the farm by Demea, comes to the city, he falls in love with a music girl, whom Aeschinus carries off to Micio's house. Demea, arriving from the country, upbraids Aeschinus for his betrayal, and ultimately he is permitted to marry. Ctesipho is allowed by his father, who has had a change of heart, to take the music girl out to the farm, and Micio marries the mother of Aeschinus' wife.

Adler Family, The. Perhaps the largest family group represented in the contemporary American theatre is that of the Adlers, founded at the turn of the century by the distinguished Jewish tragedian Jacob P. Adler, 1855-1926, who immigrated to this country from Russia. There were reputedly seventeen members of the family contributing to the theatre in 1939, the year of the fiftieth anniversary of Mrs. Sarah Adler's debut on the New York stage, among these the children of Jacob and Sarah: Julia, Florence (Flo), Francis, Stella, Luther, Jay, Abe and Charles; and the daughter of an earlier marriage, Celia Feinman Adler. Francine Larrimore is a niece of "the Jewish Henry Irving"; Lulla David (Lulla Schoengold) and her sister, Katherine Allen (Pearl Schoengold) are his granddaughters. The rosters of the Group Theatre and the New York Jewish language theatre are studded with the Adler name. Stella and Luther Adler are the best known members of the family today and Luther bids fair to eclipse the fame of his distinguished father.

Ad lib. To extemporize in a performance, or interpolate impromptu remarks between the set, prepared speeches of a play, generally because of a lapse of memory; or to capitalize on local or timely interest of an audience.

Administration. See *Management, Business.*

Admirable Crichton, The. Sir James Matthew Barrie (English). Comedy. 4 acts. 1902.

A comedy about equality and leadership. An aristocratic English family goes on a cruise with a staff of servants including Crichton the butler. He believes firmly in the superiority of his masters and the doctrine that there must be someone to command. They are shipwrecked. Crichton takes over the leadership and becomes the master of the company. They are rescued and he reverts to his inferior role.

Admiral's Company, The. Chief rivals of Shakespeare's company in the theatrical life of Elizabethan London. The company was reorganized in 1594 under the management of Philip Henslowe with Edward Alleyn as its leading actor. Its principal theatres were the Rose and the Fortune. Christopher Marlowe was the most prominent dramatist who wrote for the company.

Adrienne Lecouvreur. Scribe and Legouvé (French). Drama. 1849.

The scene is the Paris of 1730. Maurice, Count de Saxe, a former suitor of the Princess de Bouillon, has fallen under the spell of Adrienne Lecouvreur, beautiful actress of the Comédie-Française. She returns his affection, but does not know his true identity, believing him a poor soldier of fortune. Hence many amusing complications, which do not, however, detract from the play's essential unity.

Sarah Bernhardt is one of the actresses who has played the title role.

Aeschylus (525-456 B.C.). Greek dramatist. This dramatist has been called the father of Greek tragedy. He was born at Eleusis of aristocratic parents, spent several years in military service and traveled considerably. He won a prize competition in playwriting in 467 B.C. only to lose another to Sophocles in 458 B.C. Many critics agree his greatest play is *Agamemnon*. He introduced the second and third characters into drama, thus bringing about a change from the old tradition of choral odes, or of narratives addressed to the chorus, or of conversations between chorus and actor which were epic and lyric, not dramatic, to a new tradition of vivid, lively dialogue between two actors. In spite of this, he did not do away with the chorus in his own works.

Besides increasing dramatic action by a greater number of characters, Aeschylus improved the machinery of stage presentations. He is said to have written ninety plays. Only seven of these are extant: *The Suppliant Women,* about 490 B.C.; *The Persians,* about 470; *The Seven Against Thebes,* about 467; *Prometheus Bound,* about 465; and the Oresteia trilogy, which included *Agamemnon, Choephori* and *Eumenides,* about 460.

Aeschylus saw service in the Persian wars, having been present at the battles of Marathon and Salamis. After his death Athens awarded him the extraordinary honor of decreeing that his dramas might be exhibited at the great Dionysiac festival.

See also *Drama, Greek, ancient.*

Agamemnon. Aeschylus (Greek). Tragedy. The first in the trilogy of *Orestes.* c. 458 B.C.

Agamemnon, king of Argos and commander of the Greek host that went to Troy to recover Helen, wife of his brother Menelaus, is victorious and returns home with the Trojan King's daughter, Cassandra, his captive and concubine. Cassandra prophesies that Clytemnestra, Agamemnon's wife, will kill them both. Clytemnestra does so with the aid of her lover, Aegisthus, and tries to justify her deed by recalling Agamemnon's sacrifice of her daughter, Iphigenia, ten years before. The people of Argos look to Orestes, Agamemnon's son, to avenge his father.

Agatharchus (About 5th century B.C.). Greek scenic artist. The first scenic artist to conventionalize the three dimensional backgrounds.

Agents. Much of the business of the theatre is transacted through agents. Most playwrights, both professional and amateur and almost all professional actors and actresses have agents who arrange contracts, bookings and terms of employment. The standard commission is 10%. Good agents are constantly in touch with the needs of theatrical companies and on the other hand, producers ask the assistance of agents when casting, or seeking plays.

A few representative New York play agents are: Brandt & Brandt, 101 Park Ave.; Richard J. Madden, 33 W. 42nd St.; Leland Hayward, 654 Madison Ave.; Century Play Co., 522 Fifth Ave.; Samuel French, Ltd., 25 W. 45th St.

Agitstuecke. Plays performed by the "Agit-truppe," or theatrical "shock troupes," of the German Communist Party in pre-Nazi Germany (first about 1930) for the purpose of spreading the Marxian gospel.

Agit-truppe (German). Theatrical troupes in pre-Nazi Germany which were formed about 1930 as branches of the German Communist Party. It was their purpose to spread, by means of their plays, or *Agitstuecke,* the Marxian gospel.

Agon. A division in the traditional form of the ancient Greek drama, especially as expounded by Aeschylus; a dramatization debate between the principal characters of a comedy.

Ah, Wilderness. Eugene O'Neill (American). Comedy. 3 acts. 1933.

A play about a normal adolescent, reminiscent of the writer's own boyhood. Reveals a homely humor not found in his other work.

It reconstructs a typical American family and home during 1906. The family's chief concern is the youthful fervor of the boy, Richard, who is a high school senior and a rebel. He is passionately in love with a neighbor's daughter and means to marry her, but the girl's father, feeling that Richard is too wild, breaks off their relationship. In adolescent desperation the boy gets involved with a chorus girl in a saloon and becomes riotously drunk. Satisfied that no damage has been done, Richard's father forgives the boy and helps him to straighten out his affairs normally and amiably.

Ahlers, Anny (1906-1933). German actress. Born at Hamburg, she made her first appearance on the stage as a child dancer in 1913, and continued as a danseuse until 1922. After studying operatic singing, she appeared in 1924 as Venus in *Orpheus in the Underworld* at Hamburg. Turning to operetta work, she achieved rapid success both in Germany and Austria, her principal plays being *Madame Pompadour, Casanova* and *The Song of Love,* in which she co-starred with Tauber. In April, 1932, she first appeared in London at His Majesty's Theatre in the title role in *The Dubarry,* and won immediate popularity; but a year later after a sudden illness, she died tragically in a London nursing home.

Aicard, Jean François Victor (1848-1921). French poet. Born at Toulon, he was educated in Paris for the law, and while' there met Victor Hugo who admired his poetry. Having won the Vitet prize, Aicard received recognition as a poet of charm and simplicity. He also wrote a number of plays and novels. Not one of his plays was available in English translation up to 1939, however. Aicard was one of the dramatists who was given an opportunity to present his experimental plays by Antoine in his Théâtre Libre at Paris.

L'Aiglon. Edmond Rostand (French). Drama. 6 acts. 1900.
The play treats of *L'Aiglon* (The Eaglet), Napoleon's son. He dreams of regaining his father's empire. But the idea remains a dream for although he is the true heir of the Corsican, yearning for conquest, he is physically weak and consumptive. After an abortive attempt to follow in his father's footsteps he is beaten and captured at the Battle of Wagram, and eventually dies, the expiation of glory bought with human lives.

Aiken, George L. (1830-1876). American dramatist and actor. Born in Boston, Massachusetts, his first appearance as an actor was in Providence, Rhode Island, in *Six Degrees of Crime,* 1848. He was a cousin of George C. Howard, who in 1852 was manager of the Troy Museum, Boston, and whose daughter, Cordelia, was winning reputation as an infant prodigy. The part of Little Eva in *Uncle Tom's Cabin* was thought good for Cordelia, and Aiken began his playwriting career by dramatizing Mrs. Stowe's novel. He finished it in less than a week. It enjoyed a run, then unprecedented in theatre annals, of over three hundred nights. Aiken was especially skilful in adapting short stories and novels for theatre production. He also turned his hand to the creation of many ten-cent novelettes.

Air Raid. Archibald MacLeish (American). 1938.
A verse play written for radio. It depicts, both through descriptions of a radio announcer and the speeches of the people themselves, the life in a small European town early in the morning of the day when the next war breaks out. The talk of the townsfolk before the coming of the air-raiders symbolizes the confused psychology of modern warfare.
First performed in 1938 over Station WABC.

Ajax. Sophocles (Greek). Tragedy. c. 450 B.C.
Ajax, Greek warrior, loses his reason when the Greek leaders bestow Achilles' arms on Ulysses, as the warrior most worthy to bear them.
After a night of madness, in which he becomes the laughing stock of the army, Ajax takes his own life.

Akins, Zoe (1886-   ). American playwright. Born in Humansville, Missouri, in 1886 and lived most of her early life in St. Louis. She has written for newspapers and the cinema as well as for the stage. Twenty-five years ago her sophistication shocked the bourgeois, but today she is known merely as an urbane playwright with a fine flair for dramatic situations.

Her outstanding successes have been *Déclassée* in which Ethel Barrymore starred in 1919; *The Greeks Had a Word For it* (1930) ; and *The Old Maid,* 1936 Pulitzer Prize winner.

Alarcón, Juan Ruiz de (1581-1639). Spanish dramatist. Born in Mexico of noble Spanish stock; studied for a legal career, but his fame rests on his *comedias*. Was less prolific than the other great dramatists of the Spanish Golden Age (his plays barely exceed twenty). The distinguishing feature of his plays is the production of character, an intentional aim in his works, whereas it was accidental in those of Lope.

His best-known character plays are: *La verdad saspechosa* (*The Suspecting Truth*); *Las paredes oyen* (*Walls Have Ears*); *La prueba de las pomesas* (*The Proof of the Promises*).

Alarums. ". . . and excursions," signify the sounds of alarms and general movement in Shakespearean battle scenes.

Alcestis. Euripides (Greek). Tragedy. 4 acts. 438 B.C.

Admetus, sentenced to death, can be spared if he finds someone to die in his stead. He begs his aged parents to take his place, but they refuse. Finally his wife, Alcestis, offers herself, and Admetus accepts the sacrifice. Admetus' father taunts him for his cowardice.

Alchemist, The. Ben Jonson (English). Drama. 5 acts. 1612.

Considered by many the best of his plays and among the best comedies in the English language. Lovewit, during an epidemic of the plague, leaves his house in London in charge of his servant, Face. Face, with Subtle, the Alchemist, and Dol Common, his consort, use the house as a place for cheating people by holding out to them the promise of the philosopher's stone. All the men in the play are rascally or avaricious, the women vain and libertine. There is a coarseness of style that is robust and brutal. According to Millet and Bentley's *The Art of the Drama,* this play "depends mostly upon the intellectual appeal and makes very little use of sympathy or hatred, or a strong interest in the outcome of the action." According to Coleridge, ". . . one of the three most perfect plots in literature."

Aleotti, Giambattista (1546-1636). Italian architect. Designed the Teatro Farnese, the first real proscenium arch theatre, in 1618; devised methods of grooves in the floor to facilitate scene shifting.

Alexander, Campaspe and Diogenes. John Lyly (English). Prose comedy. Prologue, epilogue and 5 acts. 1584.

Alexander the Great, enamoured of his Theban captive, Campaspe, gives her freedom and engages Apelles to paint her portrait. Apelles and Campaspe fall in love. When the portrait is finished, Apelles destroys it to have occasion for further sittings. Alexander, discovering the truth, surrenders Campaspe and returns to his wars.

Alexander, Sir George (George Samson) (1858-1918). English actor and theatrical producer.

He was in business in London before becoming a professional actor. In 1880 he joined Irving's Lyceum Company, and during the greater part of the next eight years, he played under that great actor. In 1889 he took a theatre of his own, and two years later removed from the Avenue to the St. James's where he remained for the rest of his life, producing plays by Wilde, Pinero, etc. In 1911 he was knighted.

His most successful role was the dual one of the king and Rudolph Rassendyll in *The Prisoner of Zenda*. Among his most successful productions were: *Paolo and Francesca; If I Were King; The Second Mrs. Tanqueray; His House in Order; Lady Windemere's Fan; The Importance of Being Earnest; Guy Domville; Old Heidelberg; The Thunderbolt.*

Alfieri, Count Vittorio (1749-1803). Italian poet, novelist and dramatist. Born at Asti, Piedmont; at the age of fourteen, Alfieri became practically his own master with ample means. As a youth he showed little inclination for serious study. Entering the army, he for some years led a life of dissipation and intrigue, varied with travel in France, Spain, Holland and England. At the age of twenty-six he wrote a play on the subject of Cleopatra. The reception of this at Turin fired him with ambition to write poetry, and he applied himself with zeal to the study of the Tuscan dialect and to supplying in other ways the deficiencies of his education. He wrote six comedies, twenty-one tragedies, an opera, an epic, some lyrical poems and an autobiography. The success of his work was mainly due to his style, which was something entirely new to the Italians, who had been accustomed to an artificial form of drama.

Algonquin Hotel. A famous rendezvous in New York City for writers, artists, actors, etc. Scene of the Round Table where Alexander Woollcott, George S. Kaufman, Marc Connelly, Edna Ferber, Dorothy Parker, Robert Benchley and many others used to meet regularly. Frank Case, proprietor of the Alonquin, tells its story in *Tales of a Wayward Inn.*

Alias Jimmy Valentine. Paul Armstrong (American). Melodrama. 4 acts. 1909.

Based on an O. Henry short story, *A Retrieved Reformation.*

Lee Randall, a gentleman safe-breaker, released from Sing Sing through the influence of the lieutenant-governor's daughter, Rose Lane, goes straight and gets a job despite the temptations of his crook friends. His employer's little daughter accidentally gets locked in a safe. Randall has the skill to open it but must face disclosure of his past and probable disgrace. Nevertheless he opens it and all is well.

Alice in Wonderland. Eva LeGallienne and Florida Freibus; adapted from the story by Lewis Carroll (American). 1932.

Successful adaptation of the children's classic. It combines both *Alice in Wonderland* and *Through the Looking Glass.*

Alice Sit-by-the-Fire. Sir James M. Barrie (English). Comedy. 1905.

Whimsical and charming, a typical Barrie fantasy. Amy Grey is very young, just seventeen, and has learned what life means by having gone to the theatre five times in a week. But she will never be so young as her mother, Alice, who has returned with Col. Grey from India. Seeing Alice kiss Stephen Rollo, Amy suspects the worst and goes to his apartment to prevent an assignation. Her fears are not justified, and the escapade ends with her own betrothal to the young man and her mother's resolve henceforth to sit tranquilly by the fire.

Alien Corn. Sidney Howard (American). Drama. 1933.

Katharine Cornell starred in this both in New York and on the road in 1933-'34. In it she played Else Brandt, piano teacher in a mid-Western college town who stifles her dream of a concert career long enough for a sentimental interlude with the head of the college.

Alison's House. Susan Glaspell (American). Drama. 3 acts. 1930.

The poetess mentioned in this play is thought to refer to Emily Dickinson.

The story concerns the family of Alison Stanhope, a famous American poet who had died eighteen years previous, and whose home is about to be sold. Agatha, her sister and symbol of the old life, refuses to leave the house and dies just as the century turns. She bequeaths to her family poems of Alison which she had tried to destroy. They reveal the poet's great love for a married man to whom she denied herself. These verses hold a message for all humanity so the family determines to preserve them for posterity.

Allen, Kelcey (1875-). American dramatic critic. At the age of eighteen he joined the editorial staff of the New York *Clipper* where he remained for twenty years. At the same time he wrote items for the New York *Recorder.*

In 1914 he was appointed dramatic critic for *Women's Wear Daily* and the *Daily News Record,* two posts which he still holds.

Allen, Viola (1869-). American actress. Made her debut in 1882 at the Madison Square Theatre in New York; became a great stage favorite for many years; acted with Salvini in 1886; in 1893 she was a member of the Empire Stock Company under Charles Frohman; starred in *The Christian, The Eternal City, The Daughter of Heaven,* and other plays.

Alleyn, Edward (1566-1626). English actor-manager. One of the foremost actors on the Elizabethan stage and the chief rival of the great Shakespearean actor, Richard Burbage. Alleyn was the son-in-law and business associate of Philip Henslowe, manager of the Admiral's Men and the Rose Theatre. Here Alleyn appeared in the leading role in such plays as Marlowe's *Tamburlaine, Dr. Faustus* and *The Jew of Malta,* and in Greene's *Orlando Furioso.* In 1600 Alleyn built the Fortune Theatre and headed the Admiral's company there until his retirement soon after 1603. With the wealth which he had earned he founded the College of God's Gift, at Dulwich, in 1619. The college has since been reorganized as Dulwich College and is the depository for Henslowe's diaries. Graduates are proud to call themselves "old Alleynians." Alleyn was buried in the Dulwich College chapel.

See also *Alleyn and Henslowe.*

Alleyn (Edward) and Henslowe (Philip). Elizabethan actor-managers who built theatres purely as a business proposition. They were the owners of The Curtain Theatre; The Fortune Theatre; The Rose Theatre; The Hope Theatre.

See also *Alleyn, Edward; Henslowe, Philip.*

All for Love; or, The World Well Lost. John Dryden (English). Historical tragedy. Prologue, epilogue and 5 acts. 1678.

Judged his finest play. In it Dryden abandoned the rhymed couplet and adopted blank verse. It deals with the story of Antony and Cleopatra, but, unlike Shakespeare's treatment of this theme, Dryden confines the play to Antony's besiegement at Alexandria, and to the struggle between Ventidius, Dolabella, and Octavia against Cleopatra for his soul.

All for the Best (Tutto per bene). Luigi Pirandello (Italian). Drama. 3 acts. 1920.

An example of a play in which the author treats situations and characters according to mental rather than emotional considerations.

Martino Lori, after twenty years of idealization of his dead wife, discovers that she had betrayed him and that everyone knew it. After pondering many plans of revenge he realizes he must go on playing the comedy of past cuckoldry.

All God's Chillun Got Wings. Eugene O'Neill (American). Drama. 1923.

A tragic story of miscenegation. Ella, the white girl, and Jim, the colored boy, have played together as children. He idealizes her, but she scorns him and takes up with the ward bully. Only when the latter discards her and their illegitimate child dies will Ella accept Jim's protection and marry him. The union ends in tragedy and frustration because of Ella's increasing race prejudice, which leads to insanity. Her attempt to kill her husband fails, but she so torments him that he does not pass the bar examinations for which he has been studying. Ella, now completely mad, turns once more to Jim as she had as a child, and he accepts the simple, senseless devotion which is all she has to give him.

All's Lost By Lust. William Rowley (English). Tragedy. 5 acts. 1633.

To avenge the honor of his daughter, Jacinta, Julianus, noted general, joins forces with Mulymumen, ruler of the Moors, in a revolt against the King of Spain.

When Mulymumen takes the Spanish throne, he blinds Julianus, tries to marry Jacinta, and when she refuses him, cuts out her tongue. Jacinta is finally killed by her blind father.

All's Well That Ends Well. William Shakespeare (English). Comedy. 5 acts. c. 1604?

The plot derives from a tale in Painter's *Palace of Pleasure* (1566), which was in turn taken from Boccaccio's *Decameron*.

Bertram is forced by the King of France to marry Helena, whom he does not love but who has been encouraged in her suit by Bertram's mother, the Countess of Rousillon. Bertram leaves Helena at once, refusing to see her again until she can obtain the ancestral ring which he always wears and then bear him a child. With the help of Diana, a widow's daughter to whom Bertram is making advances, Helena secures the ring. Then, unrecognized, she takes Diana's place with Bertram on the night of an appointed rendezvous. Subsequently Helena is able to present both the ring and the child, and remind Bertram of his promise. He repents and promises to love her faithfully.

All Trade Union Theatre. See *VZSPS*.

Alto del teatro. The rear portion of the stage in Spanish *corrales*.

Alvarez-Quintero, Joaquin (1873-) **and Serafin** (1871-). Spanish dramatists. The Quintero brothers, genial and delightful writers of comedy, were born at Utrera between Seville and Cadiz, and spent their boyhood in the capital of Andalusia, where, in their teens, they saw performed their first farce *Fencing and Love*. Encouraged by its success, the young men went to Madrid, worked in and for the theatre and, after various experiments, won popular approval by another farce, with incidental music, *The Good Spirits*. Thereafter, they produced plays which exhibit life as they observed it, with piquant local color and fine good humor. Their plays bear some resemblance to those of the Englishman, Barrie.

Their plays include: *Fortunato; The Lady from Alfaqueque; A Hundred Years Old; The Mad Muse; The Happy Nature; The Apple of His Eye; A Sunny Morning; The Flower of Life; The Happiness of Others; The Women's Town.*

Ama (The Fisher Girl). Seami Motokiyu (1363-1444). Japanese Nō drama.

A young man discovers that in infancy he had been taken from his mother, a fisher girl, and raised at the Capitol. He looks for her at Shido. On the shore he meets a fisher girl who tells him she is the ghost of his mother, and at once vanishes. The man prays for his mother's soul who appears before him reborn as a Blessed Dragon Lady of Paradise.

This Nō drama, whenever produced on the Kōngō stage (one of the four main schools of Nō drama), undergoes a slight change in that the Dragon Lady is dressed as a man, for women have no place in Paradise.

Amateur. Anyone whose work in or for the theatre is without expectation of financial gain. The term is frequently used in a deprecatory sense by professionals as a stigma of imperfection.

Though most publicity and glamour attaches to the professional stage, the amateur theatre in the U. S. is of vast proportions. There are countless community theatres, college, school, church and camp "theatre groups." The number of participants in these amateur activities vastly exceeds the professionals.

Amateur stage, Canada. See *Dominion Dramatic Festival of Canada.*

Amazing Dr. Clitterhouse, The. Barré Lyndon (English). Comedy. 3 acts. 1936.

Dr. Clitterhouse, a famous London physician, joins a band of thieves in order to study crime at first hand. He is blackmailed and to save himself, commits murder. His lawyer, however, believes the jury will judge him insane.

Amber. Term for the soft yellow light used to simulate sunlight; the most frequently used of all stage lights.

American Academy of Arts and Letters, New York. In 1898 the American Social Science Association felt the need of an organization devoted wholly to the interests of arts and letters, and thereupon formed the National Institute of Arts and Letters with a membership of 250. In 1904 the members of the Institute decided there should be a still smaller body made up of the most distinguished of its membership, and the American Academy of Arts and Letters, with a membership now limited to fifty, was formed. Work undertaken by the Academy includes the administration of the Evangeline Wilbour Blackfield Foundation, established "to assist the Academy in an effort to determine its duty regarding both the preservation of the English language in its beauty and integrity and its cautious enrichment by such terms as grow out of modern conditions"; the Academy also offers concerts and exhibitions and issues publications.

Among its members, both living and dead, are: William Dean Howells; Booth Tarkington; George Pierce Baker; Eugene O'Neill; Deems Taylor; and Sidney Howard. Nicholas Murray Butler, president; William Lyon Phelps, secretary.

American Comedy, The. There are plays about the contemporary American scene, perhaps of no great literary merit or dramatic distinction which achieve great popular success. These are written and played for entertainment and there is no conscious striving for dramatic excellence. Their popularity and success indicate that they are "of the people," they reflect the people, habits, customs and ideas of the times. Such plays, lightly regarded by serious critics and scholars of their time, have a real importance, perhaps if not as dramas as documents, revelations of the nature of the people and the times—their innocence, their provincialism, their ideals, their lustiness, their puritanism, etc.

The plays of Charles Hoyt, Clyde Fitch, George Ade—are instances of this type of plays which are sometimes grouped as The American Comedy. But Comedy here is used in its broadest sense, embracing the entire Drama.

American Federation of Actors. See *American Guild of Variety Artists.*

American Folk Drama, The. See American Comedy, The.

American Guild of Variety Artists. An affiliate of the four A's. All actors employed in vaudeville, circus, night clubs and allied fields belong to this union since September, 1939. This organization supersedes the American Federation of Actors, the internal affairs of which almost provoked a national theatre strike in September, 1939.

American Laboratory Theatre, New York. An experimental group theatre, with an allied School of Dramatic Art, headed by Richard Boleslavsky and Maria Ouspenskaya. The group worked on plays as a unit, harmonizing all the aspects of production as a form of "collective education." With the author, Amélie Rives Troubetzkoy, they created the production of *The Sea-Woman's Cloak.* Among the plays produced were: Shakespeare's *Twelfth Night;* Miriam Stockton's dramatization of *The Scarlet Letter;* Thornton Wilder's *The Trumpet Shall Sound; Granite* by Clemence Dane; *Big Lake* by Lynn Riggs, Knut Hamsun's *At the Gate of the Kingdom;* Schnitzler's *The Bridal Veil;* and *Dr. Knock,* by Jules Romains.

American Society of Composers, Authors and Publishers, The. A body organized in 1914 by Victor Herbert, Jay Witmark, Gustave Kerker, Silvio Hein and others to protect and license performing rights of musical compositions—strictly non-dramatic rights only. It calls itself a "voluntary, unincorporated and non-profit association." Other functions are "to perform reforms in the law respecting literary property; to procure uniformity in such laws in all countries; to arbitrate differences" . . . ; to act as a benefit society. Membership is about 1,500 authors and composers, 130 publishing firms, plus 50,000 members of 20 foreign affiliates. Gene Buck has been president since 1924.

It has established the complex arrangement for collecting royalties from radio broadcasts, and is diligent in prosecuting infringements.

American Theatre Council. Composed of actors, producers, stage hands, scenic artists and playwrights. Founded in 1937 by the National Convention of the Legitimate Theatre to increase playgoing by reducing theatre prices through support of the theatre ticket code; to encourage youth in writing, acting and directing by means of the Apprentice Theatre (for admission to which Antoinette Perry has conducted thousands of auditions) and by means of playwrights' fellowships; to extend to the country at large the professional theatre chiefly centered in New York, through revival of road shows. The Council issues two bulletins for out-of-towners: one of information for visitors to Broadway; the other about attractions on tour.

American Tragedy, An. Patrick Kearney (American). Tragedy, 1926. A dramatization of Theodore Dreiser's novel of the same name.

The plot is based on an actual murder case. A poor young man, after an affair with a factory worker who is in love with him, abandons her to court a rich and socially prominent young lady. When his former sweetheart tells him she is about to have a child by him, he takes her out in a canoe and drowns her so as not to have to marry her. His guilt is eventually discovered and he is brought to trial. The sociological implications of the story are stressed.

American Way, The. George S. Kaufman and Moss Hart (American). Pageant play. 1939.

A pageant obviously indebted to Noel Coward's *Cavalcade*.

It traces the history of a German immigrant from his landing at Ellis Island to his establishment in everyday American life.

Martin and Trina Gunther, German immigrants, settle in an Ohio town, make money, lose their son in the First World War, endure the depression, and live to see their grandson about to join a Nazi bund organization. Old Martin rebels, tries to persuade his grandson not to join the bund and is killed.

Ames, Winthrop (1871-1937). American theatrical manager. Born at North Easton, Massachusetts, he was the son of Oakes Angier Ames, the American railroad capitalist. Was educated at Harvard University, did post-graduate work there, but later became interested in editorial and publishing work in connection with art and architecture. In 1904 he took over the management of the Castle Square Opera House, Boston, and in 1908 was appointed managing director of the New Theatre and Booth Theatre, New York. He retired in 1932.

Among his successful productions mention may be made of *Antony and Cleopatra; Twelfth Night; The Merry Wives of Windsor; Prunella; Justice; Will Shakespeare; Loyalties; White Wings*. He also presented revivals of *Iolanthe; The Pirates of Penzance; The Mikado*.

L'Amoureuse. See *Impassioned Wife, The*.

Amphitheatre. An edifice of elliptical shape, constructed about a central open space or arena, encircled by tiers of seats rising behind and above one another; ancient Greek and Roman as well as modern open-air theatres.

Amphitryon, or The Two Sosias. John Dryden (English). Comedy. 5 acts. 1690.

Alcmena promises to marry Amphitryon, a Theban prince, on condition that he avenge the death of her brothers. He sends his slave, Sosia, to announce his return to Alcmena. Jupiter, ordering Mercury to assume the form of Sosia, himself assumes the form of Amphitryon. The comedy, of a somewhat licentious character, consists of the complications arising from the arrival at the palace of two Amphitryons and two Sosias, and the final confrontation of the two Amphitryons. A modern treatment of this plot was to be seen in S. N. Behrman's *Amphitryon 38*, 1937, adapted from the play of the same name by Jean Giraudoux.

Anathema. Leonid Andreyev (Russian). Tragedy. 7 scenes. 1909.

Anathema, the Devil, begs for a brief glimpse of heaven, to light his path. Because his request is refused the Devil returns to earth to torture a poor Jewish shopkeeper who is finally stoned to death. Anathema again approaches the gates of heaven, and is told that the shopkeeper has gained immortality, but that he must return to eternal darkness.

Anatol. Arthur Schnitzler (Austrian). Comedy. Series of 7 one-act plays. 1893. A charming comedy of gay Vienna.

Aided and abetted by his friend Max, Anatol deals variously with six lovely ladies of Vienna who are enamoured of him. He is winding up his affairs because he has determined to marry a seventh lady. His experiences with his old loves puzzle and worry him.

And cakes. Actor's board paid by the manager.

Anderson, John (1896-   ). American dramatic critic. Joined staff of the *New York Evening Post* in 1918, became dramatic critic in 1924. Since 1928 dramatic critic of the *New York Journal* (now the *New York Journal-American*). Gives course in dramatic criticism at New York University. Author of *Box Office; The Book of the White Mountains; The American Theatre,* etc.

Anderson, Judith (1898-   ). Australian-American actress. Born in Adelaide, Australia; educated at Rose Park, Norwood, South Australia; first appearance on the stage as Stephanie in *A Royal Divorce* at the Theatre Royal, Sydney, 1915; made her New York debut in stock, 1918. Her other plays include: *Dear Brutus,* 1920; *On the Stairs* and *Crooked Square,* 1922; *Peter Weston,* 1923; *Cobra,* 1924; *The Dove,* 1925; *Behold the Bridegroom,* 1927; *Anna,* 1928; *Strange Interlude,* 1928-29; *Mourning Becomes Electra,* 1931; *Firebird,* 1932; *Conquest,* 1933; *The Mask and the Face* and *Come of Age,* 1934; *The Old Maid,* 1935; *Family Portrait,* 1939.

Anderson, Mary (1859-   ). American actress. A popular tragedienne from 1875, the date of her Louisville, Kentucky, debut, until 1890, when she married Antonio de Navarro and retired from the stage to live in Worcestershire, England. She was highly photogenic, and her pictures decorated newspapers and magazines, and advertised soap and hour-glass corsets. It was claimed that her career was unique, in that she sprang full-grown as an actress at sixteen, and retired at the height of her achievement and acclaim at thirty-one. Born in Sacramento, California; studied for the stage under the younger Vandenhoff; made her New York debut in *Lady of Lyons* at the Fifth Avenue Theatre in 1877; her first London appearance at the Lyceum in 1883. Among her outstanding roles were Juliet and Galatea in W. S. Gilbert's *Pygmalion and Galatea.* In Shakespeare's *A Winter's Tale,* she was the first to double in the roles of Hermione and Perdita.

Anderson, Maxwell (1887-   ). American dramatist. Considered by some the foremost present day American dramatist. He was born in Atlantic, Pennsylvania, the son of a Baptist minister. After he was graduated from college, he began to teach school, then turned to journalism, and finally to playwriting. His first great success as a playwright was shared with Laurence Stallings when their play *What Price Glory?* was produced in 1924. Other plays of Anderson's are *Saturday's Children; Elizabeth the Queen; Mary of Scotland; Both Your Houses,* which won the Pulitzer prize in 1933; *Winterset* which won the Drama Critics' Award in 1936 and *High*

Tor which won the same award in 1937; *Knickerbocker Holiday* (libretto by Anderson, music by Kurt Weill), 1938. *Winterset,* considered by many his best play, attempts to establish a new convention by presenting contemporary affairs in terms of tragic poetry. Mr. Anderson is a co-founder of The Playwrights Company.

Anderson, Sherwood (1876-   ). American novelist and dramatist. He was born in Camden, Ohio, and grew up with but little educational background. After serving in Cuba in the Spanish-American war he became manager of an Elyria, Ohio, paint factory, which position he abruptly and unceremoniously quit in protest against the mechanistic, and in favor of the freer, life. His writing is characterized by a preoccupation with sexual and social problems. With Dreiser, he was one of the first apostles in America of the new realism stemming from Zola. He lived in various places, including New Orleans, New York and Paris. Later he settled down to the editorship of two weekly newspapers in Marion, Virginia.

Among his best known works are: *Windy McPherson's Son* (1916); *Winesburg, Ohio,* 1919; *Poor White,* 1920; *Triumph of the Egg,* 1921; *Dark Laughter,* 1923; *Tar,* 1926; *A Story Teller's Story,* 1924; *Hello Towns!* 1929; *Beyond Desire,* 1932; and *Kit Brandon,* 1936. In 1937 Scribner's published his own dramatization of his *Winesburg, Ohio* and *Triumph of the Egg.*

And Now Goodbye. Philip Howard (American). Drama. 3 acts. 1937.
Based on the novel by James Hilton.

The Reverend Howat Freemantle falls in love with one of his parishioners, Elizabeth Garland. On the train, returning from London, they plan their elopement. There is a wreck. Elizabeth is killed, while Freemantle, injured doing rescue work, is acclaimed a hero.

Andre, Major John (1751-1780). English. America's first pageant creator. He painted scenery, designed curtains and costumes, and to him belongs the glory for the performance of the *Meschianza* given on May 18, 1778. Written by General John Burgoyne, the *Meschianza* had a grand regatta, galleys of beautiful Tory women of Philadelphia, music, ballrooms panelled with mirrors and a supper room with 300 tapers lighting the table, and 430 covers laid.

Andrea del Sarto. Alfred de Musset (French). Tragedy. 1836.

A romantic story about del Sarto, "the faultless painter," his faithlessness to his patron, Francis I; his neglect of his parents; and his weak devotion to his wife, Lucrezia.

Andreine, Francesco (Francesco del Galle) (1548-1624). He and his wife, Isabella, *The Zealous Players* (*I Gelosi*), headed the most famous of the *commedia dell'arte* companies.

While touring France in 1577, they were kidnapped and held for ransom by the Huguenots, the French King Henry III having to pay to redeem them for a scheduled performance at the Blois State Hall.

Andreyev, Leonid Nikolaievitch (1870-1919). Russian novelist and dramatist. Born at Orel and educated there and at Moscow and St. Petersburg Universities. Suffering from melancholia in his youth, he is said to have attempted suicide three times. He started life as a law reporter, but when his short stories began to appear, rapidly attained popularity as a writer. From 1901 forward, he grew increasingly popular, adding dramas to fiction and becoming one of the best known of the Russian writers. His plays sold largely in published form, being in many cases better suited for reading than for performance. Noted for the imaginative philosophy of his plays, Andreyev has been said to be a mystic striving to grasp ultimate but external reality.

His plays include: *To the Stars*, 1905; *Saava*, 1906; *The Life of Man*, 1906; *King Hunger*, 1907; *The Black Maskers*, 1908; *Days of Our Life*, 1908; *Love of One's Neighbor*, 1908; *The Bat*, 1908; *Anathema*, 1909; *Anfisa*, 1909; *Gaudeamus*, 1910; *The Ocean*, 1911; *The Sabine Women*, 1912; *Professor Storitsyn*, 1912; *Honor*, 1912; *Yekaterina Ivanovna*, 1912; *Thou Shalt Not Kill*, 1913; *Thought*, 1914; *An Incident*, 1914; *The Parrot*, 1914; *King, Law, Liberty*, 1914; *Youth*, 1914; *War's Burden*, 1915; *He Who Gets Slapped*, 1915; *Dear Phantoms*, 1916; *Requiem*, 1917; *The Waltz of the Dogs*, 1922; *Samson in Chains*, 1923.

Androboros. Governor Robert Hunter of New York (American). Political satire or biographical farce. 3 acts. 1714.

This was the first play written and printed in America. "Androboros" means "man eater." The work is a satire on Hunter's political enemies, among whom were included officials of Trinity Church who opposed him on the grounds of his refusal to grant land to the parish.

Androcles and the Lion. George Bernard Shaw (English). Comedy. Prologue and 2 acts. 1916.

Androcles, an early Christian, pulls a thorn from the paw of a crippled lion. A few weeks later, when Androcles and other martyrs are being thrown to wild beasts, he finds the same lion who saves him. Androcles with the lion wins the respect of Caesar, who pardons all the martyrs.

Andromaque. Jean Racine (French). Tragedy. 5 acts. 1667.

The subject was taken from Euripides.

Pyrrhus, in love with his captive, Andromaque, neglects Hermione, his affianced bride. Hermione, who loves him, hopes he will turn to her until he promises Andromaque that he will kill her son if she does not marry him. Andromaque agrees, planning to kill herself after the ceremony. Hermione tells Orestes, who loves her, that she will marry him if he kills the faithless Pyrrhus. Pyrrhus is murdered, but instead of marrying Orestes, Hermione kills herself on Pyrrhus' dead body while Orestes loses his sanity.

Angel. Term used to describe the financial backer of a theatrical production.

Angely, Louis (1787-1835). German dramatist. Best known as a writer of comedies. Born in Leipzig, he became an actor and then turned to writing plays.

Four of the more important of his plays are: *School Pranks; Seven Girls in Uniform; The Feast of the Artisan;* and *Travel at the Common Cost.*

Anglin, Margaret (1876-   ). American actress. Born in Ottawa, Canada, she was educated in Toronto and Montreal. She made her first appearance in the play *Shenandoah* in 1894. Her first big success was as Roxane in *Cyrano de Bergerac* in 1898.

Among the plays she appeared in are: *The Great Divide,* 1906; and *The Awakening of Helena Richie,* 1909. In 1910 she turned her attention to classical drama, appearing in *Antigone* and *Electra.* In 1916, she produced *As You Like It* in St. Louis, Missouri; and in 1927, she revived the *Electra* of Euripides.

Animal Kingdom, The. Philip Barry (American). Comedy. 3 acts. 1932.

The story of a man and two marriages, one without benefit of clergy. The thesis of the play is that a mistress is sometimes more a wife than a wife herself. Tom Collier is the hero and after trying in vain to quench his love for his mistress who behaved as a wife, while his wife acted like a kept woman, he leaves the latter for the former. The play centers around a sophisticated group in Connecticut, and the seriousness of the theme is frequently submerged by the gay humor of the piece.

Anna Christie. Eugene O'Neill (American). Drama. 4 acts. 1920.

Anna Christie, an old Swedish sea-captain's prostitute daughter, reared apart from her kin amid poverty-stricken and profligate surroundings in midwestern America, has learned bitterness against her father and the world. Coming to New York, she is united with old Chris, her father, for the first time since early childhood, and goes with him aboard his coal-barge to sea, where she meets an Irish sailor named Matt, with whom she falls in love. The resulting quarrel between Chris and Matt for possession of her leads Anna, in a fit of vindictive bitterness against both her father for his neglect and Matt for his domineering, to reveal the sordid details of her past. After a scene which drives Chris to remorse and Matt to drink the three are reunited by Anna's promise to reform. The men sign on a freighter and Anna is left to keep a home going for them until their return. This play won the Pulitzer Prize in 1921-1922.

Anne Pedersdotter. Hans Wiers-Jenssen (Norwegian). Tragedy. 4 acts. 1910.

A tragedy of witchcraft laid in the sixteenth century. The youthful Anne, married to an elderly palace chaplain, falls in love with her stepson, and seeks to draw him to her by the occult powers which she believes she has inherited. When she boasts to her husband of her triumph and wills his death, he forthwith succumbs. But after the funeral her husband's mother accuses her; the bishop demands that she touch the corpse to prove her innocence. Attempting to do this, she loses her reason, and in frenzy admits having bewitched both father and son.

John Masefield did a version of this play under the title, *The Witch.*

Annie Oakley. A free pass to a public entertainment (theatre, circus, sport). So-called because the famous woman rifle shot made a point of generously, but judiciously, distributing passes—handsomely printed with her own portrait—where the most publicity would accrue. A more current and certainly more picturesque explanation of this synonym for "punched paper" is that passes are called Annie Oakleys because they sometimes look as if the markswoman had used them for a target. Ban Johnson is supposed to have originated the expression, on seeing a thoroughly riddled baseball pass.

In carnival cant, a cardboard meal ticket, punched as it is used.

See also *Oakley, Annie*.

L'Annonce fait à Marie (The Tidings Brought to Mary). Paul Claudel (French). Medieval mystery play. 1910.

This play preaches the faith and humility that works miracles. The good Violaine, betrothed to the catch of the village, is made leprous by a lover's kiss. After many years of ostracism by the community, Violaine's sister, Marie, brings her dead child to the leper. Through Violaine's supreme faith the child is restored to life.

D'Annunzio, Gabriele (1863-1938). Italian poet, novelist and dramatist. The sensuous, emotional and the poetic elements in his plays set their author apart among modern Italian playwrights.

He was of Dalmatian extraction, his surname being Rapagnetta, and was born at Pescara. When he was about fifteen, he published his first volume of poems, *Primo Vere*. His first novel *Pleasure* developed his ruling idea that the end of human existence is joy. In 1919, after an adventurous career as an airman in the World War, dissatisfied with the delay of the Peace Conference in deciding the future of Fiume, he led a raid on the port and occupied it. He administered its affairs until 1920, when he surrendered his self-assumed authority. His first full-length play *The Dead City* was written in 1898.

Among his best known plays are: *The Parable of the Foolish Virgins and the Wise Virgins*, 1897; *The Dream of a Spring Morning*, 1897; *The Parable of the Rich Man and Poor Lazarus*, 1898; *The Parable of the Prodigal Son*, 1898; *The Dream of an Autumn Sunset*, 1898; *The Dead City*, 1898; *La Gioconda*, 1898; *La Gloria*, 1899; *Francesca da Rimini*, 1902; *The Daughter of Jorio*, 1904; *The Light Under the Bushel*, 1905; *More Than Love*, 1907; *The Ship*, 1908; *Fedra*, 1909; *The Martyrdom of Saint Sebastian*, 1910; *The Pisan Woman*, 1911; *The Honeysuckle*, 1913; *Parisina*, 1913; *Cabiria* (motion picture), 1913; *Amaranta*, 1914; *La Piave*, 1918.

Anschutz, Heinrich Eduard (1785-1865). German actor. One of the best German players, who became a pillar of the Vienna Burgtheater.

Ansky, S. A. Yiddish playwright (1863-1920). Pseudonym of Solomon Rappaport. Author of *The Dybbuk*, which was translated into English by Henry G. Alsberg and Winifred Katzin, 1926, and had a long New York run with Mary Ellis playing the heroine.

Antagonist. Adversary of the protagonist, or hero, as well as of the main idea of a play.

Anti-climax. A scene or event that is notably or absurdly less important than the preceding climax.

Antigone. Sophocles (Greek). Tragedy. c. 440 B.C.

Creon, King of Thebes, denies funeral rights to Antigone's brother, Polynices, who was slain in battle. Antigone breaks the law and sprinkles dust on her dead brother's eyes, that his ghost may find peace. As punishment, Creon orders Antigone buried alive.

Antigone. Walter Hasenclever (German). Drama. 3 acts. 1917.

A modern version, unchanged in plot, of the Greek tragedy, by Sophocles, of the same name.

Anti-masque. A comic counterpart of the masque proper in Elizabethan times, the hearty, jovial humor of the former relieving the excess lavishness and sweetness of the latter. Both were generally presented on the same occasion, the masque by members of the aristocracy, the anti-masque by actors hired from the public theatres.

Antoine, André (1858-   ). French actor, producer and theatrical manager. Founded the Théâtre Libre, in Paris, in 1887, for the purpose of producing plays interpreting the realities of contemporaneous life. Afterwards he became director of the Odéon and in 1897 opened a new theatre called the Théâtre Antoine. In 1906 he returned as director to the Odéon, and retired in 1916.

With the support of noted writers, among them Zola, he produced plays by Brieux, Curel, etc. In Berlin the Freie Buehne and in London the Independent Theatre were established on Antoine's model.

Antony and Cleopatra. William Shakespeare (English). Tragedy. 5 acts. 1606.

The play is based on Plutarch's *Lives,* although Shakespeare has completely remolded the materials to his own ends. Antony, infatuated with Cleopatra, returns to Rome upon receiving news of the death of his wife, Fulvia, and of an attack on Rome by Pompey. There he marries Octavia, sister of Octavius Caesar, but soon returns to Cleopatra. Caesar, using this desertion as an excuse to break Antony's political power, sends a fleet which defeats him. Antony blames the seductions of Cleopatra for his subsequent defeats on land, but on hearing the false report that she is dead, falls grief stricken on his own sword. He dies from his wounds after a last meeting with Cleopatra. The Egyptian queen, about to be taken by Caesar to Rome as a captive, kills herself with the sting of an asp.

Anzengruber, Ludwig (1839-1889). Austrian actor and dramatist. Acted from 1859-1869 and learned the misery connected with being a strolling player. In 1870 wrote *Der Pfarrer von Kirchfeld,* which discussed the great problems of humanity, writing only of the lower class or peasant-folk; author of *Die Kreuzelschreiber,* 1872; *Der Meineidbauer,* 1871; *Doppelsmord,* 1873; *Der ledige Hof,* 1876; *Viertes Gebot,* 1877. Was considered the only important dramatist produced by the German speaking stage in his period.

Apart, the. See *Aside, the.*

Apologie for Poesie, An (or, **The Defence of Poesie**). An essay by Sir Philip Sidney, probably written about 1580, thought to have been a reply to Gasson's *The School of Abuse,* a Puritan attack on plays and poetry. It remained in manuscript until nine years after Sir Philip's death; in 1615 two editions were printed, one for Henry Olney with title as above, the other for William Ponsonby, entitled *The Defence of Poesie.* It is a glorification of art, and its influence on the mind and conduct of human beings. Although Sidney touches various forms of literature, his remarks on the drama reveal an extensive knowledge of the classics, and of the Italian commentators on Aristotle. It was through the *Apologie* that Aristotle first became an influence in English literature.

Appia, Adolphe (1862-1928). Swiss scenic designer. A disciple of Wagner and a theorist on theatrical staging, setting and acting. His ideas were connected mainly with the German theatre. Dickinson, in his *The Theatre in a Changing Europe,* says: "He applied to the setting a space law as absolute as the time law of music; he went beyond this and indicated the manner by which the space law of the setting could be co-ordinated with the time law of the music through the medium of the living and moving actor."

His two great works are: *La Mise-en-scène du drame Wagnerien* and *Die Musik und die Inscenierung.*

Appius and Virginia. John Webster (English). Tragedy. 5 acts. Printed 1654.

Though attributed to Webster, there is evidence that it was partly written by John Heywood.

Based on an Italian *novelle,* the plot is taken from a classical legend which forms one of the stories in Painter's *Palace of Pleasure.*

The story of Virginia, daughter of the centurion, Lucius Virginius, and Appius Claudius, the tyrannous decemvir. The decemvir is enamoured of her and seeks to possess her. Therefore, she is claimed by one of his favorites as the daughter of a slave, and Appius, in the capacity of a judge, gives sentence in his favor and delivers her into the hands of his friends. Virginius kills his daughter and rouses the soldiers. They march to Rome and seize Appius. He is imprisoned and kills himself. The incident led to the abolition of the decemviral power.

Apple Cart, The. George Bernard Shaw (English). Political extravaganza. 3 acts. 1930.

Magnus, King of England, finds himself in conflict with his progressive cabinet, led by the prime minister. The cabinet demands that Magnus relinquish the right of veto. Magnus is superior in debate to his ministers. Though he defeats them in argument, he gives in to them. His Majesty agrees to abdicate the throne, but he will also as a private citizen, continue to fight the ministers of the cabinet.. He threatens to stand for Parliament from Windsor. Rather than face this embarrassing situation, the ministers withdraw their demands.

Apron. That part of the stage projecting in front of the curtain; probably deriving from the ancient Greek *orkestra;* done away with first by the Haymarket Theatre in 1843; later transformed into the orchestra.

Arbor. Part of counterweight system; frame for supporting weights.
See *Scenery*.

Archer, William (1856-1924). British author and critic. He was born in Perth in 1856, and educated at the University of Edinburgh. His career as a journalist began in Australia, then shifted to London in 1879. He was successively dramatic critic on *Figaro, The World, The Tribune, The Nation* and *The Star*.

Archer is noted for his espousal of realism and naturalism in the theatre. He was an early and ardent defender of Ibsen, whose complete works he edited.

He wrote a successful melodrama, *The Green Goddess,* 1921, in which George Arliss starred. His published works include *A National Theatre* (with Granville Barker), 1907 and *The Old Drama and the New,* 1923.

Architecture. See *Theatres, architecture*.

Arden. The family name of Shakespeare's mother, Mary. Robert Arden, the poet's grandfather, was a wealthy "gentleman of worship" living at Wilmecote, three miles from Stratford. John Shakespeare, the poet's father, was one of his tenant farmers. Mary was the youngest of eight children. She married John Shakespeare about 1577. On the basis of his Arden connections William Shakespeare applied for and received a coat of arms in 1596.

Arden of Feversham, The Tragedy of Mr. Author unknown. Tragedy. Attributed to Shakespeare by Edward Jacob in 1770, a theory now generally rejected. 1592.

The plot is based on a contemporary crime committed in February, 1550, and recorded by Holinshed. A play on the same subject was written by George Lillo. It is the first extant middle-class tragedy in English drama.

It deals with the persistent attempts, finally successful, of Mistress Arden and her paramour, Mosbie, to murder Arden, for which purpose they hire two killers, Blackwill and Shakebag. The crime is discovered and Mosbie and Mistress Arden are executed.

Arena Goldoni. A famous open-air theatre in Florence, Italy, built in 1818 by the architect Corazzi. From its founding it stood for the best in democratic theatre. In 1908 it was taken over by Gordon Craig and performances of a varied repertory were given under his direction for many years.

Aretino, Pietro (1492-1556). Italian poet. Born at Arezzo, Tuscany, he achieved notoriety as the author of the licentious *Sonetti Lussuriosi,* in which he satirically and savagely attacked many of the leading characters of the day. He is also memorable for his letters, five comedies, and a tragedy *Orazia*. He spent his last years at Venice under the patronage of those who feared his sarcasm.

Argentine. Material used in scenery for imitating glass for windows.

Arion of Methyma (7th-6th century B.C.). Greek. The most celebrated harp player of the ancient Greeks, a native of Lesbos. He lived the greater part of his life at the court of Periander, the tyrant of Corinth. His changes in the dithyramb rendered to Dionysos are credited with having led the way to the Greek drama. It was he who fixed the number of dancers in the dithyramb at fifty. He is said to have introduced "spoken verses" into the choral odes. These consisted of short conversations in verse between the leader and his fellow performers.

Ariosto, Ludovico (1474-1533). Italian poet. Born at Reggio of an old and noble Bolognese family, he devoted five years to the study of jurisprudence, which he abandoned on discovering his vocation for poetry. In 1503 he became one of the gentlemen attendants on the cardinal Ippolito d'Este, and while so employed began his poem *Orlando Furioso,* which was first published in 1516. After serving the cardinal faithfully for fourteen years, Ariosto was dismissed, and joined the household of the cardinal's brother Alfonso, duke of Ferrara. In 1522 he successfully quelled a rebellion in the Garfagnana province, of which he was later governor. He is generally recognized as a sincere and splendid artist. He wrote a number of comedies, among which are: *Il Suppositi* (The Pretenders); *Il Negromante* (The Necromancer); *Orlando Furioso.*

Aristophanes (c.448-c.388 B.C.). Ancient Greek dramatist. Known as the chief representative, the genius, of old comedy. He was born in Athens to a certain Philippus who held property in Aegina. In 427 B.C. his *The Banqueters* appeared, followed in the next year by a biting satire called *The Babylonians.* His *The Acharnians* came in 425 B.C. He is said to have written fifty-four comedies in all, but only eleven are now extant. His best known work is probably *The Frogs,* in which he satirized other dramatists and writers of his time. He was conservative in his ideas and his mind reverted with admiration to the days of Aeschylus, while he held up to ridicule the more modern Euripides. The eleven plays still extant are: *Plutus* (c.388 B. C.); *The Knights; The Clouds; The Wasps; The Frogs; The Birds; The Acharnians; Peace; Lysistrata; Priestesses of Demeter;* and *Women of Parliament.*
See also, *Drama, Greek, ancient.*

Aristotle (384-322 B.C.). Greek. The ancient Greek philosopher and poetic-dramatic analyst and theorist. At eighteen he went to Athens where he was apprenticed to the philosopher, Plato, with whom he remained for twenty years. After the death of Plato he tutored Alexander the Great for eight years. Later he kept a school in Lyceum for twelve years. He died at the age of sixty-three. He is most famous, as dramatic theorist, for his *Poetics.*
S. R. Littlewood, in his "Dramatic Criticism" (Pitman Publishing Co., New York, 1939) says: "It is one of the paradoxes of history that Aristotle's *Poetics* . . . an assortment of lecture notes, badly put together, atrociously corrupt and amounting

altogether to not much more than a modern magazine article . . . should have dominated and gone far to stifle so much dramatic effort after a score of centuries."

Brooks Atkinson, in the *New York Times* (October 1, 1939) says: "There is an air of getting something off the chest in that statement. Probably Mr. Littlewood feels better now. Certainly I do. Although Aristotle was a tremendous fellow in science, logic and knowledge, he was no artist and no prophet in the drama. He was an intellectual devising rules for an emotional subject. If the *Poetics* were not constantly turning up even today, as the holy book of the drama, his system of platitudes and blunders would not matter. But it bullies all of us every day."

See also, *Drama, Greek, ancient.*

Arizona. Augustus Thomas (American). Drama. 4 Acts. 1899.

An example par excellence of well constructed melodrama of the type popular at the turn of the century.

The dashing exterior of Capt. Hodgman of the 11th U. S. Cavalry is but a cloak for his inherent villainy. He is the father of a baby born to Lena, a waitress in the outpost, and as the play opens is trying to seduce Estrella Bonham, young wife of his middle-aged Colonel. Young Lieut. Denham learns that Estrella plans to elope with Hodgman and forbids it. He also takes back from the Captain the lady's jewels which she had given him. Her husband, discovering Denham in his wife's room with the jewels, suspects him of betrayal and theft. Denham quits the service, but stays nearby so as to be with Estrella's sister, Bonita Canby, whom he loves. Hodgman is shot on a visit to the Canby's, and Denham suspected. But matters are cleared up when Lena's fiance confesses he shot his beloved's betrayer. In the meantime Denham has been made a Captain of the First Arizona Volunteers, and Estrella Bonham has decided she loves her husband after all.

Arthur Byron was the rascally Hodgman in the play's Chicago première, and the minor role of a young officer was played by Lionel Barrymore.

Ar lé chin. The supposed source of the name Harlequin, maintained by the Harlequin himself: a cry *en langue asiatique* by his father to his ass.

See also *Harlequin.*

Arles. The town in France supposed by some to be the native place of Harlequin who was believed to be a certain wicked serving-man who later fled to Bergamo.

See also *Harlequin.*

Arliss, George (1868-   ). English actor. Notable as a character actor. Born in London, the son of William Arliss-Andrews, he adopted Arliss as his stage name. He first appeared on the stage at the Elephant and Castle Theatre, September 18, 1886, and moved to the West End in 1890. He appeared on the screen in the days of the silent films and later in sound films. Among the plays in which he appeared successfully in both England and the United States are: *The Second Mrs. Tanqueray; The New York Idea; The Green Goddess; Disraeli; Old English.* His films include: *Disraeli; Alexander Hamilton; The Working Man* and *Voltaire.*

Armin, Robert (fl. 1590-1610). English actor. A comedian with the Lord Chamberlain's Men, Shakespeare's company of actors. He apparently received his early training from the greatest of Elizabethan clowns, Richard Tarlton. After an early career as a writer, he joined Shakespeare's company in 1599 and remained with it until his retirement in 1610. Nothing is known of the specific roles he may have played.

Armored Train, The. Vsevolod Ivanov (Russian). Drama. 3 acts. 1927.
Depicts the destruction of Admiral Kolchak's *White soldiers* by Siberian peasants.

Arms and the Man. George Bernard Shaw (English). Comedy. 3 acts. 1904.
Amusing satire on war.
Raina Petchoff saves Captain Bluntschi from the Bulgarians one night by hiding him in her boudoir. When the war is over Bluntschi returns to see Major Petchoff and wins Raina from her fiance, Sergius. Sergius finds consolation by marrying Raina's maid.
Much is made of the fact that the soldiers get rations of chocolate. The operetta *The Chocolate Soldier* was based on this play.

Arnold, Matthew (1822-1888). English poet and critic. Arnold is best known as a poet, although his valuable reports on the educational systems of France, Germany and Holland, 1861-65, his essays in criticism, *On the Study of Celtic Literature,* 1867, *Culture and Anarchy,* 1869, *St. Paul and Protestantism,* 1870, *Literature and Dogma,* 1873, assured him a high position as a critic.
Born at Laleham-on-Thames, he was the eldest son of Thomas Arnold, and educated at Winchester, Rugby, and Balliol College, Oxford. He won the Newdigate prize for a poem in 1843, became Fellow of Oriel in 1845, and 1847-51 was private secretary to Lord Lansdowne, president of the council, by whom in 1851 Arnold was appointed an inspector of schools. He held this post for over thirty years, retiring in 1883.
He wrote one play *Merope* which was done after the Greek manner.

Arnould, Sophie (1740?-1802). French actress. The woman whom Garrick called the greatest actress on the French stage, was actually more noted for her love affairs than for her acting. The Comte de Lauragais, her chief protector, wrote for Mlle. Arnould a play on Clytemnestra. She sang in the operas of Gluck, the height of her fame being reached in 1774, when she took the lead in *Iphigenia in Aulis.* A famous portrait of her is that by Jean-Baptiste Greuze.

Arraignment of Paris, The. George Peele (English). Masque. 1584.
Written for and played before Queen Elizabeth.
Paris is tending his flocks on Mount Ida with Oenone his wife, when he is called upon to decide to which of the three goddesses the golden apple shall be awarded. He decides in favor of Venus, who carries Paris away, leaving Oenone disconsolate. Juno and Pallas arraign Paris before the gods, accusing him of partiality in his judgment. The case is referred to Diana. She evades the question by awarding the apple to the nymph Eliza.

Art for art's sake. An esthetic doctrine originally conceived in irritation by the French novelist, Gautier (with his *l'art pour l'art*) which defends "pure" beauty of craft and style to the general exclusion of realistic ideas or utility. Maeterlinck was a dramatic exponent of this theory, as was Oscar Wilde.

" 'Art for art's sake' was a phrase conceived in irritation and adopted as a slogan by men more anxious to startle than to explain. It was directed at the philistine (Victorian model), and it was not ill-suited to the moment which gave it currency. Taken out of its context the phrase is, however, dangerously near to nonsense and it is a pity that so flip a formula should have become fixed as the accepted designation of an esthetic doctrine persistent and more meaningful than the formula suggests." (*The Nation*, Joseph Wood Krutch, December 19, 1936.)

Burton Rascoe, in his introduction to *Mademoiselle de Maupin*, says that Gautier's preface "was a challenge to the critics and so thorough was its disposal of the irrelevant ideas of criticism that it became the handbook and the bible of the theories of art for art's sake of which Gautier was the father.

L'Art poétique (Art of Poetry). A treatise on dramatic poetry by the French writer and *avocat*, Thomas Sebillet, published in 1548. This work, says Barrett Clark in his *European Theories of the Drama*, was a "distinct departure from the Rhetorics and Poetics which preceded it." Besides showing the effects of Italian ideas on French letters, this work contains probably the first trace of the influence of Aristotle's *Poetics* in France. It was chiefly interesting because of the parallel it draws between the old French morality plays and the tragedies of antiquity. Sebillet foreshadows, in spirit at least, some of the reforms advocated by the spokesman of the *Pléiade*.

Artist's paper stump. Rolled and pointed tools for drawing lines and shadows in grease colors; used as a substitute for rounded toothpicks or make-up pencils.

Artzybashev, Mikhail Petrovitch (1878-1927). Russian author. Revolutionary writer.

A Tartar by descent, he began his career as a caricaturist, but gave up drawing for the writing of realistic short stories. His first novel *Sanine* 1907, shows his hatred of the then existing social order, and the same revolutionary strain is evident in his other works. After the Russian Revolution he fled to Poland.

His plays include: *Jealousy*, 1913; *Enemies*, 1913; *The Law of the Savage*, 1913; *War*, 1914.

As Before, And Better (Come prima, meglio di prima). Luigi Pirandello (Italian). Drama. 3 acts. 1920.

A man, still sensually in love with his wife, who had eloped with a lover, takes her back on condition that she pretend to be a second wife, even to the child. The child, worshipping her mother, hates the pretending second mother. The woman can not bear this, and telling the truth to the little girl, escapes with her.

Asbestos. See *Curtains, asbestos*.

A.S.C.A.P. See *American Society of Composers, Authors and Publishers.*

Ascent of F 6, The. W. H. Auden and Christopher Isherwood (English). Drama. 2 acts. 1936.

The British government has to cope with a native rebellion instigated by a rival nation, Ostnia. The mountain peak, "F 6", is considered sacred by the natives; and should it be scaled, the glory of the achievement would assure their control.

When the British hear that the Ostneans are attempting the climb, they send idealistic Michael Ransom and a party of four men to beat the enemy to the summit. The climb is strenuous, however, and one by one, the four men die; only Ransom reaches the top.

Asch, Sholem (1880-   ). Yiddish writer. Well-known for his stories and plays, written in Yiddish, of Jewish life in Poland and Russia.

Born in Warsaw, and lived for many years in Russia. Just before the Revolution, he came to the United States, where he has since resided.

Among his works are: *The God of Vengeance; Uncle Moses,* 1922; *Sabbati Zovi,* 1930; *The Nazarene,* 1939.

Asche, Oscar (1872-1936). English actor, playwright and producer. Born Geelong, Australia, of Norwegian descent, he studied acting at Christiania and   e his first appearance in London in 1893 at the Opera Comique in *Man and Woman.* He was in management at the Adelphi Theatre with Otho Stuart in 1904, at His Majesty's Theatre in 1907, and later at the Globe Theatre. He married the actress Lily Brayton.

His productions include: *Chu Chin Chow,* in which he played the title-role, 1916-1921; *The Maid of the Mountains,* 1917; *Julius Caesar,* in which he played the role of Casca, 1932; and *The Merry Wives of Windsor,* 1929.

Plays include: *Count Hannibal,* 1910; *The Spanish Main,* 1915; *Eastward Ho,* 1919; *Mecca,* 1920.

As Husbands Go. Rachel Crothers (American). Comedy. 3 acts. 1931.

Lucille, thirty-five and beautiful, married to a dullish good American business man, and Emmie, forty-five and prettily plump, tied down by a proper daughter, are in Europe. There they have met Ronald, twenty-nine, an English novelist, and Hippolitus, sixty and French. Over-persuaded, the women return to America bringing their would-be lovers. A series of amusing contretemps occur, but in the end, Lucille is left to her husband, Charles. Emmie marries Hippolitus and Ronald goes away.

Aside, the. An early, now obsolete, dramatic device in which a character in a play speaks directly to, with information exclusively for, the audience, while supposedly unheard by the other characters in the play. Its best-known use is to be found in *The School for Scandal* by Sheridan. The device was put to a modern psychological use in O'Neill's *Strange Interlude,* enabling the characters to express their inmost and fugitive thoughts and bearing some resemblance to the "stream-of-consciousness" technique found in novels and used, for instance, by James Joyce in his *Ulysses*.

Aspendos. The Roman theatre at Aspendos which has a roof covering the stage.

Associated Actors and Artistes of America, Inc. Parent union of the Actors' Equity Association, Screen Actors' Guild, American Federation of Radio Artists, American Guild of Music Artists, and the newly organized American Guild of Variety Artists. It traces from the White- Rats, organized in 1900, and the Actors International Union. These were amalgamated in 1910 as the White Rats Actors' Union of America. In 1919 the differences between their organization and Actors' Equity Association were composed, and the Associated Actors and Artistes of America came into existence. Frank Gillmore is international president.

Association of German People's Theatres. An organization formed to take the place of the Berlin *Volksbuhne,* which collapsed in 1918. This association comprised, in representation, about twenty different organizations. It is now dissolved.

As the Leaves. Giuseppe Giacosa (Italian). Comedy. 4 acts. 1908.
A good example of the modern social comedy, in which Giacosa links together in a very interesting way the old and the new manners in Italian drama.
The story of a family struggle in which the reversal of their fortunes serves to bring out the essential characteristics of each of the persons involved.

Assumption of Hannele, The. See *Hannele.*

Astley's Amphitheatre. One of the most beautiful and largest 19th century theatres in London; it is an egg-shaped arena; largest stage in London, 146 feet wide, used for grand spectacles, scenes of warfare and equestrian shows. It was designed in 1804 by Philip Astley, built of wood, and opened with a horse spectacle, burned down twice and rebuilt. Torn down 1895.

Aston, Anthony (Tony Aston). The first professional actor in America, of whom any record is known. He came from England, had a reckless and spectacular career as a soldier of fortune and acted in Charleston and in New York, 1703-4.

Astor Place Riot (May 10, 1849). A theatre disturbance caused by the hostility between Edwin Forrest and William Macready. Theatregoers split into factions over these two actors and the riot occurred inside and outside of the Astor Place Opera House, New York. The militia was called out. Stoned by hoodlums in the street, they fired on the crowd, killing and wounding many. An evidence of anti-British feeling of the time.

As You Desire Me. Luigi Pirandello (Italian). Drama. 3 acts. Adapted by Dimitri Ostrow. 1931.
After a ten year search, Bruno Pieri believes he has found his wife, Lucia, who is

suffering from amnesia as the result of abuse suffered in the First World War. Lucia, or the Unknown One as she is called, is able to remember the past as Bruno and his family begin to accept her and to believe in her. However, when the family discover another woman they think may be Bruno's lost wife, Lucia loses her newly found identity and security and leaves the house an unknown woman.

As You Like It. William Shakespeare (English). Comedy. 5 acts. 1599.

The play is based on the euphuistic prose romance, *Rosalinde,* by Thomas Lodge.

Frederick has usurped the dominions of the Duke, his brother, who lives with his followers in the forest of Arden. Celia, Frederick's daughter, and Rosalind, the Duke's daughter, meet Orlando at Frederick's court. Orlando and Rosalind fall in love, but Frederick, angry with Orlando, banishes Rosalind. Accompanied by Celia, Rosalind, in countryman's disguise, meets Orlando in the forest and pretends to be a youth named Ganymede. Orlando's cruel brother, Oliver, comes to the forest to kill him but becomes remorseful. He falls in love with the disguised Celia, and Rosalind tells Orlando that she will produce Rosalind at the wedding. At this ceremony Celia and Rosalind abandon their disguises. News arrives that Frederick has made restitution of the dukedom.

Athalie. Jean Racine (French). Tragedy. 5 acts. Based on a biblical story. 1691.

Athaliah dreams she will be killed by a child whom she later identifies as the boy Joash. She tries to get him out of the way or to kill him and the drama centers around the conflicts and emotions thus aroused.

Atheist's Tragedy, The. Cyril Tourneur (English). Tragedy. 1611.

D'Amville, the atheist, wants to marry his son, Rousard, to Castabella who is wealthy. She, however, is betrothed to D'Amville's nephew, Charlemont. D'Amville arranges that Charlemont go abroad on military service. During his absence, Castabella is married to the sickly Rousard. D'Amville kills his brother, the father of Charlemont, after a will has been made in his favor. Rousard dies. When Charlemont returns, D'Amville plans to kill him, but dashes out his own brains, by accident. Charlemont is united with Castabella.

Athens, Theatre of. First theatre in Greece. The collapse of its wooden seats in 499 B.C. led to the erection of a stone auditorium in which the original orchestra stood fifty feet to the south of the present orchestra and had a diameter of seventy-eight feet. This theatre had a round orchestra (*paradoi*), a rectangular *skene* and a projecting *paraskinia,* with a low platform stage.

Atkinson, Brooks (1894-   ). American dramatic critic. Born in Melrose, Massachusetts; educated at Harvard. Assistant to dramatic critic, *Boston Transcript,* 1918; literary editor of the *New York Times,* 1922; dramatic critic, the *New York Times,* since 1926; writes for London *Daily Telegraph* on American Theatre. Author of *Skyline Promenades,* 1925; *Henry Thoreau,* 1927; *East of the Hudson,* 1931; *The Cingalese Prince,* 1934.

At leisure. Term for being unemployed in the theatre.

Atmosphere. (1) The imaginative mood established in the writing of a play by its author; (2) the realization of that mood, by process of staging, lighting and performing in the production of the play.

Attic Bee, The. A title applied to the Greek dramatist Sophocles because of the sweetness (honey) inherent in his works.

At the Bottom. See *Lower Depths, The.*

D'Aubignac, Abbé François Hedelin (1604-1676). French dramatist, critic. His *Pratique du Théâtre,* 1657, a good source for the history of the 17th century drama, outlines his principles, based on reason, most dogmatically. He condemns even the greatest classics if they do not conform to his ideas, which he lays down as laws. He wrote four unsuccessful tragedies to illustrate his theories: *Cyminde,* 1642; *La Pucelle d'Orleans,* 1647; *Le Mariage de Sainte-Catherine,* 1650; and *Zénobie,* 1647.

Aubry de Montdidier's Dog, or, The Dog of Montargis (Le Chien de Montargis); or, *The Forest of Bondy.* Guilbert de Pixérécourt (French). Melodrama. 1816.

A popular melodrama, the production of which, at tht Weimar Court Theatre in 1817 caused Goethe's resignation as director. Goethe believed it beneath his artistic dignity to have anything to do with a play in which a dog was the hero.

Aubry de Montdidier is murdered by his comrade Macaire, after a quarrel over Lucille. The concealed body is discovered by Aubry's dog and later the murderer is revealed when the dog assaults Macaire. Final proof comes when Macaire's missing belt is discovered in the woods, stained with blood. Macaire escapes, but kills himself when surrounded by peasants and soldiers.

Auden, W. H. (1907-   ). English poet and dramatist. He is associated in the general mind with the poets, Stephen Spender and C. Day Lewis, with whom he attended Oxford University. He is the author of *The Dance of Death* and collaborator with Christopher Isherwood on *The Dog Beneath the Skin, The Ascent of F 6* and *On the Frontier.*

Audio (television). A term used in reference to the sound signal associated with the electrical impulses representing the television image; also to apparatus for sound transmission.

Audition. A hearing; a term used now for any tryout performance before judges, whether of singing, dancing, acting or playing an instrument, for the purpose of prospective employment.

Auditorium, horseshoe. A 17th-18th century derivation in Italy from the early semi-circle.

See also *Teatro alla Scala; Teatro San Carlo; Teatro Vecchio.*

Auditorium, ovoid. See *Theatres: auditorium, ovoid.*

Auditorium, straight-sided. See *Theatres: auditorium, straight-sided.*

Augier, Guillaume Victor Emile (1820-1889). French dramatist. Regarded as one of the founders of the modern comedy of manners.

He was born at Valence. In 1858 he became a member of the Academy. Accepting the model of Scribe, who perfected the "well-made play," Augier employed it to different ends, striving to advise and improve his audiences. He was a bourgeois realist, governed by reason; a commonsense moralist, recommending marriage for love instead of money; domestic fidelity and industrial and political honesty.

He wrote *La Cigue*, 1844; *Le Gendre de M. Poirier* (in collaboration with Sandeau), 1854; *Les Effrontés*, 1861; *Maitre Guerin*, 1864; *Les Fourchambault*, 1878.

Augustan tragedy. The term given to a form of 18th century English tragedy. It was a mixture of diverse pseudo-classic forces and heroics. Plays of this type were amorphic, chaotic and undistinguished in character portrayal. A definite interest in Asiatic themes predominated.

Aula regia. Buildings in the foreground of the stage in Italian Renaissance theatres.

Auleum. The curtain introduced into the Roman theatre; unlike modern theatre curtains, it was dropped into a hollow recess placed toward the front of the stage.

See also *Curtains.*

Aulularia. Plautus (Latin). Comedy. About 200 B. C.

The title is derived from the Latin word for "pot," and the plot concerns an old miser, Euclion, whose household god enables him to dig up a pot of gold buried beneath the hearth by his grandfather. But once he has the pot in his hand he becomes so fearful lest he be robbed that he re-buries it deeper than before. Molière's *L'Avare* and numerous other plays have used Plautus' plot.

Aunt Urikke. Gunnar Heiberg (Norwegian). Comedy. 3 acts. 1884.

Heiberg's earliest play. He thrusts good-humoredly at the new woman, selecting as his heroine a kind-hearted eccentric. She moves among amusing folk who include an idealistic girl devoted to the concept of progress, a professor scheming to become a cabinet minister, and a radical politician uttering platitudes to catch the people.

Ausschrier, der. The name given that player in early German Shrovetide drama who announced the end of the play.

Author's League of America. Organized in 1911 in New York by Arthur Train, Gelett Burgess, Joseph Vance and Lloyd Osborne. Purpose, to establish authors' rights in manuscripts and safeguard them. Subdivided into guilds with separate officers: the *Authors' Guild, Dramatists' Guild, Radio Writers' Guild* and the *Authors' League Fund* (which functions as a benefit society). The League has published a bulletin for its members during most of the period of its existence.

Auto de los reyes magos, el (The Play of the Three Wise Men). (Spanish.) Liturgical drama. 1 act. Middle Ages.
The three Wise Men enter, expressing astonishment at the sight of the new star in the East. Their paths converge, they exchange greetings. One bears myrrh, the symbol of human nature; another brings frankincense, the symbol of divine nature; the third bears gold, the symbol of kingly dignity. The magi then wonder which gift the Christ-child will prefer. Here the scene changes to Herod's palace, where the magi inform Herod that the Christ-child has been born.

Auto sacramentale. A kind of masque in the early Spanish theatre which was a combination of prologue, farce and religious allegory written to be performed on the pageant-cars during the Corpus Christi processionals and probably dealing with the Eucharist. Lope de Vega wrote many of these.

Autumn Fires. See *The Reckoning*.

L'Avare. J. B. P. de Molière (French). Comedy. 5 acts. 1668.
Harpagon, an old miser, and his son, Cleante, are rivals for the hand of Marianne. Cleante gets possession of the miser's treasure, and gives him the choice between Marianne and the treasure. The old man chooses the treasure.

Awake and Sing. Clifford Odets (American). Drama. 3 acts. 1935.
A Group Theatre presentation, this folk-drama of Jewish-American life in the Bronx is propagandist in its protest against social injustices.
It is the saga of the Bergers, a lower middle-class family. The son Ralph is ambitious and aspiring, but he loses the girl he loves because they are both too poor to defy their families' disapproval. His sister Hennie, about to have an illegitimate child, marries a childhood sweetheart whom she will never love; then leaves him to go off with Moe Axelrod, an embittered war veteran with one leg who can offer her some measure of prosperity. Other characters are Bessie Berger, drudging mother of Ralph and Hennie; Myron, their hard-working father; and Jacob, the philosophizing old grandfather who commits suicide by jumping off the roof.

Awakening of Spring, The. Franz Wedekind (German). Tragedy. 3 acts. 1891.
A thesis play presenting an analysis of puberty, it is a naturalistic study of three children, Melchior, Moritz and Wendla, and of the vividness and promise of the life

awakening in them. It shows the cruelty and tragedy of its extinguishment, for which the adult world must take full blame. This play, according to Anita Block, in her *The Changing World in Plays and Theatre,* supplies "the great link between *Ghosts,* that first effort directed toward the lifting of sexual taboos, and those more numerous contemporary plays which brought into the theatre of our own time sexual subjects that even in this age of unparalleled sex enlightenment and liberalism, still are attacked as taboo."

Ayala, Adelardo Lopez de (1828-1879). Spanish dramatist. Born in Guadalcanal, province of Seville. Dramatist who insisted on the moral thesis. Principal work: *El tanto por ciento* (So Much Per Cent), 1861, has a theme of love versus money.

Ayatsuri. See *Acting, Japanese.*

Ayrer, Jakob (? -1605). German dramatist. One of the most important and quite the most prolific German dramatist of his day.

He lived during the 16th century and passed almost his whole life in Nuremberg, where he became imperial notary. His fame, however, rests entirely on his dramatic works. In style he was the successor of Hans Sachs, but he was influenced by a travelling troupe of English actors who visited the continent at the close of the century. His plays are not now considered of very great merit.

His dramatic works number nearly seventy and were published posthumously in Nüremberg in 1618, under the title *Opus Theatricum.*

Baby spot. A small spotlight.

Bacchae, The. Euripides (Greek). Tragedy. 406 B.C.

A symbolical tragedy in the formal classic tradition, using a Chorus to comment on the action.

The god Dionysus comes with his Bacchanals to his homeland of Thebes and is rejected by his kinsmen. So he infects them all with his own Bacchanalian madness. King Pentheus imprisons the god and the holy women, then repents and agrees to go to witness the secret religious rites on Mt. Cithaera. He does so, disguised as a Maenad, is discovered and torn to bits. His mother finds his head, thinks it is a lion's, and goes wildly off, holding it and dancing as she goes. The Chorus of Maenads, horrified at the sight, turn from Dionysus. He threatens those who oppose him, then ascends to Heaven, while the mortals proceed to their doom. The significance of the story is much disputed by scholars, but it is generally conceded to be an allegory opposing the forces of instinct and those of reason and wisdom.

Bachelor Born. (The Housemaster) Ian Hay (English). Comedy. 3 acts. 1938.

Charles Donkin, middle-aged housemaster at Marbledown School in England, is faced with the problem of putting up the three daughters of the woman he had loved in his youth, and wanted to marry. Button, Rosemary and Chris Faringdon, with their Aunt Barbara Fane settle down at Marbledown, or try to, and immediately stir up excitement. Hating the headmaster, the Rev. Ovingdon, who is unjust to Donkin, the young people organize meetings of protest, but before they are through they indirectly manage to have Ovingdon removed and Donkin promoted.

Back cloth. See *Back drop.*

Back drop. Screen or curtain lowered in back of a scene, usually for vista or panorama effects. In the early theatre, a back drop was used for change of setting and to limit the confines of the stage.

Backing. (1) Unit of scenery two- or three-fold used to mask openings in the set, such as doorways; (2) the financing of a production.

Backstage. That part of the theatre which lies behind the stage and which includes dressing rooms and stage wings.

Back Stage Club (Nashville). See *Nashville Community Playhouse.*

Back to Methuselah. George Bernard Shaw (English). Philosophic fantasy. 5 parts. 1921.
A philosophical comedy regarding the need of human beings to perfect themselves to avoid being destroyed. Shaw contends that only a life measured in centuries rather than in decades can make men mature enough to order their society rationally, and that unless a life span of at least three hundred years is achieved the genus homo will be discarded in favor of a more competent species. The work, while presented as a unit, consists of five plays:
In the Beginning. Adam and Eve in Eden learn of birth and death—how Lilith was alone until she learned to procreate; how death does not matter if birth brings other Adams. Adam chooses to live a thousand years. Centuries later, he has become an agriculturist and is scorned by his warrior son Cain. Eve reproaches her boastful son for his belligerence, but he retorts that he merely serves as the agent of Death and thus fulfils a mission.
The Gospel of the Brothers Barnabas. A satire on contemporary politics. Lubin and Burge, caricatures of Asquith and Lloyd George, visit the biology professor Barnabas, who tells them of his new book on longevity. They think he has invented some new medicine and are ready to pass a law limiting its use to the best people when they find he is discussing merely a biological thesis. Disappointed, Burge still sees a possible election slogan in the idea.
The Thing Happens. The parlor of the President of the British Isles in 2170. Barnabas of the day, a great authority on human life, is intrigued by a book by an American explaining a system of breathing which will prevent deaths by drowning. Moving pictures of prominent men who have drowned reveal that the Archbishop, supposedly thus killed, has really lived three centuries. He pretended to drown, then began a new career as his own descendant.

Tragedy of an Elderly Gentleman. The long-livers are now quite numerous. They have so congested the British Isles that the capital of the Empire has been moved to Bagdad. An elderly gentleman has been driven almost mad by the strain of talking to several young long-livers. His son-in-law, the Prime Minister, consults the long-livers' oracle, and is shortly told "to go home, poor fool." The elderly gentleman, impressed, asks to remain on the island with the oracle and is killed by the latter with a compassionate lance.

As Far as Thought Can Reach. 31920 A. D. Men and women are born from eggs at seventeen, spend four years singing and dancing and mating, then become ancients and engage in abstruse study and meditation. They are almost entirely pure intellect; their bodies are so far conquered that they need neither food nor sleep.

In an epilogue the characters of the first play judge the future state. Eve is pleased that cleverness prevails; Cain is sad that war is outlawed; Adam as stupid and puzzled as ever; Lilith hopeful for the day when man shall overcome matter entirely.

Bacon, Francis, Viscount St. Albans (1561-1626). English essayist and dramatist. Considered one of the greatest prose writers in English literature.

Born at York House, London, the son of Nicholas Bacon, lord-keeper of the Great Seal, he was educated at Trinity College, Cambridge. In 1576 he accompanied Sir Amyas Paulet, ambassador to France, to Paris, where he remained until the death of his father in 1579. In 1582 he was called to the Bar at Gray's Inn, of which he became a bencher and later entered Parliament as member for Melcombe Regis in Dorset, becoming in the years that followed the confidential adviser of the Earl of Essex, favorite of Queen Elizabeth. In 1593 Bacon incurred the anger of the Queen by opposing in Parliament the levying of a double subsidy and was excluded from the court. He was, however, befriended by Essex. He regained royal favor by taking part in the accusation at Essex's first trial for treason, and he appeared at the second trial as one of Her Majesty's counsel, speaking against his benefactor, whose execution followed the trial.

On the accession of James I, 1603, Bacon was knighted. He became one of the commission appointed to settle the terms of the union of England and Scotland. Bacon advised the King to forego the most unpopular of the patents which he had created, but the advice was rejected and in 1621, Bacon was accused of bribery and corruption in Chancery. He was sentenced to imprisonment in the Tower of London and fined, then later pardoned, but his public career was ruined. He died a few years later of bronchitis.

Bacon is regarded by modern men of science as the real originator of the modern school of experimental research. His method of discovery consisted in the gradual building up of small pieces of knowledge.

The view that Bacon is the real author of Shakespeare's plays first arose in 1852, and was based upon the alleged illiteracy of Shakespeare, the similarity between the writings of the two men and the non-existence of an authoritative Shakespearean text.

Bacon's main works include: *Essays,* 1597; *Instauratio Magna,* of which only two parts were completed, (1) *De Dignitate et Augmentis Scientarum,* 1623, and (2) *Novum Organum,* 1620; *New Atlantis,* 1627.

Bacon, Frank (1864-1922). American actor and playwright. For many years before coming to Broadway Frank Bacon played stock with his wife. He is best remembered as the originator of the character of Bill Jones in *Lightnin'*, a play which he wrote with Winchell Smith, and in which he acted from 1918 until his death. After a run of several years in New York he took the comedy to Chicago, where he gave his last performance of it only a week before he died. Will Rogers later took Bacon's role in a movie version.

Baconian Theory. The theory that Francis Bacon wrote the plays generally attributed to Shakespeare. Proponents of the theory argue that a man of Shakespeare's apparently limited formal education and provincial background could not have written with such learning and insight. They argue further that Bacon, a man suitably qualified, revealed his authorship in complicated anagrams in the texts of the plays. The theory, set forth as early as 1852, has been considerably discredited by the recent discovery of the manuscript play, *Sir Thomas More,* parts of which are in handwriting identical to that of the signature on Shakespeare's will.

Baer, Arthur (Bugs). Was born as usual and at the proper age. Became older without effort in spite of popular opinion. Was educated at home by a private tutor in the language of flowers and developed my legs riding a bicycle from city to city while voting Republican for the Literary Digest. Have talked continuously because a careless doctor vaccinated me with a phonograph needle. Was born absolutely nuts and had a relapse. Mother explains it all by saying she met father in a revolving door. Anyway, my nurse put me on a merry-go-round at the age of five and forgot to take me off. That's why I had to have my hats made in a kite factory. Am known as the most reliable writer in the nation because I never carry a bundle by the string. If I ever say anything right my wife is sure to correct me. I owe it all to the little woman at six per cent. These few paragraphs ain't exactly a "Gone with the Wind." But we will bring that up with bicarb of soda. You have now read the story of the silent valleys, and the wooded hills, of the vast frozen spaces, of a maid's love for a man, she rushed up the rain-washed canyon but horse and rider seemed to have vanished in thin air. Told as only Zane Grey can tell it at all newsstands for two dollars a copy. If anything else happens, wire."

Bahr, Hermann (1863-1934). Austrian critic, editor, novelist and dramatist. Born at Linz, he studied at the University of Vienna and elsewhere, and travelled much in Europe. In 1890 he settled in Vienna as a journalist, specializing in social and literary criticism. He was afterwards assistant editor then editor of several papers, and in 1906 became manager of the *Deutsches Theater* of Berlin.

As a dramatist, Bahr is considered a lesser Schnitzler, softening the sharp edges of realism by his scrupulous art. His works include more than eighty titles, among which is to be found the earliest discriminating treatise upon expressionism.

His plays include: *The New Men,* 1887; *The Great Sin,* 1889; *The Mother,* 1891; *The Domestic Woman,* 1893; *Dora,* 1893; *From the Suburbs,* 1893; *The*

Water Sprite, 1896; *Juana*, 1896; *The Booby*, 1897; *Josephine*, 1898; *The Star*, 1898; *The Athlete*, 1899; *Viennese Women*, 1900; *Der Franzl*, 1900; *The Apostle*, 1901; *Der Krampus*, 1901; *The Master*, 1903; *Sanna*, 1904; *The Poor Fool*, 1905; *The Deliverers' Club*, 1905; *The Other*, 1905; *The Faun*, 1906; *Grotesques*, 1907; *The Yellow Nightingale*, 1907; *Ring Around*, 1907; *The Concert*, 1909; *The Children*, 1910; *The Little Dance*, 1911; *The Principle*, 1912; *The Phantom*, 1913; *The Complainer*, 1914; *The Jolly Soap Refiner*, 1914; *The Voice*, 1916; *The Moment*, 1917; *The Brute*, 1919; *Indian Summer*, 1924; *The Aunt*, 1926; *Heaven on Earth*, 1928.

Baker, Elizabeth (1879-   ). English dramatist. Born in London. It was not until 1909 that she gained public notice for her work, with her play, *Chains*. She has contributed to many periodicals.

Her other plays include: *The Price of Thomas Scott*, 1913; *Partnership*, 1917; *Miss Robinson*, 1918; *Penelope Forgives*, 1930.

Baker, George Pierce (1886-1935). American educator, author. Perhaps the best biography of the famous founder of the 47 Workship, school of the drama at Harvard, where Baker taught English and playwriting from 1905-1924, would be a roster of those of his pupils who achieved distinction in the theatre. Yet even that would be too long to be feasible, including a fair share of the men who *are* the modern American theatre: Philip Barry, Sidney Howard, S. N. Behrman, George Abbott, Eugene O'Neill, Edward Sheldon, John V. A. Weaver and many, many others. Born in Providence, Baker received his A.B. from Harvard in 1887. Later, as a professor in the university, he sponsored the Harvard Dramatic Club when it was started in 1908. It was largely due to his influence that Harvard was the first university in the country to accept a course on the practical aspect and technique of the drama as a part of its regular academic curriculum. The Workshop proper was founded as a sort of try-out theatre and critical laboratory in which the budding playwrights could test their own works before an audience. In 1925 Baker left Harvard for Yale, where he was professor of the technique and history of the drama until his retirement in 1933. During the same period (1925-33) he was also chairman of the Department of Drama, School of Fine Arts; and director of the University Theatre. When he retired in 1933 many of his former pupils, grown illustrious, assembled in New Haven from all over the world to do him homage. His published works include *The Principles of Argumentation*, 1895; *The Development of Shakespeare as a Dramatist*, 1907; *Some Unpublished Correspondence of David Garrick*, 1907; *Dramatic Technique*, 1919; etc.

Bakst, Leon (1866-1924). Russian artist. Educated in St. Petersburg, he soon made a reputation as a painter and was employed by the court as a teacher. About 1900 he began to paint scenery for plays produced in the Russian capital and his remarkable work for Greek tragedies attracted a good deal of attention. After 1908 he increased his fame by painting scenery and designing costumes for the Russian ballet of Serge Diaghileff. His décors, which created a vogue in Paris, were richly oriental in style, the best-known being the setting for *Scheherazade*. From 1909 until his death, he lived in Paris. Examples of his paintings are in the Victoria and Albert Museum, London, and in the Metropolitan Museum, New York. Many of his sketches are in the possession of his theatrical disciple, Simon Lissim, in Paris.

Balcony, The. Gunnar Heiberg (Norwegian). Drama. 3 acts. 1894.

The passionate heroine deceives her middle-aged husband and rejoices when he dies in an accident that prevents his discovering her duplicity. Then, having married her lover, and deceived him in turn, she is deserted by him.

Balcony, Elizabethan. In the Elizabethan theatre the gallery extending over the stage was used either for spectators or for actors in an expansion of set. A part of this same upper gallery, to one side of the stage, was frequently used as a *musique* room where musical interludes and accompaniments to the play were performed.

Balcony, modern. The present-day gallery is used exclusively for audience-seating, with the sole exception of "plants" to which the orchestra, as well, is sometimes subject.

Balderston, John Lloyd (1889-   ). American dramatist and newspaper correspondent. Born in Philadelphia, Pa., and educated at Columbia University. During the First World War he went to Europe as a free-lance war correspondent, and later became a representative of the McClure Newspaper Syndicate, gathering information from England and Ireland for the United States. He became editor of *The Outlook* in London, remaining in that capacity from 1920 to 1923. After that he was employed by the now defunct *New York World* as London correspondent.

Plays include: *A Morality Play for the Leisure Class; Berkeley Square; Dracula; Red Planet.*

Bald-headed row. The name given the first row of a theatre usually occupied by elderly men and playboys.

Ballad opera. Form of 18th century comedy which came into popularity with the triumph of Gay's *The Beggar's Opera,* 1728. Its greatest period of success was between 1729 and 1738 when it ousted regular tragedies and comedies from the stage. Written in one, two or three acts, these ballad operas were composed of airs, accompanied by prose, blank verse or rime; utilized nearly all the types of comedy invention from farce to sentimentalism. Satirical and burlesque in tone.

Ballerina. Originally a dancer in the *commedia dell' arte;* generally also the *cantarina;* does not really play a part in the *scenario;* introduced purely to present *intermedii* of a musical kind. This type is traced, practically unchanged, from the dancing girl as found in a Herculaneum frieze of early Roman days through the *Francischina* of Callot in the 17th century to the *Camilla Veronese* of the 18th century. Today the ballerina is the star female performer of ballet.

Ballet. Term for an artistic or dramatic dance to music by a group and used for occasional interludes in opera or as a divertissement. Outside of this merely contributory connotation the term is also used for that series of story-plots, interpreted through dance and pantomime, which makes up a complete theatre program. Arnold Haskell, in his *Ballet,* says: "Ballet, in the form that we recognise, had its beginning with the founding of *L'Académie National de la Danse* by Louis XIV in 1661. We are able to trace its development in an unbroken line of dancers and teachers from then until the present day." As to its source, Mr. Haskell says: "The germ that was to develop into ballet was brought into France from Italy by Catherine de Medici, who was eager to divert her sons while she busied herself in ruling. The spectacle was a combination of dancing, singing and recitation. Its aim was social. It constituted an elegant pastime for the monarch and his court, an opportunity for bawdy humour, for lavish expenditure, and for the fulsome flattery of court to King. The subjects chosen were largely mythological; the King played at godship, the court worshipped. Astute minds, bent on politics rather than pleasure, used the fashionable craze for purposes of national propaganda, among other things, to point out to foreign ambassadors the might of France. . . . The finest artistic minds of the day contributed to the music, the decoration, and the poetry of the spectacle. The people paid. The first dramatic ballet of importance from which the history of the art may be said to begin was *Le Ballet Comique de la Reine* in 1581."

Ballet Russe de Monte Carlo. Modeled on the Diaghilev Ballet Russe, the traveling company organized by Col. W. de Basil, former Cossack officer, and called "de Basil's Russian Ballet of Monte Carlo," is made up chiefly of young dancers. Their work has been in the main revivals of ballets by Fokine and other master choreographers, latterly ballets are being composed especially for the group. Until 1937, when a managerial rift split the company, Massine was the director. Then Fokine took over. In 1938, however, both de Basil's and Fokine's names disappeared from the program, which showed the company (minus certain dancers) as the "Ballet Russe de Monte Carlo," under Massine, and as owned by Universal Art, Inc., a predominantly American association, with Julius Fleischman of Cincinnati its head.

Balletomane. Term meaning "ballet enthusiast." As originally used in Russia, it meant the conservative and partisan theatre-goer who never missed a single ballet performance and always sat in the front row seats, which were next to impossible to obtain because of the family custom of permanent chairs.

Balloon. To go up in one's lines; to blow.

Ballroom theatre, 16th century French. See *Hôtel de Bourgogne, Hotel de Rambouillet.*

Ballyhoo. As used in the theatre, a slang term for an exaggerated form of announcement, publicity, advertisement or stunt to create interest and increase business; outside the theatre the word has a derogatory sense, often used to refer to false claims.

Bancroft, Marie Effie Wilton, Lady (1839-1921). English actress. Daughter of Robert Wilton, a provincial actor, she was born at Doncaster, and first appeared on the stage at Norwich in 1845. She made her début in London at the Lyceum, 1856, as Henri in *Belphegor,* and later achieved a great success in burlesque at the Strand. In 1865 she became joint manager with H. J. Byron of the old Prince of Wales' Theatre, where she produced *Caste* and *Society,* in which she made her reputation as a comedian. Other productions were *The School for Scandal, The Merchant of Venice, Masks and Faces,* and *London Assurance.* In 1867 she married a member of her company, Squire Bancroft, and on January 31, 1880, the pair began their management of the Haymarket Theatre with a revival of *Money,* followed by two Sardou plays, *Odette* and *Fedora,* Pinero's *Lords and Commons,* and revivals of *The Rivals* and *Diplomacy.* Retiring from management in 1885, she appeared at the Garrick in revivals of *Diplomacy,* 1893, and *Money* in 1894. She died at Folkestone, May 22, 1921.

Bands. The name given troupes of actors who roamed throughout Germany up to and during the 17th century. Germany was overrun by English, French, Dutch and Italian acting companies. From these, independent German bands were formed, made up of vagabonds, roamers, jugglers, quacks, musicians and acrobats.

Bankhead, Tallulah (1902-   ). American actress. Born in Duntsville, Alabama. She appeared first in *Squab Farm,* March 15, 1918. Next came *Foot-loose,* 1919; *39 East* and *Nice People,* 1921; then she went to London where she scored a hit in *The Dancers,* 1923, with Sir Gerald DuMaurier. Among her successes were: *Fallen Angels,* 1925; *The Green Hat,* 1925; *They Knew What They Wanted,* 1926; *The Gold Diggers,* 1927; *Her Cardboard Lover,* 1927; *Let Us Be Gay,* 1930. Next she appeared in several films, returning to New York in *Forsaking All Others,* 1933. *Dark Victory,* 1934, and a revival of *Rain,* 1935, served as a prelude to the really fine role in *The Little Foxes,* 1939, in which she has scored her greatest triumph. She is married to John Emery.

Bankside. The principal theatrical district in Tudor London, across the Thames from the City proper and a little to the west of London Bridge. The locality had long been given over to houses of ill fame and rings for the baiting of bears and bulls. Active opposition by London authorities to theatrical activities caused many playhouse managers to move to Bankside, which was beyond the jurisdiction of the city. The *Rose, Swan* and *Globe* theatres were situated in this district.

Barber of Seville, The. Pierre Augustin Caron de Beaumarchais (French). Comedy, 5 acts. 1775.

Bartolo wishes to marry his ward and pupil Rosine, but she prefers Count Almaviva, whom she knows as Lindoro. Figaro the barber interests himself in the lovers and helps them thwart the elderly guardian. The Count's attempts to outwit Bartolo form the main plot. First he enters the old man's house disguised as a soldier, asks to be billeted and gives Rosine a note telling of Almaviva's love. When Bartolo discovers the soldier making love to the girl the gallant is forced to flee. Later he returns in the guise of a music master, and the young people plan to elope. Bartolo is tricked into signing what he believes to be a marriage contract for him and Rosine, but what is really a contract for her marriage to Almaviva, and his rage is allayed by the generous Count's offer of Rosine's dowry.

In the mouth of Figaro, genial man of the people, indignantly protesting against the abuses suffered by the populace under the rule of the nobility, the author expressed his own revolutionary ideas. The play fell with the impact of a bombshell on a society which was to follow Figaro's advice and revolt against its masters fourteen years later.

Rossini's opera of the same name is based on it. Beaumarchais wrote a sequel: *The Marriage of Figaro.*

Barchester Towers. Thomas Job (American). Comedy. 3 acts. 1937.
The play is based on the novel by Anthony Trollope.

Madeline Neroni, recently returned to the English cathedral town of Barchester after eleven years in Italy where she has had a serious quarrel with her Italian husband, enters merrily into a social crisis arising over the selection of a new dean for the Barchester diocese. Madeline favors a young liberal, Arabin, whose chief opposition is a certain Mr. Slope. To embarrass Mr. Slope before the archbishop Madeline puts champagne in his ginger beer mug. Madeline also forces young Arabin to propose to her when she knows he is in love with Eleanor Bold, and before she is positive her husband has died. When she hears that her husband, obviously alive, has been seen playing cards at Monte Carlo, she is quite satisfied to turn Arabin back to Eleanor and return to Italy.

Bard of Avon. The nickname of William Shakespeare.

Bardolatry. The cult of Shakespeare exploitation, applicable to any people or organizations who have profited by the use of the name of the Bard of Avon, among these Stratford itself with its eight major hotels, numerous boarding-houses, shops, etc., the countless commentators, teachers, lecturers, theatrical producers, actors, publishers, booksellers and associations such as the British Shakespeare Society, which alone has 10,000 members. Calling it "The Shakespeare Industry" in the book of that name, Ivor Brown admits bewilderment only at the greatness of its extent, remarking that English-speaking peoples are not especially fond of poetic drama.

Bare stage. The stage proper, free of any scenery or properties.

Barker. A shouter or clamorer; one who through high-pressure talk and exaggeration induces and drums up business for his attraction. Barkers are usually used in side-shows and amusement areas.

Barker, The. Kenyon Nicholson (American). Drama. 3 acts. 1927.

Nifty Miller, barker for the Colonel Gowdy Shows, wants his son, Chris, to study law. Chris, however, falls in love with Lou, the snake charmer, and marries her.

Nifty, sick at heart, plans to leave the carnival, but changes his mind when he hears business is bad, that he is needed and that Chris has a job in a law office.

Barn Players Club, The. See *Community Players, The, San Diego, California.*

Barnabee, Henry Clay (1833-1917). American singer, actor. Born November 14, 1833, in Portsmouth, New Hampshire. He sang in church choirs, finally making his debut as a professional at the Music Hall in Boston, assisted by Annie Louise Cary. He became associated with the Boston Ideal Opera Company in 1879. He later organized the famous Bostonians, a first-rate company. His best-known role was that of the Sheriff of Nottingham in *Robin Hood.*

Barnstorm. A theatrical term meaning to give performances from town to town, originally in barns.

Barn Theatres. See *Theatres, 20th Century American.*

Barnum, Phineas T. (1810-1891). A great American showman whose originality brought him world fame; made his first bid for attention in 1835 on the stage of Niblo's Garden with an old negress, Joice Heith, whom he introduced as Washington's nurse; navigated the Mississippi with a showboat; sold Bibles; opened Barnum's Museum in New York in 1841; introduced Tom Thumb in 1842 and toured Europe in 1844 with his famous midget; managed Jenny Lind's American tour, 1850; organized a famous menagerie and circus in 1871; in 1881 merged with J. A. Bailey to form Barnum and Bailey's circus.

Barre. A rod along the walls of a dance studio, or backstage, for the convenience of dancers who use it to steady themselves when stretching or limbering up.

Barrès, Maurice (1862-1923). French novelist. Born at Charmes-sur-Moselle, Vosges. He was educated at Nancy, and began to write while still very young. He published *Huit jours chez M. Renan* in 1888 and *Culte de mer* in 1891. In 1889 he became deputy for Nancy, and retained the seat until 1893. In the following year, he published his three-act comedy, *Une Journée Parlementaire.* During the first World War, Barrès, who had long been an intense nationalist, gained a tremendous reputation with his powerful daily articles in the *Echo de Paris.*

His most popular stories include *Un Amateur d'ames,* 1899; *Le Jardin de Bérénice,* 1891; *L'Ennemi des Lois,* 1893; and the trilogy, *Le Roman de l'energie nationale,* 1897-1902.

Barrett, Lawrence (1838-1891). American actor. He first appeared in New York in 1857; played in the South, California and England; in 1887 he joined forces with Booth and toured with him; was best known as Cassius in *Julius Caesar;*

played in *Pendragon;* made his greatest hit as Lanciotto in *Francesca da Rimini.* His granddaughter, Elizabeth Barrett, is a popular actress today.

Barretts of Wimpole Street, The. Rudolf Besier (English). Historical drama. 4 acts. 1930.

The scene of the play is the Moulton-Barrett residence at 50 Wimpole St., London; the time 1845-46. Elizabeth Barrett, invalided by a fall from a horse, leads a secluded existence, virtually a prisoner, a prey to the terrible and tyrannical adoration of her father, whose affection amounts almost to incestuous love. Her life is brightened by the liveliness of her sisters and brothers and by the poetry in which she finds solace. Her interest in literature leads to a correspondence with Robert Browning, who comes to visit her and is charmed by her intelligence and sympathy. He courts her against the express desires of her father until she agrees to marry him. They are forced to elope because of her parent's selfish and unbalanced attitude. She flees with Robert to Italy, accompanied by her faithful maid Wilson and her cocker spanied Flush.

Among other sources, Besier consulted the writings of both Elizabeth and Robert Browning; as a result his play has historical as well as dramatic authority. It had its première at the Malvern Festival, after which it ran for nearly a year and a half in London, with a cast headed by Cedric Hardwicke as Barrett. It opened in New York in 1931, with Katharine Cornell as Elizabeth, and ran for a year there, then had a successful road tour.

Barrie, Sir James Matthew (1860-1937). English author. Barrie, one of the most important and prolific writers of the modern English theatre, is equally famous for his plays and his novels. He was born at Kirriemuir, Forfarshire, where he received his earliest education, going later to Dumfries Academy and Edinburgh University. In 1885 he settled in London and became a contributor to a number of papers and journals. In 1894 he married an actress, Mary Ansell; their union was dissolved in 1910. His plays are: *Becky Sharp,* 1891; *Ibsen's Ghost,* 1891; *Richard Savage,* 1891; *Walker, London,* 1892; *Jane Annie,* 1893; *The Professor's Love Story,* 1894; *The Little Minister,* 1897; *The Wedding Guest,* 1900; *Quality Street,* 1902; *The Admirable Crichton,* 1902; *Little Mary,* 1903; *Peter Pan,* 1904; *Alice Sit-by-the-Fire,* 1905; *Pantaloon,* 1905; *Josephine,* 1906; *Punch,* 1906; *What Every Woman Knows,* 1908; *Old Friends,* 1910; *The Twelve-Pound Look,* 1910; *A Slice of Life,* 1910; *Rosalind,* 1912; *The Will,* 1913; *The Adored One,* 1913; *Half-an-Hour,* 1913; *The Dramatists Get What They Want* (sketch), 1913; *Der Tag,* 1914; *The New Word,* 1915; *Rosy Rapture* (revue), 1915; *A Kiss for Cinderella,* 1916; *Dear Brutus,* 1917; *A Well-Remembered Voice,* 1918; *The Old Lady Shows Her Medals,* 1917; *Mary Rose,* 1920; *The Truth about the Russian Dancers,* 1920; *Shall We Join the Ladies?* 1921; *Barbara's Wedding,* 1927; *Young David.* The last play, written shortly before his death as a vehicle for Elizabeth Bergner, was unsuccessful. But most of them have become so well known and so often revived, in particular *Peter Pan,* that the titles alone are descriptive to most people. Barrie is noted for his whimsy and sentiment.

A Kiss for Cinderella, in which Maude Adams starred, has been compared to the writings of Hans Christian Andersen. There is a quaint humor in even his most subtle character analyses, such as *What Every Woman Knows;* in spirit Barrie is almost the direct antithesis to the cutting rationalizing of George Bernard Shaw, one of his most eminent contemporaries. The topical problems of the day failed to interest him as dramatic material; even his plays about the war are somehow removed from grim reality by their fantasy. Yet his other-worldliness is not abstruse and forbidding, but homely and familiar, as his descriptions of homely and familiar things are lifted above the realm of the commonplace by his imaginative treatment of them.

Barron, Mark (1905-　). American dramatic critic. Educated at Baylor University. Formerly associated with the press department of the Theatre Guild. For some years connected with the Associated Press as dramatic editor. Contributor to newspapers and magazines on theatre subjects.

Barry, Elizabeth (1658-1713). English actress. Supposed to be the daughter of Edward Barry, a supporter of Charles I in the Civil War, she made the acquaintance of the Earl of Rochester and through him became an actress. According to one account, he himself helped to train her. She first appeared on the stage about 1673. Her reputation was made in tragedy, and as the creator of Cordelia in Tate's version of *King Lear,* Isabella in Southerne's *The Fatal Marriage,* and Belvidera in Otway's *Venice Preserved,* she achieved immense success. Those qualified to judge, spoke of her as "mistress of all the passions of the mind." She ranks as one of the greatest of English actresses. About 1710, she retired to Acton, where she died.

Barry, Philip (1896-　). American dramatist. Born in Rochester, New York, he was graduated from Yale in 1919, and studied playwriting at George Pierce Baker's 47 Workshop at Harvard from 1919-22. His play, *You and I,* 1923, won the Harvard Prize, was successfully produced on Broadway and established him as one of the white hopes of the modern American theatre. His other dramatic works are *A Punch for Judy,* 1921; *The Youngest,* 1924; *In a Garden,* 1925; *White Wings,* 1926; *John,* 1927; *Paris Bound,* 1927; *Cock Robin* (with Elmer Rice), 1928; *Holiday,* 1928; *Hotel Universe,* 1930; *Tomorrow and Tomorrow,* 1931; *The Animal Kingdom,* 1932; *The Joyous Season,* 1934; *Bright Star,* 1935; *Spring Dance* (adapted from the play by Eleanor Golden and Eloise Barrangon), 1936; *Here Come the Clowns,* 1938; *The Philadelphia Story,* 1939.

His is the familiar case of the clown longing to play Hamlet and doomed to meet with real success only when he clings to the comedy which is his forte. For Barry's plays fall into two distinct categories, which bear striking resemblances, it is true: his gay drawing-room comedies and his more serious, inspirational, even symbolical dramas, which seek to see life's purpose and fathom its mysteries. His comedies, from *You and I* to *The Philadelphia Story,* have been strikingly successful commercially; his "significant" works, from *In a Garden* to *Here Come the Clowns,* have generally failed to be in the "hit" class. Yet the comedies might have failed without some of the qualities which characterize the dramas: the pathos, the tear beneath the laugh, the inherent integrity of the men and women whom he presents as heroes and heroines. Certainly they would have been less popular had the author not been a gifted dramatic craftsman and had they been less soundly constructed.

Barry, Spranger (1719-1777). Irish actor. Born in Dublin, where he made his first appearance in 1744. He went to London in 1746, playing Othello at Drury Lane. At the same theatre, later, he alternated the parts of Hamlet and Macbeth with Garrick, whose jealousy he so aroused that Barry moved in 1750 to Covent Garden, where he continued to challenge comparison with Garrick in leading Shakespearean roles. From 1758 to 1767 he retired to Dublin and Cork, but, having ruined himself in a theatrical venture, returned to London, where he appeared at the Haymarket Theatre, and later, again under Garrick's management, at the Drury Lane. In 1774 he returned to Covent Garden.

He was called "as handsome as a god; a silversmith turned romantic actor." Considered a great lover, Othello was thought his greatest role. His second wife, Ann Street Barry (1734-1801), whom he married in 1768, was distinguished between 1774 and 1798 as a tragic actress at Covent Garden, and as Desdemona was held to be superior to Mrs. Siddons.

Barrymore, Ethel (1879-). American actress. Daughter of Maurice and Georgiana Drew Barrymore and sister of Lionel and John Barrymore. Born in Philadelphia, her acting debut was with her grandmother, Mrs. John Drew. She made her first appearance as Julia in *The Rivals* in Montreal in 1894, and an engagement at the Empire, New York, followed. Appearing in England in 1897, when she was engaged by Henry Irving and played in *The Bells* and *Peter the Great*. She returned to America in 1898 and established herself as an outstanding actress. In 1900 she starred under Charles Frohman's management, in Clyde Fitch's *Captain Jinks of the Horse Marines,* scoring an instant success. Among the many plays in which she appeared were: *Alice Sit by the Fire; The Second Mrs. Tanqueray; Hamlet; The Lady of the Camelias; The Twelve Pound Look; Declassée; The Constant Wife; Whiteoaks.* In 1928 she opened the Ethel Barrymore Theatre, New York, where she appeared in *The Kingdom of God,* and as Lady Teazle in *The School for Scandal.*

Barrymore, Georgiana Drew (1856-1893). American actress. Wife of Maurice and mother of Lionel, Ethel and John Barrymore; and daughter of John and Louisa Drew. She was trained for the stage by her mother and appeared with her husband and other outstanding actors of the day including Edwin Booth and Lawrence Barrett.

Barrymore, John (1882-). American actor and screen star. Younger son of Maurice Barrymore and Georgiana Drew Barrymore; born in Philadelphia, and made his first stage appearance in 1903 in *Magda* at the Cleveland Theatre in Chicago. He shortly built up as great a reputation as an actor as his sister had achieved as an actress. The plays in which he appeared include: *The Fortune Hunter; Uncle Sam; The Yellow Ticket; Justice; Peter Ibbetson.* He is best remembered in London for his performance as Hamlet at the Haymarket Theatre in 1925, where he duplicated his New York success. His film career began in 1912, and since 1925, he has acted almost exclusively in motion pictures. Among the plays in which he appeared on the screen are *Sherlock Holmes; Arsene Lupin; Moby Dick; Rasputin; Reunion in Vienna; Grand Hotel; Dinner at Eight; Twentieth Century.* He returned to the stage in the late Spring of 1939 in *My Dear Children.*

Barrymore, Lionel (1878-   ). American actor. Born in London, the son of Maurice and Georgiana Drew Barrymore. Made his first appearance on the stage in Philadelphia under the sponsorship of his grandmother, Louisa Lane Drew, in 1893. He continued to play bits in companies headed by his uncle, John Drew, and made his first hit in *The Mummy and the Hummingbird.* Then in 1905 he played the title role in *Pantaloon,* Colonel Ibbetson in *Peter Ibbetson* and later played Macbeth and many other outstanding roles. After one appearance on the screen in 1909, he returned to the stage to take his place among the leading actors of his time. Later he went back to Hollywood and has been playing continuously in moving pictures.

Barrymore, Maurice (Herbert Blythe) (1848-1905). English-American actor. Father of Lionel, Ethel and John Barrymore. He was educated at Cambridge and began his stage career in 1875 with a provincial company in a production of *London Assurance.* The same year he played in the United States in Daly's *Under the Gaslight.* After his marriage to Georgianna Drew in 1876, he became a leading figure on the American and English stage and played opposite such actresses as Modjeska, Olga Nethersole, Lily Langtry and Mrs. Fiske.

Bartholomew Fair. Ben Jonson (English). Satiric comedy. 5 acts. 1614.
A robust satire on villainy and hypocrisy in London. To the Fair, among others, go Winwife, Quarlous, Justice Overdo, Dame Purecraft, Grace Welborn, the Justice's ward, and her fiancé, Cokes. After many adventures, at the end of the day, Quarlous wins a rich wife, Dame Purecraft; Grace and Winwife are betrothed; and the Justice learns that the masked bawd he was about to sentence is his own wife.

Bartós, Jan. See *Drama, Czecho-Slovak, since the First World War.*

Bat, The. Mary Roberts Rinehart and Avery Hopwood (American). Melodrama, 3 acts. 1920.
Somewhere in Miss Van Gorder's home is hidden the loot of a bank cashier who has escaped to the West. The search for this treasure brings nightly visitors to the house and leads to a murder. At last the treasure is found in a secret room, where a few of Miss Van Gorder's staunch friends wait for the murderer to return for his prize. He is finally captured, and the mystery solved.

Bataille, Henri (1872-1922). French dramatist and poet. Born at Nîmes. He won recognition as a poet with his *La Chambre Blanche* (1895) and *Le Beau Voyage* (1904). His long series of stage successes began with *Maman Colibri,* produced in 1904. His plays which are characterized by a preoccupation with erotic abnormalities include: *The Fair Leper,* 1897; *Thy Blood,* 1897; *The Enchantment,* 1900; *The Masque,* 1902; *The Declaration,* 1903; *The Wedding March,* 1905; *Resurrection* (from Tolstoy), 1902; *Poliche,* 1906; *Woman Unadorned,* 1908; *The Scandal,* 1909; *The Dream of an Evening of Love,* 1910; *The Foolish Virgin,* 1910; *The Child of Love,* 1911; *The Torches,* 1912; *The Night Moth,* 1913; *The Amazon,* 1916; *Our Image,* 1918; *Love Sisters,* 1919; *The Animator,* 1920; *The Man With a Rose,* 1921; *Tenderness,* 1921; *Possession,* 1922; *Human Flesh,* 1922.

Bateman, Mrs. Sidney F. (1823-1881). American dramatist. Born in New York, she was before her marriage Sidney Frances Cowell, daughter of the English low comedian who was so closely associated with the early history of the American theatre, and whose *Reminiscences* are filled with a wealth of anecdote. Sidney made her professional debut at about fourteen in New Orleans. In 1839 she married Hezekiah Linthicum Bateman in St. Louis, and from that time their careers are linked, for they both were actors and they both ended their days as managers of theatres in London. She began to write in 1857 and *Self* was produced in St. Louis at the People's Theatre in April of that year.

Among her other plays are *Geraldine, or The Master Passion,* 1859; *The Golden Calf,* 1857; *The Dead Secret* (adaptation of Wilkie Collins' story), 1877.

Bates, Blanche (1873-   ). American actress. Born in Portland, Oregon. She married George Creel, editor and publicist, in 1912. Her stage debut was made in San Francisco in 1894 in *The Picture;* her New York début under Augustin Daly's management in 1897 as Bianca in *The Taming of the Shrew.* Among the many plays in which she has had leading roles have been *The Musketeers,* 1899; *The Children of the Ghetto,* 1899; *Mme. Butterfly,* 1900; *Under Two Flags* (as Cigarette), 1901; *The Darling of the Gods,* 1902; *The Girl of the Golden West,* 1905; *East Lynne,* 1917; *The Famous Mrs. Fair,* 1919; *Dangerous Corner,* 1933.

Batten. Piece of 1 by 3 inch lumber; used for (1) stiffener—an edge to stiffen a flat; (2) to join two or more flats together; (3) *folding batten*—hinged parallel to stile to enable three-fold to close together; (4) used double on top and bottom of drop to stretch canvas and give it sufficient weight to hang well; (5) a round metal bar hung in from the flies on which spot or floodlights are attached.
See *Scenery; Lighting.*

Batten clamp. Metal clamp used for joining fly line to batten.
See *Scenery.*

Battle of Alcazar, The. Attributed to George Peele (English). Tragedy in verse. 5 acts. 1594.
The King of Barbary, dethroned by his uncle, persuades Sebastian, King of Portugal, to aid in recovering his throne. They are joined by Stukeley, Marquis of Ireland, and set sail for Morocco. In the battle of Alcazar, Sebastian and the two Moorish kings are killed, and Stukeley dies later of his wounds.

Baum, Vicki (1888-   ). German novelist and dramatist. Notable for her dramatic stories which have gained wide international popularity on the stage and the screen.

Born in Vienna, she studied music in that city. She began to write and made a reputation with her novel, *Grand Hotel,* which was afterwards dramatized and translated into English. As a result of this success, she became associated with motion pictures and went to Hollywood, where she established herself as a screen writer.

Her plays include: *The Divine Drudge; Grand Hotel; Summer Night.*

Bax, Clifford (1886-   ). British playwright. He was born in London, and was one of the founders of the Phoenix Society (1919-26). The plays which he has written include, among others, *The Marriage of the Soul,* 1913; *Polly* (adapted from Gay), 1922; *Midsummer Madness,* 1924; *Up-Stream,* 1925; *The Immortal Lady,* 1930; *April in August,* 1934.

Beam. (1) Hollow beam in ceiling for concealing lighting instruments for front lighting; (2) horizontal support of a platform.
See *Lighting.*

Beare and Ye Cub, Ye. Philip Alexander Bruce. Comedy. 1665.
Acted by non-professionals in Virginia in 1665. Earliest known record of a play in English being performed in the American colonies.

Bear pit theatres. See *Theatres, England, Elizabethan.*

Beat of the Wing, The. François de Curel (French). Drama. 3 acts. 1906.
An explorer who has conquered fresh territory for French colonization, after being hailed at home as a hero, has returned to the tropics fortified in pride, believing himself authorized to deal despotically with an inferior race.

Beau. Word used during the Reformation for the fop, or dandy, who frequented the contemporary playhouses in elegant apparel calculated to appeal to the ladies and make them amenable to flirting and trifling.

Beau Brummell. Clyde Fitch (American). Drama. 4 acts. 1890.
The play deals with the rise and fall of Beau Brummell, famous Regency dandy, who loves Marianne, a commoner's daughter, loses favor at court, and finally dies in poverty.

Beaumarchais, Pierre Augustin Caron de (1732-1799). French dramatist. Writer of satirical comedies, and known chiefly in England and America for the operatic adaptations of his *The Barber of Seville* and *The Marriage of Figaro* by Rossini and Mozart respectively.

Born in Paris, he was the son of a watchmaker, whose calling he at first followed. His gifts for invention led to his introduction to the court of Louis XV, and he became watchmaker to the king. He traveled extensively in Spain, and his first play of importance was based on those travels. As agent of the French government, Beaumarchais secured considerable supplies for the American colonies in the War of Independence. He was imprisoned in 1792, but was released, and after living in Holland and England, returned to Paris where he died. His best contribution to dramatic theory is to be found in his *Essai sur la genre dramatique sérieux*. Best known of his plays are: *Eugenie,* 1767 (which provided the material for Goethe's *Clavigo*); *The Two Friends,* 1770; *The Barber of Seville,* 1775; *The Marriage of Figaro,* 1784.

Beaumont, Francis (1584-1616). Elizabethan dramatist. Educated at Oxford and published his first verse in 1602. With John Fletcher he formed the famous writing combination of Beaumont and Fletcher, and is considered to have done the most important part of the work on the joint plays. He was buried in Westminster Abbey.

His own plays include: *The Woman Hater; The Knight of the Burning Pestle.* Those he wrote with Fletcher: *Philaster, or Love Lies a-Bleeding; A Maid's Tragedy; The Coxcomb.*

Beaumont and Fletcher. English dramatists. Elizabethan dramatic collaborators, associates of Ben Jonson and his cronies of the Mermaid Tavern group. They wrote together *Four Plays in One; Cupid's Revenge; The Captain; The Scornful Lady; The Beggar's Bush.*

See also *Beaumont, Francis.*

See also *Fletcher, John.*

Beautiful Despot, The. Nikolai Yevreinov (Russian). Comedy. 3 acts. 1906.

A gentleman of the old school feels co-existent within him the Liberal and the Despot. Reading the diary of his great-grandfather makes him yearn to escape to that period. Accordingly, in his country estate, he acts as if he were living in 1808. A friend, who calls to ask for an article commending the present for its economic gains, learns that the Beautiful Despot has triumphed over the Liberal in the Soul of the Master.

Beaver Coat, The. Gerhart Hauptmann (German). Satiric comedy. 4 acts. 1893.

A comedy dealing with the social rivalry between town and country housewives, shopkeepers and grocers.

The Beaux' Stratagem. George Farquhar (English) Comedy. 1707.

One of the last of the comedy of manners, written in the spirit which made Congreve famous. It is marked by spontaneity and rollicking good humor. The author wrote it in six weeks while in the throes of an illness which proved fatal. The plot concerns Archer and Aimwell, two down-on-their-luck gentlemen who disguise themselves as master and servant; the innkeeper Boniface; Scrub, servant to a brutal squire and confidant to young ladies; Lady Bountiful, the squire's mother and benefactress of the countryside, whose name has passed into the language and is used to describe a generous lady.

Beck, Martin (1868-   ). German-born American theatre manager, owner, impresario. From a poor immigrant boy, stranded in the United States when an acting company disbanded, to manager and head of all the Radio-Keith-Orpheum circuit of vaudeville houses is Martin Beck's record. It was he who, in 1899, planned and later perfected the efficient booking system of the Circuit. Built not only the New York theatre which bears his name, but the Palace and the State Lake Theatres in Chicago, and an Orpheum in Berlin. It was he who brought the D'Oyly Carte Opera Company to this country for their first engagement in 1934. He is now head of the Martin Beck Theatre Corporation. He built the Martin Beck Theatre, which is famous as being the only theatre on Broadway on which there is no mortgage.

Becket. Alfred Lord Tennyson (English). Tragedy. 4 acts. Printed 1893.
Thomas à Becket enrages Henry II of England, first, because he does not consider himself worthy of being appointed Archbishop of Canterbury; and, second, once appointed, he serves the church with complete devotion, refusing any compromise with the State. Becket is finally murdered by the King's men.

Becky Sharp. Langdon Mitchell (American). Comedy. 4 acts. Based on William Makepeace Thackeray's "Vanity Fair."
Becky Sharp is introduced as Miss Crawley's companion in London and Rawdon Crawley's charmer. She is next seen at the Duchess of Richmond's ball in Brussels on the eve of Waterloo. Back in London, she flirts with Lord Steyne and is discovered by the jealous Rawdon. Lastly, she is in lodging in Pumpernickel, bringing Amelia and Dobbin together and managing the affair with Lord Sedley.

Becque, Henri François (1837-1899). French dramatist. An exponent of the naturalistic drama in France.
Born in Paris, he began his career as a dramatist with a production of *L'Enfant Prodigue* at the Vaudeville, Paris, 1868. His works include: *Sardanapalus,* an opera, 1867; *The Prodigal Child,* 1868; *Michel Pauper,* 1870; *The Abduction,* 1871; *The Merry-Go-Round,* 1878; *Virtuous Women,* 1880; *The Vultures* (*Les Corbeaux*), 1881; *The Parisian Woman,* 1885; *Madeleine,* 1896; *Widowed,* 1897; *A Four-Handed Game,* 1897; *The Departure,* 1897; *An Execution,* 1897; *The Harlequins* (finished by Henri de Nousanne), 1910.

Beddoes, Thomas Lovell (1803-1849). British poet and dramatist. A son of Thomas Beddoes, the physician, he was born at Clifton, England, and was educated at the Charterhouse and at Pembroke College, Oxford, where he published his first play, *The Improvisatore,* in 1820. He lived much abroad, studied and practiced medicine in Germany and Switzerland and identified himself with the democratic movement. His other plays include: *The Bride's Tragedy,* 1822; *Death's Jest Book,* 1850.

Beebe, Lucius (1902-   ). American journalist, author, critic. Since 1929 on the staff of the New York *Herald Tribune,* and writer of the syndicate column *This New York.* In 1939 he became drama commentator on radio station WOR. He is the author of poems, of books on Villon and Edwin Arlington Robinson; of *People on Parade* (with Jerome Zerbe, Jr.), 1934; *Boston and the Boston Legend,* 1935; *High Iron,* 1938.

Beerbohm, Max (1872-   ). British critic, essayist and caricaturist. Beerbohm, half-brother to Sir Herbert Tree, was born in London and educated at the Charterhouse and Merton College, Oxford. For many years he was dramatic critic of the *Saturday Review.* A number of volumes of his caricatures and critical essays have been published. *Zuleika Dobson,* 1911, is probably his best known work.

Beggar on Horseback. George S. Kaufman and Marc Connelly (American). Fantastic comedy. 1924. Incidental music by Deems Taylor.

Neil McRae, exhausted by overwork and discouraged by lack of funds, is considering marrying rich Gladys Cady. Neil's doctor has advised him to do it so that he can take a rest and study music. Cynthia Mason, the girl Neil loves, agrees with Dr. Rice. Neil falls asleep and sees in a dream his marriage to Gladys. The bride's wedding bouquet is made of banknotes; her father wears golf knickers. At the reception Neil tries to play for the guests, but the music turns to jazz as his fingers strike the keys. Neil is initiated into the mysteries of Cady's "widget" factory and paid millions of dollars for doing practically nothing. His friend the doctor, who turns up as head waiter in a restaurant, tells him to murder all his new family. One by one he kills them with his paper cutter and is brought to trial. He defends his act as justifiable because the victims interfered with his music. Cynthia appears, and together boy and girl dance a love ballet. Neil is condemned to work in the Cady Consolidated Art Factory, where masterpieces are made to order behind bars. He chooses to die instead, but before he has a chance he wakes up—and Cynthia informs him she has changed her mind and will marry him.

Beggars' Bush, The. John Fletcher and perhaps Massenger (English). Drama. 5 acts. 1622.

Florez, heir to an earldom but ignorant of his rights, is in love with Bertha, an heiress who is equally ignorant of her rights. Through the intervention of a group of beggars, Gerrard, the father of Florez and a victim of a usurper together with Hubert, a nobleman, are able to adjust all matters so that the identity of Florez and Bertha is revealed and they obtain their birthrights.

Beggar's Opera, The. John Gay (English). Lyrical drama. 1728.

A musical satire, frequently bawdy, on "polite society." Dean Swift suggested that it be written, and it shows the influence of the author of "Gulliver." Its thrusts against the thieving politicians of the day won the favor of the public, and its humor and lively tunes still draw audiences, as attested by numerous recent revivals.

Thieves and bandits are its principal characters. The hero, Macheath, is the leader of a band of highwaymen, a handsome ruffian, attracted by and attractive to the ladies. His secret wife, Polly Peachum, really loves him and is constant in spite of her mother's recommendations to be less steadfast. Macheath proposes once too often to a lady, is arrested, escapes, is recaptured, brought to trial, condemned to death, reprieved. Whereupon he feels it time to acknowledge openly at last that Polly is his wife.

Beginners, please! British call-boy's request for the actors to take their places on stage for the opening scene of a play.

Behn, Aphra (1640-1689). English poet, dramatist and novelist. The first professional woman dramatist in history.

Born at Wye, Kent, she was taken when a child to Surinam, in Dutch Guiana. There she met the romantic chieftain Oroonoko, the hero of her best novel, and gathered material for this romantic tale. After her return to England in 1658, she married a Dutch merchant, Behn, after whose death she went to Holland for a short time as a diplomatic agent. She produced poems, novels and plays as coarsely exuberant, as full of wit and of amorous intrigue as she was herself. Her work was highly praised by Dryden and Otway. She was buried in Westminster Abbey.

Among her many works are *The Forc'd Marriage,* 1671; *The Amorous Prince,* 1671; *The Town Fop,* 1677.

Behrman, Samuel Nathaniel (1893-   ). American dramatist. Behrman, who was born in Worcester, Massachusetts, was attracted to the stage at an early age. While still in his teens he wrote a vaudeville skit in which he acted himself, and in which he got as near Broadway as Fourteenth St., New York City. In 1916 he received an A.B. degree from Harvard, and in 1918 an M.A. from Columbia. For a time after that he worked on the *New York Times Book Review* and contributed to a number of magazines. By 1926 he was back in the theatre, as a press agent for George Abbott's production of *Broadway.* The following year, 1927, the Theatre Guild produced Behrman's *The Second Man,* and his reputation was made. Then came (with Kenyon Nicholson) *Love is Like That,* 1927; *Serena Blandish,* 1929; *Meteor,* 1929; *Brief Moment,* 1931; *Biography,* 1932; *Rain from Heaven,* 1934; *End of Summer,* 1936; *Amphitryon 38* (adapted from comedy by Jean Giraudoux), 1937; *Wine of Choice,* 1938; *No Time for Comedy,* 1939. He has also done considerable writing for the motion pictures.

His protagonists, though intelligent, feeling members of society, are content to be tolerant observers of life rather than battlers in the fray; they prefer a compromise to a fight; are intellectual rather than emotional. Their very dispassionateness renders them somewhat unheroic: they choose the easiest way (thus the hero of *No Time for Comedy* chooses to write light comedy instead of propagandist drama); they may even laugh at injustice because unable to cope with it (thus Marian Froude in *Biography*). Because they usually find no real solution to life's problems, Behrman's plays are apt to be inconclusive, to leave the spectator up in the air. But this fault, if it be a fault, is redeemed by the scintillating brilliance of his dialogue and the fact that his heroes, in the last analysis, are the finest flower of civilization, and that for that reason alone their existence is justified. Their tolerance comes from seeing every side of a question; though they may be indifferent, they are never undiscriminating.

Belasco, David (1859-1931). American dramatist, producer, actor. Born in San Francisco. Early theatrical experience, from call-boy to play-adapter. First stage appearance, 1871, in the California Theatre in San Francisco, followed by a barnstorming tour of California and Nevada. He met Boucicault, from whom he learned much of playwriting. He acted with Booth and McCullough in 1874. His first play to attract attention was *Hearts of Oak,* first produced in Chicago in 1879. In 1880 he went to New York, where he became stage manager of the Madison Square Theatre, and later, 1886, an associate of Daniel Frohman at the Lyceum Theatre. Thereafter he grew to be one of the most powerful producers and playwrights in the history of the American stage. He was a realist in staging. His results were reached, not by suggestion, but by putting the actual thing on the stage. In Alice Bradley's *The Governor's Lady,* 1912, he put an exact duplicate of a Childs restaurant on the stage. When producing *The Easiest Way,* by Eugene Walter, 1909, with a scene laid in an Eighth Avenue theatrical boarding house, he actually bought one and used it intact—a perfect satisfaction of his passion for the literal. The best known of his numerous plays are: with H. C. De Mille, *Lord Chumley,* 1888, and *Men and Women,* 1890; *The Heart of Maryland,* 1895; *DuBarry,* 1901; *The Darling of the Gods,* 1902, with Luther Long; *The Girl of the Golden West,* 1905; *Temperamental Journey,* 1913; *Salvage,* 1925; and *The Return of Peter Grimm,* 1921. He opened the first Belasco (now Republic) in 1902; and the Stuyvesant which he built (now the Belasco) in 1907. Belasco's collection of pressbooks, photographs, prompt books and theatrical designs are in the New York Public Library.

Bell, Dame Florence Evelyn Eleanore (1851-1930). British author. The daughter of Sir Joseph Olliffe, physician, she was born in Paris, and in 1876 married Sir Hugh Bell, Bart., the ironmaster. She wrote essays, novels and plays and was created D.B.E. in 1918 for her services during the World War.

Among her plays are *L'Indécis* (in which Coquelin appeared) ; *Time is Money; The Show Room;* and *Angela.*

Bellamy, Mrs. George Ann (1731?-1788). English actress. Played Juliet to Garrick's Romeo at Drury Lane in 1750. She rivaled Mrs. Cibber who was playing at Covent Garden with Barry. Their respective merits were the subject of lively controversy.

Belle of New York. Hugh Morton (American). Musical comedy. 2 acts and 6 scenes. 1897.

Morton is a pseudonym for C. M. S. McClellan. Gustave Kerker did the music for this extravaganza about a young spendthrift who falls in love with a Salvation Army lassie, Violet Gray. Violet persuades the young wastrel to see the error of his ways. The boy is denounced by his father, a hypocritical reformer, but in the end is restored to his fortune.

The producer was George W. Lederer, the Ziegfeld of his day, who had an enormous commercial success with it and added a shining new star to the theatrical firmament by selecting an unknown chorus girl, seventeen-year-old Edna May, to play the Salvation Army lassie.

Belle's Stratagem, The. Mrs. Hannah Cowley (English). Comedy. 5 acts. 1780.

Doricourt returns from his travels to marry Letitia Hardy, whom he has not seen since his childhood. He is not particularly pleased with her. She determines to win him by first disgusting him by playing a country hoyden, and then by conquering him with her sprightliness at a masquerade. She is successful.

Bells, The. Emile Erckmann and Alex Chatrian (French). Drama. 3 acts. 1878. The story of a burgomaster haunted by the consciousness of an undiscovered murder that he has committed. It provided Sir Henry Irving, in the role of Mathias, with one of his most successful parts.

Ben-Ami, Jacob (1890-   ). Jewish actor. Born in Minsk, Russia, Ben-Ami made a great impression on New Yorkers when he appeared in that city with the Yiddish Art Theatre in 1918-19. Arthur Hopkins engaged him and had him learn English; his first English-speaking role was as Peter Krumback in *Samson and Delilah* in 1920. His career on the English-speaking stage includes roles in *The Idle Inn,* 1922; *The Failures,* 1923; *Man and the Masses,* 1924; *John,* 1927; *Diplomacy,* 1928. In 1926 he staged *The Goat Song* for the Theatre Guild. From 1929-31 he was with the Civic Repertory Theatre under the aegis of Eva Le Gallienne, and acted in *The Sea Gull, The Cherry Orchard, Camille,* etc. After that he appeared in *Payment Deferred, Evensong,* 1934 and other plays.

Benavente y Martinez, Jacinto (1866-   ). Spanish dramatist. Born at Madrid. His first play was *El Nido Ajeno,* 1894. He became the most popular Spanish dramatist, specializing in light comedies. He won the Nobel Prize for Literature, 1922. His plays include *Saturday Night,* 1903; *Vested Interests,* 1907; *La Malquerida,* 1913; *Fabricated Truth,* 1933; *Bread Eaten From the Hand,* 1934.

See *Drama, Spanish 20th Century, before the First World War.*

Benchley, Robert Charles (1889-   ). American dramatic critic, humorist, actor. Born in Worcester, Massachusetts; A. B., Harvard, 1912. Editor of *New York Tribune* Sunday Magazine, 1916; *New York Tribune Graphic,* 1917; managing editor of *Vanity Fair* 1919-20; contributed to *New York World,* 1920-29. He was dramatic editor of *Life* magazine, 1920-29; and of *The New Yorker* magazine since 1929. He has appeared as an actor in the *Music Box Revue,* 1923-24, and in numerous movietone shorts for Fox Film Company and Metro-Goldwyn-Mayer Pictures, as well as in some longer films. He is the author of a number of humorous books.

Benefit performance. The custom of giving a starring actor the receipts or "benefit" of one evening during his season with a company originated in the English theatre of the 17th century. If bad weather or other unpredictable obstacles kept away the crowds, another benefit performance was sometimes allowed. The authors always got the proceeds of the third night of a run.

Today benefit performances in New York are held chiefly by the Actors' Fund
and other organizations, and only in rare instances (as for Don Marquis) is the
benefit for one person.

Ben Hur. William Young (American). Drama. 1899.

A dramatization of General Lew Wallace's novel of the same name. Edgar Stillman Kelley did the incidental music, and Klaw and Erlanger produced it at the
Broadway Theatre, New York, the first time it was given on any stage. William Hart
played Messala.

This tale of the Christ is laid in the East at the beginning of the Christian era.
Ben Hur, the young head of a rich and noble family, lives in Jerusalem with his
widowed mother and little sister. When the new Roman governor arrives in state,
the family goes up to the roof to see the procession, and Judah accidentally dislodges
a tile which fells the governor. He is accused of murder. His erstwhile friend, the
Roman noble Messala, turns against him. He is condemned, his property confiscated,
and sent to the galleys for life. Ben Hur is converted to Christianity through the
miracles of Jesus. A chariot race and other exciting incidents punctuate the plot. The
play was sumptuously staged, with a chorus of eighty voices and one hundred and
eighty-one extras.

Bennett (Enoch), Arnold (1867-1931). English writer. Notable for his
creation of a vivid picture of life in the Staffordshire Potteries district with his novels
of the *Five Towns.*

Born near Hanley, in the Five Towns, or Potteries, and educated at the middle
school, Newcastle-under-Lyme, he studied law with his father and afterwards with
a London solicitor, but, after winning a prize in *Tit-Bits* and getting a story accepted
by *The Yellow Book,* turned to journalism. He was an editor from 1893 to 1900,
when he retired to his cottage at Fontainebleau and devoted his life to writing. Only
twice was Bennett particularly successful as a playwright. *Milestones,* written in
collaboration with Edward Knoblock and produced in 1912, ran for 607 performances, and *The Great Adventure* based on his novel *Buried Alive* (1913) achieved a
run of over eighteen months.

Benois, Alexander Nikolayevich (1870-   ). Russian scene designer and
painter. Designed scenery and wrote scenarios for several ballets of which the outstanding one is Stravinsky's *Petruchka.*

Berenice. Jean Racine (French). Historical tragedy. 5 acts. 1670.

Berenice, daughter of Agrippa I (grandson of Herod the Great), and wife of
her uncle Herod, king of Chalcis, meets Titus, who falls in love with her. After a
long struggle with his conscience, he gives up love for duty.

The heroine is the Bernice of the Bible, Acts XXV. It is interesting to note that
Corneille and Racine both wrote plays about her at the same time at the suggestion of
Henriette d'Orléans.

Bergner, Elisabeth (1900-). Austrian actress. She studied for the stage at the Vienna Conservatory, 1915-19; made her first appearance on the stage at the City Theatre, Zurich, under the direction of Dr. Alfred Reucker, in the autumn of 1919; and after playing a number of small parts made an immediate success as Ophelia in *Hamlet* with Alexander Moissi. She appeared in Vienna, Munich and Berlin, including several Shakespearean productions at the Deutscher-Volkstheater under Max Reinhardt. Her international reputation was won by her remarkable success as Joan in *Saint Joan*, 1924. Further successes included her playing of Mrs. Cheyney in *The Last of Mrs. Cheyney* under Barnovsky at the Koeniggraetzer Theater, Berlin, 1926; Tessa in *The Constant Nymph* at the same theatre, 1927; and Portia in *The Merchant of Venice*, 1927. In 1928 she made a playing tour through Holland, Denmark, Sweden, Germany and Austria. Leading parts in *Strange Interlude, Romeo and Juliet* and *Amphitryon 38* followed. After 1931 she spent two years in Paris in cinema. Her first appearance in England was at the Opera House, Manchester, November 21, 1933, as Gemma Jones in *Escape Me Never;* the part was repeated in London December 8, 1933, with tremendous success. She played the same part in New York at the Shubert Theatre, January 21, 1935, duplicating her London success. In 1937 she played the lead in *The Boy David* in London. Her first cinema part was in *Der Evangelimann*, 1923; this was followed by: *Nju; The Violinist of Florence; Fraulein Elsa; Dreaming Lips; Ariane; Catherine the Great; Escape Me Never; As You Like It.*

Bergstrom, Hjalmar (1868-1914). Danish dramatist. Born in Copenhagen, the only child of parents in moderate circumstances. His first attempt at playwriting (when he was 13) was some verse added to one of the tragedies of Oehlenschlager, the Danish dramatist. In 1893 he obtained his degree of Ph. D., and from that year until 1905 he taught in the Commercial High School at Copenhagen. At the same time he did a great deal of writing of novels, short stories, and essays. But it was not until the appearance of his first play, *Ida's Wedding,* in 1902 that he received general recognition as a writer of exceptional talent. Other plays followed in quick succession. Bergstrom was considered one of the most promising of the group of young playwrights in Denmark.

He wrote the following plays: *Ida's Wedding,* 1902; *Mint Street, 39,* 1903; *Lynggard & Co.,* 1905; *Karen Borneman,* 1907; *The Golden Fleece,* 1908; *The Birthday Party,* 1910; *In the Swim,* 1910; *The Way to God,* 1912; *The Day of Trial,* 1915; *What People Talk Of,* 1915.

Berkeley (California) Greek Theatre. Founded by the Berkeley Playmakers at the University of California in 1923; it has a national and international reputation as a short play experimental theatre and is also famous for its play contests.

Berkeley Square. John Balderston (American). Play. 3 acts. 1928.
The spirit of Peter Standish, a 1928 American is projected back into the year 1784 when his namesake and most distinguished ancestor, also an American, first visited the ancestral home of the Standish-Pettigrew family in Berkeley Square,

London. Peter, knowing the future, is constantly making *faux pas*. He falls in love with the daughter of the household in 1784 and she dies. When he returns to 1928, he still loves her and plans to live with her memory.

Berlin Court Theatre. A pre-war German theatre devoted to performances for the entertainment of the nobility. It was inferior in most respects. Later it became the Berlin State Theatre.

Berlin State Theatre (German). Until the First World War known as the Berlin Court Theatre, a playhouse redeemed from consistent mediocrity and almost total obsoleteness to a living organization by the director-producer, Jessner. Jessner was succeeded as manager by Fehling.

Bernard, Jean-Jacques (1888-   ). French dramatist. Known chiefly as the writer of subtle dramas which avoid both action and rhetoric and reduce plot and dialogue to their lowest terms. His doctrine was, "The theatre is above all the art of the unexpressed." He was born at Enghien, the son of Tristan Bernard.

His plays include: *The Journey à Deux*, 1909; *The Joy of Sacrifice*, 1912; *The House That Was Spared*, 1919; *The Fire Slow to Rekindle*, 1921; *Martine*, 1922; *The Invitation to Travel*, 1924; *The Springtime of Others*, 1924; *Denis Marette*, 1925; *The Soul of Distress*, 1926; *The Secret of Arvers*, 1926; *The King of Malousie*, 1928.

Bernard, Tristan (1866-   ). French dramatist. A writer of farces and comedies after the manner of Plautus, using disguises, concealments, mistaken identities and all sorts of impossible situations that upset any assumption of dignity.

His plays include: *The Only Bandit of the Village*, 1898; *English As It Is Spoken*, 1899; *The Touring Club Bride*, 1899; *The Mathieu Case*, 1901; *The Gang at León*, 1902; *Triplepatte* (with A. Godfernaux), 1905; *The Twins of Brighton*, 1908; *The Ambulant Flirt*, 1908; *The Ardent Artilleryman*, 1910; *The Little Café*, 1911; *The Nocturnal Visitors*, 1912; *The Soubigou Beacons*, 1912; *Jeanne Doré*, 1913; *Prince Charming*, 1914; *The Force of Lying*, 1914; *The Cheap Cravat*, 1919; *The Idea of M. Dumorel*, 1920; *The Blue Ribbon*, 1920; *Embrace Me*, 1923; *She Also*, 1924.

Bernardoniades. A type of comedy in 18th century Viennese drama in which the chief character was a Hanswurst type called Bernardon. Joseph Von Kurz was the famous low comedian who created the Bernardon and was author of many such burlesques.

Bernhardt, Sarah (1845-1923). French actress. She was born in Paris, of French and Dutch parentage and of Jewish descent. At the age of thirteen, she began the most serious training for the stage then available in Europe, and was entered as a pupil at the Paris Conservatoire. In 1862 she made her debut at the Comédie Francaise in a small part in Racine's *Iphigenie*. For this performance she received only the slight notice which the part merited, and she passed on to try her fortune in burlesque.

As she was unable to sing in tune, she could make no hit in this, and her first real success was in *Le Passant,* by François Coppée, at the Odéon in 1869. After the run of this play, France was at war with Prussia. Sarah, throughout the bombardment of Paris, worked long hours in an ambulance. When the Odéon reopened in 1872, she played Cordelia in a French version of *King Lear,* and the queen in Victor Hugo's *Ruy Blas.* She was already complete mistress of the arts of the stage. In 1874 she rose to greater heights as an artist. As Phedre in Racine's play, she scored a triumph. In 1877 as Dona Sol in Victor Hugo's *Hernani* she was acclaimed a genius. During this period she established herself as the best known of French actresses and about this time began to circulate the Bernhardt legends which were soon to become reality through her triumphant appearances in the capitals of Europe, in both the Americas, in Australia and Egypt. She made her American debut in 1880. Among her greatest triumphs were in *Fédora; Theodora,* 1884; *La Tosca,* 1887; *Cléopâtre,* 1890; *L'Aiglon; Frou-Frou* (written by herself); *La Dame aux Camelias; Hamlet.* In 1912 Bernhardt made a film *Queen Elizabeth* in which she played the title role.

At the age of fifty-five, "the divine Sarah" was impersonating young men with astounding success. In 1915 she had suffered the amputation of a leg, but she travelled to the front to give performances to the troops, made a further tour of America and, in 1922, of Italy. She was already starting to conquer fresh fields and was engaged in a film production when she was taken ill on March 21, 1923. On March 26, she died at her home in Paris.

Bernstein, Aline (1882-   ). American designer. Began her career by designing dresses at the Neighborhood Playhouse, New York, for *The Little Clay Cart,* 1924. Has since designed settings for the Theatre Guild including *Caprice* and *Reunion in Vienna;* for Gilbert Miller, *Tomorrow and Tomorrow* and *The Animal Kingdom;* for the Civic Repertory Theatre, *The Cherry Orchard; The Sea-Gull; Camille; Peter Pan; Romeo and Juliet; Liliom.* For Herman Shumlin she has designed settings for *Grand Hotel; Clear All Wires. Late Christopher Bean; Firebird; A Good Woman; For the People; Thunder on the Left; Mackerel Skies; Judgment Day; The Children's Hour; Night in the House.* Her costumes for *The Little Foxes,* 1939, have been highly praised.

See also *Museum of Costume Art, Neighborhood Playhouse.*

Bernstein, Henry Leon Gustave Charles (1875-   ). French dramatist. One of the Naturalist School of French dramatists, he is noted as a master of stagecraft. Born in Paris of Jewish parents; began writing for the stage in 1900.

He wrote *Le Marché,* 1900; *La Détour, Joujou,* 1902; *Brother Jacques* (with Pierre Veber), 1903; *The Fold,* 1904; *The Tempest,* 1905; *The Talon,* 1906; *The Thief,* 1906; *Samson,* 1907; *Israel,* 1908; *After Me,* 1911; *The Assault,* 1912; *The Secret,* 1919; *To the Heights,* 1917; *Judith,* 1922; *The Gallery of Mirrors,* 1926; *Felix,* 1926; *The Poison,* 1927; *Melo,* 1929, etc.

Bertoldo. Legendary Italian clown whose exploits led to the phrase "imperturbable Bertoldo," meaning, not to be thrown off one's guard by unexpected circumstance.

Besier, Rudolf (1878-   ). British dramatist. Born in Java, of Dutch extraction, educated at Elizabeth College, Guernsey, and Heidelberg; for some years a journalist, about 1908 he took to writing for the stage. He is noted chiefly for his play *The Barretts of Wimpole Street* which provided Katharine Cornell with a resounding success.

His plays include: *The Virgin Goddess,* 1906; *Olive Latimer's Husband,* 1909; *Lady Patricia,* 1911; *Kings and Queens,* 1915; *Kultur at Home,* 1916; *A Run for His Money,* 1916; *Secrets* (with May Edginton), 1922; *The Barretts of Wimpole Street,* 1930.

Betrothal, The. Maurice Maeterlinck (Belgian). Fairy play. 1918.

Sequel to *The Bluebird,* Maeterlinck's most popular play, and featuring many of the same characters, this really points the same moral: that happiness, though sought afar, often lies very near home.

Tyltyl is seventeen and, with the help of the fairy Bérylune, is seeking the girl he shall love. Six village maidens sent by the fairy to woo him charm the youth but leave him more perplexed than ever. So he sets forth to consult his ancestors, guided by Light and Destiny. The ancestors, a motley crew, are interested not in the six maidens, but in a silent white-veiled figure who follows in their train. But since Tyltyl is unable to remember her, he cannot see her clearly. Next he visits his unborn children, the littlest of whom again chooses the lady in white. Tyltyl awakes from his dream in his mother's cottage to greet some visiting neighbors, accompanied by their daughter Joy. In her the lad recognizes the fair unknown of his dreams and the girl to whom he gave his bird long ago.

Betterton, Thomas (1635-1710). English actor. The foremost actor of the English stage during the Restoration and also a prominent manager. In 1661 he was engaged as a leading player at the theatre in Lincoln's Inn Fields under Sir William D'Avenant. His interpretation of Hamlet was said to have stemmed from that of Joseph Taylor, who is presumed to have been instructed in the role by Shakespeare himself. (It was the recollection of Taylor's performance as Hamlet that enabled Sir William D'Avenant to impart to Betterton the examples and tradition established by the author and which provided a model that has endured to the present day.) After D'Avenant's death Betterton assumed the managership of his company, which was, however, doomed to failure. Thereafter he acted in the Haymarket Theatre, which was built especially for him and his company. He contributed much to the improvement of stage settings as a result of a trip to France at the command of Charles II and his study there of theatrical styles and the plays of Molière.

His principal performances were in *King Lear; Macbeth; Othello; King Henry VIII; Love For Love; The Provoked Wife;* and *The Way of the World.* His last appearance was on April 25, 1710, in *The Maid's Tragedy.*

Betty, William Henry West (The Young Roscius) (1791-1874). British actor. Born at Shrewsbury, of educated parents, he was taken to Ireland and appeared on the stage in Belfast with conspicuous success as Osman in Aaron Hill's *Zara,* a version of Voltaire's *Zaire,* 1803. He appeared subsequently in Dublin, Waterford, Cork, and Glasgow, augmenting his repertoire to include Hamlet. By the time he reached Edinburgh, his success was so great that a critic who denied his abilities had to leave town. His great success both in Ireland and Scotland earned for him the name of the Young Roscius. In 1804, he made his first appearance at Covent Garden, the crowd being so great that people were injured striving to gain admission. On one occasion the Commons adjourned to see him play Hamlet. His extraordinary career as a boy actor ended in 1808; after three years spent at Christ's College, Cambridge, he returned to the stage in 1811, but his success was only moderate.

An account of his life was published, and at the request of the king, he was presented to the Prince of Wales.

Beyerlein, Franz Adam (1871-   ). German writer. Born at Meissen, Saxony, he made his reputation in 1903 as the author of a novel and a play, both of which dealt in a startling manner with conditions in the German army. Of these the novel *Jena or Sedan?* was translated into English, 1904. His other works include a life of *Frederick the Great* in three volumes, 1922-1924, and two plays, *Taps,* 1903; *The Winter Camp,* 1906.

Beyond Human Power, I and II. Björnstjerne Björnson (Norwegian). Realistic drama. 2 acts in each part. 1883.

The first part deals with the problems of religion; and the second part with the struggle between labor and capital.

Pastor Sang is praying for his paralyzed wife, Clara, when an avalanche descends upon the community, and, strangely enough turns away from the church. The entire country-side believes a miracle has occurred and they come to pray at the church.

The Pastor continues to pray that his wife may walk again. Finally as the church bells ring, and before a crowd, Clara Sang rises from her bed and walks to her husband, but the strain is too great for them both. The wife dies and in a moment, her husband drops dead beside her.

Beyond the Horizon. Eugene O'Neill (American). Realistic tragedy. 3 acts. 1920. This tragedy of frustration was O'Neill's first important full length play and won the Pulitzer Prize.

Andrew Mayo is a son of the soil; his brother Robert an intellectual, a dreamer, filled with wanderlust and a love of the sea and of far places. As he is about to leave for a sea voyage with an uncle, Robert decides he loves Ruth, a neighbor, and stays on the farm to marry her. Andrew, who hoped to wed the girl himself, angrily goes off to sea in his brother's place. Three years pass. Robert is miserable on the farm and unhappy with his wife, who has come to the conclusion it was Andrew she loved. Then Andrew's return brings disillusionment to both of them: to Ruth because he has forgotten her; to Robert because he is still dull and commonplace, untouched by his experiences. Five more years go by. This time Andrew has been to the Argentine, where he has made a pile of money and then lost it speculating. Robert has tuberculosis; the child who was his one consolation is dead and the farm bankrupt. Robert chides his brother with having been untrue to himself: having made money his ideal, he has thrown even that away. Then the thwarted adventurer dies, happy at last and free to take the trip "beyond the horizon" he has always longed for.

Bibiena family. See *Galli-Bibiena family.*

Bibliothèque de la Ville de Paris. See *Drama, French, 18th century, French Revolution.*

Billboard, The. Periodical published weekly at Cincinnati, Ohio. A theatrical tradepaper with special emphasis on the amateur theatre, circus, carnival, etc.

Billboard Index. The *Billboard Index* of the New York legitimate stage since 1920 includes comparative figures of seasons in various cities; an alphabetical list of plays and casts; theatres with plays represented; theatre seating capacities; managers with plays represented; dramatists and musical players; stage directors, designers and scenic executors; composers; lyric writers; librettists; dance directors; sketch writers; length of runs; theatre awards and prizes; address lists of everyone represented in the theatre, motion pictures and radio; theatrical costume firms and theatrical transfer firms; drama critics and theatrical editors of the United States; The New York appearance of leading players; New York productions of leading managers.

Billing. An announcement or advertisement to indicate the cast, title, authorship, composer and all other persons involved in a theatrical or any amusement production, and arranged in the order of each person's importance.

Binyon, Robert Laurence (1869-   ). British poet. Born at Lancaster, August 10, he was educated in St. Paul's School, London, and Trinity College, Oxford. He entered the British Museum in 1893, and became assistant keeper in the department of Oriental prints and drawings, 1909, retiring as keeper of the department in 1933. At Oxford Binyon won the Newdigate prize and his first volume of poetry was published in 1894. Several additional volumes appeared subsequently, including *The Death of Adam and other Poems,* 1904; *The Four Years,* 1919, and *Sophro the Wise,* 1927, as well as a number of works on the history of art, including scenic design, on which he was an acknowledged authority. His best known work, however, is probably *To the Fallen,* written for Armistice Day, Nov. 11, 1918, and set to music by Elgar. Binyon is also an authority on the work of William Blake.

Biography. S. N. Behrman (American). Comedy. 1932.

Ina Claire starred in this comedy when it was first presented by the Theatre Guild. She played Marian Froude, a portrait painter of mediocre talent but great personal radiance, who views life and the many men who have loved her with amused tolerance. Her masculine visitors in Act I include Richard Kurt, a bitterly intense, almost fanatic young editor; Melchior Feydak, Austrian composer whom she has met in Europe, on his way to Hollywood, where he has been given a contract by a producer who erroneously believes him to be his dead brother, composer of a popular waltz tune; and Leander Nolan, a pompous but somehow appealing candidate for the Senate. The latter was once Marian's boyhood sweetheart in Tennessee. He is shocked at the Bohemian life Marian has led since she left him; she looks at the dignified figure he has become and insists on painting him. Kurt has come to ask her to write her autobiography for his magazine. She finds herself attracted to the bumptious young man. Nolan objects violently to the biography, afraid lest his past be revealed. He offers Kurt a position in Washington if he will withdraw his offer; Kurt, opposed to Nolan on principle, refuses. Nolan gets in touch with Kurt's employer, makes dire threats, and stirs up such a tempest that Marian is willing to let the matter drop to avoid any fuss. Kurt reproaches her for being superficial, irresponsible, and treating life "as if it were a bedroom farce." Nevertheless he loves her, and she him. Kurt quits his job rather than kill the story and is going to publish it himself; Nolan's prospective father-in-law threatens to sue him for libel. Marian settles the problem by burning the manuscript, then tells Kurt she will not marry him, nor, for the time being, anyone. Without Kurt's capacity for being aroused by the things she hates, she realizes they are temperamentally unsuited.

Bird in Hand. John Drinkwater (English). Comedy. 3 acts. Printed 1927.
Joan, the daughter of Thomas Greenleaf, the proprietor of the Bird in Hand Inn, falls in love with the squire's son, Gerald. Thomas thinks that Gerald is only intending to seduce his daughter, and Joan, a modern girl, considers her father's fears ridiculous. One night her father drags Joan home and arouses the Inn. Three of the guests sit in on the family conference and straighten matters out. The squire asks Joan to marry Gerald.

Birds, The. Aristophanes (Greek). Comedy. 414 B.C.
An early work of Aristophanes, an exuberant burlesque on the national mythology. A couple of old Athenians, weary of the corruption of the capital, determine to leave the country, and to this end seek the advice of Tereus, the king of the birds. He speaks at such length of his kingdom that they grow interested. A council of the birds is held, and the Athenians are given permission to build Cloud-Cuckoo-Land, a walled city which is to be anti-god and pro-bird. This is done. Envoys from Athens are speedily dismissed by the heroes, but a peace offer from the gods is finally accepted on condition that the birds be restored to their former rights and privileges. The marriage of the daughter of Zeus with one of the Athenians ends the fantasy.
Many topical allusions stud the play, but the main theme is timeless.

Birmingham Little Theatre (Alabama). Birmingham has its own flourishing playhouse. It meets the needs of a city with two large colleges, and a near-by state university. This theatre has been Birmingham's chief source of entertainment for fifteen years. It can do pioneer work since it works on a non-profit basis. All the work except that of director and janitor is voluntary.

Birth of God, The. Verner von Heidenstam (Swedish). Religious drama. 3 acts. 1920.

At Karnak in Egypt a Swedish merchant, who has surrendered his occupation at home to seek the true deity, encounters an ancient priest of Apollo, awaiting for centuries the moment when he might die after announcing the birth of a new god. Together the pair of questers after truth climb to a hilltop, where the merchant immolates himself upon the altar fire they have built, and the priest dies content, declaring that a fresh and universal faith is about to be born.

Birth of Merlin, The. A play printed 1662 as work of William Shakespeare and William Rowley. Shakespeare's authorship is now discredited because of the disjointed plot and inferior poetry, while Rowley's authorship is generally accepted.

The play is a medley of farce and romance. Merlin out-tricks his father, the Devil, and solaces his mother in her old age. Uter Pendragon (King Arthur) wanders through the main action from time to time.

Birthday Party, The; or, The Ladies' Tea. Hjalmar Bergstrom (Danish). Drama. 3 acts. 1922.

Presents the talk of seven old maids assembled to celebrate the fortieth birthday of one of them. Though they boast of their freedom, these bachelor women—artists, singers, secretaries and trained nurses—would all have forfeited their careers had marriage been possible. Some hint at the men they might have had. One sadly admits that no man has ever looked upon her with passion in his eyes; and one confesses proudly that the child she has adopted is really her own.

Bit part. A small role in a production, rarely with more than two or three lines.

Björnson, Björnstjerne (1832-1910). Norwegian dramatist. Distinguished contemporary of Ibsen; but best remembered for his Norwegian tales, comparable with the old sagas in vigor and beauty, and his pleas for the single standard of morality.

Son of a Lutheran clergyman, he was born at Kvikne, Osterdalen, Norway, and educated at Molde and at the University of Christiania (Oslo). He first attracted attention by his stories of peasant life. He wrote his first play, *Between the Battles,* in 1857, and two years later became the director of the theatre at Bergen. From 1861 he was director of the National Theatre in Oslo. In 1903 he was awarded the Nobel prize for literature. As a politician, he played a prominent part in the movement which led to the separation of Norway from Sweden in 1905. He died in Paris.

The best known of his plays are: *Between the Battles,* 1857; *Lame Hulda,* 1858; *King Sverre,* 1861; *Sigurd Slembe,* 1862; *Mary Stuart in Scotland,* 1864; *The Newly Married,* 1868; *Sigurd Jorsalfar,* 1872; *The Editor,* 1874; *A Bankruptcy,* 1875; *The King,* 1877; *Leonarda,* 1879; *The New System,* 1879; *A Gauntlet,* 1883; *Beyond Our Power I,* 1883; *Geography and Love,* 1885; *Beyond Our Power II,* 1895; *Paul Lange and Tora Parsberg,* 1898; *Laboremus,* 1901; *At Storhove,* 1902; *Dayland,* 1904; *When the New Wine Blooms,* 1909.

Black Crook, The. Charles M. Barres (American). Play with music. 1866. Described by its author as an "original magical and spectacular drama," this was the first successful American revue. Its première at Niblo's Garden, New York City, brought startled gasps from an audience unaccustomed to the tights and ballet costumes worn by the dancers. Spectacularly staged, and with a generous bevy of feminine pulchritude, it held the spectators entranced for five hours running and eventually made almost a million dollars for the producer.

Blackface. A stage make-up by means of which white actors impersonate Negro characters; burnt cork or charcoal is generally used.

Blackfriars Theatre. The first private theatre in London, housed in the structure of an old Dominican monastery in 1576. Unlike the public theatres, it was rectangular and roofed, resembling a long interior hall. Until 1587, when it was temporarily closed, it was the center of English production. Here performances were given by the Children of the Chapel Royal, Paul's boys, and Oxford's actors. On several of these occasions John Lyly was the playwright. It was also used in later years as the winter quarters for Shakespeare's company. In 1600 it was re-opened to child actors by Richard Burbage, the Shakespearean actor, and in 1609 the King's Men, formerly the Chamberlain's, took it over for their performances.

Black Maskers, The. Leonid Andreyev (Russian). Symbolic drama. 5 acts. 1908.
The play presents the problem of a dual personality and the evil existent in the soul of man.
Here the hero is the human soul, entrenched within its castle, the body, and yet invaded by maskers who, when it seeks to celebrate a festival, represent its involuntary thoughts of evil. Threatened by these maskers of doubt, despair and madness, the soul struggles against the nightmare, is overwhelmed, yet dies unyielding.

Blackout. The closing of a scene, act, or the play itself, usually on a particularly effective line, by a sudden extinguishing of the lights; used now largely to describe a revue sketch.

Black Sheep. Elmer Rice (American). Comedy. 3 acts. 1932.
Buddy Porter, the black sheep of his family, returns home with a friend, Mrs. Lloyd, and is recognized by a neighbor as an important young writer. Immediately the attitude of the family changes. They are delighted to see him and want to do anything they can to make his visit a pleasant one. Buddy, however, remembering how he has been treated in the past, rules the family with a rod of iron, and is finally persuaded by Mrs. Lloyd to take a trip to South America.

Black wax. A material used in blocking out the teeth where so desired; kneaded with the fingers, it is applied directly to the teeth to be obliterated, both on the inside and outside areas of the gums.

Blanchette. Eugène Brieux (French). Drama. 4 acts. 1892.
A play in which the author attacks society because it will not give young girls an opportunity of earning a living by teaching. This was Brieux's first important success.

Blank verse. A style of poetry composed of unrhymed lines, usually in iambic pentameter. The Elizabethans were among the first to use blank verse in the drama. *Gorboduc,* which appeared in 1562, was the first English tragedy and was written in blank verse. Christopher Marlowe demonstrated to what magnificent use blank verse could be put in his *Tragical History of Doctor Faustus.* After him came Shakespeare, the greatest exponent of both blank verse and drama. It was Shakespeare who introduced infinite variation into the traditional pattern of five strong and five weak stresses in alternation by shifting stresses and carrying the rhythmic movement over from line to line.

The Blind (Les Aveugles). Maurice Maeterlinck (Belgian). Allegorical play. 1890.

A symbolical and eerie allegory, poetic and appealingly human. A group of blind men and women are seated under the stars in a mystic wood. Their guide is an elderly priest returned from the dead. Gropingly they try to discover their location and destiny, and the audience gradually realizes that they represent baffled humanity, which wanders sightless in the forest of ignorance, without faith and without knowledge of the hereafter, guided by leaders and credos which have outlived their usefulness.

Blitzstein, Marc (1905-   ). American composer. Author-composer of *The Cradle Will Rock,* a play with music, which was intended to be performed by the Federal Theatre Project in June 1937 at Maxine Elliott's theatre. Due to the political ideology, and the fact that there was a strike in the steel industry, it was deemed impolitic to open it. Angered by this, the composer and company, on two hours' notice, moved to the Venice Theatre and performed it with the author at the piano, sans scenery and costume and with the actors in the audience. It was a *succes d'estime* and ran for ten performances. It was revived somewhat similarly for two Sunday nights at the Mercury during the 1937-38 season. Meeting again with success it was put on for a regular run at the Windsor Theatre in January 1938. Blitzstein was responsible for the incidental music in Orson Welles' production of *Julius Caesar,* November, 1937. He is also author of *I've Got the Tune.*

Blizzard head (television). A pronounced blonde who, because of the extreme light color of her hair, sometimes appears in the television image to have a flare of light about her head.

Bloody Brother, The; or, Rollo, Duke of Normandy. John Fletcher and Ben Jonson, and perhaps other collaborators (English). Tragedy. 5 acts. c. 1639.

The Duke of Normandy has bequeathed his dukedom to his two sons, Rollo and Otto. Rollo, the elder, in order to win the whole heritage, kills his brother and orders the execution of all those who oppose him, including his tutor. Rollo, captivated by Edith, the daughter of his old tutor, spares her. She plots to kill Rollo to avenge her father's death, but the brother of another of Rollo's victims kills him first.

Blot on the 'Scutcheon, A. Robert Browning (English). Tragedy. 3 acts. 1843.

Lord Henry Mertoun delays asking the hand of Mildred until he has become intimate with her. Her brother and guardian, Lord Tresham, consents willingly to the arrangement, but upon obtaining a confession from her of her guilt with an unknown lover, surprises Mertoun and kills him. Mildred dies of a broken heart and Lord Tresham takes poison.

Blount, Edward (fl. 1588-1623). English printer. Stationer, translator and, together with William Jaggard, printer of the first folio edition of Shakespeare's plays in 1623.

Blow the show. To leave the show; to run away from an engagement.

Blow up. To forget one's lines in a performance.

Blue Bird, The. Maurice Maeterlinck (Belgian). Symbolistic drama. 3 acts. 1908.

The brother and sister, Tyltyl and Mytyl, set out on Christmas Eve to look for the Blue Bird of Happiness, together with the souls of the Dog, the Cat, Milk, Fire, Water, Sugar, Bread and Light. On Christmas morning the children discover that their own turtle dove is blue. But no sooner is the Blue Bird found than it flies away and the search must begin again.

Blumenthal, Oscar (1852-1917). German dramatist and critic. Founder and manager of the Lessing Theatre in Berlin, 1888.

He devoted his energy to contemporary farce and comedy and tried to elevate the tone of the comedy stage, but for financial reasons was forced to abandon his ideal for the humdrum farces on current events. His plays are distinguished by the sprightliness of the dialogue. He published several columns of critical and miscellaneous essays.

Among his most successful plays are: *The Big Bell; A Drop of Poison; The Black Veil,* etc.

B. O. Theatrical parlance and abbreviation for box office.

Boadicea. See *Bonduca.*

Boar's Head Inn. A famous tavern situated in Eastcheap, London, frequently used for theatrical performances and occupied for six months in 1602 by Worcester's group of professional actors. It is thought that the Boar's Head is intended to be the scene of the tavern sequences in Shakespeare's *King Henry IV.*

Board. (1) The wooden rack in a box office used as container of tickets for the entire theatre; tickets are sometimes arranged according to the seating plan of a theatre, the board being a miniature map of such a plan; (2) a group of individuals who control the activities of the entire theatre from production to theatre management; (3) call board; see *Callboard.*

Boards, The. In theatrical parlance, the stage; "to walk the boards" is a term used by actors meaning to appear and move on the stage.

Boguslawski Theatre (Polish). An 18th century theatre in Warsaw (named for the founder) which was taken over in 1924 by Schiller and Horzyca and developed, with the later collaboration of the Polish actor-director, Zelwerowicz, into a first-rate organization.

Boileau, Nicolas (Boileau-Despréaux) (1633-1711). French poet and critic. Born in Paris. After the death of his mother when he was two he appears to have been somewhat neglected. Early in life he conceived a "hatred of dull books." He studied at the Collège de Beauvais and later at the Sorbonne, where he took up theology. This he soon gave up, as he did law, in spite of his admission to the bar in 1656. The death of his father left him a comfortable maintenance and thereafter he devoted himself exclusively to study and writing. His *Satires* was an attack on many authors who had gone before him. He was, however, friendly with Molière and Racine. The *Satires* and *Epîtres* brought him to the attention of Louis XIV, who granted him a liberal pension and later made him historiographer to the King. His contribution to dramatic theory is best to be found in his *Art Poétique,* which was primarily intended as justification for his attacks on preceding authors in his *Satires.*

Bold Stroke for a Wife, A. Mrs. Susannah Centlivre (English). Comedy. 5 acts. 1718.
Colonel Fainall, to win the consent of Obadiah Prim, the Quaker guardian of Anne Lovely, to his marriage with the latter, impersonates Simon Pure, "a quaking preacher." No sooner has he obtained the consent than the true Quaker arrives.

Boleslawski, Richard (1889-1937). Producer and director. Born in Warsaw, Poland. He acted in the Moscow Art Theatre 1906-15; then served in the War. He had been in America since 1920. In New York between 1920-28 he staged *Revue Russe,* 1922; *Vagabond King,* 1925; *White Eagle,* 1927; *Ballyhoo,* 1927; *Mr. Moneypenny,* 1928; *Judas,* 1929; and various productions of the American Laboratory Theatre, for which he was stage director in 1928-29. He has written several books, and during the past ten years he directed the production of many films in Hollywood, among them *The Woman Pursued, Men in White* and *Clive of India.*

Bonds of Interest, The (*Los intereses creados*). Jacinto Benavente y Martiñez (Spanish). Comedy. Prologue and 3 acts. 1907.
A modern satirical *commedia dell'arte,* it shows how the bonds of interest link respectability with villainy. It represents the high water mark of Benavente's dramatic achievement, and the essence of his philosophy of life, disillusioned and a little disdainful.
Leander and Crispin, a gentleman and his valet, living by their wits and escaping the law by various subterfuges, invade a small town in Spain and trick themselves through Crispin's cleverness into a comfortable state of being.

Bonduca (Boadicea). John Fletcher (English). Tragedy. 5 acts. 1647.

Based on the story of Boadicea as given by George Holinshed. The principal character, however, is Caratach, wise counsellor to the impetuous British Queen. Presents the battles in which Boadicea is defeated and killed and Caratach is taken prisoner. Richard Burbage played in this drama.

"Bones." Metal plates used for theatre tickets at the end of the 18th century which bore the names of important actors of a company together with the names of guests; permitted the holder free admission to the play.

Bones, Mr. One of the end men in a minstrel show.

Bonfils, Helen. See *Elitch's Gardens*.

Boniface, Dr. Stock character of the French farce of the 17th century, print of whom by Huret establishes similarity with stock characters of the contemporary Italian *commedia dell'arte*.

Bonstelle, Jessie (1870?-1932). Began career in a road company in *Bertha, the Beautiful Sewing Machine Girl,* a melodrama. Worked for Augustin Daly; later for the Messrs. Shubert in Syracuse. Appeared under her own management in Buffalo, Rochester and Syracuse; leased the Garrick Theatre in Detroit and opened with a stock company which ran fourteen years. In 1923, took over the Harlem Opera House in New York, and tried out plays for Broadway producers. In 1925 she purchased the Bonstelle Playhouse in Detroit and in 1928 she organized it into the Detroit Civic Theatre. She has trained Katharine Cornell, Ann Harding, Ben Lyon, Melvyn Douglas, Frank Morgan, William Powell, Kenneth McKenna, and many other prominent actors.

Book. In theatrical usage, the term used for the play manuscript; in musical productions it refers to the libretto without the music.

Booking. (1) Hiring, engaging or contracting; when a play is hired or contracted to appear in a theatre it is booked for that theatre; (2) also applicable to actors and vaudeville acts; (3) circuit booking—see *Circuit booking*.

Boomerang. (1) A platform arrangement mounted on casters with two or more levels used for painting scenery; (2) also refers to remote control gelatin change for spotlight.
See *Scenery; Lighting*.

Booth, Edwin Thomas (1833-1893). American actor.

Born at Belair, Maryland, the son of Junius Brutus Booth, he first appeared at the Boston Museum in *King Richard III,* 1849. Later he won great success as a Shakespearean actor in California and Australia, and was manager, 1863-67, of the Winter Garden Theatre, New York. In 1869 he built Booth's Theatre in New

York and managed it until 1874. In 1880 and 1882 he played in London and Germany. His Booth's Theatre was built after the burning of the Winter Garden in 1867, and cost Booth one million dollars. Every effort was made to make the house safe for actor and audience. He devoted his company to the performing of Shakespeare. When in 1874 he went bankrupt, he spent the rest of his life in starring tours in America. He was the founder of the Players' Club. His farewell performance was made in *Hamlet,* April 4, 1891, at the Brooklyn Academy of Music.

Otis Skinner in *The Last Tragedian* (1939) throws new light on his career with the annotated correspondence with the Stoddards.

Booth, John Wilkes (1839-1865). American actor; son of Junius Brutus Booth; born in Hartford County, Maryland, in 1839; went on the stage in 1856, and left it in 1864, in which year he appeared in New York as Mark Antony to the Cassius of J. B. Booth, Jr., and the Brutus of Edwin Booth. He assassinated President Lincoln on April 14, 1865; took to flight, was shot twelve days later.

Booth, Junius Brutus (1796-1852). Anglo-American actor.

Born in London, he was well educated in the classics, but became stage-struck and left home for the town of Deptford where he made his début at seventeen, 1813. Soon Booth was filling leading roles in the provinces, and it took him only three years to get a trial at Covent Garden, as *Richard III,* when he was twenty-one. Resembling Edmond Kean, he was put forward as the great actor's rival at Covent Garden and at Drury Lane. He played Iago to Kean's Othello at the latter in 1817. There were riots in the pit every time Booth appeared, since all the theatregoers took sides. Early in 1821 he married Mary Anne Holmes, although he was already married. Thirty years later his first wife came to America and sued for divorce, to the surprise and horror and dismay of his grown children. Booth made his American debut at Richmond, Virginia, July 6, 1821, in *Richard III.* From then until his death in 1852, on his way from an engagement in New Orleans to another in Cincinnati, he was an American star, save for two seasons when he made appearances at Drury Lane in London. He was always eccentric, and as the years went by his eccentricities and his fits of drinking increased. Many times he seemed insane. In his case, as in those of Cooke and Kean, there was no way of telling how much was madness and how much alcohol. As an actor, he was famous for his realism. His best-known roles included Brutus, Lear, Othello and Hamlet. His last appearance was at the St. Charles Theatre in New Orleans, November 19, 1852, in *The Iron Chest.* He was the father of the distinguished actor Edwin Booth, as well as of the assassinator of Lincoln, John Wilkes Booth.

Boothe, Clare (1903-   ). American playwright. Clare Boothe Brokaw Luce was for many years an editor of *Vanity Fair.* She divorced her first husband, George Brokaw, in 1929, and married Henry R. Luce, editor of *Time* and *Fortune,* in 1935. She is a lady of beauty and social standing, and nothing in her background would prepare one for the cutting acid of her best known play, *The Women,* 1936.

Previous dramatic works include *Entirely Irregular* (with Paul Gallico);

O Pyramids; and *Abide with Me,* 1935. More recent plays are *Kiss the Boys Good-bye,* 1938, another biting satire; and *Margin for Error,* 1939, the story of a German Consul in the United States which aroused Nazi protests.

Borden, Gail (1905-   ). American dramatic critic, editor.

Born in Houston, Texas; A.B. from Dartmouth College and A.M. degree from Harvard. Was an English instructor in the University of Chicago and then joined the staff of the *Chicago Journal* (now the *Times*) where he was dramatic critic and columnist and is now managing editor.

Border. (1) A scenery term: a drop; (2) a lighting term: the line of front stage overhead lights.

Borderlight. Strip of individual reflectors in varying lengths to light stage from overhead; used for toning and blending the other light on stage; hung on pipe or bridge.

See *Lighting.*

Borga Gard. Tor Hedberg (Swedish). Realistic drama. 3 acts. 1915.

A landed proprietor has seen his estates diminish until only one remains. His sons take little interest in the property or in him, but he marries for a second wife a keen-witted peasant girl, who shows him that he possesses hitherto unrecognized water rights, and induces one of the sons to exercise his legal talents in using these rights to the best advantage.

Boris Godunov. Pushkin (Russian). Historical tragedy. 5 acts. 1826.

Boris Godunov, appointed regent, murders the younger brother of the weak-minded Feodor and ultimately makes himself Czar; Gregory, a young monk, impersonates the dead brother, and advances at the head of the Polish army into Russia. Boris Godunov on his tottering throne, at the head of the famine-stricken land, realizes that the time of retribution has come. While the army of the pretender is still far away, he dies.

This drama was used as libretto for a grand opera of the same name by Moussorgsky, which provided the great Russian opera singer, Chaliapin, with his greatest role.

Born in a trunk. A term meaning born into a theatre family. Sometimes, *born in a dressing-room.*

Bosse, Abraham (1602-1676). French printer. Devotee of the French theatre of the 17th century whose print of a farce at the Hotel de Bourgogne established its similarity with the Italian *commedia dell'arte.*

Bostonians, The. An organization, formed in 1887 and flourishing until about 1904, which produced light opera. Among the most successful productions were *Robin Hood* and *The Serenade.*

Both Your Houses. Maxwell Anderson (American). Satire. 3 acts. 1933. A daring and forthright commentary on national politics.

The story of a hard-fighting, young and idealistic Congressman, who suddenly finds himself up against a group of old-time politicians, all at work on a big appropriations bill. The young idealist tries to draw up a relatively honest bill, but realizing that the fight seems hopeless, he turns around and makes the bill so ridiculously dishonest that he can not imagine but that it will be instantly killed. However, it is so pleasing to all parties that it goes through both houses.

Won Pulitzer Prize award for 1932-33.

Boucicault, Dion (1822-1890). Irish actor and dramatist.

Born at Dublin. His first play *London Assurance* was produced at Covent Garden, London, 1841, and he first appeared on the London stage in his own play *The Vampire* at Princess's Theatre in 1852. He wrote or adapted nearly 140 plays. He first appeared in America in 1852, on November 10, in his own play *Used Up.* Through his efforts the first copyright law was passed in 1856. He settled in America in 1876, and died in New York City in 1890.

Best known of his plays are: *The Colleen Bawn,* 1860; *The Octoroon* (an antislavery play), 1867; *The Shaughraun,* 1875.

Bound East for Cardiff. Eugene O'Neill (American). Drama. 1 act. 1919.

One of O'Neill's first plays. Frank Shay presented it in his Wharf Theatre in Provincetown, with the author himself playing a Second Mate. Records indicate his performance was adequate. The scene of the play is the seamen's forecastle of the British tramp steamer Glencairn, on a foggy night, midway between New York and Cardiff. Five sailors, including a Cockney, an Irishman and a Swede, sit on benches talking, while on a bunk the sailor Yank lies dying. There is no dramatic action properly speaking. Yank is a frustrated creature, a man who has missed his star. All his adult life has been spent in seafaring, "travelin' all over the world and seein' none of it; without no one to care whether you're alive or dead." And during all those years he has longed for a farm on which he might settle down and till the land. In his frustration he parallels the hero of O'Neill's later *Beyond the Horizon,* who contrary to Yank, yearned for the sea and lived and died on the land.

Bourdet, Edouard (1887-   ). French dramatist. More intent on treatment than theme, he interprets the post-War philosophy with bitterness. He has written *The Rubicon; The Open Cage; The Shepherd's Hour; La Prisonnière* (produced in New York as *The Captive* and closed by the police after a five-months' run); *Man Enchained; Just Appeared; Le Sexe Faible;* and other plays. Appointed director of the Comédie Française, home of the national French drama, in 1936 by Léon Blum's government. He fought a duel in 1938 with Henry Bernstein, who claimed his play *Judith* had been delayed too long in rehearsal. Bourdet received a cut on the arm.

Bourgeois Gentilhomme, Le. Molière (French). Comedy. 5 acts. 1670.

Monsieur Jourdain, a retired French shopkeeper, desires to become a great gentleman. He studies dancing, fencing, music, philosophy, and tries to have an affair with the Marquise de Montignac. In the last act, however, he unknowingly marries his daughter to a commoner, and is forced to watch his Marquise marry the Conte de Chateau-Gaillard.

Bourget, Paul (1852-   ). French poet and novelist. The author of a number of analytical and psychological novels. Two of his works which have been dramatized have been highly successful: *La Barricade* and *Le Tribun.*

Bowery Theatre (1827-1833). Once the democratic rival of the then aristocratic Park Theatre in New York. Several times destroyed by fire and rebuilt. Boasted such managers as Charles Gilbert, Thomas Hamblin and James H. Hackett. Identified with the early career of Edwin Forrest.

Box-office statement. A formal weekly account of the box-office receipts submitted by the box-office treasurer to the business manager of a play, and given by him to the producer. The playwright is entitled by his contract to have a copy of the statement. On tour, the box-office treasurer submits the account to the company manager.

Box-set. Scene composed of three walls, the hypothetical fourth wall being taken out to permit the view of the audience.

Boyle, William (1853-1923). Irish dramatist. Born in County Louth, Ireland; was since 1874 an officer of Customs and Excise. Author of the following plays, all produced by the Irish National Theatre Society: *The Building Fund,* 1905; *The Eloquent Dempsey,* 1906; *The Mineral Workers,* 1906; *The Love Charm,* 1911; and *Family Failing,* 1912.

Boy Meets Girl. Bella and Sam Spewack (American). Farce. 3 acts. 1935.

A hilarious farce lampooning Hollywood. Staged by George Abbott, it ran in New York for two seasons. Later Hollywood proved it could laugh at a joke on itself by filming it.

Law and Benson, an irrepressible writing team working for the films, have brains as fertile as their energy is boundless. Their antics distress serious C. K. Friday, a producer and their immediate superior, who is pining for a new story for Larry Toms, Western star, and is distraught by constant interruptions—midgets no one ordered, an English extra telling him what kind of hats Coldstream Guards should wear. Susie, a blonde and extraordinarily naïve waitress who serves the authors lunch, suddenly inspires them. She is about to have a natural child. It shall be called Happy—and be the star who will help Larry come back! Months pass. As it is written, so has it come to pass. Happy is born and becomes a sensation, stealing scenes from Larry, who is considering marrying the baby's mother in self-defense. But Susie is busy fulfilling a long-deferred ambition to go to high school, and besides, her heart belongs to the hat authority, the English extra. Things almost go awry when a publicity scheme cooked up by Law and Benson to enhance Happy's publicity value proves a boomerang, and on the heels of that Happy gets the measles. But a few fake phone calls fix matters up; Susie falls into the arms of her Englishman, who turns out to be a lord's son; and Law and Benson, to the music of blaring trumpets, begin a search for a baby to succeed Happy as a star.

Brace cleat. A device used to fasten stage brace to scenery. See *Scenery*.

Bracegirdle, Anne (c. 1663-1748). English actress. A member of Colley Cibber's company. In 1688 she took the part of Lucia in Shadwell's *The Squire of Alsatia,* and in 1693, that of Araminta in Congreve's *The Old Bachelor.* Her best known part, however, was Angelica in Congreve's *Love for Love,* but she also gained success as Isabella, Portia, and Cordelia in *Measure for Measure, The Merchant of Venice* and *King Lear,* respectively. Piqued at the success of Mrs. Oldfield in 1707, she left the stage, reappearing only on the occasion of Betterton's benefit, April 1709, when she played Angelica once more.

Brace jack. Right-angle triangular frame used for bracing scenery. See *Scenery*.

Brady, Alice (1892-1939). American actress. The daughter of William A. Brady, theatrical manager, Alice Brady was born in New York City and studied for grand opera at the Boston Conservatory of Music. She made her first stage appearance in a minor role in Robert Mantell's production of *As You Like It,* 1909, and her first New York apeparance in *A Balkan Princess,* 1911. She played roles in a number of Gilbert and Sullivan operettas, including *H. M. S. Pinafore,* 1911; *Patience,* 1912; *Iolanthe;* etc.; and toured with De Wolf Hopper in a repertory of the operettas in 1914. She has also acted in *Little Women,* 1912; *The Family Cupboard,* 1913; *The Things that Count,* 1913; *Sylvia Runs Away,* 1914; *What is Love?* 1914; *Sinners,* 1915; *Forever After,* 1918; *Anna Ascends,* 1920; *Drifting,* 1922; *Zander the Great,* 1923; *The Bride of the Lamb,* 1926; *Lady Alone,* 1927; *A Most Immoral Lady,* 1928; *Karl and Anna,* 1929; *Brass Ankle,* 1931; *Ladies of the Jury,* 1931; *Mourning Becomes Electra,* 1931; and other plays.

She was an actress of great versatility, equally adept in scatterbrain comedy roles and tragic parts. Since 1914 she had been in many films, among them *When Ladies Meet; Broadway to Hollywood; Gay Divorcee; In Old Chicago.* For her work in the latter film she received the 1937 Motion Picture Academy Award as the best supporting actress.

Brady, William A. (1863-   ). American theatrical manager. Born in San Francisco. He was brought to New York and educated in the public schools. He was married to Marie Rene, by whom he had a daughter, the actress Alice Brady.

His second wife was the actress, Grace George, whom he married in 1899 and by whom he had a son, William Brady, Jr. He began his stage career in San Francisco in 1882, and last acted in 1928 in *A Free Soul*. He was the lessee of the Manhattan Theatre, New York, from 1896 to its demolition; he built the Playhouse, 1911, which he managed; and became manager of the Forty-eighth Street Theatre, now known as the Windsor, in 1912. In 1917 Pres. Wilson appointed him chairman of the committee to organize the motion picture industry; and he was president of the National Association of the Motion Picture Industry, 1915-20. Among the many actors and actresses he has managed have been Grace George, Helen Gahagan, Douglas Fairbanks, Helen Hayes, Mary Nash, Kenneth McKenna, Alice Brady and Katherine Alexander. His productions include *Gentleman Jack, Mlle. Fifi, Way Down East, Uncle Tom's Cabin, The Two Orphans, Trilby, Foxy Grandpa, The Pit, Baby Mine, Bunty Pulls the Strings, Bought and Paid For, The White Feather, Alibi, The Ruined Lady, The Skin Game, Street Scene, A Church Mouse, Alice Sit-by-the-Fire, Mademoiselle*.

Braggart soldier. A dramatic type, possibly a derivation from the ancient Latin *miles gloriosus* and the *capitano* of the *commedia dell'arte,* which came into being in England with the character of Ralph Roister Doister in Udall's play of the same name. The character in England lasted until the closing of the theatres in 1642. Toward the final years of its existence the type was characterized by baseness and sensuality.

Brand. Henrik Ibsen (Norwegian). Drama. 5 acts. 1866.
Brand, a young Norwegian clergyman, contemptuous of the compromising spirit of the religion of his countrymen, goes to a town on a distant fjord. Unbending he practises his principle and enforces it on others, though it costs him the life of his child and of his wife. The people turn against him and drive him out into the snow. An avalanche overwhelms him as he makes his last appeal to God, and receives the answer, "He is the God of Love."

Brandes, Carl Edvard Cohen (1847-1927). Danish dramatist and critic. Born in Copenhagen of Jewish parents, he was educated at the university of that city. Modern Danish drama is said to begin in the Seventies with Edvard Brandes, a dramatist and critic, whose plays are practically unknown in England and America. His most famous play *A Visit* was performed in London, in a translation by William Archer, in the Nineties.

Break up. Interruption and sometimes obliteration of one actor's lines by another actor's horseplay or practical jokes in the midst of a performance.

Breakaway scenery. Scenery that breaks or changes its form in full view of the audience.

Breaking. The closing of a show.

Brecht, Bert. See *Drama, German, since the First World War and before National Socialism.*

Brederoo, Gerbrand Adriaanszoon (1585-1618). Dutch dramatist. He ranks as the greatest comic dramatist of Holland.

Born in Amsterdam, March 16, 1585, he began life as an artist. The best of his plays are *Het Moortje*, 1615, and *De Spaansche Brabander*, 1618.

Breeches parts. The Elizabethan dramatic convention of a plot's hingeing on the masquerade of female characters as boys or men, was convincing because the female characters were then played by boys. The new wave of popularity for "breeches parts" in the first half of the 18th century was due not to convincingness, but to suggestive unconvincingness—for at that time women had taken their place on the stage in all female roles. Lacking the risqué dialogue that was giving way to sentimentalism, audiences satisfied their salacious interest visually. Performances having "breeches parts" were especially advertised. Because they felt that male costume set them off to advantage, as many of them were pert and saucy, the actresses favored such roles. Burnahy, Manning, Rowe, Johnson, Banks, Breval, Moore, and other dramatists supplied this demand of actresses and audiences.

See also *Disguised Heroine; Impersonation; Male; Transvesticism.*

Bresile Household, The. Romain Coolus (Rene Weil) (French). Drama. 3 acts. 1893.

A satire on the complacence of a husband who decides, after his erring wife has left him for a night, to receive her next morning as though nothing had happened.

Breton de los Herreros, Manuel (1796-1873). Spanish dramatist. Noted as a writer of comedies.

Born at Quel, he was sub-librarian at the National Library, Madrid, 1831-40, and secretary to the Spanish Academy from 1842 until his death in 1873. He wrote 360 plays as well as a number of volumes of poetry.

Brice, Fanny (1891-   ). American actress. Born in New York; studied for the stage under James O'Neill; made her first appearance on the stage in Brooklyn in *A Royal Slave* and appeared in vaudeville in 1910; was in *The Ziegfeld Follies* of 1910, 1911. Other plays she appeared in were: *The Honeymoon Express*, 1913; *Nobody Home*, 1915 (London) ; *The Follies of 1916; The Ziegfeld Follies of 1917; Why Worry*, 1918; *Midnight Frolic*, 1920; *The Music Box Revue*, 1924; *Fanny*, 1926; *Fioretta*, 1929; *Sweet and Low*, 1930; *Ziegfeld Follies of 1934.*

Bridge. Metal platform hung immediately upstage of teaser or combined with it; for hanging light instruments and allowing working space for operator during a show; can be raised or lowered to suit proscenium opening and aids sight lines by giving the teaser added thickness.

See *Lighting.*

Bridie, James (Osborne Henry Mavor) (1888-   ). Scottish dramatist. A writer of witty comedies, often charged with intellectual excitement, sometimes enhanced and sometimes impeded in their course by unexpectd twists of fantasy.

Born in Glasgow, he served with the Royal Army Medical Corps during the World War, and upon returning to Glasgow, began to practice medicine. He began to write for the stage in 1928 and since that time devoted himself to playwriting.

Among his plays are: *The Sunlight Sonata*, 1928; *What It Is To Be Young*, 1929; *Tobias and The Angel*, 1930; *The Anatomist*, 1931; *Jonah and the Whale*, 1932; *The Sleeping Clergyman*, 1933; *Marriage Is No Joke*, 1934.

Bridle. It is used to give extra support to a long batten with only two lines. See *Scenery*.

Brief. British term for free admission into a theatre.

Brief Moment. S. N. Behrman (American). Comedy. 3 acts. 1931.

Roderick Deane at twenty-five has everything for which most men ask, yet considers himself a failure. A millionaire's son, intelligent, with time and money to indulge his every whim—if it be flying a plane or leading a jazz band—he is disillusioned and "spiritually unemployed." He has fallen in love with and wants to marry Abby Fane, night club blues singer, because she's so refreshingly elemental, unspoiled by civilization. Among Abby's other admirers are Manny Walsh, bigshot racketeer, and Cass Worthing, polo-playing man about town, but she feels Roderick has more to offer her and accepts his marriage proposal.

Six months later she has lost all of her refreshingly elemental charm and has become a perfect parvenue, aping high society and sharing in its pseudo-culture, with a veritable passion for stuffed shirts. She is now indifferent to the caresses of Cass Worthing, the man she loved when she accepted Rod, but encourages him so as to have revenge for the suffering he has caused her in the past. Rod is rendered jealous by her coquetry, and is disappointed at the change in her. They quarrel, and her husband in a fit of temper tells Abby to run off with Cass if she wants to. Angrily she prepares to follow his advice. Three weeks later they are contemplating divorce. But by now Abby realizes that she loves Rod, and he makes the best of a bad situation by agreeing to make a fresh start with her. For after all, though he is a "Hamlet married to a career woman," doomed to doubt throughout his life, he has never stopped loving the lady.

Brieux, Eugène (1858-1932). French dramatist. The chief exponent of the useful theatre, not only in France, but throughout the world.

A Parisian journalist of the middle class. His first stage venture was a slight farce *The Divorce Bureau*, 1880, written in collaboration with Gaston Salandri. It was not, however, until the early Nineties, when Brieux submitted several plays to Andre Antoine for performance at the Theatre Libre, that he began to be known. A moralist and a reformer, he was intent less upon a study of souls in conflict than upon specific evils and concrete remedies.

His *Damaged Goods* was a great sensation in this country.

"It is likely that most of his plays, in which the interest lies mainly in the propaganda they carry, will pass into oblivion along with the conditions that gave them birth; it is a safe prophecy, however, that a few will survive because of their distinctly human values and their purely artistic qualities."—C. H. Whitman.

His works include: *Bernard Palissy* (with Salandri), 1880; *Artists' Homes,* 1890; *The Nest,* 1893; *Cogwheels,* 1894; *The Blue Rose,* 1895; *The Benefactors,* 1896; *Racing Results,* 1898; *The Cradle,* 1898; *The Red Robe,* 1900; *The Substitutes,* 1901; *Damaged Goods,* 1902; *Maternity,* 1903; *Amature,* 1905; *The June Bugs,* 1906; *Simone,* 1908; *Suzette,* 1909; *False Gods,* 1909; *Citizen in the Country,* 1920; *The Child,* 1923; *The Lavolette Family,* 1926; *Because I Love You,* 1929.

Brighella. One of the two chief characters, or *zanni,* in a *commedia dell' arte;* companion to Harlequin; an entirely inhuman rascal. Costume: wide trousers, short jacket, laced with green braid.

Brighouse, Harold (1882-   ). English dramatist. Born at Eccles. His first play *Dealing in Futures* appeared in 1909. He has written a number of novels and done considerable work for the films.

Two of his best known plays are *Hobson's Choice* and *What's Bred in the Bone.*

Brignol and His Daughter. Alfred Capus (French). Drama. 5 acts. 1894.

A jolly, impecunious optimist threatened by a gaming creditor escapes from impending ruin when his daughter marries the creditor's nephew, not out of any preconceived plan, but because she chances to fall in love with him.

Britannicus. Jean Racine (French). Tragedy. 1669.

A tragedy describing the rivalry between Nero and his brother, and tracing Nero's degeneration into a murderer and tyrant. It is classed with the great French dramatist's lesser works, not on a par with *Athalie* or *Andromaque.*

British Drama League, 9 Fitzroy Square, London. An organization founded in 1919 on behalf of the development of the art of the theatre. It has served to further a harmonious inter-relation between the stage and the life of the community, aided by a theatrical library which it established for that purpose. Harley Granville-Barker was the first chairman.

Festivals are held in various centers during the year, ending with a Final Festival in London each May when the Howard de Walden cup is presented to the best of the five amateur teams appearing.

Broad (television). A type of lighting unit used in television studio illumination.

Broadhurst, George H. (1866-1937). American dramatist.

He came to the United States from London in 1886, and after managing theatres in Milwaukee, Baltimore and San Francisco, became editor of a newspaper at Great Forks, North Dakota. Later he became manager of the Broadhurst Theatre, New York.

His popular plays include: *The Coward; What Happened to Jones; Why Smith Left Home; The House that Jack Built; The Crimson Alibi; The Red Falcon.*

Broadside. A sheet printed on one side announcing play performances, etc., largely used in the 17th and 18th centuries and up to the present day.

Broadway. George Abbott and Philip Dunning (American). Comedy drama. 3 acts. 1926.

This was the first play to present realistically the life and atmosphere of the night club and set the pace in gangster tales for a decade. The story concerns Roy Lane, a cabaret hoofer, and his struggle with the cabaret owner for the love of "Billie" Moore, a "beautiful but dumb" chorus-girl. Gun-fighting and murder contribute to this sensational picture of the prohibition era.

Broken Heart, The. John Ford (English). Tragedy. 5 acts. 1633.

Scene is Laconia. Penthea has been forced by her brother, Ithocles, to marry the contemptible Bassanes, by whom she is driven crazy. She finally dies. Orgilus who has loved Penthea, kills Ithocles. Orgilus is then sentenced to death by Calantha, beloved of Ithocles. She, herself, then dies broken hearted.

Brome, Richard (?-1652). English dramatist. The servant and friend of Ben Jonson, he lived on friendly terms with Fletcher, Dekker, Ford and Shirley.

His best work is in the pathetic drama, *The Northern Lass,* 1632; and in the comedies, *The Jovial Crew, The Court Beggar* and *The Antipodes.*

Bromfield, Louis. American author and dramatist. Pulitzer Prize winner in 1926 with his novel *Early Autumn,* and author of *Possession, Twenty-four Hours, The Rains Came* (successfully filmed in 1939) and other novels. His *The Green Bay Tree* was dramatized as *The House of Women* in 1927. He wrote the plays *Times Have Changed* and *De Luxe* (in which Elsa Maxwell made her first stage appearance) in 1935.

Brooke, Henry (1703-1783). Irish author and dramatist. Born at Rantavan, County Cavan, he is said to have received his early education from Sheridan, the friend of Swift. On leaving Trinity College, Dublin, he studied law in London, where he became friendly with Pope and Lyttleton. He returned to Ireland in 1745, where he lived until his death. Brooke possessed great ability both as an author and dramatist; his poem *Universal Beauty,* 1735, is supposed to have furnished the foundation for Darwin's *Botanic Garden.*

His play *Gustavus Vasa,* 1739, banned at Drury Lane, was produced in Dublin as *The Patriot* with great success.

Brother Rat. John Monks, Jr., and Fred F. Finklehoffe (American). Comedy. 3 acts. 1936.

Bing Edwards, star pitcher on the school team, is not brilliant but he hopes to win a $200 prize on graduation as the best athlete. Bing, who has been secretly married, is told the day before the big game that he is to become a father. Since his marriage was against school regulation, he is in mortal fear of exposure and expulsion. His roommates eventually get him out of his trouble.

Brothers, The. Richard Cumberland (English). Comedy. 5 acts. 1769.

The hero, the younger Belfield, has been dispossessed of his estate by his brother and separated from his sweetheart, Sophia. His brother, having forsaken his wife, Violetta, is now courting Sophia. His designs are frustrated, however, by the unexpected arrival of the younger Belfield and Violetta after the boat on which they have embarked is wrecked off the coast. Sophia and Belfield pair off for marriage.

Brougham, John (1814-1880). English actor, later American manager. Born in Dublin, he first appeared in London in 1830 at Tottenham Street Theatre. In 1840 he became manager of the Lyceum, and going to America, managed several theatres there, in 1869 opening Brougham's Theatre. His last appearance was as O'Reilly in *Rescued,* and he died in New York, June 7, 1880. Brougham is said to have written over a hundred plays, none of which has survived.

Broun, Heywood Campbell (1888-   ). American journalist. Born in Brooklyn, New York; educated at Harvard University. Reporter on the New York *Morning Telegraph,* 1909-1912; New York *Tribune,* 1912-1921; dramatic critic New York *World,* 1921-1928; since 1928 he has written a syndicated column for the Scripps-Howard newspapers, including the New York *World-Telegram.* Played in *Round the Town,* 1924; and *Shoot the Works,* 1931, and was also responsible for the production. Was dramatic editor, *Vanity Fair;* and is well known as a lecturer on the drama. Besides books of dramatic criticism, he is also the author of various works, in which he champions the under-dog and criticizes social injustice.

Brown, David Paul (1795-1875). American dramatist. One of the Philadelphia school of dramatists, particularly known for his closet dramas.

Born in Philadelphia. His education was marked by the classical thoroughness of the time. He was descended from a line of Friends. At the age of seventeen he began the study of medicine, but with the death of his instructor he began reading law. In 1816 he passed his examinations and there followed a long legal career, during which he occupied important posts in the Supreme Court of his native state. However, by 1824, Brown had gained fame as an easy and graceful writer. He wrote four dramatic compositions of which there is record: *Sertorius or The Roman Patriot; The Prophet of St. Paul's; The Trial;* and a farce, *Love and Honour; or, The Generous Soldier.* The latter two were never acted and probably were never published.

Brown, Gilmor. See *little theatres; Pasadena Community Playhouse; National Theatre Conference.*

Brown, John Mason (1900-). American dramatic critic, author. Born Louisville, Kentucky; A. B. degree from Harvard; associate editor and dramatic critic of the *Theatre Arts Monthly,* 1924-28; lecturer at the American Laboratory Theatre, 1925-31; dramatic critic *New York Evening Post* since 1929; has conducted courses on the theatre at the University of Montana, Middlebury College, Yale and Harvard universities; member of the New York Drama Critics Circle and the London Critics' Circle.

His books include: *The Modern Theatre in Revolt,* 1929; *Upstage—The American Theatre in Performance,* 1930; *Letters From Greenroom Ghosts,* 1934; *The Art of Playgoing,* 1936, etc.

Browne, Maurice (1881-). English producer. Born in Reading, England, he came to America and he was, 1912-18, director of the Little Theatre, Chicago. As manager of the Savoy Theatre, London, he produced *Journey's End* in 1929. He produced *Street Scene* and *B.J. One,* and in January, 1931, with F. B. Fagan, *The Improper Duchess.* Browne wrote several plays, including *Wings Over Europe* (with Robert Nichols), and himself appeared successfully on the stage. His most notable performance was in *The Unknown Warrior,* 1928.

Browning, Robert (1812-1889). English poet and dramatist. Browning, born in Camberwell, lived most of his life in London and Italy. He married the poetess Elizabeth Barrett in 1846. After his death in Venice his body was taken to Westminster Abbey for burial.

While chiefly known as one of the most famous Victorian poets, Browning himself thought his strength was as a "writer of plays." His dramas include *Strafford,* 1837; *King Victor and King Charles,* 1842; *The Return of the Druses,* 1843; *A Blot on the 'Scutcheon,* 1843; *Colombe's Birthday,* 1844. Of these, only *King Victor* was a success. Yet the author shows a fine sense of the dramatic in his narrative poems; Arthur Goodrich's dramatization of *The Ring and the Book,* entitled *Caponsacchi,* 1926, ran for over half a year in New York. The poet's own romance has also inspired playwrights, notably Rudolf Besier in *The Barretts of Wimpole Street,* 1930.

Brunelleschi, Filippo (1377-1446). Florentine architect, engineer and sculptor. First of the moderns to rediscover perspective; he gave it impetus for stage use.

Brush off. Theatrical slang. To get rid of.

Brutus; or, The Fall of Tarquin. John Howard Payne (American). Drama. 1818.

A biographical play based on the life of Brutus, full of historical inaccuracies, but notable because Payne in writing the part for Edmund Kean gave the actor a part in which to regain the favor of the English public.

Bryan, George (fl. 1594-1598). English actor. An actor in Shakespeare's company, Lord Chamberlain's Men, 1594-98. Nothing is known of roles played by him.

Buchner, Georg (1813-1837). German dramatist. The strongest dramatic talent of his period. His play of the French Revolution, *Danton's Death,* 1835, retains its vitality today; it was revived in 1927 by Max Reinhart, and staged in 1938 by Orson Welles in New York.

Buck, Gene (Eugene Edward). Born in Detroit, Aug. 8, 1885. Associated for many years with Florenz Ziegfeld as librettist, producer and songwriter, collaborating with Ring Lardner, Victor Herbert, Jerome Kern, Rudolf Friml and many other celebrities. Produced *Yours Truly* in 1926, with Leon Errol as the star. President of the American Society of Composers, Authors and Publishers.

Buehnenvolksbund. A stage confederation that grew up in Germany shortly after the First World War as a rival to the *Volksbuehne,* supported by Catholic interests and carrying a Christian repertory. Its success was only moderate.

Buffalo Bill. See *Cody, William Frederick.*

Bug, The. Vladimir Maiakovsky (Russian). Social drama. 3 acts. 1929.
Endeavors to show the Russia of the future, with a reactionary and a bug both reviving in 1979 after an interval of mummification. The reactionary is converted, and the bug excites curiosity since science has already exterminated all his fellows.

Build. That accumulation and gradual acceleration of tempo, emotional intensity and action by the combined forces of dramatist, actors and director in the approach to the climax of a play.

Bulgakov, Leo (1889-   ). Russian actor, producer. Born in Moscow; studied under Stanislavsky; made his debut in *The Lower Depths* at the Moscow Art Theatre in 1911; member of that company until 1926; with it, visited America in 1923. In 1926 he began his New York career, playing in *Lovers and Enemies; Spring Song; Gods of the Lightning; Street Scene;* and *The Devil in the Mind,* which he also produced. He staged *Princess Turandot; The Seagull; Amourette; The Night Remembers,* and other plays. Directed the production of the films: *White Lies; I'll Love You Always; After the Dance.* Together with his wife, Barbara, an actress, conducts a school of acting in New York.

Bulwer-Lytton, Edward George Earle Lytton (1803-1873). English writer. Born in London, his mother was a Lytton and his father General Bulwer. He sat in Parliament successively as both a Liberal and a Conservative, was Colonial Secretary 1858-59, and was created Baron Lytton of Knebworth in 1866. In 1827 he married the beautiful Rosina Doyle Wheeler, from whom he separated nine years later.
His plays and novels, while considered dated today, were once very popular.

Among the most successful of the dramas were *The Lady of Lyons*, 1838; *Richelieu;* and *Money*, 1840, in which such stars as Macready and Irving were glad to act.

Bunyan, John (1628-1688). English author. Author of *The Pilgrim's Progress* (1678-1684). He had no direct connection with the theatre but his great work undoubtedly had a wide influence on those writing for the theatre. *Pilgrim's Progress* was arranged as a play by James MacArthur, 1907.

Burbage, Cuthbert (? -1636). Elder son of James Burbage, builder of the Theatre and brother of Richard Burbage, the Shakespearean actor. Cuthbert became proprietor of the Theatre and was instrumental in the erection of the Globe Theatre, with which Shakespeare was for so long associated.

Burbage, James (? -1597). English actor-manager. He came of a Hertfordshire family, and first appears as one of the Earl of Leicester's players, May 7, 1576. On a site between Finsbury Fields and Shoreditch, he built the first English theatre, called the Theatre. He converted a large house in Blackfriars in 1596 into The Blackfriars Theatre. A year after his death the Shoreditch Theatre was removed to Bankside, Southwark, and re-erected as the Globe. He was the rival of the theatrical manager, Henslowe, who had a playhouse, the Rose, on the Bankside. Burbage was not a particularly good business man, and while Henslowe amassed a fortune, Burbage was never more than comfortably well off.

Burbage, Richard (1567?-1619). English actor. Leading actor of Lord Chamberlain's Men, Shakespeare's company, and son of James Burbage, from whom he inherited the management of Blackfriars theatre; for many years unrivalled star of both the Globe and the Blackfriars. Richard was also a shareholder in the Globe Theatre and is credited by many with having built the Globe in 1599, which Shakespeare's company occupied. First associated with the Admiral's Men, he joined Lord Chamberlain's Men in 1594 and remained with them until his death. He is known to have played Richard III, Hamlet, Lear and Othello, probably creating those roles, and to have starred in Jonson's *Sejanus, Volpone, The Alchemist,* and Catiline, in Kyd's *Spanish Tragedy,* in Webster's *Duchess of Malfi,* and other plays. Burbage was bequeathed a memorial ring by Shakespeare in his will. Burbage was an excellent painter as well as an actor and the Felton portrait of Shakespeare is accredited to his brush.

Bureau of Fine Arts. A division of the United States Department of State initiated July 1, 1939, and devoted to the furtherance of foreign cultural relations and to the proper representation of the United States in cultural affairs.

Burgomaster of Stilemonde. Maurice Maeterlinck (Belgian). Drama. 3 acts. 1918.
Contrasts national ideals of self-assertion and self-abnegation with as little chauvinism as might be expected. When a German lieutenant is shot from ambush in an

occupied Belgian village during the World War, and the gardener of the mayor is accused, the mayor insists upon taking his place.

Burgtheater (Vienna). Playhouse dating from 1741; first known as the *Koenigliches Theater nachst der Burg.* On April 8, 1776, it became a national theatre in that its financial arrangements came under the direct control of the Crown, while its artistic leadership was left to the actors themselves; opera and ballet were abolished, and exclusive attention was now given to German drama. The theatre was renamed the Vienna National Theatre. In 1789 Schroder came to it and reformed the bombastic acting.

In 1817 the *Vienna Burgtheatre* became a court theatre under the Emperor; it banished light opera, vaudeville and all forms of the lower classes of popular play. These went into the repertory of the *Leopoldstadter Theater.*

Burian. Czechoslovakian. A theatrical family. Vlasta Burian was the leading comic actor of Czechoslovakia. He maintained his own theatre, the Burian Theatre, and company, which maintained its popularity chiefly through the acting of the star. His brother, E. F. Burian, directed the theatre.

Burlesque.
The American burlesque show came into existence during the years of 1865 and 1868, largely as a result of the craze for women's tights popularized by Lydia Thompson and her troupe of English blondes, Adah Isaacs Menken, and the Mazeppa players' and *The Black Crook* extravaganza. The performances were patterned after the lady minstrel shows, with first part and olio and variety bills. There were occasional illustrated songs.

The comedy centered around an individual comedian or a quartet of comedians, including, usually, the Dutchman, the burnt-cork colored man, the dude or sissy, and the straight man. Their humor was based on what was called *the bits,* sketches or anecdotes worked out on a set pattern, talked off and filled in, after the manner of the *commedia dell' arte,* but having always a set ending. *The bits* which were bawdy and often obscene, were known to comedians by their subject matter—*The Butcher Bit* or *The Prima Donna Bit,* or by the stage apparatus employed for the laughs; the bladders, the dentist's chair, the blush detector. Eventually, these *bits* became the material used in Broadway revues as sketches, and blackouts.

The show usually ended with what was called the *Extra Added Attraction,* often a hoochee coochee dancer, a bout, or a wrestling match. Fun and noise were rampant, the cost cheap and the girls at the stage door. Leg shows were the nirvana of the male during the 90's, but most men attended surreptitiously. Sometimes too the theatres had their entrances up alley ways to make secret entrance and egress. Most burlesque companies had a system of signaling by lights and outposts to warn them if the police were near. Arrests were frequent and the harried burlesquer lived continuously in fear of the law.

The introduction of the strip tease killed burlesque comedy and finally killed burlesque entirely, necessitating for a time the closing of all burlesque houses. The fault was largely due to the managers. They, instead of following tradition and saving their big sex act till the latter part of the program, introduced one strip dancer after another so that the audience spent most of its time applauding for encores, knowing that with every reappearance the strip artist would remove an article of dress until she was down to the G-string.

The burlesque atmosphere was similar to that of the saloon, beer drinking, and smoking, brawls, and cat calls. Yet out of the melee came most of the foremost musical comedy comedians of the present day: Leon Errol, Bert Lahr, Clark and McCullough, Fanny Brice, W. C. Fields, Jack Pearl.

For a time, burlesque was so successful that certain managers like Lawrence Weber banded together to form circuits, touring companies known as the Wheels, the Columbia and the Mutual being the most prominent. Meanwhile, Minsky's operated independently in New York, building up a reputation at the old Winter Garden on Houston Street, a place celebrated in the writings of George Jean Nathan, O. O. McIntyre, and other burlesque enthusiasts. The passing out of burlesque was attributed to its purification, permitting ladies and children to attend, and the elimination of filth. These changes together with prohibition and the invention of the cinema ruined the box office. Besides legs were no longer a treat. Fashion decreed that women should expose them to the knees at least! and the Broadway revue and music, not content with this generous display, went in for bare breasts, bare feet, and legs. At the depth of the depression, a tabloid burlesque in Detroit charged ten cents for admission, and showed, in addition, third and fourth run motion pictures, together with a notice which read: "Stay all night if you like." The burlesque theatre had turned into a flop house.

Burlesque. George Manker Watters and Arthur Hopkins (American). Melodrama. 3 acts. 1927.

Skid, and Bonny, his wife, are comedian and leading lady of a burlesque show. Skid gets a job in a big Broadway musical comedy and his interest in Bonny begins to wane, until she finally decides to divorce him. Later, Skid finds himself on the down grade and returns to the burlesque show where he meets Bonny again and they are reunited.

Burlesque, English. An adaptation of French musical parody. During the 18th century a reaction to most of the too well-known types of play extant led to a great popularity for this form. The English burlesque was a satiric play cast in the form of a rehearsal which was shown only privately and semi-publicly. Its characters were farcical and satirical. Fielding was the most important figure in the school. His *Tumble-Down Dick, Author's Farce, Tom Thumb the Great* and *Covent Garden Tragedy* are among the best examples.

Burlesque queen. Popular term for a strip-tease artist. Among the best known burlesque queens have been Rose Sydell, Vinnie Henshaw, Ann Corio, Margie Hart, Hinda Wassau, and Gypsy Rose Lee.

Burletta (Italian). Literally, "a little jest." It is confined to scenes of gayety and is always associated with humor; a short comic opera or musical farce; the use of the *burletta* died out with the abolition in 1833 of the special rights of the patent theatres.

Burleycue. Popular term for burlesque.

Burnacini, Ludovico (1636-1707). Italian theatre architect and designer. Designed the Imperial Theatre, Vienna, in 1690. An important production of his was *Il pomo d'oro,* 1667.

Burnside, R. H. American (English) dramatic author and stage director. Formerly an actor and stage-manager in London and for a number of years was the general producer at the New Hippodrome. The plays he has written include: *Private Patsy; Sergeant Kitty; A Trip to Japan; The Three Romeos; The Big Show,* 1916; *Cheer Up!* 1917; *Happy Days.*

Burnt cork. A make-up agent generally used for minstrel shows, otherwise for any spectacles requiring black-face. In application it is mixed with water and applied smoothly and thinly.

Bury the Dead. Irwin Shaw (American). Tragedy. 1 act. 1936.

An anti-war play presented through a *spot* technique. The story, recalling that of the play, *Miracle at Verdun,* concerns dead soldiers who refuse to be buried. The problem involves not only relatives, friends, and sweethearts of the dead, who come to plead with them to lie down in their graves, but also the guardians of the civilized world, generals in the army, clergymen, governors, etc. The play ends with a passionate plea by the dead soldiers for all to stand up against any more war.

Business. Action interpolated by actors; much of the "business" in standard plays is traditional. In a general sense, all action and movement on the stage apart from dialogue. In moving pictures, a bit of pantomimic action developed to point up character, comedy, or a plot clue.

Business administration. See *Management, business.*

Business is Business (*Les Affaires sont les Affaires*). Octave Mirbeau (French). Drama. 3 acts. 1903.

The portrayal of money-lust shriveling the soul of Isidore Lechat and ruining the lives of his wife and children. Isidore is the incarnation of the worship of high finance. He believes that everyone has his price, and that money is the single source of greatness for the individual, the institution and the nation. Capitalist rule has made the people happy with plenty of work and cheap products. He may drive his daughter from home and learn of the tragic end of his gambling son in an automobile, but he turns from domestic afflictions to match wits against two business partners.

Buskin. An early metonymic term for tragedy. Comes from the Greek; literally, part of the sandal worn by tragic actors to give them height. The thick sole was attached to an ornate laced half-boot and the whole was called *cothurnus,* or *kothornos.*

Bussy D'Ambois. George Chapman (English). Tragedy. 5 acts. 1607.

The most famous of Chapman's plays. It was severely criticized by Dryden. The story is the same as that told by Dumas in *La Dame de Montsoreau.* Both authors make the same alteration of actual fact, which was that the king was the person who detested Bussy and not Monsieur, and it was the former who revealed Bussy's amour to Montsoreau.

Bussy D'Ambois (in real life, Louis de Bussy-d'Amboise), a man of insolence and fiery courage, is introduced to the Court of Henry III of France. He quarrels with everyone at court, but wins the favors of Montsoreau's wife. This fact becomes known to Monsieur, who is also enamoured of the lady, and is by him revealed to Montsoreau. The latter forces his wife to send a letter to Bussy summoning him to her. On Bussy's arrival, he is slain.

Butcher. Slang term in circus and burlesque for peddler, such as candy butcher.

Butt, Sir Alfred (1878-   ). English producer. Born in London, he gave up a position as accountant to become Secretary of the Palace Theatre, of which he was made manager in 1904. He was subsequently connected with the following theatres: Gaiety (retired 1919); Adelphi (retired 1919); Empire (retired 1928); Globe; Queen's; Drury Lane, which produced under his auspices *Rose Marie,* 1925; *The Desert Song,* 1927; *Show Boat,* 1928; *The New Moon,* 1929; etc. He was knighted in 1918.

Byron, Arthur (1872-   ). American actor. Son of Oliver Doud Byron and Kate Byron, both players; and nephew of Ada Rehan.

He made his first appearance on the stage in his father's company, February, 1889; and his first appearance on the New York stage with the same company at the People's Theatre, October 27, 1890, in *The Plunger.* After a year with Sol Smith Russell and one in stock at San Francisco, he played with John Drew for successive seasons. He starred in *Petticoats and Bayonets* and *The Stubbornness of Geraldine,* 1902; and in *Major André,* 1903. Subsequently he was leading man with Maxine Elliott, Maude Adams and Ethel Barrymore. He toured with Maude Adams in *What Every Woman Knows* in 1910. He played continuously thereafter, frequently touring to Chicago and other cities, until 1932 when he entered films. His notable pictures have been: *Gabriel Over the White House; The House of Rothschild; The Casino Murder Case; Oil for the Lamps of China.*

Byron, Henry James (1834-1884). English dramatist. Born at Manchester, he achieved success in 1858 with his burlesque *Fra Diavolo* at the Strand Theatre. His most successful play *Our Boys* ran for four years, 1875-79.

Byron, Oliver Doud (1842-1920). American actor. One of the best known tragedians of the Nineties. Supported Booth, Hackett, Mrs. Scott-Siddons, and other stars. He married Mary Kate Rehan, sister of Ada Rehan, and his son Arthur is an actor. His made his debut in *Nicholas Nickleby,* with Joseph Jefferson, at the Holliday St. Theatre in Baltimore, in 1856. He starred for many seasons in the melodrama *Across the Continent.* In New York he became known as Edwin Booth's protégé. At twenty-one he starred in several Shakespearean roles, then returned to his familiar *Across the Continent.*

Later successes were in *The Plunger,* 1892; *The Man on the Box,* 1905; *The Lion and the Mouse,* 1906-9; and *General John Regan,* 1913.

Cackle. British slang term for dialogue.

Caesar and Cleopatra. George Bernard Shaw (English). Comedy. 1899.

A reinterpretation of Caesar in the light of modern history. Shaw maintains that the world of 48 B.C. was just like the world in 1907 A.D., and his historical characters therefore speak just like modern people, even using topical allusions to occurrences they could not have known. Caesar is a weary middle-aged conqueror, sick of war and desiring peace above all things. Cleopatra is a petulant little charmer, alternately a spitfire and a kitten. Frightened at the approach of the Roman legions and Caesar, whose cruelty is legendary, she flees the palace and cuddles up to sleep between the paws of the sphinx, where Caesar finds her. She invites the "kind old gentleman" to take the other paw and warns him that Caesar will probably eat him. Caesar insists that she go back to the palace and act like a queen. The Roman soldiers salute her new friend, she realizes who he is and falls into his arms, weeping with relief. Ptolemy, Cleopatra's brother and co-claimant to the Egyptian throne, is a boy of ten. Caesar's respectable British secretary is perturbed to learn that Egyptian tradition would make brother and sister man and wife. Cleopatra, like a naughty child, would chop off Ptolemy's head and poison her slaves to see them wiggle. She is imprisoned in the palace when it is besieged by the Egyptians, and gets past the guards to Caesar by rolling herself in a rug. Caesar scolds her for having had an enemy assassinated, and goes off to Rome, promising to send Marc Antony back as a present. The Queen bursts out weeping, but nevertheless expresses the hope that Caesar will never come back.

Cahill, Marie (1870-1933). American actress. She appeared in Hoyt comedies, with Augustin Daly, and in George W. Lederer musicals. Her first appearance was in Brooklyn, her native city, in *Kathleen Mavourneen.* Her New York debut was in *C. O. D.* in 1889. She also acted in *A Tin Soldier; Morocco Bound* (in London), 1894; *Sporting Life,* 1897; *Monte Carlo,* 1898; *Sally in Our Alley,* 1902; *Nancy Brown* (her first starring role), 1903; *Moonshine,* 1905; *Marrying Mary,* 1906;

Judy Forgot, 1910; *The Opera Ball,* 1912; *Ninety in the Shade,* 1915; *Just Around the Corner,* 1919; etc.

Cain's Warehouse. Going to Cain's is a synonym for a play's closing. The warehouse for many years was a storage place for old scenery, to be rented or purchased by road companies. With the decline of the road, the business dwindled. The concern ceased operations December 31, 1938.

Calderón de la Barca, Pedro (1600-1681). Spanish poet and dramatist. Born of nobility in Madrid, he wrote his first play *The Chariot of Heaven* before the age of fourteen; became official playwright and master of the revels to the court of Philip IV, for which services he was knighted in 1636; became a priest in 1651 and thereafter wrote mostly for the secular stage and produced only *autos sacramentales* for the feast of Corpus Christi. The Jesuit influence is seen in his plays and some of the most successful defend the attitude of the Jesuits toward the doctrine of freewill. Calderon was honored by royalty and the principal cities of Spain commissioned him annually to write their *autos sacramentales.* His works remained popular until the middle of the 18th century when he was singled out by the pseudo-classical critics for the butt of their attacks on the national drama. In 1763, the performances of *autos sacramentales* were forbidden by law and his plays were censured for the importance given by them to intrigue.

Among his principal cape-and-sword plays are *La dama duende* (*The Woman Ghost*); *Casa con dos puertas mala es de guardar* (*It is Difficult to Guard a House of Two Doors*). Honor tragedies: *El medico de su honra* (*The Physician of His Honor*). His philosophical drama, *Life is a Dream,* is probably the most famous of all his plays, while *La Cena del rey Baltasar* (*Belshazzar's Feast*) is one of his most popular.

Caliban. A curiously sympathetic character in Shakespeare's *The Tempest,* 1611. He is a deformed and savage monster, of subnormal intelligence, the slave of Prospero and Miranda, and is a native of the island on which they are all shipwrecked. So stupid as to mistake a drunken jester for a god, he is pitiable rather than antipathetic. His name today denotes a poor, blundering, clumsy wretch, the victim of fate and circumstance.

Call. Notice placed generally near the stage door, on which is posted information or instructions to the actors.

Call board. A bulletin board backstage on which notices and messages are posted for the information of the cast.

Call boy. Man employed in the theatre to notify actors of their cues, today rapidly being supplanted by the assistant stage manager.

Callot, Jacques (1592-1635). French engraver and designer. Born in Nancy. He studied in Rome under Tempesta and Philippe Thomassin, later entering the service of Cosimo II in Florence. Returning to France he attained a notable reputation throughout Europe under the patronage of the ducal court. His plates number, in all, over fifteen hundred. His importance to history is great as it is his sketch of Francischina which provides the necessary link in the chain of ballerinas which began with the dancing-girls on the Herculaneum frieze in the early Roman days and which, to all appearances, ended with Camilla Veronese in the 18th century. He also did many designs of the stock-characters of the *commedia dell'arte:* Scapino he represents as a brigandish type; Mezzetino as a fool; Punch, whom he calls *Cucurucu,* he pictures as boasting two enormous cock's feathers.

Calypso. A somewhat synthetic folk-song of the natives and adventuring loiterers of Trinidad. The subject-matter ranges from effective political tirade to outright pornography. The name may have taken its origin from the Calypso, the muse, as the makers of these songs affect a pseudo-classicism in titles. A primitive form of dramatic recital.

Camille. Alexandre Dumas, fils (French). Drama. 5 acts. 1852.

Marguerite Gautier, Parisian courtesan, and her young lover, Armand Duval, are living happily together in the country, when Monsieur Duval, the boy's father, begs her to leave his son.

Broken-hearted, Marguerite agrees and permits Armand to believe she has jilted him. Not until she is dying does Armand learn the truth—when he comes to her bedside to ask forgiveness, and Marguerite dies in his arms.

Though the play, book and picture versions of *Camille* are familiar to thousands, there are many facts about the author, Alexander Dumas, fils, and his original story, which the public has either forgotten or never known. He based the novel on the life of Alphonsine du Plessis, "a girl with a Dresden China figure and long enamelled eyes." He created the impression that she wore scentless camellias because she could not endure the odor of flowers. He wrote the play to pay off his debts and called it a pot-boiler. Yet the book set the pace for his entire career, a career which had an extraordinary influence on the history of modern literature. As an incorrigible exponent of the thesis or "useful" drama, he maintained: "If I can exercise some influence over society and require the law-maker to revise the law, I shall have done more than my part as a poet. I shall have done my duty as a man." He became, as a result, the progenitor of the social movement developed by Ibsen, Shaw, Brieux, Hervieu, etc. Camille started the vogue for crying—"tear-jerker"—heroines, a series that was to include Manon Lescaut, Little Eva and Madame X. William Winter's historic fight against realism in the theatre started with Camille. He declared that the theme "ought not to be obtruded in the theatre. It should be 'quietly inured.'"

Campaspe. See *Alexander Campaspe* and *Diogenes.*

Campbell, Mrs. Patrick (Beatrice Stella Tanner) (1865-   ). English actress. She first appeared on the professional stage at Liverpool, 1888, and became famous for her acting in the role of Paula in the original performance of Pinero's *The Second Mrs. Tanqueray* in 1893, which was the foundation of her career as an outstanding tragic actress. Her many notable performances included Juliet, Ophelia, and Lady Macbeth; Magda in Sudermann's play of that name; Mrs. Alving in Ibsen's *Ghosts;* Eliza Doolittle in Shaw's *Pygmalion;* and Anastasia in G. B. Stern's *The Matriarch* at the Royalty Theatre in 1929. She made her film debut at the age of sixty-eight in *Rip Tide.*

Candida. George Bernard Shaw (English). Comedy. 3 acts. 1897.

Candida's tact and intelligence are important factors in the success of her husband, the Reverend Dr. James Morrell. When Candida tries to help a maladjusted young poet, Eugene Marchbanks, Morrell becomes alarmed and says she must choose between him and Marchbanks. Candida chooses Morrell because he is the weaker one and needs her more.

Cantarina. Songstress in the *commedia dell' arte;* generally also the ballerina; does not really play a part in the scenario; introduced purely to present *intermedii* of a musical kind.

See also *Ballerina.*

Cantor, Eddie (1893-   ). American actor. Born in New York, he first appeared on the stage in vaudeville at the Clinton Music Hall, New York, 1907. After acting in many revues and musical comedies he scored a great success as an eccentric comedian in *Kid Boots* in 1923, also further successes in the *Ziegfeld Follies,* 1927, and *Whoopee,* 1928. He made his film version of *Kid Boots,* 1926, and later became, in a series of films, including *Palmy Days, The Kid from Spain* and *Roman Scandals,* one of the most popular comedians on the screen. Also a great radio favorite.

Cape and sword plays. See *Cloak and sword plays.*

Čapek, Josef (1887-1927). Czechoslovak author and painter. Although devoting himself principally to painting, Josef, brother of Karel Čapek, celebrated dramatist, collaborated with his brother in writing and in staging effectively the latter's plays. Largely through their work Czechoslovak drama has become known to the world.

Among his plays are: *The Life of Insects*—known also as *The Insect World* (by Karel and Josef), 1921; *The Land of Many Names,* 1923; *Adam, the Creator,* (by Karel and Josef), 1927.

Čapek, Karel (1890-1939). Czechoslovak dramatist. Recent Czechoslovak drama is known to the world chiefly through the plays of Karel Čapek and his brother Josef.

Karel, son of a village physician of northern Bohemia, has composed verse, fiction and critical essays. He began his theatrical career at twenty-one with *The Robbers,* an allegorical presentation of selfish youth arrayed against age. With the appearance of *R.U.R.,* he became a celebrity (1923).

Chief among his plays are: *The Robbers,* 1920; *R.U.R.,* 1923; *The Life of Insects* (by Karel and Josef), 1921 (produced by Wm. A. Brady as *The World*

We Live In); *The Makropoulos Affair,* 1922; *Loupeznik,* 1926; *Adam, the Creator,* (by Karel and Josef), 1927.

Capitano. Stock character in a *commedia dell'arte;* the *miles gloriosus* of the antique stage, made popular and more grotesque; arresting personality, full of boasts and vaunting, but coward as soon as there is fighting. Costume: suggests now Italian *condottiere,* now Spanish bravo, with long-nosed mask, fierce moustache; vaunts his way through scenario, creating terror by appearance and laughter by poltroonish cowardice.

Caponsacchi. Arthur Goodrich and Rose A. Palmer (American). Tragedy. Prologue, epilogue and 3 acts. 1926.

Based on Robert Browning's poem, *The Ring and the Book,* which in turn was derived from the story of a Roman murder case.

Count Guido Franceschini, a fortune hunter, marries Pompilia Camparini, a supposedly wealthy girl, only to find her with no money and living as a ward in the Camparini household. The Count to get rid of his wife accuses her of infidelity with a certain Canon Giuseppe Caponsacchi. She is so harassed by her husband that she persuades the Canon to take her back to the Camparinis. Guido pursues them and catches them. Pompilia is tried for adultery and sent to a convent, while Caponsacchi is banished. Later, Pompilia, her young son, and her foster parents are murdered by Count Guido. The crimes are discovered; Guido is arrested and, on the Pope's decision, executed.

Caprice. Sil-Vara (Hungarian). Translated and adapted by Philip Moeller. Comedy. 1928.

This was produced by the Theatre Guild, with Alfred Lunt and Lynn Fontanne in the leading roles. They later acted in it in London, 1929.

Counsellor Albert Von Echardt learns from an ex-mistress, Amalia, that their son Robert, now sixteen and at the age of indiscretion, is curious about life and romance and needs a father's wise advice. Moved by his old sweetheart's plea and anxious to know his son, Albert receives the boy into his home. This does not entirely meet with the approval of Albert's current flame, Ilsa Von Ilsen. In fact, so outraged is she that when Amalia and her son arrive, she flees to the Bavarian mountains. Two weeks pass. Ilsa returns. She has determined that she herself will teach Robert those things he wishes to know. Being immature and susceptible, the boy is a willing subject, and is soon in the throes of a violent puppy love for the older woman. Whereupon she confesses to him that his father is her lover. Disgusted and disillusioned, Robert leaves the house with his mother and Ilsa once again is in full command of Albert's heart and home.

Captain Applejack. Walter Hackett (American). Farce-comedy. 3 acts. 1925.

Ambrose Applejohn, a young English squire, tires of his sedentary life in Cornwall, decides to go in search of adventure, and puts his house up for sale. A few nights later some people call and Ambrose believes them to be prospective buyers. They are crooks in search of a treasure supposed to be hidden in the house. Upon learning this the squire decides to sit up all night on guard but falls asleep and dreams himself his piratical ancestor. When he wakes he beats off the crooks and at the same time realizes he is in love with a girl who has been living in the house all the time.

Captain Brassbound's Conversion. George Bernard Shaw (English). Comedy. 1899.

Shaw wrote this as a vehicle for Ellen Terry, who played Lady Cicely Waynflete, and this may account for the fact that it is less seriously satirical than most of his works and is mainly concerned with portraying a heroine of charm and graciousness, woman incarnate and delightfully so. James Carew, whom Miss Terry married, acted Captain Brassbound on tour with the star. Grace George is one of the American actresses who have revived the play.

In Morocco, Captain Brassbound, a dangerous brigand, conducts parties from the port, Mogador, to the interior, by arrangement with an Arab sheikh. Brassbound's crew consists of wastrels and ragged cutthroats. To the country there come Sir Howard Hallam, English judge, and his sister-in-law, Lady Cicely Waynflete. The latter, curious and also courageous, decides they must ascend the Atlas mountains. The clergyman of Mogador arranges for Brassbound to lead the expedition, which pleases the freebooter no end, since he has an old score to settle with Hallam. For the judge is the desperado's uncle, and it was through him that Brassbound's half-mad mother was sent to prison. Therefore the pirate ponders selling his uncle into captivity. Whereupon Cecily intervenes. A rare charmer, with the power to twist sheikhs and nobles alike around her little finger, she soon has Brassbound so smitten with her that he is willing to forego his revenge. When word comes from the captain that the pirate and his confederates are to be sent down to the coast in chains, Cecily repays her debt to Brassbound by conducting the prosecution herself.

Acting as both witness and advocate, she procures his acquittal. Having completely converted the bandit from his evil ways and left him without an occupation, it would seem as if the least the lady could do would be to marry him. But just as she grows worried lest she have to consent to this course, Brassbound is summoned to join his ship and reverts to his villainous ways. Much relieved, the lady murmurs, "What an escape!"

Captive, The. Edouard Bourdet (French). Tragedy. 3 acts. 1926.

Seeks to exploit disharmonies due to homosexual love. Represents the heroine struggling against a force too strong for her. She has conceived for another woman a passion which renders her indifferent to the advances of a male lover. Yet she would keep this lover as a screen to hide her real reason for remaining in Paris against the wishes of her father, a diplomat desirous of taking her to Rome. At first, Jacques accepts her suggestion that he merely pose as her fiance. Then, in the hope of driving out a morbid passion by one perfectly natural, he marries her. But, although the pair spend a year in travel, Irene returns as mad over her friend as ever, and Jacques is forced to recognize the wisdom of the warning given him earlier by a friend who had suffered with a wife similarly infatuated.

Capus, Alfred (1858-1922). French author. Born at Aix-en-Provence, he came to Paris from the South in order to enter the ranks of the journalists. Eventually he won fame as editor of *Figaro*, author of several novels, and member of the French Academy. In his plays, he is an ironic realist, and most of them are also devoted to drawing the new type of self-dependent heroine, philosophic in facing misfortune.

His plays include: *Brignol and His Daughter*, 1894; *Rosine*, 1897; *The Little Minxes*, 1897; *Bourgeois Marriage*, 1898; *The Husbands of Leontine*, 1900; *Money or Your Life*, 1900; *The Little Functionary*, 1901; *Luck*, 1901; *The Two Schools*, 1902; *The Chatelaine*, 1902; *The Adversary*, 1903; *Monsieur Piegois*, 1905; *The Passersby*, 1906; *The Wounded Bird*, 1908; *The Two Men*, 1908; *An Angel*, 1909; *The Adventurer*, 1910; *The Favorites*, 1911; *Helene Ardouin*, 1913; *The Beauty Institute*, 1913.

Carbon arc. Type of lighting instrument; a clear strong blue white light is obtained by the electric arc between two carbons; although outmoded by the incandescent lamp it still is used for long throw projection.

Cardinal, The. James Shirley (English). Tragedy. 1641.

The Cardinal, urged by ambition, designs that the Duchess Rosaura, the widowed daughter-in-law of the king of Navarre, shall marry his nephew, Columbo. She is betrothed to Colombo, but he leaves soon after to go to war. While he is away, she becomes betrothed to Alvarez, whom she loves. Colombo returns home unexpectedly and kills Alvarez on his wedding night. The Duchess to be revenged has the treacherous Hernando kill Colombo. The Cardinal, suspecting the complicity of the Duchess, plans to ravish and kill her. Hernando, however, kills the Cardinal, but not before the latter, by a trick, poisons the Duchess. Hernando takes his own life.

Careless Husband, The. Colley Cibber (English). Comedy. 5 acts. 1715.

Sir Charles Easy, who neglects his wife, becomes contrite when he discovers that her gentle treatment of him is due not to ignorance of his infidelity, but to her virtue and sense of duty.

Carey, Henry (1690-1743). English dramatist and musician. Said to have been an illegitimate son of George Savile, Marquis of Halifax, he wrote the words, and often the music, of many burlesques produced on the London stage between 1715 and 1737. Best known as the author of the ballad, *Sally in Our Alley*. He was credited, without much authority, with the authorship of *God Save the King*. He was the great-grandfather of Edmund Kean. He died probably by suicide.

Carolina Art Association. See *Dock Street Theatre*.

Carolina Playmakers. In 1910 Professor Frederick H. Koch founded the Dakota Playmakers at the University of North Dakota. In 1918 he was attracted by the promise of the field of mountaineer life and began his work as professor of dramatic literature at the University of North Carolina at Chapel Hill. Here he has developed something unique in playmaking. His students are concerned with the material around them, drawn from a civilization that has remained homogeneous. How much influence upon playwrights the success of the Carolina Playmakers has had it is difficult to estimate, but it is a fact that a real regional drama has been built up. Koch frequently lectures at other universities.

Carr, Joseph William Comyns (1849-1916). British author. Born in London he became an art critic, helped to found the New Gallery, and was first editor of the *English Illustrated Magazine*. He dramatized Thomas Hardy's *Far from the Madding Crowd*, 1882; wrote a blank verse play called *King Arthur*, in which Irving, Forbes-Robertson, and Ellen Terry appeared; and later was the author of several plays which Beerbohm Tree produced.

Carriage trade. A term which dates from the latter half of the 19th century when the socially élite of the town came to the theatre in their carriages. Now used to describe well-to-do audiences in New York and other cities.

Carroll, Earl (1892-   ). American producer. Born in Pittsburgh, Pennsylvania. Enlisted in the aviation corps in the First World War and was kept in the United States to teach aviators. Visited native theatres in the Orient after the war, established a flying-school in China, then returned to Pittsburgh to write plays. Wrote lyrics and music for *So Long, Letty, Canary Cottage;* author of *The Love Mill, Flora Bella, The Lady of the Lamp, Bavu.* For several seasons since 1923, produced *Earl Carroll Vanities,* many of which he wrote and composed.

Carroll, Paul Vincent (1900-   ). British dramatist. He was born on the outskirts of Dundalk, County Lough, Ireland. His father, a country schoolteacher, saw personally to his son's early education. At the age of fourteen, young Carroll departed for Dublin to enter training as a teacher. There he found the Abbey Theatre and became interested in the stage. Since 1921 has taught in a boys' school. His first play, *The Watched Pot* was produced in 1931. In 1932 he and Teresa Deevey shared an Abbey prize with *Things That Are Caesar's,* and in 1934 he wrote *Shadow and Substance.* Eddie Dowling produced it in New York City in 1938. This was followed in 1939 by *The White Steed.*

Cars of Thespis. Name of present-day touring companies in Italy which give open-air performances of plays and operas.

Carter, Mrs. Leslie (1862-1937). American actress. Born in Lexington, Kentucky; debut at the Broadway in New York in 1890 in *The Ugly Duckling*. On tour until 1893; then after two years' study appeared as Maryland Calvert in *The Heart of Maryland* at Washington. After three years in this role she made her London first appearance at the Adelphi Theatre in 1898, in the same play. A highly successful career under David Belasco's management, during which she scored in *Zaza, Du Barry* and *Adrea,* was terminated by a financial disagreement at the time of her marriage to W. L. Payne in 1906. For six years under her own management, and for four years under David Cort's, she played in New York and on tour in her tried vehicles, as well as in new plays. She made a London vaudeville appearance in 1917, then retired until 1921, when she returned to New York as Lady Catherine in *The Circle;* between 1923 and 1934 she played in old and new plays, including *Stella Dallas* and *The Shanghai Gesture,* and in her seventies played in a film *The Vanishing Pioneer,* a Western picture.

Carton, Richard Claude (Richard Claude Critchett) (1856-1928). English dramatist. Best known as a writer of farcical comedies.

The son of a surgeon, he became an actor, taking the name of Carton. His name is always associated with that of his wife, Katherine Compton (1853-1928), known to the public as Miss Compton, for whom he wrote his best plays and who was distinguished by her sonorous voice and her comic caricatures of the imperturbable aristocrat. Best known of Carton's plays are: *Lady Huntworth's Experiment,* long a favorite with amateurs; *Mr. Preedy and the Countess;* and *Lord and Lady Algy.*

Cartwright, George (17th century). English dramatist. Cartwright's one important work was *The Heroic Lover,* 1661, an heroic tragedy of the type of which Dryden was a later and greater exponent.

Case. Scene-buildings of the theatre of Renaissance Italy, corresponding to the medieval mansions.

Case Is Altered, The. Ben Jonson (English). Comedy. 1609.

Count Ferneze, who has lost an infant son, Camillo, when Vicenza was captured by the French General Chamont, sees his elder son, Paulo, go off to the wars against the same Chamont. Paulo is taken prisoner, but Maximilian, Ferneze's general, brings back Chamont captive and with him a friend, Gasper. Ferneze arranges for an exchange of prisoners—Paulo for Gasper—but Chamont learns of it, impersonates Gasper and so escapes. Chamont returns with Paulo. Then it is discovered that Gasper is Ferneze's lost son, Camillo.

Cassilis Engagement, The. St. John Hankin (English). Comedy. 4 acts. 1907.

After spending a week-end with his fiancee and her mother, Geoffrey Cassilis breaks off his engagement, convinced that marriage would be a failure. The week-end visit was arranged by Geoffrey's mother.

Cast. (1) Noun: the dramatis personae of a play; the group of actors selected to portray the dramatis personae. (2) Verb: to employ actors according to their suitability for respective roles.

Caste. Thomas William Robertson (English). Drama. 1867.

Esther Eccles, a ballet girl, marries The Honorable George D'Alroy. She receives a report that her husband has been killed in battle, but soon discovers the report is false. D'Alroy returns to England to rescue his wife and child from poverty and social snobbery.

This play is important because Robertson strives to introduce serious thought and actual living types into the theatre. His methods of looking at life and the naturalism of his stage conversation make him a forerunner of modern drama.

Castelvetro, Lodovico (1505-1571). An Italian litterateur. He was born in Modena of an old and noble family. He was educated in Bologna, Ferrara, Padua and Siena, taking a degree in law at the latter's university in deference to his father. He finally felt obliged to leave the legal profession and he returned in ill health to Modena where he took up literary pursuits. A literary quarrel begun by his criticism of the poet Caro resulted in his exile. For several years he travelled from place to place—Lyons, Geneva, Vienna, finally Chiavenna, where he died. He was well-known as a translator of Aristotle's *Poetics,* and his commentary thereon forms his contribution to dramatic theory.

Caster. Rubber-tired ball bearing wheel and support not less than 4 inches in diameter used for shifting scenery. Two types: (1) swivel, turns in all directions; (2) stationary, moves back and forth. These casters are permanently attached to the pieces of scenery that are to be moved.

See *Scenery.*

CASTING

BY A. AND S. LYONS

1. An actor enters a casting office and obtains admittance; either by being told to write to the casting director for an appointment, by having an appointment made at that time by a secretary, or by chance by being seen at once. When the actor has his appointment he is interviewed in the following manner:

He fills out a card with his name, address, telephone number, date of his registration. The actor is then asked what he has done in the theatre, in New York or outside of New York. The name of the play and the specific part the actor played is recorded whenever possible; and sometimes the name of the star of the play is put down in conjunction as an indication of the type of company with which the actor has worked. If the actor lists out-of-town experience, he is usually asked what parts and in what play.

If the actor has done radio, this experience is usually noted. If he has any particular attributes; such as a trained voice, ability to play the piano or various musical instruments, ability to dance or, what is more important, a command of any foreign language or various dialects these are noted. There is also a space on the card in which the height, weight, general appearance, i.e., brown hair, etc., is recorded.

Then, if possible, a note is made which will recall the actor to mind by saying "reminds of . . ." (usually some actor who is well-known). Some notation is made also of the quality of his voice, speech and also general appearance. In some cases the actor is asked his age, in other cases the age is written down as a range of ages which he could possibly play.

Frequently he is catalogued also as being juvenile, character, juvenile leads, second or character, as the case may be.

2. A dramatic or legitimate actor is usually not auditioned. In some rare cases, where it seems that the particular actor would be possible for a most important part, he may be asked to come in late one afternoon and read—usually a scene of his own preference. Normally, the musical or musical-comedy actor is given an audition as soon as possible; if a singer, usually by recording or by direct audition.

3. An actor's fitness in the sense of ability in the theatre is usually judged in various ways. First, by the past record of parts that he has played and the type of company in which he has played. Secondly, by the impression that one gets of the actor's authority, warmth, self-confidence or general personality. This second point is rather important, especially in the case of the unknown actor, the actor who has done nothing on Broadway and who has never been seen in so far as this particular agent is concerned.

4. From the standpoint of physical appearance, an actor is rated first in a general classification, i.e., juvenile, character juvenile, lead, second or character. As a sub-heading to this, he may be classified as good for professional types—lawyers, doctors, judges—or as rural types, small-town bankers, etc.; or as specifically a lady, a gentle-man, a mug, a tart, a laborer, etc.

(b) Actors are usually not rated according to their experience. There is no method of scoring or rating them except that some are recognized as thoroughly established, promising young people, or absolutely newcomers.

5. (a) Training in the dramatic school can be of importance to the actor as far as matters of voice, diction and posture are concerned.

(b) Summer stock usually affords a better method of training for the actor because today summer stock has become completely commercial, usually professional and the actor does have the opportunity of actual performances and working under professional methods.

(c) Amateur performances, unless seen by the agent, are not of particular value.

(d) Stock companies, other than summer stock, usually afford the same value as summer stock. In cases where the actor has worked with organizations like the Cleveland Playhouse, Pasadena Playhouse, Goodman Theatre of Dallas Little Theatre are referred to as stock companies, a definite notation is made, for these specific companies have developed to such an extent that the actor who is associated with them for a period of time usually has a better training than the average.

(e) Professional appearances outside of New York are usually only of value in that the actor has had that experience under professional conditions and also, usually from the parts played, give a more complete idea of the sort of role for which he is right.

6. There is no preliminary examination or reading of lines given in the office.

7. If an actor has registered, he is placed on the active file and on an active list which is consulted each and every time that there is a call for an actor for a specific part. If that actor seems right in quality and in age, range and specific physical re-

quirements, he is called back into the office and the agent tries to make a comparison
of the parts the actor has played with the current specific requirement, i.e., if the
agent has seen him in a similar part or in a part that has the same sort of quality, it is
much easier to point to that performance as a selling point to the producer.

8. The casting agent either (1) calls the producer, playwright or director, or
(2) is called by one of the above regarding a definite play. The agent invariably asks
to read the play so that he may have a definite idea of the various characters and, after
reading, talks with the producer, playwright or director to get their various specific
ideas about definite qualities desired in the various characters. The agent then compiles
a list of possibilities, picking five or six different actors for each of the desired characters in the play. Then the agent calls either the producer, playwright or director
and makes known his various selections. At that point the actor is sent to see the
producer at which time he is told he is a definite possibility to read or is discarded.

9. Personality is definitely an important factor as far as the actor is concerned but
this point is completely a matter of the reaction on the part of the specific agent. The
word personality is more encompassing here than in its usual use, for in this case a
matter of authority, ability, warmth and what the actor possesses also enter into the
person's natural physical abilities.

Casting, amateur. The director of amateur productions must assume most of
the burdens of presenting a play. He is dealing with people who are volunteering
their services and who frequently gain admission to the cast because their father,
mother or someone is a member of the church council or the school board. Usually
these handicaps are somewhat offset by natural enthusiasm. Everyone loves to be in a
play, and the moment that the school or the amateur dramatic club sends out a call,
the whole community get excited.

Taking then into consideration, all the social, political and personal issues that
always arise in this form of entertainment, the director starts out by preparing himself thoroughly for the task before him. He should read play catalogs and strive, above
all things, to get pieces in which the honors are equally important. This is the best
advice obtainable, because it means that no amateur will be required to carry the
burden of the show in a star role. Plays with star roles should be avoided, established
classics that are intricate in plot and character development should also be avoided.
Comedy and farce comedy are usually safe mediums for the display of amateur talent.

Having made his play selection, the director should familiarize himself with the
various roles, and then call for a tryout. Informally, then, without letting the people
know his purpose, he should talk to one person and then another, striving to see how
they measure up to the impressions he has of the various characters in the play.

Next he should ask these people, in turn, to get up and speak off something they
know or to read a scene from the play. Sometimes a director can get an excellent idea
of an amateur's ability by asking him to improvise a scene. Two players, for instance,
can be told a little story and then told to act out the story, using the proper movements to indicate a state of feeling, and words that put over the idea. An extemporaneous test of this sort will reveal almost instantly, native ability, elasticity of spirit
and above all, the player's power to project his personality before a crowd of
onlookers.

Final selections should be made in regard to the suitability of the player from the standpoint of culture, feeling, personal taste in dress and bearing, deportment and memory.

Before giving out the parts, it's a good thing to have the various players copy the part and report to rehearsal merely to read them. This method makes them unconscious, at first, of the fact that the director is observing them and permits the director to change characters without offending anyone. To be demoted in a reading doesn't hurt peoples' feelings, but giving up a memorized role causes humiliation.

When the parts are all assigned and the play learned, the director should insist on repetition. He can do marvels in giving a play a professional effect, by rehearsing big scenes and difficult bits, over and over, while the players are sitting down, standing up, and then actually going through the business of the scene.

Big parts should not be given to people who are tone deaf. At the very beginning, the players should be given a conception of the part as the director sees it. Every player should be made to believe that he is contributory to the whole story; that the effect of his character continues even after he leaves the stage. Exits and entrances should be polished so that they are swift and imperceptible. Repeat and repeat; and soon an amatur show will seem professional.

Casting agent. A go-between for both actor and producer who serves to procure engagements for actors and to supply performers for producers. Because his rate was usually 10 per cent of the salary, he came to be known as a "10 per center."

Castle Garden Theatre. A playhouse that was among New York's earliest theatres; originally a fort, it was circular in form; enjoyed great popularity when first opened as a theatre in 1845. Jenny Lind made her American debut here; now used as the Aquarium in Battery Park.

Castle of Perseverance, The. Author unknown. (English). Morality play.
A. W. Pollard, in his *English Miracle Plays, Moralities and Interludes* says of this, it is "the most primitive morality play we possess in date and type—" it "gives the spiritual history of the microcosm, Man, from his birth to his individual doom."

This is a play in rhyme, with thirteen line stanzas and is considered to have been written not later than 1425.

Castro, Guillén de (1569-1631). Spanish dramatist. A dramatist, native of Valencia, who had a career both in the army and in politics. He imitated his friend, Lope de Vega, in several comedias, but his principal contribution to the Spanish theatre of the Golden Age is the fact that he was the first dramatist to dramatize the Cid legend.

Principal works: *Las mocedades del Cid* (The Youthful Adventures of El Cid); *Las Hazanas del Cid* (The Exploits of El Cid). His plays, written in the old romantic style achieved enormous popularity. These two plays are based on the old Cid ballads. The first-named presents a dramatic conflict between love and honor and was the basis of Corneille's famous drama *Le Cid* which was the French author's first masterpiece.

Castrum. Name of a certain scene building, or mansion, of the medieval stage, meaning, literally, "castle."
See also *Mansions.*

Cathleen ni Houlihan. William Butler Yeats (Irish). Poetic drama. 1 act. 1892.

First produced as *The Countess Cathleen* in 1892, it is one of the two plays with which the Irish Literary Theatre started on its course. It treats of Ireland in old times, at a period of famine, when the people sell their souls to the demons for food. It revolves about the figure of a noble woman who is ready to sell her soul for the people.

Catholic Theatre Movement, The. Organized in 1932 to censor the theatre for Catholics, and discipline it by pressure, through recommendation and boycott. A Catholic White List is published weekly in the Catholic News, classifying plays as (A) satisfactory; (B) partly satisfactory; and (C) wholly objectionable. Examples are: (A) *Victoria Regina;* (B) *Parnell* and *Winterset;* (C) *Boy Meets Girl; Tobacco Road; Dead End.* This organization is to the legitimate stage what *The National Legion of Decency* (q.v.) is to the screen and radio.

Catiline. Ben Jonson (English). Printed 1611.

Based on the events of the year 63 B.C., when Catiline organized a conspiracy to overthrow the existing government and to renew with the aid of Sulla's veterans the scenes of bloodshed which Rome had recently seen.

Cato. Joseph Addison (English). Tragedy in blank verse in 5 acts. 1713.

The scene of the play is a hall of the governor's palace in Utica, the historical background of Cato's last desperate struggle against Caesar and his resolve either to free his country or die in the attempt. The play's success was due as much to its eighteenth century implications as to its merits as a drama per se. Whigs and Tories took each line personally. The Whigs cheered whenever "liberty" was mentioned and applauded Cato as representing Marlborough. To the Tories, on the other hand, dictatorial Caesar resembled the oppressor, Marlborough, and was fervently booed. Almost every poet of the day, including Pope, wrote verses about "Cato," and the play itself was almost as successful in a German version as in the original.

Cavea. Name given to auditorium in Roman theatre.

Cazuela. The space in Spanish theatres back of the corral, where women of the lower class witnessed performances.

Ceiling. Canvas flat, which is flown, and rests on the edges of the upright flats, to suggest a real ceiling.

Ceiling, book. Ceiling for interior sets built in two pieces which fold together at the middle, book-like. The fold is parallel to the footlights. This method is used for flying the ceiling.
See *Scenery.*

Ceiling plate. Back stage term. Holds fly line to ceiling piece.
See *Scenery.*

Ceiling, roll. A ceiling of cloth, which may be rolled for transportation or storage.

Celeste, Celine (1814-1882). The first French actress to appear in America, making her New York debut on June 27, 1827. Scored tremendous hit in *The French Spy.*

Celestina, La; or The Tragi-Comedy of Calisto and Melibea. Fernando de Rojas (Spanish). Drama.
The oldest known edition (1499) contained sixteen acts, as did the edition of 1501. That of 1502 consists of twenty-one acts. *Celestina* ranks as one of the most important dramas in Spanish literature. The double love-affairs of a master who loves a certain lady, while his confidential servant loves the servant of his lady, the intense realism, and several other features found in *Celestina* are bases of many later Spanish *comedias.*

Cenci, The. Percy Bysshe Shelley (English). Tragedy. 5 acts. 1819.
Count Francesco Cenci, head of one of the noblest and richest families in Rome, conceives an implacable hatred against all of his children, except his daughter, Beatrice for whom he has an incestuous passion. Beatrice plots with her step-mother, Lucretia, and her brother, Bernardo, to murder the Count, and it is done by two hired assassins. The Cenci are arrested and sentenced to death. In spite of general sympathy for them, they are executed by order of the Pope. These events in 1599 are the subject of the play. It is essentially of the library rather than the theatre. The single important play of the English theatre between Sheridan and Pinero, it bridges a century of British drama and is a strong expression of the romantic idealism of the time.

Censorship. In the U. S. there is legal censorship of motion pictures, but not of plays. However there are laws regarding obscenity that must be observed. There are strict penalties involved which apply to all those engaged in the play and its production, and the theatre license. In various localities there are organizations like the New York Society for Suppression of Vice, The Catholic Theatre Movement, The Watch and Ward Society, church and civic organizations that keep an unofficial but watchful eye on the theatre. Anthony Comstock and John S. Sumner have been leaders in this activity. On the other hand, the theatre has been watchful of its freedom and is prompt to defend it and attack any censorship or quasi-censorship laws.

In England there is absolute censorship and every play that charges admission or is performed in a place where liquor is sold must be first passed on by the Lord Chamberlain, the official censor. This control of the theatre goes as far back as 1545 when the official was called Master of the Revels. But Walpole's statute of 1737 was the first statutory enactment of this control. It has continued ever since and has acted as a retarding influence on the Theatre in England. During most of the 19th century the theatre in England was stagnant and stale. There was no vitality and the limitations of the censorship militated against live and new ideas.

Censorship always causes this suffocation of talent and thought and wherever there is censorship of one kind or another the result is the same. The continental countries have been definitely freer from it and have been rewarded by a brighter, more adult and sophisticated drama.

See also *Stage Jurisprudence.*

Censorship, Puritan. Synonomously, strict. From the stern morals of Puritan days the word puritan has come to symbolize any strait-laced influence. In 1698, Jeremy Collier published *A Short View of the Immorality and Profaneness of the English Stage,* which aroused great bitterness in theatre lovers. A book called *The Controversy Between the Puritans and the Stage* has been written by Elbert Thompson, tracing the long conflict between the bluenoses and the theatre, from the earliest days of Plato down to the present century.

Censorship, Roman. Morals were extremely loose in the ancient Roman theatre, more so, even, than those of the Greek devotees of the *phlyakes.* Licentious plays were a commonplace and very little restraint was exerted upon them by their producers.

Centlivre, Susannah (c. 1667-1723). English dramatist. The daughter of a Lincolnshire farmer, named Freeman. Garrick was very popular in her play *The Wonder: A Woman Keeps a Secret, 1714.* Others of her successful plays were *The Gamester; The Busy Body* and *The Basset Table.*

In 1706 she married the chef to the royal household, Joseph Centlivre, and had the friendship of Rowe, Farquhar and Steele.

Central figure. The hero or heroine or, otherwise, principal protagonist of a play.

Cervantes, Saavedra Miguel de (1547-1616). Spanish author. Author of the celebrated *Don Quixote,* born at Alcala de Henares. He was a soldier for a number of years; spent almost five years in captivity by pirates at Algiers; was ransomed, went to Constantinople, and finally returned to Spain where he married and wrote a number of plays and novels. His theories of the drama are best expressed in Chapter XLVIII of the first part of *Don Quixote.*

Chains. Elizabeth Baker (English). Play. 4 acts. 1909.
A city clerk, oppressed by the deadly monotony and narrowness of his life,

thinks of going to Australia, but never does. A shopgirl, oppressed by the equally dull routine of her life, thinks of escaping it by marrying a middle-aged widower, but never goes through with it. Both are bound by the chains of convention.

This is a play with little story, complications of incident or emotional tension. It is considered one of the most successful of those plays which avoid the ordinary and established conventions.

Chamberlain's Men, Lord. See *Lord Chamberlain's Men.*

Chances, The. John Fletcher (English). Play. 5 acts. 1611.

The plot is based on a novel of Cervantes, and the chances dealt with in the play are the coincidences which bring Constantia and the Duke of Ferrara, with whom she is eloping, into a number of complications. This work contains some of Fletcher's finest dialogue.

Changeling. Thomas Middleton and William Rowley (English). Tragedy. 1623.

Beatrice-Joanna, daughter of the Governor of Alicant, ordered by her father to marry Alonso de Piracquo, has Alonso killed by de Flores, a roué. She is in love with Alsemaro, who discovers their guilt. They are brought before the Governor, but before he can sentence them, they commit suicide.

A sub-plot affords the title of the play: Antonio disguises himself as a crazy changeling in order to get access to Isabella, wife of the keeper of the madhouse.

Chantecler. Edmond Rostand (French). Symbolic drama. 4 acts. 1910.

This satire on society is notable for its wit and poetry. According to the author it is the drama of human endeavor grappling with life. Of it Rostand said: "It is a . . . symbolic poem in which I have used animals to evoke and develop the sentiments, passions, and dreams of men . . . My cock is not, properly speaking, a dramatic hero. He is a character which I have used to express my own dreams and to make live, before my eyes, a little of myself." The tragic climax of the play comes when the vain Chantecler discovers he is not responsible for making the sun rise.

Coquelin, for whom the role of the cock had been created, was dead when the play was produced and Lucien Guitry took the part.

Chapelain, Jean (1595-1674). French poet and critic. Born in Paris, he was destined by his parents from birth for a literary career. As a friend of Racine, Corneille, Richelieu, and Malherbe he was a welcome frequenter of the Hôtel de Rambouillet. The poem *La Pucelle,* on which he spent a great number of years, was a failure and brought down upon him the venomous ridicule of Boileau. In spite of this he was still regarded as an important critic. His contributions to dramatic theory are to be found in his *Les Sentiments de l'académie française sur la tragi-comedie du 'Cid'* and the *Sommaire d'une poetique dramatique.*

Chapin, Harold (1886-1915). Anglo-American dramatist. Born at Brooklyn, New York, of Huguenot descent, he went to England and became known as a skillful playwright. He was serving with the R.A.M.C. when he was killed at the battle of Loos, Sept. 26, 1915. He was identified with the repertory movement in England.

His plays include: *Augustus in Search of a Father; The Marriage of Columbine; The Autocrat of the Coffee Stall; Art and Opportunity; It's the Poor that Helps the Poor.*

Chaplin, Charles (1889-   ). Anglo-American producer, actor. One of the greatest comedians of all time. At an early age he became a member of a juvenile troupe of actors. He played Billy the page boy in *Sherlock Holmes* with William Gillette and afterwards was a vaudeville headliner in Great Britain and the U. S. His film career began with Keystone in November, 1913. In 1918 he built his own studios in Hollywood. Among his outstanding pictures are: *The Kid; The Gold Rush; The Circus; City Lights* was a pantomimic comedy with synchronized music and sound, but no dialogue. In 1936 he produced, directed, wrote, composed music, edited and appeared in *Modern Times*. In his acting he has never departed from his original character of the pathetic little tramp with the out-pointing gait and the tiny mustache which in his philosophy epitomizes the comic spirit. He has also steadfastly refused to take a speaking part. He is now making a cinema on dictators; is President of the Charles Chaplin Film Corporation.

Chapman, George (c. 1559-1634). Elizabethan dramatist. He lived in the period that produced the artistic genius of Shakespeare, Dekker, Jonson. He was one of the most capable dramatists of his time, a trifle rough on occasion, but with a fund of humor. He was more adept with comedy than tragedy, for he lacked subtlety in the latter. He wrote in collaboration with his contemporaries as well as alone.

Among his works are: *The Blinde Beggar of Alexandria; The Gentleman Usher; Bussy d'Ambois; The Conspiracie and Tragedie of Charles, Duke of Byron; Eastward Hoe* (on which he collaborated with Jonson and Marston).

Chapman, William, Sr. Organizer of the Chapman family floating theatre, 1829, one of the earliest Mississippi showboats.

Character actors. Those players who interpret roles older or younger than themselves, or a nationality foreign to their own, necessitating changes in manner of speaking, voice, habit, walk, etc.

Characterization. (1) by dramatist: the delineation of a role in the script of a play; (2) by actor: the portrayal of a role onstage.

Charles II of England (1630-1685). Lacy was his favorite actor and Nell Gwyn one of his favorite actresses. He became literally the patron of the contemporary theatre, issuing grants, or patents, to the two major companies, D'Avenant's and Killigrew's. His taste, deriving from his years in exile, favored the artificial French drama and rejected the English drama, especially the work of Shakespeare;

and as he was patron, or more properly dictator, of the theatre, his taste was the deciding factor in the choice of material. Playwrights wrote primarily to please him. His predominant demand or interest was entertainment.

Charley's Aunt. Brandon Thomas (English). Comedy. 3 acts. 1892.

When Charley's aunt does not arrive from Brazil, Fancourt Bobberly impersonates her and chaperones Charles Wykeham, Jack Chesney, and their sweethearts at a luncheon and tete-a-tete in Charles' rooms at Oxford. Charley's aunt, who is reputed to have money, is courted ardently by the Oxford solicitor.

Chastelard. Algernon Charles Swinburne (English). Tragedy. 5 acts. 1865.

The first of three romantic dramas by Swinburne on the subject of Mary Queen of Scots, of which *Bothwell, A Tragedy* (1874), and *Mary Stuart* (1881) are the others.

Deals with Chastelard, a grandson of Bayard, and Mary Queen of Scots. Chastelard, madly in love with Mary, follows her to Scotland, where he is discovered in her room and sentenced to death.

Chatrian, Alexandre (1816-1890). French dramatist. Was the inseparable collaborator of Émile Erckmann, with whom he wrote countless plays and operas. The collaboration began in 1847, its first notable dramatic success being *L'Illustre docteur Matheus* in 1859. The two men were strongly opposed to militarism and imperialism, for which reason their *l'ami Fritz* was denounced as anti-patriotic. It scored a great success. *Le Juif Polonais,* one of the best known Erckmann-Chatrian plays has been seen in this country under the title of *The Bells.*

See also *Erckmann, Émile.*

Chatterton. Alfred Victor Vigny (French). Biographical Drama. 3 acts. 1835.

Chatterton who wrote history and poetry which he sold as old masterpieces was finally exposed as a fraud; and, poverty stricken, killed himself at the age of seventeen.

Chekhov, Anton Pavlovich (1860-1904). Russian author. Generally regarded as the greatest Russian dramatist. He contributed largely to the success of the Moscow Art Theatre and was its leading creative genius.

Born at Taganrog in South Russia, Chekhov grew up in humble circumstances. His father was a grocer, and his grandfather had been a serf. After study at a church school, diversified by work in the paternal shop and summers at an estate in the country, where his grandfather was a supervisor, Chekhov entered the medical department of the University of Moscow, from which he received his degree in 1884. Two years later appeared his first volume of stories, a collection which discloses the influence upon him of the French. His health was early impaired, however, and he was forced to move to the South. His fiction grew somber, and he began to dally with the drama, which hitherto he had regarded with contempt, having said, "The novel is a lawful wife, but the stage is a noisy, flashy and insolent mistress."

Although *Ivanov* and *The Sea Gull* were accorded a welcome by the public, their widest recognition came only when set forth by the Moscow Art Theatre, an organization which could understand the author's purposes and give these plays artistic being. The wings of the sea gull, in honor of Chekhov, were taken as the symbol of that theatre.

Threatened with tuberculosis during the latter years of his life, he lived mainly in the Crimea or abroad. He married an actress, Olga Knipper, in 1901; became a fellow of the Academy of Science in 1900, but resigned as a protest against the cancellation of Gorky's election; and died at Baden-Weiler, South Germany, July 2, 1904.

John Mason Brown says of Chekhov: "His method is an incomparably happy one for realism. It gives more than truth. It is the quintessence of truth."

Best known of his plays are: *On the High Road,* 1884; *Ivanov,* 1887; *The Bear,* 1888; *The Tragedian in Spite of Himself,* 1888; *That Worthless Fellow Platonov,* 1889; *The Swan Song,* 1889; *The Proposal,* 1889; *The Wood Demon,* 1889; *The Sea Gull,* 1896; *Uncle Vanya,* 1897; *The Three Sisters,* 1900; *The Jubilee,* 1903; *The Wedding,* 1903; *The Cherry Orchard,* 1904.

Ch'eng Yen-ch'iu. Contemporary Chinese actor. Second to Mei Lan-fang in female roles. His sweetly melancholy singing voice, expression, gait and sober costuming conjure up a wistful, demure and correct atmosphere in a Victorian sense. His superb singing is characterized by a smooth flowing voice (he is rarely shrill). His singing style, as well as his ideas about orchestra and scenery, were possibly influenced by an extensive European tour.

Cherry Orchard, The. Anton Chekhov (Russian). Tragedy. 4 acts. Produced in 1904, the year Chekhov died, by the Moscow Art Theatre.

A play about the passing of the old order in Russia, and the triumph of industrial civilization over pastoral tradition.

Facing eviction and the auction of their estates, the Ranevskys, Russian aristocrats, can do nothing but cling to the past and hope for a miracle. As the curtain falls, they hear the ring of axes chopping the cherry trees, and learn that their land has been sold to a peasant who formerly worked on the Ranevsky estate.

Cherry Sisters. American actresses. Oscar Hammerstein presented Jessie, Addie, Lizzie, and Effie Cherry to Broadway in 1896; the four sisters won "reverse fame" through audience hooting and howling. Jessie, the youngest, was seventeen; Effie, the oldest, twenty-two. Their work in *Gypsy's Warning; The Modern Young Man;* and *Americy, Cuby, and Spain,* brought them a thousand dollars a week. Dramatic critics could not agree "whether they were doing their misguided and dreadful best, or capitalizing on a rare ability to fool the most sophisticated audience." The sisters denied newspaper reports that they played behind protective wire netting. After Jessie's death in 1903, during a Southern tour, her three sisters retired to their farm at Cedar Rapids, Iowa.

Chester Cycle. A series of mystery plays in England in the 14th century written in French or Latin and only after 1350 in English, and performed in the town of Chester.

Chettle, Henry (?-1607). English dramatist. He edited Robert Greene's *Groat's-Worth of Wit* in 1592 and wrote thirteen plays, only one of which, *The Tragedy of Hoffman, or, Revenge for a Father,* is extant. His satirical pamphlet *King Heart's Dream,* 1592, is notable for its apology to Shakespeare; and his *Englande's Mourning Garment,* 1603, for its references to contemporary poets.

"Chew the scenery." A popular term, meaning to rant and rave onstage.

Chief and state plays. The name given the type of 18th century German drama in which the hero went through a series of adventures in absurd changes of scenes and with great bombast. These plays were popular, numerous and in the repertoire of all 18th century drama in Germany.

Chikamatsu Monzayemon (1653?-1724). Japanese dramatist. The greatest dramatic genius of Japan and considered the Shakespeare of his country by some Japanese critics. Recognized as the founder of the *Kabuki Shibai,* or popular theatre. Little is known of his life. Born of a *Samurai* family of the name of Sugimori at Hagi, on the west coast of Japan; nothing is known of his parents. Studied for the priesthood at Chikamatsu Temple in Karatsu, from which he derived his pen-name. He left the priesthood in 1677 and turned his attention to writing for the *Kabuki* theatre. From 1699 on he wrote for the *Joruri* and *Ayatsuri* stage in Osaka, giving these forms their highest development. His plays were produced in the *Takemoto-Za,* Takemoto Gidayu's famous Osaka theatre. Chikamatsu wielded enormous power as playwright, at one time saving the *Takemoto-Za* from bankruptcy' and at another influencing thousands of couples to commit double suicide for love, which theme he had invented in one of his plays. He wrote over fifty plays and is credited with as many more—all fully as long as Shakespeare's and containing three to five acts. His most famous plays are *The Battles of Kokusinya* and *Chiushingura.* (See *Story of the Forty-Seven Ronins, The.*)

Child Company, Chinese. A company formed by a group of Shanghai children orphaned by the present Sino-Japanese War. At first they were strolling singers of patriotic songs who sang to the inmates of various refugee camps. They soon attracted the attention of playwrights and directors and, after a short theatrical training period, were acting out a repertory of war-time propaganda plays such as, *Arrest the Traitors, Japanese Moustache, Aid Our Mobile Units* and *On the Firing Line.* Since then, they have been giving their brave little performances in many cities and villages in Central China.

Children in the theatre. There were numerous acting companies of children in England under the reigns of Elizabeth and James I. Among the most famous were the children of the Chapel at Blackfriars (1597-1603), Children of Revels to the Queen at Blackfriars (1604-1608). Children of King's Revels at Whitefriars (1603-1609) and Children to the Queen at Whitefriars (1610-1613).

Two hundred years later found a revival of this interest in children playing, particularly adult parts. The most famous was Master Betty (see also William Henry West Betty) who between 1804 and 1811 played Hamlet, Douglas, Romeo, Richard III in adult companies. Master Burke (The Irish Roscius), John Howard Payne and Miss Leesugg were others.

Toward the end of the 19th century came the children's companies which played Gilbert and Sullivan operettas. Julia Marlowe made her debut in one of them. Since then children have played themselves on stage and screen. Noted among them have been Shirley Temple, Peter Holden, Freddie Bartholomew, Jackie Coogan, Lillian and Dorothy Gish.

Children of the Chapel Royal. A group of boy-actors, drawn from the choristers of the Royal Chapel, who presented plays at court and at Blackfriars Theatre. Their principal directors were Richard Edwards and Richard Farrant. The court drama developed by them differed from the professional drama in superior refinement of plot and language and more elaborate stage effects. John Lyly wrote for them until 1584, when they were suppressed. They reappeared in 1600 as strong rivals of the professional companies, and performed successfully in plays by George Chapman and Ben Jonson at Blackfriars. The popularity of this troupe and Paul's Boys forced Shakespeare's company to close the Globe for a time, a fact to which the dramatist alludes in *Hamlet* when Rosenkrantz speaks of "an aerie of little children, little eyases," as being responsible for the players' visit to the court of Denmark.

Children of the Sun, The. Maxim Gorki (Russian). Drama. 5 acts. 1904.

The story of a wife who becomes unhappy because her husband grows too absorbed in his professional researches as a physician. She endeavors to provoke his interest by returning the attentions of a painter. The physician has aroused the admiration of a wealthy woman who offers to endow his laboratory if he will but leave his wife. In the end, he refuses this offer and responds to his wife's real love for him.

Children's Hour, The. Lillian Hellman (American). Drama. 3 acts. 1934.

A psychological study of the havoc a lie can create. Its fourteen-year-old protagonist is probably as perverse, pitiless, precocious a villainess as has ever appeared on a stage. The story was considered so shocking that, when filmed as *These Three,* it was considerably changed so as not to offend the sensitive.

Mary Tilford is a spoiled, thoroughly unpleasant child who uses her native intelligence to obtain her own selfish ends. She is a pupil at the school run by Karen Wright and Martha Dobie, two sympathetic young women of about thirty. Angry because Karen has penalized her for tardiness, Mary fakes a heart attack so as to escape punishment. Dr. Joe Cardin, Karen's fiancé, assures them she is all right, angering Mary the more. And when insult is added to injury by the directress' order that Mary change roommates, since she has had an unhealthy influence on her present ones, she flees to the home of her grandmother, Mrs. Tilford. Her tale of persecution does not convince the old lady, and the girl finds in an overheard conversation the inspiration for a more forceful tale. Martha Dobie's aunt, Lily Nortar, an elocution teacher in the school, had been quarreling with Martha and accused her of not wanting Karen to marry Joe. Mary has heard this. She tells her aunt that Martha and Karen are Lesbians, hardly knowing what she says but seeing at once that it is effective. Mrs. Tilford immediately gets in touch with the parents of every pupil in the school, and within a few hours the establishment is deserted. Karen and Martha come to protest the outrage, and so confuse Mary that her grandmother is almost convinced of her deception. Rosalie Wells, a fellow student being put up at Mrs. Tilford's temporarily, is asked to assert her innocence of the rumors. But Rosalie once stole a bracelet. Mary knows this, and Rosalie fearfully repeats whatever Mary orders so as not to be given away. Karen and Martha sue Mrs. Tilford for libel. Lily Mortar, who would be their key witness, does not appear to testify, and they lose their case. Alone in the world, they stay on at the empty school. Karen's fiancé offers to marry her, but she refuses, lest he always suspect her of that of which she was accused. Martha suddenly confesses that she, for her part, has been guilty—not in act but in impulse—although she never realized it herself before. She shoots herself. Too late Mrs. Tilford arrives with the announcement that she has found the stolen bracelet, gotten to the root of the matter and is convinced of their innocence.

Children's Theatre (Nashville). See *Nashville Community Playhouse.*

Chiton. A loose-flowing garment, extending from neck to ankles, worn in early Greek theatre.

Chiusetti. A series of formal expressions or tags of dialogue in the *commedia dell' arte,* used when leaving the stage.

Chiushingura. See *The Story of the Forty-Seven Ronins.*

Choephori (The Libation Bearers). Aeschylus (Greek). The second in the Orestes trilogy. 458 B.C.
Clytemnestra and her lover, Aegisthus, have banished Orestes to Phocis to escape his vengeance. Orestes' sister, Electra, is left to mourn their father, Agamemnon. Orestes returns to Argos and is commanded by Apollo to kill Aegisthus and Clytemnestra. Electra urges him on. Claiming hospitality as a tired stranger from Phocis, he gains admittance to the palace and tells Clytemnestra that Orestes is dead. When she sends for Aegisthus that they may question him more closely, he kills them both. Clytemnestra's murder dooms Orestes to be pursued by the Furies. As the play closes the Furies appear, visible only to their victim.

Choerilus of Athens (6th century, B.C.). Ancient Greek dramatist. A tragedian of the 6th century B.C. His numerous works, said to have rivalled those of Aeschylus, gained him the prize on thirteen occasions, but not one of them has survived.

Choregus. Term used to describe the "angel," or financial backer, of ancient Greek play-production. He shared in the selection of actors and chorus, paid the salaries and was honored with the dramatist if the play was a success.

Chorus. A group of performers in the ancient Greek theatre originally employed to intone the dithyramb in honor of Dionysos, but which later became the central element in classic tragedy and comedy. The dithyramb comprised fifty members; but by 487 B.C., the number was reduced to twelve, due to the convention of presenting at one sitting four plays (three tragedies and one satyr-drama). Among the functions of the chorus in the drama were: a sparing of the audience of every immediate sensation of physical violence, which yet might be a necessary component of the plot; the exposition of all the details of the dramatic situation; the "purging," as advocated by Aristotle, of the emotions through "terror and pity." In the works of Aeschylus the chorus was always related to the dramatic action; in those of Sophocles, with the number raised to fifteen, it was usually related to the dramatic action; but in those of Euripides the presence of the chorus was deliberately obscured, as it was here that the chorus ceased to have any connection with the dramatic action; and subsequent dramatists banished the chorus completely. In the 3rd century B.C. the comic chorus was reduced to seven; in the 2nd century B.C. the chorus in comedy was numbered four and had ceased to exist in tragedy. By the era of New Comedy the chorus no longer stood in the orchestra throughout the whole action but came on for entertainment in the intermissions. Today the term chorus is used exclusively for group singers or dancers, usually in grand opera, musical comedy and revues, while the players in crowd scenes in plays are referred to as extras.

Chorus boy. Member of the body of singers and dancers in a musical production.

Chorus girl. Member of the body of singers and dancers in a musical comedy, revue, operetta, or burlesque.

Christiansen, Arne Einar (1861-   ). Danish dramatist. Writer of comedies of manners set in a background of Copenhagen society.

He was born at Copenhagen, and after spending some years travelling, became the director of the Royal Theatre, Copenhagen, in 1899. He was also a versatile dramatist.

Chronicle history. A form of drama popular in England in the 1590's, practised by the University Wits in such plays as Peele's *Edward I,* Marlowe's *Edward II* and Greene's *James IV*. Its popularity, says Allardyce Nicoll, in his *British Drama,* was due to the fact that "it allowed of bustle and action, partly because it could mingle together thoughts serious and merry, tragic and comic, and partly because there had come over England in those years a wave of patriotic sentiment." The form, indeed, was exactly what its name implies, a history, told in more or less chronological sequence, generally of the events of a particular monarch's reign. Shakespeare wrote his *Henry* and *Richard* plays under the impress of its influence. The chronicle history is sometimes referred to as "historical tragedy."

Chronicles. Holinshed. The principal source of all Shakespeare's plays on English history. The *Chronicles of England, Scotland and Ireland* were first published by Raphael Holinshed in 1577; a second edition in 1587 is probably the one used by Shakespeare.

Church Theatres. The entire history of the drama is bound up with the church. Almost everywhere the drama began as a religious institution, and, as in Art, its subjects were almost entirely religious: the gods and legendary heroes in the Greek drama, Masques, Passion Plays, etc. When secular drama developed the church took a dual role. It has always recognized the drama as an important educational medium and gradually fostered the production of plays which though non-religious were moral. The Morality plays were a link in this development. However, the church also was keenly aware of the license and abuse possible in the theatre and therefor constituted itself as a guardian against violation of decency and against the spread of ideas inimical to itself and public morals. Except for the Catholic Theatre Movement, the church, at the present time, is rather passive in the role of unofficial censor though churchmen constantly combat, both successfully and unsuccessfully, the production of plays they consider objectionable.

The real importance of the church in the Modern Drama is in the countless theatrical performances and pageants produced by church organizations. Play productions (chiefly one-act plays) in which the members participate and take care of all features are encouraged. Many denominations have their own central play and costume bureaus which guide and assist the local congregations. The number of participants, mostly young folk, is more than 500,000.

Cibber, Colley (1671-1757). English actor, dramatist and poet. With Betterton's company at Drury Lane, 1690. His first produced play was *Love's Last Shift; or, The Fool in Fashion* (1696), in which he played a role. In 1704 he wrote, produced and with Mrs. Oldfield appeared in *The Careless Husband*. George I made Cibber Poet Laureate in 1730. Praised by Horace Walpole, Cibber was the subject of much ridicule, denunciation and criticism by Pope, Dr. Samuel Johnson and Fielding. A versatile and brilliant man, he gave a good account of himself as a business man, lawyer, critic and essayist. Goldsmith compared to Montaigne Cibber's *An Apology for the Life of Colley Cibber, Comedian, with an Historical View of the Stage During His Own Time."*

Cid, Le. Pierre Corneille (French). Romantic drama. 4 acts. 1636. Considered the most famous of Corneille's dramas.

Based on the great native folklore concerning the Cid, Spain's favorite hero, who was born about 1030 and rose to fame by his prowess in the war between Sancho of Castile and Sancho of Navarre and in conflicts with the Moors. Having been banished by the king of Castile, he became a soldier of fortune. His principal achievement was the capture of Valencia from the Moors after a siege of nine months. He died of grief at the defeat of his forces in 1099.

Cinderella. Richard Batka (Hungarian). Drama. 3 acts. 1905.

A dream play based on the folk-lore relating to the Cinderella legend, the poor step-sister who in the end triumphs over her wicked sisters and wins the Prince.

Cinema. See *Motion Pictures.*

Cinthio, Hecatomithi. A collection of Italian *novelle,* or short novels, by Giraldi Cinthio, published in 1565. Though not translated until after Shakespeare's day, they contain the sources of *Measure for Measure* and *Othello.*

Circle, The. W. Somerset Maugham (English). Comedy. 3 acts. 1921.

Lady Kitty, who had run away with Lord Porteous thirty years before, returns with him to England to visit her son, Arnold. During their stay, Lady Elizabeth, Arnold's wife, repeats the family history by running away with Edward Luton, whom she prefers to her husband.

Circus. The Latin word for "circle." Its present significance derives from the *Circensian Games,* said to have originated in the time of Romulus. These added to the circular course of the chariot race, athletic contests and combats between men and wild animals. Such entertainment is referred to in the "bread and circuses" phrase of the Roman emperors.

The circus as we know it grew out of the agricultural fairs held in England and on the continent. The modern nomadic tent circus began with Philip Astley in 1768. He wandered about England giving trick riding performances, with two fifes for music, while his wife beat a drum and passed the hat. In 1770 he built the Royal Grove—a sort of hippodrome—in Lambeth, and added three riders and two clowns. Antoine Franconi entered the field in Paris in 1793. John Robinson's circus was one of the first known in this country, and is said to have been started in 1824— but Robinson had served apprenticeship with some older circus. Adam Forepaugh established a circus in 1861. After the Civil War circuses multiplied in America, gradually expanding from the equestrian show with clown dialogue to a complex multiple-unit organism combining spectacular pageantry, trick performances by persons and animals, equestrian displays, menageries, freak shows and acrobatics. As the number of attractions increased, the clowns had less and less dialogue, becoming more numerous, but almost exclusively pantomimic.

Barnum's circus opened in 1871, absorbed the Great London Circus, Sanger's Royal British Menagerie and Grand International and Allied Shows in 1881, took Bailey into partnership in 1887, toured England in 1889, set up a British show in 1899, sold out to Ringling Brothers in 1907, but continued on the road separately until 1920. Ringling Brothers started their railroad show in 1888, bought Forepaugh-Sells in 1906. In 1920 Ringling Brothers and Barnum and Bailey in consolidation became the undisputed "Greatest Show on Earth"—and in the course of general circus reorganization in 1930 gained control of the remaining independents—Sells-Floto, Hagenbeck-Wallace, Al. G. Barnes, Charles Sparks Railroad Circus, and Home's Great London. The Wild West Show, a peculiarly American form originated in the 1890's by Buffalo Bill Cody, reproduced the life of cowboys, pioneers, and Indians. Now outmoded, some of its features live on in the American circus.

Famous European circuses have included the Circus Renz in Vienna, Mills Brothers Circus in England, and Jungman's, Hagenbeck's, Schneider's, and Helman's in Germany. For grandiose size and pretentiousness the American circus has for decades led the world.

Circus terms. A brief glossary. *Appleknocker,* a country yokel; *barker,* a box-office adjunct who harangues for a show; *beetle* (or frail), a woman; *benders,* contortionists; *big top,* main tent; *bulls,* elephants, both sexes; *butch* (or butcher), refreshment vendor; *cats,* tigers or lions or leopards; *clink,* jail; *clipped,* without money; *come-on,* inducement to attract a crowd; *cooch show,* side-show with "muscle-dancers"; *cut,* a share, or to share; *darb,* something (or someone) excellent; *dick,* detective; *dog joint,* hot-dog (frankfurter in roll) stand or booth; *double in brass,* an employee also playing in the band; *go rotary,* become enthusiastic; *grinder,* a continuous talker outside a show; *"Hey, Rube!",* the battle cry of the circus—the call to arms; *joey,* a clown; *lam,* depart hastily; *punk,* a young animal—or an adolescent, a term of derogation; *shill,* a decoy to lure customers.

City Heiress, The. Aphra Behn (English). Comedy. Printed 1682.
Sir Timothy Treat-all disinherits his Tory nephew, Tom Wilding. Wilding is courting a city heiress, Charlot, but introduces his mistress Diana to Sir Timothy as Charlot. Sir Timothy under the impression that Diana is Charlot, arranges to marry her himself. Wilding further complicates his uncle's life by disguising himself and stealing valuable papers. Wilding, however, in the end is united with Charlot, and Diana and Sir Timothy straighten out their lives.

City Madam, The. Philip Massinger (English). Comedy. 5 acts. 1632.
The wife and daughters of a rich merchant have grown extravagant. Sir John, the husband and father, in order to teach them a lesson, pretends to retire to a monastery and to hand over the management of the estate to Luke, a ruined prodigal. After a short time Luke's hypocrisy is exposed and Sir John's family is anxious to have him back home.

City Wit, The; or, The Woman Wears the Breeches. Richard Brome (English). Comedy. 1653.
The story of Crasy of easy disposition, his wife of easy virtue, and his virago of a mother-in-law, Mrs. Pyannet Sneakup. Crasy becomes tired of having his family and his friends impose on his good nature and determines to get even with them. He does so by means of disguises and the help of a faithful servant.

City Wives Confederacy, The. See *Confederacy, The.*

Civic Repertory Theatre. A theatre organization in New York City founded at the Fourteenth Street Theatre in October, 1926, by Eva Le Gallienne. Throughout the next seven seasons Miss Le Gallienne offered, at lowest rates (with usually a dollar-fifty top) works of dramatists ranging from Shakespeare and Goldoni to Chekhov, Ibsen and Benavente. Among her famous acting associates were Burgess Meredith, Nazimova, Jacob Ben-Ami.

Civic theatre. It was Percy MacKaye who first thought of the name "civic theatre." In the preface of his volume *The Playhouse and the Play*, he speaks of "thinking intensely for an apt and perfectly new name by which to call the new conception of the theatre which then filled all my thoughts—a theatre wholly divorced from commercialism." . . . He goes on to say: "In after years I came to wish that I had named it 'The Communal Theatre,' and I still think that would have been a better term for its intrinsic idea."
See also *Community Theatre movement; Theatres, 20th Century American.*

Civic Theatre, Fort Wayne, Indiana. Formerly the old Majestic Theatre. Taken over by the Old Fort Players in 1933. This group was an organization founded in 1931 to bring the theatre to the people and does noteworthy work in modern plays, the classics and stylized sets.

Civic Theatre, Indianapolis, Indiana. Developed from the Little Theatre of South Indianapolis which was founded in 1915. In 1925, the Civic Theatre Society erected its own theatre. In 1937-38 its membership was 1500.

Civic Theatre, Palo Alto, California. This is the only completely municipally subsidized community theatre in the United States, in that all expenditures are paid for by the city by an estimated budget set up in advance. All income from the theatre goes back towards the amount the city gives. The Community Players was organized in 1931 by the Palo Alto Recreation Department. In 1932 a Community Playhouse, seating 428 in comfortable upholstered chairs, with a splendid workshop, ample office facilities, etc., was given to the theatre. In 1934, another wing was added, and an outdoor Patio Theatre for open air production. The whole is probably unrivaled as an ideal set-up for community drama.

Claire, Ina (1892-   ). American actress. Real name Ina Fagan. Born in Washington, D. C.; educated at Holy Cross Academy; made her debut on the stage in vaudeville and made an instantaneous success for her impersonation of Sir Harry Lauder; continued in vaudeville until 1911 when she appeared successfully in *Jumping Jupiter* and *The Quaker Girl.* Her other plays include: *The Honeymoon Express,* 1913; *The Girl From Utah* and *The Belle of Bond Street* (London), 1913-14; *Lady Luxury,* 1914; *The Follies of 1915; The Ziegfeld Follies,* 1916; *Polly With a Past,* 1917; *The Gold Diggers,* 1921; *Bluebeard's Eighth Wife,* 1922; *The Awful Truth,* 1923; *Grounds for Divorce,* 1924; *The Last of Mrs. Cheyney,* 1925; *Our Betters,* 1928; *Rebound,* 1931; *The Greeks Had a Word for It,* 1931; *Biography,* 1932-33; *Ode to Liberty,* 1934-35; *End of Summer,* 1936-37; *Barchester Towers,* 1937.

Clamus. Outer robe worn by Greek tragic actor; long flowing robe which was an important part of the costume.

Clandestine Marriage, The. George Colman, the elder, and David Garrick (English). Restoration comedy. 5 acts. 1776.

The principal motif of the play is derived from Hogarth's pictures of *Marriage-a-la-Mode.*

A young couple, Fanny Sterling and Mr. Lovewell, having been secretly married, attempt to conceal the fact from the bride's rich father, who wants his daughter to marry Lord Oglebay, an old and impoverished member of the nobility. A second daughter is being married to Lord John, who is in love with Fanny. The secret marriage is finally disclosed and Lord John, the fiance of Fanny's sister, is released from his engagement.

Clap-trap. Critical term meaning a trick or device to catch applause; false or showy sentiment put into the lines of a play to make the audience clap. Also, formerly, a mechanical clapper to use in theatres for loud applause.

Clarence. Booth Tarkington (American). Comedy. 4 acts. 1919.

Clarence was one of the millions in the First World War, who served where he was sent, although it happened to be no farther away than Texas. As an entomologist, he found no field for his specialty in the Great War; so he was set to driving mules. When Clarence returns to civil life, he finds a job with a wealthy family and becomes guide, philosopher, and friend to the members of the distracted and irresponsible family group, to their discipline and delight.

Clark, Barrett H. (1890-   ). American author, editor. Born in Toronto, Canada; educated at University of Chicago and the University of Paris. Actor and stage manager with Mrs. Fiske, 1912-13; dramatic instructor, Chautauqua, New York, 1909-17; literary editor, Samuel French, Ltd., 1918-36; executive director of the Dramatists' Play Service, New York, since 1936; member of board of directors of the Drama League of America, 1915-26; dramatic editor, Drama Magazine.

His books include: *The Continental Drama of Today,* 1914; *British and American Drama of Today,* 1915; *Contemporary French Dramatists,* 1915; *How to Produce Amateur Plays,* 1917-25; *A Study of the Modern Drama,* 1925; *Eugene O'Neill,* 1926; *Oedipus or Pollyanna,* 1927; *Professor Clark, a Memoir,* 1928, etc. He is also the editor of the *World's Best Plays* as well as many other volumes; translator and editor of numerous foreign books and plays. See also *Drama, theories of; Theatre Library Association; Dramatists' Play Service.*

Class of '29. Orrie Lashin and Milo Hastings (American). Drama. 3 acts. 1936.

This propagandist problem play was a production of the Popular Price Theatre of the WPA Federal Theatre project. Ken, Tippy, Ted and Martin are four members of the class of '29, typical representatives of that Lost Generation which graduated into a world which seemed to have no need of their services. Ken, an architect, has spent six heartbreaking years looking for employment. His father, a Bishop finally buys him a job without his realizing it. When he finds out what has happened, his newfound confidence dies and he is spiritually and morally worse off than before. Tippy opens a business specializing in washing and walking dogs and is financially the most successful of the four. Martin, an artist, becomes a Communist, until the New Yorker buys one of his sketches and he decides it won't be necessary to change the existing order of society after all. Ted has been living, unwillingly, on the earnings of his sweetheart. But when she finds him a position as elevator operator and gives him a chance to support himself, he cannot bear to become a menial and in despair throws himself under a subway train. The authors' implication is that society needs to change radically.

Claudel, Paul (1868-   ). French dramatist. His writings show traces of the influence of the Symbolists, such as Rimbaud, but are more influenced by his profound Catholicism. He held various consular and diplomatic appointments and was ambassador at Tokyo, 1921, Washington, 1927, and Brussels, 1933.

His plays include: dramatic trilogy—*L'Otage,* 1911; *L'Annonce faite à Marie,* (*The Tidings Brought to Mary*), 1912; *Le Pain dur,* 1918, and *Le Père humilié,* 1919.

Clean house. A sold-out performance.

Clemenceau, Georges Eugène Benjamin (1841-1929). French statesman and litterateur.

The French Premier of the First World War, who became known as the Tiger of France, was a considerable writer. He founded newspapers, wrote novels, and one play *Le Voile du Bonheur,* 1906.

Clercs de la basoche. A corporation in medieval France of all lawyers within French territory and authorized to give theatrical productions in the great hall of the Palais de Justice, in Paris. Encouraged by the success of the *Confrérie de la passion* they began composing their own plays. These were the first morality plays, the comedies of the Middle Ages.

Cleveland (Ohio) Play House, The. In 1914 the Cleveland little theatre movement had its beginning. Those interested met in the house of the first president, next in an empty house, then in an attic where a temporary stage was erected, then in a barn, next in a ballroom. The 1916 Report says: "The Playhouse was founded to establish an Art Theatre; to encourage native artists and native art in all its forms; and to cultivate folk art possessed by the cosmopolitan population." In 1938 *Stage Magazine* awarded to Frederic McConnell, noted director of the Play House, its "palm" for a distinguished theatrical service of the season. William F. McDermott's history of The Play House says: "Without exception, everybody in Cleveland interested in the theatre as an art or as adult entertainment goes to the

Play House." The Cleveland Play House is a repertory company of the first order with a wide range of production and professional technique. It has its own building with two stages and two auditoriums, under one roof, one for major productions; the other for experimental or short-run productions. The playhouse is open to the general public during an eight-month season of constant playing. The production program is professionally organized with a company of thirty members. The staff is supplemented by the employment of guest actors and by students. Among the foremost activities of the Play House is its School of the Theatre which is about ten years old. It also has a children's theatre. A regular season usually includes fourteen plays, with an average run of six or seven weeks of nightly performances and Saturday matinees.

Click. A slang term for success, or to succeed (used in referring to either productions or players).

Climax. The highest point in action and emotional intensity in a play, and that toward which everything previous has "built" and after which everything declines in suspense and excitement.

Climbers, The. Clyde Fitch (American). Comedy. 4 acts. 1901.

Produced by Amelia Bingham, this "audacious comedy" and "brilliant play of social life" held the boards for many weeks at the turn of the century. The young man marrying for social prestige; the widow marrying to rehabilitate herself financially—the whole gallery of climbers won the plaudits of enthusiastic audiences. London, on the other hand, was revolted by the characters' cold-bloodedness and un-English conduct.

Richard Sterling, a lawyer, has the mania of stock speculation, and has lost his wife's fortune, of which he was custodian. Edward Worden, a friend in love with Mrs. Sterling, discovers the truth. Richard's wife is also suspicious, and makes him sign a paper promising to administer honestly the affairs of a maiden aunt who has appointed him her business agent. Fourteen months later, Sterling has broken his word to his wife, lost the estates entrusted to him, and proposes to abscond. Worden promises to make good the deficits and swears the victims to secrecy. Sterling finds Worden and his wife together and, in a fit of jealousy, accuses them of being lovers. Worden's adoration has been undeclared and unsuspected by Mrs. Sterling, but now her husband's outburst causes her to see clear into her own heart, to realize the full extent of Sterling's villainy and Worden's devotion. She is willing nevertheless to continue to be a faithful wife. But Richard, whose love for her was his one merit, seeing that he has lost it, takes an overdose of morphia tablets and dies, while those about him look and think him merely fallen asleep.

Clinching plate, steel plate; bends clout nails as they come through the wood, thus insuring a strong hold.

See *Scenery.*

Cline, Maggie (1857-1934). American actress. Variety and musical comedy actress; made her debut at the age of sixteen at Tony Pastor's Theatre. She is probably best known for introducing the song *"T'row Him Down, McClosky,"* which was written for her by John W. Kelley of Philadelphia.

Cloak and sword plays. Swash-buckling plays full of fighting and adventure. The name comes from the Spanish comedies of the 16th century dramatists.

Closed Door, The. Marco Praga (Italian). Drama. 3 acts. 1913.
A youth, who has felt unduly constrained at home by the overpowering affection of his mother, desires to join a colonizing expedition to East Africa, but is refused permission until he reveals the fact that he knows he is the illegitimate child by a friend of the family.

Closet drama. A play written to be read rather than performed. Shelley's *The Cenci* and Thomas Hardy's *The Dynasts* are examples of closet drama, though both were acted.

Closing notice. A notice hung backstage on the callboard informing the cast of the closing date of the play's run; by Equity ruling, closing notices must be posted one week before closing date (at latest 8:00 P.M. on the Monday before a Saturday closing) ; where uncertainty is involved, a closing notice may indicate that the play will continue to run but may close at any time; this special notice is called a "week to week" notice.

Clouds, The. Aristophanes (Greek). Comedy. 423 B.C.
While this has been one of the most enduring and is still one of the most widely read of the author's plays, it was a failure when first produced, being given for only one performance. Strepsiades, almost ruined by the extravagance of his son Pheidippides and seeking to re-establish himself by fair means or foul, asks Socrates how he can cheat his creditors. Just then the Clouds enter and speak in the high-flown style in vogue at the time, to Strepsiades' confusion. Socrates explains that they are not divinities, but mere clouds; however, they have great skill in idle palaver. He goes on to explain such natural phenomena as thunder. Strepsiades is shocked that he pretends that these are not caused directly by the gods, and worried that he has still received no practical advice about his debts. Socrates wastes more time teaching him rhetoric; then the Just and the Unjust appear. The Just represents tradition and old-fashioned principles; the Unjust the new sophistry and free-and-easy ways of the younger generation. The latter teaches sophistry to Strepsiades' spendthrift son, who confounds both the creditors and his father with his newly acquired logic. But when he beats Strepsiades under the pretext of behaving reasonably the old man rebels and sets fire to Socrates' house and school.
Although neglected in 423 B.C., the play was used by Socrates' enemies twenty-five years later to prove their accusations against him, and thus is historically important in that it was partly responsible for the philosopher's death.

Clout nail. A wedge-shaped lead nail used for fastening corner blocks and key-stones to scenery; the soft lead flattens out when it hits the clinching plate and permanency of connection is insured.

Clown. Term loosely applied to any funny fellow, whether he is funny by intention or by mistake. Sometimes in British usage a synonym for a rustic, or country bumpkin. Specifically, in circus connotations, the clown is the buffoon with the white-and-red painted face. He wears the traditional capacious "clown suit," with ruffs at neck, wrists, and ankles—a modification of the dress of the *commedia dell'arte* Pierrot and other stereotyped comic characters, from whom the clown in generally assumed to have descended. His tricks and essential character are based on the exaggeration of a human frailty—greed, conceit, mental simplicity, physical awkwardness, and the like.

The earliest example in English comedy is the servant fool, half jester and half saucy lacky in John Heywood's *Merry-report*. Shakespeare's clowns can be divided into five classes—the jester, the vice-clown, the Italianate Servas, the court pages and the elf. Their dramatic function was comparable to that of the French *raisonneur* and the Greek *chorus*. Will Sumner, Richard Tarlton and Will Kemp were outstanding actors of clown roles in the Elizabethan era.

Among the famous clowns of modern times are: Joseph Grimaldi (1779-1837); Joe Jackson (fl. 1905); Toto (1888-1938); Grock (Adriano Wittach), now retired to a villa in Italy; the Swedish vaudeville pair, the Arnaut brothers; and the famous Parisian trio, François, Albert and Paul Fratellini, who are training younger Fratellinis to succeed them.

See also *Gracioso; Grimaldi, Joseph; Grock.*

Clown white. A make-up foundation for clowns and harlequins laid on heavily on a cold cream base, often used for statuary effects.

Clubs. See *Theatrical clubs.*

Clue. A device for fastening sandbag to rope.
See *Scenery.*

Coburn, Charles Douville (1877-) **and Ivah** (1882-1937). American actors, managers. After playing in stock companies and touring for several years, Mr. and Mrs. Coburn organized the Coburn Shakespearean Players, which they maintained for many years. Produced *The Yellow Jacket,* in 1916, with Mr. Coburn playing the part of Chorus. In 1918, Mr. Coburn played Old Bill in *The Better 'Ole,* which continued until 1920. Played in many productions, toured in several revivals of *The Yellow Jacket.* At Schenectady, New York, in the summer of 1934, Mr. and Mrs. Coburn inaugurated the Mohawk Dramatic Festival, playing in *The Merry Wives of Windsor; Lysistrata; Rip Van Winkle; The Master of the Revels.*

See also *Mohawk Drama Festival.*

Cochran, Charles B. Manager (English). Born in Sussex 1873, was formerly an actor. Made his first appearance in N. Y. C. in 1892 with Joseph Jefferson and subsequently became the agent for Richard Mansfield. His first production as manager was Ibsen's *John Gabriel Borkman* in N. Y. 1897. In the course of his long career in New York and London he produced: *The Better 'Ole*, 1917; *The Man Who Came Back*, 1920; *Cochran's Revue*, 1926, 1930, 1931 and many other musicals. He introduced to London the Chauve Souris, the Guitrys, Eleanor Duse. He also produced *Anna Christie*, 1923; *The Road to Rome*, 1928; *Poryg*, 1929; *Paris Bound*, 1929; *Bitter Sweet*, 1929; *Grand Hotel*, 1931; *Escape Me Never*, 1933; *Conversation Piece*, 1934. During his distinguished and successful career from 1914 to 1935 he personally supervised 120 productions and has staged important boxing matches, rodeos, wrestling bouts. He has written his reminiscences under the title *Secrets of a Showman*, 1925, and *I Had Almost Forgotten*, 1932.

Cody, William Frederick (Buffalo Bill) (1846-1917). American plainsman and showman. Born on an Iowa farm, he went to the Colorado gold mines at fourteen years of age. After being a pony express rider and serving as a scout in the Civil War, he turned to the stage, producing and taking part in Western plays. In Chicago, in 1872, he played the leading role in *Scouts of the Plains,* written by his friend, Colonel Judson. In 1876 his stage career was interrupted by the Sioux War, but he returned and played to large audiences throughout the country. In 1883 he started his famous Wild West exhibition with Major John M. Burke and Dr. W. F. Carver. He divided his time between this and his ranch until 1916, when he went to Denver. In 1894 he received a large land grant in the Big Horn basin. He was buried on top of Lookout Mountain near Golden, Colorado.

Coello, Antonio (1600?-1652). Spanish dramatist. Born at Madrid. Plays attributed to him are *Conde de sex* and *Los Empenos de seis horas.* The latter was published under the name of Calderon and long attributed to him. It was adapted in English by Sir Samuel Tuke as *The Adventures of Five Hours.*

Coghlan, Charles (1842-1899). English actor. Made his American debut in 1876 under Wallack's banner; made a tremendous hit in America, playing in *Money, The Royal Box* and *Citizen Piérre.*

Coghlan, Rose (1850-1932). English actress. Made her American debut in 1872-73 under Wallack's banner; one of the best Lady Teazles ever seen on the stage; played in *Ixion, Diplomacy, London Assurance, As You Like It* and *Deburau.* Acted with Joseph Jefferson and Barry Sullivan. Sister of Charles Coghlan.

Cohan, George Michael (1878-   ). American actor, dramatist, director and producer. Born in Providence, Rhode Island, July 4. In his boyhood he appeared as a member of the vaudeville team called the "Four Cohans." The team consisted of Jerry and Helen Cohan, and their children, Josephine and George Michael. At the age of fifteen, George Cohan began writing skits, plays and songs. Before he was thirty he had lifted the Cohans out of vaudeville and into a fortune in musical comedy. Joining forces with Sam H. Harris up to the year 1920, he next became successful as manager, dramatist and stage director.

He is author of some fifty dramas and musical shows in many of which he has acted. Among them are: *45 Minutes from Broadway; Get Rich Quick Wallingford; Hit-the-Trail Holliday; Seven Keys to Baldpate; Broadway Jones; The Song and Dance Man; Pigeons and People.* In addition he has appeared notably in *Ah, Wilderness* and *I'd Rather Be Right.*

Cold Cream. Prepares the skin for application of grease paints; used as a base for powder in make-ups and serves as an aid to removing make-up.

Coleridge, Samuel Taylor (1772-1834). English writer. He was born in Devon and educated at Christ's College and Cambridge, where he met Charles Lamb, Samuel Butler, Robert Southey and other writers who were to remain his lifelong intimates. Like most of the poets of the romantic school, he also tried his hand at drama. Inspired by the French Revolution, in 1794 he wrote a historical play, *The Fall of Robespierre,* in collaboration with Southey. In 1797 *Osorio,* his next dramatic effort, was refused by Sheridan. He revised this under the name of *Remorse,* 1813, and it was presented at the Drury Lane at Byron's instigation. His plays seem artificial, his characters lack the pulsing life which can be projected successfully across the footlights, and it is through his imaginative poetry rather than through his dramas that the poet's name has lived.

Coliseo. See *Corral.*

College Theatres. See *Theatres, 20th Century American.*

Collet, Richard (1885-   ). English manager. Born at Worthing, became a bank clerk and in 1906 joined Arthur Chudleigh at the Comedy Theatre as assistant manager. Was the manager of various theatres including the New Theatre for Dion Boucicault and Irene Vanbrugh. Made general manager of the D'Oyly Carte Opera Company, 1919; director of several hotels; managing director of Savoy Theatre, Ltd.

Collier, Constance (1878-   ). English actress. Born at Windsor, she first appeared on the stage at the age of three. A distinguished and widely-varied career on the stage in England and America followed. She also had a company in London during the early 1900's, and it was in this group that Eva Le Gallienne first played.

Some of Miss Collier's notable appearances have been in *Sweet Nell of Old Drury; Twelfth Night,* with Beerbohm Tree's company, for which she acted, 1901-07; *Antony and Cleopatra; The Merchant of Venice; Trelawney of the Wells; The School for Scandal; Our Betters; Hay Fever.* She was part author with Ivor Novello, under the pseudonym of David L'Estrange, of *The Rat* and *Downhill.*

Collier Forgeries. A long series of spurious records produced after 1831 by John Payne Collier, who claimed that they were original documents pertaining to the life and works of Shakespeare. Collier never fully confessed his guilt and the taint of suspicion rests on all his work, much of which is probably genuine and valuable.

Collier, Jeremy (1650-1726). British cleric. A Tory "non-juring" preacher who violently objected to the licentiousness of the Restoration stage, and spent ten years fighting for the correction of current abuses. His importance to dramatic history lies in his having written *A Short View of the Immorality and Profaneness of the English Stage,* 1698, in which the foul language, the abuse of clergymen and the flagrant encouragement of vice in Restoration plays were bitterly attacked.

Collier, William (1866-   ). American comedian, writer, director. The son of Edmund and Henrietta Engel Collier, both actors. William Collier has led an active and varied career, from playing in Augustin Daly's company during the eighties to appearing in old Triangle Film productions under Mack Sennett and Thomas Ince. He starred in many plays in New York and in London. Was under contract at different times to Weber and Fields, Charles Frohman and George White. He was in the first *Vanities; Tickle Me* and *Sweetheart Time;* directed dialogue for the cinemas. He wrote several plays and was part author of several others.

Collin, Heinrich Joseph von (1771-1811). Austrian dramatist. As a dramatist he formed a link between the French classical style and the 19th century German romanticists.

Born in Vienna, he wrote various dramas, including *Coriolan,* 1804, to which Beethoven wrote the overture. He also wrote a collection of patriotic ballads *Wehrmannslieder* directed against the French invaders.

Collinge, Patricia (1894-   ). English actress. Born at Dublin. Made her first appearance on the stage in *Little Black Sambo* and *Little White Barbara,* 1904, at the Garrick Theatre, London. Came to America in 1908 and first appeared at the Circle Theatre in *The Queen of the Moulin Rouge.*

Other plays in which she has appeared include: *Hedda Gabler; The Importance of Being Earnest; The Lady with a Lamp; She Stoops to Conquer; Pollyanna; Tillie; Tarnish; Merton of the Movies; The Little Foxes,* etc.

Collins, Sewell (1876-1934). American dramatist. Born at Denver, Colorado, he was for a time dramatic critic on the New York *Journal* and became later a playwright and producer.

His first play *Miss Patsy* was produced in New York in 1910; others were *Shepherd's Pie,* 1922 and *Anne One Hundred,* 1927. He produced *Outward Bound,* 1923 (New York City); *The Wreckers,* 1927 (London); *The Left Bank,* 1932 (London).

Colman, George, the Elder (1732-1794). English dramatist. Born at Florence, where his father was English envoy, and educated in England. He was called to the Bar in 1757, and began to write plays while practicing law. Besides writing and adapting a number of plays and editing Beaumont and Fletcher and Ben Jonson, Colman translated the comedies of Terence, 1765.

His friend, Garrick, produced his successful comedy *The Jealous Wife,* 1761; and with him Colman wrote *The Clandestine Marriage,* produced at Drury Lane in 1766. He was manager of Covent Garden, 1767-74, and of the Haymarket, 1777-85.

Colman, George, the Younger (1762-1836). English dramatist. Succeeding his father, he became manager of the Haymarket Theatre and subsequently its owner.

His works include: the plays, *John Bull* and *The Heir-at-Law;* numerous poems of a humorous nature; and his autobiographical *Random Recollections.*

Colombe's Birthday. Robert Browning (English). Drama. 4 acts. 1844.

Prince Berthold seeks to marry Colombe, Duchess of Joliers and Cleves, and sends his advocate, Valence, to plead his case. Valence, however, pleads too well, and finally wins Colombe for himself.

Color wheel (stage apparatus). Various colored gelatins arranged in a circular frame to allow for color changes on one lighting instrument.

Columbine. Most famous of all maid-servants in a *commedia dell'arte;* pert, witty, lover or beloved of Harlequin. Costume: various, extending from ordinary maid's dress to fanciful white costume such as has been preserved in pantomime.

See also *Maid-servants.*

Columbia University. See *Theatre collections.*

Combination system. A scheme introduced in the 1860's changing theatrical procedure; abandoned resident stock companies and in part the individual star; it established the method of selecting actors in reference to play and role, each actor being chosen as to type. Joseph Jefferson claimed to be the originator and believed that towns all over the country would thus see plays done by the best companies and performed as in the big cities.

Comedia. In the Spanish *siglo de oro* (Golden Age) a play was a comedia, regardless of the seriousness or levity of its theme.

Comedian. An actor who specializes in comic or farcical roles. The French word comédien means actor and not comic actor.

Comedian, eccentric. Funnyman, as opposed to "straight" performers, who use tricks of characterization such as dialect, special make-up, personal idiosyncrasies, etc., to gain their effects.

Comedian, light. A funnyman whose humor depends largely on his sparkling repartee rather than on any physical motions of an "act." The opposite of a "low comedian."

Comedian, low. A professional funnyman whose stage deportment is vulgar or generally without appeal to the intelligence.

Comédie des Champs Élysées (French). A present-day experimental theatre in Paris, once directed by Louis Jouvet, now frequently housing Surrealist and other advance-guard plays.

Comédie des moeurs. The French comedy of manners, comprising also the problem or thesis play, and realistically treated. The school in France was founded in 1852 by Dumas fils with his *Dame aux Camélias*.
See also *Comedy of manners, Problem play, Thesis play*.

Comédie-française. The official name of the Théâtre français, a state institution devoted largely to a repertory of established French classics. It came into being in 1680 as a merger between the two rival theatrical companies, the Hôtel de Bourgogne and the Hôtel Guénégaud (the latter a merger of the Théâtre du Marais and the company left by Molière when he died in 1673). The repertory has consisted to a great extent of the works of Cornielle, Racine, Molière, de Musset, etc. Edouard Bourdet, dramatist, is the present director (1939).

Comédie rosse. French term to describe the pessimistic drama before 1880 in which all the characters are too contemptible to merit the interest of a respectable audience.

Comedienne. An actress who specializes in comic or farcical roles.

Comédiens du Roi. French dramatic company of the 17th century, which played before Henry IV, alternating with the popular Italian company, *I Gelosi*. After the death of Isabella Andreini, head of the Italian players, the French group under Valleran Lecomte became the permanent company, Les Comédiens du Roi, at the Hôtel de Bourgogne. The ensemble of the three comic actors, Gros Guilliaume, Gaultier Garguille and Turpulin was the delight and wonder of Paris.
See also *Confrérie de la Passion; Hôtel du Bourgogne*.

Comedietta. A short comedy.

Comedy. A style of drama which originated in the ancient Greek *comus* and which is generally characterized by the humorous and the amiable. Aristotle's definition, in his *Poetics*, is: "an imitation indeed of bad characters, yet it does not imitate them according to every vice (but the ridiculous only) ; since the ridiculous is a portion of turpitude. For the ridiculous is a certain error, and turpitude unattended with pain, and not destructive." Here the comic would seem synonymous with the ludicrous, the latter being defined as "some defect or ugliness which is not painful or destructive." According to Sir Philip Sidney, there are "no right comedies and no right tragedies but only a mongrel sort of tragi-comedy." Ashley Thorndike, in his *English Comedy*, says: "A comedy cannot be tragic or end too unhappily and it cannot be too continuously and obstreperously comic. To escape the banalities of farce it must have some other interest than mere amusement. It has in fact tried almost every interest."

Of this form of drama Cicero said: "It is a copy of life, a mirror of custom, a reflection of truth."

In its broader sense, however, comedy implies all of the drama.

Comedy, Greek. There were three kinds of Greek comedy: (1) the *palliata* or *tabernaria* in which actors wore Greek costumes; (2) *togato,* in which the actors wore togas; (3) the *atellana* or plays with witticisms and jokes.

Every comedy was divided into four parts: *prologos, protasis, epitasis* and *catastrophe.*

All comedies were subdivided into four classes, according to: (1) title role (e.g. Phormio, Hecyra, Epidicus); (2) scene of action (e.g. the Andria, the Leucadia); (3) the situation (e.g. eunuchus, captivi); (4) the outcome (e.g. the Adelphi).

Comedy, Greek, middle. Second form of comedy in ancient Greece; 4th century B.C.; represented best by Antiphanes; consisting of literary, philosophical criticism and parody.

Comedy, Greek, new. Third form of comedy in ancient Greece 4th and 3rd centuries B.C.; represented best by Menander; consisting of domestic life humorously drawn. Stock-characters: old man; young man; old woman; young woman; soldier; parasite; cook; doctor; many slaves.

Comedy, Greek, old. First form of true comedy in ancient Greece; 5th century B.C.; represented best and chiefly by Aristophanes; consisting of coarse, ribald plays which were a part of the worship of Dionysos; often political. Form had no specific divisions, although it usually contained seven parts: *prologos; parodos; agon; parabasis; epeisodia; stasima,* or *chorika; exodos.* Stock characters: old man; young man; old woman; young woman; soldier; parasite; cook; doctor; stupid slave; clever slave.

Comedy, Greek, satyr plays. Satyr plays, the forerunners of Greek comedy, were presented as afterpieces following tragic trilogies. The only extant text is the *Cyclops* of Euripides, but scenes appear on vases and shards. Satyrs appeared in the plays, wearing spotted costumes with tails, in representation of leopards. Silenus was always indicated as a drunken old man with a half-animal expression. The plays were not funny, but humorous characters were introduced.

In the later Greek comedies, which were more on the order of farces, characters playing real persons resembled closely the persons represented. Grotesque and extravagant masks for fictitious characters, and fantastic animal masks, were also used. Pollux's *Onomasticon* contains a description of the different typical masks in the Greek theatre, and mentions twenty-eight stereotyped character-masks for the tragedy.

Comedy, grotesque. Comedy that exceeds the bounds of realism and demands imagination on the part of the audience. It is really an outgrowth of the *commedia dell'arte* and found its master in Pirandello.

Comedy, Italian. A form of humorous drama derived from the Latin plays of Terence and Plautus. It originated in 1486 at the Court of Ferrara with a version of the *Menaechmi* of Plautus, which was the first of a series of similar translations, handsomely staged, written in Italian *terza rima,* and presented with interludes and dances. In 1508 Ariosto wrote his *Cassaria,* an Italian comedy based on a Latin model. The development of the form was carried forward by Bernardo Dovizi Machiavelli and Pietro Aretino among others. Aretino dropped classical imitation except for the external form and treated his subject-matter realistically.

Comedy, literary. An Italian form of drama which was written, as opposed to oral, impromptu, improvised style of the *commedia dell'arte* tradition. The earliest exponents of this form were Goldoni and Molière.

Comedy, realistic. A form of drama of the late 16th, early 17th centuries distinguished by a treatment of common themes, principally middle-class, and by local color, boisterous language, and action less restrained and less colored by romantic sentiment than that of its predecessors. Shakespeare's *Taming of the Shrew* and *The Merry Wives of Windsor* are among the finest examples of this type. Ben Jonson brought a richer and deeper note with a new classical restraint. *Every Man in His Humour, Epicoene, Volpone,* all of which fall, as well, into other categories, among them, satire, are yet representative of this form. Among others are: Dekker's *The Shoemaker's Holiday;* Beaumont's *The Woman Hater;* Fletcher's *The Wild-Goose Chase.*

Comedy, romantic. See *Romantic comedy.*

Comedy, sentimental. A form of drama, popularly believed to be based on the French model of Destouche and developed by Steele and Cibber. It became a protest against cynicism, libertinism, duelling, stage indecency and social vices. It failed to accomplish the desired reform and failed also to reflect effectively contemporaneous life. A good study of this is to be found in Ashley H. Thorndike's *English Comedy.*

Comedy of Errors, The. William Shakespeare (English). Comedy. 1593.
Based on *The Menaechmi,* by Plautus. Shakespeare's comedy is a series of farcical situations rising from the confusion between the twins, Antipholus of Syracuse and Antipholus of Ephesus, and their twin servants, the two Dromios. The love of the Syracusean Antipholus for Luciana, sister of Adriana, wife of the Ephesian Antipholus, adds further complications. The twin servants are Shakespeare's principal addition to his source. He also added a romantic frame, in which Aegeon and Aemilia, the parents of the Antipholus twins, are reunited after a long separation.

Comedy of Genius, The. François de Curel (French). Drama. 8 scenes. 1918.
A youth, perceiving an actress in a window rehearsing a part, supposes that she is beckoning him in. Their acquaintance thus begun inspires him to become a dramatist and to make her both his leading lady and his mistress.

Comedy of humors. A term used to describe a form of 17th and 18th century comedy which was inspired by Jonson and was based fundamentally on satire. Its best examples were written by Shadwell in the 18th century. As developed by Jonson it became the accepted model for realistic comedy and was for many years an influence on every form of dramatic expression.

Comedy of intrigue. Term used to describe a form of 17th and 18th century comedy which was related to the comedy of manners and differed from it only in its leaning toward farce. Here the laughter arises largely from the variety of the disguises and the complications of the plot. It differs from actual farce in that it does not necessarily, or even usually, employ horseplay in its development. Frequently the complications of the comedy of intrigue lead only to situations that are laughable solely for their intellectual incongruity. Its most outstanding representative in the 18th century was Mrs. Centlivre.

Comedy of manners. A term used to describe a form of 17th and 18th century comedy and still used today as a type-name. This form is characterized by a witty satire on the foibles of the contemporary upper classes. It was developed to its first and probably greatest brilliance by Molière whose method, differing from the Shakespearean one of rounded characterization, was that of presenting people as personifications of abstract qualities. Allardyce Nicoll, however, in his *Introduction to Dramatic Theory,* says the term should be "the comedy of Congreve" as that dramatist is its foremost exponent. Ben Jonson also was a master of the form. During the Restoration it was carried forward not only by Congreve but by Wycherley, Etherege and Fielding. Latterly, Somerset Maugham and S. N. Behrman are perhaps the most brilliant writers of the comedy of manners.

Comedy of sensibility. A term used to describe a form of 17th and 18th century comedy which was characterized by sympathy not with the protagonists but with actions, an artificial love of natural scenery and rural landscapes, and a deliberate enunciation of moral and social problems. Its chief exponents in the 18th century were Colley Cibber and Sir Richard Steele.

Comic epilogue. A form used in all 18th century plays. It was a well-bred protest against any kind of enthusiastic sentiment, expressed wittily, with cynicism and gentility.

Comic opera. Had its origin in Italian *opera buffa* and *inter-mezzi,* presented between the acts of regular pieces; early in the 18th century these were put together to form light or comic operas. Giovanni Batista Pergolesi was the first master of the form (about 1710 to 1736); but later the French took over the *genre* and made of it their *Opera Comique,* which they developed from musical plays given at fairs.

Its first beginning in England was Henry Purcell's production of *Dido and Aeneas* at a girls' boarding school, toward the end of the seventeenth century. At the beginning of the eighteenth century tragedies were so bad and heavy that audiences demanded after-pieces and dances and other light entertainment; it became customary to have standard *commedia dell'arte* characters burlesque in pantomime the action of a known opera. "Ballad-opera" (the first important example of which was *The Beggar's Opera,* arranged to a libretto by John Gay, with music by Finley, produced at Lincoln's Inn Fields Theatre in 1727) led to popular English comic opera, through Isaac Bickerstaff's *The Maid of the Well,* 1765; and *Lionel and Clarissa,* 1768; and Sheridan's *The Duenna,* 1775; and to the operettas of Gilbert and Sullivan.

Comic-relief. A scene or a comic actor introduced into the action of a play to cause laughter, to divert and relax the attention of the audience from the strain of the play's action and plot.

Comic, the nature of. Among the many varied theories of what constitutes the comic are: (1) That which falls below the normal ideal. (A man in walking should keep on his feet. Falling makes him ridiculous.) (2) Things are comical when they enable us to display our intellectual superiority. (To laugh at a dialect is to indicate one's knowledge of proper pronunciation.) Hazlitt says, "We laugh at what only disappoints our expectations in trifles."

Comica accesa. Young girl, character in a *commedia dell'arte,* whose lover is the *comico acceso;* usually uninteresting and subdued; often desiring marriage but curbed by hard parents; sometimes merely a kind of doll, a puppet for the plot. Frequent names: Aurelia, Ginevra, Isabella, Flaminia, Lucinda. Fashionable young person of the time without special characteristics.

Comical Revenge, The; or, Love in a Tub. Sir George Etherege (English). Restoration Comedy. 5 acts. 1669.

This play is important as the first example of English prose comedy. The serious portions are written in rhymed heroics. Etherege's familiarity with Molière's early comedies is evident from the play.

Comicer. The comedian of a comedy team; opposite of a straight man.

Comico acceso. Young lover of the *comica accesa,* character in a *commedia dell'-arte;* dressed usually in contemporary garb, he is, representative, albeit colorless, of the young men of Roman comedy—the inoffensive gallant of the age; may be called Lelio, Flavio, Orazio or Ottavio; his uninspired nature remains the same.

Coming down. Approaching the front of the stage, or that part nearest the audience; to come downstage.

Command to Love, The. Rudolph Lothar and Fritz Gottwald. Adapted by Herman Bernstein and Brian Marlow. Comedy. 3 acts. 1927.

The place is the French Embassy in Madrid; diplomats and their ladies are the dramatis personae. Of these, Gaston, Marquis du Saint-Lac, attaché to the French Embassy, is known far and wide as a lady-killer. Nor was his diplomatic appointment entirely divorced from his conquests, for his ambassador has let it be known that any effort to help his country by wooing the influential ladies of Spain will be appreciated. Unfortunately, at the moment Gaston is interested in the ambassador's wife and loath to seek further conquests. It is only when his superior practically threatens him that he regretfully turns aside from Marie-Anne and encourages the not unwilling Manuela, wife of the Spanish War Minister. His campaign is so successful that he eventually manipulates the signing of a treaty between France and Spain which Manuela's husband had hitherto stubbornly opposed, thus proving that Ministers are best reached through their wives and that the greatest victories are not always won on the battlefields.

Commedia all'improvviso. See *Commedia dell'arte.*

Commedia dell'arte. A style or school of theatre in Italy belonging to the Renaissance, flourishing particularly from the 16th to the 18th centuries, and probably deriving in some part from the ancient Greek *phlyakes* and the Roman *mimus.* The type was one of improvised comedy (sometimes known as the *commedia all'improvviso*) and represented an essentially popular form of entertainment, being usually performed on a rude platform in the public streets. It was a lusty, spirited and sheerly theatrical show, coarse and licentious while unfailingly amusing and uncynical. The stage was a platform with only a backdrop to indicate the setting. On this backdrop were usually painted two rows of houses to suggest, between them, a public street. Actors were strolling players who identified themselves with certain stock characters and continued to play their respective choices, without deviation to other types, throughout their careers. Of these types, or stock characters, there were only about a dozen, and, with the progress of the *commedia,* these tended to become standardized in dress and limited to clichés in mannerisms and speech. The most famous of these types was undoubtedly the *Harlequin,* or *Arlecchino,* which was to the Italian comedy what the clown, *Pierrot,* was later to the French: by turns a cunning valet and a blundering fool. The *Capitano* was a braggart soldier and is perhaps a descendant of the *Miles Gloriosus* of Plautus. The two old men were the *Dottore,* the comic pedant, and *Pantalone,* the foolishly deceived father or cuckolded husband. Outside of *Arlecchino* among the servants, or *zanni,* were *Brighella,* a cruel and dishonest character, and *Colombina,* a trick-devising maid. Other stock characters were: *Pulcinella, Gratiano, Scapino* and *Mezzetino.* (See under individual characters.) As the comedy was not written but improvised by the actors around the characters they played, only an outline of the plot, or a *scenario,* was provided to guide them along the main lines of the intrigue. When the action lagged, bits of "business," called *lazzi,* were used to fill in. At other times the *ballerinas* came on and danced, and the *cantarinas* sang. The line of demarcation between players and audience was not very definite and in no sense inviolable. The knowledge that a person of any kind of significance was in the audience could alter the whole procedure of the performance to include allusions and often downright caricature. Philippe Monnier, in his book *The Mask* has the following to say about the players, their performances and the relationship with the audience: "They were all as chock-full of malice as of wit. Mimes, acrobats, dancers, musicians, comedians, all at once, they were also poets, and composed their own pieces. They strained their fancy to the utmost in inventing it, and improvised it on the spot as their turn came and the inspiration took them. They were not willing, like silly school-boys, to recite only what they had learnt from a master, nor to be mere echoes, unable to speak for themselves without another having spoken before them. They did not draw themselves up in a line before the footlights, five or six in a row, like figures in a bas-relief, and wait their turn to present their tricks. Rather they were full of impatience, imagination, deviltry. They were the great artists of Laughter, the sowers of the golden grain of Gaiety, the servants of the Unseen, the kings of Inspiration. They had only to receive a scenario, which someone had scribbled on his knee, to meet their stage manager in the morning to arrange the outlines of the plot, and to hang the paper within easy reach of the wings; the rest they could invent themselves. Familiarity with the stage and their profession and their art had taught them a whole bundle of tricks and quips. They had a store of proverbs, sallies, charades, riddles, recitations, cock-and-bull stories, and songs jumbled together in their heads. They knew all sorts of metaphors, similes, repetitions, antitheses, cacophonies, hyperboles, tropes, and pleasant figures; and besides they had volumes of tirades, which they had learnt by heart, of soliloquies, exclamations of despair, sallies, conceits of happy love, or jealousy, or prayer, or contempt, or friendship, or admiration, always on the tips of their tongues, ready to utter when they were out of breath. They raised their scaffolding high into the air, and then gave themselves up to their own fertile genius and their amazing caprice. They obeyed all the intemperance and extravagance of their humors. They became nothing but retorts, sallies, conceits, paradoxes, witticisms, mental somersaults. They seized opportunity by the forelock and turned the least accident to profit. They drew inspiration from the time, the place, the color of the sky, or the topic of the day, and established a current between their audience and themselves out of which the mad farce arose, the joint product of them all. It varied at each representation, seemed different every evening, with all the spirit and warmth and alertness of spontaneous creation, a brilliant ephemeral creature born of the moment and for the moment." So popular did the *Commedia dell'-Arte* become that troupes were sent abroad, finding high favor in the courts and among the peoples of France, Spain and England. The most famous of these bands were the *Gelosi,* but the *Uniti* were not far behind in popularity. The *Commedia* ruled the Italian theatre until Goldoni made his attacks upon its clichés and counterposed his literate comedy derived from Molière.

Commedia dell' arte (dramatic form). Impromptu comedy, from which the name of the theatre derived, played with the traditional masks; sometimes called the *commedia all' improvviso.*
See also *Commedia dell' arte.*

Commedia dell' arte, in England. Introduced by Italian players in the 16th and 17th centuries; popular in London during the Restoration; in 18th century turned to pure *pantomime;* this held due to the English actor, Rich, imitator of the Italian players, who, finding he could not speak as well as he could act, turned to dumb show.

Commedia erudita. A style of humorous play established in Italy during the 1530's, graced with but negligible subsequent development. This type of comedy included contemporary stock-characters such as vain and foolish Neapolitan gentlemen and Spanish captains. Its customary features dealt with Italian national conditions, French invasions, the sack of Rome and Turkish tyrants.

Commedie sostenute. Regular written drama, belonging to the *commedia dell' arte* period, ordinarily played by the academicians; based in all essentials upon the best traditions of Terence and Plautus; 16th century to the end of the 17th.

See also *Commedia dell' arte*.

THE COMMENTATOR

BY BERNARD SOBEL

Though the commentator, jester, harlequin, master of revels or master of ceremonies—call him what you will—has only an anomalous place in the history of entertainment, his career is ancient and his place indisputable.

Technically, he embodies the continuous effort that dramatist and player have made throughout the ages to bridge the artificial breach created by separating the actor from the audience. Economically, he represents the growth of a merely social liaison agent into a champion of personal and professional rights.

His origin is dignified and picturesque, reverting from the modern Graham McNamee to the commentator of the classic Greek drama known as Chorus. His purpose has always been practically the same: to insure understanding and appreciation of the performance by establishing a favorable atmosphere; to supply relief and contrast; to sum up what is seen and to be seen; and to stimulate laughter and tears.

With the development of the stage, however, the procedure became more complex, alternating between pantomime and articulance, set speech and the extemporaneous, play-acting and propaganda.

In plays of the early Middle Ages, it was the court jester or professional fool, descendant, perhaps, of Stupidus of the Roman mimes, who functioned as a master of ceremonies.

In French and German carnival plays, and in the English mummer pieces, he had no special part in the story, but amused the audience by cutting capers and tossing off personal comments.

In the Mystery and Morality plays, he appeared under the title of Imp or Demon. And he was extremely welcome here because he often enlivened these dull and humorless works by slicing off the mystery theme and substituting topical allusions, gags, asides and horseplay.

Folly and merriment flourished and the stage benefited through the growth of Fool Companies, organizations resembling the modern fraternal order, and also through the pranks of amateur performers.

On Plow Monday, for instance, the playboys dressed up as fools, went from place to place and put on skits. And if people didn't tip them with money, they plowed up their yards, singing:

"We're not actors from London town
"We're just poor plowhands who work all
day for very little pay."

But the services of the fool, as a master of ceremonies, were not limited to play-acting. He had a much wider influence as a holiday-maker at seasonal, court and church festivals. His title varied, of course, according to nationality and period, but his procedure was largely the same whether he was called King of Beans, Mere-Folle, mock king, boy-bishop or *Prince des Sotes*. And when, as a result of economic change, he added to his powers as court jester those of the village clown, he was known in Scotland as the Abbot of Unreason and in England as the Lord of Misrule.

Elected by university students as a temporary officer to provide entertainment at Yuletide and Shrovetide, he served also as master of ceremonies in the Maypole games, wakes and sports and would lead his troupe from house to house, selling wake indulgences and drinks. Generally speaking, the Lord of Misrule was well-behaved. Nevertheless, he enjoyed reversing the established order of affairs and making sport of the rich.

Similar in character was the Master of Revels. When elected by the people, he was a gay fellow who directed the games and led his followers on predatory and amatory excursions to the fields. In court, he was subject to annual election and served throughout the year as a presiding officer at Christmas festivities and official entertainments. Eventually he grew into the Lord Chamberlain, in charge of court presentations.

Even more interesting, especially on the continent, was the master of ceremonies who rose from the clergy as a feature of the festival of the subdeacons or Feast of Fools. He was called Pope of Fools and King of Fools, and his activities were incredibly riotous. During his brief reign, he burlesqued the mass, led an ass to the altar, while the Church alternately supported or opposed his pagan rule.

Similarly satirical were the activities of the boy-bishop during the Feast of the Choir Boys, at which time the church service was ridiculed and reversed; when old shoes were burned on the altar instead of incense and mock-archbishops consecrated with farm yard sounds.

Throughout these miscellaneous activities, the fool retained a kind of symbolical significance. He was the "licensed agent for social criticism," a medium for fostering reform and revolt, and a literary influence.

But the opposition to improvisation, changed almost beyond recognition, was still active to a master of ceremonies under the general name of clown and with specific titles like the Bobo, the Vice, Badin, English John and Pickle Herring. Though still largely extraneous to the plot of a play, he bobbed on and off the stage whenever he had a chance to do so; and began to make determined efforts to establish his own personality with an individualized type of humor and characteristic comic apparel. Comedians like Pickle Herring and Will Kemp were famous for their jigs, tumbling, trick entrances and wit, which was often directed at the "masters."

The license authorities actually attempted to suppress the performance of a popular master of ceremonies, Dr. Samuel Foote, who antagonized such important men of his day as Samuel Johnson. But the jester evaded the authorities by inviting his friends to the theatre for a cup of chocolate and then presenting his players in a public rehearsal.

Notwithstanding, the Restoration dramatists eventually reduced the jester to a printed routine; forced him to recite the lines assigned to Prologue and Epilogue.

In Italy, throughout these same centuries, the master of ceremonies had been developing special faculties by way of the *commedia dell'arte,* and the character of Harlequin.

The *commedia dell'arte,* or vulgar popular comedy, one of the most fascinating forms of stage expression, was sheer theatre and extemporaneous.

Unfortunately, though, the *commedia* suddenly degenerated into obscenity and ribaldry. It introduced nude women and obscene incidents sometimes so shocking that spectators dropped their heads in shame.

Soon, as a result, the state refused to grant the players license, and the Church denied them the right to decent burial. Simultaneously the court and the academies attacked their morality.

By 1697, their disrepute spread so widely that Harlequin, in his capacity as a master of ceremonies, had to fight back, champion personal and professional liberty, defend himself and his associates against political, literary and social enemies. Through heckling, wisecracks and community singing, he turned the stage into a public forum with the audience as participant, becoming by force of circumstances, a censor, a critic, a caricaturist and the forerunner of the modern living newspaper.

With the modern era and the English variety show, the master of ceremonies became the precursor of the modern announcer of the stage and radio. His title was Chairman, and he took his place not on the stage but in the auditorium, facing the first row.

Sometimes he would turn around and watch the performance; and sometimes, when the audience grew noisy, he would take out a mallet and rap for order. Occasionally patrons would treat him to a mug of beer which he would drink with winkles, cockles, fish and chips, and sprinkle with vinegar and salt.

The English revue has frequently employed two masters of ceremonies: the commere and compere, now superseded by individual artists like Rex Evans, who does off-color songs like Dwight Fiske's, and Douglas Byng who offers female impersonations.

Meanwhile, in the United States, the master of ceremonies was developing by way of the minstrel and burlesque show. His relationship may even be traced, perhaps, to the early medicine men who introduced the Negro entertainers from his wagon in the public square as a come-on for the sale of patent medicine, a traffic similarly conducted during the formative days of the *commedia dell'arte.*

In the minstrel show, the m.c. was known as the *interlocutor,* who usually opened the show with the time-worn wheeze, "Gentlemen, be seated"; introduced the various performers; and acted as a feeder for the comics.

During the 90's, company managers of traveling repertory troupes acted as m.c.'s, explained the nature of the bills, presided at the country store raffle and distributed prizes that ranged from roosters to celluloid toilet sets.

Up until this time, the master of ceremonies had confined his activities largely to his side of the footlights. But with the growing popularity of burlesque there came a new emphasis on introductions.

John E. Henshaw in George Lederer's revue, "The Passing Show," originated the stunt of introducing people in the audience to the audience. Raymond Hitchcock introduced individuals in the audience to each other. He also greeted patrons at the entrance of the theatre. Ed Wynn bade them goodbye, assisted them in putting on their coats, and sometimes helped them into their automobiles.

James J. Morton is generally credited with being the first vaudeville announcer. Until he began introducing the performers, letters and numbers set up in frames at the sides of the stage identified them. His procedure was droll and seemingly timid. He made his explanations in abashed tones between nonsensical anecdotes and stories.

Will Rogers established the record for skill in presenting celebrities from the audience and the stage. Eddie Cantor, runner-up, gained considerable adverse criticism by addressing the present king of England as "Davy."

The Russian, Balieff, in "Chauve Souris," gained popularity with announcements in mangled English, French, German and Russian.

With the advent of the radio, the m.c. was faced with the most difficult task of his career: holding the attention of an audience while remaining unseen.

Incidentally, the modern toastmaster bears a close relation to the master of ceremonies, and also to the master of revels. For the art of the master of revels lies in setting a note of lightness, humor, revelry.

All these years the playwright has kept the m.c. accessible, and despite the present insistence on realism brings him into plays.

Barrie, for instance, fearful of losing the sympathy of his audience, stopped the action of *Peter Pan* midway so that his hero might step out of character to appeal for confidence. Obey's *Lucrèce* retained the formal male and female commentators of the French drama. Elmer Rice made these same commentators consistent characters in *Not For Children*. The Chinese play, *Lady Precious Stream,* introduced a modern woman expositor. *Our Town* revived to a degree the Greek chorus by way of its commentator.

Commercial theatre. The theatre operating as a business for profit. In America, Broadway and the road; in London, the West End; in Paris, the Right Bank, although a few on the Left Bank have had financial successes. In short, the opposite of little, arty, advance-guard, or amateur theatre.

Committee for Verse and Prose Recitation. Established in 1937 in England by John Masefield, Dame Sybil Thorndike and others for the purpose of bringing plays and poetry back to the public inn. The Taverners gave more than fifty performances during 1938 in London, sometimes acting on a platform at the end of a small room; their repertoire included Shaw and Galsworthy.

Commonwealth. A practice, frowned upon by Actors' Equity Association, wherein the receipts are pooled and after a play's expenses are taken out, each actor gets a share, larger or smaller or equal, depending on previous agreement.

See also *Hallam Company.*

Community Players, The. San Diego, California. Originally a group of players banded together under the name of the Barn Players Club in 1933. After the close of the San Diego exposition with its unique Shakespearian Globe Theatre performances, a movement to save the Globe Theatre resulted in the building of a charming, fireproofed theatre, modelled after Shakespeare's own.

Community Theatre Festival of Australia. In 1937 the Australian Drama League helped to organize a festival in the town of Wagga, near Sydney. At that time it resolved to make Wagga the centre for a pioneer Country Dramatic Festival; these festivals have continued annually.

Community Theatre Festival of Britain. The annual festival of community drama at which amateur companies compete for the Howard de Walden cup. Was organized by the British Drama League in 1926.

See also *British Drama League.*

THE COMMUNITY THEATRE MOVEMENT

BY CARL GLICK

Let a group of stage-struck Americans get together, be they bankers, lawyers, stenographers, teachers, society matrons, factory workers, and someone is bound to say, "Let's put on a play." And another Community Theatre is born.

This Community Theatre Movement that today is sweeping over America from the prairies of the Dakotas to the green hills of Vermont, from towns and cities on the Pacific Coast to winter resort colonies in Florida, is one of the most exciting adventures in the theatre that has taken place in our generation.

It is one of the most unusual, too, for it means that Mr. or Mrs. Busy-During-the-Day America, at night steps into the theatre and engages in active play production as producer, actor, scene shifter, electrician, prop boy, scene and costume designer, box office manager. Not because he wishes to make money and commercialize the stage, but because he loves the theatre and has found a new outlet for his leisure time activities. Today this Community Theatre Movement means that a new type of theatre has come into being; a non-profit making, non-professional, educational, social, and recreational theatre. It may rightly be said to be the Theatre of Democracy, for it is a theatre of the people, by the people and for the people. It represents the cooperative effort in every community of the people of that community, a cross section of the entire town; bricklayers and carpenters, stenographers and dowagers, doctors and debutantes, all drawn together by a common interest—theatre.

America has always been stage-struck. Even the early pioneers put on plays for their own amusement. As far as we know, according to Mary Austin, the first *home talent* plays in this country were given by the Spanish soldiers, with the Indians as spectators, near what is now Sante Fe, New Mexico in the year 1598. Amateur actors in Boston started play production on their own in 1750, and even though the City Fathers at that time objected, interest in the theatre did not die. Today there are some sixty non-professional producing groups in Boston, and one of them, the Footlight Club of Jamaica Plain, has been in continuous existence since 1877. In the West the first Community Theatre playhouse was built by Brigham Young in Salt Lake City in 1853. In the South amateur play production before the Civil War was an accepted part of the social life, and one of the earliest groups established in 1790 and still in existence today is the Thalian Association in Wilmington, North Carolina.

But the Movement as we know it today did not gain impetus until shortly after the turn of the century. In the gay nineties the professional theatre flourished in towns and cities throughout the country. Every city of any size had its opera house, and traveling companies of actors played one-night stands in what was known as the road. Then came the movies, and the road began to decline. The opera houses were either sold to the moving-picture magnates, or else torn down. Save for the large metropolitan centers, there was no more spoken drama in America. Then it was that these amateur stage societies began to gain strength.

About 1911 theatre-lovers in towns far removed from the white lights of Broadway, began to talk about producing their own plays. Inspired by the success of Antoine with his Little Theatre in France, the Abbey Theatre in Dublin, Reinhardt in Germany, and others, pioneers in this country, revolting against the methods and practices of the commercial theatre, began to experiment in play production. Maurice Browne started a Little Theatre in Chicago seating ninety-one persons.

Encouraged by the success of his undertaking, other cities began to have their own theatres. According to Constance D'Arcy Mackay, by 1917 there were some fifty established groups in this country. They called themselves, *Little Theatres*.

These *Little Theatres* were the subject of much laughter at first. George Kelly satirized them in his play, rightly named, *The Torchbearers*. But their lights were not dimmed, and the movement grew and spread, from the large cities into towns and villages throughout the nation.

Inspired by the writings of Percy Mackaye, who as far back as 1909, said that the theatre should be dedicated to public, not private, ends, these groups now began to call themselves *Community* or *Civic Theatres*. The reason was obvious, they were becoming the expression of the people of that community. And Percy Mackaye's definition of community drama, "There is participation; there is creative expression; there is neighborly ritual," has become the understood slogan of these various groups.

Today there are over seven hundred established Community Theatres in this country producing five or more plays each year. And there are some three or four hundred more who do at least one or two plays each season. In all, around one thousand active groups engage in community participation in creating their own theatre. The estimated number of workers in these theatres, actors, scene shifters, and so forth, non-professionals all, engaged in the production of plays for the joy of creating their own drama, is over one million participants. And the average yearly attendance at these productions is over fifteen million.

In *Curtain Going Up* (Pitman Publishing Corporation, 1939), the detailed stories of near two hundred Community Theatres, representative of groups in large cities as well as small towns, have been told; their beginnings, their early struggles, their problems, and the ultimate goal to which they are striving.

Nearly two hundred of these groups have their own playhouses. In many cities these theatres are colorful, remodeled old buildings of one sort or another; a former morgue in Dover, New Jersey; a laundry in Macon, Georgia; a barn in Fitchburg, Massachusetts; an engine house in Peoria, Illinois; and so forth and so forth.

Other cities, inspired by success, have built their own playhouses, in many instances handsome theatres that rival those on Broadway. Pasadena, California, has a theatre valued at $400,000; Cleveland, Ohio at $325,000; Dallas, Texas at $150,-000; Columbia, South Carolina at $45,000; New Orleans, Louisiana, at $175,000; San Antonio, Texas, at $104,000, (This is the San Pedro Playhouse, the first city built and city owned community theatre in the country); and so on. The total value of these community owned theatres runs into several millions of dollars.

Many groups are writing and producing their own plays. St. Louis, Missouri has a national playwriting contest, so have Columbia, South Carolina, and others. Each year there are more new plays given premieres in community theatres than are produced on Broadway. Many of these plays have been published, and some have had Broadway productions.

The destinies of these community theatres are guided by a Board of Directors, elected by the entire membership, which is open to anyone interested. In management, these theatres are thoroughly democratic. Many cities engage a full time, paid professional director. Some even have paid technical directors and business managers. But the actual play producing is done by volunteers.

The average player in these community theatres does not aspire to a professional career. Only some five percent of those who have first appeared on community theatre stages have gone to Broadway or Hollywood. The rest are content to remain at home; doing their mundane jobs by day, and play acting at night merely for the joy to be had in creating their own theatre.

The most recent trend of these various groups, scattered throughout the country, is toward regional and local organizations; one of the most outstanding being the Wisconsin Dramatic Guild, composed of some eight groups in that state with headquarters and a service bureau at the University of Wisconsin.

This then is America's theatre, a true people's theatre, the expression of their culture and their art. And ultimately from these Community Theatres there may arise in this country a real national theatre.

See *Theatres, 20th Century American.*

Compagnie des Quinze. A group of fifteen, now disbanded, which had its inception in Copeau's *Vieux Colombier,* and whose leader was Michel St. Denis. The principles were not unlike those of the Group Theatre, without the political ideology of course, and their methods of withdrawing to the country to rehearse are analogous. André Obey was identified with the Quinze and his *Noé* is his most brilliant play.

Compañía de titulo. The name applied to each of the eight royal troupes of actors in Spain organized in 1600. A typical compañia was composed of three *galanes* (lovers) and three *damas* (ladies), a *barba* for old-man parts, a *gracioso* and *graciosa,* the lovers.

Complimentary. Term meaning gratis, as complimentary ticket. Inside the theatrical profession it is the sole term used, excluding other near-synonyms such as passes, courtesies, etc., which apply to the general public.

Comrades. August Strindberg (Swedish). Naturalistic Drama. 4 acts. 1888.

Axel, a gifted artist, has for years prostituted his talent to earn money for his wife. When they both send pictures to the Salon, he attaches his number to her picture so that she will win a place in the exhibit. Hearing that his picture has been rejected, she humiliates him by having it returned during a party. When she discovers the rejected picture is her own, she tries to propitiate him, but he drives her out into the streets.

Comstock, Anthony (1844-1915). American reformer. The father of modern American censorship. He was born in New Canaan, Connecticut, served in the Civil War, and then became a worker for the New York Young Men's Christian Association. The urge to wipe out what he considered sin caused him to become a self-appointed censor of books, plays and pictures. His influence was responsible for the passage of stringent laws prohibiting the sending of pornography through the mails and otherwise safeguarding the public morality. These were the so-called Comstock Laws, 1873. He became the secretary and special agent of the New York Society for the Suppression of Vice, and in this capacity prosecuted relentlessly every questionable book to be published or play to be produced. Almost fanatically zealous and extremely puritanical, he left his lasting imprint on American arts and letters.

Comus. A mummery, or voluntary procession of the townsfolk in ancient Greece, in honor of Dionysos, ending with phallic song; the origin of comedy; the procession with its satiric cries, answered by back-chat of onlookers, developed into two choruses; became a dramatic tradition in itself, distinct from tragedy with its one chorus.

Comus. John Milton (English). Masque. 3 scenes. 1634.

Though described as a masque, *Comus* is strictly a pastoral entertainment. The name *Comus* was not included in the title in the first three printed editions, but is taken from one of the characters, a pagan god invented by Milton, son of Bacchus and Circe, who tempts travellers to drink a magic liquor which changes their faces into those of wild beasts.

Concert, The. Hermann Bahr (Austrian). Comedy. 3 acts. 1909. Adapted by Leo Ditrichstein.

Gabor Arany, a concert pianist, falls in love with Flora Dallas, a physician's wife, and takes her to a cottage in the mountains. They are followed by Mrs. Arany, the pianist's wife, and by Dr. Dallas. The affair ends when Mrs. Dallas discovers that she loves her physician husband, and Gabor Arany realizes how much he depends on his wife.

Concertatore. Manager of a *commedia dell' arte*.

Concetti. A series of formal expressions or tags of dialogue in a *commedia dell' arte* used when conversing with others in set situations.

See also *Uscite* and *Chiusetti.*

Condell, Henry (? -1627). English editor and actor. Joint-editor with John Heminges of the First Folio edition of Shakespeare's plays in 1623 and a principal actor in Shakespeare's company, the Lord Chamberlain's Men. He was a share-holder in the Globe Theatre and the Blackfriars. He is named in the 1623 Folio list of performers in Shakespeare's plays. Among other dramas in which he is known to have had roles are Jonson's *Every Man in His Humor; Every Man Out of His Humor; Sejanus; Volpone; The Alchemist; Catiline;* Webster's *Duchess of Malfi.* In Shakespeare's will Condell was bequeathed a memorial ring.

Condottiere. Italian soldier suggested by the stock character of the *commedia dell' arte,* the *capitano.*

Confederacy, The. Sir John Vanbrugh (English). Comedy. 5 acts. (Published also as *The City Wives' Confederacy.*) 1705.

An adaptation of d'Ancourt's *Les Bourgeoises a la mode.* It deals with the complications which ensue when Gripe and Moneytrap, two rich usurers, exchange their wives.

Confidenti. Famous Italian troupe of the *commedia dell' arte.*

Confrérie de la Passion. An acting company of French artisans who were given a royal privilege in 1402, of preventing all theatrical performances "in the city of Paris as well as in its suburbs and the surrounding country" if the profits were not turned over to them. They ceased to function as an acting company in 1548, but their monopoly on receipts continued (theoretically, at least) until 1677. From 1548 until 1710, the Confrérie controlled the only established theatre in Paris, the Hôtel du Bourgogne, and any company which attempted to play in another place found rough going.

See also *Hôtel du Bourgogne.*

Confréries des fous. See *Actors, medieval.*

Confréries pieuses. See *Actors, medieval.*

Congreve, William (1670-1729). English dramatist. He was born in Bardsley, Yorkshire, the son of a soldier who, during William's childhood, commanded a garrison at Youghal, Ireland, where the future dramatist was reared. He was educated at Kilkenny and Trinity College in Dublin, where he met Swift. Later he went to Middle Temple in London and studied law. After publishing in 1692, under the pseudonym, Cleophil, an almost unnoticed novel, *Incognita; or, Love and Duty Reconciled,* he became suddenly famous through the production in 1693 of his first comedy, *The Old Bachelor.* Generously sponsored by Dryden, and competing only with the much coarser work of Wycherley and Shadwell, this witty, immoral comedy of manners achieved instant success. His popularity reached its greatest height with *Love for Love* in 1695. Generally, however, his success in the theatre was varying, as his great masterpiece, *The Way of the World,* was a failure. Collier's attack on the stage did much to alienate him from the theatre, although he replied with at least one pamphlet to Collier's diatribe, he wrote nothing for the stage after *The Way of the World.* He did some travelling, and in 1710 he became blind. Though ignored by the Victorian stage, his comedies have been frequently and successfully revived in modern times.

He is also the author of *The Mourning Bride.* He was the most brilliant exponent of the comedy of manners. His dramatic theories are to be found in his *Letter Concerning Humour in Comedy.*

Conkle, Ellsworth Prouty (1899-). American educator and dramatist. Born in Peru, Nebraska, he received his Ph.D. from the University of Iowa, studied drama with Professor Baker at Yale and spent a year in Europe on a Guggenheim Fellowship. He taught at both the University of North Dakota and the University of Delaware; became assistant professor of the Department of Speech in the University of Iowa, and director of the University Theatre, one of the most progressive of the little theatres of the Middle West. As a playwright he first attracted attention in 1932 with a farce called *Forty-nine Dogs in a Meat House.* His first play to be shown on Broadway was *200 Were Chosen,* in 1936. On March 6, 1938, *Prologue to Glory,* which had been held for a time by commercial managers, was finally produced by the Federal Theatre and achieved great success.

Connelly, Marc (1891-). American dramatist. Born in McKeesport, Pa. In Pittsburgh he became a newspaperman, then turned toward thoughts of the theatre. He wrote lyrics for a musical that failed, but which brought him to New York. Here he continued writing for newspapers and magazines and doing occasional skits for revues. In 1921 he joined with George Kaufman to form a most productive and successful partnership. The Kaufman-Connelly collaborations included *Dulcy,* 1921; *To The Ladies,* 1922; *The 49-ers,* 1922; *Merton of the Movies,* 1922; *Helen of Troy,* 1923; *The Deep-Tangled Wildwood,* 1923; *Beggar on Horseback,* 1924; *Be Yourself,* 1924. At this time they parted company by mutual agreement and Mr. Connelly wrote *The Wisdom Tooth,* 1926. But Mr. Connelly's real triumph came with *The Green Pastures,* 1930, which ran for almost two years in New York and for three additional years on tour, and which won the Pulitzer Prize. For four years Mr. Connelly gave some time to motion pictures and traveling. In 1934 he collaborated with Frank B. Elser on *The Farmer Takes a Wife,* which was moderately successful. He produced and directed *Having Wonderful Time,* 1937; *The Two Bouquets;* and *Everywhere I Roam,* co-author 1938. He has also either written or collaborated on a number of motion picture scenarios.

Conquerors, The. Emile Fabre (French). Drama. 3 acts. 1908.

Deals with money as an instrument for furthering political ambition, showing a lawyer so eager to enter the ministry of state that he descends to blackmail and consents to raising a loan from the lover of his wife. He loses his son who falls in a duel with a scandalmonger.

Conquest of Granada; or, Almanzor and Almahide. John Dryden (English). Heroic play in rhymed couplets. 1672.

Besides much rant and bombast it contains some good verse and pleasant lyrics. The background is furnished by the quarrels of the rival factions of Moors under Boabdelin, the last king of Granada, and the war in which Granada fell to Ferdinand and Isabella.

Conrad, Robert T. (1810-1858). American dramatist. The son of one of the members of the publishing house that issued the works of Charles Brockden Brown, the first American novelist, and Joel Barlow. Born in Philadelphia, by the time he was twenty-two he was writing plays, his first *Conrad of Naples* being produced at the Arch Street Theatre, Philadelphia, 1832. He was educated for the Bar and early began to interest himself in local politics. He had read law with his uncle, but instead of immediately going into practice, he gave satisfaction to his interest in Journalism by publishing the *Daily Commercial Intelligencer,* later known as the *Philadelphia Gazette.* When his health failed, he turned to law, became recorder of the city, and judge of the Court of Criminal Sessions. The American party also elected him candidate for mayor. This activity did not prevent his writing. Among the plays credited to him are: *Jack Cade,* 1835; and *Conrad of Naples.*

Conscious drama. Term given to the dramaturgy of civilized man, whose emotions are so well controlled as to lend themselves easily to clear and logical expression within the precise form of a play.

Conscious Lovers, The. Sir Richard Steele (English). Comedy. 5 acts. 1730. Based on the *Andria* of Terence. Illustrates the author's views on duelling and the proper attitude of men towards women.

The story of young Bevil who is about to marry the wealthy Lucinda Sealand, but who really loves Indiana, an orphan. After many complications, in the end Indiana turns out to be a long lost daughter of Sealand by a former marriage and all ends happily, with various lovers united.

The Constant Nymph. Margaret Kennedy and Basil Dean (English). Drama. 3 acts. 1926.

This dramatization of Margaret Kennedy's popular novel of the same name ran for 587 performances in London. Its New York production the same year, however, was comparatively short-lived.

The members of "Sanger's circus," eccentric music-lovers with a dash of madness and a dash of genius, are living in the Tyrol. In addition to Albert Sanger and the seven wild, brilliant children of his two wives and his mistress, the group consists temporarily of Lewis Dodd, a disciple of Sanger; Jacob Birnbaum, manager who had arranged a ballet for an opera of Sanger's; and Trigorin, another acquaintance. All the conventions of drawing-room society are ignored in the household; the children go undisciplined; only music is sacred. Then Sanger dies suddenly, leaving his children penniless. The oldest and youngest ones are able to fend for themselves, but Dodd and Birnbaum cannot cope with the impractical vagaries of the four children of Evelyn Churchill, Englishwoman to whom Sanger was married for a time, and write to England asking what should be done with them. Robert Churchill and his niece Florence answer the summons and come to take two of the girls, Paulina and Teresa, back to England to school. Teresa, "the constant nymph," at fifteen is a child-woman, capricious, moody, at once naïve and wise beyond her years. And she loves Lewis Dodd with all the understanding of one musician for another and all the passion of an untamed heart. Lewis, talented, selfish, hiding his sensitiveness beneath an arrogant exterior, is fond of the girl—but in Florence Churchill, pink and white and proper, he sees a visitant from another world, is infatuated and marries her. They go to London, where Florence reveals herself as domineering and stuffy, and Lewis falls out of love with her. Moreover, her persecution of Teresa causes the musician to realize it is the Sanger girl he really loves. He persuades Teresa to elope to Brussels with him. On the boat going over she becomes ill, and dies of a heart attack in the pension to which they go in Brussels.

Constant Wife, The. W. Somerset Maugham (English). Comedy. 1926.

This cynical and scintillating protest against the double standard in marriage is developed in Maugham's best comedy manner. It was successful both in London and New York, where Ethel Barrymore starred.

Constance has been married for fifteen years to John Middleton, London surgeon. She is aware that he is having an almost overt affair with her best friend, Marie Louise, but refuses to admit it or to listen to gossip. She also refuses the financial independence which would be possible if she accepted her friend Barbara's offer of a partnership in her interior decorating shop. However, she does rebel to the point of receiving in her home an old sweetheart, Bernard Kersal, back in England after fifteen years in the Orient. He honorably promises he will act only as a friend in spite of his lasting affection. At this juncture the philandering husband returns and is introduced to the noble lover. Two weeks later, the suspicions of Mortimer, Marie Louise's husband, are aroused when he finds John's cigarette case under his pillow. Constance gallantly comes to her husband's defense by announcing she left the case there, and convinces Mortimer so thoroughly he goes off to buy his wife a pearl necklace in apology. When he has left, Constance finally admits she has known the true state of affairs all along. John is more disturbed by her calmness than he would have been by an outburst; Bernard offers to marry her. But she explains that she could not be unfaithful to John as long as he was supporting her; moreover, John need regret nothing, since they had five perfect years before falling out of love. Then, left alone, she telephones Barbara her acceptance of the business offer. For a year she works, at the end of which time she has paid John for her board and lodging. Independent at last, she plans to go off with Bernard for six weeks, until he sails for Japan, then return to home and husband. John is furious, but unable to object to his wife doing what he himself did, and promises to wait.

Constructivism. A counterpart of futurism with its scenic emphasis on machines and mechanical devices. In one phase of his career Meyerhold employed this form as a method of interpreting the inner meaning of the drama.

Contention betwixt the Houses of York and Lancaster, The First Part of. (1594.)

Anonymously published; a play on the same subject as Shakespeare's *King Henry VI,* and long considered the source used by Shakespeare for his work. Shortly afterward appeared *The Civil Wars between the Two Houses of Lancaster and York* (Books I-IV; also Book V), by Samuel Daniel. E. K. Chambers, the historian, holds the opinion that the *Contention* of 1594 is a pirated, corrupt version of Shakespeare's play—which Shakespeare later revised into *King Henry VI.*

Contour curtains. See *Curtains.*

Conventions, planes of. Those conditions essential and native to the times in which a play is written, like soliloquies and asides in Elizabethan drama.

Conversation piece. A term occasionally applied to a comedy, with much talk and little action.

Cook, Madge Carr (1856-1933). English-American actress. Born in England; sister of L. Morton Powell, theatrical manager. As a child of three, appeared as Fleance in *Macbeth.* In 1881 she joined an English pantomime company, and played in *Elizabeth, Pluck, No Coronet,* and other plays. In 1887, when she was thirty-one, she came to America, making her New York debut in *The Beautiful Star* at the old Niblo's Garden. Her best known role was the title part in *Mrs. Wiggs of the Cabbage Patch,* in which she played for several years, both in America and in London. Her last engagement was a tour in *If I Had the Money.* She retired in 1910. Eleanor Robson is her daughter.

Cooke, Alexander (? -1614). English actor. An actor named in the 1623 Folio list of performers in Shakespeare's plays. It is conjectured that he took all the principal female roles. Other plays in which he is known to have acted include Jonson's *Sejanus, Volpone, The Alchemist* and *Catiline;* and Beaumont and Fletcher's *The Captive.*

Cooke, George Frederick (1756-1811). English actor. The illegitimate son of an officer, he was born in a barracks. He was brought up in the town of Berwick-on-Tweed, in the north of England. He had no theatrical connections, but when about ten or eleven years old, fell in love with plays and acting. He saw Garrick in 1775, and thereafter the man was his idol. Cooke joined strolling companies and played much in the provinces. In 1800, he first appeared at Covent Garden in London, as King Richard III, where he had great success. During the season 1810-1811 he acted in America in New York, Boston, Philadelphia and Baltimore. Everywhere he went he drew crowds. He continued to stay on in the United States, although he told his friends, "I don't want to die in America. John Kemble will laugh at me." Yet he never took decisive steps about returning to England. As late as July 1812, he was playing in Providence; and there he made his last stage appearance, July 29. He died in New York on September 26, 1812, of hardening of the liver induced by alcoholism. His body was interred in the strangers' vault in St. Paul's churchyard. He is considered, after Edmund Kean, one of the most forceful actors of the English stage. Kean erected a monument to his memory, the first ever erected to an actor in America.

Coolus, Romain (Rene Weil) (1868-   ). French dramatist. Born at Rennes. His first successful comedy was acted in 1901. His later productions, noted for his ironical characterization and sympathy with the unconventional attitude towards love, include *L'Enfant Cherie,* 1906, and *Coeur à Coeur,* 1907, and a number of vaudeville sketches. He was president of the Society of Dramatic Authors and Composers.

His plays include: *The Bresile Household,* 1893; *Raphael,* 1896; *The Sick Child,* 1897; *Lysiane,* 1898; *Coeurblette,* 1899; *The Marquis de Carabas,* 1900; *The Lovers of Sazy,* 1901; *Lucette,* 1902; *Antoinette Sabrier,* 1903; *Little Pest,* 1905; *The Cherished Child,* 1906; *The Risk,* 1909; *A Woman Passed,* 1910; *The Coast of Love,* 1912; *The Week of Folly,* 1912; *The Eternal Masculine,* 1920; *Love, When You Hold Us,* 1921; *The Ostrich* (with Hennequin), 1922; *The Alarm Clock* (with Hennequin), 1923; *Jim* (with Hennequin), 1924; *The Kisses of Panurge* (with A. Rivoire), 1925. *The Alarm Clock* was adapted by Avery Hopwood and performed in New York, 1923.

Cooper, Violet Kemble (1889-   ). English actress. She has acted extensively both in England and the United States and, since 1933, in films. She made her English stage début in 1905 as Kitty Verdun in *Charley's Aunt;* her first New York appearance in 1912 in *The Indiscretion of Truth.* She has also played in *Peg O' My Heart,* 1913; *Happiness,* 1914; *The Wooing of Eve,* 1917; *Dear Brutus,* 1918; *Clair de Lune,* 1921; *The School for Scandal,* 1923; *The Servant in the House,* 1925; *The Command to Love,* 1927; *The Apple Cart,* 1930; *Lysistrata,* 1930; *He,* 1931; *Criminal-at-Large,* 1933; *The Shining Hour,* 1934; etc.; etc.

Copeau, Jacques (1878-   ). French director, actor, manager. Designed with Louis Jouvet the formal stage at the *Vieux Colombier* which was the leading experimental theatre in France. He is a first-rate character actor and he developed a well-integrated company about him. His troupe played in New York, 1917-18, as part of French wartime propaganda. He retired in 1924 and lectured in America 1926-27.

See also *Garrick Theatre, New York; Théâtre du Vieux Colombier.*

Coppée, François Edouard Joachim (1842-1908). French poet, novelist and dramatist. Born at Paris, he is known as a poetic interpreter of the commonplace realities of everyday life. Although his many poetic works, like *Le Reliquaire,* 1869, *Les Humbles,* 1872, and his novels and tales, notably *Le Coupable,* 1897, deal with such material with delicacy and sympathy, his plays belong to the romantic drama, which they helped to revive. Coppée was elected to the French Academy, 1884. His short story, *A Tragedian's Funeral,* is a charming sidelight on theatrical life.

Plays by Coppée are: *The Passerby,* 1869; *Two Sorrows,* 1870; *The Woman Abandoned,* 1871; *Do What You Should,* 1871; *The Jewels of Deliverance,* 1872; *The Lute Maker of Cremona,* 1876; *The House of Molière,* 1880; *The Treasure,* 1880; *Mme. de Maintenon,* 1881; *Severo Torelli,* 1883; *The Jacobites,* 1885; *Our Father,* 1889; *For the Crown,* 1895; *The Guilty Man,* 1896.

Copyright. Ownership of intellectual and artistic property. The word as commonly used refers to government registration and protection of the rights guaranteed in the copyright law. Application covers such creative items as books, periodicals, dramas, ballets, musical works, graphic or plastic works of art, photographs and maps, and insures exclusive ownership in this country and abroad. Copyright was first granted by the Republic of Venice in 1469, to John Speyer, who received the sole right to print letters of Cicero and Pliny for five years. Copyright at first covered books only, and has been gradually extended to its present scope. There are international copyright rules—the Berne Convention with modifications—but the United States does not adhere. However, reciprocal agreements have been signed with various nations. Procedure in the obtaining of American copyright is as follows:

A notice of copyright is placed upon the work, with the date of issuance or completion.

To copyright a play, write to the Register of Copyrights, Library of Congress, Washington, D. C., requesting an application blank. This will be received within the course of ten days to two weeks. All the information on the blank should be filled in and submitted to the Register with either one or two copies of the play, depending on the request from the Register's office. The fee is one dollar for each copy.

The copyright is in force for twenty-eight years, and may be renewed for another twenty-eight years by the original owner, his heirs or assignees only. After the fifty-six years the work becomes public property. Anyone may use it in any way.

Even in the case of non-copyrighted plays, the author has a property right provided the play has not been printed.

The copyright law protects the author. No one may produce a play whether admission is charged or not, without the permission of the copyright owner or his representatives. This also holds for a public reading of the play, or the reading of the play in any open group. The author receives his return for his work from the royalties charged for performances of his drama. Every conscientious person must be scrupulous about this. Most plays can be produced for a royalty fee of ten dollars to fifty dollars a performance. Some plays are royalty-free with only one requirement, that a copy of the play must be bought for each character in the play.

To obtain rights of production, write to the publishers, or to the persons named in the printed text of the play, as the author's agents. If there is no copyright notice, if the play has not even been printed, care should still be exercised if the work seems to be within the 28 year period. For ignorance is no defense. The Dramatists Guild of the Authors League of America, 6 E. 39th St., can be helpful in such matters.

Coquelin, Benoit Constant (Aîné) (1841-1909). French actor. Made his debut at the Comédie Francaise in 1860 as Gros-René in *Dépit Amoureux*. His first great success was in *Figaro* in 1861. He created the leading roles in forty-four new plays. He had great success in society by reciting, and also added to the reputation of new poets, particularly Eugène Manuel and François Coppée. He resigned from the Comédie-Française in 1886 because of a dispute over his right to make provincial tours. He joined in 1890 as a *pensionnaire,* but broke definitely in 1892 and toured Europe with a company of his own. In 1895 he rejoined the Renaissance Theatre in Paris, and played there until he became director of Porte Saint Martin in 1897. Here he made a sensation in *Cyrano de Bergerac.* In 1900 he toured America with Sarah Bernhardt, and continued to appear with her in *L'Aiglon* upon their return. He was rehearsing the leading part in *Chantecler* when he died. His books were valuable contributions to the history of the stage and the art of acting; among them were: *L'Art et le Comedien,* 1880; *Molière et le Misanthrope,* 1881; essays on *Eugène Manuel,* 1881, and on *Sully-Prudhome,* 1882; *Les Comédiens,* 1882; *L'Art de Dire le Monologue* (with his brother Ernest) ; *L'Art du Comedien,* 1894.

Coquelin, Ernest Alexandre Honoré (1848-1909). French author, actor. Younger brother of Benoit Constant Coquelin called "Coquelin cadet"; made his debut at the Odéon in 1867; appeared with his brother at the Théâtre Français; became a *sociétaire* in 1879. He played many modern and classic parts, and recited monologues of his own composition. Among his books are: *Le Monologue Moderne; Le Rire; Pirouettes.*

Coquette. George Abbott and Ann Preston Bridgers (American) Drama. 3 acts. 1927.

Norma Besant or Coquette loves Michael Jeffrey of whom her father Dr. Besant disapproves. In a quarrel Dr. Besant shoots Michael, and pleads not guilty on the ground of defending his daughter's honor. Since Coquette is carrying Michael's child, she has no alternative but to take her own life that she may avoid an examination and save her father.

Coriolanus. William Shakespeare (English). Tragedy. c. 1607.

Closely follows Plutarch's life of Coriolanus. Coriolanus, an excellent soldier but bitter antagonist of the common people, is made candidate for the consulship in return for his military services to Rome. The tribunes, to save their own power as representatives of the people, rouse a mob against Coriolanus and banish him from the city. Coriolanus turns to Rome's enemy and his own personal foe, Aufidius, leader of the Volsces, and joins him in a march against Rome. Only the pleas of Volumnia, Coriolanus' militantly patriotic mother, dissuade him from his purpose. Rome is saved, but Aufidius uses Coriolanus' action as an excuse to kill him.

Corker. British slang term for an actor who ruins a play. Also dead stick.

Corner block. A triangular piece of three-ply profile board used for corners in flat construction. Dimensions are 14 inches along the hypotenuse, 10 inches for other sides of the right triangle.

See *Scenery*.

Corner plate. An "L" shaped plate used for joining the corners of a flat instead of a corner block.

See *Scenery*.

Corneille, Pierre (1606-1684). French dramatist. He was born in Rouen of a middle-class family of lawyers and petty officials, of which his father was one in that city. Pierre was educated at the Jesuit College in Rouen and later studied law, becoming an advocate in 1624 and carrying on a practice for several years. He wrote his first play, *Mélite,* when he was twenty-three, the successful production of which by Mondory in Paris induced him to abandon law for the drama. For a time he was one of the five poets whose business it was to make plays out of the rough sketches or mere ideas given them by Richelieu, but from this distasteful office he was dismissed in 1634. Between this time and 1636 he wrote five comedies, a tragi-comedy and a tragedy, all being produced. In 1636 his most famous play, *Le Cid,* was produced, marking the beginning of his true, and greatest, successes. The famous controversy over *Le Cid,* involving the *Académie française,* brought him increased fame. After two unsuccessful attempts he was admitted to the Academy in 1647. Discouraged by the failure of *Pertharite* in 1653, he retired to Rouen where he occupied himself with a verse translation of the *Imitatio Christi.* Though he returned to the theatre in 1658, he never repeated his earlier triumphs. His works represent most fully the French ideal of so-called "classical" tragedy and he was the first and foremost in the group called "neo-classicists." He believed in strict observance of the Aristotelian unities of time, place, and action. The effect of these rules on the work of Corneille was the placing of exceptional importance on speeches; and it is in the eloquence of these, in the grandeur and dignity of the versification, and in the lofty moral elevation of the characters, that Corneille particularly excels.

His most important plays, aside from *Le Cid,* are: *Horace; Cinna; Polyeucte;* and *Nicomede.* His contribution to dramatic theory is scattered throughout his *Examens* and his *Discours.*

Corneille, Thomas (1625-1709). French dramatist. Born at Rouen, the younger brother of the great Pierre Corneille, he was made a member of the Academy, 1685; died at Les Andelys.

His tragedy, *Timocrate,* 1656, ran for eighty nights, a record for the century.

Cornell, Katharine (1898-   ). American actress. Born Feb. 16 in Berlin, Germany, of American parents. Her father was a theatre manager. She made her stage debut in New York on November 13, 1916, at the Comedy Theatre in *Bushida.* She was engaged by Jessie Bonstelle to play small parts, in Buffalo, but because of her lack of confidence in herself she was not at first given a long speaking part. It was not until 1921, when she played in *A Bill of Divorcement,* that she made a definite hit. In the same year she married Guthrie McClintic, who has directed and supervised every production in which she has appeared since 1925. Most notable among her early successes were *The Outsider; Candida* (which she has played twice, the revival being in 1937) ; *The Green Hat; The Letter; The Age of Innocence;* and *Dishonored Lady.* Her more recent appearances include *The Barretts of Wimpole Street,* 1931, under her own management, running for a year and subsequently going on tour; *Lucrece,* 1932; *Alien Corn,* 1933; *Romeo and Juliet,* 1934; *Flowers of the Forest,* 1935; *Saint Joan,* 1936; *Wingless Victory,* 1936-37; *Herod and Mariamne,* on tour in the fall of 1938; and *No Time for Comedy,* 1939.

Autobiography, *I Wanted to be an Actress,* with Ruth Woodbury Sedgwick.

Corporazione dello Spettacolo. A theatrical organisation, formed under Italian Fascism in 1931, which controls two great federations uniting all theatrical syndicates: (1) the Federation of the Administrators of Labor, which includes operatic and dramatic managers, leading actor-managers, theatre-editors, cinemaowners and -managers; (2) the Federation of Workers, which includes artists, actors, singers, orchestra players, mechanics, and other employees. The purpose of this corporation is to ally the interests of the different theatrical categories on behalf of the higher interest of industry and art. It has been, so far, financially successful.

Corps municipaux. See *Actors, Medieval.*

Corral (or coliseo). Name applied to the courtyard, or space between houses, which was the place for the representation of plays, and the corrales were the first permanent theatrical establishments. In the earlier days of the 16th and 17th century drama, the windows in the upper floors of houses served as box seats.

The earliest recorded *corral* of Madrid was the *Corral de la Pacheca* where performances were given as early as 1568. Later this was called the *Teatro del Principe.* The present *Teatro Español* stands on the same spot and has the oldest uninterrupted tradition of any playhouse in the world. Its rival establishment, the *Teatro de la Cruz,* dates from 1579. For over 200 years with few intermissions these two spots were the only Madrid playhouses.

Other cities had *corrales* or *coliseos.*

Coryphee. A ballet dancer; member of the corps de ballet.

Cossa, Pietro (1830-1881). Italian dramatist. Exiled to South America for his participation in the rising of 1849, he returned after a short time to Italy, and lived in poverty until 1870.

His historical tragedies, with which he achieved his first success, include: *Nero,* 1870; *Messalina,* 1876; *The Borgias,* 1878; and *Cleopatra,* 1879. His complete works appeared in 1887.

Co-starring. Billing which gives equal prominence to two performers in a theatrical production and which tops the name of play and author.

COSTUMES

BY ALINE BERNSTEIN

The clothing that an actor wears when he comes on the stage to play his part is his costume. It is not his own dress, it is the dress of the character he is representing, just as the words he speaks are not the words of his own thoughts, but the words the author has written for the character to speak.

The costume of the actor is the heightening, the translation into theatrical terms of the dress of everyday life. It is the selection of what is suitable, beautiful, and helpful to the portrayal of character, from the vast store of material of life. When this is well done, the artist is not merely a copyist of a period, even if it is the style of our own time, but he is a real creator. This principle applies to all costumes designed for the stage, whether for straight drama, comedy, tragedy, or the more fantastic forms of ballet and musical show. Naturally there must be the intention of beauty, that is the taste of the designer.

It is a fascinating art, in practice, execution, and preparation. There are two fields of study necessary to it. The first is the study of life and character, for people look the way they look because they are the way they are. Each personal variation of dress springs from some variation of character, differences that may be slight but are none the less important. A gay person and a tragic person would never be dressed exactly alike, no matter if their circumstances and position in life were identical. Had Hamlet been a well adjusted and happy prince, he would not have clung tenaciously to his inky cloak. The patches of Harlequin are the multiple manifestations of the possibilities of the actor's character, a thing of shreds and patches. It is almost impossible not to be expressive of one's self in dress, even if self is only manifest in the tilt of a hat, the length of a sleeve, or the way a collar sets around a neck. All these signs are present for study, but to make use of them the eye of the designer must be trained, and above all, interested.

The research into period and national costume is a fascinating part of the designer's work. He has the entire pageant of the arts of the world at hand. It is not only in costume books that material is found, but in all of painting and applied arts. There are hundreds of wonderful books, containing reproductions of paintings, sculpture, ceramics, and textiles, all the arts, books that are available in libraries and museums. Some excellent ones are cheap enough to buy, even for the most modest purse. Much valuable information about wearing apparel and social customs relating to apparel is to be found in writings of every time in recorded history. Sometimes in words one may get a very special flavor that is lacking in pictorial representation. For example in the letters of Lady Mary Wortley Montague written from Turkey in the early eighteenth century when her husband was Ambassador from England, there are the most fascinating descriptions of the dress and undress of the ladies of the harems. Her descriptions, too, of the court and society clothes in Vienna where she stopped on her way, are priceless for certain details of hair dress, jewelry, laces and so forth. The eighteenth century diaries are rich in material. Faithfulness to such detail is worthy of the designer's closest study, for it adds a lot to the illusion of the stage picture. I do not advise overloading any design with detail, but what detail there is should be correct.

Every script presents a new problem; every play has a new set of characters and a new approach; every actor and actress has a different temperament to deal with. We do not lack variety in our work, but we often lack hours enough in the day to get through with it.

After consultation with the director, the author and the actors, I make my drawings. I have to see to it that three estimates are submitted to the producer. There are many ways of interpreting a costume drawing, so that in getting these estimates from the costumer I go over each drawing carefully, specifying the quality and type of material, the trimmings, laces and manner of execution. This takes time, and it does not always follow that the job goes to the lowest estimate. Sometimes we know that one costume company may be better fitted to handle a certain job than another, and the difference in price is worth the money. After the work is assigned to the maker, I select every piece of material used in my costumes, even trimmings and buttons. If samples are not to my satisfaction, I shop myself until I find just what I want. The selection of material is important to the effect of the design. There is always a budget to consider, as well as the suitability of the material. I also insist on having exactly the colors I want, even if dyeing of fabrics is necessary.

I see all costumes before the first fitting, so that they are as close as possible to my idea. There are usually two fittings, sometimes three for principals. I superintend every one. I should say that is the most trying, if not the most difficult part of the work. Little time is allowed for fittings by the directors, we usually get the people early in the morning before rehearsal when they are sleepy, or in the late afternoon when they are tired and cross. An actor is himself his own instrument, he has neither violin nor piano to perform upon, he has to charm you with his own body and voice; so I think it is important to have him pleased and comfortable, as important as the design itself.

The problem with modern clothes is different, but just as particular. I sometimes design them and have them made, sometimes when possible I buy them. It is seldom that I find a suitable model in the color I want, in which case the color is selected then ordered. I watch every fitting, even at the best Fifth Avenue shops. I order wigs, shoes, stockings, gloves, bags, hats, all accessories, even jewelry; and it is part of my business to see that everything is delivered at the theatre and complete for the first dress rehearsal.

The dress rehearsal is an ordeal. In a large production we have a dress parade, a certain time set aside for the clothes to be worn and shown. In any case it is trying, for the costumes are actually worn for the first time, the actors are strange in them, and they come more or less as a surprise to everyone; often a disappointment to me. They are shown under difficult circumstances, without the proper stage lighting and all concerned in a fault-finding mood. Nobody knows how hard we work, how good we are, and what splendid people carry out my designs. When changes need to be made, they accomplish the impossible, three weeks' work is done in one day; not as a favor but as a matter of course.

Occasionally in my work I have designed costumes for the theatre when I did not design the scenery. I do not like to, I think that the designing of the stage picture should be done by one person, for no two minds think alike. It is almost unavoidable in large musical productions, where there is not time enough for one person to do all. Even that could be avoided with forethought. It is hard work, with little reward, except for the exciting moment never equalled in anything else in life, when the house lights darken, the footlights go up, the curtain rises, and magic takes place.

Costumes, Modern Designers of. Costuming has become an important element in theatre art. The excellence of the creative work produced by such artists of stage decor as Mrs. Bernstein, Donald Oenslager, Robert Edmond Jones, Jo Mielziner, Norman Bel Geddes and others traces back to the stimulus of the brilliant work more than 20 years ago of Josef Urban, the Viennese modernist who raised the standard of stage costumes and scenery to a plane of genuine artistic effort. His colorful designing for the Ziegfeld Follies and other productions was extensively publicized and the place of the costume and scene designer became definitely more important. Art in the theatre took a step forward. Diaghileff and his Ballet Russe were contributors also to this effect. They toured France and England and in 1916 they visited the U. S. They brought with them the beautiful demonstration of the value of artistic costume and scene design. So that today, even ordinary costumes of everyday people are designed with full regard to line and color values, harmony and utility, whereas in the first decades of the 20th century, costumes were merely adequate.

Costume libraries. See *Museum of Costume Art; Brooks Costume Library.*

Costumers. New York: Brooks Costume Rental Co.; Eaves Costume Co.; Veronica Blythe (long with Eaves and a well-known Broadway personality); Oscar Berner (wigs); Charles Chrisdie & Co., Inc.; Gertrude Elliot; Juliette (wigs); Lane Costume Co.; Tams Costume Emporium.
Philadelphia: Van Horn.

Costuming, English, Elizabethan. All the stage garments of the time were sumptuous, even the hirelings wearing silk and giving the appearance of gentlemen. For many plays, even those placed in other eras, the ordinary Elizabethan garb was made to serve. For others there must have been marked differences, both for historical exactitude and symbolical illusion, but little is definitely known about them. However, as contemporary audiences demanded little or nothing in the way of geographical or historical accuracy considerable latitude was the rule rather than the exception. Actors received clothes from noblemen who were their patrons which accounts for richness of costume.

Costuming, English, Restoration. Beyond an occasional toga, or turban and barbaric ornaments for Eastern personages, costuming on the English stage of the 17th century made little attempt at historical accuracy. The women's gowns, often the gift or loan of rich patrons, followed the prevailing mode; the men's costumes, regardless of the period of the play, were invariably topped off with the then fashionable periwig.

Costuming, English, 18th century. Eighteenth century audiences constantly demanded show; pseudo classic writers who cut down on scenic effects because of monetary arguments from producers made up for it by rich costuming and other externals. All historical productions were played in contemporary dress.

Costuming, English, 19th century. Under the influence of Planché, costumes became historically authentic to fit the period of the piece requiring them; this was first done in the early part of the century by the Kembles and Mrs. Siddons; *King John* in 1823 with Charles Kemble and Mrs. Faucit is notable; this established a tradition of historical accuracy.

Costuming, German, 18th century. Among the requisites in stage apparel for every actor in the 1700's were: black velvet knickerbockers, a brown cloth coat and a light silk waistcoat; These made up the conventional accoutrement of every ordinary role. For special parts: kings—scepters, gold embroidered waistcoats, and, atop a full-bottomed wig, a hat with feathers; heroes of prehistoric times—helmets in place of hats and a scarf tied around their brown cloth coats.

Costuming, Greek, ancient. In the early religious drama of all nations theatrical costume was highly symbolic. Deities, heroes and personifications of qualities such as virtue and vice had traditional colors, garments and insignia. Masks and wigs were always important.

In the Greek theatre dress was conventional in color and accessories, the sock and buskin (*soccus* and *cothurnus*) standing respectively for comedy and tragedy.

In tragedy, the costume was of two distinct types: (1) typical: long flowing dress, belted at the waist, and extending from neck to ankles, called *chiton;* similar to that worn in ordinary life with but one or two changes; over this a cloak, usually a mantle thrown over one shoulder; (2) special costumes designed for characters with special profession or in special circumstances: e. g., beggars in abject rags, kings with crowns, etc. In comedy, costumes were of two general types: (1) puffed-out, Falstaff-like garb; (2) tight, skin-fitting, flesh-colored dress, both characterized by the phallus, an emblem of the licence of the Greek theatre.

Costuming, Italian, Commedia dell' Arte. See specific stock characters, such as Harlequin, Brighella, the *dottore,* etc.

Costuming, medieval. Much fantastic dress was used in the medieval moralities, such as devil masks, while divinities were garbed in the styles of contemporary religious paintings. Medieval costuming in the main was of the following types: (1) devils: in the form of animals; (2) for ordinary characters: dress of the day. Color symbolism was generally used. For example, "Mercy" was robed in white, "Truth" in green, etc.

Costuming, Roman, ancient. In ancient Roman drama, costume was modelled on the Greek. It was symbolic and conformed to two distinct types: (1) for tragedy: long sweeping robes, or *syrmata,* corresponding to the Greek *chiton;* (2) for comedy: various short garments recalling costumes of both the *Phlyakes* and the regular literary comedy of the Greeks. Wigs (*galeri*) were worn, also buskins, corresponding to the Greek *kothornoi.* Old men wore white; young men wore purple; parasites were dressed in grey; and courtesans in yellow.

Cothurnus. Boot worn by Greek actor to give added height and stature.
See also *Kothornos.*

Counsellor-at-Law. Elmer Rice (American). Drama. 3 acts. 1931.
A character study of a successful attorney, whose reputation is threatened by the disclosure that in his earlier days he had resorted to illegal means in order to save a young client from life imprisonment. His wife and all his friends desert him and he decides to commit suicide. He is prevented from doing so by his secretary in whom he finds real love and understanding.

Counterplot. A plot or story, usually minor in key, opposed to the main plot of a play; intended to emphasize or enhance the main plot of the play.

Counterweight system. A system for flying scenery by using weights to counterbalance scenery.
See *Scenery.*

Count Julian. Walter Savage Landor (English). Tragedy. 5 acts. 1812.
Deals with the story of the vengeance taken by Count Julian, a Spanish noble, on Roderigo, the king, who has dishonored Julian's daughter. The subject is also treated in Southey's *Roderick* and in a different form by William Rowley in his *All's Lost by Lust.*

Count of Monte Cristo, The. Alexandre Dumas (French). Drama. 5 acts. 1844.
Edward Dantes is soon to become captain of the ship, Pharoon, and to marry his sweetheart, Mercedes. Dantes' hopes are wrecked, however, when his rivals succeed in having him arrested on false charges, and imprisoned for twenty years in the lonely Chauteau D'If. It is there that he learns of a hidden treasure on the Island of Monte Cristo. He escapes, finds the treasure, and becomes the fabulous Count of Monte Cristo. He then relentlessly hunts down the men who took his ship, his sweetheart, and twenty years of his life.

Country Theatres. See *Theatres, 20th Century American.*

Country Wife, The. William Wycherley (English). Restoration comedy. 5 acts. 1675.

Living in 18th century London, Margery Pinchwife, the Country Wife, although carefully guarded by her husband, succeeds in having an affair with an eligible bachelor, Mr. Horner.

Pinchwife, like other London husbands, believes Mr. Horner's friendship for his wife to be of a platonic nature. Mr. Horner is, in reality, a Don Juan, and Margery makes peace with Pinchwife when he finds that he is only one of many duped husbands, and that Horner has transferred his affections to Lady Fidget.

Coup de théâtre. A theatrical hit; hence any showy or sensational trick.

Court theatres. Built during the 16th Century to accommodate Italian *commedia dell' arte* players in demand at courts in France, Spain, Austria, Germany, England, in fact all over Europe. These were distinguished from medieval theatres by the roofing of the buildings. Gordon Craig speaks of their handsome stages. During the 17th century, court theatres were built at Versailles and in the 18th century at Trianon, Drottningholm near Stockholm, and in the Christiansborg Palace in Copenhagen among other places.

Courtesies. Seldom used term for free admission into theatres.

Courtneidge, Cicely (1893-   ). English actress. Born in Sydney, N. S. W.; made her first appearance on the stage at the Prince's Theatre, Manchester, 1901 in *A Midsummer Night's Dream*. Went to Australia for six years and returned to England and was seen in *Tom Jones*. Other plays in which she appeared include: *The Arcadians,* 1910; *The Mousmé,* 1911; *Princess Caprice,* 1912; *The Pearl Girl,* 1913; *The Light Blues,* 1916; *Oh, Caesar,* 1916. She made her first appearance in the United States in *By-the-Way,* 1925; she later appeared in *Clowns and Clover,* 1927-29, and began a long film career in 1929.

Courville, Albert de (1887-   ). English dramatic producer. He was born March 26, in London, and after a period in journalism was assistant director of the London Hippodrome until 1920. His successful revues included *Hullo, Ragtime!* 1912; *Zig-Zag,* 1917; *The Whirl of the World,* 1924; *Sky-High,* 1925. He has also produced successfully for the British Broadcasting Corporation and directed the films *There Goes the Bride* and *The Midshipmaid*.

Covent Garden Theatre, London. Opened Dec. 7, 1732, with Congreve's *The Way of the World*. The house was beautifully decorated by the Italian artist, Amiconi, who painted a magnificent ceiling, representing the gods banquetting in the clouds; the scenery was by this same artist assisted by George Lambert. It was a small theatre; the length from the stage to the back of the boxes was only fifty-one feet, and when full would only hold two hundred, which allowed only twenty-one inches to each person. The fronts of the boxes were flat, there were twisted double branches with candles against the pilasters. There were no footlights, but the stage was illuminated by four hoops of candles, surmounted by a crown hung from the borders.

On each side of the stage was an ornamental pedestal with painted figures of Tragedy and Comedy. The orchestra was of a bowed form, narrower than the house, and adapted for from twelve to twenty musicians. Rebuilt and remodeled several times. Since 1846, it has been devoted only to opera and musical performances.

Coventry Plays. A series of forty-two English mystery-miracle plays dating from the reign of Henry VII, the earliest of which was probably composed about 1416. These were purely religious plays with a suggestion of the morality play yet to come. Performances originated in, but were not limited to, the town of Coventry.

Covering material. Light, durable and easily painted cloth, such as duck, muslin, linen, or lightweight canvas, used to cover the frame of a flat.

Coviello. Stock comic figure in the *commedia dell' arte,* a "mask" who is a coward pretending to be brave; often a mountebank. His name is an abbreviation of that of his inventor, a Neapolitan called Jacoviello. He wears bells on his wrists and ankles, and plays the lute.

Coward, Noel (1899-   ). English actor, dramatic author, producer and composer. Born in Teddington, he showed an early aptitude for the theatre and made his stage debut in a children's fairy play in 1911. That same year he was engaged by Charles Hawtrey and appeared in a great variety of plays until 1917 when he joined the army. After the war he returned to acting and began writing.

Mr. Coward is a master of the theatre. As a writer his range is not easy to parallel, for he is equally successful in the writing of revues, comedies, serious drama, clever lyrics and musical accompaniments. His first great success was attained with his serious play *The Vortex* in 1924 after which he established himself as one of the leading theatrical personalities of his time. Among his best known works are *London Calling* (part author), 1923; *The Vortex,* 1924; *Charlot's Revue* (part author), 1924; *The Rat Trap,* 1924; *Hay Fever,* 1925; *Easy Virtue,* 1925; *This Year of Grace* (author and composer), 1928; *Bitter Sweet* (author, composer and producer), 1929; *Private Lives,* 1930; *Cavalcade* (author and producer), 1931; *Words and Music* (author, composer, producer and conductor for opening performance), 1932; *Design for Living,* 1932; *Conversation Piece* (author, composer and producer), 1934; *Point Valaine,* 1934; *Tonight at 8:30,* 1935; *Set to Music,* 1939. In 1934 he appeared in the film *The Scoundrel.* He is the author of several volumes of prose and poetry, among them his autobiography, *Present Indicative.*

Cowl, Jane (1890-   ). American actress and dramatic author. Born in Boston, Mass., and studied at Columbia University. She made her first stage appearance in 1903 in *Sweet Kitty Bellairs* and has been playing leading roles ever since. She has appeared in *The Music Master,* 1906; *Within the Law,* 1915; *Common Clay,* 1917; *Lilac Time,* 1917; *Information Please,* 1918; *Smiling Through,* 1919-1922; *Romeo and Juliet,* 1923; *Pelleas and Melisande,* 1924. She made her first appearance in London in 1926 in *Easy Virtue.* After returning to New York, she appeared in *Road* *to Rome,* 1926-8; *Paolo and Francesca,* 1928; *Twelfth Night,* 1930; *Camille,* 1932; *The Shining Hour; Rain from Heaven,* 1934; *First Lady,* 1935. She is part author of *Lilac Time, Daybreak, Smiling Through, Information Please, The Jealous Moon* and *Hervey House.* She is one of America's most distinguished players of lead roles.

Cowley, Hannah (1743-1809). English dramatist. Born at Tiverton. Her first play, *The Runaways,* was successfully produced by Garrick in 1776. It was followed by twelve others, of which the most popular was *The Belle's Stratagem,* 1782. Under the name of Anna Matilda she corresponded in verse with Robert Merry, who styled himself Della Crusca, and their joint poems, published in 1788, enjoyed considerable popularity.

Cowly, Richard (?-1605). English actor. An actor named in the 1623 Folio list of performers in Shakespeare's plays. He is known to have played Verges to Will Kempe's Dogberry in a 1598 production of *Much Ado About Nothing.*

Crabtree, Lotta (1847-1924). American actress. Born in New York, was taught dancing by Lola Montez and was a popular child actress in the mining camps of California. Scored a success as Little Nell in a dramatization of *The Old Curiosity Shop* in New York, 1867, and won the hearts of a large audience with her spontaneous and graceful acting. She amassed a great fortune by her lengthy tours and retired in 1891.

Cradle. A caster mounted frame for supporting strip lights used to light the base of the cyclorama.
See *Lighting.*

Cradle Song, The (Cancion de Cuna). Gregorio and Maria Martinez Sierra (Spanish). Drama, 1911.
Produced in an English version in New York in 1921, it was revived by Eva Le Gallienne in 1926. The simple, poetic, tender, devoutly pious play has also proved popular with college and other amateur theatrical groups.
At a convent of Dominican nuns in Spain, the birthday of the prioress is being celebrated. In the midst of the fete the bell of the convent door rings. No one is at the gate, but there is a basket containing a baby girl and a note asking that this daughter of an erring woman be brought up as a child of God. The novices and the stern vicaress disagree as to whether or not to keep the child. Their friend the kindly doctor offers to adopt it to conform to regulations, and they decide to lodge it with the gardener's wife until the girl is old enough to say for herself if she cares to lead the cloistered life. Eighteen years pass. The child, Teresa, is a gay, pretty young girl. She is going to be married and go to America to live; her adopted mothers are busy making her trousseau. Teresa asks that her betrothed, Antonio, be allowed personally to thank the nuns who have done so much for his beloved. Her request is granted. In a poignant scene, Sister Joanna of the Cross tells the girl how she has always felt more her mother than the others, and how she will always consider her as dear as a daughter. Antonio arrives, thanks the sisters from behind the grill, and promises to

take good care of his bride in America, where he has a position as architect. Then he asks to see the nuns face to face. The prioress graciously allows Teresa to draw the curtains. The nuns sadly kiss their protégé farewell, and the doctor, now an old man, comes to escort his adopted daughter from her girlhood home.

Cradle Will Rock, The. Marc Blitzstein (American). Musical drama. 10 scenes. 1937.

This play was written for production by the Federal Theatre in New York, but was canceled by Washington authorities. It was later staged by the Mercury Theatre in New York without scenery, costumes, or properties, the composer, Mr. Blitzstein, playing the score and serving as announcer at the piano, the actors arising on cue and doing their bits. This was the first play in the history of the theatre to be produced professionally in such a fashion.

Mr. Mister is an economic royalist who practically owns and controls Steeltown. He corrupts the press, bulldozes the church, selects his own Liberty Committee and arranges for the assassination of a labor organizer. He is, however, unable to beat the hosts of labor. At the final curtain they overwhelm him and his henchmen.

Craig, Edward Gordon (1872-   ). English designer. Born near London; the son of Ellen Terry; educated at Bradfield College and Heidelberg, Germany; made his first appearance on the stage at the Court Theatre, 1878, in *Olivia;* his acting career is associated with his mother's and with Sir Henry Irving. His great effect on the theatre has been as a visionary and a writer. As one of the pioneers of modern theatre art he urged simplification of scenery and the unity of production. As a designer his work has been largely impractical. His productions include: Purcell's *Dido and Aneas,* 1910; Purcell's *Masque of Love,* 1901; *Much Ado About Nothing,* 1903; *Das Gerettete Venedig (Venice Preserved),* 1904; Ibsen's *Rosmershelm,* 1911; *The Pretenders,* 1926; *Macbeth,* in New York, 1928; and others.

Among his books are: *Art of the Theatre,* 1905; *On the Art of the Theatre,* 1911; *Towards A New Theatre,* 1913; *Theatre Advancing,* 1921; *A Production,* 1928; *Books and Theatres,* 1930.

Craig's Wife. A drama by George Kelly (American). 1925.

Mrs. Craig's credo is that a woman should seek from marriage independence and security rather than romantic love, and her guarantee of the performance of a home for herself is "the control of the man upon which they are founded." She is a fanatical housekeeper, discourages the visits of her husband's friends and alienates him from his family. Mr. Craig bears with her patiently until an accident reveals her to him in her true colors. He leaves her, and Mrs. Craig is left alone in the house for which she has sacrificed so much.

Crash the gate. To gain free admission to the theatre.

Craven, Frank (1880-   ). Actor, dramatic author, and producer. Was born in Boston. Made his first appearance in 1887 in *The Silver King* and spent many years in traveling in stock companies all over the U. S. Has appeared in *The Writing on the Wall*, 1909; *Bought and Paid For*, 1911; *Too Many Cooks*, 1914, which he also wrote; *Under Fire*, 1915. He wrote and played in *Money From Home*, 1927; *The Nineteenth Hole*, 1929; *That's Gratitude*, 1930. He was the commentator in *Our Town*, 1938. He staged *Whistling in the Dark*, 1932; *Riddle Me This*, 1932; *Bridal Wise*, 1932. He appeared in the films in *State Fair*, *City Limits*, and has written and directed the production of other films. He is the author of *Spite Corner*, 1922; *Up She Goes*, 1922; *The Girl Goes Home*.

Crebillon, Prosper Jolyot de (1674-1762). French dramatist. Father of Claude P. J. Crebillon, who wrote the immoral novel, *The Sofa;* and author of gloomy, horrific tragedies, among them: *Idoménée*, 1705; *Atrée et Thyeste*, 1707; *Rhadamiste et Zénobie*, 1711.

Creditors. August Strindberg (Swedish). Drama. 1 act. 1890.

Thekla, the heroine, has preyed upon her first husband, Gustav, and her second, Adolph. Gustav resists Thekla's attempt to take him back as a lover, and destroys Adolph by hypnotizing him and then revealing to him Thekla's faithlessness.

Crepe hair. An artificial wool-like substitute for hair, used in making beards, moustaches, etc.; comes braided and in various colors.

Criminal Code, The. Martin Flavin (American). Drama. Prologue and 3 acts. Printed 1929.

Robert Graham, serving a prison sentence for manslaughter, is given a job as the warden's chauffeur. Later he is witness to a murder in the warden's office. When he adheres to the Criminal Code and refuses to divulge the murderer, Graham loses the privilege of working and is locked in his cell. Finally he kills a prison official who has mistreated him, and receives a life sentence.

Critics and criticism. Theatrical criticism is as old as the drama, natural and necessary to it. It governs its growth and development, for the acceptance and reaction of audiences to dramas determines to a great extent the course and nature of future acting, dramatic technique, production and writing. And, of course, the opinion and expressed views of informal or authoritative persons has had, has, and will always have an important influence on popular opinion. The source of influence of the authority may vary—emperors, kings, churches, teachers, scholars have influenced the popular opinion of plays.

The province of criticism is everyone's. The profession of criticism is, however, comparatively new. Since the days of the Greeks, scholars, philosophers and others have commented and written on dramas and dramatic theory. But only since the development of the newspaper and periodical have men been paid to report on, review or criticize plays. Perhaps the origin was in the informal institution of Fop's Corner criticism in the Restoration theatre when the public avidly awaited the decision of the "experts." Nevertheless, as newspapers and periodicals developed, expert opinion on theatre matters was recognized as an important public interest.

Because the role of critic is authoritative, expertness was required of critics and the cloak of importance was loaned to him. Thus many great men of letters have been critics and many achieved their fame as critics. William Archer, Walkley, Lemaitre, Shaw are among the famous 19th century critics abroad and William Winter, the most famous American critic. J. G. Huneker, Percy Hammond, Alexander Woollcott, Heywood Broun, George Jean Nathan are famous 20th Century American critics.

Because New York is the center of the professional theatre in America the New York critics are the most important and influential. Recently they organized themselves as the *New York Drama Critics Circle*.

Present day New York critics include: *New York Times*, Brooks Atkinson, Lewis Nichols; *New York Herald-Tribune*, Richard Watts; *New York Post*, John Mason Brown, Willella Waldorf; *New York World-Telegram*, Sidney Whipple; *New York Sun*, Richard Lockridge; *New York Journal-American*, John Anderson; *Daily Mirror*, Walter Winchell, Robert Coleman; *Women's Wear Daily*, Kelcey Allen; *Daily News*, Burns Mantle, John Chapman; *Time*, Louis Kronenberger; *Morning Telegraph*, Robert Rice; *Brooklyn Eagle*, Arthur Pollock; *Daily Worker*, John Cambridge; *Theatre Arts*, Rosamond Gilder, Edith J. R. Isaacs; *The New Yorker*, Wolcott Gibbs; *Cue*, Oliver Claxton; *Variety*, Jack Pulaski; *The New Republic*, Stark Young; *The Nation*, Joseph Wood Krutch; George Jean Nathan, various; John Gassner, various. On the radio are Lucius Beebe, Station WOR; Martin Starr, Station WMCA.

London critics include: *Times*, Charles Morgan and A. V. Cookman; *Sunday Times*, James Agate, Geo. W. Bishop; *Daily Mail*, M. Willson Disher, Harold Conway; *Daily Telegraph*, W. A. Darlington, Geo. W. Bishop; *Illustrated London News*, Ivor Brown; *Observer*, Ivor Brown, Horace Horsnell; *Punch*, Eric Keown; *Sketch*, Ivor Brown; *Sphere*, Philip Page; *Stage*, H. M. Walbrook; *Sunday Dispatch*, F. W. Connery Chappell; *Sunday Express*, Stephen Watts; *Sunday Graphic*, F. Harris Deans; *Sunday Pictorial*, Herbert Farjeon; *Sunday Referee*, Philip Page; *Daily Herald*, Hannen Swaffer; *Theatre Arts*, Ashley Dukes. On the radio for the British Broadcasting Corporation is James Agate.

See also *New York Drama Critics' Circle; Reviewers*.

CRITICS AND CRITICISM

BY JOHN MASON BROWN *

To the majority of people, and even to that highly specialized majority of theatre people, the dramatic critic seems, at best, a spiritless person who prefers the indolence of opinions to the trials of action. Because his interest leads him only into judgment and away from performance, the world can never quite forgive him or take him with that final seriousness he undoubtedly desires. It presumes, believing it to be a charitable presumption, that he must have turned dramatic critic because he is either waiting to do some real work in the theatre or because he has failed there.

---

* Reprinted from *Upstage*, 1928, by the kind permission of W. W. Norton and Company.

The critic is a figure, and often a power, in the larger cities, but his readers share with him the knowledge that the roots of his sway go no further than an opinion he happens to have formed in a crowded theatre, where everyone else may have been forming radically different opinions. When, therefore, he speaks—as he is sometimes tempted to—too confidently, too arbitrarily, as though he were the one and only chosen representative of the earthly estates of Thalia, his position is somewhat precarious and not a little ludicrous.

In daring to lift his voice above the crowd the critic may feel justified because of his delusion that what he writes so unhesitatingly is an expert opinion, whereas what they feel is only an immediate and unthinking emotional reaction. He may hope against hope that this will endow his words with their due finality. But if he has recourse to his dictionary, he only adds to his confusion. Though he may be comforted by reading that a reaction is a "responsive or reciprocal action," or the "response of an organ, etc., to external stimulus," he is disheartened to learn that an opinion is only a "judgment based on grounds short of proof," "a provisional conviction," or at best a "formal statement by an expert when consulted of what he holds to be the facts or the right course." In other words the dramatic critic is always far short of infallibility, and the sooner he learns it the better it will be for him and his profession. His truth at best is his truth to himself and his own temperament but even in his statement of this one truth that can be absolutely his, he is often fallible. His fallibility, however, leaves him once more as only a single voice raised against many.

In dramatic criticism, more than in any other form of appraisal, it is apparent that one man cannot speak with a complete knowledge of the many aspects of a production which combine to make it effective. He is faced with the sorry dilemma of speaking not only intelligently, but also authoritatively as a playwright, an actor, a scenic artist, a director, an electrician, a costume mistress, and a member of the audience. More than that, in the course of a single week of professional theatregoing he may meet, not one kind of playwriting, or one kind of scenery, or one kind of direction, or acting, or one historical period and specialized locale, but as many as six, with their corresponding styles in costume, language and demeanor. Obviously his lot is not a happy one if he attempts to muster facts towards authority. Accordingly what he does is to seek means of escape. And in means of escape his profession abounds.

For one thing he takes refuge in the highly debatable purposes of his job. He catechizes himself, with such questions as the following, and finds asylum in the easiest answers. Is he writing to tell his public what happened and who was there? Is he only an audible member of the audience whose reactions are valuable mainly as they serve as a common denominator to what the town may think? Is he trying to help the actor and the playwright by constructive suggestions, or is he merely to describe them for prospective ticket-buyers? Is he a middleman or an autocrat, a press agent or a synopsis manufacturer? Do his readers want to know what he thinks or learn about what they may like? Is he to parade his understanding or his adjectives, his knowledge or his enthusiasms? Is he to treat each production as an isolated unit, or judge it by comparative values? Is he paid to analyze technicalities or to amuse his public? Is he to turn crusader and fight for a play or a production or a group in which he believes, even when they are not ripened enough to warrant his praise, or is he to pass judgment only on the finished product? Is he to measure what he is asked to see by a general theory of the theatre, or come receptive, with his mind and body fresh for new impressions? In short, and this is more important than it may seem, is he to be a reporter, a reviewer, or a critic?

The dramatic critic differs from the reporter and the reviewer in that he is more interested in the idea behind the event than in the event itself. Sharing with them an indebtedness to another man's work, or rather in his case the work of other men, he is, like them, a lean-to in literature and cannot stand alone. He needs an incentive, if not an excuse, for his work, but he does not find it in the date which heads the page of a daily newspaper. Supposedly the reflections he has to make are not confined only to a passing interest because they are based upon eternal principles. His realm is the idea rather than the fact. He sees a play or a performance not in relation to what it may say to a prospective ticket-buyer, but in terms of what it does contribute to the theatre and to life. Even if he makes no mention of the past, its contribution and its sequence are somehow in his mind. To him the past is not dead because it is past any more than the present is alive merely because it is the present. There again he shows that his interests are timeless and transcends a mere date because to him, as Arthur Symons phrased it, "No perfect thing," of any time or period, "is too small for eternal recollection," just as "any living insignificance is already dead." To him only the first rate is important. It is that which is his ceaseless goal, and his constant standard of comparison.

Unlike the reviewer, whose copy is due the next morning and sure to be of a certain presentable length in print regardless of the merits of its subject matter, the critic has a greater latitude in rejecting what is patently beneath his notice. Even when he contemplates mediocrity, which is his tireless foe, he is attracted to it only by its relation to distinction. Because he is an essayist, not a journalist, because he writes—when and if he writes at all—for weeklies and for monthlies instead of dailies, and has the time for mulling instead of reporting, his measuring rod can be the best instead of the popular. To him news is no end in itself. It is only a demonstration of principles, a moment that is never self-sustaining nor isolated but that has come from somewhere and leads somewhere.

When the critic is a figure of any real importance he has a definite conviction of his own, a theory of the theatre, which is the springboard to many of his enthusiasms and detestations. In his littlest examples he may be merely a critic, seeing what he sees only in terms of what he has viewed in the theatre or read at home rather than what he has lived. He may exclude life from his province, and yet perform a valuable service as a technician, a rule-giver, a "professional dramatic critic" and nothing more. But the more he is a lean-to in life as well as in letters the more circumscribed is his value, because side by side with his "sense of the theatre" he must draw upon his knowledge of life to understand and appraise the thing he is asked to judge. How much more he is than a dramatic critic depends entirely upon how much more there is in him, and how thirsty his sympathies and emotions as well as his intellect have been. He draws upon his fund of personal experience as a guide to what is probable, and a means of recognizing the truth and rejecting the specious. His verdict on this score is more important than a scrubwoman's only in proportion to how much deeper is his knowledge, how much more passionate and sensitive is his range of experience and his comment on human nature.

Before a man is a dramatic critic, and not a reporter or a reviewer, he must have standards that are born of the theatre itself and not of the press-room. He must serve it, and dedicate himself to its interests rather than to his own or those of his editors or his readers. He must be the first to realize that the traditions of hard-boiled journalism which the reviewer and the reporter have held up to the stage as its final standards, have less than nothing to do with the theatre and can only harness and imprison the imagination that is its life-blood. He must know the theatre's traditions and see behind its mysteries as well as record his personal impressions. He must not limit his concern to the commerce and gossip of the rialto, or to proving that he is shrewder than the managers in guessing at successes or failures. Sitting before an art, he cannot look upon it merely as a trade, nor can he hold it as lightly as his editors are willing to confess they do by leaving it so often to the mercy of cub reporters. When all is said and done the fact remains that he is not an agent for the manager but a servant of the art which the manager exploits.

Though the critic, like the reviewer or the reporter, is only a signpost when he writes of what other men have done and are doing, it is his special duty to point the way not to one playhouse or one play but to the theatre itself. Unlike the signpost, however, if he is worthy of the title of dramatic critic, he is unwilling to point the way without going there himself. In his negative, passive way he must be something of an artist himself. Denied the divinity of creation, he must at least be blessed with the gifts of re-creation.

Critics, second-string. This descriptive term which in ordinary usage would be derogatory (as, second-rate) means, rather, in theatre parlance, the understudy to or proxy for the regular drama critic sent out by a newspaper. When two or more plays open on the same night the reserve man—the second-string critic—covers the second opening; he also goes to plays already seen by the regular critic when changes in the cast occur. The second-string critic is sometimes dramatic editor.

Critics, in the Restoration theatre. Criticism in Fop's Corner occurred during the play and was spoken aloud. When the play was over the wits remained to discuss it. The success or failure of a play was decided by these critics. The ladies often remained in their boxes after the play was finished to hear their verdict.

Croly, George (1780-1860). British author. Notable for his satires and dramas in the style of Byron. Born in Dublin, he entered the Holy Orders in 1810 and became rector of St. Stephen's, Wallbrook, in London, in 1845. He was a contributor to Blackwood's, dramatic critic of the *New Times,* and published a number of plays and satires.

His one play of importance was *Salathiel,* 1829, reprinted as *Tarry Thou till I Come,* a romance based on the legend of the Wandering Jew.

Crothers, Rachel (1878-   ). American dramatist. Her plays, notable for their craftsmanship and clever dialogue, are social comedies written from the modern woman's point of view. Beginning as an actress, she then turned, with success, to the drama, first writing one act plays. Her first play *Nora* was produced in 1904. *A Man's World* was one of the first American versions of the Ibsen suffrage ideal. Among the other plays which followed are: *The Three of Us,* 1906; *He and She,* 1911; *Mother Carey's Chickens,* 1917; *Nice People,* 1921; *Let Us Be Gay,* 1929; *As Husbands Go,* 1931; *When Ladies Meet,* 1932; *Susan and God,* 1937.

Cucurucu. The name Jacques Callot, the French etcher, gave to *Punch.* See also *Punch* and *Callot, Jacques.*

Cue. A signal, provided by the last words of the speech directly preceding an entrance on the stage or a rejoinder in dialogue, from the French *queue,* meaning the tail of a sentence, or catch word.
See also *Cues, to clip.*

Cue Magazine. A weekly periodical devoted to concise information on current amusements in New York City.

Cue sheet. Notations of light changes, props, sound effects, etc., for the use of the stage manager and the switchboard.

Cues, dragging. Popular stage expression for allowing the voice to drop in a performance so that the speeches fade into inaudibility, with the result that rejoinders and entrances, dependent on these speeches as signals, or "cues," become haphazard and not precise.

Cues, to clip. To begin to speak one's lines before the actor preceding has had time to finish the cue phrase, and thus to destroy the meaning or effectiveness of his final words. Done wilfully rather than accidentally, clipping cues is a malicious way for an actor to draw the attention of the audience.

Cueva, Juan de la (1550?-1620?). Spanish poet and dramatist. Born in Seville. He is accredited with having a marked influence on the drama by his advocacy of lack of restriction in regard to the rules of time, place, and action and his advocacy of national subjects for dramatic themes. This latter idea he expounded rather late in life and after he had produced plays based both on classic and national themes.
Among his principal dramatic works are *Trajedia de Ayax Telamón* (of classic theme); *La Muerte de Virginia* (of classic theme).
His *Cerco de Zamora, Bernardo del Carpio* and *Los siete infantes de Lara,* are virtually the first plays written in Spain which are based on national history.

Cumberland, Richard (1732-1811). English dramatist. Born in Cambridge; entered public service, becoming secretary to the Board of Trade, in 1776. His best-known play, *The West Indian,* was produced by Garrick at Drury Lane in 1771. Goldsmith, in his *Retaliation,* called Cumberland "the Terence of England," and Sheridan caricatured him as Sir Fretful Plagiary in *The Critic.* Cumberland's

formula for comedy was: a complicated plot, comedy mixed with villainy and sentimentality, all crowned with a happy ending. It was Cumberland's skillful use of this
formula which assured its general adoption. He was one of the first dramatists to
manifest interest in the under dog.

Cup, The. Lord Alfred Tennyson (English). Tragedy. 5 acts. 1881.
  Gamma, widow of Sinnatus, tetrach of Galatia, poisons Synorix, the traitor who
killed her husband, and then takes her own life.

Cure for a Cuckold, A. John Webster and William Rowley (English).
Comedy. 5 acts. c. 1640.
  A rather rowdy and ribald comedy based on a comparatively familiar situation:
Compass, a sailor, away at sea for four years, returns to find his wife the mother of a
three months old child.

Curel, François de, Vicomte (1854-1928). French dramatist. One of the
modern French classicists. Born in Lorraine, he was trained in science, but read
widely and led the life of an artistic amateur. Having written a novel which failed,
he tried his pen at plays, and in 1891 sent to Andre Antoine three of them signed by
three different names. All were accepted. Thus encouraged, de Curel from time to
time interrupted his life of gentlemanly leisure to compose dramas as the spirit moved
him without much thought of a popular audience. In spite of his early affiliations
with Antoine, his art is romantic rather than naturalistic in tendency and his last
plays even treat of the supernatural. A genius of penetrating imagination and dark
moods, he has invented unusual situations in which to place his more unusual
characters.
  His plays include: *The Other Side of a Saint*, 1892; *The Fossils*, 1892; *The
Fair Guest*, 1893; *Love Adorns*, 1893; *The Dancer*, 1896; *The Lion's Share*, 1898;
The New Idol, 1899; *The Wild Girl*, 1902; *The Beat of the Wing*, 1906; *The
Dance Before the Mirror*, 1914; *The Comedy of Genius*, 1918; *The Soul in Madness*, 1920; *The Intoxication of the Sage*, 1922; *Inhuman Land*, 1922; *The Quick
and the Dead*, 1926; *Mystical Storm*, 1927.

Curtain. A device for shutting off the scene from the audience—the concealing
drape of the stage; developed into its modern form and usage only slowly. In the
early Roman theatre something of its principle was executed by the *auleum;* in Renaissance Italy several small curtains were used in the scene itself, serving, when drawn,
to disclose something deeper on the stage, but the curtain as we know it today was
practically unknown; it was occasionally used, but drawn, not raised and dropped,
in certain Elizabethan theatres; it was used in the Court *masques* of the Elizabethan
period, usually painted with a "perspective," not drawn but dropped beneath and
before the stage like the Roman *auleum,* and at a later date raised by means of rollers;
in the Restoration theatre used only to open and close a play, never at any time in
between, so that scenes were shifted in full view of the audience. The use of the term
"curtain" first began about 1690. Type of curtain: draw, tab, roll, contour, drop (up

and down). The term used in the body of the play-script is to denote the end of an act or of the entire theatrical production, which is the curtain's major utility.

Curtain, emphatic. The closing of a play on an effective line or action; now considered old-fashioned and unrealistic.

Curtain, unemphatic. The closing of a play on a usual line without special effectiveness; now considered more realistic.

Curtain calls. Appearing before the curtain to acknowledge the applause of the audience; taking bows with the raised curtain; the habit of an actor, killed in the play's action, taking a call was exaggerated at the time of Kean's first American appearance, 1820. At the present time a "picture-ending" or "tableau" curtain is usually taken in plays of this kind, the stars later taking a call.

Curtain going up! To signify to the audience that the curtain is rising, chimes were sounded in Belasco's Theatre and are used at the Yale University Theatre. Beating on the stage with a wooden stick serves warning to spectators at the Grand Guignol in Paris. The director, Jacques Copeau, carried along this not-too-subtle device when he took his Vieux Colombier troupe abroad. A flickering of the electric lights, or a buzzer is the signal in many American theatres.

Curtains. Asbestos curtain, fire-proof required by law to be raised and lowered once for every performance. *Auleum,* name for curtain in the Roman theatre, pulled up from groove at front of stage, at end of play. *Contour curtain,* a curtain which may be draped in for desired opening; essentially a fly curtain with the top stationary; series of lines spaced evenly across the proscenium opening; each line is operated individually by motors to raise the curtain; the curtain in the Radio City Music Hall is an example. *Draw curtain,* a curtain sliding on a wire or track, drawn to the sides of the stage when opened. *Drop curtain,* a decorated canvas or muslin cloth, fastened to a batten at the top and bottom, and hung from the grid. Usually of fairly large area. Lowered between scenes and acts. *Roll ceiling,* a ceiling of cloth, which may be rolled for transportation or storage. *Roll-out,* a hinged horizontal flap let into bottom of a flat through which a performer can roll onto the stage; used in Harlequinade. *Tab curtain,* a curtain with draw-ropes strung in a curve. It divides and forms a frame for the tableau (whence "tab") revealed.

Cushman, Charlotte (1816-1876). American actress. First native born actress of top rank in the American theatre; made début in New Orleans as Lady Macbeth; New York debut in that role Sept. 12, 1836. Her most popular role was Meg Merrilies, in a dramatization of Scott's *Guy Mannering.* She was the first great tragedienne of the American theatre. Played with great success in England where her Wolsey, and Romeo (with her sister as Juliet) were highly praised. She also essayed the roll of Shylock. Called by Laurence Barrett the "greatest Lady Macbeth of her age."

Custom of the Country, The. John Fletcher and Philip Massinger (English). Comedy. 5 acts. 1619-22.

Count Clodio claims his right to "the custom of the country" whereby as an Italian governor he may spend the night with any bride he wishes. The Count chooses Tenocia, whom he sought in marriage, but who became the wife of Arnoldo. Luck being with them, Tenocia and her husband are able to escape the Count's command and board a ship for Lisbon.

Cut drop. A regular drop, cut out after painting, in whatever outline may be needed for the particular scene; by superposition of one cut drop on another a three dimensional effect is obtained.

Cyc. Cyclorama or large back-drop.

Cycles of plays. A series of dramas built around identical characters and themes. The tradition of cycles began with the ancient Greek custom of performing three plays together on a single afternoon, all written by the same dramatist about the same subject. The *Oedipus* plays of Sophocles form a cycle. O'Neill's trilogy, *Mourning Becomes Electra,* although performed as a whole, may be considered a cycle.

Cyclops, The. Euripedes (Greek). Drama. c. 440.

Ulysses in his wanderings encounters the one-eyed giant Cyclops, and by a trick, blinds the giant in order that he and his men may escape to their ship.

Cyclorama. Scenic device; a sky piece, a contrivance used in outdoor settings to simulate the sky. For best results a curved light blue drop or a permanent plaster dome is used. In large cities as well as on the road during the Nineties the display of cycloramas and sensational scenic paintings constituted a form of entertainment in itself. The most popular cycloramas of this period were to be found in *The Battle of Vicksburg* and *The Battle of the Monitor and the Merrimac.*

See also *Horizont, der.*

Cyc trough. The trough running around the base of the cyclorama for permanent installation of horizon lights; four feet from the cyclorama.

Cymbeline. William Shakespeare (English). 1609.

The quasi-historical action comes from Holinshed's *Chronicles* and the Imogen story from Boccaccio's *Decameron.* The story of Belarius is of Shakespeare's own invention. Cymbeline banishes Posthumus because the latter has married Imogen, Cymbeline's daughter, against the king's wishes. In Rome Posthumus wagers with the crafty Iachimo that Imogen would never be inconstant. Iachimo, by strategy, secures Imogen's bracelet and returns with it to win the wager. Posthumus sends orders that Imogen be killed for what he believes her inconstancy, but she escapes, disguised as a page, and goes to a cave where Belarius, a banished lord, lives with two of Cymbeline's children, formerly kidnapped by him. Meanwhile Cymbeline is preparing to undertake a war against Rome. In the course of this the complications of the plot are resolved, true identities established, and general forgiveness and concord reigns.

Cynthia's Revels. Ben Jonson (English). Comedy. 5 acts. 1601.

A satire of contemporary court types: the traveler who has drunk at the fountain of self-love; a foolish young gallant; the voluptuous woman; the impudent lady; the worshipper of money; the victim of folly. Queen Elizabeth is represented as Cynthia in the play, and Essex as Actaeon. Contains one of Jonson's most beautiful lyrics, the *Song of Hesperus*.

Cyrano de Bergerac. Edmond Rostand (French). Poetic drama. 5 acts. 1897.

Cyrano, poet, swordsman, doctor and musician, is afflicted with an enormous nose. In love with Roxane, he discovers that she loves the handsome Christian, who, knowing that Roxane expects a letter from him, is miserable in the knowledge of his own inarticulateness. Cyrano volunteers to write the love letters for him. They are letters of extraordinary beauty. Roxane's love is now transferred from Christian's looks to his supposed soul and wit. When Christian dies in battle, Cyrano still does not tell her that the letters which she has loved are his. In the convent, where she has gone to live, she learns of it many years later on the day that Cyrano is killed by an enemy.

Daikon. An actor in the Kabuki plays of Japan. Also a Japanese term to describe a poor actor; the word is used to humiliate.

Dailey, Peter (1868-1908). American actor. A born comedian, making his début at the age of eight. He later joined Weber and Fields and for many years was one of the leading stars at their Music Hall in New York.

Dalberg, Baron Wolfgang Heribert (1750-1806). German manager. Superintendent of the Mannheim National Theatre in Germany; between 1784 and 1795 he engaged the noted actor Iffland and produced Shakespeare's *Julius Caesar*. Dalberg was the first to recognize the then unknown Schiller; first produced Schiller's *The Robbers* and *Fiesko* in Germany.

Daly, Arnold (1875-1927). American actor and producer. Born in Brooklyn. His first appearance was in 1892 in *The Jolly Squire*. He appeared on the New York stage for the first time in *Puddin'head Wilson* in 1899 at the Herald Square Theatre. Not long after he played in *Barbara Frietchie* with Julia Marlowe. He was famous, as a producer, for his early presentation of Shaw's plays, among them: *Candida, Mrs. Warren's Profession,* and *You Never Can Tell*. He toured with *The Man of Destiny, Arms and the Man, How He Lied to Her Husband* and *The Monkey's Paw,* among others. He appeared in *Arms and the Man* in London in 1911. Later he played in *Juarez and Maximilian*. Burned to death in 1927.

Daly, Augustin (1838-1899). American theatre manager, dramatist. One of the greatest of American theatrical managers. Daly began as dramatic critic for several New York papers. He adapted many plays from the German and French, his debut as a manager in 1867 being with the London melodrama, *Under the Gaslight*. His productions also included Shakespearean comedies, chief among which were: *The Taming of the Shrew; A Midsummer Night's Dream; As You Like It*.

In 1869 he opened his first theatre, the Fifth Avenue, and a few years later he established his famous Broadway theatre, Daly's, with a stock company starring John Drew and Ada Rehan. E. L. Davenport, Fanny Davenport, Clara Morris, Mrs. Scott Siddons, and many other accomplished players acted for Daly.

In 1893 he established a London theatre, known later as Daly's, where he took his company annually, meeting with great success. In New York society his performances were very popular, a Daly first night being an important event.

Damaged Goods. Eugène Brieux (French). Drama. 3 acts. 1902.

A thesis play attacking society's secrecy about venereal disease and revealing the evil of its not being openly recognized and treated. It pleads for compulsory premarital examinations. It caused a furore when first produced and was censored. While the subject is that of Ibsen's *Ghosts,* Brieux is less interested than the Norwegian in the moral aspects of the malady and more in the physical ravages it effects. Georges Dupont, a young Frenchman, learns on the eve of his wedding that he has syphilis. He disregards the advice of a reputable physician and marries after six months' treatment by a quack. His child is born and inherits his affliction. Georges again consults the specialist, and is told that he may not even keep a nurse for the child, lest she and her own offspring be contaminated. He dismisses the current nurse, and it is through her that his wife learns his secret. She wants to divorce him, and his father-in-law to shoot him, but the physician intervenes once more, pleads for tolerance, and holds out hope for a cure if treatment is continued.

Dame aux camélias, La. See *Camille*.

Damon and Pythias. Richard Edwards (English). Drama. 1564.

Good example of early Elizabethan drama, morality play. Said to have been written by the choir master for the boys of St. Paul's and the Royal Chapel. Plays of this genre heralded the work of Lyly and Peele several years later.

Damon and Pythias, Pythagorean Greeks, visit Syracuse, where Damon is arrested on a baseless charge of spying. Pythias' devotion to his friend and his efforts to save him and their mutual self-sacrifice, so impress Dionysius that he pardons Damon.

THE DANCE AND THE THEATRE

BY JOHN MARTIN

The relationship between the dance and the theatre is one that has got itself curiously twisted in popular practice. Actually, the dance is the mother of the theatre arts, and both tragedy and comedy, with all their various offspring, are outgrowths of its original creative impulse. This is only logical, to be sure, for the dance deals in the movement of the body as its medium, and that happens to be the first means by which men express all their emotional experiences.

As the theatre developed, however, this fundamental medium was relegated to the background more and more until today by far the greater part of all theatrical activity consists of speech, with no more movement accompanying it than is essential for verisimilitude. The dance is allowed to enter the picture chiefly as a kind of garnish for musical comedy and revue, where it is pleasant but not indispensable. Here its functions are rhythmic, acrobatic and erotic—which, indeed, are perfectly good functions in their own way, but rather remote from the deeply felt religious and social impulses that gave rise to that kind of dance out of which the theatre grew in the first place.

Dancing, however, plays a more imporant part in the theatre than this would seem to indicate, and during the past twenty years or so this fact has become increasingly apparent. As a matter of fact, with the advent of Isadora Duncan (who was not by any means a theatrical type of dancer in the popular sense of the term) there was revealed for the first time since antiquity the principle of the elemental kind of dance from which the Greek theatre sprang. Isadora's great discovery was that movement itself, informed by emotion, can be made an eloquent means, much as music is, for expressing those concepts that are too deeply felt to be shaped in words. On this principle, there has grown up a virtually new art of the dance. Though it is tagged with the meaningless label of "modern", it is without any such restrictions as this would seem to put upon it, and is actually nothing more nor less than basic dance, as timeless, as free, and as adaptable for us as for primitive men.

Dancing as a whole falls naturally into three large divisions, according to the motives of the dancers. The first is recreational, the second is spectacular, and the third is expressional. Recreational dancing concerns the theatre only incidentally. It consists chiefly of ballroom and folk dancing, and is done not to be watched but for the pleasure of the dancers themselves. Occasionally, however, folk dances are elaborated and transferred to the stage, and exhibition teams find material in the ballroom dance that can be made interesting enough to entertain an audience.

The other types of dance are essentially of the theatre, though not necessarily of what is commonly known as "show business." The range of the spectacular dance is a wide one, extending from the most insignificant tap-dance routines to the great art of the ballet, which is a theatre form all to itself. Its range of quality is equally wide, and cuts across all classifications of style. It is possible, for example, to find within the confines of the lowly tap-dance a first-rate artist such as Paul Draper, and within the much more elevated field of the ballet, completely meretricious performers here and there, concerned only with exploiting themselves.

The ballet came into existence as an effort to restore the vital elements of the antique Greek theatre, but it would be too much to expect that the dancers, musicians and poets of the Renaissance, eager to unite their arts into the synthesis which they believed the Greek theatre to have been, could have hit upon the profound principle that actually underlay it. By putting together the materials of their own time, they achieved notable new art forms—in Italy the opera and in France the ballet—but they did not touch upon either the form or the spirit of the ancient classic art they were seeking. The dance element in their synthesis was patterned after the social practices of the day, characterized by graciousness, elegance, and display, suitable to courtiers, but without emotional or expressional connotations. These qualities it has never lost through the centuries, though it has gained many others by the way. Its highest achievements as a synthesis of the arts of dance, mime, music and décor, came about as a result of the genius of Michel Fokine, the creator of what we have come to know as the Russian ballet. Whatever its particular style or form, the ballet makes an entirely objective kind of appeal; that is, it presents sensuous beauty, charming personalities, and specialized skills, which the spectator is expected to look at and admire.

The expressional dance, on the contrary, is not concerned with admiration, with sensuous beauty, or with skills for their own sakes. Its compelling interest is in presenting some intuitive emotional concept in such a manner that the spectator will in a sense experience it himself by contagion, and be enriched thereby. It is not necessarily amusing, any more than the symphonies of Beethoven or the operas of Wagner are amusing. It is, above all, the content of the dance that is important, and not the personality of the dancer. In this type of dance there is no such synthesis of the arts as the ballet employs. Music is used merely as accompaniment, and décor to define and delimit the space in which the dancer moves.

Isadora Duncan herself was a lyric dancer, in spite of the fact that she often dealt with tragic and dramatic emotions; she made no use of the potentialities of the theatre, but poured forth her feeling quite simply and directly. Many of those who have followed her have developed the principles of the dance that she discovered toward more theatrical purposes. They have not, however, resorted to story-telling, characterization, or pantomime, after the manner of the ballet, but have rather dramatized the heroic, impersonal conflicts of life in terms of pure movement. Their theatre is not representational and mimetic, but touches the roots of the drama, in much the same way that the theatre of the Greeks touched them.

In this branch of the dance, America has definitely taken the lead from the beginning, only Mary Wigman among the Europeans having made any great contributions. The outstanding figures at present are Martha Graham, Hanya Holm, Doris Humphrey and Charles Weidman.

Dance, American stage. Early American stage dancing took root in the minstrel and variety shows and burlesque. About 1851, "Jim Crow" Rice, generally conceded to be the father of Ethiopian minstrelsy, started the rage for a song and dance number called "Jim Crow," which ran:

> Wheel about, turn about,
>   Do just so,
> Every time I wheel about
>   I jump Jim Crow.

Rice had a ludicrous limp and a peculiar step called "rocking de heel." Other early American dances were the "essence" and the "clog." The essence was performed in soft shoes and the clog in wooden ones. This latter dance was founded, it is said, on a traditional continental routine, centuries old. But the American version originated definitely in Lancashire where the mill workers still wear wooden shoes with small iron horseshoes attached to the soles. Dancing the clog was always accompanied by a brief but somewhat ostentatious ceremony. First a stagehand would step out from behind the scenes carrying in his hand a cornucopia full of sand. This he would scatter from one end of the stage to the other. Next, the performer would do a dance, emphasizing the steps to the sound of sand scraping the floor. When he finished, the stagehand would reappear, this time sweeping up the sand carefully while the audience waited patiently for him to dispose of the last grain.

Eventually, Eddie Leonard, the old minstrel man, decided to obscure this wearisome interval; so he engaged two men to step down before the footlights to sing popular ballads as the sweeping went on. Another early dance was the "buck and wing," theoretically a native composition, identified by the side vaultings into the air, "the wings," supposedly borrowed from the Negro. Soon soft shoe and buck and wing dancing began to overlap and take on new deviations; some dancers provided their own jingling accompaniments by screwing coins to the heels of their shoes, thus giving the impression of tinkling bells. Others attached metal plates to the heels and toes of their shoes. Harry Bolger had the soles of his heels extended for what was called slap-shoe numbers wherein the sound of the sole cracking on the floor created a slapstick effect. Though these so-called innovations were trivial, they created something of a furore on the Rialto. "Hand" dancing, for instance, said to have been introduced by Eddie Foy, was considered a great novelty. The performer, while progressing or coming to a complete halt, would slap his legs with his hands, sometimes strike his arms and end occasionally by aiming a grotesque thrust at his throat. To Eddie Horan belongs the distinction of being the first performer to introduce the cane dance. He was said to be so expert in tapping out a cane accompaniment to his own numbers that he gave the impression of two dancers performing simultaneously. Later, Bernard Granville and George M. Cohan became well known as cane dancers. With the transformation of variety into vaudeville, came the development of highly intricate dance numbers and effects, with acrobatic interpolations. The climax in stage novelty was the pedestal dance in which the performer stood on a high stand and danced on an area about twelve inches square from which he turned and somersaulted and then returned safely to his small platform. The pedestal number was sometimes known as the "statue dance" because, when originally performed, two dancers dressed in white make-up and white tights were stationed on stands to resemble marble statues.

Meanwhile, new professional dance numbers were gaining in popularity. One of these was the *pas mala,* which dancers themselves described as they sang and stepped. The words ran like this:

> The latest craze in town,
> Was the one that's goin' around,
> Salute your partner, all hands around,
> With a ha-ha-ha-ha,
> Everybody bow and do that pas mala.

With the success of the famous dancing teams, Williams and Walker and Cole and Johnson, the "cake-walk" came into vogue. Simultaneously, solo artists, particularly in vaudeville, began developing novelty numbers by means of electrical effects and stage equipment. Gertrude Hoffman created her picturesque but supposedly scandalous "Spring Song." Löie Fuller performed the "Fire Dance" and the "Serpentine Dance," by manipulating draperies over a trap door from which flames were reflected to give the impression that the draperies were on fire. Mary Garden's apparance and dance in *Salomé* and the subsequent *Salomé* by Maude Allan, concert dancer, precipitated Eva Tanguay's burlesque presentation of the "Dance of the Seven Veils."

During the war, America went dance mad. With the advent of Irene and Vernon Castle came the craze for the new dances—the one-step, the two-step, the hesitation waltz—and later the bunny hug, Charleston, Black Bottom, Lindy-hop, Susy-Q and swing (the addicts of which are known as jitterbugs). Among the teams who were notably popular were Gaby Delys and Harry Pilcer, Paris exponents of dance novelties; Fred and Adele Astaire, Maurice, and Florence Walton; Tony and Renée De Marco, Marjorie Moss and Georges Fontana; Veloz and Yolanda; Paul Draper; and the Hartmans, who have cruelly burlesqued their fellow dancers.

Dance, clog. A kind of dancing performed with shoes having wooden soles; some shoes have metal taps to emphasize the click, as in tap dancing.

Dance, tap. A form of terpsichorean entertainment composed of minute and intricate pedalling and accompanied by the loud clacking noise produced by the beating on the stage of toe and heel shod in footwear with special noise-making devices.

Dance directors, American musical comedy and revue. About 1910, American musical comedy and revue became dance conscious and much of production responsibility was placed on the dance director. The graceful maneuvers popularized by Edward Royce and Julian Mitchell gave way to the craze for novelty and even acrobatics. Among the dance directors who have brilliantly met the new demands were Ned Wayburn, Dave Bennett, Albertina Rasch who combined ballet with syncopation, Chester Hale, Bobby Connolly, Sammy Lee, Seymour Felix whose *Dancing in the Rain* number made dancing important on the screen, Busby Berkeley, Robert Alton, George Balanchine, etc.

Dance-drama, Russian. "The art of the perfect combination of color and line and movement and music in one harmonious appeal to eye and ear." It is a combination derived from three sources: the old time ballet, the revival of classic and aesthetic dancing and the Craig impulse to decorative staging. In: *The New Movement in the Theatre* by Sheldon Cheney.

Dance interludes. Intervals of ballet or other terpsichorean entertainment to break the monotony of a play or opera.

Dance macabre (dance of death). A term originating in a German morality play of the 14th century which presented an allegorical concept of death. This term was used many years later as a title for one of Strindberg's plays and also served the German dramatist Wedekind, in one of his works. W. H. Auden has also used this term as a title.

Dance of Death, The. W. H. Auden (English). Drama. 1 act. 1933.

The decline of the middle class told in verse, music and dancing, as its members try to escape reality through false values, and finally meet their doom in a night club.

Dance of Death, The. August Strindberg (Swedish). Naturalistic drama. 3 acts. 1901.

A Swedish captain of artillery and his wife, Alice, a former actress, have lived for twenty-five years in an isolated fort. An inexplicable hatred binds them together so that they can not separate and can see no release from torment except in the death of one. Curt, a friend comes to live with them. The captain has a stroke but his superhuman strength pulls him through. He and Alice become more devilish than before, and Curt, possessed by the evil of their house, falls in love with Alice and joins her in a plot to ruin her husband. During a second stroke a vision appears to the captain which points out how wrong his outlook on life has been. Upon his recovery he feels that he and Alice have tormented each other long enough. The play ends with his beseeching for a reconciliation.

Dancourt, Florent Carton (1661-1725). French dramatist. Born at Fontainebleau, he practiced as a lawyer, went on the stage in 1685 and produced his first play *Le Notaire Obligeant* the same year. His comedies are lively pictures of the middle class and the peasantry. He retired from the stage in 1718, devoting himself to religious poetry until his death in 1725.

Among his plays the topical comedies *Le Chevalier à la Mode,* 1687, and *Les Bourgeoises de Qualité,* 1700, are the best known.

Dane, Clemence (Winifred Ashton) (189?-   ). English novelist, actress and dramatist. She was born at Blackheath and was first an artist, but later went on the stage, appearing in 1913, under the name of Diana Cortis. She soon began to write both plays and novels. Of the latter the theatrical romance *Broome Stages* is perhaps the most popular.

Her plays include: *A Bill of Divorcement,* 1921; *The Way Things Happen,* 1924; *Naboth's Vineyard,* 1926; *Wild Decembers,* 1932; *Come of Age,* 1934; *Moonlight is Silver,* 1934.

Daniel, Samuel (1562-1619). British poet and dramatist. Born in Somersetshire, the son of a music master; attended Oxford and Wilton, became Poet Laureate in 1599, was made a groom of the Privy Chambers by Queen Anne, wife of James I.

His works include: *The Twelve Goddesses,* 1604; *The Queen's Arcadia,* 1605; *Hymen's Triumph,* 1605; *Philotas,* 1611.

Daniello, Bernardino (?-1565). Italian scholar, translator and theorist. He was born in Lucca; was known as a scholar, a translator of and commentator on the classics, and a writer on Dante. His *Poetica* embodies his dramatic theories. He died at Padua.

Danmari. The title given to the kind of *Kabuki* play that is akin to our panto-mimes. A *Danmari* play is very short, about ten minutes in length, actors are brightly costumed and it is performed in a dance manner.

Dante Alighieri (1265-1321). Italian author. The greatest and most famous of all Italian authors; poet, philosopher and theorist. He was born in Florence of poor parents of noble extraction. He first met his famous love, Beatrice, at the age of nine. She died in 1290. Thereafter he devoted himself to the study of philosophy and literature. He also had considerable business and political affiliations. In or before the year 1298 he was married. He had four children, all born in Florence. In 1302 he was exiled because of his disregard of the fine levelled against him on the basis of a false charge of corrupt dealings. For almost twenty years he wandered from place to place in poverty, now in Siena, now Verona, Padua, eventually even Paris and England. He returned at last, in 1317 or 1318, to Italy and settled in Ravenna, where he finished his great work, the *Divina Commedia*. Aside from his masterpiece his best known work is *La Vita nuova*. His theory of the drama is to be found in his *Epistle to Can Grande*. He died in Ravenna from an illness contracted on a difficult journey.

Danton's Tod. George Büchner (German). Drama. 5 scenes. 1835.

This historical drama was written when the author was twenty-one, gripped by the anti-royalist fever which was sweeping Germany. He had been threatened with arrest for his articles in a radical journal. He associated himself with his hero, and saw in the Germany of his day a parallel to revolutionary France. The time of the play is the most bloody period of the Year II, when Danton was facing defeat, between February 5th and April 5th. Desmoulins was calling out for moderation and clemency, while the rabble was tearing the very cloaks off the backs of the aristocracy. Robespierre was calling anti-Terrorists such as Desmoulins and Danton "noble sympathizers," while they protested and asked that the state be allowed to evolve liberally and without bloodshed. Danton is shown on trial before a revolutionary tribunal, proudly declaring he has dealt a death blow to royalty; outside the building a citizen rouses the mob against him, assuring them that "he wears fine clothes, eats from silver plates and, when drunk, sleeps with your wives and daughters."

Daughter of Jorio (La Figlia di Torio), by Gabriele d'Annunzio, 1904.

This is a poetic drama laid in the mountain land of the Abruzzi, primitive Italian people. Aligi, a shepherd, falls in love with Mila, the daughter of a sorcerer, much to the distress of his family inasmuch as he is already betrothed to someone else. They live together for a while, and one day while the shepherd is away his father Lazaro comes to their cave. The girl fearing that the father will do her bodily harm calls for help. Aligi returns, pleads with his father and finally strikes him dead. In order to save her beloved, Mila claims that she killed Lazaro and that she blinded Aligi to her guilt with some magic her father taught her. So she is carried away to be burned alive, cursed by all.

Daughters of Atreus. Robert Turney (American). Tragedy. 3 acts. 1936.

A retelling of the Electra story—Agamemnon, on his return from Troy, is murdered by his wife, Clytemnestra. To avenge her father's death, Electra drives her brother Orestes to kill his mother.

D'Avenant, Sir William (1606-1668). English dramatist, producer and manager. He is reputed by some historians to be a son, by others a godson, of Shakespeare. His first play *Albovine* was successfully produced in 1629, and in 1638 he was appointed Poet Laureate. In 1639 he received a patent to build a playhouse for "music, scenes and dancing," and in the same year he became manager of the Cockpit (the first theatre in Drury Lane) in London. He supported the king throughout the Civil War, and was knighted at Gloucester in 1643. Under the Commonwealth he suffered both exile and imprisonment, owing his life to Milton, whom, it is said, he in turn saved at the Restoration. With a grant from Charles II his company began to play at the Salisbury Court Theatre on November 15, 1660, under the name of the Duke of York's Company. Shortly afterwards he moved to the Lincoln's Inn Fields Theatre. His rival was Killigrew, whose company was known as the King's Company. The success of his rival, added to his own failure, which was brought about by his excessive expenditures on lavish scenery, more music and dancing, induced him to build another playhouse, the Dorset Garden. He died in 1668 before it was completed, the property going to his widow and son, Charles. With bankruptcy his company combined with the King's Company in 1682, retaining the latter title for the merger. Sir William D'Avenant is reputed to have been the first to introduce scene-shifting and operatic music on the English stage; he is also said to be the first to present women in the production of a play.

Davenport, Edward L. (1815-1877). American actor. A noted tragedian; first appeared in 1836; played with Mrs. Mowatt; made his outstanding hit in *Hamlet* and as Brutus; founder of the acting family of the same name. Married Matilda Vining of the English theatrical family, who also appeared in New York.

Davenport, Fanny Lily Gipsy (1850-1898). American actress. Made her first appearance on the stage in 1858 beginning as a juvenile actress; acted under the management of Mrs. John Drew and later for Augustin Daly from 1869-77; made her greatest success in plays by Sardou and in Shakespearean roles such as Ophelia, Rosalind, Mistress Ford and many others.

Davenport, Robert (early 17th century). English dramatist. Nothing is known of his life except that he was the author of *A Crowne for a Conqueror,* published in 1623; of *King John and Matilda,* a tragedy, 1655, and of two comedies. Other plays and several poems have been attributed to him and in *The History of Henry I* he is supposed to have collaborated with Shakespeare.

Davies, Hubert Henry (1869-1917). English dramatist. Born at Woodley, Cheshire, he spent some years in America as a journalist before he started writing for the stage. He returned in 1901 to England, where his social comedies soon became popular. They include: *Fifty Years Ago,* 1901; *Cynthia,* 1904; *A Single Man,* 1910; *Outcast,* 1914.

Davis, Owen (1874-   ). American playwright. Born in Portland, Maine, and educated at the University of Tennessee and Harvard. One of the most prolific modern authors, he is said to have written over 300 plays. His earlier efforts were sensational melodramas: *Through the Breakers,* his first play, 1898; *The Gambler's Daughter; Driftwood* and many others. His best known work is *Icebound,* 1923, which won the Pulitzer prize. He dramatized several famous novels. Among the scores of his dramas are *Alibi,* 1919; *Detour,* 1921, a serious play which won for him the respect of the critics; *The Nervous Wreck,* 1923; *The Great Gatsby,* 1926; *Gentle Grafter,* 1926; *The Good Earth* (with Donald Davis), 1932; *Jezebel,* 1933; *Ethan Frome* (with Donald Davis), 1936. In the past few years he has also achieved success in the motion pictures and radio.

Day, John (1574?-1640). English dramatist. Born at Cawston, Norfolk, he collaborated, 1598-1608, with Chettle, Dekker and others in twenty-one plays of which, until A. H. Bullen published his works in 1881, only *The Blind Beggar of Bednall Green* survived in accessible form. His most famous work is a masque or satirical dramatic allegory *The Parliament of Bees* published in 1641.

Days Without End. Eugene O'Neill (American). Drama. 3 acts. 1934.
John Loving, happily married and economically secure, has forgotten the ideals and faiths of his youth. When his wife learns he has taken a mistress, she goes out into the rain, contracts pneumonia, and is facing death. It is then that Loving goes back to his God. Finally, his wife recovers and forgives him.

Dead End. Sidney Kingsley (American). Drama. 3 acts. 1935.
The scene is a dead end slum street on the river, flanked by an expensive apartment house. Baby Face Martin, Public Enemy Number One, returns to the slums to see his family, and is shot by detectives, who were informed by Gimpy, a crippled architect.

In spite of his sister Drina's efforts to save him, Tony, leader of a gang of dead end boys, is arrested for knifing. Drina realizes that it is the slum environment that is turning her young brother and his gang into future public enemies, and that there is no hope for them until slums are eliminated.

Dead stick. British slang term for an actor who ruins a scene.

Dead wood. The unsold tickets still in the box-office after a performance.

Dear Brutus. Sir James Matthew Barrie (English). Comedy. 3 acts. 1918.

"The fault, dear Brutus, is not in our stars, but in ourselves, that we are underlings." This Shakespearian quotation, from which the play's title is derived, points its moral: that people are moulded less by circumstances than by those qualities inherent in their own characters. Fate cannot be blamed for frustrated lives, but only the individuals themselves. And Barrie proves his point in an exquisite blending of humor and fantasy worthy to stand with his masterpieces.

Mr. Lob, a sort of modern Puck, has invited a group of people to be his week-end guests. Strangely heterogeneous, they have only one thing in common, the desire for a second chance. Lob lets them visit a magic wood which appears suddenly before their eyes in quest of "what might have been." In the wood each sees what he would do if given his second chance. Mr. Purdie, unhappy with his wife and consoling himself flirting with Mabel, finds himself married to Mabel—and flirting with his "wife." Matey, the dishonest butler, is a dishonest captain of finance; and the snobbish Lady Caroline, who in real life tried to send him to jail, is his wife. Mr. Dearth, the artist, is happiest in his second chance, for he has the dream-daughter for whom he always yearned and who makes up for his wife's infidelity. As the spell wears off, the guests return to the house and a proper garden replaces the wood. Each one is chastened to find him or herself not quite such a fine fellow as he thought. But they are contented, too; one of them goes so far as to propose to his wife all over again. And the Dearths, the two who have profited most, start out on a painting expedition together.

Dear Departed, The. Samuel Houghton (English). Play. 1 act. 1909.

With their father supposedly lying dead upstairs, his two married daughters and their husbands begin with indecent haste to bargain over his effects. The sensational moment arrives when the old man suddenly appears in the doorway and discovers what is happening.

Death Takes A Holiday. Walter Ferris (American). (Adapted from the play *La Morte in Vacanze* by Alberto Casella.) Drama. 3 acts. 1930.

Death, on a holiday, visits an Italian family, and falls in love with the beautiful daughter, Grazia. When he must leave, Grazia begs to go with him, and Death takes her.

Death's Test Book; or, The Fool's Tragedy. Thomas Lovell Beddoes (English). Tragedy. 5 Acts. 1850.

To avenge their father's death, Wolfram and Isbrand enter the service of Melveric, the Duke of Munsterberg. Wolfram, however, quickly forgives the Duke, and fights with him against the Moors. Later Melveric kills Wolfram in a dispute over a woman, and is led to his own death by Wolfram's ghost.

Debayasi. A visible orchestra used in Kabuki dramas when a dance is used; its members sit stage center or stage left; the kinds of music played are Nagauta, Tokiwazu and Kiyomoto, all in the nature of an emotional recital with samisen accompaniment.

Decameron (c. 1353). Famous collection of short tales or novelettes by Giovanni Boccaccio. The tales, one hundred in number, are told by a group of Florentines who have fled to the country to escape the plague. The collection contains source material for Shakespeare's *The Merchant of Venice; All's Well That Ends Well* and *Cymbeline*. Its first tale was the origin of the Patient Griselda legend which Dekker, in England, and Molière, in France, later adapted for the stage. These pieces are the foundation of the modern short story.

Décor simultané. A setting of multiple scenery used in the 17th century French theatre for the representation of different localities in a play for the scenes to which they respectively belonged. In this setting the action of a play would move from place to place according to the demands of the plot. Its plan and design were influenced by the multiple relief settings of Serlio.

De Cordova, Rudolph (1860-   ). British dramatist and actor. Born in Kingston, Jamaica, he studied medicine in England, but went on the stage in 1884 and thereafter devoted himself to acting and writing. He wrote regularly for magazines and periodicals; also edited and acted in films and wrote scenarios.

Best known among his plays are *The Password; The Mannikin; The Mandarin.*

Deeter, Jasper. See *Hedgerow Theatre.*

Deirdre. George William Russell (A.E.) (Irish). Tragedy. 3 acts. 1929.

It is prophesied that Deirdre's beauty will bring banishment and death to heroes. Betrothed to Conchobar, King of Ulster, she falls in love with Naoise and escapes with him to Scotland. Conchobar tricks them into returning, and slays Naoise. Deirdre takes her own life.

Deirdre of the Sorrows. John Millington Synge (Irish). Tragedy. 3 acts. Printed 1911.

Deirdre, young and beautiful, is wooed by Conchubor, elderly king of Ulster, but loves the young hero Naise. When Conchubor comes to claim her she secretly marries Naise and escapes with him to the forest. For seven years, they lead an idyllic existence, before tragedy finally overtakes them.

Dekker, Eduard Douwes (1820-1887). Dutch author. Born in Amsterdam, he spent eighteen years in government service in the Dutch East Indies, and on his return published, under the pseudonym of Multatuli, a slashing exposure of the administration called *Max Havelaar.*

The one play which he wrote is a fine poetical drama, *The School for Princes,* 1852.

Dekker, Thomas (1570-1641). English dramatist. Next to Jonson, the most graphic depicter of the town life of his time.

Born in London. His wholesome humor and lyric genius contrast vividly with all that is known of his hand-to-mouth existence. His plays are remarkable for their deft delineation of female character and for the comic types found in the tavern and the street. He wrote most of his plays for specific acting companies, such as the Admiral's Men at the Rose and Fortune, Worcester's Men at the Rose. His most notable plays are: *Shoemaker's Holiday,* 1600; *Old Fortunatus,* 1600; *Satiromastix* (a reply to Jonson's *Poetaster*), *Honest Whore* (with Middleton), 1604; *Westward Ho!* (with John Webster), 1607; *The Roaring Girl* (with Middleton), 1611; *The Virgin Martyr* (with Massinger), 1622; and *The Witch of Edmonton* (with Ford and Rowley), printed 1658.

De Koven, Reginald (1861-1920). American composer. Also a conductor and music critic. Educated at Oxford; studied in Stuttgart, Florence, Paris and Vienna. Founder of the Washington Symphony Orchestra. The light operas for which he wrote music include: *Happyland,* 1905; *The Highwayman,* 1897; *The Red Feather,* 1903; *The Begum,* 1887; and *Robin Hood,* 1890.

De la Pasture, Mrs. Henry (1866-   ). British author. Born at Naples. In 1887 she married Count Henry de la Pasture, who died in 1908. In 1910, she married Hugh Clifford. Her books which have been dramatized are *Deborah of Tod's,* 1897, which was produced in Boston in 1909; and *Peter's Mother,* 1905, dramatized and produced in 1905. Her daughter became a novelist under the name of E. M. Delafield.

Her plays include: *The Lonely Millionaires,* 1906; and *Her Grace the Reformer,* 1906.

Delavigne, Jean François Casimir (1793-1843). French dramatist. Born at Le Havre, he began writing for the stage when he was in his twenties when the classical tradition was first being disturbed by the new romantic movement in France. He made his reputation as a satirist in 1818 with his *Messeniennes,* satires on the Restoration.

Two plays by which he is best known are: *Les Vepres Siciliennes,* 1819; and *La Fille du Cid,* 1839.

De Mille, Cecil Blunt (1881-   ). American film director. Born at Ashfield, Massachusetts, he went on the stage in 1900, and after many years as an actor, dramatist and producer, entered the motion picture business, forming with Jesse L. Lasky in 1913 the Famous-Lasky Corporation.

The Squaw Man, 1913, was his first film. It was followed by over sixty others which gave de Mille the reputation of being one of the most lavish directors in films. Several of these were produced by the Cecil B. de Mille Pictures Corporation of which he was founder and president.

His better known films include *The Ten Commandments; The King of Kings; Madam Satan; The Sign of the Cross; This Day and Age; Cleopatra; The Buccaneer; Union Pacific.*

Denise Marette. Jean-Jacques Bernard (French). Drama. 3 acts. 1925.

In this fantasy the playwright reacts against the naturalistic school of French playwriting.

Denise, the gifted daughter of an aging painter who has lost his touch, makes up for his failure by passing off her own work as her father's. The critics, enthusiastic, acclaim the charm of the master's second style. To salve her conscience for such a deception, the girl determines to use her earnings to endow in her father's name an artists' home, to be erected after his death. In the meantime her lover, angry at her for having abandoned their mutual studio, marries someone else. Her father dies. She has sacrificed personal fame and even love for his sake. Yet as she sits alone pondering on the course she has chosen, her parent's ghost returns, not to thank her, but to chide her for having been his inferior in talent and to boast of his own glory. Then as the girl watches she sees him transformed again into the unselfish, idealized father who was the associate of her childhood and shared in her girlish games. The vision fades, and Denise, rubbing her hands over her eyes, is left wondering if she has really seen the phantom or only imagined it, as does the audience.

D'Ennery, Adolphe Eugène Philippe (1811-1899). French dramatist. Born in Paris, of Jewish descent, he was twenty when he produced his first play *Emile* in collaboration with C. Desnoyer. In addition to novels, he produced, sometimes in collaboration, about 200 pieces for the stage.

Two of the most successful of his plays were *Marie Jeanne,* 1845; and *Michel Strogoff,* 1883. He was probably best known for his libretto for Massenet's opera *Le Cid,* 1885.

Dennis, John (1657-1734). English dramatist, critic. His *Rinaldo and Armida* in 1699 opened the way to pseudo-classic tragedy. Macauley said Dennis wrote "bad odes, bad tragedies, bad comedies." Some of his other plays are *A Plot and No Plot,* 1697; *Iphigenia,* 1700; *Liberty Asserted,* 1704; *Gibralta,* 1705; *Orpheus and Eurydice,* 1707; and *Appius and Virginia,* 1709. Other books include: *The Usefulness of the Stage to the Happiness of Mankind, to Government, and to Religion,* 1698; *A Defense of a Regular Stage,* 1703; *The Stage Defended,* 1726; *Works,* 1702, and *Selected Works,* 1718.

Dénouement. The untying of knots, the unravelling of the threads of the plot; the result of the conflict. It comes after the climax and in the last act.

Designer's drawing. A blueprint showing front of scenery in outline and used by technicians to make working drawings. Scale usually is ½ inch to the foot, and details 3 inches to the foot.

Desire Under the Elms. Eugene O'Neill (American). Drama. 1924.

Ephraim Cabot, a religious New England farmer of 70, marries Abbie, a woman half his age. His thirty-two year old son greets his step-mother with hate, for he feels that the farm rightfully belongs to him. Abbie, greedy for the land, cleverly seduces the boy and then persuades Ephraim to sign over the property to the heir in the belief that the child is his. After Abbie's son is born, however, Eben tells his father the truth. And Abbie, finding herself madly in love with Eben strangles the child to prove her love for Eben is greater than her desire for the farm. The play ends with Abbie and Eben led off to jail, happy in their absorption in one another.

Destouches, Philippe Néricault (1680-1754). French dramatist. He was popularly regarded as the founder of sentimental comedy (*la comedie larmoyante*). Destouches wrote *Le Philosophe Marié,* 1727, which concerned the exemplary virtues of a submissive wife.

His other comedies include: *Le Glorieux,* 1732; *Le Dissipateur;* and *La Fausse Agnès.*

Deus ex machina. A term used in the 4th century B.C. for a machine employed in the ancient Greek theatre for the purpose of introducing the god, whose utility in the dramatic action of a play was the solving and concluding of the plot. This utility, being a mere makeshift for a solution and usually preposterous and unrealistic, was condemned by Aristotle in his *Poetics* in an attempt to improve the uses of the device and to influence dramatists to plot play-action more naturally. Today the term *deus ex machina* is used for any unnatural plot device introduced by a playwright into his play when a truer solution eludes him. It is also used generally for any obvious trick thought up to solve a problem which is preposterously out of place in the issue.

Deutsches Theater. A private theatre in Berlin, founded several decades before the first World War; a leader in theatrical style. It had four distinguished managements: (1) under L'Arronge, whose classical historical performances carried on the Meiningen traditions; (2) under Brahm, with his naturalistic settings of Ibsen and Hauptmann; (3) under Reinhardt, with his wide variety of conceptions and unique genius for "atmosphere." (This theatre collapsed in the crisis that developed after the war); (4) revived after the Revolution of 1933, under Heinz Hilpert.

Devil, The (Ördög). Ferenc Molnar (Hungarian). Drama. 3 acts. 1907.

The devil, to amuse himself decides to create an affair between an artist and a married woman. The audience is always aware of what is going on, but the protagonists never know that the bland man of the world is the devil, who is destroying them.

Devil Is an Ass, The. Ben Jonson (English). Comedy. 5 acts. 1616.

Ridicules the promoters or monopolists, and exposes the pretended demoniacs and witch-finders of the day.

Fitzdottrel, a simpleton, is cheated out of his estate by Meercraft, a promoter, who parades various ridiculous schemes for making money before Fitzdottrel. The latter finally discovers that Meercraft has cheated him, but does not let Meercraft know this. He continues to act and behave like a fool. Pug, one of the lesser devils, who has been allowed by Satan to try his iniquity on earth for a day, finds himself completely outwitted by human knaves, as exemplified by Meercraft.

Devil's Disciple, The. George Bernard Shaw (English). Melodrama. 4 acts. Printed 1899.

The scene is New England, before the American Revolution. Richard Dungeon, the young renegade who has sworn allegiance to the devil, allows the Red-Coats to take him in place of Reverend Anderson. Dungeon is about to be hanged in Anderson's place, when he is finally granted a reprieve.

Devrient, Ludwig (1784-1832). German actor. The greatest and most original actor of the Romantic school in 19th century German drama; portrayer of many of Shakespeare's characters.

Diaghilev, Sergei Pavlovich (1872-1929). Russian ballet master. He founded the Russian journal, *Mir Isskustva,* which revolutionized all art in his country. From 1907, up to the time of his death, he devoted all of his time and energy to promoting ballet productions. His organization was known as the Ballet Russe. Their Paris seasons stimulated the French theatre before the World War. In later years he centred his activities with Monte Carlo as a base. His company included such incomparable dancers as Nijinsky, Pavlova, Mordkin, Massine, Karsavina. Bakst designed his sets. Stravinsky, Debussy, Ravel all wrote music for his ballets.

Dialect part. A character role to be spoken in some regional, or foreign, vernacular.

Dicky bird. British slang term for an actor who sings as well as acts.

Diderot, Denis (1713-1784). French scholar. Born at Langres in Champagne, and educated by the Jesuits, he turned to literature for his living, working for many years as a bookseller's hack. After Voltaire and Rousseau, he was the greatest intellectual force of his time in France. Of great importance to the dramatist is his well-known *Le Paradoxe sûr le comédien,* a discussion of the actor's art in which he laid the foundations of the serious drama of ordinary life. Here he stated that the actor will more surely move the audience when he himself remains unmoved. Ever since its first draft in 1770 this paradox has been subject to constant attack and defense. Among Diderot's plays are: *Le Fils Naturel* and *Le Pere de Famille.* He also wrote several essays in which he announced the principles of a new drama: the serious, domestic bourgeois drama of real life, in opposition to the stilted conventions of the classic French stage. Among the most important of these is his *De la Poésie dramatique.* Diderot's lessons as well as his example gave a decisive bias to the dramatic taste of Lessing, whose plays and collection of criticisms (the *Hamburgische Dramaturgie*) mark an epoch in dramatic history. Diderot is of course famous for his "Encyclopédie," which he worked on for 20 years with d'Alembert.

Dietz, Howard (1896-   ). American lyricist, librettist, publicity man. Born in New York City. Wrote the lyrics for *Dear Sir,* 1924; *Merry-Go-Round,* 1927; *Three's A Crowd,* 1930; *Follow the Sun,* 1936; *The Show Is On,* 1936; *Between the Devil,* 1937. Was librettist for *The Little Show,* 1929; *Second Little Show,* 1930; *Three's A Crowd,* 1930; *The Band Wagon,* 1931; *Flying Colors,* 1932; *Revenge With Music,* 1934; *At Home Abroad,* 1935; *Between the Devil,* 1937. He is also the director of publicity for Metro-Goldwyn-Mayer Pictures.

Diggers. Slang term for Broadway sidewalk ticket speculators who buy seats at the box office and sell them at a premium.

Digges, Dudley (1880-   ). Irish actor and producer. He was born and educated in Dublin, and had his first stage experience with the Abbey Players of that city. Subsequently made his United States debut, 1904, with Mrs. Fiske; played in *The Rising of the Moon,* 1908; *The Spitfire,* 1911; *The Squaw Man,* 1911; etc. For seven years he acted as stage manager for George Arliss. He first came into prominence when he appeared in the Theatre Guild's first production, *Bonds of Interest,* in 1919. From 1920-30 he remained with the Guild, acting and producing. He appeared in *Jane Clegg, Heartbreak House, Liliom, Mr. Pim Passes By, The Adding Machine, Hedda Gabler, Outward Bound, Volpone, Marco Millions, Dynamo, The Guardsman, The Doctor's Dilemma* and other plays. He produced for the Guild *Candida,* 1926; *Pygmalion,* 1927; *Love is Like That,* 1927; *Becky Sharp,* 1930. In 1930 he began his film career and has played character roles in many pictures. In 1938 he returned to the stage as Gramps in *On Borrowed Time.*

Dillingham, Charles B. (1868-1934). American producer and journalist. Born in Hartford, Connecticut. He became a journalist in Hartford, Washington and Chicago; then became dramatic editor of the New York *Evening Sun;* became a producer in 1898 and managed many stars including Margaret Anglin, Fritzi Scheff, Maxine Elliott, and produced all of Fred Stone's musicals for twenty years.

His productions included, among others: *Mademoiselle Modiste; Chin-Chin; Watch Your Step; Blossom Time; A Bill of Divorcement; Bulldog Drummond* and *Stepping Stones.*

Dimmer. Electrical stage device worked by resistance plates which are controlled by levers on the switchboard and by means of which the lights may be raised or lowered gradually. The device is indispensable for twilight or sunrise effects. See *Lighting.*

Dinner at Eight. George S. Kaufman and Edna Ferber (American). Drama. 3 acts. 1932.

Millicent Jordan, stylish, pretty, rather insipid, is planning a dinner party in honor of the Ferncliffes, socially prominent English visitors in the United States. This episodic drama is the story of her guests, invited for business or social reasons, and reveals what happens to them from the time they accept the invitation until the dinner "a week from Friday." Each is facing some personal crisis or financial disaster; and the threads of all their lives are momentarily entangled. Carlotta Vance, aging actress and once a famous beauty adored by Oliver Jordan, Millicent's husband, has returned from Europe, bankrupt, and wishes Oliver to buy back the Jordan shipping stock she owns. But Oliver himself is hard pressed, unknown to his wife, and can't afford to oblige. This is the explanation of his having asked Dan Packard to dinner. Dan is brash, boastful, uncouth, and married to a gum-chewing blonde straight out of a hat-checking concession, but he is a successful business man and therefore able to help Oliver. Dan promises aid, but only because he intends to gain control of the Jordan lines and ruin his supposed friend. To this end he buys the stock Carlotta wishes to sell, through a proxy. Dan's wife Kitty rails at him for his crooked business deals, and he retaliates by taunting her with her infidelity. He does not know, however, that her last lover is attractive Dr. Talbot, who is already weary-ing of her and trying to get rid of her. To keep the knowledge from Dan, Kitty sub-mits to the blackmail of her maid. Dr. Talbot, who is also Oliver's physician, realizes what is perhaps Oliver's greatest tragedy, that he is fatally ill. In the meantime Paula Jordan, daughter of Oliver and Millicent, is not so happy as an engaged girl should be. This is because she is infatuated with Larry Renault, down-at-the-heels actor, once a movie idol, now a drunkard without the price of a meal, glad to accept her mother's dinner invitation and be the extra man. Yet on the very night of the dinner be becomes so desperate that he commits suicide without taking advantage of the free meal. As the guests assemble, Paula looks around anxiously for him. Her mother is too worried about other things to bother. The Ferncliffes, the reason for the dinner, have been unable to come. Gaily chattering, the Jordans, the Talbots, the Packards, Carlotta and a couple pinch-hitting for the guests of honor move into the Jordan dining room.

Dionysos. The Bacchus, or wine god, of the Greeks, the *dithyramb* in honor of the god most historians generally agree to be the origin of tragedy. This god was the inventor of wine, and the patron of poetry and music.

See also *Drama, Greek, ancient.*

Dionysos, festivals of. Celebrations to the wine god in ancient Greece, held principally in Attica. These consisted of two principal kinds: (1) in winter, to celebrate the completion of the vintage, the harvest, and the gathering of the fruits; (2) in spring, when the wine of the past year was ready for drinking. Here was the original source of the entire Greek drama, and, by historical process, the drama of the world.

Dionysos, Temple of. Place of worship of this god in Athens near the Acrop-olis.

Dionysos, Theatre of. An arena for dramatic productions in Athens, built 67 A. D. It had no roof because performances were acts of worship. It was called the Lycurgos Theatre of Dionysos.

Direction. The co-ordination of all the elements of *the theatre* with all the elements of *the drama* is the function of direction. The skill, understanding and im-agination with which this is done will determine the effectiveness of the performance.

This work is divided between the producer and the director and the division of labor between these two is seldom clearly defined. In many cases, particularly in amateur theatres, one individual will do both jobs. In this discussion we are concerned with the work of direction, regardless of how the job may be divided.

Diseuse. Literally, a "speaker" (feminine form); a dramatic recitalist or monologist. Most famous have been Yvette Guilbert, Ruth Draper and Cornelia Otis Skinner.

Disguisings. Elizabethan vessels chartered by English royalty for nocturnal amusement.

Dithyramb. Ode sung in ancient Greece in honor of Dionysos, originally improvised and rhapsodical; under the influence of Arion of Methyma, it became poetized; a choral ode, set to brisk music, sung by a troupe of fifty satyrs dancing and gesticulating around the sacrificial altar, usually under the direction of one leader; offspring of the wine and merriment at the Dionysiac festivals; innovations by Arion, such as the spoken verses, are credited with leading the way to Greek tragedy. See also *Drama, Greek, ancient*.

Dixey, Henry E. (1859-   ). American actor. Born in Boston; made his first appearance on the stage at the Howard Athenaeum, Boston, 1868, in *Under the Gaslight*. At Chicago in 1884 he appeared for the first time in *Adonis* in which his imitation of Sir Henry Irving made him famous. Was a member of Augustin Daly's Company beginning 1894 and continued to play in America and England.

Other plays in which he appeared include: *The Sorcerer; H.M.S. Pinafore; The Babes in the Wood; Patience; Twelfth Night; Nancy and Co.; Erminie; The Devil; Becky Sharp; Personality; The Rivals; The School for Scandal*, etc.

Do a Brodie. Slang expression for falling down in a scene.

Dock Street Theatre. Successful community theatre in Charleston, South Carolina. Through an appropriation from the governor, the WPA reconstructed a theatre in the shell of the old Planter's Hotel (the site of the first commercial theatre). After the opening of the Dock Street Theatre, the management was turned over to the Carolina Art Association. Here the performances of the Footlight Players, established in 1932, are given.

Doctor Faustus, The Tragical History of. Christopher Marlowe (English). Drama in blank verse and prose. 14 scenes. 1589.

An early dramatization of the legend of a man who sold his soul to the devil. Marlowe follows general outline of a story appearing in the *Volksbuch* published at Frankfort in 1587. His conception of Faustus, however, changes him from a mere magician to a man ambitious to be a "great emperor of the world."

There is also the version by Goethe and an operatic version by Gounod.

". . . (as in Tamburlaine and the Jew of Malta) . . . the medieval conception of royalty of tragedy is here being supplanted by the Renaissance idea of individual worth . . ." Allardyce Nicoll, *British Drama*.

Doctor in Spite of Himself, The. Molière (French). Comedy. 2 acts. 1666.

A boisterous farce which makes light of the dignity of the medical profession and mocks the stupidity of professional practitioners. Sganarelle, who knows nothing about medicine, is beaten until he accedes to his tormentor's request and announces he is a physician. Whereupon his lack of knowledge is no bar to his effecting numerous and miraculous cures of the many patients who entrust themselves blindly to him. Molière revised an old farce, *The Doctor by Compulsion* (*Le Médecin par Force*) to make this comedy at a time when he was losing money on *The Misanthrope* and needed a new offering with which to recoup. Written when the playwright was beginning to suffer seriously from ill health, it reflects his preoccupation with that subject.

Doctor's Dilemma, The. George Bernard Shaw (English). Drama. 3 acts. 1906.

Jennifer Dubedat begs Sir Colenso Ridgeon, the great British surgeon, to treat her husband, Louis Dubedat. Ridgeon, terribly overworked, is forced to choose between saving Dubedat or Blenkinsop, an old friend and classmate. He saves Blenkinsop, and leaves Dubedat to die in the hands of a less skilled physician.

Doctor Jekyll and Mr. Hyde. Luella Forpaugh and George F. Fisk. Drama. 4 acts. 1897.

The story of the distinguished English physician Dr. Jekyll who discovers a drug which transforms him into Mr. Hyde, a shrunken malformed criminal. After a series of brutal crimes Mr. Hyde goes beyond Dr. Jekyll's control, and both are destroyed. Based on Stevenson's story.

Dodsworth. Sidney Howard (American). Drama. 3 acts. 1934.

Sam Dodsworth who wants to enjoy life, resigns as president of his automobile company, and takes his wife, Fran, to Europe. Fran, an essentially selfish woman, falls in love with a young German, Kurt von Obersdorf, but when he will not marry her, she goes back to her husband. However, Dodsworth, who for the first time begins to understand his wife, leaves her on a liner bound for the States and returns to a more understanding friend, Mrs. Cartright, whom he has learned to appreciate during his wife's defection. Adapted from the novel by Sinclair Lewis.

Doebbelin, Karl Theophilus (1727-1793). German actor, director. Unimportant as an actor, but directed his own company which produced Lessing's dramas. He was the prototype of the German Kulissenreisser (wing-splitter) acting—a ranting boisterous rushing about the stage—which became popular in the 18th century.

See also *Kulissenreisser.*

Doll's House, A. Henrik Ibsen (Norwegian). Drama. 4 acts. 1879.

In order to help her husband, Thorwald Helmer, who is ill and in need of funds, Nora forges her rich father's name to a check, intending to send him abroad with the money thus obtained. Although she escapes serious consequences when her guilt is disclosed, Nora is brought face to face for the first time with the realities of her social position. She realizes that her husband had been keeping her as a doll, that she had never functioned as a living, thinking person, but had been merely a kind of ornament to decorate his modern home. Small wonder that she had lost the capacity for clear thinking and an awareness of what is moral behavior and what immoral. The sawdust marionette is suddenly infused with life; she suffers; and she sees how unsatisfactory the existence she has led as Helmer's wife has been. So she leaves him and his doll's house in order to establish her own identity, escaping to she knows not where, "a moth flying towards a star."

This was one of the first and most important social dramas to deal with the problem of woman's freedom. Nora in 1879 was modern woman incarnate, daring, radical, unbelievably courageous. In a day when women walk out of their homes for less reason than she had, Ibsen appears less of an iconoclast than formerly. Yet his play has not entirely lost its vigor, as proven by a successful American revival as recently as 1937, when Jed Harris produced it in an acting version by Thornton Wilder. Among the actresses to have starred as Nora between 1880 and 1939 are Helena Modjeska, Mrs. Fiske, Nazimova, Ethel Barrymore and Eva Le Gallienne.

Dome. Type of cyclorama; permanent plaster dome-shaped structure, painted a light blue to simulate sky; sometimes known as *dome-horizont, kupola-horizont*.

Dominion Dramatic Festival of Canada. Lord Bessborough, the Governor General, launched the first festival in April, 1933. Seven provinces sent teams to the Little Theatre in Ottawa to compete for the Bessborough trophy and other prizes. In 1938 the festival was moved to Winnipeg, a more central location.

Domus. Name of a certain scene-building, or mansion, of the medieval stage, meaning literally "home" or "house."
See also *Mansions*.

Don Carlos. Thomas Otway (English). Tragedy in rhymed verse. 5 acts. 1676.
Philip II of Spain marries Elizabeth of Valois who was formerly betrothed to his son, Don Carlos. Philip fears they are deceiving him, and driven by court gossip, finally has them killed, only to learn afterward of their innocence.

Don Carlos. Johann Christoph von Schiller (German). Drama in blank verse. 5 acts. 1784.
The tragic story of Don Carlos, heir presumptive to the Spanish throne, his struggle for recognition, and his final defeat and death.
This historical drama enhanced Schiller's reputation as a poet rather than as a tragedian. In form and manner it imitates the French school of classical tragedy more than the English.

Don Juan (Le Festin de Pierre). Molière (French). Comedy. 5 acts. 1665.
Don Juan, as a joke, invites the stone statue of a Commandant to dinner, when, to the horror of his guests, the statue arrives, and is believed to be a sign of divine wrath. Finally Don Juan pretends conversion to religion and is swallowed in a flaming abyss. Everyone is avenged but his servant Sganarelle, who is left unpaid.

Don Sebastian. John Dryden (English). Tragi-comedy. 5 acts. Printed 1691.

Based on the legend that Sebastian, king of Portugal, survived the battle of Alcazar. He is presented as a captive of the Moors, together with Almeyda, a princess of the royal house, with whom he is in love. He becomes an anchorite and she takes the veil when he discovers that they have the same father.

Donatus, Aelius (middle of the 4th century A.D.). Roman writer. A grammarian and theorist of the early Roman empire. He was the teacher of St. Jerome. Barrett Clark, in his *European Theories of the Drama,* says: "His importance lies . . . in the fact that he is the last of the Latins to formulate any theory, even a derived one, of the drama." He is best known for his grammatical and rhetorical treatises. His theories of the drama are to be found in the *De Comoedia et tragoedia.*

Donnay, Charles Maurice (1859-   ). French dramatist. Belongs to the French school of the ironic realists. Born in Paris, he began his career as playwright with Phryne, 1891. The satiric gifts of Donnay were first expended for the benefit of frequenters of the Chat Noir of Montmartre in little dialogues and vaudeville skits. Their author had reached his early thirties before he set a larger audience laughing by adapting to modern conditions the *Lysistrata* of Aristophanes.

His plays include *The Family Boarding-House,* 1894; *A Mad Enterprise,* 1894; *Lovers,* 1895; *The Emancipated Woman,* 1898; *The Torrent,* 1899; *The Other Danger,* 1902; *Birds of Passage* (with Lucien Descaves), 1904; *The Return from Jerusalem,* 1903; *The Marriage of Telemachus* (with Lemaitre), 1910; *The Rise of Virginie,* 1929.

Door button. Used to hold stage door closed.

Dorset Garden Theatre. The theatre that was the last word, architecturally, among the playhouses of the English Restoration. It had a splendid stone exterior; was situated on the Thames River, with a terrace for those arriving by water; the roof was of glass; the auditorium was horseshoe in shape; and there were three galleries.

Dossennus. Forefather in the *fabula Atellana* of the *dottore,* stock character in a *commedia dell'arte.*

Dostigaev and Others. Maxim Gorki (Russian). Social drama. 3 acts. c. 1933.

The second of a series about capitalism of which *Yegor Bulichev* is the first. The proposed trilogy was not completed, owing to Gorki's death.

This play deals with political strife in the early stages of the Revolution, from the Czar's abdication in March, 1917, to the Kerenski Cabinet, which survived until November of the same year, when it was seized by the Military Revolutionary Committee.

Dottore. Stock character in a *commedia dell'arte;* companion to Pantalone; the pedant of ancient comedy, appearing as philosopher, grammarian, or medical man in variety of diverting situations; but for laughter, mocked at by wife or mistress, cheated by the servant, Harlequin or Brighella. Costume: that of professor, black with dark cloak covering black garment which falls to knees; black hat, in contrast to that of Pantalone; dark mask with red cheeks and short beard. Forefather was Dossennus in the *fabula Atellana;* later translated to literary comedy as Molière's *médecin.*

Double Dealer, The. William Congreve (English). Comedy. 5 acts. Printed 1693.

Lady Touchwood, in love with her nephew, Mellefont, attempts to prevent his marriage to Cynthia. Maskwell, the double dealer, enters her plot, which is perceived finally by her husband, Lord Touchwood.

Doubling in brass. To play two parts; originally to play in the band and a part in the play.

Douglass, David (?-1786). English actor and manager. In 1751 John Moody recruited him for the West Indies. A mediocre actor, as a manager he was "for thirty years virtually theatrical king of the Western Hemisphere." Between 1758 and 1767 he built the second, third and fourth theatres ever built in New York, and Philadelphia's second and third. His marriage to the widow of the elder Hallam brought a union of the two companies and Lewis Hallam, Jr., became the leading light of the American stage. His company toured the colonies until the Revolution forced him to abandon his enterprises. He returned to Jamaica, where he became a British government official and died worth £25,000.

See also *John Street Theatre.*

Dover Road, The. A. A. Milne (English). Mystery comedy. 3 acts. 1922.

Mr. Latimer makes it his hobby to intercept eloping couples and keep them at his house for a week in order that they may become more closely acquainted with each other before breaking an already existing marriage knot. A human and delicately ironic play.

Dowling, Eddie (1895-   ). American actor, author and producer. Born in Woonsocket, Rhode Island. He first appeared in *Quo Vadis* in Providence in 1909, then toured in England, and made his New York debut in *The Velvet Lady,* 1917. He played in the *Ziegfeld Follies* in 1918, 1919, 1920; was first starred in *Sally, Irene and Mary,* 1922, of which he was co-author; acted in *The Fall Guy,* 1926; *Honeymoon Lane,* which he wrote in part, 1926. He produced *Big-Hearted Herbert,* 1934; appeared in and managed *Thumbs Up,* 1934; produced *Agatha Calling,* 1935, and *Shadow and Substance,* 1938. Co-producer with the Theatre Guild of *The Time of Your Life,* 1939. His acting in the last-named play and in *Here Come the Clowns,* 1938, have won him prominence as one of the finest portrayers of character roles of our day, and have marked his transition from a musical comedy star and entrepreneur to a serious interpreter and producer of high-minded and poetic drama.

Downstage. The front of the stage nearest the audience.

D'Oyly Carte, Richard (1844-1901). English theatrical manager. D'Oyly Carte is noted for his presentations of Gilbert and Sullivan operettas, with which his name is always associated. He was born in London, where he started a concert and theatre agency in 1870. In 1875 he produced Gilbert and Sullivan's *Trial by Jury*, and from then on was responsible for the London productions of all of the Gilbert and Sullivan operettas. He erected the Savoy Theatre to house these productions; after his death his son Rupert succeeded him as proprietor.

D'Oyly Carte, Rupert (1876-   ). English manager. The youngest son of Richard D'Oyly Carte, producer of Gilbert and Sullivan operas, Rupert D'Oyly Carte is now proprietor of the D'Oyly Carte Opera Company which his father founded, as well as chairman of three prominent London hotel companies.

Drama. (1) That quality in communication, situation, or action which arouses interest, excitement and empathy in a listener or beholder.
". . . conflict of human wills which has ever been the mainspring of drama."— Brander Matthews. ". . . drama must reveal the human will in action."—Ferdinand Brunetière. (2) A play; dialogue for enactment. A form invented in the 18th century. Allardyce Nicoll, in his *British Drama,* calls it "simply a serious problem play where the emotions never rise to tragic height and where the *denouement* is in harmony with the general atmosphere of the plot." (3) In a general sense, dramatic art, literature, or affairs. Forms of the drama include tragedy, comedy, melodrama, opera, operetta, farce, pantomime, monologue, and puppetry.

Drama, American, fireman. A type of popular American play which followed the Yankee play in vogue. Works of this school dealt exaggeratedly with life in a big city. The origin of the type was *A Glance at New York* in 1848, in which Mose, the fireboy, was the central character.

Drama, American, Indian. A type of popular American play dating from the late 18th century. Major Robert Rogers, pioneer backwoodsmen, published *Ponteach* in 1766, soon after the uprising of the Ottowan chief of that name. This is the first Indian play as well as the earliest American problem play. In 1829 *Metamora,* another Indian play, was written by John Augustus Stone. The success of this play resulted in a run of Indian dramas from which the public suffered from 1830 to 1840, depicting the nobility of the red men. A reaction finally set in. John Brougham in 1855 wrote an extravagant parody, *Pocahontas; or, The Gentle Savage,* which dealt the Indian drama its final death blow.

Drama, American, 17th-18th century. The earliest play written by a native American was *Gustavus Vasa* by Benjamin Colman, which was produced at Harvard College in 1690. The first play presented in New York of which there is actual record was George Farquhar's *The Recruiting Officer.* This is the earliest known play to have been acted in North America by professional players. It was produced at the New Theatre on Dec. 6, 1732. In 1753 non-professionals in New Orleans

acted in a play called *Le Père Indien* written by a Frenchman, Le Blanc de Ville-
neuve. The first play to be printed in America was Robert Hunter's *Androboros,*
1714. The first dialogue was *An Exercise Containing a Dialogue and Ode Sacred
to the Memory of George II.* It was performed on May 23, 1761. In 1762 Princeton College presented *The Military Glory of Great Britain,* the performers being
the "late candidates for the Bachelor's degree at Nassau Hall." *The Prince of
Parthia* by Thomas Godfrey, Jr., was the first play written by an American and
acted professionally. It was produced in 1765. *Ponteach* by Major Robert Rogers
was printed in 1766 but was never acted. In 1771 Hugh Henry Breckinridge and
Philip Freneau wrote *The Rising Glory of America* for Princeton's commencement
program. It was anti-British propaganda. Charlotte Lennox was the first American
writer to use drama for political satire. It was she who wrote *The Adulator* and
The Group. The Contrast by Royall Tyler was the first play by an American author
on an American subject to be produced on the American stage. In this play Jonathan
was the first typical American character to be presented on the stage; the part was
a Yankee and low comedy role. Other plays sprang up in which native types were
predominant. These came to be known as "Yankee plays."

Drama, American, 19th century. No genuine masterpiece was forthcoming in
America during the 19th century, although a considerable number of plays were
written and produced. Edwin Forrest was the first to offer money prizes for scripts
by Americans, which, if accepted, he undertook to produce. This was the first real
stimulus given the national drama and no doubt accounts in large part for the
growing output of theatrical works. The American dramatist may properly be said
to date from this time. Among the plays of new playwrights that Forrest produced
were: *Metamora* by John Augustus Stone, 1829; *The Gladiator* and *The Broker
of Bogota* by Dr. Robert M. Bird, 1829; *Jack Cade* by Robert T. Conrad, 1841;
and *Francesca da Rimini* by George H. Baker, 1856. These authors became known
as the Philadelphia School of Dramatists. *Fashion* by Mrs. Mowatt, produced in
1845, was the first successful social satire and first social comedy. Dion Boucicault
and John Brougham were perhaps the foremost playwrights of the 19th century
before the appearance of Augustin Daly and Augustus Thomas. Boucicault adapted
a great many works from the French and also produced original plays like *After
Dark.* Brougham was also an adaptor, while his original plays include *Benjamin
Franklin* and *Tom Thumb, the Second.* In 1852 the celebrated and enormously
popular dramatization, by George Aiken of Harriet Beecher Stowe's *Uncle Tom's
Cabin* was first performed. Thereafter came Daly's *Under the Gaslight,* one of
the most famous of all American melodramas. Daly was the leader of the "ten-
twent'-thirt'" school of playwriting. Others of his melodramas are *A Flash of
Lightning* and *The Red Scarf.* In 1866 came the first performance of the most
famous of all American melodramas, *The Black Crook.* Then came the great box-
office attraction, Albert M. Palmer's *The Two Orphans,* in 1873; also Steele
Mackaye's *Hazel Kirke* in 1880. Augustus Thomas' greatest plays were *The
Witching Hour, Arizona, As a Man Thinks,* and *The Copperhead.*

Another important trend of this century was that of the minstrel show. This form of entertainment began about 1828 and derived from the Negro singing and dancing on the southern plantations. It eventually grew into a lampoon of the Negro and his dialect was played by white men in blackface. Today the minstrel show survives mainly in small communities and in the vaudeville revues sponsored by the recent Federal Theatre Project, 1935-39.

Drama, American, 20th century. At the opening of the 20th century an advance-guard of native playwrights set the pace for the rapid rise of American drama. This group chose to comment upon the problems of an expanding nation. In *The Great Divide,* 1906, Moody brought a poet's vision to the problem of the social amalgamation of the open West and Puritan-restricted East. In *Daughters of Men,* 1906, Klein mirrored Theodore Roosevelt's plea for arbitration in labor disputes. Broadhurst's *Man of the Hour,* 1906, exposed the evils of boss rule in city governments. Mitchell's *The New York Idea,* 1906, and Walter's *The Easiest Way,* 1908, protested moral laxity.

In this opening decade Ibsen was praised by Harrison Grey Fiske as "the apostle of truth" and decried by William Winter as "an evil to be deprecated." American critics censured Shaw as "immoral and degenerate." Cohan's *Broadway Jones,* 1910, and Sheldon's *Romance,* 1913, were romantic throwbacks to an earlier period of writing. The War brought a temporary anesthesia with such musicals as Ziegfeld's countermarching spectacle of soldiers, sailors and feminine beauty, *The Century Girl,* 1916.

The post-War theatre brought paced-to-life melodramatic pictures of American life. Hecht and McArthur's *The Front Page,* 1928, depicted the newspaper world; Cormack's *The Racket,* 1927, the gangsterland; Abbott and Dunning's *Broadway,* 1927, night clubs; Walters and Hopkins' *Burlesque,* 1927, burlesque; Anderson and Stallings' *What Price Glory?,* 1924, the First World War; Rice's *Street Scene,* 1928, the slums; and Steinbeck's *Of Mice and Men,* 1937, the brute world. Along with these serious dramas grew a steadily increasing stream of light, satiric and serious comedies. There were the popular triumphs: *Lightnin',* 1918; and Nichols' *Abie's Irish Rose,* 1922. There were Craven's *The First Year,* 1920; Barry's *Holiday,* 1928, and *The Animal Kingdom,* 1932; Crothers' *As Husbands Go,* 1931; Behrman's *The Second Man,* 1927, and *No Time For Comedy,* 1939; Kaufman and Connelly's numerous collaborations; Kelly's *The Show-Off,* 1924; Howard's dramatization of *Dodsworth,* 1934; O'Neill's *Ah, Wilderness!,* 1933; Kaufman and Hart's *You Can't Take It With You,* 1936; and Boothe's *The Women,* 1936.

While these conventionally constructed plays were lining the pockets of commercial producers, the experimental drama was being fostered by the non-professional groups. O'Neill's sea plays were produced by the Provincetown Players in 1916, opening the way for professional production of his first long play, *Beyond the Horizon,* 1920. Critics hailed it "the best serious play any American author has written for years." O'Neill's experimentation through the following ten years grew to be the most exciting thing in dramatic composition. To the sordid social themes of Ibsen he added the soul-probing and Freudian analysis of Strindberg. He experimented with elemental rhythms in *Emperor Jones,* 1920, with expressionistic symbolism in *The Hairy Ape*, 1922, with masks in *The Great God Brown*, 1926, and the aside in *Strange Interlude*, 1928. He transplanted the Greek *Oresteia* to New England soil in *Mourning Becomes Electra*, 1931. He lengthened the time of performance, and at all times re-made the theatre to fit his dramatic composition. He was the first to bring the Nobel prize to American drama.

Experimental plays soon became as numerous in the post-War theatre as the conventionally written play. Rice's *Adding Machine*, 1923, Kaufman and Connelly's *Beggar on Horseback*, 1923, and Lawson's *Processional*, 1925, all showed the influence of German expressionism. Barry's *Hotel Universe*, 1930, reverts to psychoanalysis. The growth of the folk play brought additional experimentation for a form that would suit the regional subject matter found in the plays of the Carolina mountaineers, Vollmer's *Sun-Up*, 1923, and Hughes' *Hell-Bent Fer Heaven*, 1923, or the Kentuckians in MacKaye's *This Fine-Pretty World*, 1923. Riggs added Oklahoma folk songs to *Green Grow the Lilacs*, 1930. Negro spirituals greatly enhanced the Heywards' *Porgy*, 1927, and Connelly's *The Green Pastures*, 1930, "the divine comedy of the modern theatre."

Freedom in form added to the propaganda plays Rice's *Judgment Day*, 1934; Odets' *Waiting For Lefty*, 1935, and the Federal Theatre's *one third of a nation*, 1938. Another interesting development in play form has been the addition of the musical score to the political satire, as in the Kaufman-Gershwin *Of Thee I Sing*, 1931, the Friedman-Rome *Pins and Needles*, 1937, Blitzstein's *The Cradle Will Rock*, 1937, and the Anderson-Weill *Knickerbocker Holiday*, 1938.

Film-writing has brought into prominence the short-scened episodic play form used effectively by Green in *In Abraham's Bosom*, 1926, and more recently by Sherwood in *Abe Lincoln in Illinois*, 1938. Wilder's *Our Town*, 1938, added novelistic exposition and narrative to this episodic play form. Anderson has experimented successfully with free verse in the dialogue of *Elizabeth, the Queen*, 1930, *Mary of Scotland*, 1934, and *Winterset*, 1935.

The American playwright's independence of thought and freedom in dramatic composition has led native comedy into the vein of social satire, and the serious play into the tragedy of the individual. Throughout the 20th century the dramas have been filled with native character portraits, and the choice of subject matter has reflected the mental temper of America.

Drama, Austria. Austria-Hungary was a conglomerate nation. Its various peoples had their corresponding drama; German, Polish, Czechoslovak, etc. There was however, the Viennese comedy—the one definite and peculiarly Austrian contribution. It was marked by gaiety, glamor and sophistication. Schnitzler, particularly in *Anatol*, was the shining light. Hugo von Hoffmannsthal, who wrote the librettos for several Strauss operas, was another important romanticist.

After the war Austrian drama became more serious and profound. Not only the disasters and problems brought on by the war contributed to this change. The stimulus of Freud and the live new dramatic force of psychoanalysis, which originated in Vienna, was also a factor.

Drama, British, earliest. From the 10th century when the liturgical *trope* was performed inside the church, until the early 16th century, British drama was cradled in ecclesiasticism. First came the "mystery plays," performed in the church-yard and dramatizing, very primitively, episodes of the Old and New Testament; then the "miracle plays," often performed by members of trades in cycles named for the town where they were given (as York, Chester, Wakefield), dramatizing miracles in the lives of saints; and after these, the more secular "morality plays," performed—as were some of the miracle plays, on pageant wagons. The moralities, of which *Everyman* and *The Castle of Perseverance* are the best examples, the allegorical characters illustrating moral truths. The vice or buffoon here, and Herod, who ranted in the mystery plays were favorites with the audience.

Drama, British Elizabethan, 1550-1642. The earliest form of the English national drama was the "historical tragedy," originating in a poetical play named *The Mirror for Magistrates* in 1557. Works in this form are known also as "chronicle plays" and relate in chronological order the events of a particular king's reign. Some famous chronicle plays of the period are: Shakespeare's *King John, Richard II* and those about the three Henrys; Marlowe's *Edward II;* Greene's *Scottish History of James IV.* After these came certain "blood and thunder" plays invented by Kyd which are pure melodrama and which owe much to Seneca. *The Spanish Tragedy* is the best known of Kyd's works. Marlowe, on his advent to the theatrical scene, fused these separate elements into a single unified whole in the creation of "romantic tragedy." Among Marlowe's best known works are: *Doctor Faustus, The Jew of Malta* and *Tamburlaine the Great.* Between "classical" and "romantic" comedy appeared the works of Lyly with their allusions to history and mythology. His principal comedies are: *Endymion, the Man in the Moon, Mydas* and *Gallathea.* The melodramatic school of Kyd was carried on by Peele in such of his plays as *The Battle of Alcazar.* Other predecessors of Shakespeare: Greene, with his one notable play *The Scottish History of James IV;* Lodge, with plays like *The Wounds of Civil War;* Nash, with his *Summer's Last Will and Testament.* (Shakespeare is treated independently elsewhere in this volume. The most famous dramatist after Shakespeare, Ben Jonson, with his comedies such as *Every Man in His Humour, Volpone* and *The Alchemist.* Provoked by a literary quarrel he turned in 1603 to tragedy with his *Sejanus;* another tragedy *Catiline, His Conspiracy* followed in 1611, but these were the only tragedies written by Jonson. He also composed masques. After Jonson came Chapman with both tragedies and comedies, among these: *Bussy d'Ambois* and *The Conspiracy and Tragedy of Charles, Duke of Byron, Marshall of France.* Following Chapman appeared two collaborators who were destined to become known as a famous writing team, Beaumont and Fletcher. They were among the earliest and best writers of the pastoral play. Fletcher's *The Faithful Shepherdess* is one of the finest examples of this type. Beaumont and Fletcher wrote both comedies and tragedies the most important of which are *Philaster, The Maid o' Tragedy* and *The Coxcomb.* Both Beaumont and Fletcher also wrote plays separately, of which Beaumont's *Rule a Wife and Have a Wife* and Fletcher's *The Humorous Lieutenant* are representative. The joint ventures of Beaumont and Fletcher are marked by a wide literary knowledge and a considerable acquaintanceship with languages, with particular emphasis on Spanish literature. After this noted duo come: Dekker, with his *Shoemakers' Holiday;* Webster, with his *Duchess of Malfi* and, in collaboration with Dekker, *Westward Ho!;* Marston, with his "blood and thunder" dramas and comedies such as *What You Will;* Middleton, with his political comedies like *A Game At Chess;* Heywood, with his many dramatic styles, including the "pageant," and whose best play is probably *A Woman Killed with Kindness.* Among other dramatists thereafter were: Rowley, Daniel, Massinger and Ford.

Drama, British, 1660-1800. The dramatic literature of England during the 17th century felt the influence of the pseudo-classicists. The most fanatic of these insisted on a conformity to the unities. The more liberal assented to certain modifications, such as a compromise between the law in the French theatre prohibiting the depiction of death on the stage and the love of action and excitement innate in the typical English audience. For all of these liberals certain old taboos persisted, such as that against the enactment of any passion onstage. Comedy was more popular than tragedy and fell into several categories: (1) the "comedy of manners," which was a satirical mirroring of upper class life, best represented by Congreve, Etherege (whose work was influenced by Molière), Wycherley (whose work, though he was a court favorite, yet satirized the corrupt court of Charles II), and Fielding; (2) the "comedy of humors," based fundamentally on satire, originally inspired by Jonson, and best represented at this time by Shadwell; (3) the "comedy of intrigue," differing from the comedy of manners only in its leaning toward farce, and best represented by Mrs. Centlivre; (4) the "comedy of sensibility," characterized by sympathy not with protagonists but with actions, by an artificial love of natural scenery and rural landscapes, and a deliberate enunciation of a moral or social problem, best represented by Colley Cibber and Sir Richard Steele; (5) the "genteel comedy," and adaptation of the comedy of manners but more effeminate and artificial, best represented by Cibber and brought to a contemporary triumph by the acting of Mrs. Oldfield. Restoration comedy, generally, was a reflection of the temper, if not of the actual life, of the upper classes of the period. In it were pictured the external details of living, the fashions of the time, its manners, speech and interests. For settings playwrights turned to the most interesting places they knew, which were drawing rooms, coffee houses and the streets and gardens of London. Characters were chiefly people of fashion and plots were largely love intrigues. The tendency of the plays, on the whole, is toward the licentious, and represents the reaction of the playgoing public against Puritanism. Otherwise the plays were of no social import, nor were they romantic or revolutionary in any sense. Tragedy, pseudo-classic and otherwise, did not curry the full favor of the public. Addison's pseudoclassic *Cato* was perhaps the most successful tragedy of the period. Shakespeare was the most popular tragic dramatist, and following his works, the "pathetic" dramas of Banks, Southerne, Otway and Rower, and thereafter the heroic dramas of Dryden, Settle and Lee. Outside of these two major categories came the pantomimes (influenced by classic myth, Italian *com-*

media dell' arte, earlier English farce, and contemporary satire), best represented by Lun and Weaver. Political plays were universally accepted. Continental influence, particularly that of Voltaire on tragedy, was strong. The rise of the tradesman class disclosed many playwrights in their midst, but most of these turned out to be one-play writers.

Drama, British, 1800- . The growth of the drama in the early 19th century did not take place in the two patent theatres which held a monopoly on legitimate drama (Drury Lane and Covent Garden), but in the minor theatres whose managers evaded the law by creating a new dramatic form called the "burletta." At first it was nothing more than a short burlesque opera filled with vigorous action. It attracted the public away from the patent theatres with their productions of monotonous sentimental comedies and turgid tragedies. In an attempt to win back the audience Drury Lane added lyrical ditties to the dialogue of Fielding's *Tom Thumb* and billed it as a burletta. This was a fatal step. Minor managers seized upon the right to add dialogue to their shows. A few years later the licenser of plays defined the burletta as a play of three acts including not less than five songs. This makeshift entertainment had become at once thrilling melodrama and burlesque extravaganza. In 1843 an act of parliament allotted equal license to all theatres. This gave impetus to theatrical writing but it did not elevate the low quality of drama hack writers had been turning out since the beginning of the century. Managers, with their minds on scenic display and rhetorical acting, continued to accept tawdry romantic dramas and wretched farces which were nothing more than rewrites of German and French plays. They rejected as unactable Shelley's poetic tragedy *The Cenci,* 1820.

In this early 19th century dearth of native drama there were a few distinctive exceptions. *Virginius* (Covent Garden), 1820, and *The Hunchback* (Covent Garden), 1832, established Knowles as a dramatic teller of glorified tales in the manner of the Elizabethans. *The Lady of Lyons* (Covent Garden), 1838, most often revived play of the century, proved Lord Lytton to be as adept in the construction of romantic melodrama as his French contemporaries. *London Assurance* (Covent Garden), 1841, created a stir with its comic characters and established Boucicault on his career of leading melodramatist of the age. But even these outstanding plays had rehashed themes, uninventive plots and stereotyped characters. Dramatic composition seemed hopelessly submerged in the general industry of entertainment.

Finally there appeared in 1865 Robertson's *Society,* the play that pulled British drama out of its romantic and artificial rut onto the road of realism and social reform. The audience welcomed the natural characters reflecting in word and action the follies and foibles of the time. Shortly after this the critics, William Archer and Sir Edmund Gosse, introduced Ibsen to English readers. In the eighties came a renaissance of the playwright's art and once again dramatic composition became a vital part of native literature. *The Second Mrs. Tanqueray,* 1893, proved Pinero to be a master of the problem piece and drawing room drama. Jones's *Michael And His Lost Angel,* 1896, raised domestic tragedy to a new level of literary and social importance. *The Admirable Crichton,* 1902, was Barrie's popular contribution to realism. In a majority of his plays, as in *Dear Brutus,* 1917, and *Peter Pan,* 1904, whimsy mingles with realism. Wilde's *The Importance of Being Earnest,* 1895, brought to comedy writing a rare and unmatched brilliance in dialogue. The great mid-Victorian contribution to light opera was the partnership of Gilbert and Sullivan bringing a long series of satirical and melodious operettas of which *The Mikado* is the most popular.

Shaw's decision to think on the stage gave to British drama the modern master of the play of ideas. Such plays as *Androcles and the Lion,* 1913, *Pygmalion,* 1913, *Heartbreak House,* 1919, and *Saint Joan,* 1924, have in turn shocked and captivated the world by their topsy-turvy turning of current thought and conventional play form. Granville-Barker who brought Shaw's plays to the professional stage likewise contributed to the drama of ideas with *The Madras House,* 1910. The realism of Ibsen had become the life force of British drama: the kind of realism that was near to the emotions of man and to his social problems. The most truthful revelation of the social problems of the 20th century came when Galsworthy turned to drama to depict, with excellent craftsmanship, class war in *Strife,* 1909, man against society in *Justice,* 1910, and racial pride in *Loyalties,* 1922. Ervine's *Jane Clegg,* 1913, is an incisive characterization of a member of the lower class, and Masefield's *The Tragedy of Nan,* 1908, adds restraint and imaginative power to realism.

During the First World War serious drama was replaced by trivial farces and spectacles such as *Chu Chin Chow,* 1915, which ran 2,238 performances. The post-War period brought a revival of the comedy of manners: Maugham's *The Circle,* 1921, and *Our Betters,* 1923; Lonsdale's *The High Road,* 1928; and Coward's more popular *Private Lives,* 1930, and *Design for Living,* 1933. Realism remained the paramount feature of serious drama, Sheriff's war play *Journey's End,* 1928, being a distinguished example, as is Sayers' *The Zeal of Thy House;* and Isherwood and Auden's *Ascent of F6* carries story and character into the surrealistic realm of symbolic play. Since that time, symbolism and heightened prose, if not poetry, have been evident in the dramas of Synge, Dunsany, Lady Gregory and Carroll.

Drama, Bulgarian, since the First World War. At best, modern Bulgarian drama since the First World War is still primitive by its very national traditions and popular characteristics. It depends to a great extent on historical subjects. Some of the well-known dramatists are: Ivan Vazoff, with his historical plays; Strashimiroff, with his naturalistic dramas; Todoroff, with his dramatic legends. Today dramatists are turning for material to the contemporary life of their cities.

Drama, Chinese. The Chinese spirit is in its very essence dramatic; it is alert and vivid and fond of abstractions—good drama, of course, makes visible an abstract idea; its selective power is sagacious—and the carrying quality of any play depends upon judicious choosing of incidents and situations. Thus it has been truly said about the Chinese that "to know their theatre is to know, in no small degree, the Chinese people."

The Chinese theatre is the best equipped theatre in the world from the point of view of costuming and properties. It has a higher standard of artistic finish than any Western stage, but its influence has not as yet been felt in the West, except by the Russian stage, which has begun to adopt some of the Chinese theatrical technique. In 1922, Vakhtangov produced in Moscow the play *Turandot,* using as his libretto Carlo Gozzi's fairy play of the same name which is an 18th century version of an Eastern legend. Vakhtangov, who was familiar with Chinese stage methods, presented the play in the Chinese tradition. Puccini used the same story for his last and unfinished opera, employing Chinese characters, settings, and some genuine Chinese music throughout. Goethe, Schiller, and others had also adapted *Turandot* for their own purposes. Goethe, furthermore, read an English version of a famous Chinese play called *Lao Sêng Erh* (An Heir in Old Age), and expressed deep regard from it. A Yuan dynasty play served as the groundwork for Voltaire's rhetorical tragedy *Orphelin de la Chine* (Little Orphan of China).

The first evidences of drama in China are clouded in dim legend. It is claimed that music existed there from 5400 B.C. and ceremonial dances for religious worship and military rejoicing appeared in the Hsia dynasty (2205-1766 B.C.). In the Shang dynasty (1766-1122 B.C.), this interpretive dancing spread to new ceremonies—to the gods of the harvest, rain, drought, famine—things representative of an agricultural society. A stage was used for the presentations, and thus the spirit of the people was expressed. Later speech was added and parts were acted with a new form of chanting. These *shên-hsi* or "sacred plays" of the Chou dynasty (1122-255 B.C.) in time assumed a role essentially dramatic. Thus it is evident that, like the early drama of Greece and the West, the Chinese drama was at first ritualistic.

Since the rulers had to be amused, this new drama naturally found encouragement in court. Those who performed were considered inferior members of society who had assumed their positions through lack of other opportunities. And to this day the drama as literature is ignored by Chinese scholars; actors and playwrights were so looked down upon that the dramatist often wrote anonymously.

The early emperors frowned upon a theatre for the people, and while one of them started a theatre about 700 B.C., those following destroyed all written works of his time. Emperor Ch'in Shih Huang (246-210 B.C.) had as many as three thousand actors in his famous "Ah Fang" palace. But as luck would serve the Chinese drama, the most ardent patron of the stage, music and dancing was an emperor who had an artist's exquisite taste and an unusual ability for launching and organizing the art. He was the T'ang dynasty emperor, Ming Huang, who established a school for actors under his patronage and tutelage in the 8th century A.D. Through his efforts the drama effected a lasting hold in China. Today actors are still known as "The Young Folk of the Pear Garden," a title dating back to Ming Huang's pupils who were given instruction in the emperor's Pear Garden at Ch'ang-an. Later Ming Huang was deified as the Patron Saint of Theatricals.

In consequence of such a favorable start, theatricals made great strides in China, but the interest in them probably did not extend beyond the bounds of the imperial court until the 13th century, and it was during the Yuan dynasty (1280-

1368) that the Chinese drama as it exists today took a sudden and permanent place in the land. Some experts believe that marionette shows marked the real beginning of the theatre for they can be traced to the 10th century B.C. and they were popular with all classes, their root being more among the people.

Nevertheless, the Chinese drama, as modernly constituted, falls into two main classes: the *Fun Pan Hsi*—the oldest form, expressing patriotism and filial devotion; and the *Jin Pan Hsi*—representing the greater bulk of the drama wherein are expressed civil and military subjects and differing from *Fun Pan Hsi* in method of acting and singing. A more recent development is the *Fun Min Hsi,* which is the only form in which colloquial dialects are allowed in place of the usual and more classical Mandarin speech. Several of these plays (as many as eight, which are often interpolated with shorter pieces) are presented in a single evening, and the first two types are always given. Western plays and plays in Western style have also been done, but they have never proved popular.

There is no term in Chinese for the word "drama," but the term for "play" (*hsi*) means "to make fun of," "to ridicule playfully." A Chinese saying, "those in front of the stage are fools, and those *on* the stage are lunatics," is, on the whole, true; but both actors and audience, paradoxically enough, are deeply serious about it all. The Chinese have never distinguished carefully between Comedy and Tragedy; instead, most plays are broadly classified as Civil (*Wen*) and Military (*Wu*). The latter present battles and other violent deeds while the former include the quieter aspects of social life often with a comic interpretation. Though the Chinese drama always has a moral aim, quite a number of plays are marked by buffoonery and licentiousness and these have been banished from the stage in recent years. In the 7th century B.C. the philosopher Kuan Chung said, "Owing to the rise of play-actors the morals of the people have greatly declined." Confucius was so deeply shocked once by a performance of dwarfs and buffoons that, as Minister of Justice, he ordered their instant execution.

The religious influence of Buddhism, Confucianism and Taoism add to the confusion. Buddhistic plays are in the form of fantasy, humor and burlesques of deity and demon symbols. Taoistic plays are based on superstition and spirit worship and are concerned with evils of the present. Confucian plays moralize on ancestor worship and filial piety. With so many creeds extant it is small wonder that the writers like the average Chinese became confused and worshipped at all shrines.

The Chinese fear of demons and respect for symbols is an integral part of their drama, making it doubly difficult for the Westerner to understand and enjoy performances. To eliminate this symbolism, however, would only rob the drama of its potency and the greatest part of its natural charm.

The Chinese drama of greatest importance was produced in Yuan times (1280-1368) and even this is inferior to the best poetry and novels of the period. This condition is attributed to the high state of development in which the latter literary styles basked. In China, where the writing of plays was considered but a step higher than the acting of them, the lack of impetus and subsequent belated progress of the dramatic style of literature is understandable.

Since the Khan rulers during the Yuan (Mongol) reign did not honor poets and scholars with official ranks, these retired to write plays and novels in which they could express themselves. During this ninety-year period 535 plays were produced. *Hsi Hsiang Chi* (Romance of the Western Chamber) and Chao Mei Hsiang (Intrigues of a Maid) are excellent examples of the best that this dynasty has to offer and show great beauty of expression attained by the authors. This is remarkable because the play is not at all the thing in China and playwrights were usually content to follow the monotony of tradition and the sentiments and ideals of their predecessors.

Among the greatest Yuan dramatists may be mentioned Kuan Han-ching who wrote sixty plays, Kao Wen-shiu credited with thirty, Ching Teh-hiu with eighteen, Pai Jen-fu with fifteen and Mah Chih-yuan.

About 140 major plays were produced in the Ming dynasty (1368-1643) and 246 in the Ch'ing (Manchu) dynasty (1644-1911). Among the better Ming dramatists, Kao Tse-ch'eng, T'ang Hsien-tsu and Wu Shih-chu are worthy of mention, The most important Ch'ing dramatists are: K'ung Yun-t'ing, Hung Fang-ssu, Chiang Shihchuan and Li Yu. The last mentioned, Li Yu, wrote fifteen plays and is the most modern of the Ch'ing writers, not only in his plays but also in his sound dramatic criticisms and theories. His literary works were published about 1672.

About sixty to seventy years ago, a type of local drama from Hupeh province came into prominence and gradually spread over all China. This school is known as the *Pi-huang* and is representative of the Chinese drama of today.

The characters in a play, though they are fashioned from life, actually belong to no set race or country; they are universal. In order that they may be easily recognized they conform rigorously to established tradition. The most important roles are the *Tan,* or women's parts, which were taken by men. The women were barred from the theatre quite early in its history; actresses were even classed with courtesans. Later, when women timidly began to return to the stage, they found that the female roles had become so conventionalized that they were forced to copy the mannerisms of the *Tan* female impersonators in order to compete with them and find favor with the audience. The *Shêng* are the leading male characters; the *Ching* are the villainous characters with painted faces. Another important figure is *Chou,* the clown, named for his white-painted nose. His role is allowed the greatest freedom of interpretation since Patron Saint Ming Huang sometimes played it.

All Chinese plays contain music and singing and could correctly be called *music dramas* or *operas*. Most Chinese go to "listen" to a play rather than to "see" it. To the Chinese, "music is the soul of art and the inspiration of acting." Singing parts were added to plays in the 10th century A.D. to augment and elaborate the speaking parts, and here, too, the manner in which they are sung, and not the song itself, is the most important part. Stage singing is generally done in a high falsetto; in the singing of folk songs, the natural voice is preferred. Unless we can think of singing in the drama as a kind of chanting, the singing would always seem to us a monotonous repetition of the same few themes in the same keys from play to play. The music for "new plays" is literally composed of passages already well-known in existing plays, a procedure which makes it possible for accompanists to know any number of plays and to play them by heart. The style of dramatic music varies with the type of play, and a change in style is indicative of a change in action. The style of music is named: i.e. *Erh-huang,* played during solemn action; *Pang-tzu,* played during martial action, etc.

The orchestra generally consists of from four to eight men who sit on chairs or stools onstage facing the audience. The conductor of the orchestra sits at the *tan-p'i-ku* (single-skin drum), which is the leading instrument and marks the tempo; the two-stringed fiddle and the moon guitar usually carry the melody; flutes, cymbals, flageolets, gongs and drums are used particularly in the military plays where there is fighting and much rapid action. Long apprenticeship is necessary to master these instruments. Though the accompaniment of the voice is most carefully studied and precise, the musicians are a very free lot on stage employing no music books, no stands, no regulations as to how and where they should sit and no restrictions against indulging in a smoke or an occasional stroll about the stage.

There is much hawking of wares, tea sipping, spitting, blowing of noses with the fingers and other unsightly things among the audience. The Chinese audience is not unlike that of Shakespeare's time in England, and to a foreigner half the show is the audience.

It is remarkable how quickly one forgets the distractions of the strolling musicians and performing audience and concentrates on the actors. The Chinese word for "bravo" is *hao* (good), and it can turn to hoots and jeers at the slightest *faux pas* on the part of the actor.

Chinese dramatic critics have been rather poor. There were those who praised almost everything and those who damned or wise-cracked all. But the critics, like the theatre in China, were so steeped in tradition that they never discovered the creative function of criticism. However, most Civil plays are nothing but artificial sentimentalism apparently designed to make people weep, but Civil plays display showy dresses and paraphernalia with some good singing and verse. Poets, high officials, philosophers, artists, lofty thinkers, divine men and women form the characters of the Civil plays, while a long and bewildering succession of emperors, empresses, traitors, voluptuaries, murderers, rebels, monks, bandits, etc., are to be encountered in the Military plays. Since the southern drama does not conform so rigidly to tradition as does the northern, plays of the southern drama often run beyond the four act limit, one of many revolutionary changes. *Hsi Hsiang Chi* (The West Chamber) is representative of the northern drama, while *P'i P'a Chi* (Romance of a Lute) is a typical southern play.

Acting editions of plays are either unobtainable or unreliable, because the text is so often altered by the players themselves who do not learn from books but from one another; once learned, a part is never forgotten.

The Chinese dramatists have repeatedly drawn from two main works for the plots of many of their most successful plays. Both of these works are vast Yuan dynasty products. The first, *San Kuo Chi* (The History; or, Romance of the Three Kingdoms), is a huge historical novel bursting with emperors, ministers and traitors of every degree. The second is a romantic novel called *Ts'ao Hsueh-ch'in* (The Dream of the Red Chamber), whose chief virtue is that it presents a panorama of Chinese social life with a remarkable life-likeness, detail and delineation of character.

See also *Acting, Chinese; Staging, Chinese.*

Drama, classics. The great writers, and their works, of ancient Greece and Rome; more broadly; all dramatists who expounded and upheld the strict conventions of dramatic writing, such as the three unities, the necessity of beginning middle, and end, etc., as outlined by Aristotle in his *Poetics.* The principal classic writers: (Greek) Aeschylus, Sophocles, Euripides, Aristophanes; (Roman) Menander, Terence, and Plautus. Corneille and Racine, of the 17th century French theatre, are also considered classics in their imitations of Greek and Roman tragedy, indeed were called *neo-classicists* in their time. In the broadest and most general sense, the word *classic* is today applied to any work which has retained critical as well as popular favor over a certain period of time. *Saint Joan* of Shaw is called a modern classic.

Drama, Czechoslovak, before the First World War. Romantic patriotism was a thing of the past; yet patriotic themes, such as the principle of non-violence and non-resistance in time of strife were treated. Arnošt Dvořák was a significant historical dramatist. Stroupežnicky was a popular playwright of peasant life. Plays in verse were written by Vrchlichy and Zeyer. Dramas of ideas were written by Hilbert, a dramatist deeply influenced by Ibsen.

Drama, Czechoslovak, since the First World War. The most celebrated and possibly the greatest Czechoslovak dramatist is Karel Čapek, whose *R. U. R.,* first performed in 1921, brought him world fame. His *The World We Live In,* written in collaboration with his brother Josef, is a powerful indictment of society. His last play, 1939, was *The Mother,* an anti-war drama. The next most gifted playwright of this period is Ivan Stodola, a describer of the peasantry and satirist of the Czechoslovak Babbitts. Jan Bartos, learned theatre curator of the National Museum, is another leading dramatist.

Drama, Danish. In the work of prolific Ludwig Holberg, 1684-1754, director of Denmark's first theatre (Copenhagen) and inventor of a whole set of stock comic characters, the middle-class comedy which was the first notable contribution is best exemplified. It was J. Ewald who first called attention in his plays to the untouched treasures of Scandinavian history and folk-lore ready to be used. A. G. Oehlensläger, 1779-1850, the great writer of the romantic movement drew upon these, as have subsequent Danish playwrights. The spirit of realism and naturalism touched 19th century drama in the plays of H. Drachman, 1846-1908, and later, in those of Sven Lange, 1868- . The satiric comedy *2 x 2= 5,* by Gustav Wied, 1858-1914, has been produced in New York City, in German at the New German Theatre, 1908, and in English at the Civic Repertory Theatre, 1928.

Drama, Egyptian. Actually religious ceremonials and dances. Osiris, chief Egyptian god, was the central figure of a passion play which dates from 2000 B.C. It establishes the story of the cult of Osiris worship. Drama was engendered with actual life and history of the Egyptians. The passion play was made up of a series of huge pageants, processions and floats interspersed with sham battles.

See also *Passion play, Egyptian.*

Drama, equestrian. A form of English melodrama in which the parts were played by characters on horseback, a fashion inaugurated at Astley's Amphitheatre and sustained at Drury Lane and Covent Garden in London. This form flourished at the beginning of the 19th century in England.

Drama, Finnish. Previous to Finland's independence after the First World War, there was a National Finnish Theatre at Helsingfors, devoted to patriotic drama. As Finland is bi-lingual, there are theatres playing in both Swedish and Finnish. There is a magnificent new Swedish theatre at Helsingfors. Finnish language playwrights include Eino Leino, 1878-1926, and Tenvo Pakkala, 1862-1925, who described the life of the small-town proletariat. Writing in Swedish were Runar Schildt, 1888-1925, and M. Kael Lybeck, 1864-1925, who mingled realism with symbolism. Yrjö Hirn, 1870-   , is the foremost authority on Finnish drama. The Finnish National Theatre, *Suomen Kansallisteatteri,* is a first-rate theatre producing translations of many American and English plays. Einó Kalima is the manager.

Drama, folk. A play drawn from indigenous peasant sources and usually made up of long-lived myths and legends of the popular lore.

Drama, French, 17th century. The 17th century saw in France the glorious flowering of the classic drama, for after Alexandre Hardy who gave the theatre its initial impetus, came the disciplined poetic tragedies of Corneille and Racine, written in close observance of the unities of time, place, action and tone. Corneille's *The Cid, Horace, Cinna* and *Polyeucte,* each with a man in the title rôle, all present the struggle between love and duty, with duty triumphant. Racine's beautiful *Andromaque, Phèdre, Athalie* and *Esther,* each with a woman as the dominant figure, show similar contests between will and inclination, but with greater naturalness and warmth.

Satiric pieces, ranging from plain farce to exquisite literary comedy came from the prodigal and prolific pen of Molière, and his imitators. The 17th century saw first those witty and philosophic comedies which still delight the public: Molière's *Le Misanthrope, L'Avare, Le Bourgeois Gentilhomme, Les Femmes savantes, Le Malade imaginaire, Les Precieuses ridicules,* and *Tartuffe.*

Drama, French, 18th century. French tragedy came upon lean times in the 18th century despite the efforts of Crébillon the elder, and Voltaire in *Zaire* continued the classic tradition. Chief contributors to comedy of the period were: the satirist, Lesage; Marivaux, the light wit of those lines occasioned the word "marivaudage"; Destouches and de la Chaussée who wrung tears out of the audience with their *comédie larmoyante;* Diderot, who stressed in his *tragedie bourgeois* a revulsion from the idea that tragedy should be concerned only with the high-born; and Beaumarchais. Beaumarchais' comedies, *Barbier de Séville* and *Mariage de Figaro,* animated in characterization, brilliant in dialogue, and very gay, are the high peaks of the era.

Drama, French, 18th century, French Revolution. There had been plays up to the Revolution expressing revolutionary sentiments. With the first political violence, "appropriate" plays were evident, but nothing of lasting importance. There was a sudden lack of any real theatre activity. *Charles IX* by Chenier was given in 1789 at the Comédie Française and was a tremendous success, bringing Talma to the fore. Art was not considered timely, and the drama was burdened with many prohibitions. Plays with titles of nobility in them could not be produced. *Monsieur* and *Madame* were not to be spoken. Two considerable collections of these revolutionary dramas, many of which were little more than tracts, are to be found in libraries, at the Bibliothèque de la Ville de Paris and the New York Public Library.

Drama, French, 19th century. In 1829 romantic drama, as best represented by Alexandre Dumas *père* (*Henri III et sa Cour*) and Alfred de Vigny (*Othello*), supplanted classical tragedy as the major force in the theatre. The romantic school was carried to its most brilliant success with the production of Victor Hugo's *Hernani* at the Comédie-Française in 1830. This latter, with Hugo's *Ruy Blas* established the highest peak of the romantic style. The comedy of this period is best represented by pieces like *On ne badine pas avec l'amour* and *Il faut qu'une porte soit ouverte ou fermée,* by Alfred de Musset; *Les Demoiselles de Saint-Cyr* by Dumas *pere;* and *Le verre d'eau* by Scribe, who originated the "well made" play—the play of mechanical perfection, written by studied formula. In 1843 there was a reaction against the violence and sensationalism of the romantic school, led by Ponsard with his *Lucrèce,* which play helped to establish the *école du bon sens.* The foremost dramatists of the latter half of the 19th century are: Émile Augier, with plays such as *Maître Guérin* and *Les Fourchambault;* Alexandre Dumas *fils,* with his famous *La Dame aux Camélias;* Victorien Sardou, with his two masterpieces, *Patrie* and *La Haine;* Pailleron, with his comedy of manners, an example of which is *Le Monde où l'on s'ennuie;* François Coppée, with his historical plays like *Les Jacobites;* Edmond Rostand, with his celebrated heroic tragi-comedy, *Cyrano de Bergerac.*

Drama, French, 20th century. The dramatic fare in France during the last 20 years can be roughly classified into five types: (1) the psychological drama together with the comedy of manners, as typified by such plays as *Aimer* by Paul Géraldy; *La prisonnière* by Edouard Bourdet; *Topaze* by Marcel Pagnol; *Le paquebot Tenacity* by Charles Vildrac; *Tovarich* by Jacques Deval; (2) modern tragedy and drama, as instanced by a work like *Le tombeau sous l'Arc de Triomphe* by Paul Raynal; (3) symbolical plays and plays of ideas, such as *Les ratés* by Lenormand; *Maya* by Gantillon; *Amphitryon 38* by Giraudoux; *Donogoo,* by Romains; (4) light comedy and vaudeville, exemplified by plays like *Je t'aime*—or, indeed, most of the works of Sacha Guitry, *La huitième femme de Barbe Bleue* by

Alfred Avoir; (5) plays in verse, such as *Jeanne d'Arc* by François Porche. The once popular "well-made" play has become completely outmoded.

Drama, German, 17th-18th century. Not until the second decade of the 18th century did German drama begin to assume a form and national character, the 17th century seeing mainly horror pieces and comic improvisations with Hans Wurst and Pickelhaering (modeled after the English clown) cracking ribald jokes. Caroline Neuber, head of a Leipsig theatre company, and the great G. E. Lessing did heroic service for serious drama at the start of the 18th century, she by her efforts to differentiate comedy and tragedy, and to suppress the harlequinade type of play; he by his own plays and his criticisms in the *Hamburgische Dramaturgie.* The golden names in German drama of the period, besides Lessing, are Goethe, for his choice of a German subject in *Goetz von Berlichingen,* his *Faust, Iphigenia and Tasso;* Schiller for his Wallenstein trilogy and *Wilhelm Tell;* and von Kotzebue for his domestic drama and comedy. The phrase *sturm und drang,* associated with the period, originated as the title of a play by von Klinger.

Drama, German, 19th century. With the rise of Goethe and Schiller in the 18th century German romanticism had come into its own. The literary school to which it gave rise originated in a philosophical movement which was a reaction against materialism and rationalism. This movement was founded by August Wilhelm, Friedrich von Schlegel and Ludwig Tieck and bore a dominant concern with esthetics and a belief in subjectivism, nature, solitude and mysticism. Romanticism, as a literary school, produced but two important dramatists: Heinrich von Kleist and Franz Grillparzer. The next literary movement of any considerable significance was not to appear until about 1880, with the advent of naturalism. Naturalism was the depiction of material life, especially that of the middle and lower classes, and was marked by literalness of observation with a corresponding mistrust of spiritual or mystical values. Ibsen was the predominant force in the German naturalist school. As his plays were translated into German as early as 1872 and were well-known on German and Austrian stages, every serious dramatist in the country began to show traces of his influence. Other powerful influences were felt in the plays and novels of Björnson, Balzac, Flaubert, Gogol, Turgeniev, Dostoievski and Tolstoi.

Drama, German, 20th century to the First World War. The theatrical literature of the early 20th century in Germany was dominated by naturalism, which was formulated in the 1890's. Although as a style it was frequently found wanting, it gave impetus to the genius of Gerhart Hauptmann, probably the greatest single dramatist of the whole modern period in Germany and the most powerful writing influence in its theatre. It was Hauptmann who carried the banner of the social drama in Germany even as Ibsen did in Norway. His *Weavers,* perhaps his greatest masterpiece, was a serious realistic study of the working class and carried powerful socialistic implications. Hauptmann also defended the progressivism of such men as Haeckel in his *Lonely Lives.* He was, with all his preoccupation with material and sociological ideas, not innocent of mysticism, an example of which is to be found in his dreamplay, *The Assumption of Hannele*. He also authored the fantastic *The Sunken Bell*. Next in importance to Hauptmann probably comes Wedekind, with his strenuous, frequently overwrought treatment of sexual themes. Here, too, are there social implications, but the emphasis and approach are different, marked as they are by a preoccupation with the physical to an almost total distrust of the spirit and soul. His *Erdgeist* is typical: the ruin of an entire generation of men by the unscrupulousness of a single woman. Others of his plays are: *Lulu* and *Marquis von Keith*. Following Wedekind came Sorge, who was a herald of the coming expressionism. In such plays as *Der Bettler* fantasy is predominant, possessing a weird power indicative of the author's individualistic style. Hasenclever's *Der Sohn* is a perfect example of expressionism, combining a sense, if not an experience, of revolution with some of Wedekind's tempestuousness, Hofmannsthal's lyricism, Strindberg's mystical imaginativeness and Sorge's ebullience. Perhaps the most popular, certainly the most frequently performed dramatist of this period was George Kaiser, who wrote a great number of plays. He soon became the leading exponent of expressionism, though he evidenced a wide variety of influences, ranging from inept imitations of Ibsen and Wedekind to echoes even of Maeterlinck. His most famous plays are probably *Gas* and *Von Morgen bis Mitternacht*. Among other less successful expounders of the expressionist drama were: Essig, Bronnen and Jahn. The last expressionist of the pre-War period was Kornfeld with spiritual plays such as *Die Verfuehrung*.

Drama, German, since the First World War and before National Socialism. Expressionism had left a heavy mark on the dramatists who were emerging during the period from 1917-20, and the War had served to quicken the social pulse to such a point as to abet the progress of Communism in the drama. The foremost representative of the remaining expressionism and the new Communism was Ernst Toller. His *Wandlung* was his first notable play. Here is to be found an absolute expressionism coupled with a social philosophy more journalistically than dramatically effective. In *Hoppla, Wir Leben,* Toller stylistically interpreted the seven years following the War. His *Feuer aus den Kesseln* was a depiction of the mutiny of the German navy in 1917. His most famous play is probably his allegorical revolutionary drama, *Masse Mensch*. He is also well known for his political satire, *No More Peace!* Perhaps the most skilful representative of the old expressionism conjoining with the new political tendencies in the drama was Bert Brecht. His *Trommeln in der Nacht* was an indictment of war profiteers, and served to acquaint the public with a sensuous and lyrical, through passionate and arrogant, talent. He is best known for his *Dreigroschenoper,* which was a derivation from Gay's *Beggar's Opera* and was enhanced by a musical score by Kurt Weill. In *Die Massnahme* Brecht evidenced his espousal of Communism. The most important remaining dramatist is Ernst Barlach. Plays such as *Der Blaue Boll* embodied a spirituality rising by force of will from the limitations of the body.

Drama, German, under National Socialism. Nothing can be said of German literature of the present day. No single author of importance has emerged.

Drama, Greek, ancient. The history of all the dramatic writings of the western world begins with the 5th and 6th centuries B.C. in Greece. Tragedy had its source in the choral ode known as the *dithyramb* which a group sang in honor of Dionysos at the festivals of this wine god. These choral odes were composed especially for the occasion and were later expanded into a dramatic form comprising the chorus and leader and called the "goat song" (either because of the sacrifice of a goat during the ceremony, or because a goat was given as a prize to the composer of the dithyramb, or because of the goat skins worn by the chorus), from which the word *tragedy* was derived. In the middle of the 6th century B.C., Thespis, winner of the first tragedy award, introduced the actor as such, into the dithyramb. This actor engaged in dialogue with the leader, and thus began the spoken drama. Ten years after this innovation the first great dramatist of all time, Aeschylus, was born. It was he who introduced a second actor into tragedy, but, though he began the minimizing of the chorus as a dramatic factor, it remained for Sophocles and Euripides to subordinate it to dramatic action and individual speech and to prepare its final extinction. His earliest works were composed to a great extent of long lyric speeches assigned principally to the chorus in which action is described rather than performed. It was a tradition for tragic poets to write plays in a series of three and Aeschylus was no exception. His works are characterized by an exalted religious mood and his human characters by a regal dignity. *The Suppliants* is his first known tragedy, and shows the static influence of the dithyramb with the long declamations and the slow movement of what little action there is. *Prometheus Bound,* relating of the wrath of the gods at the giving of fire to humans, is still static, but the conflict is implicit in the theme and helps to enliven the lengthy speeches. In *Agamemnon,* however, Aeschylus attained a genuinely theatrical composition, with a thoroughly delineated plot and a sense of suspense created through impending doom. This was the first play of the *Oresteia* trilogy and is still considered by many critics his great masterpiece. Sophocles was a more skilled technician than Aeschylus and was the second great dramatist of ancient Greece. It was he who introduced a third actor into tragedy and thus carried forward the torch of drama which was some day to burst into a multi-tongued flame. Sophocles wrote of the nobility of men. His plays show an increase in dramatic intensity over those of Aeschylus as well as a vaster freedom of dialogue. His greatest tragedy was probably *Oedipus Rex,* the story of a man's incestuous (though unwitting) love for his mother, in which are depicted human beings at the mercy of fate. Beside this must be placed his *Antigone,* a play with wise political overtones. The third great dramatist of the period was Euripides. If, as Aristotle says, Sophocles paints men as they should be, Euripides surely paints men as they are. In this and other senses, such as his radical questioning of the gods, his warmth of sympathy with his characters, Euripides was the first modern. It was Euripides who reduced the chorus to a thoroughly subordinate capacity and humanized the drama with his dominant individualism. He deified also the Aristotelian unity of action by daring to write an unheard of amalgam of tragedy and comedy, called today tragi-comedy, his *Alcestis.* His *Trojan Women* was an indictment of war. His *Hippolytus* was a startling (for its time) depiction of an illicit love. His *Medea* was a story of hatred and revenge so strong as to result in a mother's murdering her own children. Among others of his better known plays are: *Ion;* the *Iphigenia* tragedies; *Electra,* which has served as a basis for the Strauss opera and the 20th century O'Neill *Mourning Becomes Electra;* and *The Bacchae.* The great philosopher Aristotle came forward with the first and only contemporary study of the ancient Greek drama, the *Poetics.* This defined tragedy and comedy and formulated the laws of the three unities. Comedy was an outgrowth of the *comus,* or festive procession in honor of Dionysos, in which performers disguised as birds and animals wound their way through the streets of the town to the temple. The back-chat between the performers and the onlookers is said to be the real beginning of comic dialogue. In comedy, first called "village song," the chorus was used. The earliest writers of comedy were Cratinus and Eupolis, and even in works as primitive as theirs, comedy came to serve a purpose, such as political satire, travesty on public figures, etc. The first great comic dramatist was Aristophanes, who was the chief representative of "Old Comedy." This form was specifically personal in its references and was characterized by a bawdiness, a vitriolic carcicature and lusty buffoonery. Aristophanes' comedies are marked by a brilliant wit and a savage parody on a wide variety of public figures. *The Wasps* is a political satire, centering on the Athenian jury system. In *The Frogs* he pillories certain literary contemporaries, among them Euripides. His *Lysistrata* was a bawdy and comic protest against war. Of "Middle Comedy," whose main characteristics comprised a parody of old mythology, character sketches in place of personal and political satire, caricature of contemporary manners, and criticism of such schools of philosophy as the Platonists and the Pythagoreans, Antiphanes (about whom, and whose plays, little is known) was the foremost exponent, seconded by Alexis. The third type of comic drama of the times, "New Comedy," was impersonal in its satire and attacked types rather than specific individuals. Menander, Philemon, and Diphilus were the chief exponents of this form. Only fragments of the many plays written by this triumvirate have come down to us. Menander was an imitator of Euripides and was paid a like tribute by Plautus and Terence in having them, in their turn draw upon his works.

Drama, grotesque. A play that supersedes the bounds of strict realism through affinities with the fantastic or supernatural. Pirandello's *Six Characters in Search of an Author* is an example of one kind of grotesque play.

Drama, Hebrew. According to the Bible, Hebrew drama began with ceremonial dances. *The Book of Job* and *The Songs of Solomon* may be considered to be long dramatic poems in dialogue form. The latter, too, may be a processional rather than designed for stage presentation. Job is more dramatic in structure and deals with a man and the drama of his soul. "In the body of the work," Sheldon Cheney says, "the author has written down what remains in translation, one of the finest literary dramas of all times."

Drama, Hindu. Hindu drama is the most interesting branch of Hindu literature. No other ancient people, except the Greeks, has brought forth anything so admirable in this department. Its invention is attributed to Brahma who commanded the heavenly architect to build the first playhouse so that the sage Bharata could produce his plays. Bharata is thus the father of the Hindu drama, and the word "bharata" gradually became one of the terms for "actor." Dances combined with gestures and speech were performed before the gods by attendants of Indra's heaven; the god Siva added two new styles of dancing.

Dramatic dialogues occur in Hindu literature as early as the hymns of the *Rigveda,* which dates about 1500 B.C. It is quite possible that India had a well-developed drama even before the Greeks, though not much is known of this early period. It appears to have been a perfectly indigenous creation, a growth through the union of the lyric with the epic recitations, and independent of Greece, Persia or China. It was firmly established when some Greek influence crept in, and it had already passed into its decline when Mohammedan forms arrived. The most glorious period of Hindu drama is the fourth to the ninth century, and the decline begins before the drama of modern Europe arose.

Hindu drama selects its subjects from the rich mythology and legend of the country. But whether the drama represents the legends of the gods or the simple circumstances of ordinary life, whether it describes allegorical or historical subjects, it bears always the same character of its origin and of its tendency. Simplicity of plot, unity of episodes and purity of language unite in its formation. Prose and verse, the serious and the comic, pantomime, dancing, music and song intermingle in its presentation. Hindu verse has a particular tendency to the didactic style, embodying religious and historical knowledge, dipicting all in enchanting colors and adorning everything with all the magnificence of language and sentiment.

There are over 500 plays extant in Sanskrit, about 100 in Tamil and some in other vernaculars. The literature of India is highly polyglot, including works in Sanskrit, Prakrit, Pali, Bengali, Tibetan, Pahlavi, Arabic, Persian, Tamil, Telugu, Kanarese and Malayālam. The Indian plays of greatest merit, such as Kalidasa's and Shudraka's, are notable for their graceful blending of poetry and prose, for their life-like characterizations and sophisticated gentility. In contrast to the early Greek dramas, they shun violence, ending always upon a happy note. They were written for presentation before aristocratic audiences, both sexes participating in the performance. Since the themes were drawn largely from epic poetry, they frequently centered in the legends of Rama and Krishna, the two most celebrated incarnations of Vishnu: Rama is the seventh incarnation and Krishna the last.

The history of Hindu dramatic literature can be divided into definite periods:

THE EPIC PERIOD (500 B.C.-320 A.D.), during which were produced the two great epic poems, *Mahabharata* and *Ramayana,* the former some eight times larger than the *Iliad* and *Odyssey* combined and written in the fifth or fourth century B.C., while the latter was composed in the third century B.C. These are the two great source books of the Hindu dramatists. Also in this period is the earliest dramatist of whose work specimens are extant. He is Ashvaghosha, a Buddhist teacher who lived in the second century A.D. Only parts of three of his plays are known. One of them is *Shāriputra-prakarana.* The story, in nine acts, concerns the young Shariputra and his friend Maudgályayana who become deeply impressed with and finally converted to Buddhism in the presence of the Budda himself.

THE CLASSIC PERIOD (320-800), includes the work of the greatest masters of the Hindu drama. Only about twenty-five plays of this period are in existence today. The earliest group of thirteen (recently discovered and published in 1912), are attributed to Bhasa. Kalidasa, who is thought to have lived about 400, mentions in his play *Mālavikā and Agnimitra,* the merits of Bhasa as a playwright. Therefore Bhasa is earlier than Kalidasa and probably wrote about 350. Most of Bhasa's plays are based on epic themes. *Bālacharita* depicts the exploits of the young god Krishna who strives against and overcomes enemies. The only Bhasa play which is a drama of domestic life is *Daridra-chārudatta* (*The Poor Charudatta*), which seems to be an early version of *The Little Clay Cart.* But Bhasa's plays are inferior to Kalidasa's three plays. Kalidasa, the Hindu Shakespeare, has been called by his countrymen the Bridegroom of Poetry. According to Hindu tradition, he is reputed to have been one of the "nine gems" of the court of King Vikrama at Ujjain in the first century B.C., but Western scholars believe that he lived about 400 A.D. Kalidasa's *Shakuntala* is the masterpiece of Hindu dramatic literature. It aroused the interest of literary Europe and an enthusiastic panegyric from Goethe when it was first translated by Sir William Jones in 1789. Goethe wrote:

> "Spring's blossoms, Autumn's harvest-gold
> In one large word wouldst thou enfold?
> All that delights and satisfies
> In single phrase wouldst thou comprise?
> I "Shakuntala" name, and there
> At once speak all that's good and fair."

Shakuntala, or *The Fatal Ring,* a seven act love-idyll, takes its plot from the first book of the *Mahabharata.* (See *Shakuntala.*) Kalidasa's language is harmonious and elevated in all his compositions, uniting grace and tenderness with grandeur and sublimity.

Kalidasa's second drama, *Vikrama and Urvashī,* known as *The Hero and the Nymph,* is inferior to *Shakuntala,* though it possesses one act of incomparable loveliness. It is a five act dramatic and romantic episode of the rescue of a nymph by the heroic king with whom she falls deeply in love. This play was translated in 1827 by H. H. Wilson, and its chief interest lies in the fact that it greatly influenced the development of the Hindu theatre. Less important is Kalidasa's third play, *Mālavikā and Agnimitra,* which may have been written by the dramatist in his youth. The story concerns King Agnamitra's love for *Mālavikā,* a maiden in waiting to one of his two queens. The mistress, infuriated, imprisons Mālavikā, but the smitten king marries the girl when it is discovered that she is a princess in disguise and the queens finally consent to the match, though reluctantly. The plot is based on a Shunga dynasty story.

The charming *Meghadutā,* or *The Cloud Messenger,* also by Kalidasa, is unsurpassed in beauty of sentiment by any European poet. Although it is a lyrical monologue rather than a drama, it has often been recited on the stage in India. The story deals with a cloud which is made the envoy of an absent lover to his distant sweetheart. The poem is made up of 115 four-line stanzas. *Meghadutā* affords the poet the opportunity of describing the lands over which the cloud must sail to reach its destination. Schiller employed the same device in one of his poems. *Meghaduta* is a great lyric expression of delight in nature.

Mrichhakatika (*The Little Clay Cart* or *The Toy Cart*), is usually attributed to a legendary King Shudraka, who is supposed to have lived in the sixth century, but may have been written by a court poet, Dandin. *The Little Clay Court,* a drama of social life in ten acts, is a strikingly beautiful and impressive play which has been successfully presented in the Western theatre. (See *The Little Clay Cart*.)

To Shri-Harshadeva (606-648), a king of northern India, are ascribed three plays of considerable merit. *Ratnavali* (*The Pearl Necklace*), is a romantic piece resembling Kalidasa's *Malavika* and *Agnimitra* in plot. It tells the story of King Udayana, a legendary hero, who falls in love with an attendant of the queen. The girl is really the princess *Ratnavali*. An escaped parrot plays an important part in the drama when he repeats the princess' confession of love in the king's presence. Shri-Harshadeva's second drama is called *Priyadarsika* (*The Lost Princess*). His best known play is *Nagananda*, a *nataka,* or "dance drama," in five acts. Buddhistic in character, it tells how the hero Jimutavahana, a Boddhisattva, gives himself up to be devoured by the Garuda, a mythical vulture, in order to save the Naga, or "serpent race," which has a snake for its tribe totem. In the last act, however, the hero is miraculously restored to life, and the Nagas rejoice. The question of the authorship of this play has often been discussed. There are English, French, Italian, Swedish and German translations of Shri-Harshadeva's three dramas. Shri-Harshadeva is fond of descriptions in the conventional manner. His language is classical and precise; his speech and thought figures show restraint and good taste.

Bhavabhuti, a Brahman by birth who flourished during the late 7th century and early 8th, was called by his contemporaries the Sweet Speaking. He was the author of many dramas of distinguished merit which rank next to those of Kalidasa, though his language is more artificial, rule-bound and humorless. It is judged that he was a native of south Central India and that he spent part of his life in Ujjain. Only three of his plays have survived. *Mahavira-charita* (*The Story of the Great Hero*), a dramatic rendering of the *Ramayana,* in seven acts, from the viewpoint that Ravana has undertaken to destroy Rama rather than the reverse. The *Uttararama-charita* (*The Later Story of Rama*), which is a sequel to the *Mahavira-charita. Malati and Madhava* is a powerful melodrama which has been called the Indian *Romeo and Juliet. Malati and Madhava* (known as *The Stolen Marriage*), however, differs from Shakespeare's play in that the lovers were promised to one another by their parents from birth, and that the play has, after all, a happy ending. It is written in ten acts and is particularly interesting because of the use of a "play within a play" as a by-plot and a kind of foil to the main action. Winternitz calls Bhavabhuti "der Sprachgewaltigsten unter den indischen Dichtern." Bhavabhuti has been reproached for his over-elaborate and fantastic style and for his sentimental and lengthy descriptions.

The dramatist Bhatta Narayana (about 850, though some place him earlier than 800), is known through one six act drama, *Venisamhara* (*The Binding of the Braid*

of Hair), a theme taken from the *Mahabharata* wherein Draupadi, after a great
gambling match, is dragged by the hair by one of the Kauravas. This play is a work
marred by too much detail and conventionalization.

Of greater interest is Vishakhadatta's *Mudrārākshasha* (*The Signet of Rakshasha*), and the only known work by him. Vishākhadatta probably lived in the 9th
century, and his drama is an historical one of political intrigue dealing with the efforts
of the famous minister Chanakya to win over Rakshasha, the minister of the Nandas,
to the cause of Chandragupta who thus founds a dynasty.

POST-CLASSIC PERIOD (800-1000). Sanskrit had long ceased to be generally
spoken, but continued to survive as the language of scholars and the nobility. In the
early 9th century, Murari wrote his lone surviving play, *Anargharāghava,* a hyper-
bolical work in seven acts dealing with the favorite story of Rama, Sītā and Rāvana.

At about the end of the 9th century, Rājashekhara left four plays. Bālarā māyana
is another Rāma play, ten acts long. Bālabhārata tells the story of Draupadi and the
great gambling scene; but is only two acts, and seems to be incomplete. *Karpūramanjāri* (*The Cluster of Camphor Blossoms*), is a four act love story in which a Kuntala
princess is the heroine. This play is the only example extant of a *sattaka* (minor
heroic comedy), written entirely in Prakrit. Rajashekhara's fourth play is *Viddhās-
halabhanjikā,* also in four acts and closely resembling the plot of *Karpūramanjāri*.
The story deals with King Vidyadharamalla's love for the statue (*shalabhanjikā*) he
beholds in a gallery. The statue corresponds to a living woman who, though at first
a slave, is soon discovered to be a fitting bride for the king.

Rajashekhara's work is light and graceful. He seems to have been born in the
Deccan near Vidarbha and Kuntala, whence he came to the court of Mahendrapala,
King of Kanauj. He was a Brahman, and his wife, Avantisundari, was a Rajput
princess.

In the 10th century, Kshemīshvara wrote *Chandakaushika* (*The Angry Kau-
shika*), which concerns the story of an irascible sage who pronounces a curse upon
King Harishchandra who had unwittingly offended him. The king's misfortune
follows, during which he loses his realm, his wife and his child, but his patience
proves inexhaustible; he seems to be the Job of Hindu drama. Ultimately, through
divine intervention, all ends happily. Kshemīshvara also wrote *Naishadhānanda,* a
dramatic treatment of the story of Nala, a young prince who has a John Alden role
to play. The plot is taken from one of the episodes of the *Mahabharata*.

THE PERIOD OF DECLINE (1000-1300). The beginning of this period coincides
roughly with a series of Mohammedan invasions of India. Very early in the 11th century, Damodaramishra wrote the *Hanumānnātaka* or *Mahā-nātaka* (*The Great
Play*), which is a long and rambling monstrosity in fourteen acts dealing with the
story of Hanuman, the monkey god.

Krishnamishra's remarkable allegorical drama, *Prabodha-chandrodaya* (*Rise of
the Moon of Intellect*), written about 1100, is a glorification of the cult of Vishnu.
The six act plot concerns the circumstances of the struggle against vice and the final
triumph of justice. It is like an old English morality play, with allegorical characters
such as King Error, King Reason, Religion, Revelation, Confusion, Exegesis, Will,
etc.

This style of drama had mostly inferior followers. For the most part, the output had now become little more than reworking of old themes, artificiality of manner increasingly replacing originality of thought. There is a noticeable affected, over-elaborate style; and most of the works are tediously narrative and descriptive.

During the 12th century, Jayadeva wrote *Gita-govinda* (*The Song of the Divine Herdsman*). This long lyric poem has been called the Indian Song of Songs (Song of Solomon). Krishna represents the human soul and Radha the spirit of the intellect which frees him from the bonds of his material senses. This work is not a true drama, but it is in its form a transition between pure lyric and pure drama; really a primitive type of play in which three characters engage in lyrical monologues.

THE MODERN PERIOD (1300 onward), exhibits plays which deal chiefly with the legend of Krishna. The latest in this style is the play *Chitra-yajna,* written about 1820. Its dialogue is not complete, and this is supplemented by the actors in much the same way as in Italian improvised comedy. Besides these works are farces of often gross and indelicate humor.

During the latter part of the 19th century, the Indian theatre felt the influence of Western civilization, and an effort was made to compose plays of modern life. However, the results were not extraordinary. Today the tendency is to create a drama which will combine the classic and spiritual beauty of ancient India with modern social ideals, as in the work of Rabindranath Tagore. (See *Rabindranath Tagore.*)

About 1894, Rabindranath Tagore wrote *Chitra,* a truly great drama. *Chitra* was published in English in 1916. In 1910, *Rājā,* a profoundly moving drama was written. *Rājā* was published in English, in 1914, as *The King of the Dark Chamber.* Tagore published *The Cycle of Spring* in 1917.

The Hindu drama aimed at awakening sentiment and appealed to the cultured minority who were able to understand the Sanskrit in which most plays were written and could appreciate the Brahmanical sentiments expressed.

The collective term for dramas is *rūpaka* (or *visible form*); the minor *rūpakas* are called *uparupakas;* the highest type is the *nātaka,* which always treated of cele-brated subjects such as heroism and love, and the hero is always a god, a demigod or a king. The *prakaranas* (*e.g., The Little Clay Cart; Malati and Madhava*), are less elevated *natakas,* their stories being drawn from domestic life. Among the kinds of *uparupakas* are the trotaka (*e.g.* Vikrama and Urvashi), in which the characters are part human and part divine; the *bhāna,* a monologue of low life; and the *praha-sana,* a kind of farce.

There is no lack of dramatic theory in India. The sage, Bharata, the legendary inventor of the drama, was likewise revered as the father of dramatic criticism. Com-mentators forever cite his supposed *sūtras* or aphorisms. By the 10th century dramatic criticism had reached an advanced point—the *Dasarūpa* distinctly differentiates ten main forms of drama. Other critical works followed, most of them revealing a liking for hair-splitting. The types of heroines which have been differentiated number 384.

Unity of Action is mostly not observed; the story of the play is sometimes carried on through the recitations of a Chorus of actors or "interpreters." *Unity of Time* is such that the duration of action is usually limited to a single year. *Unity of Place* is

unknown because of the virtual abscence of scenery, since the plays were performed
in the palace halls or open inner courts. Hence, scenery is usually indicated in the
text of the play by the performer's speech and action.

There were strict conventions for both dramatist and actor—the hero could be
one of forty-eight types, for instance. Some other rules of dramaturgy are: (1) The
title of a play must be formed by compounding the names of hero and heroine; (2)
The scene must be laid in India; (3) The hero shall appear in every act; (4) The
heroine may be a lady of good family or a courtesan, or the two may share the honors,
providing they do not meet; (5) It is advised that the drama be "full of rascals";
(6) The erotic sentiment should dominate; (7) The ending must be happy, and all
deeply tragical incidents or conclusions are forbidden.

Not only must a play end happily, but biting, scratching, kissing, eating and sleeping are excluded. Yet such rules are sometimes broken as at the end of the love scene
in the third act of *Shakuntala* when the hero is about to act "the part of the bee to the
honey of the heroine's lips." But later writers are less refined.

Music is a most important part of the Hindu drama. According to the ancient
Hindu belief, all arts were bestowed upon man by the various gods: Siva gave the
dance, and music was the gift of Brahma. The hymns of the *Rigveda* (about 1500
B.C.) were intended to be sung to music.

Viewing a modern production of an ancient Hindu play usually adds nothing to
one's knowledge of the classical Indian theatre. The plays are not even presented in
Sanskrit.

Hindu plays usually open after a benediction and a prologue in which the manager and an actor or two discuss the play to follow. The plays are divided into acts
and scenes. Seven is the common number of acts; some have as many as fourteen.
Thus the higher class of Hindu play is about as long as an Aeschylus trilogy. Farces
are only two acts long, and close with a prayer. Recognition of lost loved ones—particularly recognition between parents and children—frequently gives rise to scenes of
pathos rivaling Euripedes (*e.g. Shakuntala; Uttararama-charita*). The device of a
"play within a play" is employed with great success by that Master of Eloquence,
Bhavabhuti.

Indian drama indicates freer relations between the sexes than is found in the
Mohammedan plays which were introduced into India. Male characters are usually
drawn with considerable skill. The courtesan is not a low type but one comparable to
the Greek *hetaerae.* Among the lesser characters there are the *vita,* or parasite, and
the *vidushaka,* the buffoon, always a Brahman or the pupil of a Brahman (the priestly
cast came in for their share of ridicule), and who jokes pointlessly and harmlessly,
acting as a foil and contrast to the king or prince.

Only the principal characters speak in Sanskrit; women and the less important
characters use Prakrit, more or less refined according to their rank. Whatever may
offend propriety, whatever may produce an unwholesome excitement is excluded.
Propriety of costume seems always to have been observed. The introduction of a
parasite or a buffoon on stage is usually opened by an apologue, or fable containing
a moral, and always concluded with a prayer.

Actors' companies were common in India quite early in the theatre's history. The player's social status shows a gradual rise, and the actor later enjoyed a widespread reputation. The managers or directors were highly-cultured Brahmans.

Indian drama has been the entertainment of the literary and aristocratic classes; hence, it was never a truly national drama. Its ethics are lofty; its pathos blends with resignation; its humor is delicate; its diction eloquent and figurative; its poetry is fanciful and flowery and fragile, replenishing itself from a seemingly inexhaustible garden, yet able to depict admirably the grander aspects of nature.

The charm of *Shakuntala,* for instance, lies in the exquisite description of natural scenery and the atmosphere of religious calm, austere and serene, which is typical of the hermit life of India. To the supernatural and to Fate is sometimes ascribed a power to which gods and mortals must bow. Thus the central action of *Shakuntala* hinges on the fact that the heroine, absorbed in thoughts of love, neglects to welcome with due respect a great holy man. He blights her with a curse which results in all the unhappiness of the drama, and which is only ended by the intervention of a more powerful being. Thus the characters are reduced to mere shadow creations, delicate as arabesques and tinted light as porcelain. Humanity is dwarfed and its powers rendered inoperative by the host of supernatural creatures that control its destiny.

The literary merit of Kalidasa's work is unquestioned. Hindu verse, at its best, is of great idyllic beauty. It is remarkably exquisite in coloring; its fancy is rich and luxuriant, its feelings true and tender. Verses from the players were often published apart for a widespread audience. The Hindu drama depended upon its literary qualities as well as on familiar themes of the divine for success, clothing itself in a language always ornate and tropical, where, as Goethe expressed it, words became allusions, allusions similes and similes metaphors.

Drama, humanist. Humanism was the literary movement of the late Middle Ages and the Renaissance whose object was the revival of pagan learning of classical antiquity. English drama at this time was being influenced by foreign drama and literature. The plays show attempts at imitation or translation of the humanists' writings in Latin and in English. Nicholas Grimwald produced *Christus Redivivus* in 1543. *A Briefe Comedy or Enterlude of Johan Baptystes* in 1577, *Archipropheta* in 1547 and *Kynge Johan,* written before 1548, are all examples of the humanist drama in England.

Drama, Hungarian. Directly after the Armistice, and for several years following, social themes were the predominating fashion. The best known playwrights are: Herczeg, with his plays that united past and present, used historical material in a polished esthetic style, and demonstrated a spiritual ideology; Ferenc Molnar, the Hungarian dramatist best known abroad, with his scintillating comedies like *The Guardsman,* his fable play *Liliom* and his plays of abstraction such as *Everyone;* Moricz, a novelist as well, with his plays of peasant life. Other dramatists: Zilahy, Bibó, Alexander Brody, Szomory, Melchior Lengyel, Alexander Hunyadi, Lazlo Bus-Fekete, Lazlo Fodar.

Drama, Italian, commedia dell'arte. As the *commedia dell'arte* was not a written but an improvised form there exists no body of plays by which we might judge the actual skill in the wording of lines or the delineation of plot. It is, however, generally understood that the comedies of this theatre were lusty, exuberant, consistently bawdy pieces to be put, perhaps, on a level with the humor of our latter-day vaudeville and burlesque. In them, nevertheless, are agreed to be the sources from which emerged many of the qualities of the infinitely more polished literate comedies of Molière and Goldoni.

See also *Commedia dell' Arte.*

Drama, Italian, 15-16th centuries. See *Drama, Italian, commedia dell'arte; Commedia dell' Arte.*

Drama, Italian, 17th and 18th centuries. Tragedy in Italy was imitative of the French strict classicism in pattern. The subjects, generally historical, were treated without regard to history; remote scenes, Spain and Asia, were the vogue. The *commedia dell' arte* improvised dialogue between *Harlequin* and other stock characters, charmed the public both in Italy and in Paris (where an Italian troupe introduced it). But the rapid descent of the *commedia dell'arte* to a more scandalous than literary plane brought a violent reaction.

The 18th century saw the development of comedy upon classical models, by G. B. della Porta, and G. A. Cicognini; the flowering of romantic comedy under those two quite opposite rivals, Goldoni, 1707-1793, who drew his characters from middle-class life and let them speak in Venetian vernacular rather than in literary phrases; and C. Gozzi, 1722-1806, who "rescued" comedy from the middle-class subjects by reviving masked comedy without its former obscenity. *Opera bouffe* and *opera serio,* which had grown out of efforts to put on Greek plays with musical accompaniment and had changed to a native Italian invention, was popular at home and greatly imitated abroad.

Drama, Italian, 19th century. The great acting of Salvini inspired Niccolini's *Arnaldo da Brescia,* Morelli's *l'Arduino d'Ivrea,* Giacometti's *Michelangelo* and *Sophocles,* D'Aste's *Moses* and *Samson.* All of these plays depicted "a champion of a humanity with his head in the clouds."

Realism received from the 19th century Italian theatre little more than a struggling start. The quieter well-made play was slight competition to the established romantic drama which held its supremacy in Italy long after realism and naturalism reigned in Europe. The chief representative of the romantic school was Manzoni who followed in the footsteps of Alfieri as a powerful advocate of freedom, but broke from the bonds of formalism in play form. The *Countess of Carmagnola,* 1819, and *Adelchi,* 1822, added depth of character to the usual typed roles but the dialogue was still heavy with long declamatory speeches.

Comedies genuinely represented Italian life and manners. They held to Goldonian principles, even when built on imitation of French models. Dialect dramas became more popular. Ferrari's comedies in Modenese (*La Medicina d'una ragazza amma-*

lata and *Il Codicillo dello Zio Venanzio*) were the most popular and are still being performed in Italy. His best play, *Goldoni,* traced the life of the great playwright and brought a vivid picture of Venetian life of the 18th century. Ferrari's later plays stressed social conditions and psychological problems, but he rarely tried to solve these problems. *Il Ricicolo, Il Duello* and *Il Suicidio* are too superficial to measure up to the realism in the dramas of Giacosa.

There was no common viewpoint, moral standard or aesthetic preparation in divided Italy to bring to flower a school of realistic writers. The transition period between the old and the new drama was marked by Giacosa who was influenced by Becque and Augier to use material drawn from contemporary life. He was soon recognized as the chief exponent of the naturalistic school in Italy. *Luise,* 1883, was his first problem play. It had been preceded by the idyllic verse-play *A Game of Chess,* 1871, which established the craftsmanship of Giacosa.

The close of the century showed the interest in drama divided into two camps: the romantics and the naturalists, who came to be called Verists. Praga was iconoclastic, affecting disbelief in goodness, purity and faithfulness in his plays *The Enamoured Woman* and *The Ideal Wife.* Vega, author of *Cavalleria Rusticana, In the Porter's Lodge* and *The Fox Hunt,* wrote with power and honesty on the questions of lust and violence. Romanticism was strengthened by D'Annunzio's attempt to force the fashion of lyrical tragedy in the productions of *Citta morta,* 1898. But he, along with the realists Bracco and Fogazzarro and the experimentalist Pirandello, wrote the majority of their works for the 20th century stage.

Drama, Italian, 20th century to the First World War. Dramatic fare was varied, showing a wide range of influences, from that of brittle French comedy to that of the heroic tragedies of D'Annunzio, such as *La città morte* and *Francesca da Rimini.* This theatre included such dramatists as Enrico Annivale Butti, Roberto Bracco, Sem Benelli. There was an attempted revolution in Marinetti's futurism, but it contributed little of value to the stage.

Drama, Italian, 20th century, since the First World War. The predominant characteristic of early post-War Italian plays was tragic, embodying a bewilderment, desperation, or terror before a cruel and hopeless world. Pirandello began his theatrical career shortly after the close of the War, although he had been known since the beginning of the century as a writer of tales; he has practically dominated the Italian theatre ever since. Other dramatists: Rosso di San Secondo, Luigi Antonelli, Enrico Cavacchioli, Massimo Bontempelli.

Drama, Japanese. The Japanese drama can really be considered an offshoot of the Chinese drama, carefully cut and transplanted by the Korean Scholars, for Japan received its culture from China by way of Korea. It is very likely that marionettes drifted into the Japanese line of vision from China, and these energetic people, always eager to assimilate the improvements of others, took the dolls to their hearts and did not let go until the middle of the 19th century.

It is said that at the close of the 6th century, a man of Chinese extraction called

Hada Kawatsu was ordered to arrange entertainments for the nation and, as a result, was supposed to have created about thirty-three plays. However, the Japanese claim that the drama originated from the dance *Sambāso* which was first employed as a charm against a volcanic disturbance in the year 805. At the beginning of the 12th century, a woman called Iso-no-Zenji was known to have performed certain *Otokomai* (dances in male attire), so that she is regarded as "the mother of the Japanese drama." But the introduction of the drama proper is universally ascribed to the impressarioship of Saruwaka Kanzabusō, who in 1624 opened the first theatre at Yedo (later called Tōkyō).

The classic age of Japanese literature closes in the 12th century and is followed by a period which, though called the Dark Age of Japanese letters, is notable for the rise of the *Nō* drama and its accompanying comedies or interludes (*Kyōgen*). The *Nō* was closely associated with pantomimic religious dances called *Kagura,* which were used in Shinto ceremonies. Later, stories were added to these dances in the Buddhist ceremonies, and the *Nō,* as it exists today, was born. Though Buddhistic in origin, soon the aristocratic and warrior classes of feudal Japan were practising it for entertainment, and many monks and doctors became playwrights.

The credit for composing the earliest specimens of the *Nō* is given to Kwanami Kiyotsugu (1333-84), a member of the priestly class, and to his son, Seami Motokiyu (1363-1444), who, by revising the *Saru-gaku,* which means "monkey music," and referring to juggling feats and comic remarks of earlier stage presentations, created a type of drama that was performed by highly trained masked male dancers, a chorus, and musicians. Seami wrote over ninety of the 235 Nō plays extant; his father wrote fifteen.

From its beginning, the *Nō* has had four main schools: Kwanze, Komparu, Hōshō and Kōngō, all of which are still in existence. Later, the Kita school won official recognition, while today, still another school, Umewaka, has many followers. The various schools differ but slightly. Though the leading actors enjoy great popularity and high salaries, the class is looked down upon, for the companies were formerly recruited from the lowest sources.

During the Muromachi period (14th century), Japanese taste was further influenced by China through the importation of such gentle arts as the tea ceremony, incense judging and flower arrangement. Also, chanting began in Japan about this time. Chanting developed from recitations of stories of an epic or heroic nature and was at first accompanied merely by taps of a fan, but within two centuries the Japanese had added the music of a three-stringed guitar, the *Samisen.* This form of drama was known as *Joruri.* At about the same time some producers began to use puppets in their presentations of *Joruri.* This innovation won immediate popularity and the combination of Joruri and puppets was known as *Ayatsuri.* It was performed in such a way that while the chanter told the story, the puppets acted it out. *Joruri* thus became a designation of the story or libretto, and the entertainment came to be called *Ayatsuri* (manipulation). These doll theatres were called *Ningyo Shibai.*

Both the *Joruri-Ayatsuri* and the *Kabuki* reached their highest development in the plays of Chikamatsu Monzayemon (1653?-1724) and Takeda Izumo (1688-1756). Before this, a few stories of heroic proportions had appeared under the patronage of the Emperor Go Yōzei, and these were utilized by the chanter Satsuma Jōun. But it was not until Takemoto Gidayu, who in 1685 began a theatre in Ōsaka and employed Chikamatsu to write plays, that the modern drama began.

Chikamatsu, who had turned from studying for the priesthood to writing plays, had first written for the Kabuki theatre. From 1699 on he wrote *Joruri* and *Ayatsuri* for Takemoto's Ōsaka theatre. In him the *Ayatsuri* reached its highest development. Chikamatsu Monzayemon was a voluminous writer who created over fifty plays and is credited with as many more. Each is of about the length of a Shakespearean play, and has from three to five acts.

Chikamatsu began to have a powerful influence on the people. It was he who brought into Japan the Chinese sagas and stories and who began the dramas of double suicide for love. (The increase in the rate of these suicides, which became popular tradition in Japan after the invention of this form of drama, was alarming.) So great was his fame that he has been called by the Japanese, "the Shakespeare of Japan," and such was his power, that his most famous masterpiece *The Battles of Kokusinya* saved the theatre Takemoto-Za from bankruptcy at one time. A rival theatre headed by an educated doctor named Kaion soon sprang up in Ōsaka, and the rivalry did much to make this period the greatest in Japanese drama. Under Chikamatsu, drama was divided into historical plays and plays of social life and manners. Most of his plays are written in prose intermixed with poetry.

The themes of both the *Ayatsuri* puppet play and the *Kabuki* popular play are extremely diversified, embracing historical, legendary, domestic and poetically fantastic material, and representing the manners, dress and customs of "Old Japan." The comedies have a tendency to immorality. Whereas the *Nō* is a highly condensed type of drama, several complete plays being included in the same performance, the *Kabuki* is usually of many acts and in some cases requires several days for complete presentation. It makes use of all the dramatic modes and swings from extreme realism to extreme conventionalism. For the most part, however, it leans toward what the Western world calls operatic effect. Many of the earlier *Nō* plays were popularized and elaborated into *Kabuki* forms.

The dramatic instinct is truly alive in the Japanese people. The drama is passionately loved by the lower classes, and it would not be an exaggeration to state that the Japanese constitute the most theatre-loving public in the world. The Japanese spirit is the truly artistic one of an instinctive effort to achieve the beautiful. Everything connected with their stage is a fine art. Such a spirit is greatly lacking in the West where the dramatic idea is to cram as much realism and detail into a scene as possible. Three small potted pine trees, symbolizing heaven, earth and humanity, and a spreading pine painted at the back of the stage, symbolizing faithful endurance, constitute all the scenery for a *Nō* drama. The Western craving for realism has only made the Western stage a technical imitator no better than the efforts of a counterfeiter of paper money. Forgotten are the words of Goethe: "Art is art because it is not nature." In Japan the spectator is made to feel that he is actually living in the atmosphere of the play. The dramatist purposely aims at this, dragging everyone into the heart of his pageant. The Kabuki theatre, furthermore, is built with one or more projections of the stage into the auditorium. Such a runway is called *Hanamichi* (flower path), and is used by the actors when representing someone starting on or returning from a journey, connoting a much closer contact between audience and play. In the West, this device, except for some experiments of recent years, is absent so that the scenes are limited by or hemmed into a frame. The prompter and property men of the Japanese stage never bother to conceal themselves. The property men are robed in black to indicate invisibility, and are busy arranging costumes, slipping stools under actors, and bearing away used props in full view of the audience. Thus, like the Chinese theatre, the theatre of Japan is untrammeled by any fetters of realism; time and space are servants of the playwright, not his masters. If all the world's a stage and all of us are the players, then the Far Eastern ideal of uniting the two parts of actors and audience is essentially correct.

A program of plays in Japan usually lasts from morning until midnight, and the playgoers make preparations to attend the theatre as if starting out on a picnic, by taking baskets of food along; they partake of their meals with the same regularity as at home. Since the Western theatre has lost most of its festive attributes since Shakespeare's time, foreigners attending the Japanese popular theatre, are entertained by the audience as much as by the actors—the audience scoring an amazing success in the disposal of food. The women are usually seated by themselves. There is a good deal of pipe smoking going on and, between the acts, the servants from the tea houses appear, bringing lacquered trays loaded with rice, tea, hard-boiled eggs, sweets, and fruit, all of which vanish like magic.

There are four types of Japanese drama. The *Nō* dramas, which consist of chanting and dancing, developed from the old folklore of China and Japan. They have a chorus where the dialogue leaves off, resembling the ancient Greek plays in this extent. The *Joruri,* or epical music dramas, are the second type, an example of which is the famous feudal suicides of the Forty-seven Ronins in the beginning of the 18th century. (See *Story of the Forty-Seven Ronins, The.*) The *Joruri* began in the Yedo period, a peaceful age lasting from 1615 to 1866, during which time the arts made remarkable progress among the masses. Before this, the culture of each period had been monopolized by the court nobles, military aristocrats, or Buddhist priests; commoners scarcely benefited. In the course of these peaceful years the plebeians accumulated wealth, while the military men, with no wars to fight and a diminishing income, gradually became so poor that they could not partake of comforts and amusements. The *Joruri* were built of alternate five and seven syllable lines, with music, a good plot, and spectacular effects. A variation of *Joruri* was *Ayatsuri,* which introduced puppets in the performance. Later, the puppets' roles were easily adapted for regular actors who acted out the roles in pantomime while the narrative was recited by a chanter chorus. The third type of Japanese drama is the *Kabuki,* a word meaning "the art of song and dance." *Kabuki* is the popular theatre of Japan. The fourth type is the New School which presents Western drama in translation and drama in Western style. The New School reveals the influence of Shakespeare, Ibsen, Strindberg, Maeterlinck, Wilde, Shaw and O'Neill. Shakespeare even influenced a writer named Shoyo, who, in 1885, wrote an essay entitled *The Essence of the Novel,* after which the novel became a new form of literary expression in Japan. While the New School is popular with the younger generation, it is the old epical dramas that hold the nation at large spellbound. It is an interesting fact that William Butler Yeats, Irish poet-dramatist, wrote many plays 1916-39 which were based on the short singing and dancing *Nō* dramas whose unrealistic charm appealed to him. Some of these plays he entitled: *Four Plays for Dancers; The Cat and the Moon; The Dreaming of the Bones.*

The chanting of heroic and historical material is once again very popular in Japan, and there are 150 variety halls today in Tōkyō in which women again compete with men for acting honors. Women were once barred by law from performing in the theatre because their singing and dancing was thought to contribute to the breakdown of public morals. But today this law has relaxed its vigil somewhat. However, the drama, on the whole, has a good moral effect upon its patrons, with good triumphing over evil and model examples held up before them for emulation. Though actors have always been looked down upon by the leisured classes, a few performers gain great fame and command handsome salaries. Two of the leading stars of the Japanese stage are Onoe Kikugōrō and Nakamura Kichiemon.

Most Japanese drama is not as well executed "literature," in a technical sense, as Western or even Chinese drama. In the Kabuki theatre, the actors often behaved in such a monstrously overbearing manner that no independent writer of merit would offer his services. Further, Japan has for centuries held on to a form of marionette theatre, even placing it before the legitimate stage. Finally, the Japanese have of recent years adulterated their drama with Western forms, which may ultimately lead to a loss of freshness and individuality.

See also *Acting, Japanese; Staging, Japanese; Nō drama; Drama, Kabuki.*

Drama, Javanese. As in Hindu literature, the two great Javanese epics are the *Ramayana* and the *Mahābhārata*. The Javanese *Ramayana* was written in the 13th century or earlier, but its author did not know Sanskrit and derived his material from other sources apart from the Hindu *Ramayana.* Of course, the story of *Ramayana* had wide currency and is to be found today throughout the Malay Archipelago. The prose translation of the *Mahābhārata* was made during the reign of *Dharmavaṁśa* (c. 10th century). Most of the Javanese plays are based on these two great works of the Old-Javanese literature.

The poetical works of the Middle-Javanese literature (after the 16th century) employ new kinds of metre as opposed to the Sanskrit metre of Old-Javanese, and are known as *kidung.*

Many *kidungs* are used for the Javanese stage. One of the most important of these works is the Panji cycle (those books dealing with the romantic adventures of the famous hero Panji). The best known work of this series is *Malat.* It is as voluminous as the *Ramayana* and forms the source of all later Javanese and Malayan works of the Panji cycle. The crown prince of Kahuripan, the hero of this cycle of legends, is known by various names and represented as a wonderful stranger and young lover wandering about on horseback in search of his beloved Candra Kirana of Daha. This enigmatic and shadowy figure's character is full of contradictions. On the one hand he is a sentimental lover, almost on the verge of madness for his long

lost loved one, but on the other, he is fully alive to the charms of other women and
only too eager and unscrupulous in gaining them. He changes his name and forms,
gets involved in endless complications, and plays his role sometimes among mortals
on earth and sometimes among gods in heaven. This story is purely Javanese without
any Indian elements and apparently originated in Java and spread over all Indonesia,
Indo-China and the Malay Peninsula. The story is subject matter for the *wajang
gedog* and *wajang topeng* plays.

Next to the Panji cycle may be mentioned the folk-tales and fables known as
tantri. Some of these works are written in poetry. They are found also among the
Balinese, the Siamese and the Laotians. The stories are told by a queen, the last of a
long series who were daily married and put off for a new one, reminding us of the
introduction of the Arabian *Thousand and One Nights*.

Among mythological tales which have been applied to the theatre in Java is the
Bhimasvarga which describes the journey of Bhīma to hell in order to release the soul
of his father Pāndu. One of the most popular *kidungs is Shrī Tanyung*. It relates
how Sidapaksa, son of Nakula, married his cousin Shrītanyun, how the king sent him
to heaven in order to seduce the bride and how, on his return, Sidapaksa killed her
on the suspicion that she had committed adultery, but was convinced of her innocence
by the fragrance emitted by her blood. Shrītanyun was then restored to life by
Durgā.

The *kidung, Kuntī-Yajnya,* describes the exploits of the Pāndavas and Arjuna in
particular who was twice married and twice killed. The second time, in a fight with
his son by Suprabhā, both were killed. But Suprabhā restored them to life and revealed their relationship.

The various types of Javanese drama are readily classified. The *wajang* (pronounced *vayang*) or puppet show, so popular in Java today, existed in East Java as
early as the first half of the 11th century. Some experts trace the *wajang* back to the
7th century, and it is not at all impossible that this unique form of drama is a good
deal older and may have derived from the Chinese shadow-plays. The *wajang* shows
are played exactly the same way as in ancient times; that is, by a *dalang,* who has the
shadow silhouettes of flat, skilfully-cut, leather puppets thrown on a white screen
which is faintly illuminated by a hanging oil-lamp. The puppets (*wajang purwa*)
have sharp, grotesque profiles, thin arms and curved fingers, and are manipulated by
means of wooden sticks attached to the arms. They are held by the seated *dalang*
(show master) above his head and their shadows fall upon the screen so that the audience sees the moving shadows and not the puppets themselves. Without motion pictures, one cannot convey the delightfully agile and ghostly movements of these skilfully operated loose-armed marionettes. The *dalang,* who is the successor of the pre-
Hindu priests, not only operates the puppets but also speaks in their place, provides
a running commentary of the story and conducts the orchestra. The whole action of
the *dalang,* which takes up a whole night, is called *lakon* in Central Java, a word
which has exactly the same meaning and etymological construction as the Greek term
"drama." The form of a *lakon* is defined by the traditional character of the performance. The oral tradition of the *lakon* has exercised an enormous influence on the style
of the written literature, especially since quite often the same persons acted as poets

and *dalangs*. This condition is especially true for the literature of Central Java, and is not at all impossible for East Java as well, which may serve to explain why one of the oldest and most characteristic works of Javanese poetry, the *Arjunawiwaha* (Arjuna's Marriage) has a construction which is essentially that of a Javanese *lakon*. The *Arjunawiwaha* was written in thirty-six cantos by Mpu Kanwa about the year 1030. It is to be found in a Balinese version also. The fact that it has often been represented on temple reliefs and in paintings and drawings indicates how highly later generations valued the poem. The story treats of the fortunes of Arjuna, of the unsuccessful attempts of three nymphs to seduce him on Mount Kailāsa according to Indra's command, and of his meeting with Siva who is disguised as a Kirata hunter and who, as a mark of favor, gives him some magical weapons which prove useful later. Purified and strengthened by becoming proof against all worldly temptation, Arjuna then defeats, at the request of the gods, the demon Niwātakawaca, the unconquerable, who had been threatening the gods with ruin, but whose fortune takes a new turn at the moment when the beautiful Suprabhā, together with Arjuna, purloins the secret of his invulnerability. After the victory, Arjuna enjoys in Indra's heaven the company of the nymphs which he had denied himself before, on the occasion of the temptation on Mount Kailāsa.

A further development of the *wajang purwa* or flat puppets was the *wajang klitik,* puppets carved out of soft wood, half-rounded and in double-sided relief, which appeared directly before the audience. Next came the *wajang golek,* puppets in the full round and capable of being shown from all sides. These puppets were clothed only from the waist down and were operated by means of a rod which passed through the body and by sticks attached to the hands.

Out of fear-filled imitation of nature, through the charm of rhythm, under the impulse of an instinctive yearning, grew the earliest (the magical) form of dancing. From such far origins are the dramatic dances, which form so inherent a part of the life of the Javanese, traced. The story of the links between the present-day dances of Java and their distant Indian prototypes is well known. But it is from the 18th century revival of the *wajang wong* (the *wajang* performed by living actors, not by puppets) at the court of Prince Mangkunagoro the First, that one traces the recent history and development of the Solonese and Jogjanese danced drama and dramatic dances. For the example of the Mangkunagoro court of Solo came soon to be followed by that of Sultan Amangkubuwana the First of Jogja, who introduced the performance of *wajang* by unmasked actors.

In the *wajang topeng,* the living actors wear costumes and masks, and dance in imitation of the puppets. The masks are made of wood or leather and are held to the face by means of a strap on the inside which is gripped in the performer's teeth. The actor does not speak; his lines are spoken by a reciter. Though revived through court patronage in the 18th century, this form of drama originated in the 11th century.

In the *wajang gedog,* though the actors do not wear masks, they are likewise mute and really dance rather than act. Spoken parts were added under Western influence, and this new form came to be known as *wajang orang.*

The Javanese playhouse is a simple affair called a *pendoppo.* It is a pillared hall open on two or three sides to the outdoors and surmounted by a pointed roof. Travel-

ing troupes are known, for the comic drama is represented in Java and other parts of
the Malay Archipelago by small strolling groups consisting usually of two men and a
woman.

The content of the Sundanese dances of West Java is rather more secular and its
traditions more popular and less aristocratic than those of Central Java and East
Java where the ancient Hindu tradition has remained an honored practice, requiring
that "the dancer should be handsome, of sweet speech, learned, capable, eloquent, of
good birth, learned in the *sastras* of art and science, of sweet voice, versed in song,
instrumental music and dancing, self-confident, and ready of wit," according to
Ananda Coomaraswamy in his *Mirror of Gesture* (1916). It is a fact that the most
famous actors and dancers of Java were usually of aristocratic birth and included
many sons of rulers or great nobles.

One of the best known *wajang gedog* (play with human actors without masks) is
The Adventures of Dewa Sukma, or *How Petruk becomes King of Madura.* Petruk,
who has the leading part, usually appears as a clown; however, there are various features which reveal that he is considered to be of noble or even royal birth. The same
applies to the characters Semar and Nala Gareng, who, with Petruk, are most probably personifications of the original Javanese princes who ruled the people before the
advent of the Hindus. Subsequently they took inferior roles in the *wajang.* This is
also evident in the story, for notice how one fool is exposed by two others. The story
goes that the King of Darawati has been asked by the neighboring King of Mandura
to send help, for Mandura is being attacked by the enemy hosts of the Army of
Giants. As usual, before help can materialize, Mandura is conquered and Dewa
Sukma proclaimed king. In the meantime, a man named Angkavidjaja has been
searching high and low for his servant Petruk who has apparently disappeared. Dewa
Sukma is challenged by Gatot Katja, an ally of Mandura. Dewa Sukma gets his
Head Commander to fight him but the Commander loses; whereupon the usurper
king himself challenges Gatot Katja and is victorious. However, other allies of Man-
dura in the persons of Semar and Nala Garong fight and finally vanquish Dewa
Sukma, tear off his clothes and prove that the enemy king is none other than Petruk,
the lowly servant.

The element of *semadi* forms an essential part of every *wajang* drama. *Semadi*
means the method of searching after the spiritual power, a power not to be achieved
until one is fully qualified to wield it purely, nor to be granted unless the aim for
which it is sought is deserving. The music of the *gamelan* (Javanese orchestra) is a
tangible aid towards the practice of *semadi,* for the attentive following of a *wajang*
performance during the whole course of a night is not only a high artistic joy, but for
the mystic who practises *semadi* also a means of obtaining enlightenment and achieving exaltation.

Drama, Kabuki. A type of Japanese drama based on singing and dancing; a
play more like a revue but classical, with a very complicated plot. Popular with the
masses. The singing and dancing occur during the course of the development of the
story characterized by dramatic elements and performed artistically.

The *Kabuki* drama originated over 250 years ago. A *Kabuki* play is a spectacle, colorful in presentation and mystical in form. The chief writer for this form of drama was Chikamatsu Monzayemon.

Most *Kabuki* plays are historical dramas. Civil war between clans, as in *The Story of the Forty-Seven Ronins,* an authentic tale which furnished the basis for more than fifty plays, is the representative and most popular type. Second in popularity are love stories in which the "Lady Courtesan," a distinguished and sympathetic figure of great filial piety, is a favorite heroine. Also popular are the dramas dealing with the tribulations of great families.

The Japanese audiences loves melodrama with plenty of pantomime. The principle of unity is not observed, but action and sentiment are essential.

Kabuki Zyuhatban is the collective name for the eighteen best *Kabuki* plays, only ten of which are now staged. *Sukeroku, Kenuki, Yanone, Kanzintyo, Sibaraku, Narukami* and *Kamahige* are the plays of greatest merit.

Zidaimono is the general name for *Kabuki* plays with historical background; of puppet play origin. *Chiushingura* is best known; written in many acts, but when performed is abridged.

Sewamono is the general name for love dramas and plays of everyday life. *Sinzyu Ten-no-Amizima* and *Meido-no-Hikyu* are the best examples.

See also *Acting, Japanese; Drama, Japanese; Staging, Japanese; Story of the Forty-Seven Ronins, The.*

Drama, Korean. The sources of the drama of Korea, as of all countries, lie so deep that the search for them inevitably leads to folk psychology and metaphysics. In its rudimentary aspects, the Korean religious festival in the temple was the first link in a chain of development of which the stage is the last. Strictly religious at first, the drama originated in the Buddhistic processional chantings of the temples. Through a process of secularization, these services gradually developed into solemnly chanted renderings of historical events which were performed with ultra slow movements to ultra serious music and without stage settings. This phase is still kept alive in the *Nō* plays of Japan.

The first Korean form of drama was a kind of morality play dealing with ancestor worship and sung and acted in epic style. This early form was the *Sohkiungkok,* which was revived in the 15th century of the Yi dynasty and is still performed today.

The Korean village playhouse is usually a temporary one of poles with bamboo mats spread overhead for a roof. A small platform and very little in the way of stage setting complete the outfit. A few rough benches or mats accommodate the audience who smoke and eat while the show is going on.

The Korean drama is mostly a matter of monologue recitations of events extracted from popular histories, with a single performer representing the successive roles and a few others acting merely as necessary accessories. He usually improvises a great deal.

In the higher type of theatre, a program of plays lasts for hours and sometimes consumes a whole day. The plays are shown consecutively and the leading actor uses his own judgment as to presentation. Music and theatricals developed greatly under the patronage of the Korean ruler, Pyun-wun-wang. The next great friend of Korean music and drama was the king Sejong (15th century), who ordered the great musicians of the land to study music history and music technique with the thought of developing new forms. It was Sejong who deemed it wise to exclude female performers from the stage, believing that they contributed towards immorality. From this time on, the female impersonator becomes a familiar figure in the Korean drama.

The Silla dynasty (57 B.C.-935 A.D.) was the most glorious period of Korean history and expansion for the country included parts of Manchuria and Siberia. The Koryu dynasty (918-1392) was the bloom of Korean culture during which the Koreans enjoyed the fruits of Silla.

It was at the beginning of the Koryu dynasty, in the 10th century, that there began a persecution of Buddhist priests which drove them into the mountains to live as hermits away from civilization. In this inquisition, the drama played a very important part, for plays were used as propaganda which attempted to show that the monks and priests were politically and morally corrupt. Buddhism never quite recovered from the blow that the propaganda play dealt it. These plays were performed for hundreds of years and some are still to be seen today.

But the drama itself, though usually serving a much nobler function, has always been despised by the scholars and sponsored by the nobility. Like the Chinese plays, Korean plays are classified as Civil and Military. *Kuk* is the word for "stage performance." A very recent classification is *Hikuk* (Comedy) and *Pikuk* (Tragedy), the result of Western influence. However, regardless of classifications, Korean plays show a complete dramatic formula with a hero, heroine, villain and comic person usually in the guise of a messenger or servant.

Korean drama is very difficult to translate. In translation one loses a great deal of the humor which lies hidden in puns and word plays. However, the essence may be gleaned from a few synopses.

About 1440, a celebrated monk named Kasan wrote *The Adventures of Hong Kil-dong*. Later, another monk, Ha Jong, wrote *The Adventures of Kyong-op*. Both of these were successfully dramatized and the first is extremely popular in Korea. Its story concerns Kil-dong, the son of Prime Minister Hong's concubine, who is despised and abused by the Prime Minister's first wife because he is a beautiful child and wise, and because the father is growing fonder of him than of the first wife's two sons. The boy grows to manhood and leaves his family to make his fortune. He finds crushing disillusionment because a world disproportionate to his own compassionate spirit refuses to recognize the son of a concubine as a social equal. Through a series of fantastic adventures, Hong Kil-dong becomes the leader of a band of thieves who rob corrupt priests and government officials only to give their loot away to the oppressed in the most approved Robin Hood fashion. Finally, Hong Kil-dong forces the king to remove the stigma of his birth by getting himself conferred with his father's official title. Shortly after, he rescues a beautiful maiden from a band of savages, falls in love with her, marries and lives happily ever after with his wife and his aging concubine mother. Thus Good triumphs over Evil, as in most, if not all, Korean dramas.

Around 1760, Yi Munjong wrote a novel bearing the Aristophanean title of *The Frogs* which was dramatized. Also in the 18th century was written *The Adventures of Yi Ha-ryong*. The most famous history is really an historical novel called *The Story of the Long North Wall*, dealing with the Great Wall which Korea once had which extended from the Yellow Sea to the Sea of Japan. This history of the Three Kingdoms was written by Kim Pu-sik, the greatest writer of the Koryu dynasty (918-1392).

Perhaps the best known classical play is *Chunhiangchon* (Story of Chunhiang), written in Korean, instead of the traditional Chinese, by Lie Kiuhiung in the 16th century. The play is composed in an ornate yet delicately beautiful song style, filled with the most exquisite love poetry. The story tells of Toh Ryong, a handsome young scholar and son of a Minister, who is about to compete in the government examinations, and who falls in love with a *kisang,* Chunhiang, whom he meets at a banquet. Despite the knowledge that his father will object to the match, he marries the dancing-girl. He is away for several months dispatching his scholarly and official duties, and meanwhile, little Chunhiang is thrown into jail and tortured because she will not yield to the advances of the new City Magistrate and remains faithful to her Toh Ryong. He returns finally, having been promoted to the rank of Government Inspector, and, learning of his wife's fate, determines to get to the bottom of the case by disguising himself as a beggar. He manages to free Chunhiang and punish the corrupt Magistrate, as the countryside rings with praises for the faithful wife.

An interesting work is *Hwasa* (History of Flowers), which is rather like a collection of stories and ancient legends of flowers wherein flowers symbolize human personalities. The original *Hwasa* was edited by a Chinese writer of the Ming dynasty called Chung who published it in Chinese in twenty-seven volumes. Late in the 16th century, Lim Ch'e wrote a novel from this vast work which was later produced as a play.

The Story of Sim Chung is also well known as a play. It treats of a scholar and his talented wife who are childless for fifteen years. One night she dreams that a star has descended to her from heaven. It isn't long before they have a child, but to their dismay it is only a girl. The mother soon dies and the father gradually goes blind. Sim Chung (our heroine) grows into a beautiful creature who is extremely dutiful to her blind parent.

The blind man hears from a priest-prophet that if he makes an offering of 300 bags of rice to the Buddha of his temple, his sight will be restored. The blind man is poor, but he agrees that if the priest furnishes the rice, he will pay him back in installments. When the daughter discovers the pact he has made, she is greatly distressed and, in order to pay back the debt, she plans to have herself cast to the evil spirit of the sea, the dread of mariners, as a maidenly sacrifice, for which she receives in advance the 300 bags of rice necessary to pay the debt. When the father discovers the fate that awaits his daughter, a very passionate and touching scene of fatherly love and filial piety ensues. Sim Chung is thrown into the sea and finds herself in the submarine palace of the King of the Sea. The King tells her that once she was a star in heaven who fell in love with another star, and through an action which made the King of Heaven angry with her, the lovers were banished to Earth. Fearing a recurrence of the affair on earth, he sent her lover first, keeping her imprisoned for a long time, after which she was sent as daughter to her former lover. He is the man she claims as father. Heaven has seen her filial piety, however, and repents. Sim Chung ascends to the surface of the sea concealed within a giant flower. In this state she is taken aboard the same ship off which she had been cast. The wonderful flower is brought to the King's palace and there presented to him. The King keeps it in a glass house inside the palace grounds. Every night, Sim Chung creeps forth from her hideaway unobserved except for one night when the King spies her, falls in love and, after elaborate preparations, makes her his Queen. But Sim Chung, always thinking of her poor blind father, is unhappy. One day the King sees her weeping and discovers she is desirous of helping all the blind men of the country. The King summons the blind to a great feast at the palace. Among the gathering she locates her father. He, in despair because he cannot see her, tears at his sightless eyes and, to his amazement and joy, the scales fall away and he sees once more.

Drama, left-wing. Plays of social consciousness and generally marked by more than a little Marxist ideology. Clifford Odets is perhaps the most brilliant member of this school. His definitely left-wing plays include: *Waiting for Lefty; Till the Day I Die; Awake and Sing* and *Paradise Lost.* John Howard Lawson's *Processional;* Elmer Rice's *The Adding Machine;* Ernst Toller's *Man and the Masses* and John Wexley's *They Shall Not Die* (on the Scottsboro case) are all illuminating works of this school. In 1933 a producing organization called the Theatre Union was founded in New York for the express purpose of performing leftist plays. Here were put on such plays as *Peace on Earth* by Sklar and Maltz, *Stevedore* by Peters and Sklar, *Black Pit* by Maltz and several others. The Federal Theatre's productions of the *Living Newspaper,* Auden's *Dance of Death, Haiti, The Life and Death of an American,* the Mercury Theatre's *The Cradle Will Rock,* and *Pins and Needles* and others are all signs of the vitality of the left-wing theatre. Other left-wing plays like Auden and Isherwood's *The Dog Beneath the Skin* and *The Ascent of F 6* and Spender's *Trial of a Judge* have been produced in England, but not yet professionally in the United States.

Drama, liturgical. A short play or dramatic scene in Latin performed as part of the service in the Roman Catholic church. This form was developed by the clergy in its desire to present the salient facts of Christ's life more realistically to the congregations. The two great festivals of the church, Easter and Christmas, provided the principal occasions for plays of this type. Roughly, the form lasted from the 10th to the 13th century A.D. Latin hexameters, especially from Virgil, were introduced. Between 1100 and 1200 A.D. vernacular languages were substituted for Latin. Also during this time various Old Testament and New Testament stories from the lives of the saints were introduced. Gradually more ambitious effects were attempted and laymen began to join in with priests as actors. Comic elements were interpolated into predominantly serious plays, and those who played the parts of devils contributed most of the humor. Finally these plays, at least many of them, grew unsuitable to the churchly setting and were forced to move to the market-place.

See also *Drama, medieval.*

Drama, medieval. A form of theatrical presentation that sprang from the liturgical dramas performed in Latin in the Roman Catholic church. The next stage was the separation of these dramas from the body of the church service to accommodate the increasingly large audience, performed on the steps of the church. With the growing popularity of these dramas the clergy, feeling them too great a force in the lives of the people, issued edicts restricting them, finally prohibiting all the clergy from taking part in their performances. Hereupon the dramas were taken over by the town guilds, which made up the greatest social force of the day. While the subject-matter remained Biblical the plays were worked into mystery or miracle cycles, dealing with the entire Old and New Testaments, and including some of the Apocrypha. After a time these miracle plays gave way in turn to morality plays.

Drama, modern. Assuming the beginnings of the "modern" era to be in the first days of Ibsen, and proceeding with Chekhov, Strindberg and Hauptmann, through Shaw, Galsworthy, and O'Neill up to and including Rice, Anderson, Lawson and Odets, the prevailing characteristics of modern dramaturgy may be properly said to be the following: (1) a powerful new realism, stemming from the intimate, middle-class naturalism of Ibsen (in such plays as *A Doll's House* and *Hedda Gabler*) and Chekhov (in *Three Sisters; Uncle Vanya; The Sea Gull* and *The Cherry Orchard*) through the peasant themes of Hauptmann (in *The Weavers*), to the strikingly naturalistic New York of Odets (especially in *Waiting for Lefty; Awake and Sing; Paradise Lost* and *Golden Boy*); (2) the priority of ideas over action, a trait of which Shaw is easily the prime example (in such static works as *Back to Methuselah; Heartbreak House; Man and Superman*) and one also manifested in the near-closet quality of T. S. Eliot's poetic plays *Murder in the Cathedral* and *The Family Reunion* and the sparkling polemics of S. N. Behrman's *Rain from Heaven;* (3) an emphasis on revolt, a quality absent from the work of no single modern playwright of major importance, but most notable in the plays of Ibsen (in their progressive pioneering, all), Hauptmann (especially in *The Weavers,* also in other plays such as *Lonely Lives*), Shaw (in all his works bearing more than his usual socialist slant, among them *Man and Superman; Mrs. Warren's Profession* and *Heartbreak House*), Ernst Toller (in all his plays, the best known of which are *Man and the Masses* and *No More Peace!*), Odets (especially in his *Waiting for Lefty* and *Till the Day I Die*), Maxwell Anderson (particularly in his two plays on the Sacco-Vanzetti case *Gods of the Lightning* and *Winterset* and his exposé of political graft *Both Your Houses*), John Wexley (with his picture of the Scottsboro case *They Shall Not Die*), and John Howard Lawson (with his indictment of the Ku Klux Klan and picture of labor conflict in *Processional*); (4) the prevalent concern with sex, which is exemplified by Ibsen (in *Ghosts*), Strindberg (in many of his plays, particularly *The Father*), Wedekind (in practically all his works, most notably in *The Awakening of Spring; Earth-Spirit* and *The Box of Pandora*), O'Neill (in *Desire Under the Elms, Strange Interlude* and *Mourning Becomes Electra*), Bourdet (with his treatise on Lesbianism, *The Captive*), and Mordaunt Shairp (with his depiction of male homosexuality in *The Green Bay Tree*). Characters in these plays are typically restless, emotionally tortured and searchingly introspective. Through the shifting fashions of symbolism, naturalism, expressionism, impressionism, futurism and surrealism the emphasis of morality has been completely altered and action has given way to suspense or mere polemic. A major trend during the last thirty years has been the revival of the comedy of manners, which served the social-revolutionary themes of Shaw (particularly in such plays as *Too True to be Good*) although the witty Irishman had previously learned much about the comedy of manners from Wilde, and gave impetus to Somerset Maugham's satirical commentary on the upper and middle classes in such plays as *The Circle* and *The Constant Wife*. In later years S. N. Behrman in America has been the most brilliant exponent of the modern comedy of manners, evidencing his skill in such brilliant tracts as *Rain from Heaven; End of Summer* and *No Time for Comedy*. What was at the time considered a new trend was the introduction of a surrealist note in the recent (Spring, 1939) Saroyan play, *My Heart's in the Highlands,* which was also considered to have a social commentary. During the season of 1938-39 on Broadway the dramatists rediscovered America as a dramatic subject, notably in Kaufman and Hart's *The American Way,* Sklar's *Life and Death of An American,* Sherwood's *Abe Lincoln in Illinois,* Rice's *American Landscape* and Anderson and Weill's *Knickerbocker Holiday.*

Drama, neo-Latin. Latin plays and themes introduced into England under the quickening influence of the Renaissance and Reformation.

Drama, Nō. See *Nō drama.*

Drama, Norwegian. In the latter half of the 19th century Björnson and Ibsen came to the front in Norwegian literature through their dramatic treatment of characters and episodes of the saga period. Björnson's trilogy *Sigurd, the Bastard,* 1862, and Ibsen's *The Pretenders,* 1864, are the best of this group. In the Seventies they left their contemporaries far behind by turning to the field of social drama. In 1874 Björnson's *A Bankruptcy* caused a sensation in Europe. As one who turned earliest to the theatre for the discussion of social problems, he is considered by his countrymen as the founder of their national drama.

Ibsen inaugurated his realistic period with *The Pillars of Society,* 1877, a title emblematic of the great social dramas to follow. Two years later came *A Doll's House,* prophesying the realistic Ibsen and the modern theatre that was to be rooted in his work. Then followed *Ghosts* in 1881, rousing the fury of Europe to which Ibsen retorted with *An Enemy of the People,* 1882, an attack on the stupid majority who preferred disease to the acknowledgment of their fault.

The following year Björnson made a plea in *A Gauntlet* for the abolition of the double standard, and that same year completed the symbolic drama *Beyond Our Power,* dealing with the abnormal features of religious ecstasy. Ibsen had already produced the poetic dramas *Brand,* 1866, and *Peer Gynt,* 1867, which early emphasized the playwright's major theme of the supreme importance of the development and enrichment of the individual. Lyrical beauty came again in *The Wild Duck,* 1884, along with devastating satire. While Björnson turned to the novel and poetry to preach his liberal doctrines, Ibsen continued an almost yearly attack from the theatre. In *Rosmersholm,* 1886, he reached his greatest height in pure tragedy. *Lady from the Sea,* 1888, was the first of his plays in which the masculine character was as strongly delineated as the woman. *Hedda Gabler,* 1890, is one of the finest examples of modern dramaturgy with a character portrayal of classic Greek proportions. In 1892 Ibsen returned to poetic symbolic expression for *The Master Builder.* The two plays written in 1894 *Little Eyolf* and *John Gabriel Borkman* were further comments on the conflict between love and the claims of other desirable things. His last play *When We Dead Awaken,* 1900, was his final statement of the poet's creed that he who loses love loses all.

Ibsen's plays have influenced the modern theatre more than the works of any other single playwright. From them stems the play of ideas, the fearless outspoken realism of playwrights with a purpose on the Continent and in America. He brought elasticity to the well-made play of the French, dealt deftly with exposition, established the value of the catastrophic play and strengthened mental climaxes to equal the physical in excitement for intelligent playgoers.

Since Ibsen's last play at the turn of the century, Norwegian dramatists have produced little of lasting worth. Heiberg's *The Balcony,* 1894, and *Love's Tragedy,* 1904, are perhaps the strongest social dramas. Klinck's *The Cattle Dealer,* 1908, has been compared to *Peer Gynt* by some critics, and his *Agilulf, the Wise,* 1910, is interesting for its unconventional rhythm and poetic form.

Drama, pastoral. A form of drama that was largely Elizabethan and which took as subject matter themes of rustic life. In this type the main story is always one of unrequited love and the chastity motif is rarely absent. The same plot devices are used again and again—the inconstant lover, the untrue friend, the lovers' merry-go-round in which everybody loves somebody who does not love him, identity concealed through disguise or ignorance, the discovery of gentle birth, supernatural betrothal, assault upon innocence by deity or one of the nobility—all these changes are rung over and over. Arcadia, or some similar forest, is the setting. Among the foremost examples must be counted Ben Jonson's *The Sad Shepherd;* Daniel's *Queen Arcadia;* Shirley's *A Pastoral Called the Arcadia;* and Fletcher's *The Faithful Shepherdess.* The finest writers of this type were Jonson and Fletcher.

Drama, plays within plays. A piece performed, as in a theatre, and forming part of the larger play in the real theatre. The play arranged by Hamlet to "catch the conscience of the king" is one example. The piece written by Fanny, the character of Shaw's *Fanny's First Play,* is another.

Other examples include: Middleton and Rowley's *The Spanish Gipsy,* Massinger's *The Roman Actor,* Sheridan's *The Critic;* Rice and Barry's *Cock Robin;* Kelly's *The Torch-Bearers.*

Drama, poetic. The very roots of theatrical writing are in verse, from Aeschylus, Sophocles and Euripides through the Elizabethans in England, Corneille and Racine in France, W. B. Yeats in Ireland, to the present with such dramatic poets as Auden, Eliot, MacLeish and Anderson. The poetic play during the last century or two, however, has acquired connotations of the closet drama, and in fact all works belonging to this school have been generally more literary than dramatic. Shelley's

The Cenci is perhaps the foremost example of a poetic closet play. Coleridge's *Remorse* was performed, but still it is better read than played. Byron, of all poets not primarily theatrical, achieved the greatest success in the drama. His *Manfred, Werner* and *Sardanapalus* are all powerful dramatically. Walter Savage Landor should be mentioned for his effective *Count Julian,* which is the greatest of his several poetic dramas. Though no writer of specifically cadenced verse, J. M. Synge must be included for the cogently poetic cast of his plays, particularly his *Riders to the Sea,* generally credited with being the greatest one-act play ever written. His *Deirdre of the Sorrows* is also genuinely poetic, a drama taken from Celtic lore and used also by W. B. Yeats. Yeats is perhaps the greatest exponent of the poetic drama of the last century, having produced works with an explicit use of verse, as against the poetic prose of Synge, coupled with a predominant flavor of mysticism. His *Cathleen Ni Houlihan* is probably his greatest dramatic masterpiece. He is remembered also for his *The Land of Heart's Desire, The Shadowy Waters* and *Deirdre.* Other poetic dramatists of the early 20th century are John Masefield, with his *Philip the King* and *Good Friday,* Thomas Hardy, with his closet drama *The Dynasts,* and James Elroy Flecker, with his *Hassan.* In the last few years, generally through the 1930's, there has been a renaissance of this school with T. S. Eliot's *Murder in the Cathedral* (produced in America by the Federal Theatre) and *Family Reunion* (produced in London), MacLeish's *Panic* (produced on Broadway by the short-lived Phoenix Theatre) and his two radio plays *The Fall of the City* and *Air Raid,* Auden's *The Dance of Death* (produced in New York by the Federal Theatre), Auden and Isherwood's *The Dog Beneath the Skin* and *The Ascent of F 6,* Spender's *Trial of a Judge,* and MacNeice's *Out of the Picture.* Of course Maxwell Anderson has long been crusading for the poetic play, of which *Winterset, High Tor, The Masque of Kings* and *Wingless Victory* are best known. Producers are generally wary of plays in verse as they are not considered good box-office, but the trend would seem to be toward a larger public for them in the future.

See *Dramatic Poesy, Poetics, Aristotle, Poetics, Scaliger.*

Drama, Polish. Creating a body of Polish drama has been Sisyphus' work, for hardly have the dramatists had a breathing spell and an audience than war has destroyed both. The result has been not to kill Polish plays, but to make writers choose strongly nationalistic themes. Fredro (1783-1876), with his *Maiden's Vows* and other brilliant pieces was—and has remained—the preeminent master of comedy. Contemporaneous with him Slowaki, Mickiewicz, and Krasinski wrote tragedy. Stanislaw Wyzpiánski, most notable of pre-world war playwrights, sounded prophetic notes in his tragedies and sympathetic portrayals of the ignorant peasantry. The chapter of new burgeoning and great hopes in the theatre after the World War will have to be written all over again, for again war has blotted it out.

See also *Wyspiánski, Stanislaw.*

Drama, Polish, since the First World War. There was a rebirth of theatrical traditions and ideas following the war which, pursuing a middle course between outright political tracts and mere depictions of manners, embraced the expressionism already established in other places in Europe. Zeromski, the novelist, turned to the theatre, carrying into it his strong social views. Rostworowski wrote poetic dramas on ethical and religious subjects; he also wrote expressionistic plays and other works which manifested the turn to the new realism. Szaniawski's works propounded a poetic realism. Other dramatists have been: Nalkowska, with her subtle psychological plays; Jasnorzewska-Pawlikowska, with her concrete, albeit poetic, works on social themes; Nowaczyński, with his social and political satires. The general tendency in the post-War Polish drama had been the treatment of current social or political problems against an earlier historical background for the purpose of contemporary analogies.

Drama, problem plays. See *Problem play.*

Drama, religious. In the elaboration of liturgical responses given in the church, drama grew. Thus the first dramas of any kind were of church, often by the church (i.e. its priests), and for the purpose of teaching vividly the lessons of the church. Though liturgical plays may be traced as far back as the founding of the Church of Rome, it was not until about the 12th century that they became drama to the extent of having costuming, properties and business. The mystery, miracle and morality plays, drawing upon Scriptures for their subjects, were the chief types, and with certain changes they persist even today in such productions as the *Passion Play of Oberammergau;* the *Pilgrimage Play* of Los Angeles; *The Miracle* of Max Reinhardt, and numerous less spectacular presentations.

See also *Church Theatres, drama, British, earliest; drama, Spanish, 15th-17th century; miracle plays; morality plays; mystery plays; passion plays.*

Drama, religious (children's). Among the themes more frequently used are: The First Christmas; Easter Morn; A Thanksgiving Service (Miriam); The Good Samaritan; The Secret of Success (Nehemiah); The Value of Preparation (Ten Virgins); A Search for a Wife (Isaac and Rebecca); A Woman who Dared (Esther); A Mother's Faith (Moses); In Quest of a Great Treasure (Naaman); David Livingstone; The Building of the Temple (Solomon); The Parable of the Talents.

Drama, Roman, ancient. The Romans followed the suit of the Greeks in their theatrical output, but were not nearly so rich in the quality of their works nor so passionate in their theatre going. The most significant dramatists were Terence and Plautus in comedy and Seneca in tragedy. Roman drama, like its Greek counterpart, originated in rituals performed in honor of rustic divinities, for the goddess Victoria in particular. Comedy derived largely from the early Fescennine Verses, which were lyrical dialogues, marked by coarse banter, sung at harvest festivals, and the *saturae,* which supplanted the Fescennine Verses in public favor, and which were composed of short comic sketches, without much plot but showing improvement in dramatic skill. In the domain of comedy the rustic Atellan farces, brought to Rome from Atella in Campania, are the most distinctive. Their subject-matter is generally rural and the actors in them are presumed to have exercised a free improvisatory hand. This type reigned supreme in popular favor from late in the 3rd century B.C. until the not dissimilar *mimus* usurped its throne. These Atellan farces were usually made up of two distinct kinds: (1) the *palliatae,* which were based on Greek models; and (2) the *togatae,* which were more native and treated of indigenously Roman themes. The *mimus,* or mime, which followed these Atellan comedies, was destined to be so popular as to hold sway in Rome until the very end of the Empire. It was a pantomimic farce dealing with subjects of low life and marked by an occasional crudeness which today would be considered licentious. When, in the 3rd century B.C., with Plautus, true literate comedy came into its own in Rome, it was the New Comedy of Greece that was the predominant model. The influence of this form, indeed, was so strong that the characters in Plautus' plays were performed as Greeks and dressed in Greek garb. Because of the scant attention or respect paid the theatre of his time Plautus was hard put to it to attract the interest of the crowd and yet maintain the criterion of his art. For this reason he is not to be too severely dealt with for catering to the tastes of this crowd. Furthermore, admission was free, inducing the audience to depreciate something to be had for nothing. That Plautus borrowed copiously from the Greeks is a fact for which we have the dramatist's own substantiation. He expressed a Greek point of view and did not hesitate to refer to his own people as barbarians. He coined new words in Latin form out of Greek derivations. His works abound in references to Greek, rather than Roman, places and figures. The mixture of Greek material and viewpoints with Roman background and temperament is, indeed, so pronounced as to confound almost any historian of the ancients. Among the most famous plays of Plautus are: the *Menaechmi,* a story of complication and mistaken identity between twins, each of whom is unaware of the other's presence in the same locality; the *Aulularia,* a portrait of a miser; the *Captivi,* a play without female characters and telling of the heroic self-sacrifice of a slave; the *Pseudolus,* a play of intrigue, again centering about a slave; and the *Bacchides,* a comedy of great complications and handled with unusual skill. In all of these, perhaps because of his untutored audiences, Plautus evinces a strange amalgam of culture and crude vulgarity. If Plautus was the virile dramatist of ancient Rome, Terence was certainly the elegant one. Where Plautus' work was distinguished by its vigor and sharp individualism, that of Terence was marked by a refinement and subtlety of insight. Where Plautus showed the impress of Greek "New Comedy," Terence evidenced an interest in keeping alive the qualities of Menander in a smoothly polished Latin style. Much of his enduring fame rests on his pre-eminent quotability, for more household expressions than are commonly realised derive originally from his plays. The best known of Terence's plays is *The Eunuch,* which is a fable of slavery and prostitution in which the seduction scene most clearly shows the contrast between Terence and Plautus in its delicacy and restraint of treatment. Among his other plays are: *Andria* and *Adelphoe.* In tragedy Seneca was the one great name. Many other dramatists wrote in the form during his time, but Seneca alone reached major stature. He was perhaps the first writer of closet drama as a deliberate form, and most of his works bear the scholar's intention to be read rather than the vital dramatist's concern with being performed. His tremendous influence in the Italy of the Middle Ages and the

Renaissance as well as upon many of the Elizabethan dramatists, including Kyd, Shirley and Shakespeare, accounts perhaps in large part for his surviving fame. Among plays generally accredited to him are: *Phoenissae; Hercules Furens; Troades; Medea; Phaedra; Oedipus* and *Thyestes.*

Drama, Rumanian, before the First World War. Cathon Theodorian wrote plays of middle class problems, such as *Bujorestii;* A. de Herz wrote facile, well-constructed light comedies like *Paiajenul;* Victor Eftimiu wrote plays in many popular styles, but remained most attached to the romantic fairy-tale.

Drama, Rumanian, since the First World War. The present day dramatic literature in Rumania is best represented by Camil Petrescu with his social and psychological dramas like *Suflete Tari;* the poet Ion Minulesco with his grotesques. Others include: Popa, Sîn-Giorgiu, Musatesco and Blaga.

Drama, Russian, 18th century. Few names figure in the history of Russian drama of this period, for neither theatre nor drama flourished. Such mystery and morality playlets as continued to be given in schools were imitative. Alexander Sumarokov, author of a tragedy in the French classic style, in 1747, however, gave a start to original Russian drama.

Drama, Russian, 19th century to the Revolution. The beginning of the 19th century found a fresh force influencing the drama. In the audience a healthy middle class was clamoring for bourgeois drama. Kotzebue, who was living in Russia at the time, gave the initial impetus by permitting his plays to be translated. There followed a Russian school of "Kotzebuists" extolling the calm life of the average family in hugely popular plays. Typical was Illin's *Magnanimity; or, The Conscription,* 1803, which tells of peasants noble on the battlefield and prompt in their payment of taxes.

After the War of 1812, the public demanded patriotic plays. Prince Shakhovskoy's operetta *The Cossack Poet* was the most popular of these and remained in repertory until the close of the century. A majority of the early plays were unoriginal in theme and treatment, following in almost every instance the French classic style. A brilliant exception was Griboyedov's verse satire upon Russian official society *Trouble from Reason,* 1821. It represents one of the classic peaks of Russian comedy and is historically interesting in that its hero speaks the liberalism of the young generation which reached its climax four years later in the military insurrection against Tsar Nicholas. During his reign there was a strict censorship of drama. Playwrights were constantly suspected of trying to spread republican ideas. There was nothing to do but revert to melodramas and romantic tales.

In 1831 Pushkin introduced the Shakespearean pattern for historical drama with his verse-tragedy *Boris Godunov.* It became a popular form in the Sixties and Seventies in close association with Russian opera. It was at Pushkin's suggestion that Gogol wrote *The Inspector General,* 1836, a brilliant satire on bureaucracy that escaped the persecution of censorship only because of its unbounded humor. It is one of the most skilfully constructed dramas in Russian literature with true proportion and forceful characterization; it greatly influenced the playwrights of the day who referred to the author as "our great Gogol."

Russian drama increased in realism when Turgeniev denied the dramatic to bring to the stage simple people who lived inert and lazy lives. *A Month in the Country,* 1853, has a subtly woven poetic atmosphere. The characterizations, particularly those of the women, are marked by elaborate naturalness, in line with 19th century taste. The accession of Alexander II brought leniency in censorship and permitted a prolific writing career to Ostrovsky, who created a new type of dramatic realism based on character drawing and local color. There is epic serenity and psychological character development in his tragedy *Live Not As You May but As God Wills,* 1854. In the exceptionally beautiful fantasy *The Snow Maiden,* 1873, Ostrovsky retold in verse a favorite national legend.

Realistic tragedy in the tradition of Gogol was continued by Pisemski, whose *Bitter Fate,* 1863, depicts peasant and gentry life. With A. K. Tolstoy's trilogy *Death of Ivan the Terrible,* 1866, *Tsar Fedor Ivanovich,* 1868, and *Tsar Boris,* 1870, the historical epic returned in all its logical detail. Heavy and slow moving, these plays are nevertheless intensely interesting through unsparing characterizations of the three tsars. Tolstoy wrote a valuable introduction to the second in the trilogy indicating to directors the *mise en scène,* character delineation, and basic idea of the play.

At the end of the 19th century, Chekhov carried the Russian tradition of inactive drama still further. The principal thing became not the action but the emotional accompaniment to the action. In avoiding the traditional theatrical effects Chekhov introduces a new kind of atmospheric effect. There is no central figure in *The Seagull,* 1896, but the characters have more or less equal rights. For this reason the play lends itself to ensemble playing. This play is the poet's cry against the hack writer, and a plea for the right to "depict life not as it is, and not as it ought to be, but as we see it in our dreams." Chekhov's last play *The Cherry Orchard,* 1904, depicts the conflict of a useless but artistic past with a useful but inartistic present. It holds the characteristic rhythms of Russian life, is filled with beautiful symbolism and represents a lyric naturalism that has not been achieved by any other playwright.

At Chekhov's insistence Gorky turned to dramatic composition. He adds no more action to his play than he puts in his novels. Philosophy becomes the action, his characters the tapestry woven background for this questioning of the meaning of life in his one great drama *The Lower Depths,* 1902.

A third Russian master of naturalism, Leo Tolstoy, avoids dramatic form. There is no selectivity in his development. Rather than beginning catastrophically as did Ibsen, Tolstoy elaborates the details of exposition. His plays *The Power of Darkness,* 1886, and *The Living Corpse,* 1912, are valuable because of their remarkable pictures of Russian life made vividly alive by accurate characterizations.

Andreyev turned from naturalism and realism to what he termed the "theatre of the soul," which should represent the inner action of the spirit. Thought was the most dramatic thing to him. His *Life of Man,* 1906, is the pageant of man's life. The fears, hopes and joys of man are dramatized through symbolic stage effects as well as voiced in rhythmic dialogue. The characters are abstractions, and the entire play is a symbol of worldly suffering. *He Who Gets Slapped,* 1915, is a tragedy of disillusionment. Both Strindberg and Maeterlinck have influenced Andreyev. Block introduces the mystic and grotesque in *Little Booth,* 1906, the pathetic story of Pierrot's love for Columbine who assumes now the mask of death, now the mask of a beautiful maiden. The essence of theatricality, it lent itself to Meyerhold's abstract staging in which the masked actors could achieve that statuesque quality and become, as Craig believed all actors should, an integral part of the scenic design.

Evreinov is another symbolist who has had many theories he changes at will with the exception of his invention of the "monodrama" which removes reality from the stage and replaces it with man's dreams. *The Theatre of the Soul,* 1915, shows the soul broken in its rational, emotional and subliminal entities. Then the different concepts of the dancer and the wife and the professor lecture on this dissection of man's soul.

The growth of Russian drama from realism through naturalism to expressionism and symbolism has at all times revealed the Russian creative genius, the individual detailed approach, with emphasis always upon character, be it real or an abstraction.

Drama, Russian, since the Revolution. The literature of the Russian theatre since the Revolution can be roughly divided into six categories or periods: (1) plays about imaginary revolutions, such as the *Mystery-Bouffe* produced in 1918; (2) plays about actual historical revolutions, such as *Stenka Razin,* written in 1919; (3) plays dramatizing the Russian Revolution, such as *The Days of the Turbins* in 1927 and, in the cinema, Eisenstein's *Ten Days That Shook the World* (known in Russia as *October*) ; (4) plays about peasant life and problems since the Revolution, such as *A Window on the Village* in 1928 and, in the cinema, Eisenstein's *Old and New;* (5) plays about industrial workers, their life and problems since the Revolution, such as *The Rails are Humming* in 1928; (6) plays about general, and variegated, social problems, such as *Squaring the Circle* and *Fear.*

Gorky, in *Yegor Bulitchev and Others* and *Dostigaev and Others,* continues the essentially realistic method. Afinogenov (author of *Fear*) is the leading younger Russian dramatist. The most exhaustive treatment of the Soviet period is to be found in H. W. L. Dana's *Handbook of Soviet Drama,* published by American Russian Institute, New York, 1938.

Drama, Scandinavian. See *Drama, Danish; Drama, Norwegian; Drama, Swedish.*

Drama, sentimentalism in. In English drama by 1800 sentimentality came to include errant wives who are forgiven; all sorts of checks to virtue, peace and happiness; poverty; robbers; death sentences; imprisonment; excitement and showy sentiment which were relieved only by comic interims and sidelights.

Drama, social. Plays embodying a philosophy of civilization. Ibsen was probably the first great social dramatist. In his treatment of what came to be known as "feminism" (in *A Doll's House*) and the necessity of candid sex education (in

Ghosts), he was the theatrical herald of a new order. Beside him, in his native land of Norway, if not equalling his stature, is Björnson, who wrote plays of peasant life with a deep realism and political plays from a pronounced liberal viewpoint. Gerhart Hauptmann was also engrossed in social themes; his play, *The Weavers,* is a great study of the working class. After these came George Bernard Shaw, with a different dramatic approach, but with a social cause his predominant master. In *Major Barbara* he treated munitions, in *Mrs. Warren's Profession* prostitution. During the last few years, through the upsurge of the left-wing theatre, social dramatists have had a new lease on life and consequently have been numerous. Among the finest of these are: Elmer Rice, with his *Street Scene* on city penury, his *Judgment Day* on the burning of the Reichstag in Germany; John Howard Lawson, with his *Processional,* a study of strikes, with a reference to the Ku Klux Klan; Maxwell Anderson, with his two plays on the Sacco-Vanzetti case, *Gods of the Lightning* and *Winterset,* and *Both Your Houses,* his muck-raking study of political intrigue and corruption in congress; Clifford Odets, with *Waiting for Lefty,* his play in one act on the taxi strike, his two studies of middle class poverty, *Awake and Sing* and *Paradise Lost,* and his short play indicting Nazi Germany, *Till the Day I Die;* and John Wexley, with his brief for the Scottsboro boys, *They Shall Not Die.*

Drama, Spanish, 15th-17th century. The theatrical literature of this time bears strong reminders of the Middle Ages with their liturgical dramas. From the modern standpoint, the origins of Spanish drama date from 1492, the year in which Juan del Encina presented on Christmas Eve, in the palace of the Duc de Alba two of his *Representaciones,* but its derivations extend far into previous years. Spanish drama, like the drama of all Europe, sprang from the church ritual. The parallelistic lyric poetry of the Hebrews, in which each thought was repeated in varied language, formed the basis of the church liturgy. Such poetry contained the germ of the drama, but it was not until the 9th century that actual acting was introduced into the church service. Early in the 10th century Tutilo, a monk of the Swiss monastery of St. Gall, invented the *tropus,* a dialogue introduced into the introitus, or first part of the mass. Thus was taken the first step toward the dramatization of the church ritual. This *tropus* consisted of an interview which was made up of scriptural passages in Latin between the angel guarding Christ's tomb and three priests who came to seek the body. Though Tutilo added no new language, this *tropus,* used in connection with the Easter service, marks the beginning of the European drama. The genre soon passed on to the other churches and monasteries and became more elaborate, including *The Harrowing of Hell.* This dramatization of Biblical events served as an excellent means of instruction in the tenets of the faith. Tutilo also wrote a Christmas *tropus* which portrayed the Annunciation, the Nativity and the Massacre of the Innocents. Thus were born two of the great cycles of liturgical drama: the Christmas cycle and the Easter cycle. The Epiphany cycle, which developed shortly after, was the most important of all. Three priests, representing the three magi, came from different parts of the church, exchanged greetings, and followed a star which slid along a rope until they were guided to the manger. Then came the adoration scene. To the Liturgical influence was added a colorful and heroic strain to form what became known as the drama of the Golden Age. The outstanding characteristics of this drama were: a fervent Catholicism, patriotism, realism, the predominant importance of plot over characterization, the part prose, part verse style, the disregard of the classical unities and, in general, a disregard for the vast scope of themes. The Golden Age of Spanish literature is represented mainly by four great dramatists: Lope de Vega, Gabriel Téllez (better known as Tirso de Molina), Calderón de la Barca and Ruiz de Alarcón. Of these de Vega and Calderón were the most prolific. The dramatist known as "the father of Spanish drama," Juan del Encina, was born in 1468 or 1469, yet all that we know of his works is a collection of brief dialogues, pastoral or religious, and not intrinsically important. The Spanish drama properly begins with Lope de Rueda, who, besides being a dramatist, was an actor-director of a company of strolling players. The best known of his works is *The Olives*. Cervantes wrote for the theatre but without success conspicuous enough to measure up to his other literary distinctions. Lope de Vega wrote his plays with the express purpose of pleasing the public, and perhaps for that reason has left no single work that has lived through the years. He wrote 1500 plays as well as more than three hundred dramatic sketches, religious processionals and many minor miscellaneous works. Everything he has written is full of swift action and color, but lacks the deeper values of intellect and contemplation. Besides pleasing secular audiences, Lope de Vega flattered the Church with his *autos sacramentales*. Other dramatists of his time were: Ruiz de Alarcón, Guillen de Castro, Perez de Montalvan and Tirso de Molina. Lope de Vega was perhaps surpassed in dramatic mastery by Pedro Calderón de la Barca, who is better known as Calderón. He was less spontaneous, inventive and prolific than de Vega, but more deeply and richly imaginative. His poetry reached the greatest heights known to the contemporary theatre. After Calderón, standards declined, only the cheapest and most popular attractions held sway, and with no new dramatist of the first magnitude to maintain a criterion, the writers of the theatre pandered to the low level of public appreciation. In Spanish literature the one-act play is to be found for the first time in *El auto de los reyes magos,* which is the oldest dramatic work still extant in this country. The tradition of the one-act play is sustained in the dramatic productions of Juan del Encina, and in the *pasos* of Lope de Rueda. The latter used the word *entremés* to mean a comic, irrelevant episode inserted in the main body of a play, though the term *paso* is applied to these today. By the last decade of the 16th century the *entremés* became the fixed term applied to a one-act farce written to be played between the acts of a longer and more serious play. The *entremés,* like the *paso,* could be made up from the merest comic incident and had practically no plot. At the same time that the *entremés* and the *paso* were being developed, many of the best dramatists of Spain were writing drama, which, like the *Auto de los reyes magos,* frequently were composed only of one act. Among the authors who composed *entremés* during the Golden Age, Cervantes and Quinones de Benavente deserve special mention.

Drama, Spanish, 18th century. Spanish literature of the 18th century produced few masterpieces as the period was emasculated by the baneful influence of French neo-classicism. A restricted group of intellectuals frowned on the Golden

Age drama, but the people generally remained loyal to their national drama of the Golden Age. During this century the one-act play was sustained by Ramon de la Cruz (1731-1794) in his *sainetes,* and by Arniches, Vital-Aza and the Quintero brothers in *sainetes* and *zarzuelas.* These latter two forms of dramatic production are termed *genero chico* (the small type) in modern Spanish. In this way the one-act play has continued with few, if any, interruptions from the origins of the literature up until our present day.

Drama, Spanish, 19th century. Romanticism in Spain begins approximately in 1833, the year of the return of many liberals, who were also men of letters, from exiles in various European countries. Romanticism in the Spanish theatre was marked by the same lack of restrictions and rules that had marked the Golden Age drama. Fatalism was a dominant feature. Scenes in tombs, nocturnal landscapes, wild storms and unusual scenery marked the stage settings. The main characters were unusual persons driven on by a fatalism against which they were powerless.

Romanticism stressed the ego, was subjective and emphasized a return of nature. The exotic and local color were emphasized. The romantic drama was emotional, melodramatic. However, Spanish romanticism really contained much realism in the subject-matter of its theatre.

Many liberals were exiled during the reign of Fernando VII and some spent their exiles, at least in part, in London and Paris. This gave them the opportunity to become acquainted with Byron, Scott, Hugo and other famous authors of the time. In Spain the romanticists rehabilitated Spain's glorious past.

Drama, Spanish, 20th century before the First World War. The pre-War Spanish drama, like much of that of the post War period, was dominated by the dramatist Jacinto Benavente. He helped to bring a greater realism, a finer drawn satire, a greater attention to ideas into the theatre. Echegaray, a member of the old neo-romantic school, adapted himself to some extent to the new realism but kept an essentially romantic cast to his plays and brought about something of a school of his own. The plays of Galdos were among the most substantial of all, embodying certain strong and profound social convictions. With the rise of the Quintero brothers the expression "the theatre of kindliness" came into conception; their plays always expressed a belief in the natural goodness of man. Sierra appeared with plays of optimistic tenderness.

Drama, Spanish, 20th century since the First World War. Since the World War the prestige of Benavente has increased and his influence has been powerful. The popularity and influence of the Quinteros have continued. The plays of Sierra, once full of optimistic tenderness, have now leaned toward social apostleship. All these have had their various imitators.

Drama, static. A style of playwriting expounded by the Belgian dramatist, Maurice Maeterlinck, in which inner, spiritual meaning, as against outward conflict in action, is presented. The nearest approximation of this interior action, according to Maeterlinck (says Hugh Allison Smith in his *Main Currents of Modern French Drama*), is "the brief action of the Greek theatre," and the attempt in some of Ibsen's plays "to suggest or evoke symbolically a deeper and more mysterious tragedy, or a dramatic dialogue, without actually putting it in words."

Drama, subjects (viz. plays about a person or subject) for the guidance of those seeking to produce plays on a chosen subject or historical personage. The selection of plays arranged by subject include only those which have been consulted. All of these lists could and should be amplified. It is intended to offer this experimental list in the hope that if it is found useful a way of continuing it will be discovered. Plays about a few historical or literary persons are also included. This also holds true for examples listed under each sub-division of the heading.

For subjects not found here (such as Christmas, Easter, etc.) substantial bibliographies may be found in most public libraries under the heading: U. S. Works Progress Administration (Federal Theatre Project), National Service Bureau Publications; Lists 1936-1939.

Drama, subjects, actors and acting. Examples: *Wise Tomorrow* (Powys); *Mr. Booth* (Thomsen); *Homespun* (Koenigsberg); *The Sea Gull* (Chekhov); *Accidental Family* (Gross); *The Shannons of Broadway* (Gleason); *Excess Baggage* (MacGowan); *Bonnet Over the Windmill* (Smith); *At the Theatre* (Taylor); *Drama at Inish* (Robinson); *Straw Hat* (Unkelbach); *Reflected Glory* (Kelly); *In Theatre Street* (Lenormand); *Catch a Comet by Its Tail* (Woodbury); *Love and How to Cure It* (Wilder); *Let the Mare Run* (Grant, Perry); *Stage Door* (Kaufman, Ferber); *Nine Sharp* (Farjeon); *Sing, Sweet Angels* (Forrest); *Ruby Morn* (Landstone); *Dearly Beloved* (Beahan-Buckner); *Comedienne* (Novello); *The Fabulous Invalid* (Hart, Kaufman); *A Woman's a Fool—To be Clever* (Bennett, Hannah); *The Lady from Broadway* (Ballard); *The King of Nowhere* (Bridie); *The Nutmeg Tree* (Sharp); *Pamela* (Carole); *Rhyme Without Reason* (North, Gow); *Goodness, How Sad!* (Morley); *Le Comedien* (Guitry); *Duet in Floodlight* (Priestley); *Central Casting* (Cosentino); *I Must Love Someone* (Kirkland, Georgie); *A Moral Entertainment* (Maibaum); *Failures* (Lenormand); *Royal Family* (Kaufman, Ferber); *The Torch-Bearers* (Kelly); *Here Come the Clowns* (Barry); *Trelawney of the Wells* (Pinero); *The Play's the Thing* (Molnar); *The Rehearsal* (Sheridan); *The Critic* (Sheridan); *The Flattering Word* (Kelly).

See also *Theatre; Cinema*.

ADOLESCENCE. Fata Morgana (Vajda); *Ah, Wilderness* (O'Neill); *Merton of the Movies* (Tarkington); *Seventeen* (Tarkington); *Young Woodley* (Van Druten); *The Jazz Age* (Hall); *Dame Nature* (Birabeau); *Mirror for Children* (Rogers).

ADULTERY. The Circle (Maugham); *Old Music* (Winter); *Even as You and I* (Cole); *The Second Mrs. Tanqueray* (Pinero); *Stork on Skis* (Acton); *Sweet Sorrow* (Swift); *Trois et Une* (Amiel); *Madame Bovary* (Levy, Baty, Flaubert); *Alte Liebe Rostet Nicht* (Bock, Giannini); *Banana Ridge* (Travers); *Alien Earth*

(Catto); *All Fools' Night* (Vernon); *All Through the Night* (Washburne); *Batoche* (Ferdinand); *The Road to Rome* (Sherwood); *The Devil* (Levy); *The Latitude of Love* (Richman, Weil); *Lot's Wife* (Blackmore); *Gallivanting Lady* (Prideaux); *Hatters Castle* (Cronin, Knoblock); *Where Do We Go From Here?* (Bowers); *Mr. and Mrs. Phipps* (Hamilton); *The Monument of Memory* (Wertheim); *Pardon, Madame* (Coolus, Rivoire); *Le Peché* (Orna); *Goodness, How Sad!* (Morley); *Land's End* (Lucas); *Septembre* (Coline); *This Sheltered Life* (Turney); *Thou Shalt Not* (Zola); *Fata Morgana* (Vajda); *Where There's A Will* (Guitry); *Black Corners* (Flack); *Les Parents Terribles* (Cocteau); *Mamba's Daughters* (Heyward); *The Primrose Path* (Buckner, Hart); *I Must Love Someone* (Kirkland, Georgie).

ALBERT, PRINCE CONSORT. *Vickie and Albert* (De Reyes); *Victoria* (Housman); *Victoria, Queen of England* (Housman); *Victoria Regina* (Housman); *The Friend of a Queen* (De Reyes).

AMERICANIZATION. *One Flight Down* (Stromm, Freund, Friedman); *The American Way* (Kaufman, Hart); *Life and Death of An American* (Sklar); *America* (Bartholomew); *America, Yesterday and Today* (Lamkin); *Americans* (Schoonmaker); *Awake and Sing* (Odets); *Melting Pot* (Zangwill); *We Americans* (Gropper, Siegel).

ANNE OF ENGLAND (1665-1714). *A Glass of Water* (Scribe); *Viceroy Sarah* (Ginsbury).

ANTI-WAR. *Lysistrata* (Aristophanes); *What Price Glory* (Anderson, Stallings); *For Services Rendered* (Maugham); *Journey's End* (Sherriff); *No More Peace!* (Toller); *Wings Over Europe* (Nicholas, Browne); *Miracle at Verdun* (Chlumberg); *Peace on Earth* (Sklar-Maltz); *Paths of Glory* (Howard); *If This Be Treason* (Holmes, Lawrence); *Johnny Johnson* (Green); *Idiot's Delight* (Sherwood); *Flowers of the Forest* (Van Druten); *Bury the Dead* (Shaw); *Sacrifice* (Tagore); *This Seat of Mars* (Bartlett); *Bila Nemoc* (Capek); *Last Full Measure* (Musmanno); *Till the Cows Come Home* (Kerr); *Peace Prize* (Boretz); *The Ghost of Yankee Doodle* (Howard); *The Good Soldier Schweik* (Hasek-Schweid); *Blocks* (Thatcher); *Trojan Incident* (Homer, Euripides); *Robert's Wife* (Ervine); *Napoleon* (Trench); *Out of the Picture* (MacNeice); *Siege* (Shaw).

ARNOLD, BENEDICT. *The Treason and Death of Benedict Arnold* (Chapman); *Arnold and André* (Calvert); *Benedict Arnold* (Emerson); *Arnold* (Orton); *A Point of Honor* (Eisinger, Van Gluck).

AUTOMOBILES. *Retreat From Folly* (Gould-Russell); *The Star-Wagon* (Anderson); *Can We Tell?* (Gore, Browne); *Man and Superman* (Shaw).

AVARICE. *Volpone; or, The Fox* (Jonson); *Return to Sanity* (Rushton, Mack); *Smash* (Walshe); *The Late Christopher Bean* (Howard); *Peace in Our Time* (Walshe, Balchin); *The Soul of Nicholas Snyders* (Jerome); *The Little Foxes* (Hellman).

AVIATION. *The Ghost of Yankee Doodle* (Howard); *Air Raid* (Hutteroth); *A Great Day* (Kirshon); *Night Sky* (Peach); *Distinguished Gathering* (Parish); *Official Secret* (Dell); *Flight* (Cozine); *Ceiling Zero* (Wead); *Flight* (Saul and Lantz); *Georgia Transport* (Andrews).

BABIES. In the Best of Families (Hart, Braddell) ; *Strange Rhythm* (Bolton, Vagliano) ; *Life Begins* (Axelson) ; *Dame Nature* (Birabeau).

BASEBALL. Triple Play (Roos) ; *Brother Rat* (Monks, Finklehoffe) ; *Elmer the Great* (Lardner).

BIBLE. Seed of Adam (Williams) ; *Spark in Judea* (Delderfield) ; *Sulamith* (Goldfaden) ; *Chorus Angelorum* (Morrah) ; *The Cup of Trembling* (Carlton) ; *Ruth* (Blum) ; *Thou Art The Man* (Hood) ; *King Saul* (Parry, Rich) ; *Tobias and the Angel* (Bridie) ; *Eve Serves a Term of Childhood* (Abell) ; *Jonah and the Whale* (Bridie) ; *The Eternal Road* (Werfel, Weill) ; *Die Frau Des Potiphar* (Holenia) ; *Hieram und Salomo* (Steffen) ; *Susannah and the Elders* (Langner) ; *The Prophecy* (Hatch) ; *Herod's House* (Masterman) ; *Jeremiah* (Zweig) ; *The Unveiling* (Downes).

BLINDNESS. The Inner Light (Miner, Csergo) ; *A Blind World* (Wolf) ; *The Blind* (Maeterlinck).

BOARDING HOUSE LIFE. Spring Tide (Billam, Goldsmith) ; *Women Without Men* (Ellis) ; *39 East* (Crothers) ; *Women Go on Forever* (Ruben).

BOOTH, JOHN WILKES. Mr. Booth (Thomsen) ; *Gentlemen Unafraid* (Kern-Hammerstein, Harbach, Boykin) ; *Man Who Killed Lincoln* (Harris) ; *Audacious Mr. Booth* (Ford).

BORGIA, LUCREZIA. Lucrezia Borgia's Little Party (Talbot) ; *Les Borgia* (Josset).

THE BRONTE FAMILY. Charlotte, Emily and Anne (Sangster) ; *Moor Born* (Totheroh) ; *Wild Decembers* (Dane).

BROWN, JOHN (1800-1859). *Gallows Glorious* (Gow) ; *Battle Hymn* (Blankfort, Gold).

BURBAGE, RICHARD. Sing, Sweet Angels (Forrest) ; *Un Amour de Shakespeare* (Auzanet).

BUSINESS. It Happened Today (Hallatt) ; *Straight Scotch* (Hart) ; *Big Business* (Waller, Tunbridge, Browne, Lee, Carter) ; *The Tailor Becomes a Storekeeper* (Pinski) ; *Peace in Our Time* (Walshe, Balchin) ; *The Little Foxes* (Hellman).

BYRON, GEORGE NOEL GORDON, LORD. Bright Rebel (Young) ; *Fallen Angel* (Bodeen) ; *His Heart Was Not Burned* (Laver) ; *Lord Byron* (Ferber) ; *Glorious Martyr* (Pike) ; *Crede Byron* (Lea) ; *Love and Lord Byron* (Rice) ; *Bitter Harvest* (Turney) ; *Immortal Byron* (Glick, Sobel).

CAPITAL PUNISHMENT. The Dead Hand (Fraser-Hemmerde) ; *The Last Mile* (Wexley) ; *The Criminal Code* (Flavin).

CATHERINE II OF RUSSIA (1729-1796). *The Great Catherine* (Shaw) ; *Empress of Destiny* (Lee, Walsh) ; *Catherine Empereur* (Rostand).

CATHOLICISM. White Steed (Carroll) ; *Father Malachy's Miracle* (Doherty) ; *Shadow and Substance* (Carroll).

CELLINI, BENVENUTO (1500-1569). *Cellini* (Walsh) ; *The Firebrand* (Mayer).

CHARLES I OF ENGLAND. Charles, The King (Colbourne) ; *Stubble Before Swords* (Dornhurst-Jordan).

CHARLES II, KING OF ENGLAND. *Thank You Mr. Pepys* (Lipscomb); *Ninety Sail* (Bryant, Lipscomb); *Thomas Ken* (Cropper); *Loves of Charles II* (Skinner).

CHILD LABOR. *Sunup to Sundown* (Faragoh); *But for the Grace of God* (Atlas).

CHILDREN. *Mirror for Children* (Rogers); *But For the Grace of God* (Atlas); *Children's Hour* (Hellman); *Children's Tragedy* (Schoenherr); *Dead End* (Kingsley); *Fly Away Home* (Bennet, White); *Remember the Day* (Higley, Dunning); *Seen But Not Heard* (Baumer, Berkeley); *Thunder on the Left* (Pryce); *Wednesday's Child* (Cady); *The Women* (Brokaw); *Little Stranger* (Hilliker, Caldwell); *Tony Draws a Horse* (Clark); *The Secret Garden* (Burnett); *Schoolhouse on the Lot* (Fields, Chodorov); *The Golden Cage* (Smith, Blake).

CLASS STRUGGLE. *Pins and Needles* (Rome-Arent, Blitzstein, Eisenberg, Friedman, Rome); *Tornado* (Egri); *I'm a Stranger Here* (Priestley); *Paradise Lost* (Odets); *People at Sea* (Priestley); *Philistines* (Gorky); *Truth* (Korneichuk); *Earth* (Virta).

CLERGY. *Father Malachy's Miracle* (Doherty); *First Legion* (Lavery); *A Village Priest* (Grundy); *Murder in the Cathedral* (Eliot); *Roseanne* (Stephens); *The Parson Said No* (Powell); *Robert's Wife* (Ervine); *Professor Bernhardi* (Schnitzler); *Ascent of F 6* (Auden Isherwood); *On the Rocks* (Shaw); *The Bishop Misbehaves* (Jackson); *She Had to do Something* (O'Faolain); *The Silver Jubilee* (O'Daly); *The White Steed* (Carroll); *Thomas Ken* (Cropper); *Yes and No* (Horne); *The Zeal of Thy House* (Sayers); *Shadow and Substance* (Carroll); *The Char-lady and the Angel* (Shipp).

COLLEGES AND UNIVERSITIES. *Delightfully Yours* (O'Neill); *The West Point Cadet* (Billand, Barre); *Fool's Hill* (Wetzel); *Goodbye, Mr. Chips* (Hilton, Burnham); *Where Do We Go From Here?* (Bowers); *Sorority House* (Chase); *Reunion* (White); *Curriculi Curricula* (Gilmore, Farrow-Fleischer, Reisman, O'Bryen); *And For Yale* (Davis); *The Old Suit* (Brown); *Brother Rat* (Monks, Finkelhoffe).

COMMUNISM. *Tornado* (Egri); *Today in America; The Plough and the Stars* (O'Casey); *Waiting for Lefty* (Odets); *Distant Point* (Afinogenov, Griffith); *To Quito and Back* (Hecht); *Kiss the Boys Goodbye* (Boothe); *Leave It to Me* (Porter-Spewack); *Les Evenements de Boetie* (Berr, Verneuil); *Suzanna and the Elders* (Langner, Marshall); *Leonidas* (Verneuil); *Time and the Hour* (Kennington, McElwee); *Close Quarters* (Lennox, Somin).

CORDAY, CHARLOTTE. *Charlotte Corday* (Kingsley & Benedict); *Charlotte Corday* (Klein); *Charlotte Corday* (Montesquieu); *Charlotte Corday* (Jerome).

CRIME. *The Gangster* (Hemingway); *Warsaw By Night* (Siegel, Levin); *Alias the Deacon* (Hymer, Clemens); *Think of a Number* (Hoare); *Something for Nothing* (Essex, Schwartz); *Criminals* (Bruckner, Auerbach); *The Front Page* (Hecht, MacArthur); *Death on the Table* (Beauchamp, Pertwee); *Thanks for Tomorrow* (Bailey); *Das Horoskop Seiner Lordschaft* (Loder, Wilde); *The Green Pack* (Wallace); *Jail for Sale* (Park); *Money Talks* (Armont, Marchand); *Le Bal des Voleurs* (Anouilh); *Snow Train* (Carpenter); *But For the Grace* (Otway); *The*

Gentle People (Shaw); *Worth a Million* (Sylvaine); *Alias Jimmy Valentine* (Armstrong).

CRITICS. *The Critic* (Sheridan); *The Guardsman* (Molnar); *Fanny's First Play* (Shaw).

DANCING. *White Poppy* (Marlow); *She Had to do Something* (O'Faolain); *Balalaika* (Maschwitz); *Laura Garnett* (Stokes); *The Three Set Out* (Leaver).

DAVID. *The Boy David* (Barrie); *Thou Art The Man* (Hood); *King Saul* (Parry, Rich).

DEATH. *Road Crash* (Hutteroth); *Merely Murder* (Thomas); *Brand* (Ibsen); *The Last Trump* (Bridie); *Outward Bound* (Vane); *On Borrowed Time* (Osborn); *Our Town* (Wilder); *Little Earthquake* (Mayor); *The Bridge* (Adair); *Volpone, or The Fox* (Jonson); *The Intruder* (Maeterlinck).

DENTISTS. *One Sunday Afternoon* (Hagan); *Rocket to the Moon* (Odets); *Ruby Morn* (Landstone).

DETECTIVES. *Ten Minute Alibi* (Armstrong); *The Ninth Guest* (Davis); *The Wooden Kimono* (Floyd); *Sherlock Holmes* (Gillette); *Criminal-at-Large* (Wallace).

See also *Crime.*

DEVILS. *A Comedy of Good and Evil* (Hughes); *God's Jailer* (Thomas); *Madame Fears the Dark* (Irwin); *The Virgin and the Clerk* (Porter); *Faust* (Goethe); *Doctor Faustus* (Marlowe); *The Devil* (Levy); *Here Come the Clowns* (Barry); *The Witch of Edmonton* (Dekker).

DICTATORS. *Power and Glory* (Capek); *Lorelei* (Deval); *Waltz in Goose Step* (Garrett); *Sejanus* (Jonson); *Trial of a Judge* (Spender); *The Dogs of War* (Watson); *Swing Along* (Broones-Bolton, Thompson, Furker); *Dux* (Conway); *Julius Caesar* (Shakespeare); *Save Me The Waltz* (Dayton); *Punch and Judy* (Gielgud); *Judgment Day* (Rice); *Glorious Morning* (Macowan); *It Can't Happen Here* (Lewis); *Geneva* (Shaw); *The King of Nowhere* (Bridie).

DISEASE, EPILEPSY. *Step Into My Parlor* (Risjean).

DISEASE, TUBERCULOSIS. *The Switchback* (Bridie); *The Straw* (O'Neill); *Rovina* (Baines); *Mountain Sunshine* (Hunyady).

DISEASE, VENEREAL. *Damaged Goods* (Brieux); *Ghosts* (Ibsen); *Maya* (Gantillon-Boyd); *Mrs. Warren's Profession* (Shaw); *Moral* (Thoma); *Paths of Glory* (Howard); *Spirochete* (Sundgaard); *Flight into Darkness* (McDonagh-Hill).

DISEASE, YELLOW FEVER. *Yellow Jack* (Howard).

DIVORCE. *Imitation By Design* (Laidlaw, Lively); *Retreat from Folly* (Gould, Russel, Anglin); *Gay Divorce* (Porter, Taylor); *The Circle* (Maugham); *Reno* (Haggart); *Excuse Me* (Hughes); *Sarah Simple* (Milve); *Strange Rhythm* (Bolton, Vagliano); *Dearly Beloved* (Beahan, Buckner); *On the Rocks* (Shaw); *As Husbands Go* (Blow, Whitehead); *The Animal Kingdom* (Barry); *Co-Respondent Unknown* (Harris, Goldman); *La Chaleur Du Sein* (Birabeau); *Lightnin'* (Smith, Bacon); *The Innocent Party* (Harwood, Kirk); *Laughter in Court* (Mills); *The Philadelphia Story* (Barry).

DUNCAN, ISADORA. *Diana* (Davis); *Laura Garnett* (Stokes).

EDUCATION. Topaze (Pagnol) ; *Bachelor Born* (Hay) ; *Wandering School* (Auslaender, Kassil) ; *The Corn is Green* (Williams) ; *Goodbye, Mr. Chips* (Hilton, Burnham) ; *What A Life* (Goldsmith) ; *The Children's Hour* (Hellman) ; *Children in Uniform* (Winsloe) ; *These Days* (Clugston) ; *Remember the Day* (Higley, Dunning).

See also *Colleges and Universities.*

EDWARD VIII, KING OF ENGLAND. See *Drama, subjects, Windsor, Edward, Duke of.*

ELIZABETH OF AUSTRIA. Masque of Kings (Anderson) ; *The Queen Was Young* (Branden, Branden) ; *Elizabeth of Austria* (Sprigge).

ELIZABETH, QUEEN OF ENGLAND (1533-1603). *The Virgin Queen's Daughter* (Whalen) ; *The Lost Colony* (Green) ; *Merrie England* (German, Hood) ; *The Tragedy of Queen Elizabeth* (Browne) ; *The Boy of Bisley* (Clemens) ; *Le Comte D'Essex* (Coutier) ; *Leicester* (Craigmyle) ; *Elizabeth of England* (Hammond) ; *The Great Elizabeth* (Hay) ; *Kring Drottningen* (Horn) ; *Amy Robsart* (Hugo) ; *The Prince* (John) ; *Clipt Wings* (Leigh) ; *Marie Stuart et Elisabeth* (Marford) ; *To Kill the Queen* (McColvin) ; *Le Testament de la Reine Elisabeth* (Nus) ; *If You Know Not Me, You Know No Bodie; or, The Troubles of Queen Elizabeth* (Heywood) ; *Rebell in England* (Schwarz) ; *Elizabeth, Königinn von England* (Mueller) ; *Elizabeth of England* (Shaler) ; *Essex* (Stainer) ; *Elizabeth of England* (Tagger) ; *Elizabeth of England* (Tullidge) ; *The Princess and the Players* (Watts) ; *Queen Elizabeth; or, The Origin of Shakespeare* (Gregg) ; *Queen Elizabeth* (Hole) ; *The Albion Queens* (Banks) ; *Gloriana* (Bruckner) ; *Elizabeth, La Femme Sans Homme* (Josset) ; *Young Elizabeth* (Rives) ; *Elizabeth of England* (Bruckner) ; *Elizabeth the Queen* (Anderson) ; *Mary of Scotland* (Anderson) ; *The Tudor Wench* (Thane).

ESPIONAGE. No Sleep for the Wicked (Ames) ; *The Panama Canal* (Lazarain) ; *Lady at Large* (Goodman) ; *The Toss of a Coin* (Hackett).

ESSEX, EARL OF. Gloriana (Bruckner) ; *Elizabeth, La Femme Sans Homme* (Josset) ; *Elizabeth and Essex* (Anderson) ; *Elizabeth of England* (Bruckner).

FAITH. Ben Hur (Wallace, Young, Kelley) ; *The Christian* (Caine) ; *The Eternal Road* (Werfel, Weill) ; *The First Legion* (Lavery) ; *The Fool* (Pollock) ; *The Joyous Season* (Barry) ; *The Last Days of Pompeii* (Fitzball, Bulwer-Lytton) ; *The Last Days of Pompeii* (Oxenford, Bulwer-Lytton) ; *The Last Days of Pompeii* (Buckstone, Bulwer-Lytton) ; *The Miracle* (Vollmoeller, Humperdinck) ; *Many Mansions* (Goodman, Goodman) ; *Mary of Magdala* (Heyse) ; *Mary Magdalene* (Hebbel) ; *Mary Magdalene* (Maeterlinck) ; *The Ladder* (Davis) ; *Nydia, The Blind Girl of Pompeii* (Fox, Bulwer-Lytton) ; *Quo Vadis* (Strange, Edwards, Sienkiewicz) ; *Passing of the Third Floor Back* (Jerome) ; *St. Elmo* (Holcombe, Evans) ; *Susan and God* (Crothers) ; *Faith Healer* (Moody) ; *Jean de la Lune* (Achard) ; *Shadow and Substance* (Carroll) ; *Father Malachy's Miracle* (Doherty, Marshall) ; *King Argimenes and the Unknown Warrior* (Dunsany).

FAMILY LIFE. Daybreak (Cowl, Murfin) ; *Four Fierce Women* (Garth) ; *Fame* (Gusev) ; *Farfalle* (Bagno) ; *Invaded Retreat* (Single) ; *The First Year* (Craven) ; *Love My Dog* (Pierce, Miller) ; *Famille* (Amiel, Amiel-Petry) ; *Miscast* (Gillam) ;

The Patriot (O'Callaghan) ; *You Can't Take It With You* (Hart, Kaufman) ; *March Hares* (Gribble) ; *The Parson Said No!* (Powell) ; *No Laughter in Heaven* (Pittenger) ; *The Prodigal Father* (Barry) ; *Never Trouble Trouble* (Hilliker, Caldwell) ; *This Money Business* (Campion) ; *Two Time Mary* (Davis) ; *Trouble for Two* (Burden) ; *Trois et Une* (Amiel) ; *Yes and No* (Horne) ; *Western Union, Please!* (Goodrich, Hackett) ; *Widow Jadzia* (Tuwim-Ruszkowski, Tuwim) ; *Women of Property* (Wuolijoki) ; *Asmodée* (Mauriac) ; *American Wing* (Jennings) ; *Black Swans* (Kerr) ; *Famille* (Amiel) ; *The Good* (Erskin) ; *Dear Family* (Frank, Rosenthal) ; *Honey* (Greene) ; *I Can't Help It* (Goodrich) ; *Can We Tell?* (Gore, Browne) ; *Dear Octopus* (Smith) ; *Grandpa* (Morgan) ; *Hatter's Castle* (Cronin, Knoblock) ; *Mad Hatters* (Perdue) ; *Mademoiselle* (Deval) ; *Sixième Etage* (Ghéri) ; *Soubrette* (Deval) ; *Too Large A Family* (Birabeau) ; *And Niobe Wept* (Wilmot) ; *Tony Draws a Horse* (Clark) ; *Bird's Nest* (Robinson) ; *Peace and Goodwill* (Bowen) ; *Summer for Seven* (McNair) ; *A Ship Comes Home* (Fisher) ; *Uncle Harry* (Job) ; *We The Willoughbys* (Kanin, Ingram) ; *The Primrose Path* (Buckner, Hart) ; *Week-End at Stormes* (Smalley) ; *Wind From the West* (O'Callaghan) ; *The London Prodigal* (author unknown) ; *The Oldest Son* (Galsworthy) ; *Hindle Wakes* (Houghton) ; *Magda* (Suderman) ; *Little Stranger* (Hilliker, Caldwell) ; *Yes and No* (Horne) ; *George and Margaret* (Savory) ; *The Royal Family* (Kaufman, Ferber) ; *Three Cornered Moon* (Tonkonogy) ; *Our Everyday Lives* (Prescott) ; *Whiteoaks* (De la Roche) ; *Palm Beach* (Hunter, Danning) ; *The Prize Novel* (Mitchell) ; *The Dear Queen* (Canley) ; *The Little Foxes* (Hellman) ; *Awake and Sing* (Odets) ; *A Party for Christmas* (Hunter) ; *The Maitlands* (Mackenzie) ; *Saturday's Children* (Anderson) ; *Craig's Wife* (Kelly).

FARM LIFE. *The Touch of Silk* (Davies) ; *Two Fields* (McKee) ; *Mid-West* (Hagan) ; *A Man, A Wife, And A Horse* (Xantho) ; *In Clover* (Scott) ; *Down on the Farm* (Tailby) ; *The New Gossoon* (Shiels) ; *Because We're Here* (Irving) ; *Everywhere I Roam* (Sundgaard, Connelly).

FASCISM (ANTI-FASCIST). *Private Hicks* (Maltz) ; *Auf Wiedersehen* (Cowan) ; *Till the Day I Die* (Odets) ; *Heil Hitler* (Walinsky) ; *The Crooked Cross* (Carson) ; *The Shattered Lamp* (Reade) ; *Rain From Heaven* (Behrman) ; *It Can't Happen Here* (Lewis) ; *We Shall Conquer* (Blake) ; *The Jewish Wife* (Brecht) ; *Pastor Hall* (Toller) ; *The Sun and I* (Stavis, Stavis) ; *Bitter Stream* (Wolfson) ; *Judgment Day* (Rice) ; *Racconti d'Autunno* (Forsano) ; *To Quito and Back* (Hecht) ; *Siege* (Shaw) ; *The Frodi* (Kennedy) ; *Trial of a Judge* (Spender).

FASCISM (PRO-FASCIST). *I Figli* (Mughini) ; *Mid-West* (Hagan) ; *The Hundred Days* (Mussolini and Forzano) ; *On the Rocks* (Shaw).

FASCISM, GERMANY. *Spell Your Name* (Kortner) ; *Borderline* (Gansert) ; *Crooked Cross* (Carson) ; *Waltz in Goose Step* (Garrett).

FASCISM, ITALY. *Victory* (Munk).

FASCISM, SPAIN. *Alcazar* (Mdivani).

FASCISM, U. S. *American Landscape* (Rice) ; *It Can't Happen Here* (Lewis, Moffett).

FATHERS. *Banana Ridge* (Travers) ; *The Prodigal Father* (Barry) ; *Bird's Nest* (Robinson).

FIREMEN. *One of the Bravest* (McCarthy) ; *The Streets of New York* (Boucicault) ; *The Still Alarm* (Arthur) ; *The Fireman's Flame* (Krimsky).

FIRST WORLD WAR 1914-18. *Maid of France* (Brighouse) ; *Miracle at Verdun* (Chlumberg) ; *Nurse Cavell* (Roberts) ; *Paths of Glory* (Howard) ; *Sailors of Cattaro* (Wolf) ; *Searchers* (Pilcher) ; *The Sorrows of Belgium* (Andreyev) ; *Der Tag* (Barrie) ; *The Unknown Warrior* (Lewis-Reynal) ; *What Price Glory* (Anderson, Stallings) ; *Draw the Fires* (Toller) ; *O'Flaherty, V.C.* (Shaw) ; *The Brothers Ashkenazi* (Shlionsky, Schwarts, Singer) ; *Johnny Johnson* (Green) ; *Barbara's Wedding* (Barrie) ; *The Better 'Ole* (Bairnsfather) ; *Bill of Divorcement* (Dane) ; *The Conquering Hero* (Monkhouse) ; *In the Zone* (O'Neill) ; *Journey's End* (Sherriff) ; *Louvain* (Roberts).

FRENCH REVOLUTION. *Danton's Death* (Buchner) ; *Madame Capet* (Havrette) ; *Six Women* (Cammer) ; *Danton* (Rolland) ; *The Game of Love and Death* (Rolland) ; *La Patrie en Danger* (Goncourt, E. and T.) ; *The Only Way* (Wills).

FRONTIER. *Davy Crockett* (Murdoch) ; *Horizon* (Daly) ; *Sue* (Harte, Pemberton) ; *The Danites in the Sierras* (Miller) ; *Forty-nine* (Miller) ; *Tally Ho* (Miller) ; *An Oregon Idyll* (Miller) ; *My Partner* (Campbell) ; *The White Slave* (Campbell) ; *Green Grow the Lilacs* (Riggs) ; *Night Over Taos* (Anderson).

FUTURE LIFE. *Liliom* (Molnar) ; *Green Pastures* (Connelly) ; *The Glittering Gate* (Dunsany) ; *The Bridge* (Adair) ; *The Last Trump* (Bridie) ; *Johnson Over Jordan* (Priestley) ; *Outward Bound* (Vane).

See also *Supernatural.*

GARIBALDI, GIUSEPPI (1807-82). *Garibaldi in Sicily* (Sawyer, Hatton, Calcott) ; *Garibaldi* (Taylor).

GLADSTONE, WILLIAM E. *Mr. Gladstone* (Williamson) ; *Parnell* (Schauffler) ; *The Uncrowned King* (MacNamara, Pearn).

GOSSIP. *The New Gossoon* (Shiels) ; *Women's Gossip* (Goldoni) ; *Spreading the News* (Gregory) ; *Forty-Nine Dogs in a Meat House* (Conkle) ; *The Jailbird* (Shiels).

GWYN, NELL (ELEANOR). *Sweet Nell of Old Drury* (Kester) ; *Thank You, Mr. Pepys* (Lipscomb) ; *Ninety Sail* (Lipscomb) ; *The Loves of Charles II* (Skinner) ; *Thomas Ken* (Cropper).

HEROD, ANTIPAS (d. A.D. 39). *John The Baptist* (Barry) ; *Herod's House* (Masterman) ; *Salomé* (Wilde) ; *Herod and Mariamne* (Hebbel, Dane).

HOLLYWOOD. *Hey Diddle Diddle* (Cormack) ; *Schoolhouse on the Lot* (Fields, Chodorov) ; *Boy Meets Girl* (Spewack) ; *Greatest Find Since Garbo* (Birchard, Bard) ; *On Location* (Wiley) ; *Dearly Beloved* (Beahan, Buckner) ; *Kiss the Boys Goodbye* (Boothe) ; *Hollywood Be Thy Name* (Fagan) ; *Stars in Your Eyes* (McEvoy) ; *Limelight* (Jerome).

See also *Moving Pictures.*

HORROR. *The Old Women* (DeLovde) ; *Congratulations* (Palmer) ; *Something More Important* (Maltby) ; *Eight O'Clock* (Berkeley) ; *E. and O. E.* (Crawshay,

Williams) ; *Frills* (Joyce, Roberts) ; *Night Must Fall* (Williams) ; *Love from a Stranger* (Vosper).

ILLEGITIMACY. Jenny Frensham (Robinson) ; *The Winter's Tale* (Shakespeare) ; *The Old Maid* (Akins, Wharton) ; *It's a Wise Child* (Johnson) ; *Stork on Skis* (Acton) ; *Trois et Une* (Amiel) ; *Let's Never Change* (Davis) ; *The Corn is Green* (Williams) ; *L'Embuscade* (Kistermaeckers) ; *Hatter's Castle* (Cronin, Knoblock) ; *Mademoiselle* (Deval) ; *La Pouponnière* (Verdun, Oberfeld, Pujol, Pothier) ; *Purgatory* (Yeats) ; *The Silver Jubilee* (O'Daly) ; *Soubrette* (Deval) ; *This Sheltered Life* (Turney) ; *Where There's a Will* (Guitry) ; *Melodrama* (Stuart) ; *Mademoiselle* (Deval) ; *Union Forever* (Gale) ; *Das Wespennest* (Hansen) ; *Twenty Shadows* (Maude) ; *What Every Woman Wants* (Kling, Forbes) ; *He Believed in Marriage* (Parrish) ; *Bachelor Father* (Carpenter) ; *Annie Green; or, The Girl Who Died Twice* (   ) ; *Greatness Comes to the Maronies* (Page, Forrester) ; *Sweet Aloes* (Mallory) ; *Scarlet Letter* (Hatton).

IMAGINARY COUNTRIES. Arms and the Man (Shaw) ; *Marriage Royal* (Wallsten) ; *Punch and Judy* (Gielgud) ; *The Wise Cat* (Heyermans, Val Diaz, Gibson, Cowan) ; *Glorious Morning* (Macowan) ; *Brave New World* (Walinsky, Huxley) ; *Les Evenements de Boetie* (Berr, Verneuil) ; *Surprise Item* (Brooks) ; *Leonidas* (Verneuil) ; *O Mistress Mine* (Travers) ; *Storm Over Europe* (Jerrold, Agar, Chilton).

IMMIGRATION AND EMIGRATION. Everywhere I Roam (Sundgaard, Connelly) ; *The American Way* (Kaufman, Hart) ; *The Melting Pot* (Zangwill) ; *Mrs. O'Brien Entertains* (Madden).

INHERITANCE. Thirty Days Hath September (Gaumont, Sobell) ; *Neal Maquade* (Shiels) ; *Where There's A Will* (Guitry) ; *Das Wespennest* (Hansen) ; *Week-End at Stormes* (Smalley).

INSANITY. Ghosts (Ibsen) ; *The Island* (Hodge) ; *The Second Mrs. Tanqueray* (Pinero) ; *Satyr* (Leslie) ; *Step Into My Parlor* (Risjean) ; *This Same Love* (Ford Imman) ; *The Case of Constance Kent* (Box) ; *La Sirena Varada* (Casona) ; *Small Hotel* (Clark) ; *The New Gossoon* (Shiels) ; *Henry IV* (Pirandello) ; *Should a Mother Tell?* (Freiman) ; *Twenty Shadows* (Maude).

IRISH. Mrs. O'Brien Entertains (Madden) ; *Fiddler's House* (Colum) ; *King and Hermit* (Corkery) ; *Clan Falvey* (Corkery) ; *Passing of Dana's People* (Craig) ; *Full of the Moon* (Herrick) ; *For Ireland's Sake or, Under the Green Flag* (Muldoon) ; *Birthright* (Murray) ; *Piper* (O'Riordan) ; *Patriots* (Robinson) ; *Robert Emmet* (Tietzelieve) ; *Cathleen ni Houlihan* (Yeats) ; *King's Threshold* (Yeats) ; *Rising of the Moon* (Gregory) ; *Spreading the News* (Gregory) ; *White Cockade* (Gregory) ; *Playboy of the Western World* (Synge) ; *Riders to the Sea* (Synge) ; *Deirdre of the Sorrows* (Synge) ; *Shadow of the Glen* (Synge) ; *Well of the Saints* (Synge).

JACKSON, ANDREW. The Awful Mrs. Eaton (Benet, Ferrar) ; *Everglades* (Alexander) ; *Rachel's Man* (Foote).

JAMES II OF ENGLAND. Ninety Sail (Bryant, Lipscomb) ; *Thank You, Mr. Pepys* (Lipscomb) ; *Sweet Nell of Old Drury* (Kester).

JEALOUSY. The Winter's Tale (Shakespeare); *Othello* (Shakespeare); *Daybreak* (Cowl, Murfin); *I am Different* (Hatvany); *Illusion* (Bernard, Boyd).

JEANNE d'ARC. The Maid of Orleans (Benson); *The Maid of Orleans* (Calvert); *The Maid of Orleans* (Schiller); *The Lily of France* (Parker); *Maid of France* (Brighouse); *Joan la Romée* (Harris); *Joan the Maid* (Ould); *Joan of Arc* (Julley); *Joan of Arc* (Stevens); *Trial of Jeanne d'Arc* (Garnett); *Saint Joan* (Shaw); *Joan of Arc* (McLaren); *The Lily of France* (Brougham).

JESUS CHRIST. The King of Glory (Shiner); *Publican and Sinners* (Andrewes); *Family Portrait* (Coffee, Cowen); *Trial of Jesus* (Masefield); *Oberammergau Passion Play; Jesus of Nazareth* (Hulley).

JEWS. Escaped (Steen); *We Never Die* (Ginsburg); *What's In A Name?* (Einstein); *His Eyes* (Feinstein); *They, Too, Arise* (Miller); *The Four Corners* (Landa); *Uriel Acosts* (Gutzkow); *The Golem* (Leivich); *The Eternal Road* (Lewisohn, Drake); *Adam* (Lewisohn); *Loyalties* (Galsworthy); *Cohen and Son* (Goller); *The Jew* (Cumberland); *The Eternal Jew* (Pinski); *The Golem* (Leivick); *The Bells or, The Polish Jew* (Erckmann, Chatrian); *The Wandering Jew* (Thurston).

JEWS IN AUSTRIA. Professor Bernhardi (Schnitzler).

JEWS IN GERMANY. Requiem For An Idiot (Menon); *Crooked Cross* (Carson); *Prof. Mamlock* (Wolf).

JEWS IN ITALY. The Merchant of Venice (Shakespeare).

JEWS IN PALESTINE. Sad (Batador); *Family Portrait* (Coffee, Cowen); *Soil* (Rodell, Rost).

JEWS IN POLAND. The Brothers Ashkenazi (Shlionsky, Schwartz, Singer).

JEWS IN RUSSIA. Herschelle Ostropoler (Gershenson); *Highwayman Boitre* (Kulbak).

JEWS IN U. S. The Russian Jew in America (Gordin); *Having Wonderful Time* (Kober); *The Melting Pot* (Zangwill); *Unto This Day* (Winer); *Processional* (Lawson); *Where Do We Go From Here?* (Bowers); *Union Forever* (Gale); *Round the Family Table* (Stutchkoff); *Prejudice* (Selwyn); *Awake and Sing* (Odets); *Who is Who?* (Aleichem); *Potash and Perlmutter* (Glass, Klein); *Abie's Irish Rose* (Nichols).

JOHN THE BAPTIST. Herod's House (Masterman); *Salomé* (Wilde); *The King of Glory* (Shiner).

JUAREZ, BENITO PABLO. Coronation (Segal); *Juarez and Maximilian* (Werfel).

JUDAS ISCARIOT. The King of Glory (Shiner); *Family Portrait* (Coffee, Cowen); *Judas* (Rathbone, Ferris).

JUSTICE. Trial of a Judge (Spender); *Justice* (Galsworthy).

KIDNAPPING. Kind Lady (Chodorov); *Too Many Heroes* (Schary); *The Little Man* (Galsworthy); *One Thing After Another* (Noble); *Death on the Table* (Beauchamp, Pertwee); *Come Across* (Beauchamp, Pertwee); *Post Road* (Steele, Mitchell); *Leaning on Letty* (Steele, Mitchell).

LABOR. Stevedore (Sklar, Peters); *Plant in the Sun* (Bengal); *Processional* (Lawson); *Press Time* (Bookman, Coles); *Gymnazisty* (Trenyev); *Strife* (Galsworthy) ; *Waiting for Lefty* (Odets) ; *Days to Come* (Hellman) ; *Pins and Needles* (Rome, Arent, Blitzstein, Eisenberg, Friedman) ; *They, Too, Arise* (Miller) ; *The Cradle Will Rock* (Blitzstein) ; *The Frodi* (Kennedy) ; *American Landscape* (Rice) ; *Sixth Avenue* (Bryan) ; *Jobs, Inc.* (Shreiber) ; *Close Quarters* (Lennox, Somin).

See also *Child Labor*.

LINCOLN, ABRAHAM. *Follow Me Ever* (Horgan) ; *Gentlemen Unafraid* (Kern, Hammerstein, Harbach, Boykin) ; *Abe Lincoln in Illinois* (Sherwood) ; *Abraham Lincoln* (Drinkwater) ; *If Booth Had Missed* (Goodman) ; *The Lonely Man* (Koch) ; *Prologue to Glory* (Conkle) ; *Gallows Glorious* (Gow) ; *Mantle of Lincoln* (Dalton) ; *Child of the Frontier* (Levinger) ; *Gettysburg* (Masters).

LIQUOR. *Daybreak* (Cowl-Murfin) ; *No Laughter in Heaven* (Pittenger) ; *The Plough and the Stars* (O'Casey) ; *White Cargo* (Gordon) ; *Juno and the Paycock* (O'Casey) ; *Susan and God* (Crothers) ; *Ned McCobb's Daughter* (Howard).

LOTTERIES. *Delila* (Molnar) ; *Whatever Goes Up* (Lazarus) ; *Sheppy* (Maugham).

MARIE ANTOINETTE, QUEEN OF FRANCE. *The Austrian Woman; Marriage a la King* (Shields, Sprague) ; *Six Women* (Cammer) ; *Antoinette* (Konjati, Bertuch, Herz, Scanto, Szecsen, Harmath) ; *Madame Capet* (Maurette).

MARRIAGE. *Sarah Simple* (Milne) ; *To Have and to Hold* (Brown) ; *Susan and God* (Crothers) ; *The Orchard Walls* (Hodge, Fodor) ; *Maitre Bolbec et Son Mari* (Beer-Verneuil) ; *Men Are Unwise* (Gow) ; *Innocent Party* (Harwood-Kirk) ; *Goodbye Again* (Scott, Haight) ; *But Not Your Heart* (Francis) ; *The Constant Wife* (Maugham) ; *Almost a Honeymoon* (Ellis) ; *Amitie* (Mourguet) ; *I Have Been Here Before* (Priestley) ; *The Animal Kingdom* (Barry) ; *Springtime for Henry* (Levy) ; *Batoche* (Ferdinand) ; *Her Master's Voice* (Kummer) ; *A Woman's A Fool—To Be Clever* (Bennett, Hannah) ; *Les Cadets* (Duvernois) ; *Dear Family* (Frank, Rosenthal) ; *Domino* (Achard) ; *The Latitude of Love* (Richman, Weil) ; *Lot's Wife* (Blackmore) ; *Lightnin'* (Smith, Bacon) ; *Illusion* (Bernard, Boyd) ; *A Million Dollars* (William) ; *Mr. and Mrs. Phipps* (Hamilton) ; *People of Our Class* (Ervine) ; *Plan for a Hostess* (Browne) ; *Run for Your Wife* (Golden) ; *Gentlemen Unknown* (Milne) ; *They Fly By Twilight* (Dornhorst) ; *Tomorrow's Dream* (Sirota) ; *Quiet Wedding* (McCracken) ; *Angela Is 22* (Lewis, Wray) ; *The Birds Stop Singing* (Coffee) ; *This My Life. . .* (Lennard, Plowden) ; *Retreat from Folly* (Gould, Russell) ; *Two by Two* (Taber) ; *Unfaithfully Yours* (Pomeroy) ; *When We Are Married* (Priestley) ; *Design for Living* (Coward) ; *The Philadelphia Story* (Barry) ; *Blow Ye Winds* (Davies) ; *Men Are Unwise* (Gow) ; *Miserable Sinners* (Balchin) ; *This Same Love* (Ford Inman) ; *Convalescence* (Sandeman Kohn).

MARY, MOTHER OF JESUS CHRIST. *Our Lady* (Sinclair) ; *Family Portrait* (Coffee, Cowen).

MARY, QUEEN OF SCOTS. *Mary Stuart* (Drinkwater) ; *Mary Stuart* (Schiller) ; *Mary of Scotland* (Anderson) ; *Royal Scapegoat* (Erskine) ; *Maria Stuart* (Schiller) ; *The Rival Queens* (Shaler) ; *The Coronation* (Shaler) ; *A Tragedy of Queen Elizabeth* (Browne) ; *The Great Elizabeth* (Hay) ; *Marie Stuart et Elisa-*

beth (Marford) ; *The Albion Queens* (Banks) ; *Queen Elizabeth; or The Origin of Shakespeare* (Gregg).

MAXIMILLIAN, EMPEROR OF MEXICO AND ARCHDUKE OF AUSTRIA. *Juarez and Maximillian* (Werfel) ; *Coronation* (Segal).

MEDICI, CATHERINE DE. *Medea* (Walkridge) ; *Catherine de Medici* (Silver).

MEDICINE. *The Wind and the Rain* (Hodge) ; *Case History* (Bardoly) ; *Pasteur* (Guitry) ; *Tuberin 5* (Mueller) ; *The East Side Doctor* (Dymow) ; *Robert's Wife* (Ervine) ; *Professor Bernhardi* (Schnitzler) ; *Bila Nemoc* (Capek).

See also *Physicians.*

MIDDLE CLASS. *Paradise Lost* (Odets) ; *Petty Trumps* (Ardov) ; *Return to Sanity* (Rushton, Mack) ; *The Stepmother* (Balzac) ; *Trouble for Two* (Burden) ; *Wolves and Sheep* (Ostrovsky) ; *People of Our Class* (Ervine).

MISCEGENATION. *Mulatto* (Hughes) ; *All God's Chillun Got Wings* (O'Neill) ; *In Abraham's Bosom* (Green) ; *Prejudice* (Selwyn) ; *Jordan* (Kennedy).

MISTAKEN IDENTITY. *As You Like It* (Shakespeare) ; *Comedy of Errors* (Shakespeare) ; *Corsican Brothers* (Dumas) ; *Masqueraders* (Jones) ; *Prisoner of Zenda* (Hope) ; *The Prince and the Pauper* (Twain) ; *Twelfth Night* (Shakespeare) ; *Nuts in May* (Bolton, Millar) ; *Bei Kerzenlicht* (Katscher, Farkas) ; *The Man from Cairo* (Yvan-Noe, Goldberg) ; *The Winter's Tale* (Shakespeare) ; *Mirabelle* (Boulton) ; *She Stoops to Conquer; or The Mistakes of a Night* (Goldsmith) ; *The Good Fairy* (Molnar) ; *You Never Know* (Porter, Katscher-Leigh, Porter) ; *Lady Windermere's Fan* (Wilde) ; *Broken Threads* (Greenfield) ; *The Boys from Syracuse* (Rodgers, Abbott) ; *La Mauvaise Conduite* (Variot) ; *Princess, Ltd.* (Glass) ; *Le Roi Masque* (Romains) ; *The Two Gentlemen of Verona* (Shakespeare) ; *Friday at Four* (Holmes) ; *Soubrette* (Deval) ; *Moses in the Bulrushes* (Benton) ; *The Importance of Being Earnest* (Wilde) ; *Libel* (Wooll) ; *Pariserinnen* (Armodt, Gerbidon, Benatsky) ; *Rupert of Hentzau* (Hope).

MONEY. *Ride A Cock-Horse* (York, Bruhl) ; *This Money Business* (Campion) ; *The Millionairess* (Shaw) ; *Dear Relations* (Hare) ; *Money* (Bulwer-Lytton).

MORE, SIR THOMAS. *Traitor's Gate* (Stuart) ; *Master of the Revels* (Marquis).

MOTHERS. *Mamba's Daughters* (Heyward) ; *The Primrose Path* (Buckner, Hart) ; *Long Live America* (Blum) ; *Living Hours* (Schnitzler) ; *Cap des Tempêtes* (Bernstein) ; *Ghosts* (Ibsen) ; *Mothers and Children* (Wolf) ; *Satyr* (Leslie) ; *Apron Strings* (Davis) ; *Lady Windermere's Fan* (Wilde) ; *Her Master's Voice* (Kummer) ; *Consider Lily* (Kauffman) ; *A Spark of Genius* (Shale) ; *And Niobe Wept* (Wilmot) ; *The Prodigal Mother* (Shute) ; *Should a Mother Tell?* (Freiman) ; *Jennie Frensham* (Robinson) ; *The Silver Cord* (Howard) ; *Yvelle* (Scott-Fernald) ; *Autumn* (Surguchev, Kennedy, Ratoff) ; *Time and the Conways* (Priestley) ; *Craig's Wife* (Kelly).

MOVING PICTURES. *Double Features* (Julian Weinberg) ; *The Meal Ticket* (Mankiewicz) ; *Man and Wife; In Theatre Street* (Lenormand) ; *Stage Door* (Kaufman, Ferber) ; *Le Corsaire* (Achard) ; *New Use for Old Husbands* (Lewis) ;

Gentlemen Need a Shave (Washburn, Gross) ; *Kiss the Boys Goodbye* (Boothe) ; *Goodness, How Sad!* (Morley) ; *7-11* (Cain) ; *Hollywood Pirate* (Achard) ; *Stars in Your Eyes* (McEvoy) ; *Storm Song* (Johnson) ; *Work for the Giants* (McCormick); *Central Casting* (Cosentino) ; *O.K. For Sound* (Weston and Lee). *Schoolhouse on the Lot* (Fields, Chodorov) ; *Once in a Lifetime* (Hart, Kaufman). See also *Hollywood.*

MURDER. *The Invincibles* (Hunt, O'Connor) ; *There's Always a Breeze* (Caulfield) ; *Black Limelight* (Sherry) ; *Flood Tide* (Bohnell, Herbert) ; *The Last Straw* (Percy, Denham) ; *Macbeth* (Shakespeare) ; *Man at Liberty* (Anderson, Morrice) ; *Murder at the Seven Stars* (Downing) ; *Murder Intended* (Beeding) ; *Murder Tomorrow* (Harvey) ; *Pay Day* (Brown) ; *One Flight Down* (Stromm, Freund, Friedmann) ; *Satyr* (Leslie) ; *Step Into My Parlor* (Risjean) ; *The Case of Constance Kent* (Box) ; *Strange Barrier* (Pollard) ; *Suspect* (Judd) ; *Angel Island* (Angus) ; *Mile Away Murder* (Armstrong) ; *And the Music Stopped* (Scott) ; *Merely Murder* (Thomas) ; *The Playboy of the Western World* (Synge) ; *Distinguished Gathering* (Parish) ; *The Dead Hand* (Fraser-Hemmerde) ; *In The Train* (Hunt, O'Connor) ; *The Second Shot* (Meyrick) ; *The Bridal Crown* (Strindberg, Bjorkman) ; *The Day is Gone* (Chatham-Strode) ; *Murder Sails at Midnight* (Gordon) ; *Wanted for Murder* (Robinson, De Marney) ; *Who Killed the Count?* (Coppel) ; *Alien Earth* (Catto) ; *Thanks for Tomorrow* (Bailey) ; *The Devil Takes a Bride* (Smith) ; *Night Must Fall* (Williams) ; *The Burglar* (Williams) ; *Come Across* (Beauchamp, Pertwee) ; *Nether-World* (Smith) ; *Escape* (Galsworthy) ; *Conjur* (Freeman) ; *Grandpa* (Morgan) ; *The Green Pack* (Wallace) ; *No Traveller Returns* (Goddard) ; *Ringside Seat* (Ide) ; *Purgatory* (Yeats) ; *Le Simoun* (Lenormand) ; *7-11* (Cain) ; *Thou Shalt Not* (Zola) ; *They Fly by Twilight* (Dornhorst) ; *But For the Grace* (Otway) ; *Murder Tomorrow?* (Harvay) ; *Dearly Beloved Wife* (De Casalis) ; *Murder Without Tears* (Kilpatrick) ; *Open Verdict* (Wolseley) ; *London After Dark* (Hackett) ; *Her Affairs in Order* (Bolton) ; *Murder on Account* (Talbot, Hayden) ; *Maria Marten, or the Murder in the Red Barn; No Sharper Spur* (Watling) ; *Pay Day* (Brown) ; *Strange Incident* (Desmond) ; *Suspect* (Denham, Percy) ; *The Thinking Butler* (Ireland) ; *The Toss of A Coin* (Hackett); *Uncle Harry* (Job) ; *Mamba's Daughters* (Heyward) ; *Gentle People* (Shaw) ; *What Really Happened* (Lowndes) ; *Within Seven Hours* (Paumier) ; *The Little Foxes* (Hellman) ; *Close Quarters* (Lennox, Somin) ; *They Walk Alone* (Catto) ; *The Trunk* (Wood) ; *Black Limelight* (Sherry). See also *Suicide.*

MUSICIANS. *The Songmaster* (Drakeford-Springer) ; *The Music Master* (Klein) ; *The Concert* (Bahr) ; *Whiteoaks* (De La Roche) ; *Mariette* (Strauss-Guitry) ; *Roter Mohn* (Herzog) ; *Concert* (Faiko) ; *And Now Good-Bye* (Hilton) ; *Bitter Root* (Ceough) ; *Milan in May* (Torriani, Berg) ; *Music at Evening* (Nathan) ; *Orchester* (Reich) ; *Mamba's Daughters* (Heyward) ; *Romance* (Sheldon).

NAPOLEON BONAPARTE. *The Two Napoleons* (Fulop, Miller, Gregor) ; *Napoleon Intrudes* (Hasenclever) ; *Madame Sans-Gene* (Sardou, Moreau) ; *Napoleon* (Trench) ; *Napoleon Unique* (Raynal) ; *The Washerwoman-Duchess* (Anspacher); *The Man of Destiny* (Sham); *Lazarre* (Catherwood); *Napoleon's Barber* (Caesar); *No More Peace* (Toller); *Hostage* (Claudel); *L'Aiglon* (Rostand); *The Man of Destiny* (Shaw).

NEGROES. *Mamba's Daughters* (Heyward); *In Abraham's Bosom* (Green); *Green Pastures* (Connelly); *All God's Chillun Got Wings* (O'Neill); *Emperor Jones* (O'Neill); *Deep River* (Stallings); *Never No More* (Millen); *Porgy* (Heyward); *Darker Brother* (Seiler); *Divine Comedy* (Dodson); *Kiss the Boys Goodbye* (Boothe); *Big Blow* (Pratt); *Conjur* (Freeman); *Front Porch* (Hughes); *Share Cropper* (Howard); *Harlem* (Blatt); *Lulu Belle* (Sheldon, MacArthur); *Out of Bondage; Trial of Dr. Beck* (Allison); *Roseanne* (Stephens); *Mulatto* (Hughes); *Stevedore* (Peters, Sklar); *Brown Sugar* (Angus); *How Come, Lawd?* (Heywood).

　　See also *Miscegenation.*

NEWSPAPERS. *Gentlemen of the Press* (Morehouse); *Five Star Final* (Weitzenkorn); *Freedom of the Press* (Lewis); *The Ghost of Yankee Doodle* (Howard); *Power* (Arent-Wainer); *Suspect* (Judd); *Strange Rhythm* (Bolton, Vagliano); *Roaring Girl* (Moffit); *The Squeaker* (Wallace); *The Front Page* (Hecht, MacArthur); *Kiss the Boys Goodbye* (Boothe); *Chase a Comet* (Robinson); *Leave it to Me* (Porter, Spewack); *The Machine* (Cook); *Qualchi Cosa Di Me* (Tieri); *Press Time* (Bookman, Coles); *'Mid Pleasures and Palaces* (Knight); *The Newspaper Doctor* (Miller); *Run, Sheep, Run* (Knight).

NIGHT CLUBS. *Night Hostess* (Dunning); *All for Love* (Schoop); *Night Alone* (Dell); *One Thing After Another* (Noble).

OLD AGE. *King Lear* (Shakespeare); *Goodbye, Mr. Chips* (Hilton, Burnham); *Dump Heap* (Axelson); *The Sun Rises in the West* (Murray, Vale, Pezman); *The Gentle People* (Shaw); *The First Fifty Years* (Myers); *Whiteoaks* (De la Roche); *Back to Methuselah* (Shaw); *Three Wise Fools* (Smith); *Swan Song* (Chekhov); *The Circle* (Maugham); *Grumpy* (Hodges, Percyval); *Old English* (Galsworthy); *Old Lady Shows Her Medals* (Barrie).

　　See also *Youth and Age.*

ORPHANS. *The Kingdom of God* (Sierra); *Daddy-Long-Legs* (Webster); *The Two Orphans* (D'Ennery, Cormon).

PAINTING. *Biography* (Behrman); *Van Gogh* (Burke); *Fulfilment* (De Vaux); *Where is Bohemia?* (Jarvis); *The Late Christopher Bean* (Howard).

PARNELL, CHARLES. *Mr. Gladstone* (Williamson); *Parnell* (Schauffler); *The Uncrowned King* (MacNamara, Pearn); *Moses' Rock* (O'Connor, Hunt).

PHYSICIANS. *Robert's Wife* (Ervine); *Professor Bernhardi* (Schnitzler); *Knock* (Romains); *Bila Nemoc* (Capek); *Madame Bovary* (Levy, Baty, Flaubert); *The Switchback* (Bridie); *Love of Women* (Stuart); *Convalescence* (Sandeman-Kohn); *The Orchard Walls* (Hodge, Fodor); *Uncle Vanya* (Chekhov); *Waters of Jordan* (Steele); *Case History* (Bardoly); *Men in White* (Kingsley); *Mountain Sunshine* (Hunyady); *Amazing Dr. Clitterhouse* (Lyndon); *Tuberin 5* (Mueller); *Mèdecin Malgré Lui* (Molière).

POLITICAL LIFE. *On the Rocks* (Shaw); *Salvage the Best* (Urban); *What Every Woman Knows* (Barrie); *A Lady's Gentleman* (Cleaver); *Storm Over*

Europe (Jerrold, Agar, Chilton) ; *Waste* (Granville-Barker) ; *Mrs. O'Brien Entertains* (Madden) ; *Glory for All* (Perrin) ; *Hulda, Daughter of Parliament* (Wuolijoki) ; *Bees on the Boat Deck* (Priestley) ; *Both Your Houses* (Anderson) ; *Of Thee I Sing* (Gershwin-Kaufman Ryskind) ; *Put Up Job* (Baker).

POTEMKIN. *The Great Catherine* (Shaw) ; *Empress of Destiny* (Lee, Walsh).

POVERTY. *Keep Going, Pal* (Kreymborg) ; *The Lower Depths* (Gorki) ; *Love on the Dole* (Gow, Greenwood) ; *Tobacco Road* (Kirkland) ; *By Bread Alone* (Zunzer, Singer) ; *Poor House* (Driscoll) ; *Poverty Is No Crime* (Ostrovsky).

    See also *Slums; Unemployment.*

PRISONS. *Criminal Code* (Flavin) ; *Chalked Out* (Lawes, Finn) ; *Blind Window* (Boross) ; *The Sheriff* (Park-LaVerne) ; *Men at Liberty* (Anderson) ; *Bystander* (Brennan) ; *Out of Sight* (Stokes) ; *Ladies and Gentlemen* (Hunter).

PRIZE FIGHTERS. *Celebrity* (Keefe) ; *Golden Boy* (Odets) ; *Plain Jane,* musical; *Ringside* (Paramore, Dobb, Abbott) ; *The Big Fight* (Gropper, Marcin) ; *Cashel Byron's Profession* (Shaw).

PROSTITUTION. *House of Assignation* (Dukes) ; *Fickle Women* (Brown) ; *Even as You and I* (Cole) ; *All That Glitters* (Baragwanath-Simpson) ; *L'Abito Nuovo* (Pirandello, de Filippo) ; *Madame Bovary* (Levy, Baty, Flaubert) ; *Jean de la Lune* (Achard) ; *Anna Christie* (O'Neill) ; *The Cradle Will Rock* (Blitzstein) ; *Story to be Whispered* (Hurlbut) ; *Tortilla Flat* (Kirkland, Steinbeck) ; *Waterloo Bridge* (Sherwood) ; *Chase a Comet* (Robinson) ; *The Kingdom of God* (Sierra) ; *The Primrose Path* (Buckner, Hart) ; *The Easiest Way* (Walter) ; *Rain* (Colton, Randolph) ; *Morals* (Howard) ; *Mrs. Warren's Profession* (Shaw) ; *Animal Kingdom* (Barry) ; *Camille* (Dumas) ; *Behind Red Lights* (Shipman-Brown) ; *The House of Kuvalsky* (Bein) ; *Now You've Done It* (Chase) ; *Young Madame Conti* (Frank, Griffith, Levy) ; *Censored* (Seiler, Marcin) ; *Night Hawk* (Oliver) ; *Warsaw by Night* (Siegel, Levin) ; *Dutch Courtesan* (Marston) ; *The Honest Whore* (Dekker) ; *Maya* (Gantillon) ; *The Kingdom of God* (Sierra).

RACE PREJUDICE. *Professor Mamlock* (Wolf, Bromberger) ; *Kultur* (Phillip) ; *Birthright* (Maibaum) ; *The Shattered Lamp* (Reade) ; *Races* (Bruckner) ; *Heil Hitler* (Walinsky) ; *Mulatto* (Hughes).

RADIO. *Howdy Stranger* (Sloane, Pelletier, Jr.-Leslie Burke) ; *If I Were You* (Fox, Levy, Smith) ; *I've Got the Tune* (Blitzstein) ; *Power* (Arent, Wainer) ; *Come Blow Your Horn* (Wendell) ; *We Are All Your People* (Lavri, Rust) ; *Remote Control* (North).

RALEIGH, SIR WALTER. *The Lost Colony* (Green) ; *Merrie England* (German, Hood) ; *The King's Pirate* (Thompson) ; *Thankless Errand* (South).

RELIGION. *The God Innis* (Williams, Dowell) ; *A Man Who Has Nothing* (Flannery, Browne) ; *Robert's Wife* (Ervine) ; *Professor Bernhardi* (Schnitzler) ; *Seed of Adam* (Williams) ; *Shadow and Substance* (Carroll) ; *Brand* (Ibsen) ; *Divine Comedy* (Dodson) ; *Susan and God* (Crothers) ; *Many Mansions* (Goodman) ; *Father Malachy's Miracle* (Doherty) ; *The Seal of Confession* (Holweck) ; *A Comedy of Good and Evil* (Hughes) ; *The Empress of Rome* (Masefield) ; *The First Legion* (Lavery) ; *Kingdom of God* (Sierra) ; *Here Come the Clowns* (Barry) ; *The White Steed* (Carroll) ; *Traitor's Gate* (Stuart) ; *Publican and*

Sinners (Andrewes) ; *Thomas Ken* (Cropper) ; *Waste* (Granville-Barker) ; *Androcles and the Lion* (Shaw) ; *Family Portrait* (Coffee, Cowen) ; *Hearts Enduring* (Erskine) ; *Outward Bound* (Vane) ; *Pawns* (Wilde) ; *Prize Money* (Wilson) ; *Monsignor's Hour* (Lavery) ; *The Great Choice* (Eastman) ; *He Came Seeing* (Hamlin) ; *Tidings of Joy* (McFadden) ; *The Trail of the Dragon* (Field) ; *The Lord's Prayer* (Coppee) ; *Twentieth Century Lullaby* (Mount) ; *Peace I Give Unto You* (Wilson).

RICHELIEU. Richelieu (Bulwer-Lytton) ; *Richelieu* (Payne).

ROBBERY. Roseanne (Stephens) ; *Four Knaves and a Joker* (Gordon) ; *Il Ladro Sono Io* (Cenzato) ; *The Black Spider* (Dawe) ; *The Burglar* (Williams) ; *Cognac* (Langer) ; *Come Across* (Beauchamp, Pertwee) ; *Lady With Designs* (Middleton, Gregory) ; *Marcia Gets Her Own Back* (Darlington) ; *The Jailbird* (Shiels).

ROYALTY AND NOBILITY. Lèse-Majesté (Beanes) ; *Tovarich* (Deval) ; *The King's Breakfast* (Weiman, Marks) ; *Wolves and Sheep* (Ostrovsky).

RUDOLPH, CROWN PRINCE OF AUSTRIA-HUNGARY. Masque of Kings (Anderson) ; *The Crown Prince* (Akins-Vajda).

SACRIFICE. Let the Mare Run (Grant, Perry) ; *Robert's Wife* (Ervine) ; *Sacrifice* (Tagore) ; *Story to be Whispered* (Hurlbut) ; *Ethan Frome* (Davis-Wharton) ; *Alcestis* (Euripides) ; *Brand* (Ibsen).

SAILORS. See *Sea and Sailors.*

SALOME. Herod's House (Masterman) ; *Salomé* (Wilde) ; *The King of Glory* (Shiner).

SAUL, KING. The Boy David (Barrie) ; *King Saul* (Parry, Rich).

SCHOOL LIFE. Blue and Rose (Bruschtein) ; *Honor Bright* (O'Hara) ; *Schoolhouse on the Lot* (Fields, Chodorov) ; *What a Life* (Goldsmith) ; *Bachelor Born* (Hay) ; *Brother Rat* (Monks, Finklehoffe) ; *Your Number's Up* (Wright-Morgan-MacDermot) ; *Wandering School* (Auslaender, Kassil) ; *Where Do We Go From Here?* (Bowers) ; *Sorority House* (Chase) ; *Women Without Men* (Ellis).

See also *Colleges and Universities.*

SEA AND SAILORS. Bees on the Boat Deck (Priestley) ; *Anna Christie* (O'Neill) ; *The Frodi* (Kennedy) ; *Blow Ye Winds* (Davies) ; *Where the Cross Is Made* (O'Neill) ; *Riders to the Sea* (Synge) ; *S.S. Tenacity* (Vildrac) ; *H.M.S. Pinafore* (Gilbert, Sullivan) *Pirates of Penzance* (Gilbert, Sullivan) ; *Moon Over the Caribbees* (O'Neill) ; *Ile* (O'Neill) ; *Marius* (Pagnol) ; *Excursion* (Wolfson).

SHAKESPEARE, WILLIAM. Red, Bright and Blue (Blatt, Soutter, Frankau, Ayer, Van Thal, Crick) ; *Will Shakespeare* (Dane) ; *Sing, Sweet Angels* (Forrest) ; *The Lost Colony* (Green) ; *The Wooing of Anne Hathaway* (Carlton) ; *Un Amour de Shakespeare* (Auzanet) ; *William's Other Anne* (Brown) ; *Fortune and Men's Eyes* (Peabody) ; *Mousetrap* (Darmady) ; *Dark Lady of the Sonnets* (Shaw) ; *Women of Shakespeare* (Bartholomew) ; *Master Skylark* (Burrill) ; *Mr. Shakespeare at School* (Duer) ; *Gloss of Youth* (Furness) ; *Master Will of the Stratford* (Garnett) ; *William Shakespeare, Pedagogue and Poacher* (Garnett) ; *Queen Elizabeth—or, The Origin of Shakespeare* (Greggs) ; *Hour of Prospero* (Lawrence) ; *The Day Will Shakespeare Went to Kent* (Lord) ; *Caliban by the Yellow Sands*

(MacKaye); *Good Theatre* (Morley); *Rehearsal* (Baring); *The Mousetrap* (Darmady); *Death of Shakespeare* (Blair).

SLUMS. *Nether-World* (Smith); *The Lower Depths* (Gorki); *Land of Plenty* (Holland); *". . . one-third of a nation . . ."* (Arent); *Winterset* (Anderson); *Dead End* (Kingsley).

SMALL TOWNS. *Our Town* (Wilder); *Run Sheep Run* (Knight); *The Parson Says, No!* (Powell).

SMUGGLING. *Night Alone* (Dell); *Invaded Retreat* (Single); *A Spot of Bother* (Sylvaine).

SOCIAL CONTRAST. *The Admirable Crichton* (Barrie); *At Your Service* (Eisman); *Heartbreak House* (Shaw); *Eye on the Sparrow* (Selser); *Petty Trumps* (Ardoy); *Pygmalion* (Shaw); *The Silver Box* (Galsworthy); *Once Is Enough* (Lonsdale); *A Lady's Gentleman* (Cleaver); *Wuthering Heights* (Bronte); *The Cherry Orchard* (Chekhov); *You Can't Take It With You* (Kaufman, Hart); *An · American Tragedy* (Kearney).

SUICIDE. *The World is an Eight Ball* (Swerling); *Catch a Comet by Its Tail* (Woodbury); *Ladies and Gentlemen* (Hunter); *Crisis* (Horler); *The Dead Hand* (Fraser, Heyn, Hemmerde); *Madame Bovary* (Levy, Baty, Flaubert); *Fulfilment* (De Vaux); *Great Possessions* (Douglas, Home); *This For Remembrance* (Neale, Urbant-schitsch); *Fool's Hill* (Wetzel); *The Good* (Erskin); *Thou Shalt Not* (Zola); *Too Large a Family* (Birabeau); *Tomorrow's Dream* (Sirota); *Outward Bound* (Vane); *Masque of Kings* (Anderson); *Romeo and Juliet* (Shakespeare); *Antony and Cleopatra* (Shakespeare); *Julius Caesar* (Shakespeare); *Wild Duck* (Ibsen); *Hedda Gabler* (Ibsen); *The Happiest Days* (Armstrong); *The Living Corpse* (Tolstoy); *Rain* (Colton, Randolph); *Things is That-a-Way* (Conkle); *Miss Tassey* (Baker); *Winter's Night* (Boyce); *Last Straw* (Crocker); *Spark of Life* (Brunner); *Cocaine* (King); *Facing Death* (Strindberg).

SUPERNATURAL. *On Borrowed Time* (Osborn); *Our Town* (Wilder); *I Have Been Here Before* (Priestley); *Father Malachy's Miracle* (Doherty); *That Fell Arrest* (Scott); *A Comedy of Good and Evil* (Hughes); *The God Innis* (Williams, Dowell); *The Virgin and the Clerk* (Porter); *Carmilla* (Longford, Lefanu); *Doctor Faustus* (Marlowe); *The Glory of the Sun* (Brandon, Thomas); *Conjur* (Freeman); *No Traveller Returns* (Goddard); *The Tempest* (Shakespeare); *Here Come the Clowns* (Barry); *The Undiscovered Country* (Robinson); *Outward Bound* (Vane); *Johnson Over Jordan* (Priestley); *The Tempest* (Shakespeare); *Liliom* (Molnar); *Faust* (Goethe); *Mima* (Molnar); *The Assumption of Hannele* (Hauptmann).

TEACHERS. *What a Life* (Goldsmith); *Remember the Day* (Dunning); *Goodbye, Mr. Chips* (Hilton, Burnham); *Topaze* (Levy, Pagnol); *Children's Hour* (Hellman).

See also *Colleges and Universities; Education; School Life.*

THEATRE. *It Can't Last Forever, Comedienne* (Novello); *Trelawney of the Wells* (Pinero); *The Fabulous Invalid* (Hart, Kaufman); *Jean III* (Guitry); *Juliet in the Rain* (Lenormand, MacLiammoir); *The Land That God Remembers* (Ayres, Montgomery); *The Torch-Bearers* (Kelly); *Pamela* (Carole); *Goodness,*

How Sad! (Morley); *The Red Velvet Goat* (Niggli); *Le Comédien* (Guitry); *Duet in Floodlight* (Priestley); *Spring Tide* (Billam, Goldsmith); *Two-a-Day* (Stone, Robinson); *I Must Love Someone* (Kirkland, Georgie); *We the Willoughbys* (Kanin, Ingram); *A Moral Entertainment* (Maibaum); *The Storm Must Go On* (Kanin, Ingram); *You've Got Something There* (Sherman, Garland); *Dramatic School* (Deval); *Straw Hat* (Unkelbach); *Drama at Inish* (Robinson); *The Jesters* (Tunkel); *First Night* (Donisthorpe); *The Meal Ticket* (Mankiewicz); *Sing Sweet Angels* (Forrest); *Behind Your Back* (Landstone); *At the Theatre* (Taylor); *In Theatre Street* (Lenormand); *Stage Door* (Ferber, Kaufman); *The Royal Family* (Kaufman, Ferber).

TIME. *On Borrowed Time* (Osborn); *Our Town* (Wilder); *The Star Wagon* (Anderson); *Berkeley Square* (Balderston, Squire); *Time and the Conways* (Priestley); *I Have Been Here Before* (Priestley); *Le Corsaire* (Achard); *The Man in the Tree* (Woodworth).

See also *Supernatural*.

TRAMPS. *Tortilla Flat* (Steinbeck); *The Young Go First* (Martin, Scudder, Freeman); *Young Hoboes; Broken Threads* (Greenfield); *Hobo* (Squire).

TRIALS. *Ladies of the Jury* (Ballard); *Justice* (Galsworthy); *Cynara* (Harwood, Gore-Browne); *Libel* (Woolf); *Ten-Minute Alibi* (Armstrong); *Young Madame Conti* (Levy, Griffith); *The Trial of Mary Dugan* (Veiller); *The Night of January 16th* (Rand); *Trial of Dr. Beck* (Allison); *Ringside Seat* (Ide); *Murder on Account* (Talbot, Hayden); *Madame X* (Bisson); *On Trial* (Rice); *We The People* (Rice); *Judgment Day* (Rice); *They Shall Not Die* (Wexley); *Gods of Lightning* (Anderson, Hickerson); *American Holiday* (Barker); *Trial by Jury* (Gilbert, Sullivan); *The Missing Witness* (Reach); *It Might Happen To You* (Lord); *Saint Joan* (Shaw); *Trial of a Judge* (Spender).

UNEMPLOYMENT. *But for the Grace of God* (Atlas); *Class of '29* (Lashin, Hastings); *1931* (Sifton); *Blessing on The Little Man* (McColl); *His Jewels* (Harris); *Castle of All on 23rd St.* (Smith); *Jobs, Inc.* (Schreiber); *Private Hicks* (Maltz); *End of a Cycle* (Smith); *Moonlight Flitting* (Thomson).

VICTORIA, QUEEN OF ENGLAND (1819-1901). *The Friend of a Queen* (De Reyes); *Mr. Gladstone* (Williamson); *The Queen's Image* (Bower); *Victoria* (Housman); *Vickie and Albert* (De Reyes); *Knights of Song* (Alviene); *Victoria Regina* (Housman); *The Friend of a Queen* (De Reyes).

VILLON, FRANCOIS. *The Poet Thief* (Anderson); *The Vagabond King* (Friml-McCarthy, Post, Hocker); *If I Were King* (McCarthy).

WASHINGTON, GEORGE. *Washington, or The Revolution* (Allen); *Washington, The Man Who Made Us* (MacKaye); *Washington, the Statesman* (Gue); *Washington Marches On* (Price); *Valley Forge* (Anderson); *Washington and Betsy Ross* (MacKaye); *English Gentlemen* (Lambe).

WILDE, OSCAR. *Oscar Wilde* (Stokes); *Knights of Song* (Alviene); *Le Procès D'Oscar Wilde* (Rostand); *Patience* (Gilbert, Sullivan).

WINDSOR, EDWARD DUKE OF. *Sovereign* (Zimmerman); *God Save the King* (Murray); *The Duchess Goes to Baltimore* (Reade); *Knights of Song* (Alviene).

WRITERS. Time Plays the Devil (Hons, Works); *Accent on Youth* (Raphaelson); *No Time for Comedy* (Behrman); *Second Man* (Behrman); *End of Summer* (Behrman); *Madame Sand* (Moeller); *Alison's House* (Glaspell); *Merrily We Roll Along* (Kaufman, Hart); *You Can't Take It With You* (Kaufman, Hart); *Barretts of Wimpole Street* (Besier); *Angela is 22* (Lewis, Wray); *Prize Novel* (Mitchell); *Literature* (Schnitzler); *The Stepmother* (Bennett); *Best Sellers* (Bourdet, Bennett); *A Spot in the Sun* (Murray).

YOUTH AND AGE. Septembre (Coline); *Fata Morgana* (Vajda); *Angela is 22* (Lewis, Wray); *Remembrance of Things Past* (Ackland); *Milestones* (Bennett, Knoblock); *Accent on Youth* (Raphaelson); *The Running of the Deer* (Meany); *The Prodigal Parents* (Jerome); *Heartbreak House* (Shaw); *The Dangerous Age* (Ellis-Michaelis); *Fulfilment* (De Vaux); *Young Society* (Clements); *Asmodée* (Mauriac); *All Fool's Night* (Vernon).

Drama, Swedish, 19th century to the First World War. The first half of the 19th century in Sweden was almost wholly lacking in dramatic literature. Atterbom's *Isle of Bliss,* 1824, though in dramatic form is in no real sense a drama. Von Beskow's historical dramas after the manner of Schiller were of little importance, and the plays of Stagnelius and Almquist were of even less value.

Blanche was more successful in his imitation of Scribe during the middle part of the century. Borjesson showed the influence of Shakespeare, whose works were being translated about this time by Hagberg. The last quarter of the century brought Agrell, Molander and Didring, a more talented group of playwrights (none of their plays are available in English), but they were completely overshadowed by Strindberg, Sweden's one great dramatist.

The production of *The Father,* 1887, established him as a writer of great power. The succeeding *Comrades,* 1888, *Miss Julia,* 1888, *Creditors,* 1890, and *The Stronger,* 1890, brought to the modern theatre a new kind of naturalism of a highly sensational order. In contrast to photographic naturalism, Strindberg sought "the true naturalism which seeks out those points in life, where the greatest conflicts occur, which loves to see that which cannot be seen every day, rejoices in the battle of elemental powers . . . which cares not whether a subject be beautiful or ugly if only it be great." He applied analysis to the conflicts of human minds and brought bitter personal hatred to a ruthless bearing of the feminine mind and soul.

Through all of these naturalistic dramas runs an undertone of personal suffering. He became concerned with the transcendental and expressed his reaction against the unfathomable mystery of life in the so-called (for want of a better term) expressionistic dramas: *The Dance of Death,* 1901; *Easter,* 1901; *The Crown Bridge,* 1902; *Swanwhite,* 1902; *The Dream Play,* 1902. The great allegorical trilogy *To Damascus* (1898-1904), showed Strindberg's transports of asceticism in the symbolization of the soul's battle with itself and the devil. His *Spook Sonata,* 1907, and other shorter plays written for the *théâtre intime* which he established in Sweden, carried expressionism to new symbolic heights and at times to the grotesque.

Strindberg has proved an original force in the development of dramatic technique; he is a master of sensational naturalism, and at the same time, a herald of the new expressionism. However, his greatest contribution to the modern theatre lies in his conception of character resulting in men and women who are alive and constantly changing in ceaseless response to the pressure of modern existence.

The 20th century has brought a number of Swedish dramatists of repute: Hedberg, Sodderberg, Hallstrom and Bergman, but only Hedberg is available in translation.

Drama, Swedish, since the First World War. The Riksteatern (Swedish National Theatre), founded in 1934, is perhaps unique in that its scope extends through a nationwide subscription organization, to seventy-five separate localities. Dramatists include: Pär Lagerkvist, symbolist-expressionist; Vilhelm Moberg, grim realist; Ragnar Josephson, subtle sophisticate; and Sigfrid Simertz. Per Lindberg is one of the most progressive directors and designers; others are Olov Molander and Erik Wettergren. Prominent actors include Lars Hansen, Tora Leje, Anders de Wahl, Olof Winnerstrand and Inga Tidblad.

Drama, symbolic. A form of playwriting marked by allegory and mysticism and generally associated with the end of the 19th century when the French school of symbolists (predominantly poets, not dramatists) was at its height. Its leading exponent was Maeterlinck, in none of whose plays is there any observance of realism. *Pelleas et Melisande, L'Oiseau Bleu* and *Les Aveugles* are all romantic, fanciful, dreamlike and static. Pirandello has adopted much of Maeterlinck's symbolic method, but in him its otherworldliness is not so pronounced.

Drama, theories of. Full information and discussion of *Theories of Drama* may be found in Barrett Clark's *European Theories of the Drama* and Allardyce Nicoll's *The Theory of Drama*. The reader is also referred to many books and publications mentioned in this article.

Of all philosophies pertaining to the theatre, the first in point both of time and importance is that embodied in the *Poetics* (4th century B.C.) of the Greek philosopher, Aristotle. Outside of a passage on tragedy and comedy attributed to Antiphanes, another brief passage attributed to Simylus, and the incidental dramatic criticisms in Aristophanes' *The Frogs,* this was the sole work of criticism of its time and is the father of all dramatic theory, influencing every critic of the art down through history. In the *Poetics* are declared: the importance of the "unities" (of time, place and action), the necessity of "beginning, middle, and end" in the drama, the two prime components of tragedy ("terror and pity"), the meaning of "imitation" (the essence of theatre and differing in "the means, the objects, or the manner"), and "purgation" or "catharsis" (the refining effect on the emotions by the "terror" and "pity" of true tragedy). Following this great work was Horace's *Epistola ad Pisones* (written between 24 and 20 B.C.) and representing, according to Professor Saintsbury, "the only complete example of literary criticism that we have from any Roman." Here was stated the famous theory of "pleasure and profit" (to the effect that to please and inform should be the dual object of a writer) and dogmatically emphasized the importance of the formal side of writing, including close observance of the conventions of the five acts, the chorus, the respective meters, the segregating of characters into types, the selection of action proper to the public stage, the limitation of simultaneous speaking presences onstage to three, and, especially, the Greek canons of dramaturgy. This work had almost as much influence as Aristotle's *Poetics,* but is now considered cut-and-dried where the Greek philosopher's work is still a bearer of enlightenment. In the 4th century A.D. the Roman Donatus came forward with his *De Comoedia et Tragoedia,* which was the last dramatic theory in Latin and which was a derivation from Horace. Donatus, says Clark, was "the connecting link between Horace and Dante." Dante's principal contribution to ideas on the drama is to be found in the brief *Epistola XI* (to Can Grande), about 1318, in which he defined comedy as, in its work derivations, a "village song," "mild and humble," with a "happy termination," and tragedy as a "goatish song; that is, foul like a goat," "lofty and sublime," and "in its ending or catastrophe foul and horrible." The *Poetica* (1536) of Daniello is the next considerable contribution to dramatic theory, indeed, says Clark, "the first work of its sort since antiquity," and one that shows a mixture of the influences of Aristotle and Horace. Here are references to Aristotle's concept of ideal imitation and Horace's theory that "pleasure and profit" form the objective of poetry. Minturno's *Arte poetica* (1563) is a dialogue on poetic and dramatic properties, and includes definitions of dramatic poetry ("imitations"), and three kinds of subjects treated in the theatre, or definitions of tragedy, comedy and satyric drama (1—"serious and grave happenings and concerning those of high rank," 2—"the middle strata of society," and 3—"humble persons, mean and ludicrous," "all those in fact who seem most fitted to provoke merriment"), and ideas on time-limitation. Scaliger's *Poetices Libri Septem* (1561) was a violent and dogmatic interpretation and misinterpretation of Aristotle, "the first work," says Clark, "to attempt a standardisation of literary form and content," and one later to enjoy wide-spread fame. Castelvetro's *Poetica d'Aristotele vulgarizzata e esposta* (1570) was a translation of, with frequently misinterpretive commentary on, Aristotle's *Poetics.* In France Sebillet promulgated his ideas on the drama in his *Art poetique* (1548), a "distinct departure," says Clark, "from the Rhetorics and Poetics which preceded it." This work is interesting chiefly because of the parallel made between the old French *moralité* and the tragedies of antiquity. Here is likewise contained not only evidences of the effect of Italian ideas on French letters but also what is probably the first trace of the influence of Aristotle's *Poetics* in France. Sebillet foreshadows, in spirit at least, some of the reforms advocated by the spokesman of the *Pléiade.* Sebillet's work was followed by the *Art de la tragédie* in Jean de la Taille's *Saül le furieux* (1572), which formulated the third unity, that of place, supported the dignity of tragedy, attacked the enactment of violence and bloodshed on the stage, and all in all was a complete acceptance of Aristotle's *Poetics,* filtered perhaps through certain "interpretations" of Castelvetro. In Spain Cervantes came forward with his *Don Quixote* (1605), which, among other things, carried on illuminating commentary on dramatic canons, comprising an attack on nationalism (possibly motivated by a resentment against Lope de Vega, whose plays were pre-eminently nationalist) and a restatement of the value of the unity of time. De Vega himself produced a tract called *Arte nuevo de hacer comedias en*

este tiempo (1609), in which, voicing the sentiments of the majority of the dramatists and public of his time, he championed the "free and unclassic romantic drama
of the Golden Age of Spain." Following him came Tirso de Molina with his
Cigarrales de Toledo (1624), which, partly written in dialogue form, defends the
free romantic *comedia* as well as Spain's greatest writer in the form, de Vega, and
goes on to a general acceptance of the Aristotelian conventions. Among the Elizabethans in England about the first dramatic theorist (in point of time), and during
a period of scant criticism, was Sir Philip Sidney, whose *Apologie for Poetrie* (1595)
was an attack on certain prevalent Puritanisms in the theatre and the first entrance of
the Aristotelian influence into English literature. Ben Jonson followed him with the
various commentaries in *Every Man in His Humour* (1598), *Every Man Out of
His Humour* (1599), and *The Poetaster* (1601), as well as his various critical
essays, among which *Timber; or, Discoveries Made upon Men and Matter* (1641)
is perhaps his most important. Here Jonson discusses the parts of comedy and
tragedy, the ideas of Aristotle, Socrates, Plato and Homer, the works of Aristophanes
and Plautus, and the necessity of form and proportion in dramatic writing. In
France during the 17th century Ogier was among the first of the dramatic theorists.
His *Preface au lecteur* to Schelandre's play *Tyr et Sidon* was published in 1608
and was, perhaps, ahead of its time in its commonsense and liberality, emphasizing, as it did, the injustice and fruitlessness of subjecting the creative dramatist to rules, and criticising the rigid conventions of the ancients. After him came
Jean Chapelain, whose *Sentimens de l'academie française sur la tragi-comedie du Cid*
(1637), though it perforce supported Richelieu in his jealous condemnation of
Corneille's *Le Cid*, yet drew attention to its peculiar beauties and restated the
Aristotelian canons. Here, as well as in his *Sommaire d'une poetique dramatique*
and his letters, he went far in making possible the subsequent verdict upon him as
the dogmatic apostle of "Good-Sense and Reason, the corner-stones of Neo-classicism." Hedelin followed him with his one notable work, the *Pratique du theatre*
(1657), which, composed of much that is ridiculous and pedantic, yet manages to
re-state Aristotle's laws and to establish the importance of the playable, as against
the merely readable, qualities of a drama. Corneille's various *Prefaces* and *Epitres*
bore many of his neo-classic ideas, but it was the *Examens* and *Discours* (1660) which
best embodied his theoretical ideas on the drama, which in short, were: "to please, but
please according to the Rules," an idea which grew up out of the conflict between
a powerful individualism and a deep awe for, and respect of, the ideas of Aristotle.
Moliere, differing, as did Racine in this sense from Corneille, preferred to write
plays rather than to argue about their structure, and so left little critical theory
outside of the Prefaces to certain of his plays and his reply to critics of *Ecole des
femmes, La Critique de l'Ecole des femmes* (1663). This latter was a dialogue
setting forth the merits of pleasing and not worrying about the Rules, a view which
places him squarely among the moderns. Racine vouchsafes us certain insight into
his literary beliefs and methods in his *Prefaces* (1660-1680), showing a pure classic
strain and a devotion to the canons of Aristotle and Horace, but there is nowhere
the formal, lengthy, and ponderous essay on objective theory as would be appropriate to one claiming to be a major critic. One of the most important of all

French critics of poetry was Boileau, and his *Art poetique* (1674) is now generally considered a classic. This contains many strictures on the theatre, among them a warning against pedantry, a defense of disciplined emotion, a re-statement of the unity of place, and commentaries on the substance and meaning of tragedy and comedy. This work comprised, indeed, a kind of historical summary of the theatre, with specific mention of many dramatists and critics, from Aeschylus to Ben Jonson. It was primarily Boileau's justification of the savage attacks he had made on certain of his contemporaries in his *Satires*. After him came Saint-Evremond with his several important treatises on kinds of tragedies and comedies, and on operas. Perhaps his finest single contribution to dramatic theory is his *De la tragedie ancienne et moderne* (1672), which evidences an impartiality unusual for his time and is perhaps the first embodiment of that "comparative system of criticism" by which authors are related to, and explained by, their respective times. Here, in the works of Saint-Evremond, says Clark, "are probably the earliest specimens of the modern essay." In England, meanwhile, such writers are Dryden, Milton, Congreve, Farquhar and others were offering, or beginning to formulate, their respective dramatic creeds. Dryden, unlike men such as Molière and Racine, who were first of all creative writers and only secondarily critics or theorists, was, besides a successful dramatist a highly significant critic. He left a large body of theoretical writings, much of which is to be found in his prefaces to his own plays and those of others. His greatest single critical work is doubtless his *Essay of Dramatick Poesie* (1668), which, in dialogue form, illumines the controversy between the neo-classicists who saw only Corneille and Racine in France and the more liberal critics able to appreciate Shakespeare. Here Dryden is sufficiently daring and original to suggest a possible fallibility in Aristotle, who drew his theories from the dramatists only of his own time, and who, could he have known those of the more recent past and of Dryden's present, might well have modified some of his views. Dryden maintains here as well that "to instruct delightfully is the general end of all poetry." Milton, though not primarily a dramatist but a poet and only thirdly a critic, yet left one treatise on the drama, a work entitled *Of that sort of Dramatic Poem which is call'd Tragedy* (1671), a defense of the form used in his "unactable pseudo-Greek play" *Samson Agonistes* (to which the essay was a Preface), a drama whose ideas derived from Italian Renaissance, rather than essentially Greek, principles. Following Milton came Rymer who, throughout his several tracts, but especially in his *Short View of Tragedy, Its Original Excellency and Corruption, With Some Reflections on Shakespeare and Other Practitioners for the Stage* (1693), gave proof of the strict neo-classicism that so severely, and usually unjustly or absurdly, pilloried Shakespeare. The great English master of the comedy of manners, William Congreve, wrote several theoretical tracts on the drama, some of which are to be found in his various prefaces and dedications to his own plays. Congreve was a believer in the Aristotelian unities, though he was not one always and consistently to abide, in practice, by the principles of his own theory. Among his most important contributions to dramatic theory is the essay, *Concerning Humor in Comedy* (1696), which is a study of the constituency and meaning of comedy, its many interpretations, false and otherwise, and is crowned with the admission of preference for English

humor. Farquhar, aside from his several prefaces and letters, was practically catapulted into dramatic criticism from playwriting by Jeremy Collier's famous attack
on the presumed "immorality of the stage," which he felt obliged to answer. Thus
was provoked the *Discourse upon Comedy in Reference to the English Stage* (1702),
which, besides being a reply to Collier in defense of the drama, was a light essay
that rejected the classic canons embodied in the Aristotelian unities. Addison, the
entertaining collaborator (with Steele) on the *Spectator* papers, contributed in 1711
several articles to that periodical on the estate of the drama, displaying a general
practicality of approach based on firm neo-classic principles, summing up "the
rationalistic tendency of criticism in the early 18th century," denouncing English
tragedy for being insufficiently moral and tragi-comedy for being insufficiently
classical. Following more or less in the footsteps of the Spectator, Johnson's *Rambler*
was a periodical containing essays on contemporary manners, among which were
several on the drama, one in particular carrying what Professor Saintsbury has
called "this single utterance" with which "all the ruling doctrines of sixteenth,
seventeenth, and eighteenth century criticism receive notice to quit, to wit: "It
ought to be the first endeavor of a writer to distinguish nature from custom, or
that which is established because it is right from that which is right only because it
is established; that he may neither violate essential principles by a desire of novelty,
nor debar himself from the attainment of beauties within his view by a needless
fear of breaking rules which no literary dictator had authority to enact." Johnson, in
short, though he was orthodox in his acceptance of the classic canons, was also
liberal in his tolerance for those who demonstrated the need of breaking
them, as witness his appreciation of the tragi-comedy of Shakespeare, a form not
then conventionalised or wholly accepted. Goldsmith, though he wrote comparatively little on dramatic theory, did write one important work of this kind, the
Essay on the Theatre; or A Comparison between Laughing and Sentimental Comedy
(1772), which was an attack on the over-seriousness of that contemporary form of
drama, the sentimental comedy and a plea for a lighter and more genuinely comic
play. In other works, such as his *Enquiry into the Present State of Polite Learning*
(1759), Goldsmith defends a more natural and liberal attitude in dramatic writing,
unhampered by stiff moral posturing and more honest in its depiciton of lower class
life. Dramatic criticism in the Italy of this era was led mainly by Goldoni, whose
many prefaces, his essay *Il Teatro comico* (1751), and his Memoires (1787) serve
amply to inform of his dramatic creed. In *Il Teatro comico* Goldoni treated of the
attributes, actual and theoretical, of comedy, remarking its basis on character, and
differentiating two fundamental species: pure comedy (which "can be written with
the unity of place") and comedy of intrigue (which "cannot be thus written without
crudity and incongruity"). In his *Mémoires* Goldoni treated of a variety of topics:
praise for, and admission of his own emulation of, Moliere; his ideal of the theatre
as "a school for the prevention of abuse and the consequences resulting from it";
an acknowledgment of the importance of the classic unities combined with a plea
for a liberal challenge of them when necessary; a defense of his new comedy as a
corrective or supplanter of the old Italian *commedia dell' arte* with all the stiff and
outworn clichés with which the latter had become burdened. In Germany the

great dramatic critic of the time was the dramatist Lessing. His *Hamburgische Dramaturgie* (1769), a collection of the papers he wrote during the two years he was critic of the new National Theatre in Hamburg, insists on an abiding by the Aristotelian rules but, by a broader interpretation of the Greek critic than shown by some of his predecessors, shows that Shakespeare was fundamentally a follower of his principles. Classicism was also the lofty banner of Voltaire in France, but he was lacking in the essential liberality and circumspection of the German's Aristotelianism. Clark refers to Voltaire, in respect to his criticism at least, as "a reactionary classicist" and quotes Faguet as calling him a "Classic who understands practically nothing of antiquity." His rigid regulationism stemmed from a firm belief in the unities, in rhymed verse in tragedy, and in precision of form and clarity of thought, was often unjust to neo-classicists such as Corneille and Racine. His theories are scattered throughout his many *Préfaces,* letters and discourses, best known of which may be said to be his *Préface* to *Hérode et Mariamne* (1725) a tribute to Racine and a defense, on the basis of certain ancient Greek models, of his own play, to which this is an introduction; his *Lettre au Père Porée, Jesuite* (1730), an examination of the three unities and their importance, and his *Discours sur la tragedie, à Mylord Bolingbroke* (1731), an examination of the unity of action. One of the great critics in France during this period was Diderot, whose demand for a "return to nature" was in keeping with revolutionary sentiments of Rousseau. He left several critical works, among which his treatise, *De la poésie dramatique, à Monsieur Grimm* (1758) is perhaps his finest. This is a study "of the various kinds of drama," "of serious comedy," "of a sort of moral drama," "of a sort of philosophic drama," "of simple and complex dramas," "of the burlesque drama," "of the plot and the dialogue," "of the first sketch," "of the incidents," and "of interest," the whole being an indictment of over-stiff traditionalism and a plea for a new liberalism. Beaumarchais did much to further the cause of Diderot, from whom his critical ideas were, in the main, derived, but he differed from Diderot in that he was first and foremost a dramatist. His significance as a critic lies in his insistence—perhaps the first explicit point in this respect in the history of dramatic theory—on the prime importance of action in drama. The duty of comedy, he opines, is to "inspire, move, transport, and strike" the spectator. Among his several works on dramatic subjects, including letters and prefaces, his *Essai sûr le genre dramatique sérieux* (1767) stands out as the most rewarding. This is a largely personal commentary, inspired by the controversy over one of his plays, on the serious, as opposed to the comic, drama, a category to which the work under discussion belonged. Here are to be found an attack on oppressive rules ("In what branch of art," he asks, "have rules ever produced masterpieces?") and a plea for greater truth of observation and depiction and a greater vitality of real, rather than merely dramatically simulated, emotion. Beaumarchais' *Lettre modérée sur la chute et la critique de Barbier de Séville* (1775) was, as its title implies, a defense of his play *The Barber of Seville* against certain critics. In the latter part of the 18th century Schiller in Germany was writing his aesthetic essays which contain the cream of his dramatic theories, although many of his critical ideas are to be found among his divers reviews and prefaces. One of his two most significant treatises on dramatic subjects was his *Ueber den Grund des Vergnuegens an tragischen Gegenstaenden* (1792), which was an attempt according to Clark, to prove that the sole end of tragic art is to give pleasure. The other, his *Ueber die tragische Kunst* (1792) is divided between theory and proof, and gives, without benefit of a knowledge of Aristotle's *Poetics,* definitions of, and remarks on, tragedy. As to Schiller's theories of acting, it was his belief a player should strive for truth coming not from nature but art, and for beauty depending not on art but on nature. Following Schiller came the greatest of all German writers, Goethe. His criticism is scattered over a heterogeneous body of material, from passages of his novel, *Wilhelm Meister* (first published in its entirety in 1830), to his divers prefaces, letters and articles. It is perhaps his famous *Gespraeche* (Conversations) with Eckermann and Soret (1836-1848) that contains the passages of richest theoretical commentary on the drama. These are best prefaced with the remark by Calvin Thomas in his Goethe (1917) to the effect that Goethe's simple creed was "that the artist as such must have no creed; that is, no creed derivable from the intellect or accountable to it. Rules, conventions, theories, principles, inhibitions of any sort not born of his own immediate feeling, are no concern of his. They proceed from an inferior part of human nature, being the work of gapers and babblers." Consequently, it is best to look upon the *Gespraeche* as the personal reflections of a great, broad-minded, deep-hearted, liberal man of the theatre rather than as formal, objective tracts on the canons of the dramatic art. Here Goethe touches upon the warm, vital emotionalism of tragedy, the proper meter of dramatic verse, the plays of such writers as Kotzebue, Schiller, Molière, Lord Byron, Calderon, the ancient Greeks, and Shakespeare, and of the famous thirty-six dramatic situations of Gozzi. His significant essay, *Ueber epische und dramatische Dichtung* (1797) is a study of two main kinds of poetry, on describing "an action as being altogether past and completed," the other representing it "as actually occurring," followed by an analysis of "five different varieties" of motives ("progressive," "retrogressive," "retardative," "retrospective," and "anticipatory"), and the three "worlds which are to be represented to view" and which are "common to both" ("the physical," "the moral," and "the world of phantasies, presentiments, apparitions, accidents, and fatalities"). After Goethe came Schlegel with his *Vorlesungen ueber dramatische Kunst und Literatur* (1809-1811), which was a collection of lectures on dramatic art and literature. Here he examines the nature and meaning of the dramatic, the theatrical, the tragic and the comic. He comes, among others, to the following conclusions: that "visible representation is essential to the dramatic form," that a work of the theatre must be judged on two counts, the "poetical" and the "theatrical," and that the tragic tone of true drama is to be found in the very substance of our lives, the disappointments, dangers, fears and passions, and that by these alone are we fitted to write or judge great tragedy. Wagner followed Schlegel with ideas on the drama which show how predominantly was he a dramatic poet and how secondarily, for all his great music, a composer. For him, sounds were an expansion of the emotional meanings which mere verbal language, even when supported by stage action, were powerless fully to convey. Perhaps his clearest single statement of his theatrical creed is his *Ueber dis Bestimmung der Oper* (1871), in which he delineated the purpose of the opera, or music-drama, as he was wont to call his own work. Here he emphasised the importance (in vitality of inspiration) of improvisation, both for the interpreter and the creator, and the supreme value of theatricalism for its emotional effect and appeal. Freytag contributed to dramatic theory at about the same time as Wagner, giving considerable insight into the working methods of one who was himself, a practising dramatist. His *Die Technik des Dramas* (1863) is, as Clark calls it, "a handbook of practical advice" for playwrights, limited in its applicability because of the narrow range of its models—Sophocles, Shakespeare, Lessing, Goethe, and Schiller being practically the only dramatists mentioned. In France dramatic criticism was enunciated by a writer who remained first of all a poet and dramatist, Victor Hugo. His ideas are to be found in his *Préfaces* to his several plays, and one of these stands out as of especial moment, the *Préface* to Cromwell (1827), which clearly evidences his overweening romanticism and the inspiration, as against logic, which was its keystone and mainstay. Here a defense is made of a kind of turgidity and abandon in dramatic writing, with re-marks upon the "grotesque" as a kind of comic relief in tragedy ("a halting-place, a mean term, a starting-point whence one rises toward the beautiful with a fresher and keener perception") and an out-and-out defiance hurled in the teeth of the rigid regulationism of the Greeks, with their unities, etc. Dumas *fils* was not far behind Hugo in his espousal of romanticism, but he was an impassioned devotee of the "useful drama, of the theatre as an instrument of social, civic, or political progress. His didacticism is borne out in the *Préfaces* to his many plays. The Préface to his play, *Un Père prodigue* (1868) may be taken as representative. Here he declares the importance of a sure technique, but he also declares the higher value of an idea which that technique should serve. He ends with the conclusion that "the dramatist who knows *man* as Balzac did, and the theatre as Scribe did, will be the greatest of the world's dramatists." Sarcey, appearing in the latter half of the 19th century, was for sometime the despot of French criticism, being able to make or break a play or writer. He was, though narrow, clear-sighted, logical and consistent. In his *Quarante ans de théâtre* (published 1900-02) he reveals the mind that was so strict a believer in the "well-made play" (drama that follows the classic unities of Aristotle, represented contemporaneously by Scribe and Sardou) and such dramatic properties as the *scène à faire* (called by William Archer the "obligatory scene"). Sarcey's *Essai d'une esthétique de théâtre* (1876) is a plea for less rigidity of dramatic rules at the same time that it is a body of "directions or guide-posts" to the value of the audience to a play and to the importance of the unity of action, by which, for all the actual mingling of tears and laughter in real life, the necessary tone, predominantly tragic or predominantly comic, is achieved. (This latter argument was an issue he took with Victor Hugo over the latter's defense of the introduction of the "grotesque" into tragedy.) The great social novelist, Zola, contributed a considerable body of critical theory which showed the prevalent naturalism of his approach. This appeared among his several *Préfaces* and essays. His best and clearest statement of his dramatic theories is to be found in the *Préface* to his play *Thérèse Raquin* (1873). Here Zola ably championed the cause of progressivism in the theatre, attacking the old school of the "well-made play" and the overdone romanticism of the historical or heroic drama, and defending the naturalism of which he was the greatest French exponent. A figure in France more properly a critic than a creative writer was Brunetière, a contemporary of Zola. Among his large number of writings on the drama he is best known for his *La Loi du théâtre* (1894), a preface to the *Annales du théâtre et de la musique* for the year 1893, which expounded the law of *will* as the central force of drama. Brunetière himself says: "In drama or farce what we ask of the theatre is the spectacle of a will striving towards a goal and conscious of the means which it employs. The general law of the theatre is defined by the action of a will conscious of itself; and the dramatic species are distinguished by the nature of the obstacles encountered by this will, and that one drama is superior to another drama according as the quantity of will exerted is greater or less as the share of chance is less and that of necessity greater." William Archer translates, in his *Play-making* (1912), a summary of Brunetière's theory as follows: "Drama is a representation of the will of man in conflict with the mysterious powers or natural forces which limit and belittle us; it is one of us thrown living upon the stage there to struggle against fatality, against social law, against one of his fellow mortals, against himself if need be, against the ambitions, the interests, the prejudices, the folly, the malevolence of those around him." The Belgian Maeterlinck appeared with his strangely delicate, subtle criteria, for the expression of which he invented the so-called "static drama," later discarding it. He has written several essays concerning dramatic topics, and of these perhaps the best or most representative are his *Le Tragique quotidien* (1896) and his *Préface* to *théâtre I*. Here he supports the inner meaning of the soul as against outward action in the drama, the conflict of the conscious and subconscious minds, and the struggle between the infinite or supernatural and common, material human life. In England during the 19th century theory was led by Coleridge, whose analysis, though not directed primarily at acted drama, belongs to the great criticism, dramatic and otherwise, of all time. The cream of his critical work is to be found in his *Literary Remains* (1836-1839), in which are included his *Lectures on Shakespeare* and other assorted pieces on Greek dramatists and the English poets. Coleridge, not primarily concerned with the theatre, necessarily treats all of these as pure poets, apart from dramatic or stage considerations. Withal he is capable of mentioning the "willing suspension of disbelief" necessary to a full enjoyment of theatre, and he analyses as follows what is to the average playgoer theatrical experience: "The true stage-illusion in this and in all other things consists—not in the mind's judging it to be a forest. . . . For not only are we never absolutely deluded, or anything like it, but the attempt to cause the highest delusion possible to beings in their senses sitting in a theatre, is a gross fault, incident only to low minds, which, feeling that they cannot affect the heart or head permanently, endeavor to call forth the momentary affections." Coleridge's interpretation of *Hamlet* is also celebrated. Another critic not primarily concerned with the theatre was Charles Lamb, a contemporary of Coleridge. His *Essays of Elia* (1823) contain several pieces concerned with the drama. Of these, *On the Artificial Comedy of the Last Century,* though it contributes neither theory nor genuinely new ideas, is the most important. One of the greatest critics of literature of all times, Hazlitt, lived and wrote in England during this same period. He differs from both Coleridge and Lamb in that much of his criticism has been directed toward acted plays. This is marked neither by the brilliance of Lamb nor the profundity of Coleridge, but is highly valuable for his clear, commonsense approach to all matters he chooses to discuss. His *Lectures on the English Comic Writers* (1819) is a study of the "comic muse" and a criticism of various comic writers, including Etherege, Wycherley, Congreve, Steele, Addison, Farquhar, Mrs. Centlivre, Colley Cibber, Fielding, Goldsmith and Sheridan. His other essays on dramatic topics include *On Modern Comedy* (1815), *A View of the English Stage* (1818), and *On Dramatic Poetry* (1820). In the late 19th century and early 20th century in England the banner of dramatic theory was borne by the playwright, Pinero. Though more important in the creative capacity, he yet wrote criticism which is both interesting and rewarding. Among his several essays on dramatic topics, that on Stevenson as a worker in the theatre—*Robert Louis Stevenson: The Dramatist* (1903)—is perhaps most significant, for it offers his explanation for the failure of Stevenson's plays with the corresponding theory of how else plays should be written. Here is ample evidence of Pinero's emphatic belief in form and technique in playwriting. The contemporary of Pinero, Henry Arthur Jones, though belonging to the same school of dramatic thought, was perhaps more significant in his critical utterances than his colleague. He explains the large number of essays he wrote on the drama by the lack he found in England of "any tolerable school of drama" and the necessity he felt of making it "possible for an English dramatist to produce his best work without the almost certain result that it would be slighted, or hooted off the stage." His *The Renascence of the English Drama* (1895) was a pointing-out of the new direction the drama was to take. Outside of this, perhaps his greatest single discussion of the drama is to be found in his *Introduction to Brunetière's "Law of the Drama"* (1914). (See: *Loi du théâtre, La—Brunetière*.) Taking Brunetière's law of the will as a starting-point, Jones formulates a new "universal law of drama" as follows: "Drama arises when any person or persons in a play are consciously or unconsciously "up against" some antagonistic person, or circumstance, or fortune. It is often more intense when, as in *Oedipus,* the audience is aware of the obstacle, and the person himself, or persons, on the stage are unaware of it. Drama arises thus, and continues when or till the person or persons are aware of the obstacle; it is sustained so long as we watch the reaction, physical, mental, or spiritual, of the person or persons to the opposing person, circumstance, or fortune. It relaxes as this reaction subsides, and ceases when the reaction is complete. This reaction of a person to an obstacle is most arresting and intense when the obstacle takes the form of another human will in almost balanced collision." The great social dramatist, Shaw, also had much to contribute in the way of dramatic theory. In general his sentiments are against the "well-made play" (as represented by Scribe and Sardou, the school which he has called "Sardoodledum") and for the thesis play. For Shaw the theatre is not an end in itself and entertainment is not its principal object; for him the theatre is the means of spreading a message, and he has used it in precisely that sense, as a pulpit of Socialism and social progress. His *The Author's Apology* (1902), from an edition of his play *Mrs. Warren's Profession,* is at once an attack on old-fashioned romanticism and sentimentality and a defense of the drama of ideas. His contemporary, William Archer, wrote several treatises on modern theatre and drama, which, while demonstrating no single important new theory, served to illumine and appraise theories that had gone before. Of these, *Play-making* (1912) is undoubtedly his most important work. Here he studies much of the large body of dramatic theory in existence, and offers many reservations and suggestions of his own; in one place, for example, he attempts to disprove the validity of Brunetière's famous law by counterposing *crisis,* not *conflict,* as the first requisite of drama. In general it was Archer's belief that "any representation of imaginary personages which is capable of interesting an average audience assembled in a theatre" is worthy of the term "dramatic."

See also *Freytag's pyramid; Malevinsky's Algebraic Formula of Dramaturgy, 1925.*

Drama, Yugoslav, before the First World War. Before the First World War most of what is now known as Yugoslavia was under Austrian rule. In the Catholic parts of the country mystery and miracle plays were performed. Influences of Molière, Schiller and Shakespeare had previously been very strong. Now Ibsen and Strindberg showed their effects. The best-known play was probably *The Death of the Jugovići Mother* (from the Kossova cycle) by Ivo Vojnović. Others: *Hasanaginica* by Ogrizovic; *The Building of Skadar* by *Korolija;* the Marko trilogy by Dimović; and *Fair Vida* by Ivan Cankar.

Drama, Yugoslav, since the First World War. Serbian audiences clung to their liking for historical-patriotic plays and colorful folk-lore works like *Koštana* by Stankovic. Nusic has had the greatest success with his comedies. Other talented Serbian playwrights: Milošević, Nikolajevic, Vesnić, Manojlović. Among Croatian dramatists the most important is still Ivo Vojnović, who has felt the influence of many recent theatrical trends, from naturalism to symbolism, but has retained his individual style. His masterpiece is *The Death of the Jugovići Mother.* Milan Begović has also felt the touch of modern trends and is attracted by erotic themes. Zagreb has the finest opera, and Ljubljana the finest theatre proper.

Drama Critics' Circle. See *New York Drama Critics' Circle.*

Drama of fate. The chief contribution made by the German romanticists in the 19th century. This was a cross between romanticism and classic tragedy. The fates were introduced into modern life. Zacharias Werner's *The Twenty-fourth of February, 1809,* is characteristic of this school.

Drama of ideas. A play in which characters and events serve not only a story but also a philosophy.

Dramatic Art and Literature. A series of lectures by August Wilhelm Schlegel written in 1808 which became the basis for historical judgment in the German theatre.

Dramatic criticism. See *Critics and criticism.*

Dramatic editor. One who assembles and edits material for the daily and Sunday drama sections of his newspaper. He also arranges layouts and determines what photographs and drawings shall be used, with an eye to their artistic worth and suitability. The job is a practically continuous one as he must keep in touch with press agents, artists and managers, read copy day after day, call for copy, answer routine and emergency telephone calls, and relate his page to the news of the day.

Dramatic Index. Formerly edited by the late Frederick Winthrop Faxon; the volumes edited by Mary E. Bates begin with 1936.
An index to periodicals—quarterlies, monthlies, weeklies—concerning the stage and its players. It includes stage portraits, scenes from plays, articles about the theatre —critical, historical, biographical—notices of production, information about dramatists and librettists. It is also an index to published plays and the synopses of plots. One volume yearly beginning with 1909, to date.

Dramatic Poesy. This essay by John Dryden, 1668, was one of the epoch-making critical pronouncements of the centuries. It discussed the unities, defined the play, the value of variety and regularity, and matters of plot and characterization together with commentaries on Shakespeare, Beaumont, Fletcher and Ben Jonson.

Dramatic readers. In the 19th century and in the provincial cities public readings of plays became popular. Among the famous practitioners were Fanny Kemble, S. H. Clark, Leland Powers, Henry Southwick and others.

Dramatic recital. A program of monologues or scenes from plays spoken, generally not in costume.

Dramatis personae. Latin, meaning, in our present day term, "cast of characters"; literally: "persons of the play."

Dramatists' Guild (first called Association of Dramatists). To protect their rights, a group of 131 playwrights in New York City drew up and signed a "defensive" agreement, September 1, 1926, and under the leadership of George Middleton, confronted theatre managers with the following basic contract: "A manager shall not accept a play except from members of the Guild, who agree not to submit the play to any manager failing to enter the agreement; the control of cinema and foreign rights; a competitive market must be conserved for cinema rights; and no secret dealing or indirect profit shall be made by a manager." The Guild's contract has been established, British authors joining with Americans. The Guild is part of the Author's League of America, but is affiliated with no labor union. The executive-secretary for both organizations is Luise M. Sillcox.

Dramatists' Play Service. A New York organization founded and headed by Barrett H. Clark, which provides plays and makes royalty arrangements for amateur players. This is a subsidiary of The Dramatists' Guild of the Authors' League of America. Located at 6 East 39th Street, New York.

Drame d'Adam et d'Ève. The most important play of the 12th century, a link between the liturgical drama and the mystery play, and the first religious play written in French. It is divided into three parts: (1) the fall of Man; (2) the murder of Abel; (3) the appearance of the Prophets as the forerunners of the Savior.

Draper, Ruth (1889-   ). American *diseuse* and monologist. Sister of the late Paul Draper, vocalist, and aunt of the younger Paul Draper, dancer. Since her first appearance in 1915, she has toured the United States, Europe and South Africa. Among the best-known of her character sketches, many of which are satiric, and all of which she writes, are: *In a Railroad Station on the Western Plains; Opening a Bazaar; Three Women and Mr. Clifford;* and *In a Church in Italy.*

Draw curtain. See *Curtains.*

Dream Play, The. August Strindberg (Swedish). Drama. 3 acts. 1902.
An imaginative romance expressing the author's familiar aversion to the female sex and embodying his conception of life as a waking dream. The daughter of Indra, king of the gods, visits the earth to see how men live. She finds that Maya, the world-mother responsible for propagation, has created only sin and sorrow, strife and misery. Man's senses have obscured and fettered his spirituality; only when he has won the eternal war against love and womankind can he free himself and conquer evil. The daughter of Indra leaves the earth by entering a castle which catches fire as a bud on the roof opens into a giant chrysanthemum. Strange symbols like this abound throughout the play, the meaning of some clear, of others dubious. Thus there is an officer imprisoned in a castle surrounded by hollyhocks; a quarantine officer disguised as a blackamoor; a girl filling in all the cracks of a house until its inhabitants suffocate; and other figures as wildly fanciful as those of a modern surrealist painting. And interspersed among these scenes are telling lines conveying the author's philosophy of life and his personal maxims: "Duty is everything you dread." "At the heart of happiness grows the seed of disaster."

Dreiser, Theodore (1871-   ). American author. Notable in the theatre for the adaptation of his famous novel *An American Tragedy* to the stage. A single performance was given in London in 1927. It has since been produced as a motion picture. His play *The Hand of the Potter* was staged in 1921.
Born in Terre Haute, Indiana, he adopted a journalistic career, being an editor-in-chief of the Butterick Publications in New York from 1907 to 1910. His first novel *Sister Carrie,* 1900, attracted considerable attention, though it was suppressed.
Among his other works are: *Jennie Gerhardt,* 1910; *The Financier,* 1912; *The Titan,* 1914; *Chains,* 1927.

Dressler, Marie (1869-1934). American actress. She was born in Ontario, Canada, her real name being Lelia Koerber. She made her American stage debut in

1886, after which she toured extensively. She appeared in London from 1907-09 and again in 1923 with marked success. For twenty years before her death she devoted herself almost exclusively to the motion pictures, however, achieving fame as a portrayer of comedy and pathos in such films as *Anna Christie, Min and Bill* and many others. When she died she was one of America's best loved and most popular character actresses. Her autobiography, *The Life Story of an Ugly Duckling,* was published in 1925. Her stage roles include Cigarette in *Under Two Flags* and Katisha in *The Mikado.*

Drew, John (1827-1862). American actor-manager. Born in Dublin. He made his debut in 1846 at the Bowery Theatre, New York, afterwards touring throughout the country. His career was principally with the Arch Street Theatre, Philadelphia, where he maintained a famous stock company with his wife as co-star. His wife, Louisa Lane Drew, on her husband's death, assumed management of the Arch Street Theatre, carrying on its standard of excellence. Their three children, John, Sidney and Georgiana Drew, were distinguished figures of the American stage.

Drew, John (1853-1927). American actor. Eldest son of John and Louisa Lane Drew; began his career in their stock company in Philadelphia. In 1875 he joined Daly's Company, New York, supporting Fanny Davenport in plays adapted from the German. Later he co-starred with Ada Rehan in *The Taming of the Shrew, As You Like It, The School for Scandal,* etc. In 1893 his *Twelfth Night* ran in London for one hundred consecutive performances. In 1892 he left Daly's and played in modern comedies. Drew's last appearance was in George Tyler's all-star revival of *Trelawney of the Wells,* in which he was touring in 1927. He occupied a unique place on the American stage. A robust actor in Shakespearean comedy, a suave interpreter of society drama, he was easily the leading actor in his own type of plays throughout his long career.

He wrote *My Years on the Stage* (1922). A memorial theatre at East Hampton, Long Island, was erected in his honor.

See also *Harvard Universiy.*

Drew, Mrs. John (Louisa Lane Drew) (1820-1897). American actress-manager. Born in London, she came to the United States in her childhood, made her debut in Philadelphia with Junius Brutus Booth in *Richard III.* She became one of the first actress-managers of the American stage. On her husband's death in 1862 she assumed control of the Arch Street Theatre in Philadelphia, maintaining the high standard of the theatre and her reputation as a portrayer of character parts. She gave Philadelphia one of the most brilliant periods in its theatrical history. She was a distinguished actress in her own right, famous for her portrayals of Mrs. Malaprop, Lady Teazle, Peg Woffington, Lydia Languish. Her three children, John and Sidney Drew and Georgiana Drew (Georgiana Drew Barrymore) had their training under their mother. She published *Autobiographical Sketch,* with an introduction by John Drew, 1899. See also M. J. Moses, *Famous Actor-Families in America,* 1906.

Drinkwater, John (1882-1937). English dramatist. His biographical plays are his most notable achievements. Born at Leytonstone, he was one of the founders of the Pilgrim Players, 1907, which subsequently developed into the Birmingham Repertory Theatre. His first publication was a volume of verse, 1906, followed in 1911 by his first play, also in verse, *Cophetua.* His most successful play has been *Abraham Lincoln,* 1919. As an actor he played various parts, including the title-role of *Abraham Lincoln, Mary Stuart,* 1922; *Oliver Cromwell,* 1923; *Robert E. Lee,* 1923.

Droeshout, Martin (fl. 1620-1651). English engraver. Engraver of the portrait of William Shakespeare prefixed to the Folio edition of the dramatist's works published in 1623. The Droeshout engraving is generally regarded as the most authentic one of the poet.

Drop. (1) Applies to any material used as backing for a scene: there are battens on top and bottom to stretch and hold the drop taut. Types include: (a) translucency; (b) leg drop; (c) cut drop. (2) To let a scene down, or drag, by slowing up tempo and relaxing intensity.

Drop curtain. See *Curtains.*

Drottningholm Theatre. An 18th century court theatre on Queen's Island, just outside of Stockholm. This Swedish theatre now houses the Drottningholm Theater museum. For full information consult *Theatre Collections in Libraries and Museums* by Rosamond Gilder and George Freedley.

Drums in the Night. Bertolt Brech (German). Drama. 1922. The scene is Germany after the First World War. The play deals with the fury of a German soldier returning from the trenches to find the war profiteers in possession of everything.

Drury Lane, Theatre Royal. A famous theatre in London, first built in 1663; burned down in 1672; rebuilt, on designs by Christopher Wren, in 1674. The great actor David Garrick first appeared here in 1742 (later became manager and played in his own house until 1776). Mrs. Siddons first appeared here in 1775, but had to wait until 1782 for her success; she remained until about 1804, later playing in Covent Garden. Garrick, as manager, was succeeded by Sheridan who presented his *School for Scandal.* The theatre was again rebuilt in 1794, with considerable increase in seating capacity. In 1809 it was again burned down and in 1812 was built on the same site as the present Theatre Royal. Alterations were made in 1814 and 1821 to improve the acoustics. It was Edmund Kean in 1814 who restored prosperity to the theatre after a lean period following the rebuilding.

Dry up. To forget one's lines in a performance, thereby causing an embarrassing pause and frequently leaving the other actors onstage without a proper cue.

Dryden, John (1631-1700). English dramatist. A great critic, poet and satirist of Restoration days, Dryden was greatly admired by his contemporaries, Congreve, Vanbrugh and Addison and became the literary dictator of his day. Born at Aldwinkle, Northamptonshire, he was the son of a small landowner and was educated at Westminster School under Dr. Busby, and at Trinity College, Cambridge. On his father's death in 1654 he inherited an income of sixty pounds a year, and three years later, went to London and adopted the career of letters. His first efforts were the *Heroic Stanzas on the death of Oliver Cromwell,* 1659, which were followed by *Astraea Redux,* a poem celebrating the Restoration.

It was necessary for the young poet to supplement his small income, and the easiest way which presented itself to him was by writing for the stage, a pursuit for which he had no special aptitude and, as far as comedy was concerned, no personal inclination. His early efforts met with little success. It was not until the performance of *The Indian Queen,* 1664, that he gained real popularity. This was a tragedy in heroic verse written in collaboration with Sir Robert Howard.

In 1668, he published his classic *Essay of Dramatick Poesie,* and in the same year his *Defence of an Essay of Dramatique Poesy,* an introduction to his play, *The Indian Emperor.* For fifteen years, 1666-81. Dryden's output was entirely for the theatre.

His other works include: *Secret Love; or, The Maiden Queen,* 1667; *Sir Martin Mar-all; or The Feigned Innocency,* 1667; *Marriage a la Mode,* 1672 (revived in 1930 at the Lyric Theatre, Hammersmith, England); *Tyrannic Love; or, the Royal Martyr,* 1669; *The Rehearsal,* 1675; *Aurungzebe,* 1675; *All for Love; or The World Well Lost,* 1678; *Don Sebastian,* 1690.

Dual personality. A dramatic theme based on the idea of the *alter ego,* or the split in character, and used most notably by Ibsen, Pirandello, Benavente and most spectacularly in Stevenson's *Dr. Jekyll and Mr. Hyde.*

Ducats. Broadway slang term for theatre tickets.

Duchess of Malfi, The. John Webster (English). Tragedy. 5 acts. c. 1614.
The story is taken from one of Bandello's *Novelle,* Painter's *Palace of Pleasure* and from Spenser's *Arcadia.* Considered Webster's masterpiece.

The Duchess, a widow, secretly marries the steward of her court, despite warnings by her brothers that she must not marry again. They hope to inherit her share of the estate. Her secret marriage is discovered and she and her two sons are killed. One brother goes mad, the other brother is killed by the betrayer of the Duchess's secret, who, in turn, is killed by the mad brother, Ferdinand.

Dudley, Bide (1877-   ). American dramatic critic and author. Born in Minneapolis, Minnesota, and the father of Doris Dudley, actress. Was drama critic for N. Y. *Evening World;* and has recently done dramatic articles for the New York *Sunday Enquirer.* He is the author of the following plays: *Odds and Ends* (with John Godfrey), 1917; *The Little Whopper* (lyrics), 1918; *Sue Dear,* 1922; *The Matinee Girl,* 1926; *Bye Bye Bonnie* (with Louis Simon), 1927; *Come Along All,* 1928;

Oh, Henry, 1928; *Borrowed Love,* 1929. Has been critic of the drama for radio stations WOR and WHN.

Du Harlay, Hachille. Supposed source of the name Harlequin: an early patron of the theatre who gave his surname to the type.
See also *Harlequin.*

Duke of York's Company. The theatrical company, during the Restoration, of Sir William D'Avenant; first began performances in 1660; drew a large public because of its spectacular presentations with ornate settings and new machines; it soon, however, became bankrupt because of expenditures, which increased yearly due to the many new and expensive devices; in 1682 it combined with the King's Company of D'Avenant's rival, Killigrew, retaining the title of "King's," the merger was not a success and in 1687 Charles D'Avenant, son of Sir William, assigned his patent to Alexander D'Avenant, who in 1690, sold it to Christopher Rich, an unscrupulous lawyer, thereby finally terminating the union.

Dukes, Ashley (1885-). English dramatist. Born at Bridgwater, he made an early reputation as a dramatist and critic. Of his critical works, *The World to Play With* is most popular. He married Marie Rambert, dancer and teacher of dancing. He is also English editor of *Theatre Arts.*
His plays include: *The Man With a Load of Mischief,* 1924; *One More River,* 1927; *The Dumb Wife of Cheapside,* 1930; *Matchmaker's Arms,* 1930. Among his skillful adaptations are *The Machine Wreckers,* 1923; *Mozart,* 1926; *Jew Suess,* 1929; *Elizabeth of England,* 1931.

Dulcy. George S. Kaufman and Marc Connelly (American). Comedy, 3 acts. 1921.
With her bromides and endless blunders, Dulcy almost ruins her husband's chance to put through an important merger. By some miracle, however, she finally blunders on to success, and saves her husband's business.

Dumas, Alexandre (fils) (1824-1895). French author and dramatist. It has been said that Dumas *fils* was first a moralist and secondly a writer.
Born in Paris, a natural son of the author of *The Count of Monte Cristo* and *The Three Musketeers* by whom he was acknowledged and legitimated. His school days left painful memories, which he utilized in his *Affaire Clemenceau.* As a young man he shared his father's alternations from penury to extravagance. Determined to be independent, he turned author, issuing a volume of verse and half a dozen novels, of which only one had any vitality. This was the *Lady of the Camelias,* published in 1848. It was dramatized by its author and ultimately performed in 1852. It has held the stage not only in France, but all over the world, for more than sixty years. Its success caused its author to give up novels for drama. He was made a member of the Academy in 1874. His next play was a dramatization of his own novel *Diane de Lys.* In 1855 he brought out a wholly original play,

the *Outer Edge of Society*. This was followed by *Ideas of Madame Aubray; Denise; Francillon,* 1887; *L'Etrangère*. In the first performance of this last play Mmes. Bernhardt, Croizette and Brohan, and Mm. Coquelin, Got and Febvre, all appeared, while Aimée Deselée created the heroine in *Une Visite de Noces, Princesse Georges* and *La Femme de Claude*. His contribution to dramatic theory is best found in his various *Préfaces* and his letters.

Dumas, Alexandre (*pere*) (1802-1870). French author and dramatist. The famous creator of *D'Artagnan* and *Monte Cristo*.

Dumas was descended from Alexandre Davy de la Pailleterie, an illegitimate son of the Marquis de la Pailleterie by a Negress, Marie Cessette Dumas. Born at Villers-Cotterets, the young man was brought up by his mother in straitened circumstances. He early showed a taste for writing, and left a solicitor's office to seek his fortune in Paris in 1823. A liaison with a dressmaker, Marie Labay, resulted in the birth in 1824 of a son Alexandre who is known as Dumas *fils*.

His play, *Henri III et sa cour,* produced by the *Comédie-Française* in 1829 marked a new epoch in the French theatre, being a complete departure from the sterile and decadent classical tradition, its brilliance, historical and romantic setting secured it a triumph, established the reputation of the author, won for him the friendship of Victor Hugo, and brought him the librarianship of the Palais Royal under Orleans.

For a time Dumas' prosperity knew no limits, but his excessive extravagance, his lack of business acumen and his number of hangers-on quickly burdened him with a load of debt from which he never escaped.

Much has been written on the question of Dumas' staggering output. He himself claimed that he had written twelve hundred works, and the number can not be much less, but such an amount could not have been produced without considerable help. Among his collaborators were Auguste Maquet, Paul Lacroix, Paul Bocage and J. P. Mallefille. It is significant, however, that none of these ever, under his own name, produced a work comparable with any of those which appeared under the signature of Dumas.

He joined Garibaldi in Italy in 1860, and worked enthusiastically in his cause, staying in Naples for four years, but on his return to France his position became deplorable. His failing health placed him at the mercy of his creditors, and he was never out of the clutches of one actress or another. His son and daughter came to his rescue, and he died at his son's house near Dieppe, December 5, 1870.

His plays include: *Henri III et sa cour; Christine; Charles VII; La Tour de Nesle; Mademoiselle de belle isle; Antony* (containing the famous and melodramatic line *Elle me resistait, je l'ai assassiné*).

Of his novels which have been dramatized the following are the most famous: *Les Trois mousquetaires; Vingt ans après; Le Vicomte de Bragelonne; Le Comte de Monte Cristo*.

Du Maurier, George Louis Palmella Busson (1834-96). Born in Paris, the son of a Frenchman who became a British subject. In 1856 he studied art, first in Paris, then Antwerp. As a member of the staff of Punch he did a series of social satires.

In 1881 he was made a member of the Royal Society of Painters in Water Colors. Towards the end of his life, his eyesight failed him and he turned to writing novels. His first, *Peter Ibbetson,* 1892, is a prose poem that is a skillful blend of romance and realism. *Trilby,* 1894, perhaps his best known and most successful work, is the story of the English and Continental art and literary life of Du Maurier's student days. His last book, *The Martian,* which was published posthumously, is a genial story of bohemian friendship and love.

Du Maurier, Sir Gerald (1873-1934). English actor, producer. Son of George Du Maurier, author of *Trilby,* brother of Guy Du Maurier. Author of *An Englishman's Home* and father of Daphne Du Maurier who has described him in *Gerald, A Portrait.* He played in: *Trilby; Interference; Brewster's Millions; Hamlet; The Daring Girl;* and many other plays.

Dumb act. The first act in a vaudeville show that can not be spoiled by late arrivals, usually one of acrobatics, dancing, or with trained animals.

Dumb show. A dramatic sketch or part of a play which presents plot-action without speech and which is often, though not invariably, accompanied by music; pantomime.
See also *Pantomime.*

Dumb show, Elizabethan. Pantomimic representation inserted between the acts of a play to summarize, interpret or foreshadow action elsewhere in the drama. The pantomime was generally accompanied with appropriate music. The only example of the form in Shakespeare is the dumb show preceding the play within the play in *Hamlet.*

Dumbfounding. The name given to an inane and vulgar manner of hoaxing during the Restoration, possibly the comic source of American burlesque or leg show.

Dumping seats. The selling of tickets under box office price by ticket agencies just before curtain time.

Duncan, Isadora (1878-1927). American dancer. Born at San Francisco, she made her first appearance at Chicago, in 1899, without much success. Struggling against hardships of all kinds, she made her way to Europe with her family, determined to impress upon the theatre her personality and her ideals of dancing. These derived through nature from Greek art. In an age devoted only to the ballet, she acquired a large body of adherents, and through Fokine considerably influenced the development of the Diaghileff ballet. She attained great popularity throughout Europe and set up dancing schools at Paris, at Grunewald near Berlin, in Moscow and in the United States, where she was not generally appreciated. She spent her last years in unhappy circumstances in Europe. She was killed in a motor accident near Nice, September 14, 1927. A memorial school to her was set up at Neuilly. She developed the art of classical dancing by drawing inspiration from the rhythm of nature and from the Greek ideal that "all gestures have a moral resonance and thus can directly express every possible moral state."

Dunlap, William (1766-1839). American dramatist. "Father of the American drama," a title given him because he is the first American man of letters who made playwriting a profession. He wrote and adapted sixty plays. His first play was *The Modest Soldier; or, Love in New York,* written in 1787 but never produced. His first production was *The Father; or, American Shandyism,* at the John Street Theatre, New York, September 7, 1789.

His *History of the American Theatre,* published in 1833, is one of his most valuable contributions. Among his other works, *The Life of George Frederick Cooke,* published in 1815, is well known. Besides his writings, a series of paintings place him as one of the best American artists of the period.

Dunning, Philip (1890-   ). American actor and playwright. Born in Meriden, Connecticut. He first appeared in *Pomander Walk* in 1911, then toured in vaudeville and stock. For several seasons he was stage manager at Poli's Theatre in Hartford, Connecticut. In New York he played in *Ruggles of Red Gap,* 1915; *Object—Matrimony,* 1916; *The Dancer,* 1919; *For All of Us,* 1923; etc. He is the co-author of *Broadway* (with George Abbott), 1926; *The Understudy* (with Jack Donahue), 1927; *Lilly Turner* (with George Abbott), 1932; *Kill That Story* (with Harry Madden), 1934; *Page Miss Glory* (with Joseph Schrank), 1934; etc. In 1931 he went to Hollywood as author-director with the United Artists Corporation. While his name is not so well known as that of the Spewacks and George Abbott, his sometime collaborator, he exploits the same vein of hearty comedy.

D'Urfey, Thomas (1653-1723). English dramatist. Born at Exeter, he wrote both tragedies and comedies, but the latter were the more popular. They include: *The Fond Husband,* 1676; *Squire Oldsapp,* 1679; and *Sir Barnaby Whig,* 1681.

He was a prolific writer of songs, of which two series were published: *New Collection of Songs and Poems,* 1683; and *Wit and Mirth; or, Pills to Purge Melancholy,* 1719-20.

Duse, Eleonora (1859-1924). Italian actress. She was a *figlia del arte,* a child of the theatre, the daughter of an actor, Alessandro Duse, and granddaughter of Luigi Duse, a Venetian player of some fame. She was born in a third-class railway carriage, October 3, 1859, when her father and mother were on tour between Venice and Vigevano. Eleonora remained with the company and made her first appearance on the stage at the age of four in the part of Cosette in *Les Miserables,* the performance taking place in a booth at Chioggia near Venice, a village from which her family had sprung.

Her early life was one of great hardship, accompanied by the incessant travelling of the strolling players and saddened by the premature death of her mother. The first important landmark in her career was her playing of Juliet in Verona at the age of fourteen, a performance of which there exists some record. It is said that the child actress discovered for herself to what purpose flowers might be put in sensitive and skilful hands, a theatrical asset of which she made full use throughout her career. Her first real success was made in 1878 when she appeared in the leading part in *Les Fourchambault* by Augier. In the following year the great Rossi engaged her as leading actress for his company, and from that date her true career may be said to have begun. She had triumphant tours throughout Italy, and earned an international reputation. Her repertoire at the time consisted of such plays as *Théodora, Divorçons, Fedora,* Goldoni's *La Locandiera,* Dumas' *The Princess of Bagdad.* She toured South America in 1885, and in 1892 she was in Vienna electrifying her audiences in *La Dame aux Camélias.* When playing in London in 1895 occurred that clash between her and Sarah Bernhardt, which made theatrical history. Both elected to play Sudermann's *Magda* and the challenge to comparison was taken up, notably by George Bernard Shaw. He gave the palm unhesitatingly to Duse. She created Gabriele D'Annunzio's fame as a dramatist when she acted in his plays *La Gioconda, Francesca de Rimini* and *La Citta Morte.* She began her association with D'Annunzio when she was about forty. The companionship was largely intellectual, and pledged her anew to a devotion to the poetic drama presented to her by the work of her beloved poet. In poor health and on the verge of nervous prostration, Duse retired shortly before the First World War. However, in 1923, she appeared for a series of matinees in London and then she appeared for eight matinees in New York at the Metropolitan Opera House. Nearly five thousand people rose and cheered her at each performance. Her failing health was insufficient to meet the onslaught of a severe chill, from the effects of which she died in Pittsburgh, Pennsylvania, April 21, 1924. Mussolini, who had offered her a pension for her declining years, which she refused, ordered that her body should be sent back to Italy at the public expense and she was buried with great honor at Asolo.

See also *Theatre, Italian, 19th century.*

Dutchman. Thin strip of canvas or duck, five inches wide, glued on the face of two flats at the point where they are hinged; used to cover up opening between flats. See *Scenery.*

Dutch Treat Club. Established in 1905. Membership includes among other notables, men who have had a book published or a picture hung. The annual party is celebrated by the publication of a book written and designed by members and includes such contributors as John La Gatta, Russell Patterson, Burns Mantle, Fairfax Downey, George S. Kaufman, Otto Harbach, one of the most prolific Broadway librettists, Roy Chapman Andrews, Brooks Atkinson, critic and author of *The Cingalese Prince,* with sidelights on the oriental theatre, Rupert Hughes and William Lengel. Prominent members include Clarence Budington Kelland, author of *Mr. Deeds Goes to Town,* Gene Buck, Stanley Rinehart, John Chapman, John O'Hara Cosgrave, Edward Ziegler, Metropolitan Opera Assn. official, Harry Hanson, critic, and Marc Connelly.

Dybbuk, The. A play by S. Ansky. 1926.

The people in this play belong to a very religious Russian Jewish sect. In a synagogue some prayermen and students are chanting the Talmud and waiting for the news that Sender, a wealthy merchant, has found a suitable bridegroom for his daughter, Leah. Channon, a student, drops dead when the news comes that a bridegroom has been found. The day of the wedding, Leah, instead of accepting the groom her father has chosen, cries out a refusal in a strange voice. It is then decided that a Dybbuk has entered the bride, and in order to exorcise the invading spirit, certain ceremonies must be performed by the holy men. During the proceedings it is discovered that Channon and Leah had been betrothed at birth, but her father, on growing rich, had greater aspirations and had broken his pact. Therefore he is responsible for Channon's death and must be punished. Meanwhile the exorcism is completed and in a moment when she is alone, Leah hears the soul of Channon call to her and joins him in death.

This play is based on an old superstition that when a young person dies before his time, his soul returns to earth and enters the body of a person in the form of a Dybbuk. Then this invading spirit must be exorcised.

Dynamo. Eugene O'Neill (American). Tragedy. 3 acts. 1929.

Against the hum of the dynamo, this play on the deification of the machine is presented.

A hard and fast Christian and an atheist are neighbors, but are equally contemptuous of one another. Their children fall in love. The atheist and his daughter play a joke on the son of the Christian, who takes it seriously and is upbraided by his father for his naïvete. The son forswears religion and goes out into the world to seek knowledge. Many years later he returns, convinced that Electricity is the only god. He finds, however, that he is still in love with the daughter of the atheist, who again tricks him. In expiation of his sin, he kills her, throws himself upon the Dynamo and is executed.

Dynasts, The. Thomas Hardy (English). An Epic-Drama of the War with Napoleon. 3 parts, 19 acts and 130 scenes. 1904-08.

This panorama of Napoleon's life and conquests overleaps all theatrical barriers. Regarded as a curiosity by most critics. The play is an unsuccessful example of the experimental theatre. Part I opens with the year 1805 and Napoleon's threat of invasion. It presents the House of Commons discussing the repeal of the Defense Act, Napoleon's Coronation at Milan, the preparations at Boulogne for invasion, the battles of Ulm and Austerlitz, Trafalgar, the death of Nelson, and the death of Pitt. In Part II the Prussians are defeated at Jena, Napoleon and Alexander meet at Tilsit, Josephine is divorced and Napoleon marries Marie Louise. Part III treats of the Russian expedition of 1812, the British victories in the Pyrenees, the Battle of Leipzig, Napoleon's abdication, the return from Elba and Waterloo. By the side of the major scene are smaller episodes. One of them is an unconscious Force and Will that moves the world. This Force and the Spirits introduced are to give a universal significance to the particular events recounted.

Each in His Own Way (*Ciascuno a suo modo*). Luigi Pirandello (Italian). Drama. 3 acts. 1918.

A man has committed suicide because Delia deceived him. Doro gives an indulgent explanation of Delia's deceit; Francesco, a slanderous explanation. The two quarrel, but during the quarrel change their minds and resume the quarrel on opposite sides. Delia, ignorant of the change, thanks Doro for his defense. Touched, he returns to the indulgent explanation. Delia is worried when she hears of bad judgments passed upon her. The man for whom Delia betrayed the suicide enters, and he and Delia decide to run away again.

Earth. Karl Schoenherr (Austrian). Drama. 3 acts. 1908.

A crusty old innkeeper, past seventy, refuses to allow his son, nearing fifty, to marry or to take a man's place at the inn, even though warned by the village doctor that he must die. The old fellow orders a coffin to be placed at his bedside, and lies ailing all winter awaiting his end.

Easiest Way, The. Eugene Walter (American). Drama. 4 acts. 1908.

Laura Murdock, the mistress of a wealthy man, falls in love with a newspaper reporter. An attempt to "go straight," proves too hard and she attempts to return to her lover, but instead loses both men.

East Lynne. Mrs. Henry Wood (English). Drama. 5 acts. 1861.

The story of this lachrymose drama concerns Isabel turned out by her husband "never to darken the door again." She returns under the guise of a servant for her child, and is caught and rebuffed once more. All of this domestic tragedy is because of a fancied infidelity. This typical melodrama of the heart throb variety is perhaps the first theatrical translation of "the woman pays" theme, and one of the most popular melodramas ever written.

Eastward Hoe. George Chapman, Ben Jonson and John Marston (English). Comedy. 5 acts. 1605.

Gitred, daughter of a city goldsmith, and married to Sir Petronel Flash, is persuaded by her husband to sell an estate. Sir Petronel had planned to run away with the proceeds, but circumstances prevented his flight, and he is finally forgiven.

Eaton, Walter Pritchard (1878-   ). American author, professor and critic. He was born in Malden, Massachusetts, and completed his education at Harvard, where he received his A.B. degree in 1910.

He was then dramatic critic on the New York Sun, 1907-08; on the American Magazine, 1909-18. In 1933 he was appointed associate professor of playwriting in Yale University. Among his many published works are *American Stage of Today,* 1908; *At the New Theatre and others,* 1910; *Plays and Players,* 1916; *Queen Victoria* (play with David Carb), 1923; *The Actor's Heritage,* 1924; *The Theatre Guild, The First Ten Years,* 1929; *The Drama in English,* 1930.

Ecclesiazusae, The; or, The Women in Politics. Aristophanes (Greek). c. 393 B.C.

This rollicking satire on Hellenic feminism and Utopianism dramatizes the taking over of government by women. It is one of the dramas which had a great influence on subsequent satirical comedy.

Ecclestone, William (-1625?). English actor. An actor named in the 1623 Folio list of performers in Shakespeare's plays. He is known to have assumed roles also in Jonson's *Alchemist* and *Catiline* and in a large number of plays by Beaumont and Fletcher.

Echegaray, José de (1832-1916). Spanish dramatist. He was a professor of mathematics, engineer, statesman, as well as a dramatist who dominated the Spanish stage for some twenty years after 1873. He was a neo-romanticist who produced tragic scenes from everyday life.

Principal works: *O locura o santidad* (Either Madness or Saintliness), 1882; *El hijo de don Juan,* 1892, inspired by Ibsen's *Ghosts* (a study of the effects of inherited disease). *El gran galeoto* (The World and His Wife), 1881, is his best-known work and has been acted in America and every European country; the message is that the world with its calumny can ruin even the virtuous.

Eckenberg, Johannes Karl von (1685-1748). German manager. Famous strong man and acrobat of the 18th century, who started a company of court comedians and acrobats. He can be said to represent the link between the juggler of the fairs and the theatrical manager in the German theatre; his company received the patent of Royal Prussian Court Comedians.

École du bon sens. A school of dramatic writing which came into existence in France, 1843, as a reaction against the sensationalism of the romantic school as expounded by Dumas *père,* de Vigny and Victor Hugo.

Edwards, Gus (1881-). American producer. Famous vaudeville headliner and manager, song writer, publisher, film and radio performer, best known for his discoveries of new talent. With his brother, Leo, he toured with John L. Sullivan, singing between knockouts. Began his professional career with the Newsboy Quintet at the old Gaiety Theatre in Brooklyn, New York. Wrote the song hit *School Days,* and opened his own music publishing business. Other hits were *By the Light of the Silvery Moon* and *In My Merry Oldsmobile.* His revue *School Days* opened in 1916, and ran season after season. The title song after decades, is still a sentimental classic. He produced the vaudeville units *Kid Kabaret, The Blonde Typewriters* and the *Band Box Revue,* and when cabarets were novelties in America opened three in New York. He has appeared in several films and radio programs since 1929, and in 1936 tried to revive two-a-day vaudeville in New York with *Broadway Sho-Window.* Among the successful performers he discovered are Joe Cook, Jr., Groucho Marx, Lila Lee, Mae Murray, Earl Carroll, George Price, Eddie Cantor, Milton

Berle, Eddie Buzzell, George Jessell, Mervyn Le Roy, Herman Timberg, the Duncan Sisters and Helen Menken. He was the subject of the 1939 film, *The Star Maker*.

Educational Commission. A university theatre existing in pre-Nationalist Spain. It produced plays performed by its own student actors and developed an extensive travelling theatre.

Edward II. Christopher Marlowe (English). Historical drama. 5 acts. 1593.
Deals with Edward II's recall of his favorite, Gaveston; the revolt of the barons and Gaveston's capture and execution; the period in which Spenser became the king's favorite; Queen Isabella's estrangement from the king and her revolt; the capture of Edward, his abdication and his murder. Generally regarded as the finest historical drama before Shakespeare.

Edward III. An English chronicle history play. Printed 1596.
Attributed to Shakespeare by Edward Capell in 1760. Shakespeare's authorship is now generally denied, although a number of critics argue that the scenes describing Edward's love for the Countess of Salisbury and her triumph over this passion are authentic Shakespeare. The remainder of the play deals with Edward's wars in France.

Egmont. Goethe (German). 5 acts. 1787.
Emperor Charles V abolished the constitutional rights of some of the Netherland provinces, and introduced the Inquisition in order to stamp out Protestantism. Prominent among his officers was the Fleming, Lamoral, Count Egmont, upon whom he lavished honors and opportunities of service. By his victories over the French at St. Quentin, 1557, and Gravelins, 1558, Egmont became the idol of his countrymen. The people hoped that Egmont would be appointed Regent, but Philip II who had succeeded Charles V appointed his half-sister Margaret. Persecution of the Protestants followed and Egmont though a Catholic was martyred.

Einschrier, der. The name given one of the players in early German *Shrovetide* drama who announced the arrival of his comrades at the beginning of the play.

Ekhof, Konrad (1720-1778). German dramatist. Called "The true father of German drama"; started acting with the Schoneman Company and began a new, more realistic and natural school of German acting devoid of strutting and bombast; first theorist of the German stage; founder of the Academy of Actors in 1753.
See also *Academy of Actors*.

Ekkuklema. A stage device used in the ancient Hellenistic and Graeco-Roman theatres: a semi-circular, revolving platform on which the throne is set, the purpose of which was to reveal interior action.
See also *Machines*.

Electra. Euripides (Greek). Tragedy. c. 414 B.C.

Agamemnon on his return from Troy is murdered by his wife, Clytemnestra. After many years of inward bitterness Electra their daughter drives her brother Orestes to murder their mother. After the murder, the brother and sister run from the house and are stricken with remorse. The play ends with the appearance of Castor and Polydeuces, two gods who denounce the evil deed of the brother and sister. Differs from the Electra of Sophocles in that the characters are treated psychologically rather than "heroically."

Electra. Sophocles (Greek). Tragedy. c. 450 B.C.

When Agamemnon is murdered by his wife, Clytemnestra, their daughter, Electra, sends her young brother, Orestes, away for safekeeping. Electra remains with her mother for many years enduring all kinds of insult and humiliation until Orestes reaches manhood and makes a secret return. Then with the help of Electra, Orestes murders Aegisthus and Clytemnestra. Electra then marries Pylades.

Electrician. The technician who is responsible for the actual switching on and off of lights, dimming, focusing of spotlights, wiring of instruments, placing of equipment, etc. The artistic aspects of lighting are plotted by the designer, director and stage manager. The last is responsible for the accuracy of the electrician's light area in a performance. The electrician should work with a light-plot which should provide him with cues, detailed and precise instructions on each change in the lighting during the performance.

See *Lighting, Light Plot.*

Eliot, T. S. (1888-   ). American poet and dramatist. Born in St. Louis, Missouri, and educated at Harvard, the Sorbonne and Oxford. He has lived for the past 25 years in London, where he was editor of the monthly *The Criterion.* His plays include *The Rock, Murder in the Cathedral* and *The Family Reunion,* all in verse. His critical works include *An Essay on Poetic Drama* and *Essays in Criticism.* As a critic he is an opponent of romanticism and advocates a return to the austere classicism of the 18th century poets.

Elitch's Gardens, Denver, Colorado. Opened in 1890 by John Elitch as a pleasure resort with zoo and vaudeville. A stock company was organized by his widow, opening May 30, 1897, with *Helene* by Martha Morton; George R. Edeson, director. Since that time players have included George Arliss, Sarah Bernhardt, Cecil de Mille, Minnie Maddern Fiske, Lewis Stone, David Warfield, Douglas Fairbanks, Helen Menken and Frederic March. Many important players received their first professional training at the Gardens. John Mulvihill succeeded to management in 1916; Arnold B. Gurtler in 1930. The present managers are George Somnes and Helen Bonfils (Mrs. Somnes).

Elizabethan Stage Society, The. An organization founded by William Poel in London in 1875 for the purpose of giving public readings of Shakespeare's plays.

Elizabeth the Queen. Maxwell Anderson (American). Drama. 3 acts. 1930.

This historical drama, written in alternate scenes of blank verse and poetic prose, is the author's version of the love story of Elizabeth of England and the Earl of Essex, those lovers "whom a kingdom kept apart." Presented by the Theatre Guild with Lynn Fontanne and Alfred Lunt in the leading roles, it had a long and prosperous run.

Elizabeth has almost reached middle-age; she is imperious, moody, and in love with Essex with the ardor of a sixteen-year-old. There are those at the court who are displeased with the favor she has been showing the Earl, a handsome blade of thirty— Lord Cecil, for instance, and Sir Walter Raleigh, who plot to oust Essex by making him seem a rebel. And whenever the Queen and Earl meet there is a clash, in spite of their love for each other. For Essex is ambitious and a natural soldier, while Elizabeth would have peace abroad. Even if there were war, she tells him, she would hesitate to let him go, convinced at heart that he is more poet than soldier. The Council meets; the crafty Cecil proposes an expedition to Ireland under Raleigh as Lord Protector. Essex, infuriated, cries out against this and insists on being in command himself. It is what Cecil and Raleigh have been playing for. Once he is abroad, they intercept his letters to the Queen and hers to Essex. It is therefore not hard to convince Elizabeth of her favorite's treachery. Essex returns to England with his army; the people rise up and acclaim their hero; according to Cecil, he intends to usurp the throne. This the Earl denies when he obtains an audience with the Queen, and explains about the letters. She yields to the ecstasy of seeing him once more; there is talk of marriage. Again differences separate them. Essex would be King, not merely consort, but Elizabeth would not give up an iota of her power. Does he love and trust her enough to disband his army if she gives in to him in this? Yes. He dismisses the soldiers as proof. The shrewd Queen's trick has worked; he has lost his supporters; she has him arrested. He is condemned to death. The day set for his execution arrives without his having sent word to her. And since she cannot bear to see him die, loving him almost as much as she loves her realm, she summons him to give him a chance to beg forgiveness and mercy. But this he will not do. Once free again, still a popular idol, Essex realizes that inevitably he would play once more for power, almost in spite of himself, for he now knows the Queen's peaceful policy is more salutary than his warlike one. Even as she entreats him to ask her pardon, he goes off to die.

Elliott, Maxine (1871-   ). American actress. Born in Rockland, Maine. Among her early vehicles on the New York stage were *The Middleman, A Fool's Paradise, The Prodigal Daughter,* etc. In 1895 she was engaged by Augustin Daly and appeared in his theatres in New York and London in many plays. From there she went to Miner's Fifth Avenue Theatre, then toured Australia. In 1903 she went under the management of Charles B. Dillingham to become a star, in *Her Own Way, The Chaperon* and a number of other plays. In 1908 she opened the Maxine Elliott Theatre; appeared there in *The Inferior Sex, Lord and Lady Algy,* etc. She also appeared in the moving pictures, 1916-17, in *The Eternal Magdalen* and *Fighting Odds.* In the early 1920's she retired, and has been living since then in England and France.

Elocution. Recitation with dramatic emphasis. Public speaking of memorized verse or prose. Although outworn and ridiculous as parlor entertainment, it has still a value on the stage that might be indicated by the words "finding shades of emphasis or emotion."

Emancipated Woman, The. Maurice Donnay (French). Drama. 5 acts. 1898.
A philosopher proclaims his right to cease loving when he will and advises perfect frankness, but he is daunted to find that the widow he still adores has stopped loving him because she prefers an artist. This artist has opposed the philosopher's theory of frankness. He regards it as futile and dangerous to tell women everything. The philosopher denounces feminism. What need have women for freedom, since already they are masters? Why should they lose their childlike charm by coping with men as creatures of thought and will?

Embates. See *Kothornos*.

Emerson, John (1874-   ). American actor, dramatist. Born May 29, 1874, he went on the stage in 1904 and began an association with Mrs. Fiske's repertory company in the same year. He was later stage-director for the Shuberts, 1908-11, and for Charles Frohman, 1911-15.
His writings, in collaboration with his wife, Anita Loos, include *Gentlemen Prefer Blondes,* 1926, and *The Social Register,* 1931.

Emperor Jones, The. Eugene O'Neill (American). Tragedy. 1 act. 1920.
Brutus Jones, a former pullman porter, rules a small island in the West Indies. He claims supernatural power, exploits his subjects, and accumulates a fortune through taxes and graft. Finally the natives rebel and Jones escapes to the jungle at night, where he is tortured by fear and finally captured by his rebellious subjects.

Empire Theatre. Opened January 25, 1893, with *The Girl I Left Behind Me.* This theatre, one of the oldest still in use on Broadway, was the home of Charles Frohman's stock company, which John Drew headed. Maude Adams was the leading woman and Ethel Barrymore, the ingenue. Primarily a theatre of comedy and elegance. The Empire has always had the "carriage trade." In its lobby hang a series of fine theatrical portraits.
In the outer lobby are: portrait enlargements of Gertrude Lawrence, Katharine Cornell, Leslie Howard, Helen Hayes, and a full-length oil photograph of Katharine Cornell, by Florence Vandamm; portraits of Otis Skinner by Abbe; Ethel Barrymore by Charlotte W. Fairchild; Maude Adams by Otto Sarony Co.; and a full-length oil of Margaret Anglin.
In the inner lobby are seven oil portraits: Viola Allen by Hi Hintermeister; Ina Claire and Leslie Howard by Nikol Schattenstein; Billie Burke and Ethel Barrymore by S. de Jvanowski; Judith Anderson by M. V. Rusko; and Otis Skinner by Victor D. Hecht.

Enchaînement. A ballet term meaning step-sequence.

Encina, Juan del (1469-1529?). Spanish dramatist. He is called "the father of the Spanish drama" and is the first outstanding personage in its history. The early part of his life was devoted to dramatic production. These early plays contain serious parts, based on the Christmas, Good Friday and Easter plays. After some time spent in Rome, attached to the chapel of Pope Leo X, he produced several mythological and allegorical plays. One of his productions was presented at the court of Leo X. His lasting contributions to the evolution of the Spanish stage are (1) the "bobo" or simpleton, pictured in the rustic shepherd who made his audience laugh by his efforts to use words that belonged to more cultured classes; (2) his secularization of the drama, by taking it from the market-place to private audiences, and making it popular in these groups.

His works usually have little plot. Encina's plays, usually called *églogas* (literally, ecologies), were written for courtly audiences rather than for the masses. At the age of fifty he abandoned his dramatic career, received final ordination and devoted the rest of his life to the priesthood.

Among Encina's best-known plays are: *Egloga de Placida y Vitoriano Egloga de tres pastores,* and *Egloga de Cristino y Febea.* One of his plays was presented before a brilliant audience at the court of Pope Leo X.

End of Summer. S. N. Behrman (American). Play. 3 acts. 1936.

Leonie, a wealthy and impressionable divorcée becomes interested in a fortune hunting doctor who is in love with her daughter, Paula. He is tricked by Paula into confessing his love for her before Leonie, who puts him out of the house. Paula, in love with a penniless, social-conscious writer, leaves home to marry him.

End man. The performer seated at either side of the stage in the course of a minstrel show, who has most of the jokes. Generally addressed as Mr. Bones.

Ending, emphatic. The closing of a play on an effective or "strong" line or action; now considered old-fashioned and unrealistic.

See also *Curtain, emphatic.*

Ending, unemphatic. An unspectacular termination to a play, opposed to the final "punch" of the Scribe-Sardou school, but no less pointed because of its slyly quiet disguise. Barrett Clark, in his *Study of the Modern Drama,* says: "The unemphatic ending contains a sting, a satirical touch that sums up the act, or, in some instances, illustrates the theme of the entire play." William Archer, in his *Play-making,* calls it "a deliberate anti-climax, an idyllic, or elegiac, or philosophic last act, following upon a penultimate act of very much higher tension." An excellent example is to be found in the final curtain of *The Cherry Orchard.*

See also *Unemphatic curtain.*

Endymion, or The Man in The Moon. John Lyly (English). Comedy. 5 acts, Prologue, Epilogue. Printed in 1591.

Tellus, jealous of Endymion, who loves Cynthia, casts a spell which puts Endymion into a supposedly everlasting sleep, and changes him to an old man. Cynthia, however, breaks the spell with a kiss, and restores his lost youth. One of the most important plays in English literature because of the subsequent influence that Lyly had on style.

Enemies. Mikhail Artzybashev (Russian). Drama. 3 acts. 1913.
Elaborate analysis of the difficulties that attend marriage.
An elderly professor resents his wife's devotion to housekeeping and her meddling with his studies. When she dies, he finds himself lonely and conscience-stricken. The unhappy marriages of his daughter and his son, added to his own, make up the play. The son, a composer deficient in vitality, is wed to a woman who requires it and for that reason takes an officer of the guards, though she recognizes him to be a fool.

Enemy of the People, An. Henrik Ibsen (Norwegian). Drama. 5 acts. 1882.
A stinging indictment of corrupt society. Dr. Stockman, whose idea it was to construct Baths, using the beneficent water of his native town, discovers that the water, badly pollued by refuse from the tanneries, is spreading typhoid fever. In his fight to remedy the situation, which will cost the taxpayers many thousands of pounds, the mayor, the newspaper publishers, together with the majority of the townspeople turn against him and denounce him as an enemy of the people.

Enfants Sans-Souci, Les. A theatrical company in medieval France, composed of men from solid bourgeois families.

English Traveller, The. Thomas Heywood (English). Drama. 1623.
A young traveller, returning home after a long journey, finds his sweetheart married to an elderly man. Out of loyalty to her husband, he refrains from making love to her, and they agree to marry after the old man's death. He discovers later that she is the mistress of one of his best friends. When he denounces her as an adulteress, she dies in despair.

Enter above. A stage direction used by actors, directors and playwrights of the Elizabethan theatre to apply to that part of the gallery extending over the stage and used either by spectators or performers.

Entr'acte. French for intermission, a term taken over to a large extent into English terminology.
See also *Intermission.*

Entrance. Appearance onstage.

Entrechat. A ballet term meaning a leap in the air during which the feet change position in a scissor-like movement from four to eight times, and, as a feat, ten times.

Entremés. A term applied for many decades to short plays used to entertain the audience between the acts of the principal play.

Epeisodia. Episodes, histrionic action in ancient Greek drama, especially Old Comedy, as expounded by Aeschylus.

Ephesus, Theatre of. An ancient Greek auditorium built on Hellenistic lines with an imposing stage-building, or *skene*.

Epicharmus (540?-450 B.C.). Greek dramatist. Born in Cos, he early went to Megara, in Sicily, where he lived until its destruction in 483. He then moved to Syracuse where he lived until he died.

He was the chief representative of the Dorian or Sicilian comedy, and his thirty-five plays written in the Doric dialect of which only scanty fragments remain, dealt chiefly with mythological subjects. They were distinguished by rough humor, some satire, and by rapidity of action.

Epicoene; or, The Silent Woman. Ben Jonson (English). Comedy. 5 acts. 1609.

Morose, a self-centered bachelor with an aversion to noise, decides to disinherit his nephew, Sir Dauphine, and to marry a Silent Woman, if he can find one. He chooses Epicoene. Immediately after she is married, however, she recovers the use of her tongue. Morose finds this noise, increased by that of the wedding party, intolerable. He accepts Sir Dauphine's offer to rid him of her for five hundred pounds a year. Whereupon Sir Dauphine pulls off Epicoene's disguise and reveals that she is a boy he has trained for the part.

Epidaurus, Theatre of. A famous auditorium in ancient Greece built at the end of the 4th century B.C. Here the traditional semi-circle was prolonged on lines curving into the beginnings of a new circle with a different radius.

Epilogue. A speech written for one or more actors to be spoken at the end of the play, occasionally an apology or explanation of the author's intentions.

Episkenion. Two-story building (or, upper story of such a building) at the back of the Greek stage, and part of the permanent setting before the three entrance doors of which the action took place. Stage machinery was cached in the second-story part.

Erckmann, Émile (1822-1899). French author and dramatist. Born at Phalsburg, Lorraine, he began in 1848 to collaborate with Alexandre Chatrian in the writing of novels. Under the signature of Erckmann-Chatrian a large number of novels and plays was produced over a period of some forty-two years. A severe difference of opinion over money dissolved the partnership in 1890.

Among the most notable of their plays are: *Le Juif Polonais* (The Polish Jew), 1869, famous to all English playgoers as *The Bells* (adapted by Leopold Lewis in 1874) ; and *L'Ami Fritz,* 1876.

See also *Chatrian, Alexandre.*

Eretria, Theatre of. Dates from the 4th century B.C. On two occasions the building was altered, first about 300 B.C., and, second, during the 1st century B.C. These changes were made in the *skene,* the erection of additional *columns,* etc.

Erlanger, Abraham L. (1860-1930). American producer. Born in Buffalo, N. Y., he became the most powerful manager of the American stage. His firm (Marc Klaw and himself) controlled the principal theatres in the U. S. during the first decades of the 20th century. In addition to producing on his own, he formed a managerial triumvirate with Dillingham and Ziegfeld, and produced hundreds of plays including *The Wandering Jew, The Perfect Fool, Honeymoon Lane* and several Ziegfeld Follies.
See *Klaw and Erlanger Syndicate, Theatrical syndicate.*

Ernst, Paul Carl Friedrich (1866-1933). German author. Born at Elbingerode, Harz, he obtained a post in 1905 at the Dusseldorf Theatre, for which he wrote several historical tragedies. At first a professed socialist, as described in his books on Marxism, 1918, and German idealism, 1920, he turned gradually to extreme conservatism. Influenced by ancient models, he stressed classic restraint as being essential in drama.
His plays include: *Demetrios,* 1905; *Canossa,* 1908; *Brunhild,* 1909; *Ninon de Lenclos,* 1911; *The Soul of Prussia,* 1915; *Manfred and Beatrice,* 1918.

Ervine, St. John Greer (1883-   ). Irish dramatist, critic. Born at Belfast, he became known as a playwright of distinction, a novelist and a forceful writer on the theatre and other subjects. His early plays were produced at the Abbey Theatre, Dublin, but he rapidly interested a wider public. He also wrote studies of Sir Edward Carson, Parnell and General Booth (*God's Soldier*), and dramatic essays such as *The Organized Theatre* and *The Theatre in My Time.* He was dramatic critic of *The Morning Post* and now of *The Observer.* An outspoken partisan of those causes to which he attached himself, he was always ready to take part in controversy both in the press and on the platform. During the season of 1928-29, he was guest critic on the old New York *World.*
His plays include, among others: *Jane Clegg,* 1913; *John Ferguson,* 1915; *The Wonderful Visit* (with H. G. Wells), 1921; *The Lady of Belmont,* 1927; *The First Mrs. Fraser,* 1928; *Robert's Wife.*

Escape. John Galsworthy (English). Drama. Prologue and 9 episodes. 1926.
Captain Denant is conversing with a young woman in Hyde Park when a policeman arrests her as a prostitute. He gets into an argument with the policeman who falls down, strikes his head against an iron rail and dies. Denant is sentenced to five years' imprisonment for manslaughter.
He makes his escape from prison and in the various episodes of the play he meets many people, some of whom befriend him and others want to turn him in. He finally reaches a church and when there is a knocking at the door, the parson hides him. Denant gives himself up to avoid incriminating the parson and is sent back to prison.

Escapist. Term used to describe any form of literature or art not concerned with social issues, especially when emphasizing romantic or mystical traits, or dealing with historical eras that have few, if any problems, or ideas in common with the present, or frank amusement which is intended to provide an escape from reality.

Eslava Theatre. See *Teatro Eslava.*

Esmond, Henry Vernon (Henry Vernon Jack) (1869-1922). English dramatist. He was born at Hampton Court, and went on the stage in 1885. His numerous plays, some of which enjoyed considerable popularity, include: *Bogey,* 1895; *One Summer's Day,* 1897; *The Wilderness,* 1901; *Under the Greenwood Tree,* 1907; *Eliza Comes to Stay,* 1913; *The Dangerous Age,* 1914.

Essex Rebellion, The. In disgrace after the failure of his Irish expedition, Robert Devereux, Earl of Essex and favorite of Queen Elizabeth, sought, with the help of Shakespeare's patron, the Earl of Southampton, and others, to overthrow Elizabeth's government. Shakespeare's company revived *King Richard II* at a performance at the Globe Theatre on February 7, 1601, the eve of the rebellion, to prepare the public for the enforced abdication. The rebellion failed, however, and Essex was executed. Southampton was imprisoned but eventually released, and Shakespeare and his company, apparently unaware of the part they had played in the plot, escaped without punishment.

Estal. A scene-building, or mansion, of the medieval stage.
See also *Mansions.*

Estate Theatre, Prague. The *Stavoské divadlo* was the first national theatre in Prague, opened in 1783. Known also as the *Národni divadlo.*

Ethan Frome, play adapted by Owen and Donald Davis from novel of same name by Edith Wharton. 1936.
This is a tragedy of a New England farm. Because of her imaginary ailments, Ethan Frome's wife, Zenia, makes their life a lonely and a bitter one. A young girl cousin of hers comes to live with them and brings life and cheer to Ethan's existence. Zenia goes away to see a doctor and Ethan and the girl, Mattie, are very happy together. On Zenia's return she announces Mattie must leave. Helpless to oppose Zenia and heartbroken at their forced separation Ethan and Mattie declare their love for each other. When he takes her to the station they decide to take one more coast down a long hill with a great elm at the foot of it. On the way down, they decide to run into the elm and die together. But the fates are against them, and they survive, she with a broken back, and he, embittered, to be tied down to Zenia and the desolate farm.

Etherege, Sir George (1634?-1691). English dramatist. Little is known of his early life except that he was a law student who gave his time mainly to being a gentleman of fashion. In 1685 he was knighted and made ambassador to Ratisbon, the

Upper Palatinate. He left that city after three years, and passed most of his later life in Paris.

He may be described as the originator of the comedy of social life, which reached such perfection in the hands of Congreve. His knowledge of the gay life of his time was abundant, and his portraiture of its gallants, ladies, and their surroundings was done with great realism.

His plays include: *The Comical Revenge; or, Love in a Tub,* 1664; *She Would if She Could,* 1667; *The Man of Mode,* 1676.

Eumenides (*The Benign Ones*). **Aeschylus** (Greek). Tragedy. c. 458 B.C. The third in the Orestes trilogy.

Orestes, pursued by the Furies, throws himself on Apollo's mercy, since it was at the god's command that he murdered his mother. Apollo commands him to observe the purification rites and to appear at Athens. Athena, goddess of wisdom and justice, summons a jury of Athenian citizens to hear his case, with the Furies as complainants and Apollo stating Orestes' defense. Athena casts the deciding vote in favor of Orestes, and the angry Furies threaten to devastate the land with plagues. Athena, to placate them, promises that if they will settle down peacefully in Athens, the citizens will build them a shrine and worship them as kindly divinities. The Furies change character and are thereafter worshipped as "The Benign Ones."

Eupolis (?-410 B.C.). Athenian dramatist. A contemporary and chief rival of Aristophanes and Cratinus. Among his comedies of which twelve fragments remain, were: *Kolakes* (the *Flatterers*), ridiculing wealthy patrons of learning; *Marikas,* an attack on the demagogy; *Demoi,* a criticism of democracy; and *Baptae,* an exposure of the licentious practices of Alcibiades.

Euripides (486-407 B.C.). Greek poet, dramatist. He is one of the three masters of Greek tragedy, of whom Sophocles and Aeschylus are the other two.

Born on the day of the great naval victory of Salamis, 486 B.C., according to tradition, the date of his birth given on the Parian marble differs only by two years. His father was a merchant and his mother of very high family. His birthplace was Phyla in central Attica. When young, he was an athlete who won prizes at Athens and Eleusis, and a painter, some of his work having been found by later antiquarians at Megara.

His earliest tragedy was a play on the *Daughters of Pelias,* produced in 455. He was credited with over ninety plays in all, of which eighteen survive. It is significant of the mixed reception which his work received at the hands of his contemporaries that he gained the first prize only five times. His vogue increased, however, after his death and he has been the favorite dramatist of many of the world's great poets, notably Virgil, Horace and Milton. Commentators of today are as much occupied as were his contemporaries, with the complexity of his characters. A reputed misogynist, he has, however, portrayed women as fine as any to be found in all literature. In dramatic construction his work stands high, and is the most human of the three tragedians, which probably accounts for his comparatively greater popularity.

The brilliant atmosphere of Athens in the 5th century was favorable to his questioning spirit. There was nothing particularly incongruous in the poet taking part, as an hereditary cup-bearer, in the worship of the Delian Apollo and in his own mind cultivating and adopting an intellectual agnosticism. Religion was a ritual, the theatre was part of the ritual, over which the priest of Dionysus presided. Form and subject were more strictly imposed upon the dramatist than on any other practitioner of the arts. Euripides obeyed the convention even more strictly than Sophocles or Aeschylus. His originality lay in the daring nature of his plots, in his forceful delineation of character, and in his courage in allowing those characters to develop along purely natural lines, even though their utterances might shock the orthodox.

The extant plays of Euripides are: *Alcestis; Medea; Hippolytus; Hecuba; Andromache; Ion; The Suppliants; Heracleidae; The Mad Heracles; Iphigenia Among the Tauri; The Trojan Women; Helen; The Phoenician Maidens; Electra; Orestes; Iphigenia at Aulis; Bacchae and Cyclops.* The last is the only extant specimen of a satyric drama.

See also *Drama, Greek, ancient.*

EUROPEAN THEORIES OF THE DRAMA

BY BARRETT H. CLARK

(The essential facts in this paper are based on the latest revised edition [1929] of *European Theories of the Drama*).

It is interesting to imagine what would have happened to the drama of Europe if Aristotle's *Poetics* had never been written, or if it had not been rediscovered during the Renaissance. Thousands of playwrights would doubtless have been spared infinite trouble trying to square their practice with the Greek theory, and probably a still greater number of critics would either have remained silent (which is not likely) or would have had to find other matters to discuss.

We know very little about the effect of the celebrated Greek treatise from the time it was written in the Fourth Century, B.C., until the end of the Middle Ages, because references to it in existing works are extremely rare. The most influential treatise on drama in antiquity was Horace's *Art of Poetry,* which dates from a few years before the Christian Era. This was known, studied, and analyzed from the very earliest days, but when in the late Middle Ages Aristotle's work was again made known and published it was that, rather than Horace's, that became the source of wisdom to the scholarly world on all matters pertaining to dramatic form and subject matter. Nevertheless, the *Art of Poetry* was studied and analyzed and to a certain extent looked upon with respect and even awe by playwrights and critics alike. Edition after edition of the *Poetics* was printed between 1498 and 1600, and then the commentaries and analyses followed, first in Italy, then in France, Germany, and Spain. As we study the musty pages of such editors and commentators as Robortello, Minturno, and the rest, we of today are amazed at the lack of critical independence, the slavish acceptance, as gospel, of remarks made by a professor hundreds of years before. How the actual, or derived, or almost wholly imagined "Rules" of Aristotle ever managed to spread through Europe and be accepted as inspired precepts is hard to explain. Many a playwright (Corneille is a good example) wrote reams of apologies, essays and even whole books explaining how he had observed this Unity or that, or how—in departing a little from what Aristotle said or was said to have said—he had none the less preserved the spirit of the master.

Once in a great while some really original playwright had the courage not only to disregard the sacred rules but to admit it publicly. The Spanish Lope de Vega, for example, boldly declared that when he sat down to write he securely locked up the pedagogue's works, and Molière—in a famous passage—frankly said that the greatest of all rules was to please the audience.

As the drama of Europe developed we find that critical discussion kept pace with it, and though the 18th- and 19th-century Germans and French felt free, for the most part, to write as they pleased, the critics (and some of the playwrights) went right on discussing Aristotle and to a greater or less extent follow his precepts.

To this day the arguments persist. To what extent did Aristotle foreshadow the "Unity of Place?" What is the meaning of *Katharsis?* To what extent is the *Poetics* still valid, either as a practical guide for writers or simply as an exposition of the principles practiced by the ancient Greeks?

But no longer, fortunately, does any playwright feel the necessity of adhering to the Rules. Consequently our modern playwrights are in a position to read the *Poetics* in a detached mood, and on occasion a Eugene O'Neill, a Maxwell Anderson, a Shaw, or a Galsworthy is able to profit by some remark in the famous treatise without feeling any obligation to follow the rules.

Today we look upon Aristotle's treatise as one of the soundest and most suggestive contributions to the subject ever written. No longer driven by an almost religious compulsion to follow the Rules, our writers can, and do, benefit sometimes from the Greek's wisdom.

Of course we do not know whether he wrote the *Poetics* as a guide to playwrights, or simply as a historical summing-up of what the best writers of the Golden Age had done, but the fact remains that this celebrated fragment, while calling forth an immense amount of written and spoken nonsense, has probably helped rather than hindered the playwright in his long pilgrimage down through the ages.

Eva (Little Eva). Character in Harriet Beecher Stowe's *Uncle Tom's Cabin;* the little mistress and child friend of Uncle Tom, whose death forms one of the famous scenes in the novel and the play versions of the same. A favorite role for the road repertories of actresses whose work is satirized in Kenyon Nicholson's play *Eva, the Fifth.*

Evans, Maurice (1901-   ). English actor-manager. Formerly engaged in music-publishing. His first professional stage appearance was at the Festival Theatre, Cambridge, 1926, in *The Orestia* of Aeschylus. He played first in London in 1927, and appeared in twenty-four plays of various kinds until 1934, when he joined the Old Vic-Sadler's Wells company, playing six Shakesperean roles and two of Bernard Shaw's. Came to America in 1935, and in October toured with Katharine Cornell as Romeo to her Juliet. His first New York appearance was with her in the same role at the Martin Beck Theatre, December 23, 1935. He produced and played the title role in Shakespeare's *Richard II,* which ran 171 consecutive performances in New York in 1937. Of this role John Mason Brown wrote: "As Richard he may lose his kingly crown, but in doing so he gains another as an actor which is no less full of glory." Evans was awarded the Drama League medal for 1937; and has played the Dauphin in *St. Joan* by Bernard Shaw, and Napoleon in *St. Helena.* He played the first unabridged Hamlet to be seen in New York, October, 1938.

Evening at the Front, An. Henry Kistemaeckers (Belgian). Drama. 3 acts. Printed 1918.

Tells the story of a German long naturalized in France, who leaves at the outbreak of the World War, but returns as a spy. When he is apprehended, his wife begs his life of an officer whom she has saved from death. Although the officer yields, the spy is duly punished otherwise.

Everyman. Author unknown (Dutch origin). First printed about 1529.

When Everyman is summoned by Death to appear before God for judgment, he begs help of his friends—Strength, Beauty, Knowledge, Good Deeds, Fellowship. Only Good Deeds, however, will accompany him to the judgment seat.

One of the oldest in the English language, this morality play is being constantly revived and produced.

Every Man in His Humor. Ben Jonson (English). Comedy. 5 acts. 1598.

This was Jonson's first play, the others preceding it having been written in collaboration. Drawing upon Roman comedy of manners and upon realistic observation Jonson created in this play and the one following *Every Man Out of his Humor* a new type of comedy. The object of his play is social criticism; the method is caricature, each man's foible being brought to the foreground as the essence of his character. Jonson's genius, however, went beyond mere inventory of idiosyncrasies William Shakespeare performed in this play.

Through the complications of the plot Kitely, a jealous man, and his wife are brought face to face at a house which each thinks the other is frequenting for an immoral purpose. The kindly Justice Clement clears up the misunderstandings.

Although the plot is a trivial one this play contains some of the most memorable characters in all literature such as the servant Brainworm, the cowardly braggart Bobadill, Cob the water carrier and many others. In the prologue, Jonson expounds his dramatic theories.

Evirati, The. Male prima donnas of the 17th century; musical eunuchs, taken from church choirs and trained for opera and concert. Combined male artistry with the sweetness of the female voice. Among the most "sublime eunuchs" were Gizziello, Caffarelli, Senesino, Guadagni (chosen by Handel to sing in the *Messiah*), Bernacchim Carestubu and Tenducci.

"Farinelli," says C. J. Bulliet in *Venus Castina,* "is still reckoned, by all odds, the finest singer who ever lived."

Evreinov, Nicolas. See *Drama, Russian, 19th century to the Revolution; Theatre, Russian, 19th century to the Revolution.*

Excursion. Victor Wolfson (American). Comedy, 3 acts. 1937.

After thirty years on the route from Battery to Coney Island, Captain Obadiah Rich's excursion steamship Happiness is about to be taken out of service and made into a garbage scow. The compassionate captain rebels at the idea and on the final cruise heads his antique tub straight for a magic island south of Trinidad, where his oddly assorted passengers can begin existence anew under luxuriant tropical surroundings. The Coast Guard is called out and the ship is forced to turn back and the romanticists return to their basement rooms and dull jobs.

Exiles, The. James Joyce. Drama. 3 acts. 1915.

This frank play by the author of *Ulysses* was not given on the stage until ten years after it was written. When it was produced at the Neighborhood Playhouse in New York in 1925, critical opinion about it was divided. The hero was described as a psychopathic subject or a noble and honest superman, according to the reviewer.

Richard Rowan, a writer, has run away from Ireland nine years before with Bertha. As the play opens they have returned with their son Archie, still without a marriage certificate. Rowan has the mad idea, under the delusion that he is giving Bertha her freedom, to thrust on her the attentions of Robert Hand, journalist, whose intentions are strictly dishonorable and entirely unwelcome to the lady. But she obediently accepts Robert's caresses, then gives all the details to the curious Dick. She even makes a rendezvous at night at Hand's house with her lover's consent. After she has filled her engagement as directed, Hand tries to assure Dick that Bertha is his alone still, and leaves town. Bertha pleads with Dick to trust her, but he prefers uncertainty. For he is an "exile from happiness."

Exit without lines. An undistinguished departure from the scene, marked by no speech.

Exodos. Part of ancient Greek drama, especially of Old Comedy as expounded by Aeschylus; final song by *chorus,* often addressed to audience directly, pointing out salient features of play.

Exostra. A stage device used in the ancient Hellenistic and Graeco-Roman theatres: a low platform on wheels or rollers, operated in connection with the *ekkuklema.* See also *Machines.*

Expressionism. A school of thought that developed in Germany in the late 19th century. It is really an extension of impressionism and is opposed to realism and naturalism. The expressionists are concerned with producing an inner emotional, sensual, or intellectual reaction. It is this inner emotion that they try to express and they maintain that it does not necessarily bear a relation to the outer aspect of life. Thus, shocking news may be accompanied by an electric flash or a sudden loud clap of thunder; a haunted house may be expressed by an exaggerated distorted twisted structure that conveys the idea of terror and fear.

Extempore acting. Impromptu performing, without preparation and with general "ad libbing."

Exteriors. Flats painted to represent the façades of buildings, wood-wings, back drop with a scene depicting country, street, castle, etc.

Extra. Person hired to supplement the cast of a company in scenes requiring additional characters. An extra has no individual lines to speak, but may take part in crowd noises if the action calls for it.
See also *Walk-on*.

Extravaganza. A lavish and fantastic composition; a musical burlesque marked by floridness and exaggeration.

Eye shadow. A small compressed form of grease color used to shade eyelids.

Eyvind of the Hills. Johann Sigurjonsson (Scandinavian). Tragedy. 4 acts. 1930.
Eyvind, an outlaw, marries the beautiful Halia and they escape to live in the hills. They are happy for a time, but finally the long Icelandic winter closes in and they become lonely and desperate. Halia goes mad and walks out into the storm and Eyvind follows her.

Fabula Atellana. A rustic type of Roman drama of small-town and village life, of a coarse humorous tone. It flourished in Campania, and took its name from the small town of Atella (now Aversa). It had for stock characters an old man, a soldier, a buffoon, and a learned man. It followed the *fabula palliata* (adaptations of Menander, written by Terence and Plautus) ; the *fabula togata* drama with Italian instead of Greek mannerisms, costumed in togas, and *fabula tabernaria* scenes of business life, or life of artisans, with the characters in the costumes of the provinces.

Fabula palliata. Most famous of all types of Roman comedy; patronized by Terence and Plautus; based on the New Comedy of Greece. Stock-characters: (1) testy old men; (2) *miles gloriosus,* or boasting soldier; (3) comic slaves; (4) pedants.

Fabula riciniata. See *Mimus.*

Fabula tabernaria. A type of Roman drama preceding the *fabula Atellana* and following the *fabula togata.* It was a presentation of the manners of people dwelling in the city.

Fabula togata. A type of Roman drama preceding the *fabula tabernaria* and following the *fabula palliata*. It was a presentation of manners.

Fagan, James Bernard (1873-1933). British dramatist. Became an actor in the companies of Frank Benson and Herbert Tree. He began to write plays in 1899, but returned to acting in 1913. He also produced many plays in London, the provinces, and in New York.

His plays include: *The Rebel,* 1899; *The Prayer of the Sword,* 1904; *Under Which King,* 1905; *The Earth,* 1909; *A Merry Devil,* 1909; *And So to Bed,* 1926; *The Greater Love,* 1927; *The Improper Duchess,* 1932.

Failures, The (*Les Ratés*). Henry René Lenormand (French). Drama. 3 acts. 1920.

A man and his wife succumb to the power of evil through the pressure of adversity, each compromising with worthy ambitions and ideals in order to gain a momentary advantage, and each believing that such violation of the sanctities may be indulged in with impunity. They sink lower and lower, however, until the man in drunken madness slays the woman and then himself.

Faire Em. A romantic comedy published before 1593. It has been attributed to Shakespeare on the flimsiest of evidence and the majority of critics deny his authorship. There are two plots; one concerns William the Conqueror's love for one lady, passing interest in a second, and return to the first. The other plot concerns Faire Em's relations with three rival lovers.

Fair Quarrel, A. Thomas Middleton and William Rowley English. 1617.

A fellow officer insults Captain Agar in a manner which reflects on his mother's virtue. Agar, not wishing to fight a duel unless the cause is just, tells his mother of the accusation. At first she denies it, but then admits it to be true in order to prevent the duel. Agar refuses to fight and is called a coward. Now, feeling he has a just cause he fights and wins the duel. They become reconciled and the play ends happily.

Faithful Shepherd, The (Il Pastor Fido). G. B. Guarini (Italian). Comedy. 5 acts. Translated by Richard Fanshawe. 1648.

An elaborate and laborious literary effort to meet the critical demand for a pastoral tragi-comedy following the division of Vitruvius of the classical stage into three kinds of scenes for "tragedy, comedy and satyr," the last being "decorated with trees, caverns, mountains and other rustic objects delineated in landscape style."

Faithful Shepherdess, The. John Fletcher (English). Drama. 5 acts. Printed before 1610.

Various shepherds and shepherdesses have complicated and involved love affairs which are finally resolved to everyone's satisfaction. Although the plot is a weak one, there is great beauty in many of the poetic passages.

Fake. To improvise speeches in place of forgotten ones; to "ad lib."

Falcone, G. A. (17th-18th century). Italian theatrical architect. Designed and built the *Teatro Falcone* in Genoa.

See also *Teatro Falcone*.

Fall of the City, The. Archibald MacLeish (American). Radio drama. 1 act. Printed 1937.

The voice of the studio director describes the waiting crowd gathered in the central plaza of the city. The voice of a dead woman warns the people that a new master will take over the city. Then a messenger announces the coming of a dangerous and violent conqueror and he warns them to beware. The orator urges the people to keep their freedom, scorn conquerors and let reason and truth be their weapons. Another messenger brings news of the approaching conqueror, the crowd grows frantic and the priests urge them to turn to their gods. A general urges them to fight, but the people destroy their arms, shouting freedom is for fools, the city is doomed and men must have a master. The conqueror enters the city dressed in full armor. The people, cowering on the ground before him, faces covered, don't see that the armor is really empty and that they have really subjected themselves to a master, and so caused the fall of the city.

This play, in verse, was written exclusively for radio production and it is hailed as the forerunner of a new form of literary expression.

False Saint, A (or The Other Side of a Saint). François de Curel (French). Drama. 3 acts. 1892.

The author's first important play. A woman, many years before, has tried to kill a rival who took her sweetheart from her. Since then she has served her church faithfully as a nun, abandoning the world and its vanity. Upon her emergence from the convent she meets the daughter of the woman she hated and the man she loved. Suddenly her old resentment, which she thought long since overcome, flares up, this time directed against the girl, on whom she is tempted to wreak deferred vengeance. But when she hears the girl, Christine, repeat her dead father's dying message of love, it stirs her like a voice from beyond the tomb, and her nobler instincts prevail. She will encourage Christine to find the happiness she herself has missed, then go back again to the convent to continue making amends for the attempted murder so long ago.

Family Boarding-House, The. Maurice Donnay (French). Satire. 5 acts. 1894.

The dramatis personae are amusing middle-class characters. A landlady is pleased to find that one of her tenants is a man who had once been her lover. She is likewise happy to discover that the man's wife is unfaithful to him. And in the hope of gaining her own selfish ends she breaks the news of his wife's disloyalty to him. He confronts his wife with his information, not too seriously, and she replies not merely by confessing the truth of the accusation, but by announcing that she plans to divorce her husband and marry her lover. All of which her accredited spouse takes in good stead, and plans to seek consolation where it will be willingly given. An apt illustration of

Donnay's theorem that love, while delightful and indispensable, is not irreplaceable; in fact, its very charm lies in its transitory nature and, if one's beloved prove unfaithful, the only thing to do is to seek another object for one's adoration.

Falstaff, Sir John. Character in Shakespeare's *King Henry IV, Parts I and II,* and in *The Merry Wives of Windsor.* His death is described by Mistress Quickly in *King Henry V,* though he does not appear as a character. Based on the life of Sir John Oldcastle.

Familienkatastrophe. Name given to the kind of plays which dealt with a family tragedy; a theme which became popular in German drama with the rise of naturalism during the last half of the 19th century.

Family Portrait. Lenore Coffee and William Joyce Cowen (American). Drama. 3 acts. 1939.

The life of Jesus of Nazareth as seen through the eyes of His family—the inability of His brothers to understand Him, their shame when he is tried and crucified, Mary's worship of her Son. At the end of the play, when Mary is talking of her grandson whom she hopes will be called Jesus, she says, "It's a nice name. I'd like Him not to be forgotten."

Family Reunion, The. T. S. Eliot (English). Drama. 2 acts. 1939.

Gerald Piper, suspected of murdering his wife, returns to his home in England, and for the first time sees the Eumenides, the Greek Furies that are driving him as they drove his father.

He is comforted by a favorite aunt, formerly his father's mistress, who tells him it is impossible to escape the Furies, and that he must seek them out. Only then can he expiate the family curse.

Fantasy. A play unrestricted by literal or realistic conventions of the theatre and usually distinguished by imaginative uses of the supernatural and the mythological. Molnar's *Liliom,* Maeterlinck's *The Blue Bird,* Saroyan's *My Heart's In The Highlands* are fantasy plays.

Far Away Princess, The (*La Princess Lointaine*). Edmond Rostand (French). Drama. 4 acts. 1895.

The story of Rudel's passionate quest for the far-away princess, who is in reality a very human woman, weak and selfish, but who becomes strong through Rudel's idealization. Rudel finds his princess only as he is dying.

Farce. A comedy designed only for entertainment and laughter. There is no serious or sincere attempt to depict character nor is there genuine concern with probabilities or realities. A farce does not intend to be convincing—only amusing. It bears the same relation to comedy that melodrama bears to drama.

According to Dryden "farce is that in poetry which grotesque is in a picture, the persons and actions of a farce are all unnatural and the manners false."

Farce, French. The counterpart of the Italian *commedia dell'arte,* with its characters of *Michau, Dr. Boniface,* etc., corresponding to the Italian *Pantalone* and others.

Farce-comedy. A form of play halfway between farce and comedy and containing elements of both.

Farjeon, Eleanor (1881-   ); **Joseph Jefferson** (1883-   ); **Herbert** (1887-   ). British dramatists.
The three Farjeons are the grand-children of the famous American actor, Joseph Jefferson. Herbert has been dramatic critic for *Vogue, The Sphere, The Graphic* and other publications. His plays include: *Advertising April,* 1922; *Many Happy Returns,* 1928; *The Little Revue,* 1939; and, in collaboration with his sister Eleanor, *Kings and Queens,* 1932; *Two Bouquets,* 1937; *An Elephant in Arcady,* 1938. Joseph Jefferson Farjeon's plays include: *No. 17,* 1925; *After Dark,* 1926; *The Green Dragon,* 1929; *Philomel,* 1932.

Far Off Hills, The. Lennox Robinson (Irish). Comedy. 3 acts. 1928.
Marion Clancy has always longed to become a nun, but responsibility to her blind father and sisters has kept her at home; while her suitor, Harold Mahony is unable to marry again because of his insane wife. At last both find themselves free. Strangely enough Marion has lost interest in the convent, and Harold would prefer to remain single. The problem is settled satisfactorily, however, when Marion finds another husband, and Harold is relieved of his promise to Marion.

Farquhar, George (1678-1707). English dramatist. One of the best known of the Restoration dramatists; a writer of "merry comedies." Born at London-derry in Ireland. Became an actor in Dublin before 1697; but after accidentally stabbing a fellow actor in a stage duel, gave up acting and went to London, where his first play, *Love and a Battle,* was produced at Drury Lane in 1699. In 1700 he served as a lieutenant in Holland, and wrote *The Constant Couple,* in 1701 a sequel, *Sir Harry Wildair.* In 1702 he published *Love and Business,* with a discourse on comedy in reference to the English stage. That year his *The Inconstant* and *The Twin Rivals* appeared. In 1704 in collaboration with Motteaux, he wrote *The Stagecoach.* His *Beaux' Stratagem,* 1707, gave the characters Lady Bountiful, and Boniface, the innkeeper, to the language as types. His were the last authentic Restoration comedies. Farquhar's comic heroes, considered autobiographical in character, were early prototypes of Tom Jones, in Fielding's famous novel.

Farrell, Frank T. (1909-   ). American journalist. Born in New York City. In 1925 he became a reporter on the *Brooklyn Standard Union,* then transferred to the *Brooklyn Times.* Received his B.S. at New York University, and later his L.L.B. from the same institution. In 1933 he became a reporter on the *Chicago Herald-Examiner.* Since 1935 he has been connected with the *New York World-Telegram* for which paper he is now amusement editor.

Fashion; or, Life in New York. Mrs. Anna Cora Mowatt Ritchie (American). Play of manners. 5 acts. 1845.

Mr. and Mrs. Tiffany, though of obscure provincial origin, are haughty New Yorkers who desire to marry their daughter to the Count Jolimaître, who is, without their knowing it, a French imposter. They are rather cruel to the lovely Gertrude, a dependent and a music teacher, and they catch her seemingly guilty with the Count in her bedchamber. Mr. Tiffany is a forger at the mercy of Snobson, his bookkeeper, who proposes silence in exchange for the hand of Miss Tiffany. Gertrude is proved to be the long lost granddaughter of rich and chin-whiskered old Adam Trueman from Cattaraugus, and the Count is discovered to be an ex-barber, "a false jewel on the finger of society." Further, he is disclosed as the betrayer of Mlle. Millinette, the Tiffany's French housemaid.

Fashionable Follies. Joseph Hutton (American). Comedy. 5 acts. 1815.

The scene is laid on the borders of Lake Champlain, in New York. Charles Delaney, while pretending to be in love with Miss Charlotte Positive, is planning to carry off Maria Dorriville, daughter of a gambler and ward of Charlotte's brother, Peregrine. He entices her into the woods under guise of meeting a benefactor who will help her restore her father's fame and fortune, and then declares his love. Maria is saved by the sudden appearance of her brother who has just returned from the wars, and the villain flees. Maria goes off to find her benefactor at the farmer Ploughby's cottage, and her brother meets his loved one, Fanny Ploughby, in the woods only to be torn from her arms by the Bailiff who puts him in prison when he is unable to meet a note Delaney holds against him. In the meantime the old Dorriville returns, realizes the plight of his son and daughter and straightens matters out. Since fleeing from America he has lived in India where he amassed a great fortune. Captain Dorriville is reunited with Fanny, Marion is betrothed to the son of her benefactor, and Charles Delaney is compelled by his conscience to confess all and make amends for his evil deeds.

Fashions for Men. Ferenc Molnar (Hungarian). Comedy. 3 acts. 1915.

Peter's wife misappropriates funds and then runs away with his star salesman, Oscar. Peter takes the blow in a manner which any saint might envy. Then his best saleswoman, Paula, uses his bankruptcy as a mask to cover up her becoming the mistress to his Excellency, the Count. On the farm of Gerelypuszta the impositions on Peter's saintliness multiply. But his spirit of love drives him on. He does everything to save Paula and finally falls in love with her himself. But he rushes away from a field in which he can no longer fight for mere goodness. However, the last act leaves Peter and Paula presiding over the haberdashery which has been made prosperous by Peter's reputation for saintliness.

Fat. A good, telling speech; easy lines to get over; sure-fire stuff; sometimes hokum.

Fata Morgana (Mirage). Ernest Vajda (Hungarian). Comedy. 1924.

The playwright names his heroine Mrs. Fay because of her resemblance to Morgan le Fay or Fata Morgana, pupil of Merlin, who created mirages more potent than reality. Mathilde, a Budapest coquette, arrives in the country to spend the night with relatives and attend the local Anna Ball. She finds the house deserted except for George, eighteen-year-old student. Her telegram was not delivered, and the rest of the family have already gone to the ball. George falls head over heels in love with the older woman. She is flattered and leads him on, even jokingly promising to divorce her husband and marry the boy, and finally going to him after he has retired to his room for the night. The next morning the other members of the household return, accompanied by Mathilde's husband Gabriel, who presents her with a check just received from a client with which she can purchase new clothes and a trip abroad. Excited and pleased, she plans to leave with Gabriel at once. George, still under the spell of her enchantment, protests and announces that Mathilde is engaged to him. She indignantly denies this, and appeals to his chivalry not to make her pay with a lifetime of unhappy poverty for a single night of madness. Gallantly the boy tells Gabriel he has imagined things and has lied to him. Reconciled, husband and wife depart. George, his mirage having vanished, disillusioned, no longer a child, goes back to his text books.

Father, The. August Strindberg (Swedish). Naturalistic drama. 3 acts. 1887.

The play which established Strindberg's reputation in Europe as a powerful dramatist. His bitterness against women is given an outlet in a picture of a woman who is a fiend incarnate. The drama as a whole is a trenchant and forceful portrayal of the duel between the sexes, relying on horror rather than on pity for its effect.

A wife who wishes to get full control of their child insinuates to her husband that he is not the youngster's father. The man, nervous and high-strung, becomes more and more so as she works on him ceaselessly. Then, when his nerves are on edge, she makes use of a letter he has written declaring that he is crazy and threatens to get the doctor to testify to his insanity. Thus she will be able to educate the child in her own way. Cruelly she tells her husband that he is no longer needed as a bread-winner, that he has proven himself the weaker of the two in both will and intelligence, and may as well get out. Really driven to insanity at last by her machinations, he throws a lighted lamp at her and tries to escape. But an old nurse lures him into a straitjacket and, thus imprisoned, he sits powerless in his own home while his wife rules the household. His outcries are futile, and eventually he dies of apoplexy brought on by his impotent rage.

Father Malachy's Miracle. Brian Doherty (Canadian). Comedy. 3 acts. 1937.

Father Malachy becomes involved in miracles when he prophesies that the Garden of Eden Night Club will be moved from Edinburgh to Bass Rock, off the Scottish coast. The miracle occurs on schedule. However, in order to appease the church, and to avoid exploitation, Father Malachy prays that the night club may return to Edinburgh. This miracle also occurs on schedule, much to Father Malachy's relief.

Fat part. A colloquial expression for a substantial role in a production.

Faust. John Wolfgang von Goethe (German). Drama. 2 parts. 1808, 1831.

The prologue takes place in Heaven where Mephistopheles gains permission to try to ruin the soul of Faust. God grants it, confident that though Faust may fall, he will through trial and error attain the clearer vision.

In the first part of the play, Mephistopheles presents himself to a discontented, despairing and disillusioned Faust. They enter a compact wherein Faust promises to forfeit his soul if the devil can give him one moment of perfect contentment. Mephistopheles tries various means of pleasing Faust, ending in the incident of Margaret. Faust seduces this innocent young girl and when attacked by the girl's brother kills him and flees the city. The girl becomes insane, drowns her child and finally dies.

The second part of the play is symbolic and complex. Here (Part 2) Faust meets the world of public affairs and aesthetic beauty as opposed to the world of sensual pleasures (Part 1). Here Helen of Troy, symbolizing ideal beauty, is recalled from Hades to be wooed and won by Faust. They have a child, Euphorion, who represents the spirit of poetry. He soars into the air and disappears as does Helen. Faust now feels ennobled and desirous of serving mankind. He reclaims a piece of submerged land with the help of Mephistopheles, as an abode for contented people. Near the end of this task, old and blind, he realizes the only real satisfaction in the world is in serving others and pronounces himself perfectly contented and falls dead. And although he has lost his wager with the devil his soul is taken to heaven.

See also *Doctor Faustus.*

Faust and the City. Anatoli Lunacharsky (Russian). Drama. 3 acts. Translated by Leonard Magnus. 1923.

Faust, believing that a benevolent despot will best ensure the happiness of his people, rules them firmly. But when they revolt, and after he is forced from the throne and discovers they can govern themselves, Faust rejoices in their joy.

Favart, Charles Simon (1710-1792). French dramatist, producer. Born in Paris, he produced his first vaudeville *Les Deux Jumelles* in 1734, but wrote anonymously until the production of his *La Chercheuse d'esprit* in 1741. He became a director of the *Opèra Comique,* where his wife, Marie Justine Duronceray (1727-1772), achieved success in many of his productions, including *Ninette à la cour,* 1753, and *Les Trois Sultanes,* 1761. Favart and his wife took a company to perform for the troops of Marshal Saxe in Flanders, and were so popular that battles were stopped to let the opposing force attend their performances.

Faversham, William (1868-   ). English actor. Born in London. For a time he served in the Yeomanry Cavalry Regiment. He made his first appearance on the stage at the Vaudeville Theatre in *Retained for the Defense,* 1885. His first play in New York was *Pen and Ink* at the Union Square Theatre, 1887. He played with Mrs. Fiske for two seasons. In 1893 he was engaged by Charles Frohman and appeared in many plays with the Empire company. In 1901 he made his début as a star in *A Royal Rival*. He has played in many Shakespearian roles, and appeared in *The Prince and the Pauper, Lord and Lady Algy,* etc. In 1934 he toured in *Tobacco Road,* and also made some motion pictures.

Feast of Fools. The first expression in dramatic form in the church, introduced in 990 in the Greek churches in Constantinople. Its object was to wean the minds of the populace from the prevalent pagan ceremonies, especially the Bacchanalia, by using their identical licentious means in the service of Christianity. The custom flourished in France in the 11th century and later was to be found in England.

Feast of Ortolans, The. Maxwell Anderson (American). Drama. 1 act. 1926.
Involves several French aristocrats and intellectuals gathered together for the last time on the eve of the French Revolution. The climax comes when a representative of the old order commands a servant to come to him; the servant refuses, the master leaves the room to punish him, and is found shortly after with his throat cut.

Feast of the Boy-Bishop. A form of religious festival popular in England in the 13th century, at which time plays and interludes were performed.

Featured. Billing secondary only to starring, concerning the main actor or actors in a production; in the programme or advertising, the name, or names, of featured players follow directly *after* the title of the piece.

Fechter, Charles Albert (1824-1879). French actor. Played in English in England and America. He was the original Armand of *La Dame aux camélias* and was the foremost romantic actor of his time. After a great success in England, particularly, in the *Ruy Blas* of Victor Hugo, he came to America in 1870, where, after a tour, he became the manager of the Lyceum Theatre. Here he made many innovations in staging, such as the abolishment of the ancient grooves, trapdoors and flats by which scenery had previously been raised and lowered. He was also the first builder of solid ceilings in plays, ceilings formerly having been represented by hanging cloths, and walls by open wings.

Federal Theatre Project. An American experiment in federal subsidy of the theatre growing out of an attempt to include the cultural occupations in the work relief program of the Works Progress Administration. Set up in 1935 to solve unemployment in the theatre under the national direction of Mrs. Hallie Flanagan of Vassar College. It was planned as a theatre for the people with a fifty-five cent top and the booking of large groups at lowered prices was sought. The units were scattered over half of the states of the country and did yeomen work in bringing back the living theatre to the road. New Orleans, Atlanta, Boston, Philadelphia, Chicago, Denver, Seattle, San Francisco and Los Angeles were producing centers outside New York. Important productions were made including, among others, Eliot's

Murder in the Cathedral; the Negro *Macbeth, Swing Mikado; Androcles and the Lion;* the Orson Welles-John Houseman *Horse Eats Hat* and *Doctor Faustus;* the experimental "living newspaper" technique of *Triple A Plowed Under, Power, . . . one-third of a nation . . .* ; the children's play *Pinocchio* (an adult success). Other than those listed above, the following important theatre names have been associated with the project: Elmer Rice, Gilmor Brown, Rosamond Gilder, James Ullman, Jr., Philip Barber, Morris Ankrum, Halstead Welles, Helen Arthur, Agnes Morgan, Alexander Lefkovitch. During June, 1939, partly as the result of the testimony before the Dies Committee, the project was blackened in the eyes of the Congress. Despite the efforts of a theatre delegation led by Tallulah Bankhead, daughter of the Speaker of the House, and mass demonstrations throughout the country, the Federal Theatre Project ceased to exist July 31, 1939.

Feed. To speak lines in a performance to an actor to enable him to make effectual a certain necessary rejoinder; to prompt an actor on the stage in such a way that the audience is unaware of it.

Feeder. A straight actor or actress whose lines give the comedian a chance to put over his jokes or comic lines.

Feigning. Pretending onstage, for dramatic purposes, whatever is necessitated by author and director for the character in a play. The quintessence of acting; as "to feign death" by lying motionless.

Femmes Savantes, Les (The Learned Ladies). Molière (French). Comedy. 5 acts. 1672.
Chrysale's wife and daughters spend their days affecting learning, a vogue popular among ladies at court. His youngest daughter, Henriette, finds a sweetheart and old Chrysale finally musters courage to brave his wife's anger, and champion Henriette's marriage and escape from affectation.

Ferber, Edna (1887-   ). American author, dramatist. Born in Kalamazoo, Michigan. Since 1911 she has published a score of novels, including *So Big, Show Boat* and *Cimarron,* all filmed. Her plays include *$1200.00 a Year* (with Newman Levy), *Our Mrs. McChesney* (with George V. Hobart), *Show Boat* (with Oscar Hammerstein II); four productions with George S. Kaufman, *Minick, The Royal Family, Dinner at Eight* and *Stage Door.*

Fernald, Chester Bailey (1869-   ). American dramatist. Born in Boston, Massachusetts, he became a prolific author and play-translator. His translation of *The Mask and the Face,* which was first performed in London in 1924, was probably his greatest success.
Original plays include: *The Cat and the Cherub,* 1897; *Always Afternoon* (a collaboration), 1929; *Tomorrow,* 1931.

Ferrier, Paul (1843-1920). French dramatist. Born at Montpellier, he wrote and collaborated on a great many operas, comic operas and comedies. He was particularly noted for his gaiety and humor.

Best known of his plays are: *Josephine vendue par ses soeurs*, 1886; *La Belle Mère*, 1898; *Tabarin*, 1884; *La Fille de Tabarin*, 1901.

Fescennine Verses. A form of farce in ancient Etruria in the 3rd and 4th centuries B.C., paralleling the Athenian comedy. This form developed from what originally was no more than a chant into a kind of humorous give-and-take or banter. It derived from the rituals of an agricultural people at harvest and vintage time.

Feuchtwanger, Lion (1884-). German author and dramatist. Born in Munich, he first became known as a dramatist. His international reputation is based, however, on his novels, the most famous of which, *Jew Suess*, first published in 1924, and translated into English in 1926, was dramatized by Ashley Dukes and produced in London in 1929. A film based on the book was first shown in London in 1934. Feuchtwanger, a Jew, was compelled to leave Germany after the advent of the Nazis to power in 1933.

His plays include: *Warren Hastings*, 1916; translations of *The Persians of Aeschylus*, *The Peace of Aristophanes*, and the Indian legend, *Vasantasena;* and a translation of Marlowe's *Edward II*, 1924.

Feuillet, Octave (1821-1890). French author and dramatist. Born at St. Lô in La Manche, he became an assistant to Dumas *père*. Elected to the Academy in 1862, he was later made librarian at Fontainebleau.

His comedies are marked by their sentimentality and include: *The Man of Success; The Romance of a Poor Young Man*, 1859; *The Sphinx*, 1881; *Led Astray*, adapted by Dion Boucicault from his *La Tentation*, 1873.

Feydeau, Georges (1862-1921). French dramatist. Born in Paris, he was a contemporary of Georges Courteline, Tristan Bernard, Alexandre Bisson and H. R. Lenormand. The Plautine influence, supplemented by whimsicalities of character and plot, is evident in the farces of Feydeau.

His first play, *Tailleur pour dames*, 1888, was followed by *The Free Exchange Hotel*, 1894; *La Dame de chez Maxim*, 1899, which had a long run in London as the *Lady from Maxim's; The Duchess of the Fôlies-Bergère*, 1902; *Look Out for Amelie*, 1908; *A Cathartic for Baby*, 1909; *The Flea in the Ear*, 1910; *But Don't Go About Without Your Clothes*, 1911; *I Don't Deceive My Husband*, 1915, etc.

Feyntes (or *secrets*). Machines or other theatrical devices used on the medieval French stage. By the Italians these were called *ingegni*. They were derived from the Greek drama via the *Onomasticon* of Pollux, which described the Greek machinery for stage-effects, as well as masks. The *feyntes* included iron girdles supporting angels, clouds of cottonwood, contrivances to shake the stage in simulation of earthquake, and bolts of lightning that destroyed houses. There were concentric wheels fitted with lights to represent stars, which revolved at the top of the stage as "the ten circles of the heavens"—reminiscent of Ezekiel's vision of wheels within wheels turning in the air.

Field, Nathan (1587-1619 or 1620). English actor. An actor in Shakespeare's company, the Lord Chamberlain's Men, 1615-19. He is listed in the 1623 Folio as one of the performers in Shakespeare's plays and is known also to have acted in Jonson's *Cynthia's Revels, The Poetaster, Epicene* and *Bartholomew Fair,* and in plays of Beaumont and Fletcher, notably *The Queen of Corinth, The Knight of Malta, The Mad Lover* and *The Loyal Subject.* As a writer he produced two plays, a defense of the stage and several dramas in collaboration with Massinger, Daborne and Fletcher.

Fielding, Henry (1707-1754). English novelist, dramatist. Born near Glastonbury, a scion of the Denbigh family, he was educated at Eton and at the University of Leyden, studying civil law. At about the age of twenty he went to London and began to work for the stage. He wrote a number of farces and other light pieces which, unfortunately, because some of them were the finest plays of the later years of the era, have passed into the limbo of literary curiosities. Called to the Bar in 1740, he was appointed justice of the peace for Westminster in 1749 and proved a conscientious and painstaking magistrate.

The author of *Tom Jones,* which many critics consider the greatest novel ever written, is remembered for two plays: *Love in Several Masques,* 1727-28; and *The Debauchees,* 1732.

See also *Stage; jurisprudence.*

Fields, Lew (1867-   ). American actor and producer. He made his first appearance on the stage in partnership with Joseph Weber in juvenile Dutch sketches. In 1885 they formed their own company and then became owners of Broadway Music Hall, which was soon generally known as Weber and Fields. Then came a series of burlesques which made them both famous and extremely popular. In the years that followed he dissolved partnership and later rejoined Joe Weber. Mr. Fields has had a tremendous success alone and with Weber in a great variety of plays. In addition, he has produced a number of successful musicals such as *The Girl Friend, Hit the Deck, A Connecticut Yankee,* etc.

Figurantes. Female ballet dancers.

Finale. The final number; chiefly in a musical show.

Fireproof curtain. The asbestos shield dropped at the front of the stage before the doors are opened, which must remain down until five minutes before the performance is to begin.

See also *Curtains.*

Fireproofing. According to standardized fire laws all scenery must be flame-proofed; frames can be brushed with a solution of one pound of borax, one pound of sal-ammoniac, dissolved in three quarts of water.

Fireside, The. Octave Mirbeau and Thadée Natanson (French). Drama. 4 acts. 1908.

An attack against mismanaged philanthropy, this drama of reform pictures the patron of an orphan's home, hypocritically seeking the respect of the community, who helps himself to the funds which he collects while the girls in the home are half starved. And the pious rogue has been so successful in hiding his misappropriations that he has been elected both senator and academician. Mirbeau's socialist and anti-clerical views are obvious in this drama.

First Lady. Katharine Dayton and George S. Kaufman (American). Comedy. 3 acts. 1935.

Lucy Chase Wayne has presidential ambitions for her husband, Stephen Wayne, now Secretary of State, while her worst enemy, Irene Hibbard is sponsoring a young senator from the West. To draw attention from the western senator, Lucy starts a boom for Irene's aging Supreme Court Justice husband. The boom gets out of hand, however, and it takes all of Lucy's political strategy to defeat the Supreme Court Justice and promote her husband's nomination.

First Little Show. First, 1929, of a series of three revues on Broadway, presented by Dwight Deere Wiman and the late William A. Brady, Jr. This set a mark of sophistication which helped to change the trend of musical production from the lavish to the intimate as a general style. The *Grand Street Follies,* the *Garrick Gaieties* and *Americana* preceded the *Little Show* in this genre.

First Mrs. Fraser, The. St. John Ervine (English). Comedy. 3 acts. 1928.

A drawing room comedy in the polite tradition. Marie Tempest created the title role in London and Grace George in New York; both runs were prosperous. Janet and James Fraser had been married for twenty years when they were divorced so he could marry Elsie, nineteen at the time, completely hard-boiled and interested only in his money. Five years later the young gold-digger is already seeking greener fields— to be exact, Lord Larne, who is older than James and less attractive, but richer and more gullible. For she is having an affair with Mario, night club dancer, and needs an easily deceived spouse. James, however, who was stricken from the honors list at the time of his first divorce, hesitates about a second, and goes to the first Mrs. Fraser to ask her advice. Janet Fraser is in her forties, still attractive, and, to James' discomfiture, being wooed by one Philip Logan, a handsome and personable bachelor. She is inclined to let James muddle through on his own, although she does hint that Elsie would be sensible to elope with Lord Larne and let James divorce her afterward. James is shocked at the suggestion. Not long after he has left Elsie arrives, also desirous of counsel. Janet practically forces her to elope with Larne by threatening blackmail. For Logan has seen Elsie and Mario register in a hotel and can prove they are lovers. So that Janet won't tell James or, more important, Lord Larne about it, Elsie agrees to go off with Larne at once. She does, and James divorces her. In the meantime he has been seeing a great deal of his first wife, to Logan's displeasure. On the day when the divorce becomes final, both men propose. Janet does not accept either at once, and James presses his suit by the gift of a pearl necklace. She puts it on dreamily, remarking to her son, "Your father's beginning to court me all over again, and I rather like it."

FIRST NIGHTS

BY LUCIUS BEEBE

From time to time, with a certain regularity and usually by well meaning but pretentious amateurs of the legitimate theater, the thesis is advanced that it would be a good thing to do away with first nights as an institution. Generally speaking, this movement, if it achieves the support of more than one nominee derives from one of two circumstances: either a premiere has been characterized by some particularly hideous form of outrage, a row one debutante has fallen in an ungenteel moment into the traps, or a reviewer from one of the morning papers has demonstrated his distaste for the proceedings by an attack of noisy nausea into his opera hat, or else the audience at a given opening has been so much more spectacular, witty or attractive by comparison with the doings on the stage as to arouse the vindictive fury of actors and management alike.

For the woman scorned is a docile housepet to the ham ignored, and when some baldpated has-been with his blood pressure up to Union League proportions is found kicking the cuspidors up and down the bar at the Lambs or Players and demanding public execution for the entire Sam Harris first night list, it's a safe bet that the night before's audience at the Music Box gave a better performance than he did.

Not that occasional provocation to pique on the part of performers is not on the record. There have been inexcusably late arrivals of large and noisy groups, wafting before them an aroma of Old Taylor and affectionately saluting acquaintances in the aisle seats by kicking them in the shins and disarranging their hairdress as they climb uncertainly, but determinedly to their seats. There have been occasional reviewers who have contrived to tie on a lovely brannigan at Sardi's before fumbling their way down front to pass out with snores and belches at highly inappropriate moments. There is the record of one scholarly critic not so many seasons ago who arrived at an Empire opening handsomely attired in tailcoat, glace gloves and chapeau claque but quite lacking in stockings or other footgear, and there was another who, at a notable Shubert premiere was afflicted with a sudden rush of food to the face so that a bemused dowager nearby was heard to observe it was a pity that these reviewers couldn't wait till they got to the office to write their notices.

But if these infrequent and often enough hilarious lapses in taste are true of audiences, the same can be said for the performers on the other side of the footlights. Several supposedly lady actresses have been known to stop the show to denounce audiences in terms that would have interested the fishwives of Billingsgate; one American actress is on record as slapping a British reviewer because of an unfavorable notice and at least two artistes of the American theater have been known to fall flat on their faces during performances, lapses which have usually been ascribed to vertigo, the altitude or malnutrition, but which connoisseurs in the front rows have said were accompanied by a pawing at the prop furniture and a variety of uncertain footwork usually associated with Saturday night and the family entrance.

It is a serious mistake to imagine that the glitter, superficiality of some of the Broadway regulars, smash and hurrah of a fashionable first night are anything but an asset to the launching and successful promotion of any show. The top hats and sables, the extra policemen and bright lights of the marquee, the attraction of traffic-snarling crowds and even the nuisance value presence of film celebrities, panhandlers and autograph urchins, all serve to add to the occasion a panache of excitement and, to use a much overworked word, glamor that could be contrived through no other form of advertising and that no variety of promotion, no matter how ingenius and costly, could evolve. That managers and producers in general believe this, despite their occasional outbursts, is evidenced by a first night list ranging in inclusiveness from the Orson Munns, the Grand Duchess Marie and Jock Whitneys to Tommy Manville, Jack Dempsey and the leading saloon keepers of Fifty-second Street, not to mention a press list of 170 odd pairs of seats, maintained from year to year and varied only by the mutations of death and success in the professional and social worlds.

The most successful producers of the current decade of the theatre: Sam Harris, Brock Pemberton, the brothers Shubert, Gilbert Miller, Jed Harris, Winthrop Ames, Dwight Deere Wiman and Vinton Freedley specialized in snob appeal first nights. They populated their premieres with chinchilla and opera cloaks, Rolls Royces, titled columnists, Vanderbilts, Morgans and professional celebrities. They dressed their carriage starters in regal liveries and turned the reporters and photographers loose in the lobby. They invested their every venture with whatever chic and opulence the most expensive press agents could contrive and a very fine thing they made of it too. Don't sneer at the carriage trade; there's gold in them thar swells!

First Pantomime. A dance ballet based on the fourth act of Corneille's *Horace* and presented in Paris in 1706.

First Year, The. Frank Craven (American). Comedy. 3 acts. 1920.
Dick Loring, an old suitor comes to dinner and nearly wrecks Tommy's business deal to sell land to the railroad. Tommy and Grace have their first serious quarrel over Dick, with Grace going home to mother. Tommy follows, later, gives Dick a thrashing and wins Grace back. Peace is restored, and Grace admits she is expecting a baby.

Fiske, Minnie Maddern (Mary Augusta Davey) (1865-1932). American actress. Born in New Orleans, the daughter of Thomas Davey, a western manager, and his wife Lizzie Maddern, an actress. She was brought up in the theatre and began her professional career as an infant-in-arms, but was soon graduated to speaking parts in support of many notable stars. She made her first New York appearance at the age of four with J. K. Emmet and was in steady demand as a child actress. In 1874, she played Prince Arthur in an all-star production of *King John* at Booth's Theatre. By 1880 she had become a soubrette and ingenue. At sixteen she starred in *Fogg's Ferry*. Later she played in *In Spite of All, Caprice* and *Featherbrain*. She made her greatest success as an ingenue in *Caprice,* in which she sang "In the Gloaming" and made the song popular. She married Le Grand White about 1882, but before long divorced him. Before she was twenty-five, she married Harrison Grey Fiske and gave up the stage. He was editor and owner of the *New York Dramatic Mirror* and was a playwright and dramatic critic. Mrs. Fiske wrote several one-act sketches which she later produced. She returned after four years to acting. She spent a great deal of time studying, particularly Ibsen, and finally, in 1894, gave a special matinee of *A Doll's House* in New York. Without profit, she put on plays, one after another for three years. In 1897, she gave *Tess of the D'Urbervilles* and won the critics' acclaim. In the early 1900's Mrs. Fiske said she was in her second incarnation. Her first had been as Minnie Maddern. But as Mrs. Fiske she had come back to the stage to do plays of far greater import than any with which Miss Maddern had beguiled her public. "Realistic" was the word she never applied to the kind of acting she believed in. She called it merely "natural, true acting." She played in *Hedda Gabler, Rosmersholm, Pillars of Society* and *Ghosts, Becky Sharp, Salvation Nell, The New York Idea, Mrs. Bumpstead-Leigh* and *Mis' Nelly of N'Orleans*. She is considered one of the most distinguished actresses ever to have played the American stage, and its chief portrayer of Ibsen roles.

Fitch, William Clyde (1865-1909). American dramatist. Fitch, although he has not worn extremely well, was very prolific and an enormously successful playwright in his day. Born in Elmira, New York, he was graduated from Amherst in 1886. In 1889 Richard Mansfield asked the author to write *Beau Brummel* for him. The author complied, and the play was an instant hit. Some of his other plays were *The Climbers,* 1901, a social satire which was sensationally popular when first produced; *Captain Jinks of the Horse Marines,* 1902, which gave Ethel Barrymore one of her first opportunities in light comedy; *Girl with Green Eyes,* 1902; *The Truth,* 1907; *The City,* 1909; *The Moth and the Flame; Barbara Frietchie; Nathan Hale; The Cowboy and the Lady,* adapted for the films in 1938 by S. N. Behrman and others; *The Last of the Dandies; The Woman in the Case;* etc.; etc. There is a room in the Amherst College Library devoted exclusively to his plays, manuscripts and letters; and the holograph copy of *The Girl and the Judge* is in the New York Public Library.

Many of his dramas were produced in England, where as a rule they were less favorably received than here, the characters in such a work as *The Climbers* being considered unbearably crude and ill bred by British critics. Yet though the playwright drew on the United States for his character types, his style and treatment were inspired by Europe. His comedies are good examples of craftsmanship, well constructed and polished, in which they are related to the French and English dramatic output of the period. It is perhaps because they are period pieces, lacking in vitality and robustness and content to follow tradition rather than to make it, that today, when they are no longer daring or original, they are seldom revived. They are interesting chiefly as museum pieces and as an indication of popular tastes at the turn of the century.

Fit-up stage. During the Middle Ages the stage consisted of a few boards on trestles which the players of Interludes carried so that the crowd might see those who appeared thereon. A form of this stage is still in use.

Fit-ups. British slang term for touring companies which carry their own equipment of sets for transforming a plain platform into a suitable stage.

Fizzer. British slang term for a sure-fire hit, applied both to a show and a performance.

Flag. The curtain.

Flanagan, Hallie. Professor of drama, Vassar College; author of *Shifting Scenes in Europe, 1928;* university theatre innovator. National Director, Federal Theatre Project, 1935-39.
See *Federal Theatre Project.*

Flat. An effect of scenery painted in perspective on flat canvas, boards, or ordinary cloth to simulate three-dimensional solidity. It is usually 5 feet 9 inches wide, and 12 to 20 feet high. The width of a flat is determined by the door of a freight car, which is 6 feet wide.

Flavin, Martin (1883-). American dramatist. He started out on a commercial career but turned to playwriting. He has written a number of interesting plays and three very successful ones, *Children of the Moon,* which appeared in 1923 created a minor sensation. *The Criminal Code* and *Broken Dishes,* both in 1929, were successes. Other of his plays are *Cross Roads,* 1929; *Achilles Had a Heel,* 1935; *Tapestry in Gray,* 1935; *Around the Corner,* 1936. Recently he has written a number of scenarios for the films.

Flers, Robert de la Motte-Ango, Marquis de (1872-1927). French dramatist. He made his reputation as a collaborator with G. A. de Caillavet in a series of light and witty comedies. Among them are *Les Trauvaux d'Hercule,* 1901; *Primerose,* 1911; *L'Habit vert,* 1912; *La Belle Aventure,* 1913. He became editor of *Le Figaro* with Alfred Capus in June, 1914.

Fletcher, John (1579-1625). English dramatist. A son of Dr. Richard Fletcher, Bishop of London, he was born in Sussex, and began writing for the stage in 1596. He appears to have begun about 1607, with *Philaster,* his association with Francis Beaumont, with whom he lived in Southwark, near the Globe Theatre. To what extent Fletcher was responsible for the quasi-Shakespearean plays *King Henry VIII* and *The Two Noble Kinsmen* remains an open question. He wrote beautiful lyrics and brilliant dialogue, but his inattention to meter and his failure to carry over the sense from one line to another tend to make his blank verse slow and uneven. He died of the plague and was buried in St. Saviour's, Southwark, August 29, 1625.

Among his plays are: *The Faithful Shepherdess,* 1609; *The Maid's Tragedy* (with Beaumont), 1611; *The Knight of the Burning Pestle* (with Beaumont); *Bonduca; Valentinian; The Loyal Subject; The Wild-Goose Chase; A Wife for a Month.* He was also joint-author of other plays with Massinger, Middleton, Rowley and Field.

Flies (always used in the plural). In a theatre, the space over the whole stage, above the proscenium.

Floating. Lowering a covered flat by placing the foot on the bottom rail and allowing the flat to float down; the flat provides enough resistance and falls slowly.

Floating stage. A steel stage, motor-powered, which rides on two steel arms upward at a 45° angle which holds a revolving stage, enabling the stage manager to make four or five changes in succession. It has the advantage of going offstage, upstage, escalator fashion, so that another stage could come into view.

Floating stages. In 1936 a floating stage was built as a civic project on Zack's Bay, Jones Beach, New York, fifty yards off shore, with an amphitheatre on shore seating 10,000. A San Carlo Opera Company performance of *Carmen* opened the theatre on June 27, 1936.

The *Casa Mañana* that Billy Rose built at the Frontier Days Celebration in Fort Worth in 1936 had a stage which opened to reveal water on which gondolas floated. His marine restaurant and cabaret at the Cleveland Great Lakes Exposition in 1937 had a stage "5½ times the size of Radio City Music Hall" floating in Lake Erie. It was floated up to the shore when performances to be heard by the audience were given, and moored at a distance off shore to make way for aquatic spectacles. His Aquacade at the New York World's Fair (1939) had a fixed stage; the aquatic spectacles taking place in a large pool of water in front of it.

In the Roman era, a stage not *on* water, but *of* water, floated the performances. Renaissance engravings by Jacobus Laurus Romanus picture *Naumachia*—flooded amphitheatres—of Nero and Domitian, in which naval battles were staged. The Colosseum is believed to have been flooded for this purpose at one time.

Floating theatre. Another term for show boat.
See also *Floating stages.*

Flood-lighting. Created by means of a group of bunch lights that are placed to provide a higher intensity of light on a particular part of the stage. They are best used for selective illumination. They should not be used for general illumination, to flood the stage with light, because of the undesired shadows and the flatness of illumination that result.

Flop. A theatrical production that fails.

Florence, Malvina Pray Littell (1830-1906). American actress. Married William Jermyn Florence in 1853. She was one of the first American actresses to appear before the English public. She played with great success in *The Mighty Dollar,* which was repeated more than 2,500 times in England and America. Their *The Irish Boy and Girl* also greatly pleased the London public.

Florence, William Jermyn (1831-1891). American actor, dramatist, comedian. Played Irish and Yankee subjects. Wrote songs, including "Bobbing Around." Best roles included O'Bryan in Brougham's *Temptation; or The Irish Emigrant* and *Handy Andy.* Toured through many American cities with his wife, Malvina Pray Littell, with universal success. Also played in London and the provinces. Some of Florence's best roles were: Bardwell Slote in *The Mighty Dollar;* Bob Brierly in *Ticket-of-Leave-Man;* and Sir Lucius O'Trigger in *The Rivals.*

Florodora Sextette. To the tinkling tune of "Tell Me Pretty Maiden," six lovely girls appeared in a chorus of the popular *Florodora* in 1900. They became the toast of the town overnight and their marriages and love affairs were national objects of interest. Jack Kirkland and Leyla Georgie celebrated their careers in a fictional play, *I Must Love Someone,* 1939. The names of the famous six were: Marjorie Relyea, Agnes Wayburn, Vaughn Texsmith, Marie L. Wilson, Margaret Walker, and Daisy Greene.

Flower path. See *Hanamichi.*

Flowers, The (Las Flores). Serafin and Joaquin Alvarez Quintero (Spanish). Comedy. 3 acts. 1901.
An early work of the exceptionally productive Quinteros, this sentimental comedy was originally a failure, but posterity has reversed the decision of its first audiences and still enjoys seeing it in repertory. The authors' thesis is that women are like flowers, languishing or flourishing according to the care they are given and the earth in which they are planted. This is illustrated by three sisters who spend most of their time in a Seville garden, and whose sheltered lives put them in the class of hothouse or garden flowers, delicate and lovely.

Flowers Are Not for You to Pick, The. Tyrone Guthrie (English). Drama. 3 acts. Printed 1931.
A missionary facing death sees his life unfold before him. He recalls incidents of babyhood, boyhood, school days, university days, right up to his saying good-bye to friends before embarking on the fateful trip. Throughout his entire life, he

realizes, he has been continually thwarted in his desires. As a baby he was forbidden to pick the flowers. As a man he is refused by the girl with whom he fell desperately in love. The play unveils the soul of that mediocrity which means well but is foredoomed to failure.

Flown. A term used where backdrops and other scenic effects are raised out of sight on pulleys by means of the counterweight system.

Fluff. To speak indistinctly when uncertain of the exact words; also to blow, that is to forget one's lines entirely.

Focusing control (television). An adjustment for bringing the electron beam to its smallest dimensions at the point of contact with the fluorescent screen in the receiving tube, thus causing a sharp, clear image.

F. O. H. Front of the house, that is, all that lies in front of the footlights in a theatre.

Fokine, Michel (1880-   ). Russian Dancer. A dancer of the Imperial Ballet in St. Petersburg, he became an important force in the revolution of ballet as choreographic director of Diaghileff's company and toured with them in Europe and London. He innovated a new ballet style under the influence of Isadora Duncan. He composed many ballets and is still active as a choreographer with the Monte Carlo company, and as a teacher.

Folger Shakespeare Library. See *Theatre collections*.

Folio, Shakespeare. The term, refers to the size of the book, generally employed to describe the early one-volume editions of Shakespeare's collected plays. The First Folio was published as a memorial to the poet in 1623 by John Heminge and Henry Condell. Besides the plays it contained a portrait of Shakespeare by Martin Droeshout, eulogies by a number of poets, including Ben Jonson, and a descriptive foreword by the editors. Subsequent editions of the Folio appeared in 1632, 1663 and 1685. A number of non-Shakespearean plays were included in the Third and Fourth Folios.

Follow. To keep the spotlight trained on an actor as he moves on the stage.

Follow spot. A spotlight on a movable joint operated to follow a character on the stage.

Foltz, Hans (?-1515). German dramatist. With Rosenpluet, one of the two precursors of Hans Sachs. He was a barber-surgeon and a *meistersinger* from Worms. He wrote farces, *Fastrachtspiele,* riddles, New Years Greetings and *Meisterlied* (Master Songs).

Folwell, Arthur (1877-   ). American dramatic editor. A great scholar and the dean of New York dramatic editors. He has aided scores of press agents and artists with constructive criticism, has sat patiently with them working over articles, and has consistently offered invaluable advice. He began his writing career as a contributor to *Puck* and to *Collier's Weekly* in 1904. He became the editor of the *New York Tribune* Sunday magazine section in 1921, and in 1927 was made dramatic editor of the same paper, now the *Herald-Tribune*. He has held other important editorial posts and has contributed to the old *Smart Set,* the *New Yorker* and many other publications.

Fontanne, Lynn (1882-   ). Anglo-American actress. With her husband, Alfred Lunt, Miss Fontanne forms America's most celebrated acting couple and is known throughout the United States and England. Born in London in 1882, she made her début with Ellen Terry in *Alice-Sit-by-the-Fire,* 1905, after which she appeared in pantomime at the Drury Lane. Then she played, sometimes in London and sometimes in New York, in *Lady Frederick,* 1909; *Billy's Bargain,* 1910; *Mr. Preedy and the Countess,* 1910; *Dress,* 1914; *Milestones,* 1914; *Searchlights,* 1915; *The Wooing of Eve* (the first of several seasons with Laurette Taylor's company), 1916; *The Harp of Life,* 1916; *Out There,* 1917; *Happiness,* 1917; *A Pair of Petticoats,* 1918; *Someone in the House,* 1918; *Chris,* 1920; *Dulcy,* 1921; and other plays. *Sweet Nell of Old Drury,* 1923, marked her first stage appearance with Alfred Lunt, whom she married the following year. Since 1924 she and her husband have been mainstays of the Theatre Guild and have redeemed seasons which would otherwise have been unprofitable to the Guild by their performances. As co-stars they have achieved world fame, and have acted in New York, London and on the road. Their vehicles include: *The Guardsman,* 1924 (filmed in 1931); *Arms and the Man,* 1925; *The Goat Song,* 1926; *At Mrs. Beam's,* 1926; *Pygmalion,* 1926; *The Brothers Karamazov,* 1927; *The Second Man,* 1927; *The Doctor's Dilemma,* 1927; *Strange Interlude,* 1928; *Caprice,* 1928 (in London, 1929); *Meteor,* 1929; *Elizabeth the Queen,* 1930; *Reunion in Vienna,* 1931; *Design for Living,* 1933; *Point Valaine,* 1935; *The Taming of the Shrew,* 1935; *Idiot's Delight,* 1936; *Amphitryon 38,* 1937; *The Seagull,* 1938. Mr. Lunt did not appear in *Strange Interlude.*

Fool, The. Channing Pollock (American). Drama. 4 acts. 1922.
Daniel Gilcrest, a young rector, is ousted from his pulpit because he urges the adoption of Christ's ideas to the conduct of business affairs. He attempts to mediate a coal strike, but is unsuccessful, and departs to establish a mission house in the slums. Once again his God-like simplicity is misunderstood and a mob turns on him. He is saved only by the miraculous healing of a crippled girl.

Foote, Samuel (1720-1777). English actor. Having wasted his early years and failed to earn a degree at Oxford, Foote went on the stage in 1744. At first barely successful, from 1747, at the Haymarket Theatre, London, he became widely popular for his imitations of other actors and of celebrities in his programs *Diversions* *of the Morning.* He wrote and adapted many plays, appeared in most of them, but it is as a wit that he is remembered. He was buried in Westminster Abbey.

See also *Tea parties.*

Footlights. Series of lights placed along the front of the stage near the floor with reflectors to throw light back upon the stage and actors. Usually, three different colors are used—amber, white and blue. This makes possible almost any general light effect. For special effects, of course, red, green or any other bulbs may be used. Footlights provide sharply-angled general lighting. In general, the factors of shadows, brilliance and unusual direction require the use of some additional, complementary and supplementary lighting.

See *Lighting.*

Footmen's gallery. The top balcony in the playhouse of the English Restoration, to which lackeys and the general lower classes were consigned. It was abolished in 1737.

Fops' alley. A place in the Restoration theatre on the fore-stage, or apron, where the wits paraded while criticizing the play.

Fops' corner. A corner near the stage in the Restoration theatre where dramatic criticism of the spectacle was discussed.

Forbes-Robertson, Sir Johnston (1853-1937). English actor. Born in London, eldest son of John Forbes-Robertson, art critic and journalist, of Aberdeen, he studied art at the Royal Art School, but, taking to the stage, studied under Phelps. He made his début, March 5, 1874, at the Princess' Theatre, London, as Chastelard in *Mary Queen of Scots.* Associated in turn with Charles Calvert, the Bancrofts, Henry Irving, Wilson Barrett and John Hare, he achieved his first notable success as Geoffrey Wynyard in *Dan'l Druce* at the Haymarket, 1876. His first venture as an actor-manager was at the Lyceum, 1895, when he appeared as Romeo to the Juliet of Mrs. Patrick Campbell. In 1900 he married Gertrude Elliott, sister of Maxine Elliott. His farewell season in London was opened at the Drury Lane in 1913. He was knighted in that year. He toured America several times, chiefly in Shakespearean roles; his final professional performance took place at Harvard University, April 26, 1916. Of the many parts he played his Hamlet and Dick Heldar in *The Light That Failed* were the most memorable.

Ford, John (1586-1639). English dramatist. Charles Lamb placed Ford, an associate of Thomas Dekker, in "the first order of poets." His somber genius is at its best when he portrays human passions, but his great defect is that the problems which he places before his audience are left unsolved. As a student of the tragedies of domestic life, and in his sympathetic interpretation of the situations they create, he still stands unsurpassed.

Born at Ilsington, Devon, he became a lawyer and then a dramatist. His reputation rests on: *'Tis Pity She's a Whore,* 1626; *The Broken Heart,* 1629; *Perkin*

Warbeck, 1634. He collaborated with Dekker in *Sun's Darling* and with Dekker and Rowley in *The Witch of Edmonton,* 1621?; and with Webster in a lost play, called *A Late Murder of the Son upon the Mother.*

Formal stage setting. A type of scenery belonging to the 16th century. The setting was fixed and before it all plays were given. Serlio and Palladio were the foremost architects of formal stage settings. Another name for this stage setting is the sculptured setting.

See also *Sculptured stage.*

Forman, Dr. Simon (1552-1611). English astrologer. Astrologer and quack-doctor whose manuscript *Booke of Plaies* contains accounts of performances of *Macbeth* in 1610, *Winter's Tale* in 1611, and of *Cymbeline.* The *Booke of Plaies* has been regarded by some critics as a forgery by the 19th century Shakespearean student, John Payne Collier.

Foro. The rear space on the stage of the theatre in Renaissance Italy.

Forrest, Edwin (1806-1872). American actor. Made his début November 6, 1826, at the Bowery Theatre where he became a great favorite with the gallery in the role of Othello, and became one of the most dominant personalities the stage had known. During his career he played in every city in the United States. He also appeared in London. His quarrel with Macready, the English actor, led to the Astor Place riot. He was the first person to offer substantial money prizes for plays by American authors and produced those which were chosen. This marked the real beginning of a native American drama.

See also *Astor Place Riot.*

For Services Rendered. Somerset Maugham (English). Drama. 3 acts. 1932.

An evening in the life of the Ardsleys is given to show the effect of the war fifteen years after the Armistice on a typical English family. Their home, where the action takes place, is in Kent. The son, Sydney, has been blinded in the war, and compensates for his consequent morbidity by catering to his unmarried sister, whose sweetheart was killed in action. Another sister, Eva, is reaping the harvest of the "struggle for democracy." Her husband is a drunkard, and she is only waiting for him to die so she can wed Collie Stratton, whom she loves. But Collie has been a business failure since his discharge from the navy, and in the course of the evening shoots himself, which causes Eva to lose her mind. Lois, the third sister, is being courted by a war profiteer, married, who promises her money to burn and a winter in France if she will let herself be seduced. She accepts the offer and runs away with him.

Fortune Theatre, The. A public playhouse built in 1599 by Edward Alleyn for the Admiral's Men to compete with the Globe theatre, where Shakespeare's company, the Lord Chamberlain's Men, was located. The Fortune was situated on the London city boundary across the Thames from Bankside, the principal theatrical district.

Fortuny, Mariano (1838-1874). Italian lighting expert. Founder of the "Fortuny System"; indirect lighting using spotlights focused on colored silk fabrics; the silk redirects the light to the stage; it is shadowless, diffuse and allows for subtle color changes. It is impractical because of its expense and the space it requires.

Fossils, The. François de Curel (French). Drama. 4 acts. 1892.

A duke, living in a lonely castle in the Ardennes, has found consolation in a secret intrigue with the governess. She has yielded to his importunities chiefly through fear, not loving him. Then she falls in love with his son, becomes his mistress and bears him a child. The rivalry of father and son is revealed when they quarrel over little Henri's education. When the son realizes what the father's interest in the boy is, he is shocked to the core. Under the circumstances, there is no solution but for him or his father to die, he feels, and decides to be the martyr himself. A tuberculosis victim, he has been living on the Riviera for his health. So, having married his mistress to legitimatize the child and arranged that his devoted sister should help his wife rear the boy, he leaves for the frozen North, where Death will certainly visit him soon.

Foundation. A make-up term. The preliminary cleansing with cold cream, and application of flesh color to the face which precedes the main details of the stage cosmetic method.

Four A's. See *Associated Actors and Artistes of America, Inc.*

The Four P's. John Heywood (English). Interlude. Printed 1543-7.

A Palmer, a Pardoner, a Potycary and a Pedler having met and started to tell stories arrange to give a wager for the greatest lie. The Pardoner tells of cures and the Potycary of medicines. Finally the Pardoner tells of seeking a lady in Hades. Satan decides to let her go if he will pardon all women on earth, women being so vexatious in Hell that the place is impossible. The Palmer interrupts to say he has never known an impatient woman and wins the wager.

Four Saints in Three Acts. Gertrude Stein (American). Opera. Music by Virgil Thomson. 4 acts. 1934.

In spite of the title, this "opera" has not four, but fifteen, saints, excluding those in the chorus, and is written not in three, but in four, acts, which are preceded by a prelude. There is no story, no plot, no development. The principal personages are a dual Saint Theresa, Saint Ignatius, and Saint Chavez. Burns Mantle says of the work: "Colored cast against a cellophane setting representing visionary Spain. Libretto incomprehensible."

Four stars. Term devised by the *Daily News* of New York City to indicate superlative worth of a play, with fewer stars and fractional stars attesting the various degrees of the critic's esteem; also used by the motion picture critics.

Four walls. A theatre rented on lease, without staff.

Fourth wall. The name given to the hypothetical line of separation between the stage with its illusion and the audience with its actuality.

Frame (television). One complete television image. Thirty are transmitted every second.

Framing control (television). A device of which the usual receiver has two: one for regulating the horizontal centering of the image, another for the vertical centering.

Francesca da Rimini. Gabriele D'Annunzio (Italian). Tragedy. 4 acts. Printed 1902.
The scene is the Italian Renaissance. Francesca, wife of Giovanni Malatesta, lord of Rimini, falls deeply in love with her husband's younger brother, Paolo. When Giovanni learns the truth he orders the lovers put to death.

Francischina. A ballerina of the 17th century; sketched by Callot; belonging to the long line of ballerinas beginning with the dancing-girls (as found on a Herculaneum frieze of the early Roman days) and culminating with Camilla Veronese of the 18th century.

Frankenstein. John Balderston (American). 1932.
Adapted from the novel by Mary W. Shelley.
Frankenstein, a student of philosophy, discovers a method of giving life to inanimate matter. He creates a revolting-looking creature of supernatural size and strength which inspires terror and disgust in anyone who sees it. Unhappy and lonely, the monster murders his creator's brother and bride. Frankenstein pursues the creature to the Arctic regions to do away with it, but is himself killed by it.

Free People's Stage. See *Freie Volksbuehne.*

Free Stage Society. See *Freie Buehne.*

Freedley, George Reynolds (1904-   ). American theatre historian, librarian. Born Richmond, Va.; A.B., University of Richmond; M.F.A., Yale University; studied under George Pierce Baker; stage manager for Theatre Guild, 1928-31. Played bit parts in *The Grey Fox,* 1928; *The Camel Through the Needle's Eye,* 1929; *Everything's Jake,* 1930. Organized the theatre collection and established the reference theatre service of the New York Public Library, 1931; first Curator of Theatre Collection, 1938. Co-author with Rosamond Gilder of *Theatre Collections in Libraries and Museums,* 1936 (reference work on theatre cataloguing).
See also *Societé Universelle du Théâtre, Theatre Collections, Theatre Library Association, Richmond Theatre Guild.*

Freiburg Passion Play. This German version of the life of Christ, beginning with the Entrance into Jerusalem and ending with the Crucifixion, has been periodically produced in Freiburg, Germany, every three years since 1760, members of the Fassnacht families taking the principal roles. Produced in New York in 1929 at the Hippodrome under the aegis of Morris Gest.

Freie Buehne (1889). German experimental theatre. Founded in Berlin, on model of the Parisian *Théâtre Libre,* as the first great art and experimental theatre in Germany, the founders including Theodor Wolff, Maximilien Harden and Otto Brahm, the first director. Opened Sept. 29, 1889, with Ibsen's *Ghosts,* and subsequently produced plays of the naturalist school by Hauptmann, Sudermann, Zola, Edmond de Goncourt and Tolstoi. After 1894, the theatre company merged with the *Deutsches Theater,* and under the name of the latter, both companies as one were eventually directed by Max Reinhardt.

Freie Volksbuehne. After the success of the *Freie Buehne* many little and experimental theatres opened in imitation throughout Germany and Austria; the *Frei Volksbuehne* was one of the most powerful ones; opened in 1890 and by 1908 had a subscription list of 1200; founded by Dr. Bruno Wille.

French Without Tears. Terence Rattigan (English). Comedy. 3 acts. Printed 1937.
The Honorable Alan Howard and others are studying French at the villa of Maingot in the South of France, with some thought of entering the diplomatic service. A fellow student is Diana Lake who is flirtatious. Diana lures them in turn and, having enjoyed the satisfaction of conquest, practically tosses them over and turns to Lieutenant Commander Rogers, a newcomer. Rogers is in turn disillusioned. Whereupon all her victims conspire to teach Diana a lesson by individually and severally leading her on and then tossing her over. Diana is hurt, but immediately begins laying plans for the subjugation of Lord Heybrook, who is on his way to the villa. When his lordship arrives he is discovered to be a sturdy young lad of eleven years.

Freud, Sigmund (1856-1939). Austrian psychoanalyst. His discoveries concerning the structure and nature of the mind were that there is an "unconscious" which sharply affects the consciousness; that the mind is split thus because of certain conflicts or "repressions"; and that sexual impressions are received earlier and are more significant than has been realized. Freud called the unconscious conflicts of love and hostility in a child's attitude toward his parents, the "Oedipus complex" (strictly speaking, the phrase refers to the son's affection for his mother, a sort of parallel to Oedipus's guilty passion for his mother, Jocasta, described in Sophocles' tragic trilogy). Freud's work in psychoanalysis (the interpretation of dreams, etc.) was made known to the public in this country through the explanations of Brill and other disciples of the scientist.
The effect of Freudian doctrine and terminology is easily discernible in con-

temporary art and writing. The art movement of surrealism takes Freud as its source. The stream-of-consciousness novel—James Joyce's *Ulysses,* for example— is another reflection of Freudian influence. In the drama, psychoanalysis (or the popular vogue for it) was at first ridiculed, as in the one-act comedy with which the Provincetown Players launched their career, *Suppressed Desires,* 1915, by Susan Glaspell and George Cram Cook; or W. W. Jacobs' one-acter, *Establishing Relations,* 1925. Alice Gerstenberg, in her playlet *Overtones,* 1915, showed the Freudian differentiation between a character's words and thoughts by having two actors portray the same person, one speaking the controlled, polite words, the other fiercely speaking the quite opposite thoughts or overtones. Eugene O'Neill's *Strange Interlude, The Great God Brown, Emperor Jones* and *Mourning Becomes Electra* among others, reflect their author's interest in Freudian principles.

See also *Psychoanalysis in the drama.*

Freytag's pyramid. Gustav Freytag (1816-1895) made a diagram of a dramatic plot which was reproduced in his *Technik des Dramas;* it is also reproduced in Arthur Edwin Krows' *Playwriting for Profit* (1928).

Friar Bacon and Friar Bungay, The Honorable History of. Robert Greene (English). Comedy. 1594.

Based on a prose pamphlet embodying legends relating to Roger Bacon and Thomas Bungay. Bacon with Friar Bungay's help makes a head of brass; the Devil promises him the head will speak within a month. After watching for three weeks, Bacon leaves his servant Miles on duty and falls asleep. The head says, "Time is." Miles is afraid to wake Bacon. The head says "Time was," and finally "Time is past," then falls and breaks.

The Friars. A theatrical club, founded by Charles Emerson Cook, Channing Pollock, Col. John S. Flaherty, John W. Rumsey and others as The Press Agents Association, in 1904. Their public and private performances are known as *Frolics,* their clubhouse the *monastery,* their chief officer is the *abbot.* Wells Hawks was the first abbot. Among others who have been so honored are: Charles Emerson Cook, William Collier, Sr., and George M. Cohan, who has held the chair almost continuously since 1912.

Friml, (Charles) Rudolf (1881-   ). Bohemian pianist, composer. Studied at the Prague Conservatory and toured with Kubelik. He is best known as composer of light operas among which are: *The Firefly; High Jinks; Katinka; Rose Marie; The Vagabond King.*

Frogs, The. Aristophanes (Greek). Comedy. 405 B.C.

Because so many of the Greek dramatists had died, Dionysus dresses as Hercules and with his slave Xanthias crosses into Hades to bring back Euripides. He is greeted by a chorus of frogs with their famous chorus of Brekekekex, ko-ax, ko-ax. In Hades he finds that there is a dispute between Aeschylus and Euripides as to who is the greater dramatic poet. A public contest is held in which each poet parodies the style of the other. Aeschylus is declared the winner and Dionysus leads him back to Athens.

Frohman, Charles (1860-1915). American manager. Born at Sandusky, Ohio, he was a leading theatrical manager in America and after 1897, also in London, where he sponsored the first productions of *The Admirable Crichton,* 1903, and *Peter Pan,* 1904. He was the first to realize the possibility of an extensive interchange of New York and London productions. While Frohman worked on the New York *Daily Graphic,* he sold tickets at night at Hooley's Theatre, Brooklyn, New York. In 1877 he took charge of the company that was sent west to play *Our Boys.* In 1888 he saw *Shenandoah* at the Boston Museum, organized a company and bought the rights to the play. In 1890, he organized the Charles Frohman Stock Company. Among those who owe much to his management are Maude Adams, Ethel Barrymore, Otis Skinner, May Robson, Margaret Anglin. He was drowned in the sinking of the Lusitania, May 7, 1915.

Frohman, Daniel (1850-). American manager. He assumed direct control of the Lyceum Theatre in 1887. This marked the beginning of the managerial careers for the Frohmans. His first stock company was made up of such members as Henry Miller, William Faversham, Effie Shannon, Henrietta Crosman, May Robson and James K. Hackett. He secured David Belasco for stage manager, and the first play of the newly formed stock company was a composition by David Belasco, *The Wife.* It was produced on November 1, 1887. This marked the beginning of one of the most remarkable and leading play producers of the time. For the more than fifty years' history of the Actors' Fund of America, he has been associated with it and responsible for its benefits.

From Morn to Midnight. Georg Kaiser (German). Expressionistic drama. 7 scenes. Translated by Ashley Dukes. 1920.
Desiring to escape the deadly routine of his existence, a German bank clerk steals sixty thousand marks and goes on a prolonged debauch, endeavoring in his own way to test humanity. He ends up thoroughly disillusioned, and finally shoots himself.

Frons scaenae. Stage architectural term meaning a façade with doors, at the back of the Roman stage. Adapted from the *episkenion* (two-story building) of the Greek stage.
See also *Episkenion.*

Front of house. The auditorium of a theatre; often used to mean the audience in the auditorium.

Front Page, The. Ben Hecht and Charles MacArthur. Comedy-melodrama. 3 acts. 1928.

Conceded by reporters themselves to be atmospherically authentic, this newspaper melodrama was one of the most popular of the Hecht-MacArthur collaborations. Fast-moving and uproariously funny, it was filmed with Adolphe Menjou. Lee Tracy created the stage role of Hildy Johnson, Examiner reporter of the old school, happy-go-lucky, hard-drinking, combination buffoon and d'Artagnan. The scene is the press room of the Criminal Courts Building in Chicago, where a group of typical reporters await news of the Earl Williams execution for the murder of a negro policeman, scheduled for midnight. Last word is that radical sympathizers are surrounding the jail and threatening trouble, and that a new alienist hired by friends is examining the convict. Hildy is late in arriving on the scene because on his way to get married and go to New York, but postpones quitting his job when there is a fusillade of shots, considerable attendant excitement, and the news that Williams has made a jail break. Hildy, by bribing the assistant warden with his fiancée's money after the others have left, gets the exclusive story. The convict escaped with the gun given him by the alienist so he could reenact the crime. A dragnet has been thrown around Williams' old house in Clark Street. The governor has sent him a reprieve, but the mayor, furious at this being done before election, has paid the messenger not to deliver it. Then into Hildy's arms through the window falls Williams, exhausted. He is followed by Molly, a prostitute he once befriended, and she and Hildy lock Williams in a desk. Hildy's boss, Walter Burns, who has gotten his ace reporter's phoned story, arrives, enthusiastic. Hildy has gotten hold of dynamite; he can upset the whole administration. As they are about to lower the desk on pulleys and send the reprieved man to safety, trouble really starts. The Tribune reporter enters and wants his desk; the Sheriff and his posse, suspicious, want Hildy's scalp. Williams' gun is recognized; they realize where he is hiding and prepare to shoot into the desk. Whereupon the governor's messenger arrives, very drunk, and spills the beans about the reprieve. Hildy has saved an innocent man's life. After listening to a touching farewell speech by Burns and accepting the latter's gift of his watch, the newspaperman at last leaves for New York with his bride. Burns picks up the phone, and asks the New York police to arrest Hildy and send him back as soon as he arrives. Why? "The son of a bitch stole my watch."

Fulda, Ludwig (1862-   ). German dramatist. Born at Frankfort-on-Main, he became a popular dramatist. His plays include *Talisman*, 1893; *Jugen-freunde*, 1898; *Des Esels Schatten*, 1921. He also translated *Cyrano de Bergerac* and Ibsen's *Peer Gynt* into German.

He is the closest to Sudermann, and began in the Eighties, as a disciple of Paul Heyse, writing *Beneath Four Eyes* and *The Wild Chase*, satirical comedies intended to reprove those who would seek happiness as social climbers. Then he felt the spell of naturalism, and wrote *The Lost Paradise*. From this he drifted to romanticism, of which *The Blockhead* is a good example.

His other plays include: *Honest Folk*, 1883; *Woman's Right*, 1885; *A Meteor*, 1887; *The Comrades*, 1894; *The Son of the Caliph*, 1896; *Herostrat*, 1898; *The Twin Sisters*, 1901; *Master and Servant*, 1910; *Evening Sun*, 1914; *The Shadow of the Ass*, 1920; *High Sun*, 1927; *The Enchanted Princess*, 1929.

Full set. The use of the entire stage.

Funeral; or Grief-a-la-Mode, The. Richard Steele (English). Comedy. 5 acts. 1701.

Because of the misinterpretations of his young wife, Lord Brumpton disinherits his son, leaves his property and the care of his two wards to his wife. At the opening of the play Lord Brumpton, believed to be dead, is persuaded by his servant Trusty to remain in concealment. Thus he discovers his wife's unscrupulous plans and deeds. The widow is exposed, the son reinstated, and the two wards allowed to marry their true lovers.

The importance of the play is that it marks a change of moral tone in the drama after the Restoration period.

Furtenbach, Joseph F. (1591-1667). German engraver, designer. Furtenbach's engravings record a good summary of scenic art of his time. His *Architecture Civilis,* 1628, shows the various machines for changing scenery (revolving *periakti*) and rotating wave machines.

Futurism. A school of art, especially Italian, affecting scenic design, distinguished by mechanistic forms.

Futurist Manifesto of 1909. A declaration of ideals by a group of Italian artists devoted to new mechanistic styles and headed by Marinetti and Prampolini. Dickinson says of them in his *The Theatre in a Changing Europe:* "However much they might be actuated by high ideals they were at least equally urged by the desire to be sensational." Their own expression of their faith, says Dickinson, was as follows: "After innumerable battles, experiments, work achieved, victories inconceivable, we feel the need of delivering ourselves from old sensibilities, in order to create definitely the new plastic art inspired by the machine."

Gabriel, Gilbert Wolf (1890-   ). American critic, author. Began his career as a reporter on the *New York Evening Sun,* 1912; subsequently he was drama critic of the *New York Telegram-Mail, New York Sun, New York American.* He collaborated on a play *Clap Hands,* 1934; is a contributor to various magazines; has lectured on the drama and criticism; and is the author of: *The Seven-Branched Candlestick; Jiminy; Brownstone Front; Famous Pianists and Composers; Time Was; I, James Lewis;* etc.

Gag. Slang term generally applied to a highly noticeable twist of comedy. A "two-line gag" is a cue with a gag rejoinder.

See also *Gagging; Ad lib.*

Gagging. Slang term meaning the unauthorized improvisation or revision of lines by an actor, or joking with the audience or other players during the performance of a play. The Italians of the *commedia dell' arte* improvised whole acts of dialogue, and even plot. By the Elizabethan period, when plays were planned and written, the common practice of extemporizing often imperiled successful production—even though stage directions often called for actors (particularly clowns) to "gag." Shakespeare protested against the abuse, in Hamlet's speech, "Let those that play your clowns speak no more than is set down for them." Today "gagging" is a grave offense—yet often clever "gags" have been retained in subsequent productions. The term and practice also extend to radio.

See also *Ad lib.*

Gaige, Crosby (1882-   ). American producer. Born in Nelson, New York; attended Columbia from 1899-1903. He became a play broker in 1903. In 1905 he started as director for Edgar and Archibald Selwyn, an association which lasted until 1923. Since 1926 he has been an independent producer. His productions include: *Within the Law,* 1912; *Beware of Widows,* 1925; *Silence,* 1924; *The Butter and Egg Man,* 1925; *The Enemy,* 1925; *The Good Fellow,* 1926; *The Road to Happiness,* 1927; *The Shannons of Broadway,* 1927; *Little Accident,* 1928; *The House Beautiful,* 1931; *I Loved You Wednesday* (with Jed Harris), 1932; *A Hat, A Coat and Glove,* 1934; *Time and the Conways; Accent on Youth,* 1934; *Whatever Goes Up,* 1935. He is also known as an epicure and has written several books on cookery.

Gale, Zona (1874-1939). American dramatist and novelist. Born in Portage, Wisconsin, author of the Pulitzer Prize winning play *Miss Lulu Bett* (1920) taken from her novel of the same name. Also wrote *The Neighbors,* 1916, *Mr. Pitt,* 1924, and many novels and short stories.

Galeri. Wigs in the Roman theatre.

Gallery. The balcony or the upper or second balcony in a theatre; also used to mean the audience occupying such a place.

Galley Slaves, The (Los Galeotes). Serafin and Joaquin Alvarez Quintero (Spanish). Comedy. 4 acts. 1900.

An episode in Cervantes inspired this comedy about Don Quixote, who becomes the victim of the galley slaves whom he set free. It was the first major success of the Quinteros, authors of several hundred plays, and illustrates their belief in man's essential good will. The whole spirit of the play is one of benevolence and kindliness, characteristic of the playwrights.

Galli-Bibiena family. Members of this Italian family of artists include: Ferdinando, 1657-1743; Francesco, 1659-1739; Giovanni Maria, 1625-1665; Guiseppe, 1696-1756.

See also *Teatro Ducale Nuovo, Teatro Filharmonico.*

Galliari, Bernardino (1707-94). Italian scenic designer. Galliari, his brother Fabrizio, and his two nephews, Giovanni and Guiseppe Galliari, followed the Bibienas in their rich baroque architectural style of scenic design which dominated the Italian and European stage for over a century.

Gallo, Fortune (1878-   ). American impresario. Born at Torremaggiore, Italy; came to America in 1895. Formerly the owner and manager of various opera companies. President and treasurer of San Carlo Grand Opera Company, Jones Beach Summer Operetta and Randall's Municipal Stadium Summer Opera, Fortune Gallo Musical Comedy, and others. With Arthur M. Oberfelder head of The Legitimate Theatre Corporation which sponsored national tours of *What A Life, Hedda Gabler, Golden Boy, On Borrowed Time* and *The Master Builder* during the season of 1939-40.

Galsworthy, John (1867-1933). British novelist, dramatist. Notable for his realistic portrayals of the English upper middle class and for his championship of the working man.

Born at Coombe in Surrey, he came of an old and well-to-do family and was sent to Harrow and to Oxford. He studied for the Bar, but never practised. He traveled a great deal and on one of his journeys met a young Polish merchant officer, now the famous Joseph Conrad, who gave him a manuscript which was later published as *Almayer's Folly*. Conrad always acknowledged this early encouragement.

Galsworthy was forty years old before he gained recognition. His first works were published under the pseudonym of John Sinjohn. These were *From the Four Winds, Jocelyn, Villa Rubein* (1900) and *A Man of Devon*, 1901. His great year came in 1906 when the first of the Forsyte novels *The Man of Property* was published and his play *The Silver Box* was produced.

Other plays followed: *Strife*, 1909; *Justice*, 1910; *The Pigeon*, 1912; *The Island Pharisees, The Mob*, 1914; *The Skin Game*, 1920; *Loyalties*, 1922; *Escape*, 1926; *The Roof*, 1930.

Galsworthy refused a knighthood but was awarded the Order of Merit in 1929.

Gammer Gurton's Needle. Attributed to William Stevenson (? -1575) (English). Farce-comedy. 5 acts. c. 1566.

The second extant English comedy. It is written in rhymed long doggerel. Long attributed to John Still (1543?-1605).

The story has to do with Gammer Gurton who loses her precious needle while mending Hodge's breeches. Diccon tells her that it has been stolen by her neighbor, Dame Chat, and ultimately the whole village is set by the ears. The needle is finally found sticking in Hodge's leg.

There is a modern version of the play by Colin Clements.

Gaol Gate, The. Lady Augusta Gregory (Irish). Drama. 1 act. 1906.

An Irish mother goes to inquire about the welfare of her son, and learns that he was hanged a few hours earlier.

Garbage Man, The. John Dos Passos (American). 3 acts. 1930.
This impressionistic story deals with funerals, bankruptcy, millionaires, press agents, elopement, love and reunions, etc. It was one of the typical Greenwich village experimental dramas of the period.

García Gutiérrez, Antonio (1813-1884). Spanish dramatist. Born in Chiclana, province of Cádiz. His best known work is *El Trovedor* (The Troubadour), 1826. It forms the basis of Verdi's opera *Il Trovatore*.

Garguille, Gaultier. Stock-character in French farce.

Garland, Robert (1895-   ). American dramatist and newspaperman. Born in Baltimore; dramatic editor, critic and columnist, *Baltimore Daily Post;* dramatic critic, *New York World-Telegram;* motion picture critic, *New York American;* public relations counsel New York Federal Theatre Project.
His plays include: *The Double Miracle; Importance of Being a Roughneck; Calling All Men* (with Leonard Sillman). Also the author of short stories and articles.

Garnett, Constance (1862-   ). British translator. The wife of Edward Garnett and mother of the author, David Garnett, has translated into English the novels, plays and other works of the chief 19th and 20th century Russian writers, including Dostoevsky, Tolstoi, Ostrovski, Gogol, Turgenev, and Chekhov.

Garnett, Edward (1868-1937). English author and dramatist. The son of Dr. Richard Garnett, English author, he married Constance Black, who under her married name published many translations of the great Russian novelists. Garnett was a well-known critic and edited *Letters from Conrad.* He was also associated with the publishing firm of Jonathan Cape. His plays include *The Breaking Point,* 1908 (refused a licence by the Lord Chamberlain) ; *The Feud; The Trial of Jeanne d'Arc.*

Garnier, Robert (1534-1590). French dramatist. Important in the history of the development of French classical tragedy. His works are eloquent but dull. However, his masterpieces were widely acclaimed in their day. Their inherent interest is slight, but they do show considerable poetic and dramatic technique. Having practiced at the Paris bar, he became one of the royal councillors for Le Maine.
His plays include: *Porcié,* 1573; *Cornélie,* 1573; *Antigone,* 1580; *Bradamante,* 1582; *Les Juives,* 1583.

Garrick, David (1717-1779). English actor. Foremost actor of his century. He was born at Hereford and made a debut as Harlequin in 1741, in a pantomime in Goodman's Fields Theatre. In 1742 he played Hamlet at Drury Lane with Peg Woffington. He was noted as a great interpreter of Shakespeare, his roles including King Lear, Hamlet, etc. He altered many plays for his own acting editions. For the most part he emasculated Shakespeare. For thirty years he was manager of the Drury Lane

Theatre. He was a great inventor of scenic effects and was the first person to introduce new lighting effects. His school of the theatre was essentially realistic and enlivened his auditors. The famous love story *David Garrick* is founded presumably on the facts of his life.

Garrick Club. Theatrical club (located at 13-15 Garrick Street, W.C. 2, London). Founded in 1831 at 35 King Street "for the purpose of bringing together the patrons of the drama and its professors, and also for offering literary men a rendezvous." The club houses an important collection of theatrical portraits in oil, as well as a considerable library.

Garrick Theatre, London (1830-1875). In Leman Street, Whitechapel. Wyman and Conquest were managers. House burnt and rebuilt 1845. Renamed the Royal Albert in 1873 or 1874 by J. B. Howe, whom it bankrupted. It was presumably destroyed in 1875.

Theatres of the same name were subsequently built in New York, Chicago and Philadelphia.

See also *Garrick Theatre, New York.*

Garrick Theatre, New York (1895-1932). Built 1890 as the Harrigan by Edward Harrigan, on 35th Street, east of Sixth Avenue. Reopened 1895 by Richard Mansfield as the Garrick with pretentious alterations, including elaborate basement lounges and a Pompeiian Room dispensing coffee, tea, ices—an innovation in New York. First offering, G. B. Shaw's *Arms and the Man,* Mansfield playing Bluntschli. The same year, typhoid and threat of bankruptcy forced Mansfield to relinquish the venture. Charles Frohman took over and introduced many famous plays there. In 1915, New York's first all-night moving picture house. Sold in 1916 for razing. But in 1917 Otto Kahn established Jacques Copeau's *Théâtre du Vieux-Colombier* in it. In 1919, birthplace of the New York Theatre Guild, which in 1925 moved to its new Guild Theatre. After this, Guild successes were occasionally transferred to the Garrick. Used by the Provincetown Players in 1929. Burned and torn down in 1932.

See also *Garrick Theatre, London.*

Gauntlet, A. Björnstjerne Björnson (Norwegian). Drama. 3 acts. 1883.

Well-defined example of the thesis play. The author attempts to prove that a woman has a right to demand of her fiancé the same sexual purity that he demands of her. It is a plea for the abolition of the so-called "double standard."

Sava breaks off her engagement to her betrothed upon learning of his previous love affairs and despite her parents' plea to alter her decision and avoid a scandal she remains adamant. Alf and his parents call on his former fiancée to talk things over. Sava slaps his face with her gauntlet. Alf's father plans to ruin Sava's father in business and drive him from the community in revenge for this insult, but his son prevents him from carrying out such a plan. The play ends with Alf begging for a sign from Sava before she goes that she will wait for him and perhaps some day realize his faithfulness. Hopefully Sava extends her hands to him in recognition of the happiness that once existed between them and still may be reborn.

Gautier, Théophile (1811-1872). French author and dramatic critic. Born at Tarbes, he gained admittance to Hugo's circle through his clever essays. He was a notable member of the romantic regiment which fought for Hugo in the "battle of Hernani," and soon gained further notoriety with two brilliant but licentious romances: *Albertus,* 1830, in verse; and *Mlle. de Maupin,* 1835, in prose. He was dramatic and art critic of *La Press.*

Gay, John (1685-1732). English poet, librettist. Born at Barnstaple, Devonshire, he began life as a silk mercer, but became a frequenter of literary doorsteps in London. He remained unknown until he gained the friendship of Pope, to whom he dedicated his *Rural Sports,* 1713. His first real success came with a pastoral *Shepherd's Week,* 1714, written at the suggestion of Pope. He wrote many unsuccessful comedies, burlesques and verse, but was finally saved from poverty and made well-to-do by *The Beggar's Opera,* 1728. This opera is said to have made Gay rich and Rich gay, since Rich was the producer of the work. *Polly,* a sequel, was published, in book form in 1729, but prohibited from the stage on account of its political references. Gay also wrote the libretto of Handel's opera *Acis and Galatea,* produced after his death in 1732.

Geddes, Norman Bel (1893-   ). American scene designer. His first production was *Nju* at Little Theatre, Los Angeles, 1916. First production he designed in New York was *Shanewis* for the Metropolitan Opera. For Max Reinhardt he designed *The Miracle* and *The Eternal Road.* Other productions include *Divine Comedy,* 1920; *The Rivals,* 1922; *The School for Scandal,* 1923; *Jeanne d'Arc, Arabesque* and the *Ziegfeld Follies,* 1925; *Lysistrata,* 1930; *Flying Colors,* 1932. Designed and produced *Hamlet,* 1931; *Dead End,* 1935; *Iron Men,* 1936; *Siege,* 1937.

He designed the settings for the films *Feet of Clay,* 1924, and *The Sorrows of Satan,* 1926; and he published a book on Dante's *Divine Comedy,* 1924. His futurama "Highways and Horizons" was one of the highlights of the New York World's Fair.

Geisha (Geisya). A favorite role as performed in Japanese drama by the *onnagata* (female impersonators); represents a beauty of the pleasure quarters and is more delicate in character than the *oiran,* even excelling that of the real life character in beauty of form and manners.

Gelatine. Color in stage lighting may be achieved by means of gelatine slides placed over the spotlight lens. A fair range of colors is available and is essential to any well-equipped theatre. These slides, however, fade quickly and care must be taken of them.

See *Lighting.*

Gelosi. A famous Italian troupe of the *commedia dell' arte.*

Gemier, Firmin (1866-1934). French actor, producer. Director of the Odéon and founder of the Shakespeare Society of France. Brought his own company to New York for a three weeks' engagement. He opened with a performance of *L'Homme qui Assassina,* November 10, 1924. He produced five more plays during this visit. According to Burns Mantle, Gemier introduced Eugene O'Neill to the French stage by way of *Anna Christie.* Founder of The Société Universelle du Théâtre in 1927.

Género chico. The name given to a short musical farce in Spanish drama.

Género ínfimo. The name given to a kind of vaudeville revue, in Spanish drama.

Gentleman Dancing-Master, The. William Wycherly (English). Comedy. 5 acts. 1673.
Hippolita, engaged to her cousin whom she dislikes, is discovered with her lover, Gerald, who pretends he is her dancing master. Hippolita's aunt sees through the trick, but her father is too conceited to admit he can be duped. Later, when a parson arrives, the lovers are married.

Gentleman Usher, The. George Chapman (English). Comedy. 1602.
The Duke Alphonso and his son, Vincentio, are both in love with Margaret. She loves the son, and when the father hears of this he banishes his son. Heartbroken, Margaret disfigures herself. The Duke then realizes his mistake, but Margaret refuses to marry the son because of her lost beauty. However, a doctor is able to cure her and all is happily resolved.

Gentle People, The. Irwin Shaw (American). Drama. 3 acts. 1939.
Two old friends, a Jew and a Greek, whose great pleasure is fishing, plan to buy a boat large enough to travel to the Gulf. Their hopes are jeopardized when they are threatened by a gangster in an extortion racket. Rather than lose their only pleasure in life, the two men lure the gangster into their boat, row out into Sheepshead Bay, and drown him. Their crime, however, is not discovered.

Georgette Lemeunier. Maurice Donnay (French). Comedy. 5 acts. 1898.
The wife of a successful inventor leaves her husband who has been unfaithful, but returns to rescue him from a mistress who is using the inventor to promote her own husband's business schemes.

Gershwin, George (1898-1938). American composer. Deems Taylor has called him "a link between the jazz camp and the intellectuals." Made his name as a composer of dance-music and jazz with tunes written for George White's *Scandals,* 1920 to 1924. His famous *Rhapsody in Blue* was written in 1924. He composed the music for *Lady Be Good,* 1924; *Stop Flirting* and *Tell Me More,* 1925; *Funny Face,* 1927; *Girl Crazy,* 1931; *Of Thee I Sing,* 1932; *Let 'em Eat Cake,* 1933; and *Porgy and Bess,* 1935. He died in Hollywood, of a brain tumor.

Gest, Morris (1861-   ). American producer. Born in Vilna, Russia. He is married to Renée Belasco, daughter of David Belasco, with whom he was occasionally associated in the theatre. He began his career in 1903 and in 1905 formed an association with F. Ray Comstock which lasted for twenty years. They were responsible for: *Chu-Chin-Chow; Aphrodite; The Rose of China; Very Good, Eddie; Afgar; Oh, Boy!* In 1924 he produced *The Miracle,* which had great success in New York and elsewhere in America. In 1922 he brought to America Nikita Balieff's *Chauve-Souris* for the first of many engagements. In 1923 and 1924, he managed the engagements of the Moscow Art Theatre in New York and on the road. In 1929 he imported the Freiburg Passion Players for an engagement at the New York Hippodrome. In 1936 he produced Hsiung's *Lady Precious Stream.*

Get the bird. To be jeered at and ridiculed; razzed.

Get the hook. A theatrical term meaning to be driven from the stage by hissing for a poor performance; coming from the literal use of a hook on a pole to remove performers on amateur nights in vaudeville houses, late 19th century.

Getting Married. George Bernard Shaw (English). Satirical comedy. 1911.
The original Haymarket program described this merely as "a conversation"; elsewhere Shaw calls it a "drama of ideas." But though lacking in dramatic action, as these appellations would indicate, it is a thoroughly amusing satire ridiculing the inconsistencies of the marriage system in England.
Alfred Bridgenorth, Bishop of Chelsea, who believes in always letting the devil speak for himself, thinks that the institution of marriage is a creation of Satan in its present form and that sooner or later there will be a strike against it. He warns the Prime Ministers, although he realizes that the strike will begin with the propertied classes and that the government will not dare interfere. The Prime Ministers agree about the imminence of a strike, but won't institute the reforms which might prevent it for fear of losing the next election. The Bishop, who has married off several daughters, thankfully prepares to give the only remaining one away before marriage is outlawed. But on her wedding day the bride receives a pamphlet in the mail and goes on strike herself. For in it she reads that one cannot divorce one's husband for having committed a murder. In vain the groom pleads that he has no intention of murdering anyone; the girl will not sign a marriage contract which countenances such barbarism. The contract must be revised. The Bishop's Chaplain is called in, and after lengthy consultation draws up a new contract which actually is no better than the old one, although they think they have allowed for all contingencies. Moral: marriage at best is a makeshift, but one cannot hope for perfection and so must get along with makeshifts for the time being.

Geza. *Nō* plays. A music box on the opposite side of the stage from the *tyobo* players. Inconspicuously placed, a number of specialized musicians operate it; these box men signal for the entrance and exit of actors and are responsible for the effects used in a play such as rain, thunder, bells, water, fire.

Gherardi, Evaristo (1670?-1700). Italian actor, dramatist. Author of *commedia dell' arte;* known especially as a collector of plays written by French authors for the *Commedia dell' Arte,* in France *Le Théâtre Italien.*

Ghetto, The. Herman Heijermans (Dutch). Drama. 4 acts. 1898.

A powerful picture of sordid life in the Jewish quarter of Amsterdam, Holland. It was with this play, his fifth, that Heijermans first won distinction as a dramatist.

Sachel, a merchant who is rich and blind, has as servant, Rosa, a Christian girl of good birth who is beloved by his son, Rafael, a musician. Sachel wishes to marry his son to Rebecca, daughter of Aaron, a brother merchant, for the dowry she will bring. Rafael, who abhors the spirit of avarice which dominates the ghetto, refuses to be a party to the bargain. His ideas have made him an object of suspicion and hatred and he is stoned and reviled by his fellow Jews. On the steps of the synagogue he halts and in bitter irony offers his soul at auction, and clasping Rosa in his arms, accepts her, with only her heart to offer, as the highest bidder. They are married civilly and in the final act Rosa is hounded by Aaron and Sachel with alternate curses and cajolings. She is persuaded that Rafael has deserted her, and so she throws herself into the river. Rafael returns and his father dares not tell the truth. Rosa, apparently drowned, is carried in. Standing over her Rafael denounces his father and his race. The play ends with Rosa coming to life and being borne by Rafael to a happier world.

Ghosal, Mrs. (1857-1932). Hindu author. The sister of Rabindranath Tagore, she wrote under the name of Srimati Svarnakumari Devi. By editing the *Bharati,* a Bengali magazine, she became the first woman editor in India. She wrote novels, plays, farces, short stories, poems, and children's books. Some English translations of her works are available.

Ghost (television). A second, and undesirable image in the television receiver, due to the reception of two or more signals over different routes from the transmitter. The time difference causes the ghost image to be slightly displaced from the position occupied by the brighter image.

Ghost of Yankee Doodle, The. Sidney Howard (American). Drama. 3 acts. 1938.

Another war has broken out. Sara Garrison and her family, all liberals, hold out for neutrality, although it spells financial bankruptcy for their factory. Sara is about to marry James Madison Clevenger, owner of a chain of newspapers, but breaks off the engagement when Clevenger's son, who is an aviator, is killed, and Clevenger uses his son's death as pro-war propaganda.

Ghost plays. Plays in which ghosts figure. Whether the ghosts actually appear to the audience, or only to the other characters, depends upon a producer's interpretation of many such plays. A multitude of devices are used for showing ghosts to the audience. The actor may simply reappear in person after his stage death; or he may be shown as transparent, or in the air, or piecemeal—either by means of trick lighting, screens, mirrors, or trap doors. Sometimes only a voice is heard, or a light shown to suggest the presence.

Shakespeare's *Hamlet, Julius Caesar,* and *Macbeth* have ghosts; his *King Richard III* has eleven in one scene. Flecker's *Hassan* has three ghosts.

Ghosts appear in costume in Balderston's *Berkeley Square.* All the characters but two in Sutton Vane's *Outward Bound* are ghosts. Two ghosts in Otway's *Venice Preserved* rise up and sink back wordless. A production of Dickens' *Christmas Carol* bathed Marley's ghost in a ghastly green light, and three others in rosy hues. Ghosts appear in the casts of *The Persians* of Aeschylus; *Death Takes A Holiday,* by Walter Ferris; *Sheppey,* by Somerset Maugham; *Supper for the Dead,* by Paul Green; Walter Hasenclever's *Beyond;* Belasco's *The Return of Peter Grimm; American Landscape,* by Elmer Rice; Irwin Shaw's *Bury the Dead;* and Thornton Wilder's *Our Town.* The weirdest ghost effect of modern times is thought to be in W. W. Jacobs' *The Monkey's Paw.* The most wholesale instance occurs in *Miracle at Verdun,* by Hans Chlumberg, in which millions of soldiers killed in the war arise and return to their homes, creating dramatic consternation until they go back to their graves.

Ghosts. Henrik Ibsen (Norwegian). Drama. 3 acts. 1881.

Mrs. Alving, widow of a dissolute, diseased captain, welcomes her son, Oswald, home from Paris with the hope that he will marry and take over the management of the estate. She finds, to her horror, that Oswald has inherited his father's disease and is facing insanity—that he is the ghost of his father. When Mrs. Alving sees his approaching insanity she gives him an overdose of a drug and lets him die.

Perhaps Ibsen's greatest play, *Ghosts* has the intensity and fatalism of a Greek drama. It is also the first play to deal with the modern understanding of heredity.

Ghost walks. Pay day for a theatre company.

Gibbs, Wolcott (1902-   ). American dramatic critic. Born in New York City. Worked for various Long Island newspapers before going to the *New Yorker* in 1925. Has been with that magazine in various capacities, now associate dramatic critic. Author of *Bird Life At The Pole,* 1927, and *Bed of Neuroses,* 1938. Contributor to magazines including the *New Yorker.*

Gielgud, John (1904-   ). English actor and producer. Born in London; first appearance on the stage at the Old Vic, November, 1921, as the Herald in *Henry the Fifth.* In 1923 played Felix in *The Insect Play;* June, 1923, the Aide-de-camp in *Robert E. Lee;* Charles Wykeham in *Charley's Aunt,* 1923; was with J. B. Fagan's company, 1924; played Romeo in 1924. His other plays include: *The Orphan, The Vortex, The Cherry Orchard, The Sea Gull, Gloriana,* 1925; *The Tempest, The Three Sisters, Katerina, The Constant Nymph,* 1926; *The Great God Brown,* 1927; first appearance in New York in *The Patriot,* 1928; *Ghosts, Holding Out the Apple, The Skull, Fortunato,* 1928; *Red Rust; The Lady with a Lamp; Red Sun-*

day; The Merchant of Venice; The Imaginary Invalid; Julius Caesar; The Importance of Being Earnest; Henry IV (Part I) ; *Antony and Cleopatra; Twelfth Night,* 1930; *Arms and the Man, The Good Companions,* 1931; *Musical Chairs, Richard of Bordeaux, Strange Orchestra,* 1932; *Sheppey, Spring, 1600,* 1934; produced *Queen of Scots,* 1934. In 1934 he again played *Hamlet,* also producing the play, which then achieved the second longest run on record for this play; brought *Hamlet* to New York in 1936; *He Was Born Gay; Romeo and Juliet; The Three Sisters,* 1937; *The School for Scandal; The Merchant of Venice; Dear Octopus,* 1938; *Hamlet* at Elsinore; *The Importance of Being Earnest* (the first play to be reopened after the closing of the theatres due to the Second World War), 1939. He is the subject of Rosamond Gilder's *John Gielgud's Hamlet,* 1937, to which he contributed a chapter on the staging of his productions of Hamlet. He is also the author of *Early Stages,* 1939.

Gift of the Wise Bees, The. Feodor Sologub (Russian). Drama. 3 acts. 1908.
The story of Laodamia, praying for the return from Hades of her husband Protesilaus. The author preaches no lesson of self-control as does Wordsworth in his poem dealing with this subject, but portrays instead the wrath of Laodamia's father that led him to fling into the fire a waxen image of her lord, whereat, as the wax melts, the life of the faithful Laodamia dwindles until she joins her husband in death.

Gilbert, Douglas. American dramatic critic, journalist. Born in Rochester, N. Y., educated at Columbia University. Entered journalism in 1918. Since 1929 he has been feature writer and for a season dramatic critic of the New York World Telegram.

Gilbert, Mrs. George Henry (1822-1904). American actress. Called the "grand old lady of the stage"; was a public favorite for fifty years; played under Daly's banner; made her American debut in Chicago in 1851 as a dancer and in 1857 as an actress. She was famous for her aristocratic dowager roles. Among her important parts were characters in *Dollars and Cents; Macbeth; She Stoops to Conquer; Caste; A Celebrated Case; Frou-Frou; David Copperfield; Granny; The School for Scandal.*

Gilbert, John Gibbs (1810-1889). American actor. He first appeared as Jaffier in *Venice Preserved* in 1828; acted for over sixty years and was identified throughout his career with the excellence of his portrayal of old men.

Gilbert, Sir William Schwenk (1836-1911). English dramatist, librettist. The son of a novelist, he was born in London. From 1857 to 1861, he was a civil servant, and in 1863 was called to the Bar. He began his career as a humorist by contributing to *Fun.* His first dramatic work was a Christmas burlesque in 1866. This was followed by half a dozen more burlesques, including a travesty of Tennyson's *The Princess,* and by three fairy plays, *The Palace of Truth,* 1870, *The Wicked World,* 1873, and *Broken Hearts,* 1875; a classical romance, *Pygmalion and Galatea,*

1871; and two farcical comedies, *Tom Cobb,* 1875, and *Engaged,* 1877. Gilbert also wrote plays of serious interest, among them *Dan'l Druce,* 1876; *Gretchen,* 1879; *Comedy and Tragedy,* 1884; and *Brantinghame Hall,* 1888. The unforgettable series of operas, in the production of which Gilbert was associated with Arthur Sullivan as music composer and Richard D'Oyly Carte as theatrical manager, started at the Royalty with *Trial by Jury,* 1875; and was continued at the Opera Comique, London, by *The Sorcerer,* 1877, *H.M.S. Pinafore,* 1878, *The Pirates of Penzance,* 1880, and *Patience,* 1881; and at the Savoy by *Iolanthe,* 1882, *Princess Ida,* 1884, *The Mikado,* 1885, *Ruddigore,* 1887, *The Yeoman of the Guard,* 1888, *The Gondoliers,* 1889, *Utopia Limited,* 1893, and *The Grand Duke,* 1896.

The wit and finish of his dialogue and lyrics, the urbanity of his satire, and the topsyturviness of his humor contributed to the success of the Savoy operas as much as the grace and charm of Sullivan's music. Revival after revival cannot dim their charm. For twenty years Gilbert and Sullivan worked in harmony. Then, after the production of *The Gondoliers,* a dispute arose between them—it is said, over a carpet which Gilbert considered too expensive for the theatre. Two more operas were produced, but about three years before Sullivan's death, 1900, the breach widened, and music for Gilbert's last libretto *Fallen Fairies* was written by Edward German. It was produced in 1909, and two years later Gilbert met a tragic death by drowning at Harrow, Middlesex, May 29, 1911.

Gilburne, Samuel. An actor named in the 1623 Folio list of performers in Shakespeare's plays. Nothing is known of his life or of roles played by him.

Gilder, Rosamond. American dramatic critic, author, editor. Born in New York City, the daughter of Richard Watson Gilder. Her first published work was the *Life and Letters of Richard Watson Gilder,* 1916. Editorial secretary of *National Theatre Conference,* 1933-36; director of The Playwrights Bureau of the *Federal Theatre Project,* 1935-36; since 1936 dramatic critic and associate editor of Theatre Arts. Among the most notable of her other books is *Enter The Actress,* 1931; *A Theatre Library,* 1932, to date the really outstanding short theatre bibliography; (with George Freedley) *Theatre Collections in Libraries and Museums,* 1936; *John Gielgud's Hamlet,* 1937.

See also *Theatre Arts; Theatre collections.*

Gillette, William (1855-1937). American actor, dramatist. Born in Hartford, he made his first stage appearance in 1875. On June 1, 1881, he appeared at Madison Square Theatre in the dual capacity of actor-dramatist in *The Professor.* After playing in Shakespeare and in light comedy, he brought out, in 1899, *Sherlock Holmes,* the play of which he was co-author and in which he constantly reappeared in revivals until 1932. *Clarice,* 1905, and *Too Much Johnson,* 1894, were two other plays, written and acted by himself and frequently revived. He was also the author of a version of *The Private Secretary, Esmeralda,* and *Secret Service.*

Gillmore, Frank (1867-   ). American actor. Made his debut on the stage at Maidstone in 1879 in pantomime, *Jack And The Beanstalk.* For three years he appeared in the company of his aunt, Sarah Thorne, at Margate. He made his first London appearance January 19, 1888, in *Fascination*. Among his other London appearances were: *Joseph's Sweetheart; Clarissa* and *Captain Swift.* He played first in America in St. Louis in *Settled Out of Court,* in 1892. His New York debut came February 16, 1893, in *The Better Part.* Among the long list of his plays are *Romeo and Juliet* with Sir Johnston Forbes-Robertson, *A Bachelor's Romance, The Gay Lord Quex, Becky Sharp, Tess of the D'Urbervilles, Mary of Magdala, Glorious Betsy, Vanity Fair, The Piper, Bella Donna.* He was first secretary and then in 1929 appointed president of *Actor's Equity Association.* In 1937 he became International President of the *Associated Actors and Artistes of America, Inc.* He has been prominent in promoting the affairs of The American Theatre Council and The American Section of The Société Universelle du Théâtre.

See also *Associated Actors and Artistes of America, Inc., Actors' Equity Association.*

Gioconda, La. Gabriele D'Annunzio (Italian). Tragedy. 4 acts. Printed 1898.
This play is typical of most of the author's work. It is a revelation of the artist at odds with a practical world. The problem is posed as to whether the artist is to be bound by the moral conventions, to submit himself to the laws which govern the rest of humanity, or whether he is to create a world for himself.

Lucio, a sculptor, attempts suicide because he has reached an impasse in his love for his wife, Silva, and his fascination for his model, Gioconda. His attempt is unsuccessful. Silva, confronting Gioconda in Lucio's studio, attempts to convince the girl that Lucio is through with her. Gioconda, in a rage, would smash Lucio's latest work, and Silva's hands are crushed when she tries to save it. The hands have to be amputated. Finally Lucio deserts Silva to live with Gioconda.

Giraldi, Giovanni Battista (1504-1573). Italian novelist, dramatist. Born in Ferrara, he was professor of natural philosophy there, 1525-37, and then professor of belles lettres. He also taught at Pavia. His writings include several tragedies on the Senecan model, but he is best remembered as the author of the *Hecatommithi,* a collection of novels or short stories which attained European fame. The plots of Shakespeare's *Measure for Measure* and *Othello* were drawn from this work.

Giraudoux, Jean (1882-   ). French novelist, dramatist. He was born in Bellac (Haut Vienne) and educated at the École Normale in Paris. A play of his called *Siegfried* was played by Eva Le Gallienne at the Civic Repertory Theatre in 1930. In 1937 *Amphitryon 38,* an adaptation by S. N. Behrman of Giraudoux's play, was produced by the Theatre Guild in New York. It duplicated the Paris success of the previous year.

Gish, Dorothy (1898-   ). American actress. Born in Massillon, Ohio, she made her first stage appearance in *East Lynne* in 1903. After 1912 she devoted her time to cinema work. Her best known films are: *An Unseen Enemy; Hearts of the World; The Orphans of the Storm; Nell Gwyn; Romola;* and *Madame Pompadour.* In 1928 she returned to the New York stage in *Young Love*. Since then she has been seen in *The Inspector General*, 1930; *Getting Married*, 1931; *The Streets of New York*, 1931; *The Pillars of Society*, 1931; *The Bride the Sun Shines On*, 1931; *Foreign Affairs*, 1932; *By Your Leave*, 1934; *Comedienne*, 1934; and *Brittle Heaven*, 1934. Her last play on Broadway was *Missouri Legend*, produced at the Empire Theatre, in 1938.

Gish, Lillian (1896-   ). American actress. Born in Springfield, Ohio; educated in private schools; first appeared on the stage in 1902 in *The Little Red Schoolhouse*. After taking a course in dancing she was engaged as one of the fairy dancers in Sarah Bernhardt's company and remained with Bernhardt for two years. In 1913 she played with Mary Pickford in *A Good Little Devil*. Her film career began in 1912. After many years in Hollywood she returned to the legitimate stage in 1930 as Helena in *Uncle Vanya*. Her plays include: *Camille; Nine Pine Street; The Joyous Season; Within the Gates; The Star-Wagon; Dear Octopus; Hamlet;* etc.

Her films include: *The Birth of a Nation; Broken Blossoms; The Orphans of the Storm; Way Down East; The White Sister.*

Glaspell, Susan (1882-   ). American dramatist, novelist. Born in Davenport, Iowa, she became a political reporter and short story writer. Among her plays are *Trifles*, 1916; *Suppressed Desires*, 1917; *Inheritors*, 1921; and *Alison's House*, with which she won the Pulitzer prize in 1930. Since 1933 she has withdrawn from the stage and has confined herself to writing novels and short stories.

Glass, Montague Marsden (1877-1933). Anglo-American dramatist. Born of Jewish parents at Manchester, England, he was taken to America when a child. Became famous as the author of *Potash and Perlmutter*, which was dramatized and produced in 1913. He also wrote *Abe and Mawruss*, 1915, and several plays with J. E. Goodman, including *Business Before Pleasure* and *It's Never too Late*.

Glass crash. Box filled with glass and used back stage during performances, to create the sound of breaking glass.

Glick, Carl (1889-   ). American author, dramatist. Born in Marshalltown, Iowa; was graduated from Northwestern University. Well-known for his contributions to the community theatre. He was Director of the Community Theatre at Waterloo, Iowa, the Little Theatre of San Antonio, Texas, the Little Theatre of York, Pennsylvania, The Players Club of Sarasota, Florida, and others. His plays include: *The Fourth Mrs. Phillips; Outclassed; Ten Days Later; It Isn't Done; The Devil's Host; The Immortal* (with Bernard Sobel), etc. In collaboration with Albert McCleery, he is the author of *Curtains Going Up*, a book about the community theatre.

Globe Theatre, The. The Elizabethan public theatre most closely associated with Shakespeare's career as playwright and actor. It was erected in 1599 on the

Bankside by a syndicate headed by Cuthbert and Richard Burbage. Shakespeare himself was one of the original shareholders in it. In plan it followed the general pattern of the 16th century public playhouse, with polygonal walls and no roof. Destroyed by fire in 1613 during a performance of Shakespeare's *King Henry VIII,* it was immediately rebuilt and stood until 1644. The Globe was the home of Shakespeare's company, the Lord Chamberlain's Men, and probably most of his plays after 1599 were first performed by them in this theatre.

Its structure: a round auditorium with a bare main floor (or "yard") and two galleries with rude seats, the stage jutting into the yard and separated from the spectators who crowded all about it by a railing along the rim; the platform equipped with trap-doors; at the rear of the stage a columned wall broken, as well as flanked, by doors. Above, the upper gallery continued over the stage and was used either for audience or for actors in an expansion of set.

Go on. To enter upon the stage.

Goat Song. Franz Werfel (German). Tragedy. 3 acts. Printed 1921.

In southern Serbia, there is a monster, half man, half goat, who escapes and becomes the symbol of a peasant uprising. Juvon, leader of the peasants, agrees to release the beast to the bride of a young nobleman. When the monster is finally killed, the bride confesses that she is carrying his child.

Gobo (television). A shield used in studio lighting to deflect glare from the camera lens.

Godfrey, Thomas, Jr. (1736-1763). American dramatist. The author of *The Prince of Parthia,* the first American tragedy and the first American play to be acted professionally. It was produced at the Southwark Theatre, Philadelphia, April 24, 1767.

God of Vengeance, The. Sholom Asch (Yiddish). Drama. 3 acts. 1918.

The tragedy of a brothel keeper who learns that his own daughter is a prostitute. It is deeply religious in conception; the God of vengeance is the God of the Old Testament, who believed in visiting the sins of the fathers upon the children. In spite of its Biblical inspiraton, the subject was considered not fit for innocent ears, and when the drama was given in New York in 1924 there was an attempt to ban it. The case was brought up before the Supreme Court of the State of New York with Rudolph Schildkraut and others connected with the production as co-defendants.

Gods of the Lightning. Maxwell Anderson and Harold Hickerson (American). Drama. 1928.

A drama based on the Sacco-Vanzetti case and crying out against the injustices wrought by the courts of law in the name of justice. Anderson's more successful *Winterset* was later to treat the same theme more competently.

Macready and Capraro are arrested for killing a payroll messenger. Macready is a labor organizer who has called a strike in a small town; Capraro a peaceful and passive individual, but with anarchistic leanings. On the basis of these two facts the men's trial is framed, witnesses bribed to commit perjury, and they are condemned to death. As they go to die their companions sadly read the bulletins confirming the execution.

Gods of The Mountain, The. Lord Dunsany (Irish). Drama. 3 acts. Printed 1911.

A group of beggars exploit the public by pretending to be gods. Fate punishes the beggars, however, by turning them into the very idols they have represented.

Goethe, Johann Wolfgang von (1749-1832). German poet, dramatist. What Shakespeare is to England, Goethe is to Germany. Credited with being the greatest poet in Teutonic literature, and leader of the Storm and Stress school of writers. His approach to life was tempered with a practical wisdom and colored with poetic imagination. He paralleled the classical ideal not only in mind but in body; his life itself displayed a harmony which to Carlyle seemed the very embodiment of all that was finest in the spirit of man. There was for him no mental death at sixty or seventy. Scientist, art critic, philosopher, soldier, financier, statesman and poet, Goethe may claim to rival Leonardo da Vinci in his splendor. His great achievements, however, constituted the sign rather than the substance of his character, and his greatest memorial will for ever be the three words of Napoleon, *"Voilà un homme."*

He was born at Frankfort-on-Main, of good family, received a liberal education at the hands of tutors, and studied law at the University of Leipzig and subsequently at Strasbourg.

After writing a number of poems while in Leipzig, and later while a lawyer in Frankfort, he went to Italy. In the course of the years in Italy, 1786-88, he wrote the dramas *Iphigenie auf Tauris,* 1787; *Egmont,* 1788; *Torquato Tasso,* 1790. Returning to Germany, he became friends with Schiller and began to write novels.

The last period of his life was comparatively uneventful, although he did a great deal of writing. His principal works were *Faust,* 1808; *Die Wahlverwandtschaften,* 1809; *Der Westostliche Divan; Wilhelm Meisters Wanderjahre,* 1821 (a continuation of an earlier novel). In 1811 he commenced the publication of his autobiography, *Aus meinen Leben; Dichtung und Wahrheit,* which, however, was not carried beyond the year 1775, although other works such as *Die Italienische Reise,* 1816, may be regarded as a continuation. In the very last years of his life he added finishing touches to the second part of Faust, 1832.

His contribution to dramatic theory is best found in his various *Gespraeche* (conversations).

Goetz Von Berlichingen. Johann Wolfgang von Goethe (German). Historical drama. 1773.

This is important in that it is Goethe's first major dramatic opus, the first of the Shakespearian type of drama to be written by a German, and the first example of the commonly called Sturm und Drang (Storm and Stress) school of German playwriting.

An autobiography of his hero and title character published forty years previously was the historical source of Goethe's play. Goetz is not depicted, as he had generally been considered, as a rascally robber baron of the Middle Ages, but as an idealist, humanitarian and defender of liberty. The poet-dramatist creates most of his characters and situations, as did the Bard in England, without undue regard for historical accuracy: thus we have such original personages as the vacillating Weisslinger and the two women, gentle Maria and heartless Adelheid.

Gogol, Nikolai Vassilievitch (1809-1852). Russian novelist and dramatist.

Considered one of the greatest Russian writers of comedy and the novel. Born at Sorochintsky, Poltava. In his boyhood he attempted writing but his first published work, an idyll which appeared pseudonymously in 1829 was unsuccessful. He entered the Russian civil service, later the subject of his keenest satire, and in 1831 published *Evenings at a Farmhouse near Dikanka,* a collection of stories set in Little Russia. It foreshadowed the type of humorous description of Russian provincial life of which Gogol was to become the greatest exponent. *Taras Bulba,* a Cossack romance, followed in 1834. It was this work which, recast in 1842, was the foundation of the Russian novel. It was widely translated. Two years later Gogol produced his dramatic masterpiece, *The Inspector General.* This brilliant satire did for Russia what the episode of the burgomaster of *Kopenick* did for the German bureaucracy.

The works of his latter years show a sad decline in power. His melancholy became more pronounced, and he developed a religious mania in which he was persuaded that his writings were sinful, and so burned his remaining manuscripts.

Going clean. All tickets for a performance being sold out.

Going up. Approaching the rear of the stage, or that part farthest from the audience; to go upstage.

Golden, John (1874-   ). American dramatist and producer. Originally an actor he later turned author and wrote many plays either alone or in collaboration, including several musical comedies for which he wrote the music. He has produced many notable plays including *The First Year, Lightnin', Seventh Heaven, Let Us Be Gay, As Husbands Go, The Bishop Misbehaves.*

Golden Boy. Clifford Odets (American). Drama. 3 acts. 1938.

Joe Bonaparte, born to play the violin, gives it up to become a prizefighter, partly because of Lorna, whom he loves, and partly because of a drive for money and power. The renunciation is too great, however; and after Joe has killed his opponent in the ring, he and Lorna go for a wild drive in the country, and finally crash.

Goldoni, Carlo (1707-1793). Italian dramatist. Born in Venice, he was the son of a physician who later moved to Perugia, where he abandoned his young son to his own devices. There Carlo joined a company of actors and returned to Venice, where he studied law. Expelled for a satire on Pavian nobility, he returned to Venice, where he produced his first plays, a number of unsuccessful tragedies. He then turned to comedy and replaced the antiquated buffooneries that disgraced the Italian stage with vivid plays reflecting Venetian life in all its aspects. He wrote in the *commedia dell' arte* tradition even though he opposed the pure *mime* with the literary comedy. The fertility of his invention was amazing. He produced scores of brilliant comedies, writing sixteen in one year alone. His plays, in all, total more than 150. The dubious morality of many of his comedies offended the purists, however, and a dispute with Count Gozzi, his rival, led him to leave Italy for Paris in 1761. There he enjoyed equal popularity and received a pension from Louis XVI but suffered extreme privation during the Revolution. Among his best comedies are: *La Donna di Garbo; Pamela Nubile; I Rusteghi; Gli Innamorati, L'Adulatore.* His contribution to dramatic theory is best found in his many prefaces, but especially in his *Teatro Comico* and his Mémoires.

Goldsmith, Oliver (1728-1774). Irish author, dramatist. The son of a poor Protestant curate of County Longford, he spent the greater part of his boyhood in the little village of Lissoy in West Meath. Attended the village schools but neither there nor at Trinity College, Dublin, did he give any promise of future greatness. In fact, while at Dublin, he was consistently at the bottom of the examination lists but finally received his degree in 1749. Through relatives he was sent to Edinburgh to study medicine but left there with no more knowledge than he had obtained at Dublin, and for two years wandered about the Continent, playing his flute for a room or board at some country cottage.

He returned to England in 1756 and for a time was a bookseller's hack. This he gave up to teach and act, but he was a success at neither. In 1761 Goldsmith made the acquaintance of Dr. Johnson and was admitted to the literary circle which included Garrick, Sir Joshua Reynolds and Burke, and he was one of the nine members of the Club. In 1764, *The Traveller* was published and his fame was established. This poem was followed by *The Vicar of Wakefield* in 1766, and *The Deserted Village* in 1770; then by two comedies, *The Good-Natur'd Man,* 1768, and the celebrated *She Stoops to Conquer,* 1774. Notwithstanding the sums which these works brought him and the wealth he obtained from booksellers for hack compilations which he continued to produce, he left debts amounting to two thousand pounds. He was a man of infinite good humor and was both loved and despised by his friends. Garrick, his severest critic, said of him, "Noll wrote like an angel and talked like poor Poll." Goldsmith was a rebel against the prevalent sentimentalism of the age, and his works reflected the idealism which was beginning to be manifested in a new realistic era. Although he considered strict realism impossible, he saw the world in essentially realistic terms.

His play *She Stoops to Conquer* clearly illustrates this idealism, while its humor is warm, though subdued. His contribution to dramatic theory is best found in his *Essay on the Theatre.*

Goncourt, de. Edmond Louis Antoine Huot and Jules Alfred Huot (1822-1896; and 1830-1870 respectively). French novelists, essayists, dramatists. Known familiarly as the brothers de Goncourt, they are among the most famous collaborators in French literature. They belonged to a Lorraine family; Edmond was born at Nancy, and Jules in Paris. They were chiefly interested in French and Japanese art of the 18th century, and their first works were historical. Later they wrote a number of novels and collaborated on the play *Henriette Marechal,* 1865. After the death of Jules, Edmond continued to write alone, publishing monographs on art and writing a few novels as well as *A bas le progrès,* 1893. Edmond left his estate to form the *Academie des Goncourts* to help struggling authors.

Gondoliers, The. W. S. Gilbert and Arthur Sullivan (English). Operetta. 2 acts. 1889.

One of the most finished of the Gilbert and Sullivan libretti. The brilliance and wittiness of its dialogue and the tunefulness of its music make it a favorite with every self-respecting Gilbert and Sullivan repertory company; and "The Duke of Plaza-Toro," "Take a Pair of Sparkling Eyes," etc., are among the best known of the composer's songs.

The rather complicated plot hinges on the marriage in infancy of the daughter of the impoverished Duke of Plaza-Toro to the son of the King of Barataria. The baby boy was put in the care of a Spanish nurse, then later transported by the Grand Inquisitor to Venice, where he was lodged with a gondolier. The King of Barataria being dead, the Duke and his train arrive in Venice to find their daughter's husband and claim the throne. There is some confusion, since the gondolier foster-parent of the princeling long ago lost track of which child in the house was his and which the stranger. Moreover, both boys, now grown to manhood, are married to native girls, making one of them an unintentional bigamist. While waiting for the matter to be clarified the two gondoliers go to Spain and rule jointly in exceedingly democratic fashion, making every cook a Lord High Cook and every scullery maid head of her own department. The Spanish nurse who originally cared for the prince is finally found, and confesses that she kept the royal baby and sent her own son to Italy. Both gondoliers are therefore commoners and free to retain their brides. And by a coincidence, the real prince is the musician whom the Duke's daughter loved and wanted to marry all along.

Gonzaga, Pietro (1751-1831). Italian architect and scene designer. Studied under Canaletto; his designs were strongly architectural in quality, being drops of an open landscape with a towered city on a hill in the background. Many of his designs are to be found in the *Museo Teatrale alla Scala* in Milan.

Good Hope, The. Herman Heijermans (Dutch). Naturalistic play. 4 acts. 1900.

Probably the best play written by any modern Dutch dramatist. A virile revolutionary document setting forth the doctrine of social freedom.

The play presents a two-fold theme: That the sea is victor in man's struggle to snatch a living from it, and that man is cruel to man in the eternal struggle for gold.

The story deals with the fisherfolk in a town in Holland, the tragedies which come to them in gaining a living from the sea, and their great exploitation by the greedy shipowners. Because of its powerful exposé of conditions, the play was an important factor in bringing about the passage of new maritime laws in Holland in 1910. Clemens Bos is a hypocritical shipowner whose cupidity wrecks a whole family, leaving only the mother and niece who was betrothed to one of the drowned sons, in an agony of bereavement.

Goodman, Mr. (fl. 18th century). American actor. Said by some authorities to have been the first native born actor to appear on the American stage. Others claim John Martin as the first. Goodman appeared with the Douglas Company at the Southwark Theatre, Philadelphia, in 1768.

Goodman, Jules Eckert (1876-   ), American dramatist. A journalist; wrote his first play in 1906. His chief work has been done in collaboration with Montague Glass in the plays in which Potash and Perlmutter figure, such as *Partners Again, Business before Pleasure,* and *His Honor, Abe Potash.* His other plays are mainly adaptations and include *The Man Who Came Back, Treasure Island,* and *Simon Called Peter.* He collaborated with his son, Eckert Goodman, on *Many Mansions,* 1937.

Good Natured Man, The. Oliver Goldsmith (English). Comedy. 5 acts. 1768. Young Honeywood is too bashful to tell Miss Richland of his love, and to press his suit, until after his uncle has him arrested for debt, to "teach him a lesson." Honeywood is finally released from prison, however, and reunited with Miss Richland.

Good theatre. Dramatic term; applied to a piece of business or play which clicks, or communicates easily and surely with an audience. Examples of usage: "Blank's death scene is good theatre"; "Fritz Leiber's candle-snuffing during Hamlet's soliloquy is good theatre."

Goose Hangs High, The. Lewis Beach (American). 3 acts. 1924. When the Ingals family faces a financial crisis, the daughter and two sons rebel at losing the things they have always taken for granted. Grandmother Ingals brings them around.

Gorboduc, or Ferrex and Porrex. Thomas Norton and Thomas Sackville (English). Tragedy. 5 acts. 1561. Two princes, Ferrex and Porrex, quarrel over the division of their father's kingdom. Ferrex is killed, and Porrex is later murdered by his mother to revenge the death of Ferrex. Later, the Duke of Albany tries to seize the kingdom and civil war breaks out.

Gordon, Max (1892-   ). American producer. Born in New York City; was first active in vaudeville; formed a partnership with Albert Lewis and later Sam Harris, with whom he produced *The Family Upstairs, The Jazz Singer* and *Easy Come, Easy Go.* Alone he produced *Three's A Crowd,* 1930; *The Band Wagon, The Cat and the Fiddle,* 1931; *Flying Colors,* 1932; *Design for Living, Her Master's Voice, Roberta,* 1933; *The Shining Hour, Dodsworth, The Great Waltz, Spring*

Song, The Farmer Takes A Wife, 1934; *Jubilee, Pride and Prejudice,* 1935; *Ethan Frome, The Women, St. Helena,* 1936; *Othello,* 1937; *Sing Out the News,* 1938 (with Moss Hart and George Kaufman); *Missouri Legend,* 1938 (with Guthrie McClintic); *The American Way,* 1939. He is also a film producer and since March, 1939, has been general production director of television for the National Broadcasting Company.

Gordon, Ruth. American actress (1896-). Born in Wollaston, Mass., she made her first stage appearance in 1915 as Nibs in *Peter Pan.* In 1918 she returned to New York as Lola Pratt in *Seventeen.* Since then she has appeared in many outstanding plays, including *Clarence, Saturday's Children, Serena Blandish, Hotel Universe, Three Cornered Moon* and *The Country Wife.* She is considered one of America's outstanding actresses.

Gordon, Will (1898-). American dramatic editor. Born in New York City; attended the University of California; at one time was an engineer for the United States Government. Became a dramatic editor for *The New York Clipper* and *Zit's Weekly.* Was press agent for A. H. Woods and several night clubs and is at present dramatic editor for the *Morning Telegraph,* New York.

Gorky, Maxim (Alexei Maximovitch Pyeshkov) (1868-1936). Russian author, dramatist. One of the greatest exponents of the Russian naturalist school of literature. Born at Nizhni-Novgorod. His father, a dyer, left him an orphan to make his own way from the age of nine. He served as many masters as Gil Blas, working in a bootshop, helping a surveyor, acting as cook on a river steamer, as peddler and laborer and wandering with tramps. Having educated himself by reading, Gorky secured a position as secretary to a lawyer at Nizhni, met the novelist Korolenko, and by him was inspired to write short stories. From 1892 to 1900 he published four volumes of tales which attracted the attention, not only of his own countrymen, but also of English, French and German translators. For the stage, Gorky wrote fourteen plays, only one of which stands on the level of his best work in fiction. This is the chaotic yet striking drama *The Lower Depths,* 1903, everywhere recognized as one of the finest examples of dramatic naturalism.

Other plays include: *The Smug Citizen,* 1900; *A Country House,* 1903; *Children of the Sun,* 1904; *Vassa Zheleznova,* 1904; *Summer Folk,* 1905; *The Barbarians,* 1906; *The Enemies,* 1906; *The Last,* 1908; *Odd People,* 1910; *The Zykovs,* 1913; *Children,* 1913; *The Judge* (*The Old Man*), 1915; *Cain and Artema,* 1921; *The Counterfeit Coin,* 1926; *Yegor Bulitchev and Others,* 1932; *Dostygayev and Others,* 1935.

Gosse, Sir Edmund William (1849-1928). English author. Equally distinguished as poet, critic, translator and biographer. His father was Philip Henry Gosse, a naturalist and zoologist, and his mother was a Hebrew and Greek scholar. Edmund Gosse is important dramatically as the translator of Scandinavian writers, including Ibsen and Björnson, and for his series of biographies, now standard, of Congreve, Donne, Jeremy Taylor, Gray (the poet), Ibsen and Swinburne.

Gosson, Stephen (1554-1624). English dramatist. Born probably at Canterbury, he went to London, where he became an actor and playwright, and gained a high reputation for his pastoral verse, none of which survives. In 1579 he published *The Schoole of Abuse,* an attack on the immorality of the stage, which, like its sequel, *An Apologie of the Schoole of Abuse,* 1579, was dedicated, without permission, to Sir Philip Sidney. The latter took up the challenge in his famous *Apologie for Poetrie,* 1581. Gosson was rector of St. Botolph's, Bishopgate, from 1600 until his death.

Got, François Jules Edmond (1822-1901). French actor. He won prizes for his work in both comedy and tragedy. Made his debut at the Comédie-Française and remained a member for half a century. Exponent of the classical school of acting and author of the libretto for *François Villon* and *L'Ésclave.*

Gottlieb, Christian and Stephanie. Austrian actors. Famous theatrical brothers of 18th century Vienna. Christian Gottlieb was a tragedian and was the principal actor of this new era of dramatic art in Vienna; his acting style was bombastic, realistic and pompous. Stephanie Gottlieb was a leading comedian; a monotonous actor but pleasant in manner; popular as a dramatist, his military plays were played all over Germany.

Gottsched, Johann Christoph (1700-1766). German critic. Born near Koenigsberg, he went to Leipzig in 1723, where, as professor of poetry and metaphysics, he remained for the rest of his life. As a critic he was the founder of the pseudo-classical school of imitators of the French which dominated German literature until the romantic revival. In his *Versuch einer Kritischen Dichtkunst fuer die Deutschen,* 1730, he introduced into Germany the artificial regulations laid down for poetry and drama by Boileau. From 1740 to his death he engaged in a famous controversy with J. J. Bodmer of Zurich. The battle between Leipzig and Zurich—between the classicists and those who wished to abolish literary rules—ended in victory for the latter.

Gottsched was the first organizer of the German theatre. He also made an alliance with the Neubers, who were the most prominent actors in Leipzig in 1727. He was the author of *The Reasonable Censors,* a critique which was the first theatrical review in Germany, 1724.

Goughe, Robert (?-1625). English actor. An actor in Shakespeare's company after 1603, when the group was known as the King's Men. He is listed among the performers in the 1623 Folio but nothing is known of his roles.

Goulding, Edmund (1892-). English dramatist, motion picture director. A native of London, he was first an actor, but abandoned the stage for writing about 1915, and later went to Hollywood as a film director. His writings include the play *Dancing Mothers,* 1924, and *Fury,* a novel, and the scenarios for many American films. As a director he has been responsible for *Grand Hotel* and *Blondie of the Follies.*

Gozzi, Count Carlo (1720-1806). Italian dramatist. A native of Venice, he made a reputation with his satirical and farcical plays and fairy pieces in the Venetian patois. They were written to ridicule his playwright rivals, Carlo Goldoni and others, and their success contributed to driving Goldoni from Venice. *Re Turandote,* the best known of these, was the basis of an opera by Puccini. Vakhtangov in 1922 at his theatre in Moscow, did a splendid revival of this piece. The Provincetown Players in New York in 1926 were considerably less successful in an English translation of the Russian version. It was Gozzi who undertook to discover the number of plot types possible in the drama, which he determined was thirty-six; the body of these is now commonly known as *The Thirty-six Dramatic Situations.*

Gracioso. Freely translated "clown," an evolution of the *bobo* of Encina and the *simple* of Rueda. He is frequently the confidant of his master and the means through which his master works out his plans.

Graham, Harry Joscelyn Clive (1874-1936). English author. Born in London, he entered the army, serving in South Africa and in the First World War. He began his literary career with the publication of *Ruthless Rhymes for Heartless Homes,* 1899, and continued with much humorous verse, several novels, lyrics and books for numerous musical comedies.

He is part author of the plays *A Southern Maid, Katja the Dancer* and *By Candle-Light.* He also adapted *White Horse Inn, The Land of Smiles* and *Casanova* for the English stage.

Grand Guignol (1897-). French theatre in Montmartre, Paris, founded in 1897; headed by Oscar Metenier, its programs consist of one-act plays, farce alternating with terrifying horror pieces. The blood-curdlers which have made the reputation of the theatre, and are its distinction, have given rise to the expression, "the Grand Guignol style."

The repertory has included *Au Rat Mort, Cabinet No. 6, Le Crime de la Rue Morgue, Sur le Banc, Au Coin Joli.* In 1923, several members of the Parisian Company, appearing as the Grand Guignol Players, offered ten weeks of hair-raisers in New York City.

See also *Grand Guignol Players.*

Grand Guignol Players. A French theatrical company which appeared in New York in October, 1923. Some of the plays offered were: *A Night in a Den; The Short Circuit; On the Bench; At Dead Rat-Room No. 6;* and many others. During one week Nazimova played with them. Grand Guignol players included: Robert Keller; Maurice Henriet; Marcel des Mazes; Simone Hermann; Paul Bernier; Louis Defresne. The run continued ten weeks.

See also *Grand Guignol.*

Grand Hotel. Vicki Baum (American). Drama. 3 acts. 1927.

The play covers thirty-six hours in the lives of guests at Grand Hotel. Grusinskaia, an aging dancer, finds new life in her love for Baron Von Gaigern. When she leaves the hotel the following morning she does not yet know he has been killed.

Flaemmchen, a stenographer, escapes from Preysing, a manufacturer, and goes to Paris with Kringelein, a provincial clerk, dying of heart trouble and ready to spend his savings to enjoy life while he may.

As the curtain falls new guests are registering at Grand Hotel, and life goes on.

Granville-Barker, Harley (1877-   ). English producer, dramatist, actor. Born in London, he was at first an actor, making his stage debut in 1891. He toured with Ben Greet's company and was for a time associated as actor and producer with the Stage Society. In 1904 he entered with J. E. Vedrenne on the management of the Court and later the Savoy theatres. The Barker-Vedrenne management marked a new epoch on the English stage, since under its auspices new methods of presentation, scenery and lighting were tried out, and most of the plays of Shaw and a number of Ibsen's appeared under its aegis.

Granville-Barker's own plays are: *The Voysey Inheritance,* 1905; *Waste,* 1907; *The Madras House,* 1910; *The Weather Hen* (with Berte Thomas); *Prunella* (with Laurence Housman).

He made a number of successful adaptations from the French and German for the English stage. These include *Dr. Knock* and *Anatol.* His adaptations from the Spanish of Martinez-Sierra, undertaken in collaboration with his second wife, Helen (*née* Huntington Gates), include *The Kingdom of God, The Lady from Alfaqueque,* and *A Hundred Years Old.*

In collaboration with William Archer, he also wrote *Scheme and Estimates for a National Theatre,* 1907. His other works include *The Exemplary Theatre,* 1922, and *Prefaces to Shakespeare,* 1927 and 1930.

Grease paint. A composition of oil, spermaceti and wax used in theatrical make-up. It is available in all shades from white to black.

See *Make-up.*

Great Adventure, The. Arnold Bennett (English). Drama. 3 acts. 1913.

Based on Bennett's novel, *Buried Alive.* It is an impossible fantasy, partly satirical. partly farcical.

Ilam Carve, famous artist, allows himself to be thought dead. His valet, Albert Shawn, is buried with full honors in Westminster Abbey in his name, and the artist takes lodgings in Putney and leads a tranquil existence with Janet Cannot. Unfortunately he meets an old acquaintance, the Bond Street art expert Ebag. Ebag recognizes him as Carve, and Westminster Abbey is on the point of being disgraced. Just in time Lord Leonard Alcar remedies the situation. Ebag is reconciled with the American collector Texel, and promises to be silent about the fraud. And Carve's past disagreements with his cousin are smoothed over by the diplomatic lord.

Great Divide, The. William Vaughn Moody (American). Drama. 4 acts. 1906.

Ruth Jordon marries a westerner, Ghent, who saves her from desperadoes. She grows tired of western life, however, and finally returns to her native New England. Later, Ghent follows, and after a child is born they are reconciled. Ruth begs Ghent to teach her his way of life. The native American drama gained importance with this play.

Great Galeoto, The. José Echegaray (Spanish). Drama. 3 acts. 1881.

A husband, listening to the false gossip of neighbors, accuses his wife of taking a lover. The wife, who has been innocent up to this time, decides to live up to the accusation, and seeks out the man whom her husband and the good people of the village have named as her lover.

Great God Brown, The. Eugene O'Neill (American). Drama. 1925.

An experimental play in which the various characters wear masks which represent the faces they present to the world. It is only when they meet people who understand them or when they are soliloquizing that their true faces are presented.

Greeks Had a Word For It, The. Zoe Akins (American). Comedy. 3 acts. 1930.

The play concerns three former Follies beauties, Schatz, Jean and Polaire, veritably three musketeers of the evening, who make a pact of "all for one and one for all" and no poaching on staked out territory. Then Dey Emery, attractive and a millionaire's son besides, arrives on the scene, and both Polaire and Jean gaze on him covetously and almost forget their vow of friendship. When it becomes clear that he prefers Polaire, however, Jean consoles herself by promising to marry his father and become respectable. But after a few drinks, preceding the ceremony, her pals seem dearer than ever, so she deserts her aged groom at the altar and flies off to Paris with her friends to join a party of aviators.

Green, Paul (1894-   ). American dramatist. Born at Lillington, North Carolina. He was educated at the University of North Carolina and is associated with Prof. Frederick Koch in the Carolina Playmakers and the Drama Department there.

He is author of the following plays: *The No 'Count Boy,* 1924; *Fixin's* (with Erma Green), 1924; *In Abraham's Bosom,* 1926 (awarded the Pulitzer Prize, 1927); *The Field God,* 1927; *The Last of the Lowries,* 1927; *The House of Connelly,* 1931; *Roll, Sweet Chariot,* 1934; *Johnny Johnson,* 1936; *The Lost Colony,* 1937. He has written also stories, novels and other plays.

Green Bay Tree, The. Mordaunt Shairp (English). Drama. 3 acts. 1932.

The story is that of a middle-aged man, Mr. Dulcimer, rich, brilliant, skillful and utterly selfish, and the young Julian, whom he adopted at the age of eight. Since that time, the two have shared a life of exquisite luxury. When Julian falls in love with a very clear-headed young woman, Mr. Dulcimer, jealously enraged, cuts off Julian's allowance. The young man attempts to break away from the luxury to which he has become accustomed. Julian's father kills Dulcimer but his hold extends even after death and the young man returns to live as Dulcimer did.

Green Cockatoo, The. Arthur Schnitzler (Austrian). Drama. 1 act. 1899.

It is the eve of the French Revolution, and a group of French aristocrats are whiling away the time in a Paris café. A player bursts in and, in order to thrill the idlers, announces that he has killed a certain duke for stealing his bride. The spectators approve his make-believe deed as highly laudable. Then, to his consternation, the comedian finds out that his jest is true and that he has really beeen wronged by the duke. The latter enters, and the man he has wronged leaps on him, dagger in hand, and makes real the second performance of the drama he has simulated. As the noble-man lies on the floor, the mob of patriots return from storming the Bastille and hail the player as their champion and the enemy of the aristocracy.

Green Grow the Lilacs. Lynn Riggs (American). Comedy. 1930.

The setting is the prairie country, then Indian territory, which shortly afterward was admitted to the Union as the state of Oklahoma. The hero is Curly McLain, a sweet-swinging cowboy and an A-1 bull-dogger and bronc-buster. Laurey Williams, eighteen, pretty and spoiled, is superficially unimpressed by Curly, though she is really more interested than she lets on. She accepts the invitation of sinister Jeeter Fry, hired hand on the Williams place, to escort her to the party which is to take place that evening. Curly, vexed, pays Jeeter a visit in the barn and questions him about his past. Suspicious, he even hints Jeeter may be a murderer. In a rage Fry fires at him; the shot goes wild. Curly proves his own superior markmanship by shooting straight through a knothole in the wall. The commotion and the sound of firing brings Laurey anxiously running to the barn; she begins to realize how dangerous Jeeter can be. That evening, when he grows angry because he isn't seeing enough of her, she becomes afraid, and asks Curly to protect her. He comforts her with kisses; a few minutes later they are stealing away to be married. The crowd, when it finds out, comes to their new home, gets them out of bed in their night-clothes to celebrate and seat them on top of a haystack. Jeeter's jealous attempt to set fire to the stack is thwarted when the flames are extinguished, and he pull a knife. In the subsequent struggle with Curly, Fry falls on his own knife and is killed. Curly is arrested, but breaks out of jail before the trial to visit his wife. The Marshal, overtaking him, allows him to stay with Laurey until morning. And Curly announces that he is going to become a farmer after his acquittal, and help build the United States of America, of which Oklahoma is destined any day to become a part.

Green Hat, The. Michael Arlen (Anglo-Armenian). Drama. 1925.

Based on Arlen's novel of the same name. Katharine Cornell made a personal hit in the play in New York in the role of Iris.

The lady in the green hat, Iris Fenwick, was born a March, and "the Marches are never let off anything." Her stern father disapproves of both Iris and her twin brother Gerald, whom he wanted to make rich marriages and settle down. Accord-ingly he broke off Iris' romance with Napier Harpenden, whom she loved. She married Boy Fenwick on the rebound, because she was hungry for the adoration he had to give her. On his wedding night Boy jumped out of the window of their hotel bedroom. Iris has protected his memory by ambiguously announcing that he died for "purity," letting it be supposed he was disillusioned in her, whereas actually the "beloved young man" was a weakling and diseased. Gerald, who idolized Boy, thinking his sister has wrecked his hero's life, takes to drink and will have nothing to do with her. Four years later she marries Captain Storm, who is killed by Sinn Feiners in Ireland. About this time the unhappy Gerald commits suicide. Iris is now considered déclassée, beyond the pale. She meets Napier again; he is about to marry Venice Pollen. He learns from Iris of Boy's unworthiness, and knows he still loves her. But it is too late to call off his wedding. Iris falls ill shortly afterward; Napier, on his honeymoon, visits her in a Paris nursing home. When she recovers she plans to elope to Venice with Napier; his understanding wife is agreeable. But Iris' father intervenes once more, and there is a stormy scene. Iris goes off in her car and smashes into a tree. Her death, which gives Napier back to Venice, has been made to seem accidental.

Green Pastures, The. Marc Connelly (American). Drama. Two parts, 18 scenes. Based on Roark Bradford's *Ol' Man Adam and his Chillun*. 1930.

A Louisiana Negro preacher's idea of the story of the Bible when the Lord walked the earth as a natural man. After the prologue the play opens with a scene in heaven with colored mammy angels attending a fish fry. The Angel Gabriel smoking "ten cent seegars" and the Lord presented as a dignified colored pastor. Then follows in many scenes the story of the Bible as it would appear in the mind of the simple backwoods preacher. The Garden of Eden, the Flood, the drowning of the "no count" Babylonians and the leading of Moses to the promised land.

This is one of the great and most beloved plays of our time. It was the winner of the Pulitzer Prize for the season 1929-30.

Green room. A waiting or reception room, behind, near, or under the stage, used by authors, actors, directors and sometimes visitors from the audience. So called because the first "retiring room," in Covent Garden Theatre, was all in green. Most professional theatres no longer have green rooms, but university and little theatre groups usually have them.

See also *Acting, Chinese; Staging, Japanese*.

The Green Room Club, 46 Leicester Square, W.C. London. Founded in 1877, for the association of members of the dramatic profession. Membership limited to five hundred.

Greene, Robert (1558-1592). English author, dramatist. Born at Norwich, received his M.A. at Cambridge and went to Oxford in 1588. His writings are unequal in quality. They comprise pamphlets, really short novels largely autobiographical, which contain most of his verse and plays.

His story *Pandosto; or, The Triumph of Time,* 1588, provided Shakespeare with the plot of *A Winter's Tale*. As a dramatist, Greene probably had a hand in many of the composite productions of his day. Four plays, however, are his own: *The Comical History of Alphonsus, King of Aragon;* the *Honorable History of Friar Bacon and Friar Bungay;* the *History of Orlando Furioso;* the *Scottish History of James IV*. Plays attributed to him are *George-a-Green*, the *Pinner of Wakefield*. This last play and *Frior Bacon and Friar Bungay* are among the best of early English comedies. He did a series of pamphlets of the darker side of Elizabethan life that are valuable social documents, and his autobiographical pamphlets are of great interest.

Greenwich Village Theatre. New York (1917-1929). Opened at 220 West 4th Street, near Washington Square, November 17, 1917, with *Behind a Watteau Picture* by R. E. Rogers; *Efficiency* by R. H. Davis and Perley Poore Sheehan; and *The Festival of Bacchus,* by Arthur Schnitzler. Frank Conroy was director; its purpose was "to establish a home for the art of the theatre, and to gather a company of players and craftsmen who recognize the theatre as an art medium." The war pressure forced the company to relinquish the theatre for the duration of the war; the Coburns took over, and in 1918 were playing *The Better 'Ole* there. In 1923-25 the theatre was operated jointly with the Provincetown Playhouse. Eugene O'Neill, Kenneth Macgowan and Robert Edmond Jones were the triumvirate that controlled its destinies. Some of New York's most interesting productions were staged there, including: *Desire Under The Elms; Spook Sonata; Love For Love; Fashion; All God's Chillun Got Wings; The Saint;* etc.

As The Irish Theatre it opened in 1929 with *The Silver Lassie.* It was closed in 1930, and torn down.

Greet, Sir Philip Ben (1856-1936). English actor-manager. Born in London; he made his stage debut in 1879, and his first venture in management in 1886 with a series of open air performances. After that he toured, mostly in Shakespearian productions throughout the United Kingdom and America, settling in New York, 1902-14. He was associated with the Shakespeare seasons at the Old Vic, 1914-18, and in the production of English plays in Paris, 1924-26. A convinced believer in the educational value of good plays, he produced and acted at many schools and local community centers. He was knighted in 1929, the year in which he celebrated his fiftieth year on the stage. He was associated as Master of the Greensward with the production of Shakespeare's plays at the Open Air Theatre, Regent's Park, 1933-34.

Gregory, Lady Augusta (1859-1932). Irish dramatist. Born at Roxborough, County Galway; she early devoted her attention to Irish legend and folk-lore, and after her marriage in 1881, to Sir William Gregory became the chief associate of W. B. Yeats in the foundation of the Abbey Theatre and the Irish Players. She wrote a large number of plays which were acted there, including the tragedies, *The Rising of the Moon* and *The Goal Gate.*

Her Irish legends in dialect include *Cuchulain of Muirtemme,* 1902, and *Gods and Fighting Men,* 1904. She also translated three plays of Molière, published as *The Kiltartan Molière,* 1910. Other plays include *The Workhouse Ward, The Spreading of the News,* etc.

Grein, Jacob Thomas (1862-1935). British drama critic. Born at Amsterdam, he became a naturalized British subject in 1888. He was dramatic critic on the *Sunday Times,* 1897-1918, and also for the *Illustrated London News* and the *Sketch.* He founded the Independent Theatre, 1891; the People's Theatre, Mile End, 1923;

and the Cosmopolitan Theatre, 1929. Largely responsible for the introduction of Ibsen's plays into England, he organized the Ibsen centenary celebration in 1928. Five volumes of his dramatic criticism were published in 1899-1905; he also wrote *The World of the Theatre*, 1921.

Grid. A loft or skeleton roof over the stage from which are suspended the battens by means of the counterweight system.

Griffith, David Wark (1880-   ). American motion picture director. Born in Kentucky, he became an actor, appeared in a film *The Eagle's Nest* in 1907, and directed his first picture *The Adventures of Dolly* in 1908. A pioneer in the full-length film, he secured his first triumph with the epic *The Birth of a Nation* in 1915. For many years connected with United Artists, he directed, among other motion pictures, *Way Down East; Abraham Lincoln* (both silent and sound); *Orphans of the Storm;* and *America.* He is one of the great innovators and is largely responsible for the technical and artistic advance of the cinema.

Grillparzer, Franz (1791-1872). Austrian dramatist. Born in Vienna and at the age of twenty-five made his first great dramatic hit with *Die Ahnfrau,* a ghost tragedy. This was followed by a succession of pieces that brought him an international reputation. His other early plays included *Sappho,* 1819; a trilogy on *Das Goldene Vliess,* 1821; two historical plays, *Konig Ottokar,* 1825, and *Ein treuer Diener seines Herrn,* 1828. He was deeply influenced by the tragic tenor of his own life, heightened by an extreme pessimism. As a dramatist he took a great deal from the Spanish school.

Among his plays are: *Des Meeres und der Liebe Wellen,* 1831, the story of Hero and Leander; *Der Traum ein Leben,* 1834; *Libussa* (unacted and perhaps his masterpiece), 1872.

Grimaldi, Joseph (1779-1837). English clown and dancer. Known as "Joey." Born in London, he belonged to an Italian family of clowns and dancers, danced as a juvenile at Drury Lane and Sadler's Wells and made a great success in the pantomime of *Mother Goose* at Covent Garden in 1806. His singing of such ditties as *Tippety-Witchet* and *Hot Codlings* aroused great enthusiasm. His memoirs were edited by Charles Dickens in 1838.

He made his debut on April 16, 1781, as a one year old baby clown in the part of a monkey in *Robinson Crusoe.* He was not a great actor, but is regarded as the last and greatest of the clowns.

Gringoire, Pierre (Gringore) (1480?-1539). French dramatist. French poet and author of *soties,* famous because of his attack on the church and king.

Having produced *Le Chasteau de Labor,* a morality play, in 1499, he was frequently commissioned to write plays for Philip of Austria, and was made Prince de Sots. In this, the highest office of the Société d'Enfants sans Souci, he had a great influence on contemporary drama, and in his entertainments also embarked on considerable political propaganda. Known as the French Aristophanes, he attacked the

Pope and the Church on many occasions. His best known play was *Jeu de prince des sots*. He also wrote polemics and allegorical poems.

Grip. Term for any stage-hand who assists the chief carpenter in a production.

Grock (Adrian Weltach). French clown. He made his first appearance in a circus in Switzerland at the age of seven. In 1912, with a partner, he tried the variety stage and first appeared in England at the Palace Theatre. An accomplished musician, his acts invariably ended with a musical finale. He was a headliner at the Palace Theatre, New York, in 1919.

After twenty-seven years as an international favorite, he retired in 1932.

Gros-Guillaume. Stock-character in the French farce, similar to the English Falstaff, but difficult to place in any affinity to stock-characters in the Italian *commedia dell' arte;* appearance: huge stomach, short trousers, bearded face.

Grosses Schauspielhaus. German theatre for the masses. Designed by Max Reinhardt and Hans Poelziof, in 1919, to accommodate five thousand persons, thus enabling all Berlin to afford seats for the spectacular productions of classic plays. The huge warehouse of a building opened with *Orestes. Lysistrata, Faust, Goetz von Berlichingen, Hamlet* and *Julius Caesar* were among the Reinhardt productions.

Ground cloth. Large piece of cotton cloth or canvas to cover acting area during performance.

Ground plans. Layout of the stage showing location of set, properties and lights for a production.

Ground row. Low flats set on stage floor upstage of acting area, used to complete scenic background and, occasionally, to make the cyclorama lights.

Grouping. The disposition of the cast about the stage.

Group Theatre. A lusty, kicking offspring of the Theatre Guild of New York, this organization has supplied the New York stage in the 1930's with much of its vigor and excitement. Like its parent company, it has steered a course somewhere between the purely commercial theatre and the experimental, purely propagandist laboratories. It was called the Theatre Guild Studio when it gave *Red Rust* at the Martin Beck Theatre in 1929. Its first independent productions were experimental, Waldo Frank's *New Year's Eve* and Padraic Colum's *Balloon*. It really achieved maturity with Paul Green's *The House of Connelly,* which had its première in September, 1931. By this time Cheryl Crawford, Lee Strasberg and Harold Clurman had taken charge of the destinies of the group; after *The House of Connelly* it was to break away from the Guild entirely and direct its program from its offices at 234 West 44th St., New York City. Robert Ardrey's *Thunder Rock,* 1939, was its twenty-first production. It was preceded by the following plays, among others:

The Siftons', 1931, a play of the depression; Maxwell Anderson's *Night Over Taos,* 1932; John Howard Lawson's *Success Story,* 1932; Elmer Rice's *Counsellor-at-Law,* 1931; Sidney Kingsley's *Men in White,* 1933, which won the Pulitzer Prize; Irwin Shaw's *The Gentle People,* 1939; and William Saroyan's *My Heart's in the High-lands,* 1939. This list, while containing the names of several important older play-wrights as well as some of the theatre's white hopes, would be as incomplete as it is misleading without mention of the plays of Clifford Odets, who, since 1935, has come to be the laureate of the group and has added both to its prestige and its profits. Starting out as an actor, in which career he was inconspicuous, Odets turned to play-writing with *Awake and Sing,* but was unable to peddle his opus. While awaiting a producer for it, he turned out a one-acter, *Waiting for Lefty,* and submitted it for the annual award offered by the New Theatre Magazine for a play of "social significance." It was successfully produced, and the Group went on to present his *Till the Day I Die, Awake and Sing, Paradise Lost, Golden Boy* and *Rocket to the Moon. Golden Boy,* which was also filmed, had the greatest popular appeal and laid less emphasis on a possible message. On the whole, the Group list of productions is an honorable one. Its firebrands have simmered down somewhat—*Golden Boy* is less controversial than *Waiting for Lefty*—but their popularity is rather heightened thereby. And they have succeeded more often than the average group in giving a good show.

This is largely due to its actors and direction, without which good plays would have been doomed. Originally dedicated to the principles of group acting as set down by Stanislavsky in the Moscow Art Theatre, it has built up a permanent repertory troupe which does it honor. Some of its early members have been lured to Holly-wood—Franchot Tone, who returned in 1939 to act in *The Gentle People,* John Garfield and J. Edward Bromberg. It has had some fairly recent recruits, fresh from the Gold Coast, such as Frances Farmer and Sylvia Sidney. But the actors and actresses who have been its mainstay—Morris Carnovsky, Luther Adler, Ruth Nelson, Art Smith, Elia Kazan, Roman Bohnen, Lee J. Cobb, etc.—have been associated with the Group throughout all or most of its history, and have added to its lustre by their reliability and versatility.

Grundy, Sidney (1848-1914). English dramatist. Born at Manchester, he was called to the Bar and practised, 1869-76. He became known later as a playwright, chiefly associated with skilful adaptations from the French.

His works include: *The Bells of Haslemere* (with Henry Pettitt), 1887, and *A Pair of Spectacles* (from *Les Petits Oiseaux* of Labiche and Delacour), 1890. They were extremely successful. He also wrote *Sowing the Wind,* 1893, and *The Mus-keteers,* 1899.

Guardsman, The. Ferenc Molnar (Hungarian). Comedy. 3 acts. 1911.

The story of an actress who grows tired of her actor husband. He, therefore, disguises himself as a Cossack soldier and makes love to her. Fearing to discover she is unfaithful, the actor admits the disguise. The actress, however, takes it calmly, and tells her husband she recognized him from the start.

Guarini, Giovanni Battista (1537-1612). Italian poet, dramatist. Born at Ferrara, he was for some time a professor at the University there, and was in the service of the Duke of Ferrara, 1567-81. He is chiefly remembered as the author of *Il Pastor Fido,* a pastoral drama first produced in 1585, which was written as the result of his own experiences at court. It has many faults as a play, but for the brilliance of the writing alone it is one of the masterpieces of Italian literature.

Guerrero-Mendoza Company. A theatrical company formed in Spain in 1896 by the actress Maria Guerrero and the actor Fernando Díaz de Mendoza (who came from the private theatre of the Marchioness of Castellón, his first wife), whose performances, raising the actor to a high level, were among the finest in Europe. This company endured until 1924 and its repertory included comedy and tragedy, modern as well as classical, native and foreign.

See also *Teatro de la Princessa; Teatro Español.*

Guest artist. A star or featured player who assumes a limited engagement of guest performances with some stock or repertory company. In recent years this custom has been a popular radio procedure.

Guest performance. The acting of a well-known actor or actress in a limited engagement with a stock or repertory company with which he or she has had little or no previous association.

Guggenheim Fellowships. Annual fellowships of about $2,000 awarded since 1925 by the John Simon Guggenheim Memorial Foundation, for the purpose of fostering creative and research work in various fields. Application blanks and details may be secured from Henry Allen Moe, Secretary General, care of the Foundation, 551 Fifth Avenue, New York City.

In the theatre field, the Guggenheim fellows include: Angna Enters, dance mime, 1935 and 1936; Mordecai Gorelik and Charles Norris Houghton, stage designers, 1936; Robert Ardrey and Robert Turner, playwrights, 1937; Stewart Chaney, scene designer, 1937; Arthur Arent, managing editor of *The Living Newspaper,* 1938; Samuel Selden, associate director Caroline Playmakers, 1938; Joseph Leon Edel and Frederick Millet Salter, play editors, 1938.

Guignol. A stock character in the puppet show in France. As the performances of this puppet show, which dates from the 18th century, were frequently of a gruesome nature, plays of like cast were given the name, generally "Grand Guignol." This name also applies to the theatre in which they are performed.

See also *Grand Guignol; Grand Guignol Players.*

Guilbert, Yvette (1868-   ). French *diseuse,* dramatic teacher. Born in Paris, she made her stage debut at the Varietés, Paris, subsequently gaining an immense reputation by her gift of witty impersonation and her skill as a singer of songs of lower-class Parisian life. She first appeared in London in 1905, and later opened a school of dramatic diction in New York. She reappeared in London in 1928 and 1929. She was seen in the motion picture *Pecheur d'Islande* in 1934.

Her works include two novels, *La Vedette* and *Les Demi-Vieilles,* 1902; and her reminiscences, *La Chanson de ma vie,* 1927.

Guild. Known in medieval times as "gild"; an early trade-union of varied craftsmen who performed the mystery and miracle plays. Through the various gilds the morality plays were kept alive, buoyed by professional rivalry. Gilds performed plays according to their respective professions.

Guild Theatre, New York. The Theatre Guild, Inc., was formed in 1919, opening on April 14 at the Garrick with Benavente's *Bonds of Interest.* The new Guild Theatre was opened April 13, 1925, with G. B. Shaw's *Caesar and Cleopatra.* It titles itself, "Home for all the Arts of the Theatre," and exists "for drama, for beauty, for ideas." The playwright, the player and the public receive equal consideration. Since 1925 the Guild has worked on a limited five week run for its subscribers and has successfully expanded to include other cities. The New York run is extended if returns warrant it. Frankly experimental, the Guild lost money on Shaw's *Back to Methuselah,* and made it back on O'Neill's *Strange Interlude.* Helen Hayes, Helen Westley, Lynn Fontanne, Alfred Lunt, Ina Claire, Judith Anderson are among the first-rate actors who have been cast in Guild productions.

See also *Theatre Guild.*

Guimera, Angel (1847-1917). Spanish dramatist. Guimera Perez Galdos and José de Echegaray best represent the modern Spanish drama as it developed before the advent of Benavente, the Quintero brothers and Martinez Sierra.

Though born in the Canary Islands, he came of Catalan stock and spent his life in Barcelona. His earliest ventures were made in the realm of lyric poetry, and it was not until he was thirty-two that he captured the stage with *Gala Placidia,* first of a long line of dramas. Critics have grouped these in four chronological periods. The earliest were influenced by Guimera's reading of Shakespeare and Hugo and consist of historical tragedies of love in the romantic epic style; the second group consists of realistic plays of contemporary life dealing with the loves and hates of fishermen, peasants, or folk of the middle class; the third group demonstrates the author's attempts for the most part unsuccessful, to follow the northern playwrights, Ibsen, Björnson, Strindberg, Hauptmann and Sudermann; the fourth group, dramas written between 1902 and 1917, reverts to his earliest manner, as *The Path of the Sun* and *Andronica.*

He wrote: *Judith de Welp,* 1884; *The Son of the King,* 1886; *Sea and Heaven,* 1888; *The Daughter of the Sea,* 1889; *King and Monk,* 1890; *The Dead Soul,* 1892; *Don Powder,* 1893; *Maria Rosa,* 1895; *Harvest Home,* 1896; *Water Which Flows,* 1902; *The Path of the Sun,* 1904; *La Miralta,* 1905; *The Holy Thorn,* 1907; *Sanet Trist,* 1910; *The Young Queen,* 1911.

Guitry, Lucien (1860-1925). French actor, manager. Born in Paris, he made his stage debut in *La Dame aux camelias* in 1878. He became famous as an actor-manager at the Théâtre de la Renaissance, Paris, 1902-09, where he appeared in a wide variety of plays, including Anatole France's *Crainquebille,* and Zola's *L'Assommoir.* In versatility he had, after Coquelin's death in 1909, no male rival on the French stage. He appeared in London in 1902, 1909 and 1920.

Guitry, Sacha (1895-   ). French actor, dramatist, director. Born in St. Petersburg, he became famous both as an actor and as an author of witty, sparkling and often cynical comedies. He wrote several of the plays in which his father, Lucien Guitry, acted, including *Pasteur, Jacqueline, Le Grand Duc,* and *Un Sujet de Roman,* in which Sarah Bernhardt played the leading female role.

After his marriage to Yvonne Printemps, he acted continuously with her until their separation in 1932. He was very popular with English audiences, appearing in London in many of his own plays, including *Mon Pere Avait Raison,* 1920; *Mozart,* 1926; and *Écossaise;* and *Désiré,* 1932. He appeared in New York in 1926 in *Mozart.*

He has acted and directed a great number of motion pictures, among them, *Le Roman d'un Tricheur* and *Les Perles de la Couronne.*

Gustav den tredge. Per Hallström (Swedish). Drama. 5 acts. 1918.
A biographical play based on the career of Gustavus III of Sweden (1746-1792).

Guthrie, Tyrone (1900-   ). English producer, actor. Born at Tunbridge Wells. After an apprenticeship with the British Broadcasting Company and at the Festival Theatre, Cambridge, he made his reputation as a producer with a series of productions at the Westminster Theatre, 1931-32, including *The Anatomist,* and *Six Characters in Search of an Author.* He later produced *Dangerous Corner,* 1932, and in 1933-34 he was producer to the Old Vic-Sadler's Wells company.

Gutzkow, Karl Ferdinand (1811-1878). German writer. Born in Berlin; he published in 1835 *Wally die Zweiflerin,* a sceptical attack on marriage and divine revelation, the style and matter of which earned him three months' imprisonment and inspired the "Young Germany" literary movement, of which he was a leading figure.
His play *Richard Savage,* 1839, was acted throughout Germany.

Gwenn, Edmund (1875-   ). British actor. Born at Glamorgan, he made his London debut in *A Jealous Mistake,* 1899. He later became famous for his portrayal of lower middle class characters in many plays, including *The Twelve Pound Look; The Voysey Inheritance; The Skin Game;* and *Laburnum Grove.* He also appeared in various films, among them *The Good Companions* and *Friday the Thirteenth.*

Gwynn, Nell (Eleanor) (1650-1687). English actress and mistress of Charles II. Born either in an alley in Drury Lane, London, or at Hereford, she early attracted notice as an orange seller at the Theatre Royal, Drury Lane, where in 1665 she made her first stage appearance as Cydaria in Dryden's *Indian Emperor.* She played a variety of parts and was especially successful in broad comedy and in daring prologues and epilogues. Dryden in particular wrote many parts peculiarly suited to her talents.

She became the mistress of Charles II in 1669 and remained his favorite until his death in 1685. At no time a snob, she was devoid of social or political ambitions, and by her good-natured recklessness and lively temperament became a universal favorite, at the expense of her rival, the dour Duchess of Portsmouth. She died in London of apoplexy and was buried at St. Martin's-in-the-Fields. Of her two sons by Charles, the elder was created Duke of St. Albans in 1684.

Gyp (Sybille Gabrielle Marie Antoinette de Riquetti de Mirabeau) (1850-1932). French author, dramatist. Born in Brittany, a direct descendant of Mirabeau. She was married in 1870 to Count de Martel de Janville, and shortly afterwards, under the pseudonym of *Gyp,* began a long series of novels and sketches which made her famous. She also produced some clever theatre pieces and caricatures, under the name of *Bob.* In politics she was connected successively with the Boulangist, anti-Semite, and nationalist movements.

Habima Theatre. A Hebrew language Jewish group now in Tel-Aviv, Palestine; organized by N. L. Zemach in Moscow, Russia, shortly after the 1905 revolution. They were forced "underground" in 1911 by Czarist persecution. Stanislavsky, director of the Moscow Art Theatre, helped them, and his pupil, Eugene Vakhtangov, became their director for a period. For a time, after the Bolshevist revolution in 1917, there was pressure against them for their use of the Hebrew language, but they were saved by support from influential well-wishers. Their first world tour, begun in 1925, in two years took them to twenty-two countries, including the United States, where they opened in November, 1926, at Jolson's Theatre, New York, with a repertory consisting of *The Dybbuk,* by Ansky; A. Berger's *The Deluge;* D. Pinski's *The Wandering Jew;* and *Jacob's Dream,* by Richard Beer-Hoffman. The American venture was not a success. A second tour covered most of Europe, and ended with their first London appearance, at the Phoenix Theatre. In 1928-29 they removed to Palestine, where Gnessin (a Stanislavsky pupil) merged his Hatai players with them; their new theatre at Tel-Aviv, built at a cost of $150,000, raised from contributions, has become the center of drama in the Zionist colony.

Hachi-no-Ki. Seami Motokiyu (Japanese) (1363-1444). Nō drama.

A very popular Nō drama relating the story of a priest on a pilgrimage to the capitol who seeks shelter during a snowstorm at a house he has come upon in the woods. The lady of the house refuses to let him in until her husband comes home, so the pilgrim waits outside. When the husband, Tsuneyo, returns he regrets that there is barely room for two in the house and must refuse the priest lodging. The priest goes on his way, but is recalled when the man and his wife feel sorry for him; besides they would be breaking a Buddhist ordinance if they refused hospitality to a priest. They feed him with what little they have and even sacrifice their three favorite and only dwarf trees to the fire to keep him warm. Tsuneyo confesses he is of noble birth and ashamed of having sunk so low in life. When he is able to find his way again, the priest leaves.

Six months later, the priest, who was really Lord Tokiyori, becomes ruler of Japan and orders all of noble birth to hasten to the capitol. He asks that the shabbiest of the lot be brought to him. The shabbiest is the man Tsuneyo who had sheltered him the night of the blizzard, fed him and kept him warm. The ruler restores to Tsuneyo the fortune he had lost to usurpers.

Hachi-no-Ki is the only Nō play that lacks a *Mai* (a dance of slow steps and solemn gestures simulating the movements of cranes).

The character of Lord Tokiyori is taken from an actual ruler of Japan of the same name who ruled 1246-56 and who became a priest and travelled through the country incognito, acquainting himself with the needs of his subjects.

Hackett, James Henry (1800-1871). American actor. The first native-born American actor of conspicuous talent; made his first appearance in New York, March 1, 1826; first American actor to cross the Atlantic and appear on English stage as a star. He first played Falstaff on May 31, 1832, in Philadelphia, and his triumph was such that he was considered the best Falstaff ever to have played that role.

Hackett, James K. (1869-1921). American actor-manager. Son of the actor James Henry Hackett, first player of Rip Van Winkle. The younger Hackett's success was in romantic leads. Under Augustin Daly, in 1892, he played leading Shakespearean and Sheridan roles; for Charles Frohman, whose company he joined in 1895, he was a dashing Rudolf Rassendyl in the Zenda pieces, and others of similar appeal. Later he toured in the United States, and then played under his own management, at Hackett's Theatre in New York. He starred in *Monsieur Beaucaire,* 1912; *The Crook,* 1914; *Craig Kennedy,* 1915.

Hadda Padda. Godmundur Kamban (Icelander). Drama. 4 acts. 1914.
Hadda, madly in love with a youth who cares nothing for her, tries to kill him by dragging him over a cliff. She fails, however, cuts the rope, and plunges to her own death.

Haggin, Ben Ali (1882-   ). American painter and scene designer. Planned and directed the Metropolitan Balls. Designed the famous *tableaux vivants,* consisting of half-nude girls, in a setting of elaborate draperies and baroque scenery (now considered out of date and generally discarded), which helped make the *Ziegfeld Follies* a success for several decades. In 1935 he staged *Field of Ermine* for Crosby Gaige, New York producer, at the National Theatre—his first essay at legitimate theatre direction.

Hagoromo. Seami Motokiyu (Japanese) (1363-1444). Nō drama.
One of the most beautiful of Nō plays. It is primarily the delicate beauty of the dance which makes this Nō.

A moon-maiden (angel) has been dancing in lonely delight on the beach by the pine forest of Mio and has hung her magic feather-robe on a tree. A rude fisherman, Hakuryo, spies the robe, steals it and refuses to listen to the moon-maiden's pleadings. She cannot fly into the sky without her magic cloak:

> "How shall I tread
> The wing-ways of the air?"

As she droops slowly before him like a dying flower, he softens and agrees to restore the garment on the condition that she dance for him the Heavenly Dance, "which mortal eyes have never seen." She, happy again, asks for the cloak which is a necessary part of her performance. But he thinks she will fly away without dancing. She rebukes him with the words:

> "Doubt is for mortals.
> There is no deceit in heaven."

Whereupon he returns the cloak and she begins a gentle, delicate, almost imperceptible dance. The chorus accompanies the dance, calling on the wind to "build cloud-walls about the sky, lest the vision leave the world to empty day."

The theme of Hagoromo is widely spread, existing in India, China, and even Sweden. The story of Hasan in the *Arabian Nights* is an elaboration of the same theme.

Hairy Ape, The. Eugene O'Neill (American). Tragedy. 8 scenes. 1921.

Yank, called the Hairy Ape, a coal stoker on an ocean liner, searches desperately to find some place "where he belongs." The shipowner's daughter recoils from him; Fifth Avenue church-goers don't even notice him; and he is refused admission to the I.W.W. Yank finally dies in a gorilla's cage in the Bronx Zoo, asking the question, "Where do I go from here?"

Hale, Louise Closser (1872-1933). American actress, author. Born in Chicago; made her first appearance on the stage in 1894, in *In Old Kentucky;* appeared with Arnold Daly in *Candida,* 1903-04; *The Straight Road* and *Mills of the Gods,* 1907; played Miss Hazy in *Mrs. Wiggs of the Cabbage Patch* in London, 1907. In addition to her stage work she wrote short stories and dramatic pieces and dramatized her own story, *Her Soul and Her Body.*

Hales, Thomas (1740?-1780). Anglo-French dramatist. Born of a Gloucestershire, England, family. He settled in Paris about 1770. There he acquired a facility in the French language and a mastery of the stage which admitted him as a dramatist to the most exclusive theatre in Europe. He wrote *Le Jugement de Midas, Les Fausses Apparences; ou, L'Amant jaloux,* and *Les Evénements imprévus,* which were for long in the repertoire of the *Théâtre français.* In France, Hales was generally known as D'Hele or D'Hell.

Halèvy, Ludovic (1834-1908). French dramatist. Born in Paris, he started to write, in collaboration with Henri Meilhac (1831-1897) operettas, vaudeville sketches, and comedies. Their work includes *Orphée aux enfers,* 1861, and *La Belle Helène,* 1864, both to the music of Offenbach; *Froufrou,* 1869.

Halèvy also published volumes of his collected short stories, notably *Monsieur et Madame Cardinal,* 1873, and several novels, of which the best is *L'Abbé Constantin,* 1882. He was elected to the French Academy in 1884.

Half-hour. Warning by call boy or stage manager a half-hour before the curtain is to go up.

Hall, John (1575-1635). English physician and son-in-law of William Shakespeare. He married at Stratford-on-Avon, June 5, 1607, Susanna, Shakespeare's elder daughter. She and her husband inherited New Place, Stratford, under Shakespeare's will. In the attacks on the authenticity of Shakespeare's plays, it has been pointed out that Hall's faither-in-law, Shakespeare, was never one of his patients, and that when Hall died in 1635, he left his property to his son-in-law, Thomas Nash. Nash's legacy, which should have included Shakespearean manuscripts, did not, and there is neither record nor trace of them.

Hallam, Lewis (1755-1808). American actor. Presented *The Citizen* on August 24, 1785, opening the John Street Theatre in New York for the first time since the Revolution. The edict against plays was not yet recalled, but Hallam met with no opposition. The law was repealed in 1789. Hallam and John Henry became partners and thus began a new era in the history of the American theatre, an uninterrupted monopoly that continued for seven years.

Hallam Company. An acting company which came to America from England in 1752. Its arrival marked the beginning of dignified drama in America. The company played in Williamsburg, New York, etc. Lewis Hallam was the founder of this company and he was the first theatrical manager to send a company from England to America. His brother, William, financed the venture.

The Hallams introduced the sharing system, by which actors were partners in the enterprises.

Hall of Fame, Actors in the. Edwin Booth, selected in 1925, is the only stage personality in the Hall of Fame at New York University. Theatre folk are not included in the fifteen classifications defining eligibility except as "other distinguished men and women."

Haly Blude, The. Anonymous. Scottish mystery play. Not printed.

First produced in Scotland at Aberdeen, about 1440. It is the earliest drama known to the Scottish stage. It lasted eight or nine hours and took from two to three days for performance. The play was based on Biblical characters and situations with allegorical figures introduced to illustrate the dramatic point, as well as ribald dialogue to amuse the masses who made up its audience.

"Ham." An actor who is bad or pretentious, or both.

The Hamburg Dramaturgy. A collection of dramatic criticism, wit and learning by Gotthold E. Lessing. The origin of all German theatrical criticism; written during 1767 and 1768, Lessing's period as paid critic for the Hamburg National Theatre. Lessing denounced French tragedy and pleaded for a German drama.

Hamburg National Theatre. Playhouse in Germany. Built July, 1765, by Konrad Ernst Ackermann, who had the best company of actors in Germany at that time. In 1767 leased to an organization of citizens headed by Seyler and Loewen as manager and director respectively, it became the first German National Theatre. Gotthold E. Lessing was engaged as critic. The opening play was *Olint und Sophronia,* by an obscure young German author whose name Lessing fails to mention. Financial failure ended the enterprise November, 1768, after fifty-two plays had been produced, of which only eighteen were by German authors.

Hamilton, Cicely (1872-   ). English dramatist, actress. A journalist turned actress; toured in 1898 in *The Gamekeeper;* for twenty-six years thereafter played, chiefly in London, in such plays as *Fanny's First Play, Esther Waters, The Twelve Pound Look,* and *The Great Gamble,* 1914. Since 1906 she has written a score of plays, among them *The Sixth Commandment, Diana of Dobson's, The Human Factor, The Old Adam, The Beggar Prince,* and an adaptation, *Caravan,* 1932. She has been a contributor to many periodicals; has lectured, chiefly on topics of feminine interest; and is the author of a number of books on various subjects, including *Life Errant,* 1935, her reminiscences.

Hamilton, Cosmo (1879-   ). English author and dramatist. Brother of Sir Philip Gibbs; assumed his mother's name in 1898. Editor of *The World,* 1905-06. Author of many short stories, plays, and novels (some of which have been dramatized). Among his plays are: *The Wisdom of Folly; Arsène Lupin; Gentlemen, the King!; Pickwick* (with Frank C. Reilly); and *The Aunt of England* (with Anthony Gibbs). His reminiscences, Unwritten History, appeared in 1924.

Hamlet. William Shakespeare (English). Tragedy. 5 acts. 1603.
In the First Folio, 1623, *The Tragedie of Hamlet* stands between *Macbeth* and *King Lear,* occupying pp. 152-280 in the division named "Tragedies." The Folio text has lines not given in the Second Quarto and omits lines given there. It is plain that these two texts are from separate stage manuscripts which, for acting purposes, have been cut differently. The Folio text, in the light of its omissions and additions, may be described as "more theatrical, but less literary than that of 1604," according to Dowden. The Second Folio, 1632, corrects many of the misprints of the First Folio, and this corrected text is repeated with few changes in the Third Folio, 1663-64, and in the Fourth Folio, 1685.
Act 1: Hamlet, Prince of Denmark, is advised by the sentinels of the royal castle at Kronborg at Elsinore that an apparition resembling his father has appeared on the battlements. Hamlet encounters the Ghost and in an interview learns that

Claudius, the late King's brother who has ascended the throne and married Hamlet's mother, the widowed Queen, poisoned Hamlet's father, the late King, while he slept. Hamlet is sworn to secrecy. Act 2: Because of the news and the tremendous responsibility put upon him, Hamlet is distraught. He writes passionate letters to Ophelia, daughter of Polonius, a court dignitary. A company of players arrive at the Castle and Hamlet engages them to give a certain play in order to make sure of the truth of the Ghost's accusation. ("The play's the thing wherein I'll catch the conscience of the king.") Act III: Hamlet is torn by conflict. He gives the "To be or not to be" soliloquy, interrupted by Ophelia, placed there "as 'twere by accident." They are observed by Polonius and the King. The players arrive and the play selected by Hamlet parallels the circumstances of his father's death. Hamlet watches his uncle's face intent. As the player poisons his victim, the King rises screaming, "Give me some light, away!" Hamlet has proof of the crime and resolves on action. A chance comes to kill his uncle, but he does not wish to commit the murder while his uncle is praying. The Queen sends for Hamlet to reproach him. When he upbraids his mother she is overwhelmed with remorse. Polonius, spying on the interview, is slain. Act IV: The King and Queen decide to banish Hamlet to England and plan for his death. He departs. Laertes, brother of Ophelia, returns home after a long absence to find Ophelia mad with grief. He is incited by the King to seek revenge against Hamlet, who has slain his father. Act V: Hamlet returns to Denmark at the moment Ophelia's funeral is being held. The gravediggers prepare to receive the body. The funeral procession arrives and when Hamlet discovers that it is Ophelia's funeral he leaps into the grave and contests with Laertes the place as chief mourner. Seeing the hatred of Laertes for Hamlet, the King urges him to engage Hamlet in a fencing match. The foil is poisoned. The King prepares a poisoned drink should Hamlet escape the foil. The Queen toasts Hamlet unwittingly with the poisoned cup. Laertes wounds Hamlet. In the ensuing confusion they exchange rapiers. Hamlet also wounds Laertes with the treacherous blade. The Queen dies. Laertes falls, asking pardon of Hamlet. Hamlet turns upon the King, stabs him, and dies saying, "The rest is silence." Allardyce Nicoll says of Hamlet, "There is here . . . the same union of fate and human failing which is to be discovered in Sophocles." Similar characters and plots have been found in many literatures and in *The Latin History of the Danes* (written about 1200 by Saxo-Grammaticus; published in a French translation, by Belleforest, 1570, in the fifth book of the *Histoires tragiques*). It was probably through Belleforest's version that the story of Hamlet reached the English stage.

According to John Masefield, it is a part of this play's ironic teaching that life must not be baffled; but when wrenched from her course she must either be wrenched back to it or kept violently in the channel into which she has been forced. In the history of the stage, the part of the hero of this play has been the test of great actors—from Shakespeare's friend, Richard Burbage, to Edwin Booth and beyond, to Forbes-Robertson, Barrymore, Gielgud and Evans. Although the philosophy is profound, the language is simple and was comprehensible to the unscholarly audiences of Shakespeare's day.

Hammerstein, Oscar (1847-1919). American impresario. Born in Berlin, he emigrated to America at the age of sixteen. In the course of a checkered career he built the Manhattan Opera House, New York, in 1906, where he ran successful seasons of grand opera until 1910, when he sold his interests to the long-established Metropolitan Opera Association. Among his other enterprises were the building of the London Opera House, 1911, which after its failure became the Stoll Picture Theatre, in Kingsway; the Philadelphia Opera House, 1908 (now called the "Met"); and the American Opera House, 1912, which became the Lexington Theatre, New York.

Hammond, Aubrey Lindsay (1893-   ). English artist, scene designer. Born at Folkestone, 1893, he became noted as a designer of stage settings and as a black-and-white artist. Productions for which he designed scenery included *The Rose and The Ring,* 1924; *The Man with a Load of Mischief,* 1925; *The White Chateau,* 1927; *Jew Suess,* 1929; *The Shining Hour,* 1934; and various Shakespearean productions at Stratford-on-Avon.

Hammond, Percy (1873-1935). American dramatic critic. Born in Cadiz, Ohio, he was first engaged as a newspaper reporter for the Chicago Evening Post, 1898. He was an editorial writer and dramatic critic on that paper until 1908, when he became the dramatic critic of the Chicago Tribune. He stayed with that paper until 1921. From that time until his death in 1935 he was dramatic critic of the New York Herald Tribune. He was one of the most influential of critics. Though most of his reviews had to be written under the pressure of the deadline, they were notable for style, freshness of language and the use of unusual words.

Hampden, Walter (Walter Hampden Dougherty) (1879-   ). American actor. Born Brooklyn; educated at Brooklyn Polytechnic Institute, Harvard and in Paris; made his stage debut in Sir F. R. Benson's company at Brighton, England, in 1901 where he remained until 1904 playing in the old comedies and in Shakespeare. Appeared in London until 1907 when he made his debut in New York opposite Alla Nazimova in *The Comtesse Coquette.* In 1925 he leased the Colonial Theatre, New York, which he renamed Hampden's Theatre, and played in and produced revivals of Ibsen and Shakespeare. He is probably best known for his portrayal of the characters of Ibsen and Shakespeare and as Cyrano in Rostand's famous play, *Cyrano de Bergerac.* He has been president of The Players since the death of John Drew.

Hampton, Louise (1862-   ). English actress. Born at Stockport, England, she made her stage debut at Manchester in 1881. Plays in which she made successful and widely varying appearances are: *The Second Mrs. Tanqueray; The Importance of Being Earnest; Nine till Six; Payment Deferred; Late Night Final;* and *The Late Christopher Bean.*

Hanamichi (flower path). A construction in Japanese Kabuki theatres akin to a runway leading to the stage through the left section of the theatre; has been used for about two centuries, furnishing the actors with additional means of access to the stage and allowing for valuable additions to dramatic possibilities. Popular actors make their exits and entrances by this means and it was customary to show appreciation of their work by throwing purses and flowers to them.

See also *Drama, Japanese; Acting, Japanese; Staging, Japanese; Kabuki.*

Hand properties. Hand props are items which actors carry on stage with them, or with which they have important business, as letters, pistols, cameras, tea trays, etc. Fans, monocles, etc., are considered part of the costume.

Handbill. A printed sheet giving title of play, cast, theatre, date and time of performance.

Handy Green Book. Small paper-backed directory of the New York theatrical industry published since 1936 twice yearly, in February and August, by the Handy Green Book Company, 250 West 57th Street, New York City. It lists, with addresses and telephone numbers: theatrical advertising agencies; booking managers; costume designers; drama critics; radio critics; photographers; concert managers; motion picture producers; play agents; radio broadcasting stations; newspaper columnists; ticket brokers; and many other items of theatre interest.

Hanging the show. Putting up the sets of a play, hanging lights, etc.; so called because originally the show was set with wings and drapes which had to be hung.

Hankin, St. John E. C. (1869-1909). British dramatist. A dramatist of ideas, all of his works throw a revealing light on the society of his time. While his plays lack naturalism, they have an amusing cynicism. Among his better plays are *The Two Mr. Wetherbys,* 1903; *The Return of the Prodigal,* 1905; *The Cassilis Engagement,* 1907; *The Last of the De Mullins,* 1908.

Hanna Jagert. Otto Erich Hartleben (German). Drama. 5 acts. 1893.

Hanna, a girl of the people, experiments first with Socialism and then with individualism, but finds small satisfaction in either. She then sells her garment shop and marries a baron, as a means of securing greater freedom.

Hannele. Gerhart Hauptmann (German). 1893. 2 parts. Drama. (The Journey to Heaven of Hannele.)

A child tries to drown herself to escape the brutality of her step-father. She is rescued by a woodcutter who carries her into an almshouse. In her delirium, the girl believes she is being taken into heaven and is exultant with joy. The child is surrounded by a schoolmaster, policeman, magistrate, physician and nurse. The child in her dream-like trance identifies the nurse with her dead mother and feels her protective influence. In the course of her dream she sees the schoolmaster reprimanding her stepfather for his harsh treatment of her. Soon, the schoolmaster takes on the gentle heavenly mien of the Savior Jesus. He entrusts her to the tender care of the angels in soft, accented verses. The scene dims and then is brought back to sharp reality when we see again the anxious physician hovering over her and we know that the child is dead.

Hannen, Nicholas James (1881-). English actor. Born in London, he made his stage debut in 1910. He became noted in the post-War years for his portrayals of English gentlemen. Plays in which he appeared are: *The Dover Road; The Conquering Hero; The Madras House; Many Waters; The Skin Game; Escape; To See Ourselves;* and *On the Rocks.* He is particularly well-known in America for his fine performance in *Accent on Youth,* 1934-35.

Hanswurst. The name given the comic actor in the German plays of the 18th century; plays of this period were void of talent but approached art in humor and the Hanswursts who became the national type of German clown.

Hapgood, Norman (1868-1937). American author. Born in Chicago; received his A.B., A.M. and LL.B. degrees at Harvard; was drama critic of the New York *Commercial Advertiser* and the *Bookman;* editor of *Collier's Weekly; Harper's Weekly;* and Hearst's *International Magazine.* He was Minister Plenipotentiary from the United States to Denmark in 1919.

Books include: *The Stage in America,* 1901; *Why Janet Should Read Shakespeare,* 1929; etc.

Harakiri (or **Seppuku**). The name given to the act of suicide in Japanese dramas as performed by a Samurai, or a member of the nobility, whose ethical ideal was to give up his life for his lord and master, to "save face," or as a protest against a world that refuses to accept his ideals.

Hardwicke, Sir Cedric (1893-). English actor. Born at Lye, Stourbridge, he was trained at the Royal Academy of Dramatic Art and made his first appearance on the stage at the Lyceum Theatre in 1912, in *The Monk and the Woman.* He was a member of the Benson and Old Vic companies. In 1922 he joined the Birmingham Repertory Company, where he played many parts and laid the foundation for his brilliant career. He appeared in London during the long run of *The Farmer's Wife* and achieved many successes in first productions at the Malvern Festival and elsewhere, most notably as King Magnus in G. B. Shaw's *The Apple Cart.* He made a great impression, 1930-31, as Moulton Barrett in *The Barretts of Wimpole Street,* and as Dr. Haggett in *The Late Christopher Bean,* 1933-34. In New York he is known for his fine performances in *The Amazing Dr. Clitterhouse,* 1937, and *Shadow and Substance,* 1938. He has appeared in films, including *Dreyfus* and *Rome Express,* and more recently in *Stanley and Livingstone* and in *On Borrowed Time.* He married Helena Pickard, the actress, and was knighted in January, 1934.

Hard wood. Substitute tickets used for cut-rate admissions.

Hardy, Alexandre (1570-1631). French dramatist. Connected with the Hôtel de Bourgogne Company. He wrote over five hundred plays, of which about forty are extant, including *Marianne, La Mort d'Achille* and *Frédégonde*. Hardy was important as the first to give life and movement to the classic drama. He is important in the history of the French drama, not for the plays themselves, but for the prestige and popularity they gave to the theatre, and for their development in stagecraft.

Hardy, Thomas (1840-1927). English novelist. Born at Upper Bockhampton, near Dorchester, where he lived quietly for the greater part of his life. Although Thomas Hardy is most famous for his novels, stories, and poems, dramatically he is important for his epic-drama *The Dynasts*. This is an epic of the Napoleonic Wars, and began to appear in 1904; two further instalments came in 1906 and 1908. As poetry, drama and history, it is a noble contribution to world literature.

Hare, Sir John (1844-1921). English actor-manager. Born in Yorkshire, he first appeared on the London stage in 1865. After an apprenticeship with the Bancrofts, he became manager of the Court Theatre, 1875. He was joint manager with Kendal of the St. James's Theatre, 1879-88, establishing his position as a leading actor, and in 1889 he became sole manager of the Garrick Theatre, where he produced many of Pinero's plays, and made a great personal success in *A Pair of Spectacles,* 1890. His other outstanding success was at the Globe Theatre (where he became manager in 1897) in Pinero's *The Gay Lord Quex,* 1899. Equally popular in England and the United States, he was knighted in 1907. His last appearance was in a revival of *A Pair of Spectacles* in 1917.

Hare's foot (rabbit's foot). A so-called good luck charm, used for the application of dry rouge by actors.

Harle (or **herle**). Supposed source of the name Harlequin, which, it is maintained, is a diminutive; means a gaily colored water-bird.
See also *Harlequin.*

Harlequin (also Arlecchino, Arlequin). Chief character or one of the two *zanni* in a *commedia dell' arte;* originally, rascally beggar; in 16th century acquired the diamond patch costume which he has retained to the present day. His mask is a mixture of stupidity and cunning, for he can be deceived as well as deceive.
See also *Arléchin; Ailes; Bergamo; Du Harlay, Hachille; Mercury; Phalliphoric Negro slaves.*

Harold. Alfred Lord Tennyson (English). Drama. 5 acts. 1877.
It deals with the later years of the reign of Edward the Confessor, the short reign of Harold, and Harold's love for Edith the Fair. Harold is prevented from marrying her because the church prohibits it. Edith urges him to marry Aldyth, sister of Eadwine and Morkere—two important earls of the north. This marriage Harold accepts only because of political expediency. Hilda, a Saxon renowned as a seer, has

prophesied their eventual union and when Harold dies on the field at Senlac, the prophecy is fulfilled, for Edith finds him and dies beside him.

This was the seventh of Tennyson's historical dramas and his most famous.

Harrigan, Edward ("Ned") (1845-1911). American dramatist, actor, manager, theatre-owner. Ned Harrigan, son of a ship calker, was born on New York's East Side, but his first acting was done far from home in San Francisco and Chicago. The gifted comedian teamed with an Irishman named Rickey, and later with Anthony Cannon, whom he renamed Tony Hart. Harrigan and Hart, with the musical collaboration of David Braham (whose daughter Harrigan married) produced numberless comic successes, mainly about "The Mulligan Guards." In New York, after the fire of 1884 destroyed Theatre Comique which the partners had built, the men parted company, Harrigan later building the Garrick Theatre. Among Harrigan's best works are: *Old Lavender, Reilly and the 400,* and the Mulligan Guard pieces.

Harris, Sir Augustus Henry Glossop (1852-1896). British manager. Born in Paris, he made his first appearance as an actor at the Theatre Royal, Manchester, in 1873. In 1879 he became the lessee of the Theatre Royal, Drury Lane. With Meritt and Pettit he wrote *The World,* 1880, the first of the spectacular melodramas for which the house became famous. He also staged splendidly produced pantomimes at Drury Lane. He was knighted in 1891, and died at Folkestone.

Harris, Frank (1856-1931). British journalist, author, dramatist. Born of Welsh parentage in Galway, he emigrated to Canada when fifteen, and on his return to England began in 1881 to write for *The Spectator.* In 1882 he became editor of *The Evening News,* which he left to edit *The Fortnightly Review,* 1888-93. Proprietor and editor of *The Saturday Review,* 1894-98, he afterwards edited *Vanity Fair.* He was a figure of considerable notoriety, a man of mercurial temperament and as an editor he was singularly outspoken. He was a Shakespearean critic, playwright and author of some notably good short stories.

His works include: *Elder Conklin,* 1894; *Montes the Matador,* 1900; *The Bomb,* 1908; *The Man Shakespeare,* 1909; *The Women of Shakespeare,* 1911; *Oscar Wilde, His Life and Confessions,* 1916; *My Life,* 1926; and the plays, *Mr. and Mrs. Daventry,* 1900, and *The Bucket Shop,* 1914. Harris came to the United States during the World War and, adopting violent pro-German views, was not again seen in England. His book on Bernard Shaw, 1931, was controversial, but showed genuine psychological insight.

Harris, Sam H. (1872-   ). American manager. Born New York City; first theatrical venture was *The Gay Morning Glories,* a burlesque which toured the United States. In association with George M. Cohan produced *Little Johnny Jones; Forty-Five Minutes from Broadway; Get-Rich-Quick Wallingford.* As individual producer, presented: *Welcome Stranger; Little Old New York; The Music Box Revues; Rain; Icebound; Cradle Snatchers; Chicago; Once in a Lifetime; Dinner* *at Eight; You Can't Take It With You,* Pulitzer Prize winner of 1936-37; *The American Way,* etc.

Harrowing of Hell, The. The earliest dramatic composition in the English language. A dialogue poem of religious cast, written in the early south of England dialect, and often mistaken for a miracle play. Authorities place its date variously from 1250 A.D. to 1327 A.D., most opinions favoring the 13th century.

Hart, Charles (? -1683). English actor. Grandson of Shakespeare's sister, Joan, he was first heard of as playing women's parts at the Blackfriars. After the Restoration he was in 1660 the original Dorante in *The Mistaken Beauty,* adapted from Corneille's *Le Menteur.* In 1663 he went to the Theatre Royal in Killigrew's Company, and until 1682 took parts there in Dryden's, Jonson's, and Beaumont and Fletcher's plays. He was praised as Othello and Brutus, and often mentioned by Pepys. Betterton refused to play Hotspur until after Hart's retirement. Hart is said to have been Nell Gwyn's first lover and to have trained her for the stage.

Hart, Moss (1904-   ). American librettist, dramatist. Worked for Augustus Pitou, manager and dramatic director, to whom he sold his first play. Within ten years he made a remarkable rise to fame. His first real success came with *Once in a Lifetime,* upon which he collaborated with George S. Kaufman, 1930. Among his most successful works are *Face the Music* (with Irving Berlin), 1933; *The Great Waltz* (adaptation), 1934; *Merrily We Roll Along* (with George S. Kaufman), 1934; *Jubilee* (with Cole Porter), 1935; *You Can't Take It With You* (with George S. Kaufman), 1936; *The Show Is On,* 1936; *I'd Rather Be Right* (with George S. Kaufman), 1937; *The American Way* (with George S. Kaufman), 1939; *The Man Who Came To Dinner* (with George S. Kaufman), 1939.

Hart, Tony (1857-1891). American actor. Real name Anthony Cannon. Born in Worcester, Massachusetts. Female impersonator, as the Dutch girl in *Little Fraud.* Partner of Edward Harrigan in numerous comedy turns, especially *The Mulligan Guards.*
See also *Harrigan, Edward.*

Harte, Francis Bret (1839-1902). American author, dramatist. Born at Albany, New York. Spent his early life in California as a gold seeker, school teacher and journalist; then began to write sketches of his experiences. He was appointed secretary of the mint in San Francisco and at the same time contributed popular verse and stories to newspapers and was editor of the *Overland Monthly.* In 1871 he settled in New York and was later United States consul in Germany and Scotland. In 1885 he settled near London and remained there for the rest of his life.

His stories of pioneer life in America have become famous (*The Heathen Chinee; The Outcasts of Poker Flat,* etc.) and have been the bases for dramatization and filming.

His plays include *Two Men from Sandy Bar; Ah Sin* (with Mark Twain);
and *Sue* (with T. Edgar Pemberton).

Harvard Dramatic Club. Organization at Harvard University. Founded in
1908 by a group of men interested in playwriting who conceived the idea of
organizing a club whose main purpose would be to stimulate an interest in dramatic
composition. Wrote and produced its own plays until the Spring of 1917. From
1919 it has produced no undergraduate plays. Its production schedule now includes
outstanding foreign plays to which it gives their initial American performances, such
as Aulden and Isherwood's *The Dog Beneath the Skin;* Saki's *The Watched Pot;*
Robinson's *Ever the Twain;* Johnston's *A Bride for the Unicorn;* Hughes' *A
Comedy of Good and Evil;* Cocteau's *La Machine Infernale,* etc.

Harvard University. Professor George Pierce Baker organized the dramatic
class which took the name informally of 47 Workshop from his English 47 course.
He was the pioneer in the field of teaching the principles of playwriting and dramatic
construction (as was Frederick Koch at the University of North Dakota). A distinguished group of men and women studied under Baker, including Eugene O'Neill,
Philip Barry, Sidney Howard, Lee Simonson, Robert Edmond Jones, Donald
Oenslager, John Mason Brown, Mary Morris, Dorothy Sands. This work was later
transferred to Yale University in 1925. A more complete listing of all personages
both at Harvard and at Yale is to be found in the manuscript prepared by Virginia
Vaughn Tryon, in the New York Public Library.

In 1903 John Drew bought the Robert W. Lowe Collection and presented it to
the Widener Library; the fine Robert Gould Shaw and Evart Janesen Wendell
Collections of rare English and American playbills, engraved dramatic portraits,
prompt books, plays, biography, etc., were given to Harvard.

See also *Theatre Collections; Harvard Dramatic Club; Hasty Pudding Club.*

Hassan. James Elroy Flecker (English). Drama. 1922.

A sumptuous spectacle as staged, with gorgeous ballets and considerable incidental music. The setting is the far East. It is thus in the tradition of such works
as Edward Knobloch's *Kismet* (1912). which used the triple appeal of exoticism,
spectacular staging and sensational action and which were popular in the United
States and England in the first twenty-five years of the century. Among the colorful
and romanesque figures in Flecker's drama are the savage Haroun; the rapt poet
Ishak; Rafi, King of the Beggars; and the slave girl Pervaneh.

Hasty Pudding Club, The. A dramatic organization at Harvard University.
It was begun in 1770 as the Hasty Pudding Institute and later adopted the present
name. Now produces only musicals in which all members of the cast are enlisted
from the student body. First production was December 13, 1844.

Haunted Inn, The. Perez Hirschbein (Yiddish). Folk play. 3 acts. 1911.

A play of Jewish life in Eastern Europe. Bendet, a headstrong, wilful man, becomes obsessed with the idea that his daughter's sweetheart, Itsick, has stolen one of

his horses. So in his anger he orders her to marry a neighbor's son. In the general excitement preceding the wedding, Itsick comes for the girl and she flees with him. Bendet is certain that her flight is his punishment for having torn down a haunted inn near his home in order to build a new home for his daughter and the man he had chosen as her husband. The inn is supposed to be a trysting place for evil spirits, and Bendet is convinced he has offended the spirits by leaving them homeless. A few accidental mishaps confirm his belief. To pacify them he rebuilds the inn. But bad fortune still hounds him, and he realizes that they are still not appeased. So in despair he burns both the inn and his own house.

Bendet is a typical Lithuanian peasant, to whom evil spirits are as real and powerful as the gods were to the ancient Greeks. The inn, which houses the satanic hosts, is his Olympus; and in his struggle to escape from the supernatural forces which plague him, he resembles the heroes of Greek tragedy pursued by the anger of the gods.

Possibly because of the difficulty of recreating this simple superstitious spirit in a translation, *The Haunted Inn* was a failure when given in English on Broadway.

Haupt Aktion. The name given the principal play of the performances of the strolling players in early German drama. The bill was in two parts: the *Haupt Aktion* and the *Nachspiel*.

Hauptmann, Gerhart (1862-   ). German dramatist. The foremost German dramatist of the present day, Hauptmann was born at Obersalzbrunn, Silesia, in 1862. His early schooling was received in his native town and in Breslau. The youth wanted to become a sculptor, and attended art schools in Breslau, in Jena and finally in Italy. In 1885, after his first marriage, he settled in Berlin, where he joined the Free Stage group. In 1891 he retired to Silesia.

His first play *Before Dawn* was produced by the Free Stage in 1889, and was hailed at the time as one of the first important examples of naturalism in the German drama. *The Weavers* created a profound impression; it was the most ambitious play yet written in the Nineties. Hauptmann has written about thirty plays, including historical dramas, folk plays, prose comedies, fairy plays and festival pageants. Two paradoxical distinctions are to be found in the case of Hauptmann. He won the Nobel prize in 1912 for his humanitarian play *The Weavers,* and he was the model of the renegade playwright who, in the face of German National Socialism, deserts the cause of humanity in S. N. Behrman's *Rain from Heaven*.

Nevertheless his initial prestige is remembered and we may say of him, that if Ibsen was the founder of the Social drama in its more general aspects, Hauptmann, in his pristine glory, was the founder of that kind of social drama which presented the workers, *as such*, rather than separate individuals, as the chief protagonists in the conflict between capital and labor.

Among his plays are: *The Festival of Peace,* 1890; *Lonely Lives,* 1891; *The Weavers,* 1892; *The Beaver Coat,* 1893; *The Assumption of Hannele,* 1893; *Florian Geyer,* 1894; *Drayman Henschel,* 1898; *The Red Cock,* 1901; *Poor Heinrich,* 1902; *Griselda,* 1909; *The Rats,* 1911; *The Festival Play,* 1913;

Winter Ballad, 1917; *Indipohdi,* 1920; *Dorothea Angermann,* 1926; *Witches' Ride,* 1930; *The Golden Harp,* 1933.

See also *Drama, German, 20th century to the First World War.*

Having Wonderful Time. Arthur Kober (American). Comedy. 3 acts. 1937.

Teddy Stern, a stenographer, meets Chick Kessler during her vacation at Camp Care-Free. Chick is a law graduate who is waiting on table at the camp. They fall in love, and in order that they may be married, Teddy, much as she hates a typewriter, promises to support Chick until he gets a job.

Hawtrey, Sir Charles (1858-1923). British actor-manager. The leading comedian of his day, he created a style of playing which was widely imitated.

Born September 21, 1858, the son of a schoolmaster at Eton, and the grandson of Rev. E. C. Hawtrey, its headmaster. Made his first stage appearance under the name of Bankes. In 1884 he produced *The Private Secretary,* in which as Douglas Cattermole he achieved an extraordinary success. The play ran until 1886. He became manager of Her Majesty's Theatre, 1885, and of the Comedy, 1887. In New York in 1901 he appeared in *A Message from Mars,* which he took to London in 1905. He was knighted in 1922.

Hay, Ian (Ian Hay Beith) (1876-   ). British novelist, dramatist. He became language master at Fettes College, but soon began to write, publishing under the name of Ian Hay, his first novel *Pip* in 1907. This was followed by *The Right Stuff,* 1908; *A Man's Man,* 1909; *A Safety Match,* 1911; *Happy Go Lucky,* 1913; *A Knight on Wheels,* 1914, and others.

His experience at the front in the First World War gave him the material for *The First Hundred Thousand,* 1915, a vivid and humorous description of the training of a Highland battalion. Dramatizations of Hay's novels were *Tilly of Bloomsbury,* 1919, and *The Safety Match,* 1921. Other plays in which he collaborated were: *A Damsel in Distress; The Middle Watch; Leave it to Psmith; The Midshipmaid; Orders Are Orders; The Sport of Kings,* 1924; and *Housemaster,* 1937 (*Bachelor Born,* in New York) was an original play.

Haydon, Julie (1911-   ). American actress. Real name, Donella Donaldson. Born in Oak Park, Illinois. First appeared in Los Angeles in January, 1934, in *Autumn Crocus.* She made a brilliant success with Noel Coward in the film, *The Scoundrel,* 1935. This was followed with Barry's *Bright Star* in the same year. Her next Broadway appearance fixed her among the important younger actresses because of the excellence of her performance in *Shadow and Substance,* 1938. In the 1939-40 season she appeared in Saroyan's *The Time of Your Life.*

Hayes, Helen (1902-   ). American actress. Born in Washington, D. C., she made her first appearance on the stage in Washington in *The Babes in the Wood,* 1908, where she caught the attention of Lew Fields. Subsequently she appeared with him in New York in *Old Dutch,* 1909. From 1913-16 she played with the Columbia

Players in Washington. In 1918-19 she toured in *Pollyanna*. She played the ingenue roles in *Penrod* and *Dear Brutus*, 1918, with great acclaim. Among her successful plays are *To the Ladies*, 1922; *Dancing Mothers*, 1924; *What Every Woman Knows*, 1926; *Coquette*, 1927; *The Good Fairy*, 1930; *Mary of Scotland*, 1933; *Victoria Regina* (in which she created one of the greatest successes of modern times); *Ladies and Gentlemen*, 1939. In 1931 she began her career in motion pictures and has won further acclaim in *Arrowsmith, Farewell to Arms, Another Language*. She is one of America's greatest and best beloved actresses.

She is married to Charles MacArthur, the playwright.

Hay Fever. Noel Coward (English). Comedy. 3 acts. 1925.

A week-end with Judith Bliss, retired actress, and her family. Life must always be dramatic for Judith and the week-end becomes a series of scenes in which she plays a neglected wife, a sacrificing mother, and a sad but glamorous woman—all without provocation.

Haymarket Opera House. A theatre in London built in 1705. In this house, in 1705, the first opera in the Italian style was performed. The house was burned in 1789; rebuilt and reopened in 1791; operas, including those of Mozart, were performed.

Haymarket Theatre. A small theatre in London erected in 1720; originally a kind of chapel-at-ease to Drury Lane and Covent Garden. First performances to be given here were those of French comedy. Fielding produced here, in 1730, his once-famous burlesque *The Tragedy of Tragedies; or, The Life and Death of Tom Thumb the Great*. The theatre was demolished in 1820, giving way the following year to a new house, the present one, which opened with *The Rivals*. This is a carriage-trade theatre devoted to drama and comedy.

Hays, Will H. (1879-   ). American attorney. Became president of Motion Picture Producers and Distributors of America, Inc., in 1922. As such he is the arbiter on all points at issue, on all questions of regulation within the industry. Formerly Postmaster General of the United States under President Harding.

Hazel Kirke. Steele MacKaye (American). 4 acts. 1880.

Hazel, a miller's daughter in rural England, has an iron willed father who has promised her in marriage to old Squire Rodney, the family benefactor. She loves a young lord in disguise; they elope but the ceremony is not exactly legal, and when Hazel hears of this she throws herself into the mill race at her old home. She is saved and there are reconciliations all around.

Hazel Kirke went on tour in 1880 under the title of *The Iron Will*, then opened at the Madison Square Theatre, playing 486 consecutive performances, a record at that time.

Headliner. A theatrical term for a star or leading player; as used in vaudeville, the main act or actor.

Heart of Maryland. A melodrama, by David Belasco, 1895. (American).

The locale of this drama is the old Calvert homestead in Maryland, at the time of the Civil War. The big scene is one in which the heroine hangs to the iron tongue of the bell to silence it, for the clang of the bell would reveal to the Confederate sentries the escape of a northern prisoner, who is her sweetheart.

The importance of this play is that it turned the tides of fortune for Belasco and established him as a playwright and also established Mrs. Leslie Carter, the heroine, as one of the stage's leading actresses.

Heartbreak House. George Bernard Shaw (English). Drama. 3 acts. c. 1914.

Although written on the eve of the first World War, this uncannily prophetic drama was not produced until 1919. In the play Shaw imagines that the war has already begun. Heartbreak House is the country home of 88 year old Capt. Shotover, a grand old man who potters around the household inventing instruments of death. He drinks, oddly enough, to escape from a world of dreams and gain a sense of reality. Assembled are Boss Mangan, a business executive; Hector Hushabye, a philandering husband, various other social parasites. What plot there is concerns a fresh young girl's romance with the rich businessman who is years older, and her attempt to decide whether or not she should marry him so as to stave off financial ruin for herself and her father. Her advisor in the matter is Mrs. Hushabye, Capt. Shotover's daughter, who feels that the match would be a grave mistake. She has invited Mangan to the house so as to show him up in his true colors. One typically Shavian creation is a burglar who purposely makes a noise so as to be caught, then tells his sad story and passes around a hat. At the end of the play, when bombs drop from the skies, the burglar and Mangan are killed, the others escape. Shaw himself, when asked the meaning of the play, pleaded ignorance, explaining "I am only the author." But if its plot is rambling and its general significance obscure, its dialogue is scintillating and its social and political analyses brilliant.

Heavens. A term used in Elizabethan drama to identify a wooden, canopy-like roof extending over the outer stage and supported by two heavy columns. It served partly to protect the players from the weather, but primarily to sustain the machinery used to lower properties to the stage.

Heavy. Theatrical term for the villain in a play.

Hebbel, Christian Friedrich (1813-1863). German dramatist. Born at Wesselburen, Holstein, he was the son of a mason. He was educated by friends who were impressed by his early poems. He studied Schiller intensively. He moved to Hamburg and began to write in the 1830's. His first tragedy *Judith,* 1839, brought him immediate fame and is regarded as the first modern German drama. He died in Vienna. Considered one of the greatest German dramatists since the classic writers. His *Maria Magdalena,* 1844, began the social drama of the present day, and foreshadowed German naturalistic drama.

The most important of his plays are: *Judith,* 1839; *Genoveva,* 1840-1841; *Der*

Diamant, 1841; *Maria Magdalena,* 1844; *Die Nibelungen,* 1862 (a trilogy considered his masterpiece).

Hecht, Ben (1894-   ). American author and dramatist. Began his career as a newspaper reporter. Was on several newspapers. In 1912 he wrote several short plays with Kenneth Sawyer Goodman which appeared under the name of *The Wonder Hat.* Among his better known plays are *The Egotist,* 1922; *The Front Page* (with Charles MacArthur), 1928, which had a tremendous success; *The Great Magoo* (with Gene Fowler), 1932; *Twentieth Century,* 1932; *Jumbo* (with Charles MacArthur), 1935; *To Quito and Back,* 1937; *Ladies and Gentlemen* (with Charles MacArthur), 1939. In 1933 he started writing for the movies and has done many successful pictures, e.g., *Design for Living, Scarface, Topaze,* and in collaboration with MacArthur, *The Scoundrel,* and *Crime Without Passion.* He is also the author of many short stories and novels.

Hecuba. A tragedy by Euripides (Greek) c. 450 B.C.
During the siege of Troy, Hecuba's youngest son, Polydorus, was placed under the care of Polymnestor, King of Thrace. Later, she discovers that her son has been murdered and in revenge she blinds Polymnestor and kills his two sons. Later she is turned into a dog and her grave becomes a mark for ships.

Hedda Gabler. Henrik Ibsen (Norwegian). Drama. 4 acts. Printed 1891.
This is one of Ibsen's most powerful plays. It is a continuation of his philosophy to "be yourself"; that is: emphasis on individual action. However, in Hedda Gabler we see the evils of selfish individualism. Hedda is a cool, disdainful woman, a woman who is unscrupulous and unrelentless. She marries George Tesman only for security and then proceeds deliberately to plot to destroy a former admirer and scholar, Eilert Lävborg. She is irked by his loyalty to a dull, good woman, Mrs. Elvsted. Also he is her husband's competitor in the university and finally it is a test of her ability to maneuver the fate of another. She works it out by getting Lävborg drunk and sending him to a gay party. When he returns bewailing the loss of a manuscript involving his life's work and reputation, she suggests suicide and gives him one of her pistols. She then burns the manuscript which her husband had found and feels triumphant. This is short lived. Eilert dies. She realizes she is implicated by the damaging evidence of the pistol. She has no way out except to submit to a blackmailing, libertine judge. This solution is so repulsive to the unyielding Hedda that she commits suicide.

Hedgerow Theatre. American repertory company established and directed at Moylan-Rose Valley, Pennsylvania, by Jasper Deeter, in 1923, for the purpose of giving actors a chance to play varied roles and of providing a public for brand-new plays as well as for those already known. A permanent company of approximately thirty members performs in a repertory of 150 plays. Occasionally the company tours but more usually performs in the converted mill playhouse, thirteen miles from Philadelphia. Among plays given their debut at the Hedgerow Playhouse are Lynn Riggs' *Rancour,* 1928; *The Cherokee Night,* 1932; and Maria Coxe's *Kit Marlowe,*

1936. Players at one time members of Mr. Deeter's group include: the motion picture actress, Ann Harding; Alexander Kirkland; John Beal; Herbert Biberman; and Rose McClendon.

Heiberg, Gunnar (1857-   ). Norwegian dramatist. Born in Christiania, he was theatre director at Bergen, and, for a while, a newspaper correspondent in Paris. He began his writing career with a philosophical poem, *The Genesis of Man*. He wrote a group of light, satirical comedies, as well as serious plays on sex. He is also the author of critical volumes, the best of which is *The Norwegian Theatre*. Among his comedies are *Aunt Ulrikka*, 1884; *Love Your Neighbor*, 1902; *The Council of the People*, 1897; and among the serious plays *The Balcony*, 1849; *The Tragedy of Love*, 1904.

Heijermans, Hermann (1864-1924). Dutch dramatist. Born in Rotterdam of Jewish parents. Wrote under the name of Samuel Falkland and gained his reputation for his play *The Good Hope*, 1900, which was translated into several languages.

His other plays include: *Ahasuerus*, 1893; *Ghetto*, 1898; *Bonheur*, 1919; *A Case of Arson* and *The Rising Sun*, 1922. He wrote several novels but created the greatest notice with his play, *The Good Hope*, played in Paris and England. In his one-act play, *A Case of Arson*, Henry de Vries created a tour de force of acting by portraying all seven characters who appear as witnesses in the play. Heijermans lived in Berlin for a few years but returned to Holland 12 years before his death to manage a players' group.

Held, Anna (1873-1918). French-American actress. Her first appearance on the stage was in London at the Princess Theatre. At the Herald Square Theatre in New York City, 1896, she made her first American appearance in *A Parlor Match*. Her songs with a French accent, her wickedly rolling eyes, and the famous milk baths which an enterprising press agent publicized for her, made the imported beauty the darling of this country. She played in one musical comedy after another, among them *Miss Innocence, The Little Duchess* and *The Parisian Model*. She was married to Florenz Ziegfeld, Jr., but her one daughter, Liane Carrera, is the child of an earlier marriage.

Hellas. Percy Bysshe Shelley (English). Drama. 1822.

Shelley patterned this play in form after *Persae* by Aeschylus. Devoted to the cause of Greek independence he wrote the play after they had proclaimed their independence. The main character is the Sultan Mahmud who receives information of the revolt in different sections. Ahasuerus, an old Jew, calls up a strange sight for the Sultan—namely the fall of Stamboul. The play has a Greek chorus of captive women and their lines are distinguished lyrical poetry.

Hell-Bent for Heaven. Hatcher Hughes (American). Drama. 3 acts. 1923. Winner of the Pulitzer Prize in 1923-1924 season.

Rufe Hunt, a religious fanatic with criminal tendencies, falls in love with a mountain girl and tries to kill her lover. The mountain folk finally realize that his piety is false, and they drive him out of the community.

Hellman, Lillian (1904-   ). American dramatist. Born in New Orleans, she received her education at New York University and Columbia College. She started her career by reading plays for Herman Shumlin, and has done book reviewing, scenario reading, short story writing and articles for the better magazines. Her play, *The Children's Hour,* 1934, was a tremendous hit in New York and on tour. Her other plays include *Days to Come,* 1936, and *The Little Foxes,* 1939.

Heminge, John (?   -1630). English editor. Joint-editor with Henry Condell of the first collected edition of Shakespeare's plays, the 1623 Folio. He was associated with Shakespeare's company, the Lord Chamberlain's Men, from 1594 to the time of his death, sometimes as an actor, but for the most part as chief director and business manager of the company. He appeared in Shakespeare's plays and in Jonson's *Sejanus, Volpone, The Alchemist,* and *Catiline.* He was a shareholder in both the Globe and Blackfriars Theatres.

Henderson, John (1747-1785). English actor. Began his theatrical career at Bath, 1772, as Hamlet; first appearance in London, 1777, as Shylock; caused much criticism for his breaking away from the traditional business in Shakespeare's plays; from 1778 until the end of his career, he played at Covent Garden. He was an actor of the first rank and was regarded as second only to Garrick. His was an analytical mind that studied a character and gave a finished portrait of his idea. There is some doubt as to whether or not he was poisoned by his wife.

Besides Hamlet he was outstanding in roles which included Falstaff, Richard III, Iago, Macbeth, Sir Giles Overreach, etc.

Henrietta, The. Bronson Howard (American). Comedy. 1887.

For many years this was one of the most popular American comedies. At the time of the first performance the New York *Herald* called it "the first genuinely American comedy, pure and simple, produced in this country in the past ten years"; and the Advertiser described it as "perfectly refreshing, positively inspiring." Its stars, Robson and Crane, revived it frequently, and it was a success in London when given there in 1891. In 1918 Winchell Smith and Victor Mapes brought it up to date and presented it as *The New Henrietta.*

Nicholas Van Alstyne, the Napoleon of Wall Street, has two sons. The elder, Nick Jr., is a thorough rogue. The younger, Bertie the Lamb, is a good-natured nonentity. Nick Jr. deceives his wife concerning an escapade with another woman and throws the brunt of the onus on Bertie's shoulders. Bertie allows himself to be blamed and burns the letters which would reveal Nick's guilt, although it means losing the girl he adores. Then Nick proves he is incapable of any loyalty by deserting the mistress who depends on him. Not satisfied with that, he manipulates stocks secretly in the hope of ruining his father and getting control of all the Van Alstyne wealth. Bertie is only vaguely conscious of what is going on, but with a stroke of luck which amounts to sheer genius he achieves a financial coup himself and maneuvers things so that Nick shall have nothing and their father everything. Nick is so astonished and enraged by this unexpected turn of events that he drops dead of heart disease. The chief comic effect of the play, of course, is derived from Bertie, guileless and timid and unfitted for business, yet somehow, and to his own surprise, accomplishing miracles. The Henrietta of the title is a mining corporation in whose stock they speculate.

Henry IV (Enrico IV). Luigi Pirandello (Italian). Tragedy. 3 acts. 1922.
A young man is at last recovering from insanity in which he believes himself to be Henry II, and tells the good news to his sweetheart. However, the shock and change are too much to bear, and the mania returns. Months later, when he is again recovering, he guards the secret, and remains Henry II to his friends.

Henrye the Fyft, Famous Victories of. Anonymous. Elizabethan. This was produced before 1588 and deals with the early escapades of Prince Hal, his military exploits as king, and his wooing of Katherine of France. Shakespeare used the play for episodes relating to Prince Hal in his *King Henry IV* and for material in *King Henry V*. From the character, Sir John Oldcastle, mentioned in the *Famous Victories,* Shakespeare developed his great comic creation, Falstaff.

Henslowe, Philip (? -1616). English manager. Chiefly associated with his son-in-law Edward Alleyn, and the Admiral's Men; built the Rose Theatre, 1587, the Fortune, 1600, and the Hope, 1613. He managed several companies of actors and had financial dealings as impresario and money lender with many of his contemporary dramatists. His celebrated diary, now in the college library at Dulwich, is a complete daily record of receipts and expenditures, including sums paid to authors for every one of his productions, 1592-1609.
Joseph Quincy Adams in his *Shakespearean Playhouse* calls him "the greatest theatrical proprietor and manager of the Tudor-Stuart age."
See also *Alleyn and Henslowe.*

Hepburn, Katharine (1909-   ). American actress. Born in Hartford, Connecticut, she made her first appearance on Broadway in *These Days,* November 12, 1928. She next acted with Jane Cowl in *Art and Mrs. Bottle,* in 1930; then, in 1932, in *The Warrior's Husband,* a production which led to her Hollywood engagement. Among her best known pictures have been: *A Bill of Divorcement; Little Women; Morning Glory; Christopher Strong; The Little Minister; Alice Adams; Mary of Scotland; Quality Street; Bringing Up Baby;* and *Holiday.* She made several attempts at a success on the legitimate stage (*The Lake* on Broadway during the 1933-34 season; *Jane Eyre,* Helen Jerome's adaptation of the Bronte novel, on the road during the 1936-37 season) but had to wait until the spring of 1939 for her real success, which was provided by Philip Barry's comedy *The Philadelphia Story.*

Herbert, Victor (1859-1924). Irish-American composer, conductor. Attended Stuttgart Conservatory; was 'cello soloist at the Metropolitan Opera House, New York; soloist and conductor of Seidl's, Thomas's, and the Pittsburgh Symphony

Orchestras. He is best known in the theatrical world for his operettas, which include: *Babes in Toyland; Mlle. Modiste; Little Nemo; Naughty Marietta; The Madcap Duchess; Princess Pat;* etc.

Hernani. Victor Hugo (French). Tragedy. 5 acts. 1830.

Young, beautiful Doña Sol de Silva and her uncle and guardian, the aging Don Ruy Gomez de Silva, are betrothed. She, however, is in love with the outlaw Hernani, with whom she arranges a secret meeting. They are just completing their plans for running away when a stranger slips out of the closet. Don Ruy returns, and it is revealed that the stranger is King Charles of Spain. The next evening the king, having overheard Doña Sol's discussion of her elopement, seizes her as she is about to escape. Hernani arrives, but, realizing that defiance of his king would be useless, bids her marry her uncle as intended. Hernani goes to the ancient castle of Don Ruy. The old man pledges the guest safety before he knows who he is and hides him from the king and his troops. The king in the meantime has taken Doña Sol along with him. Don Ruy and Hernani determine to rescue her. To prove his sincerity and loyalty, Hernani vows that whenever Don Ruy shall blow a horn the young man will end his own life. The king is made Emperor of Germany and pardons Hernani, found to be the noble Don Juan of Aragon. Once more the young man plans to marry Doña Sol. Then on his wedding night he hears the blast of the horn and kills himself. His bride, unable to face life without him, joins him in death.

This is Hugo's most successful play, with the possible exception of *Ruy Blas,* and was the first drama of the romantic school to be presented at the Théâtre Français. The classicists were shocked at the innovation, the presentation of the play became the topic of the day in Paris, and men went so far as to fight duels in defense of their opinions for or against *Hernani.* For the forty-five days during which performances of *Hernani* were given the war raged, and came to be known as "les batailles d'*Hernani.*" When the excitement had died down, a new precedent had been established, and the way was cleared for romantic playwrights.

Herne, James A. (1839-1901). American playwright, actor and stage manager.

The author of *Shore Acres; Margaret Fleming; Mary the Fisherman's Child; The Minute Man; Sag Harbor; Hearts of Oak; Drifting Apart; Griffith Davenport;* etc. Herne was serious about his work, and believed that a play should improve the morality of the members of the audience and send them away better than they had come in. A contemporary, J. J. Enneking, said of him that his credo was "truth for art's sake." *Hearts of Oak,* a melodrama, was enormously popular, but Herne felt that it was not instructive and turned resolutely from such facile and profitable efforts to more elevating dramas, although for the most part he earned less money from them. He was a staunch disciple of Henry George, for whose single tax he fought in his writings; and his theatrical gods were Ibsen and the other realists of his school. He also was an actor and stage manager for his company. The years have dimmed his reputation, but such eminent contemporaries of the playwright as Hamlin Garland deemed him one of the greatest dramatists of his day.

Heroic mood. A style of playwriting popular in the early part of the Restoration in England, in which ridiculous (to us) scenes were written solely for the purpose of arousing the emotions of awe and pity. It is a style noted for its crudities, its violent ranting, its fantastic psychology and exaggerated realism. Dryden was probably the first and greatest of this school.

He Who Gets Slapped. Leonid Andreyev (Russian). Tragi-comedy. 4 acts. 1922.

A defeated and lonely man joins a circus and becomes one of the clowns. He falls in love with Consuelo, a lovely bare-back rider, and rather than see her married to a degenerate millionaire by her money-seeking guardian, he poisons her and then commits suicide. It is an effective and moving play with much philosophy and symbolism. Though it seems profound it is actually rather superficial and not properly motivated.

Heyward, Du Bose (1885-   ). American novelist and playwright. Born in Charleston, South Carolina, he started out in the insurance business. He began writing for the better English and American magazines and organized the Poetry Society of Charleston. He is the author of many books, *Carolina Chansons* (in collaboration with Hervey Allen), *Mamba's Daughters, Porgy,* etc. With his wife, Dorothy Heyward, he dramatized *Porgy,* which was the outstanding hit of the 1927 season. With the help of George and Ira Gershwin, *Porgy* was made into an American folk opera, 1935. Other of his plays are *The Brass Ankle,* 1931; *Mamba's Daughters* (in collaboration with Dorothy Heyward), 1939.

Heywood, Thomas (? -1650). English dramatist. He became an actor in Henslowe's company in 1598 and, after the accession of James I, a member of the Queen's Company of players. About 1596 he wrote his first play *The Four Prentices of London* and in 1633, in a prefatory address to *The Traveller,* he claimed to have had "either an entire hand, or at the least a main finger" in 220 plays. Of these only thirty-five are known to exist.

He also wrote various prose works, including: *An Apology for the London Mayor,* 1631-39; *Several Actors,* 1612; *Nine Books of Women,* 1624; and a *Life of Queen Elizabeth,* 1631. Of his plays, *Edward IV,* 1600, and *A Woman Killed with Kindness,* 1603, are perhaps the best examples.

Hichens, Robert Smythe (1864-   ). British novelist and dramatic author. Born at Speldhurst, Kent, he gave up a musical career to write many successful novels. He has also written a number of plays some of which are adapted from his novels. Among his plays are *The Real Woman,* 1909; *The Garden of Allah,* 1911; *Press the Button,* 1918; *The Voice from the Minaret,* 1919.

Hicks, Sir Edward Seymour (1871-   ). British actor, dramatist, producer. Born at St. Helier, Jersey, he first appeared on the stage at the Grand Theatre, Islington. He was engaged by the Kendals and toured with them in England and America. He built the Aldwych Theatre, which he opened December, 1905, with

Blue Bell in Fairyland, and in December, 1906, opened the Hicks (later the Globe) Theatre, appearing in the musical play *The Beauty of Bath.*

Among the plays in which he appeared are: as Andrew McPhail in Barrie's comedy *Walker, London; Scrooge; The Man in Dress Clothes; Sleeping Partners; The Gay Adventure; Vintage Wine.*

He was author of *Blue Bell in Fairyland; The Gay Gordons; The Beauty of Bath; The Catch of the Season.*

He married Ellaline Terriss in 1902.

High Tor. Maxwell Anderson (American). Comedy. 3 acts. 1937.
Received the Drama Critics' Circle award in 1937.

Two realtors endeavor to force Van Dorn to sell High Tor, a mountain top above Haverstraw overlooking the Hudson River. That night a storm engulfs the mountain, and Van meets a phantom crew of Dutch sailors who have been lost for three hundred years. He falls in love with their ward Lise, the ghost of a beautiful Dutch girl.

In the morning, however, when the phantoms have gone, Van faces reality and realizes he will be forced to sell his mountain.

Hill, Aaron (1685-1750). British dramatist. Translator and adapter of Voltaire. Wrote farce, domestic tragedy, classical tragedy, heroic tragedy, and opera and made a whole-hearted attempt to lift the status of the 18th century stage. His plays include: *Elfrid,* 1709; *The Fatal Vision,* 1716; *Alzira,* 1736.

Hindle Wakes. Stanley Houghton (English). Drama. 3 acts. 1912.

Fanny Hawthorn and the mill owner's son Allan have been lovers. She has very unconventional ideas much to the chagrin of this small provincial Lancashire town. She refuses to marry Allan, her lover. She makes it clear by explaining that she has refused because she doesn't wish to ruin "her" life not "his"; that she does not approve of "forced marriages" and that she never loved him in the first place. Allan is shocked at this last revelation but Fanny explains that she cannot understand why she should be condemned for pleasurable temporary dalliance while he, a man accepts it as a matter of course.

Hippolytus. Euripides (Greek). Tragedy. c. 450 B.C.

Aphrodite, furious with Hippolytus, a young mortal, because he worships only Artemis, plans his death. This is brought about when Hippolytus' stepmother Phedre falsely accuses him of making love to her, and he is driven into exile. Riding near the sea, Hippolytus' horse stumbles, dashing him against the rocks. As he lies dying in the presence of his father Theseus, Artemis appears in a cloud and explains that Hippolytus is an innocent victim of Aphrodite's jealousy and desire for vengeance.

Hirschbein, Perez (1880-   ). Yiddish playwright. Hirschbein was born in Lithuania, in the country. As a young man he moved to town and studied the Talmud and other subjects required of an orthdox Jew. Although he outgrew the dogmas of orthodoxy, his best plays depict just such people as the pious men who had educated him and raised him, and picture a religious way of life which is fast disappearing. His ambition was to write plays which would give a poignant picture of the Jewish poor— the farmers, peddlers, etc., of rustic Lithuania. Their poverty he knew from experience, for he himself had been a poor boy; their superstitions fascinated him, for he had been brought up to believe in them. His idols were Gorki and Hauptmann. Since his plays were primarily folk-plays, the atmosphere was more important than the plot or even character delineation. Perhaps it was due to the difficulty of transposing this atmosphere in an English version that his *The Haunted Inn* was a failure on Broadway.

Others of his plays, which have been given in Yiddish theatres in the United States and Europe, are: *Eva; Babel; Wayside Nook; The Snowstorm; The Stranger; When the Dew Falleth; In the Dark; On the Threshold; Twilight; The Carcass; Downhill; Across the River.*

His Majesty's Theatre. London playhouse. At Haymarket and Charles Street; built as *Her Majesty's Theatre* (Victoria being the ruler) by Sir Herbert Beerbohm Tree; opened 1897 with Gilbert Parker's *The Seats of the Mighty.* Sir Herbert spent money freely, and with his sumptuously staged Shakespearean revivals made it the most important center of theatrical art in Great Britain. The house was sold in 1918 to Joseph Benson, who leased it for twenty-eight years to Messrs. Grossmith and Laurillard.

Histrion. Name for an actor or buffoon in the early Roman theatre. Three kinds: those who, in the words of Thomas de Chabham, Sub-Dean of Salisbury (14th century) (1) "transform and transfigure their bodies with indecent dance and gesture, now indecently unclothing themselves, now putting on horrible masks"; (2) "who have no definite profession, but act as vagabonds, not having any certain domicile"; who "frequent the Courts of the great and say scandalous and shameful things concerning those who are not present so as to delight the rest"; (3) "who play musical instruments for the delectation of men, and of these there are two types": (a) those who "frequent public drinking-places and lascivious gatherings, and sing there stanzas to move men to lasciviousness"; (b) those who are called *jongleurs, . . .* sing of the *gestes* of princes and the lives of the saints."

Hit. A box-office success.

Hobson's Choice. Harold Brighouse (English). Comedy. 3 acts. 1916.

Maggie Hobson is the daughter of a Lancashire shoemaker and serves as her father's bookkeeper and clerk—without pay. She is a purposeful miss, and no one gets out of the store without buying if she is on the premises. In fact, she is so bossy that her father has resigned himself to her being an old maid—she is about thirty— and is occupying himself with seeking husbands for her two younger sisters. Even marriage is not beyond Maggie's powers, however, when she sets her mind to it. A grand dame of the village admires the handiwork of one William Mossop, a cobbler in Hobson's shop, and Maggie decides he shall be her future husband. He is engaged to someone else, but that fact does not faze her. Soon they are married, and have set up store in a cellar, while Maggie bosses her spouse all over the place. She sees that her two sisters are married as she wishes, and bullies their father into presenting them with suitable dowries. Then Hobson comes on troublous times, due to drink and business competition. His younger daughters, prosperously married, will not help, but Maggie returns home to him, leaving Will to handle the business. This he does successfully, having learned Maggie's lesson and become as bustling and efficient as she. And at the end of the play Hobson is signing papers which will establish the new firm of Mossop and Hobson.

Hofmannsthal, Hugo von (1874-1929). Austrian dramatist, poet. Noted for his adaptation of Sophocles' *Elektra,* 1902, which was set to music by Richard Strauss, and for his *Das Spiel von Jedermann,* 1912, an adaptation of *Everyman.* His original librettos for operas include: *Der Rosenkavalier* (music by Richard Strauss), 1911; *Ariadne auf Naxos,* 1912; *Die Frau ohne Schatten,* 1920. Born in Vienna, he was extremely receptive to the influences of any number of leading literary lights from Hugo to D'Annunzio, and even though his writing is colored with a palette taken from other men's work, nevertheless he gave impetus to the whole neo-Romantic drama of Germany. Richard Strauss was his friend and wrote music for some of his plays and Reinhardt produced them at Salzburg.

Hokum. Accepted sure-fire stock situations considered good for a laugh or a heart throb.

Holberg, Ludwig, Baron (1684-1754). Danish dramatist. Born in Norway, he supported himself by teaching. He traveled to a great extent, then returned to Copenhagen in 1716 to teaching.

From 1722-27 he became interested in the drama, and devoted himself to directing the new Danish theatre at Copenhagen. He produced numerous comedies and became known as the Moliere of Denmark.

In the third phase of his life, he produced a large number of historical, biographical and philosophical works.

He was among the first to write literature in the Danish tongue and is known as the founder of Danish literature.

Holcroft, Thomas (1745-1809). British dramatist. Prompter in a Dublin theatre, actor in strolling companies, until 1778, when his first play, *The Crisis* was produced at Drury Lane. Became the Paris correspondent for the London *Morning Herald.* Having seen Beaumarchais' *Le Mariage de Figaro* until he had it memorized, he did a successful translation from memory. It was produced as *The Follies of the Day* at Drury Lane in 1784. Also the author of novels and verse, his most successful melodrama was *The Road to Ruin,* 1792.

Holding up the back drop. Term applied to the show girls who do nothing on stage but wear costumes—or not wear them as the case may be.

Holiday. Philip Barry (American). Comedy. 3 acts. 1928.

Johnny Chase believes that life is made to be enjoyed and that holidays should be taken while one is young. This point of view does not satisfy his fiancée, Julia, or her father, who believe that business and power should be a man's goal. Holidays, however, do appeal to Julia's older sister, Linda. Johnny transfers his love to Linda, and they start on their honeymoon.

Holinshed, Raphael (? -1580?). English historian. Born of a Cheshire family, he came to London early in the reign of Elizabeth and was employed as a translator by Reginald Wolfe, the printer and publisher. While in his employ he planned the *Chronicles* (1577). These are known by his name but are by several hands. The *Historie of England* was Holinshed's own work. Other parts were translations, adaptations and the work of others. A few passages in the history of Ireland offended the Queen and were expunged. Holinshed's work was utilized by Shakespeare and other dramatists.

Honest Fellow. Holger Drachmann (Danish). 1898. Romantic drama. 4 acts.

The author, shortly before he wrote this play, had had a passionate experience with a music hall artist. This is a dramatic treatment of his own life story, with the time changed to the Middle Ages and the heroine's name changed to Gerda. The influence of Byron and other nineteenth century romanticists is evident.

Honest Whore, The. Thomas Dekker (English). Drama. 2 parts. 5 acts in each. 1604.

The play was written in two parts. Middleton is noted as collaborator of the first part. This play has some of the most famous lines of 17th century playwriting dealing with marital infidelity. Count Hippolito, discovering that Bellafront is a harlot convinces her to change her mode of life. She reforms and falls in love with Hippolito. He marries Infelice, daughter of the Duke of Milan and she marries Matheo, the man who originally seduced her. She is a loyal wife but Matheo, a roue, wishes her to return to harlotry as a source of income for him. Hippolito tries to force his attention on her but she resists. Orlando Frisiobaldo, her father, comes to her assistance. It is in his character portrayal that we see the great dramatic power of Dekker best exemplified.

Hoofer. A dancer; also known as a *heel-beater*.

Hook-up. To budget a show by close scrutiny of the production cost beside the operating cost.

Hope Theatre, London. Elizabethan theatre built on the site of the Paris Garden, later known as the Bear Garden, in 1613. It had a movable stage, so as to enable the building to be used also for baitings. Otherwise it was patterned after the Swan. In 1614 the Lady Elizabeth's company played in it. One day a fortnight was reserved for baiting. It changed occupants several times; in 1632 it was spoken of as "a building of excellent hope for players, wild beasts, and gladiators." Bear-baiting was suppressed in 1642, and in 1656 the house was dismantled.

Hopkins, Arthur (1878-   ). American producer and dramatist. Born in Cleveland, Ohio; started his career in journalism. Began as producer with *The Poor Little Rich Girl*, 1912. Produced: *On Trial, Good Gracious Annabella, Redemption, The Jest, Richard III, Macbeth, Hedda Gabler, Anna Christie, The Hairy Ape, Hamlet, What Price Glory, Burlesque, Paris Bound, Machinal, The Man On Stilts, Blow Ye Winds*, etc. Author of *How's Your Second Act* and *To A Lonely Boy*. He has also written several plays. His play *Conquest*, produced in February, 1933, was not a popular success but has fine dramatic quality. In collaboration he wrote *Burlesque*, which had a highly successful run on Broadway.

Hopkins, Miriam (1904-   ). American actress. Born in Bainbridge, Georgia, she made her first appearance in New York as a dancer in the *Music Box Revue*, 1921. First attracted attention in *Little Jessie James*, 1923. She appeared in numerous plays such as *Excess Baggage*, 1927; *The Camel Through the Needle's Eye*, 1929; *Lysistrata*, 1930; *Jezebel*, 1933. She began her moving picture career in 1930 and has appeared in a great many films, among them, *Fast and Loose, The Smiling Lieutenant, Becky Sharp, Barbary Coast, The Old Maid*.

Hopper, De Wolf (William De Wolf Hopper) (1858-1935). American singer, comedian. Was with the Weber and Fields Company after gaining prominence in New York in the 1880's and achieved fame in Gilbert and Sullivan roles. He will always be remembered for his recitation *Casey at the Bat* and the title role in *The Mikado*. Some of his more popular appearances were in *Patience; Iolanthe; The Yeoman of the Guard; The Better 'Ole; Erminie;* and *The Student Prince*. He is also co-author of the book *Once a Clown Always a Clown*.

He was married to (1) Ella Gardiner; (2) Ida Mosher; (3) Edna Wallace; (4) Nellie Bergen; (5) Ella Furry; (6) Lilian Glaser.

Hopper, Edna Wallace (Mrs. Albert O. Brown) (1864-   ). American actress. Born in San Francisco, California; made her debut as Mabel Douglas in *The Club Friend* at the Star Theatre, New York, 1891; was with Charles Frohman's Stock Company in musical comedy with De Wolf Hopper; appeared as Lady Holyrood in *Floradora*, 1900; became associated with the Lew Fields Company, 1906; played the leading role in *Girl o' Mine*, 1918; later in vaudeville; is now vice-president of the Edna Wallace Hopper Corporation and known for her youthful appearance.

Horace (Latin: Quintus Horatius Flaccus) (65-8 B.C.). Roman poet. Born at Venusia. He was educated in Rome and Athens. His friendship with Maecenas, Varius and Virgil laid the foundation for his adoption of literature as a career. He is most famous for his *Satires* and *Odes*. His *Ars poetica* (*Epistle to the Pisos*) is his principal contribution to dramatic theory.

Horizont, der. Continental theatres are roughly divided into two classes: those using the old fashioned painted wings and borders (*die Gassenbuehne*); the modern ones using *der Horizont*, or cyclorama.

See also *Cyclorama*.

Horniman, Annie Elizabeth Fredericka (1861-1937). British theatrical producer. Born in London, she became private secretary to William Butler Yeats. She was first connected with play production in 1894, and opened the Abbey Theatre, Dublin, in 1904. In 1907 she managed the Midland, and Gaiety Theatre in 1908. Some of the more than 200 plays she produced include: *Hindle Wakes; The Mob; The Younger Generation.*

Horseshoe Robinson. Clifton W. Tayleure (American). Drama. 3 acts. 1857. A story of the American Revolution in which Horseshoe Robinson, a soldier adventurer, captures Curry, the spy. "Lie there, where every mother's son ought to be— under an American freeman's boot," declares Robinson who finally leads a victorious American army.

This play forms a link between the early period of the pioneer story and the mid-period of American drama.

Hostage, The. Paul Claudel (French). Drama. 3 acts. Translated by Pierre Chavannes. 1911.

Sygne can save Pope Pius VI, Napoleon's hostage from death only by breaking her engagement with a cousin worthy of her love and by marrying a villain who has slain her parents. When the outraged cousin would shoot her wicked husband, Sygne steps between them, protecting the latter at the price of her life.

Hot light (television). Concentrated studio lighting.

The Hot Mikado. Swing version of Gilbert and Sullivan's *The Mikado* by Dan Goldberg. Produced in New York in March 1939 by Michael Todd. Not printed.

An all-Negro cast starring Bill Robinson "swing" the music of Sullivan to a rewritten book. After closing on Broadway the show reopened at the Music Hall of the New York World's Fair.

Hôtel de Bourgogne. A famous theatre in France during the 16th and 17th centuries, leased, as their second theatre after the Hôpital de la Trinité, by the Confrérie de la Passion. The Hôtel did not greatly resemble a theatre; it had a wide, lengthy, but low hall, a deep stage which was lighted by a row of candles at the front, two galleries at either side of the auditorium and the central pit where the audience stood or wandered about. Here was the home of the French farce. During its visits to Paris the Italian *commedia dell' arte* troupe gave their performances in this theatre. A sketch of a performance of a French farce here by the French printer, Abraham Bosse, helps to establish the close affinity of the French farce with the Italian *commedia dell' arte*. It was here that the *décor simultané* was first used. Tragi-comedy, recognizable as a distinct form, also saw its beginnings in this theatre. Tragedies were part of the repertory. (Generally its repertory consisted of moral tragedies, allegorical and political plays, tragi-comedies, tragic histories, farces, *soties* and mysteries.) With the Hôtel Guénégaud (the latter a merger of the Théâtre du Marais and the company left by Molière when he died) it became the Théâtre Francais or Comédie Française.

Hôtel de Rambouillet. The most famous meeting-place and salon of Parisian high society in the 17th century. Here plays were frequently performed before select gatherings.

Hôtel Guénégaud. A merger of the Théâtre du Marais with the company left by Molière when he died and later merging with the Hôtel de Bourgogne to form what is now known as the Comédie Française.

Hotel Universe. Philip Barry (American). Drama. 1 act. 1930.

In a villa in southern France, a noted physicist has as his guests a set of thwarted, unhappy people. Through his knowledge of life forces they are able to regain mental health by turning back to someone they have loved. The actress remembers her father; the Catholic, his priest; the sophisticate, his first romance.

Houdini, Harry (1874-1926). American magician, author. Born Harry Weiss, in Appleton, Wisconsin, the eventual Houdini progressed from trapeze performer to master escape artist (releasing himself from handcuffs, chains, etc., was his most notable feat) and President of both the Society of American Magicians and the Magicians' Club of London. Wrote *Handcuff Secrets; Spooks and Spiritualism; Rope Ties and Escapes.*

Hour Glass, The. William Butler Yeats (Irish). Drama. 1903.

Really a modern morality play. The characters even take the names of the dramatis personae of medieval morality plays: they are called simply a Wise Man, his Pupils, a Fool. The Wise Man represents reason without faith; the Fool, blind impulse and trust; the Pupils are those who accept unquestioningly whatever they are told. The Wise Man, a rationalist and a materialist, denies the existence of an unseen world of the spirit and teaches his Pupils to be skeptical. Then they come across a contrary opinion in their readings and ask the Wise Man for an explanation. His confidence in himself is momentarily shaken. At that moment the world of the spirit takes shape and becomes visible to him—in the form of an angel who warns the Wise Man that he must die when the sands of the hour glass run down, unless, before that time, he has found one person who believes. The Wise Man searches, but in vain. His pupils, faithful to his own teachings, are hopeless. Only the Fool believes, and he is concerned with foolish things, too indifferent to bother to state his belief. But he is finally aroused, and the Wise Man saved. This ending is like that in the old legend which was Yeats' inspiration. In 1912 the Irish poet revised the end of his play, however, and had the Wise Man, unable to save himself, submit meekly to the will of the Lord. It is this revised version of the play which is generally given when it is revived now.

Technically and stylistically flawless, this has been called by some Yeats' finest play.

House. Term used to indicate the audience and used in reference to the size of the audience.

House boards. The boards, or frames, outside a theatre where the posters, or painted boards, are placed; these carry the information concerning title, star, theatre and time of performance.

House full of paper. An audience admitted altogether, or largely, on passes.

House lights. Term applied to the lighting equipment in the auditorium proper, as differentiated from stage lights.

House of Connelly, The. Paul Green (American). Drama. 2 acts. 1931.

A picture of the decadent but proud aristocracy of the old South, forced to make way for the representatives of the new democracy. The Connelly's are a typical Southern family: two old maid sisters, inhibited and repressed; Uncle Bob, run-down and dissolute, with a jollity born of drink; his nephew Will, spineless, unable even to shoot straight. As Will says: "The great Connellys are all dead. The fools and the weak are left alive." Patsy Tate, a tenant on the plantation, is poor white trash, but she has the brains and determination Will lacks. Will is attracted to the girl, and associates with her despite his aunts' reminders that there "never was anybody good enough for a Connelly." At a Christmas Eve party, their relations reach a climax. His aristocratic fiancée notices Will's indifference and is piqued by it. And dissolute Uncle Bob makes love to Patsy. Will comes to her defense and knocks the old man to the ground. Patsy asks if she can help him reorganize the plantation, confesses that she loves him. As the months pass Will becomes an active landlord, parceling out work to the tenants and improving the farm, with Patsy's counsel. Then his mother warns him the girl is a schemer, caring only for the land, and in his disillusionment Will takes to drink and lets the farm go. Finally Patsy upbraids him. When he accuses her of loving not him but his land, she admits that that was the reason she encouraged him at first, but that she has grown to love him. In a righteous mood again, Will gives Uncle Bob a violent tongue-lashing for his immorality, and the old man shoots himself. As another Christmas rolls around Will and Patsy are married. Will's aunts leave the house rather than receive the girl as its mistress, the servants are refractory, but Will and Patsy, undaunted, are ready to make an uphill fight and finish the task which they have begun, of bringing back prosperity to the house of Connelly.

Housman, Laurence (1867-   ). English novelist and playwright. He first attracted attention as an artist by his illustration of some works of Shelley, Meredith and Christina Rossetti. He is the author of many books of verse and prose as well as plays. Among his better known plays are *Lysistrata* (adaptation), 1910; *Bird in Hand*, 1918; *Mr. Gladstone's Comforter*, 1929; *Palace Plays*, 1930; *Victoria Regina*, 1935, which was one of the best plays of its season and had an exceptionally long run in New York and on tour.

Howard, Bronson (1842-1908). American dramatist. Began writing plays while a newspaper reporter. *Saratoga,* his first serious play, produced by Augustin Daly in 1870, made managers change their attitude towards the native drama. American drama was at a low ebb and plays by Americans on American themes virtually did not exist. The theatre was then crowded with foreign dramas, mostly French and English. Howard's success with *Saratoga* gave new impetus to the native drama and paved the way for native playwrights like Clyde Fitch, Augustus Thomas, William Gillette and others. His greatest success came in 1887 with *The Henrietta,* a satire on American business. His *Shenandoah,* taken over by Charles Frohman in 1889, established Frohman as a producer, and made a fortune for both Frohman and Howard. Founder of the first society for dramatic authors. His library is housed in the offices of the Dramatists' Guild.

Howard, Leslie (1893-   ). British actor. Born in London, he started out as a bank clerk, then joined the army. After his discharge he made his first appearance on the stage in 1917 when he toured in *Peg O' My Heart* and *Charley's Aunt.* He first appeared on the London stage in *The Freaks,* 1918. After many successful roles he came to New York to play in *Just Suppose,* 1920. He became a very popular matinee idol. Some of the plays he appeared in are *Outward Bound,* 1924; *The Green Hat,* 1924; *Her Cardboard Lover,* 1927; *Berkeley Square,* 1929; *Candlelight,* 1929; *The Animal Kingdom,* 1932; *The Petrified Forest,* 1935; *Hamlet,* 1936. He has produced and staged a number of the plays he has appeared in.

He has also had great success in the moving pictures which he entered in 1930. Among the films he has made are *Outward Bound, Berkeley Square, Of Human Bondage, The Scarlet Pimpernel, The Petrified Forest.*

He is also the author of a play, *Murray Hill,* produced in London, 1928, under the title, *Tell Me the Truth,* and later rewritten as *Elizabeth Steps Out.*

Howard, Sidney Coe (1891-1939). American dramatist. Born at Oakland, California; graduate of the University of California and student in Baker's 47 Work-shop, Harvard. He served in the First World War. In 1919 he joined the staff of *Life,* of which he became the literary editor. Shortly thereafter, he began to write plays. His first play was *Swords,* 1921. Then followed *S. S. Tenacity* (from the French); *Casanova* (from the Spanish), 1923; *Sancho Panza* (from the Hungarian), 1923; *Bewitched,* 1924; *They Knew What They Wanted,* 1925, which won for him the Pulitzer prize. These plays were tremendously successful. Then followed *Lucky Sam Carver; Ned McCobb's Daughter; The Silver Cord,* 1926; *Half Gods,* 1929; *Marseilles* and *The Late Christopher Bean* (both from the French), 1932; *Alien Corn,* 1933; the stage adaptation of Sinclair Lewis' novel, *Dodsworth; Yellow Jack* and *Ode to Liberty,* 1934. In 1935 he wrote the adaptation of *Paths of Glory* for the stage. Some of his better motion pictures are *Bull Dog Drummond; Condemned; Raffles; A Lady to Love; Free Love; The Greeks Had a Word for It;* Sinclair Lewis' *Arrowsmith;* and screen versions of his own plays *The Silver Cord* and *Christopher Bean.* He was tragically killed when a tractor ran into him. On the day of his death he had put in a morning of work on a new play based on Carl Van Doren's *Benjamin Franklin*. He was one of the country's major playwrights, and a leading force in the contemporary theatre.

Howard, Willie (1883-   ). American actor and vocalist. Made his debut in 1897 as a boy soprano at Proctor's 125th Street Theatre, New York. In 1902 was in vaudeville doing imitations; with his brother Eugene toured the United States until 1912 when he began appearing for the Messrs. Shubert at the Winter Garden, New York. He was with them over a period of ten years. Appeared in *Sky High* at the Apollo Theatre, New York, in 1925; played in George White's *Scandals* from 1926 to 1931, in *Ballyhoo of 1932* at the 44th St. Theatre and in *The Ziegfeld Follies* at the Winter Garden in 1934. He is famous as a comedian and in recent years has appeared in several motion pictures.

Howells, William Dean (1837-1920). American author. He was the leader in the realistic treatment of familiar life; his example, inspiration and critical judgments guided and encouraged Harrigan, Herne, Thomas and Fitch, who have expressed their obligation to him directly and implicitly. From his editorial chair on the *Atlantic Monthly* and from his "Editor's Study" and "Easy Chair" in *Harper's Magazine*, 1866-1920, he preached the doctrine of truth to life in all art, and when he touched the drama his judgment was sane and discriminating.

In his earlier plays he introduces his characters by delightful touches of description in which he anticipates both Barrie and Shaw, to mention only two of his many successors. As Clyde Fitch has said, the Eighties and Nineties were "the Howells age." and many who do not acknowledge it were affected by his unending struggle for truth in art. His plays include: *A Counterfeit Presentment*, 1877; *Yorick's Love* (from the Spanish), 1884; *The Garroters*, 1886; and *The Mouse Trap*, 1889. The best collection of Howells' books is in the library of the University of Southern California, Los Angeles.

How He Lied to Her Husband. George Bernard Shaw (English). Farce. 1 act. c. 1905.

A one-act burlesque of the author's own *Candida*. Henry, young society blade, is frankly and desperately in love with Aurora, an older woman and married. He has even written any number of poems to her. Unfortunately Aurora's husband's sister finds the verses and proceeds at once to give them to Edward, the faithful husband. Aurora is at her wits' end. She pleads with Henry to lie to her husband, to say that he wrote the poems to some other Aurora—anything to avert suspicion. Whereupon Edward arrives, flourishing the poems. Henry immediately proclaims his innocence, announces that the Aurora celebrated in the lyrics is none other than the rosy-fingered dawn. What is more, he would never think of writing verses to Edward's wife; she is positively distasteful to him. Her husband grows furious. How dare the young pup be so insolent? Cabinet ministers have fought for the honor of making love to Aurora. The young man is forced to use his fists to defend himself. Arising from the floor, he proclaims that he does in truth find Aurora attractive above all women. Edward, delighted, promises to publish the poems at his own expense, with a dedication to "Aurora, wife of Edward Bumpus, Esq."

Hoyt, Charles Hale (1860-1900). American dramatist. Born in Concord, New Hampshire, went into cattle business in Colorado; became a newspaper man, then started to write plays. His satires on contemporary events made him one of the most successful writers of his day. Typescripts of most of his plays exist in the New York Public Library. His plays include: *A Bunch of Keys; A Parlor Match; A Rag Baby; A Tin Soldier; A Hole in the Ground; A Brass Monkey; A Midnight Bell; A Texas Steer; or, Money Makes the Mare Go; A Trip to Chinatown; A Milk White Flag; A Temperance Town; A Contented Woman; A Black Sheep; A Stranger in New York; A Day and a Night; A Dog in a Manger; A Runaway Colt.*

Hrotsvitha of Gandersheim (born about 935). German playwright. Hrotsvitha's exact dates are unknown. Presumably she was of gentle birth, and she became a nun of the Order of St. Benedict when about twenty-three years of age. In the convent of Gandersheim where she lived, this medieval German nun wrote a number of plays. She wrote in Latin, the language of educated people of the period, but without publicizing her work. It was not until the end of the fifteenth century that her manuscripts were discovered; the plays were first printed in 1501.

They are *Gallicanus; Dulcitius; Callimachus; Abraham; Paphnutius; Sapienta.* They are all based on religious legends of the saints; chastity and virginity were glorified in them. The author is endearingly pious and naïve; her conscience troubled her that she should even have to mention, albeit in derogatory terms, things "which should not be named." She is a believer in miracles, a primitive who is to literature what Cimabue and Giotto are to painting. Yet strangely enough, the form of her plays was that of the bawdy Latin comedies of Terence.

Hughes, Archie (-1860?). Actor. A player who had the distinction of being the first performer to do a monologue on the stage in the form of "gags" told between the verses of a song, in this case a song called *George, the Charmer.*

Hughes, Elinor (1906-). American motion picture and dramatic editor. Born in Cambridge, Massachusetts; received an A.B. from Radcliffe College. Reviewed films and wrote a daily column for The Boston Herald; motion picture and dramatic editor for the same paper since 1934; is the author of the two books *Famous Stars of Filmdom* (*Men*) and *Famous Stars of Filmdom* (*Women*).

Hughes, Hatcher (1883-). American playwright. Born in Polkville, N. C., he taught English at the University of North Carolina, then went to Columbia for post-graduate work and then went into the drama department. Since 1912 he has become a professor and has been teaching playwriting at Columbia. He collaborated with Elmer Rice on *Wake Up, Jonathan,* 1921. In 1924 he wrote *Hell Bent for Heaven,* the choice of which as the Pulitzer prize play for that year caused an outbreak against the award. He has also written *It's a Grand Life,* 1930, with Alan Williams; *The Lord Blesses the Bishop,* 1934.

Hughes, Margaret (1643?-1719). One of the earliest English actresses. Like Mary Betterton, she is accredited with being the first woman to play the role of Desdemona, at the Theatre Royal (subsequently Drury Lane) in 1663. Before she left the stage as mistress to Prince Rupert, she played Theodosia in Dryden's *Evening's Love* and Panura in Fletcher's *Island Princess*. She returned to the theatre in 1676, playing in the dramas of D'Urfey, Aphra Behn, Charles Sedley and others. There is a fine portrait of her by Lely.

Hugo, Victor Marie, Viscount (1802-1885). French dramatist, novelist, poet. In his Preface to his drama *Cromwell,* 1827, he showed his allegiance to The Romanticist School, and soon became the greatest exponent of that school. The production of his tragedy *Hernani,* 1830, caused a minor riot between the Classicists and the Romanticists. It shattered the three unities and other conventions which had held the French stage since about 1636. Irving Babbitt said: "The total impression *Hernani* produces is that of a *parvenu* melodrama."

Other plays include *Marion Delorme,* 1831, and *Ruy Blas,* 1838. His great novels, *Nôtre Dame de Paris* (*Hunchback of Notre Dame*) and *Les Miserables* have been made into moving pictures.

Hull House Players. A play-producing group at Hull House, the Chicago settlement house. This famous settlement house stressed the importance of social recreation and diversion. The group emerged from the "club" system instituted in social settlements formed among people of similar interests. The great impetus of the "Little Theatre" movement emerged from Chicago and these groups became centres of great experimentation and originality.

Human Flesh. Henri Bataille (French). Drama. 3 acts. 1922.

The story of a man enriched by the World War who learns from a mistress long since abandoned that the son she bore him has fallen at the front. Hitherto he has kept his legitimate son out of fighting, but now he enters the conflict and wins distinction. Then his half-brother, supposedly dead, returns alive, released from a German prison. Although urged by his mother to claim a share of his father's estate, he declines. He will withdraw with his mother to the country, while the father and the legitimate son will continue to live in town. *Human Flesh* was Bataille's last play.

Hundred Years Old (The Centenarian). Serafin and Joaquin Alvarez Quintero (Spanish). Comedy. 3 acts. 1909.

At the celebration of his one hundredth birthday, Papa Juan is busy making peace in his large quarreling family, and in uniting two lovers. He has led a full colorful life, striving and succeeding in his successive aims. He is not discouraged by derogatory jibes of his neighbors when at the age of 76 he builds himself a new home. He is not ready for the tomb. His goal is to reach his hundredth birthday. He does attain this dream and gathers around him his large family. It is a family of mixed fortunes. His new idea is to unite his favorite great-granddaughter to her cousin a rollicking adventurer type. The family is split over his arrangement resenting the old man's lack of differentiation between his well fixed descendants and the poor or ne'er-do-wells. Papa Juan triumphs and ends the celebration by bestowing his blessing on the contented couple—Papa's new aim being a great-great-grandson.

Huneker, James Gibbons (1860-1921). American critic. Born in Philadelphia, he began studying law, but gave it up to study music. He became music and dramatic critic for the New York Recorder and The Morning Advertiser in about 1890, and for the New York Sun in 1902. In 1912 he left the Sun to write for the New York Times, where he worked from 1912-1919. In that year he returned to the Sun. In February 9th, 1921, he died in Brooklyn.

He is noted as a stylist and keen critic. His sophistication, and familiarity with the continental drama served to widen the horizon of the American theatre.

The Huntington Library. See *Theatre collections.*

Huret (17th century) French printer. His print of *Michau* and *Dr. Boniface,* stock-characters of the contemporary French theatre, is taken as an indication of the close affinity between the French *farce* and Italian *commedia dell' arte.*

Huston, Walter (1884-). American actor. Born in Canada, he made his first appearance on the stage at Toronto in 1902. In 1905 he appeared in New York in a drama called *In Convict Stripes,* toured in another play, and then left the stage for many years. In 1909 he returned to appear in vaudeville with his first wife as Whipple and Huston. 1924 saw his return to the legitimate stage, from which time on he has appeared successfully in a great number of plays. Among them are *Desire under the Elms,* 1924; *Kongo,* 1926; *The Barker,* 1927; *Dodsworth,* 1934, in which he scored a tremendous success both in New York and on tour; *Knickerbocker Holiday,* 1938. In 1928 he embarked on a motion picture career which has also proved successful. He has appeared in *Gentlemen of the Press, Abraham Lincoln, The Criminal Code, Rain, Kongo, The Prizefighter and the Lady,* etc.

Hutton, Joseph (1787-1828). American actor, dramatist. There are few records of facts about the life of Hutton. However, it is generally conceded that he was a much better dramatist than an actor. Born in Philadelphia, his play *The School for Prodigals* was given at the Chestnut Street Theatre in 1808. His next effort was a musical afterpiece *The Wounded Hussar; or, Rightful Heir,* 1809. Then followed *Fashionable Follies,* 1809, and *The Orphan of Prague,* 1810. Various theatrical sources reveal that Hutton's experiences as an itinerant player were wide, and if known, they would no doubt be full of color. In 1823, he moved to Newbern, North Carolina, where, tired of the road, he lived with his family until his death. He devoted himself to teaching and became a regular contributor to the Newbern *Sentinel.*

Hyacinth Halvey. Lady Augusta Gregory (Irish). Comedy. 1 act. 1906.
The theme is based upon a simple and universal philosophical truth: that reputation is in a great measure a matter of "a password or an emotion."

Hyacinth Halvey boasts of his crime of stealing a sheep from a butcher shop. However, to his dismay, he is congratulated by the butcher, who saved prosecution by a government inspector by having the meat disappear.

Hypodorian. See *Modes.*

Hypophrygian. See *Modes.*

Hyposcenium. Name given to stage in Roman theatre.

Ibsen, Henrik (1828-1906). Norwegian dramatist. Born at Skien, Norway, he spent some years at the small town of Grimstad as apprentice to an apothecary. In 1850 he entered the University of Christiania. It was at this time that he began writing plays—poetic dramas on historical and legendary subjects more or less in the pseudo-classical style of the day. After traveling in Denmark and Germany, he became director of the Bergen Theatre, where he remained for five years. He then went to Christiania as manager of the theatre, a position which he left in 1862, becoming "aesthetic adviser" to still another theatre. In 1864 he went to Italy and Germany. Ten years later he returned to his native land for a short period after which he took up his residence in Germany, remaining there until 1891. From that time until his death in 1906 he lived in Christiania. Isben's international reputation is due not so much to his technical achievements as to his popularization, in play form, of the social problem.

He was one of the most important influences in the Modern Theatre. His departure from the stilted Victorian Drama, his insistence on treating contemporary problems openly and frankly were radical for a playwright of this era. Pinero, a popular contemporary of his, dealt with the drama of secrecy, the woman of mystery, hiding her misdeeds. Ibsen brought her problems out in the open. Ibsen not only had a story to tell but he had an idea behind it. His audience was to reflect as well as to feel. He had no hesitancy in dealing with sociological problems never before brought out in the open. He found opposition among the critics but persisted, then turned to the use of symbolism in some of his later plays but this did not detract from their sense of realism. He had a profound influence on stagecraft and was the great precursor of realism in drama with his emphasis on moral and social truth.

His plays include: *The Pretenders,* 1864; *Brand,* 1866; *Peer Gynt,* 1867; *The League of Youth,* 1869; *The Pillars of Society,* 1877; *A Doll's House,* 1879; *Ghosts,* 1881; *An Enemy of the People,* 1882; *The Wild Duck,* 1884; *Rosmersholm,* 1886; *The Lady from the Sea,* 1888; *Hedda Gabler,* 1890; *The Master Builder,* 1894; *John Gabriel Borkman,* 1894; *When We Dead Awaken,* 1899.

Icebound. Owen Davis (American). Drama. 3 acts. 1923.
Winner of the Pulitzer Prize award for 1923.
The Jordans are northern New Englanders, Puritans as stern and uncompromis-

ing as the rockbound coast on which they live. The clan is composed of Henry, middle-aged, weary and resigned; his wife Emma, fat and forty and formidable; Nettie, her daughter by her first marriage, a shallow coquette; Sadie, Henry's sister, a widow; her young son Orin. Ella, an unhappy spinster. As they sit waiting greedily for Mother Jordan to die in her upstairs room so they can split her money, they are joined by Ben, the black sheep of the family, who fled many years before when under indictment for arson and has not visited them since. He is dissipated and arrogant. While he is quarreling with his brother Henry the old lady dies. Jane Crosby, a distant relative who has been caring for the woman, and who has summoned Ben to be at her deathbed, is left the whole estate. The Jordans are furious but can do nothing. And Jane proceeds to order things in her own way. First, she is determined to reform Ben, the dead woman's favorite son. When the sheriff comes for him, she agrees to stand bail for Ben if he will stay on the farm and help work it until the trial. To the others Jane is less kind, obdurately refusing all requests for loans. Yet association with Ben gradually almost mellows her, and when her birthday comes she actually plans a party and buys a pretty new blue dress in which to surprise Ben. Vain Nettie finds the dress in Jane's room and puts it on. When Jane comes upon them Nettie is in Ben's arms kissing him. But the thought of loving a jailbird frightens Nettie, and the affair peters out. Several months afterward Jane calls another family meeting and informs the gathering she is turning the icebound farm and other assets over to Ben. She has persuaded the judge to convince the plaintiff against Ben to drop the arson charge; moreover, his mother always had loved Ben and wanted him to have her money, but had instructed Jane to look out for him until he was worthy of it. The drudge, her work done, is ready to leave the farm, but Ben realizes that the feeling he has felt for her is love and begs her to remain. She consents to stay on as his wife.

Ice Drift, The. Max Halbe (German). Drama. 3 acts. 1892.

The conflict between an old school father and a son with ideals of social justice, who treats his workmen well. Ironically the men desert him to carouse in a tavern, when the dikes need protection and later break, flooding the land.

Most of Halbe's plays deal with the struggles of individuals against conditions which keep them enslaved and although most of his heroes end up as embittered or disillusioned men his dramas have great power and stamina. Later he wrote a play called *The Stream* which was reminiscent of this earlier play.

Iconoscope (television). Camera tube, developed by Dr. Vladimir K. Zworykin.

Ideal Husband, An. Oscar Wilde (English). Comedy. 1895.

One of Wilde's highly epigrammatic comedies, so studded with bons mots, particularly in the first act, that the dialogue becomes a veritable tour de force.

The plot concerns the machinations of a Mrs. Cheveley, "A genius in the daytime and a beauty at Night." As the play opens this brilliant adventuress is attending a soiree given by Lord and Lady Chilton in their London home. Lady Chilton recognizes her as a schoolmate who was expelled for theft. Robert Chilton knows her too, though he does not mention it to his wife. Robert, at forty is Under-Secretary of Foreign Affairs, famous for his probity. But eighteen years previously he committed one grievous error. Anxious at that time for wealth and the power that goes with it, he made money by selling a state secret. Mrs. Chevelv has Chilton's incriminating letter and uses it now to blackmail Robert. She is anxious for Robert to report favorably on a project. He is strongly against this but he agrees in order to save his reputation. When his wife learns of his volte-face, for which she does not know the reason, she shows such disappointment that he writes Mrs. Cheveley that he cannot keep his promise. The next day Mrs. Cheveley calls on Lady Chilton. The women quarrel and Lady Chilton learns of her husband's dishonesty. But everything ends happily and Robert is offered a Cabinet post to cap his good fortune.

Ideal spectator. A term applied to the Greek chorus as medium for the introduction of extraneous musical and poetic passages in the performance of a drama. It went out of usage as the chorus declined in importance in the theatre.

Ideal Wife, The. Marco Praga (Italian). Drama. 5 acts. 1890.
An ironic study of feminine disloyalty in the manner of Henry Becque and the French naturalists. The play is a character study of Guilia, who is fond of her husband, and therefore manages her affair with his friend skillfully enough to avoid even the slightest suspicion.

Idiot's Delight. Robert E. Sherwood (American). Drama. 3 acts. 1936.
An Alpine hotel has as its guests a young English couple, a German scientist, a French munitions man, Harry the American vaudevillian with his troupe, and the mysterious Irene. While the war has been threatening, the guests are isolated in the hotel. The dialogue turns on the useless idiotic waste of war and yet the ineffectualness of "the little people," the average citizens, to do anything about it. One by one the guests depart leaving only Irene and Harry, who recapture their almost forgotten love. They decide to carry on their own lives in their own way, regardless of the major events.
This play was awarded the Pulitzer Prize for 1936.

I'd Rather Be Right. Book by George S. Kaufman and Moss Hart; lyrics by Lorenz Hart; music by Richard Rodgers. (American). Musical comedy. 2 acts. 1937.
Phil Barker and Mary Jones cannot get married until Phil receives a raise which his employer cannot grant until business improves. Phil dreams he meets President Franklin D. Roosevelt in Central Park and tells him his dilemma. The President, determined to help Phil, decides to balance the budget. This task becomes the President's platform for re-election.

If. Lord Edward Dunsany (Irish). Fantasy. 4 acts. 1921.
One morning John Beal, a prosaic little clerk living in the London suburbs, misses the 8:10 train to work. For ten years he is haunted by the thought that his life might

have been changed into something exciting and wonderfully different if he had only caught the train that day. So when he is given a chance to look into a crystal globe and wish for whatever he desires, he asks for another start, to be permitted to catch that train which went to London ten years previously. Immediately he finds himself in an unmapped and mountainous land in the wilds of Persia. He is the country's swashbuckling ruler, living adventure after adventure, breaking idols, slaying kings, steeped in gold and blood, surrounded by conspirators and voluptuous Oriental dancers. Yet through it all he remains a clerk at heart. His fortunes change and he returns to London, penniless, begging crusts at his own door. Whereupon he wakes up, cured of regrets for what might have been, and is contented to resume his placid, humdrum existence.

Iffland, August Wilhelm (1767?-1814). German actor, dramatist. In 1794 he became superintendant of the Berlin Royal Court Theatre, and in 1784-95 acted at the Mannheim National Theatre. For his time, he wrote unparalleled plays with simple, unsophisticated characters and well-invented plots. He reached his highest peak in fame as an actor in Weimar in 1796 and was best in those roles which required coolness and reserve.

His plays include: *Der Jager; Crime;* and *Ambition.*

If I Were King. Justin Huntley McCarthy (American). Drama. 1901.

One of the most enduring romantic dramas. E. H. Sothern, who was originally starred in it, revived it frequently. It was also the basis for a popular musical comedy, *The Vagabond King.*

The plot concerns an imaginary incident in the life of François Villon, fifteenth century French poet and scoundrel. Villon is roistering with friends in a tavern and reading them his verses expressing contempt for Louis XI and stating what he would do if he were king when the monarch himself enters incognito, and hits on a novel punishment for his critic. In a brawl the poet has killed the King's Constable, who was in disfavor with the high-born Katherine de Vaucelles. So when Villon is drunk with much wine, the King has him transported to the palace and announces when he awakes that he has been made Grand Constable of France in the place of the man he has slain. He is to have full power for one week; after that he is to be executed. The days pass. The King, piqued at the indifference of the lady Katherine toward himself, decides to avenge himself on her. He tells Villon that if he can win the lady's hand before his time is up, he will be pardoned and allowed to live. Villon wins the lady's heart, and then reveals his true identity. She is horrified that she has been so weak as to listen to the wooing of the rough fellow who went to her defense in the tavern, and her love turns to hate. Villon makes good the boast expressed in his poem and leads the French troops to victory at the gates of the city, where they rout the Burgundians who were besieging them. Then he returns to the palace to be executd as ordained. The people hail him and demand his life, and the King asks for a substitute. Katherine, unable to see her lover die, comes forward. The King banishes both her and Villon, and, having cheated the gallows, the happy couple go forth together into exile.

Ike. See *Iconoscope*.

Ikria. The wooden benches arranged in a semi-circle on the slope of the ancient Greek amphitheatre.

Ile. Eugene O'Neill (American). Drama. 1 act. 1916.

The captain of a whaling boat faces mutiny but refuses to return home until the hold is full of oil. His wife, slowly going mad from loneliness, finally persuades him to turn back, but a whale is sighted and the captain resumes the chase. His wife goes insane.

Illustre Théâtre. A French acting company formed in 1643, whose chief claim to distinction seems to be the fact that Molière was with them for a brief time and thus received his first experience as a player. The company performed in Paris and its environs.

I Married an Angel. Richard Rodgers and Lorenz Hart (American). Musical comedy. 2 acts. 1938.

Count Palaffi, weary and disillusioned, vows he will marry no mortal woman, only an angel. Immediately an angel descends from heaven and they are married. Believing that "truth is beauty, and beauty is truth," the angel all but wrecks her husband's business and alienates his affections. However, a wise countess friend, formerly a prima donna in "Blossom Time," teaches the angel deception, and helps her win back her husband.

Imitation. A fundamental principle of Aristotle's *Poetics,* easily susceptible of misinterpretation. It refers not to mere copying or reporting of life, but to creation through re-creation. The poet, drawing component elements from life, makes from these fragments a repatterned whole; forming from the inconsistencies of life a clear picture revealing an ideal or universal truth. Thus the actor, aping no one person, but borrowing mannerisms and characteristics from many, synthesizes them into a convincing whole—a real character.

Imitation des anciens. An expression used in France in the 17th century to describe the neo-classicist school of Corneille and Racine; means "imitation of the ancients," or emulation of the early Greek and Roman dramatists, such as Aeschylus, Sophocles, Euripides, Terence and Plautus.

Immortal Jew, The. Sidney Royce Lysaght (Irish). Drama. 3 acts. 1901.

A character study of Stephen, a wandering Jew, stressing his courage; the weakness which causes duplicity and the betrayal of a friend; his remorse; and always, his uncertainty and fear.

It is a moving work, but really more a poem in dramatic form than a poetic drama. Thus Lysaght, a successor to Synge and Yeats and the older Irish playwrights, inherits their lyricism but fails to be as effective on the stage.

Impassioned Wife, The (L'Amoureuse). Georges de Porto-Riche (French). Drama. 5 acts. 1891.

An intellectual and scientific husband has married only to secure calm and tranquillity in order better to work out his research in medicine. He finds, much to his distaste, that his wife is attracted by his coolness and is determined to make him love her. He gladly relinquishes her to a former lover but she returns determined to stay with him. Georges de Porto-Riche wrote most of his plays in this vein, his forte being mostly plays of passion.

Imperial theme. Term coined by George Wilson Knight in his book *The Imperial Theme* to represent all manifestations in Shakespeare's plays of the "vital spark." Mr. Knight says of his book that it is "concerned primarily with what I have termed 'life' themes. By this I intend themes which are positive and optimistic and consistently related throughout Shakespeare to images suggestive of brightness and joy."

Impersonation, male. Women appearing as men; breeches parts as in *The Country Wife, As You Like It,* etc. were popular in the 17th and 18th centuries; many actresses assayed men's roles including Sarah Bernhardt, Eva LeGallienne, Nellie Holbrook, Anna Dickinson, Esmé Beringer as Hamlet; Rebekah Deering, Kate Bateman as Richard III; Charlotte Cushman as Romeo; the same actress, as well as Lucille Laverne as Shylock; Maude Adams, Eva LeGallienne as Peter Pan; Marguerite Clarke in *The Prince and the Pauper,* etc.

Impersonators, female. Include Charles Hart, Edward Kynaston, James Nokes, Charles Heywood, Bothwell Brown, George B. Pettengill, Tony Hart, Henry E. Dixey, the Russell Brothers, McIntyre and Heath, George Munro, Bert Savoy, Harry Rogers, Karyl Norman, Francis Renault, Albert Carroll, Peter Joray, etc.; among the famous Chinese female impersonators are Mei Lang-fang and Ch'en Gen-chòiu.

Importance of Being Earnest, The. Oscar Wilde (English). Comedy. 3 acts. 1895.

Jack Worthing invents an imaginary younger brother, Earnest, who demands attention whenever Jack needs a convenient alibi or escape for a week-end holiday. Cicely, Jack's ward, becomes interested in this brother, but the lie gets out of hand when Algernon Moncrieff, Jack's friend, introduces himself to Cicely as Earnest. Jack tells Algernon he is going to propose to Gwendolyn, Algie's cousin, who knows him as Earnest. Gwendolyn says she will marry Jack emphasizing her great fondness for the name "Earnest" and her feeling that she was fated to marry an "Earnest." Gwen's mother, Lady Brackwell, does not consent to the marriage, due to Jack's dubious paternity. In the interval Cecily and Algy have become engaged. Cecily, too, has a predilection for the name Earnest. Jack returns to the country deciding to kill off the now troublesome imaginary Earnest only to hear he is in the house. Jack and Algy decide to be rechristened. Gwen and Cecily find they are presumably engaged to the same man, "Earnest Worthing." When the young men return everything is cleared up and upon hearing their desires to be re-named they forgive all. Lady Brackwell arrives and discovers that Jack is really Algy's lost brother Earnest and all ends well. Mr. Wilde's comedies are more important than his serious plays and of all his comedies *The Importance of Being Earnest* is probably his most popular.

Impressionism. A theory of art that naturally has important bearings on the drama. In general, impressionism is the theory that artistic production of any kind should be concerned with *appearances* rather than with *realities*. A brown tree will look blue under certain conditions. Thus on canvas it may look more like the tree, if blue pigment is used rather than brown, though it is not blue at all. Obviously, this principle is very important in scenic design and costume in the theatre where the conditions of light, space, etc. are so vastly different from the actualities portrayed. Belasco's realism was faulty for this reason. The exact real things cannot be reproduced: in reality we see the things in a room when we are in the room and we see only part of it—that part within the orbit of our eyes. Whereas in the theatre the audience is at a distance, sees all the room on the stage which is either above or below the level of the eyes.

Therefore on the stage the factor to be borne in mind is not how things are but how they will appear to the audience. The use of make-up is elementary impressionism.

But the principle of impressionism is easily extended to the other facets of the drama: acting, playwriting, etc. In playwriting impressionism is akin to symbolism and expressionism.

Impressionism was a revolt from realism to appearances. Expressionism was an extension of impressionism. It is concerned not only with producing the proper vision on the eye of the beholder but with producing the proper inner vission. And if this can be achieved by symbols, fantasies, scenes or dialogue that bear no resemblance to actual externals, the expressionist does not hesitate to use them. The simplest example of impressionism-expressionism is the beating of the tom-tom in O'Neill's *Emperor Jones*. It conveys the impression, the feeling of Jones' heightened pulse-beat.

See *Expressionism*.

In Abraham's Bosom. Paul Green (American). Drama. 7 scenes. 1926. Won the Pulitzer Prize 1927.

Abraham McCranie, son of a black mother and white father, discovers in himself yearning for education. He also realizes that only through education can the Negro be truly emancipated. At last, his white father helps him establish a primary school over the opposition of other planters and the apathy of the Negroes. But the white father dies and Abraham and his wife and child are turned out. Abraham turns his hopes to his son, but the lad is only shiftless and fun-loving. Abraham returns to his native community hoping his white half-brother will help him establish another school. But the white man turns him away and robs him of his land, and so Abraham in a frenzy kills him.

Incident, An. Leonid Andreyev (Russian). Drama. 3 acts. 1914.
Reveals the influence of Tolstoy.

A merchant, repenting of having murdered a girl long before, is urged by his wife to make confession, but the police official to whom he speaks proves to be a legalist pure and simple. Since the crime has been outlawed for eleven years according to the Russian code, and since the prisons of Siberia are already overcrowded, the official refuses to arrest the conscience-stricken merchant. If the latter insists upon being punished, let him confess to having committed a crime more recent for whose perpetrator the police are now looking.

Incidental music. A definite music form written and played for effect during the action of a drama. Elizabethan drama included incidental music; later standard composers of all nations began to devote themselves seriously to the writing of this form of music. Beethoven composed the Egmont score; Webster the *Preciosa* score; and Mendelssohn, the famous *Midsummer Night's Dream* music. Sir Arthur Sullivan was first known for his incidental music for *The Tempest*.

Independent Means. William Stanley Houghton (English). Drama. 4 acts. 1909.

Faced with financial ruin a father takes to drink and eventually dies; while his son Edgar, who has had a gentleman's education, and is at first a hopeless weakling, learns a lesson from the catastrophe, and finally makes good.

Indian Emperor, The (or The Conquest of Mexico by the Spaniards). John Dryden (English). Drama. 5 acts. 1665.

The scene is Mexico during the Spanish conquest. Montezuma's daughter, in spite of her love for Cortez, is condemned to death with her father. The histories of Gomára, Cortez and Mariana have been used as source books. The play itself is of the love and honor school, heroic, somewhat bombastic. The hero is a superman in strength and purity; the heroine the most faithful and beautiful of women. Some rather violent battle scenes lighten the leaven of such heavy virtues. And one song: "Ah Fading joy, how quickly art thou past," is noteworthy for its haunting appeal.

Ingegni. Machines, or other theatrical devices, used on the medieval Italian stage.

Ingenue. The young girl in a play, usually providing the love interest.

Ingomar the Barbarian. Frederich Halm. Drama. 5 acts. 185?.
Parthenia, a Greek maiden, falls in love with Ingomar, a barbarian who overcomes patriotic opposition to their marriage by making his countrymen allies of the Greeks. This play was a great stock favorite for half a century.

Inner stage, Elizabethan. An alcove or recess directly back of the outer stage and under the upper stage or balcony. It was separated by a curtain from the outer stage, and was flanked on either side by doors leading to the retiring room. Scenes requiring properties were played here, as were scenes of restricted locality, tableaux, and other episodes demanding a more versatile stage than the outer stage.

In Old Kentucky. Charles T. Dazey (American). Melodrama. 4 acts. 1893.

A very popular play that served as a standard vehicle for stock and road companies for 30 years. Madge, an illiterate but loyal mountain girl helps her unfortunate blue blood sweetheart out of his financial difficulties by riding (disguised as a jockey) his famous race horse Ashland Oaks to victory. This restores the family's fortune and the hero responds by telling his love to his mountain sweetheart. The plot is interspersed with constant underhanded villainies which the two leading characters must constantly foil.

Inset. A small scene inside a larger one.

Inspector-General, The. Nikolai Gogol (Russian). 1836. Comedy. 5 acts.

Ivan Khleskatov, a poor clerk, passing through a Russian village, is mistaken by local officials for the Inspector General. To cover their graft the officials fete him and pay him generous fees. The clerk enjoys himself thoroughly, and succeeds in escaping before the real Inspector General arrives.

Instituto Nazionale del Dramma Antico. A theatrical organization founded in Italy by the Hellenist Romagnoli, now directed by the archeologist Pace, and devoted to solemn performances of the Greek and Roman classics.

Intendant General of the Royal Stage Plays. Title given to directors in chief of the German playhouses of the 19th century when the theatres came under systematized Court control.

Interior dialogue. A modern counterpart of both the soliloquy and the aside but too fragmentary and generally too long to be either. Essentially a device borrowed from the "stream-of-consciousness" technique as used by James Joyce and other novelists. Its most famous use came in O'Neill's *Strange Interlude*.

Interiors. Sets representing indoor scenes.

Interlacing (television). A system of scanning alternate lines to reduce the flicker apparent to the human eye.

Interludes. Rude 16th century farces developing out of English morality plays, their object ostensibly being to teach a lesson but actually to make the audience laugh. The interlude may get its name from being a play between several actors or from being inserted between parts of longer productions. John Heywood, the chief author of this type of play, wrote *The Four P's* and *The Merry Tale of Johan-Johan, Tyb, and Sir Jhan*.

Interludium de Clerico et Puella. (An Interlude of a Clerk and a Girl.)
A medieval English play consisting of two scenes: (1) that in which a girl repulses a clerk who has offered love to her; (2) that in which the clerk goes to Mome Helwis and begs her to aid him. This is a fragmentary dialogue version of a popular tale *Dame Scriz* and represents the sole survival from the repertory of the medieval *mimi* and *histriones* whose plays were rarely more than dancing and general buffoonery but which nevertheless sustained a tradition of acting, an appreciation of comic situation and possibly some skill in constructing actable plays.

Intermedii. Fragments, not properly "intermissions," of dancing and singing performed for the diversion of the audience during the change of scene in a *commedia dell'arte;* often the introduction to the *commedia* as well.

Intermission. The space (usually of ten to fifteen minutes) which elapses for the relaxation of audience and cast between two acts of a play, also permits scene shifting, costume and make-up changes without an audience wait.

International Alliance of Theatrical Stage Employees and Moving Picture Machine Operators of the United States and Canada (the I.A.T.S.E.). Formed 1893 in New York City by eleven local unions, as the National Alliance of Theatrical Stage Employees; in 1898 the word "National" changed to "International."
In 1914 the American Federation of Labor granted it unequivocal jurisdiction over motion picture operators, and the remainder of the title was added, although the A. F. of L. charter maintains the pre-1914 name. Many controversies on jurisdiction have occurred as recent changes in the theatrical world, and expansion of the film industry, have raised numerous new problems.

International Theatre Society. See *Société Universelle du Théâtre.*

Interpolation. (1) A speech or piece of business added to a play by author or director after the completion of the script; (2) a passage of "ad-libbing" by an actor; (3) a musical phrase or chorus added in a selection for purposes of contrast or elaboration.

Interval. British equivalent of "intermission."

In the Grip of Life. Knut Hamsun (Norwegian). Drama. 3 acts. 1910.
Juliana, once a great singer, now passé and facing poverty, marries a wealthy man of seventy. Later, she falls in love with a young art dealer whom she supports by buying his material through an agent. He finally grows tired of Juliana and leaves her to find consolation from a Negro servant.

In the red. Losing money on a show.

In the Shadow of Evil. Henry Rene Lenormand (French). Drama. 3 acts. 1882.

A French official stationed in an isolated post in Africa treats the natives with unbelievable cruelty. A local chieftain accused by another unjustifiably is punished by order of the official. The guilty man is scot free. The official knows he is unjust but persists in his treatment because he himself had once been victimized by a superior and his actions now bear the imprint of that injustice. He has become tinged with evil and this breeds evil. When the wife of the official's assistant goes to dress the wounds of the whipped chieftain she is killed by a jealous mistress. Lenormand deals with the power of evil in many of his plays, of the perverse pleasure of doing the forbidden, and he is a devotee of the Freudian school of Drama.

In the Shadow of the Glen. John M. Synge (Irish). Drama. 1 act. 1903.

A sketch of Irish peasant life, at once poignant and bitter. The setting is a solitary little cottage in a glen. Nora, the wife, is actually relieved when Dan Burke appears to be on his deathbed, for her husband is aging and suspicious. Moreover, her vocation is not to be a homebody, but to respond to the spell of the wild moors and the open road. So she gives her love to the tramp who represents these things, and they joke and plan the future in the very room in which Nora's sick husband lies. But if the tramp is a symbol, Nora's friend Mike Dara is an attractive man of flesh and blood, and she encourages him when he comes to call. Before the flirtation has reached its climax, however, Daniel, supposedly dead by now, sneezes. He had tricked his wife by pretending to be dead (a classical device used by Molière and the Latins before him), and now has his worst suspicions confirmed. Angry, he orders his wife out of the house. She goes willingly, for the road is wide and the tramp is waiting around the first turn.

There were political repercussions when the play was first produced, the Irish esteeming it indelicate and pro-British of Synge to intimate that all Irish wives were not loyal.

The Intruder. M. Maeterlinck (Belgian). 1 act. 1862.

"The Intruder" in this play is really Death. He enters the family group quietly. All vainly try to resist him especially the husband of the dying wife expecting to give birth. A cry of a new born baby is heard. The nurse enters the room, makes her announcement to the anxious family and tells them the mother has died.

Invitation to Travel (*L'Invitation au Voyage*). Jean-Jacques Bernard (French). Drama. 3 acts. Translated by Ernst Boyd. 1924.

Marie Louise, wife of Oliver Mailly, falls in love with Philippe just before he sails for the Argentine, and for years is haunted by his memory. When she finally learns he has returned she hurries to see him only to find, either that Philippe has changed, or that he never was the person she imagined him to be.

Iolanthe, or the Peer and the Peri, by W. S. Gilbert; music by Sir Arthur Sullivan (English). Operetta in 2 acts. 1882.

Iolanthe has been banished by the queen of the fairies for marrying a mortal. Her son, Strephon, a shepherd, is half mortal and half fairy and is in love with Phyllis, a ward in Chancery. After the usual Gilbertian plot complications, the members of the House of Lords are changed into fairies and fly off into Fairyland.

Ion. Euripides (Greek). Tragedy. 423 B.C.

Ion is the son of Apollo and Creusa. Apollo decided to take him to be reared at his temple in Delphi as an attendant. Through a series of circumstances the play evolves around Creusa seeking to kill Ion, her own son, ignorant of the fact that he is her son. Many have called this Euripides' finest play and it is especially noteworthy for the creation of Ion—a fresh, new portrayal for Greek drama of that era.

Ionic. See *Modes.*

Iphigenia in Aulis. Euripides (Greek). 407 B.C.

Iphigenia is the daughter of Agamemnon and Clytemnestra. Diana, the goddess, demands Iphigenia be sacrificed by Agamemnon and since his ships are delayed by contrary winds, he decides to do so to appease the Goddess. Just as the sacrifice is about to be consummated Iphigenia disappears and in her place is found a goat. Diana has taken her to the temple at Tauris and placed her in charge. One of her duties is to sacrifice all strangers who arrive. Twenty years go by and Iphigenia begins to yearn to see her beloved Greece. Two strangers are taken, Orestes and Pylades. When she discovers Orestes is her own brother she plans for their escape. This part of the play is marked by some of the finest Greek dramatic poetry in literature.

Ireland Forgeries. Deeds, signatures and two plays, *Vortigern and Rowena* and *King Henry II,* purporting to be in the handwriting of Shakespeare, but which are the confessed forgeries of William Henry Ireland, made by him in 1794 and 1795.

Irène. François Marie Arouet de Voltaire (French). Tragedy. 5 acts. 1777.

A tragedy written when the author was eighty-three years of age, and the last work which he completed before his death. Its Paris première was in March, 1778, and he attended it shortly afterward (two months before his death). It was his first public appearance in Paris after an absence of twenty-eight years. He was crowned with laurels and smothered with roses amid the plaudits of the audience and thus got a foretaste of immortality.

The play, which is set in Constantinople, adheres to the rules laid down by the Greeks and followed by Corneille. The action takes place in the Emperor's palace. Irene, the Emperor's wife, has loved Alexis, Prince of Greece, since childhood, but has married the Emperor at her father's orders. Alexis visits the palace, is accused of treachery, and later kills the Emperor in combat. Irene is unable to bring herself to marry her husband's slayer. Finally she convinces herself it was really she who was responsible for his death and kills herself with a dagger to expiate her crime.

Iris. Sir Arthur Wing Pinero (English). Drama. 5 acts. 1901.

A tragedy by a playwright better known for his comedies. Iris Bellamy is a woman born to trouble. Supine, pleasure-loving, she drifts downward step by step to her own destruction despite her husband's attempt to safeguard her by making certain conditions in his will. She forges a check. When her boy lover learns of her disgrace, he leaves her, and she is driven to the streets. And throughout the action the relentless Maldonado pursues her, loving her in his own way, but cruelly. "It is women like you who send men like me to the gallows," he accuses her. And even when she flees far away to Caderabbia, he turns up, like a shadow of evil constantly darkening her pathway.

Irving, Sir Henry (1838-1905). English actor, producer. Real name, John Henry Brodribb. The son of a small shopkeeper of yeoman stock, he was born at Keinton Mandeville, Somerset, England, and at the age of fourteen became a clerk in London. Four years later he was engaged for the stock company at the Lyceum, Sunderland. After acting for two years and a half under R. H. Wyndham at Edinburgh, in 1860 he joined Charles Calvert at Manchester, where, at the Theatre Royal and the new Prince's Theatre, he remained for nearly five years. He was brought to London in 1866 to play the villain in Boucicault's *Hunted Down*.

He played at the new Queen's Theatre, Long Acre, 1867-69, where he first met Ellen Terry, appearing as Petruchio to her Katharine. His success procured him the position of leading man at the Lyceum, where as Mathias, in *The Bells* (English version of Erckmann-Chatrian's *Le Juif Polonais*), 1871, he at length achieved fame. From 1872 to 1878, he acted in *Hamlet, Macbeth,* and *King Richard III*.

In 1878, he began his own management of the Lyceum, playing Hamlet to the Ophelia of Ellen Terry, who thus commenced a famous association of twenty-four years with him. For the next twenty-three years he remained at the Lyceum. He acted in and produced *The Merchant of Venice;* Goethe's *Faust* (Wills's version); Tennyson's *Becket*. The last is considered his greatest artistic triumph. In 1903 he staged *Dante* (a play written for him by Sardou) at the Drury Lane. He also revived *Becket,* and because of its great success, he went on tour with it in 1905. On October 13 of that year, on reaching his hotel at Bradford, he collapsed and died. He was buried in Westminster Abbey.

Irving married Florence O'Callaghan in 1869, daughter of a surgeon, by whom he had two sons, Henry and Laurence. Irving was knighted in 1895, the first actor to receive this honor.

Irving, Henry Brodribb (1870-1919). English actor. Born in London, the elder son of Sir Henry Irving. He made his stage debut at the Comedy Theatre in 1891, and appeared with George Alexander, 1896-1900.

His later successes include the title role in Barrie's *The Admirable Crichton,* 1902-04; *Hamlet,* 1904. He visited the United States in 1906, as well as Australia, 1911, and South Africa, 1912-13. He was manager of the Shaftesbury Theatre in 1908 and lessee of the Savoy from 1913.

A student of criminology, he wrote various books on the subject, including *A Life of Lord Jeffreys,* 1898; and *The Trial of Mrs. Maybrick,* 1913. In 1896 he married Dorothea Baird, the original *Trilby*.

Irving, Laurence Sidney (1871-1914). English actor. Born in London, the younger son of Sir Henry Irving, he made his name as Hialmar Ekdal in Ibsen's *Wild Duck*, 1894. Later, in addition to writing plays for his father, which included *Peter the Great*, he became a leading character actor appearing in *The Unwritten Law*, 1910; *The Lily*, 1911; *Typhoon*, 1913. He was drowned May 29, 1914.

Isaacs, Edith J. R. (1878-　). American editor, dramatic critic. Born Edith Sidenberg in Milwaukee, she is married to Lewis Isaacs. Dramatic critic *Ainslee's Magazine*, 1913; editor of *Theatre Arts*, 1918 to date. She is editor of *Essays on the Arts of the Theatre*, 1928; *Plays of American Life and Fantasy*, 1929; etc.

Isherwood, Christopher (1904-　). English poet and dramatist. One of the younger English writers who have achieved prominence in the 1930's. His name is usually associated with those of Auden and Spender, his compatriots and contemporaries. It is Auden who has collaborated with him on his dramatic works, which are *The Dog Beneath the Skin; The Ascent of F 6;* and *On the Frontier*. Isherwood has also written a number of non-dramatic works, including *The Inch and the Ell; Goodbye to Berlin;* and *Journey to a War* (with Auden).

Israel. Henri Bernstein (French). Drama. 3 acts. 1908.

A Catholic youth, having publicly insulted a Jewish banker, is about to respond to the latter's challenge to a duel when he learns from his mother that he is the banker's son. Congratulated by his father on being a Jew, he takes his life rather than face his anti-Semitic friends.

Istri. Name given to the actors in the Etruscan *saturae*. This term, through the Latin *istriones,* developed eventually into our present-day term "histrionic."

Isutzu. Seami Motokiyu (Japanese). (1363-1444). *Nō* drama.

A *Nō* drama about a boy and girl who played together as children near a well and who refuse to marry the choices of their parents now that they are grown up. They write each other love poetry and finally marry. After a few years the girl's parents die, leaving them without support. The young man goes daily to a distant town to earn a living while she stays home. Because she never shows signs of grief whenever he leaves, he thinks she doesn't love him any longer. One morning, instead of going directly to the town, he conceals himself behind a hedge near his home and hears the girl singing a song which reveals to him that she still cares for him. He resolves never again to seek a livelihood far from home.

In the play, a wandering monk meets a village girl who is really the ghost of the girl in the story.

The text of *Isutzu* is taken from the *Ise Monogatari,* which is a collection of the love adventures of Narihira (825-880) in 125 episodes and supposedly written by Narihira himself.

It Can't Happen Here. Sinclair Lewis and John C. Moffitt (American). Drama. 3 acts. 1936. Adapted from the novel by Sinclair Lewis.

The play deals with the question—is it possible for America to succumb to a widespread campaign by a fascist dictator and how would America respond. The play opens in a small Vermont town where a fascist movement begins, spreads like wildfire and controls the population in its viselike grip. A few courageous citizens, led by Editor Doremus rebel against this Unamerican procedure and it is this spark of Americanism and tolerance the author wishes to extol. The play was produced by the Federal Theatre and also in translation.

Ivanov. Anton Chekhov (Russian). Drama. 4 acts. 1887.
Warned that the neglect of his wife will shorten her life, Ivanov nevertheless spends his evenings with Sasha, daughter of a friend, who defends his poverty. A year after his wife's death, when Ivanov is about to marry Sasha, he learns that a physician will denounce him at the wedding. Ivanov shoots himself.

Jack Cade. Robert T. Conrad (American). Drama. 4 acts. 1835.
A study of the heroic Jack Cade, leader in the English insurrection of 1450. The first general rising of the English Commons. This was one of the plays given a prize by Edwin Forrest and Conrad then became one of the Philadelphia school of dramatists.

Jackknife stage. A method of shifting scenery by use of wagons on pivots.
See *Scenery.*

Jacksonville Little Theatre, Florida. This little theatre is the outgrowth of an organization started during the First World War to provide entertainment for soldiers. The Community Players was formed in 1920. In 1926 the name was changed to the Little Theatre of Jacksonville. This theatre has contributed toward American literature by sponsoring playwriting contests.

Jacob's Dream. Richard Beer-Hoffman (German). Drama. 3 acts. 1918.
The play is based upon the story of Jacob and his dream. Esau, returning from the chase, learns his father, Abraham, is dying and that Jacob has received his blessing. Esau is enraged and goes in pursuit of Jacob despite the protestations of his wives and comes upon Jacob in the mountains where the lad is treating a wounded lamb. Esau attacks repeatedly, but Jacob is protected by the God of the Mountains, but at last he yields and humbles himself by breaking his vow and accepting the mess of pottage. Jacob then dreams that the rock and the stream as animated and that Gabriel, Raphael, Uriel, Michael, two other angels and Semal (Satan) appear to him. After a struggle Semal is conquered and slinks away.

Jaggard, William (1568-1623). English printer, publisher. Printer of the First Folio of Shakespeare's plays. It is due to him, in spite of his blindness, that eighteen of the plays were preserved and that the errors in the text of the plays printed in the earlier edition were corrected. He died shortly before the First Folio was finished.

Previous to his work on the folio Jaggard had been in Shakespeare's company as a printer of playbills, and was also responsible for the printing of *The Passionate Pilgrim*.

James II of England. See *Duke of York's Company*.

Janauchek, Mme. Francesca Romana Magdalena (1830-1904). Czech actress. Born in Prague; made her debut in 1846 at the Royal Theatre there in the comedy *Ich Bleihe Ledig*. At eighteen she was the leading actress of the Frankfort Stadt Theatre, where for ten years she played classic dramas; on her vacations she toured Germany, Austria and Russia. Later, as female star of the Court Theatre at Dresden, she scored in such tragic roles as Medea, Iphigenia, Marie Stuart and Lady Macheti. In 1867 she toured the United States. She studied English, and in 1873 began to play parts in that language, principally as Deborah, Brunhilde and Marie Stuart, as well as Shakespearean and other roles. She suffered a stroke of paralysis in 1900, and in 1904 died at the Actor's Fund home.

Jane Clegg. St. John Ervine (Irish). Drama. 3 acts. 1913.
A drama that deals with the depressing side of lower middle-class life. Jane Clegg is a stern realist and although she is weighed down by her sordid surroundings in the presence of disaster she rises to be master of the situation. She watches the slow disintegration of her weak-willed, depraved husband, bears with his meanness and base ways, until she discovers that he has tried to steal her money and failing that, plans to elope with another woman. Realizing her duty, she orders him to leave the house, never to return.

Janis, Elsie (1889-). American actress and mimic. Born in Columbus, Ohio, she made her first appearance on the stage as a boy in *The Charity Ball*, 1897. 1900 saw her first New York appearance on the stage in vaudeville as *"Little Elsie"* under the management of E. E. Rice, and for the next three years she toured the United States. She made her first real hit in 1905 in *When We Were Forty-One* where her imitations of popular artists created a sensation. In 1906 she appeared in *The Vanderbilt Cup* which ran a full season and had a long tour. Among the many plays she has appeared in are *The Slim Princess*, 1910-1911; *The Passing Show*, 1914; *Miss Information*, 1915; *Elsie Janis and Her Gang*, 1919 and 1922; *Oh, Kay*, 1927, etc.

She first appeared in the movies in 1920, and among the pictures she has made are *A Merry Madcap, A Regular Girl, Nearly a Lady*, etc.

She is the author of *A Star for the Night*, 1911; *It's All Wrong*, 1920; *Puzzles of 1925* (in all of which she appeared) and of a movie *Close Harmony*. She is also the author and composer of many songs and several works of prose. She also staged *New Faces*, 1934.

Jannings, Emil (1886-). German actor. Born of German parents in Brooklyn, New York, he was taken to Germany while a child. He first appeared on the screen in 1915, but it was only with the celebrated film *Variety,* 1926, that he began to enjoy world-wide reputation. Thereafter he became famous as the interpreter of, at first, sinister roles, as in *Waxworks, Peter the Great,* and *Faust,* and later of touching portraits of dignified but pathetic old age, as in *The Last Laugh,* 1925 (a film without subtitles). Of these latter characters the best known were the chief parts in the American films: *The Way of All Flesh; The Last Command; The Patriot.* With the advent of sound films, Jannings returned to Germany from Hollywood. In Germany he made possibly his greatest picture *The Blue Angel* with Marlene Dietrich. *The Tempest,* with Jannings and Anna Sten, was shown in England in 1932.

Jealous Wife, The. George Colman the elder (English). Comedy. 1761. A comedy based on *Tom Jones,* the novel by Fielding.

Mrs. Oakly has an unreasoning jealousy of her husband and falls into tantrums on the slightest provocation. Oakly, genuinely fond of her but powerless to cope with her whims, generally cowers before the storm of her wrath and says nothing. When one young lady under suspicion, seeking understanding, throws herself in the hapless Oakly's arms, Oakly's bachelor brother urges him to take a firm stand against his wife and proclaim his innocence of any weakness for the lady. Thus encouraged, the worm turns ever so little. Eventually it is discovered that it is Oakly's nephew with whom the young lady is in love, and that she has run away from home because her father wants her to marry someone else.

Jealousy. Mikhail Artzybashev (Russian). Drama. 3 acts. 1913.

This play centers about a seductive, pursuing woman who tries to fascinate every man she meets. Her husband, who is extremely jealous, discovers through a friend that she is having an affair with a prince. When he accuses her, the wife admits that she has had many lovers, besides the prince. Thereupon, the husband, in a rage, strangles her.

Jeans, Isabel (1891-   ). English actress. Born in London, she made her first appearance on the stage at His Majesty's Theatre in 1909, in *Pinkie and the Fairies.* During 1915-16, she toured in the United States with Granville-Barker's company. She has acquired a reputation as a classic actress in many productions for the Phoenix and Stage Societies. Her first husband was Claude Rains; her second, Gilbert Wakefield. She later appeared in numerous plays, including: *The Man Who Married a Dumb Wife,* 1917; *Fanny's First Play,* 1922; *Hassan,* 1923; *The Rat,* 1924; *The Man with a Load of Mischief,* 1925; *The Amorists,* 1929. Among the films in which she also appeared are: *The Rat; Easy Virtue* and *Sally Bishop.*

Jeans, Ursula (1906-   ). English actress. Born at Simla, India, she studied at the Royal Academy of Dramatic Art. Her first stage appearance was made at the Theatre Royal, Nottingham, 1925, and she played in London at Wyndham's Theatre in 1926.

Later plays in which she has appeared are: *Escape,* 1927; *The Fanatics,* 1927;

Passing Brompton Road, 1928; *The First Mrs. Fraser,* 1929; *Grand Hotel,* 1931; *I Lived With You,* 1932.

Jefferson, Joseph (1829-1905). American actor. Born in Philadelphia, he made his stage debut at the age of three. He was a child of exceptional talents, and was dancing and doing imitations when he was four. He belonged to the fourth generation of actors named Jefferson, his great-grandfather having played with Garrick. His grandfather, a comedian of skill,. was highly regarded in New York and Philadelphia. His father, however, led his family from one poverty-stricken theatrical enterprise to another through the Middle West and the South. An actor and manager with a taste for scene painting, he had no sense of money. Once when he had gone bankrupt, his friends found him sitting cheerfully on the bank of a river, fishing. He said he had lost so much that he could no longer afford to worry about anything. There was a touch of this sunny disposition in his son's *Rip Van Winkle* years later, the play with which Joseph Jefferson is said to have had almost a lifetime partnership.

Joseph's vagrant upbringing gave him hard training, both in life and in acting. He played children's parts, sang and danced, ground colors in the paint room. At fourteen, he was utility man in the stock company at Mobile, Alabama. At last he rose to be a comedian. By the time he was twenty-one he had played a season or two in Philadelphia and had appeared in New York. His first outstanding success as a comedian was in the role of Asa Trenchard in *Our American Cousin,* 1858.

His reputation grew steadily from 1850 until he first thought of *Rip Van Winkle.* He did his own version of the story, which he first acted in 1859, and in which he subsequently appeared in 1865 for 170 nights. On September 3, 1866, at the Olympic Theatre, New York, he presented the play, which had been redrafted a year earlier by Dion Boucicault. It was extremely successful. He played Rip to several generations of theatre-goers. He was on the stage for seventy years.

He is the founder of the *combination system.*

See also *Combination system.*

Jessner, Leopold (1878-   ). German director. Jessner departed from the use of regular scenery and instead used levels in space or stairways, *Jessner-treppen* (Jessner-steps). He was Director of the State Theatre in Berlin, 1919-25. He was an expressionist and in 1922 was considered the most radical director of the German theatre.

Jest, The (Cena delle beffe). Sem Benelli (Italian). Melodrama. 4 acts. 1919.

A colorful poetic melodrama of hatred, love and vengeance, in which the artist and the man of action are contrasted. Neri and Gabriello, brothers, attempt to kill the mild-mannered Giannetto while he is on the way to see Ginevra, his betrothed. Then the brothers buy the girl from her father and make her Neri's plaything. But Giannetto escapes the death intended for him and Neri lands in a dungeon from which Giannetto kindly releases him. Neri appears at Ginevra's house determined to kill Giannetto for certain, but slays his brother by mistake. The play ends with Neri a raving lunatic and Giannetto praying for his soul.

Jewish Cultural Society. A Jewish theatrical organization in present-day Nazi Germany devoted to performances of plays by Jewish dramatists, acted and directed by Jews, and exclusively for the Jewish public now prohibited from entering Aryan theatres; it has branches almost entirely throughout Germany.

Jew of Malta, The. Christopher Marlowe (English). Drama. 5 acts. 1592.
Anticipates *The Merchant of Venice* in plot. The Jew of the title is Barabas, the thief who was released by popular demand in place of Jesus. The Grand Seignior of Turkey having demanded the tribute of Malta decides that it shall be paid by the Jews of the island. Barabas, a rich Jew, who resists the edict has his possessions impounded and his house made into a nunnery. In revenge he poisons Abigail, his daughter, and procures the death of her lover, among others. Malta is besieged by the Turks. He betrays the fortress and as reward is made Governor. He plots the death of the Turkish commander, but is himself betrayed and hurled into a cauldron.

Jig, Elizabethan. A dance by the players which generally concluded the performance of a play in the Elizabethan playhouses. Foreign costumes, musical accompaniment and farcical dialogue comprised such entertainment.

Job. Anonymous 400-350 B.C. Hebrew.
The well known book of Job is considered one of the earliest forms of drama. It is based on an ancient Hebrew legend, and to all appearances is the work of several people.

Jodelle, Etienne, Siuer de Lymodin (1532-1573). French dramatist. Founded the modern form of French tragedy with his *Cléopâtre,* 1552, a play of little value but one which employed for the first time the Alexandrine verse scheme for dramatic composition—a form which French tragic dramatists followed for a hundred years. He also was the founder of modern French comedy with his farce *Eugène* the same year. Through the miscarriage of a pageant, he lost favor at court.

Joe's. The agency of the late Joe Leblang, which sells theatre tickets at cut-rate. This is now operated by his widow, Tillie. Also known as Gray's, since the entrance is through Gray's Drugstore.

Jog. Small piece of scenery usually under 2½ feet wide.

John. Philip Barry (American). Drama. 5 acts. 1927.
A Biblical drama based on the life of John the Baptist. It is a story of the heart and mind of the great prophet and takes us through the most important episodes of his career. It ends with John proclaiming the coming of the Messiah who hovers in the background as the ruling influence of John's last days.

John Bull. George Colman (English). Comedy. 5 acts. 1803.
The main character Job Thornberry, generous and kind-hearted, but irascible under a sense of injustice, is supposed to typify the national character. It is the story

of a young man who runs away to sea, and later, with ten guineas to start on, amasses a fortune and becomes an important philanthropist.

John Bull's Other Island. George Bernard Shaw (English). Comedy. 4 acts. 1904.

A satire on Ireland, in the days before it became autonomous. Two friends, Broadbent and Doyle, arrive in a rural spot in Roscullen, Doyle's native village. Broadbent is typically English—a Gladstonian liberal, efficient, bent on regenerating the land. In short, he might as well be called John Bull. Doyle is as characteristically a son of Erin—witty, erratic, mocking, a citizen of the world come back home after eighteen years. They enter politics, and the blundering Englishman, with an eye to the main chance, wins out and gains a seat on the Irish bench by virtue of his earnestness and ability to get things done. The simple Irish peasants see through him, but decide that, in spite of his faults, he is less of an ass than their present representative. Parallel to the political plot runs a love story. When Doyle left Ireland eighteen years before to become a practical scientist, he was in love with Nora Reilly. She has waited patiently ever since, and he has stayed in love with her. But with Celtic perversity he now shuns her and flouts her love. So Broadbent, efficient as always, catches the lady on the rebound and wins out in love as well as in politics.

The moral, of course, is that it is Ireland's fate to be absorbed by the practical British. There is a great deal of talk in the comedy, and the plot frequently stands still while the characters discuss the Tariff Reform League, home rule, the progressive tariff and a hundred and one other controversial topics. These digressions were criticized by American reviewers when the play was given in the United States in 1905. Thus Alan Dale found the comedy a "thick, glutinous and imponderable four-act tract"; and Acton Davies described the audience as "bored to utter extinction."

John Ferguson. St. John Ervine (British). Tragedy. 1915.

This play is a story of middle-class life. John Ferguson allows his farm to be taken from him in order to save his daughter from a loveless marriage with James Caesar. Meanwhile fate brings added misery to him. His daughter is seduced by his worst enemy, Witherow. One night, Caesar, weak in character though he is, announces that he is going to get revenge and kill the seducer. The next morning he returns, cringing, to say that he lost his nerve in the darkness. Witherow is found murdered, and Caesar is arrested. For a while peace seems to come to the household of John Ferguson but not for long. Andrew, Ferguson's son, announces that it was he who killed Witherow and that he cannot allow Caesar to die for a crime he did not commit. The play ends with Hannah and Andrew leaving on the mission of confession. This play is an outstanding example of domestic drama.

John Gabriel Borkman. Henrik Ibsen (Norwegian). Drama. 1896.

The tragedy of a man who gives up love to satisfy his ambition, and learns too late the folly of materialism. John Gabriel Borkman does not marry Ella Rentheim, whom he loves, because her sister is more prosperous. The sister, wed to him, grows bitter and disillusioned because she is neglected in his mad struggle to obtain gold and more gold. Both unhappy women refuse to concern themselves with his son. Even when Borkman has suffered imprisonment for his pains, he still clings to the hope of material gain. Symbolically, Ibsen shows at the end of the play that love should be considered all-important: without it, there is no real life. Borkman, Ella and Gunhild, who have not known it, find that they have been dead all along; only the old clerk Foldal has really lived.

Johnny Johnson. Paul Green (American). Drama. 3 acts. 1936. Music by Kurt Weill.

Johnny Johnson, a pacifist, allows his girl to persuade him to enlist in the war to end all wars. He suffers many disillusionments in the army, is wounded and hospitalized. He escapes from the hospital with a tank of laughing gas which he sprays over the French High Command and thus persuades them to sign a decree ending the war. Before the order can be given, Johnny is put into an asylum. The only sane man there, he organizes a debating society which proves very funny. When he finally gets out he is reduced to selling toys on a street corner and singing pacifist songs. This imaginative, expressionistic tragi-comedy was hailed as originating a new form in the drama: A serious play in which the music is an integral part.

John Street Theatre, New York. The fourth theatre built in New York. Erected near Broadway in 1767 by David Douglass. The audience was accommodated inside the red wooden structure by two rows of boxes (for ladies) a pit, (for gentlemen), a gallery and balconies over two proscenium doors on stage. A continuous row of curved metal shields concealed candle footlights. *The Beaux' Stratagem* opened the house on December 7, 1767. During the next thirty years such players as William Hallam, Joseph Jefferson, James Fennell, Maria Stover, John Hodgkinson, Mrs. Morris and Mrs. Kenna acted in such plays as *Alexander the Great, Robinson Crusoe, She Stoops to Conquer,* several by Sheridan and many of Shakespeare's. *The Contrast,* by Royal Tyler—the first outstanding drama by a native American author to be produced—was performed here April 18, 1787. In off seasons horse-riders, dancers, rope-walkers and rudimentary circuses entertained the public. The house was pulled down in 1798.

Jolson, Al (1886-). American actor. He made his first appearance on the stage as one of the mob in *Children of the Ghetto.* For several years he appeared in various circus companies and also with Lew Dockstader's Minstrels. After several years in vaudeville he was engaged for the Winter Garden in New York where he appeared in *La Belle Paree,* 1911. Among the shows he has appeared in since are *Honeymoon Express,* 1913; *Robinson Crusoe, Jun.,* 1916; *Sinbad,* 1918 (which ran for two years) ; *Bombo,* 1921 (on tour 1922-24) ; *Big Boy,* 1925; *Wonder Bar,* 1931.

He began his film career in 1927 with his appearance in the first "talkie," *The Jazz Singer.* Some of the other pictures he has made are: *The Singing Fool, Mammy, Wonder Bar, Go Into Your Dance.*

Jones, Henry Arthur (1851-1929). British dramatist. Born at Grandborough, Buckinghamshire. His first play, *Only Round the Corner,* was produced in 1878. Four years later he made his first great success with the melodrama, *The Silver King,* 1882. Then, in 1884, he found his true métier with the social comedy, *Saints and Sinners.* Other plays include *Breaking a Butterfly,* an adaptation of *The Doll's House,* 1884; *The Middleman,* 1889; *The Profligate,* 1889; *Judah,* 1890; *The Dancing Girl,* 1891; *The Crusaders,* 1891; *The Bauble Shop,* 1893; *The Tempter,* 1893; *The Masqueraders,* 1894; *The Case of Rebellious Susan,* 1894; *Michael and His Lost Angel,* 1896; *The Triumph of the Philistines,* 1895; *The Physician,* 1897; *The Liars,* 1897; *Carnac Sahib,* 1899; *The Maneuvers of Jane,* 1899; *Mrs. Dane's Defense,* 1900; *Whitewashing Julia,* 1903; *Mary Goes First,* 1913; *The Lie,* 1914; *Cock o' the Walk,* 1915; *The Pacifists,* 1917; etc.

He also wrote several books on the theatre: *The Renascence of the English Drama,* 1895; *Foundations of a National Drama,* 1913; *Theatre of Ideas,* 1915; etc.

Jones' plays vary considerably as to subject and style. Some of them are pure melodramas; some serious dramas of a high moral tone; some comedies of manners of the type popularized by Oscar Wilde. The best known of his works is *Mrs. Dane's Defense,* which was revived in New York as recently as 1928. Although the problems underlying such plays as this seem somewhat dated to modern audiences, the playwright's great technical skill and facility have kept them alive. The same cannot be said of the more ponderous dramas, which have fallen into partial oblivion.

Jones, Inigo (1573-1652). English architect, scene designer. Made a thorough study of the remains of Roman architecture and Palladio's Renaissance buildings. From 1605-13 he was engaged as architect to James I and designed the settings for the court masques. He was the originator of the classic architecture of the late Renaissance and Georgian periods in England. He was the founder of scenic design in the English theatre. He also designed *Albions Triumph,* 1609 and *Florimène,* 1635.

See also *Webb, John.*

Jones, Dr. Joseph Stevens (1809-1877). American dramatist. One of the chief exponents of the Yankee type of American play. The form of entertainment, which encouraged such Yankee delineation as James H. Hackett was accustomed to give, was probably suggested by the success of Charles Mathews, the English actor, in this country. But the character of the Yankee was indigenous to the soil.

Born in 1809, Dr. Jones was an actor in his early life and at various times proprietor and manager of the Old National and Tremont Theatres in Boston. In 1843 he graduated from the Harvard Medical School and practiced medicine in Boston for several years. He then began the management of the Tremont, and in that capacity met Mill and Marble, and was importuned to write for them.

As a writer, he was particularly active, and to his credit, a staggering, but incomplete list of plays might be assembled. Among them are: *The Liberty Tree; The Fire Warrior; The Siege of Boston; Moll Pitcher; The Mask of Huguenots; Paul Revere; The Wizard of the Sea; The Wheelwright; The Green Mountain Boy; The Last Days of Pompeii; Plymouth Rock; The People's Lawyer.*

Jones, Robert Edmond (1887-   ). American designer, director. One of the foremost American designers, beginning in 1911, his design of *The Man Who Married a Dumb Wife* in 1915 gave the impetus to the modern era of scene designing. From 1925 onwards he was associated with Kenneth MacGowan and Eugene O'Neill in the production of several plays at the Greenwich Village Playhouse. He staged many of Eugene O'Neill's plays, including *Mourning Becomes Electra; Ah, Wilderness!; Night Over Taos*. Other important productions were: *Hamlet,* 1922; *The Green Pastures,* 1931; *Camille,* 1932; *Othello,* 1936; *The Sea Gull,* 1938; *The Philadelphia Story,* 1939.

He has done designing in Hollywood and helped to develop technicolor there. He is author (with Kenneth MacGowan) of *Continental Stagecraft.*

Jongleurs. Performers in the Middle Ages considered synonymous with the *histriones* (or actors), although today the word means juggler or acrobat. Later in the Middle Ages, and thereafter, they were known also as *ministri.* With the troubadours and minstrels of their time they were the progenitors of the strolling players. In other words, wandering entertainers who danced jigs, sang, walked the tight rope, did acrobatic horseback riding, performed tricks and presented interludes. Places of performances were usually inns, fairs or palaces.

Jonson, Ben (1573?-1637). English dramatist. The greatest Elizabethan dramatist after Shakespeare and Marlowe. He was born in Westminster and was educated at the famous school there and thereafter at Cambridge, remaining only a few weeks at the University but nevertheless obtaining his Master of Arts degree. After a period in the army he was engaged as actor in Henslowe's company. In 1598 he wrote his greatest comedy *Every Man in His Humour.* An "accident" in a duel—his killing of another actor—threw him into prison and the arms of the Catholic faith, whereafter, for twelve years, he was a member of the Church. Although he is known mainly as a writer of comedy he wrote two tragedies *Sejanus* and *Catiline, His Conspiracy,* the former provoked by a literary quarrel in 1603.

Aside from those mentioned his best-known works are: *Volpone; Epicoene; or, The Silent Woman* and *The Alchemist.* His dramatic theories were influenced by Sidney's *Apologie for Poetry; or, A Defence of Poesie* and are best expressed in his *Timber; or, Discoveries,* in which many of the entries are translations of extracts from the classic authors. Jonson was the center of a younger group of playwrights and an outstanding literary leader of his time. He and Shakespeare were intimate friends.

Jordan, Dorothy (1762-1816). Irish actress. Born near Waterford, the daughter of an actress, she played for the first time in London at Drury Lane as Peggy in *The Country Girl,* 1785. Remaining at Drury Lane until 1809, she became recognized as an admirable performer of breeches parts, but her chief successes were in such comedy roles as those of Letitia Hardy, Lady Teazle, Miss Hardcastle and Lydia Languish. She made her final appearance on the stage at Covent Garden in 1814, as Lady Teazle, and died at St. Cloud. From 1790 to 1811 she was the mistress of the Duke of Clarence, afterwards King William IV, and bore him ten children. She was the subject of some of the most beautiful portraits by Reynolds, Gainsborough and Romney.

Joruri. A species of Japanese dramatic ballad based on legendary or historic tales of epic proportions which was at first performed by a chanter chorus while the narrative was recited by a reader. The *Joruri* rose in the Muromachi period (14th century) but it was not until the 16th century that it was played to the accompaniment of the *Samisen,* a three-stringed guitar. In the same century the addition of puppets proved a popular innovation. This new form was known as *Ayatsuri* (manipulation) and the *Joruri* referred to the story or libretto. The puppets used were almost life-size and were not manipulated by strings but by actors on stage who were clothed completely in black to indicate invisibility. The *Ningyo Shibai,* or doll theatres, have all but disappeared today in Japan, but *Joruri* chanting is gaining in popularity. The most famous doll theatre is one in Osaka, reputed to be the oldest in the world. The best known *Joruri* theme is the feudal suicide of the Forty-seven Ronins. The greatest *Joruri* and *Ayatsuri* writer is Chikamatsu Monzayemon.
    See also *Drama, Japanese; Story of the Forty-seven Ronins, The.*

Jourdain, Monsieur. The principal character of Molière's *Bourgeois Gentilhomme*—the *nouveau riche* type of middle-class individual who makes himself ridiculous by his obviously strenuous efforts to acquire social graces. His most famous remark was that which denoted his surprise on discovering that he had been talking prose all his life without knowing it.

Journey's End. R. C. Sherriff (English). Drama. 3 acts. 1928.
    Cross-section of life in a British dug-out in the First World War. Young Raleigh has always looked up to Captain Stanhope as a hero, but when he joins Stanhope's company in the trenches, he finds him changed into a disillusioned, ruthless soldier. He realizes that this is Stanhope's way of enduring the war, but there is an estrangement between them which is erased only when Raleigh is shot and Stanhope comforts him before he dies.

The Joy of Living. Hermann Sudermann (German). Drama. 1902.
    Discovering that her husband and her lover, Baron Richard, have become friends, Countess Beata puts an end to her love affair. Still devoted to the Baron, she wants their children to marry and persuades her husband to resign from the Reichstag so that the Baron can take his place. During the political campaign, Richard's opponent brings to light the old scandal. Richard is elected and Beata's husband wants to sue the slanderer. On finding out that the story is true, Beata's husband realizes that he should fight a duel but to do so would confirm the suspicion. After much conferring between the families, Richard promises to do away with himself. He sets his affairs in order and delivers a speech in the Reichstag on the sanctity of the home. The slanderer, hearing the speech, returns to Richard the compromising letters. Beata in order to show that all is well gives a luncheon at which her two men are very

friendly. She drinks a toast to the joy of living, then falls dead. The guests think she has had heart failure, but she has really taken poison.

Juarez and Maximilian. Franz Werfel (German). Drama. 13 scenes. 1924.
To further his own ambitions, Napoleon III sends Maximilian from Europe to rule Mexico. Maximilian, an idealist, believing the Mexicans want him as a ruler and blind to the fact that they want Juarez as their leader, is cajoled into signing the death warrant of certain civil prisoners, and so seals his own fate. Carlotta, his wife, makes him keep the throne, while she returns to Europe to seek the aid of the Emperor, all in vain. Maximilian, finally realizing his fight is hopeless, goes from his cell to die before a firing squad.

Julius Caesar. William Shakespeare (English). Tragedy. 5 acts. Printed 1623.
The play is based on Plutarch's lives of Caesar, Antony and Brutus. The action covers the conspiracy led by Cassius and Brutus against Caesar, the assassination of Caesar, the defense of Caesar and discrediting of the assassins in the remarkable funeral oration of Antony, the subsequent conflict between the consiprators, and their defeat at the battle of Philippi at the hands of the triumvirs, Octavius Caesar, Antony and Lepidus.

Jumbles. A mixture of tragedy, opera and farce, devised by George Colman, 1762-1831.

June Moon. Ring Lardner and George S. Kaufman (American). Comedy. Prologue and 3 acts. 1929.
Freddy, young song writer from Schenectady, spends all the money from his first song hit on an industrious blonde. Finally he realizes his mistake, and goes back to his first love, a small town girl.

"Jung Wien" movement. See *Bahr, Herman; Hofmannsthal, Hugo von; Schnitzler, Arthur.*

Juno and the Paycock. Sean O'Casey (Irish). Tragedy. 3 acts. 1925.
One of the great tragedies of the Abbey Theatre repertory. Captain Jack Boyle, nicknamed the "Paycock" because of his tendency to brag and strut, lives in a two-room flat in a Dublin tenement with his wife Juno and their two children, Johnny and Mary. Jack is called "Captain" because he once spent a short time on the water in a collier; he now spends most of his waking hours frequenting public houses in the company of his crony Joxer Daly, a lazy but engaging wastrel whom Juno detests. Johnny Boyle is a cripple, wounded while still little more than a child during the disturbances of Easter Week and having lost an arm later in another Irish uprising. Mary and Juno work for their men; as the play opens Mary is on strike. The girl is being courted by Jerry Devine, a would-be labor leader, but prefers Charlie Bentham, a schoolteacher who is studying law. Bentham brings news of a

legacy which he assures the Boyles Jack is due to receive soon, and they celebrate by buying new furniture and giving a party for the neighbors. The festivities are interrupted by the funeral of the son of a resident of the house. All except Johnny go to attend the rites of this young man who has been killed for Ireland. Johnny is visited by a messenger who summons him to a Battalion meeting. He protests that he has already done enough for his country, but finally is persuaded to answer the summons. Time passes. Bentham has gone to England, and the fictitious legacy has failed to materialize. The creditors take all the Boyles' fine new belongings. Mary learns from the doctor that she is to have a child by the schoolteacher. The faithful Jerry deserts her when he finds out, and her father and brother will have nothing to do with her. Johnny is accused of being a spy, responsible for the death of his chum, the young man buried in the previous act. He is led away to be executed. Juno, her son dead, her daughter betrayed, her husband a drunkard, rises above her misfortunes and bravely plans to build a new life on the ashes of the old.

Jury. A first night audience.

Justice. John Galsworthy (English). Drama. 4 acts. 1910.

William Falder, a junior clerk in a solicitor's office, falls in love with a married woman who is cruelly treated by her husband. To rescue her from her husband he commits forgery. As he is about to sail with her for South America, he is apprehended. At the trial his counsel pleads guilty but asks the jury for leniency on the ground that Falder acted under great emotional stress, not realizing what he was doing. The judge sums up against this plea and Falder is committed to 3 years penal servitude. On his release from prison he is unable to keep a job because of his past. Finally his old employers offer him his old job if he gives up the woman he loves. He refuses. His employers relent but just then a detective comes to arrest Falder for failing to report himself. Falder commits suicide by jumping out of a window.

So great was the impression this play made that certain important reforms in prison administration can be traced to it.

Juvarra, Filippo (1676-1736). Italian architect, scene designer. Superintendent of the private theatre in Rome of Cardinal Ottoboni. Known for the richness of detail in his work. His designs are now, among other places, in the National bibliotek in Vienna; the Victoria and Albert Museum in London; the Bibliotica Nazionale Vittorio Emanuele III in Turin.

Juvenile. A player of youthful male parts up to the age, roughly, of twenty-five.

Kabuki-Zyuhatiban. The name given to the eighteen most successful plays of *Kabuki* origin in Japanese drama.
See *Drama, Kabuki.*

Kaiser, Georg (1878-). German dramatist. Born in Germany, son of a merchant he spent his early life in business. In 1903 he wrote *Schoolmaster Kleist,* a tragi-comedy, *The Jewish Widow, King Cuckold,* after the legend of Tristan and Isolde, and a ballet-drama based on the fable of Europa and the bull. *Alcibiades Saved* contrasts the mores of the Greek warrior and the famous philosophers. *Gilles and Jeanne* followed in a serious vein with a basis of fact. *The Flight to Venice* concerns itself with George Sand and her literary loves. *The Burghers of Calais* treats a historical episode most successfully. The more romantic plays are *Woman's Sacrifice, Juana, Friedrich and Anna* and *Claudius.* His unusual contributions to the theatre are his more abstract plays such as *The Conflagration of the Opera House, Literary Trash, From Morn to Midnight.*

Side By Side, Noli Me Tangere and *The Phantom Lover* are his more realistic plays.

Kalamazoo Civic Players. Founded 1929 in Kalamazoo, Michigan. Erected and donated by Dr. William E. Upjohn, the Civic Auditorium is one of the most complete and best equipped theatres in America. Plays were first presented in the Central High School Auditorium. The Civic Players were instrumental in bringing about the idea for the auditorium which was opened in 1931.

Kamerny Theatre. A theatre in Moscow established in 1914 on the principles of Tairov, who is its director, and maintaining an international repertory, with plays of O'Neill, Sophie Treadwell, Shaw, Dos Passos, Chesterton, among others, but specializing in political plays among the native works. This theatre has never produced more than four plays a year and has kept a high dramatic standard against all attempts to force it to give more plays of Soviet ideology.

See also *Tairov, Alexander.*

Kamisino. A costume dating from feudal times in Japanese drama; it is worn by the musicians, or *Tyobo* players.

Karagoz. The Turkish *Punch,* present descendant of the *mime* tradition in the Near East.

Karen Borneman. Hjalmar Bergstrom (Danish). Drama. 4 acts. 1907.

The play evolves around the conflict between Karen and her father, a theological professor. The old father sincerely believes in the traditional virtues and holds to the accepted morality of his code . . . that women shall marry, have homes and children. He believes that is their destiny. Chastity before marriage and fidelity during marriage are part of this code. Karen exemplifies the modern woman in her revolt from this strict moral code. She has had a lover, a novelist, who died. She has gone to Paris and had an affair with a sculptor who philandered. When she learns of his infidelity she returns to Copenhagen where she has formed an attachment to a liberal physician whom she truly loves. The reappearance of the sculptor in Copenhagen and the revelation of her past cause the physician to withdraw his proposal of marriage. When the father learns of Karen's past he is shocked and embittered while she tries to justify her actions as a modern adult and emotionally honest woman.

Karson, Nat (1910-   ). American scene designer. Born at Zurich, Switzerland and attended the Chicago Art Institute. His Broadway career began with *Waltz In Fire*, 1934. Since then he has designed the sets for the Negro production of *Macbeth;* painted murals for the Chicago World's Fair, 1933; and is now art director for Radio City Music Hall.

Kataev, Valentin (1897-   ). Russian dramatist. Kataev, one of the younger Soviet writers, has written the following plays: *The Embezzlers*, 1928; *Squaring the Circle*, 1928; *Department Store*, 1929; *Vanguard*, 1930; *The Million Torments*, 1931; *Time Forward*, 1932; *Under the Circus Tent*, 1934; *Path of Flowers*, 1934; *The Rich Bride*, 1936; *Lonely White Sail*, 1937; *I, Son of the Working People*, 1938. They treat some of the most serious problems of the day—the farm problem, the White Russian problem, the labor problem, the problem of the younger generation—but they do so with a chuckle. Primarily a writer of farce, Kataev believes in purging with laughter and not with tears. His earlier comedies, *The Embezzlers* and *Squaring the Circle*, are the ones best known outside of the U. S. S. R.

Kaufman, George S. (1889-   ). American dramatist, journalist. Born in Pittsburgh, Pa., November 16th, 1889. He conducted a daily humorous column in the Washington Times 1912-13, and the New York Evening Mail, 1914-15. He was subsequently on the dramatic staffs of the New York Tribune and the New York Times. He is co-author of *Dulcy*, 1921; *Merton of the Movies*, 1922; *To the Ladies*, 1922; *The Royal Family*, 1927; *Beggar on Horseback*, 1924; *The Butter and Egg Man*, 1925; *Animal Crackers* (musical), 1928; *June Moon*, 1929; *The Channel Road*, 1929; *Strike Up the Band* (musical), 1930; *Of Thee I Sing*, 1931; *Dinner at Eight*, 1932; *Let 'Em Eat Cake*, 1933; *First Lady*, 1935; *Merrily We Roll Along*, 1934; *Stage Door*, 1936; *You Can't Take It With You*, 1936; *Fabulous Invalid*, 1938; and *The American Way*, 1939; *The Man Who Came To Dinner*, 1939. Known as the "Great Collaborator." He has written most of his plays with the exception of two or three in collaboration (Marc Connelly, Edna Ferber, Morrie Ryskind, Moss Hart). He is sole author of *The Butter and Egg Man, Cocoanuts*. He also directs; and produces an occasional play that he is interested in such as *Of Mice and Men* and *The American Way*. He is famous for his comic and bitingly satiric dialogue.

Kean, Charles John (1811-1868). English actor. Born at Waterford, the second son of Edmund Kean, he played Iago to the Othello of his father at Richmond in the latter's tragic final performance, March 25, 1833. He made his first appearance as Young Norval in *Douglas* at Drury Lane in 1827, and his last as Louis XI at the Theatre Royal, Liverpool, 1867. He died January 22, 1868, having made his greatest successes in a carefully produced series of Shakespearean revivals. He married in 1842 Ellen Tree, 1805-1880, with whom he played until the end of his life. After his death she conducted an acting school.

Kean, Edmund (1787-1833). English actor. One of the foremost actors of all time. Born in London, March 17, 1887, he was the son of Anne Carey, an actress, and granddaughter of Henry Carey, his father being probably an architect's clerk named Kean. His character suffered much from his mother's neglect of him in his childhood, and he became a wayward and uncontrollable youth. Adopted by various benefactors, he ran away from them all, once to sea, and later to a theatre, where he played children's parts and appeared as a ventriloquist and circus acrobat, having both legs broken in a tumbling act. On one occasion he recited before George III at Windsor. By 1807 he had advanced sufficiently in his profession to act opposite Mrs. Siddons, and in 1808 he married Mary Chambers, a Waterford actress.

Eventually he attracted the notice of the stage manager of Drury Lane Theatre, who offered him a three years' engagement. On his arrival in London, his appearance was delayed by his contract to appear for Elliston at a minor theatre. This matter adjusted, his début, in the part of Shylock, 1814, was memorable for the tremendous ovation which was accorded him by the audience prepared to receive him with indifference. He also appeared successfully in: *Richard III; Hamlet; Othello; King Lear; Macbeth; Henry VIII; Brutus; Coriolanus; King John;* as Sir Giles Overreach in Massinger's comedy *A New Way to Pay Old Debts* and as *Young Norval* in Home's *Douglas,* and Rolla in Sheridan's *Pizarro.* He visited the United States in 1820 and 1825. Taken ill during a performance of *Othello,* just after he had uttered the words, "Othello's occupation's gone," March 25, 1833, he was removed to his house at Richmond, where he died, May 15.

Keane, Doris (1885-   ). American actress. Born in Michigan, she made her debut in New York in 1903 and in London in 1907. Her early successes include: *The Happy Marriage,* 1909; *The Lights o' London,* 1911; *Anatol,* 1912; and *Romance,* in which she played the lead as Margherita Cavallini, 1913-15. She scored a further success with this play in London, when it ran from 1915 to 1918. She revived it in London, 1926-1927.

Keen, Malcolm (1887-   ). English actor. Born in Bristol, he first appeared in 1902, in London. He played in Martin Harvey's Shakesperean season in 1916; in *The Skin Game,* 1920; *R.U.R.,* 1923; as Rev. Alfred Davidson in *Rain,* 1925; and in 1932 joined the Vic-Wells Shakesperean Company. In 1934 he scored a success as Sir Mark Loddon in *Libel.* He was the Claudius in Gielgud's *Hamlet* in New York, 1936-37.

Keene, Laura (1826-1873). English-American actress producer. The first actress-manager in America; brought to America in 1851 by Wallack; toured around the world and then opened own theatre in New York; produced light comedies and dramas. It was her company that played *Our American Cousin* at Ford's Theatre, Washington, 15 April, 1865, the night of the assassination of Abraham Lincoln.

Keeper hook. S-shaped hook for temporary battening of unit. See *Lighting.*

Keith, Benjamin Franklin (1846-1914). American vaudeville manager. The youngest of eight children, B. F. Keith, wearied of farm chores at home in Hillsboro, New Hampshire, and at the age of eleven he ran away to join a circus. As an employee and proprietor he was associated with first P. T. Barnum's and then Forepaugh's Circus until 1883, when he joined Col. Williams Austin in opening a Boston theatre. In Keith's Theatre of Boston he introduced Edison's "vitascope," the earliest movie, showing a play called *The Milk White Flag.* At this time Keith began the "continuous performance" policy which is distinctively his. In 1906, with F. F. Proctor, he formed the Keith and Proctor Amusement Company, a theatre chain which at the time of his death in 1914 included over 400 playhouses. These became eventually a part of the Radio-Keith-Orpheum circuit.

See also *Vaudeville.*

Kelly, George (1890-   ). American actor, producer and author. George Kelly was born in Philadelphia, Pa. His plays are a decided contribution to the American theatre and he is also noted for his discrimination in casting and direction. His first long play (he had previously been connected with vaudeville) was *The Torchbearers,* 1922, a satire on the Little Theatre Movement. *The Show-Off,* 1924, which followed, narrowly missed the Pulitzer Prize but the next year, 1925, saw *Craig's Wife,* which did win the Pulitzer award. In 1926, he did *Daisy Mayme,* a comedy which failed. This was followed by *Behold, the Bridegroom,* a very fine psychological study of a neurotic rich girl who disintegrates when she cannot get what she wants. This was written with candor and was not too well liked by the theatre-going public. In 1929 he reappeared with *Maggie, the Magnificent,* quite frank and unsparing in its treatment of a "coarse mother" and ambitious daughter. In 1931 he wrote *Philip Goes Forth,* which was not very successful. *Reflected Glory* in 1936 enjoyed a moderate success.

Kemble, Adelaide (1814-1879). English actress. Second daughter of Charles Kemble. She studied singing and appeared in public in 1835. She later appeared in Paris, after which she visited Italy. There she studied and sang with marked success in Venice and also at Covent Garden until her retirement at the end of 1842.

Kemble, Charles (1775-1854). English actor. Another son of Roger Kemble; he appeared first on the stage at Sheffield in 1793. He acted in *Macbeth* in London in 1794, and played a number of successful parts, chiefly in comedy, until 1840, when he retired. At the time he was joint proprietor of the Covent Garden Theatre and later was an examiner of plays. He married an actress, Maria Theresa de Camp, 1774-1838, and their eldest daughter, Frances Anne, 1809-1893, became famous as Fanny Kemble. His American engagements, 1832-1834, with his daughter, were extremely successful.

Kemble Family. A family of famous British actors.

The founder of this family, perhaps the most famous in the history of the stage, was **Roger Kemble,** 1721-1802, a strolling player and manager. He married in 1753

Sarah Ward, an actress, by whom he had twelve children, nine of whom followed the theatrical profession. The eldest, Sarah, was married in 1773 to William Siddons, and as Mrs. Siddons (see *Siddons*) was the most famous actress and beauty of her day.

Kemble, Fanny (Frances Anne) (1809-1893). English actress. Eldest daughter of Charles Kemble. She was born in London, and made her first appearance on the stage at Covent Garden, October 5, 1829, as Juliet to her father's Mercutio. So successful was she during the season in a number of tragic roles, such as Belvidera in *Venice Preserved,* and Mrs. Beverly in *The Gambler,* that she re-established her father's managerial fortunes. She married in 1834 an American, Pierce Butler, but divorced him, 1849, after returning to the English stage. She began at Willis' Rooms in 1848 the first of her Shakesperean readings. She was also the author of several plays and poems, and in addition wrote several volumes of reminiscences.

Kemble, John Mitchell (1807-1857). English actor. He was the eldest son of Charles Kemble and was born in London. He studied at Cambridge and under the Grimm brothers at Gottingen. He wrote several historical works, and *Beowulf,* 1833-1837, and was examiner of plays from 1840 until his death, March 26, 1857.

Kemble, John Philip (1757-1823). English actor. Eldest son of Roger Kemble; he was born at Prescot, Lancashire, and was educated for the Roman Catholic priesthood, but went on the stage instead. He made his debut at the age of ten, his first adult appearance in 1776, and his first London appearance at Drury Lane, September 30, 1783, as Hamlet. He was manager of Drury Lane for many years, and of Covent Garden from 1803 to 1817. At the former theatre, he played in Shakespearean tragedy, except for *Brutus,* acted at Covent Garden, 1812. His Coriolanus, Brutus, Cato, Hotspur and Hamlet were considered his most successful roles. He played Lear to Mrs. Siddons' Cordelia, at a benefit, thereby enhancing his growing reputation. He challenged comparison with Edmund Kean in a series of revival performances. He was an exponent of realistic costume. He died at Lausanne, February 26, 1823.

Kemp, Will (?-1603). English comedian. First a member of the Earl of Leicester's Company, he became in 1594 principal comedian of Shakespeare's company, the Lord Chamberlain's Men, and one of the leading clowns in the Elizabethan period. He played such parts as Dogberry, and Peter in *Romeo and Juliet.* In 1600 he created a sensation by dancing from London to Norwich, a feat which he described in his pamphlet, *Kemps Nine Daies Wonder.* He left Shakespeare's company to join another company of actors, the Earl Worcester's men, in 1602, remaining with the latter group until his death in 1603.

Kendal, Dame Madge (Margaret Robertson) (1849-1935). English actress. She was born at Cleethorpes, Lincolnshire, and was a sister of T. W. Robertson, the dramatist. She made her London debut, July 29, 1865, as *Ophelia* at The Haymarket. Here she also first revealed her rare sense of comedy in *New Men and Old Acres,* 1874, while at the Old Prince of Wales' she showed her unique powers of pathos in *Peril,* 1876, and *Diplomacy,* 1878. She reached the height of her reputation in 1879-88, when she displayed her wide emotional range in plays produced at The St. James' under the Hare and Kendal management, more particularly *The Squire; The Ironmaster; A Scrap of Paper;* and *Clancarty.* Her greatest triumph in her later years was in *The Elder Miss Blossom.* After her retirement in 1908 she devoted herself largely to charitable works, receiving the D.B.E., 1926. Her husband, William Hunter Kendal, 1843-1917, whose real name was Grimston, was Madge Kendal's leading man during his management with Hare of the St. James' Theatre. They were married in 1869.

Kennedy, Margaret (Mrs. David Davies) (1898-　). English novelist, dramatist. Educated at Cheltenham and Somerville College, Oxford. Came into prominence for her book and play *The Constant Nymph.*

Her plays include: adaptation with Basil Dean of *The Constant Nymph,* 1926; and *Come With Me,* 1928; *Escape Me Never,* 1933; *Autumn,* 1937.

Kern, Jerome David (1885-　). American composer. Born in New York City, he studied music under his mother and later studied piano at the New York College of Music with Alexander Lambert, Paolo Gallico and harmony with Dr. Austin Pierce and under private tutors in Germany from 1904-1905. While in England in 1903 he began to compose. He specializes in the application of the modern school of harmony to the lighter forms of opera and musical plays. He is the composer of *Very Good Eddie,* 1915; *Theodore & Co.,* 1916; *Follies,* 1916; *Oh Boy,* 1917; *Have a Heart,* 1917; *Oh, Lady, Lady,* 1918; *Rock-a-Bye Baby,* 1918; *Sally,* 1920; *Show Boat,* 1927; *Sweet Adeline,* 1929; *Music in the Air,* 1932; *Roberta,* 1933; *Very Warm for May,* 1939.

Kerr, Frederick (1858-1933). English actor. Born in London, he was the son of Grinham Keen, and in 1881 went to America, appearing in New York, 1882, in *The School for Scandal.* First appearing in London in the same year, he rapidly made a reputation, and in 1895 became manager of the Vaudeville Theatre. Kerr was on the stage almost continuously for nearly fifty years, and in 1930 commenced his film career, appearing in *Raffles; The Midshipmaid;* and other films.

Key a role, to. The tone which an actor gives to his part. "Mansfield's Brutus was keyed very low."

Key city. A town outside of New York such as Chicago, Boston, Philadelphia, which presents world premieres, or important shows, usually with the original cast intact or with some members of it.

Keystone. Three-ply profile board cut into the shape of a trapezium; used for joining the toggle to the style.

See *Scenery.*

Killigrew, Thomas (1612-83) (The Elder). Page to Charles I and companion and favorite of Charles II. He became "master of revels" in 1679, and built a playhouse in London in 1663—now the site of the Drury Lane Theatre. His most popular play was the *Parson's Wedding*—played in 1637—printed in 1664. He also wrote *The Prisoners, Claracilla, The Princess, Cecilia and Clorinda.*

Kinescope (television). A special type of cathode ray tube developed for home television receivers by the Radio Corporation of America laboratories.

A King And No King. Beaumont & Fletcher (English). Drama. 1611.

Tigranes, king of Armenia, and Arbaces, king of Iberia, end a long war by engaging in personal combat. Arbaces wins and demands that Tigranes marry his sister Panthea to gain his freedom. Tigranes, in love with the Armenian damsel Spaconia, refuses. When Arbaces, Tigranes and Panthea, meet both men are smitten by her Arbaces had not seen his sister for years. Feeling guilty, he vainly tries to smoulder this passion which Panthea reciprocates. Gobrias, who has been ruling the kingdom under a protectorate, confesses that Arbaces is his son. He had permitted his adoption by the Queen when she thought she would never have children. Panthea was born 6 years later and is now the rightful Queen of Iberia, she is not related to Arbaces, and the lovers are united. Tigranes marries Spaconia and is released.

Kingdom of God, The. G. Martinez-Sierra (Spanish). Drama. 3 acts. 1916.

Three scenes in the life of a nun. First, as a girl of eighteen, just before taking her final vows. Second, as a woman, repressing her love for a young doctor. Third, as an old woman who stops a revolt of hungry orphans, and tells them they must work and pray for "The Kingdom of God."

King Henry the Fourth (Part I). William Shakespeare (English). Drama. 5 acts. 1598.

This historical play is based largely on the account of Henry IV's reign in Holinshed's *Chronicles.* Shakespeare also drew on an older play, *The Famous Victories of Henry V,* for episodes relating to the youthful escapades of Prince Hal. It was this source, indeed, which, in its character of Sir John Oldcastle, suggested to Shakespeare the creation of Sir John Falstaff. The action of the play depicts Henry's suppression of a rebellion against his rule by the Percys of Northumberland. The rebels are led by young Henry Percy, surnamed Hotspur, who, in the ensuing Battle of Shrewesbury, is killed in single combat by Prince Hal, Henry's son. The escapades of Falstaff with Prince Hal and a company of tavern frequenters comprise a comic sub-plot which reaches a climax with Falstaff's comic faint-heartedness in battle.

King Henry the Fourth, Part Two. William Shakespeare (English). Drama. 5 acts. 1598.

Published in quarto form in 1600. The chief source is Holinshed's *Chronicle,* with suggestions from the older play, *The Famous Victories of Henry V.* The Earl of Northumberland and the Archbishop of York join in a new rebellion against

Henry which is crushed by Prince John, younger son of the king. Henry, dying, draws from Prince Hal a promise that the latter will leave his riotous tavern life. Hal is crowned Henry V and banishes Falstaff and his companions from his company. The comic sub-plot centers in Falstaff's wooing of Doll Tearsheet and his selection of recruits for the army.

King Henry the Fifth. William Shakespeare (English). Drama. 5 acts. 1599.

It is based on an earlier play, *The Famous Victories of Henry V,* and partly on Holinshed's *Chronicles.* The play deals with Henry's campaign to seize the French throne, which he believes to be rightfully his. The action covers the surrender of Harfleur to the English, the privations and weakness of the English army, and their eventual brilliant victory over the French at Agincourt. Henry secures the succession of the throne of France to his son and the hand of the French princess Katherine in marriage for himself. He is portrayed in heroic terms as England's ideal king. Fluellen, a Welsh officer, and Pistol, Nym and Bardolph, three soldiers, supply interludes of comedy.

King Henry VI, Part I. William Shakespeare (English). Drama. 5 acts. 1592.

Based on materials found in Holinshed's *Chronicle.* Only II, iv, v; IV, v, vi, vii; and V iii can be definitely assigned to Shakespeare; remainder of the play is generally considered to be by an unknown dramatist. The action opens with the funeral of Henry V, when his successor was an infant, and closes with Suffolk's departure for France to bring back Margaret of Anjou as a bride for Henry. The beginning of the Wars of the Roses between the houses of York and Lancaster is depicted. Other episodes include the loss of Orleans and Bordeaux to France under the leadership of Joan of Arc, the capture of Rouen from Joan, and the subsequent execution of the French heroine, who is here portrayed as a witch.

King Henry VI, Part II. William Shakespeare (English). Drama. 5 acts. 1590-1.

Based on Holinshed's *Chronicles. The Contention between the Houses of York and Lancaster,* long considered a source play used by Shakespeare, has been shown to be a corrupt version of the play pirated from Shakespeare's own work. The action covers Henry's reign from his marriage to Margaret of Anjou to the victory of York over the king at the battle of St. Albans'. It includes the ruin of Gloucester at the instigation of Margaret and Suffolk, the execution of the last for his treason, the rebellion led by Jack Cade and fomented by York, Cade's pretenses to the throne and his subsequent defeat by Clifford, and the battle of St. Albans, in which the York faction triumphs over the house of Lancaster.

King Henry VI, Part III. William Shakespeare (English). Drama. 5 acts. 1590-1.

Based on Holinshed's *Chronicles. The True Tragedy of Richard Duke of York,* long considered a source play used by Shakespeare, has been shown to be a corrupt version pirated from Shakespeare's own work. The action opens with the death of

York after his plot to seize the throne after the battle of St. Albans has failed. His son, however, carries on the cause of York and soon forces Henry into hiding while he assumes the crown as Edward IV. Henry's queen, Margaret, secures aid from Warwick and the French, defeats Edward, and restores Henry. Edward returns, defeats and imprisons Henry, and resumes the title of Edward IV. Henry and his son are murdered by the Duke of Gloucester, later Richard III, Edward's brother.

King Henry VIII. William Shakespeare and John Fletcher (English). Drama. 5 acts. 1613.

Written about 1613 and published in the Folio of 1623. The play is based on the account in Holinshed's *Chronicles*. The action opens with the execution of Buckingham at the instigation of Cardinal Wolsey. Wolsey, hoping to marry the king to the French princess, suggests a divorce from Katherine of Aragon. Henry is willing to have the divorce, but has picked Anne Boleyn instead of the French princess for his second wife. When Wolsey learns of this, he secretly delays the divorce. But Henry's discovery of this, and of the wealth amassed by Wolsey, causes the Cardinal to retire. Anne is crowned queen after a secret marriage to Henry. Cranmer, Archbishop of Canterbury, now becomes a powerful influence at court and arouses the jealousy of other nobles. He is about to be convicted by the latter in a farcical trial when Henry takes justice into his own hands, rescues Cranmer, and makes him godfather to the newly-born princess Elizabeth.

King Hunger. Leonid N. Andreyev (Russian). 1907.

At a meeting of workingmen in a cellar, where they are toiling before an open furnace, King Hunger emerges from the fire. He has promised them Death and Time to aid them and urges them to revolt. When the proletariat hold a mock trial to judge a man who stole a loaf of bread and a woman who did away with her child because she could not see it starve, he condemns them both to death. The wealthy citizenry dancing upstairs become alarmed as the hungry mass threatens them. They are reassured by an engineer who tells them he has an invention that will vanquish the poor. They turn back to their dancing and King Hunger appears telling them the poor have fallen. The rich are well pleased with this until King Hunger again turns to the starving and urges them to rebel.

King John. William Shakespeare (English). Tragedy. 5 acts. 1596.

Written about 1596 and first published in the Folio of 1623. The play is based on an older drama, *The Troublesome Reign of King John,* which in turn is drawn from Holinshed's *Chronicles*. John, having seized the throne from young Prince Arthur, is about to defend himself against France and Austria, who support Arthur's cause, when a marriage between John's niece, Blanche of Castille, and the Dauphin of France, brings a peaceful settlement. The war is resumed, however, when John is excommunicated for refusing to obey the Pope's commands. John's own lords turn against him and join the Dauphin when Prince Arthur is found dead and John is suspected of murdering him. The war is indecisive, but John is poisoned by monks at Swinstead abbey, the Dauphin returns with his army to France, and peace is restored.

King Lear. William Shakespeare (English). Tragedy. 5 acts. 1605.

Written about 1605 and published in quarto form in 1608. An older play, *King Leir,* provided materials for Shakespeare's play, as did Holinshed's *Chronicles.* The Gloucester sub-plot is from Sidney's novel *Arcadia,* 1590. Lear, king of Britain, divides his realm between Goneril and Regan, his flattering daughters, and leaves their sister Cordelia, who really loves him, with nothing. She marries the king of France and goes abroad, while Lear is treated with abuse and disrespect by the remaining daughters. Turned out by both, with only his fool and the distinguished Earl of Kent attending him, he encounters Edgar, son of the Duke of Gloucester, who has been unjustly banished by his father at the instigation of Edmund, Gloucester's bastard son. Gloucester arrives to do kindness to Lear, who has gone mad, but for this act has his eyes put out by Regan's husband Cornwall, inspired by Edmund. Edgar, unrecognized, saves his blind father from suicide, while Cordelia, who has arrived with an army from France, tries to solace Lear. Cordelia and Lear are defeated by an English army under Edmund and taken captive. Edmund in turn is killed in single combat by Edgar before an order for Cordelia's death can be countermanded. Lear dies of grief trying to revive her. Meanwhile, Goneril, jealous of her sister's love for Edmund has poisoned Regan and killed herself. The Duke of Albany, Goneril's husband, who has never countenanced Goneril's behaviour, succeeds to the throne.

King Leír. Anonymous (English). Drama. 5 acts. Printed 1605.

An Elizabethan play with the same basic plot as Shakespeare's "King Lear"— the old man, abused by two of his three daughters, for whom he has divided his kingdom, but (unlike Shakespeare's Lear) finally victorious and restored to his throne.

King Richard II. William Shakespeare (English). Tragedy. 5 acts. 1595.

Published in quarto form in 1597. It is based on the account in Holinshed's *Chronicles.* Bolingbroke, banished by Richard, leads an army against the king, forces him to abdicate, and brings about his murder. The usurper succeeds to the throne as Henry IV. The weakness and self-pity of Richard contrast with the practical and efficient character of his rival. For fear of offending Queen Elizabeth, who often compared herself to Richard II, the abdication scene was omitted from published versions of the play until 1608. The play was revived in a performance at the Globe on February 7, 1601, the eve of Essex's rebellion, in order to inspire the rebels.

King Richard III. William Shakespeare (English). Tragedy. 5 acts. 1592.

Written about 1592, published in quarto form in 1597. It is based on accounts in Holinshed's Chronicles. Richard, who had murdered Henry VI, continues his march to the throne, held by his brother Edward IV. He has the Duke of Clarence, another brother, murdered and further secures his position by marrying Anne, widow of Henry VI's son. Upon the natural death of Edward IV, Richard has the young princes, Edward V and his brother, killed, and manipulates public opinion into demanding his coronation. Thereupon he comes to the throne as Richard III. After a series of tyrannical executions of Hastings, Rivers and Grey, the Duke of Buckingham rebels, supporting the Earl of Richmond. Buckingham is captured and executed. But Richmond marches on and engages Richard III in battle. Richard is defeated and dies at Bosworth. Richard, as a dramatic character, is drawn as ruthless and ambitious, cruel and unrelenting, yet he is renowned for his valor and shrewdness.

King's Company. The theatrical company, during the Restoration, of Thomas Killigrew; with a patent from Charles II it first began performances in 1660; it opened in a new theatre in 1663, and, with the burning of this, moved in 1674 to the Theatre Royal in Drury Lane, later to become known as the Drury Lane Theatre; not long afterwards it lost its patronage; in 1682, with the bankruptcy of D'Avenant's rival company, the Duke of York's Company, the two combined for mutual benefit with a new patent from the King, retaining the title of King's Company; the merger was not successful.

The King's Henchman. Edna St. Vincent Millay (American). 1927. This play served as the libretto for Deems Taylor's opera.

Eadger, king of England, surrounded by his court of henchmen, is awaiting the arrival of Aethelwald, his foster brother and most trustworthy henchman. He is to go on a mission for Aelfrida, daughter of Thane of Devon, and if she is really beautiful he is to woo her and bring her back with him.

The evening of All Hallow Mass finds Aethelwald in the forest of Devon. Aelfrida has come into the forest to find out who her lover will be. She comes upon the sleeping Aethelwald and they feel destined for each other. They marry and he sends a perfidious message to the king saying she is worthless. A messenger arrives one day telling Aethelwald the king is coming to see him. He tells his wife all and instructs her to dress up as a hag. When the king arrives, she emerges dressed in her most costly and beautiful garments. Realizing her self-love and his mistake Aethelwald stabs himself—the king denounces her as unworthy of his friend.

Kingsley, Sidney (1906-   ). American dramatist. Graduate of Cornell University, member of the Dramatic Club. He appeared with the Tremont Stock Co. and took a small part in *Subway Express,* a Broadway production. He had, in the interval written a play called *Crisis.* In 1933 it was produced by the Group Theatre, the title changed to *Men In White.* It won the Pulitzer award, played over 300 performances and was done on the continent as well as England.

In 1935 he wrote *Dead End.* This play was even more successful and won the Theatre Club award. In October, 1936, he wrote, financed and produced *Ten Million Ghosts.* It dealt with the conspiracy and hypocrisy of the munitions manufacturers.

Kingston, Gertrude (1868-   ). English actress, author. Born in London, she made her London début in 1888, appearing thenceforth in a long series of comedies and other plays. In 1910 she planned and built the Little Theatre, John Street, London, appearing there with success until 1913, as well as in America. Miss Kingston translated and produced several plays and illustrated children's books. George Bernard Shaw wrote *Great Catherine,* 1913, for her.

Kirkland, Alexander. American actor. Studied for the stage under Jasper Deeter, Louis Calvert and Rouben Mamoulian; made his first appearance on the stage at the Ramshed Playhouse, Washington, 1925, in *L'Aiglon;* first appeared in New York later that year as Nanning Storm in *The Devil to Pay.* Has since appeared as Stephen Bartan in *The Right Age to Marry;* Wu-Hoo-Git in *The Yellow Jacket;* Aleksei in *A Month in the Country;* Marius in *Marseilles.* Joined the Group Theatre, New York, 1933, and appeared as Dr. Ferguson in *Men in White;* Lon Firth in *Gold Eagle Guy;* Ernst Laussig in *Till the Day I Die;* Danny Stowe in *Weep for the Virgins.* Founded the Berkshire Playhouse, Stockbridge, Massachusetts, 1933, and was manager for three years, playing roles as well. In 1939 became associated with Frank Carrington in the management of The Paper Mill Playhouse, New Milburn, New Jersey.

See also *Paper Mill Playhouse.*

Kismet. Edward Knoblock (American). Drama. 1911.

The action consumes a day in the life of Haji the beggar of Bagdad, beginning with early morning when he awakes from sleep on the Mosque steps. He invokes Allah's blessing on the head of his old enemy, the sheikh Jawan, and thus tricks the man who has robbed him of his wife and son into throwing him a bag of gold. Thus Haji starts his day accursed but wealthy. Slyly he robs the tailors in the bazaar of their wares, is arrested and brought before the Wazir. The latter promises to let Haji go free if he will do him the favor of killing the Caliph. For the Wazir has been stealing the city's funds and fears exposure. In return for this service the Wizar promises to marry Haji's daughter Marsinah, "fair as the lotus bloom," who, unknown to her father, is secretly in love with the Caliph. Haji's attack on the Caliph is unsuccessful, and he is thrown into a dungeon—right next to the wicked Jawan. Haji strangles the sheikh to death, dons the dead man's clothes and escapes. In the city once more, he learns that the Wazir wanted Marsinah only as a concubine, and goes to the harem to rescue her. There he learns that the Wazir is, by a happy coincidence, Jawan's son. He now has two reasons to hate him, because he is related to the sheikh and because he has mistreated Marsinah. So Haji drowns the gentleman. The Caliph claims Marsinah for his bride, but is obliged to banish Haji for his sins. Unperturbed, the beggar decides to make a pilgrimage to Mecca. As the curtain falls, he is lying snoring on the Mosque steps in the same attitude he had taken when the play began.

This play was a great success when first given. The spectacle was colorfully staged so as to have considerable visual appeal, and Otis Skinner made a personal hit as Haji the beggar, that "gorgeous rogue," that "gay and gaudy adventurer."

A Kiss For Cinderella. J. M. Barrie (English). 1916.

Little "Miss Thing" is a slavey employed in a studio building. A policeman enters the building to warn against showing so much light with German airplanes abroad and overhears Jane, Miss Thing, expressing her romantic desires to go to a ball at Buckingham Palace. The policeman follows her home and finds that at night she runs a penny shop. She is also doing her share of the war work by keeping a group of four war orphans. She feeds the children, going hungry herself, and amuses them by relating the Cinderella story. Sitting on the steps of her tumbledown home, she falls asleep and dreams that she is Cinderella. The policeman tenderly puts his muffler around her. In her dream, the Prince is the policeman and of course the glass slipper fits her. Miss Thing awakens to find herself in a hospital sick from exposure and undernourishment. The policeman writes her a letter proposing and Miss Thing has been vindicated in her loyalty to the Cinderella story.

Klaw and Erlanger Syndicate. Part of the theatrical enterprise which had been secretly gaining control of the theatres of the country. During the season of 1895-96, they openly organized a powerful trust which closed its doors to all actors who refused its terms. A. L. Erlanger, Marc Klaw, Liebler and Company were partners to it.

Kleist, Heinrich von (1777-1811). German dramatist. Born at Frankfort-on-Oder, he wrote many plays, and strove for a new national drama in harmony with the spirit of the age. He possessed an independent originality. Largely neglected during his lifetime and embittered by failure, he shot himself November 21, 1811. Subsequent performances of his plays gained him posthumous recognition as the chief Prussian dramatist of the romantic period. Of his stories, *Michael Kohlhass*, 1808, is considered the best novelette in the German language.

Best known of his plays are *Die Hermannschlacht*, 1809; *Kaetchen von Heilbronn*, 1810; *Der Zerbrochene Krug*, 1812; *Der Prinz von Homburg*, 1821. The first is regarded as one of the best comedies in German literature.

Knight of the Burning Pestle. Beaumont & Fletcher (English). Satire. 1607.

A satire designed to poke fun at knight errantry, and London's manners. A play is being performed by a group of players for a grocer and his wife. Their interest is in Ralph, their apprentice, for whom they have secured the leading role. He as Grocer Errant undertakes very adventurous errands, with a burning pestle on his shield.

The thread of the real plot is interspersed with that of Jasper, apprentice to a merchant, who wishes to marry Luce, his master's daughter. The master prefers another. Jasper, pretending he is dead, intimidates the father by feigning to be a ghost and ends up by getting consent to the marriage. All through the play, the grocer and his wife keep up a barrage of remarks commenting on the play.

Knights, The. Aristophanes. Comedy. c. 424 B.C.

A satire on the demagogues and militarists of the times, notable for its invectives against prominent contemporaries, mainly against Cleon. In a previous play Aristophanes had denounced Cleon and continues to do so here. An old man, Demos, symbolic as the "State," falls into the scheming, unscrupulous hands of a Paphlagonian steward. Meanwhile two slaves of Demos's are plotting against the steward. They mark out a plan whereby the steward shall be supplanted by a friend of theirs, a sausage vendor. Demos soon realizes what has been going on and comes to his senses in time to retain his prestige.

Knoblock, Edward (1874-). Anglo-American dramatist. Born in New York, April 7, 1874, he was naturalized as a British subject in 1916. His numerous and successful plays include: *The Shulamite* (with Claude Askew), 1906; *Kismet,* 1911; *Milestones* (with Arnold Bennett), 1912; *My Lady's Dress,* 1914; *London Life* (with Arnold Bennett), 1924; *The Good Companions* (with J. B. Priestley), 1931. He did the English stage version of Vicki Baum's *Grand Hotel,* 1931; and *Evensong,* with Beverley Nichols, 1932.

Knock. Jules Romains (French). Farce. 3 acts. 1924.

In the tradition of Molière, Dr. Knock, a sharper, takes over a legitimate practice in a small French town. He promptly votes all the population on the sick list and collects fees for writing patent medicine recipes as prescriptions. The play is written in the satiric vein showing how this quack has regimented the whole village into a medical army following his somewhat ridiculous medical orders.

Knock-out. A sure-fire hit.

Know Thyself. Paul Hervieu (French). 1909.

An officer consults the general about his wife's infidelity. The officer feels that it is perhaps wiser to do nothing about it. The general disagrees and tells him he cannot face such a situation with honor—he must divorce his wife and challenge his rival. Soon the general learns that this rival is his son and that his wife has been unfaithful with his ward. The general thinks things over and resorts to no such radical conduct as he advised the officer to follow. He admits neglect of his wife and forgives her, rationalizing human frailty and the power of temptation.

Komisarjevsky, Theodore (1882-). Russian director, designer. Russian producer, scenic and costume designer, born in Italy. He became a naturalized British subject in 1932. He made his first production at his sister's theatre, the Komisarjevsky, Petrograd, in 1907. During the management of his own theatre from 1910, and as director of the Imperial and State Theatres in Moscow, until 1919, produced more than twenty operas, besides many plays by Shakespeare, Molière, Shaw, and others. His first production in London was Borodin's *Prince Igor* at Covent Garden, October 1919. Since then worthy productions have been: (1) In London: The *Government Inspector,* 1920; *Six Characters in Search of an Author,* 1921; *Uncle Vanya,* 1921; *The Three Sisters,* and *The Cherry Orchard,* 1926; *Escape Me Never,* 1933; *Hatter's Castle,* Edinburgh, 1932. (2) In Paris: *The Dover Road, The Duenna, Siegfried, Walkure, La Maitresse du Roi.* (3) In New York: *The Lucky One, The Tidings Brought to Mary, Peer Gynt,* 1922-23; *The Sea Gull* and *Antony and Cleopatra,* 1936. He has produced also in Italy and in Riga, Latvia. He is author of a play, *The Brass Paperweight* (which he produced in London in 1928); and of *Theatrical Preludes, The Costume of the Theatre, The Actor and the Theory of Stanislavsky, Myself and the Theatre, The Theatre,* etc.

Korusi. The name given to the kind of *Kabuki* drama in which the murder scene presents a sight less cruel than in reality and more artistic.

Kothornos. Variously known as *embates* and *okribas*. Boots with heavy wooden sole, used in ancient Greek theatre to give actors height; used only for the important (from the viewpoint of both the play and the class to which, in life, they would belong) characters; in *chorus* non-existent.

Kotzebue, August Friedrich Ferdinand von (1761-1819). German dramatist. He composed 218 dramatic pieces in the form of fairy dramas, historical plays, social problem plays, operas and comedies. Due to the enormous popularity of his plays, he dominated the boards in Germany during his lifetime and for several decades thereafter. His works were translated into most of the civilized tongues of the world and his plays were performed in every corner of the globe. After 1815 many regarded him as a Russian spy and believed he was trying to amalgamate Russia and Germany. In 1790, under an assumed name, he published the obscene play, *Dr. Bahrdt mit der sesernen Stirn,* and his immorality became notorious. He was killed by the fanatic Karl Ludwig Sand. Kotzebue laid his spell upon the English dramatists and taught them how to express new problems. Sheridan adapted his *Pizarro* for the English stage. In the Manheim Theatre in Germany the library administration has brought together a collection of works by and on the playwright.

Kronenberger, Louis. American author, dramatic critic. Author of the plays, *Nobody's Business* (with Leane Zugsmith) and *Deer Queen* (with Lillian Hellman); drama critic of *Time Magazine.*

Krutch, Joseph Wood (1893-   ). American dramatic critic, author. Born Knoxville, Tennessee, B.A. University of Tennessee, M.A. Columbia, instructor of English and journalism, lecturer, and drama critic of *The Nation.*
Edited, *The Plays of William Congreve* and *Nine Plays by Eugene O'Neill.*

Kulissenreisser (wing-splitter). The name given the type of 18th century German acting in which the characters rushed about the stage wildly, boisterously and thundered their speeches. Karl Theophilus Doebbelin was the portotype of this form.

Kurogo. The prompter in the Japanese theatre; dressed and hooded in black so as to be invisible; aids the actor in a new play by standing behind him and prompting him; sets the chair or *aibiki* used by leading players.

Kurz, Joseph Felix von (1715-1784). Austrian dramatist, actor. Created the *Berdardon* character, which competed with *Hanswurst,* created by his rival, Gottfried Prehauser, 1699-1769; von Kurz directed a troupe of his own.

Kyd, Thomas (1558-1594). English dramatist. An Elizabethan dramatist who was educated at the Merchant Taylors School in London; there is some evidence that he proceeded to a university. He was associated with Marlowe, and got into trouble because of a mixture of Marlowe's "atheistic" papers with his own, for which he was imprisoned. He died intestate in the parish of St. Mary Colchurch. His most famous play is *The Spanish Tragedy*. Among others are: *Cornelia* and *The "Ur-Hamlet."*

Labiche, Eugene Maria (1815-1888). French dramatist. Born in Paris, he produced his first play, *L'Avocat Loubet,* in 1838, and thereafter until 1877 produced, in collaboration with other writers, nearly 100 comedies and vaudeville sketches, including *Le Chapeau de paille d'Italie*, 1851; *Le Voyage de M. Perrichon,* 1860; and *La Cagnotte,* 1864. Although farcical in intent, his plays show in addition considerable gifts of observation and witty dialogue. Labiche raised French farces to a high level of merit, which was not sustained after he ceased to write. He became a member of l'Académie française in 1880. His *Le Chapeau de paille d'Italie* was made into a motion picture by Rene Clair, under the title *The Italian Straw Hat*. Orson Welles and John Houseman produced the play for the Federal Theatre Project in 1936 as *Horse Eats Hat*.

Labor Stage, Inc. The theatrical producing unit of the International Ladies Garment Workers Union. Established during season of 1935-36. This group took over the former Princess Theatre, 104 West 39th Street, and renamed it the Labor Stage. In the spring of 1939 the Windsor was leased and renamed Labor Stage Windsor Theatre. Their most notable production is *Pins and Needles*.

The Labyrinth. Paul Hervieu (French). Drama. 5 acts. 1903.
Marianne who is divorced and remarried, is called to watch with her first husband over the bed of their sick child. She returns to her parents, and her Catholic mother who does not recognize the second marriage as legal, forgives her her sin. The second husband, however, pursues her and threatens to kill his rival. Marianne, in an attempt to escape both husbands goes to the country. Both husbands follow and in a struggle, they both fall over the edge of a cliff to die.

Lacy, John (1660-85). British dramatist. Wrote *The Old Troop,* an anti-puritan satire, and *Sir Hercules Buffoon*. His plays have a noteworthy farcical and robust quality.

Ladder, The. J. Frank Davis. 1926.
A play dealing with reincarnation, nominally produced by Brock Pemberton. Edgar B. Davis, no relation to the author, financed the play. He was a millionaire oil man and was anxious for the public to hear the play's message. Usually admission was free. It ran 640 performances.

The Lady from the Sea. Henrik Ibsen (Norwegian). Drama. 4 acts. 1888.

For the sake of having a home, Ellida marries the physician, Wangel, but soon yearns for the freedom of her girlhood at the lighthouse and recalls the fascination of a stranger with whom she feels she has a mystic union. Pregnant with Wangel's child, she is haunted by the thought that she has been untrue to the stranger. The stranger returns and Wangel at first forbids Ellida to have anything to do with him. Finally he gives her freedom of choice. She dismisses the stranger who disappears and she becomes Wangel's true wife. The play is symbolic in that the stranger is the externalization of Ellida's desire for moral freedom.

Lady of Lyons, The. Edward Bulwer-Lytton (English). 5 acts. 1838.

This play enjoyed quite a vogue for over 60 years. It is patterned after an old story called *The Bellows-Mender* and deals with the post-revolutionary period of 1795-1798. It is written in blank verse and was published anonymously. The critics hailed it but reserved their opinion when they learned the authorship, because of a feud that had been going on between them and Lytton.

Lady Precious Stream. See *Wang Pao Ch'uan*.

Lady Windermere's Fan. Oscar Wilde (English). Drama. 4 acts. 1892.

Because she believes her husband is paying attentions to another woman, Lady Windermere quarrels with him. She does not know that the woman, Mrs. Erlynne, is her own mother whom she believes dead and that Lord Windermere is just trying to help her. When he brings the woman to their house, however, Lady Windermere decides to run away with her lover, Lord Darlington, and leaves a letter to her husband to that effect. Mrs. Erlynne finds the letter, destroys it and follows her daughter to Lord Darlington's quarters and persuades her to return to her husband. Mrs. Erlynne waits for Lord Darlington who returns with Lord Windermere. When the latter discovers Lady Windermere's fan on the floor, Mrs. Erlynne says that she took it by mistake and gives the impression that she had a secret rendezvous with Lord Darlington. The Windermeres are reconciled and Mrs. Erlynne marries Lord Augustus Lawton and promises to leave England.

Lamb, Charles (1775-1834). English author. Wrote *John Woodvil*, a poetic tragedy, which although it has a strong poetical quality is lacking in coordinated central power. His great fame lies in his essays which contain his contribution to dramatic theory. Together with his sister Mary, he paraphrased Shakespeare's plots as Lamb's Tales from Shakespeare.

Lambs, The. Taking its name from the London organization, the New York club was organized in 1874, being originally a supper club. The charter members were George H. McLean, Henry T. Montague, Edward Arnott, Henry Beckett and Arthur Wallack, son of J. Lester Wallack. In 1877, the club incorporated under the laws of the State of New York; and in 1904 moved into its present home at 128 W. 44th St. Among the Shepherds were Clay M. Greene, Thomas W. Clarke, Augustus Thomas, William Courtleigh, R. H. Burnside, Thomas Meighan, Thomas A. Wise, Fritz Williams, A. O. Brown, Frank Crumit and William Gaxton. The club's historic functions include the Lambs Wash, Seidel Nights, annual public and occasional road Gambols and Crazy Pool Nights. The Lambs dedicated the opening of the Earl Carroll theatre with a parade and ceremonies. The clubhouse boasts a collection of masks, portraits of famous stars of the past like John Philip Kemble, bronze busts of De Wolfe Hopper and David Warfield and original paintings by Howard Chandler Christy, James Montgomery Flagg and Frederick Remington. The Lambs Immortals are Charles H. Hoyt, Joseph R. Grimer, William Morris, Winchell Smith, Frank W. Kitching, Clay M. Greene and Augustus Thomas.

Lambs Gambol. The Lambs Club Gambol, a seasonal event, consists of sketches with songs and vaudeville numbers by members of the club without pay.

Lanchester, Elsa (1902-). British actress. Born at Lewisham, she started the children's theatre in Soho, 1918, and subsequently opened the Cave of Harmony, where she presented several plays. She made her first appearance on the stage in 1922 in *Thirty Minutes in a Street*. Since then she has appeard in *The Way of the World,* 1924; *Riverside Nights,* 1926 (in which she achieved fame as an eccentric comedienne) ; *The Outskirts,* 1930; *Payment Deferred,* 1931, etc. She made her first New York appearance in *Payment Deferred,* 1931, then joined the Old Vic-Sadler's Wells Company, 1933, and during the season played in *The Cherry Orchard, The Tempest, Love for Love* and others.

She made her film début in 1932, and has appeared in several pictures, such as *The Constant Nymph, David Copperfield, Naughty Marietta, The Ghost Goes West,* and *The Private Life of Henry VIII,* in which she appeared with her husband, Charles Laughton. She is also the author of *Charles Laughton and I,* 1938.

Land of Hearts Desire. W. B. Yeats (Irish). A poetic drama in one act based on an old Irish fairy tale. 1894.

A fairy in the guise of a child enters an Irish home where Michael, an old farmer, John, his son, Bridget, his wife, sit. The fairy weaves her spell over the young wife and lures her away.

Land of Many Names. Joseph Čapek (Czechoslovak). Drama. 3 acts. Translated by Paul Selver. 1923.

A new continent, just discovered, becomes everyone's dream state. To the boy, it is escape; to the young lovers, an Eden; to the socialist, Marxian, to the capitalist, a new market for exploitation. Everyone is disillusioned, however, when the new continent sinks back into the ocean.

Lang, Alexander Matheson (1879-). British actor. Born in Montreal, he first appeared on the stage at Wolverhampton in 1897 and, having joined Sir F. R.

Benson's company, appeared at The Lyceum, London, 1900, as Mountjoy in *King Henry V*. After touring with Mrs. Langtry and Ellen Terry he scored successes in Shakespearean and other parts, and during 1909-12 toured in America, Australia, South Africa and India. He reappeared in London at His Majesty's in 1913, and made his great success as Mr. Wu in the play of that name. In 1915 he reappeared in the title-role of *Pete;* and, in 1920, created the leading part in *The Wandering Jew*. After 1916 he appeared in the motion pictures *Carnival; The Wandering Jew; Mr. Wu,* and other films made from his plays. He also played in *Christopher Sly,* 1922; *The Tyrant;* and *Jew Suss*. He married Hutin Britton, who appeared with him in many productions.

Langner, Lawrence (1890-   ). American dramatist. Born in South Wales; co-founder and director of The Theatre Guild, New York.

His plays include: *Another Way Out; The Family Exit; Matinata; Don Juan* (an adaptation from the French) ; *Henry Behave; These Modern Women; Moses; The Pursuit of Happiness* (with his wife, Armina Marshall) ; etc.

Langtry, Lillie (Emily Charlotte Langtry) (1852-1929). British actress. Born in Jersey, she was the daughter of W. C. E. Le Breton, dean of the island. She made her London début at the Haymarket in 1881 as Kate Hardcastle in *She Stoops to Conquer*. Known as Lillie Langtry she became an immediate favorite because of her great beauty and her considerable talent. She toured in the provinces and in America under her own management. In 1874 she married Edward Langtry, who died in 1897. In 1899, she became the wife of Sir Hugo de Bathe. Greatly interested in racing, she at one time kept a large stable of race-horses, and was one of the most famous owners.

Lardner, Ring (1885-1933). American humorist. He began his career as a reporter and editor, writing mostly sport news. He is best known for his short stories of simple, uneducated ordinary American people. Though light and amusing they were barbed with satire or based on profound pity. *June Moon,* with George Kaufman, was his only play. It is typical of his style.

Larra, Mariano José de (1809-1837). Spanish novelist, dramatist. Born in Madrid, he was an able critic of drama and customs. Used the pseudonym Figaro. *Macias* is his most important play, based on the love story of the famous Galician troubadour, Macias.

Larrimore, Francine (1898-   ). American actress. Born in Verdun, France, 1898, the niece of the famous Jewish actor, Jacob P. Adler. Made her first appearance as a small child in *A Fool There Was* and has played in *Where There's a Will,* 1910; *Fair and Warmer,* 1917; *Parlor, Bedroom and Bath,* 1918, and many other productions. Recently she has appeared in *Brief Moment,* 1931; *Spring Song,* 1934. She is also a skilful designer and was responsible for the settings of the production of *Scandal*.

Last Mile, The. John Wexley (American). Tragedy. 3 acts. 1929.

Based in part on a short play, *The Law Takes its Toll,* written by Robert Blake, a condemned murderer, and in part on the records of actual prison mutinies. The entire action of the drama takes place in the death house of a state penitentiary. Its inmates are Richard Walters, young, tall and handsome, scheduled to die in a few hours; a large psalm-singing negro; a hard-boiled badman; an insane fanatic; Fred Mayor, high strung, cruel; Killer Mears who lives up to his name. Walters is choking over his last meal while the hum of electricity is heard outside (the chair is being tested) and Eddie, the insane man recites in a singsong, poems on death. D'Amoro, up for the murder of a policeman, joins the group and is led to the empty cell. Amidst a bedlam of noise the priest gives Walters the last rites and the guard shaves him. He is taken to the death chamber; offstage the hum of the hot seat is heard.

Two weeks later. Mayor is due to die this time. He has more reason to live than Walters, for he has a wife who is about to have a child. Mears decides to take charge and engineer a break. He overpowers the guard. Three of the convicts overpower the priest and four guards who are in the adjoining office, and lock them in the death cells. The window bars are chopped down. Mears delivers an ultimatum to the cops gathered in the yard. When the deadline arrives, Mears, true to his word, shoots a guard. At ten another will follow, he warns. It is the keeper who is shot next. Then Mears warns the priest his hour is near. Some of the other convicts are weakening by now, however. Moreover their ammunition is low, and a charge of dynamite is being set up in the yard. Realizing they are licked Mears walks out into a volley of machine gun fire.

The Last of Mrs. Cheyney. Frederick Lonsdale. Comedy in 3 acts. 1925.

Mrs. Cheyney yearns for luxury and becomes an accomplice to a certain Charles in an attempt to steal Mrs. Ebley's pearl necklace. Lord Dilling falls in love with her, discovers her secret and foils her plan at a fashionable house party. When she decides to tell the truth she discovers that the other members of the house party are even more disreputable than she. She produces written evidence of their guilt. In order to silence her, a bargain is struck and she is given a 10,000 pounds check which she promptly destroys. She thus rehabilitates herself in the eyes of everybody and then agrees to marry Lord Dilling.

Late Christopher Bean, The. Sidney Howard (American). Comedy. 3 acts. Adapted from Rene Franchois's *Prenez Garde á La Peinture.* 1932.

After his death, Christopher Bean is acclaimed a great artist and his paintings are sought after. His relatives try to cheat Amy, Christopher Bean's maid, out of especially valuable paintings, but she proves that she is Bean's widow, their legal owner, and donates them to an art museum.

Lauder, Sir Harry (1870-   ). Scottish comedian. The son of a humble potter, he was born at Portobello, and while a boy worked in a flax mill at Arbroath and in several of the coal mines of Lanarkshire. His professional début was made in Hamilton, and in 1900 he made his first London appearance at Gatti's. He quickly made a reputation in variety at the old Oxford Theatre, the Tivoli and the London Pavillion, and made numerous tours through the provinces. London critics considered him the greatest living Scottish comedian. During the World War he riased large sums for charity by organizing concerts, and in 1919 he received a knighthood for his services at home and at the front. He toured all over the world, during his long career, becoming the highest paid music-hall or broadcasting artist. He made his twenty-fifth tour of America and Canada in 1932. Some of the songs he made famous include: *I Love a Lassie; Roamin' in the Gloamin'; It's Nice to Get Up in the Morning; Tobermory;* and *Stop Yer Tickling, Jock.*

He also acted on the screen. His films include: *Huntingtower* and *Auld Lang Syne.*

Laughton, Charles (1899-   ). English actor. Born at Scarborough, he made his stage début at the Barnes Theatre in *The Government Inspector* in 1926. Within a few years, in a series of parts, including Ephikhodov in *The Cherry Orchard,* 1926; Mr. Pratt in *The Happy Husband,* 1927; Mr. Crispin in *A Man with Red Hair,* 1928; Hercule Poirot in *Alibi,* 1928; and William Marble in *Payment Deferred,* 1931; he built up for himself an outstanding position on the contemporary stage. His mastery of dramatic technique and ability to sink his personality in the parts he played made him unrivalled as an actor of character parts. He also appeared in: *Macbeth; Love for Love;* and *Measure for Measure;* in the Vic-Wells season, 1933-34. He achieved immediate fame in a succession of films, including *Devil and the Deep; The Sign of the Cross; The Private Life of Henry VIII; White Woman; The Beachcomber; Mutiny on the Bounty.* He is married to Elsa Lanchester.

Laurent, Michel (fl. 1673). French stage mechanic, scene designer. Successor to Laurent Mahelot, Michel Laurent completed Mahelot's *Memoire du plusieurs decorations.*
See *Mahelot, Laurent.*

Lautrec, Henri de Toulouse (1864-1901). French lithographer, illustrator. Noted for his many poster designs, book illustrations and valuable lithographs taken from the music halls, Montmartre, and other night spots of Paris. He was the greatest painter of theatrical posters and the first to give them importance.

Lawrence, Gertrude (1898-   ). English actress. Born in London; educated at the Convent of the Sacré Coeur, Streatham; studied dancing under Mme. Espinosa and acting under Italia Conti; made her first appearance on the stage at the Brixton Theatre, 1908, in the pantomime *Dick Wittington;* appeared as a feature dancer in *Fifinella,* 1912. Plays she has appeared in include: *All Aboard; Miss Plaster of Paris; Some; Cheep; Tabs; Buzz-Buzz; The Midnight Frolics; Aladdin; A to Z; Dédé;* made her New York début in *André Charlot's Revue of 1924; The Charlot Revue,* 1926; *Oh, Kay!,* 1926; *Icebound; Treasure Girl; Candle-Light,* 1929; *The International Revue,* 1930; *Private Lives,* 1930; *Moonlight and Silver,* 1934; *To-Night at 8:30,* 1935-37; *Susan And God,* 1937-39; *Skylark,* 1939.

Lawson, John Howard (1886-   ). American dramatist, critic. Born in New York, he has been writing plays since he graduated from Williams in 1914. He is also the author of critical books on the theatre and the technique of playwriting. Among his plays are *Processional,* 1925; *Nirvana,* a discussion of universal religion; *Loudspeaker,* a farce on the American political set-up; *The International,* a conflict between capitalism and the workers; *Success Story,* 1932; *The Pure in Heart,* 1934; *Gentlewoman,* 1934; *Marching Song,* 1937. For the most part he has been interested in liberal causes and social problems. He was the co-founder with Emjo Basshe, Francis Faragoh, etc., of the New Playwrights' Theatre.

Lay 'em in the aisles. To be so funny on stage as to make the audience roar with laughter.

Lazarus Laughed. Eugene O'Neill (American). 1927.
Lazarus is resurrected by Jesus and all the followers of Lazarus come to Bethany to hear what message he will have. He tells them there is no death and he himself knows nothing but "God's Laughter." His followers dance and sing and his home is known as the "house of laughter." Finally Tiberius Caesar sends for him in the hope that Lazarus has some mysterious power to restore his youth. He has heard reports about the strange power of Lazarus' eyes—the eyes that make you forget sorrow. Caligula encounters Lazarus and feels his power. Unconvinced, he has Lazarus' followers trapped by the Roman Legions but he sees only that they die with laughter on their lips. Tiberius, meanwhile, incensed that he cannot learn the secret of youth from Lazarus has him burned in the amphitheatre. Tiberius wishing a reassuring word asks Lazarus about hope for himself. Lazarus says "There is hope for man." Caligula arrives to save Lazarus, stabs Tiberius and then Lazarus, believing that he, the mighty, has killed God and restored Death. Caligula in remorse asks forgiveness of Lazarus and asks to be saved from the horrors of fear. Lazarus tells him "Fear not," but Caligula cannot trust and remains tormented.

Lazzi. Theatrical turn or trick, name for any piece of comic business, usually interpolated impromptu in a *commedia dell' arte.*

Lead. The principal role in a play, or the actor or actress playing the role.

Lead sheet. Set of cues, or leads, to guide the musical director.

Learned Ladies, The (Les Femmes Savantes). Molière (French). 1672.
A brilliant satire which involves Chysale, an honest bourgeois, Philaminte, his pretentious wife, Belise, his stupidly romantic sister and Armande, his pedantic child. The plot is long and involved. It is the character portrayals that drive home Molière's scathing condemnation of pretentious learning and idle vanity.

Le Bargy, Charles Gustave Auguste (1858-   ). French actor and dramatist. Born at La Chapelle, Seine, he became a leading actor at the Comédie Française. *Une danseuse est morte* is his one notable play.

Lecouvreur, Adrienne (1692-1730). French actress. Born at Damery, Marne, she first appeared at the Comédie Française in 1717 in the title-role in Crebillon's *Elèctre,* and as Angelique in Moliere's comedy, *Georges Dandin,* and at once became celebrated for her powers as a tragic actress and for her refusal to emulate the stilted style of her predecessors. She became the mistress of Maurice de Saxe in 1721. She was the subject of Scribe and Legouvé's *Adrienne Lecouvreur,* a favorite role for Rachel and Bernhardt. John Oxenford, Fanny Davenport, Sir Theodore Martin, and Henry Herman all made adaptations into English.

Lederer, Francis (1906-   ). Czechoslovak actor. Born at Karlin, in Prague, Czechoslovakia, he established a reputation on the continent in a wide variety of parts before first appearing in London in 1931 in *My Sister and I.* He won fame in England with his performance in *Autumn Crocus* in the same year, and also appeared in *The Cat and the Fiddle* in 1932. He was introduced to Broadway in *Autumn Crocus* and was speedily contracted by Hollywood. He made his film debut in *Man of Two Worlds* in 1933. His next picture was the film version of *The Pursuit of Happiness* in 1934. Among his subsequent pictures have been: *The Gay Deception; My American Wife; It's All Yours; Confessions of a Nazi Spy.* Early in the summer of 1939 he appeared in Chicago with his wife, Margo, in a stage revival of *Seventh Heaven.* Later in the same summer he took over the leading-man role vacated by Laurence Olivier in Behrman's *No Time for Comedy,* starring Katharine Cornell. He went on tour with this play, October 1939.

Lee, Nathaniel (1653-92). English dramatist. Elizabethan playwright educated at Trinity College. Author of *Rival Queens, Nero, Emperor of Rome, Sophonisba, Gloriana* and *Theodosius.* His plays are too extravagant and tumultuous but possess many individual passages of great beauty.

Left Bank, The. Elmer Rice (American). Comedy. 3 acts. 1931.
This play is a clever satire on the life led by American expatriates in Paris. It relates the trials and tribulations of two ill-matched couples. Finally the couples decide to get divorces and marry again with an exchange of husbands and wives.

Leg drop. A drop from which center has been cut out leaving an inverted *U.*

Leg show. A burlesque, or revue with scantily-clad chorus girls.

LeGallienne, Eva (1899-   ). American actress, producer. Born in London, the daughter of the poet, Richard LeGallienne, and a Danish authoress and critic, Julie Norregaard LeGallienne, she came to New York in 1915, appearing in *Mrs. Boltay's Daughters.* Constance Collier was her first instructor, and it was in Miss Collier's London company that, as a fifteen-year-old girl she first appeared on the stage. In 1921, she made a conspicuous success as Julie in *Liliom.* She toured with Ethel Barrymore and appeared with Elsie Janis. She was the founder and director of the Civic Repertory Theatre, New York City, which opened in 1926.

This repertory company continued under her management until its dissolution in 1933. Since that time she has appeared in: *L'Aiglon; Rosmersholm; Madame Capet.* In October 1939 she began a tour in *Hedda Gabler* and *The Master Builder.*

Légende de Robert le Diable, La. The most famous of the *Miracles of Notre Dame.*

Legit. A popular abbreviation of legitimate stage.

Lehman, Adelaide. See *Niblo's Gardens.*

Leiber, Fritz (1883-   ). American actor. Born in Chicago, made his first stage appearance there in 1902. Toured with Julia Marlowe and Robert B. Mantell. From 1929-32 directed and played with the Chicago Civic Repertory Society. Toured with his own company 1934-35. In the course of his career he has played over 100 Shakespearean parts.

Lemaître, Fréderic (1800-1876). French actor. Born at Le Havre, July 21, 1800, he became famous both as a tragedian and comedian in the romantic drama of the day. Among the plays specially written for him was Hugo's *Ruy Blas.*

Le Maître, Jules (1853-1914). French critic and dramatist. Born at Vennecy, he was first a university instructor and later became dramatic critic of the Journal des Debats and the Revue des Deux Mondes. His plays include *Révoltée,* 1889; *Le Député Leveau,* 1891; *Le Mariage Blanc,* 1891; *Les Rois,* 1893; *Le Pardon,* 1895; *L'age Difficile,* 1895; *La Massiere,* 1905; and *Bertrade,* 1906. His plays have a strong ironic realism and show a very varied influence. He was elected to the French Academy in 1896.

Lengyel, Melchior (Menyhert) (1880-   ). Hungarian dramatist. His first play *The Great Chieftain* was produced in 1907 by the Thalia—a Hungarian experimental theatre which lived only three years. His *Typhoon,* with Walker Whiteside; *Czarina;* and *Sancho Panza* were New York successes. He visited New York in 1920, and in 1925 returned to write scenarios in Hollywood. His *Antonia,* later filmed, and other plays, have since been produced on Broadway.

Lennox, Charlotte (Ramsay) (1720-1804). American novelist. Considered by many the first woman playwright in America. She wrote *The Female Quixote,* 1752, her most famous novel; *The History of Henrietta,* 1758; *The Sister,* 1769; *Shakespear Illustrated,* 1753.

Lenormand, Henri-René (1882-1938). French dramatist. Born in Paris, May 3, 1882, he became known by his play *Les Possédées,* 1909, but his reputation was not firmly established until the staging by Georges Pitoëff of *Le Temps est un Songe,* 1919; and *Les Ratés,* 1920. Subsequently he became recognized as one of the leading exponents of the psychological drama of which *Le Mangeur des Rêves,* 1922, is a notable example.

Among his plays which have been translated into English are: *White Madness,* 1905; *Dust,* 1914; *The Failures,* 1920; *Simoon,* 1920; *The Devourer of Dreams,* 1922; *The Red Tooth,* 1922; *Man and His Phantoms,* 1924; *In the Shadow of Evil,* 1924; *The Coward,* 1925; *The Magician Love,* 1926; *Mixture,* 1927; *The Innocent,* 1928; *A Secret Life,* 1929; *Theatre Street,* 1936.

Leontovich, Eugenie. Russian actress. Born in Moscow and studied there at the Imperial School of Dramatic Art; made her first appearance on the stage in *Taming of the Shrew* and was a member of the Moscow Art Theatre before the Revolution. After the revolution she played on the continent and made her first appearance on the New York stage in *Revue Russe.* She has played in *Grand Hotel, Twentieth Century, Bitter Oleander.* She first appeared on the London stage in *Tovarich.* She is the author of *The Laughing Woman.*

Leopoldstadter Theater. Viennese playhouse which in 1817 became the home of light operas, light plays and vaudeville when they were banished from the Vienna Burgtheater.

Leris, Claire-Joseph (1723-1803). French actress. Known as La Clairon, she was born at Condé-sur-Escaut, January 25, 1723. She made her first stage appearance at the Comédie Italienne in 1736, and took the title role of *Phèdre* in 1743 at the Comédie Française, where for twenty-two years she played all the great roles of classical tragedy.

Leslie, Fred (Frederick Hobson) (1855-1892). English actor. Born at Woolwich, he became a baritone vocalist, making a great success as Rip Van Winkle in Planquette's operetta *Rip,* at the Comedy, London, in 1882. Developing as a comedian, and finding a colleague in Nelly Farren, he became for the last seven years of his life the chief mainstay of the Gaiety in a series of costume burlesques, beginning with *Little Jack Sheppard* and ending with *Cinder-Ellen up too Late.*

Lessing, Gotthold Ephraim (1729-1781). German author, poet dramatist. Born at Kametz, Saxony, he was educated at Leipzig university, where officially he studied theology, but where his enthusiasms were for philology, and particularly for the philosophical discourses of A. G. Kaestner. He became literary critic to the *Vossische Zeitung* in 1751. From 1760 to 1765 he was secretary to the governor of Breslau. On his return to Berlin in 1765, he could find no employment, for previous criticism of Voltaire had turned Frederick the Great against him. However, he began during that year some of his finest writing in criticism and in drama. His *Hamburgische Dramaturgie,* 1767-68, has been called the first modern handbook of the dramatist's art. The final period of his life was marred by the death of his wife and by the violence of his theological controversy with Pastor Goetze. This gave rise to his play *Nathan the Wise,* 1778-79, a unique plea for religious toleration. Lessing was a pioneer of the modern German study of Greek literature and a champion of Shakespeare. He maintained that the ultimate goal of all art is the imagination through the senses. His critical studies served to overcome the numbing influence of French neo-classic orthodoxy and to stimulate native German art and criticism.

Chief among his dramatic works are: *Der junge Gelerte,* 1748; *Miss Sara Sampson* (the first German comedy of low life), 1753; *Minna von Barnhelm,* 1767; *Nathan the Wise,* 1778.

Let Us Be Gay. Rachel Crothers (American). Comedy. 3 acts. 1929.

Kitty Brown discovers that her husband has been unfaithful with another woman. This revelation is so shattering and disillusioning that they are divorced. Her husband thinks this is a ghastly mistake, protesting his sincere love for her and his faith in their marriage even though he has committed a fleeting indiscretion. Kitty remains unmoved and they separate. Three years later they meet again at a Westchester house party. Kitty has been invited to rescue the grand-daughter of the house from taking an impulsive step with a certain man. The certain man turns out to be the former Mr. Brown, much to her surprise and chagrin. She carries on an intrigue with another house guest which shocks the ex-Mr. Brown. After some bedroom confusion and boudoir talk Mr. and Mrs. Brown are reconciled, a wiser and more tolerant pair.

Levy, Benn W. (1900-   ). English dramatist. Was born in London and educated at University College, Oxford. Author of *Mrs. Moonlight,* 1928; *The Devil,* 1930; *Springtime for Henry,* 1931; *Accent on Youth,* 1934. His work is especially noteworthy for its masterly dialogue and light touch.

Lewis, Lloyd (1891-   ). American dramatic critic. Born in Spring Valley, Indiana, educated at Swarthmore College; feature writer for the *Philadelphia North American* and for the Keely-Handy syndicate; film critic for the *Chicago Herald* and *Examiner;* became dramatic critic, dramatic editor and motion picture editor of the *Chicago Daily News,* which posts he now holds. He is the author of several books and one play, *Jayhawker* (in collaboration with Sinclair Lewis).

Lewis, Sinclair (1885-   ). American author. Wrote *Jayhawker* with Lloyd Lewis and a dramatization of his book *It Can't Happen Here* with John C. Moffitt. His novels *Elmer Gantry* and *Dodsworth* have been dramatized. He has recently played in *It Can't Happen Here* and *Angela is 22,* on a road tour.

He won the Nobel Prize for Literature, 1930, and is regarded as one of the foremost American novelists.

Lewisohn, Irene. See *Museum of Costume Art; Neighborhood Playhouse.*

The Liars. Henry Arthur Jones (English). Comedy. 4 acts. 1897.

Resentful at her husband's neglect, Lady Jessica has a flirtation with Edward Falkner who adores her. She has a dinner appointment with her lover and is discovered by her brother-in-law who threatens to disclose the affair to her husband. To get out of the situation Lady Jessica and her friends invent a whole maze of lies, but her lover tells the wrong lie and then the truth. Lady Jessica, annoyed, decides to elope with her lover, but is finally persuaded by an old family friend to be reconciled with her husband, and the lover goes to Africa.

Libation Bearers. See *Choephori.*

Library of Congress, The. See *Theatre collections.*

Libretto. The text, aside from the music, of an opera, operetta or musical comedy.

License commissions. The Lord Chamberlain is the official censor to whom all plays must be submitted in writing and a license given, before they can be produced. "He shall have the right to prohibit any play whenever in the opinion of the Lord Chamberlain it is necessary for the preservation of good manners and decorum, or of the public peace."
See also *Stage, jurisprudence.*

Life is a Dream (La Vida es Sueno). Pedro Calderon de la Barca (Spanish). Romantic drama. 5 acts. c. 1636.
One of the hundred and twenty plays left by Pedro Calderon de la Barca, one of the chief dramatists of Spain. *Life is a Dream* may be regarded as the most universal in its theme. It is a philosophical and moralistic romance. Representative of the medieval quality of the 17th century Spanish theatre.
A son, destined, according to oracle, to prove violent toward his parents, is kept by them in solitary confinement and made the very beast they feared.
A modern parallel exists in Franz Werfel's *Goat Song.*

Life of Man, The. Leonid Andreyev (Russian). Tragedy. 5 acts. 1906.
This is a symbolic play depicting the rise and fall of man. The prologue is spoken by a Being in Gray who forcasts the spectacle to come. The cry of a mother and the wail of a baby are heard and the Being in Gray lights a candle and announces Man is born. The scene changes, years have passed, and Man, poor but happy, defies the Being in Gray who holds the candle, now burnt down one-third. In the third scene Man has achieved success, and in the fourth poverty has overtaken him. His son is dying as the result of an accident. Man prays to the Being in Gray, but when his son dies, he curses him. The last scene shows Man, ragged and disheveled, still defiant of the Being in Gray, whose candle flares and goes out. Man is dead.

Lifting jack. A caster mounted lever attached to unit scenery to facilitate shifting; the lever lifts the scenery off the floor and it is then rolled on the casters.

Lighting. Modern stage lighting is designed not only for illumination but also for illusion. Proper equipment, control and planning of lighting are required.

Lighting equipment may be classified into general and spot lighting. General lighting is achieved by means of footlights and border lights. The border lights are suspended on battens overhead, 7 or 8 feet apart. A counterweight system is used to permit raising or lowering of these battens at will. Battens are placed over each entrance, spanning the entire width of the stage. The No. 1 batten should be as far down stage as possible so that the light will be cast on the actors' faces. Border lights and footlights are usually arranged with individual reflectors and in color groups.

Spot lighting is achieved by means of bunch or flood lights, spotlights, etc. Most of these are suspended on bridges placed in various locations all about the stage. There should also be an alcove or cradle just below the ceiling as far downstage as possible. In addition there is portable apparatus which can be carried or rolled on casters to the desired location. In professional productions it is usual to light from spot lights on the front of the first balcony, and from unused boxes, or from beams in the ceiling. In musical productions the lights should be placed at the highest level possible—the back of the gallery or top balcony. For it is important to avoid the shadows cast on the scenery by a horizontal or only slightly angled beam.

Flexibility is essential because of the variety of light requirements and this flexibility applies to color as well as to the amount of lighting. Gradual changes should also be possible. Therefore, a sufficient number of bulbs of all colors with adjustable reflectors must be distributed throughout the stage area. These should be subject to central control so that the quantity of lights and their color may be regulated at will. This central control board where all switches, dimmers, etc., are located is called the Dimmer Board. The electrician operates it according to a light-plot which is prepared after the light changes in the particular performance have been determined. The angle of reflection however cannot be controlled entirely from the dimmer-board. In the case of stationary lights the reflectors must be fixed at the desired angle. Where, however, a number of different angles is required, various reflectors may be placed at the various angles. The corresponding lights may then be regulated from the dimmer. In the case of movable lights the variation of angles is naturally simplified. Color variations may be achieved not only by means of bulbs of different colors but also by means of slides of gelatin or glass.

With this equipment some of which may be rented, it is a simple matter to provide illumination.

But the stage is a shallow box, which will continue to look like a shallow box if it is merely illuminated. An illusion must be created. What the eye sees is light—not actors or scenery. Light must be employed to delude the eye and to suggest the scene. With ordinary scenes, such as living rooms, offices, etc., there is little difficulty. But sometimes scenes of great dimensions must be presented (temples, forests, palaces, etc.). Scenery, of course, is the first requisite, but if merely illuminated it will still look like scenery, unless the variations in light intensities and directions create the semblance of reality. Planes of light, cutting each other, eliminate the distance between them—the eye instantly moves from one to the other. Thus, the appearance of Pyramids directly behind a palm tree will give the illusion of great space. Sharp shadows produce a greater suggestion of solidity than solidity itself. Intensity of light in front and a gradual reduction towards the rear will make the background seem distant. A curtain or drop, hung in folds, may be used to suggest a forest by means of an intelligent light-and-shadow effect. Shadows, as used in Emperor Jones, may be used to suggest greater scale and dramatic importance. Likewise, the concentration of the lighting on an important scene will make it dramatic whereas a diffusion of lighting will cause a diffusion of interest.

Lighting is a highly technical matter. It should be discussed with the electrician who should participate in rehearsals.

Lightnin'. Winchell Smith and Frank Bacon (American). Comedy. Prologue and 3 acts. 1918.

With the co-author, Frank Bacon, playing the leading role, this play ran for 1291 performances on Broadway. This is the third longest run of any play produced in New York; only *Tobacco Road* and *Abie's Irish Rose* have bettered its record. Bacon then took the comedy to Chicago, where he was playing in it just before he died in 1922. The homespun humorous appeal of Lightnin' Bill Jones undoubtedly accounts in large part for the play's success. Lightnin' owns a hotel on the Nevada-California state line. Half of the property is in one State, half in the other. This leads to complications when the sheriff is trying to capture John Marvin on a Nevada warrant; every time the officer approaches Marvin jumps into California and saves himself. Lightnin' turns down the offer of two scheming rascals who are attempting not only to purchase the hotel with fraudulent stock, but also to arrest the log-chopping young lawyer sweetheart of Lightnin's attractive daughter. Mrs. Jones wants Lightnin' to sell to the railway sharks, and is so outraged when he defies her that she sues for divorce on grounds of "intemperance, cruelty and failure to provide." When accused of being a liar in court, Lightnin' takes the law into his own hands and challenges those concerned to prove that his story about driving a swarm of bees across the plains in the dead of winter without losing a bee is false. His wife soon realizes that she does not wish a divorce after all; and Lightnin's young lawyer friend exposes the villains who had been trying to buy the hotel.

Light O' Love. Arthur Schnitzler (Austrian). Tragedy. 3 acts. 1894.

Christiane, the daughter of a poor violinist, falls in love with Fritz, a man of the world. To him she is just a passing diversion, a refuge from the dangers of an affair with a married woman. But his love means everything to her. Fritz has to fight a duel with the lady's husband and is killed. Christiane, desolate, goes forth to die on his grave.

Light-Plot. The electrician's cue-sheet. There are various types with essentially the same characteristics. The light-plot is prepared after the lighting scheme has been determined. A diagram is made of the stage area and each light is keyed by number or letter. Then the sequence of light-changes, from beginning to end, is charted. The lines or business that immediately precede the changes are given as cues and the notations indicate which lights are changed and whether on, off, dimmed, etc.

Likes of 'Er, The. Charles McEvoy (English). Drama. 3 acts. 1923.

A realistic play laid in Bridewell Court, Stepney, in the East End of London. Sally Winch, a pretty waitress in a cheap coffee house, is waiting for her sweetheart George to return from the war. She turns a deaf ear to the proposals of his friends Alf and Jim, and gives up her job when her elderly employer would imitate the turtledove. When George finally shows up, he is horribly mutilated, with a single eye, a single arm, a single leg. He had stayed away so long because he did not think himself good enough for the "likes of 'er." But the faithful Sally assures him she loves him anyway, and proves it by falling into his one arm.

Liliom. Ferenc Molnar (Hungarian). Drama. 7 scenes and prologue. 1908.

Liliom, a barker at an amusement park, flirts with Julie and is consequently discharged. Her admiration for him attracts him and they live together. Liliom, never having learned a trade, is idle, unhappy, and beats Julie. But she understands. When she tells him she is going to have a baby, he is delighted and plans to get money by means of a hold-up so that they can go to America. The hold-up fails and Liliom stabs himself to escape capture by the police. Before he dies, he tries to justify himself to Julie and she understands.

Presently two policemen from Heaven come to have Liliom give an account of himself. Defiant, he refuses to express any regret for his actions and he is condemned to hell for sixteen years, at the end of which time he will be allowed to return to earth for one day to expiate his sins. The final scene shows his return to earth in the guise of a beggar. Because he speaks ill of Liliom, Julie orders him from the house. He tries to give his daughter a star he has stolen from the heavens but she points to the gate. In despair, he slaps her and is again taken away for regeneration.

Lillie, Beatrice (1898-   ). Canadian actress. Born in Toronto. Made her first stage appearance at the Alhambra Theatre, London, October 1914, in *Not Likely*. Among her better known productions have been *Oh! Joy,* 1918; *Up in Mabel's Room,* 1921; *The Nine O'Clock Revue,* 1922; her first New York appearance in Andre Charlot's Revue of 1924; *Oh, Please,* 1928; *This Year of Grace,* 1928; *The Third Little Show,* 1930; *Too True To Be Good,* 1932; *At Home Abroad,* 1935; *Set To Music,* 1939. She married the late Sir Robert Peel, Bart.

Lillo, George (1693-1739). English dramatist. Author of *The London Merchant, or the History of George Barnwell,* which was the first English tragedy dealing with middle class characters. Because of its significant moral lesson to apprentices, it had a long run.

Lincoln and the American Theatre, Abraham. Though many American presidents have been interested in the theatre as an amusement, Abraham Lincoln has had a definite posthumous influence on the theatre itself and on plays and characters. The immediate effect of his assassination was a vengeful attack on the American theatre, so violent that it almost resulted in its suppression. For scarcely had the tragedy taken place than reformers and cranks throughout the country endeavored to make the entire acting profession responsible for the crime of one of its members. On the morning of April 15, 1865, hundreds of people, eager to avenge Lincoln's death, rushed into the lobby of the Burnet House in Cincinnati hunting for Junius Brutus Booth, a tragedian, entirely innocent of the crime, who had to remain hidden in a friend's room for days until he could be smuggled out of town. Almost simultaneously, in Boston, Columbus and Cleveland, mobs hissed and injured local actors, and held mass meetings for the purpose of closing the playhouses. And even in New York, a gang of street boys hooted at an actress and pinned her against the rails at Trinity churchyard until a policeman and a naval officer came to her rescue. "In Pittsburgh," says Thomas Beer, "a committee of the pious rode through the town, trying to get signatures on a petition which demanded the closing of every theatre in the state of Pennsylvania." To all this unjust persecution, the actor has made valiant response. No sooner had the critical days passed than he proceeded to make Abraham Lincoln, the indirect cause of his sorrows, his favorite hero. Time after time, as a result, the martyred President returns to the scene, lovingly recreated in stage and screen characterization.

Lind, Jenny (Johanna Maria Lind) (1820-1887). Swedish singer. Born in Stockholm. As a child, she appeared on the stage in plays, making her opera debut in 1836. She earned immediate success in the following five years, being admitted a member of the Swedish Academy of Music. She first came to America in 1850, and her debut was made in Castle Garden under the direction of P. T. Barnum. Ticket speculation first appeared at this concert. She toured the country, after her New York appearance, giving ninety-five concerts, and the enthusiasm with which she was greeted was remarkable. She married Otto Goldschmidt while in America. The "Swedish Nightingale," as she was called, was probably the greatest soprano the world has ever heard.

Line (television). A strip across a television image, varying from point to point in its light intensity. Four hundred forty-one vertical lines constitute a complete frame.

Line of business. The type of role or roles in which an actor may specialize.

Lines. Speeches in a play.

Lining. (1) Using straight edge and lining brush to paint architectural details. (2) A make-up term meaning the dark rimming of the eyes; the emphasizing of wrinkles on the face; the continuing of the eyebrow line, etc.

Lining colors. Grease materials in sticks, small jars, compact cases for drawing lines, shadows, highlights, scars and other items including shading of eyelids. Put on directly with fingers, paper stumps, rounded toothpicks or orange sticks.

Linnebach, Adolphe. German designer. A native of Munich and Dresden. His famous contribution is the Linnebach projector, a form of stereopticon, that allows scenes or parts of scenes to be projected on a drop. It has a wide angle of projection and thus enables large scenes to be projected.

Lion Tamer, The; or, English as It is Eaten. Alfred Savoir (French). Comedy. 3 acts. 1925.

Derived from a story by Jacques Thery. Concerns the ridiculous contrast between a brutal lion tamer who believes in absolute discipline and a philosophic Englishman who upholds the freedom of the will. It is the lion tamer whose tyranny wins the circus lady they both love, and the philosopher who is eaten by the animals he pities.

Little Cafe, The. Tristan Bernard (French). Comedy. 3 acts. 1911.

A waiter inheriting a fortune, is pledged to forfeit most of it unless he consents to serve his master for a term of twenty years. He feigns madness to secure release, but acts quite sane before witnesses when threatened with the asylum. Finally, after posing in his leisure hours as a fine gentleman at a big cafe, he resigns himself to his humble office at the little cafe and marries his master's daughter.

Little Church Around the Corner. Church of the Transfiguration. 1 East 29th Street, New York. In 1870 the rector of a fashionable church refused to bury the veteran actor George Holland, whereupon one of Holland's orphaned sons said: "There is a little church around the corner where you may get it done." Since then this church has been a favorite place for theatrical weddings and funerals. The denomination is Episcopal. Rev. Randolph Ray is the pastor.

Little Clay Cart, The. Shudraka (Hindu). Drama in Sanskrit. c. 900 B.C.

This play, which deals with a ruined merchant and introduces a comparatively virtuous courtesan, combines a love plot with a story of political change. The characters are drawn more warmly and more humorously than usual. Deserting the usual theme of its time, that is, the aristocracy, this early work is an outstanding example of Indian drama.

Thought to have been written either in the eighth or the tenth centuries B.C. A drama of invention going from farce to tragedy, and from satire to pathos. Attributed to King Shudraka.

Little Foxes, The. Lillian Hellman (American). Drama. 3 acts. 1939.

Regina Giddens outwits her two brothers, and permits her husband to die of a heart attack without receiving medical aid in order that she may gain the controlling interest in a cotton mill. After her husband's death, Regina for the first time is frightened and lonely, and seeks the companionship of her daughter only to find that she hates and fears her mother.

Little Lord Fauntleroy. Frances Hodgson Burnett (American). 3 acts. 1889.

This dramatization of the author's novel of a little American boy who is discovered to be the heir of a noble English family, goes to live with them and cures them of their snobbishness and dislike of Americans, was a great sentimental success. Mothers dressed their uncomfortable little boys as "Little Lord Fauntleroy," curls and all. Elsie Leslie and Tommy Russell alternated in the role. United Artists filmed the story in 1921 with Mary Pickford and in 1936 with Freddie Bartholemew.

Little Man, The. John Galsworthy (English). Comedy. 1 act. 1915.

While waiting for a train, the Little Man tries to help a mother by holding her baby. In the confusion of boarding the train, he leaves the mother on the station platform and, after the train has started, finds he is still holding the baby. He is arrested, but finally vindicated.

Little Minister, The. James M. Barrie (English). Comedy. 1897.

A dramatization of Barrie's novel of the same name. The title character is Gavin Dishart, twenty-one year old preacher who has established his influence in Thrums, a small weaving town in Scotland. His youth, shortness of stature and occasional gayety encourage the village to exert a maternal sort of vigilance over him. They watch everything he does and then interfere or criticize with neighborly efficiency. The plot concerns the little minister's romance with Babbie the gypsy. From the day when she enters his life, with her gypsy dress, dancing feet, madcap tricks and dazzling eyes, Gavin is a lost man. Although he tries to resist and preaches three castigating sermons on "woman," it is to no avail. The village is outraged by the infatuation and Babbie nobly decides to give him up. She will marry the elderly Lord Rintoul. But on the eve of her marriage she hears a false report that Gavin is dead and seeks him out in alarm. They decide on a quick marriage ceremony, but are thwarted by the arrival of Lord Rintoul and others anxious to prevent the marriage. Gavin and Babbie are separated. Gavin once more wins the affection of his people and their support, and the way is finally smoothed for his union with Babbie.

Little Ol' Boy. Albert Bein (American). Drama. 3 acts. 1933.

Robert Lockett, in a reform school, writes a letter to the governor protesting conditions. When Red Barry, his friend, is accused of writing the letter, Lockett confesses. Later Red and Lockett try to escape but they are unsuccessful. Lockett is killed and Red is sent to the penitentiary.

Little Theatre of Houston, Texas. Directed by Henning Nelms; sponsors a workshop which presents everything from melodrama to Gilbert and Sullivan. This is one of the best equipped theatres of the Southwest.

Little Theatre Tournament (American; national; 1923-1931). Under the auspices of the Manhattan Little Theatre Club and the general managership of Walter Hartwig, a one-act play tournament for Little Theatres throughout the United States (and England) was held in New York City for nine years. Prizes of $100 were given to the three best productions each year, with the Belasco Cup going to the top-ranking play of the three. This cup became the permanent property of the Dallas Little Theatre after being won three times hand-running at the outset of the tournaments. Samuel French Ltd., also gave a publication prize for rights to the best play each year.

Little Theatres. Among the best known little theatres of America are: The Cleveland Playhouse (Ohio); The Playmakers (Berkeley, California); Padua Hills Players (Padua Hills, California); Pasadena Community Playhouse (California); The Wayfarers (San Francisco, California); Hedgerow Theatre (Moylan-Rose Valley, Pennsylvania); Players Club (Santa Barbara, California); Theatre League and Plays and Players (Philadelphia, Pennsylvania); Birmingham Little Theatre (Alabama); Civic Theatre (Palo Alto, California); Community Players (San Diego, California); Community Players (Colorado Springs, Colorado); Civic Theatre (Denver, Colorado); Community Players (Pueblo, Colorado); Community Little Theatre (Quincy, Illinois); Civic Theatre (Fort Wayne, Indiana); Civic Theatre (Indianapolis, Indiana); Jacksonville Little Theatre (Florida); The Players (Sarasota, Florida); Macon Little Theatre (Georgia); The Playhouse (Savannah, Georgia); The Players (Peoria, Illinois); The Players Workshop (Burlington, Iowa); Community Players (Burlington, Iowa); Community Players (Cedar Rapids, Iowa); Community Theatre (Des Moines, Iowa); Little Theatre Company (Louisville, Kentucky); Le Petit Théâtre du Vieux Carré (New Orleans, Louisiana); Little Theatre (Shreveport, Louisiana); Vagabond Players (Baltimore, Maryland); Footlight Club (Boston, Massachusetts); The Workshop (Fitchburg, Massachusetts); Civic Theatre (Kalamazoo, Michigan); Duluth Little Theatre (Minnesota); Resident Theatre (Kansas City, Missouri); Community Playhouse (Omaha, Nebraska); Reno Little Theatre (Nevada); Dover Little Theatre (New Jersey); Studio Theatre Players (Buffalo, New York); Civic Theatre (Dobbs Ferry, New York); Community Players (Great Neck, Long Island, New York); Amateur Comedy Club (New York City); Community Players (Rochester, New York); Charlotte Little Theatre (North Carolina); Little Country Theatre (Fargo, North Dakota); Civic Theatre (Cincinnati, Ohio); Civic Theatre (Cleveland Heights, Ohio); Players Club (Columbus, Ohio); Repertoire Little Theatre (Toledo, Ohio); The Very Little Theatre (Eugene, Oregon); Civic Theatre (Portland, Oregon); Community Players (Erie, Pennsylvania); Footlight Players (Charleston, South Carolina); Town Theatre (Columbia, South Carolina); Chattanooga Little Theatre (Tennessee); Memphis Little Theatre (Tennessee); Community Theatre (Nashville, Tennessee); Dallas Little Theatre (Texas); Fort Worth Little Theatre (Texas); Galveston Little Theatre (Texas); Houston Little Theatre (Texas); Oak Cliff Little Theatre (Texas); San Antonio Little Theatre (Texas); Logan Little Theatre (Utah); Lynchburg Little Theatre (Virginia); Civic Theatre (Seattle, Washington); Mobile Little Theatre (Alabama); Pittsburgh Playhouse (Pittsburgh, Pennsylvania); Richmond Theatre Guild, Inc. (Richmond, Virginia).

Of community participation in the drama, Gilmor Brown in the foreword to *Curtains Going Up* says, "This is American Theatre! It is the non-commercial and community producing groups, existing all across the country, that are responding to the desire of the American people for a non-merchandized, personal theatre. It is very largely through them that a national theatre is coming into being. They are closer to the people than any professional theatre can be and, therefore, at their best they present a truer and more fundamental reflection of American life and thought." The Community theatres of America as we know them today have developed in this country since 1900. At the outset, they were just what the name implies. Today, many of them are no longer little. Of 105 theatres analyzed in *Curtains Going Up,* McCleery & Glick, thirty-four call themselves "Little Theatre." The next group, numerically, include "Players," in their title. Others include "Community" or "Civic" in their name. The great number of theatres were started in 1933-1935. In these years of depression people had leisure and turned within themselves for pleasure. In California the first community participation was at Santa Barbara, and the first performance was about 1873. One of the most valuable reference books on university and little theatre is Jean Carter and Jean Ogden's *Everyman's Drama,* 1938.

See *Community Theatres.*

Little Women. Drama in 4 acts by Marion de Forest. 1912.
This dramatization of Louisa May Alcott's famous novel exploits the problems of Jo, Meg, Amy, Beth, Marmee, Lawrie, Professor Bhaer and John Brooks. It recounts the main incidents of the book—the writing and rehearsing of the Christmas play, Jo's courtship and marriage and the love affair of Meg and John Brooks.

Lius. A kind of scene-building, or mansion, of the medieval stage, meaning, literally, *place.*
See also *Mansions.*

Live talent (television). Performers, or a performance, given in a studio for instantaneous transmission to the receiver, as distinguished from film transmissions.

The Living Corpse. See *Redemption.*

Living Newspaper. This is a highly effective form of drama that has been popular in Russia since the Revolution, but new to America. The topics in the headlines of newspapers are put into a dramatic form of entertainment. The WPA Federal Theatre put on several of these productions in New York. Among them were *Ethiopia,* 1936 (in which undiplomatic references to European dictators caused a furor in Washington) ; *Power,* 1937 ; *one third of a nation,* 1938.

Lobsterscope. Circular disc with large slots cut in it and attached to the front of the spotlight to give flickering effect when rotated.

Loca (locus). See *Mansions.*

Local Railway, The. Ludwig Thoma (German). Comedy. 3 acts. 1902.
A group of burghers send their mayor to intercede with a high official regarding the building of a railway. When he returns and reports the interview, the mayor

magnifies his importance and claims to have flouted the minister. The burghers organize a parade for their champion. After sober reconsideration, they decide the next day that he has hurt their interests by arousing ill feeling in high quarters and they come back to assail him. The mayor retracts his story and the people have another parade in his honor.

Locke, Robinson (1856-1920). American critic. Former dramatic critic *Toledo Blade,* whose dramatic collection at the New York Public Library covers American theatrical life, 1870-1925.

See also *Robinson Locke Dramatic Collection,* New York Public Library.

Lodge, Thomas (1557-1625). English dramatist. He was educated at the Merchant Taylors School in London, later at Oxford. He took several long voyages, such as one to South America and the Pacific, became a physician, then was converted to Catholicism. He had but slight knowledge of the stage. His literary style was influenced by Lyly and Greene. His best known plays are: *The Wounds of Civil War* and *A Looking Glass for London and England* (on which he collaborated with Greene).

Loew, Marcus (1870-1927). American producer. Born in New York's East Side, he started to sell newspapers when he was eight. Worked at many other jobs, including the fur business; then developed the "penny Arcades." His Automatic Vaudeville Co. gave way to a new firm exploiting *nickelodeons,* in association with the noted actor David Warfield. Rented various stores and old theatres, giving pictures with vaudeville acts. Picked new theatres in strategic spots, and by 1919 he had one hundred theatres, and his Loew's Inc. had become a $25,000,000 asset. Bought the distributing company called Metro in 1920, and in 1924 acquired control of Goldwyn Pictures, and the same year Metro-Goldwyn was consolidated with interests of Louis B. Mayer to form Metro-Goldwyn-Mayer. At the death of Marcus Loew, Nicholas M. Schenck became president of Loew's Inc. and Arthur Loew, son of Marcus, took charge of the newly organized international department.

Loftus, Cecilia (1876-). British-American actress. Born in Glasgow; made her first appearance on the stage at the Alhambra, Belfast, 1892, singing the ballad *Molly Darling;* appeared at the Oxford Music Hall in London, 1893, making an immediate success; appeared in vaudeville in America in 1895; went back to the music halls of London, 1897; returned to America in 1900 to make her debut in comic opera; joined Madame Modjeska's company, then worked for Daniel Frohman at Daly's Theatre, next was with E. H. Sothern as leading lady. From 1902 to 1915 she alternated between England and America, vaudeville and burlesque. Since 1915 has appeared in many plays, including: Mrs. Rimplegar in *Three-Cornered Moon;* Aunt Chloe in *Uncle Tom's Cabin;* Frau Lucher in *Reunion in Vienna;* Mrs. Riley in *Merrily We Roll Along.*

Has appeared in films, including: *Abide With Me; East Lynne; Doctors' Wives; Young Sinners,* etc.

Logeion. The slightly-raised stage of the ancient Greek theatre; sometimes used also for the *theologeion*.

See also *Theologeion*.

Lokalstueck. See *Volkstueck*.

London Prodigal, The. A Jacobean comedy of domestic life attributed to Shakespeare on the title page of the 1605 quarto edition and included in the Third and Fourth folio editions of the poet's works in 1664 and 1685 respectively. The play differs greatly in method and style from authentic works of Shakespeare, however, and his authorship here is generally denied. The action concerns the trials placed on the faithful Luce by her husband to test her fidelity.

Lonely Way, The. Arthur Schnitzler (Austrian). Tragedy. 3 acts. 1904.

Wegrath, a student, takes his friend, Julian Fichtner, to visit his fiancée, Gabrielle. The girl and Julian fall in love with each other and plan to elope. At the last moment, Julian forsakes her, not wishing to be tied down by marriage. Gabrielle marries Wegrath, who becomes a professor of art, and has two children, the oldest of whom is Julian's son. The play opens just before Gabrielle's death. Julian, who has spent his life in the pursuit of his own pleasure, returns to claim the love of his son, only to be spurned. Von Sala, a middle aged poet, who has lived the same type of life as Julian, points out to him that he has no right to his son, because love is service and for those who do not serve but think only of themselves, there is only the "Lonely Way." Johanna, Gabrielle's daughter who is in love with Von Sala, drowns herself and he commits suicide.

Lonsdale, Frederick. English dramatic author. Born in Jersey Channel Islands, England, 1881; was formerly a private in the English army and an able-bodied seaman. Has written many plays but is best known for *Spring Cleaning* (1923) and *The Last of Mrs. Cheyney,* 1925, both comedies of manners and satires on modern life.

Lopez de Ayala, Adelardo (1828-1879). Spanish dramatist. Born in Guadalcanal in the province of Seville. His plays all have a moral thesis. His principal drama is *El tanto por ciento (So Much per cent),* 1861, which has a theme of the struggle between love and money.

Lord Chamberlain. Censor of the English stage whose present power goes back to 1737. All plays must be submitted to him for a reading. For this service a fee is charged. He may then grant a license or veto the play. Although his reasons may be moral, religious or political, he need not state them. He can close plays and prevent them from opening, and there is no repeal after he has made a decision.

Lord Chamberlain's Men (Shakespeare's Company). The company of professional actors with whom Shakespeare was associated for the greater part of his career. They were organized in the early years of Elizabeth's reign as Lord

Leicester's Men. Thereafter they came successively under the patronage of, and took the names of, Lord Strange, the Lord Chamberlain, and King James. Shakespeare probably joined the company between 1587 and 1590. Its leading actor was Richard Burbage and its principal theatres the Globe on the Bankside and Blackfriars in London.

Lorne, Marion (1888-   ). American actress. Born in Pennsylvania, she made her stage debut in New York in 1905. She first appeared in London in 1915 and became known for her portrayals of fluffy-minded women, in a series of comedies written for the most part by her husband, Walter Hackett. These plays included: *Ambrose Applejohn's Adventure,* 1921; *Other Men's Wives,* 1928; *77, Park Lane,* 1928; *Sorry You've Been Troubled,* 1929; *Road House,* 1932; *Afterwards,* 1934; *Hyde Park Corner,* 1934.

Louvers. A series of parallel or concentric thin metal shields used for directing the light from an instrument.

Love Adorns. Francois de Curel (French). Drama. 3 acts. 1893.
This is the story of a wealthy widow and her suitor who is too shy to ask her to marry him. Finally, hoping to force a proposal out of him, she pretends the need of a husband in order to save her from disgrace. Aware of the ruse, he is ready to act out his part. She advises him to rehabilitate his honor through suicide, never believing he will do it, and he doesn't, but she finally gets him to propose.

Love and Lord Byron. Cale Young Rice (English). Drama. 4 acts. 1936.
The story of Lord Byron's love affairs with Lady Carolyn Lombard and with Annabella Millbanks, and finally, his departure to Greece where he is killed.

Love for Love. William Congreve (British). Comedy. 5 acts. 1695.
Valentine, a seventeenth century dandy, is in disgrace with his father because he is besieged by creditors. His father, Sir Sampson, offers to pay his debts if he will sign over his inheritance to his brother. Valentine to escape embarrassment agrees. Later, realizing what it will mean to him, he pretends to be insane and unable to sign the final deed. Angelica, with whom Valentine is in love, but who has not yielded to his suit, intervenes. She induces Sir Sampson to propose to her and gets possession of Valentine's bond. When Valentine discovers that Angelica is about to marry his father, he declares himself ready to sign. Then she reveals her scheme, tears up the bond and declares her love for Valentine.

Love-interest. Term meaning the couple (or either one, singly) who supply the romantic intrigue in a play.

Love of One's Neighbor. Leonid Andreyev (Russian). Drama. 3 acts. Translated by Thomas Seltzer. 1908.
The proprietor of a mountain hotel, in order to advertise his hostelry, has hired a man to pose upon a cliff as though he were unable to get either up or down. The

guests of the hotel are duly thrilled at the stranger's peril, secretly hoping he may fall. But the stranger, tied there day after day grows weary of his vigil, and exposes the proprietor's fraud.

Lover, The. Gregorio Martinez-Sierra (Spanish). Drama. 4 acts. 1912.

Out of romantic devotion for his queen, a man of the people sells his factory in order to follow her in her travels. He cherishes a hairpin, a pair of gloves, a feather blown from her hat. He follows her everywhere she goes, and she is extremely flattered by his adoration. When he saves her from an overturned carriage she offers him any favor he may ask. His request is a pass over the state railways so that he may always be near her. She is delighted by this survival of romance.

Lovers. Maurice Donnay (French). Comedy. 5 acts. Translated by Barrett H. Clark. 1895. Donnay's first marked success.

The mistress of a count, making an excursion to Italy with a younger charmer, is aware that they must part since their life together would soon become as matter-of-fact as marriage. They say farewell, and later they meet in Paris as excellent friends, Claudine felicitates her ex-lover upon his approaching marriage with an heiress, and prepares to retire with her count to the country, now that he has loosed the bonds that tied him to an uncongenial wife.

Love's Labour's Lost. William Shakespeare (British). Comedy. 5 acts. c. 1588.

This play, one of Shakespeare's earliest, is a satire on Utopias. Ferdinand, King of Navarre, and his three attendant lords decide to form themselves into a monastic academy of study. They swear to fast, eat only one meal a day, study and not look at a woman for three years. The arrival of the Princess of France and her three ladies alter their attitude however. Ferdinand will not allow them in the palace, but has pavilions put in the park. At first glance each man falls in love with one of the ladies. On finding each other out, each pretends severity with the other until he himself is discovered. To entertain the ladies, the gentlemen devise a masque. The ladies exchange tokens and costumes so that the lords woo the wrong ladies. While the fun is at its height, news of the death of the princess' father comes to interrupt the gaiety. The lords ask for the ladies in marriage but the latter impose a year's penance on their lovers. If the lords remain true, the ladies will have them. So for the present love's labor is lost.

Lower Depths, The (Also called *At the Bottom* and *Night Lodging*). Maxim Gorki (Russian). Drama. 4 acts. 1902.

The scene is a Russian tramp lodging-house and it presents the scattered talk of the various unfortunates. The wife of the proprietor intrigues with a thief and when he kills her husband in a brawl her sister charges that the two of them have plotted the murder and sends them to prison.

There is very little action in the play; its significance is in its portrayal of character, e.g., Luka, the pilgrim, who urges these derelicts to remember they are men and to have faith in the will to believe.

Lowin, John (1576-1658?). English actor. An actor named in the 1623 Folio list of performers in the original productions of Shakespeare's plays. Associated at first with another company of actors, Worcester's Men in 1603 and remained with them for the rest of his life. His great versatility as an actor is indicated by the large number and wide variety of plays in which he is known to have acted.

Loyalties. John Galsworthy (English). Drama. 3 acts. 1922.

Ferdinand De Levis, a Jew, discovers that he has been robbed of nearly a thousand pounds at a house party. The guilt evidently settles on Captain Dancy, another guest, but the host refuses to believe that an English gentleman and an officer could be a thief, and De Levis is persuaded to drop the matter under threat of social ostracism. At length, however, he voices his suspicions. Dancy reluctantly brings civil action against De Levis, but first attempts to force a duel by calling him "a damned Jew." After that De Levis is unmerciful; he is fighting for the honor of his race, as his antagonists are fighting for "the honor of an English gentleman." At the trial Dancy is proved guilty, and shoots himself before he can be arrested.

Luce, Claire. American actress. Born in New York; studied dancing at the Denishawn School; received her stage training with Florence Colebrook Powers; appeared as Clair in *Dear Sir,* 1924, at the Times Square Theatre. The plays she has been in include: *The Music Box Revue,* 1924; *Palm Beach Girl,* 1926; *No Foolin',* 1926; *The Ziegfeld Follies of 1927; Burlesque,* 1928 (London); *Vintage Wine* (London); *The Gay Divorcée; Of Mice and Men,* 1937-39.

Luck of Francoise, The. Georges de Porto-Riche (French). 4 acts. Translated by Barrett H. Clark. 1888.

A wife endeavors to keep her light-o'-love husband from making a fool of himself. She forgives his petty infidelities, induces the other woman's husband to forego a duel, and finally accepts him when he returns home.

Lucy, Sir Thomas. English nobleman. A wealthy landowner near Stratford on whose estate, according to tradition, Shakespeare as a young man was caught stealing deer. Lucy's anger forced Shakespeare to leave Stratford for London, where his career as a dramatist began. There is little evidence to support this story, or the associated tradition that Shakespeare, in retaliation against Lucy, satirically portrayed him as Justice Shallow in *Merry Wives of Windsor.*

Ludi scaenici. Secular *farces* of the early Roman theatre.

Ludiones. The Etruscan actors who, in 364 B.C., first performed at the *Ludi Romani,* the *satura,* the verses which supplanted the Fescennine Verses, and which were destined to constitute the second form of primitive Roman comedy.

Ludus. Term used by Aquinas in his *Summa Theologiae* to mean *dramatic show.*

Ludwig, Emil (Emil Cohn) (1881-   ). German author, dramatist. Born at Breslau, he early began to write novels and plays. Before the World War, he had produced a number of his plays, but after the success of his *Goethe,* a biographical novel, 1920, he devoted himself mainly to biography. His works include *Genius and Character,* 1924; *Napoleon,* 1925; *Bismarck,* 1927 (a play was based on this novel) ; *Lincoln,* 1930. His play *Versailles,* containing vivid portraits of Clemenceau, Lloyd George and other protagonists of the Peace Conference, was seen in London in 1932.

Ludwig, Otto (1813-1865). German dramatist. Studied music with Mendelssohn; wrote novels influenced by Tieck and Hoffman. His famous novel, *Zwischen Himmel und Erde,* published in 1856, struggled for a realistic and psychological depiction of life. Ludwig tried to determine from Shakespeare laws of dramatic construction and of character delineation. His *Der Erbfoerster,* 1850, a study of bourgeois life, and *Die Makkabaer,* 1852, an apocryphal drama, are his best-known plays.

Lunt, Alfred (1893-   ). American actor. He was born at Milwaukee, Wisconsin, and made his stage debut in 1913. He became known in London, with his wife, Lynn Fontanne, by his witty and polished acting in *Caprice,* 1929; *Reunion in Vienna,* 1934; and in the film *The Guardsman.*

When Booth Tarkington saw Alfred Lunt, he chose him for the title role of *Clarence.* It put the young actor on the highroad to fame, in 1919, when Lunt was still with the Castle Square Company. Petruchio in *The Taming of the Shrew* was his first Shakespearean role. The production was arranged by Lunt and his wife, and was one of the great successes of the 1935-1936 New York season. Alfred Lunt played also in *Ned McCobb's Daughter; Marco Millions; Volpone; Meteor; Design For Living; Amphitryon 38;* and *The Sea Gull.* He and his wife constitute the foremost acting couple of the modern stage.

Luria. Robert Browning (English). Poetical drama. 5 acts. 1846.

It deals with an episode of the struggle between Florence and Pisa in the 15th century. Luria, a moor, is the hired commander of the Florentine forces, but the Signoria distrust him and plan to overthrow him after he has gained victory. After victory is his, he discovers the conspiracy and though he has Florence and Pisa at his mercy, he refuses to take advantage of his power, takes poison and dies.

Lyceum theatre. A theatre in London built originally as an exhibition hall in 1765; the theatre interior built in 1794; in 1802 Madame Tussaud used it for her first exhibition of wax figures; in 1809 it finally became a regular theatre; in 1810 its name was changed to the English Opera House; ballad operas, musical farces and melodramas were performed; a renovated house (with gas) opened in 1816; Edmund Kean and the company from Covent Garden played here during 1828 because of an explosion of gas at the other house which necessitated its closing for the season; it was destroyed by fire in 1830; the present building was finished in 1834. Henry Irving and Ellen Terry played here from 1871 to 1902. Torn down 1939.

Lycurgos. See *Dionysos, Theatre of.*

Lyly, John (1554-1606). English dramatist. An Elizabethan dramatist, known in France as the inventor of Euphuism, in England as a creator of an intermediate type drama between Classical and Romantic Comedy. He was educated at Oxford and thence went to live in London. He wrote plays for specific acting companies, such as the Paul's Boys. Lyly introduced *Endymion, the Man in the Moon; Mydas;* and *Gallathea.*

Lysistrata. Aristophanes (Greek). Farce. 2 acts. 411 B.C.

Aristophanes wrote this anti-war satire during the twenty-first year of the Peloponnesian Wars, during the events which led to the revolution of the Four Hundred. It followed the author's *Peace* and *The Acharnians,* two other anti-militaristic comedies.

Lysistrata of Athens, wife of Lycon, is wearied of the long war and assembles the young women of the city, and also the young women of Corinth, Thebes and Sparta, to suggest that they deny themselves to their husbands until peace is declared. There are strenuous objections from some of the more loving of the fair sex, but the stronger members of the assembly bolster their resolve, and they agree to Lysistrata's proposal. There is considerable amusing discussion as to what should be done if the men force their attentions, but conditions are finally drawn up. In the meantime the old women and the men too old for war are having a private set-to. The old women storm the Acropolis, are driven out by the graybeards, and then get the upper hand again by dousing the men with water until they retreat ignominiously. Lysistrata and her cohorts join in the fun, truss up the President of the Senate on a litter and give him a mock funeral, then ensconce themselves in the Acropolis. Five days later, the frailer of the young women have grown weary of virtue, and are trying all sorts of subterfuges so as to escape from their quarters and return home. Kalonika, for example, hits on the idea of concealing a helmet beneath her gown and pretending to be pregnant. Lampito, leader of the Amazons, supports Lysistrata, and they persuade the slackers and the others to renew their pledge in wine. The warriors return. The women don their prettiest clothes and lure them to the very edge of the nuptial couch, only to withdraw. Kalonika alone weakens and goes off with her husband's friend Polydorus, since her husband has not returned. The frustrated warriors in desperation agree to any peace terms the women wish to impose.

Lytton, Sir Henry (1867-   ). English actor. Born in London, he spent most of a long theatrical career interpreting the leading comic roles in the Gilbert and Sullivan repertory. His first appearance was made at the Royalty Theatre, Glasgow, in 1884, in the chorus of *Princess Ida.* He appeared in the Gilbert and Sullivan operas in all the principal towns of the British Isles, in America, and in Canada. His most famous parts were Ko-Ko in the *Mikado,* the Duke of Plaza-

Toro in *The Gondoliers,* and Jack Point in *The Yeomen of the Guard.* He was knighted in 1930. He wrote the autobiographical *Secrets of a Savoyard,* 1922, and *A Wandering Minstrel,* 1933.

M.C. An abbreviation of master of ceremonies.
See *Commentator.*

M.O.S.P.S. The Moscow Trade Union Theatre, one of the two organisations (the other: the V.Z.S.P.S.) which branched off from the Theatre of the Revolution.

Ma'Lien-liang. Chinese actor. With T'an Fu-ying is considered one of the few contemporary Peiping actors who can give most male roles full justice. His sensibility and mimetic powers are unexcelled.

MacArthur, Charles (1895-   ). American dramatist. He is primarily a collaborator with other writers. With Edward Sheldon, he wrote *Lulu Belle;* with Sidney Howard, *Salvation;* with Ben Hecht (a long and fruitful association), *The Front Page, Twentieth Century, Jumbo,* and *Ladies and Gentlemen,* based on a play by Ladislas Bus-Fekete. He is married to Helen Hayes.

Macbeth. William Shakespeare (English). Tragedy. 5 acts. 1606.
Written about 1606; published in the Folio of 1623. It is based on an account in Holinshed's *Chronicles.* Some critics suggest that the accession in 1603 of Scottish James I, who claimed descent from Banquo, turned Shakespeare's attention to the story.
Moved by his own ambition and that of his unscrupulous wife, Macbeth murders Duncan, king of Scotland, and takes his crown, thereby fulfilling a witches' prophecy that Macbeth will be king. Duncan's sons escape to England. But the prophecy had also stated that the sons of Banquo, a general, would succeed Macbeth. To prevent this Macbeth orders the execution of the general and his sons, but one of the latter, Fleance, escapes. The return of Banquo's ghost at a banquet shatters Macbeth's nerves. Warned by the witches to beware of Macduff, he orders the execution of Lady Macduff and her son when he learns that that lord has escaped. The crimes, meanwhile, have affected Lady Macbeth's mind and she dies. Macduff and Malcolm, a son of Duncan, return with an army against Macbeth. The army, screened behind boughs from Birnam wood, led by Macduff, overcomes Macbeth, thereby fulfilling the prophecy that he would be safe until Birnam wood came to Dunsinane. Macbeth rushes out to meet Macduff, since the prophecy foretold that "none of woman born" could harm him. Macbeth learns that Macduff had a caesarian birth and was therefore really not of "woman born." Thus the prophecy is fulfilled and Macbeth is slain. This is one of Shakespeare's greatest tragedies showing the devastation of character which is wrought by overwhelming ambition. Lady Macbeth, unusual

study of a courageous, ruthless woman, disintegrates morally and mentally before our eyes as does Macbeth, her husband. One murder has led to another until the paths of blood threaten to overtake them in retribution and eventually do so. Shakespeare piles one horror on another, leading them to their inexorable fate.

Macco. Stock-character in the *Phlyakes,* connected with the *Maccus* of the Roman *fabulae Atellanae.*
See also *Maccus.*

Maccus. Character in the Roman *fabulae Atellanae,* a foolish gull, connected with the *Macco* of the *Phlyakes,* and to which the character of *Punch* in a *commedia dell' arte* is traced.
See also *Macco.*

Macgowan, Kenneth (1888-   ). American author, producer. Born in Winthrop, Massachusetts. He was graduated from Harvard University in 1911. Dramatic critic for the *New York Globe,* 1919-23; *Vogue,* 1920-24; dramatic critic, vice-president and editor of *Theatre Arts Magazine,* 1919-25. Later was a director of the Provincetown Players, 1924-25; Greenwich Village Theatre, 1925-27; and the Actors Theatre, 1927. Among the plays he has produced are: *Fashion; All God's Chillun Got Wings; Desire Under the Elms; The Great God Brown; Outside Looking In; Bride of the Lamb; The Marquise.* He is the author of *The Theatre of Tomorrow,* 1921; *Continental Stagecraft,* 1922; *Masks and Demons,* 1923; *Footlights Across America,* 1929. Mr. MacGowan has also done directing and producing for the motion pictures.

Machiavelli, Niccolo di Bernardo (1469-1527). Florentine statesman, author. The greatest prose writer of the Italian Renaissance; held high political offices; represented his government abroad. Upon the return of the Medici to power in 1512 he was imprisoned and tortured for his supposed conspiracy against the Medici, but was restored to favor under Pope Leo X. While in exile he wrote *Il Principe* (*The Prince*), which was not translated until 1640 but was frequently referred to in Elizabethan plays. The ideal of *The Prince* was incorporated in the villain-hero protagonist best exemplified in Shakespeare's *King Richard III* (See *Villain as Hero,* by Boyer.) "His *Prince,*" says Allardyce Nicoll, "is a summing of regular Renaissance ideals of conduct; it is the culmination of that individualism which marks off the newly awakened Europe from the anonymity and communal ideals of the Middle Ages."

Machinal. Sophie Treadwell (American). Tragedy. 10 episodes. 1928.
The Young Woman works in an office. Her employer, Mr. Jones, is repellent to her, but through sheer indifference she marries him. They have a child, but she takes no pleasure in it. Then in a speakeasy she meets an attractive young man who takes her home with him. He tells her of his adventures in Mexico—how, with a stone, he killed some bandits who had captured him. He is the Romance she has missed, and

she gives herself to him. Then she kills her husband by striking him with a bottle filled with pebbles. In court her story about some mysterious stranger attacking Jones does not hold water. And her lover, who has tired of her and whom she has been pestering, tells of their affair. Breaking under the weight of evidence against her, she confesses. "A sin—a mortal sin—all I know of heaven," is her summary of the love affair which has spelled her doom. At the appointed time, she is led off to be executed.

The Ruth Snyder-Judd Gray murder case is supposed to have suggested this play. But its characters are obviously supposed to be symbolic, more universal than any individual man or woman. They are not even named, except for Jones; they are called simply Young Man, Young Woman, etc. They are products of a machine age—frustrated by the mechanical devices around them, without the standards and sense of values familiar to the horse-and-buggy age. The impressionistic settings carried out the mood of the drama.

Machina versilis. See *Periaktoi.*

Machine per ogni ascione. Machines for every action, or scene in the theatre of Renaissance Italy.

Machines. Scenic and dramatic devices used in the Hellenistic and Graeco-Roman theatres: (1) *ekkuklema,* semi-circular revolving platform on which throne is set, device to reveal interior action; (2) *exostra,* associated with the *ekkuklema,* low platform on wheels or rollers; (3) *mechane,* in hook and pulley set at top of *skene* by which divinities could be raised or lowered; (4) *deus ex machina,* most famous of all, employed to introduce the god.

Machines, Elizabethan theatre. (1) A crane, probably a descendant from the ancient Greek *deus ex machina;* (2) a kind of *ekkuklema* to thrust beds or similar objects necessary to a scene onto the stage; (3) trapdoors; (4) instruments producing thunder and lightning.

Machines, medieval theatre. From all evidence, many ingenious machines were used to introduce saints, to give realistic effects of clouds and other natural phenomena, to simulate fire (as of Hell), etc.

Machines, Renaissance Italian theatre. (1) For the raising and lowering of divinities; (2) trapdoors; (3) for thunder and lightning. Other scenic devices: (1) lights: (a) sometimes in the streets or on house roofs or towers; (b) sometimes overhead facing the audience; (c) sometimes placed behind the houses or skyborders; (d) Sabbatini: side-lighting gives the best brightness and shade which aids theatrical illusion; (e) footlights, also suggested by Sabbatini; (f) colored lights, by means of candles or lamps behind bottles filled with colored liquids; (4) the heavens: (a) "entire," with cloth stretched over frame; (b) "cut," for purposes of swallowing up a certain disappearing divinity, raising, or other kinds of machines; (5) curtains, rarely used.

Mackay, Constance D'Arcy (Mrs. Roland Holt). American author. Since 1905 she has written, produced and directed many pageants, among which were *The Pageant of Patriotism,* 1911; *The Historical Pageant of Schenectady, New York,* 1912; *The Historical Pageant of Portland, Maine,* 1913. She was also a director of pageantry and drama and has written books about the theatre as well as plays for children. She is also the author of the play *Benjamin Franklin, Journeyman.*

Mackaye, Percy (1875-). American dramatist. The son of Steele Mackaye (1842-1894), the founder of the Madison Square and Lyceum Theatres, New York, and the inventor of numerous theatrical improvements, he was born in New York, March 16, 1875, and began life as a teacher. His first play *The Canterbury Pilgrims,* a comedy, was produced in 1903, and thenceforward he devoted himself to dramatic and other writing, and to the delivery of lectures on themes connected with the theatre. His plays included *Jeanne d'Arc,* a tragedy, 1906; *The Scarecrow, a Tragedy of the Ludicrous; Anti-Matrimony,* a satirical comedy, 1910; and *A Thousand Years Ago,* a comedy, 1914. He was also the author of many poems and essays on the drama.

Mackaye, Steele (James Steele Mackaye) (1842-1894). American dramatist and producer. He studied art, but was attracted to the stage in Paris where he studied with Francois Delsarte and Regnier. In 1873 he played *Hamlet* in London. At the same time he collaborated with Tom Taylor and Charles Reade in playwriting. From 1867-79 he produced several plays that had a fair success. In 1880 his play *Hazel Kirke* created a sensation in New York. It had a two year run and was a repertory piece for the next thirty years. His chief contributions to the theatre, however, were devices for overhead lighting, first used in 1874; the invention of the first moving or double stage, 1877; and his many improvements both for stage and auditorium, including folding theatre seats.

Macklin, Charles (Charles McLaughlin) (1697?-1797). Irish actor, dramatist. He made his first appearance at Drury Lane under the name of Mechlin, October 31, 1733. He acted at the Haymarket and Covent Garden, also in Dublin, and achieved enormous success as Shylock, Peachum, Polonius and Iago. His own plays included the farce *Love à la Mode,* 1759; and the comedy *The Man of the World,* 1781. Notorious for his quarrels and lawsuits, he retired in 1789. With Garrick he did much to reform the style of acting in his day, and was an excellent comedian.

MacLeish, Archibald (1892-). American poet, dramatist. Educated at Yale; studied law at Harvard; practised in Boston; in 1923 left law to write poetry. In 1926 published *Nobodaddy,* a poetic play not meant for production. His sixth book of verse, *Conquistador,* won the Pulitzer Prize in 1933. The Monte Carlo Ballet Russe in 1934 produced his *Union Pacific,* a strictly American ballet. Nathan Zatkin and John Houseman produced his experimental play, *Panic,* at the Imperial Theatre in March 1935, with Orson Welles in the leading role. Only three performances were given, by plan. In 1937 Poet in Residence at Princeton; his radio play, *The Fall of the City,* broadcast over CBS. In 1938 Columbia broadcast his *Air Raid;* that year he was adviser to the Harvard Poet's Theatre, and resigned his contributing editorship of *Fortune,* a position held for several years. In 1939 he helped form a Radio Workshop at Harvard, and in June was appointed Librarian of Congress.

MacNeice, Louis (1907-   ). English poet, dramatist. Educated at Oxford and having some association with the group of poets including Auden, Spender, C. Day Lewis, and Christopher Isherwood. He is author of the verse-play *Out of the Picture.*

Macready, William Charles (1793-1873). British actor. Born in London, the son of an Irish actor-manager, he made his first appearance at Birmingham as Romeo, 1810, and his London debut at Covent Garden, 1816. In 1819 and 1820 he rose to the front rank with his performances of Richard III, Coriolanus and Hamlet. He acted in the United States in 1826-27, and in Paris in 1828. He was the first to present Bulwer-Lytton's *The Lady of Lyons,* 1838. He was manager of Covent Garden, 1827-39, and of Drury Lane, 1841-43, where he made his final appearance as Macbeth, February 26, 1873. His later years were made melodramatic by a feud with Edwin Forrest, which culminated in the Astor Place Riot in which seventeen or more people were killed. An actor of great talent, painstaking and conscientious almost to a fault, who did much to purge the Shakespearean drama from Restoration alterations and interpolations, Macready had a sincere desire to elevate his profession.

See also *Astor Place Riot.*

Madame Sans-Gêne. Victorien Sardou and Emile Moreau (French). Comedy. Prologue and 3 acts. 1893.

Caterina Hubscher, a spirited French washwoman, becomes a Duchess in Napoleon's court. She retains her old blunt crudities, and is finally ordered by Napoleon to divorce her husband and retire from court. She reminds him of the days of struggle and triumph in which she shared, and also of his unpaid laundry bill of that time. The Emperor relents and reinstates her.

Madame X. Alexandre Bisson (French). Drama. 3 acts. 1908.

A famous tear-jerker.

Two years before the start of the play, Jacqueline has run away from her husband, Floriot, to join a lover. She is a weak woman rather than a wicked one, and when, two years after her fatal misstep, she learns that the infant son whom she abandoned is ill, she returns home to inquire about him. Her lover has died. Her husband will not let her see the baby and orders her from the house. Then a sympathetic family friend makes him see the error of his ways and warns him that, by his cruel conduct, he may have started her on the downward path to ruin. Repentant, Floriot starts a long and fruitless search for his wife.

Twenty years have passed. Jacqueline has taken the easiest way predicted by her husband's friend. She is hard, bedizened, old before her time, but with a certain haunting sadness in her face. When in her cups she sometimes hints that she has known prosperity and social position. These random confessions interest two blackmailing friends of her current lover, Laroque, and they persuade him to try to discover the secret of her past. He does so, and finds out that she was married to a deputy general, and had money in her own name which she left for her son, Raymond. Laroque threatens to visit Floriot and blackmail him into handing over this money. Rather than see her son lose his inheritance, Jacqueline shoots Laroque.

When arrested, Jacqueline refuses to talk. For want of a better name, she is called Madame X. Raymond, now a rising young lawyer and engaged to a charming young girl, is appointed to defend her. It is not until the trial that Jacqueline realizes who he is; she almost collapses on the stand. But she pulls herself together long enough to accuse the two blackmailers, whom she sees in the courtroom, of the real responsibility for Laroque's death. Raymond's defense of her is brilliant, and she is acquitted. Floriot, who has been attending the trial and has recognized her, tells her son who she is and leads him off to meet his mother. There is a joyful reunion of the trio. But the strain has been too much for Jacqueline. After having had the exquisite pleasure of hearing Raymond call her "Mother," she dies.

Maddernmarket Theatre. An amateur theatre with an Elizabethan stage in Norwich, England. Designed by Nugent Monch. Built 1921.

Made an ascension. Went up in his lines.

Madras House, The. Harley Granville-Barker (English). 4 acts. 1910.

The Madras House is a large shop which has women as its chief clientele. The new executives of the shop discuss the effect women have, and their place in society. First, Mr. Huxtable is shown surrounded by his six daughters. Unfortunately their preoccupation with nursing, foreign missions and water color sketching is insufficient to fill their lives and the conclusion is that nothing can take the place of husbands and homes. A young member of the firm, Philip Madras, has just realized the difficulties his employees have especially in the case of a young unmarried mother which has just been brought to his attention. An American millionaire has offered to buy the store, and at a conference to discuss this, the conversation turns to women. Mr. Chas. Madras, head of the firm, so resents the modern woman in business and politics that he has decided to retire to a Mohammedan country where the women are segregated. Th parade of the models in their new gowns is illustrative of the exploitation of sex. Finally Jessica is introduced, the interesting, attractive modern woman, wife of Philip, and we hear the idea of the play resolved in the conversation on the emancipated woman.

MAGAZINES

BY BERNARD SOBEL

American magazines played a great part in sustaining an interest in the stage during the 1890's and early 1900's. Few plays were published at that time, and the Little Theatre was just coming into existence. So those people who did not live in theatrical key cities or in towns that were large enough to support one night stands had to depend entirely on newspapers and magazines for information about players, plays, and playwriting. For them the *Theatre Magazine* filled a need for decades. Published by Paul and Louis Meyer and edited by Arthur Hornblow, Sr., this publication symbolized quality in the playhouse and the heightened glow of the footlights. The contents were comprehensive, but the emphasis was on pictures rather than subject matter, the treatment being somewhat superficial rather than deeply scholarly. Other magazines of the same period which gave space to the theatre was the weekly *Vanity Fair,* a white paper version of the pink *Police Gazette* which delighted barber shop patrons with pictures of girls in tights; the trade publications, the *New York Clipper, The New York Dramatic Mirror,* and *Variety* and varied periodicals like *The Bohemian, Judge, Puck* and *Harper's Weekly.* Substantial were the reviews in *Munsey's Magazine* and the original *Smart Set Magazine.* When George Jean Nathan succeeded Channing Pollock as the critic of this latter publication the hopes for a literate theatrical public rose suddenly. Nathan introduced the American public to the continental drama. He discussed the new technique. He exposed the drolleries and inadequacies of our provincial drama from the standpoint of subject matter, characterization, and dialogue. His influence pyramided. After a time, publishers began to be more active in publishing plays. *Poet Lore,* an expensive magazine, known to a limited number, published plays by Andreyev, Strindberg, Maeterlinck and other continental dramatists. Eventually also, The Drama League did the same in a pretentious magazine called *The Drama.* Simultaneously, the League's comments on plays caused controversy. By the time that the road died out and the cinema had begun to supplant the theatre outside the key cities, nearly every important magazine had a drama department. *The Green Book,* a popular priced monthly, catered openly to the interests of casual theatregoers, while other magazines like *The Literary Digest,* the new monthly *Vanity Fair,* and *Life* carried serious criticism. The appearance of Burns Mantle's yearbook gave continuity to theatrical accomplishment. Today the theatre has a place in practically every monthly and weekly magazine. *Newsweek, The New Yorker, Mademoiselle, Cue, Time* and *Life,* all go in for criticism. The standard publication is *Theatre Arts.* Established in 1916, it is edited by Edith J. R. Isaacs. From the outset this handsome magazine has upheld the highest ideals of the theatre and inspired readers, writers and actors with its scholarly articles, provocative photographs, stage designs, and excellent criticism.

Magda (Heimat). Hermann Sudermann (German). Drama. 4 acts. 1893.

Magda leaves home at an early age because her father insists on a marriage which she opposes. She returns as the great singer engaged for a music festival, but her free attitude toward life causes nothing but trouble. When her father finds out that she has an illegitimate child he is beside himself. Von Keller, the father of the child, offers to marry Magda, but she refuses him. Magda's father is about to shoot her in a fit of rage when he suffers a stroke which kills him.

Magi, The. Anatoli Lunacharsky (Russian). Drama. 13 scenes. 1918.

This is a fantasy with symbolic landscape and colors, white for purity, blue for wisdom and red for passion. When Manessa arrives on the scene, Sempronius, in order to possess her, kills the leader of the Magi, Andromenes. Sempronius, jealous of a humble hunchback for whom the lady has shown pity, taunts him. The spirit of the slain Andromenes returns to help him, but when the spirit kisses the lady, Sempronius kills him again and returns to taunting the hunchback. The next scene shows all the people ascending a mountainside. Sempronius, aided by the ghost of Andromenes, recognizes in him his double. The slayer and the slain are one. No individual can injure another without injuring himself.

Magic. The theatrical art of magic is extremely ancient and has been popular at all times with all people. It includes sleight of hand, legerdemain, all phases of conjuring. Such a variety of men as Cagliostro, Robert Houdin, Heller, Keller, the Herrmanns, Houdini, Ottokar Fischer, Horace Goldin, Fred Keating, and the practical magician and scholarly historian, John Mulholland, grace its records. The official American organization is the Society of American Magicians and its magazine is *The Sphinx,* published monthly, John Mulholland, editor.

Magic lantern. A lantern by means of which small images are represented on a screen, a wall or a sheet on a dark room, magnified to any size. Popular before the introduction of the motion picture but now used only to illustrate lectures. The innovation of this machine is attributed to Athanasius Kircher, a German Jesuit archeologist.

Mahelot, Laurent (fl. 1634). French stage-mechanic, scene-painter. Mechanic, and probably designer, for the Comédiens du Roi—the sole theatrical troupe in France from 1633 to 1678, performing at the Hotel de Burgogne. Mahelot has been called the first Renaissance scenic artist in France. The *Memoire de plusieurs decorations,* begun by him and completed by Michel Laurent, his successor, in 1673 (or 1678), showed scenery and mechanical arrangements for many 17th century plays. Mahelot's influence on design was great in both France and England.

Mai. An old style of dancing done by the First Actor (*Shite*) of the Japanese Nō stage. The *Mai* is a dance of slow steps and solemn gestures simulating the graceful movements of cranes. It is very popular with the upper classes.

The Maid of Orleans. Schiller, Johan (1759-1805). German drama. 1801.
The traditional story of Joan of Arc, the maid who led the French troops against the English to raise the siege against Orleans and who led Charles VII to his coronation at Rheims. She accomplished both these tasks although illiterate and untutored. She maintained she received her "call" from the "voices," presumably of her patron saint. She was taken by the Burgundians and turned over to the British. She was tried by French clerics who condemned her as a witch and the English burned her at the stake at Rouen.

Maid servants. Attendants of the young ladies of *commedia dell' arte,* most famous of which are Columbine, Ricciolina, Nina, Betta, Olivetta.

Maid's Tragedy, The. Beaumont & Fletcher (English). Tragedy. 1609.

The king of Rhodes has taken as his mistress the young and beautiful Evadne. In order to make everything appear in order he commands a young courtier Amintor to wed her. Amintor is in love with Aspatia but feels it his duty to obey his monarch. They are married and Amintor really feels smitten by Evadne's charm. On their wedding night she discloses her relationship with the king and in a sneering and haughty manner tells him it will be a marriage in name only. Melantius, Evadne's brother, realizing something is amiss, wrings the truth from Amintor. Melantius, shocked, decides on revenge. He organizes his friends, decides to seize the fortification and compels Evadne to kill the king. Meanwhile Aspatia, the rejected, having nothing to live for disguises herself as a boy, calls on Amintor, claims to be her own brother, and challenges him to defend her sister's honor. Reluctantly Amintor fights and mortally wounds her.

Evadne returns and urges Amintor to accept her as a true wife. He refuses and she kills herself. Then the dying Aspatia reveals who she is and the lovers have a few fleeting happy moments. After her death Amintor has no wish to live. Milantius, on discovering all this wishes to die also, but is prevented by force although he vows to die slowly of starvation.

Major Barbara. George Bernard Shaw (English). Comedy. 1907.

Like many of Shaw's plays, this is really a dramatized discussion or debate, attacking the problem of organized charity.

Barbara Undershaft, feeling that the evils of the present social system must somehow he remedied, joins the Salvation Army. On the opposite side of the fence is her father, Andrew Undershaft, a munitions king and armament manufacturer, who foments the war spirit and encourages the development of a capitalistic society indifferent to spiritual values. Once in the Army, Barbara is entirely carried away by spiritual fervor and becomes anti-capitalistic to the core. So she is doubly dismayed to learn that capitalists support even the charity organizations on which she depends. And finally she is practically ready to admit the truth of her father's dictum that poverty alone is shameful, that it is responsible for crime and is in itself the only sin.

Make the rounds. A term used by actors meaning to go from producer's office to producer's office.

MAKE-UP

Sidelights of Make-up

BY WILLIE HOWARD

The art of make-up has changed greatly since the days when I was first an actor. It is not so serious a matter now as it used to be. The movies have simplified the process and the stage is already benefiting by their methods.

In days gone by, make-up had a great deal to do with an actor's success. Particularly was this true of the now forgotten Protean artist. This gentleman was a feature of the golden days of vaudeville, and among the most famous were Willie Zimmerman and Albert Chevalier. Both men were lightning-change artists and they used to dazzle audiences by changing their entire appearance from top to toe, almost before the eyes of the audience. One minute they would appear as Abraham Lincoln, the next as an Irish washerwoman, and the next as U. S. Grant or George Washington. The resemblances were astonishing, but they were accomplished with the aid of trick makeup, eyebrows, beards, false noses and trick teeth, all tied together so cleverly that they could be put on or taken off in a second.

And the comedian today has to be almost equally speedy in his changes. Revue sketches are numerous and characters are as varied as the writer's imagination can make them. But after many years of experience, my brother Eugene and I have learned several ways of meeting these requirements. In the first place, I depend largely on my natural features rather than on make-up for my stage characterizations. First I cover my face with greasepaint—the foundation, then I put a little black on the brows. I never use any lines on my face, preferring to let the natural contours create the effect desired. Besides I have learned, I believe, to use my features so that I can look like an old man, a foreigner or an eccentric. When necessary, I can change the shape of my nose by building it up with putty.

Most of my character make-ups are founded on general observations. They are taken from life with little exaggeration and are based on the people I meet. They are based also on Italian, French and German cartoons or photographs that I pick up here and there. Often when I walk down the street and see an odd or an amusing face I say to myself, "Gee, I believe that I'd look funny with a make-up like that." So I store the impression in my memory and when I get to the dressing room I strive to duplicate it.

Funny pictures from newspapers and magazines I hide in my trunk and they come in handy when George White, for instance, says, "I want you to play the Frenchman in the *Scandals,*" I dig into my trunk and usually find what I want—a Frenchman, a Mexican or an Indian. The tenor whom I imitate in the burlesque quartet from *Rigoletto* is based on the real picture of a former opera singer; and my impersonation of Professor Pierre Ginsberg is a copy of a former French phrenologist's. Sometimes the make-up requires a beard and sideburns. In such a case I turn over the cartoon or photograph to the wigmaker and ask him to copy these facial decorations. Wigs and beards, of course, must come on and off quickly because of revue speed. But wigs made for the legitimate stage these days are so perfect that all that can be seen of them is a bit of hairline. They're fitted to the head and blended with the skin imperceptibly.

My brother Eugene works more slowly than I and with more details. In his characterization of John L. Lewis, in the current *Scandals,* he accentuates his eyebrows and creates life-like resemblances with pigments and powder. Then too, his features bear a certain resemblance to Lewis's.

Both of us, as young players, learned many points about make-up from Wilton Lackaye. He was an expert and like a portrait painter worked patiently at crow's feet, baggy eyes and wrinkles; knew how to shade browns, maroons and white for life-like effect. His Svengali make-up in *Trilby* was extraordinary.

But the time for this sort of labored effort has passed. In the movies in particular, specialists build up synthetic casts of a face or head and all the actor need do is put the cast on and attach it. Paul Muni's cheeks, for instance, in *Juarez* were built out with rubber and blended with grease paint. These make-ups have a certain permanency. They don't melt under heat. Any actor can eat with his make-up on now without spoiling it. Better still, he can use the same make-up, day after day, knowing that it is accurate and not spoiled.

Today, even backstage, most actors use manufactured standard brands of make-up. You take a little sponge. You put a little water on it, and you're made up in two minutes. That's all there is to it. The leading man perhaps, blackens his brows, reddens his lips, uses a bit of rouge and then goes on.

For the girls it's still difficult, if they don't use this prepared make-up. They use cold cream first as a base, and then grease. Yes, they even make-up with grease-paint these days, the old-fashioned idea of the theatre. Cold cream first; then grease-paint—what is called panchromatic make-up. You can put it on in two minutes. Then apply rouge and lipstick. The eyes come next, but even they're quicker to do, thanks to modern methods. Girls used to bead the eyes—a long, slow process—but now they simply put on false lashes in a jiffy.

I would advise actors and students of make-up to watch human nature all the time, because it is there that you find the funniest character. You can see more funny characters off the stage than on. But enough of this for the present. I hear them calling "Curtain!"

Make-Up. Make-up is the art of the application of cosmetics to produce the appearance of the character. The appearance must be regarded from the point of view of the audience. Therefore, lighting and distance must be taken into consideration.

The factors in successful make-up are: Smoothness of Base; Evenness of Foundation; Proper Application of Lines, Highlights and Shadows; Proper Blending.

The Base is used to protect the skin, to enable easy application and easy removal. Cold cream is the almost universal base but any pure vegetable shortening will do.

The Foundation is the colored grease paint. Grease paints are available in a great variety of colors and are supplied both in sticks and in tubes. There are a number of standard brands, all governed by the U. S. Pure Food and Drugs Act and are quite safe to use.

The Lines are used for wrinkles, scars, etc., and to accentuate eyebrows, eyelashes and other features.

The High Lights are bright spots needed to give roundness to a part of the face and to complement a wrinkle or shadow. Light-colored grease paints are used.

Shadows are furrows or sunken areas on the face. Eye-shadow is used.

Blending is the final smoothing out, chiefly by means of face powder.

Lining is applied with eyebrow pencils, orangesticks, stumps of pointed rolls of paper. Thin sticks of lining grease paints, slightly harder than base grease paints, are used as well as cream base eye shadow.

Rouge, of course, is an important material for cheek and lip make-up and face powder is essential in blending. But theatrical face powder must be used. It has a different adhesive quality from ordinary powder and is available in a wide variety of colors which match the grease paints. Wool powder puffs are used. There are many other materials for special purposes: crepe hair and spirit gum; corn starch for graying hair; burnt cork and minstrel black; metallic powders for hair coloring; nose putty; black wax for blocking out teeth; etc. Facial tissues are used with cold cream for the removal of make-up. The above mentioned materials are available at many drug and department stores as well as at theatrical supply houses.

There are various methods of employing them. The type used depends on the particular problem. Many actors avoid make-up whenever possible because they believe it conceals the face and interferes with the play of the facial muscles. Eleanora Duse, in her later years, never used it at all. Furthermore, under modern lighting conditions, the audience may see the paint and not the complexion. On the other hand, the lighting arrangements may require correction of features that do not show up correctly: eyebrows and lips may require accentuation, cheeks may have to be highlighted.

The only sure way to judge the effectiveness of the make-up is to have it viewed from a point midway in the orchestra, under the lighting conditions that will prevail during the performance. Professionals and persons with experience in make-up, of course, do not require this test. They do, however, use mirrors framed in bright lights to give the approximate equivalent of the stage lighting. However, less expert performers will realize that the appearance from close up will be vastly different from the appearance from a distance.

"The Last Word in Make-up," by Rudolph G. Liszt, is a comprehensive book on the subject.

Make-up, straight. Greasepaint as applied by an actor to his face so that his features can be visible, and using enough color to offset the footlights and at the same time emphasizing his natural features.

Make-up box. The container of cosmetics applied to cheeks, lips, eyebrows, etc., of an actor or actress when making ready to appear on the stage in a theatrical part.

Make-up pencil. Like an ordinary lead pencil but has compressed grease material for a core. Used for lining eyes, darkening and defining eyebrows and for making wrinkles.

Malade Imaginaire, Le (The Imaginary Invalid). Molière (French). Comedy. 5 acts. 1673.

Argan, a hypochondriac, is completely under the influence of M. Purgon, his physician. The doctor urges him to marry off his daughter Angelique to a young doctor although she is in love with Cleante. Beline, his second wife, wants Argan to make his daughters become nuns so that she will inherit his property. Argan's brother, Beralde, pleads for Cleante, tries to convince him that the doctor is a charlatan and his wife has selfish designs. Because Argan asks him to postpone a medical treatment, the doctor refuses to treat him further. Toinette, a maid, disguises herself as a doctor and tells him Purgon's diagnosis was wrong. Argan feigns death, to discover the true character of his wife and his daughter's love.

He consents to Cleante's marriage with Angelique, if he promises to be a doctor. Beralde suggests that Argan, too, become a doctor. He consents and is made a member of the faculty by a crowd of carnival masqueraders.

Maladie de Chrétienté, La. A 16th century French play, satirizing the Christian church and clergy.

Malaprop, Mrs. Character in Sheridan's *The Rivals.* The name has become a word meaning inappropriate.

Malcolini, Amalie (1780-1851). German actress. Leading tragedienne at Goethe's Weimar Court Theatre after the early death of Christiane Neumann; acted in *Die Braut von Messina;* played Iphigenia, Antigone and Ophelia.

Malevinsky's algebraic formula of dramaturgy, 1925. A formula for the construction of a play as expounded by Moses L. Malevinsky:

A: A basic emotion or an element in or of a basic emotion constituting a theme; plus

B: Personified by character; plus

C: Motivated through . . . (1) crucible, (2) conflict, (3) complication, (4) crisis, (5) climax; plus

D: Progressed by narrative, plot or story; plus

E: Compartmented by derivated situations; plus

F: Dressed up by incidental detailed construction;

G: The underlying idea orientated through its constituent elements dramaturgically expressed;

H: Articulated by words;

I: Imagined by artistry.

Malone, Edmund (1741-1812). Irish scholar. Born in Dublin, he settled in London in 1777, becoming an intimate friend of Johnson, Boswell and Sir Joshua Reynolds. He produced his great work, an edition of Shakespeare in ten volumes, in 1790. He detected the Shakespearean forgeries of William Henry Ireland and was also one of the first to deny the authenticity of the so-called Rowley poems of Chatterton.

Maltz, Albert (1908-   ). American dramatist. Deeply concerned with social problems of the masses. Collaborated with George Sklar on *Merry-Go-Round,* 1931, a satiric commentary on the Tammany political machine in New York City; and *Peace on Earth,* 1933, an anti-war play which was the initial production of Theatre Union. In 1935, alone, he wrote *Black Pit,* a drama of the West Virginia coal mines; and *Private Hicks,* winner of the New Theatre League's one-act play prize. He is married to Margaret Larkin, formerly of Theatre Union.

See also *Sklar, George.*

Malvaloca. Serafin and Joaquin Alvarez Quintero (Spanish). 3 acts. 1912.

The cracked convent bell in an Andalusian village is to be remolded by two brothers Salvador and Leonardo. Malvaloca, who once had an affair with Salvador, but then repented, comes to visit him when he is ill. She tells Leonardo that she bears Salvador no ill-will despite the fact that she has been abused because of her folly. She grows to care deeply for Leonardo and he loves her and wants to see her forgiven and respected as she deserves. After the bell is recast, Salvador resolves to go away. While they all watch the religious procession as the recast bell rings out, Leonardo tells Malvaloca that he will recast her life by the warmth of his love. She consents to his plea and the bell breaks forth into a happy song.

Maly Theatre. The oldest theatre in Moscow, long famous for its classical repertoire. Since the Revolution, it has given a great deal of attention to plays of Soviet ideology.

Mamoulian, Rouben (1898-). Director. Born in Russia. Attended Lycée in Paris and University of Moscow. Came to the United States and became director at the Eastman Theatre, Rochester, New York. Then came to the Theatre Guild where he did *Porgy* in 1927, then *Marco Millions, Wings Over Europe, R. U. R., Farewell to Arms,* and *Porgy and Bess* in 1935. Went to Hollywood in 1930 and has directed many successful films.

Management, business. The production of a play is a business as well as an artistic enterprise. The conduct of this part of the affairs of a company is generally divorced from the production and left to a business manager.
See *Manager.*

Manager. Term usually applied to the company manager in charge of the personnel and business of the company during rehearsals and subsequent performances in contradistinction to the producer and general manager of the theatrical firm. The essential duties of a manager are to "watch the gate" as tickets are taken at the door; to count the tickets with the treasurer or house manager; to pay salaries on Saturday afternoon; and to balance a weekly statement on Saturday night. Very much the same duties fall to a house manager, but, in addition to similar tasks, he is responsible for cleaners, ushers, etc., in brief the personnel of the theatre quite apart from the company playing there, except in the case of repertory and stock theatres where one manager usually takes entire charge.

Managers. Among various types of managers are: *manager,* that is a producer; *house manager,* who is responsible for all the details in the management of a theatre building; *business manager,* who handles monies, payrolls, accounts, etc., for the producer; *company manager,* who performs the duties of the business manager for an individual company, usually on the road; *stage manager,* who, with his assistants, is responsible for the running of the performance during the run of a play; *personal manager,* who acts as representative for an author, actor, or manager.

Man and His Phantoms. Henri René Lenormand (French). Drama. 1924.

In this play, the leading character is called the "Man," although he really typifies a modern version of Don Juan. The Man has gone through life, thirsting for new thrills in his relationship with women. He does not have a fine or lasting relationship with them but discards them quickly, seeking new titillation. He seduces a peasant girl in the Alps; a Russian girl who burns the child she bears him; a neurotic wife in Algeria. Soon he sinks to the lowest street walkers. Finally, a psychoanalyst tells him that though he has a long record of amorous adventures, none of them were satisfactory because in his greedy desire to experience many he has really had none and his conquests were defeats. He remains alone, masculine in appearance, feminine in soul. As he lays dying, in a burning room, the phantoms of his victims come to haunt him and he dies in fear, haunted by their accusations.

Man and Superman. George Bernard Shaw (British). Comedy. 3 acts. 1903.

Ann Whitfield, a pretty English girl, decides to marry Jack Tanner. She has him appointed her guardian by her father's will. He objects to this responsibility and when he discovers the girl's real intentions, he is panic-stricken. Deciding his only hope for escape from marriage is flight, he rushes off to Europe in his car. Ann, however, follows and overtakes him in the mountains in Spain. At first he refuses to marry her, but finally succumbs, for she is Everywoman, the Life Force which cannot be denied.

Manfred. Lord Byron (English). A dramatic poem. 1817.

Manfred, living in the Alps, has been tortured by his conscience because of some mysterious crime he has committed in the past. He calls upon the spirits of the world, seeking the one thing he wants—oblivion—but he cannot get it. He goes to the hall of Arimanes, resists submission to the evil spirits but bids them call the vision of Astarte, his former sweetheart. She appears and tells him he will die on the morrow. At the time foretold the spirits appear to take him. He resists them, they disappear, but Manfred dies.

The Man from Cairo. Dan Goldberg (American). Comedy. 3 acts. 1938. Adapted from the French of Yvan-Noë.

At a Budapest night club, the lovely Leni meets and is captivated by a romantic-looking young man, Istvan Kovat. They agree to meet outside the club, but he disappears. The next day Leni learns his address and goes to find him. There she meets Henrietta who denies any knowledge of Istvan Kovat, but says her husband is Leon Kovat and perhaps Istvan is a distant cousin. After Leni has left, Leon Kovat enters, a commonplace government clerk, and he is Istvan minus the glamor. Henrietta accuses Leon of deception and he admits he has sought outside the gaiety and companionship his home lacked. Henrietta says she will leave him. Meanwhile, on learning that Leni is to return, Leon is delighted and orders a banquet. Henrietta, curious, agrees to serve the meal. Leni comes, sees Leon and recognizing that she has been deceived upbraids him. He says that his invention of Istvan, the man from Cairo, has helped brighten his life, that one can be happy if one believes in dreams. He helps effect a reconciliation between Leni and her fiance. Leon and Henrietta, left alone, sit down to the banquet and there is promise that their life together from now on will be a happier one.

Mannering, Mary (Florence Friend) (1876-   ). English actress. Educated privately; studied for the stage under Hermann Vezin; first appearance on the stage at the Prince's, Manchester, 1892, as Zela in *Hero and Leander*. Other plays in which she appeared include: *A Night in Town; The Wife of Dives; Called Back;* first appearance in New York at Hartford, Connecticut, in *The Courtship of Leonie,* 1896; *Trelawney of the Wells; The Ambassador; Janice Meredith,* 1900; *Step by Step,* 1909; *The Truant; Kiddie,* 1909; *A Man's World,* 1910; *The Garden of Allah,* 1910.

Mannheim National Theatre. German playhouse which dates from 1778; founded by Elector Karl Theodor of Bavaria; Baron von Dalberg was Theatre Superintendent who brought the theatre to its heyday between 1784-95 because of the noted actor, Iffland, who became Superintendent of the Berlin Royal Court Theatre.

Man of Destiny, The. George Bernard Shaw (English). Comedy. 1 act. 1897.
The time is May, 1796. Corporal Napoleon, aged twenty-six, has just been victorious at the bridge of Lodi. "An original observer, he has perceived that a cannon ball, if it strikes a man, may kill him." Now, wearied from his victory, he has taken shelter at a little inn at Tavazzano, on the road between Lodi and Milan. There is a very charming lady staying at the inn; the little corporal's susceptibilities to her attractions do not blind him to the fact that she is probably a spy. Napoleon's orderly arrives with a tale of having had important papers stolen by a young soldier who wormed his way into the orderly's friendship and then betrayed him. The traitor, he observes, looked exactly like the lady. Her twin brother, she assures him glibly. Napoleon is not deceived, and, after the orderly has left to find the soldier with the papers, deftly retrieves the documents from the lady's bodice. But he will learn some scandal about Josephine if he reads them, she warns. Let him keep the political plans and return only the personal ones to her. The orderly returns. He has not found the soldier, and is willing to undergo the disgrace Napoleon has promised him. The lady feels sorry for him. It takes only a few minutes for her to return as her twin brother and save the hapless orderly from permanent dishonor. Napoleon nobly throws the papers in the fire. The lady is indifferent, for she has already read the contents. "So have I, in the garden a little while ago," says the future general, and leads the way to his bedchamber.
This amusing comedy, which includes a discussion of England in Shaw's best manner, should be classed with *Caesar and Cleopatra* as one of the dramatist's works which do not hesitate to humanize and even ridicule the men who have made history. Napoleon is both sympathetic and clever, but he is in no wise idealized.

Man of Mode, The; or Sir Fopling Flutter. Sir George Etherege (English). Comedy. 5 acts. 1676.

A pre-Congreve Restoration comedy. Its characters include Dorimant, the perfect fop, supposed to be modeled after Lord Rochester; Belair, a flowery poet; Sir Fopling Flutter, king of the dandies; and the ladies of these pleasure-loving dudes and beaux. The plot consists of their complicated love affairs, particularly those of Dorimant. He successively deserts two mistresses, Mrs. Loveit and Belinda, in order to court an heiress. The latter's mother hesitates at first to let her daughter wed him, but he overcomes her scruples and wins the young lady's heart at the same time. The dialogue is brilliantly handled. The courtiers reflect those of Molière and foreshadow those of the later Restoration dramatists.

Mansfield, Richard (1857-1907). American actor. Born May 24, 1857, in Berlin, he was the son of Madame Erminia Rudersdorff, a distinguished soprano in grand opera and oratorio, who had married Maurice Mansfield, a London wine merchant. He began his professional career doing monologues. From 1878-81 he advanced to touring in minor Gilbert and Sullivan companies, singing Sir Joseph Porter and John Wellington Wells. He had a few months' experience in a dramatic company, and in 1882 he sailed for New York, where he at once applied to the most important theatrical managers, A. M. Palmer, Augustin Daly and Lester Wallack. They refused him, so he made his first New York appearance in a comic opera, *Three Black Cloaks,* September, 1882. By December, A. M. Palmer gave him a small part in *A Parisian Romance.* When the actor who had the best part in the play resigned, Mansfield got it. When the play opened in 1883, Mansfield was made famous. His career was a fact by 1893. He had some astounding hits to his credit, including, *Prince Karl; Dr. Jekyll and Mr. Hyde;* and *Beau Brummell,* which was especially written for him by Clyde Fitch; and *Cyrano de Bergerac.* In 1894 he introduced Shaw to the American stage with *Arms and the Man.* Mansfield's last season, 1906-07, was devoted to a production of *Peer Gynt,* the first given in this country, or in fact, in English. All during that time he was suffering from cancer, and later in March, 1907, he was too ill to go on. He died in August. His widow, the distinguished actress of Ibsen roles, is Beatrice Cameron.

Mansions. Buildings of all kinds represented on the medieval stage, including: *lius* (place), *loca* (places), *domus* (home or house), *sedes* (seat), *castrum* (castle), *thronus* (throne), *palatium* (palace), *tentum* (tent), *estals, sieges,* and others; several usually on stage together and the scene of action would move variously from one to the other.

Mantell, Robert Bruce (1854-1928). British-American actor.
He made his first appearance on the stage with Boucicault in England in 1876. In 1878 he played juvenile roles in the United States with Modjeska. From 1880-83 he toured England. He supported Fanny Davenport in *Fedora* in New York. With his own company he toured the United States playing Shakespeare. He was practically the last of the great Shakespearean actors in the old tradition.

Mantle, Burns (Robert Burns Mantle) (1873-   ). American author, dramatic critic. Born in Watertown, New York; educated at public school and normal college;

dramatic editor of *Denver Times*, 1898-1900; *Denver Republican*, 1900-01; *Chicago Inter-Ocean*, 1901-06; *Chicago Tribune*, 1906-07; Sunday editor, *Chicago Tribune*, 1907-11; dramatic editor *Evening Mail*, New York, 1911-22; dramatic editor New York *Daily News*, since 1922. Editor of the *Best Plays* and *A Treasury of the Theatre* (with John Gassner) ; *Year Book of the Drama in America* (annual volume 1920 to date) ; author of *American Playwrights of Today;* co-author with Garrison P. Sherwood, *The Best Plays of 1909-1919.*

Manuscript. The written or typed play, or the book of a musical play; usually used in rehearsal.

Man Who Came to Dinner, The. George S. Kaufman and Moss Hart. Comedy. 3 acts. 1939.

The plot of this play is relatively unimportant, but its brilliant, mirth-provoking dialogue and the portrait etched in acid of Sheridan Whiteside, raconteur, radio town crier, essayist and critic, made it one of the outstanding hits of the 1939-40 New York dramatic season.

Whiteside is visiting a small middle-Western town on a lecture tour when he slips on the ice in front of his hosts' home and is incapacitated. The neighbors rally round to hear the oracle utter gracious words of wit and wisdom. Instead, he insults his admirers, bullies his hosts, swears at his nurse and makes life generally disagreeable for those forced to associate with him. He gets people to do as he wills by fair means or foul: by hypocritically promising to publish a book or sternly threatening to divulge a murderer in the family. When his secretary, Maggie Cutler, wishes to leave him in order to marry a local newspaper editor, he is particularly demoniacal. Whiteside, knowing that the editor has written a play which he is anxious to have produced, develops a vicious plot involving an actress, an English lord and a celebrated mimic. But finally, realizing he has lost in any case, resolves to make amends. With the aid of a zany actor from Hollywood, one of the famous persons who are continually dropping in to visit the great man, he imprisons the actress in a mummy case, a gift which he has just received, and ships her off to parts unknown. Maggie, radiant, goes off with her editor. Whiteside, long since recovered, also takes his leave and goes out the door, brandishing his cane. There is a crashing sound, a muffled curse, and he is carried back into the room. He has slipped on the ice again!

Man With a Load of Mischief, The. Ahsley Dukes (English). Comedy. 3 acts. 1924.

A lady, a nobleman and Charles, a servant, come to an inn called The Man with a Load of Mischief. The nobleman, desiring to humble the lady, decides that his valet will make love to her. Charles, who had heard the lady sing years before, has always adored her. Now free of the bonds of servility, he woos her and they find the beauty of life together.

Manzoni, Alessandro (1785-1873). Italian author, dramatist. Born at Milan, he became the leader of the romantic and medieval reaction in Italian literature. His tragedies, *The Count of Carmagnola,* 1820, and *Adelchi,* 1822, mark an epoch in Italian drama by their adoption of Shakespearean methods, and his novel of the 17th century describing Milan life under Spanish rule. *I Promessi Sposi,* 1825-27, established a world-wide reputation and created a school of Italian historical novelists.

Marching Song. John Howard Lawson (American). Drama. 3 acts. 1937.

A propagandist pro-labor play which was the last production of the socially conscious Theatre Union.

The action takes place in an abandoned factory near the large Brimmer Company plant around which the life of the city revolves. The evicted Russell family have taken refuge in the factory. Pete Russell was on strike against unfair labor conditions in the plant where he worked when the bank holding the mortgage on his home showed its disapproval of his policies by throwing him, his wife and baby out of their home. The Russells' plight and the oppression of workers generally leads to another strike; the strikers set up headquarters in the factory with the Russells. Thugs and informers sent to break up the strike tell Pete he can have his old job back if he will betray the leader of the labor forces. He refuses, and strikebreakers kill the leader. In the meantime the strike has been spreading through the Brimmer plant and many other large industrial organizations. With their activities so seriously curtailed, the heads of the factories are obliged to come to terms with the workers.

Marco Millions. Eugene O'Neill (American). Comedy. Prologue, 3 acts and epilogue. 1927.

This was produced by the Theatre Guild with Alfred Lunt as Marco Polo.

The play is based on the actual trip taken by the famous Venetian traveller. Marco is treated satirically. He is an up-and-coming businessman, a go-getter, a thirteenth century hustler, endowed with acumen about business but no imagination where romance is concerned. In honor of the fact that he is almost grown and ready to be initiated into business, Marco is allowed to accompany his father Nicolo and his uncle Maffeo on a sales trip to the court of the great Khan. There the Princess Kukachin falls madly in love with the travelling salesman from Italy, who is unaware of her passion. He acts as her convoy to Persia, as requested by the Khan, and amasses a fortune through shrewd business deals, then returns to Venice to marry his sweetheart Donato. Kukachin, heartbroken at his indifference, dies for love of him.

Margaret Fleming. James A. Herne (American). Drama. 4 acts. 1890.

Philip Fleming, a prosperous mill owner, learns that his mistress Lena Schmidt has had a child by him. His wife Margaret, waiting for him at home, finds out from her maid that her sister has been betrayed by an unknown lover. It is revealed that it is Margaret's sister with whom Philip had an affair. Not suspecting her husband's duplicity, Margaret goes to visit Lena, only to see her sister die as a result of childbirth. Before her demise Lena names Philip as her seducer, stating however that he has always loved his wife and felt only passion for her sister. She entrusts her baby son to Margaret, who at first regards the child with horror. Then her maternal instincts are aroused, and Philip arrives to find her nursing his illegitimate baby. She sends him away angrily. Margaret, whose vision has been failing for some time, grows totally blind as a result of the shock of the experience she has undergone. Philip, thinking he has lost the woman who made his life worth while, attempts suicide. Margaret realizes that she needs him as much as he needs her and takes him back.

This serious play had a critical but not a popular success. Herne paid for its production himself, and sank into it most of the fortune he had made with his melodrama, *Hearts of Oak*. Although the general public appeared to prefer his more frivolous manner, Hamlin Garland, Thomas Bailey Aldrich and other eminent men of letters were so impressed by *Margaret Fleming* that they cited it as an example of a "strictly American theatre . . . where Drama shall be considered a Work of Art."

Maria Stuart. Johann Schiller (German). Tragedy. 5 acts. 1800.

A historical drama of Mary Stuart's last days. She is imprisoned in England. Parliament has pronounced her guilty and is waiting for Elizabeth to pronounce her death sentence. But Mary has a few supporters in Albion, among them young Mortimer, her keeper's nephew. Leicester, the favorite of the Queen, also pretends to support her, but in reality is playing a double-dealing game and is acting as a spy in both camps. Mary is given an audience by Elizabeth, and the latter makes it clear she fears the Scottish Queen too much to free her. Yet she would prefer to see her murdered by private individuals than to have Mary's blood on her hands. Since this seems a futile hope, she orders Leicester to see to Mary's execution. Mortimer's treachery is discovered and he commits suicide, but the crafty Leicester justifies his own action to the Queen and is excused. On the day set for her execution, Mary goes with dignity to her death on the scaffold.

Marinetti, Filippo Tommaso (1878-   ). See *Futurist Manifesto of 1909*.

Marion DeLorme. Victor Hugo (French). Tragedy. 5 acts. 1831.

Marion De Lorme, a courtesan, falls deeply in love with Didier who knows nothing of her past. The affair ends tragically, however, with the intervention of an old lover, the Marquis de Soverney.

The play is noted for the skillfulness with which it is woven. Always behind the scenes, but dominating the action is the figure and will of the Cardinal Richelieu. Originally the play was forbidden by the Bourbon censors and had to wait until the revolution of 1830 overturned the Bourbon throne before it was produced.

Marionette Plays. Dramatic sketches and scenes performed by man-worked dolls. The voices are those of actors or puppeteers who are unseen by the audience. To all evidence they originated in the 13th century and performances were given all through the middle ages. They were developed by Gordon Craig into an art form through the movement of richly dressed puppets in suggestive settings amid changing lights. Craig's theory was that the director must have absolute control of his stage, therefore there could be no living actors.

See *Puppet Show*.

Marlowe, Christopher (1564-1593). British dramatist and poet. Born at Canterbury, he became attached as playwright to Lord Admiral's company of players. Later he was introduced to the circle of Sir Walter Raleigh with whom he was accused of atheism in 1593. Shortly after he was killed in a tavern brawl.

He is considered the greatest pioneer in English literature and is credited with the introduction of true blank verse into drama. He is the author of the first great tragedy in English, *Tamburlaine the Great,* 1588; and the first great English historical drama, *Edward the Second.* Among his other well known plays are *Dr. Faustus* and *The Jew of Malta.*

Marlowe, Julia (Sarah Frances Frost) (1866-). American actress. Born near Keswick, Cumberland, she was taken to the United States as a child and made her New York debut in 1887. Her first appearance on any stage was in Vincennes, Indiana, October, 1878, under the name of Fanny Brough, in a juvenile *H.M.S. Pinafore* company. Later she turned to Shakespearean roles, her best known being Rosalind, Ophelia, Juliet and Beatrice. However she appeared with equal success in both Shakespearean and modern plays, and for many years held a high position on the American stage, especially after her marriage in 1911 to E. H. Sothern, the celebrated actor. She first visited England in 1907 and in 1926 presented, with her husband, a series of Shakespearean plays at Stratford-upon-Avon.

Marquis de Priola, The. Henri Lavedan (French). Drama. 5 acts. 1902.

The Marquis is a philanderer who is divorced by his wife but he still holds a spell over her. She interests him only when it becomes necessary to win her back. His protege, Pierre, who has been devoted to him, turns against him when he learns he is the illegitimate son of the marquis. As Pierre berates him for his debauchery, the Marquis suffers a stroke. A hopeless invalid, he is now forced to depend completely on the care of the son he had disgraced.

Marriage a la Mode. John Dryden (English). Comedy. 1672.

Rhodaphil and Doralia, having been married two years, find that the early rapture has worn off. Subscribing to the view that it is sheer hypocrisy to pretend, they unconsciously seek other company. It happens that Palamede, a friend of Rhodaphil's, after a long absence returns and falls in love with Doralia, ignorant of the fact that she is his friend's wife. Although he has been ordered by his father to marry Melantha, a girl infatuated with French words and fashion, he sternly refuses. Rhodaphil has now turned his attention to this very Melantha, not knowing her to be betrothed to Palamede. These intrigues go on apace with amusing amorous byplay until the friends discover that they are involved with each other's women. This leads to jealousy and quarrels. Rhodaphil feels that he has perhaps neglected and overlooked some hidden charm in his wife and Palamede feels that Melantha must have some attraction he has not noticed. They make up, deciding never again to interfere with other people's property.

Marriage of Figaro. Beaumarchais (French). Comedy. 1776.

Sequel to the *Barber of Seville*. Figaro, servant of Count Almaviva and Suzanne, waiting woman to the countess, are engaged to be married. The Count in promoting and paying the dowry demands a reward. He asks Suzanne to be secretly his mistress. She immediately confides this to Figaro and the Countess. They conspire to dupe him. They decide to dress Cherubin, a young susceptible adolescent, in Suzanne's clothes and then surprise them together. This plan is frustrated by the unexpected arrival of the Count. He doesn't know what is happening but he gets suspicious. The Countess decides to keep the rendezvous herself to win back the Count's love. Meanwhile, the Count has decided out of perversity to have Figaro marry Marceline. The basis of this choice is that Figaro has borrowed considerable money from her, promising marriage if he cannot repay her. Figaro cannot produce the money and it looks bad for him, especially since Marceline seems to be well along in years. It is soon discovered that not only is she old enough to be his mother but she *is* his mother. The plans for the marriage of Figaro to Suzanne are resumed and the Countess urges Suzanne to arrange a meeting (secretly) with the Count. Figaro, not told of this, spies on Suzanne. Then follows a series of recriminations, mistaken identity and comedy of errors situations. Everything is finally cleared up—the Count and Countess are reconciled, Figaro and Suzanne married—Figaro expounds on aristocratic hypocrisy and smugness, an important sidelight in a drama which preceded the revolution.

Marrying of Ann Leete. Harley Granville-Barker (English). Drama. 4 acts. 1916.

George Leete, son of a decadent Eighteenth Century family, marries a farmer's daughter, arousing the wrath of his relatives. Inspired by her brother's example, his sister, Ann, renounces her opportunity of a satisfactory marriage with Lord John Carp, and marries the gardener.

Mars, Mlle. (Anne Françoise Hippolyte Boutet) (1779-1847). French actress. She was born in Paris, and during the greater part of her career, was a member of the Comédie Française, creating between 1795 and 1839 no fewer than 109 roles there. An actress of great dramatic power, she was particularly famous for her interpretation of ingenue parts.

Marshall, Herbert Brough Falcon (1890-   ). English actor. Born in London, he made his first stage appearance at Buxton in 1911. He lost a leg in the First World War, but nevertheless returned successfully to the stage. His acting in such plays as *Aren't We All?* 1923; *The Pelican*, 1924; *Interference*, 1927; *Michael and Mary*, 1930; *Tomorrow And Tomorrow*, 1931; and *There's Always Juliet*, 1932, won him a great reputation. He began his equally successful film career in Hollywood in 1927. He married the actress, Edna Best, in 1928 (now divorced) and appeared with her on both stage and screen.

Marston, John (1575-1634). British dramatist and satirist. Educated at Oxford, he wrote two tragedies, *Antonio and Mellida; Antonio's Revenge,* 1602.

In 1604 appeared *The Malcontent;* 1605, *Eastward Ho* (on which he collaborated with Chapman and Jonson and for which he spent a short time in prison). Other of his plays are *The Dutch Courtezan,* 1605; *What You Will,* 1607. He gave up playwriting in 1607 and took holy orders.

Martin, John (1893-   ). American dance critic. Member of the faculty of the New School for Social Research; author of *The Modern Dance,* 1933; *America Dancing,* 1936; *Introduction to the dance,* 1939; contributor to the *Encyclopaedia of the Social Sciences,* the *National Encyclopedia,* and various magazines; lecturer both in the United States and Europe; present dance critic of the *New York Times.*

Martin, John E. (1770-1807). American actor. One of the first native actors to appear on the American stage. Appeared on March 13, 1790 in Home's tragedy *Douglas.*

Martin-Harvey, Sir John (1863-   ). English actor, manager. Born at Wyvenhoe, Essex, England, and though intended for his father's profession of naval architect, he studied for the stage, making his début at the Court Theatre in 1881. In the following year, he was engaged by Henry Irving, with whose company he remained until 1896, playing leading parts on tour. His first venture in management was at the Lyceum in 1899, where he produced *The Only Way,* the play in which, as Sidney Carton, he became famous. With a repertory company which included his wife, N. de Silva, he toured the British Isles, Canada, and the United States many times in this play, adding from time to time such romantic melodramas as *The Lyons Mail; The Corsican Brothers; The Bells; A Cigarette Maker's Romance; The Breed of the Treshams; The Last Heir; David Garrick; The King's Messenger;* and *The Burgomaster of Stilemonde.* Several of these were from Irving's repertory. Harvey may be said to have become in the popular mind the successor of Irving. He acted also in Shakespeare, notably as Hamlet and Richard III, and in a number of Shaw's plays—*The Shewing-Up of Blanco Posnet* and *The Devil's Disciple.* He was knighted in 1931.

Martinez de la Rosa, Francisco de (1787-1862). Spanish dramatist. A native of Granada; poet, novelist and dramatist, statesman; he suffered several years of exile because of his political views. His principal work was *La conjuracion de Venecia* (The Conspiracy of Venice), the first romantic drama presented in Spain (1834). With this, the author became the innovator of Romanticism in Spain.

Martinez Sierra, Gregorio (1881-   ). Spanish dramatist, novelist, poet. Born in Madrid, he began his literary career with writing prose and poetry, and not until later did he become known as a dramatist. He first collaborated with his friend Rusinol in a comedy *Life and Sweetness,* and began writing alone with *The Shadow of the Father* and *The Friend of the House.* In 1911 *The Cradle Song* attracted a good deal of attention. In 1916 he became director of the Eslava Theatre in Madrid and organized his own stock company. He is a very prolific author and has written in almost every dramatic form. Others of his better known plays are *The Two Shepherds; The Romantic Young Lady; The Lover; Madame Pepita; The Kingdom of God.*

Maruhonmono. A Kabuki play which features a young girl of high social position known as an *ohimesama,* comes under the calling of *Maruhonmono,* a form of musical drama performed by dolls and in Japanese drama created more than two hundred years ago.

Marxism in the theatre. The infiltration of Socialist or Communist doctrine, along the principles of the revolutionary social economist, Karl Marx, in the literature of the drama, and having as its foremost exponent, George Bernard Shaw, and such latter-day disciples as Ernst Toller, Clifford Odets, John Howard Lawson, W. H. Auden, Albert Maltz, George Sklar and Stephen Spender.

Mary Baker Eddy. Ernst Toller (German). Drama. 5 acts. 1935. Translated by Edward Crankshaw.

This biographical play is an unsympathetic study of the life of the famous healer. Mary Baker is introduced to Quimby, a hypnotist and mental cure-all, and adopts Quimby's philosophy. Later she abandons Quimby and goes on alone until she meets Eddy, who becomes the pupil. She fights her way to the top and acquires a vast following. Eddy's death, because of lack of proper medical care, and her own failure are carefully kept from the public.

Mary Magdalene. Anonymous (English). Drama. 51 scenes. 15th century.

A late miracle play, which combines material from the old saints' legends with material borrowed from contemporary moralities. It has Biblical characters such as Jesus and Herod; legendary characters such as the King and Queen of Marsylle; abstractions such as Wrath and Lechery. Some of its many scenes show the resurrection of Lazarus; the pagan ritual in the temple of Marsylle; the conversion to Christianity of the country's King and Queen; the miraculous childbirth and death of the Queen; her resurrection; the assumption of the Magdalene. Comic scenes are scattered through those showing Mary Magdalene's progress from degradation to salvation.

Mary of Scotland. Maxwell Anderson (American). Drama. 3 acts. 1933.

Mary of Scotland arrives to rule her country. She is met by the Earl of Bothwell, a blunt, brave and loyal admirer. Queen Elizabeth, reigning in England, fears Mary —she knows that with her beauty and legitimate claim on the throne of England she constitutes a menace to Elizabeth's safety. Elizabeth plots to dethrone her without the expense of a war. She will use women's weapons, scandal, intrigue, spying. Elizabeth, by objecting, throws Mary into the arms of the Catholic Darnley, a weak stupid man. In the second act, Mary expects an heir to the throne and Darnley has proved to be a boor and a drunkard. Then the Earls of Scotland have Darnley murdered and Bothwell returns from exile. Elizabeth lets the earls know she approves the marriage of Mary and Bothwell so that she may better spread the rumor of the queen's perfidy and Bothwell's murderous treachery. Elizabeth's plan works. Knox, the fanatical anti-Catholic rouses the army against Mary and they deliver her to the Earls. They hold her captive. Bothwell offers to leave the kingdom and give up his earldom providing the queen's powers remain intact. The earls agree. Bothwell escapes but Mary is held captive. She escapes to England for aid and is held captive there. Elizabeth finally comes to see Mary and asks her to abdicate in favor of her son. Mary begins to see the hand of Elizabeth in everything that has happened to her. Elizabeth admits that she feared her from the first and had to destroy her to win. Mary refuses to abdicate though she rot in her cell and tells the Queen that she, Mary, has been victorious as a woman, for she lived and loved and bore a child but that Elizabeth has only schemed and hated and has borne no heir.

Mary Rose. Sir J. M. Barrie. Fantasy. 1920.

Mary Rose, the only daughter of Mr. and Mrs. Moreland, has been asked in marriage by Simon Blake, a young midshipman. The parents consent but tell him that some years ago when Mr. Morland was on a fishing trip he left Mary Rose on an island called "The Island that likes to be visited." When they came to pick her up she had disappeared and did not reappear until thirty days had passed. She apparently remembered nothing that happened and the parents never told her. Simon and Mary Rose marry and have a baby, Harry. They revisit the island on a picnic and Mary Rose vanishes again. Twenty-five years elapse. Harry has grown up and runs away to sea and Simon is an established captain. A telegram announces that Mary Rose has returned. When she arrives she is still twenty-three and asks for her baby. She cannot understand why everyone is so old. She is shocked to discover what has happened and the assumption is that the shock kills her. After the great war Harry returns to his old deserted home in London. He looks into his small room and finds Mary Rose. He takes her in his arms and then takes her on his knee. This breaks the spell of her peculiar thralldom as she had always wished for the moment when her son would be big enough to hold her as she had held him. The island beckons to her again and she goes—this time never to return.

Mary Stuart. John Drinkwater (English). Drama. 2 acts. 1921.

The play opens with a modern scene in which a young husband is telling a friend that his wife, although she loves him, seems to love many others as well. The next scene goes back to the time of Mary, Queen of Scots, who is just such a woman. She craves strength, beauty and passion and unable to find them in one person, has many lovers. She is not fickle, but simply has ideals too high for one person to attain.

Mascara. Used for coloring of eyelashes, eyebrows and touching up the hair.

Masefield, John (1878-). British playwright and novelist. At the age of fourteen he ran away to sea, and went to America where he had several odd jobs. He returned to England to become a journalist, then settled in London to write verse. Among the many plays he has written are *The Tragedy of Nan; The Tragedy* *of Pompey the Great; Good Friday; The Daffodil Fields; Reynard the Fox; Melloney Holtspur;* etc. His plays are diverse in style, including tragedy, poetic fantasies, mysticism as well as realism. He has been poet laureate of England since 1930.

Mask and the Face, The. Luigi Chiarelli (Italian). Comedy. 3 acts. 1915.

The first of the plays to be written in the manner of the modern Italian "Grotesque" school. It satirizes conventional views on marital fidelity.

When Count Paolo Grazia learns his wife has been unfaithful, he orders her to leave the country and informs the police he has killed her. During her supposed funeral, the Countess returns and again the Count is unable to punish her. The play ends with their reconciliation.

Mask and Wig Club. Theatrical organization at the University of Pennsylvania. Founded in the spring of 1889 by the undergraduates of the University. Plays are acted by the students and are restricted to musicals. First production *Lurline,* 1889.

Masks, in ancient Greek theatre. Greatest characteristic of Greek tragic actor, rendering indication of age, station and prevalent mood. Derived from religious ceremonies. Made of linen, cork, or wood. In *tragedy:* thirty masks described in the *Onomastikon* of Pollux, among which are: six men, eight young men, three servants, eleven women. In *comedy:* nine old men, eleven young men, seven servants, seventeen women.

See also *Comedy, Greek; Satyr plays.*

Masks, in ancient Roman theatre. Originally not used, but later became routine accoutrement of actor; sometimes natural, sometimes highly exaggerated. White hair, symbol of age; black hair, youth; red hair, slaves.

Masks, in the commedia dell'arte. See specific stock characters, such as *Harlequin, Brighella,* the *dottore, etc.*

Masks, manitou. Manitou signifies to the American Indian a spirit or a being with supernatural power. A manitou mask, grotesquely carved, worn by medicine men in ceremonial dances, gives them power over the devils of disease.

Masque. An early dramatic presentation in which actors impersonated mythological deities, shepherdesses, or like characters, or personified popular virtues. Four settings used: (1) the *Hôtel de Bourgogne decór simultainé;* (2) the triangular machine or *scaena versilis* (the Greek *periaktoi*); (3) the two-sided and stationary flats with movable shutters at the back; (4) the completely movable series of flats and shutters—the final evolution of the *scaena ductilis.* Masques came into greatest use in the 17th century, in the courts of James I and Charles I, thereafter becoming identified as special court entertainment. They were presented by members of the court themselves and had as their central feature an elaborate dance, which members of the audience were invited to join. Ben Jonson was the most successful and prolific creator of masques. Shakespeare introduced examples of the type into *Love's Labour Lost, A Midsummer Night's Dream; Timon of Athens; Henry VIII;* and *The Tempest.* The masque is said to have had its origin in the *disguisings,* or the pleasure boats of the royalty.

Masque, The. Henry Bataille (French). Drama. 3 acts. 1902.

A neglected wife, out of consideration for her husband, justifies their separation by pretending to be unfaithful. Her departure, however, revives his interest, and her continued devotion finally leads to a reconciliation.

Masque of Kings, The. Maxwell Anderson (American). Poetic drama. 3 acts. Printed 1937.

A dramatization of the Mayerling tragedy when Crown Prince Rudolph of Austria and Baroness Mary Vetsera were found shot to death in a hunting lodge. In the play, Crown Prince Rudolph is a liberal who joins a revolt against the tyranny of his father, but accepts defeat rather than resort to a purge and the endless brutality necessary to hold his power.

Massemensch (Man and the Masses). Ernst Toller (German). Drama. 7 scenes. 1921.

An attack on war and on mechanical civilization. The principal figure is a woman who leads a rebellion against the war which the State is waging. She wants to set free all the slaves working in the coal-mines and munition factories. Her revolt is too successful. The rebels, intoxicated by their victory, want to start another war—against the State itself. The woman pleads with them to desist, but in vain. When the rebellion is finally crushed, the woman herself is made the scapegoat and is sentenced to execution.

Massey, Raymond (1896-   ). Canadian-American actor. Born at Toronto, he became an outstanding actor first in sinister and neurotic parts, notably in a revival of *The Constant Nymph,* 1928; *Spread Eagle,* 1928; *Late Night Final,* 1931; *The Rats of Norway,* 1933. He was also an accomplished light comedy actor, as was shown in *The Second Man,* 1928; *The Man in Possession,* 1930; and *Never Come Back,* 1932. In 1938-39 he gave one of the finest character portrayals in recent times when he played Lincoln in *Abe Lincoln in Illinois.* He also produced a number of plays of the Everyman Theatre.

Massinger, Philip (1593-1640). British dramatist. Born at Salisbury, he went to Oxford for a short while and soon earned a reputation as a playwright. He was a voluminous writer and a lot of his work was done in collaboration with Beaumont, Dekker and Fletcher. It is believed that a number of his plays were lost in the 18th century when they were accidentally burned. Two of his best satirical comedies are *A New Way to Pay Old Debts,* 1625; *The City Madam,* 1632. Others of his plays are *The Duke of Milan,* 1618; *The Maid of Honour,* 1621.

Master. Master switch on switchboard; controls every circuit on stage; thus all lights can be put on or off at once.

The Master Builder. Henrik Ibsen (Norwegian). Drama. 5 acts. 1892.

Solness, the Master builder, has won success at the expense of his wife and business associates. His conscience finally bothers him when he realizes that to better himself he has been unduly unjust to old Brovik and his son, has captured the affections of the latter's sweetheart and that he has willed the destruction of his wife's mansion, the burning of which has caused the death of his own children. Superstitious, he feels the Higher Powers are mocking him in giving him success at the cost of his happiness. Hilda Wangel personifying the younger generation, persuades him to be valiant and change his attitude towards the Broviks. So inspired, Solness goes up to the tower on his own new house and falls to death.

Master of ceremonies. The director, head or manager and introducer of other actors and acts of a variety program. An American development of the English Chairman of the music halls; the *compère* of the *pierrot* troupes.

See *Commentator*.

Master of Revels. This title was conferred on the stage censor. Sir Henry Herbert was Master of the Revels during the Restoration period. In 1737 the Licensing Act abolished this office. In the matter of censorship, Sir Herbert was a mere figurehead, his attempts at enforcing his power having come to nothing after much quarreling with D'Avenant, who persistently ignored Herbert, claiming his authority came from the king in stage matters.

See *Censorship; Commentator*.

Maternity. Eugene Brieux (French). Drama. 4 acts. 1903.

A petty government official preaches the importance of an increased birth rate for France. He himself demands a child of his wife every year but he condemns women who bear illegitimate children. He sends from his house his young sister-in-law whose lover refuses to marry her. The girl, despairing over the disgrace, goes to a quack and dies. The rest of the play is taken up with the trial of the quack who argues in favor of birth control and indulgence to unmarried mothers.

Matinee idols. Term applied to male actors who through personal charm, physical beauty and acting ability have a great audience following, especially of female admirers.

Matthews, Charles James (1803-1878). English light comedian. It was said of him that "when he imitated characters he not only copied their outward man, but seemed to take upon himself, for the time being, their own individuality." The son of Charles Matthews, he made an amateur appearance in London, April 26, 1822, playing two parts, under two separate names, one as M. Perlet, a well known French actor, and the other under his own. He lived in Italy for a time and wrote several little farces, acting as a Prince Charming at the homes of the great, and doing little work. He made his professional debut at the Olympic, November 6, 1835, in *The Old and Young Stager*. He played more than two hundred roles, but always played himself. He made his debut in America before an audience made up mostly of men, the results of false reports which labeled him anti-American and ready to insult the Americans from the stage. On his return to England, he met with many personal and financial losses. A second tour of America netted him box office successes, and while in this country he married Mrs. Davenport, an excellent actress. They appeared together in a series of entertainments at the Bijou Theatre, called *Mr. and Mrs. Matthews at Home*.

Matthews, James Brander (1852-1929). American author and educator. Born in New Orleans, graduated from Columbia University, 1871. He taught at Columbia 1891-1924 holding chairs of English and dramatic literature. He held a famous "Sunday Night Salon" for many years. He was founder of several clubs (Authors, Players) and was chancellor of the American Academy of Arts and Letters. He contributed his dramatic data and books to Columbia. Among his books are *The Development of Drama, Studies of the Stage, Molière, Shakespeare as Playwright, Principles of Playmaking, Essays on English*. He wrote several plays.

Maugham, William Somerset (1874-   ). English novelist, playwright and short story writer. Educated at Heidelberg University and St. Thomas' Hospital. He studied medicine but never practiced it, although he utilized his knowledge of medicine in two of his novels, *Liza of Lambeth,* 1897, and *Of Human Bondage,* 1916. He served in the secret service during the World War, later writing *Ashenden,* based on these experiences. He wrote, 1917, *Our Betters,* a brilliant theatrical gem, witty, cynical, daring and very successful. One of his short stories was dramatized as *Rain,* 1921. In 1922, he wrote *East of Suez. The Letter* and *The Constant Wife,* 1927, were patterned after the Restoration *Comedy of Manners,* tinged with a slight underplaying of the importance of love. All of his writings have extreme dramatic qualities. He cannot be identified as belonging to any particular school because of his versatility, but in the theatre he strives for naturalism. He himself has said "the foundation of living drama is actuality."

Mavor, Osborne Henry. See *Bridie, James*.

Maya. Simon Gantillon (French). Drama. 3 acts. 1927.
A symbolical study of a Marseilles prostitute. It had a successful run in Paris, but the District Attorney stopped the New York production after the play had been given for fifteen performances in an adaptation by Ernest Boyd in 1928.
Maya lives in Marseilles in the quarter reserved for ladies who sell love at a low price. As presented by the playwright she is not a tawdy waterfront prostitute. Instead, as her name suggests, she is a sort of earth mother bearing comfort and escape to men. For each man she is a reflection of his own desires; each sees in her the woman he adores. In successive scenes her visitors make love to her or, in some cases,

simply pour out their hearts to her. Since she lives in a port where ships from many lands dock, most of her callers are far from home and lonely. A Norwegian finds in her the blue-eyed freshness of a girl from his own North woods; to another she gives the affection of a mother; to still others she represents the romance for which they yearn and which they have somehow missed as they sailed the seven seas. At the end Maya has no clearly defined personality of her own; she is, like Pirandello's hero, what men have desired her to be.

Mayo, Margaret (Lilian Clatten) (1882-   ). American author, dramatist, actress. Born in Illinois; made her first appearance on the stage in *Thoroughbred,* 1896; toured in *Charley's Aunt* and *Secret Service;* played in *Because She Loved Him So* and *Pretty Peggy* and toured in *Arizona.* In 1903 she retired from the stage and devoted her time to writing. The plays she has written include: *Baby Mine; Under Two Flags; The Jungle; The Marriage of William Ashe;* etc.

McCarthy, Lillah (1875-   ). English actress. Born at Cheltenham, she made her stage debut in 1895. Her reputation as a dramatic actress was established by her performances in *The Sign of the Cross,* and later in many of the plays of Shakespeare, Bernard Shaw, Galsworthy, and others.

McClendon, Rose (1885-1936). American actress. She was the most distinguished negro actress in America. She appeared in: *Deep River,* 1926; *In Abraham's Bosom,* December, 1926, at the Provincetown Playhouse; *Porgy,* 1927; *The House of Connelly* (first play of the Group Theatre), 1931; *Never No More,* January, 1932; *Black Souls,* March, 1932; *Roll, Sweet Chariot,* 1934; *Panic,* 1935; *Mulatto,* 1935-36. Illness forced her out of the cast of *Mulatto* in 1936.

The Rose McClendon Players, under the direction of Dick Campbell, were organized as a memorial to her in 1937.

See also *Hedgerow Theatre; Theatre Union; Negro, American, his relation to the stage.*

McClintic, Guthrie (1893-   ). American producer, actor, manager. Born in Seattle, Washington. Acted in various Broadway productions. In 1918 was with Jessie Bonstelle in Buffalo. Became assistant stage manager to Winthrop Ames and then became an independent producer. Among the plays he produced are *The Dover Road,* 1921; *The Way Things Happen,* 1924; *The Green Hat,* 1925; *Shanghai Gesture,* 1926. In 1927, appointed director of the Actor's Theatre and produced *Saturday's Children.* For Gilbert Miller, he produced *The Age of Innocence* and *Dishonored Lady.* For his wife, Katharine Cornell, he staged *The Letter* (Messmore Kendall was the producer), *The Barretts of Wimpole Street, Lucrece, Alien Corn, Romeo and Juliet, Saint Joan, Candida, The Wingless Victory,* and *No Time for Comedy* (produced in association with the Playwrights' Company). On his own, he has produced among others, *Yellow Jack, The Old Maid, Winterset, High Tor, Parnell, The Star-Wagon, Missouri Legend.*

McCullough, John Edward (1837-1885). Irish-American actor. Came to the United States in 1847; made his American stage debut in 1857 in *The Belle's Strata-*

gem; he supported Edwin Booth and also Edwin Forrest; then became manager of the California Theatre. He toured throughout the country in such roles as Richelieu, Richard III, Othello, Lear, Iago.

McIntyre and Heath (James McIntyre and Thomas Heath). American actors. Famous minstrels, vaudeville headliners and later musical comedy stars. Formed their partnership in 1874 and continued till 1934. The *Ham Tree* was the most successful of the vehicles used by the pair. They were reunited briefly in minstrel shows in 1934 and 1935. McIntyre died August 18, 1937; Heath died August 19, 1938.

Measure for Measure. William Shakespeare (English). Tragedy. 5 acts. Printed 1623.

The source is a tale by Cinthio, adapted into English in both dramatic and prose forms by George Whetstone, in his *Promos and Cassandra* and *Heptameron of Civil Discourses,* respectively. Mariana is Shakespeare's addition to the story.

Angelo, deputy in the absence of Vincentio, Duke of Vienna, imprisons Claudio on charges of immoral conduct. He offers to release Claudio if Isabella, the youth's sister, will keep a rendezvous with him. Isabella agrees, but sends Mariana in her place, and although Angelo is none the wiser, he does not keep his promise. He asserts that he has had Claudio executed, and produces the head of another criminal which Isabella believes to be that of her brother. At this point the rightful Duke, who has watched the proceedings from behind a disguise, intervenes. He sentences Angelo to death, but Isabella pleads for mercy, and when Claudio is produced unharmed, Angelo is released and betrothed to Mariana.

Mechane. A stage device used in the ancient Hellenistic and Graeco-Roman theatres: the hook and pulley set at the top of the *skene* by which divinities could be raised or lowered; means, literally, machine.

Medea. Euripedes (Greek). Tragedy. 431 B.C.

Creon, King of Corinth, urges Jason to get rid of his wife, Medea, so that Jason can be his son-in-law. Jason consents and Medea, ordered to exile, is allowed one day of grace to make arrangements for her children. Outraged, she plans her revenge. She sends her children to carry to the new bride a gift steeped in poison. The bride dies together with her father who has tried to save her. Medea then kills her two children and Jason finds her laughing over their bodies. Realizing she will never know happiness again, she departs in her dragon chariot.

Médecin Malgré Lui, Le. See *Doctor In Spite of Himself, The.*

Medicine man. Held street corner shows and put on performances of magic, songs and story as a free come-on to selling patent medicine. Method said to have its origin in the *commedia dell' arte* open air performance.

Mei Lan-fang (1894-   ). Chinese actor. Born 1894, Peiping. Father and grandfather were famous actors before him. Debut at thirteen as a female impersonator. Acclaimed "King of Actors" and "Foremost of the Pear Orchard" through a popularity contest. He is well versed in the old literature of China and this knowledge helped him to restore the long-forgotten dance to its former importance in the drama in spite of great opposition by Chinese fundamentalists. At the age of twenty-five he was engaged by the Japanese Imperial Theatre—the first time in Chinese history that a Chinese actor had appeared on a foreign stage. Later played in England and successfully toured the United States in 1930. Appeared in Moscow and Leningrad in 1935.

His repertoire consists of over 400 plays of which about one-third are his own production. His wardrobe and ornaments are valued at over $100,000. He designs his own costumes.

Mei Lan-fang's gestures and actions on stage are of great beauty and refinement; his every pose is a perfect picture. His dances, tied up in form and symbolism, are in no sense impeded thereby but show remarkable adroitness, skill, and grace, and contain a clarity and persuasion which can not be approached on the more naturalistic and cruder Western stage. He possesses a clear, penetrating singing voice and his stage presence is at once gentle and very dignified. He always takes female roles (for women were long barred from the Chinese stage); in these he is the idol of 500 million souls. The feminine side glance, the smile, the dainty, tripping walk—all are most carefully studied. Though at the height of his success, he continues to study his art.

He is a collector of old books on music and dancing.

Meiningen Company. The name given the court players of the Duke of Saxe-Meiningen, who in Berlin, 1874, put on *Julius Caesar* in a production that fully realized the aims of the writer; every device of dramatic art and modern stage technique was used to make these aims supreme; began conscientious observance of scenery costume and mass movement in the German theatre. The Meiningen group provided individual plays with these requisites; drove out the star system; travelled throughout Germany from 1874-90 giving 2591 performancees, including modern writers in their repertoire, such as Ibsen, Björnsen. They travelled in Russia and were thus indirectly responsible for the Moscow Art Theatre.

See also *Saxe-Meiningen, George II, Duke of.*

Melloney Holtspur. John Masefield (English). Drama. 4 acts. 1922.

A curious fantasy in which ghosts and living people share the stage with one another, with the ghosts acting as the dei ex machina. The scene is Holtspur House, and the phantoms are those people who walked through its halls twenty-two years previously. At that time young Melloney Holtspur was very much in love with Lonny Copshrews. Lonny was a talented painter and a fascinating charmer, but a faithless and philandering lover. Unknown to Melloney, he had had affairs with any number of local servant girls and village maidens. Althuogh not fundamentally dishonest, he had also stolen the Holtspur family jewels when in a jam. And he had married a Frenchwoman in Paris by whom he had had a child. When Melloney found out, she died of a broken heart. In the meantime Lonny had destroyed some of his most valuable drawings and gone off to the Isles of Greece.

Twenty-two years later, Melloney's nephew Bunny Mento is in love with Lonny's daughter Lenda. Bunny's mother has never forgiven Lonny for breaking her sister's heart, and wishes to prevent her from marrying Bunny. In this she is abetted by Melloney's ghost, who seeks to revenge herself on Lonny by ruining his daughter's life. When Lenda is ready to give Bunny up, the jewels are found in a suit of armor, where Lonny placed them when he returned them to the house. Then some of the dead painter's mistresses appear in phantom form to plead his case. And Melloney forgives him, and allows the young lovers to wed.

Melodrama. A form of drama, originally with songs. It originated in France, became important in Italy in the 18th century, especially as popularized by Metastasis. It was also popular in England and in the U. S. *A Tale of Mystery* is an English example and *After Dark* is a later American example. Latterly, however, the term is applied to an exaggerated, romantic, exciting and improbable play without music. Incident and situation are important, characterization is not.

Melodrama, Drury Lane. Sensational melodrama similar to that offered by Dion Boucicault at the Adelphi Theatre; deep-dyed villainy, but happy endings with the hero victorious. Thrills, scenery and plots were especially written to suit the vast stage.

Melopoeia. Greek term used by Aristotle in his *Poetics*, meaning the making, composition of melody or music.

Mémoire de plusieurs decorations qui servi aux piece contenus en ce present livre (1673 or 1678).

Begun by Laurent Mahelot and completed by his successor, Michel Laurent. The book, according to E. K. Chambers, is "One of the most valuable documents of theatrical history which the hazard of time has preserved in any land. It treats of the scenery and staging of the plays of the *Comédiens du Roi,* and contains notes of the scenery required for seventy-one plays in the theatre's repertory—in forty-seven cases, drawings, showing the way in which the requirements were to be met.

See also *Mahelot, Laurent.*

Menace. An antagonistic force in the drama; overshadowing evil; considered a necessary plot ingredient.

Menaechmi. Plautus (Roman). Comedy. c. 200 B.C.

Two twins have been separated in childhood. Menaechmus was stolen from his family and found his way to Epidamnum, where he lives with his wife. Sosicles was renamed Manaechmus after his lost brother and raised by his family. He has been searching the world for his twin, and finally arrives in Epidamnum. The mistakes resulting from the resemblance of the two Manaechmi make a side-splitting farce. The stranger in town is offered hospitality by his brother's mistress, reprimanded by his brother's wife for his infidelity, and chided by his brother's parasite for failing to recognize him. When he sees them all so perturbed at his non-recognition of them, he feigns madness to get rid of them. The doctor is summoned, and captures the brother, who is rescued by Sosicles' servant. The whole town is about to go crazy when the brothers finally meet and find they are long-lost twins.

This comedy probably suggested Shakespeare's *A Comedy of Errors.*

Menander (342-291 B.C.). Greek dramatist. A native of Athens, he is said to have written 105 comedies of manners and everyday life. Only fragments of his works were known until the 20th century when more than a thousand lines from his plays were brought to light in Egypt. Among his works are *Andria and Perinthia; Eunochos and Kolax; Adelphor.*

Mencken, Henry Louis (1880-). American author, editor and critic. Born in Baltimore, he embarked on a journalistic career. From 1914 to 1923 he was co-editor of the *Smart Set,* and from 1925-33 he was editor of the *American Mercury.* He is noted for his pungent criticisms which served to stimulate American writers to a broader view and toward a more sophisticated and vital literature. Among his works are *George Bernard Shaw; His Plays,* 1905; *The Artist* (play), 1912; *The American Language; In Defence of Women,* 1917; *Treatise on the Gods,* 1931.

Men In White. Sidney S. Kingsley (American). Drama. 3 acts. 1933.

Dr. George Ferguson, interne in a great hospital, is forced to choose between marriage with the prospect of a comfortable practice, and his desire to become a surgeon. The death of a young nurse who has comforted him brings Ferguson closer to humanity, and he leaves for Vienna to study surgery.

This play had instantaneous success and was the Pulitzer Prize play for 1933-34.

Menken, Adah Isaacs (Real name: Dolores Adios Fuertos) (1835-1868). American actress. Began her professional career as a child actress, created the role of Mazeppa in the play of the same name, and started the Mazeppa craze throughout the country by appearing half-nude, strapped to the side of a running horse. Her subsequent career was sensational and covered two continents.

In 1868, while rehearsing in Paris, she was taken violently ill. When she did not report to her producer for several weeks, the management went to court to compel her to return to the cast. But when officers forced their way into her apartment, they found her lying dead.

Menken, Helen (1901-). American actress. Made her first appearance at Astor Theatre, New York, in *A Midsummer Night's Dream,* 1906. Next she played in *Humpty-Dumpty; The Pied Piper of Hamelin,* 1908; *Mr. Hamlet of Broadway,* 1909; *The Silver Star,* 1910; *Sinners,* 1915; *Major Pendennis,* 1916; *Parlour, Bedroom and Bath,* 1918; *Three Wise Fools,* 1921; *Seventh Heaven,* 1926; *The Captive,* 1926; *The Beaux Stratagem,* 1928; *Congai,* 1929; *Mary of Scotland,* 1933; *The Old Maid,* 1935. She produced and appeared in *Saint Wench* in 1933.

Merchant of Venice, The. William Shakespeare (English). Comedy. 5 acts. 1597.

Published in quarto form in 1598. The "pound of flesh" plot comes from *Il Pecorone* by Giovanni Fiorentine, 1558, and the casket story from Boccaccio's *Decamerone*. To help his friend Bassanio in his suit for the hand of Portia, Antonio arranges a loan from Shylock, a Jew, promising to forfeit a pound of flesh if the money is not repaid at a certain date. Bassanio wins Portia, but the vessels which Antonio was counting on to return with the money are reported lost, and Shylock claims the pound of flesh from Antonio. Portia, disguised as a lawyer, appears at the trial, argues that Shylock can have the flesh, but must not shed a drop of blood, and thereby saves Antonio's life. In return for her services Portia, still in disguise, demands and receives from Bassanio a ring which, as Portia, she had made him promise he would never relinquish. Then, as Portia, she upbraids him for parting with the ring, but finally reveals the true situation and forgives him.

Merchants of Glory. Marcel Pagnol and Paul Nivoix (French). Drama. 3 acts. 1925.

A father whose son is supposed to have died on the battlefield a hero is very upset to have the son turn up alive. For the father is running for a political office on the strength of his son's record and the son's wife is happily remarried. The returned soldier is induced to keep under cover until after the election, but later demands recognition. For the sake of others, however, he is persuaded to assume a different identity and act as secretary to his father, now a cabinet minister. At the close of the play, all bow in respect to the idealized hero, unaware that the humble original stands among them.

Mercury Theatre. See *Welles, Orson.*

Meredith, Burgess (1911-   ). American actor. His stage training started in 1929, when he entered the apprentice group at Eva LeGallienne's Civic Repertory Theatre. In 1932 he appeared in the disguise of the Duck with Miss LeGallienne in *Alice in Wonderland,* also contriving to be the Dormouse and Tweedledee. Summer theatres gave him opportunities when he could find none in New York. In 1933, he played Marchbanks to five Candidas in various rural localities. The Broadway role which really gave him his start was in *She Loves Me Not.* Other plays in which he has appeared are *Flowers of the Forest* (with Katharine Cornell); *Winterset,* 1935; *High Tor; The Star-Wagon.* He has also appeared in motion pictures.

Meres, Francis (1565-1647). English author. English divine and author whose *Palladis Tamia,* 1598, contains some of the earliest references to Shakespeare and his works.

Merivale, Philip (1886-   ). English actor. Born in India, attended St. Edwards school at Oxford. Went on the stage in England in 1905. Came to America in 1914 with Mrs. Patrick Campbell and appeared in *Pygmalion.* In 1919 he toured with George Arliss, played in *The Merchant of Venice,* 1922, and in *The Swan,* 1923. Appeared in *The Road to Rome, Death Takes a Holiday, Cynara, Mary of Scotland, Valley Forge, Othello, Macbeth* and many other roles.

Mérope. François Marie Arouet de Voltaire (French). Tragedy. 5 acts. 1748.

After many years, Aepytus, rightful heir to the throne of Massenia, returns to his native land and slays Polyphontes, his father's murderer and usurper of the crown. In this work, Voltaire carried out his belief that a love interest must either be the very soul of the piece or must be excluded entirely. Although he takes credit for excluding it from the play, the fact remains that the audience's emotional interest finds, as a main theme, Mérope's great love for her son, and the tragic situation in which mother and son are placed.

Merrily We Roll Along. George S. Kaufman and Moss Hart (American). Drama. 3 acts. 1934.

The story of the decline of Richard Niles is told in reverse. Thus the play begins in 1934, when he is a fashionable playwright, but one who has sold his birthright for a mess of pottage. His Long Island home is luxurious, his latest play a hit, the guests at his opening night party the pick of café society. But as his wife, Althea Royce, a slightly passé actress, tells him, he is nonetheless a "money-loving, social-climbing, second-rate hack." Niles' one remaining friend of his younger days, Julia Glenn, is even more disgusted to see what he has become. In fact, she gets drunk, makes a show of herself, and has to be escorted from the party. After most of the guests have gone, Althea accuses Richard of having an affair with Ivy Carroll, glamorous leading lady in his new play, and throws iodine in the young actress' face.

1927. A stylish restaurant. Althea Royce, a popular star, is meeting Richard, her new husband. Julia Glenn and Jonathan Crale enter. Crale is a painter, sloppily dressed but with a sympathetic and vivid personality, in love with Julia. He wishes to apologize to Richard for the unflattering portrait he has painted of him. Instead of listening to his apology, Richard strikes him.

1926. Richard is recently divorced; he has a five-year-old son. His friend Crale accuses him of being untrue to his ideals and turning out carbon-copy plays. He also advises Richard to give up Althea, tells the playwright Julia has always loved him. Althea arrives. She has just told her faithful husband she intends to divorce him, and he has shot himself. Richard comforts her.

1925. Julia and Crale buoyantly prepare to welcome Richard home from a yacht trip. But Richard, when he puts in an appearance, stays only long enough to inform them that he won't be living with Crale any more and that he has given up the serious play on which he was working to do a farce.

1924. Richard obtains his divorce. Julia and Crale suggest that he go off on a yacht trip, thus paving the way for his change of spirit.

1923. Althea is giving a party to celebrate her opening in Richard's latest play. Richard comes with his wife, a sweet, clinging-vine sort of woman, and the star flirts with him outrageously.

1922. Richard, a struggling playwright, is living with his wife's family. Julia and Crale are his buddies. His first play has been produced in Provincetown.

1918. Richard, very young, very sweet, very idealistic, is courting Helen.

1916. The scene is a college chapel. Richard is delivering the valedictory address, concluding with the quotation from Polonius: "This above all, to thine own self be true . . ."

The Merry Death. Nikolai Evreinov (Russian). Harlequinade. 1914.

Harlequin is destined to die at midnight. He has stolen the affections of Pierrot's wife, Columbine, and when Pierrot seeks revenge, argues that to do so is foolish. Pierrot agrees and decides to be gay and play for Columbine and Harlequin to dance. Since Harlequin is supposed to die on the day he sleeps longer than revels, in vain he tries to turn back the clock, etc., but he is doomed. In the midst of the revelry, Death appears in guise of a lovely woman. Harlequin welcomes her and hands her a lamp which flickers and goes out. Pierrot announces the end of the play.

Merry Devil of Edmonton, The. A comedy written about 1607, printed 1608, and attributed to Shakespeare by a book-dealer in 1633. The play has a joyous vitality, hearty humor and occasional graceful charm, but its complete dissimilarity to unquestioned Shakespearean works has led critics to deny his authorship in this case. The farcical actions concern a trick by which the hero, Peter Fabel, discomfits an unkind father.

Merry-merry. The chorus.

Merry Widow, The. Franz Lehar (Hungarian). Operetta. 1905.

As children, Sonia and Prince Danilo were in love, but she married someone else and Danilo swore never to have anything more to do with her. Sonia's husband dies, and, a gay and still young widow, she meets Danilo in Paris, where he is attached to the Marsovian embassy. Having made up his mind not to be twisted around the lady's finger again, he flirts with the pretty French girls and otherwise attempts to discourage her. But the widow has weapons of her own with which to counterattack, and men's minds, even as women's, are made for changing.

The charm of this operetta lies in its lively and lilting tunes, which have made it popular wherever light opera is sung. "The Merry Widow Waltz" is the most famous of its melodies. In the United States it has been given in English versions on both stage and screen, Jeanette MacDonald and Maurice Chevalier having acted in a recent film version. It was first seen on a New York stage in 1907, when a young singer named Donald Brian made his first striking success as Prince Danilo. In 1931 the operetta was revived, and the same actor appeared as its leading man.

Merry Wives of Windsor, The. William Shakespeare (English). Comedy. 5 acts. Printed 1602.

Written in 1600 and according to tradition, at the command of Queen Elizabeth, who wished to see Falstaff in love. There is no known source for the play. The action concerns Falstaff's advances to Mistresses Ford and Page and their devices to ridicule him. In his first rendezvous with Mistress Ford Falstaff is hurriedly carried out in a clothes basket and dumped into the river when Ford enters upon the scene. Undaunted, Falstaff makes a second appointment with Mistress Ford, and again Ford's entrance necessitates a hurried exit, this time in the disguise of an old woman. The ladies now reveal to their husbands their motives in entertaining Falstaff, and all join in the last plot to confound him. Disguised as fairies they pinch and taunt him. Finally revealing themselves, they mock, reproach, but finally pardon Falstaff. A sub-plot deals with the wooing of Anne Page by Slender, Sir Hugh Evans, Dr. Caius and Fenton, the last of whom wins her.

Merton of the Movies. George S. Kaufman and Marc Connelly (American). Comedy. 4 acts. Printed 1925.

Based on the novel of the same name by Harry Leon Wilson.

Merton Gill, serious young grocery clerk, leaves Simsbury, Illinois, for Hollywood, to become a great star. He succeeds, not as a matinee idol, but as a comedy cowboy in two-reel western travesties.

Metenier, Oscar (1859-1913). French novelist, dramatist. Once secretary to a commissioner of police, he brought to the theatre the underworld he knew at first hand. One of the French naturalistic school, his plays were tragedies of terror, and were produced at the Théâtre Libre. His plays include: *En famille,* 1887; *La Casserole,* 1889; *Les Frères Zemganno* (after Goncourt's novel), 1891; *Monsieur Betsy,* 1890, with Paul Alexis; *Très russe,* 1893, with Jean Lorrain; *Mademoiselle Fifi* (from Maupassant's book), 1896; *He* (Lui), 1898; *Son Poteau,* 1901. He founded, in 1897, the Grand Guignol, of which he remained director until 1899.

Meteor. S. N. Behrman (American). Comedy. 3 acts. 1929.

Raphael Lord marries the daughter of a famous psychologist whose work has inspired him with an indomitable determination. He has a quick rise to wealth and power in the world of high finance. When failure threatens him, his wife forsakes him, as do his friends because of his egotism. But he doesn't let that bother him, and at the end of the play is planning a new career.

Mexicana. The musical revue from Mexico produced in New York City in 1939; unique because it was sponsored by the Mexican government.

Meyerhold, Vsevolod Emilievich (1873-   ). Russian producer. He studied law and music, and for four years was an actor with the Moscow Art Theatre. After the Russo-Japanese War he left Stanislavsky and the Moscow Art Theatre in order to perform independently in southern Russia. In 1908 he became régisseur of the two imperial theatres, the Mariinsky for opera and the Alexandrinsky for drama. Influenced by the Chinese stage, the Italians and by Max Reinhardt, he regarded the theatre as a place of make-believe, and he no longer darkened the auditorium and threw the action of the play into a lighted picture frame. Rather, he preferred a stage projecting into the auditorium, and sometimes dispensed with a curtain.

Increasingly, he favored a bare setting with ladders, flights of steps, platforms at different levels, and machine-like appurtenances to express the new industrial civilization. In 1913 he published *The Theatre,* expounding his ideas on stagecraft. In 1918 he organized the theatre department of the People's Commissariat for Education and conducted a theatre of the Revolution at Moscow. He has adapted plays by Schiller and others to communistic ends. In 1923 appeared his play *The Death and Destruction of Europe* which he adapted from a German novel.

See also *Theatre, Russian 19th Century to the Revolution.*

Mezzanine. Sometimes the first balcony of a theatre having more than one; the first few rows of the balcony and separated from the balcony proper.

Mezzetino. Stock character in a *commedia dell' arte;* possibly associated with *Scapino.* Costume in early 17th Century, loose garments; in 18th Century, valet's clothing with red and white lace; possibly belonging to the *Pedrolino* (or *Pierrot*) class than to that of *Brighella* as, in Callot's designs earlier, he seems to be a fool.

See also *Scapino; Brighella; Pedrolino.*

Michael and his Lost Angel. Henry Arthur Jones (English). Drama. 5 acts. 1895.

Before his congregation, Michael, a clergyman, compels a girl to confess herself guilty of committing what he terms a sin of the flesh.

Later, Michael has the same experience, but holds no regret, and is far from penitent. However, Michael plays the part of a sinner and makes a confession before his congregation.

Michael and Mary. A. A. Milne (English). Drama. 3 acts. 1930.

Mary, deserted by her husband and contemplating suicide, is rescued by Michael, a young writer, who marries her. Several years later, when Michael is wealthy, Mary's lost husband returns to blackmail them. In a quarrel with Michael, he dies of a heart attack, and they are able to hide his identity from the police.

Michau. Stock character in the French theatre of the 17th Century; Huret's print shows resemblance to *Pantalone,* the stock character of the contemporary Italian *commedia dell' arte.*

Michel Auclair. Charles Vildrac (French). Drama. 3 acts. 1923.

Michel, a bookseller, returns to his home town after a year's absence to find his former sweetheart has married a stupid, dishonest soldier. Willing to sacrifice himself for the love of Suzanne, he studies the character of his rival and goes about making him over into a husband worthy of the girl.

Mid-Channel. Sir Arthur Pinero (English). Drama. 4 acts. 1909.

An uncompromising picture of the tragedy wrought by a selfish marriage.

Theodore and Zoe Blundell are a middle-class English couple who have been married for fourteen years. At the beginning they agreed to have no children. Now, grown fairly prosperous, without serious worries of any kind, they are both at loose ends. He has become jealous, tyrannical and surly. She is fascinating, and impulsive, and amuses herself by entertaining some of her husband's friends. He objects, and they quarrel until he leaves the house. Zoe is indiscreet enough to let one of his friends escort her through Italy. Their relationship is platonic until Zoe learns that Theodore has been flaunting a liaison with a shameless woman in London; then she has an affair with her guide. Both she and Theodore soon weary of sowing wild oats, however. He pays his mistress a large sum of money to get rid of her, and Zoe dismisses her lover. Husband and wife are together once more, ready for a reconciliation, when Theodore learns Zoe has been unfaithful. She is willing to forgive him his trespasses, but he will not overlook hers. Angrily, he tells her to divorce him and marry her lover. Equally furious, she goes to the young man to tell him she will be his wife. But he has become engaged to someone else in the meantime. Heartsick, realizing that children might have saved her from her present despair, Zoe jumps from a balcony and is killed.

Middleton, Thomas (1570-1627). English dramatist. Born in London, he became a playwright about 1600. He wrote alone as well as in collaboration with Dekker, Rowley and others. He was the author of many satirical and romantic comedies as well as tragedies. His best tragedy is *Women, Beware Women*. His satirical play, *A Game of Chess*, 1624, was an instant success. Others of this plays are: *A Mad World, My Masters*, 1608; *A Trick to Catch the Old One*, 1608; etc.

Midgets. Their part in the world of entertainment has been varied. In the medieval and Elizabethan periods they served as private entertainers in the capacity of jester and monstrosity. Victorian society admired General Tom Thumb. In the modern world they developed from side show freaks into vaudeville troupes. A recent Ziegfeld revue featured an entire group of them and the film, *The Wizard of Oz*, 1939, employed hundreds.

On the legitimate stage they frequently played child parts when children were not available or the Gerry Society forbade them to play. One of the most interesting midget roles Philip Barry provided recently in *Here Come the Clowns*. For interesting aspects of midgets read *Memoirs of a Midget* by Walter de la Mare. That they hold popular interest today is shown by the fact that Morris Gest had *Little Miracle Town* at the New York World's Fair of 1939.

Midsummer Night's Dream. William Shakespeare (English). Comedy. 5 acts. 1596.

Written about 1596, probably to celebrate a wedding at the court, and first published in quarto form in 1600. The scene is laid in Athens. Lysander and Demetrius love Hermia; Helena futilely loves Lysander, until Puck, servant to the fairy king Oberon, directs Lysander's love to Helena by means of a love potion. The same potion is used by Oberon to punish his queen, Titania, for her wandering affections; by means of the potion she is made to fall in love temporarily with Bottom, one of a troop of tradesmen who are preparing a play, *Piramus and Thisbe,* to celebrate the wedding of Theseus, Duke of Athens, to Hippolyta. By morning the spells wear off and the right relationships are restored.

Mielziner, Jo (1901-   ). American scene designer. Appeared as an actor in *The Failures,* 1923, and *Saint Joan,* 1923. Has designed the sets and costumes for many productions, beginning with *The Guardsman* in 1924. Some of his other shows include: *Anatol; Dodsworth; Yellow Jack; Winterset; Hamlet* (the John Gielgud production) ; *Pride and Prejudice; High Tor; On Borrowed Time;* etc.

The Mikado. W. S. Gilbert (English). Music by Sir Arthur Sullivan. Operetta in 2 acts. 1885.

Nanki-Poo, son of the Mikado of Japan runs away from court to escape from marrying the elderly ugly Katisha. He falls in love with Yum-Yum the ward of Ko-Ko, a tailor who has risen to the rank of Lord High Executioner. Yum-Yum returns Nanki-Poo's love but cannot marry him without Ko-Ko's permission. Ko-Ko refuses permission as he intends to marry Yum-Yum himself. However, he is warned by the Mikado that unless an execution takes place soon, the Mikado will have him beheaded. Nanki-Poo is about to commit suicide when Ko-Ko lets him marry Yum-Yum for one month on the condition that he be beheaded afterward. When the Mikado arrives the execution has not yet taken place, but all pretend that it has. When it later develops that the beheadee is the Mikado's son there are further complications, but all is finally resolved to the lovers' satisfaction.

Miles gloriosus. Name taken from the play *Miles Gloriosus* by Plautus to mean a certain type character in a *commedia dell' arte;* usually a boasting soldier; best typified by *Capitano,* the stock-character in a *commedia dell' arte.*

Milk it dry. To squeeze the utmost laughs out of a line or situation.

Milk jump. A town in the hinterlands reachable only by a difficult train-trip, often early in the morning.

Milky Way, The. Lynn Root and Harry Clork (American). Comedy. 3 acts. 1934.

In a street fight Burleigh Sullivan, a milkman, is erroneously credited with having knocked out Speed McFarland, middleweight champion; McFarland's manager trains Burleigh to fight the champion in the ring, which he does and wins.

Miller, Gilbert William (1884-   ). American producer. Son of Henry Miller. Born in New York City, but started producing in London. First production was *Daddy-long-legs,* 1919; *Monsieur Beaucaire, Peter Pan,* 1920; *Green Goddess,* 1924; *The Last of Mrs. Cheyney,* 1925; *Her Cardboard Lover,* 1927; *The Play's The Thing,* 1927; *Berkeley Square,* 1928. In London he produced *Strange Interlude,* 1931; *The Late Christopher Bean,* 1931 (also in New York) ; *Another Language,* 1932; *Reunion in Vienna, Men In White,* 1934; *Tovarich,* 1935 (also in New York).

Mr. Miller retains two producing offices, one in London and one in New York.

Miller, Joe (Joseph or Josias) (1684-1738). English actor. A comedian who played at Drury Lane Theatre for many years and was very popular. He is remembered primarily for his joke-book which was published a year after his death as "Joe Miller's Jests." It has run through many editions. Today when an actor cracks an old joke it is referred to as a "Joe Miller."

Miller, Marilyn (1898-1936). American actress, dancer. Born in Evansville, Indiana; made her debut at five as one of *The Columbian Trio,* the other two members being her mother and step-father. For ten years she toured all over the world. Lee Shubert saw her at the Lotus Club, London, in 1913, and engaged her for the Winter Garden, New York. She appeared there as Miss Jerry in *The Passing Show of 1914;* in *The Passing Show of 1915; The Show of Wonders; The Passing Show of 1917.* She appeared in *The Ziegfeld Follies of 1918;* as Sally in the musical show of that name, 1920, and continued in it until 1923; played Peter Pan in the play of that name, 1924; Sunny Peters in *Sunny,* in 1925, in which she continued until 1927; Princess Rosalie in *Rosalie,* 1928; at the Ziegfeld Theatre, 1930, as Smiles in the play of that name; in 1933, appeared in *As Thousands Cheer.* Began film career, 1929, in *Sally;* then appeared in *Sunny; Her Majesty, Love;* and others.

Of her beauty and grace, John Mason Brown says: "Dégas figure, turned American. . . . Titania of the jazz age; . . . the smiling embodiment of grace."

Milne, Alan Alexander (1882-   ). English author and playwright. Born in London; attended Trinity College. Assistant editor of Punch, 1906-14, after which he served in the war. His plays include *Wurzel-Flummery,* 1917; *Belinda,* 1918; *The Boy Comes Home,* 1918; *Make-Believe,* 1918; *The Camberley Triangle,* 1919; *Mr. Pim Passes by,* 1919; *The Romantic Age,* 1920; *The Truth About Blayds,* 1921; *The Dover Road,* 1922; *The Lucky One,* 1922; *The Great Broxopp,* 1923; *Success,* 1923; *To Have the Honour,* 1924; *Ariadne,* 1925; *The Ivory Door,* 1927; *The Fourth Wall,* 1928; *Michael and Mary,* 1929; *Other People's Lives,* 1932; *The Perfect Alibi,* 1932; etc.

For the most part they are light, charming whimsies. Milne, a sentimentalist at heart, sees life through rose-colored glasses. And his deft comedy technique keeps the sentimentality from being too cloying.

He has also written novels, and is perhaps best known for *When We Were Very Young* and his other children's books.

Milton, John (1608-1674). English poet. He was born in London. He was educated at St. Paul's and Cambridge. His earliest poems are traced to the year when he was twenty-one. He gave up an intention to enter the church because of a disagreement with its main tenets and gave himself over to the pursuit of literature. While in the country (at Horton) with his father he wrote *L'Allegro, Il Penseroso, Comus,* and *Lycidas.* He travelled on the continent and on his return became embroiled in several different religious controversies. He was married in 1643 but shortly after deserted by his wife. In 1652 he became blind and in the following year his wife, who had returned to him after two years' time, died. His position as Latin Secretary under Cromwell, assumed in 1649, lasted until the Restoration when, because of his political pamphlets, he was arrested as a menace to the government. Following his release his second wife, whom he had taken in 1656, died and he married a third time in 1663. The writing of his greatest work, the long poem *Paradise Lost,* occupied him for five years and was published in 1667. His contribution to dramatic theory, slight though it is, is to be found in the preface to his unactable pseudo-Greek play, *Samson Agonistes.*

Mime. See *Mimus.*

Mime, Dorian. A type of *comedy* originating in Doria shortly after 581 B.C.; not choral drama like the works of Aristophanes; certain traits in common with *Old* as well as *New Comedy* and the southern Italian *Phylakes.*

Mime, Greek. Type of early comedy, practiced by Epicharmus; full of licentious appeal, actors wearing the traditional phallus; type to which the *phylakes* belonged. See also *Phylakes.*

Mime, Roman. Comedy belonging to the *mime* tradition; came to occupy position more and more debased; action licentious; actor and actress social outcasts.

Mimed mystery. A mystery play towards the beginning of the 14th century which was a kind of dramatic pantomime intended as celebration of a certain national victory or a sovereign's entry into a city and performed on a scaffolding specially set up along the path of the *cortège.*

Mimics. See *Impersonators.*

Mimo-drama. A type of wordless play whose stories are worked out by flesh-and-blood actors. It is the drama that appeals to the senses by visual beauty of line, mass and color, and chiefly of moving figures. Reinhardt brought the mimo-drama to its most effective proportions in *Sumurun* and *The Miracle.*

Mimus. Form of popular comedy among the ancient Greeks (the *Phlyakes*) and Romans; sometimes called *fabula riciniata;* first definite appearance of that theme, so common later, of the doltish cuckold, the frail wife, and the intriguing gallant; scenes of common life were represented with imitative gestures and dancing, and with jocose dialogue more or less freely improvised. No doubt many points of correspondence between the Atellan and mime farce: in both, adultery was a stock jest, indecent phrases used to evoke laughter. Also, the actor in such; hence, mimic; clown; buffoon.

Ministri. See *Jongleurs.*

Minna Von Barnhelm. Gotthold Ephraim Lessing (German). Comedy. 5 acts. 1767.

Zellheim, a discharged army officer who loses his fortune, refuses to marry his sweetheart, Minna Von Barnhelm, because he is penniless and she is wealthy. To punish Zellheim for his pride, after he has recovered his fortune, Minna tells him she is penniless and refuses to marry on the same grounds of inequality. Eventually she tells him the truth and they are married.

Minor business. Details in the production of a play which are of minor or less importance than the main action of the principal players. Such would be the arranging of flowers on a table, the straightening of curtains at a window or the whispering of two persons in a corner.

Minsky Brothers. The original burlesque producers included from time to time Billy, Morton, Herbert and Abraham. Herbert and Morton exploited the fact that they were graduates of Columbia University. "Billy," the most colorful of all these brothers, took over the management of the National Winter Garden in 1912, building up a burlesque house that was notorious for its bawdiness. Later, on assuming management of the up-town Republic Theatre, he created a weekly scandal with his double entendre electric light show titles. Through the ingenuity of their press agent, Harry Davies, the Minsky brothers put over a publicity stunt at Washington where they appeared before the Dickstein committee urging that only American strip tease dancers be permitted to appear in Broadway theatres. The stunt, termed the brassiest of the year, brought about, directly or indirectly, the complete collapse of burlesque and the temporary closing of burleycue theatres.

Minstrels. See *Jongleurs.*

Minstrel show. An American form of entertainment which began about 1828. It had its origins in the Negro singing and dancing on plantations. Thomas D. Rice or "Jim Crow" Rice, a New Yorker, was one of the first white men to imitate a Negro. He first appeared in Negro character in Louisville, Kentucky. Minstrel shows developed a definite pattern with a white man as Interlocutor, two endmen in blackface—generally called Bones, Sambo and occasionally Rastus, and a chorus in blackface.

Mirabeau, Sybille Gabrielle Marie Antoinette de Riquetti de. See *Gyp.*

Miracle, The. Karl Vollmoeller (German). Spectacle. 9 scenes. 1910.
The legend of a young nun, Megildis, is presented in pageant form. Max Reinhardt brought the spectacle to New York in 1924, when the eye-filling splendor of the production enchanted spectators. Engelbert Humperdinck composed the music with Fritz Schirmer; and Norman Bel Geddes designed the sumptuous costumes and sets. These were important contributions, for the spectacle relies on music, dance, pantomime and visual appeal for its effectiveness. The drama itself is wordless.
In a cathedral, a miracle is accomplished and a cripple cured. After the crowd has dispersed the nun Megildis sits beneath the statue of the Virgin and Child dreaming of the world. The former cripple returns, this time playing a tune on pipes, and lures her forth from the church. Throughout the play he continues to appear and play weird music whenever the action becomes critical. He represents the appeal of sensual

things, of all those carnal pleasures which Megildis has forsworn. As the nun departs the Virgin descends from the pedestal and takes her place. The other nuns, returning, are shocked to see the vacant pedestal.

In the succeeding scenes the adventures of Megildis are depicted. They are perhaps only a dream; the régie book of the play calls them "as endlessly long as an intense dream, as horribly short as a full life." She flees with a Knight to a Forest, where they meet a Count who kills the Knight and takes her off with him. At a banquet, the Count plays cards for Megildis with a Prince, and loses. He stabs himself. She is married to the Prince at a mock wedding. Her husband's father, the Emperor, come to warn her about the Prince, kills his son by mistake and goes mad. The Emperor is crowned. Then the ragged mob overpower him, try him and put him to death. The Nun is liberated and finds her way to the manger. She picks up the infant lying there and flees to the forest, where she is visited by three Kings who have the forms of the Prince, the Emperor and Death. Weary, broken, the nun prays. At last she arrives back at the cathedral. The Madonna steps back on her pedestal and takes the infant, which has turned to a statue. The nuns hail Megildis as having restored the lost image of the Virgin.

Miracle at Verdun. Hans Chlumberg (German). Drama. 7 scenes. 1930.

An English adaptation of this play by Julian Leigh was given by the Theatre Guild in 1931. The drama inspired Irwin Shaw to write his one-act *Bury the Dead*, 1936.

The author looks ahead to the year 1934. Heydner, who was a German soldier during the World War, has come to visit the battlefields of France in honor of the twentieth anniversary of the beginning of that war. In the cemetery at Verdun, Frenchmen and Germans are buried together under a single shaft erected to the unknown dead. Here Heydner has paused to reflect on the past when an angel appears and tells him that the dead are about to rise. He stands watching as the soldiers get out of their graves and go away to resume life where they left off. To Paris, London and Berlin the resurrected dead journey happily, only to find the world getting along very well without them, contented that they are dead. In fact, the diplomats of the world feel that their unheralded return has precipitated an international crisis and are much alarmed. So the soldiers return to the battlefield, and Heydner awakes from his dream and starts back to Paris to celebrate.

Miracle plays. Sacred plays of the Middle Ages, popularly referred to as "miracles" because of their ecclesiastical, deistical cast.

See also *Mystery plays; Drama, Liturgical; Drama, Medieval; Towneley Cycle.*

Miracles of Notre Dame. Name given to the religious plays in France in the 14th century. They were characterized by a miraculous intervention of Our Lady.

Mira de Amescua, Antonio (1574?-1644). Spanish dramatist. Born in Guadix. As a priest he attained high position in the ecclesiastical world. As a poet, he was fertile and original but inclined toward the fantastic. Principal work: *El esclavo* *del demonio* (The Slave of the Devil) based on the legend of San Gil de Santarem, a kind of Portuguese Faust. In Mira de Amescua's play the hero makes a pact with the devil.

Mirbeau, Octave (1850-1917). French dramatist. Playwright primarily concerned with the struggle of labor and the working class. Among his plays are *The Epidemic,* 1897; *Bad Shepherds,* 1897; *Old Menage,* 1901; *Fair Lover,* 1901; *Scruples,* 1902; *The Portfolio,* 1902; *Business is Business,* probably his best, 1903; *The Fireside,* 1908.

Misanthrope, The. Molière (French). Comedy. 4 acts. 1666.

While a failure at the time it was first produced, this play has been hailed by posterity as one of Molière's masterpieces. It is more serious than the general run of his comedies. Its central character is somewhat laughable, but he is also pathetic. In 1660, Molière, a man of forty, married Armande Béjart, a coquette young enough to be his daughter, whose flirtations made him miserable. Undoubtedly the misanthrope's love for the frivolous young widow Celimène was suggested by its parallel in the playwright's own life.

Alceste is a man of uncompromising virtue and probity who has conceived a hatred for all mankind because he finds most men dishonest flatterers, cheats and thieves. In this he is contrasted with his friend Philinte, a sensible fellow who sees men's frailties but excuses them, who takes people as they are. He is a conformer, a believer in expediency. He stands for moderation in all things; in short, he is a perfect gentleman. When the posturing poet Oronte reads a very bad sonnet, Alceste frankly declares that it is terrible, while Philinte is more kindly. Oronte challenges Alceste to a duel unless he will apologize; Alceste will not retract, but bloodshed is averted. In view of his nature, the worldly widow Celimène is the last person in the world Alceste should fall in love with; the upright prude Eliante is much more suited to him. But the perverseness of his heart is something the misanthrope cannot control. He knows that Celimène is vain, a flirt, a hypocrite, a gossip, destined to make him miserable—and he adores her. He sees her receiving all the foppish nobles of the court, and forgives her for it. He intercepts a love letter which she has written to Oronte; she indignantly refuses to defend herself, and acts so hurt that he immediately appears in the wrong for having suspected her. Then Alceste learns that Oronte's rivalry has lost him a lawsuit; the poet has influence at court and has been able to defeat his enemy. Disgusted, Alceste prepares to retire from the world. He begs Celimène to accompany him into solitude if she loves him. She refuses to give up society for him, and as the play ends Philinte and Eliante, who have decided to marry one another, are trying to persuade the choleric misanthrope to reconsider and stay in the city for a while longer.

Miss Julie. August Strindberg (Swedish). Drama. 2 acts. 1888.

Miss Julie, a bored and willful lady, sick of love in her own class, has an affair with a worthless lackey. This time she becomes the slave, and he the master, and their passion soon turns to hate. He forces her to steal money from her father and when he suggests that she cut her throat, she obeys as if hypnotized.

Mistress. About 1661, English actresses used this term for stage purposes, "miss" being at that time the equivalent of "concubine."

Mistress of the Inn, The. Carlo Goldoni (Italian). Comedy. 1752.

A gay comedy by Italy's most famous comic dramatist. It concerns a resourceful mistress of an inn who uses all her wiles to attract guests to her hostelry, and then every ruse she can think of to pick their pockets. While the plot complications are manifold and complex, the chief comedy derives from the character of the heroine.

Mithridate. Jean Racine (French). Tragedy. 1673.

Mithridate, King of Pontus, sworn enemy of Rome, has strangely disappeared. His two sons, the untrustworthy Pharnaces and the gallant Xiphares, are making plans to seize the crown. Both become attached to Monima, the king's betrothed. The old king reappears, finds out that Monima favors Xiphares and swears vengeance. The king has made an ingenious plan for a march on Rome—he will attack from the north. Pharnaces opposes the scheme, Xiphares supports it. The Romans and rebels join forces and Mithridate is defeated and wounded. Before his death he sanctions the union of Xiphares and Monima.

Racine's study of Mithridate as a character, showing his cupidity and acuteness, his vices and his virtues, ranks with his best portrayals.

Mitiyuki. Which means "travel"; a favorite feature of *Kabuki* puppet plays; in character more like a dance, the *mitiyuki* scene is one which represents lovers billing and cooing. This is used to serve as a relief from the intricacies of the drama, helping the audience's mind to "travel" from the main currents.

Mixed Marriage. St. John Ervine (Irish). Drama. 1911.

A controversial play dealing with the Catholic-Protestant question. It was first produced at the Abbey Theatre shortly after there had been religious riots in the streets of Belfast, and its subject was considered a daring one to be treated dramatically.

John Rainey Sr. is an Orangeman, a bigoted and uncompromising member of the older generation. His son, John Jr., on the other hand, is modern in his outlook. He has undergone the influence of Michael O'Hara, a young labor leader, and has come to believe that religious differences should not count; that all men should unite to help better working conditions. He announces his engagement to a Catholic girl, Nora Murray, and arouses all his father's latent prejudice against Papists. There is a heated conflict between the two, and then a force beyond their control solves their problem. The populace becomes unruly in an attempt to better labor conditions, and riots. The police are called, and Nora is killed by a stray bullet.

Mixolydian. See *Modes*.

Mob, The. John Galsworthy (English). Drama. 1914.

The hero of this tragedy is Stephen More, an anti-militarist politician, ready to give up everything, even his life, for the sake of his anti-war policy. In his idealism he is opposed not only by the men in the street (the mob), but also by the so-called right-thinking people. At the time the play opens England has just declared war against a small state which it wishes to annex. A false patriotic fervor has gripped the populace; they support the government in its plea for national unity and go forth to battle unflinchingly. More rises in the House of Commons and cries out against the un-righteous struggle. His brothers-in-law, relatives and friends have been called to the front, and he knows that his protests will encourage the enemy to shoot them down, but his conscience will not let him desist. For six weeks, while the British army is suffering reverses on the battlefield, he stumps the countryside, but with slight success. His erstwhile friends cut him cold; even his wife and children, holding him re-sponsible for the death of his relatives, shun him. Finally he dies at the hands of an angry mob. In an epilogue, a statue is erected to him in honor of his unselfishness and bravery. Its inscription reads: "Faithful to his ideal."

Like *Loyalties, Justice* and most of Galsworthy's other plays, *The Mob* castigates prejudice and injustice and pleads for a better world.

Modes. Styles of Greek music used in ancient Greek theatre, most commonly employed in *tragedy:* (1) *Dorian,* majestic and dignified; (2) *Mixolydian,* pathetic. Also used in tragedy: (1) by Aeschylus, *Ionic,* severe and sober; (2) by Sophocles, *Phrygian,* passionate and enthusiastic. Used in songs of actors on stage, not in choral odes: (1) *Hypodorian,* (2) *Hypophrigian,* both styles better suited to realistic acting than to choral singing.

Modjeska, Helena (1844-1909). Polish actress. Born in Cracow. She began to act in 1860. In 1876 she came, with her second husband, to America. Her enormously successful American debut was at San Francisco in *Adrienne Lecouvreur,* December 22, 1877. She starred with Booth in 1889-90, and was thereafter considered one of the greatest actresses on the English-speaking stage. This was followed by trans-continental tours with Otis Skinner and Maurice Barrymore. She played Lady Mac-beth, Cleopatra, Ophelia and Viola in Shakespeare's plays. In 1905, a farewell testi-monial was given at the Metropolitan Opera House.

Moeller, Philip (1880-   ). American author and producer. Attended New York University and Columbia University. One of the founders of Washington Square Players 1914. A founder and director of the Theatre Guild. Among his pro-ductions are *Saint Joan,* 1923; *Fata Morgana,* 1924; *The Guardsman,* 1924; *They Knew What They Wanted,* 1924. He has produced over 60 plays and has written and adapted several, including *Caprice.*

Mohawk Drama Festival. Held at Union College, Schenectady, New York, each summer since 1935. Mrs. Charles Coburn assisted her husband in the direction until her death in 1937. The plays are produced and principal parts played by pro-fessional artists, while supporting roles are more often acted by students. Charles Coburn is the nucleus of the whole festival.

Moissi, Alexander (1880-1935). German actor. Moissi was born in Austria of Italian-Albanian parents. When he first started to act on the Berlin stage he spoke with such a pronounced Italian accent that the audience jeered at him. The producer Max Reinhardt was convinced, however, that the young man had talent, and coached and featured him until Moissi had become one of the foremost actors in Germany. As might be expected, he was almost as well known in Italy as in his native land, and was greatly admired there. Duse praised him highly when she met him in 1912, and the Italians mourned his death almost as if it were a national loss. Moissi also toured the United States.

Among the plays in which he appeared were *As You Like it* (as Jacques) ; *Romeo and Juliet; Ghosts; The Doctor's Dilemma; The Living Corpse; Everyman; Turandot; Hamlet* (a famous role) ; etc.

Molière (1622-1673). French comic dramatist. Born as Jean Baptiste Poquelin, eldest of five children, in Paris on January 15, 1622. As a child he evinced a gift for mimicry. At fourteen he studied at the Jesuit Collège de Clermont in the Rue St. Jacques. He also pursued lessons in philosophy and law. He joined a company of amateur actors collectively known as the *Illustre Théâtre*. In the 1640's he changed his name to Molière to assuage the resentment of all the Poquelins that there should be one of their family on the stage. In 1646, after the collapse of the *Illustre Théâtre* he left Paris to become, in the company of certain former associates, a strolling player. By successive patronage of the nobility he and his troupe eventually were commanded for performances before the King, in Paris, in 1658. Here the near failure precipitated by his company's indifferent playing of tragedy (Corneille's *Nicomède*) was turned to success by an impromptu performance, preceded by a speech by Molière to the nobility, of one of Molière's earliest farces, *Le Docteur Amoureux*. After this success Molière was requested to establish his company in Paris under the title of *Troupe de Monsieur* or *Troupe du Roi*. This he did, maintaining it for fourteen years at the Palais-Royal. Meanwhile he wrote farces, satires and comedies which were subsequently performed by his company. Altogether he wrote thirty plays. Among his most famous are: *Le Misanthrope; Tartuffe; Les Femmes Savantes; L'Avare; Les Précieuses Ridicules; Le Bourgeois Gentilhomme; Le Malade Imaginaire; Le Médecin Malgré Lui*. He did but little theorizing on the drama, and what he did was included in his prefaces to his plays. His answer to the critics of *L'École des Femmes*, "La Critique de l'École des Femmes" carries most clearly his expounding of dramatic ideas.

He was the greatest French comic dramatist of all time and one of the greatest in the world.

Molina, Tirso de (Tellez, Gabriel) (1571-1648). Spanish dramatist. Born in Madrid and educated at the University of Alcala, in 1613 he took orders. Much of his life was spent in travel and soldiering.

Tirso de Molina excelled in the play based on scenes placed in the palace (*comedia palaciega*). His female characters, like those of Lope de Vega, are frequently good.

His comic force is strong and his *graciosos* are the wittiest of his epoch. Is perhaps best known as the creator of the character of Don Juan.

Among his best known *comedias* are the historical play *La prudencia en la mujer* (*Prudence in the Woman*); and the lighter *comedias, El Vergouzoso en palacio* (*The Timid Fellow in the Palace*); and *Don Gil de las calzasverdes* (*Don Gil of the Green Trousers*). *El condenado por desconfiado* (*The Doubter Damned*) is more serious in tone and teaches the necessity of faith for justification. *El burlado de Sevilla* (*The Rake—Libertine of Seville*) is the first dramatic representation of the Don Juan legend.

Molnar, Ferenc (1878-   ). Hungarian playwright. Born in Budapest, Hungary. Attended the universities of Budapest and Geneva where he studied law. He attracted attention as a journalist but achieved his first wide literary notice with a play called *The Devil,* produced in England, France and America. *Liliom,* his next play and far superior to *The Devil,* is probably his most famous work. It is far more profound than any of his other works and can be ranked among the gems of the theatre. *The Guardsman* and *The Wolf* followed, dealing with the romantic flirtatiousness of women. In *The Swan* Molnar writes of a Princess and a tutor and the vicissitudes of their mutual attraction. *Fashions for Men* deals with a simple noble hero who by his very naivete and generosity wins out in the end over his more scheming adversaries. *Carnival* was written for an opera singer Molnar was in love with and whom he later married. This marriage was dissolved when he fell in love with Lily Darvas, an actress. For her he wrote *Heavenly and Earthly Love, The Red Mill and The Glass Slipper. The Play's the Thing* is an amusing play utilizing to good advantage the ingenuity of a dramatist. Having little plot it depends largely on its good dialogue. *A Matter of Husbands* (one act) and *Olympia* are more cynical in treatment.

Molnar is not especially concerned with social or political problems but is chiefly interested in being entertaining. In this he succeeds admirably, using his gifts of imagination, wit and sophistication to great advantage.

Monde, Abus, les Sots, Le. One of the most famous of satirical farces, or *soties,* in the Middle Ages. The principal characters were: *Sot-Dissolu,* representing the clergy; *Sot-Ignorant,* personifying ignorance; *Sot-Corrompu,* standing for the magistrates; *Sotte Folle,* an embodiment of the whole feminine gender. After an attempt to destroy the world and build a new one they find it best to fall back on the present world they know.

Monna Vanna. Maurice Maeterlinck (Belgian). Drama. 3 acts. 1902.

To save the starving city of Pisa, Monna Vanna gives herself to its enemy general. When she goes to him, instead of a villain she finds a romantic lover who gallantly offers to forego the bargain. To save him from treachery, she brings him home. Her husband, mad with jealousy, accuses her of doing it for revenge and by his lack of faith drives her into her lover's arms.

Monogatari. Or narration in a scene of *Kabuki* dramas, by means of which an important matter is narrated to another; it is a stage convention considered to be a difficult piece of *Kabuki* acting.

Monologist. A unique player who performs sketches in soliloquy or scenes of several roles, all of which he or she assumes. The best-known monologists in America are Cornelia Otis Skinner (an actress as well), Ruth Draper, Dorothy Sands, Elsie Janis and Cecilia Loftus.

Monologue. Originally what is now known as an aside—a character saying his thoughts aloud. Now a protracted speech by one person, sometimes in a play but generally as a separate recitation or entertainment.

Monsieur Poirier's Son-in-Law, The. Émile Augier and Jules Sandeau (French). Satire. 4 acts. 1854.
M. Poirier, a wealthy shop-keeper, marries his daughter to a penniless aristocrat, the Marquis de Presles, to satisfy his political ambitions. The young husband, through shiftlessness and pretensions manages to get himself into trouble, and his wife on two occasions saves his honor. His idle carelessness continues, however, and the wife, whose character has developed with his hardships, takes the reins into her own hands in a self-sacrificing attempt to establish her husband's self respect. Regarded as a masterpiece of French social satire.

Month in the Country, A. Ivan Turgenev (Russian). Drama. 4 acts. 1850.
Natalia Petrovna is bored with her husband and with life in an isolated community. She is thankful for the diversion offered by Mikhail Rakitin, a friend of her husband, but his platonic friendship does not suffice to fill her empty existence. Then a young tutor, Aleksei Bieliaev, is engaged for her son, and the lonely woman, with so much affection to spare, falls in love with him. When Natalia realizes that her protégée, Viena, is also attracted to the young man, she becomes exceedingly jealous and confesses her love to Aleksei. He is both confused and frightened to learn of her unrequited ardor and leaves at once for Moscow. Her one consolation, Mikhail, goes away too, and Natalia returns to her routine existence.

Month of Roses. Otto Erich Hartleben (German). Drama. 3 acts. 1900.
A young officer, separated from his sweetheart by the lies of his comrades, finally shoots her, and then takes his own life, because of the false ideals of military class built in Germany.

Moody, William Vaughan (1869-1910). American dramatist. Born at Spencer, Indiana. Graduated from Harvard and taught there as well as at the University of Chicago. He wrote *The Great Divide,* 1906, which was then hailed as the "Great American Drama." Among his other plays are *The Faith Healer,* 1907; *The Masque of Judgment,* 1900; *The Fire Bringer,* 1904. Moody's poetry and plays are noteworthy because of their richness of rhythm and beautiful lyric quality.

Moon in the Yellow River, The. Denis Johnston (Irish). Drama. 3 acts. 1931.

The title is inspired by the Chinese poet Li Po, who died by drowning while pursuing the moon in the yellow river. For the hero of this drama of the Irish Revolution is just such a futile dreamer, ardently and idealistically devoted to the welfare of Ireland, but unable to reconcile his dreams with reality. A member of the citizens' army, he opposes the building of a power plant on the Irish coast by the German electrical engineer Tausch. Such a plant, he and his fellow idealists in the army believe, will cause technological unemployment and be very bad for Ireland. When the rebellion of these patriots seems to be growing serious, Tausch calls in the government forces to protect him, and the unfortunate ringleader is shot, without having caught the moon. Tausch, who has wished protection but not bloodshed, is outraged by the murder, and protests. In the confusion which follows, the plant is blown up, and Tausch leaves the country. The dead man has won after all.

Moon of the Caribbees. Eugene O'Neill (American). Drama. 1 act. 1917.

The S.S. Glencairn is anchored in a West Indian harbor on a moonlit night. The sailors, a motley crew of many nationalities, joke and reminisce. Then a group of native women come aboard, bearing rum, and the laughing sailors take them down to the cabins to dance with them and make love to them. Only Smitty refuses to join in the merriment, and sits by himself at the forecastle brooding over a love letter. Then the lyric mood is shattered as his noisy companions come back. There is a brawl, the sound of shots, then a tense silence. A man has been killed. An officer boards the ship to discipline the sailors and send the women away.

This play, together with *Bound East for Cardiff, 'Ile,* etc., belongs to the group of short sea dramas which O'Neill wrote for the Provincetown group. Its characters are the same ones as are to be found in *Bound East for Cardiff,* for instance. These plays were written after the playwright himself had spent some time on the sea, and reflect his experiences. Their plots are negligible, but they marked him as a writer of promise, with an original literary style and the ability to create a mood or an atmosphere with a few strokes of the pen.

Moore, George (1852-1933). Irish author. The eldest son of an Irish Catholic landowner, he was born at Moore Hall, County Mayo, and spent the years from 1872-1882 studying art in Paris. Doubtful of his ability, he went to London, where he lived for a while in poverty, publishing his first novel, *A Modern Lover,* 1883, and his second, *A Mummer's Wife,* 1885. Both these works provoked a storm of criticism, and both in matter and treatment, they broke entirely fresh ground in Victorian literature. His first autobiographical work, *Confessions of a Young Man,* appeared in 1888. This was followed by the greatest of his naturalistic novels, *Esther Waters.* In 1905, he was high sheriff of County Mayo. He became a Protestant before his return to London in 1911. In his last few years he turned to playwriting. Among his plays are: *His Making of an Immortal,* 1928; *The Passing of the Essenes,* 1931; and *Aphrodite in Aulis,* 1933. He was revising the end of the last play when he died, January 21, 1933.

A dramatization of *Esther Waters* was produced in 1936.

Moral. Ludwig Thoma (German). Comedy. 3 acts. 1909.

When a certain lady of easy virtue is arrested, the president of the society for the Prevention of Vice tries to have her released from custody, because his own name as well as those of other prominent citizens appears on her list of callers. He succeeds in stealing the list and a police official arrives to berate his subordinates whose zeal has almost compromised so many important people. The affair is smoothed out after the lady is paid off.

Moral Demand, The. Otto Erich Hartleben (German). Comedy. 3 acts. 1897.

A minor comedy which was popular in Germany about 1900. It concerns a lady singer who has scoffed at conventional morality. Since her voice has enabled her to make her way in the world, she has felt no need of the financial security a husband has to offer, and has enjoyed herself to the fullest extent. And when an ex-lover actually tries to tie her down by proposing marriage to her, she laughs at him and continues to go on her merry way unhampered by the bonds of matrimony and the chains of respectability.

Morality plays. Type of drama in the Middle Ages following some centuries after the *mystery-miracle plays;* abstract qualities were the *dramatis personae;* most famous of all *morality plays, Everyman.*

Moral of the Fable, The. Marco Praga (Italian). Drama. 5 acts. 1904.

A woman who has taken a lover is ready to break up her home for him. However, he proves himself unworthy and deserts her. She is forced to return to her husband and try to keep secret from him her disloyalty.

More, Sir Thomas (1478-1535). English statesman. Spent two years at Oxford where he became interested in humanism. Studied law. Colet, Lilly and Erasmus were his close friends. At the fall of Wolsey (1529) he was made Lord Chancellor by Henry VIII, who had been attracted to him. Disapproving Henry's divorce from Katherine of Aragon and saying so, he retired in disfavor. He was sent to the tower and beheaded on a charge of treason. His *Utopia,* a book dealing with the ideal state, is a classic and extremely famous. It is believed, in the light of recent research, that a trilogy of farces generally attributed to Heywood were contributed to in a large measure by More. They are important in that they show a departure from the morality play and deal with more secular matters. *The Pardoner and the Frere,* a comedy farce; *Johan Johan* and *The Foure P. P.* are especially distinguished for dialogue and humor.

Morehouse, Ward. American dramatic critic. Drama editor of the New York *Sun;* contributor to many newspapers and periodicals. His columns on *Broadway of the Past* are read and cherished by a large audience. He is the author of *Forty-Five Minutes Past Eight,* 1939, and is considered one of the best historians of the stage and its people in America.

Morgue. Theatre with poor attendance. File of clippings, pictures and information.

Morris, Clara (Clara Morrison) (1846-1925). American actress, author. It is believed that she was born in Toronto, Canada. Her first stage appearance was in the ballet of *Seven Sisters* at the Cleveland Theatre when she was about fifteen. Extravagant in gesture and crude in speech, she was one of the most individual players America ever produced. In 1870 she took New York by storm with her debut under Daly's banner in *Man and Wife*. She was notable also in *Divorce; Wives as They Were; Maids As They Are;* and *L'Article 47.* Compelled to retire from the stage in 1885, she devoted much of her time from 1889-1904 to literary writings. In 1904 she returned to the stage in a revival of *The Two Orphans* and appeared the following year in vaudeville.

Moscow Art Theatre. The outstanding theatre of all time of ensemble acting came into being through the famous discussion in 1897 between Constantin Stanislavsky and Vladimir Nemirovich-Danchenko, a talk which lasted all day and most of the night. Influenced by the fineness of the productions of the Meiningen Company, when they played in Moscow, the founders hoped to catch that quality for Russia. The first production of the Art Theatre took place in October, 1898, when Tolstoy's *Tsar Fyodor Ivanovitch* was presented. Next came Chekhov's *The Sea Gull* and soon their repertoire included: Tolstoy's *Power of Darkness;* Chekhov's *Three Sisters; The Cherry Orchard; Uncle Vanya;* Turgeniev's *Month In The Country;* Gorky's *Lower Depths;* etc. Meyerhold (for four years), Olga Knipper-Chekhova (Chekhov's widow), Vassily Kachalov, Ivan Moskvin, Alla Tarasova, Leo Bulgakov, Maria Ouspenkaya are among the great actors who belong to the company, many of whom are still acting with it. Stanislavsky cared for the production and Nemirovich-Danchenko for the literary aspects of the theatre. It has survived the Revolution, has weathered the suspicions of the government that it was a bourgeois theatre, has made several tours abroad including 1906 to Berlin, the United States, 1922-23, 1923-24, Paris, 1937. The occasion of the fortieth anniversary in 1938 provoked a large, official celebration, which was worldwide. (The New York Public Library opened an appreciative exhibition forty years to the day of *Tsar Fyodor's* performance.) The association of Gorky with the theatre has brought about the inclusion of his name so that officially it is the *Moscow Art Academic Theatre in The Name of Gorky.*

Moses, Montrose J. (1878-1934). American author. Drama critic, editor, translator and lecturer. His works include *Francesca da Rimini,* a critical study; *Famous Actor-Families in America; Henrik Ibsen; The Man and His Plays; The American Dramatist; Maurice Maeterlinck,* a study; *The Fabulous Forrest; The Record of an American Actor; The American Theatre as Seen By Its Critics* (with John Mason Brown), 1934.

Mosqueteros. In the Spanish theatre, those who stood in the *corrales* to witness performances of plays and who constituted the turbulent element.

Mothers, The. Georg Hirschfeld (German). Drama. 1916.

Marie, a girl of the people, takes as her lover a prosperous middle-class musician. She is made to realize that if he is to achieve success in his art, she must give him up. So she returns to her tenement to bear his child, without letting him know.

THE MOTION PICTURE: PRODUCTION AND DIRECTION

BY HUNT STROMBERG

Competent motion picture direction requires perfect coordination. One of the most obvious reasons therefore for having a producer in charge of the making of a motion picture is that he be able to prevent the confusion and discord which might arise during the creating of screen entertainment. Nevertheless, if this were a producer's only function he would be merely an astute business manager, skilled in the mechanics of film making and capable of supervising cost. That he have this sort of practical knowledge is, of course, important, but a competent producer should know much more. He should be able to write a complete script, if necessary, direct the picture, and edit it satisfactorily. He must be hard to fool also on commercial work, set design and the thousands of technical details attendant on production.

The first task which confronts the producer is choosing suitable material for his star. If, for example, the star is Norma Shearer, he must determine what sort of story is best for her. Should it be a period or a modern picture? Should it recreate authentic historical characters as in the cast of *Marie Antoinette,* or should it be purely fictional? Should the background be modern, sophisticated or sentimental? Then too, there are other questions—should she be a married woman, a glamour girl, a society woman or a working girl?

Miss Shearer, being a versatile player, can do almost any type of story, but what would be best for her just now? If her last three pictures were costume or period stories, the new one must provide a contrast, for a star's abilities must not be limited nor can the public be permitted to feel that it is seeing a familiar background.

When all these values have been weighed and considered, the producer starts search for a story that fulfills the desired requirements. Then, if the ideal plot cannot be found either in the book or play form, it must be written to order. At this point, he calls in the writers, describes to them the specific character desired and the exact nature of the comedy or drama. Then follows a discussion of the treatment; and gradually a detailed synopsis of the complete story is drawn up. But only a synopsis. No actual dialogue; no scenes; no camera set-ups; no technical descriptions of any kind. Merely the story is outlined in perhaps a few pages or several hundred pages.

The treatment thereafter is basically the story conception; and the visualization determines, far more than the public realizes, the success or failure of the picture. It is this faculty for conceiving this treatment that qualifies the producer for the position he occupies.

The Great Ziegfeld for instance was originally imagined as a vast panorama that would encompass the entire life of Florenz Ziegfeld from his earliest days in Chicago to his last days as Broadway's most illustrious musical comedy impresario. The picture as a story was to have magnitude—sweeping scope, but also a warm personal story woven into a colossal stage spectacle. At the same time the important decision was made that one phase of the story would not be more far-reaching than the other. For if the picture had been top-heavy with spectacle, its human side would have suffered. Similarly, overstressing the personal story would have meant sacrificing the settings and embellishments, their appeal to the eye and ear, the motion and the melody. That one phase should not be greater or more far-reaching than the other was a momentous decision.

In the instance of *The Women,* it was decided that a picture composed of lightning scenes, depending chiefly upon sophisticated conversation of a risque nature, such as the play itself contained, would fail to become a thorough story of human beings in every day human circumstances. The story, first of all, had to dramatize the problems and experiences of women easily recognizable to the women and men composing an average audience.

Hence the sentimental and emotional side of Mary Haines' life, her character, was given equal importance with the dialogue. Here again the aim was correct balance in production. We did not employ one-sided sophistication, nor did we use an overabundance of scenes that might be termed "sex scenes."

The conception of just what the screen play should embody has always been the foundation upon which every picture is built. It can absorb value from a story which seems impossible to make.

I recall the doubt expressed when I decided to produce "The Thin Man." The book was heavy with risque dialogue and scenes, seemingly its chief charm. But the screen conception included an amusing, sophisticated, happy life of a married couple who had plenty of fun. The usual screen romance was at that time only between boy and girl before marriage and marital stories stressing divorce. This new treatment, it so happened, created a new and popular formula.

After the screen conception has been determined, the next step is the actual writing of the play. The selection of the writers is all-important; for they must be temperamentally suited to the particular story and skill in screen mechanics. Their first step on starting work is to break up the general story and the characterizations into individual shooting scenes. Then each scene must be dialogued; that is, the words created which are spoken by the actual characters.

The next step is the writing of the screen play. The selection of the men for this work is all-important. The producer must cast his writers in the same manner he casts actors. Failure to know the abilities and the limitations of each writer may mean failure of the picture itself.

The first task of the writers is to break up the general story form and the individual shooting scenes and characterizations. Each scene then is dialogued with the actual words which the character must speak. Once the dialogue is completed and the entire script finished the producer starts editing. He must be able to tear down and build up, modify and correct, provide a remedy for existing faults. Any producer worthy of the name must be creative and inventive, have a kind of omniscient understanding of the picture in its entirety.

The next task is to appoint a director who by mood, technique and experience is ideal for the star, the supporting players, and the story, who can make all live for the enjoyment of an audience. He must select cameramen too who are capable of making both the players and the backgrounds pictorial. Mood is important in photography also, and most photographers have a specialty. Nor does the producer's task end here. He must plan sets and wardrobe minutely, working always toward the basic conception. This is what counts, the original conception and the preparation therefor. If these are planned wisely actual production becomes merely a matter of guidance.

The work of the director comes in next for consideration. He must have the ability of a born creator to assimilate the spirit of the story and to interpret it in terms of mood and action. I use the word born in connection with director advisedly for direction, coming as it does under the heading of art, can depend on no rule and no line. Most of the foremost directors of the motion picture are men without the kind of background or training generally associated with skilled craftsmanship. They have been through no college; they have taken no courses, but theirs is a gift, a natural gift, the unique and peculiar ability to understand and feel how human beings think and act under circumstances that may be comical, dramatic, or tragic; how far to go, or not to go.

Experience, of course, also plays its part in the *mechanics* of direction; proper knowledge of camera composition, and grouping of players to effect the most pictorially attractive scenes. These subjects fortunately can be learned through instruction or through association with those who know.

The following is the average daily routine of the average director: He will read with his actors the certain scene to be staged that day. This is called "running lines." He determines if the lines written in the script are "playing" on the set. Do they seem convincing? Do they have the proper tonal quality? Are any speeches too long? Is the tempo right? For if any speech is too long, or if many lines are too long, the scene itself will run too long and prove slow or possibly dull in its enactment. The director must evaluate the story, judge the conviction of each individual scene, and of the story as a whole, as he goes along.

I have known many directors to halt production in the middle of a schedule and complain of a weakness in story if the motivations seem implausible. I have known many of our best pictures to have had faults of this sort corrected during actual production.

After the lines are rehearsed, the director puts his actors through what is called "going through the mechanics." There is no attempt to turn on the emotion. No attempt to inject little bits of business into the scene. The positions of the characters, how they will enter and how they will exit; where they will stand, or sit, or kneel at a given point in a scene—these are the things decided upon. Such rehearsals make the actors familiar and comfortable with their lines; give the director the opportunity to judge the general effectiveness of the scene. Then, when positions and groupings are decided upon, the little touches and incidents which must accompany each scene are discussed, business described in the script. Facial expressions—little bits of business—mannerisms—characteristics—use of props and wardrobe—these too are considered and made a part of a scene. Then when all such details have been discussed and tried out in these rough rehearsals (during which, by the way, the cameraman and his staff are arranging the lights) a real try-out of the scene takes place. The time is past now for fishing for lines; no more uncertainty on positions or groupings; no more unfamiliarity with the main dramatic point which the director is striving for. All the preliminaries are over and the actors are asked to "put their heart and soul" into the playing of the scene. The director must judge the scene for its effectiveness and its conviction as story. Then he must judge it from the viewpoint of each individual actor's performance. Are they overplaying or underplaying? More wrinkles are ironed out until, after strenuous effort, the scene is regarded as ready to photograph. This same procedure takes place before and during every scene.

Many directors have the ability to enact the scene themselves—as illustration or example for the player. Others never attempt to have the player ape them. They prefer the actor's personality and individualism intact. Some directors have very few, if any, rehearsals. They think that spontaneity—actors and actresses doing things impulsively without preliminary trial—provides the best results. Many directors, working exactly the opposite way, run their players through hours of rehearsal until every little detail is thoroughly seen and heard.

A director arrives on the set before any of his actors.

He first sees that the set is dressed properly, and he has previously seen that the set has been constructed properly to fit the action he has in mind.

He then consults with his cameraman on the first set-up of the day, informing the cameraman of his proposed action. If a particular mood is required, he will talk this over with his cameraman.

He will then consult his script with his conception of how the scene is to be staged already in mind.

When the actors appear, he calls them together and the lines are rehearsed. Then the mechanics of the scene are rehearsed and photography begins.

Many directors like to explain in full detail the psychology behind each scene, each line, each bit of action. Others do not delve so deeply into the fundamentals of a scene, preferring to have the actors express themselves without any previous examination. Each method produces its own results, according to the style of the director.

Tempo is extremely important in the direction of each scene. Some directors can shoot a scene in fifty feet that would take another director ninety. Generally the scene in fifty feet is much the best, for there is nothing that handicaps a picture so much as slow tempo.

With these few words I speed these comments to those who love and puzzle about pictures, hoping that I have made clear some of their mystery.

Motion Picture Producers and Distributors of America, Inc. This organization was founded in March, 1922, under the presidency of Will H. Hays. The home office is at 28 West 44th Street, New York City, and branches are located in Hollywood, Washington and Paris. Its aim was and *is* to emphasize the necessity of the public's support in order to improve production standards. After eight years of progressive improvement in film standards, the self-regulative principle was aided by the Production Code of Ethics (adopted in March, 1930) and the Advertising Code (adopted in June, 1930), both of which are still in force. Mr. Hays has interested thousands of community leaders in the industry's efforts at self-improvement.

Activities of the organization include: self-regulation of advertising, community service, conservation (elimination of fire hazards), foreign markets, public information, theatre service and title registration.

Motivation. For effective and convincing drama, the playwright must prepare the action of the play by disclosing the causes, the forces impelling the action. This preparation is called the "Motivation." The skill with which the characters and the incidents are motivated will determine the quality of the drama.

Mounet-Sully, Jean (1841-1916). French actor. Born at Bergerac, Mounet-Sully reached great fame in Paris, first as leading man at the Odéon where he made his debut in 1872, and later in the Comédie Française, where in 1874 his initial role was Orestes in Racine's *Andromaque.* Oedipus, Orosmane (opposite Sarah Bernhardt in *Zaëre* and Didier in *Marion Delorme* are among the most celebrated parts which he played with great fire and classic style. His performances of Hamlet and Othello were also acclaimed by the French. He was the outstanding classic tragedian of his day.

Mountjoy, Christopher. A Huguenot tire-maker at whose house in Cripplegate ward, London, Shakespeare was lodging in 1604. In a deposition which he made in 1612 Shakespeare revealed that he had been instrumental in arranging the marriage of Mountjoy's daughter to an apprentice, Belott, in 1604.

Mourning Becomes Electra. Eugene O'Neill (American). Tragedy. A trilogy in 13 acts. 1931.

One of O'Neill's most ambitious dramas, this is really a trilogy, consisting of three full-length plays: *Homecoming; The Hunted; The Haunted.* The theme of the Electra legend is borrowed from Aeschylus, but the playwright has modernized the story and placed it in a New England setting. Whereas the Greek characters were hounded by the Fates, O'Neill's New Englanders are haunted only by their own consciences. Thus the tragedy becomes internal rather than external. To some critics this heightens its effectiveness for a modern audience and renders it even more moving than its classic counterpart.

The time is the end of the American Civil War. The Mannons are a strong, proud, exclusive family. General Mannon married a passionate, exotic foreigner, Christine, whom the villagers distrust because she is so different from them. The couple have two children: Orin, who adores his mother almost fanatically; and Lavinia, who detests the mother who bore her and loves her father with an overwhelming love. A brother and sister who live nearby, Hazel and Peter Niles, are in love with Orin and Lavinia respectively, but have not received much encouragement. The other character important to the action is Adam Brant, a darkly mysterious sea captain with whom Christine has been having an affair while her husband was away at the front. Lavinia has found this out, and hates her mother the more for it. The girl forces Brant to admit what she has dimly suspected: that he is the illegitimate son of her Grandfather Mannon, his child by a French mistress. He began making love to Christine to revenge himself on the Mannons for mistreating his mother. General Brant returns. Christine is panic-stricken. Adam has told her that Lavinia now knows everything and will certainly inform her father. Christine poisons her husband and goes to join her lover.

Lavinia finds the poison tablets and convinces Orin of Christine's guilt. He is reluctant to believe at first that his idol has feet of clay, but when he is persuaded becomes so furious that he shoots Brant, her seducer, while Christine looks on helplessly. Unable to stand the strain of having killed a husband and lost a lover, Christine commits suicide.

Lavinia and Orin go away to the tropics to recover from their experiences. Lavinia loses her inhibitions, becomes as loving and passionate as her mother, returns radiant and ready to marry the faithful Peter. But Orin has transferred to her the affection he once felt for Christine, and will not let her marry. After threatening to accuse her of murder if she goes against his wishes, Orin shoots himself. Lavinia once again becomes a stern Puritan, ready to do penance for her sins. She locks herself up in the lonely house and prepares to live with her remorse until she dies. No weakling, she has chosen the harder way.

Mourning Bride, The. William Congreve (English). Tragedy. 5 acts. 1697.
Alphonso, Prince of Valencia, and Almeria are united in secret wedlock. But the young couple are soon separated. Alphonso is imprisoned, and his bride has a narrow escape from death. Then the people revolt and release the Prince, and he is able once more to join his bride.

This is the only tragedy written by Congreve, who is famous for his Restoration comedies. His mastery of the tragic muse is less complete than his mastery of the comic one; he is deficient in the art of arousing pity and portraying high passion. However, the work is intelligently written. The opening line is one of the most famous in literature: "Music hath charms to soothe the savage breast."

Mouth-to-mouth. The form of publicity deemed the best by producers, and one that has in many instances redeemed a prospective failure. Not infrequently it has enabled a production to triumph over poor notices.

Mowatt, Anna Cora (Mrs. A. C. Mowatt Ritchie) (1819-1870). American dramatist, actress. Of her acting Edgar Allan Poe, who was then a dramatic critic in New York, wrote, "The greatest charm of her manner is its naturalness." It was contrary to the "teapot acting" of the time, a term which applied to the habit actors had of standing with either one or the other hand on a hip, making a sort of human teapot, while going through the conventional business of the play.

In 1845, Mrs. Mowatt's comedy, *Fashion,* was presented at the Park Theatre, New York. It made a great hit, and was the first successful social satire and comedy of manners of American native drama. Following the success of this play, she went on the stage herself, making her début at the Park Theatre in June 1845, supported by the company that had played her comedy. She was twenty-six at the time, a writer for popular magazines, a novelist, and an amateur actress. In Paris she had seen Rachel, the great French tragedienne, and without taking herself too seriously, Mrs. Mowatt had her own ideas about acting. She made her professional début in London in 1845 in *The Lady of Lyons,* playing the part of Pauline. Her performance ended with an ovation, and she was soon booked for a season's tour. In her first year on the stage she played two hundred nights. Among the parts she played were Juliet; Mrs. Haller in *The Stranger;* Lady Teazle; and the heroine of her own play, *Fashion.*

Mr. Pim Passes By. A. A. Milne (English). Comedy. 3 acts. 1919.

A charming widow, Olivia Telworthy, has been married for five years to George Marden, member of a highly respectable family. Her first husband was a no-account promoter from whom she had been separated for years before the newspapers announced his death in Australia. Dinah, George's niece, wants to marry Brian Strange, a young artist, but George disapproves. One day a Mr. Pim arrives from Australia with a letter of introduction, and in the course of conversation announces that Telworthy is still alive. George is horrified at the thought that his marriage is unhallowed by the church and the law. After much to-do, George sends for Mr. Pim to learn further details, and Mr. Pim says now that he heard that Telworthy died recently. George, happy again, asks Olivia to go to London to be married. She agrees after he promises to consent to Dinah and Brian's marriage. Mr. Pim returns once more to tell Olivia that he never knew anyone by the name of Telworthy, that the whole story was an invention of his fancy.

Mrs. Dane's Defense. Henry Arthur Jones (English). Drama. 4 acts. 1900.

Probably Jones' best known and most popular play. While the problem it treats is somewhat dated, it is still occasionally revived for audiences who appreciate its technical skill and expert craftsmanship.

Mrs. Dane is a lady with a past, at least according to rumors which have never been denied. Lionel Carteret, though, because he is passionately in love with her, is only too willing to be convinced of her innocence. And because Mrs. Dane returns the gentleman's affection, she is silent about her former escapade and lets Lionel believe the best of her. Lionel's stepfather, Sir Daniel Carteret, is unwilling to let the matter rest there, however. He exposes Mrs. Dane and reveals to his foster-son what she really is—a woman who has sinned. She and her lover have a showdown, and agree that her position in society is forever jeopardized. So they resign themselves to giving each other up, and not going through with the contemplated marriage.

Mrs. Warren's Profession. George Bernard Shaw (English). Drama. 3 acts. 1898.

Mrs. Warren, a child of the slums, has become the operator of a chain of brothels scattered throughout Europe. Her daughter Vivian has been educated in England in ignorance of her mother's profession. The girl, a promising mathematician, loves and is loved by the worthless son of a prominent clergyman. Mrs. Warren visits her daughter, accompanied by two hangers-on, Praed and Crofts. The latter, a dissolute baronet, wishes to marry Vivian, but is afraid she may be his own daughter. Then they meet the clergyman, and he is revealed also to be an ex-lover of Mrs. Warren. So Crofts decides the minister is probably the girl's father, and breaks up her match with her sweetheart by telling Vivian he is her stepbrother. The girl confronts her mother, who confesses her shame. Her daughter is understanding and forgiving, blaming the older woman for nothing. Vivian's sweetheart also learns from his father of the clergyman's past indiscretions, and to console himself asks Mrs. Warren to go on a jaunt to the Continent with him. Vivian, her romance shattered, departs for London to earn her own living.

This play shocked two continents. Clergymen and editorial writers, women's clubs and dramatic societies all harangued against its immorality. The London production was suppressed, as was the American try-out in New Haven. Nevertheless, the American producer determined to present it in New York. In 1905 it had its première, one of the most publicized events of the year. People paid as high as thirty dollars for a seat to the première; crowds stormed the entrance of the theatre on the opening night. Anthony Comstock stopped the play after a single performance and took the case to court. The drama was allowed to reopen, but by the time it was again shown the public had lost interest and the attendance was not overwhelming.

Mucedorus, The Comedy of. Author unknown (English). Printed 1598.

It was included in a volume with the title of *Shakespeare* in Charles II's library and it belonged in the repertoire of the company at the Globe. These facts have led some critics to assign the play to Shakespeare but the attribution has been almost universally rejected. It deals with the wooing of the daughter of the king of Aragon by Mucedorus, prince of Valencia.

Much Ado About Nothing. William Shakespeare (English). Comedy. 5 acts. 1598.

Written about 1598; published in quarto form in 1600. The main plot is based on a novel by Bandello. Beatrice and Benedick, Dogberry and Verges are Shakespeare's own creations. The love of Claudio and Hero of Messina is threatened when Don John, bastard brother of the Prince of Aragon, makes Claudio think Hero unfaithful to him with Borachio, an accomplice of Don John's. In reality, Claudio has seen Margaret, whom he mistakes for Hero, addressing Borachio from Hero's balcony. Claudio dramatically denounces Hero as they are about to be married. Hero faints and it is given out that she is dead. When Dogberry and Verges of the local constabulary, who discover the ruse, reveal Don John's villainy, Claudio agrees to marry Hero's cousin to atone for the death of Hero. At the altar the "cousin" is revealed to be Hero. In a sub-plot Beatrice, cousin to Hero, and Benedick, a young lord, spend most of the time railing at one another with wit and repartee. Friends lead them to believe that each is actually in love with the other, and eventually they agree that this is an acceptable arrangement.

Mugging. Excessive facial contortion in performance.

Mulligan's Guards. One of a series of plays about Irish-American life in New York City, written by Edward Harrigan. He produced it and played the title role. Tony Hart appeared as Mrs. Mulligan.

Mummer. One who took part in a mummers' play. The play was a rural product, its actors were farmers and small villagers, some of them wore masks and the clowns often blackened their faces. Mummers' plays came into being throughout the British Isles during the 15th century.

Munday, Anthony (1553-1633). English dramatist. Very little is known either of Munday's life or of his work. However, he was highly praised by his contemporaries for his comedy and for his skilful plotting. He is also credited with having exerted a definite influence on the dramatists of his time. The three plays definitely attributed to him are: *John a Kent and John a Cumber, The Downfall of Robert, Earle of Huntington,* and *The Death of Robert, Earle of Huntington.*

Munden, Joseph Shepherd (1758-1832). English actor. Born in London, he joined a strolling company, making a reputation as a comedian before coming to London in 1790. At Covent Garden, the Haymarket, and from 1813 at the Drury Lane, he became the most popular comedian of his time. He retired in 1824. Munden was the subject of an essay by Lamb and was highly praised also by Hazlitt and Leigh Hunt.

He is considered by Cecil F. Armstrong, "perhaps the best English broad comedian of any day." He was one of the "rebellious eight" who complained about the theatrical monopoly in London, in a letter criticizing Harris, manager of Covent Garden. His son, Thomas Shepherd Munden, wrote his biography.

Muni, Paul (1895-   ). Actor. Born in Austria. As Muni Weisenfreund made his first appearance on the stage in 1908 in New York in Yiddish Theatre Stock Co. He toured over the U. S. A. and remained on the Jewish Stage until 1926. Made his English speaking debut in *We, Americans.* Later he appeared in *Four Walls, This One Man,* 1931; *Rock Me Julie, Counselor-at-Law.* Went to Hollywood and started his film work in 1929. He is recognized as one of the greatest actors in motion pictures. He returned to the stage in Maxwell Anderson's *Key Largo,* 1939.

Municipal Theatre, Prague. Once the Vinohrady Theatre, a playhouse in Prague made municipal in 1922. Subert, once of the National Theatre, was its first director.

Munro, C. K. (1889-   ). Irish dramatist. Born in Ireland 1889 and educated at Harrow and Pembroke College, Cambridge. He wrote *Rumour,* a significant play because of its early use of expressionistic technique in the English theatre. He has also written *At Mrs. Beams,* 1923; *Progress,* 1924; *Storm,* 1924; *The Mountain,* 1926; *Cocks and Hens,* 1927; *Veronica,* 1928; *Mr. Eno,* 1930; *Bluestone Quarry,* 1931; *Bletheroe,* 1931; *True Woman,* 1932; *Ding and Co.,* 1934.

Murder, in early Greek theatre. Tabooed because of religious cast of early Greek plays; introduced only by messenger, dramatically ineffectual device; later: (1) behind closed doors, e.g., the cry of a Clytemnestra; (2) actor standing at door of chamber telling in broken words what he sees inside; (3) with *ekkuklema,* dead body of victim could be shown, wheeled, as tableau, into full gaze of audience.

Murder in the Cathedral. T. S. Eliot (English). Poetic drama. 2 acts. 1935.

After a serious quarrel with Henry II resulting in exile to France, Thomas a Becket, Archbishop of Canterbury, finally returns to his beloved Cathedral, knowing that the king desires his death. He nevertheless exposes himself—refusing to flee from the king's henchmen who come for his life. He thereby gains martyrdom and immortality.

By a clever trick in the writing, the murderers step out of character and present their side of the story to the audience.

Murray, Sir George Gilbert Aimé (1866-   ). English scholar, dramatist. Born in Sydney, New South Wales; D.Litt. from St. John's College, Oxford; LL.D., Glasgow, 1900; Fellow of New College, Oxford, 1888; Professor of Greek, Glasgow University, 1889-99; Regius Professor of Greek, Oxford University, since 1908; F.B.A., 1910. He has written a number of books on English politics, and has made numerous translations from the Greek and a history of Ancient Greek literature. He is one of the great authorities on ancient Drama.

His plays include: *Carlyon Sahib,* 1899; *Andromache,* 1900; the *Hippolytus* of Euripides (translation), 1904; *The Trojan Women* (translation), 1905; the *Electra* of Euripides (translation), 1906; *Oedipus Rex* (translation), 1912; etc.

Muses, The. The muses were daughters of *Jupiter* and *Mnemosyne* (memory). In Greek and Roman mythology they presided over song and aided the memory. Nine in number, each was assigned to care over a particular department of literature, art or science. The three that presided over phases of the drama are: Melpomene, muse of tragedy; Thalia, muse of comedy; Terpsichore, muse of choral dance and song.

Museum of Costume Art. Organization located at 630 Fifth Avenue, New York. Founded in 1937 by Irene Lewisohn and Aline Bernstein for the purpose of permanent costume exhibits available to research workers; also available is a library of books and documents that serve as source material for the study of costume design and history.

Museum of the City of New York. See *Theatre collections.*

Music, Shakespearean. In accordance with Elizabethan taste, music is used extensively in Shakespeare's plays. In general, it is of three sorts, fanfares, used chiefly in battle scenes and royal pageants, dances and incidental background music, especially in the masques and entertainments inserted in the plays, and in songs. In the text of the plays Shakespeare shows an unusually accurate knowledge of the art, technique and uses of music. Thomas Morley's settings of *It was a lover and his lass* (*As You Like It*) and *O mistress mine* (*Twelfth Night*) are the only tunes employed in the original productions which have survived.

Musical comedy. The history of this form of entertainment is as involved as it is interesting. It developed from the old *Opera Buffa,* which was originated by Logroscino, Cimarosa, and other operetta writers of the period, and the French *Opéra Buffe,* as well as the German counterpart. Definitions and distinctions of operetta, musical comedy, light opera and *opéra comique* usually overlap. It is enlightening to read, in J. Walker McSpadden's *Light Opera and Musical Comedy,* of their separate characteristics and their respective forms. McSpadden says: "In Italy it was the *Opera Buffa.* In France, the *Opéra Buffe.* In Germany, the sentimental opera, or that of the Viennese type. In Russia, folk lore. In England, the ballad opera. In America, a little bit of everything, with emphasis on Musical Comedy." It is not generally regarded as a serious dramatic form though occasionally a musical comedy such as *Of Thee I Sing* has genuine merit apart from its music. In such a case, as in the case of the Gilbert and Sullivan operettas, it is generally labelled *Operetta play with music,* etc.

Music Box, New York. Playhouse built by Sam H. Harris and Irving Berlin in 1921, with Howard Crane of Detroit as architect. Since the *Music Box Revues* which held the stage for the first four years of the theatre's history, there have been many comedies and musical shows at the Music Box. William Collier, Fannie Brice, Grace Moore, William Gaxton, Frank Morgan, Victor Moore and Beatrice Lillie are only a few whose successes were scored in this theatre on West 45th Street.

Music hall. Name for any theatre specializing in a *pot-pourri* of popular musical presentations, with song, dance and variety acts; closely akin to the vaudeville theatre; became popular in the Restoration and 18th century theatres and reached its apex in modern theatres, where such presentations are interludes between showings of motion pictures. The Radio City Music Hall in New York City is most famous of all today.

Musique room. A small chamber in the upper gallery of the Elizabethan playhouse, usually to one side of the stage proper, reserved for the players of incidental music.

Musset, Alfred de (1810-1857). French author, dramatist. Born in Paris, December 11, 1810, having dabbled in law and medicine, he decided to devote himself to literature after he made the acquaintance of the circle of romantics of whom Victor Hugo was the chief. Early in 1830 he published *Contes d'Espagne et d'Italie,* which met with a cordial reception. His first comedy, *La Nuit Venitienne,* was not successful and he was plunged into depression. He continued to write, however, and *La Coupe et les Levres* and *A quoi revent les Jeunes Filles,* two short plays, were published in 1832. The following year two comedies, *Andre del Sarto,* and his greatest work,

Les Caprices de Marianne, were produced. These met with great success. From 1833 dates de Musset's passion for George Sand. They set out in December for Venice, but separated in anger after only a few months. Although much depressed, de Musset returned with redoubled vigor to writing, and some of his best work belongs to the years 1835-38. His play, *Il ne faut jurer de rien,* was written during this time. After his appointment as librarian at the home office in Paris, he wrote his proverb play, *Il faut qu' une Porte soit ouverte ou fermee,* 1845, and in 1847, his *Un Caprice* made a notable stage success. He died May 2, 1857.

Great alike as poet, dramatist, and story writer, de Musset combined fervent passion and great lyrical genius with the finest wit and rare dramatic ability. As a dramatist, he still figures in the repertory of the Comedie-Française.

Mustapha. Sir Fulke Greville Brook (English). Tragedy. 5 acts. Printed 1609.

Rossa, wife of the Turkish Emperor Solyman, persuades her husband that Mustapha, his son by a former marriage, seeks his life. She endeavors thereby to advance the prospects of her own children. Camena, the virtuous daughter of Rossa, however, defends Mustapha in vain. Mustapha refuses to seek safety in the destruction of Rossa and her faction and is finally executed.

My Heart's in the Highlands. William Saroyan (American). Drama. 1 act. 1939.

A poet, his son, and an old Armenian woman live in poverty in California, coaxing food from a nearby grocer. Into the family comes an old actor who plays the trumpet so beautifully that the whole countryside comes to hear him play, bringing gifts of food and listening quietly. However, the old actor dies, and the poet and his family are evicted. As they are leaving, the poet's boy says, "I'm not mentioning any names, Pa, but something's wrong somewhere."

Mystère d'Adam, Le. See *Adam.*

Mystery of Abraham and Isaac. The second specimen of dramatic composition in the English language dating from about the middle of the 14th century and written in the early vernacular.

Mystery plays. Sacred plays of the Middle Ages, deriving from the early Medieval liturgical dramas; so called because performed by guilds of craftsmen. (Middle English *misterie,* from the old French: *mester* and the Latin *ministerium*—meaning trade.)

See also *Miracle plays; Drama, medieval; Dramas, liturgical; Chester Plays; Drama, British, earliest.*

Nachapiel. The name given the little comic afterpiece of the strolling players' bill in 18th century German drama.

Nakamura Kichiemon (1888-   ). Japanese actor. Born in Tokyo. Debut at age of eleven. Afterwards played in *Kotomo Shibai* (Children's Theatre), becoming very widely appreciated. Appeared co-starred with Onoe Kikugoro several times. Lives in suburbs of Tokyo. Well known Japanese *Kabuki* actor who is skillful in the performance of *Mie* (the climax posing in a drama).

See also *Acting, Japanese*.

Naked. Luigi Pirandello (Italian). Tragedy. 3 acts. 1922.

Ersilia has come from a hospital where she recuperated after drinking poison in a fit of despair. She had been deserted by Franco and accused of negligence when the consul's child, to whom she was governess, fell off the roof and was killed. She was trying to make a new life, but the truth of her affair with the consul has leaked out and Franco, who had come back for her, full of remorse, again takes his leave. Ersilia is left with the full knowledge that she can never reach the respectable position she so earnestly desires.

Nanine. Voltaire (French). Comedy. 5 acts. 1762.

This play is based on Richardson's *Pamela*. It was commended by Rousseau.

Nanine, the heroine, is a helpless woman who carries on her frail shoulders much of the world's sorrow, but little of its responsibility.

The plot is not complex, resting mainly on a letter Nanine writes to her peasant father. It is mistaken for a missive to her lover.

Voltaire points out in a foreword that in his belief, tragedy should be kept on a high social plane.

Nashe, Thomas (1567-1601). English poet, playwright and pamphleteer. Educated at St. John's College, Cambridge, and settled in London. Became a friend of Greene and Marlowe. He hated puritanism and bitterly attacked its defenders in numerous pamphlets. In 1592 he wrote the satirical masque *Summer's Last Will and Testament*. After Marlowe's death in 1596 he prepared his friend's unfinished tragedy *Dido* for the stage. He was partly responsible for the now lost play *Isle of Dogs* which because of its seditious and slanderous matter landed Ben Jonson and him in jail.

Nashville Community Playhouse (Tennessee). In 1935 an organization of people who had been active in the Little Theatre, 1926-1936, and a number of younger people, organized the Playhouse. Its annual budget is made public. It has affiliated groups such as the *Children's Theatre,* the *Vanderbilt Masque Club, Peabody College Dramatic Club,* etc. It has a *Back Stage Club* and publishes monthly *The Off-Stage Noise*.

Nathan, George Jean (1882-   ). American editor, author, dramatic critic. Born in Fort Wayne, Indiana. Received his A.B. from Cornell University, 1904; attended University of Bologna. For over thirty years he has been attending New York first nights and writing about them. After two years on the New York Herald, 1906-08, he became dramatic critic and associate editor of Bohemian Magazine and

Outing. Magazines for which he has since written dramatic criticisms include Harper's Weekly; Smart Set, of which he also became an editor in 1914; The Saturday Review of Literature; Esquire; Scribner's; Newsweek; The New Freeman; Puck; Judge; Life; Vanity Fair; etc. He was founder and editor (with H. L. Mencken) of The American Mercury, 1924-30; and founder and editor (with Eugene O'Neill and others) of The American Spectator, 1932.

His many published works include *Mr. George Jean Nathan Presents*, 1917; *The Popular Theatre*, 1918; *Comedians All*, 1919; *The Theatre, The Drama, The Girls*, 1921; *The Critic and the Drama*, 1922; *The Testament of a Critic*, 1931; *The Morning After the First Night*, 1939; etc. He was an editor of *The Theatre of Today Dramatic Library;* and president of the New York Critics Dramatic Circle, 1936-39.

Probably no other contemporary American critic has so greatly influenced public taste during a third of a century. At the beginning of his career he was a staunch advocate of the continental realists such as Ibsen and Strindberg, and protested against the lack of taste and intelligence in much of the current American dramatic output. He urged both his fellow critics and the public to insist that national playwrights raise their standards. He was no critic of polished comedies or light works in general, but he was against foolish ones which lacked even the grace of urbanity.

In his book, *Two on the Aisle,* John Mason Brown says: "The importance of being Nathan . . . hell-bound to be the one contrary-minded member of the jury . . . a wretched guide but an excellent diagnostician . . . Part Columbus, part Fouché . . . symbol of impudence, gayety and irreverence." Many of the causes for which Nathan fought have been won, thanks in part to his prodding. But he is continuing to prod, and still to be as often as not "the one contrary-minded member of the jury."

Nathan the Wise. G. E. Lessing (German). Drama. 3 acts. 1783.

A plea for religious tolerance, reflecting the social idealism of the 18th century.

The scene is in Jerusalem. A certain Christian knight woos Recka, the supposed child of a Jew. Nathan has concealed the fact that she is a baptized Christian. When this is discovered, he is brought before the Sultan. Nathan relates to the Sultan the beautiful story of "The Father and the Ring," an allegory which pleads for religious tolerance. This play is a classic of German literature.

National Theatre. See *State Theatre.*

National Theatre Conference. An association of college and university theatres begun as a subscription organization for all in the amateur theatre field or who were interested in it. Since 1936 it has become an organization whose membership is only increased by a vote of the board. Certain people who are outstanding in related fields may be elected to membership. The Conference meets annually. Gilmor Brown of the Pasadena Community Playhouse is president; E. C. Mabie of the University of Iowa, vice-president; Barclay Leathum of Western Reserve University, secretary; Frederic McConnell of The Playhouse, Cleveland, treasurer.

Naturalism. Partakes of the same external form as realism, but emphasizes the natural function in life, as opposed to realism which is more selective. In the novel and drama, Zola is the most imposing example; in the theatre Stanislavsky and the Moscow Art Theatre uphold this form, particularly in Gorky's *The Lower Depths.*

Naumachia. An ancient Roman amphitheatre with lake centers designed for spectacular enactments of sea fights.

Nautical Drama. Melodrama which glorified the British navy and which employed large tanks filled with water for the playing of certain scenes showing drownings, battles and rescues.

Nazimova, Alla (1879-). Russian-American actress. Born in Yalta, Russia; educated in Switzerland and Odessa; studied music and dramatics in Moscow, toured the provinces and was leading lady at St. Petersburg. She made her English-speaking debut as Hedda in *Hedda Gabler* in 1906. Has played continuously both in the United States and Europe and has been successful in the motion pictures. Among her outstanding performances have been those she has given in Ibsen's and Chekhov's plays.

John Mason Brown says of her, "One of the rarest talents of our stage. Her nerves are charged with that special sort of electricity which is known as theatricality."

The plays she has appeared in include: *Hedda Gabler; A Doll's House; The Cherry Orchard; Katerina; A Woman of the Earth; Dagmar; War Brides;* etc.

Ned McCobb's Daughter. Sidney Howard (American). Comedy. 3 acts. 1926.

Left with a worthless husband and two children, Ned McCobb's daughter, Carrie, trys to earn a living by managing a small restaurant in a New England town. She becomes involved with a gang of rum runners, nearly loses her investment, but through her Yankee shrewdness, finally outwits the gang, and saves her business.

Negro, American, his relation to the stage. During his brief residence on the American stage the Negro has had to fight against race prejudice and tradition to win his place behind the footlights. Naturally talented, however, and loving music and dance, he has carried on smilingly, giving pleasure to those liberal enough to recognize him. His effect on the American stage has been scattered and exciting, but particularly noteworthy from the standpoint of acting, and popular song and dance music. For many years, the Negro was just the old minstrel man. Then during the Nineties Cole and Johnson, and Williams and Walker emerged into comedy teams that gained popular approval. But when Bert Williams, bereft of his partner, appeared as one of the stars of Ziegfeld's *Follies of 1911,* the public was scandalized, or pretended to be; and it was not until six to ten years had passed before mixed casts were received without exceptional comment. Only then did dramatic editors of New York newspapers include photographs of colored players in their layouts. Meanwhile it had become possible to observe the Negro's development in all forms of art, particularly those related to the stage.

There has been, of course, an effort to claim great things for the Negro in relation to American music. But syncopation, sometimes claimed as his specific contribution to musical composition, is as old as Lizst; and the Spiritual, long praised so solemnly, is now considered a rewriting of old hymns rather than an importation from primitive Africa. But even when working in his own medium of popular music, the Negro can claim only part honors for accomplishment. White composers from Irving Berlin and his *Alexander's Ragtime Band,* through George Gershwin, have employed the Negro's own idiom, and made it their own. Thus coon song, ragtime and swing have come to be representatively American rather than specifically African.

The Negro is a born actor, who ranks consistently high with the greatest members of the acting profession. During the last few years, thanks to more plays about colored folk, the Negro is coming into his own. Among the outstanding artists are: Paul Robeson, who is something of a superman—an actor, a singer, a linguist and an athlete; Charles Gilpin, of *The Emperor Jones;* the incomparable Florence Mills; Harrison, De Lawd in *Green Pastures;* Wesley Hill, the Angel Gabriel in the same play; Ethel Waters, inspired star of *Mamba's Daughters;* Julius Bledsoe; Rose McClendon; Abbie Mitchell; Fredi Washington; Marion Anderson, phenomenal concert artist; and Bill Robinson, the perfect embodiment of the dance; Duke Ellington, Cab Calloway and Jim Europe head the small army of gifted bandleaders. Among the recent productions that gave the Negro welcome stage opportunities were: *Green Pastures; All God's Chillun Got Wings; Run Little Chillun* by Paul Johnson, 1933; *Porgy* by Du Bose Heywood; *Porgy and Bess; Showboat* by Jerome Kern and Oscar Hammerstein with its modern American folk song, *Ol' Man River; Deep River* by Laurence Stallings, 1927; *Roseanne* by Nan Bagby Stephens, 1923; the Harlem version of *Macbeth; The Hot Mikado;* and *Kykunkor* by Asadata Daford.

In musical comedy and revue which began their Broadway history consciously about fifteen years ago with Lew Leslie's *Blackbirds; Shuffle Along,* with Sissle and Blake; *Strut Miss Lizzie;* and with the Franklin D. Roosevelt Jones number, *Sing Out the News,* the public had the opportunity of judging the Negro as a librettist, a composer of light musical entertainment, and as a dancer and comedian. He rates lowest as a writer, his comedy being commonplace, seldom above colored burlesque. But as a singer, comedian and dancer his talents are indisputable and provocative. Prominent among Negro composers are: Gussie L. Davis, author of such popular ballads of the Nineties as *The Baggage Coach Ahead* and *My Creole Sue;* James Bland, author of *The Mocking Bird;* Eubie Blake; Noble Sissle; Harry T. Burleigh; James Weldon Johnson and J. Rosamond Johnson; Shelton Brooks, writer of *Some of These Days;* Wilbur Sweatman; Bill Vodery; Duke Ellington; Ford Dabney; W. C. Handy, originator of the *Blues* and author of the *St. Louis Blues.*

The Negro is gradually finding himself also in pictures. Individual players are already well established, but not entire colored cast productions. Notable films, which were not financially successful, were: *Hallelujah; Emperor Jones; Green Pastures.*

Indefatigable has been the work of Lew Leslie in discovering and developing Negro talent and presenting musicals here and abroad. Laudable and generously helpful to the cause of all art have been Carl Van Vechten's confirmations, recognition and appraisals of Negro talent and growing culture.

See also *Negro Authors and Composers of the United States*. Pamphlet published by Handy Brothers Music Co., Inc., 1587 Broadway, New York. *The Negro Actors Guild. They All Sang*, E. B. Marks; *Blues*, An Anthology, edited by W. C. Handy; *Negro Musicians and Their Music*, Maud Cuney-Hare.

Neighborhood Playhouse. Built and endowed in 1915 by the Misses Alice and Irene Lewisohn, at 466 Grand Street, New York, where for the first five years an amateur group put on ballets and new plays. Later a professional company performed the work of Shaw, O'Neill, Percy Mackaye and others, the *Grand Street Follies*, and musical-dramatic experiments. Since 1927, when the Neighborhood Playhouse as a theatre closed, the Neighborhood Playhouse as a corporation sponsoring occasional artistic productions has presented several musical programs and, on its 20th anniversary in 1935, a Spanish play, *Bitter Oleander*, at the Lyceum Theatre. Offices of the organization, and of the Neighborhood Playhouse School of The Theatre are at 16 West 46th Street, New York City.

Neilson, Adelaide (1848-1880). English actress. A noted Shakespearean actress, famous for her Juliet and Viola; made her American début in 1877 and acted under Daly's banner.

Neithart Play. The name given to the longest German Shrovetide play; it exceeds 200 verses; author unknown.

Nemirovich-Danchenko, Vladimir. See *Moscow Art Theatre; Theatre, Russian, 19th Century to the Revolution*.

Neo-classicists. Name given to the French school of dramaturgy in the 17th century known for its *imitation des anciens* and represented by Corneille and Racine. All their themes were drawn from Greek and Roman history and mythology and their methods of dramatic construction and style followed the Aristotelian precepts of the unities, the law of beginning, middle and end, etc.

The Nest (*Les Noces D'Argent*). Paul Geraldy (French). Drama. 4 acts. 1917.
A simple story of children who grow up and leave the nest—of the young bride, much more interested in her own home than in the parents she left—of a young son whose main interest is his "affairs."

The mother fights back when she feels she is losing her children, but as in all other such cases, her fight is a losing one.

She finally realizes that, just as they have become independent of her, so she must become independent of them.

Neuber, Frederika Caroline (1697-1760). German actress. Manager of a company at Leipzig. With Johann Neuber, formed an alliance in 1727 with Johann

Gottsched, which completed the reformation of the German stage. The plays in which they appeared were mostly translated from the French and were complete texts.
See also *Drama, German, 17th-18th century; Actresses, earliest.*

Neue Freie Volksbuehne. Great free folk stage in Berlin founded by Dr. Bruno Wille; opened November 1892 and by 1914 had a membership of 50,000. In 1913 it became affiliated with the *Freie Volksbuehne* to erect a playhouse and the first real people's theatre of modern times was thus founded; it was called the *New Free People's Stage Society.*
See also *New Free People's Stage Society.*

Neumann, Christiane (1778-1797). German actress. Appeared in Goethe's Weimar Court Theatre. Acted in: *Die Jager; Die Rauber; Kabale und Liebe.*

New Free People's Stage Society. The name of the first real people's theatre of modern times; formed through the affiliation of the *Freie Volksbuehne* and the *Neue Freie Volksbuehne* when in 1913 they broke ground for their theatre building.

New Game, The. Henri Lavedan (French). Drama. 5 acts. Printed 1906.
A worldling takes a wife on a bet, and then drops her for the lady who had driven him into the marriage. His short-term wife has accepted him merely to be in the mode and, when they quarrel, finds consolation in another. Reproved by the divorce judge for having committed such facile matrimony, the hero explains that marriage resembles spinach: "In order to know if you dislike it, you must first taste it."

New Idol, The. François de Curel (French). Drama. 3 acts. 1899.
The title refers to science. A physician believes it to be his duty to sacrifice the individual in experiments calculated to save the many. He has inoculated with the virus of cancer a girl already doomed, as he believes, by tuberculosis. When unexpectedly she recovers from that malady, and learns that she must die as a result of the physician's experiments, she consoles him by accepting cheerfully for the sake of humanity the sacrifice he has imposed.

Newington Butts Theatre. A public theatre built soon after 1576 at Newington, a village one mile from London Bridge. It was occupied briefly in 1594 by the combined Admiral's and Lord Chamberlain's Men under Philip Henslowe's management.

Newspaper columnists. For the last twenty years, columnists have had a tremendous influence and importance in American affairs. Among the most famous columnists interested largely in theatre and cinema have been: Walter Winchell; O. O. McIntyre—Chas. B. Driscoll now carries on the McIntyre tradition; F.P.A. (Franklin Pierce Adams), the modern Samuel Pepys and *Information Please* standby; Lucius Beebe, WOR's drama commentator and conductor of the *This New York* column; Bugs Baer; Heywood Broun; John Chapman (Mainly about Manhattan); Mark Hellinger, who is a film producer and writer of books and plays as well; Damon Runyon; the Hearst Syndicate's Louella Parsons, one of the first and greatest movie arbiters; Leonard Lyons (The Lyons Den), of the New York Post;

Ed Sullivan (Hollywood), who is a stage headliner; the Journal-American's Louis Sobol, who is also a novelist and dramatist; Jimmy Fidler, who conducts the widely syndicated *Jimmy Fidler in Hollywood* column; Ward Morehouse (Broadway After Dark); Gail Borden, a pioneer Chicago columnist; Irving Hoffman (Tales of Hoffman); Danton Walker, of the Daily News; George Ross, Jr., of the World-Telegram; Sidney Skolsky, whose Times Square Tin Types are nationally known; Dorothy Kilgallen, of the Journal-American; Mark Barron, of the Associated Press; June Provines, of the Chicago Tribune.

New Way to Pay Old Debts. Philip Massinger (English). Comedy. 1633.
Frank Wellborn loses his property to Sir Giles Overreach, his avaricious uncle. Lady Allworth, a wealthy widow, consents to help him by pretending she would marry him, and Overreach changes his attitude. Tom, Lady Allworth's stepson and a page to Lord Lovell, is in love with Margaret, Overreach's daughter, but Overreach wants his daughter to marry Lord Lovell. The young couple are aided by Lord Lovell who leads Overreach to believe that Margaret and he will be married. Overreach becomes insane upon discovering the deceit and is confined to Bedlam, and it develops that he is not entitled to Wellborn's property.

New York Drama Critics' Circle. An informal organization of the leading newspaper and magazine drama critics was formed during the 1935-36 season to select the best American play produced on Broadway for the first time. Since the 1937-38 season the best foreign play has also been chosen.

New York Drama Critics Circle Award. An annual award given to the American play produced for the first time on Broadway which is judged best by the majority of the members of the circle, who come together usually in April to vote. An opportunity is given the dissenters to make their votes known at the dinner given late in April, when the silver plaque designed by Henry Varnum Poore, depicting *The Contrast* at the John Street Theatre, is presented to the author. Up to now a nation-wide broadcast has been a feature of the dinner. The award to the best foreign play produced on Broadway (originated 1938) is also presented.

New York Public Library, The. Though rivaled by the *Library of Congress,* probably the most exhaustive theatrical resources exist here. In 1925, after the theatre interests of the Library had been kept alive through the alert mind and watchful cherishing of Florence Overton, Supervisor of Branches, a circulating drama collection was assembled and organized under Eunice Comstock Wilson at the 58th Street Branch, 127 E. 58th St. Miss Wilson remains in charge of a largely augmented collection which has a devoted theatrical public. In 1931, under the initiative of George Freedley, Curator, a reference Theatre Collection was organized. There are approximately 100,000 volumes, 5,000,000 clippings, 500,000 photographs, 450,000 programmes and playbills in this collection. These are available for *reference* in the Central Building, Fifth Avenue and 42nd Street.
See also *Freedley, George Reynolds; Theatre collections; Theatre Library Association.*

N. G. Letters signifying "no good," which were painted on front of the Buckingham Theatre drops, which closed in on a performer when an audience didn't like his act.

Niblo's Gardens. First known as *Sans Souci,* 1828-1895. For sixty years almost every artist of consequence identified with the American stage appeared here. Niblo's was a fashionable public entertainment garden, opened at Broadway and Prince Street in New York, by the restaurateur and impresario, William Niblo. At first summer programs consisting of gala concerts, fireworks, and tight-rope walking made the place popular; later, plays took over the stage. Its most famous and oft-revived production was a dance extravaganza—America's first "leg" show—called *The Black Crook.* Twice burned down (1846, 1848), Niblo's Gardens rose like the Phoenix, more glorious than ever. Among the distinguished performers on its roster were Adelaide Lehman, Charles Kean, the Ravel family, Edwin Forrest, Anna Cora Mowatt, Dion Boucicault, Charlotte Cushman, and E. L. Davenport.

Nichols, Anne. American dramatist, producer. Primarily known as the author of *Abie's Irish Rose,* which held the record for the longest run any play ever had. She was also manager for the 1924 production of French repertory with Madame Simone.

Other plays she has written include: *Linger Longer Letty,* 1919; *The Gilded Cage,* 1920; *Love Dreams,* 1921; *Just Married* (with Adelaide Matthews), 1921.

Nichols, Lewis. American dramatic critic. Drama editor of the New York *Times,* critic, contributor to the *New York Times Magazine* and other publications.

Nicholson, (John) Kenyon (1894-   ). American dramatist. Born in Crawfordsville, Indiana. Studied at Columbia University, Wabash College and Cambridge University; has been an instructor in dramatic composition at Columbia University (Extension Department) since 1921. Author of the following plays: *Honor Bright* (with Meredith Nicholson), 1923; *Garden Varieties,* 1924; *Sally and Company,* 1925; *The Meal Ticket,* 1926; *Revues,* 1926; *Here's to Your Health* (with Charles Knox), 1927; *Tell Me Your Troubles,* 1928; *Taxi,* 1929; *The American Scene* (with Barrett H. Clark)—words and music, 1930. His plays which have been produced on Broadway are: *The Barker, Civilized People, Love is Like That* (with S. N. Behrman), *Eva the Fifth* (with John Golden), *Before You're Twenty-five, Torch Song, Stepdaughters of War, A Place in the Sun, Sailor, Beware!* (with Charles Robinson), *Swing Your Lady, June Night.*

Nicoll, Allardyce (1894-   ). British historian. Scottish-born authority on theatrical subjects. Chairman of Department of Drama at Yale University since 1933, and founder of the collection of unique theatre iconography in that institution. Author of *A History of Restoration Drama; Early 18th Century Drama; Late 18th Century Drama; Early 19th Century Drama; The Development of the Theatre;*

Studies in Shakespeare; The English Stage; British Drama; The Theory of the Drama; Masks, Mimes and Miracles; The English Theatre; Theatre and Film. See also *Yale University.*

Nigger, The. Edward Sheldon (American). Drama. 3 acts. 1910.
A case study of the Negro problem in the United States. This was one of the first American plays to deal with an important social problem. It anticipated by years the development of the Social Theatre in America.

Night at an Inn, A. Lord Dunsany (Irish). Drama. 1 act. 1916.
Five sailors steal a great ruby from the eye of the Hindu god, Kish. Late one night they are drawn one by one out of an inn and murdered by avenging priests of the god. The play, although simple in plot, is a tense little drama of horror and suspense which is very popular with amateur theatre groups.

Night Must Fall. Emlyn Williams (English). Melodrama. 3 acts. 1936.
Danny, bellhop in a summer hotel, and criminally insane, makes friends with old Mrs. Branson, goes to live in her cottage and finally murders her. The play is simple in plot and its dramatic value depends on the sinister development of Danny's psychopathic mind.

Night Over Taos. Maxwell Anderson (American). Drama. 3 acts. 1932.
The last stand of the Montoyas, feudal lords of Taos, against the drive of American democracy and conquest. Pablo Montoyas tries to lead a revolt against the American settlers, but when he is betrayed by his own son, he takes poison rather than accept defeat.

Night Watchman, The (*Le Veilleur de nuit*). Sacha Guitry (French). Drama. 3 acts. 1911.
A professor, discovering that his mistress entertains a second lover, accepts the situation philosophically. He offers his generous aid and assures her that only unfounded suspicion is detestable. The play is a witty satire on convention.

Nijinsky, Vaslav (1892-   ). Russian dancer. Born in Warsaw and received his training in the Russian Imperial Ballet in St. Petersburg. He was considered the outstanding male dancer of all time and was connected with Diaghileff's Ballet Russe. A quarrel with Diaghileff brought about a separation. He headed his own company until worry brought on by the First World War caused a mental collapse. His most famous creations were: *Le Spèctre de la Rose; Petrushka; Carnival; Les Sylphides* and *L'Après midi d'un faune.*

Ningyo-zyoruri. The proper name for a play which is performed by puppets in Japanese drama. Zyoruri means the telling of the puppet play by a chanter.

Nippers, The (Les Tenailles). Paul Hervieu (French). Drama. 5 acts. 1895.
A husband refuses to allow his wife a divorce. She turns for consolation to a scholar who is in love with her and has a child by him which the husband thinks is his own.

After many years, when the scholar is already dead, their quarrels break out anew, and she throws in his face the fact that he is not the father of the child.

Infuriated, he demands proof, which she refuses to give. He then demands a divorce, which she also refuses, explaining that now they have an obligation to the child and can no longer think only of their own wishes.

Noctes Atticae. A treatise on drama and the theatre by the ancient Roman author, Aulus Gellius. This work, says Barrett Clark in his *European Theories of the Drama,* "is the last of the Latin writings with any pretension to originality" concerned with the subject of dramatic theory.

Nō drama. The oldest living form of Japanese drama, practically unchanged since its origin late in the 14th century. Written in prose and verse of high nobility and subtlety, and employing choral music and dancing. Its traditions are religious and symbolical developing from the *Saru-gaku* dance and song representations of the earlier centuries. The *Nō* appealed to the upper classes and the literary. There are two kinds of *Nō:* visual and auditory. They were formerly based on the One Actor theory but at the last stage of development the Second Actor grew in importance almost to surpass the First. The names of the first two players are always: (1) *Shite,* (2) *Waki.* Each is accompanied by companions called *Tsure,* or a boy called *Ko-kata.* A program of *Nō* plays usually consists of five plays but programs of three are also popular. It is customary to place the *Kyōgen,* or comic interludes between the plays; that is, a program of five plays contains three *Kyōgen,* which relieves the emotional strain of the main plays. There are 235 *Nō* plays extant and 133 of these are common to all schools. *Nō* plays fall into six groups: (1) The *God Piece* (*Kami-mono*) or the Second Actor's *Nō* (*Waki-Nō*), in which the principal theme praises the virtue and dignity of a god. *Tagasago, Oimatsu, Kamo* are typical plays. (2) The *Battle Piece* (*Shura-Mono*), in which pathetic scenes of the battlefield are described. *Tamura, Yashima, Tsunemasa* are examples. (3) The *Wig Piece* or *Woman Piece* (*Katsura-mono*) wherein men impersonate females and are introduced as beautiful young women, or very old women, or as spirits of plants, and dance gracefully. *Toboku, No-no-miya, Hagoromo, Yohiki* are representative. (4) The *Lunatic Piece* (*Kurui-mono*) and the "Revenge Piece" (*Onryo-mono*) in which a lunatic plays a man or a woman who has gone mad through the loss of a child. *Sauragawa, Fuji-Daiko, Hana-gatami* are typical plays. In the Revenge plays, strong emotions which are aroused in a woman against a man for his infidelity are depicted. *Dojo-ji, Kinuta, Funabashi* are examples. (5) The *Earthly Piece* (*Genzai-mono*). In most *Nō* plays, ghosts of the dead are the leads, but in this group the living take the leads and are realistically treated. *Hachi-no-ki, Kogo, Shozon* are representative. (6) The *Last Piece* (Kiri-Noh-mono)—wherein supernatural beings appear and perform their special dances. *Kurozuka* and *Kokaji* are typical. In this group are also plays in which gods appear who have a mysterious power though without godly virtues. *Kuzu, Kenjo, Tani-ki, Ama, Shari* are examples.

Iwao Kongo is reputedly the most distinguished living exponent of the Japanese *Nō* drama.

The *Nō* is unexcelled for poetic subtlety, high idealism, artistic aspirations and nobility. For centuries it has constituted the principal form of entertainment among the upper classes. L. Adams Beck in *The Ghost Plays of Japan,* 1933, wrote: ". . . The *Nō* play, as it has come down to us, owes all to Buddhism; and the better the Buddhistic attitude to life and death is understood, the more certainly will this be felt.

"This perhaps is the reason why the *Nō* plays, like all Far Eastern art, appear so strange to us at first. The belief at the base of them is alien—we do not know what they are driving at. We depict life in the studio, or on the stage, in relation to ourselves. To our minds all beauty exists for man. It pleads at his judgment bar—it is his lovely slave. But to the artist influenced by Buddhistic teaching, man himself is but a small part of nature—a part of it only in the same sense as a tree or a flower; animated by the same spirit, no more, no less; passing to the same goal; subordinate, subjected to Law, as is a bough waving in the wind; a mountain-peak lost in drowning vapors. This belief has, of course, made Far Eastern artists the greatest landscape and flower artists of the world, for they have recognized that the essence of nature differs in no kind from their own, and have therefore painted as they knew.

". . . the ghosts [of the *Nō* plays] are dim wistful voices, wandering unsatisfied in lonely air. . . . The Japanese ghosts are the most insubstantial in all the world. . . . Homer's ghosts, blown like dead leaves in hell, drinking the blood of beasts, are tangible in comparison. Dante's suffering in singeing flames and glacial hells, are solid beside them; for these are the tortures that conquerors inflict and the reason of man denies; but the *Nō* ghosts, inexpressible as an odor,—a faint dream gone with the dawn—are to me the most real and terrible ghosts I know. For we have all felt them; we carry them, each of us, in our own bosom."

For synopses of some typical *Nō* plays see *Ama; Hachi-no-ki; Hagoromo; Isutsu; Ominameshi.*

See also *Acting, Japanese; Drama, Japanese; Staging, Japanese.*

Noises, off-stage. Sound effects performed off stage in relation to the stage action and to enhance the realism of that action. There are six general characteristics. Intensity of volume; pitch; quality-relationship in intensity and pitch; direction; distance; form—real or apparent reverberation.

No More Peace. Ernst Toller (German). Comedy. 2 acts. Lyrics by W. H. Auden. 1937.

The play is a satiric comedy in 2 acts. It opens in Mt. Olympus where Napoleon and St. Francis are arguing as to whether mankind really wants peace. They turn to the imaginary state of Dunkelstein to prove their theories. A peace festival at Dunkelstein is interrupted by a fabricated telegram from Napoleon. At once Dunkelstein is thrown into a militarized state. In short scenes the behaviour of mankind at war is brilliantly satirized. Socrates attempts to restore peace by reason and fails. Peace is restored only when an angel guided by selfish notions betrays the fact that the war is a trick of the Olympians.

Northward Hoe. John Webster and Thomas Dekker (English). Comedy. 5 acts. Printed 1607.

As revenge, because he has been repulsed, Greenfield claims to have had intimate relations with Mayberry's wife. Mayberry, at first enraged, is finally convinced of his wife's innocence.

Notices. Reviews; dramatic criticisms; clippings.

No Time for Comedy. S. N. Behrman (American). Comedy. 1939.

A production of the Playwrights' Company, starring Katharine Cornell. In it the playwright admittedly dramatizes his own dilemma: Should a writer with a gift for light comedy be content to devote himself to inconsequential plays during a time of crisis, or should he attempt to attack the problems uppermost in men's thoughts? His answer is: Let each man do what he can do best, whether it be provoking mirth or creating high tragedy.

Gaylord Easterbrook is the playwright of the comedy; his facile pen has fashioned a number of vehicles for his attractive actress-wife, Linda. When Linda finds him turning from comedy to a drama about Spain and death and immortality, she is sure he must have a new Muse. She is correct. The name of the Muse is Amanda Smith, whose husband calls her "a Lorelei with intellectual patter." Without talent herself, Amanda prides herself on her ability to bring out greatness in others. And Gaylord is her latest victim. Linda visits Amanda to plead with her to give Gaylord up ("Sleep with him if you must, but don't spoil his style"), but is unsuccessful. So she uses the time-honored method of throwing her husband in her rival's arms. Let him divorce her, marry Amanda and take her off to the wars in Spain. She respects Gaylord's idealism, even though she disapproves of his tragic style. It is because the respectable banker who is in love with her lacks that sympathy for the anonymous little people of the world which is Gay's that she refuses his proposal. Then, while Gay is packing for his trip, Linda has an idea. Why not dramatize their own triangle? It is the sort of a play Gay could write perfectly. He catches fire; enthusiastically they work out the plot but can not find an ending. Amanda, waiting for Gay, telephones to see what is detaining him. He picks up the phone with an agonized expression and does not answer her. It is his dénouement.

NOVEL AND PLAY CHARACTERIZATIONS

BY LOUIS BROMFIELD

As a novelist it has always been the characters which have interested me most. Plot, as an artificial contrived affair about which a story is built, is, except in the case of detective and crime stories, a dangerous and specious element in any book, play or picture. Plot as a means of carrying along the interest of spectator or reader is both justifiable and necessary. In the case of a novel, play or picture, the primary emphasis is upon entertainment, and to entertain the audience it is above all necessary to interest it. Plots can be of many kinds, those which grow out of the juxtaposition of certain characters, out of the clash or accident of events; they may even grow out of the atmosphere itself. Such plots are good ones. Of the three varieties the best is the plot which grows out of character.

This is so not only because, as the Greeks knew, the most interesting of all things to the public is a human individual. The only more interesting thing is the conflict which arises out of placing two or three or more individuals within the frame of a play or book and permitting them to work out their own story. I say "permitting" because that is what a writer must do. The choice is not with him; he can imagine, crystallize and even create his characters. After that they must take command over him. The moment they do take command over him the hardest part of his task is done. But as every veteran writer knows, the invoking and creation of character is not a quick or easy business. One may imagine a character in a second, a minute, an hour. Then comes the long, slow process of coming to know him, what he is like, inside and out—what he thinks—the way he walks and talks—what are his ambitions, his weaknesses, his mannerisms—how even do his glands function. There comes presently a moment when the character achieves a reality for the writer, as sound a reality as the existence of one's wife or neighbor or best friend. I have known characters of my own creation to become more real than anyone in the physical world about me, possessed of a reality that is beyond reality. When this happens with a character, half the struggle is over. The other half consists in conveying to the audience the creator's own sense of the character's reality; and of the truth of his relationship to the other characters in the story. A writer has to have a good deal of equipment and knowledge and skill to achieve this; not to mention a capacity for work.

From the point of view of putting across to the public the writer's ideas, conceptions and emotions, I should say that the medium of the theatre is the most difficult and hazardous, the medium of the talking picture comes a close second and the medium of the novel the easiest of all three. I have practised all these crafts—that of the theatre with dubious success, that of the talking picture with a good deal more success and that of the novel, in the sense at least of character and story telling, with a high degree of public response. Perhaps that is why I think novel writing the easiest of all. Certainly in the sense of character portrayal it offers unlimited opportunities and very little hazard from outside influence and interference.

The playwright must be skillful indeed, for he is limited to dialogue and a few paltry stage directions to put across his idea of a character and its relations to other characters. He must present his portrayal, his plot, his ideas within the more or less arbitrary limits of two hours. Therefore, whatever he writes must be terse and effective, and every word must lead toward the crisis, tragic or comic, of the play.

Economy in writing is not easy. Most writers only achieve it after years of work and practise. It is the first necessity of the playwright. The playwright is cursed too by the intervention of countless outside elements any one of which may utterly ruin the author's effort at characterization. A director has the power of utterly destroying a character; miscasting may blur the outline out of all recognition by the author; the miscasting of another role in conflict with the characters in question may change the emphasis and alter the whole idea not only of the character but of the play. The playwright unless he is so famous and successful as to have the powers of a dictator, is always at the mercy of the producer, actor, director, even at times of weather bad enough to jaundice both audience and critics.

A good many of the same limitations and disabilities apply to the realm of the talking picture. There are perhaps even more elements which intervene. There are the technical advisers, who frequently manage to inject imbecilities into the story and lead a character to do some bit of business utterly out of keeping with the characterization. There is the camera man and the star system and the false emphasis occasionally achieved by lighting effects. On the other hand, the camera can be of the most enormous help in characterization. By means of close-ups, of special angles, of symbolism and the "photography" of psychology, it provides a whole range both of tricks and honest technical achievements, which are outside the realm of the more rigid and clumsy limitations imposed on the theatre.

It has always seemed to me that a good talking picture follows the technique neither of the novel nor of the play. It lies somewhere between the two. It is not the dramatization of the novel, nor the novelization of a play, but rather a narrative told in terms of the theatre. It must "move" and its characters must "move" and develop and progress. The talking picture manages to inject into the play form some of the elements of the novel. It can produce atmosphere by means of the camera as the novelist does it with his pen. It can present facets of characterization which are beyond the means of the theatre. Like opera, it is in one sense a bastard art, and like the opera it has created about itself a certain set of conventions to indicate passing time, change of mood, even change of scene—convention, sometimes nearly as rigid as those of the Chinese theatre, which are puzzling and sometimes incomprehensible to the individual who does not go to the pictures frequently enough to know and accept them.

In characterization, the novelist has everything on his side. There is no arbitrary time limit, and in these days very little convention as to form. It might almost be said today that anything, even some of our books on international politics, may be called a novel. The novelist has a free hand in presenting and developing his character, and if he fails to convey his conception to his audience, he has no one to blame but himself. He need not writhe to see an actor, a director or a producer twisting his conception out of all recognition. Nor does he have the luck of having a brilliant performance by actor or director turn what is essentially a mediocre play into a brilliant success. He stands utterly on his own, with all the advantages and disadvantages of such a position. And he can, if he chooses, devote pages to the workings of the mind of a character—something infinitely more difficult to do by acting and dialogue than by the pen.

In our time only one notable playwright has striven to overcome and even destroy the convention limitations of the theatre. Eugene O'Neill has tried by the use of masks, by spoken interior thoughts, by plays which require eight hours to present. All of these devices have been attempted, I think, in a desire for a freer hand and a wider scope for characterization than is permitted in the theatre as it exists. All of these are evidence of an effort to burst the bonds of theatrical convention and achieve the happy freedom in characterization which belongs only to the novelist.

Novelle. A collection of short prose stories by Matteo Bandello published in 1554 and translated in both France and England. The *Novelle* contains Shakespeare's sources for *Romeo and Juliet, Much Ado About Nothing,* and *Twelfth Night.*

Novels on the stage. In general, dramatic adaptations of novels have been only moderately successful because following the novel closely has often meant including too many characters and scenes, or too many themes. Adaptations which have bridged the difficulties well and were theatrical successes include: *Becky Sharp,* in which the broad canvas of *Vanity Fair* was cut down to only what related to Becky; *Pride and Prejudice* and *Little Women,* in which the limited scene, small group of characters, and wit and freshness of dialogue were exactly suitable to play form; *The Green Pastures* (from Roark Bradford's *All God's Chillun*) and *Tobacco Road,* in which the atmosphere was important and effectively reproduced; *Of Mice and Men* and *The Old Maid,* where the taut situations as well as the small set of characters made the novel readily adaptable to the stage.

Nurseries, of the Restoration theatre. Two small theatres brought into existence by Charles II in 1663 as training schools for young actors.

Nut. The cost of producing a show.

N.V.A. The National Variety Artists; a club for vaudeville performers; once a great rendezvous in the heyday of variety (this organization was formerly known as the National Vaudeville Artists).

Oberammergau. A town in Germany where, in a theatre especially built for the purpose, performances of the *Passion Play* are given; once planned for every ten years, performances are now given somewhat irregularly; the actors are amateurs, recruited from among the simple laboring folk; Anton Lang, once a famous Christus, is now followed by his son, Alois.

Oboler, Arch (1907-   ). American radio dramatist. Educated University of Chicago. Experimentalist in writing drama to be broadcast. He has written sketches for outstanding players such as Maurice Evans, Walter Huston, Brian Aherne and Joan Crawford. He scored an outstanding success with *Rich Kid,* 1936. His *Alter Ego,* 1938, was chosen as the best original radio drama of that year. He is co-author, with Mrs. Tex Rickard, of *Everything Happened to Him,* 1936, a life of the late sports promoter.

O'Casey, Sean (1894-   ). Irish dramatist. Born in Dublin, he began work at fourteen as a laborer. Although first known as a writer of essays on labor questions and political ballads, he came into prominence as the author of the play, *Cathleen Listens In,* produced at the Abbey Theatre, Dublin, 1923. *Juno and the Paycock,* perhaps the best known of his plays, was awarded the Hawthornden prize in 1926. This play was followed by: *The Plough and the Stars,* 1926; *The Shadow of a Gunman,* 1927; *The Silver Tassie,* 1929; and *Within the Gates,* 1933. Most of his work is remarkable for realism, rich and varied dialogue, and mingled humor and pathos, although he did experiment in expressionism in *The Silver Tassie* and *Within the Gates.*

Octoroon, The. Dion Boucicault (American). 5 act melodrama. 1859.

Zoe, the octoroon daughter of a plantation owner and a slave, is given her freedom by her father. Jacob McClosky, the villain, plots against and murders innocent people in order to get the beauty in his clutches.

He does manage to get her, after she loses her freedom, and is sold to him from the auction block for $25,000.00. But by the grace of Salem Scudder, a benign overseer, and an Indian who is seeking vengeance against the villain, Zoe is saved and the play has a happy ending.

Odell, George C. D. (1866-   ). Theatre historian. Born in Newburgh, New York. Educated at Columbia University, M.A. and Ph.D. Professor of Dramatic Literature at Columbia since 1924. Author of *Shakespeare from Betterton to Irving,* 1920; *Annals of the New York Stage* (1927-   ), of which eleven volumes have been published.

Odets, Clifford (1906-   ). American actor and dramatist. Born in Philadelphia and educated in New York. His first play did not appear until 1935, but on the other hand, for more than ten years before that date he had been acting, first in stock, then with the Theatre Guild and the Group Theatre. As a Thespian he was inconspicuous, and his parts were not so taxing but that he had time to indulge his secret passion, writing, during his leisure hours. After experimenting with the novel form, he turned to the drama with a full-length play, *Awake and Sing.* This he offered to the Group Theatre, with which he had been associated since its conception and with which his name has become inextricably associated. The organization was not overly enthusiastic. While trying to peddle his opus elsewhere and collecting option money on it, Odets noticed an announcement that the New Theatre magazine was offering an award for the best short play of "social significance." Odets dashed off *Waiting for Lefty,* a one-act play about a taxicab strike. The New Theatre League produced it in a series of Sunday night presentations at the Civic Repertory Theatre, and the Group suddenly realized that they had a playwright in their midst. In 1935 they brought the play uptown and presented it together with *Till The Day I Die,* a short anti-Nazi drama by Odets. The production won critical acclaim, and from that day on Odets was the Group's mainstay and poet laureate.

In 1935 they gave his *Awake and Sing,* which they had previously refused, and *Paradise Lost; Golden Boy* in 1937; *Rocket to the Moon* in 1938. *Golden Boy,* which has since been filmed, was the most financially successful of his plays, and brought the Group out of the red after a somewhat disastrous season. It was written during a sojourn in Hollywood, where Odets met and married Luise Rainer, the actress.

Opinions about Odets' dramas are divided, but most people agree that, whatever his faults as a dramatist, his is one of the most vital and exciting talents to be revealed during the 1930's. His plots are often inconclusive, and some find the lower middle-class characters whom he depicts uninteresting. Yet because he writes of the sort of people with whom he is familiar, his dramatis personae are true-to-life and, to most, poignant. And because he so often cries out against injustice and defends, by implication at least, the rights of the little man and of the underdog, each new play is eagerly awaited by an ever-growing public.

Oedipus Colonus. Sophocles (Greek). c. 450 B.C. Tragedy.
This play has little action but is famed for its lyrical and poetic beauty. It is a hymn in honor of Athens and depicts the end of Oedipus who finds refuge in Attica, there to become the protecting hero of the land.

It is Sophocles' last tragedy, the mystical conclusion of the saga of Oedipus.

Oedipus complex. According to Freud, a child's unnatural love for a parent, usually with more or less definitely morbid and sexual implications. The term derives from the incestuousness apparent in Sophocles' *Oedipus Rex*.

Oedipus Rex (Oedipus the King). Sophocles (Greek). Tragedy. c. 450 B.C.
In the opening scene the Theban people are calling on their gods and king to save them from the plague that is ruining their city. Creon returns from Delphi to say the plague will continue as long as the slayer of Laius, the former king, goes unpunished. Oedipus vows to investigate the crime. He finds that one of the men whom he had slain in a quarrel was Laius. Further—he finds that Laius was his own father. He had murdered his own father, but worse than this he was married to his father's wife and he had children by her. When the truth comes to light, Jocasta, his wife-mother, hangs herself and Oedipus puts out his eyes.

This play, perhaps the most dramatic of the author's works, has been imitated by many writers in many languages.

Oenslager, Donald Mitchell (1902-   ). American designer. Associate Professor of Drama, Yale University, and author of *Scenery Then and Now*. He designed: *Sooner or Later*, 1925; *First Lady*, 1935; *Johnny Johnson, Stage Door* and *You Can't Take It With You*, 1936; *The American Way*, 1939; *The Fabulous Invalid*, 1938; *Of Mice and Men*, 1937; and many other plays.

Of Mice and Men. John Steinbeck (American). Drama. 3 acts. 1937. Based on the author's novel of the same name.
George and Lennie are on their way to a ranch to take jobs as grain buckers. George is short, wiry, smart, but Lennie is a big powerful simple-minded man. Lennie sticks to George as a dumb dog to its master and George feels responsible and

protective towards him. He cautions Lennie not to talk, nor get into fights, and to stick to this job and maybe they will get the only thing they have ever wanted—their own little place with their own chickens, rabbits, cows, etc. Lennie is particularly intrigued by the rabbits as he has a mania for petting soft things. He means to be gentle but he invariably kills all his pets because he doesn't realize the terrific strength in his hands. At the ranch, Candy, the crippled bunkhouse man, has been let in on their plans. He has saved $340.00. They need about $600.00 but George thinks with their coming salary they can swing the deal in a month. They are elated. Curley, the boss's son, an unpopular, scrappy dude, has tangled up with them but the men side with George and they are not fired. The men have a difficult time keeping Curley's amorous wife away from them. Since the men consistently avoid her she decides to run away. She comes to the barn to hide for a while and encounters Lennie. They get into a harmless conversation until she tempts Lennie to pet her hair. Once he does so, she screams in fear. In order to keep her quiet he shakes her and breaks her neck. When it is discovered everybody knows Lennie did it. He runs to the brush to hide and wait for George. The men go hunting Lennie, but George knows where Lennie is hiding, finds him and shoots him.

Off the nut. Term signifying the initial profit-making from a show.

Office actor. One who puts on a performance when talking to a producer in order to secure an engagement.

Of Thee I Sing. George S. Kaufman and Morrie Ryskind (American). Musical play (Lyrics by Ira Gershwin). 2 acts. Music by George Gershwin. 1932.
"Love is Sweeping the Country" and John P. Wintergreen is elected President of the United States on that platform. He is about to be impeached when Congress learns that his wife is about to be a mother. For this reason Congress permits Wintergreen to remain in the White House, explaining that "Posterity is just around the corner."
Winner of the Pulitzer prize for the season 1932-33.

Ogier, François (?-1670). French critic, poet, ecclesiastic. Ogier is presumed to have been born in Paris. At an early age he entered the church and later became *predicateur du roi*. He is known by his poems, sermons, and various criticisms of literature. His contribution to dramatic theory is to be found in his *Preface* to Schelandre's play, *Tyr et Sidon*. He died in Paris in 1670.

Ohimesama. Characters of young girls in *Kabuki* plays of Japan; the name means a daughter of a family of high social position; the actor playing the part is an active participant in the play; *Onnagata* or young male actors usually take these parts.

Oiran. The name of the character of a courtesan in Japanese *Kabuki* drama and one of the chief parts.

Okribas. See *Kothornos.*

Okuni-no-Izumo (Okuni of Izumo). A Japanese dancing girl of the shrine of Kzuki who performed on a makeshift open air stage built on the dry bed of the river Kamo. These performances gave rise to the Kabuki plays which originally were a type of religious dancing called *Nenbutsu Odori* or "prayer dance in praise of Buddha."

Okuni was at the height of her popularity in 1603-4, when she established stages in various parts of Kyōtō.

Old Bachelor, The. William Congreve (English). Comedy. 5 acts. 1693.

Heartwell, a pretended woman-hater, falls in love with Silvia, not knowing that she is the forsaken mistress of Vainlove. Inveigled into marrying her, he discovers her true character too late. The parson, however, was really Vainlove's friend, who assumed the disguise for the purpose of an intrigue. Heartwell is relieved to discover that the marriage was a pretence. The success of this play was due in part to the acting of Betterton and Mrs. Bracegirdle.

Old English. John Galsworthy (English). Drama. 3 acts. 1924.

Sylvanus Heythorp, although he is over eighty and confined to a wheel chair, still wields almighty power over the creditors and stockholders of the Island Navigation Co. His associates call him "Old English" because of his tenacity and shrewdness. In order to insure the financial security of Phyllis and Jack, children of his illegitimate son, he persuades the company to buy four ships from his friend, Joseph Pillin, for sixty thousand pounds, gets his friend to give him a commission of 10% and have it settled on Rosamond Larne, mother of the children, until they are of age. Mrs. Larne, unable to maintain secrecy in the matter, because she is pressed by bills, calls her lawyer, Charles Ventnor, to borrow money on her expectations. Mr. Ventnor, a creditor of Heythorp's, realizing what has transpired, goes to Heythorp and demands his money. If Heythorp refuses Ventnor will expose him. On the day before the scandal is to break he orders a good dinner with champagne, port and brandy to drink it down though this has been forbidden to him. He dies of apoplexy. Phyllis enters and does not disturb him as she thinks Old English is just sleeping.

Oldfield, Anne (Nance) (1683-1730). English actress. A member of Colley Cibber's company, her early successes were in the comedies *The Careless Husband* and *The Tender Husband.* Her portrayal of Cleopatra in *Caesar in Egypt* and of Sophonisba caused Pope to eulogize her. She has also been the subject of several novels and plays.

Other plays in which she had leading roles include: *Cato; Jane Shore; Lady Jane Grey.*

Old Fortunatus. Thomas Dekker (British). Comedy. 1600.

Fortunatus, a beggar, meets Fortune who offers him the good things of life. However, he must make his choice between wisdom, strength, long life, health, beauty or riches. Fortunatus chooses riches. His choice is granted. He receives a bag of gold from which he can draw 10 pieces of gold whenever he wishes. He starts his travels and succeeds in getting the wondrous hat of the Soldan of Turkey, a hat which will transport him any place he wishes to go. Just as everything is becoming marvellously enjoyable, Fortune puts an end to Fortunato's life. Andelacia, his son, continues with his father's purse, has a series of adventures at the Court of Athelstane but finally expires miserably, not having profited by his father's fate.

Old Homestead, The. Denman Thompson (American). Drama. 4 acts. 1887.
A small-town lad makes good in the big city and returns in time to save his family and pay off the mortgage on the old homestead.
This drama stimulated a vogue of such plays in the last decades of the 19th century.
The author also acted the lead and it was his excellent acting which established the success of his vehicle.

Old Lady Shows Her Medals, The. J. M. Barrie (English). Drama in one act. 1917.
The story of Mrs. Downey, a poor old charwoman who in order to impress her charwoman friends, in the days when the war fever was at its height, invents a son who is supposed to be fighting at the front. The son comes to life in the person of a soldier on leave who at first is very resentful over her actions but later is softened by her pathetic need for some one to lean on. As he is alone in the world, matters are arranged to the satisfaction of all.

Old Maid, The. Zoë Akins (American). Drama. 3 acts. 1935. From the novel of the same name by Edith Wharton.
Charlotte Lovell has an illegitimate child, Tina, whom Delia, Charlotte's sister, brings up. Charlotte stands by to see Tina fall in love and finally marry, never guessing that Charlotte, whom she regards as an old maid, is really her mother.
The plot is simple but the play is interesting because it reconstructs a picturesque era of society and capably dramatizes a difficult and unnatural relationship. The play won the Pulitzer Prize for 1934-5.

Old Man, The. Georges de Porto Riche (French). Drama. 6 acts. 1911.
A reformed roué falls in love with an attractive girl, Brigitte, as does his son. At his wife's request the father agrees to withdraw his suit but asks for one final rendezvous with the girl. When the son discovers his father's rivalry, he is so shocked he commits suicide. Although the mother holds the father responsible for his son's death, she cannot leave him for she still loves him.

Old Soak, The. Don Marquis (American). Comedy. 3 acts. 1926.
This typically American play deals with a character who is representative of all those genial alcoholics, winning failures and domestic derelicts with weak characters but good hearts, who have been written about since the days of Bacchus.

The law having closed his beloved saloon, the "old soak" devotes his life to the major task of obtaining enough liquor to keep him happy.

His wife loves her reprobate of a husband and has a few gilt edged bonds put where he can't lay his hands on them. Their son, a model lad, gets himself involved with an expensive chorus girl and steals the bonds.

The old soak attempts to shield the boy and takes the blame on his own shoulders but everything is eventually cleared up.

Old Vic. Opened as the Royal Coburg, London, May 11, 1818, under the patronage of the Duke of Saxe-Coburg. A minor house largely devoted to melodrama. Later the Royal Victoria and Royal Victoria Hall. Reopened February 6, 1928, by the late Lilian Baylis and carried on as a repertory house largely devoted to Shakespeare.

See also *Sadler's Wells.*

Old Wives' Tales, The. George Peele (English). Fantasy, 1595.

Two brothers who attempt to rescue their sister, Delia, from the magician, Sacrapant, are in turn captured themselves. They are all finally rescued by a knight with the help of a ghost who by this act shows his gratitude for the knight's paying his funeral expenses.

This is the first dramatic literary satire in English.

Oliver Cromwell. John Drinkwater (English). Historical drama. 8 scenes. 1923.

Oliver Cromwell, known for his firmness and singleness of purpose, headed the Puritan Revolution which caused the death of Charles I. He rose to the post of Protector of the Commonwealth of England and was offered the Crown, which he refused.

Olivette. Floodlight type of lighting instrument, a bunch-light.

Olympe's Marriage. Émile Augier and Jules Sandeau (French). Drama. 3 acts. 1854.

A Courtesan, Olympe, tricks a young man into marriage and is recognized by his family. A yearning for her past life overcomes her, and from sheer wantonness, she sells herself to a lover.

Discovered by the head of her husband's family, she threatens to begin a scandal about an innocent girl. To prevent this, the grandfather kills Olympe.

Omaha Playhouse (Nebraska). Organized in 1924 as a non-profit corporation and registered under Nebraska laws. The Playhouse was built and opened in its fourth season. It operates on 1500 season tickets, with the balance secured by a subscription campaign each Fall.

Ominameshi. Seami Motokiyu (1363-1444). Japanese. *Nō* drama.

A Japanese *Nō* drama telling the story of a man who comes to the capitol and takes unto himself a mistress. Suddenly he leaves her and she distractedly searches for him in his home town region. The neighbors tell her that he has married another. She leaps into Hojo river. When the man learns of the girl's suicide he takes the girl's body, and weeping, he buries her. From her grave springs a flower which he thinks is her soul. But he fancies it is angry with him, for whenever he touches the flower it droops and turns aside.

In the play, the ghosts of the lover and the girl tell the story.

On Borrowed Time. Paul Osborn (based on the novel by Lawrence Watkin). American comedy. 3 acts. 1937.

The play concerns Gramps, an amiable old gentleman, and his grandchild Pud, a boy of six. Pud's mother and father are killed in an auto accident and this draws Gramps and Pud closer than ever. Granny (Grandma) is concerned over this relationship as Gramps is free with his language. The boy imitates him, of course, and Aunt Demetria (Granny's sister), an interfering woman, is determined to send him to a God-fearing school. Demetria visits, much to the disgust of Gramps and Pud, and discovers Pud's father has left $55,000.00. She thinks she'll adopt him. Mr. Brink (symbolic of death) appears to Gramps. Gramps chases him off but when he appears to Granny in her bedroom, it is apparent that Granny is going to die.

Pud climbs the apple tree one day and cannot get down when Gramps tells him to. Gramps thinks it a game but Pud is in earnest as he tells him he really cannot get off. When Mr. Brink appears again a week after Granny's death, Gramps, unwilling to leave Pud, gets Mr. Brink up the apple tree through a ruse and keeps him there. He starts to build a fence around it. His neighbors begin to agree with Aunt Demetria that he is crazy. Gramps proves that he isn't by the fact that all death has been suspended while Brink is in the tree. Dr. Evans, realizing the menace, signs the orders for Pud's adoption by Aunt Demetria. Pud has an accident and falls off the tree. Finally Gramps calls Mr. Brink down, realizing that both he and Pud are to die together and are not to be separated.

Once In A Lifetime. George S. Kaufman and Moss Hart (American). Comedy. 3 acts. 1930.

May, George and Jerry are vaudeville performers "at liberty" in New York. Jerry, after seeing the first talking picture, decides that the three of them must go to Hollywood at once and cash in on this new idea. May decides to open a voice school. In Hollywood they meet the big producer Glogauer. The school is not a great success and they are just about to be kicked out when George insults Glogauer. Glogauer, having never been spoken to in this manner before, decides George is a genius and makes him manager over everything. George manages by sheer stupidity to blunder into the position of dictator of the new industry.

One-act play. While a play of any length may have only one act, the one-act play form is short. In construction it differs from a play as a short story differs from a novel: it is not a condensed play but an incident or a characterization only without the development and detail of the longer form.

O'Neill, Eugene (1888-   ). American dramatist. Born in New York, the son of James O'Neill, Eugene O'Neill was formerly an actor and a journalist. He was educated at Princeton and Harvard and studied with George Pierce Baker. From 1923-25 he was associated with Kenneth Macgowan and Robert Edmond Jones in the production of several plays at the Provincetown Playhouse and the Greenwich Village Theatre. Since 1934 he has been engaged in writing a series of dramatic productions, as yet unpublished, He was winner of the Nobel Prize for Literature in 1936, the first American dramatist to be so honored. Barrett Clark in his excellent *Eugene O'Neill,* 1926, says: "O'Neill is not merely a dramatist, if he were, this book would never have been attempted; he is an artist who uses the theater as a medium for the expression of his feelings and his ideas on life." The truth of this statement has grown even more apparent in the past years. He has not been represented in the theatre with a new play since 1934, but between then and 1926, his three greatest plays were published. Of these, *Lazarus Laughed* has not seen Broadway production though Gilmor Brown gave it a spirited playing at Pasadena. The two which partake of the essence of Greek tragedy in their spareness are *Strange Interlude* and *Mourning Becomes Electra,* which the Guild enhanced with brilliant casting and the American public took to their minds and hearts. The brilliant penetration of feminine psychology which marked the former has never been equaled in our drama. Only in the masters of Greek theatre is the poetic beauty and true *Katharsis* of his Electra to be found.

O'Neill has always been an innovator. He brought the one-act play to a high point of development. In *The Emperor Jones,* he made use of the continuous moving technique of the film. In *The Hairy Ape,* he employed expressionism. In *Desire Under The Elms,* he explored the potentialities of visible simultaneous action. In *The Great God Brown,* he employed the mask to differentiate the actions of his people, and in *Strange Interlude* he re-introduced the aside to reveal the true thoughts of his characters as well as demanding the full attention of his auditors for nearly five hours. He is the outstanding dramatist in the world today.

Among his plays are: *Thirst,* 1914; *Beyond the Horizon,* 1920; *The Emperor Jones,* 1920; *The Straw,* 1921; *Gold,* 1921; *The First Man,* 1922; *The Hairy Ape,* 1922; *All God's Chillun Got Wings,* 1924; *Desire Under the Elms,* 1924; *The Great God Brown,* 1926; *Lazarus Laughed,* 1926; *Marco Millions,* 1928; *Strange Interlude,* 1928; *Mourning Becomes Electra,* a trilogy, 1931; *Ah, Wilderness!,* 1933; *Days Without End,* 1934.

O'Neill, James (1847-1920). American actor. Born in Ireland; was brought to the United States in 1850. He played with Adelaide Neilson and Edwin Booth, and in 1875-77 was leading man at the Union Square Theatre, New York. His portrayal of Edmond Dantes in the dramatization of *The Count of Monte Cristo,* which ran for years in cities all over the country, is O'Neill's chief claim to fame, though he played Hamlet, Othello and Virginia and successfully produced a dramatization of *The Three Musketeers.* Eugene O'Neill is his son.

One night stand. A single out-of-town performance of a show.

one third of a nation. A Living Newspaper. Written and produced 1938 by the Living Newspaper Division of the Federal Theatre of the W. P. A. Arthur Arent, Managing Editor.

A classic example of the Living Newspaper technique, *one third of a nation* delves deeply into the problem of housing, bringing to view the evils that are caused by one third of the nation being poorly housed. It shows both sides of the question, showing also why private builders cannot supply good homes for people in the low income brackets and offers as a solution a larger government housing program. The most successful of the Living Newspaper series it ran for a year on Broadway.

Onkos. Lofty headdress used in ancient Greet theatre; towered over the *mask;* used to enhance or emphasize the importance of a character.

Onnagata. Japanese actors who take the part of women in the *Kabuki* plays; all plays are acted by men who have refined the art of playing women on the stage to a peak of unparalleled perfection. *Onnagata* are trained from early childhood.

Onoe Kikugōrō (1885-   ). Japanese actor. The bright star of the Tokyo theatre. Born 1885, Tōkyō. Début at age of thirty-six after long training. Comes from family of actors going back five generations. Considered best in Japan as *Mai* and *Odori,* tragedian and subtle pantomimist. Adept at both warrior and female roles. Is the Principal of a School for Actors which he founded in 1930. Lives in Tokyo.

Onomastikon. Greek dictionary in ten books compiled by *Pollux;* mainly dictionary of synonyms and phrases, chiefly intended to furnish reader with Attic names for individual things; supplies much rare and valuable information on many points of classical antiquity, including the ancient Greek theatre.

See also *Comedy, Greek, satyr plays; Pollux.*

On the Frontier. W. H. Auden and Christopher Isherwood. Verse-play. 3 acts. 1939.

Two adjoining countries, one fascist, one democratic, are preparing for war. However, the love of peace is so great in both countries that the people, as represented by a boy and a girl, break down the barriers and unite for peace.

On The Rocks. George Bernard Shaw (English). Drama. 2 acts. 1933.

Shaw's main character is the liberal Prime Minister of a coalition English government. His mind is stimulated by a rest cure, during which he reads the writings of Karl Marx and Lenin.

When he returns from his cure he is a new man with a Program. He plans to save England from the havoc of the depression by a semi-fascist program, but is met by the opposition of his cabinet. The final curtain finds the unemployed chanting *England Arise* outside his window while he wonders what ever would happen if England really did arise.

The play has very clever dialogue—so clever that at times it obscures its own meaning. The play has been labelled both Fascist and Communist by opposing groups.

Open cold. To give the first public performance of a production on Broadway without an out-of-town tryout.

L'Opéra de Campagne, Farce written by a French author for the *commedia dell' arte* in France and included in Gherardi's *Le Théâtre Italien.*

Orange Girls. Women in the Restoration theatres who sold refreshments. *Orange Moll* was an older woman who directed the *orange girls.* These girls sold fruit and nuts to spectators and at the same time were induced to flirt with the beaux in the pit and boxes. Nell Gwyn is said to have begun her famous career as an orange girl.

Orange, Theatre of. An ancient Roman auditorium distinguished by a stage-building (or *skene*) of imposing façade, still standing at Orange in the south of France.

Orangewood sticks. Used in making-up to line the face or to shape and model putty on the face.

Orchestra. Originally a circle, where the *chorus* was to perform, marked out at the base of the slope of the ancient Greek theatre. In the center of this circle was usually the *thymele,* or altar, erected in honor of the god. With the gradual passing of the *chorus* as a dramatic property this circle became a part of the auditorium as we know it today. The English equivalent is *stalls.*

Orchestra leader. Conductor of the band of musicians in a musical, revue or opera. Along with the prompter he serves as a signaller of cues to performers on stage, the while keeping them in time with the playing of his men in the pit by the beat of his baton.

Orders. English name for free admissions.

Oropos, Theatre of. A theatre in ancient Greece dating from the 4th-3rd century B.C.

Orphan, The. Thomas Otway (English). Tragedy in blank verse. 1680.
Monimia, orphan girl, has been brought up by a friend of her father's, Acasta. He has twin sons, Castalio and Polydore, devoted to one another but both in love with Monimia. She favors the love of Castalio but he, to spare his brother, feigns indifference. Chamont, an honest soldier and Monimia's brother, comes to visit her. He pries into her life by questioning her and finally Castalio and Monimia are secretly married. Polydore eavesdrops and overhears plans for a secret night meeting. Not knowing of their marriage he takes Castilio's place undetected. Castilio is shut out when he arrives and is furious with his wife. When the truth becomes known, the brothers kill themselves. Monimia cannot survive the tragedy and takes poison.

Osborn, Paul (1901-   ). American dramatist. Born in Evansville, Indiana, he received his education at the University of Michigan. He studied playwriting with George Pierce Baker at Yale and taught English at the University of Michigan. His career as a playwright began in 1928 when Brock Pemberton produced a comedy of his called *Hotbed*. Two more plays followed: *A Ledge* and *Oliver Oliver*, but neither was particularly successful. In 1930, however, his *The Vinegar Tree* was a box office success. *On Borrowed Time*, based on the novel by Lawrence Watkin, was produced in New York in 1937 and as a motion picture in 1939 by Metro-Goldwyn-Mayer. His latest play, 1939, is *Morning's at Seven*.

See also *Yale University.*

Oscar Wilde. Leslie and Sewell Stokes (English). Drama. 3 acts. 1937.

The tragic history of Oscar Wilde, beginning at the height of his success in London, through the notorious trial at Old Bailey, and ending when Wilde is old and broken, living in Paris.

Ostler, William (?-1612). English actor. An actor named in the 1623 Folio list of performers in Shakespeare's plays. After an early career with the Children of the Chapel Royal, a company of boy actors, he joined Shakespeare's company in 1610, when they were known as the King's Men. He appeared in: Jonson's *Alchemist* and *Catiline;* in Webster's *Duchess of Malfi;* and other plays. He was a shareholder in the Globe and Blackfriars theatres.

Ostrovsky, Alexander Nicholaievitch (1823-1886). Russian dramatist. Born in Moscow. He wrote many comedies dealing mainly with the lives of the small trader class. These included: *The Bankrupt,* 1850; *Everyone In His Own Place,* 1853; and *The Storm,* 1860. In 1874 he organized the Society of Dramatic Authors and Composers, and in 1882 Ostrovsky secured the abandonment of the theatrical monopoly. In 1884 he became director of a Moscow Theatre, which he had helped to establish. He also founded the Russian Academy of Dramatic Art. More than 800 performances of his plays were given during two decades.

Othello. William Shakespeare (British). Tragedy. 5 acts. 1604.

Written in 1604, the story is taken from Cinthio's Il Moro di Venezia. Othello, a Moor, has married Desdemona, and sailed to Cyprus, followed by Roderigo, who loves Desdemona. Iago hates Othello for choosing Cassio as his chief lieutenant and vows revenge. He involves Cassio in a drunken brawl for which he is dismissed. At the suggestion of the crafty Iago, Cassio, despairing, appeals to Desdemona to intervene for him. Iago, meanwhile, instills suspicious thoughts in Othello's mind about Cassio and Desdemona. He also has his wife, Emilia, steal a handkerchief, which Othello gave Desdemona as a talisman, and puts it in Cassio's room. Finally, when Othello sees Cassio with the handkerchief and is told by Iago that Cassio has confessed an affair with Desdemona, the tortured Moor resolves on death for the supposed lovers. Cassio is only wounded and Desdemona killed by Othello. Later, when Iago's villainy is revealed by Emilia, she is stabbed to death by him. Othello kills himself and Iago is led away to torture and death.

Other Danger, The. Maurice Donnay (French). Tragedy. 4 acts. 1902.

A woman, unhappily married, takes a lover. Much to her distress she discovers her daughter in love with the same man. Reports of the mother's affair have come to the daughter, and the older woman sacrifices her love in order to discredit the rumors, at the same time realizing that she must lose out in the long run to her daughter's youth.

Otway, Thomas (1652-85). British dramatist. Born in Sussex, he was educated at Christ Church, Oxford. He played unsuccessfully on the stage and his unrequited love for Mrs. Barry, the actress, was common knowledge. He died destitute at 33. His three great plays are *Don Carlos,* 1676; *The Orphan,* 1680; *Venice Preserved,* 1682. Among his others are *Alcibiades; Titus and Berenice, Friendship in Fashion* and *Soldier's Fortune.*

Our American Cousin. Tom Taylor (English). 1859. Comedy. 3 acts.

The daughter of a baronet is, against her will, betrothed to the attorney who drove her father to bankruptcy. If she marries him, the attorney promises to cancel all the baronet's liabilities. The baronet's daughter is saved from this marriage by a lowly clerk in the attorney's office.

On the night of April 14, 1865 this play was being shown at Ford's Theatre in Washington, D. C. The guest of honor was the president of the United States, Abraham Lincoln. During the performance the shot was fired which caused Lincoln's death.

Our Betters. W. Somerset Maugham (English). Comedy. 3 acts. 1917.

Pearl Saunders, New York heiress, who has become Lady George Grayson of London, seeks to arrange an English marriage for her younger sister, Elizabeth. However, after seeing Lady Grayson's friends, and witnessing her affair with Gilbert Paxton who belongs to the Duchess de Surennes, Elizabeth revolts and returns to her American sweetheart, Fleming Harvey.

Our Town. Thornton Wilder (American). Drama. 3 acts. 1938.

Won the Pulitzer Prize for 1937-8. It is played without scenery, the stage manager acting as narrator. It is the simple tale of the humdrum lives of humble citizens in Grover's Corners, New Hampshire. The first act (May, 1901) shows "A day in our Town." The characters are introduced by the stage manager. We see Mr. Morgan's drug store, the meeting place of the town. The whole physical layout of the town is simply described. We meet Dr. & Mrs. Gibbs and their children, George and Rebecca Gibbs. We see their neighbors, M. & Mrs. Webb, the local editor and their children, Emily and Wally. We are carried through an average day with them. The next act is called "Love and Marriage"—it is three years later. Emily and George are to be married. We see why and how they fell in love, and hear their dreams and ambitions. We feel the fears and apprehensions of their parents. They are married. Nine years have now elapsed. The scene is in the cemetery of Grover's Corners. We see those that have died sitting in chairs. The stage manager tells the audience to stop and remember what they already know, that "something" is eternal, that that something is a human being. The dead have lost interest in the living, they are waiting, waiting for the essence of eternity. A funeral procession approaches and Emily joins the dead. She has died in childbirth. Emily wishes to go back. They advise her against it. She does go back for her 12th birthday. She is saddened by it. She realizes how unseeing the living are, how rushed, how troubled and how blind. George comes and throws himself on Emily's grave. She is sorry he doesn't understand, sorry that the living carry with them the tragic grief of their dead.

Outer Edge of Society, The (The Demi-Monde). Alexandre Dumas Fils (French). Satire. 5 acts. 1855.

The character study of a designing woman in slightly off-color society.

Suzanne d'Ange, who calls herself a Baroness, but whose past is doubtful, attempts to forget that past and find security by way of a respectable marriage.

M. de Narijoc, a young soldier, falls in love with her and is about to marry her, when through a despicable trick his eyes are opened by his friend, M. de Jolin, who has excellent reasons to doubt the lady's worthiness.

Outer Stage, Elizabethan. A rectangular, uncurtained platform projecting into the central open yard of the theatre. It was generally strewn with rushes. A heavy column on each side supported a canopy-like roof over it. The greater part of the action of the play took place on the outer stage. There was no scenery, however, no indication of locality, and no properties.

Out front. In theatrical parlance, the auditorium or any area occupied by the audience.

Out of the Picture. Louis MacNeice (English). Tragi-comedy. 2 acts. Printed 1937.

The principal exponents are a young man who plays with art really seriously and happily and a young woman who, for love of him, kills him before he can be conscripted or before her failure is complete and self-acknowledged.

Outward Bound. Sutton Vane (English). Drama. 3 acts. 1923.

The scene is laid on board a ship, which the characters discover is bound for the hereafter. All of the people are dead but two, a young man and woman, suicides, still on the borderline who are finally able to return to life. All the other passengers on the ship are judged by the Chief Examiner and allotted to their proper place in the Afterworld.

Oxford Theory. The theory that Edward Vere de Vere, Earl of Oxford, wrote the plays generally attributed to Shakespeare. Proponents of the theory argue that the plays show a familiarity with court circles which only a member of the court could possess. The facts that Oxford was a capable poet and that he was for a time associated with the playwright, John Lyly, have been strongly dwelt upon by supporters of the theory.

Pace. Term meaning rate of speed and one that is to the theatre what *tempo* is to music. In acting and direction it refers to the timing of lines and actions.

Packing the house. Filling a theatre for performances.

Pageant. Originally the term used for the theatre of the English miracle plays: a portable wooden structure consisting of two floors with a room occupying each, only one of which was open at a time to the view of the audience. This rude stage was drawn through the streets and set up in the open for performances. The term *pageant* was also used for a style of English play—a kind of allegorical spectacle performed as a procession and serving as celebration of some sovereign's visit. This type of play corresponded to the *mimed mystery* of France and dates from about 1236. In our modern usage, of course, *pageant* connotes an elaborate and brilliant spectacular display or exhibition.

Pagnol, Marcel (1895-   ). French dramatist. Born at Aubagne, France. Formerly a schoolmaster and professor of English, his plays include: *Les Marchands de Gloire* (with Paul Nivoix), 1925; *Jazz,* 1926; *Topaze,* 1928; *Marius,* 1929, a new translation of which was produced at the Pasadena Playhouse in the summer of 1939; *Fanny,* 1931; *Phaeton,* 1932. Pagnol has also written directly for the motion pictures.

Palace of Pleasure. A popular collection of tales translated from classic Italian and French authors by William Painter in 1566. Many of the tales from Boccaccio, Cinthio and Bandello, used by Shakespeare as sources, came to the dramatist through Painter's versions.

Palais-Royal. The theatre in Paris that housed Molière's *Troupe du Roi* which was suppressed after his death.

Palatium. Name of a certain scene building, or mansion, of the medieval stage, meaning, literally, palace.
See also *Mansions.*

Palladio, Andrea (1518-1580). Italian architect. His Teatro Olympico at Vicenza, completed by Scamozzi in 1584, became a model for the Renaissance theatre, as well as many of those of later periods. The first indoor theatre, it preserved the Roman stage form with the five doorways, with streets in perspective behind the arches. The stage provided for the introduction of scenery.

Palmer, Albert M. (1860-1905). American manager. One of the great producers of his era. As manager of the Union Square Theatre, 1872-83 he had a series of triumphs. Under his banner such stars as Richard Mansfield, Clara Morris, Stuart Robson appeared. Many new and rising American playwrights came into their own under Palmer. He presented plays by Augustus Thomas, Steele Mackaye, William Gillette, William Young.

In 1884 Palmer assumed the managership of the Madison Square Theatre. The greatest triumph of Palmer's career was the production of *The Two Orphans* which ran almost continuously for twenty years.

See also *Union Square Theatre.*

Palmer, John Leslie (1885-   ). English dramatist, critic. Born at Oxford. Dramatic critic *The Saturday Review* and *The Evening Standard.* Author of *The Censor and the Theatres,* 1912; *The Future of the Theatre,* 1913; *Studies in the Contemporary Theatre,* 1926; *Molière,* 1930; *Timothy,* 1931; *Ben Jonson,* 1934; *The Hesperides,* 1936; *Peter Paragon; The King's Men; The Happy Fool; Looking after Joan;* and *Jennifer.* His *No More Bachelors* was produced in 1933 at East Hampton, Long Island. Since 1920 Mr. Palmer has been attached to the permanent Secretariat of the League of Nations.

Panic. Archibald MacLeish (American). Drama. 1 act. 1935.

It concerns itself with Wall Street in the few hours before the bank closings in 1933. McGafferty is desperately trying to persuade his fellow financiers to pool their resources in order to avert the panic, but he is unsuccessful.

Panning (television). A horizontal sweeping of the camera.

Pantalone. Stock-character in a *commedia dell'* arte; most important among the old-men types; Venetian merchant, avaricious, fearful of violence, inclined to meddle in high politics, cuckold, cheated father—always a source of cruel merriment. Costume: originally a long, red cloak, later changed to black; Turkish slippers, red cap. Mask: dark, with prominent curved nose, white hair, long beard.

Pantomime. A type of silent performance said to have originated in Egypt but first definitely found in the early Roman theatre. The intrigue was acted or danced, not spoken, except for occasional singing to serve the turn of plot. Mythology called Proteus the first pantomimus because of his power to change swiftly into various characters. The term pantomimus was thenceforth frequently used to describe any actor who belonged to a secret society, was something of a contortionist and often made his entrance walking on his hands. In later times the pantomimic ballet, play or pageant became an established form.

John Rich or "Lun" is usually credited with originating the form, but John Weaver, a dancing master, claimed to be the true innovator. It was influenced by classic myth, Italian *commedia dell' arte,* previous English farce and contemporary satire. It was a common practice to have the pantomimists combine with reciters or singers who moved alongside the dancers and acrobats.

Early examples are: Weaver's *Love of Mars and Venus,* 1717; Lun's *The Rape of Proserpine,* 1726.

The silent motion picture is a type of pantomime.

Pantomime-ballet. A form of, and part of, the ballets which were popular in the Courts of Europe up to the French Revolution. Courtiers and monarchs themselves liked to participate in the productions and were costumed as mythical and allegorical characters who acted out the story of their production in pantomime as interludes between the actual ballet dancing. This turned the entire production into the form of a grand pageant.

Paolo and Francesca. Stephen Phillips (American). Tragedy. 4 acts. 1897.

The story of Francesca, wife of elderly Giovanni Malatesta, Lord of Rimini. She falls in love with her husband's younger brother, Paolo. Lucrezia, a widowed cousin, embittered by life, warns Giovanni of this infatuation. Paolo asks to be sent away to rejoin his troops and does everything in his power to stem his growing attachment for Francesca, but Giovanni refuses to let him leave. Lucrezia relents of her hateful conduct and decides to help Francesca resist temptation. The lovers cannot be kept apart and are discovered by Giovanni locked in each other's arms. He kills them both. Though Paola's kiss to her was fatal, yet "it was on her lips ere she was born."

Paper. Term used for general free admissions into a theatre; as: a papered house.

The Paper Mill Playhouse. New Millburn, New Jersey. In 1932 a group, headed by Frank Carrington, organized the Newark Art Theatre and played in the Newark Art School and at the Montclair Theatre. Their subscription audience was drawn from a large radius and in 1934 a century-old paper mill was chosen as an ideal location. The theatre within and without is unique and satisfying. The productions are designed solely by the director and playhouse staff. The Playhouse is a non-profit-making corporation. Alexander Kirkland became associated with this theatre in 1939.

Paper the house. To fill a theatre with free-admission spectators to make it appear to those who have paid that the show is a success.

Parabasis. Part of ancient Greek drama, especially Old Comedy as expounded by *Aeschylus,* in which the *chorus* comes forward to address the audience.

Paradise Lost. Clifford Odets (American). Drama. 3 acts. 1936.

The Depression enters the two family house which is shared by Leo Gordon, his wife, Ben and Julie, their children, and Sam Katz and his wife. Leo and Sam are partners—Leo conservative and weak, Sam radical and strong. The constant conflict between them ruins their business. Ben, the son, marries Libby who takes up with a taxi racketeer. When Ben finds out, he deliberately enters a career of crime and puts himself in the way of a policeman's bullet. The daughter, Julie, thwarted because her lover cannot afford to marry, remains a frustrated old maid. His whole world crashing about him, Leo Gordon still finds that there is hope left. Through suffering, he feels, people will learn to rebuild a world suited to their needs.

Paradoi. The altar of Dionysus in the center of the orchestra.

Paradoxe sur le comédien, Le. A study by the great French scholar of the 18th century, Denis Diderot, in which were laid the foundations for the new serious drama of ordinary life. Here also is stated the theory that the actor will more surely move the audience when he himself remains unmoved. Ever since its first draft in 1770 this paradox has been subject to constant attack and defense.

Parasites, The. Camilla Antona-Traversi (Italian). Drama. 3 acts. 1899.

A satirical attack on unscrupulous men who organize charity rackets that provide their subsistence. The men's methods are legal and cannot be fought on the basis of any mere technicalities. But their dishonesty brings suffering to those associated with the unscrupulous grafters. Social climbers and other disagreeable members of society are also exposed.

Paraskenia. Projecting wings at either end of the stage in the classical Athenian theatre; introduced about 425 B.C.; development of the *skene*, showing the progress toward the scene building.

Paris Bound. Philip Barry (American). Comedy. 3 acts. 1927.

A comedy written in the light, sophisticated manner in which Barry excels. Its thesis is expressed by the hero's father in the first act: "Any two people who marry for love . . . and live before the world as man and wife create between them something they can never get away from." In Act I Jim and Mary Hutton, young and intelligent, are marrying. They are very much in love, but modern enough to agree not to be jealous if Jim sees other women and Mary other men. Mary even leaves Jim alone with Noel Farley, a girl who is very much in love with him, to say goodbye and persuade Noel not to make a scene at the wedding.

Act II is five years later. Jim and Mary are still blissfully happy, so much so that it does not occur to Mary to worry about his going alone on his annual business trip to France. Vacations are good for married people, she thinks. And she will be occupied helping Richard Parrish, a young composer, with the modernistic ballet he is composing. Then she learns from a friend who lets drop a chance remark that Jim lived on the Riviera with Noel Farley during his stay in France a year previously. Shocked, she bids her husband farewell. Jim, not realizing she knows of his affair, does not dream that it may be their last goodbye kiss.

Act III is six weeks later. Mary has decided to divorce Jim, who is due home that day. Jim's father asks her not to ruin both her and Jim's lives, not to accept defeat, to distinguish between a mere sexual attraction, such as Jim feels for Noel, and love. But she is adamant, and allows Richard, the composer, to make love to her for the first time. When Jim arrives the apartment is filled with people and Mary has no opportunity to break her news. And by the time they are alone, she has been so impressed by his joy at seeing her again and his anxiety to see their children that she has made up her mind not to mention Noel.

Parker, Henry Taylor (H. T. P.) (1867-1934). American dramatic critic. Left Harvard without a degree because he had no interest in subjects outside the field of English literature. His career as a critic was brilliant: New York correspondent for the *Boston Transcript*, 1892-98; London correspondent for the *Tran-*

script and *New York Commercial Advertiser,* 1898-1900; drama and music critic for *New York Globe* until he returned in 1905 to Boston, where for the remaining twenty-nine years of his life he was drama and music critic for the *Transcript.* The trenchant comments of H. T. P., individualist among critics, commanded respect from artists and managers as well as the public.

Parnassus Plays. A trilogy of plays, *The Pilgrimage to Parnassus* and *The Return from Parnassus, Parts I and II,* presented at Cambridge University, 1598-1602. They are packed with allusions to contemporary literary figures and contain extended references to Shakespeare and his works. These references, for the most part disparaging, chiefly concern the poems *Venus and Adonis* and *The Rape of Lucrece.* Kempe and Burbage, the Shakespearean actors, are introduced, and the latter recites the opening lines of *Richard III.* The general attitude of the writer is the slightly contemptuous one of a university man toward a professional actor, playwright and poet.

Parnell. Elsie T. Shauffler (American). Drama. 3 acts. 1936.
The story of a man's loyalty to a woman at the cost of his career and at the price of his national cause. Parnell, Irish leader, meets and falls in love with Katherine O'Shea. His love is returned but the lady has a blackguard of a husband who has been using her merely as a source of money. Parnell and Katherine live together and together they work for the cause of Irish freedom. But just as Gladstone is about to recognize Parnell's demands, the husband brings a suit for divorce and begins such a scandal that Gladstone is able to take advantage of the situation, and refuses to deal with Parnell. Shortly after his political defeat, Parnell dies.

Parodos. (1) Passageway, on either side of the stage, between the auditorium and the *skene* in the ancient Greek theatre; (2) entrance-song, part of the ancient Greek drama, especially *Old Comedy* as expounded by Aeschylus, sung by chorus, when it first comes on the scene.

Parquet. Term, now obsolete, for the orchestra floor of a theatre.

Part. The character assigned to an actor in a play; the scenes in which an actor appears; the typewritten portion of a play which pertains to an actor's scenes and containing all his lines and cues.

Parterre. The pit in the French theatre.

Party claps. A term used in 18th century drama as a result of the increased abuse in which bodies of gay blades took it upon themselves to make as much noise and tumult as they liked, to indicate their displeasure at what occurred on stage. This was common on opening nights; the din often prevented a single word of the play from being heard. An author who once offended was likely doomed forever. These demonstrations were the result of political and personal reasons. To escape the abuse of these rioters and to win over the first night audience, authors packed the house with friends or party claps.

Pasadena Community Playhouse. In November 1918, Gilmor Brown organized the Pasadena Community Playhouse Association on an amateur basis, with a Board of Directors of responsible citizens and a group of actors. From a tiny theatre this carefully thought out enterprise grew into a group which fills the superb theatre on El Molino Avenue. More than twenty productions were presented in 1939. The Pasadena Playhouse gives a rich and varied repertory. Every two weeks throughout the year either a new production by an unknown playwright or an experimental production by seniors of the School of the Theatre is presented. The Laboratory Theatre of the Playhouse is perhaps one of the most valuable additions to the American theatre movement. For ten years or more, the Playhouse has conducted an important school which has given admirable training to young people. The equipment, variety of subject matter and scope of theatre instruction are unique.

Paso. A term originally referring to short pieces frequently of one act in the Spanish drama, but today referring to comic interludes inserted in, even though irrelevant to, the main body of a longer play.

Passerby, The. Alfred Capus (French). Drama. 3 acts. 1906.
Capus believes that both husband and wife should be indulgent in marriage and more tolerant of each other's extra-marital diversions. *The Passerby* is a good example of this credo. The husband is the straying kind, and the wife, knowing of this weakness, reproves but forgives him. She has just hurdled the affair he has had with a milliner and now finds that he has run off with their governess to Le Havre. She follows, not for recrimination, but simply to bring him back home again, explaining that she after all is his comrade for life.

Passion Flower, The (La Malquerida). Jacinto Benavente (1866) (Spanish). Tragedy. 4 acts.
Acacia, a peasant girl, hates her stepfather, Estiban. She has never analyzed this antipathy, her feeling being that she is loyal to her dead father's memory. On the night of her betrothal, her lover is killed. Her cousin, whom she jilted, is tried and acquitted of the crime. He discovers that it was done by a servant of Estiban's. It develops that this servant has known that his master is in love with Acacia. In the last act, it is revealed that Acacia has been deceiving herself and everybody else. She and Estiban are madly in love with each other. The mother is shocked and outraged. When they are determined to flee together the mother blocks their path. In a moment of fury Estiban shoots her. The mother, dying, says that Acacia no longer can be harmed. She knows that he dare not marry the daughter of a mother he has murdered.

Passion Play, Egyptian. According to Sheldon Cheney we have evidence of one form of Egyptian religious drama. The purpose was exactly the same as in our present day passion plays. Egyptian plays centered about Osiris, chief god. The document dates from 2000 B.C. and the drama explains the establishment of the Egyptian cult of Osiris-worship.

Passion Play, Germany, Oberammergau. World famous decennial production of the dramatization of Christ's Passion and most important of all survivals of the medieval theatre. Situated in the Bavarian Alps, the theatre is rude and wooden, but receives more pilgrims and more praise for its performance by all classes of theatre goers, than any other in the world. The actors are all natives, craftsmen and peasants of the town.

Pasteboard Crown. Jean Sarment (French). Drama. 3 acts. 1920.

Because an actress, whom he adores, regards him as a commoner masquerading as royalty, an authentic prince tries to live that part. He succeeds so well that he is forced to send the actress away in order to return to his real position as a prince.

Pasteur. Sacha Guitry (French). Biographical drama. 5 acts. 1919.

Dramatic incidents in the life of Pasteur reaching a climax when a child is brought to him with arms and legs lacerated by a mad dog. It is then for the first time that Pasteur tests his serum, and saves the child's life. The play ends at the Sorbonne, with Pasteur, an old man, receiving the acclaim of his countrymen.

Pastor, Tony (Antonio) (1837-1908). American manager. "Symbolized all the lively arts of the American theatre . . . all the light and gay and daring and mystifying amusements below the straight comedy line." (Montrose Moses). His career began in 1846, as a minstrel tambourine player, and when he made his first variety appearance in 1860 he had been with at least eight circuses as clown, jester, comic singer, bareback rider, tumbler, ringmaster, low comedian and burlesquer. In Paterson, New Jersey, and then in New York in the Bowery, he established in 1865 "legitimate" vaudeville, the first to bid successfully for the patronage of respectable women and family groups. He became a manager in that year, and exploited his specialty of topical songs through a period of intense change. Three moves and a fire brought him to the building of his own house, Tony Pastor's Theatre, in 1888 on Union Square. Pastor was an innovator and a discoverer. He laid the basis for Koster and Bial's Music Hall and for Weber and Fields; he claimed to have initiated the farce-comedy in America. He introduced the attractions of the freak museum and the circus into the theatre; composed dozens of songs, sang them, and built up other singers, among whom was Lillian Russell. He was the first to establish vaudeville road shows, and the first to import London Music Hall talent.

See also *Vaudeville.*

Pathélin. A character (who later became a stock type) of medieval French farce: a crafty individual who uses sweetness to attract those he would deceive.

Pathélin, or Patélin, Maître Pierre. Author unknown (French). Farce. c. 1469.

Patelin dupes a draper out of a bolt of cloth, and later, feeling pleased with himself, gives a young shepherd some shrewd advice on how to avoid paying his debts. Later, the shepherd turns this advice back on Patelin by refusing to pay him a solicitor's fee.

Paths of Glory. Sidney Howard (American). Drama. 16 scenes. 1935.

An adaptation of the novel of the same name by Humphrey Cobb. It failed on the stage, possibly because the dramatization of the novel presented too many difficulties.

The story concerns a regiment of French soldiers during the first World War. They have just returned from battle and are taking a deserved rest when their generals, de Guerville and Assolant, order them back to the front. The generals are ambitious and ruthlessly cruel, not caring how many human lives are lost if their own reputations are enhanced thereby. The soldiers find the Germans whom they are forced to attack holding an almost impregnable position, and retreat under the enemy's devastating fire. Assolant and de Guerville decide that some of the first company shall be punished as an example. The soldiers draw lots. Three of the bravest are chosen, court-martialed and sentenced to death.

Patience. W. S. Gilbert. Music by Arthur Sullivan (English). Operetta. 1881.

Apparently a satire on Swinburne and Oscar Wilde, it is based on an early Bab Ballad called The Rival Curates.

Reginald Bunthorne, a fleshly poet, is adored by twenty love-sick maidens but his affections are only for Patience, a milk maid who does not love him. She in turn loves Reginald Grosvenor, an idyllic poet, but they cannot marry as they decide their love is selfish because of Grosvenor's perfection. Patience consents to wed Bunthorne, but Grosvenor decides to become a "Matter-of-fact young man." He loses his perfection and he and Patience are united. The twenty maidens meanwhile are captivated by members of the Heavy Dragoons and Bunthorne, deserted by all, finds solace in "vegetable love."

Patsy. An assistant who does all the work.

Paul Among the Jews. Franz Werfel (German). Drama. 3 acts. 1926.

Paul, returning to Jerusalem a Christian, visits his old teacher, the patriarch Gamaliel, and seeks out Peter, Barnabas, and James, who can give him first hand information of the crucified Jesus. Paul believes that orthodox Judaism has been transcended by the new faith and gospel of love. In the meantime, Jewish fanatics have afforded to the Romans a pretext for denying the liberty hitherto accorded them. Peter finds satisfaction in these distresses since to him they afford infallible witness of the speedy second coming of the Christ.

Paul's Boys. A group of boy actors drawn from the choristers of St. Paul's Cathedral. They presented plays at court and in the singing school attached to the Cathedral. Like the Children of the Chapel Royal, they developed a court drama superior to the professional drama in refinement and stage effects. John Lyly wrote for them after 1584. Suppressed in 1590 they re-emerged in 1599 to offer competition to the professional companies with plays by Marston and Dekker. Shakespeare refers to this competition of child actors in *Hamlet* when Rosenkrantz speaks of them as "an aerie of children, little eyases," responsible for the players visiting the court of Denmark.

Pavlova, Anna (1885-1931). Russian dancer. Born in St. Petersburg, she entered the Imperial Ballet School at the age of 10 and was trained by Michel Fokine. She became the prima ballerina at the Mariinski Theatre at the age of 16. After her appearance at the Imperial Opera House she went to England. She made her debut in London in 1910 and her popularity kept her there several years. Assisted by Michail Mordkin she did her most famous dance *Le Cygne*. *Les Papillons* and *The Valse Caprice* were also very popular. She went to Paris, joined Diaghilev's Ballet Company, where she starred in *Les Sylphides*. She toured the U. S. and for many years was renowned as the foremost ballerina in the world.

Payne, Ben Iden (1881-   ). English actor, producer. Made his first appearance on the stage in *She Stoops to Conquer,* 1899; with F. R. Benson's company; director and producer at the Midland and Gaiety Theatres, Manchester; came to America in 1913 and became a producer for Charles Frohman and others; in charge of the School of the Drama at Carnegie Institute of Technology; was director of the Goodman Repertory Theatre, Chicago. Is the author of the plays *Poe* and *Dolly Jordan*.

Payne, John Howard (1791-1852). American actor, author, dramatist. Born in New York City, he developed at an early age those two characteristics which were constantly to the fore during his entire life—a love for drama and for journalism. As a school boy he edited a little paper *The Thespian Mirror,* which was published in Wall Street. When he went to Union College, he started another periodical, *The Pastime,* in which he received the encouragement of Charles Brockden Brown. However, he turned to the stage upon being graduated and in 1809 made his professional appearance in the role of Young Norval at the Park Theatre, New York. He was an immediate success, but he found that there was little hope of future advancement. When George Frederick Cooke arrived in America, he offered Payne the part of Edgar, to play opposite Cooke's Lear. Payne accepted the offer and sailed for London in 1813, where he remained for many years. When he found that there was also little hope even in England for the advancement of the actor, he began to adapt Continental plays for English consumption, residing in Paris for the purpose. Among his adaptations are *Maid and Magpie; Accusation; or, The Family of d'Anglade*. From adapting plays he began to write original ones. For Edmund Kean he wrote *Brutus; or, The Fall of Tarquin,* and *Virginius* (which the actor tossed aside when it was finished).

Payne returned to New York in 1832. He wrote *Home, Sweet Home,* with music by Sir Henry Bishop, based on a Sicilian song which Payne had heard a peasant girl sing, and which came out in the opera *Clari*. This brought him some prominence in America. His friendship with Washington Irving resulted in their writing *Charles the Second,* and in Payne's writing, alone, *Richelieu* and *Therese; or, The Orphan of Geneva*.

He died in Tunis and in 1883 his body was transferred to Oakhill Cemetery, Washington, D. C.

Peace, The. Aristophanes (Greek). Comedy. 421 B.C.

The play was written to advocate peace with Sparta. Trygaens, an Athenian who is worried about the war, journeys to Olympus on a beetle's back. He sees the gods hammering away with mortar and pestle. He inquires about this activity and finds they are busy crushing the Greek states. The Goddess Peace has been held captive in a well. Trygaens frees her. Thereupon the gods refrain from further pounding, peace is restored and Trygaens marries one of the Peace's handmaidens.

Peace on Earth. George Sklar and Albert Maltz (American). Drama. 3 acts. 1933.

A young professor becomes deeply involved in a strike of stevedores who refuse to handle munitions. He is later accused of murder and sentenced to death. In prison, he learns that war has been declared and that his struggle for peace has been in vain.

Peanut gallery. The top gallery, where the cheapest seats are located. It derived its name from the custom, associated particularly with the gay Nineties, of eating peanuts and throwing the shells on the stage.

Peasant actors. Performers recruited from the common people of the country to appear in some indigenous production, as those of Oberammergau who form the cast of the famous Passion Play.

Pedrolino. See *Pierrot*.

Peele, George (1558?-1598). English poet, dramatist. The son of a London silversmith, he was educated at Christ's Hospital and Oxford and then went to London, where he joined the dissolute circle of the University Wits. His life is described in *The Merrie Jests of George Peele,* 1607, most of the stories in which, however, are apocryphal. Peele's chief plays were *The Arraignment of Paris,* 1584; *Edward I,* 1593; *The Old Wives' Tale,* 1595; *David and Bethsabe,* 1599; *Sir Clyomon* and *Sir Clamides,* 1599.

Peep hole. The small crevice in the stage curtain through which actors and stage managers can see the audience before the play begins, the use of which is fast becoming obsolete.

Peer Gynt. Henrik Ibsen (Norwegian). Drama. 5 acts. 1867.

The parable of Peer Gynt is the most poetic and imaginative of Ibsen's plays. Its hero is related to the characters of Norwegian folk-lore. While the doctrines expounded in the drama are familiar to Ibsen—that one cannot compromise with virtue; that the worst sin is the renunciation of love—the manner of treatment is far removed from the harsh realism of most of the author's dramas. Edvard Grieg, the Norwegian composer, wrote a Peer Gynt suite which is as famous as the play itself and has made the name of Peer Gynt known throughout the world.

Peer Gynt is a worthless, dissipated egoist. At a wedding he steals the bride just to show off, and becomes an outlaw. After a series of adventures in the mountains, he forsakes Solveig, the young, virtuous girl who has followed him, and goes off to America to seek his fortune. He becomes wealthy, and seeks further adventure and dissipation in Africa. His whole philosophy of life is egotism. Returning to Norway, the rogue is shipwrecked but escapes death by pushing another man off the boat. Death is waiting for him in the guise of the Button-Molder, but Hell refuses to take him because he is unworthy. He finally achieves redemption through the pure love of Solveig, who has waited faithfully for him all the years he has been away.

Peg o' My Heart. J. Hartley Manners (American). Comedy. 3 acts. 1912.

After the death of her father, Peg, an Irish girl, inherits a fortune and goes to London to live with a conservative aunt. Life is grim for Peg until she succeeds in saving her snobbish cousin, Ethel, from a scandal and finally falls in love with a promising young Englishman.

Pelléas and Mélisande. Maurice Maeterlinck (Belgian). Tragedy. 5 acts. 1893.

A play of symbolic fairy tale characters. Melisande, asleep in the woods, is found by Goland, the hunter. He marries her. She soon falls in love with his younger brother, Pelleas. They are innocent and child-like in their love. Goland becomes suspicious when he notices that Melisande no longer wears her wedding ring. He sends Pelleas and Melisande to look for it. He spies upon them and watches them make love in the moonlight. He comes upon them when they are bidding each other a last farewell, and slays Pelleas. Melisande dies in childbirth.

Pemberton, Brock (1885-   ). American producer. Born in Leavenworth, Kansas, he was educated in Emporia, Kansas, and at the University of Kansas, from which he was graduated in 1908. He married Margaret McCoy in 1915. He was a reporter for the *Emporia Gazette* from 1908 to 1910; dramatic editor of the *New York Evening Mail*, 1910-11; assistant dramatic editor of the *New York World* and *New York Times*, 1911-17. He began producing plays with Arthur Hopkins in 1917 and continued the partnership until 1920. Since that time he has been an independent producer.

He was the producer of *Enter Madame;* Zona Gale's *Miss Lulu Bett* and *Mister Pitt;* Sidney Howard's *Swords;* Pirandello's *Six Characters in Search of an Author* and *The Living Mask;* Maxwell Anderson's *White Desert;* Preston Sturges' *Strictly Dishonorable;* Clare Boothe's *Kiss the Boys Goodbye.*

People's Lawyer, The. Dr. Joseph Stevens Jones (American). Drama. 2 acts. 1856.

Robert Howard, a young lawyer, refuses to take the unscrupulous Hugh Winslow as his client. Later, with the aid of Solon Shingle, a Yankee, Howard succeeds in convicting Winslow of forgery.

People's theatres. Organizations in several different countries dedicated to the service of popular interests as a whole and frequently distinguished by an emancipation from the technical traditions of playwriting and production.

Pepys, Samuel (1633-1703). English diarist. Theatrically, Pepys' diary is a gold mine as a source of information for the social and political life of the period. He was an inveterate playgoer and his diary is filled with anecdotes about the theatre.

Pérez-Galdós, Benito (1845-1920). Spanish dramatist. He was born at Las Palmas, in the Canary Islands. At an early age he went to Madrid to study law, but finding this unsuited to his tastes, he turned to journalism and soon began writing fiction, which was to be his life-work. In two vast series of novels, the so-called *National Episodes,* he described and analyzed the Spain of the 19th century. Over half a century ago he made an unsuccessful effort to become a dramatist, but it was not until late in his career that he turned seriously to the theatre. As a dramatist his chief importance lies in the fact that he refused to allow himself to be dominated by traditional technique. He wrote the following plays: *The Duchess of San Quentin,* 1894; *The Condemned,* 1894; *Dona Perfecta,* 1896; *The Dragon,* 1896; *Electra,* 1901; *The Grandfather,* 1904; *Reason in Unreason,* 1915; *Saint Joanna of Castile,* 1918.

Periaktoi (or *scaena versilis*). Triangular prisms, properties of the ancient Greek theatre as described by Pollux and Vitruvius; on each of their three sides was painted a certain scene; placed on a central pivot, they could be revolved in order to display a change of scene; probably fitted with a small ledge which could, if there was need, accommodate the god; position probably in or by the two side doorways; this corresponds with the conventional significance of these doors, as the *periaktos* on the left displayed distant country scenes, that on the right, parts of the city.

Pericles, Prince of Tyre. William Shakespeare (English). 5 acts. 1608.

A dramatic romance attributed to Shakespeare, written about 1608; published in quarto form in 1609. Shakespeare is generally credited only with the story of Marina, the remainder of the work being assigned to George Wilkins. The chief source of the story was Gower's *Confessio Amantis,* although the legend is Greek in origin. The wandering, episodic plot deals with the adventures of Pericles, who is forced to flee the wrath of Antiochus, king of Antioch. Landing in Pentapolis, Pericles wins Thaisa as a bride. On their voyage to Tyre Thaisa dies during child-birth and is buried at sea. The child Marina is left with Cleon, governor of Tarsus, to be raised. Eventually her great beauty arouses the jealousy of Cleon's wife, and Marina is taken by pirates to Mytilene, where she preserves her innocence in a house of ill-fame and later becomes a popular singer and dancer. Pericles rediscovers her and in his joy goes to offer thanks at the shrine of Diana. There he finds Thaisa, who has been cast ashore and restored after her apparent death at sea.

Peripeteia. Greek term (Anglicized by William Archer as "peripety"), meaning a reversal of fortune in a play which leads to an unexpected conclusion. According to Gilbert Murray it is associated with *anagnoris,* or recognition, descending from the ritual wherein originated the whole Greek drama, and finally acquiring a special meaning—a sudden decline from prosperity to adversity.

Permanent stock-companies. Term used to describe Restoration companies like Colley Cibber's in which parts were assigned according to the actor's fitness for the role rather than for his physical appearance.

Perry, Antoinette. American actress, manager, producer. Stage appearances include roles in *Mr. Pitt,* 1924; *Minick,* 1925; *The Dunce Boy,* 1925; *Engaged,* 1925; *Caught,* 1925; *The Masque of Venice,* 1926; *The Ladder,* 1926; and *Electra,* 1927. Since 1928, with Brock Pemberton, has produced and staged: *Goin' Home* and *Hotbed,* 1928; *Strictly Dishonorable,* 1929; *Three Times The Hour,* 1931; *Christopher Comes Across,* 1932; *Personal Appearance,* 1934; and *Ceiling Zero,* 1935. Conducts auditions for the Apprentice Theatre of the American Theatre Council.

Persians, The. Aeschylus (Greek). Tragedy. 472 B.C.

This play is the only record of Greek historical drama we have. The plot is rudimentary, most of the exposition is done lyrically by the chorus.

The queen and her people are concerned about the fate of Xerxes and the army. A messenger arrives and describes the battle of Salamis (in which Aeschylus is supposed to have participated). The passages containing this description including the sea battle are probably the most famous in Greek poetry. The play was written to glorify Athens' victory over Persia.

PERSONALITIES OF THE THEATRE

Bull Street to Broadway

BY WARD MOREHOUSE

When I first set eyes on Tallulah Bankhead she was sprawled on the floor of her little house in London, sipping brandy, and saying that she longed to play again in America, but she'd never do it without a good play! That was years before anybody had ever heard of Lillian Hellman or a play called *The Little Foxes.*

I first met Katharine Cornell when she was scraping grease paint from her face in her dressing room at the Times Square Theatre, a few weeks after her triumphant opening in *A Bill of Divorcement.* "Nice isn't it?" she said quietly. "I only hope it all lasts. I wonder."

I went backstage to see David Warfield soon after the premier of his and David Belasco's production of *The Merchant of Venice.* That was in 1923. It was a costly affair, a painstakingly done production, but not particularly successful. "I don't think," he said, "that I'll ever act in another play." And he never has. His is one of the few retirements that have stuck. He lives in New York and enjoys his serenity— and his pinochle games at the Lambs. When he said he was quitting he meant it, although there've probably been moments when he was strongly tempted to return. Maude Adams couldn't stay in retirement; neither would William Gillette.

I seem to have known a million-odd people of the theatre. I genuinely like them. There's warmness and humanity in most of them. There used to be a fellow named William Seeskind, who managed the Savannah Theatre, fronting on Bull Street,

Savannah, Georgia. In my extreme youth it was my impression that there was an ogre if there ever was one. But later, when some actors were talking in the Lambs grill about their touring days in the South, one of them said: "Now take Bill Seeskind, down in Georgia. There's a fellow who has a heart."

Somehow, although I've never really been in the theatre, I seem to have been meeting people of it, and knowing them, ever since *Mrs. Wiggs of the Cabbage Patch* barnstormed its way below the Rappahannock. My memory is supposed to be good, and I've always felt that my first impressions are clear-cut. I wonder if I ever enjoyed a performance more than the one given by a road star named Fred Niblo in *The Fortune Hunter*. We never got Jane Cowl in the South—I don't think we did— but we did get Clara Joel, and she did the weeping for Mary Turner in Bayard Veiller's *Within the Law*. A bareback rider, plus actress, named Ida St. Leon, captured the Southland, in *Polly of the Circus*. One of my young friends was so overcome by her, he ran away from home and joined the troupe as a super. I don't think he ever came back. An actress named Jeanne Eagels, little known at the time, came south in *Outcast*. After her first performance in Atlanta the Capital city was hers for the asking. The name of Emma Bunting spelled money and magic at any Southern box-office and the best vaudeville playlet that ever hit Georgia—the theatre was the Forsythe and it played the top bills—was Alan Dinehart in *The Meanest Man in the World*.

Let's move northward and move up a few years. To the immediate past and the present. One of the picturesque showmen of our time was Lincoln A. Wagenhals, partner in the hit-production firm of Wagenhals & Kemper. Wagenhals died some years ago; Colin Kemper is today a first citizen of Peekskill. In Charles Dillingham's last year—a famous showman who died penniless—he asked me several times to meet him at the Astor and go with him to the ball game. "You don't mind," he'd often say, "if we go on the subway, do you? The game's just as much fun." I never met Maxine Elliott and know few people who did. I've always wanted to call upon the brilliant and inspiring Edward Sheldon, author of *Romance* and so many other plays, who has been an invalid for years.

Helen Hayes and Charles MacArthur have promised to take me there, and they probably will. I've heard about the great beauties of the past. The word "beauty" in the theatre has always seemed to imply dullness and lack of talent. But as for sheer prettiness, I wonder if the girls in the musical pieces of today, and those performing in the night spots, are not as pretty as any crop Broadway ever had in any season. Bring on your *Florodora sextette!* The New York stage of 1939-40 could put them to shame.

I've been asked about the chances of young people getting started on the stage in New York. I've tried to help many and have helped a few. Getting started is tough, all right. If a girl has looks, and can act, and has means of staying in New York to stand the siege—that all helps. The trouble is, there are always about one hundred— make it a thousand and you'd still be safe—ingenues available for every role. There are not, certainly as production activity goes at the moment, enough parts to go round. Perhaps there never were. But as you prowl Broadway these days you wonder what ever is to become of all the youngsters making conquest of the stage. Nothing, to most of them. But just when you're in the mood to say some hopeful, "If I were you I'd just forget it and go on back to Albuquerque," along comes a Uta Hagen, or a Julie Haydon or a Mary Martin. Take Miss Martin as a success story! She got a plane in California. She flew to New York. She had never been on a New York stage in her life. She sang one song in an audition during the strenuous rehearsals of the musical show called *Leave It To Me*. She was engaged in ten minutes. Several weeks later she was the hit of the season with the singing of *My Heart Belongs to Daddy*.

Well, that's just one instance. There are others somewhat similar. But they are the rare exceptions. Just how, please Mr. Producer, does a girl get a start? How does she get past Miss Levy at the Woods office? Does she make the rounds of the offices daily? Does she go to Equity for daily casting information? Does she sit forlornly in an agent's office?

If you're asking me, I'd forget the dreary job hunt. Let somebody else do the pavement pounding. Skip Equity. Just put on your nicest clothes, decide either to be demure or animated or both, and get somebody to take you to Twenty-One around cocktail time. Get a good table where you can see everybody and be seen—try to get near as possible to George Jean Nathan's corner—and just sit there. In an hour you'll see more managers (and even critics and columnists) than you've ever set eyes on in a month. Or a season. And if you'got what it takes to get a part, and to get on in a heartbreaking business, you'll be noticed, and by showmen who'll give you an immediate appointment. It's a rather expensive method of job-hunting, but one tried and perfected years ago by Kay Francis at Tony's, just down Fifty-second Street apiece. At all events, I suggest trying it. If you're another Miss Hayes or Miss Hepburn you can't miss. And even if you don't get a job in the first few tries you'll soon be calling the dashing Jack Kriendler by his first name. Which is one of the privileges of New York shared by both stars and debutantes.

Peruzzi, Baldassare (1481-1536). Italian architect, designer. Peruzzi followed Vitruvius; his successor was Serlio. In 1513 he designed Calandria which was one of the first shows of the Renaissance to use complete scenery with all the new mechanical tricks and lighting effects.

Peter Pan. Sir James M. Barrie (English). Fantasy. 3 acts. 1904.

Peter Pan, the boy who never grows up, flies in the nursery window and takes Wendy and her two brothers with him to exciting adventures in the Never-Never land. He teaches the children how to fly and they have a series of very stirring adventures. They encounter Indians and Capt. Hook and his pirates. Capt. Hook has lost one hand to a crocodile who keeps trailing him in the hope of completing his meal. Unfortunately he will never catch up to him for he once swallowed an eight-day clock and his tactics are betrayed by his tick-toks. Peter has a fairy friend, Tinker Bell, who saves Peter's life and is in turn saved only when an appeal is made to the audience to believe in fairies. The children get possession of a pirate ship and make the pirates walk the plank. Finally Wendy must return home but she promises to return every spring to do Peter's annual cleaning in this treetop home.

Petite Amie, La. Eugène Brieux (French). Drama. 3 acts. 1902.

A plea for unfortunate girl-mothers. It is not one of Brieux's best plays. Logerais, the proprietor of a fashionable shop, is ambitious and money-mad. He is anxious that his son André should make a wealthy marriage, and also wishes the boy to become a lawyer. André, however, falls in love with a pretty but poor employee of his father. They have an affair, and the girl finds that she is going to have a child. Logerais is furious when he hears the news and threatens to cut his son off without a sou if he marries his mistress. So in despair the young couple drown themselves.

Pétit Théâtre du Vieux Carré, Le. This New Orleans theatre is a corporation. It is one of the most beautiful theatres in America, set in the Vieux Carré near the Cabildo. There is an excellent library for the members, and the organization has become an integral part of the cultural life of New Orleans. Renée Gavinet Bowie is the administrative secretary.

Petrified Forest, The. Robert Emmett Sherwood (American). Drama. 2 acts. 1935.

Alan Squire, footloose and weary, who belongs to the *lost generation* stops in a lunch room near the Arizona Desert, and falls in love with the proprietor's daughter, Gabby, who wants to see the world. He secretly deeds his life insurance policy to Gabby and spends all his time with her. Then, when Duke Mantee and his gang are shooting it out with the law, Squire steps in front of a machine gun bullet, glad to die.

Phalliphoric Negro slaves. Players in the ancient Roman *mime* to whom is traced *Harlequin's* black mask.

See also *Harlequin*.

Phantasmagoria. A London magic lantern exhibit of skeletons and frightening figures (1802).

Phantasms. Roberto Bracco (Italian). Drama. 4 acts. 1906.

A tormented professor, dying of tuberculosis, makes his wife, Julia, promise that she will never re-marry. He suspects that his pupil, Lucianos, is infatuated with his wife. After his death, Julia opens a home for widows who will never marry again, but she finds it difficult to keep this up as she responds to Luciano's love and is on the verge of breaking her pledge. But she is haunted by her husband's presence and finds she cannot be untrue to her vow.

Phèdre. Jean Racine (French). Drama. 5 acts. 1677.

One of the finest tragedies by the playwright who shares with Corneille the honor of being France's greatest tragic dramatist. The subject is that of Euripides' *Hippolytus*.

Phèdre, the wife of Theseus, King of Athens, is ill, possibly dying. She confesses to her confidante Oenone that she has been guilty of feeling love for her stepson,

Hippolytus, Theseus' child by his first wife, the Queen of the Amazons. Realizing that such a love could never be consummated, she has pretended to hate the Amazon's son and has sent him into exile. Now she learns that Theseus has been reported killed, and has hopes that she may reveal her passion and win Hippolytus' proud, unconquered heart. But unknown to her, it has already been conquered, by Aricie, Athenian princess, who returns Hippolytus' love. Hippolytus has an audience with the Queen to discuss who shall rule the country, now that his father is dead, and she tells him of the love she bears him. He is horrified.

Phèdre is informed that her son has been chosen King. Then Theseus, the report of whose death was false, returns. Oenone, his wife's confidante, in her desire to protect her mistress, lets him understand that it was Hippolytus who made advances to Phèdre, not the other way around. Theseus accuses his son of ingratitude, and Hippolytus decides once more to flee the land, this time in the company of his beloved Aricie. Oenone, remorseful at the wrong she has done him, drowns herself. Before Hippolytus can elope, he is drawn into battle with a gigantic sea monster and killed by his own horses, who drag him along the ground. Phèdre admits to Theseus her own guilty passion and exculpates Hippolytus, then dies of poison which she has given herself.

Racine's influential enemies were responsible for the original failure of this great love tragedy. They commissioned Nicolas Pradon to write a rival *Phèdre*, and its competition was such that Racine's play had to close after a short run.

Philadelphia School of Dramatists. The name given to the group of writers whose works were produced by Edwin Forrest after he offered prizes to unknown playwrights. These men were: John Augustus Stone, *Metamora*, 1829; Dr. Robert Montgomery Bird, *The Broker of Bogota; The Gladiator, Oraloosa*, 1829; Robert T. Conrad, *Jack Cade*, 1841; George H. Boker, *Francesca da Rimini*, 1856.

Philadelphia Story, The. Philip Barry (American). Comedy. 3 acts. 1939.

The story of Tracy Lord, a priggish divorcee, who, intolerant of the weaknesses of others, finds that she too is capable of lapses during which she can become warmly human.

Reversing the usual procedure the play shows a man risen from the ranks who turns out to be a bounder, and a man from the top niche of society proves himself to be valiant and understanding.

Philaster, or Love Lies a-Bleeding. Beaumont and Fletcher (English). Romantic drama. 5 acts. Printed 1620.

Anethusa, Princess of Calabria, loves Philaster, rightful heir to the throne of Sicily. Their love survives all manner of court intrigue, and they are finally married. Later the King, who has listened to false testimony, orders Philaster and Anethusa put to death. They are saved, however, by an uprising of the people.

Phillips, Augustine (?-1605). English actor. An actor named in the 1623 Folio list of performers in Shakespeare's plays and a member of Shakespeare's company, the Lord Chamberlain's Men, from 1594 until his death. He is known to have acted also in Jonson's *Every Man In His Humor, Every Man Out of His Humor* and *Sejanus.* He receives praise in Heywood's *Apology for Actors,* 1612.

Phillips, Stephen (1864-1915). English poet, dramatist. Born at Somertown, near Oxford, he was the son of Dr. Stephen Phillips, precentor of Petersborough Cathedral. He went on the stage and played many parts in Sir Frank Benson's company. A volume entitled *Primavera,* containing poems by him and by his cousin, Laurence Binyon, 1890, brought him much popularity. His *Poems,* appearing in 1897, contained his famous *Marpessa.* His imaginative language and warm coloring took his readers by storm, and he was commissioned by George Alexander to write a poetic drama. This was his famous and best known work *Paolo and Francesca,* 1899, produced in 1901. Later verse dramas were *Herod,* 1900; *Ulysses,* 1902; and *Nero,* 1906. He died in comparative obscurity.

Philoctetes. Sophocles (495-406 B.C.) (Greek). Tragedy. 408 B.C.
Based on the conflict between cynical statesmanship and the generous idealistic impulses of youth Philoctetes, a renowned archer and famous warrior, is left on an island at Thasas because of a wound in his foot. Ten years have passed and Philoctetes has become embittered by his neglect. Because of a prediction that only through the bow of Philoctetes could the war be won, Adepseus reluctantly permits him to leave the island. Through the divine intervention of Heracles, whose bow he uses, and the urging of a young warrior, Philoctetes consents to fight. He sails for Troy and is instrumental in the taking of the city.

Both Aeschylus and Euripides wrote on this theme but it is conceded that Sophocles has handled it most convincingly and plausibly.

Phormio. Terence (Roman). Comedy. 161 B.C.
A Roman father returns home to find his son married to a slave girl. The dilemma is finally straightened out with the aid of Phormio, a comedy villain.

The play is a study in intrigue as conducted by two bunglers and a master. Phormio is the master who delights in each new intrigue for it's own sake but who, on the whole, is a benevolent intriguer.

Phrygian. See *Modes.*

Phylakes. Type of ancient *comedy,* first Greek, later Roman; popular, farcical; became popular when it combined with an Oscan *mimi-farce* which originated in Atella; often performed on a small wooden platform, supported by wooden props; scenes depicted on paintings on ancient Greek vases. Action licentious. Stock-characters: (1) old man, (2) old woman, (3) baldhead (or parasite), (4) cook, (5) doctor, (6) *Macco* and other comic slaves.

Phallika—Origin of comedy (Greek) processions usually or dances honoring Dionysos or fertility.

Pickford, Mary (Gladys Mary Smith) (1893-   ). Canadian-American actress. Born in Toronto, April 8, 1893, she appeared on the stage as a child but achieved her great success in the films. She joined the old Biograph Company in 1912, and her first film was called *Her First Biscuit.* Extremely successful in ingenue parts, she made a great many motion pictures, including *Tess of the Storm Country, Rebecca of Sunnybrook Farm, Pollyanna,* and *Secrets.* After her divorce from Owen Moore, she married Douglas Fairbanks in 1920. She has been divorced from him and is now married to Charles (Buddy) Rogers.

Picon, Mollie (or Molly) (1903-   ). American Yiddish actress. Born on the New York East-Side; began her stage career at five in the Philadelphia Yiddish Arch Street Theatre and played juvenile roles until 1918, when she married Jacob Kalish, playing for two years in his Boston Yiddish Theatre. He then took her to Europe, where she became internationally famous, returning to New York in 1922. Since then she has played Yiddish comedies at the Twelfth Street and Second Avenue Theatre (Molly Picon's) of which she is part owner. She had a vaudeville engagement with RKO in 1929, and one in 1932 with Loew's. Made a moving picture *Yiddle with his Fiddle* in 1937, and started on a world tour with her husband the following year.

Picture-frame stage. In the 18th century the apron was growing less in importance and the picture-frame stage began. This stage called for action within the proscenium arch and the line of demarcation between stage and audience became more pronounced.

Picture settings. Renaissance stage settings in which vistas were added beyond doorways. Stages sometimes formed a single vista. Inigo Jones combined the Roman walled platform with the vista into one stage composition. The evolution of the picture scene brought the decorated stage wall of the classic theatre forward to become the proscenium frame of the modern theatre, while the vista, once visible through the central doorway, became the full stage scene, with curtains and changes between plays or between acts.

Piece of the show. Part ownership in a production.

Pierrot (or Pedrolino). Stock-character of a *commedia dell'arte;* originally a valet; similar to the slave in the comedies of Plautus and Terence; later the clown and fool.

Pigeon, The. John Galsworthy (English). Fantasy. 3 acts. 1912.
A middle-aged artist takes in a group of social outcasts and people "who haven't got on" and tries to make them a little more adequate and aware of themselves. His daughter claims that they are rotters and events seem to bear her out. One drinks the artist's liquor in payment for his kindness; another, a flower girl, has an affair with the third derelict and, in despair, throws herself into the Thames. She does not get off so

easily for she is fished out by the police and taken to the station. The artist is not discouraged by his sad experiences and continues to remain a pigeon—one to be plucked.

Pillars of Society, The. Henrik Ibsen (Norwegian). Drama. 4 acts. 1877.

Consul Bernick, a supposed pillar of society, is really a philanderer and is dishonest in business; yet he keeps within the law. He throws suspicion of embezzlement on a friend and also allows that friend to take the blame for an intrigue in order to save himself. Knowing that one of his ships is unseaworthy, he allows it to sail hoping that it will go down with his injured friend on board. When he discovers that his son is on the ship he comes to his senses. He confesses his sin and finds that Providence has rewarded him by keeping the ship safe. He finds that the pillars of society are truth and freedom.

Pinafore. W. S. Gilbert. Music by Sir Arthur Sullivan. Operetta. 1878.

Ralph Rackstraw, a seaman, is in love with Josephine Corcoran, the daughter of the ship's captain. She is also loved by Sir Joseph Porter, First Lord of the Admiralty.

This first full-length operetta by the famous pair is typical of so many of their works—babies changed in cradles, the lovers separated and a final re-union in which all ends happily.

Pinakes. Painted boards (singular *pinax*) placed between the pillars of the *proskenion*.

Pinero, Sir Arthur Wing (1855-1934). English dramatist. Born at London in 1855, he was trained at first for the law, and remained in his father's law office until he was nineteen, when he became an actor. For a year he played minor roles with the Wyndhams in Edinburgh. In 1876 he went to London, and soon after entered Irving's company, remaining at the Lyceum for five years. During this time the young actor had been trying his hand at plays, the first of which, *£200 a Year*, was produced at the Globe in 1877. *Daisy's Escape* and *Bygones* followed soon after at the Lyceum. The success of *Daisy's Escape* and the conviction that he was not destined to become a great actor, induced Pinero to devote himself altogether to the writing of plays. Throughout the Nineties Pinero shared with Jones the supremacy of the English theatre, and to the present day, he is regarded by certain critics as the best equipped and most skilful playwright of the English-speaking world.

He is the author of the plays *The Money-Spinner*, 1880; *The Squire*, 1881; *Dandy Dick*, 1887; *The Schoolmistress*, 1886; *The Magistrate*, 1885; *Sweet Lavender*, 1888; *The Weaker Sex*, 1888; *The Profligate*, 1889; *The Second Mrs. Tanqueray*, 1893; *Trelawney of the Wells*, 1898; *Iris*, 1901; *His House in Order*, 1906; *The Thunderbolt*, 1908; *Mid-Channel*, 1909; *The Mind-the-Paint Girl*, 1912; *The Big Drum*, 1915; *Quick Work*, 1919; *The Enchanted Cottage*, 1922; *A Seat in the Park*, 1922; *A Private Room*, 1928; *Child Man*, 1930; *A Cold June*, 1932.

Pinski, David (1872-   ). Jewish-American author, editor and dramatist. He was born in Russia and was educated at the University of Berlin. He also did post-graduate work at Columbia University, New York, 1903-04. He came to the United States in 1899. He was editor of *Der Arbeiter, Der Kaempfer, Die Wochenschrift, Daily Socialist-Zionist, De Zeit* and President of the Jewish National Workers Alliance, and the Jewish Theatre Society of New York.

His plays include *The Treasure* (comedy), 1919; *King David and His Wives* (drama), 1923; *The Final Balance,* 1928. He is also the author of five volumes of dramas and three volumes of stories in Yiddish.

Pirandello, Luigi (1867-1936). Italian dramatist. Won the Nobel Prize for Literature, 1934. He was born at Girgenti in Sicily and, having studied in Rome and at Bonn, returned to Italy to become a teacher in the Rome high school for girls. He began his literary career as a poet, publishing three volumes of verses, 1889-95, but he soon turned to the novel, which was better suited to the cynicism and realism of his temperament at that time. Of his novels *Il fu Mattia Pascal,* 1904, is significant since it foreshadows the theme of most of his plays. In 1912, Pirandello's first play, the one-act drama *La Morsa* was produced, and thenceforth the stage was his main preoccupation. It is as a playwright that he became world-famous. His plays include: *Se non cosi,* 1917; *Cosi e se vi pare,* 1918; *Tutto per bene; L'imbecille; Enrico IV; Come tu mi vuoi;* and *Ciescuno a suo modo.* Among those produced on the English stage are: *And That's the Truth; The Mock Emperor; The Man with the Flower in His Mouth; Six Characters in Search of an Author;* and *As You Desire Me.* His *Better Think Twice About It* appeared in 1933. Pirandello opened his own theatre in Rome in 1925, forming a company which toured Europe. His real importance in modern drama derives from his ability to create middle-class characters of universal significance. The main theme of his plays is the power and prevalence of illusions. Man, he maintains, constructs an identity for himself, sometimes deliberately and sometimes unconsciously, in an attempt to escape from the emptiness of existence. However, this artificial construction is seldom of help to him, and he is slowly compelled to realize that he stands alone in the universe, that apart from his own individuality there is no reality.

Piranesi, Giovanni Battista (1720-78). Italian designer. He spent most of his life at Rome, where he worked on the buildings and monuments of the ancient and modern city. In his scene designs he achieved a skilful manipulation of deep blacks contrasted with strong light.

Pirates of Penzance. W. S. Gilbert. Music by Sir Arthur Sullivan. 1879.

This charming operetta about Frederic who was apprenticed to a pirate instead of to a pilot because of the deafness of his nurse, bears the distinction of being the only Gilbert and Sullivan operetta to have its premier in the United States. The song "Come Men Who Plough the Sea" in the form of "Hail, Hail, The Gang's All Here" from this operetta has become an American folk-song."

Pirouette. A ballet term for a full turn of the body on one leg.

Piscator, Erwin (1893-   ). German scenic artist, director. One of the leaders of the Left-Wing Theatre in Germany, and director of the Volksbuehne, 1924-27. His most famous production was *The Good Soldier Schweik*. His settings are of the constructivist type and he combines moving pictures with his plays to speed up the action and give added dimensions.

Pisemsky, Alexei Feofilaktovich (1820-1881). Russian novelist, actor, dramatist. He was born near Moscow, was given a liberal education and turned when young to the writing of novels. Becoming interested in the stage he began to do small parts. However, he soon discovered that his real forte lay in writing for the theatre. His plays were successful and possessed enough universality of meaning to be included in the repertory of the Moscow Art Theatre during the first years of its existence.

Among his plays are *The Hypochondriac*, 1852; *The Division*, 1853; *The Veteran and The Recruit*, 1854; *Bitter Fate*, 1859; *Lieutenant Gladkov*, 1867; *Experienced Falcons*, 1868; *Rapacious Beasts*, 1873; *Baal*, 1873; *Enlightened Times*, 1875; *A Financial Genius*, 1876; *The Last Fledgelings*, 1886; *The Miloslavskis and Naryshkins*, 1886; *The Family Whirlpool*, 1886; *The Fighters and the Temporizers*, 1886; *The Rival Mothers*, 1886. In 1928, *Baal* was translated by F. O. Dempsey under the title, *The Worshippers of Baal*.

Pit. (1) A deep sunken space in front of the stage, used for musicians, probably supplanting the earlier apron. This is the orchestra pit of the present theatre. (2) A section at the back of the lower floor (stalls) of English theatres, where seats are unreserved and patrons must queue up to secure them.

See also *Yard*.

Pitoëff, Georges (1896-1939). Franco-Russian actor, producer. Born at Tiflis, he made his stage debut at St. Petersburg in 1912. He formed a company of his own and played at Geneva in 1915. After the war he returned to Paris, where he settled, playing at the Theatre des Arts, the Comedie des Champs Elysees, and others. As a producer he specialized in plays of a high intellectual standard by authors such as Shaw, Pirandello and Lenormand, staged in simplified but artistic settings. As an actor he was best in the portrayal of neurotic characters, such as Henry IV in Pirandello's play of that name. His wife, Ludmilla, born at Tiflis, 1896, acted with him after 1917. Together they have performed in Paris, such plays as Shaw's *Saint Joan;* Schnitzler's *Reigen;* and Andreyev's *He Who Gets Slapped*.

Pizarro. Richard Brinsley Sheridan (English). Tragedy. 5 acts. 1799.

Pizarro, leader of the Spaniards, ambitious, cruel, and ruthless wishes to become ruler of Peru. Alonzo, one of his aides, has deserted him to join the ranks of his enemy Ataliba, King of Onito. He has married Cora beloved of Rolla, valiant commander of the army. Rolla's only wish was to make her happy. Cora and Alonzo have a son. In the Spanish Camp we see Elvira, Pizarro's mistress, voicing her disillusion in her lord and master. She pleads with him to put an end to this useless war against an honorable and peaceloving people but Pizarro, impelled by greed does not heed her. The two armies meet and Pizarro is defeated. He learns, however, that Alonzo is a prisoner. He is delighted to wreak vengeance on him. He orders his death at dawn. Rolla hears of this, visits him dressed as a friar and effects his escape. He is given a dagger by Elvira to kill Pizarro. He enters Pizarro's tent and finds him sleeping fitfully. He spares his life to show him what it means to be magnanimous. Pizarro amazed, relents a bit and gives him free conduct home. Two soldiers enter with Alonzo's baby. Rolla recognizes it. When Pizarro hears it is his escaped enemy's child, he insists on keeping it as a hostage. Rolla though wounded escapes with the child and reaches Quito in safety. Pizarro follows and is killed. Cora, Alonzo and the child are reunited and happy. Rolla dies of his wounds and they all mourn their great warrior.

Places, please! Signal given by the stage manager to the cast for the assumption of respective positions preparatory to the rise of the curtain.

Plagiarism. To appropriate and declare as one's own the literary or artistic work of another. In the theatre and especially in the motion pictures, there have been frequent disputes and suits about the plagiarism of a plot. One of the most famous was the case of Aurelia Bachman and George L. McKay against David Belasco. They wrote a play, *Etelle,* which they claimed Belasco and Edward Locke, author of *The Case of Becky,* had plagiarized from reading the manuscript. They denied it and the two plays were performed for the court. Belasco won. Another noted case was that of the actress Georges Lewys, against Eugene O'Neill and the Theatre Guild. She claimed *The Temple of Pallas Athenae* had been robbed to make *Strange Interlude* a successful play. She lost the suit.

See *Copyright.*

The Plain Dealer. William Wycherley (British). Comedy. 1674.

Manly, a ship's captain, has lost faith in everyone except his friend Vernish and his love, Olivia, to whom he has entrusted his money. He goes off to sea and Fidelia, who is secretly in love with him, follows him disguised as a man. Returning from a sea voyage, Manly finds Olivia has married someone else and makes excuses for not returning his money. Manly discovers that Olivia's husband is his trusted friend, Vernish. In an ensuing scuffle, Fidelia, still in disguise, is wounded in an attempt to save Manly. Her true identity is then revealed and Manly, touched by her love, marries her.

Plant. A member, properly speaking, of the acting company of a play who is put in the audience for purposes of fostering the illusion that the audience is taking part in the performance; he speaks his lines from the auditorium, sometimes the orchestra, sometimes the balcony. Perhaps the earliest evidence of this technique, or trick, lay in the ancient Greek *comus;* it has been used in *The Shoemakers' Holiday,* the Elizabethan comedy, and such modern plays as Odets' *Waiting for Lefty* and Wilder's *Our Town,* as well as frequently in present-day burlesque.

Platea. The stage in the medieval theatre.

Platform theatre. A rude form of playhouse in Elizabethan times which consisted of no more than a stage on wheels and which was moved about the streets of towns for performances.

Plautus (Titus Maccius) (254-184 B.C.). Roman comic poet, dramatist. A popular actor born at Sarsina, Umbria, he made a great reputation with his plays which are the standard Latin comedies. The author had no hesitancy in lifting whole pages from the original Greek but he was such a master of the Latin of society that his plays were acclaimed in Rome. The pungent and often coarse wit, the rapidity of action, and the shrewd knowledge of human nature have insured their continued popularity. Of some 130, only 21 survive: *Amphitruo* (Amphitryon); *Menaechini* (The Twin Brothers); *Persa; Captivi; Epidicus;* etc. Shakespeare, Goldoni, Udall, Jonson, Ariosto, Fielding, Shadwell, Molière and Dryden have all based plays on his works.

Play. A piece representing life on a stage before an audience and usually divided into acts and scenes. The term "play" came into use about 1800 to describe that form in England, Germany and France which did not lend itself easily to immediate identification as either comedy or tragedy, since it belonged to neither tradition.

Playbill, The. The programme of the New York legitimate stage and published weekly. The New York Theatre Program Corporation began publishing *The Playbill* in the form of programmes for the season of 1934-35. It is now the only form in the field, and in 1937 it was publishing programmes, uniform in size, format, advertising and features, for all legitimate theatres in New York except the Manhattan Opera House. Even the Metropolitan Opera House participates. An important feature is *Who's Who in the Cast,* written by John Dow from publicity supplied by each production's press agent, giving biographical data concerning the members of the cast for each play. Barbara Blake, editor, does a fashion column signed "Nell Gwynn"—*Audience on Parade*—a timely report of the important openings of the previous week with names and descriptions of the costumes of the well-known women in the audience; Alfred Bryan ("Beau Nash") writes *What the Man Will Wear; After the Theatre,* an outline of the New York hotels and night clubs, is written by John A. Thomas; a bridge column is written and edited by The Four Aces.

Playbills, collections of. These are to be found at The Players; Museum of The City of New York; New York Historical Society; Harvard College Library; Library Company of Philadelphia; The New York Public Library; The Folger Shakespeare Library, and others.

Playboy of the Western World, The. J. M. Synge (Irish). Comedy. 3 acts. 1907.

Treated as a spineless good-for-nothing by his tyrannical father who tries to marry him off to an old widow, Christopher Mahon, enraged, strikes down his father. Christy runs off to County Mayo, relates his troubles to a poor publican and his handsome daughter, Pegeen, who shelter him. He becomes a hero to her as well as to the community. His hardheaded father turns up and Christy wins his respect when he makes a second attempt to kill him.

Play doctor. An authority on dramatic writing who is called in to make revisions on a play script for production purposes.

The Players. An American club formed in 1888 by Edwin Booth, Lawrence Barrett, Augustin Daly and Albert M. Palmer, who conceived the idea of establishing a club for actors similar to the Garrick Club in London. Booth donated the house at 16 Gramercy Park, New York City, to the organization.
See also *Theatre collections.*

Playgoing, Elizabethan. Performance in the Elizabethan theatres were afternoon affairs, usually beginning at 2 or 3 o'clock and lasting two or three hours. Meager bills announcing details of a performance were posted the day before, and the company flag was hoisted an hour before to indicate a show. Admission ran from a penny to a shilling, depending on the particular theatre and particular class of seat. The audience arrived early, ate, smoked and played cards while waiting, and often continued eating and drinking after the performance had begun.

Playing to the gas. A miserably small audience, not sufficient to pay for the lighting.

Playmakers, The (Berkeley, California). A short-play experimental theatre, whose life of more than fifteen years stamps it as the outstanding example of this type of community theatre. It sprang into being after the last lecture given at Berkeley by Professor George Pierce Baker inspired students and embryo playwrights; The Playmakers came into being as a result. The Playmakers' schedule consists usually of four programs produced each season, each program containing four one-act plays selected from a previous contest. This group enjoys a national and international reputation.

Play of the Three Wise Men, The. See *Auto de los reyes magos, El.*

Play Pictorial. Published on the fifteenth of each month, London, Arundel St., Strand, W.C. 2.
A magazine devoted to the theatre; with it are incorporated *The Play, The Play Souvenir, Plays and Players.* Edited by John Bourne.

Play publishers. Among them are: The Walter H. Baker Company, 178 Tremont Street, Boston. Banner Play Bureau, Inc., 111 Ellis Street, San Francisco.

A. S. Barnes, 67 West 44th Street, New York City. Beckley-Cardy Company, 1632 Indiana Avenue, Chicago. The Berkeley Playmakers, 2127 Ashby Avenue, Berkeley, California. The Willis N. Bugbee Company, 428 South Warren Street, Syracuse, New York. The Catholic Dramatic Movement, 1511 West Wisconsin Avenue, Milwaukee, Wisconsin. T. S. Denison and Company, 623 South Wabash Avenue, Chicago. The Dramatic Publishing Company, 59 East Van Buren Street, Chicago. Dramatists' Play Service, 6 East 39th Street, New York City. Eldridge Entertainment House, Inc., Franklin, Ohio. The Fitzgerald Publishing Company, 11 East 36th Street, New York City. A. Flanagan Company, 920 North Franklin Street, Chicago. Samuel French, 25 West 45th Street, New York City. Ivan Bloom Hardin Company, 3806 Cottage Grove Avenue, Des Moines, Iowa. Fred B. Ingram, Gansert Building, Rock Island, Illinois. Jewish Publication Society of America, S. E. Corner Broad and Spring Garden Streets, Philadelphia. Johns Hopkins University, The Playshop of, Baltimore, Maryland. Little Brown and Company, 34 Beacon Street, Boston. Longmans, Green and Company, 114 Fifth Avenue, New York City. Meigs Publishing Company, 805 Occidental Building, Indianapolis, Indiana. Mid West Debate Bureau, 511 North Fayette Street, Jacksonville, Illinois. New Theatre League, 55 West 45th Street, New York City. The Northwestern Press, 2200 Park Avenue, Minneapolis, Minnesota. Paine Publishing Company, 40 East 1st Street, Dayton, Ohio. Penn Publishing Company, 925 Filbert Street, Philadelphia. Row, Peterson and Company, Evanston, Illinois. The Southwest Press, 2007 Bryan Street, Dallas, Texas. The Van Dyke Workshop, Box 106, Fallbrook, California.

See also *Drama, published.*

Playreader. One who is employed by a manager to read plays in order to assist in selecting suitable ones for production.

Plays, budget. Those plays usually listed in publisher's catalogues as "budget plays" may be produced by amateurs for one performance only without the payment of a royalty fee, provided the intending producer purchases as many copies as there are speaking parts in the cast.

Plays, court. Plays written from the time of the Italian Renaissance to the French Revolution for and to please the monarchs and their courts. These plays included ballets, interludes, improvisations and pantomimes. Often members of the nobility and the rulers themselves participated as actors and as pantomimists. Almost all drama of the time was given in the court of these rulers. The masques of the court of Charles and James I in England were particularly famous. Inigo Jones was the foremost designer of this phase of the theatre.

Plays, symbolism in. *Pelleas et Melisande, The Blue Bird,* Maeterlinck; *La Nouvelle Idole,* de Curel; *La Femme de Claude,* Dumas; *Cyrano de Bergerac,* Rostand; *The Assumption of Hannele,* Gerhart Hauptmann; *Peer Gynt, Brand,* Ibsen; *Faust,* Goethe; *Servant in the House,* C. R. Kennedy; *Liliom,* Molnar;

Shadowy Waters, Yeats; *Peter Pan,* James Barrie; *Makroupoulos Secret,* Karel Capek.

Play's the Thing, The. Ferenc Molnar (Hungarian). Comedy. 3 acts. 1920.

Albert Adam, a young composer, is engaged to the actress, Llona Szabo. He and two playwright friends visit her earlier than they are expected at her castle in the Italian Riviera. Having adjoining apartments, they hear a very compromising conversation between Llona and a supposedly ex-lover actor. Adam is shattered and Lurai the playwright decides to save the situation by writing a one-act play for the next evening's concert. He incorporates the lines they overheard. When the fiancé hears these lines being rehearsed, he believes as they wish him to believe, that he had been listening to a rehearsal on the previous evening. Adam feels relieved, the playwright feels philanthropic, the actor is grateful and Llona is more affectionate to her fiancé than ever.

Playwright. See *Dramatist.*

Playwrights' Company, The. This company was founded in 1938 to produce the plays of its members: S. N. Behrman, Elmer Rice, Robert E. Sherwood, Maxwell Anderson and the late Sidney Howard. As stated by Maxwell Anderson, its aims are "to make a center for ourselves within the theatre, and possibly rally the theatre as a whole to new levels by setting a high standard of writing and production." The members are joint producers of each play written by one of their number. Thus they do not have to depend on the ordinary commercial producer, and can share, as producers, in any profits made by one of their plays. Each playwright collects author's royalties on his work in the customary manner. In honor of Sidney Howard, who died in 1939, the Company has established a Memorial Award of $1500 annually for the best first play produced in New York by an American author.

Their productions of the 1938-39 season were Sherwood's *Abe Lincoln in Illinois,* Pulitzer Prize winner and outstanding success; Anderson's *Knickerbocker Holiday,* which had a moderate run; Rice's *American Landscape,* a failure; and Behrman's *No Time for Comedy,* a hit.

PLAY WRITING

BY ARTHUR RICHMAN

"In the soul of the writer, the drama gradually takes shape out of the crude material furnished by the account of some striking event. First appear single movements; internal conflicts and personal resolutions, a deed fraught with consequence, the collision of two characters, the opposition of a hero to his surroundings, rise so prominently above their connection with other incidents, that they became the occasion for the transformation of other material."

"In the broadest sense, a play is a complete and unified story of human life acted out on the stage in a series of motivated incidents so arranged as to excite the greatest amount of interest and pleasure in the spectator by means of novelty, variety, contrast, suspense, surprise, climax, humor, and pathos."

The first is a quotation from a chapter by Gustave Freytag which he calls "The Idea," the second a quotation from a chapter by Alfred Hennequin which he calls "What Constitutes a Play" and I give both to you in order to show that the writing of a play is in part an unconscious process and in part a conscious one.

The unconscious part which, as Freytag indicates, constitutes the selection of a story, comes first. Something—what he calls "the crude material furnished by the account of some striking event"—makes its appearance and starts a train of thought in the author's mind. Why this particular incident and not another should start the train of thought no one can say—since the process is unconscious and the result of innumerable events that have preceded it only the psychologist is entitled to guess. But it happens and the train of thought, usually accompanied by some degree of mental and spiritual excitement, becomes The Idea.

There follows a period of incubation and I think that what goes on during this period is partly conscious and partly unconscious. Again ideas come but now they are not stray ideas as at first but ideas related in some way to The Idea. Some are rejected at once, some after deliberation, some are accepted exactly as they appear, some are transformed into something different from their original shape yet resembling it— and this last process is a wholly conscious one.

It is interesting to note that the duration of this incubating period varies greatly among the writers. Some, the more fortunate, see their story full-blown almost at the moment it first appears; others carry the pieces of their story about with them a long time before they are made to fit. The time comes however when they *do* fit (assuming, that is, that they do) and then the actual writing of the play begins.

Here again we come upon a great variance in the time it takes. Some writers write quickly, others slowly, but it is not always those whose stories came easily who now do the fastest work. As often as not some of the details necessary to the writing of the play were left out—motivations are not adequate, characters have not been clearly visualized, other lapses have occurred—and either the writing is held up until those errors are rectified or the author tears up what he has written and starts over again. I even suspect that a long incubation in most instances presages an easier birth, since so many ideas about characters and situations and even bits of dialogue have occurred to the author during the weeks or months it involved.

When the actual writing takes place, the author has to think of a great many things. Some authors are more conscientious than others, some themes from their nature demand more logical treatment than other themes, but in every case he is conscious of the need for stating his idea as clearly as his plan for the play permits, for having the situations properly motivated, for giving them dramatic interest, for making the characters consistent and the things that are said fit the people who say them. But here I want to make an explanation. I have mentioned the need for making the characters consistent whereas what I really mean is that they should *not be inconsistent*. A great many plays, especially of earlier days, have suffered from the fact that characters *were* consistent. The effort to make them so, to have them express the same thoughts and prejudices and predilections throughout a play as often as not resulted in repetition and took from characters the resemblance to human beings which they should have had. Even when I say that characters should not be inconsistent I should like to add the adverb *too*.

A question which is frequently asked, both by people in the theatre and out of it, is whether an author writes his play with any particular actors in mind. This of course is impossible to answer, since some authors do and some do not. It is safe, however, I think, to say that in most cases nowadays an author does not, and for this there are several reasons. One is that, while the star system still obtains, it is not so essential to the success of a play that a star be in it as it once was; another is that with the competition of Hollywood you can't tell whom you can get and whom you can't; a third is that plays are so well acted today that an author sits down to his work with the mystical sense that, though the search may be arduous and long, the right person is somewhere to be found. How there happens to be so much good acting on the stage at a time when everybody who makes a hit is immediately tempted to leave it I don't know, but it seems to me, although there are comparatively few outstanding personalities, that plays in general are better acted than they ever were before.

This brings me to another point it may be worth while to consider. Although an author may not write his play with any particular actor or actors in mind, there are very few who do not hope for one more than for another and who do not picture that actor in a role because of the help it gives him to write it. Characters are ephemeral things during the writing of a play and the more solidity you give them, the easier it is to see them move about and hear the things they say.

Plays are of many kinds and although the drama has reached out into fields it never touched before and the technique of playwriting is much less circumscribed than it formerly was, it is probably more difficult today to find the kind of material from which plays are made than at any previous time. It isn't because dramatic events aren't happening, Heaven knows, but because the kind of dramatic events that are happening don't lend themselves easily to stage representation. A play is based upon conflict and conflict used to be inherent in the ordinary relationships of individuals and the conventions which governed them. Could the squire's son marry the farmer's daughter, would the leading lady be invited to the duchess' garden party, would the hero marry a woman who had a past or thrust her back into it—these were the materials from which plays were made, but they serve no longer. The squire's son would marry the farmer's daughter if he wanted to badly enough and nobody would care, the leading lady might be chagrined for a few moments not to receive the duchess' invitation but on the other hand she mightn't go if she did, and if the hero didn't marry the woman with a past merely because she had one he would be a "heel" and the play would become a farce instead of a problem-play, something the author never intended when he began. Instead of this the conflicts today are mass conflicts, oppositions of groups, and these it is difficult to put upon the stage. I don't say it can't be done—it has been, sometimes successfully—but I say it is difficult. It is difficult because it is almost impossible to symbolize the prejudices or aspirations of a group in one person or a few and yet keep those symbols human beings as well. Too often we encounter such over-simplification in the statement of the theme that it invalidates the philosophy it purports to express, or the characters are so twisted to meet the exigencies of the theme that they do not possess the traits without which they cannot become recognizable human beings, or the characters are human but the philosophy is superimposed on the play and not inherent in the incidents of which the play was made up. It is this same mass-nature of present-day conflicts that is responsible for the "institutional" type of play—the play which depicts a man's conflict with a special environment rather than with other men, and it explains why so many biographical plays are written and so many plays are laid in the past. It also explains why so many playwrights are adopting metaphysical themes. Like other men, a playwright wants to escape the miseries of a world created by these conflicts, and metaphysics is the road he takes. Nevertheless, in spite of the difficulties, plays are written and will continue to be and from the whole question of writing them only one fact stands out. A play is the product of two things, the imagination which tenders material and a selectivity so developed as to be able to shape the material into proper form. Without them there can't be any play at all.

Plot. The planned action or intrigue of a play. Referring to it as "fable," Aristotle calls plot "the principal part, and as it were, the soul of tragedy."

Plot of the Empress, The. Alexei Tolstoy (Russian). Drama. 3 acts. 1925.
The play deals with the rise of Rasputin and his relations with the Czar and Czarina—shortly before the Russian Revolution.
Though Russia is at war with Germany, the Empress, with Rasputin's advice and assistance, communicates with the enemy.
Supposed by many to be the lover of the Empress Rasputin is finally assassinated by a group of young blue-bloods whom he had ousted from royal favor.

Plough and the Stars, The. Sean O'Casey (Irish). Tragedy. 4 acts. 1926.
A sharp comment on Irish temperament and human failings during the abortive Dublin rebellion of 1915-16. The plot of the play is somewhat rambling, but individual scenes are gripping and impressive. A moving tragedy, this play was received with fury by the Dublin audience, which resented its picture of the misery, ignorance, hypocrisy, and pugnacity of the people of the slums.
The play deals with the struggle of one of the leaders of the Irish Revolution, who is finally killed, and his wife driven insane, after her baby was born dead.

Plug. A piece of scenery fitted into a permanent architectural set-up of a skeleton set.

Plutarch's Lives. The principal source for Shakespeare's plays on Greek and Roman history. The dramatist used an English translation made by Thomas North in 1576, from a French translation of the original by Jacques Amyot in 1559.

Poel, William (1852-1920). English actor-manager. Born in London, he made his first stage appearance in 1876, and was the first modern producer to revive *Hamlet* without scenery, at St. George's Hall, London, 1881. He managed the Old Vic, 1881-83, and was stage manager for Sir F. R. Benson, 1883-84. He founded the Elizabethan Stage Society in 1895, reviving plays by Marlowe, Ben Jonson,

Beaumont and Fletcher and others. Poel was the first to point out that, in characterization and in the delivery of verse, modern actors adopt the traditions of the 18th century as distinct from those of the Elizabethan open platform period. He dramatized Baring-Gould's *Mehalah,* 1886, and wrote *Shakespeare and the Theatre,* 1913.

Poelzig, Hans (1869-   ). German designer, architect. He designed the Grosse Schauspielhaus in Berlin for Max Reinhardt. In 1921 he did the scenery for a motion picture version of *The Golem.*

Poetaster, The. Ben Jonson (English). Comedy. 5 acts. 1601.

The scene is the court of Caesar Augustus. The poet Crispinus maligns the writings of Horace. He is tried by Caesar Augustus and found guilty of unjustly criticizing the works of Horace. The arrangements are read in verse. Horace is released honorably and Crispinus is given a mild emetic to rid him of chronic verboseness. The play really deals with the literary feuds of Jonson's own day. It is commonly believed that Horace is Jonson, Vergil is Shakespeare, Crispinus supposedly Marston and Demetrius is probably Dekker.

Poetics (Aristotle). A presentation of poetic-dramatic theory and an analysis of poetic and dramatic laws by the Greek philosopher and critic, Aristotle. In this work Aristotle defines: (a) comedy ("an imitation indeed of bad characters, yet it does not imitate them according to every vice, but the ridiculous only; since the ridiculous is a certain error and turpitude unattended with pain, and not destructive") ; (b) tragedy ("an imitation of a worthy or illustrious and perfect action, possessing magnitude, in pleasing language, using separately the several species of imitation in its parts, by men acting, and not through narration, through pity and fear effecting a purification from such like passions") ; (c) the laws of composition necessitating a beginning, middle and end in a drama, an observance of which makes for what has come to be known as a "well-made play"; (d) the three unities (of time, of place, and of action). This work has had a far-reaching effect on most major dramatists and drama critics since it was written, being viewed by some as the Bible of the dramatic writing profession. It has also proved an invaluable source of information on the classic Greek writers as it was the only work of its kind of that era, although its sometimes ambiguous or obscure phrasing has given rise to much speculation and controversy since its appearance.

Poetics (Scaliger). A work written by the poetic-dramatic theorist of the Italian Renaissance, described by Barrett H. Clark as an "attempt to reconcile Aristotle's Poetics not only with the precepts of Horace and the definitions of the Latin grammarians, but with the whole practice of Latin tragedy, comedy, and epic poetry." It presents the Aristotelian theories as the strictest and narrowest of rules.

Poetomachia; or, the War of the Poets. A personal and literary quarrel between Ben Jonson on one side and Thomas Dekker and John Marston on the other. The war originated in 1599 in a private quarrel between Jonson and Marston. Jonson attacked his foes satirically in his play *The Poetaster*, 1601, and Dekker retorted with *Satiromastix*, 1601. Shakespeare's Ajax in *Troilus and Cressida* has been thought by some to be a satirical thrust at Jonson, since it is known that Shakespeare was involved in the quarrel on the side of Dekker and Marston.

Point d'honneur. A French term meaning point of honor, a motive used in the old French dramas of Corneille, Hugo and Sardou. The characters were moved to defend their affronted honors.

Pollock, Arthur (1886-   ). American dramatic critic. Born in Brooklyn, New York; contributor of dramatic articles to magazines since 1912; dramatic critic of the Brooklyn *Daily Eagle* since 1917; New York theatre correspondent for *The Christian Science Monitor;* author of the English version of *Melo*, 1931.

Pollock, Channing (1880-   ). American author, dramatist. Born in Washington, D. C., he studied at the Polytechnique, Prague. In 1906 he married Anna Marble, a press agent and author. He was dramatic critic on the Washington *Post,* 1898; Washington *Times*, 1899-1900; and general press representative for William A. Brady, New York, 1900-04; press representative for Sam S. and Lee Shubert, 1904-06, when he retired to devote attention to dramatic writing. He was regular dramatic critic of *Ainslee's, The Smart Set,* and *The Green Book* successively from 1905-19.

He is the author of *Stage Stories*, 1901; *The Footlights—Fore and Aft*, 1909; and of the plays, *Ziegfeld Follies*, 1915 and 1921; *Roads of Destiny*, 1918; *The Sign on the Door*, 1919; *The Fool*, 1922; *The Enemy*, 1925; *Mr. Moneypenny*, 1928; *The House Beautiful*, 1931.

Pollux. Greek grammarian and sophist of Egypt (2nd century A.D.) ; he and Vitruvius are the only two writers who retained ancient Greek traditions; both gave to Renaissance architects almost all that was known of the classical stage. His *Onomastikon* is an invaluable source of information on ancient Greek theatre.

See also *Comedy, Greek, satyr plays; Onomastikon.*

Pompeii, Theatre of. (1) A large ancient Roman auditorium, built about 200-100 B.C. on the natural slope of a hillside and seating about 5,000 persons. (2) A smaller auditorium built near the larger with the semi-circular plan cut on two sides by rectangular boundaries.

Pong. British slang term for *ad lib,* generally used when an actor forgets the lines he has rehearsed and must fill in with improvised lines.

Ponsard, François (1814-1867). French dramatist. Born at Vienna, he published a translation of Byron's *Manfred* in 1837. His *Lucrece*, 1843, scored a great success. Ponsard is now remembered chiefly for his admirable comedy of manners, *L'Honneur et l'Argent.*

Pope, Thomas (fl. 1594-1603). English actor. An actor named in the 1623 Folio list of performers of Shakespeare's plays. He joined Shakespeare's company, the Lord Chamberlain's Men, in 1594, and became a shareholder in the Globe Theatre, but retired before the company passed under royal patronage in 1603. Besides his Shakespearean performances, he is known to have played in Jonson's *Every Man In His Humor* and *Every Man Out of His Humor*. He receives praise in Heywood's *Apology for Actors,* 1612.

Poquelin, Jean Baptiste. See *Molière.*

Porgy. Du Bose and Dorothy Heyward (American). Folk play. 3 acts. 1927.

Scene is laid in Charleston in an old cobblestone court called "Catfish Row." Porgy, a cripple earns his livelihood by begging. His avocation is shooting dice at which he has uncanny luck. One night, during a game, Crown, a stevedore, quarrels with Robbins, another player and kills him. Crown escapes before the police arrive. Everybody denies any knowledge of the crime except old Peter who breaks down under the questioning and tells the police that Crown did it. When old Peter is taken to jail as a witness, Porgy who used to rely on him to get around, buys a goat wagon and continues his begging. Crown's girl, Bess, comes to look for him and lives with Porgy when she hears of his prosperity in gambling. "Sportin' Life" a ne'er do well tempts Bess with her old vice, dope. She succumbs, seeks Crown in the thicket and gives herself to him. She tells Porgy all and says she is going to leave with Crown when the cotton comes in. Porgy asks if she could be happy without the influence of Crown hanging over her. She says yes and begs Porgy to keep him away. But Crown turns up and Porgy stabs him. Porgy is wanted to identify the man but lacking the courage to do so he disappears. He is sent to jail for contempt. On his release he returns to Catfish Row, only to find that Bess has gone North to New York with Sportin' Life. Porgy sets out for New York in his goat wagon, determined to find her.

Porta regia. Large open arch, a theatrical property of the early Greek and Roman theatres as analyzed and described by Vitruvius.

Portae minores. The lesser doors to be found on either side of the *porta regia* in the theatre of Renaissance Italy.

Porter, Cole (1892-   ). American composer, lyricist. Born in Peru, Indiana. One of the ablest of the present day sophisticated lyricists. Writes his songs frequently by doing the last line first and building up to it. Believes in using a rhyming dictionary as an aid to composition. He has composed the scores for *See America First,* 1916; *Hitchy-Koo 1919,* 1919; *Greenwich Village Follies of 1924,* 1924; *Paris,* 1928; *Wake Up and Dream,* 1929; *Fifty Million Frenchmen,* 1929; *The New Yorkers,* 1930; *Gay Divorce,* 1932; *Nymph Errant,* 1933; *Anything Goes,* 1934; *Jubilee,* 1935; *Red Hot And Blue,* 1936; *The Sun Never Sets,* 1938; *Leave It To Me,* 1938; *Dubarry Was A Lady,* 1939.

Porto-Riche, Georges de (1849-1923). French dramatist. Born at Bordeaux, he began his career in the Seventies with the writing of four romantic plays. He then turned to writing comedies and his *The Luck of Françoise,* produced at the Theatre Libre, 1888, was very successful. He was associated with Bataille, Coolus, Wolff, Guitry, Tristan Bernard, and others of the erotic and comic French school, most of whose plays first saw the light of day in Antoine's Théâtre Libre. Porto-Riche is considered the least extreme of the erotic school, although deception is the normal expectancy of every man or woman in his plays.

He is the author of the plays *Vertigo,* 1873; *A Drama Under Philip II,* 1875; *The Two Faults,* 1879; *The Impassioned Wife,* 1891; *The Past,* 1898; *The Malefilatres,* 1904; *The Old Man,* 1911; *Zubiri,* 1912; *The Merchant of Prints,* 1918.

Position. An actor's place on the stage as set by the director.

Post, Guy Bates (1875-   ). American actor. Born in Seattle, he began his career studying law. In 1893 he made his first professional appearance in *Charlotte Corday.* For a while he played Shakespearean repertoire and in 1901 made his first New York appearance in *My Lady Dainty.* In 1905 he played the lead in *The Heir of the Hoorah.* From 1907-8 he was Mrs. Fiske's leading man. He played the leading role in *Omar, The Tentmaker* from 1914-16 with great success. For many seasons afterward he toured in various plays such as *The Masquerader* and *The Nigger.* In 1927 he appeared in London in *The Climax.* He returned to America to play in *The Play's the Thing,* 1928; *Three Men and a Woman,* 1932; *The Shattered Lamb,* 1934.

Posters. Shortly before the middle of the 19th century, posters announcing plays, their casts, theatre and time of performance, began to add pictures of scenes from the production. These gradually grew more lurid so that at the end of the century the most harrowing incident was more or less truthfully pictured. A man tied to a railroad track, or on a sawmill, or a girl swinging across a chasm were favorites. *Under the Gaslight, After Dark, The Octoroon,* were advertised in this fashion. Gradually the poster changed character and became artistically representative of the show.

POSTERS

BY CLARK KINNAIRD

Least inhibited of all forms of *commercialized* art are posters, stage decor and children's book illustration.

How many great patrons of designers, as well as of composers and dramatists, there have been among the drama, opera, ballet and musical comedy impresarios is well known. There is little less realization and appreciation of how many notable and uncompromising graphic artists have been kept from starvation and accorded their only real recognition during their lives by theatrical producers.

Poster art, for which as great a case as our most influential modern trail-blazer and popularizer of new genres can be made, came to us from the theatre. It began, and was established, in fact, with Chéret, a Frenchman; Frederick Walker, an Englishman; Ludwig Hohlwein, a German; and Leon Bakst, a Russian. The name of the latter is well known to moderns for his contributions to the theatre. The others should be.

Jules Chéret's production of a poster for a Sarah Bernhardt play, *La Biche au Bois,* is as important and significant a milestone in art as the historic 1911 London exhibition of Cezanne, Van Gogh and Gaugin. Toulouse-Lautrec's genius was emblazoned on the theatrical programs and hoardings of Paris long before it entered the galleries.

Walker's first notable poster was done for a production of *The Woman in White,* in London. Hohlwein's posters for German theatrical producers were collector's items even in his own day. Poster art's beginnings in the United States must be identified with Matt Morgan's work for the theatre and circuses.

Just as we owe the inception and development of this art form to the theatre, we must credit the theatre with keeping alive the most precious form of graphic realism—the caricature. The only substantial encouragement given in our time to such American masters of caricature as William Auerbach-Levy, Al Hirsch-field, et al., has come from theatrical exploiters making use of their art for the Sunday theatrical sections. What little we see of Al Freuh's work is in his theatrical commentaries for the New Yorker. What, except the theatre, ever gave Ralph Barton the unbridled opportunities he deserved? What discriminating theatre-goers will ever forget his celebrity curtains?

Potter, Cora Urquhart (Mrs. Brown-Potter) (1858-1936). American actress. Born in New Orleans; one of the first American society women to go on the stage, or to use her name for cosmetic testimonials. Began by reciting *Curfew Shall Not Ring Tonight, The Charge of the Light Brigade* and other poems in drawing rooms. Her career was notable for her bad acting and attendant publicity, as well as for the extent of her tours, which took her to India, Australia, China, and South Africa. She made her professional debut in England in 1887, and left the stage in 1912. She was the mother of the erstwhile Mrs. James (Fifi) Stillman, who after her sensational divorce married Fowler McCormick.

Powder, aluminum. A powder used for gray hair effects, applied with a hare's foot or puff.
See *Make-up.*

Powder, blending. A theatrical powder for use as a foundation in dry make-up and for blending over a grease foundation.

Powder, bronze. Same as aluminum powder but used to give an auburn metallic effect. Both powders are used for statuary work; when mixed with glycerin, olive oil or cooking oil, it is painted on bodies with paint brushes or sponges. May be worn by performers as long as desired without any ill effect.

Powder, gold. Similar to aluminum powder; used to give light golden blonde effect to the hair.

Powder, hair. A powder used for changing or graying the hair or beard.

Powder, liquid. Used for foundation when a liquid make-up is desired. Powder in suspension in liquid which serves as a base. Most practical for concert and evening make-up.

Power, Tyrone (1798-1841). Irish actor. Son of a strolling Irish player, romantic leading man who had great success in the English provinces, later in London and in New York. Was drowned in the sinking of the America on his return to England where he was engaged to appear at Covent Garden.

Power, Tyrone (1869-1931). American actor. Grandson of the first Tyrone, son of Harold Power, he was born in London. He made his first appearance on the stage at St. Augustine, Florida, November 26, 1886, in *The Private Secretary*. He was a leading player in Augustin Daly's company, 1890-98; he appeared with Sir Herbert Beerbohm Tree, Mrs. Fiske, Sir Henry Irving, Mrs. Leslie Carter, Henrietta Crosman. In his later years he was principally associated with Shakespearean roles.

Power, Tyrone (1913-   ). American actor. Great-grandson of the first Tyrone Power, he was born in Cincinnati, Ohio. He played bit parts on the stage. He was appearing with Katharine Cornell in *Saint Joan,* when in March, 1936, he signed a contract with Twentieth-Century Fox. His work with Simone Simon in the film *Girls' Dormitory,* 1936, catapulted him to fame. He has since appeared in the cinemas, *Marie Antoinette, Suez, Alexander's Ragtime Band, The Rains Came,* etc.

The Power of Darkness. Leo N. Tolstoy (Russian). Tragedy. 5 acts. 1886.
Nikita, a young laborer, who has been carrying on an affair with his master's wife, has a pious father and a conniving mother who induces the master's wife to kill the rich husband. Nikita then marries the woman and soon after makes love to her half-witted step-daughter. The girl bears a child and Nikita's mother urges him to kill the child so that they can marry off the girl and hush up the affair. Nikita does so, but soon repents the horrible deed, and at the girl's wedding breakfast makes a full confession. Nikita's God-fearing father, delighted at his son's repentence assures him God will forgive him.

Pozzo, Andrea (1642-1708). Italian designer, architect.
Prospettiva dei Pittori e Architetti contains many sketches of the theatre, generally, as well as of many specific theatres. His sketches of a theatre, published in 1692, reveal: (1) auditorium almost a semi-circle; (2) seats disposed, not according to the ancient Roman style of the *cavea* but into tiers of five galleries separated into compartments by pillars or partitions; (3) on the stage six wings on either side

oblique to the front and tapering to the rear; (4) deeper on the stage, two sets of "shutters" or cloths backed by a space for even further and more elaborate perspective effects.

Practice Teacher, The. Max Dreyer (German). Drama. 5 acts. 1899.

The plight of a young teacher who must either cater to the prejudice and bigotry of his superiors or else lose his job and face poverty. Ironically enough, his aging mother derives her greatest satisfaction from the knowledge that her son is a teacher.

Précieuses Ridicules, Les (The Affected Young Ladies). Molière (French). Farce. 1 act. 1659.

Madelon and Cathos, two country girls, who arrive in Paris are saturated with the affected notions of the times. They reject two suitors because of their lack of extreme gallantry. The rejected suitors clothe their valets, Mascarille and Jodalet, in rich dress and send them to the ladies. Madelon and Cathos are completely taken in until the masters come and demand their clothes. In this extravagant farce, Molière satirized the preciosity prevalent in his time. The play still stands as a brilliant satire of this human foible.

Preparation. Event(s) or speech(es) established to introduce a subsequent character, occurrence, or theme in a play.

Presentational. Term used to describe one of the two general species of a play: that in which characters, events and things are introduced for their symbolical, rather than their intrinsic, values.

See also *Representational*.

Press agent. A person concerned with the promotion of publicity in the press. In New York, however, the activities of a press representative are essentially different from those of the press representative, or agent, travelling in advance of a show. The New York press representative when helping to launch a new production is dealing, like the producer, with an uncertainty, and must create for the dramatic editors exclusive stories about author, leading man, ingenue, or chorus girl, as the case may be, in addition to general stories as to the nature of the piece. A definitive book on this subject is *Press Agentry,* by Charles Washburn (National Library Press), 1937.

Press agent, road. A person concerned with the promotion or publicity for a production on tour. Unlike the New York press agent, the road press agent usually has on hand, except in the case of a try-out, a large batch of material as a result of the prolonged New York season. His press work, particularly if the bookings are for the most part for one day or one week, is comparatively simple as the same stories can be used in succeeding cities. But in addition he has such advance work as the railroad schedules for the company, hotel reservations, and all arrangements with the local manager in regard to the scale of prices, amount of money for advertising, ad copy, press copy, billing, if any, and mailing, if any.

Press agentry. Among the first recorded instances of the conscious use of Press Agentry was the maintenance of the footmen's gallantry (abolished in 1737) in the London theatre. Here the servants of the rich saw and heard the play free, in order that they might hold seats until the arrival of their master. In many cases the nobility and gentry never claimed their seats, so on returning home the servants would commend the play to their masters, thus furnishing what is considered the best type of press agentry—"mouth to mouth" praise.

By the time that "Lydia Thompson and Her Blondes" invaded the American amusement field in 1868, public press agentry had attained a standard comparable to that of P. T. Barnum's vaunted power. Extravagant speech, innumerable adjectives, and encomia stimulated the imagination and attracted patrons to the box office. The history of press agentry since then has been checkered. The work has been regarded with humor and contempt, seldom with the respect it merits, despite the ingenuity it requires and the influence it has had in all the arts. At the time of the Great War, with the development of modern business methods press agentry attained dignity and became one of the first national forces. But the term was straightway changed; leaders like Edward Bernays and Ivy Lee calling themselves publicity directors, propagandists, and counsellors in public relations; simultaneously theatrical publicity changed its quality. The stunts once perpetrated by Harry Reichenbach, Will Page, Dexter Fellows and Walter Kingsley and the marvels of the amusement world were practically abandoned for the sake of literary ballyhoo and by-line piece. Samuel Hoffenstein inaugurated a literary era with his pseudo-interview with A. H. Woods and Arthur Kober. Press agents in spite of their neglect have become leaders in the world of literature, the drama, and motion picture pictures, their social and cultural influence being incalculable. These include the following authors, dramatists, scenario writers, producers, etc.: Herman Shumlin, producer of *Grand Hotel, Children's Hour, The Little Foxes;* Jed Harris, producer of *Broadway* and *Coquette* and the protagonist in *Meteor,* by S. N. Behrman, once a press agent and author of *The Second Man, Rain From Heaven,* etc.; Willard Keefe, author of *Celebrity;* Howard Dietz, author of *The Little Show, The Band Wagon;* Ben Hecht, author of the cinema, *The Scoundrel* and many books, plays and pictures; Samuel Hoffenstein, author of *The Gay Divorcé;* Howard Benedict, magazine articles; Emanuel Eisenberg, poetry and feature pieces; Oliver M. Sayler edited the plays of the Moscow Art Theatre; O. O. McIntyre, author of famous columns and several books; Edward Bernays, editor of *Contact;* Kenyon Nicholson, author of *The Barker;* Michael Goldreyer, co-producer with Michael Mondlin of *The Last Warning;* Manuel Seff, author of *Blessed Event;* Lillian Hellman, author of *The Little Foxes;* Arthur Kober, author of *Having a Wonderful Time* and *Thunder Over the Bronx;* Richard Maney, author of magazine articles; Charles Washburn, author of *Press Agentry;* William A. Fields, author of magazine pieces; Barrett McCormick, author of *The Racket;* Dexter Fellows, author of *The Big Top;* Harry Reichenbach, author of *Phantom Fame;* John Peter Toohey, author of *Jonesy* and numerous magazine pieces; Nat Dorfman, author of Lew Leslie's *Blackbirds* and *Errant Lady.*

PRESS AGENTS

BY WILLIAM FIELDS

The roster of successful producers, in our time and of the past, unsurprisingly contains the name of *not one* showman who hasn't appreciated the futility of risking a fortune in the playshops without first insuring that his enterprise would be safe-guarded by the persistent exercise of publicity.

The mouse-trap adage, a highly questionable piece of wishful theory in *any* undertaking even remotely involving the exchange of cash for commodity, was never more incongruous than in the transitory environs of the theatre.

It is the traditional lament of the press agent that his services are never properly evaluated: that his show, if a hit, is accredited with success because of its own intrinsic merits, and through no assistance of publicity; if a flop, is invariably left lifeless on his doorstep with the lugubrious requiem that it was cut down in infancy by his criminal neglect.

There are, of course, no self-respecting press agents who really believe such specious twaddle. They only suspect that the producers believe it.

As a matter of fact, the press agent is under no less obligation with a hit than with a flop, for (the seasonal production mortality rate being what it is—i.e., some-thing to make your hackles rise) it is of paramount importance to keep a hit running to the very limit of its staying power. This staying power is an indeterminate factor with a hit, but it may be reckoned moderately at from half to two or three times the duration of its "natural momentum" if given proper and assiduous advertising and publicity promotion.

So-called word-of-mouth advertising gains its greatest effectiveness not from the necessarily limited number of people who actually have seen a production and can go forth to proselytize, but from the wider thousands, or hundreds of thousands, who —thanks to unremitting emphasis and re-emphasis in all the various media of public information—can and certainly do disseminate propaganda that is not lacking in equal value for all its indirect origin. "Going to a show? I understand 'Hail and How Now' is very good."

"They say" is one of the most powerful preambles in the English language, and it is to put those words on myriad tongues that the whole purpose of the press agent is concentrated.

In the case of flops, the objective is precisely the same, with intensive labor required to repel a swift closing. There is always a bare possibility that the playwright has had something exciting or enthralling to say, and has said it ineptly; that this actor or that one has pulled the fabric of the performance awry, or that the direction has been out of key with the substance of the play. Given a fighting chance, a reprieve of a precious week or two, the playwright is enabled to revise his ineffective scenes, the actors whose performances require adjustment are pulled into truer perspective or replaced, and the director approaches the staging with a clearer perception of the play's requirements. It is no exaggeration to say that adroitly executed publicity has given many a play failure this reprieve.

Press agents, if they are competent, definitely have something to contribute to the theatre, and, in my opinion, their most important contribution is in creating news. Thus they serve the newspapers and press associations as well as their own employers.

As an illustration of how a press agent realized the news value associated with a production he handled, and furthered it to its maximum limit, take the recent case of George M. Cohan's impersonation of the nation's chief executive in *I'd Rather Be Right*. Prior to the Boston premiere of the piece, John Peter Toohey, who was the press agent involved, sent scripts of the play to the news services and to certain weekly magazines that feature spot news. It was an astute stunt. Mr. Toohey realized that he had a timely and newsworthy entertainment and he figured that reviewers would wish to use direct quotes from the Kaufman and Hart dialogue. It would be better, Mr. Toohey reasoned, to provide them with copies of the play so that they could get their quotes precisely as they were delivered during the performance rather than forego this courtesy and perhaps have garbled versions of the speeches appear in the press throughout the country.

The foregoing certainly provides an instance of where the intelligent action of a press agent contributed to making news if indeed did not actually inspire the news itself.

There is, too, in a more trivial vein, the case of the Summer theatre press agent in Maine a few months ago who had long been a friend of a certain well known feminine picture star who was barnstorming in the resort theatre that employed him. He knew that the star was engaged to be married to an equally well-known play-wright who was soon to pay her a visit at the Maine playhouse. He went to her.

"When your fiance comes here next week," said the press agent, "you can do me a hell of a big favor if you'll get married while you are still appearing at this theatre."

"But we didn't plan to be married until the Autumn," remonstrated the lady.

"Yes, I know that," countered the press agent, "but since you are going to get married anyway, why don't you move up the date by a few weeks and give *me* a break. Furthermore, I'll handle it right for you."

The outcome was that the actress obliged, the marriage resulted in widespread publicity which reacted to the favor of the theatre operator, and the press agent created news where there was none or perhaps simply accelerated what destiny had in store anyway. True, there is the possibility that had not the press agent hastened the wedding, the principals involved might have tarried the nuptials for so long that it is conceivable the blending might never have come about. That angle, however, belongs in a realm of conjecture and guesswork that will not be investigated here.

Gilbert Miller, to cite another example of how a press agent can be of great service to newspapers as well as to the individual who engages him, is a theatrical producer of international reputation. He is said to have made more than 100 Atlantic crossings in the conduct of his New York and London undertakings. Gilbert Miller IS news. And it is of interest to the public of New York City to know of Mr. Miller's plans. His press representative, Richard Maney, attends to this admirably. Mr. Maney's scholarly and amusing, always accurate and truthful, essays about the people who employ him, one of whom is Mr. Miller, are welcomed with genuine relish and enthusiasm by every newspaper in New York City; likely indeed by every newspaper in the entire United States.

Most theatrical press agents err, and again I add in my opinion, in the biographies and stories they prepare about actors appearing in their plays. Unless material of this sort is written in the lively and tremendously amusing manner that is the exclusive talent of the aforementioned Richard Maney, it can be pretty deadly stuff. To begin with, not one actor in twenty has a life story or experiences interesting enough or important enough to rate the space in any newspaper that his press agent seeks to wangle for his contribution. It follows, then, that unless the press agent has the skill, the humor, and the literary ability to make his subject alive and vital and interesting, he is asking for something that he rightfully shouldn't have when he seeks to unload his yarn on the editor.

It might be mentioned in this connection that the current trend of publicity, it would seem to this observer, is in the direction of attractive and timely art, by which is meant photographs, and away from the stereotyped and trivial press releases and stories that once made dreary the drama sections of many newspapers.

In addition to Richard Maney, names most familiar to you among press agents are Karl Bernstein, Bernard Simon, Leo Freedman, Charles Emerson Cook, Theron Bamberger, Joe Heidt, Arthur Levy, Nat Dorfman, James Proctor, Philip Stevenson, Harry Forwood and the already mentioned Mr. Toohey. Among the feminine members of our craft there are Phyllis Perlman, Ann Ayres, Martha Dreiblatt, Helen Hoerle, Lorella Val-Mery, Marian Byram, Jean Dalrymple and Mary Ward in the legitimate field and numerous other competent women engaged in motion picture publicity. Many promising fledglings are in our ranks and they will be the Broadway press agents of tomorrow.

There are two essential attributes, I believe, that a person must have who contemplates, for a reason best known to himself, a career as a press agent. He must be accurate and he must be truthful.

If the facts contained in his stories are invariably accurate he'll be rendering a great favor to the editors who are required to read his copy. After a time they'll appreciate his accuracy and know that they can depend upon him for checking facts, thus relieving them of a boring, time wasting, and thoroughly uncalled for chore.

If only for self-preservation, a press agent should be truthful. There is no point whatever in willfully endeavoring to delude an editor in order to get away for a day —sometimes for only an edition—with counterfeit or phoney news or fabricated claims of one sort or another. Press agents who follow such tactics don't last long, at least not profitably. An editor who has been taken in by a press agent never forgets the incident, and shouldn't. Sooner or later the press agent who gives out false, or even questionable information to newspapers comes to the end of his rope, as well he should.

In conclusion, it is pretty safe to venture that in amusement publicity generally, not alone in the legitimate theatre, hokum is on the way out. Largely responsible for this happy exit are the motion picture press agents whose screaming exaggerations, frequently made in behalf of their studios' worst performers, have finally surpassed all bounds of good taste and are now actually offensive to people who feel that there are better things to do in the present day world than to sit in a picture house and have their intelligences raked by the Hollywood thinkers who provide the extravagant and frequently ridiculous trailer text that goes to describe some future fourth rate film.

Press book. Collection of newspaper and magazine clippings, in scrapbook form, pertaining to a production or player.

Pretenders, The. Henrik Ibsen (Norwegian). Drama. 5 acts. 1864.
Haakon, through his great belief in himself and his ideals, forges to the front. It has been thought that Ibsen was attempting to paint his contemporary, Bjornson, in Haakon, and himself in Skule, the uncertain hesitant one, who has the inspiration, but fails simply because of his lack of self-confidence. The period of the play is the thirteenth century and Haakons victory over Skule makes him the king of a united Norway.

Preview. A performance, sometimes a dress-rehearsal, given before an invited audience and prior to the opening night, as a test to obtain audience reaction to the presentation.

Pride and Prejudice. Helen Jerome (American). Drama. 3 acts. 1935.
Dramatization of Jane Austen's novel of the same name. Mrs. Bennet has three marriageable daughters, Jane the beauty, Elizabeth the clever, and Lydia the dashing. The family has no particular position or money. This makes it a little more difficult for Mrs. Bennet to marry off her daughters. Elizabeth, her father's favorite, is backed up by him when she refuses the hand of a pompous relative who will inherit their estate. A rich neighbor, Charles Bingley, and his friend D'Arcy are quite the catches of the season. Charles falls in love with Jane but is lured away by his sister and D'Arcy from such a mediocre marriage. D'Arcy, superior and superficially a snob, falls in love with Elizabeth. She refuses him, much to his surprise. Lydia elopes and D'Arcy settles a dowry on her. Charles returns to woo his languishing Jane and finally Elizabeth breaks down and admits her love for D'Arcy. Mrs. Bennet is elated at the splendid marriages of her daughters.

Priene, Theatre of. An ancient Hellenistic open air auditorium. Bieber, in her *History of the Greek and Roman Theatre,* says: "The theatre of Priene is the earliest and, since it is well preserved, the most important among the new theatres which were erected in Hellenistic times." This theatre was part of the original plan of the city itself. It was built about the middle of the 4th century B.C.

Prince d'Aurec. Henry Lavedan (French). Drama. 5 acts. 1892.
A drama of manners and of character. An impoverished nobleman is at the mercy of a Jewish banker. The prince is aided by his mother, a sensible woman of the middle class enabled by her money to marry a great name. She perceives that the aristocracy can be saved only by regeneration from without, and secures the promise of amendment from her volatile son who has lost all he had at gambling.

Prince of Homburg. Heinrich Von Kleist. 1810.

The Prince of Homburg, a lover and dreamer, is a general in the army which is defending Berlin from the Swedes.

His orders are not to advance, but dreaming of his loved one, he disobeys orders and his advance turns out to be instrumental in the great victory for his army.

His superior, to make an example of his disobedience, condems him to death. The prince becomes pitiable and adject as he grovels—begging for his life. He even offers to forego Natalie, his loved one, if he is spared.

He is told that he must judge himself. If the verdict is unjust it will not be carried out. His manhood restored, he admits his guilt and asks for death. As a reward he is pardoned.

Prince of Wales' Theatre. A theatre in London built originally as a concert room early in the 19th century; shortly after its inception it became a small circus, then was called the Regency Theatre of Varieties, then in 1826 the West London Theatre, as which it became the home of visiting French companies; in 1829 the Tottenham Street Theatre; in 1831 the Queen's Theatre; in 1833 the Fitzroy, alternating again with the title Queen's; in 1865 it was finally christened the Prince of Wales'. Ellen Terry acted in this theatre.

Princess Ida. W. S. Gilbert. Music by Sir Arthur Sullivan. Operetta. 1884.

Hilarion, son of King Hildebrand, was betrothed to Princess Ida when they were two and one years old respectively. Twenty years later when he goes to claim his bride he finds that she and a group of young ladies had secluded themselves in Castle Adamant and had determined to renounce all men. Hilarion and two of his friends dress in women's clothes to secure admission to the castle and finally succeed in making the princess foreswear her vows.

Problem play. A play built around a difficulty of society. Its characters personify the various forces and their conflict is the subject matter of the play.

Processional. John Howard Lawson (American). Drama. 3 acts. 1925.

The story of a West Virginia coal mining town in the grip of a strike. The mine owners make use of troops to shoot the strikers and of the Ku Klux Klan to terrify them. In this setting Sadie Cohen, the jazz-bitten daughter of the general store keeper is seduced by Dynamite Jim, a powerful but ignorant young miner. Jim is jailed and blinded in the course of a fight but though he cannot see, his eyes are opened to the true state of the struggle. Sadie becomes pregnant and in the finale suggests that the son she is carrying will carry on the struggle.

Lawson has placed the play within a framework of jazz, giving it a semi-vaudeville feeling.

Proctor, Frederick Francis (1851-1929). American theatre owner. Known as the "dean of vaudeville theatre chain owners," he was a pioneer in that field. He also operated motion picture houses. His greatest rival was once B. F. Keith, later his partner in the Keith and Proctor circuit.

Producer. The entrepreneur of a theatrical production is called the producer. He selects the play, appoints the director, decides or assists in deciding on the scenic designer, the costumer, the cast. He is generally assisted by a staff, general manager, company manager, press representative, etc.

THE PRODUCER
BY BROCK PEMBERTON

What is a producer? The question is not wholly a rhetorical one posed as a tee for the kickoff of this ball of wisdom. It is justified by the general ignorance both in and out of the theatrical profession as to the identity and function of this most shadowy of individuals in the theatre. "The fifth wheel" is one of the most complimentary appellations hurled at him in the heat of conflict.

The producer is not quite this inconsequential. He may be the least important of the theatrical triumvirate but without him in some form, however submerged, there can be no play. There may be a manuscript complete to the last detail and actors ready to translate it through the spoken word, but until the producer has come forward and directly or indirectly coordinated the various elements there can be no play in the full meaning of the term, which is a dramatic work interpreted by actors before an audience.

The producer, then, is the man or woman who causes the author's words, strung together in dramatic form, presumably to emerge from the typed page. It is his job first to decide that a play should be produced, to provide the capital for the highly costly experiment, to engage the director, actors, scene and costume designers and other necessary technicians, to provide a business staff, arrange for a theatre and procure an audience. The degree of accomplishment of the last-named duty reflects his skill in the other departments and measures his success, for unfortunately the theatre is such an expensive enterprise it must pay its way as it goes.

The producer's lot is not a happy one. (Words by Gilbert, music by T. Pan Alley.) An individualist at heart he is notably deficient as a group worker and so finds himself constantly alone confronting or caught in between various groups, all of whom are highly organized. He may be the most peace-loving, law-abiding, justice-worshipping of citizens and still be forced to carry on in a state of constant turmoil because of the goings-on of less thoughtful brethren. This is the group picture.

Between strikes and lockouts he may function as an individual if he has anything to function with. His chief problem, granted a modicum of ability, is a worthy script. As motors, movies and radio have destroyed the former monopoly of the legitimate theatre and restricted its sphere of influence critical standards have been elevated, making the dramatist's task still more difficult. This causes a constant shortage of material and until a producer has found a script he believes in he cannot move. A favorite fiction is that every producer's desk is loaded with classics. Many good plays do not win production but usually there is a valid reason. The chief of these is not the obtuseness of readers, since most scripts pass through many hands, but the odds of success. Most producers die broke; those who pick plays without regard to their probable popularity live broke.

When a producer has discovered a script he thinks audiences will pay to see performed he finances the venture. Few provide all the money themselves. There were more who did this in the golden days when the legitimate theatre had no competition, but since 75% of today's productions fail most producers spread their capital thinly and operate on O.P.M. (other people's money). The task of procuring backing for a production is not always an easy one due to the highly speculative nature of the enterprise and the specialized skill required to judge manuscripts.

Most marketable scripts can be financed, though, and when the producer has the money in the bank he chooses his director (unless as in a few instances he is his own), his actors and all the other specialists necessary for modern stage production. If he knows his stuff he should be able to spot the weak points, if any, in the manuscripts before or during rehearsals and to detect deficiencies and make replacements in his cast. He should hover over rehearsals, be able to contribute to the constructive criticism which rends the early morning hours after every preliminary performance, and still be concerned about the quality of the show when it is 500 times old. He must know that it is as important to get the curtain down with dignity as to get it up.

Who is a producer? Anyone may be. It is the only job in the theatre that doesn't call for union membership. A group of persons may combine as a unit and produce, a dramatist may bring forth his own play, an actor may set himself up in business as an actor-manager, an office boy, a press agent, a newspaper man, a prize-fight manager, a song writer, in fact, anyone may announce to the world "I am a producer," and if he causes a play to be presented he is one. Whether or not he continues to be one will depend on how much instinct, knowledge and love backed by determination he brings to his job.

Professional matinee. Matinee given on another day than that regularly chosen for matinees, to enable actors playing in other theatres to attend. The practice has altered since the turn of the century, when it began, so that matinees in New York now are given on off-days more to draw holiday visitors and out-of-town audiences than to accommodate fellow-actors. Sunday night performances for the benefit of the Actors' Fund or the Stage Relief Fund are the nearest contemporary approximation to the professional matinee.

Professor Bernhardi. Arthur Schnitzler (Austrian). Drama. 3 acts. 1912.

Into Bernhardi's private clinic comes a priest to administer the last sacrament to a dying girl who believes herself completely cured. In order not to destroy her last happy illusion, Bernhardi refuses the priest admission to the ward. Since Bernhardi is a Jew, this fact is seized upon as a motive for persecution and Bernhardi is condemned for religious obstruction in a Christian state.

Program. The playbill or printed folder (or pamphlet) without advertising given to the audience attending a performance. The cast of characters, author, producing credits, and occasionally biographies of the players are given. The passage of time elapsing between scenes and acts, together with location of the scenes, is mentioned.

Cost to audience: given free in American theatres but sold abroad, even in England and France, whereas in this country advertisements are carried.

Souvenir programme: specially illustrated and annotated programmes, sold in the theatre for charitable benefits, or profit to the starring actor or a concessionaire. Among companies for whose productions there are almost always such programmes are those of Katharine Cornell, Maurice Evans, and the Monte Carlo Ballet. One of the most unusual ever published was entitled "Reception to Miss Lydia Thompson" (the woman who fostered the leg show in America) by her brother and sister artists, Saturday, March 24, 1877. Henry Irving appeared and W. S. Gilbert wrote a farewell address, and among the players who appeared in the various scenes from plays or presented readings and songs were Cyril Maude, Charles Wyndham, Lily Langtry, Sir Beerbohm Tree, Edna May, Fred Terry, Marie Tempest, George Grossmith, Charles Hawtrey, Albert Chevalier, Sydney Grundy, Kyrle Bellew, Martin Harvey, Lawrence D'Orsay, Carlotta Nillson, Fay Compton, Constance Collier, Gerald Du Maurier, Ellis Jeffreys and Lena Ashwell.

Projection booth. Booth located at back of auditorium as operating position for spot light, stereopticon, etc.

Projector. Lighting instrument; high intensity, narrow angle beam, soft edge.

Proletarianism in drama. Proletarian drama (or literature) deals with the working class, exclusive of "white collar" workers, representing individuals or groups as conscious of the opposition of their interests to the interests of another class; it deals with the worker in process of becoming aware of his proletarianism, and of turning to the militant or revolutionary way out of his predicaments.

Galsworthy in his *Strife, The Silver Box* and other social plays writes sympathetically of the proletarian. For dramas of labor, strikes, and related subjects, see *Drama, subjects, labor.*

Prologos. Prologue, part of the ancient Greek drama, especially Old Comedy as expounded by Aeschylus, in which the general outline of plot of the ensuing play was recited.

Prologue. (1) A single scene, usually separated by a considerable space of time from the action proper, intended to clarify future action. (2) A speech concerning the play, or its circumstances of presentation, recited by an actor.

Prologue to Glory. E. P. Conkle (American). Biographical Drama. 8 scenes. 1938.

The story of the young Abraham Lincoln, the poor, uneducated rail-splitter, and of his love for Ann Rutledge. The play follows the young Abe from his father's farm to the village of Salem, through Ann's death; ending when Lincoln, a lonely man, starts for Springfield, with a volume of Blackstone's law in his satchel.

Prometheus Bound. Aeschylus. Tragedy. c. 465 B.C.

The second play of the Prometheus trilogy and the only one that has survived. In it, Prometheus, having roused the anger of the gods by bringing fire to mankind is chained to a rock. He remains defiant until the end when he is engulfed by an earthquake.

Prometheus Unbound. Percy Bysshe Shelley (British). Drama. 4 acts. 1820.

Chained to a rock and subjected to torture, Prometheus defies the threats of Jupiter, the spirit of evil and hate. Thoughts of Asia, his bride, the spirit of nature, and his mother, Earth, give him support. Finally Jupiter is driven from his throne by Demogorgon, the Primal Power of the world, and Prometheus is released by Hercules. The reign of love follows and man becomes king over himself.

Prompt book. The book of a play used by the prompter to aid actors with their cues and lines.

Prompt corner. The place backstage where the prompter stands or sits during the performance, usually downstage right (to the right of the actors as they face audience).

Prompter. One who stands in the wings or out of the audience's sight and assists actors with their lines and cues; when an actor on stage forgets his lines, the prompter usually finds it sufficient to utter only the first few words of the lines that are forgotten.

Propaganda in the drama. Provides information, accurate or not, and points of view, with the intention of influencing thought or action of the audience. Thus, Ibsen, Shaw, and almost every serious dramatist who has had a "thesis," might be considered to have written propagandistically. Plays of recent years in which the propaganda for reform (of housing, labor conditions, and the like) include most productions of the Theatre Union and some of the Federal Theatre.

Properties (props). All objects on stage exclusive of scenery are the properties. (1) Trim props—set or hung on scenery; drapes, pictures, etc. (2) Set props—stand on stage floor; furniture, rugs, telephone, etc.

Property of Others, The (Le Bien d'Autrui). Emile Fabre (French). Drama. 3 acts. 1897.

This play was suggested by Diderot's *Conversations of a Father with his Son* (Entretiens d'un Père avec son Fils). In it the upright hero discovers that property which he has received under the terms of a legacy is not really his. The deceased man who willed it to him left a later will turning it over to someone else. But since it seems impossible to make restitution to the proper person, the lucky heir decides to make restitution to the state. His wife, daughter and son-in-law all turn against him and accuse him of madness, of being a crazy idealist.

Property room. The room or space backstage devoted to the properties of a show, in which they are kept or stored when not in use.

Prop plot. List of properties used in the play.

Props. See *Properties.*

Proscenium. In ancient theatres, the part where actors performed, now the stage; in modern theatres the front part of the stage where the drop scene or curtain separates the stage from the audience and at times includes the arch or frame which encloses the curtain.

Proskenion. A file or wall of columns in the ancient Greek theatre, usually containing three doorways as entrances and exits for the performers, and serving as background for the play.

Protagonist. The hero of a play, or that character which carries its principal idea.

Provinces. Anywhere outside of New York.

Provincetown Playhouse, New York. Located at 139 Macdougal Street in Greenwich Village; opened by the Provincetown Players in 1918. Since the Players moved out in 1929, the house has been the scene of many efforts to recapture the glories of the past, with varying but usually small success.

Provincetown Players, Provincetown, Massachusetts; and New York. An experimental group of playwrights, actors and other artists, organized informally in Provincetown, Massachusetts, in 1915. The opening performance was of Neith Boyce's *Constancy* and *Suppressed Desires* by Susan Glaspell and George Cram Cook. The two latter, with Hutchins Hapgood (at whose house they first played), John Reed, Wilbur Daniel Steele, E. J. Ballantine, the William Zorachs, David Carb, Robert Edmond Jones, Mary Heaton Vorse, and Joseph O'Brien, constituted the original groups. In 1916 they had a wharf theatre in Provincetown, and that autumn moved to New York, where, on Macdougal Street in Greenwich Village, they established the Playwrights' Theatre. After two seasons there they moved a few doors along Macdougal Street, converting a former stable into the Provincetown Playhouse; there they remained from 1918 to 1929. Meanwhile they skipped one year, underwent reorganizations, and for a time operated jointly with the Greenwich Village Theatre. In 1929 they moved uptown, establishing "The Provincetown Playhouse in the Garrick Theatre." But the historic stock market collapse of that autumn caused such withdrawal of financial backing that the project had to be abandoned, and in December, 1929, the group was officially disbanded. The purpose of the Provincetown Players was "to give American playwrights a chance to work out their ideas in freedom." Among the playwrights who found opportunity in this experimental theatre were (besides those previously mentioned) Theodore Dreiser, Virgil Geddes, Edna St. Vincent Millay and Paul Green. Early in its career the group brought Eugene O'Neill's plays to public notice, and he in turn made the Provincetown Players and Playhouse famous. The records of this theatre are to be found in the New York Public Library.

Provok'd Husband, The. Sir John Vanbrugh. Comedy. 1728.

Lord Townly, desperate because of his wife's extravagance and dissipation, announces that he is going to leave her. Immediately, his wife becomes contrite and comes to her senses and a reconciliation is effected with the aid of Manly, Lord Townly's friend. There is also a secondary plot involving a country gentleman and his wife who wants to become a fine lady.

Provok'd Wife, The. Sir John Vanbrugh. Comedy. 1697.

Sir John Brute mistreats his wife, who although she is courted by Constant, remains true to her husband. Heartfree, Constant's friend, falls in love with Lady Brute's niece, Belinda. One night when the two ladies have a rendezvous with Heartfree and Constant, they are discovered by the jealous Lady Fanciful. The latter tries to make trouble by getting Sir John angry, but all ends happily.

Pseudo-classicism. A term used to describe a form of 18th century drama which combined the classic system of unities with certain compromises for contemporary audiences. This form was, thematically historical, and in style, cold and austere.

Psychoanalysis in the drama. With the advent of Sigmund Freud, the Viennese trail-blazer of modern psychology, drastically new interpretations of human conduct and character penetrated every branch of literature, art and science. In the domain of the novel the Freudian theory was a major factor in such works as Proust's *Rmembrance of Things Past,* Joyce's *Ulysses* and *Finnegan's Wake,* and Lawrence's *Sons and Lovers* and *Women in Love.* The effect of the theory on biography has been extraordinary, and today few, if any, biographical works appear without some reference, at least, to the subject's "subconscious" life. Numerous critical tomes have been written re-evaluating letters of the past in the light of the new discoveries. In art Freudianism has been the central force of Surrealism, represented by such men as Dali and Ernst. A school of Surrealism has also appeared in modern writing, but although staunchly fostered by the well-known continental American-English magazine *Transition,* which is still occasionally issued, it has had no such notoriety as it found in painting. In the light of his vast influence, therefore, Freud is definitely one of the handful of major figures of modern times. His fame has served to popularize such terms as libido, Oedipus complex, mother-fixation, sublimation, and repression until today they are a part of the common man's vocabulary. "Freud's work," says Thomas Mann, "is one of the great foundation-stones of a structure of the future which shall be the dwelling-place of a free and conscious humanity." Although there have been secessions from the school he heads, such as those of Adler (the popularizer of the terms "inferiority complex," "superiority complex") and Jung, Freud still remains the dominant force of modern psychology. His influence on modern drama has been incalculable, certainly equally as great as upon any other province of human endeavor. Eugene O'Neill is the foremost dramatist whose works bear the impress of his ideas; indeed he owes a major part of his approach to human character and themes to Freud. The most remarkable of his plays bearing a more than usual Freudian slant are: *Strange Interlude,* the delineation of a woman's life and the respective traits of her three loves; *Mourning Becomes Electra,* which, as the title suggests, is a re-telling in modern terms of the Electra legend; *The Great God Brown,* in which was adopted the use of masks in order to express the duality in human nature and the disparity of selves. Freudianism has also appeared in the outspoken treatment of the homosexual theme in plays like Bourdet's *The Captive* and Mordaunt Shairp's *The Green Bay Tree.* Philip Barry's *Hotel Universe* deserves some mention for its Freudian fantasy. Aside from these there have been a vast number of miscellaneous plays, successes and otherwise, treating of psychological themes from a Freudian viewpoint. Today Freud is considered to rank with Marx as an apostle of a new social era, in spite of the fact that there is at present a movement on foot to re-examine, critically, the validity of his theories. Perhaps typical of such re-examination is a remark made by Havelock Ellis in his *From Rousseau to Proust* in the passage devoted to a summation of the theories of Taine: "Man is an organized mechanism, a system, not a mere pile of unconnected fragments. All parts are governed by a few forces, sometimes only one force. (It is a revolutionary idea, perhaps questionable, but it is the idea on which Freud seized.)"

Publications, theatrical. Periodicals and trade papers on the theatre have had an enormous influence in keeping the theatre alive throughout the country. They have brought stage news to the outlying districts which had no theatre; and when the road shows thrived, they prepared the way educationally for oncoming productions by furnishing information concerning original productions together with critical reports.

In the Nineties *Munsey's Magazine* carried a monthly department of the theatre. From time to time, also various weeklies, like the naughty *Vanity Fair,* brought the theatre to the barber shop, while the *Dramatic Mirror,* and the *New York Clipper* catered to the professional reader.

Substantial was the service of the old *Green Book,* and Channing Pollock's reviews in the old *Smart Set.* But when George Jean Nathan became the critic for *Smart Set* he set up a new order of thinking. Insofar as the country at large was concerned, his accomplishments were inestimable. He was the first nationally read critic to point out the necessity for a mature American drama. He was the first critic to call attention to the continental drama, the Ibsen School, the Viennese playwrights, Shaw and the various newcomers. He emphasized the value of poise, detachment and relativity. He made his influence felt in school, university, theatre, library club and dressing room.

Other early cultural and educational influences were the early Drama League publications, especially the *Drama Quarterly, Poet Lore,* little known but early to publish (and make accessible through translation) Maeterlinck, Strindberg, Andreyev, and other continental dramatists. For many years the *Theatre Magazine,* with Arthur Hornblow, Sr., editor, popularized the theatre with pictures, light interviews and criticisms. At the time of the boom all the class magazines had theatre departments, including the new *Vanity Fair, Vogue,* the *Literary Digest* and the *Metropolitan Magazine,* the latter one of the first to publish dialogue. *Theatre Arts,* edited by Edith Isaacs, brought the new spirit of the theatre to students and players eager to keep pace with the finest aspects of the art. Here John Mason Brown first demonstrated his brilliance as a critic. Here the first people of the theatre presented articles and led the way to fresh ideals and the understanding of changing techniques. With Mrs. Isaacs as editor, the *Theatre Arts* remains the foremost publication of the theatre. Rosamond Gilder is associate editor.

Today almost every class magazine has its stage and sceen departments, and doubtless will soon make place for television. The new *Life* and *Newsweek* are noteworthy for their photographic studies, and *Newsweek* has, besides George Jean Nathan, who is its drama critic, Burton Rascoe as its book critic.

Theatre and movie schedules, originated by the timely new magazine, *Cue,* are now a feature of the *New Yorker, Info* and others. Meanwhile the trade publications have done a fine work. The most colorful of all the stage magazines has been *Variety,* which has a notable history.

Publicity. See *Press agentry, Press agents.*

Pulcinella. See *Punch.*

Pulpitum. Friezes in the ancient Roman theatre.

Punch (or Pulcinella). Stock character in a *commedia dell' arte;* according to many, the descendant of the Maccus of the *fabula Atellana;* owes its name possibly to the pullus gallinaceus or "cock," which was presumably a name for Maccus; Callot in the 17th century depicts him as boasting two enormous cock's feathers, calls him *Cucurucu.* Characteristics: pugnacious, vicious, cunning; looks: humpbacked, hooked-nosed, deeply wrinkled mask, vicious eyes; nearest kin: *Brighella.*

Puppet show. A dramatic performance on a miniature stage with puppets, or small images, in human or animal form. The jointed limbs are manipulated from above by means of strings or wires held by operators, kneeling or standing on a platform. They accompany the movements of the puppets with spoken dialogue, song or jest, and achieve presentations of a grotesque, burlesque, or artistic nature. For generations, in France, Italy and England, puppetry, the art of manipulating puppets or marionettes, has brought joy to young and old. There have been two especial kinds of puppet shows in the New York World's Fair, one electrically operated and another synchronized with recordings of the voices of the actual people represented. See *Marionettes.*

Purgation. As used by Aristotle in his *Poetics:* that refining brought to bear on the emotions by the terror and pity induced by tragedy.
See also *Catharsis; katharsis.*

Puritan; or, The Widow of Watling Street, The. A farcical comedy published in 1607 and assigned to "W.S." on the title page. It was included in the Third and Fourth Shakespeare folio editions in 1664 and 1665 respectively. Crudities of style and construction have led critics to reject the play as authentic Shakespeare. It is now credited to another, perhaps Marston. This farce is a coarse caricature of the "respectable" middle class and a comedy of London manners.

Pushkin, Alexander Sergeyevitch (1799-1837). Russian poet, dramatist. Born at Pskov, a member of an old noble family, he published his first poems at the age of fifteen. Entering the civil service in 1817 he lived as a young man of fashion in St. Petersburg. He was banished in 1820 to Bessarabia on account of his *Ode to Liberty,* circulated in manuscript among his acquaintances. Again banished in 1824 on account of an intercepted letter in which he spoke slightingly of religion, he finally returned to his father's estate in Pskov and there wrote his great tragedy *Boris Godunov,* 1825, which had a great influence on the later development of Russian letters.

Pygmalion. George Bernard Shaw (English). Comedy. 3 acts. 1914.
Shaw's most poignant play. Eliza, a guttersnipe from London's Covent Garden, is transformed, on a bet by Professor Higgins, who teaches her correct speech. The bet is won when Eliza is passed off as a duchess without discovery but she has then to struggle for a place in the society to which Higgins has elevated her. It is a satire on the ruling class of England, and depicts the superficiality of class distinctions. Eliza is an illiterate Cockney girl but very receptive to education and quick at learning the new tricks of her elevated station. She is also receptive to her instructor, Prof. Higgins. Their constant proximity and his cold, detached manner have made her fall in love with him. He tries very hard to resist his affection for her. His mother reproaches him for giving her a taste of the finer things of life and his lack of consideration for her future. When Eliza tells him she will accept the proposal of a young simple but rich man about town, Higgins shows his disgust but he is also a little disturbed. He realizes this is only a frantic gesture on her part to avoid going back to her old life. The play ends with the feeling that Higgins will never really let her go. Shaw has built a fascinating play around this old Cinderella theme, bringing it realistically up-to-date.

Quality Street. Sir James M. Barrie (English). Comedy. 3 acts. 1901.
Phoebe Throssel, finding that her long-absent lover, Valentine Brown, thinks her greatly changed on his return, dresses herself as an imaginary niece, Livvy, and sets out to win him all over again. She succeeds.

Quarto, Shakespearean. The term, referring to the size of the book, generally employed to describe the early printed versions of individual plays by Shakespeare. Some sixteen plays, often in more than one edition, appeared in this form before the poet's death.

"Bad Quartos" refers to certain Elizabethan editions of separate plays by Shakespeare, which are characterized by badly corrupted texts. The plays so printed are Parts Two and Three of *King Henry VI, Romeo and Juliet, King Henry V, Hamlet* and *Merry Wives of Windsor*. Omissions, inversions, paraphrases, bungled meter and word substitution make the texts in many cases unintelligible. These editions are believed to be pirated versions made from memory or shorthand notes of a performance and published without the authority of the playwright or his company.

Queen Mary. Alfred Lord Tennyson (English). Drama. 5 acts. 1875.

Presents the main events of the reign of Mary Tudor; Wyatt's rebellion, the marriage with Philip, the submission of England to Cardinal Pole as the Pope's legate, the death of Cranmer, the loss of Calais and the death of Mary.

Queer a manager's pitch. An English term for disappointing a manager.

Queue. The line of ticket purchasers at a box-office, specifically those waiting for entry to the pit or gallery.

Quick study. Hurried and technical memorization of a part and its business by an actor, usual in an emergency when a part must be learned at a moment's notice.

Quinn, Arthur Hobson (1875-   ). American author, university professor. Born in Philadelphia, Pennsylvania. He studied at the University of Pennsylvania, receiving the degrees of Litt.D. and Ph.D. there; studied modern philology at the University of Munich. He teaches at the University of Pennsylvania and has lectured at the University of Chicago, Columbia University, New York University, and University of California. He belongs to several learned societies and has been a member of the Board of the American National Theatre since 1923. Notable books on the theatre which he has written are: *The Early Drama* (in Cambridge History of American Literature), 1917; *History of the American Drama from the Beginning to the Civil War,* 1923; *History of the American Drama from the Civil War to the Present Day,* 2 vols., 1927 (rev. to one vol., 1936). He edited: *Representative American Plays,* 1917 (rev. 1938); *Contemporary American Plays,* 1923; *Harper's Plays and Playwrights Series* (general editor). He was contributor and advisor on American Playwrights to the *Dictionary of American Biography.*

Quintero, Serafin and **Joaquin Alvarez.** See *Alvarez-Quintero.*

Race, A. Fritz von Unruh (German). Drama. 3 acts. 1918.

Nightmare scenes pass in a graveyard where, while a battle rages at a distance, a Mother, aided by her daughter and a young son, has just interred their brother slain in the conflict. No sooner have they placed a rude cross above the dead than two other sons of the Mother are bound by soldiers to either side of the graveyard gate in punishment for misdemeanors.

Race for Pleasure, The. Enrico Annibale Butti (Italian). Drama. 3 acts. 1900.

One of a trilogy of plays: *The Atheists*. The other two dramas in the series are *Lucifer* and *The Tempest*. *The Race for Pleasure* is the first of the group. It makes a plea for the religious and unselfish life, and shows how futile is a life the end of which is pleasure alone. The hero is a hedonistic skeptic who sees the error of his ways and reforms when he loses his adored mother. Butti was a disciple of Ibsen, but more conservative in his philosophy.

Rachel (Elizabeth Felix) (1821-1858). French actress. She was born at Mumpf, Switzerland, the daughter of poor Jewish peddlers. She sang in the streets as a child, displaying so much talent that Étienne Choron, the musician, undertook her training until he died in 1833, when she was admitted into the Paris Conservatoire. She made her debut at the Théâtre Français June 12, 1838, and soon became the idol of Paris. In 1843 she won her greatest triumph as Phèdre, in Racine's tragedy, and in 1849 she created the part of the heroine in Scribe and Legouve's *Adrienne Lecouvreur*. She created a sensation in London in 1841 and 1842, and won immense applause all over Europe as a tragic actress of great genius. The French critics acclaimed her the greatest actress who had ever appeared at the Comédie Française. She toured America in 1855, making her first appearance here in Corneille's *Horace*. While in Philadelphia, she caught a severe cold which aggravated her tubercular condition, and she died at Cannet, January 3, 1858.

Racine, Jean (1639-1699). French dramatist. He was born at La Ferté-Milon, where he was baptized, December 22, 1639. Left an orphan when young, he was brought up by his grandmother, Marie Desmoulins, a woman of strong Jansenist leanings. Through her influence he was admitted to the school of Port Royal, where he acquired that love of Hellenism and the serenity of classical feeling which was to give purity to his art. When he finished at the Collège d'Harcourt, he went to Paris, made the acquaintance of La Fontaine, Chapelain, Boileau and Molière. He wrote sonnets and madrigals in the fashion of the epoch. His *Nymphe de la Seine,* an ode written on the occasion of Louis XIV's marriage, drew praise from Chapelain and a hundred louis from the king's privy purse. That he might avoid a life of pleasure and dilettantism he was sent, in 1661, to his uncle, Antoine Sconin, vicar-general of Uzes, in Languedoc, to study theology, with the possibility of a living in the near future; but Racine did not care for it and returned to Paris in 1663. Drawn to the theatre, he wrote *La Thébaide,* 1664, which was played by Molière's troupe, and the following year his *Alexandre* was given by the same company. These plays, poor works of his apprentice years, led to his rupture with

Port Royal, a break made the more complete by his acrimonious controversy with his old master Nicole. The glory of Racine dates from the production of *Andromaque* in 1667. In the next ten years he wrote *Britannicus, Bérenice, Bajazet, Mithridate, Iphigénie, Phèdre,* as well as a satirical comedy, *Les Plaideurs.*

Suddenly, at the height of his fame, he resolved to abandon the theatre, and it was not until many years later that he was induced by Madame de Maintenon to write *Esther,* for performance by the girls whose education she superintended at the St. Cyr. This encouraged Racine to write his last play, *Athalie,* published in 1691, considered by many the finest in perfection of style. Thereafter, Racine published only four *Cantiques Spirituels* and a history of Port Royal. His last years witnessed a decline in the favor shown him by the king, who disliked his Jansenism. He died April 21, 1699, and was buried at Port Royal.

He ranks with Corneille and Molière among the greatest French dramatists. A play by Racine may be summed up as the evolution of a crisis in the smallest possible boundaries of action, space, and time.

Racket, The. Bartlett Cormack (American). Melodrama. 3 acts. 1927.

A cross-section of city politics. Captain McQuigg fights it out with Nick Scarsi, a powerful criminal, wins.

Radio City Music Hall. This marvel of mechanical equipment and seating space wonderfully handled was designed by the regular Radio City architects, Feinhard and Hofmeister, Hood and Fouilhoux, and Corbett, Harrison and Mac-Murray, all in collaboration with Roxy (S. L. Rothafel). The semi-circular auditorium accommodates 6,200 patrons for whose convenience there are thirty-one public rooms. The stage is tri-sectional, revolves, goes up and down, and is lighted with every kind of effect available in 1932. The art objects in the great lobbies, the murals, the breath-taking arch of the proscenium, and of course the precision dancing of the Rockettes are only a part of what impresses the visitor. Opened December 27, 1932, as a music hall with a great assemblage of talent. Became a film house in January, 1933.

Radio firsts. First radio program November 2, 1920, when presidential returns were broadcast by Station KDKA, Pittsburgh. First sports broadcast, April 11, 1921, Station KDKA. First theatrical broadcast, May 9, 1921, Station KDKA from the stage of the Davis Theatre, Pittsburgh.

First commercially sponsored program, September 7, 1922, Station WEAF, New York.

RADIO HISTORY

BY LEIF EID

Although we usually associate the beginning of radio with the name of Guglielmo Marconi, the scientific discoveries which underlie radio had been accumulating for centuries before Marconi transmitted the first feeble wireless signals across the estate of his father at Bologna. Dr. William Gilbert, physician to Queen Elizabeth, had made painstaking investigations into the nature of magnetism. Galvani discovered the principle of the electric battery and Alessandro Volta made a crude battery, thus enabling Oersted to discover the relationship between electricity and magnetism. Michael Faraday contributed numerous discoveries to the foundation of radio, including the indispensable alternating current.

James Clerk Maxwell announced the theory of ether waves. Heinrich Hertz produced and identified these electro-magnetic waves. Numerous other scientists also added to the knowledge necessary before wireless telegraphy could come into being.

Marconi took out an English patent on his system in 1896 and for several years thereafter the development of wireless telegraphy was closely linked to his name. In 1897 he had so improved his original apparatus as to be able to transmit, and receive, wireless messages between Bath and Salisbury, a distance of thirty-four miles. The company which was formed to exploit his inventions dominated the field of wireless communications down to the World War.

Marconi's feat in 1901 of transmitting a wireless signal across the Atlantic Ocean gave final proof of the utility of the new wireless system of communication. In the years before the World War, wireless was being used increasingly for communication between ships at sea and shore stations.

Radio-telephony, the transmission of voice, music and other sounds, however, was impossible with Marconi's system. R. A. Fessenden, an American, gained his first success in voice transmission, over a distance of one mile, in 1900. Six years later he transmitted voices and music over a distance of twenty-five miles. Quickly the range was increased to 500 miles.

The development of modern radio, however, awaited the introduction of the three-electrode valve by Dr. Lee de Forest in 1906. Edison had discovered the curious phenomenon of transmitting a current through a vacuum from a heated filament to a positively charged plate. Dr. de Forest inserted a grid between the filament and the plate. Using the signal arising from a telephone transmitter to charge the grid either positively or negatively, de Forest facilitated or hindered the flow of current from filament to plate. It was thus found possible, by the use of very small amounts of current, to control the passage of very much larger amounts of current and to magnify tiny impulses to almost any degree of intensity.

De Forest's tube, of course, has been greatly improved and numerous types of multi-electrode tubes have since been developed for special purposes. The World War and the demands it made for communication across the seas were largely responsible for the extremely rapid development.

Radio broadcasting really began in Pittsburgh in 1920. Dr. Frank Conrad, a Westinghouse engineer, had a small amateur station over which he frequently broadcast phonograph records. Interest grew and finally a local department store began offering receivers for sale. Dr. Conrad's employers decided to build a station and conduct broadcasting for the prestige it would give the company. The first publicly announced broadcast was on November 2, 1920. It consisted of press bulletins on the Harding-Cox presidential election. In a short time hundreds of other stations were on the air. The first network program, originating in the studios of Station WEAF, now the key station of the National Broadcasting Company's Red Network, was broadcast January 4, 1923. NBC itself was formed in 1926, the first American radio broadcasting network.

The Columbia Broadcasting System was formed in 1927; the Mutual Broadcasting System was not founded until 1934.

RADIO WRITING

BY ARCH OBOLER

Writing for radio always reminds me of one of those nightmares in which you dream that you are chained to a sausage grinder with your life dependent on feeding frankfurters to the ever-grinding jaws. You know that you are dreaming and yet at the same time you have a certainty that if you fail to keep pace with the whirling gears you die, so you yank frankfurters out of the ether and throw them into the machine until finally your exertion awakens you and in a cold sweat you thank the heavens that it was all just a fantasy. And then you start to write for radio and your dream sausage grinder takes on the body of a radio studio, and the whirling gears become the ticking of the deadline clock, and the open mouth of the dream grinder becomes the insatiable maw of a microphone and there is no release but death, a nervous breakdown, or Hollywood.

It all adds up to the fact that radio as an art medium has little permanency but a great and never-ceasing appetite for words; as a temporary fugitive from the microphone I might state, herewith, a few of the thoughts which occurred to me about this terror of the typewriters.

First, the plush-lined bathrooms in radio writings are not accumulated by good writing, or clever writing, or off-the-path writing; the upper income brackets among radio scriveners are almost invariably with those writers who fill the morning and afternoon airs with the wish-fulfillment dramas beloved to the housekeeper. But since the readers of this are obviously more interested in their artistic souls than they are in tax evasion, here's the story of mature radio drama.

First, the need is there, and with television, will be increasingly there. Radio stations and networks need new ideas for thir programs and definitely consider all material submitted by writers, both known and unknown. For example, the National Broadcasting Company has a special section of its script division which does nothing but consider the work of new writers, examining each manuscript with the fond hope of a robin puncturing a watered lawn.

So eager are the networks for prestige drama that there are few taboos; in my plays over NBC I have had the characters concerned with everything from childbirth to the dirge of the dispossessed without the slightest objection from listeners or officials; on the air, very definitely, it's not what you say but how you say it that spells the difference between paean or protest.

The seriously written radio drama has, of course, borrowed from many other literary forms; the short play on the air, for example, is generally so much like the printed short story that it is usually an obvious form; the use of flash-backs, etc., are also not unique to the radio medium. Yet, unlike the printed short story, the radio play must get attention right from the start because with a touch of the dial the bored listener can go elsewhere for his entertainment.

Getting the listener's attention, however, does not necessarily mean doing it in the manner one novitiate radio writer tried. Having been told the need of an attention-getting beginning, his first play went something like this: the daughter says, "Mother, I think I'll get married." The mother says, "Why, daughter?" The daughter answers, "I think I'm going to have a baby."

It is in the use of sound and dramatic pauses and music that the radio drama has broken away from other art forms; a word, a strain of music, a sound effect, and in an instant the scene can be shifted, in the listener's mind, from past to present to future, from air to earth to water, in an attention manner which no other medium can express.

Naturally it is impossible, in anything short of a lecture course, to even begin to discuss the many, many techniques of radio writing; far more important than any discussion of "how" is "what can we write about?" The answer to that lies with the writer; if radio drama has not been at a commendable level, the fault lies with the playwright, not with the medium. The broadcast drama, particularly on a non-commercial basis, can speak as maturely as the playwright's own intellectual maturity permits. The idea that all of the radio audience has a mental age of a small boy writing on back fences is a bit of folk-lore nurtured by some of our advertising agency men to hide their own sub-level courage and imagination. The vital human problems which are the basis of good drama can all be made clear and understandable to the average listener.

The great excitements of radio to the writer, excitements which far out-shadow the gold of Goldwyn and the pearls of Paramount are that here is a medium of expression which makes the listener emotionally part of what you are saying, makes the words and ideas reality in a manner no other medium can possibly approach, and in the twinkling of an eye gives you, for what you want to say, a greater audience than could have heard Shakespeare's words in a hundred of his lifetimes.

There are important things to be said on the air these days; the more writers who take the time and trouble to say them well, the more opportunities there will be in which to speak.

Raimund, Ferdinand (1790-1836). Austrian author, actor. Viennese actor, author and genius of the light popular drama; author of *The Spendthrift, The Peasant as Millionaire.* He developed the vaudeville type of theatre into a highly characteristic feature of Viennese drama; worked at the Leopoldstadter Theater.

Rain. John Colton and Clemence Randolph (American). Drama. 3 acts. Based on W. Somerset Maugham's short story, *Miss Thompson.* 1922.

The scene is the Island of Pago Pago in the South Seas. The Reverend Davidson, trying to save the prostitute Sadie Thompson's soul and send her back to San Francisco and prison, falls in love with her, but, tortured by a sense of guilt, kills himself. Sadie and her sweetheart, a marine called "Handsome," leave for Sidney in hope of finding a happier life.

Rain from Heaven. S. N. Behrman (American). Drama. 3 acts. 1934.

A German-Jewish music critic and an American aviator wage a war of ideals during a weekend at an English country house. Their hostess, a liberal and wise English woman, serves as mediator. An American millionaire, who hopes to unite the youth of England and the United States toward Fascism, also plays an important part in the intelligent and intellectual discussions.

Rains, Claude (1889-). English actor. Born in London; first appearance on the stage at the Haymarket Theatre, 1900, in *Sweet Nell of Old Drury;* was call-boy, prompter, and assistant stage-manager at His Majesty's Theatre; then went to the Haymarket Theatre as assistant stage-manager under the Harrison French regime; in 1913 he toured in the United States as general manager for Granville-Barker. The plays he appeared in after 1918 include: *Uncle Ned,* 1919; *Reparation,* 1919; *Julius Caesar,* 1920; *The Government Inspector,* 1920; *The Jest,* 1920; *A Bill of Divorcement,* 1921; *Will Shakespeare,* 1921; *Napoleon's Barber; Volpone; Marco Millions; The Camel Through the Needle's Eye,* 1929. Now in Hollywood.

Raising the dead. Name given to a custom, which originated in Drury Lane and was later introduced to Covent Garden by Macready, of coming before the curtain and announcing the program for the following week.

Ralph Roister Doister. Nicholas Udall (English). Comedy. 5 acts. c. 1553.

Usually considered the earliest known English comedy. Perhaps played by Westminster boys while Udall was headmaster of that school.

A silly braggart makes suit to Widow Custance and upon being rejected makes a display of force, getting soundly beaten by the widow and her maids.

Modelled after the comedies of Plautus, this play opened up a new field of comedy for English men of letters.

Rank theatres. Name given by Thomas H. Dickinson in his *The Theatre in a Changing Europe* to any "caste" theatre, usually built in the Italian Baroque style, with royal boxes, tiers of horseshoes overlooking onlookers of lesser social importance below (except when they had been relegated to inferior places above).

Rant. To deliver lines in a shouting, melodramatic and extravagant manner.

Rastus. In minstrel shows end man paired with Sambo.

Raueber, Die (The Robbers). Johann Christoph Friedrich von Schiller (German). Drama. 5 acts. 1781.

A story of Karl von Moor, the heroic robber, who takes to the woods to redress the evils of his father's court and who is contrasted with the stage villain, his wicked brother, in a series of extravagant incidents. The outstanding example of the period known as *Storm and Stress* (*Sturm und Drang*).

Schiller was obliged to publish the play at his own expense but when it was presented for the first time in 1781, it made a tremendous impression on his contemporaries. The directness with which *Die Raueber* gave voice to the most pressing problems of the day made it one of the most vital dramas of the 18th century.

Rave. The highest praise by a critic; slang term for critical enthusiasm.

Raymond Joseph T. (1836-1887). American actor. In 1879 he created the role of Ichabod Crane in *The Legend of Sleepy Hollow*. He developed and continued an interest in the dramatic representation of distinctly American types as the *Yankee, Rip Van Winkle* and *Mose, the Fireboy*.

Razullo. Stock character in a *commedia dell' arte*.

Reader. Member of a theatrical producer's staff whose duty it is to read manuscripts of plays and pass judgment on them as to their suitability to his requirements.

Realism. In art and literature, realism is fidelity to nature or real life; it is representation without idealization; adherence to actual fact. In drama, Ibsen is an outstanding example of this form of art.

The place of realism has always been challenged, but modern critics are usually downright in their endorsement.

"What is, is," says Brooks Atkinson, critic of the *New York Times*, "and if we ever get anywhere with the enlightened civilization we must know the full truth about it. Whether it is flattering or distressing, inspiring or depressing, is beside the point; and the need is not for temperate speaking but for complete frankness about everyone and everything, for none of the ills of humanity can be cured until it is understood."

Realistic speech. This has had a long and difficult fight to gain its place in the drama and general literature. Certain subjects were taboo in certain countries and during certain historical periods, on the theory that they were sacrilegious, indecent or corrupted public morals. With Ibsen, however, and the development of the realistic school, frank statement became possible with subjects like the single standard of morality and social disease winning a reputable place through serious works, like *Ghosts, Damaged Goods,* and *Hindle Wakes*.

Rebound. Donald Ogden Stewart (American). Comedy. 3 acts. 1929.

A man and girl fall in love on the rebound—each after what has seemed to be their one and only big affair. Though written with a fine sophisticated touch the play handles the difficulties and problems of young married people with sympathy and understanding. The clever handling of dialogue sugar coats its rather serious implications.

Reckoning, The. Gustav Wied. (Danish). Drama. 2 acts. 1902.

Translated into English as *Autumn Fires*. Two inmates of an old men's home, first cousins to the pair in Lady Gregory's *Workhouse Ward*, united by long affection and their common love of quarreling. Each boasts of his strength and derides the other's infirmities. Each insists upon keeping inviolate his part of the room that both occupy. One talks continually of his little grandson, and the other, a bachelor, grows angry, until he can no longer refrain from revealing a secret long hidden. He has been the lover of his friend's wife. Since that wife's daughter was really his, the grandson is his as well. At first the disillusioned rival is horrified; then he says: "When men are young they see red and kill for that sort of thing. But when they are old, it's different. I can't even be very angry with you, my friend."

Recruiting Officer, The. George Farquhar (English). Restoration comedy. 5 acts. 1706.

Deals with the humours of recruiting in a country town. It presents Captain Plume making love to the women in order to secure their followers as recruits. Sylvia, who is in love with Plume, is the daughter of a sheriff. She runs away from home and disguised as a man, gets herself arrested for scandalous conduct. She is brought before her father and by him delivered to Captain Plume as a recruit.

Redemption (abridged edition of *The Living Corpse* in 6 acts). Leo N. Tolstoy (Russian). Drama. 2 acts. 1912.

Fedya is unhappy at home. He leaves Lisa, his wife, and is believed to be dead. Discovered in the midst of the depths to which he sinks, Fedya kills himself rather than have Lisa arrested and tried on a charge of having committed bigamy.

Redoutensaal. A theatre in Vienna taken over by Reinhardt in 1922 and used by him for several years.

Red Robe, The. Eugéne Brieux (French). Drama. 3 acts.

Considered perhaps the finest of Brieux's plays. This deals with a group of judicial officials and their wives in a town in southern France. All are eager for promotion or are looking for political preferment. They have lately had few convictions in their courts, so when a murder is committed some one must be singled out as the law's victim. An innocent man is accused and arrested and the remainder of the play is concerned with the utter ruin which befalls him through the legal methods with which his trumped-up case is conducted.

Red Rust. V. Kirchon and A. Ouspensky (Russian). Drama. 3 acts. 1927.

The "red rust" of the title refers to the skepticism and corruption attached to revolution. The story deals with a soldier who lives on his reputation as a champion of the people, and who, after imposing on them for a long time, is exposed and punished.

Reduta Theatre. A theatre operating in Warsaw, 1919-24, devoted exclusively to Polish plays. This theatre was influenced by the theories, particularly as to the actor "living the part," of Stanislavsky. Its director was Schiller, formerly of the Teatr Polski.

Régie. The general production plan of a play.

Régisseur. The director in charge of a play. See *Director*.

Rehan, Ada (1860-1916). American actress. Born in Limerick, Ireland, she came when a young girl to America. She made her first stage appearance at Newark, New Jersey, in 1874. She showed her versatility as a comedy actress in over two hundred parts in Augustin Daly's company from 1879-99. Her fame rested chiefly on her Shakespearean roles, notably for the first time in London in 1884, returning in 1886, 1888, 1890, 1893, and 1895. She also gained distinction in such classic revivals as *The School for Scandal*. She presented her bound playbills for Daly's Theatre 1879-97 to the New York Public Library.

Rehearsal. Repetition or practice in private, preliminary to a public performance and for the perfection of that performance. Rehearsals are informal at the beginning of the rehearsal period and may be of parts or separate features. The rehearsal period is the training period for a performance and should be thorough. The dress rehearsal is formal and the performance is given exactly as if it were a public performance.

Rehearsal, The. Attributed to George Villiers (English). Farce. Comedy. 5 acts. Printed 1672.

Probably written by him in collaboration with others. The play, designed to satirize the heroic tragedies of the day, consists of a series of parodies strung together in an absurd heroic plot. There are satiric thrusts at Dryden. Bayes takes two friends, Smith and Johnson, to see the rehearsal of his play and the farcical comments make excellent reading.

Rehearsal Club, New York. A residence club for girls with theatrical ambitions, founded in 1913. Since the charge for room and meals does not pay expenses, the continued success of the club has been due to a philanthropic board of directors interested in helping young artists. Has supposedly formed a background for plays such as *Stage Door*.

Reicher, Emmanuel (1849-1924). German actor, director. After considerable success as an actor and director in Germany he came to America and produced plays in New York. He was the organizer of the American People's Theatre and the Modern Stage, and was director of the Jewish Art Theatre. His most outstanding production was the English version of *The Weavers*.

Reinhardt, Max (Max Goldmann) (1873-   ). Austrian theatrical producer. Born at Baden, near Vienna, Reinhardt became a successful character actor. In

Berlin he managed the Kleine Theatre's cabaret *Schall und Rauch,* in 1902, and at the same time the Neues Theatre. Two years later he took over the Deutsches Theatre, and afterwards the Kammerspiele, for the production of intimate plays. From 1915 to 1918 he managed the Volksbuehne, in 1918 the Kleines Schauspielhaus. He handed over these last three theatres to his collaborator Felix Hollaender in 1920, and resumed management in 1924 of the Deutsches Theatre, the Kammerspiele and the newly opened Komoedie. Reinhardt also undertook the management of the Josefstadt Theatre in Vienna, and during the summer months controlled the Salzburg Festspielhaus. With the advent of Hitler to power, Reinhardt left Germany and worked in England and America, signing a contract in 1934 to direct films in Hollywood. In 1937, he produced *Eternal Road,* in New York City.

One of the greatest modern theatrical producers, he was the first to offer collaboration to famous painters and musicians, and was the pioneer of most of the modern theories of stage production. He elevated Berlin to the capital city of the European theatre; at the Kammerspiele, his intimate experimental theatre, actors from every part of the world came to give performances.

His most memorable achievements were *Sumurun, The Miracle* and *Oedipus Rex.* He regularly produced the old mystery play *Everyman* each year at Salzburg, and in 1933 staged the outdoor production of *A Midsummer Night's Dream* for the Oxford University Dramatic Society. He founded, at the castle of Schoenbrunn, Vienna, the first school for producers.

Réjane, Mme. (Gabrielle Charlotte Réju) (1857-1920). French actress. During her first year as an actress (1875) she scored a tremendous success at both the vaudeville and the Odeon. By 1883 her great versatility and disciplined technique had earned her recognition as the outstanding French comedienne. In 1894 she appeared as Catherine in *Mme. Sans-Gêne* at the Gaiety Theatre in London and played the same role for a memorable run in New York the following year.

In 1896 she opened at the Theatre Réjane in Paris, in a series of comedies; and in 1909 she made a South American tour.

She played at intervals, mainly in London, until 1915 and died at the age of 63.

Relapse, The; or, Virtue in Danger. Sir John Vanbrugh (English). Comedy. 5 acts. 1696.

Vanbrugh's first play, and very well received. It is an avowed continuation of *Love's Last Shift* by Colley Cibber, the characters being retained, though more effectively presented. The play was adapted by Sheridan and produced as *A Trip to Scarborough,* a satire on affectation and foppishness.

It contains two plots, very slenderly related to each other. Loveless, a reformed libertine living in the country with his wife, Amanda, is obliged to go with her to London where he meets Berinthia, an unscrupulous young widow. Worthy, a former lover of Berinthia, prevails on her to favour Loveless' suit and to persuade Amanda of Loveless' faithlessness, in order to promote his own chances of seducing Amanda. But Amanda, though resenting her husband's infidelity, remains faithful.

Relief. A relaxing of the tension after an especially dramatic scene, usually by the insertion of comedy.

René. Emile Zola (French). Drama. 5 acts. 1887.

A melodrama which is among Zola's minor works. The heroine has been betrayed by a man who has abandoned her. She contracts a platonic marriage with a husband much older than herself, who is willing to save her reputation by giving her his name in exchange for the payment of a sum of money. Then the young wife falls in love with her husband's son. The latter is in love with a Swedish girl, but his father believes him to be a rival and threatens to kill him. The heroine saves the son from death at his father's hands, and then shoots herself.

Repertory. Collection of plays, operas, or parts which may be readily performed because of familiarity with them on the part of a cast or an actor. Repertory is sometimes used synonymously with stock. A repertory company is one which instead of performing one play continuously has several productions ready, varying the performances each night or each week. The same actors have parts in the several productions.

Rep show. Company playing repertory.

Répétition générale. French for general dress rehearsal with complete and full equipment of costumes, scenery and make-up, given at the termination of the rehearsal period immediately previous to the opening performance of a new production.

Representational. Term used to describe one of the two general species of play; that in which characters, events, and things are ends in themselves and symbolize nothing beyond their aspect.

RESEARCH

BY GEORGE FREEDLEY

Almost all plays that are written and staged require research at some point before the first night audience asssembles. Those of us with theatre interests and knowledge scattered in the libraries and museums throughout the country have a heavy responsibility to the authors, directors, designers, press-agents, and critics. We must make sure that the facilities of our institutions are known to those in the theatre who must make use of them. The sitting back and waiting attitude has never made libraries cultural centers of a community, so we must take advantage of every opportunity to draw attention to our resources so that they may be used for the betterment of the American theatre.

Nearly any type of question can come up in theatrical research. Some times busy authors employ qualified persons to come to the library and document the history, customs and living habits of people in a given country and period. This is essential in a period play if the dramatist wishes to display to his audience a true picture of the people and times of which he is writing. Language changes. Expressions become outmoded. Oil lamps replace candles, and, are in turn superseded by illuminating gas, which in turn is supplanted by electricity. This may seem obvious enough but the author needs to know these dates exactly so that no anachronisms may appear in speech. Just as lighting changes, methods of transportation alter. "Order the carriage," is replaced by "Call my car." And every amateur group knows that it must change such lines if the play of a past period is being set in the present. There are however innumerable other points the careful playwright must guard against or make his play ludicrous.

Once the author has completed his research (a large library such as the New York Public Library, which has an extensive theatre collection, has many dramatists as readers), the script goes to the producer. There may be many points in the text on which he as a director knows he needs more exact information. If he is staging the "bundling scene" in *The Pursuit of Happiness,* he must know more about the history of bundling than the dramatist's lines can indicate. To the Library at Fifth Avenue and 42nd Street, he must go and consult esoteric volumes on the subject.

Should the play deal with aviation as in *Ceiling Zero,* the stage director would be tremendously handicapped if he were not, at least superficially, conversant with the problems of flying and had some idea of the technique and a thorough understanding of the terminology of this field. The play may have a modern setting but some piece of business may require special knowledge which the director may lack. I recall that in producing *Karl and Anna* for the Theatre Guild, Philip Moeller needed some piece of recorded music popular in Berlin just after the war, which would be likely to be played in a workingman's home and yet could be used to build the suspense of an important entrance. It was essential to create the proper mood and Moeller was determined that the music also should be accurately chosen. Had he selected a piece written after that time many in the audience would have recognized the fact and the effect the director was building would have been destroyed. Who will ever forget the importance of the cheap phonograph in *Rain?*

All of these are problems which bring the person to the source of information, which may be a library, museum, factory, business office or foreign consulate. For *The Camel Through the Needle's Eye,* Lee Simonson needed to know what milk bottles looked like in Prague. After examining many books of pictures on Czecho-Slovakia at the Library, none of them, alas, showing the delivery of milk, the Czech consulate informed me that they were just like New York milk bottles. Wasted time, you say? Not if we had guessed wrong and the whole point of the third act had been lost.

As a man, to whom persons pursuing research approach, I receive many kinds of questions. I was once asked by a budding designer for a college show how to build a stage rock. At that time there was no technical manual to offer, so I did him a rough working sketch. Later he showed me a photograph of the set. The rock looked gratifyingly real. On another occasion I was asked how a campfire was built on the Oregon trail; how the covered wagons were drawn up against an Indian attack. Our American History division was able to provide answers to both of these questions.

The designer of a historical show must of necessity consult books and fashion periodicals of the period, or if he is fortunate, a costume in a museum dating from the past era which his designs must recreate.

At first glance you may have wondered why the dramatic critic was included in those who must do research in advance of the first night. It would have appeared more natural for the critic in preparing volumes of historical criticism to have come in later. Well, so he does, of course. But the conscientious play-reviewer also must have some special knowledge of a period when an important play is opening. Occasionally he wishes to read a dramatist's earlier plays which he has not seen. Few of us can afford the private drama collections we should like to possess and so must turn to the theatrical repositories in our public and university libraries.

No matter where in the country a production is being made there is likely to be some library or museum not too distant to be consulted. Rosamond Gilder and I found in preparing our handbook, *Theatre Collections in Libraries and Museums,* that the widespread interest in theatre in the United States has made most libraries drama-conscious. As one result of this the Theatre Library Association was formed in 1937. This is an organization of all those interested in the preservation of the records of the theatre, whether local or national, whether in library, museum or private collection.

Too much care cannot be taken in research. A play which reaches a wide audience has among its auditors many whose pleasure would be destroyed by anachronisms or historical mistakes if those responsible for its production had not safeguarded that in advance.

The Resident Theatre, Kansas City, Missouri. The Jewish Community Center Association sponsored the theatre in 1932 and it started in the auditorium of their Center Building. This was finally renovated and converted into a comfortable, beautiful theatre. Strong competition from New York road companies forces it to be commercial in an artistic, enthusiastic, non-profit manner.

Resting. An actor out of a job.

Return from Jerusalem, The. Maurice Donnay (French). Tragedy. 5 acts. 1903.

A gentile, tired of his wife, and a pretty Jewess, equally bored with her husband seek refuge from their boredom in an affair. The intrigue leads to mutual love but the difference in religion intervenes. The opposition of race, religion and tradition places a yawning gulf between them and they are forced to separate.

Return of Peter Grimm, The. David Belasco (American). 3 acts. 1911.

Peter Grimm returns from death to visit his beloved grandson and to unite two lovers separated by family opposition. During the course of his visit and using his grandson, William, as his spokesman, he saves the family property and his beloved "Botanic Gardens" from his scheming nephew. The deep and great affection which had existed between grandfather and grandson is continued. Peter takes William with him as he returns to the dead at the finish.

Reunion in Vienna. Robert E. Sherwood (American). Play. 3 acts. 1931.

Deals with the situation which arises with the return, after ten years, of a banished Hapsburg to Vienna for a family re-union. He meets his ex-mistress, Elena, now happily married to an internationally famous psychiatrist. Happy and secure as her life is, Elena nevertheless succumbs to the blandishments and enthusiastic attacks of the rather wild young prince. The affair of ten years before is resumed as though it had never ended—but only for one night. Morning brings reality and she returns to her husband, he to his taxicab in Nice.

Revamp. To give a play or scene a new form by using old materials; or to revise it by bringing it up to date.

Revenge play. A form of drama in the 16th and 17th centuries. Allardyce Nicoll, in his *British Drama,* says: "The popularity of the revenge play is probably due to two forces, usually antagonistic to one another—the romantic love of incident and the neo-classic desire to follow Greek and Latin models." Among the best-known plays of this type are: Shakespeare's *Hamlet;* Kyd's *Spanish Tragedy;* Marlowe's *The Jew of Malta;* Chapman's *The Revenge of Bussy d'Ambois;* and certain of the works of John Webster.

Revenger's Tragedy, The. Cyril Tourneur (English). Tragedy. 5 acts. 1607.

Deals with the revenge of Vendice for the murder of his mistress by the licentious duke and for the attempt by the duke's son, Lussonoso, to seduce Vendice's sister, the chaste Castiza. He accomplishes his revenge by dressing the skull of his dead mistress in a lady's garments, then after smearing it with a deadly poison, he places it in a darkened room and after enticing the amorous duke within, represents it as "a country lady—a little bashful."

Swinburne favorably compared Tourneur's work with Shakespeare.

Revolving stage. A turn-table stage invented in Japan during the 17th century. Introduced into the Western theatre in the latter half of the 19th century.

Revue. A musical production, more like a variety show except for its fixed cast, made up of a series of sketches, songs and dances; a revue is akin to a musical comedy but lacks any given plot.

Rhenish Rebels. Arnold Bronnen (German). Drama. 3 acts. 1925.

The vain struggle of the Rhineland to break from the Reich at the end of the War. Concerned with a hero torn between love of his fanatical Rhineland mistress and a fair advocate of imperialism who finally lowers the Rhenish banner and raises that of the Reich.

Rhodes, John (1640-1720?). British theatrical manager. One of the first managers to become active after the Restoration in England. He was a picturesque figure, emerging for a few months' activity in London and thereafter returning to obscurity. In 1660 the Commonwealth had ended, the theatres were just on the point of reopening, and London was in tense excitement. The first to get a company together was John Rhodes, a printer and bookseller, erstwhile wardrobe keeper at the Blackfriars, the winter playhouse of the Globe company. The Blackfriars theatre had been demolished, the Rhodes' performances were given at the Cockpit in Drury Lane. Among his actors were Thomas Betterton, James Nokes, Edward Kynaston, William Betterton, Cave Underhill, Angel, Floyd and Moseley.

Rhodes' Boys (after 1660). British actors. Female impersonators, long members of Rhodes' company, who were pitted against the real women of D'Avenant's company in a war that resulted ultimately in the establishing of actresses permanently on the English speaking stage and in the elimination of their male rivals.

THE RIALTO

As long as almost anyone can remember, the Garden of Eden for theatregoers was represented by the words "Broadway" and "The Great White Way." Here, electric signs enticed patronage with the names of plays and stars .Here, thousands and thousands of New Yorkers, tourists and sightseers crowded the streets and sidewalks, voracious for a glimpse of hit shows and footlight favorites, seeking that recreation which only the theatre can give.

Lush was the enthusiasm, tense the movement, and rich the spoils. Everyone took the street at its face value. The tinsel and pasteboard were accepted as real jewels and pure gold. Papier mache was marble. People believed because they wanted to believe, especially during the Nineties when life seemed to fit a pattern.

And perhaps if the war hadn't come and the Depression, the same point of view would have prevailed, day after day and night after night: stars would have skyrocketed to prominence; authors would have written the same romantic plays, and galleries would have been filled with young folk never to be designated as the Lost Generation.

But the War did come, and the Market Crash, and the Depression. And the change was marked by cynicism, exposé and realism.

G. K. Chesterton, the English author and playwright, visiting here, took a first glance at the Rialto electric signs, then said: "What a wonderful sight for a person who cannot read!"

Consistently, thereafter, disillusion set in. And Prohibition, having closed the saloons, there was no going out now, between the acts, to forget a bad performance under the mellowing influence of a Manhattan cocktail.

By this time, too, the columnists came along, specialists in reality. They began to call a spade a spade and gained many readers thereby. For them, young as they were, the illusion was already gone. The Great White Way was now, "The Main Stem," "Orange Juice Gulch," and "The Queerialto."

Where once "the carriage trade" gave pomp to a premiere, taxis now squawked; lurched up to the patrician Empire Theatre. Next day, the Globe Theatre became a picture house; and the New Amsterdam, once iridescent with the glow of the glorified

American girl, become, alas, a cinema grind house. Burlesque shoved the Gaiety into ignominy. Vaudeville and the Palace went into oblivion. Circus banners, sandwich men and barkers desecrated the highway, and the old-timers began to say, "Broadway is just another Coney Island!"

Then something really sad happened. The actor began to totter on his pedestal. Newspapers shouted the lowdown about his gilded life. They exposed the tricks of backstage, the sacred mysteries of the world of make-believe. Players stopped dining at the Algonquin and Sardi's. The big stars and the important writers retreated to Hollywood. The Friars closed down; and for a time there were rumors that the Lambs were having difficulties. Actual want threatened the small theatre folk. Even the Actors Dinner Club folded; and the players, hungry, slipped off to the mean streets, some to be lost there forever.

Broadway was no longer the same. Theatre after theatre became dark, and those that remained open offered cruel competition with their free radio entertainments and Federal Theatre Project presentations at low rates.

Then came the year 1939, and with it the Second World War and the simultaneous necessity for escape from its tears and grief. Lavishly, as always, the theatre offered a haven for troubled souls. The dark theatres re-opened, premieres increased; and now, at this moment, Broadway is itself again. Gay crowds fuss and fume at box offices. Announcements of forthcoming productions manifest a new Broadway continuity. Success is in the air.

How does one learn these matters? Who has written the message on the wall? The answer is apocryphal yet certain. The news emanates from Broadway iteslf: out of the high places and out of the low places; from bar, dressing room, lunch stand and the alley; from the manager's office and the capitalist's desk.

For paradox is Broadway's nutriment. The illiterate manager brings forth a lofty play. The hack newspaper writer turns into a discriminating critic. The usherette steps into the chorus of the very theatre in which she passed out programs. Everyone senses vague things specifically. Hushed whispers and I-told-you-so's make history. The hanger-on confers with the confidential secretary. Everything is an open secret:

Anyone can tell you who is responsible for a bad musical; who found the new tenor; who ghost-writes a certain author's comedies; who provides the money to keep a flop running; how much the leading lady gets a week.

Ignoble chatter, perhaps, but it spurs on the Rialto; keeps the action going; heightens the spirit. No one is too obscure to do his part and no one too rich or powerful. Jock Whitney and the Algonquin doorman figure in the same discussion. And though names are numerous, Broadway knows their value: Toni Grasso, the bootblack whom Marc Connelly and George S. Kaufman lifted bodily into a play. Goldie Stanton, Ziegfeld's famous secretary and Alice Poole, the telephone girl who had all New York at her finger tips; Clara Bell Walsh, an inspired Mrs. Thrale, helping actors get jobs, with advice, and a humane checkbook; Bernie McDonald, technical director for a world of plays; Steve Hannagan, man-about-town; Gilmore Parker, the Knox councillor on male headgear; Alix Gard, creator of the nationally known cartoon gallery of theatrical celebrities; Kelcey Allen, raconteur and prophet;

Leo Newman, of days gone by who rode on horseback into the lobby of the New Amsterdam just to bring the new revue some luck.

How have all these furthered Broadway production? The answer is necessarily vague; the concatenation of circumstances elusive. But this is the way things happen:

Martin Beck steps into Sardi's and exchanges a word or a glance with Renee Carroll, the hat check girl. This communication, by means of facial expression, is transferred, half an hour later, to a ticket office where blustering Broadway Sam Roth gets an impression. He, on his way through Shubert Alley, happens to see J. J. Shubert talking with Pulaski, and his impression is confirmed. Naturally, he passes it on to Louis Sobol. And that night, at Leon and Eddie's or the Stork Club, Louis discusses his hypotheses with Dr. Leo Michel, Irving Hoffman and Norman Light.

By this time, Yetta Cohen, the Little Mother of the Ties, who's been selling haberdashery backstage for decades, carries the threads of gossip to the various dressing rooms; and when the curtain goes up that night, Lillian Duffy, veteran usherette, conveys the glad news to the Katzenbergs, record-breaking first-nighters, and by the end of the first act, Tommy Manville, playboy, repeats the details to "Bill" McBride. Rumor turns into definite statistics. Dates become specific. Names are spelled out, and a week later a complete, authentic story appears in Zolotow's column.

Thus the new play is born, the unknown author recognized, the missing angel produced, the understudy made a star and a Broadway hit established. The Rialto has worked its magic.

Ricciolina. Stock-character in a *commedia dell' arte*.

Rice, Alice Caldwell Hegan (1870-   ). American novelist. Born at Shelbyville, Kentucky, January 11, 1870, she became famous as the author of *Mrs. Wiggs of the Cabbage Patch,* 1901, which was produced as a play both in England and the United States.

Rice, Elmer (Elmer Reisenstein) (1892-   ). American dramatist, producer. Born in New York City, September 28, 1892, and was graduated *cum laude* from the New York Law School in 1912. He married Hazel Levy of New York in 1915. He was dramatic director of the *University Settlement* and chairman of the Inter-Settlement Dramatic Society, and on the executive committee of the Authors' League of America. He was admitted to the New York Bar in 1913, but did not practice to any degree.

He is not primarily an innovator in drama though *The Adding Machine* and *American Landscape* point in that direction. His plots are sometimes melodramatic; his interest in the theatre is in its power to influence thought. His viewpoint is that of the reformer; he is concerned with the social injustices inherent in the modern world. In *We The People, Judgment Day* and *American Landscape* he sets forth his views on labor conditions, fascism and democracy, and the affairs of the world in general. He is a member of the Playwrights' Company.

His plays include *The Adding Machine,* 1923; *A Voyage To Purilia,* 1930;

On Trial, 1914; *Iron Cross,* 1917; *Wake Up Jonathan,* 1921; *It Is the Law,* 1922; *Close Harmony,* 1924; *Cock Robin,* 1928; *Street Scene,* 1929 (winner of the Pulitzer Prize); *The Subway,* 1929; *See Naples and Die,* 1929; *Counsellor-at-law,* 1931; *The Left Bank, We, the People,* 1933; *Judgment Day,* 1934; *Between Two World's,* 1934; *American Landscape,* 1938.

Rice, John (fl. 1607-1629). English actor. An actor named in the 1623 Folio list of performers in Shakespeare's plays. He was apparently a protegé of John Heminge, and appeared with Richard Burbage in a pageant before King James in 1610.

Rich (18th century). English actor. Imitator of the Italian players of the *commedia dell' arte;* alleged to be the cause of the *commedia dell' arte* in England turning to pure pantomime: finding he could not speak so well as act, turned to dumb show.

Rich, Christopher (?-1714). English theatrical manager. At one time in control of Drury Lane, the Dorset Theatre, and The Haymarket, he was notorious for his meanness to his actors. His son John (1652-1761) after his father's death in 1714 opened his father's projected theatre in Lincoln's Inn, where he was the first to introduce pantomime to the English stage. He founded the Beefsteak Society.

Richelieu; or, The Conspiracy. Sir Edward Bulwer-Lytton (English). Historical play in blank verse. 5 acts. 1839.
Treats of the life of Cardinal Richelieu who outwits King Louis XIII and his henchman Baradis, and defends a maiden's honor satisfactorily.

Richman, Arthur (1886-   ). American dramatist. From 1925-27 president of Society of American Dramatists and Composers, and from 1928-30 president of the Authors' League of America. His plays include: *Not So Long Ago,* 1920; *Ambush,* 1921; *A Serpent's Tooth,* 1922; *The Far Cry,* 1924; *All Dressed Up,* 1925; *A Proud Woman,* 1926; *Heavy Traffic,* 1928; and a translation from the Hungarian *Antonia,* 1925.

Richmond Theatre Guild, Inc., Virginia. Founded 1934, with the active support of the mayor, it has a large membership and interest is growing rapidly. This group grew out of the former Little Theatre League, once headed by Louise Burleigh (Mrs. John Powell); and the Richmond Community Theatre founded by Charlotte Wheeler DeCourcy, Mrs. Frank Woodworth, George Freedley and others. Classes are conducted and training given.

Riders to the Sea. J. M. Synge (Irish). Drama. 1 act. 1903.
Deals with the tragedy of a mother who loses her two sons to the sea. Considered by many critics to be his best play. Although the setting in the Aran Islands is strongly localized, the author has transformed a merely local catastrophe into an event universal in meaning.

Maurya has lost all but one of her sons as well as her husband at sea. Now the last son is about to go out in his boat, but he is drowned before he has scarcely got away from the shore. With this last loss, a great peacefulness settles on Maurya, for she knows now that the sea has taken from her all that it can and she no longer need fear the wind and the tide.

Riggs, Lynn (1899-   ). American dramatist. His first Broadway production was *Big Lake,* done at the Laboratory Theatre, conducted at that time by Richard Boleslawski of the Moscow Art Theatre. It was received without enthusiasm.

In 1930 Arthur Hopkins gave his *Roadside,* a colorful production, but the audience response was not sympathetic.

In 1930 the Theatre Guild produced *Green Grow the Lilacs* and though its reception was not highly enthusiastic Riggs received many fine compliments on his inventiveness and poetic writing. *Russet Mantle,* 1936, his latest work, was also his most successful, having run 117 performances on Broadway.

Right You Are, If You Think You Are (Cosi e, se vi pare). Luigi Pirandello (Italian). Drama. 4 acts. 1916.

A metaphysical study of identity. The question is posed: "What is reality?" The answer the author gives is that truth is largely a matter of seeming, that there is "nothing right or wrong but thinking makes it so."

A husband whose wife died in an earthquake marries again, but the mother of the first wife believes the second wife to be her lost daughter. The second wife refuses to disillusion the old woman by telling her the truth.

Rinehart, Mary Roberts (1876-   ). American author. Born at Pittsburgh, Pennsylvania, she became an immensely successful writer of detective fiction, her numerous books including *The Circular Staircase,* 1908; *The Window at the White Cat,* 1910; *The Amazing Interlude,* 1917; *The Red Lamp,* 1925. Her plays include *Double Life,* 1907; *Cheer Up,* 1913; *The Bat* (in collaboration with Avery Hopwood), 1920.

Ring down. Term based on an old theatrical custom of ringing a bell to denote the closing of a show, but meaning, in general parlance, to bring a subject to an end. Used commonly in the expression "ring down the curtain."

Ring up. To pull up the curtain so that a performance may begin.

Rising of the Moon, The. Lady Augusta Gregory (Irish). Comedy. 1 act. 1907.

The charm and passion of Irish nationalism in a comic setting. One night, on the wharf of an Irish seaport town, a policeman foregoes his chance of reward and permits an Irish nationalist to escape, because he has charm. The nationalist promises to remember the policeman,

> "When we all change places,
> At the risin' of the moon."

Ristori, Adelaide (1822-1906). Italian actress. A celebrated Italian tragedienne who first visited New York in 1866; toured the country with great success; famous for such roles as Medea, Lady Macbeth, Mary Stuart, Queen Elizabeth. See also *Theatre, Italian, 19th century.*

Rivals, The. Richard Brinsley Sheridan (English). Comedy. Prologue, epilogue and 5 acts. 1775.

This was the first of Sheridan's plays, and he was only twenty-two when he wrote it. It was not a success on the first night, due to the poor performance of the part of Sir Lucius. Captain Absolute, Sir Anthony's son, is in love with Lydia Languish, the niece of Mrs. Malaprop. Being romantic Lydia prefers a half-pay lieutenant to the heir of a baronet, so Captain Absolute assumes the character of Ensign Beverley, and is well received in his courtship, though Mrs. Malaprop refuses to allow them to marry. Sir Anthony, arriving at Bath, proposes a match between his son and Lydia, and Mrs. Malaprop likes the idea. Meanwhile, Captain Absolute, afraid to tell Lydia of his deception, has a rival in Bob Acres, who, at the instigation of Sir Lucius, asks Absolute to carry a challenge to Beverley. Sir Lucius himself challenges Absolute. But when Acres discovers that Ensign Beverley is his friend Absolute he happily calls off the match and renounces all claim to Lydia, who, after a pretty quarrel with Absolute for shattering her hopes of a romantic elopement, finally forgives him. Mrs. Malaprop has become the symbol for anyone who, in using very long words, gets them just wrong enough to be amusing.

Rivas, Angel de Saavedra, Duke of (1791-1865). Spanish politician, writer. Born in Cordova, he was prominent in the revolution of 1820, fleeing from Spain in 1823. Minister of the interior in 1835, he was again forced to flee, but in 1837, having joined the moderates, was prime minister, and later ambassador in Paris and Naples. His works include verse, such as *Ensayos poeticos,* 1813; and *El Moro exposito,* 1834; and several dramas such as *Don Alvaro o La Fuerza del Sino,* 1835.

Road, the. General term for all localities outside New York City which a touring company may visit for performances.

Road apple. A theatrical term used for a touring player.

Road show. (1) A theatrical production which tours in various cities and towns throughout the country. (2) In motion pictures, a "special" which travels with an expert salesman who books it for the large theatres at advanced prices and exploits it extensively. A picture that is "road shown" is not exhibited in the local theatres until about a year after its release.

Road to Rome, The. Robert Emmett Sherwood (American). Comedy. 3 acts. 1926.

Amytis, the beautiful wife of Fabius Maximus, a Roman senator, journeys to Hannibal's camp to persuade him to spare Rome.

Her beauty and her intelligent plea for peace win Hannibal and he returns to Carthage.

This brilliantly written satire offers as good a reason as any thus far advanced for Hannibal's historic retreat after crossing the Alps, when Rome seemed within his grasp.

Roar China! S. Tretiakov (Russian). Drama. 3 acts. 1926.

When an American business man falls from his boat and is drowned during an argument with a Chinese, the press and white population clamor for reprisal. The captain of a British warship demands that the Chinese either find the murderer or slay two other men in his stead, or the city will be bombed. Terror-stricken, the coolies are forced to draw lots to save their city. Two are then strangled to death.

Roaring Girl, The. Thomas Middleton and Thomas Dekker (English). Comedy. 1611.

Modeled after a notorious thief of the time, Moll Cutpurse is an amiable rogue who helps two lovers in distress. There are many scenes of contemporary London life which give an excellent insight into the era.

Robert Frank. Sigurd Ibsen (Norwegian). Political play. 3 acts. Translated by Marcia Hargis Janson. Printed 1914.

Paints the portrait of a prime minister who opposes a general strike of syndicalists, yet plans to bring workers and employers together by a profit-sharing arrangement as the only safeguard for the modern industrial state.

The only play of importance written by the son of Henrik Ibsen.

Robert E. Lee. John Drinkwater (English). Drama. 6 scenes. 1920.

The play reveals a series of dramatic episodes in the life of Robert E. Lee from the time he takes command of the army of the Confederacy to a meeting with President Jefferson Davis, when Lee is at the height of his success; and finally, his surrender to Grant at Appomattox.

Robertson, Thomas William (1829-1871). English dramatist. Born in Newark, the eldest of a large family, Dame Madge Kendall being the youngest. Nicoll in *British Drama* says: "Any account that traces the course of modern drama must include Robertson's name, and even although he kept himself to the sphere of comedy he must head the list of those who strove to introduce serious thought and actual living types into the theatre." He was the essence of Victorianism and preached its credo. Despite this the naturalness of his stage dialogue and the fact that he brought ordinary life into the theatre renders him of importance to English drama.

His many successful comedies include: *David Garrick,* 1864; *Society,* 1865; *Ours,* 1866; *Caste,* 1867; *School,* 1869; *M. P.,* 1870. All his best known plays except *David Garrick* were for the Bancrofts' productions at the old Prince of Wales Theatre.

Robeson, Paul (1898-   ). Negro actor, singer. Born at Princeton, New Jersey, he was graduated in law from Columbia University. Abandoning a legal career, he went on the stage and appeared in several plays by Eugene O'Neill, notably in *Emperor Jones.* As a concert singer his rich bass voice and fine interpretation of Negro spirituals soon brought him fame. He visited England for the first time in 1922, playing with Mrs. Patrick Campbell in *The Voodoo* at the Opera House, Blackpool. He appeared in London in 1925 as Brutus Jones in *Emperor Jones,* and as Joe in *Show Boat* in 1928. He has also appeared in motion pictures, among them *Sanders of the River.*

Robinson, Richard (?-1648). English actor. An actor named in the 1623 Folio list of performers in the plays of Shakespeare. Jonson praised him for his success in impersonating women. Plays by dramatists other than Shakespeare in which he appeared included Webster's *Duchess of Malfi;* Massinger's *Believe As You List;* and Fletcher's *The Wildgoose Chase.*

Robinson Locke Dramatic Collection, New York Public Library. A collection of 494 bound scrapbooks and over 4,700 portfolios of unmounted material, gathered by Mr. Locke, dramatic critic and publisher for many years of the *Toledo Blade.* It covers American theatrical life, 1870-1925, and represents a lifetime of devotion to the stage.

Robson, Eleanor (Mrs. August Belmont) (1879-   ). American actress. Born in England; received honorary degrees from New York University, University of Rochester and Moravian Seminary and College; made her stage debut in San Francisco, 1897; became a success as Bonita in *Arizona;* also starred in *She Stoops to Conquer,* 1905, *The Dawn of Tomorrow, Merely Mary Ann,* and *Salomy Jane;* retired from the stage, 1910; was chairman of the Metropolitan Opera Guild, 1935; and is now a member of the executive board of the Motion Picture Research Council.

Robson, Frederick (1822?-1864). English actor. Revealed his histrionic abilities as a child by giving imitations of Edmund Kean. After an unsuccessful debut at the Standard Theatre, London, he came into sudden popularity at the Grecian Saloon Theatre in the City Road. In 1850 he became the principal comedian for the Queen's Theatre, Dublin. Once, when an audience mistook a word for "priest," he was accused of insulting religion and was made the scapegoat for a riot. Later at the Olympic, he was regarded as one of the finest comedians of his day as well as one of the greatest tragedians. He was thought of as a consummate artist.

Roca. Spanish wagon stage.

Rock and the Monuments, The. Rosso di San Secondo (Italian). Drama. 3 acts. Printed 1923.
Sets forth the ancient conflict between desire and duty, the rock symbolizing instinct and the monuments the result of applying to basic instinct the chisel of the will.

Rocket to the Moon. Clifford Odets (American). Drama. 3 acts. 1938.

A modern, normal young woman finds herself torn between an unhappily married young man, a dentist, and an older man. There is very little plot to the story, but, as in all of Odets' plays, there is a searching analysis of people at odds with their environments.

Rodenbach, Georges (1855-1898). Belgian author. Born at Tournai, July 16, 1855, he published his first verses *Le Foyer et les champs,* in 1877. Other volumes included *Les Tristesses,* 1879; *Le Regne du Silence,* 1891; and *Les Vies encloses,* 1896. His poetry reflects the quiet melancholy of the towns and country of Flanders, and his novel *Bruges-la-morte,* 1892, is a striking study of that city's life. He wrote a number of plays of which *The Veil* is the best known, and the only one to be translated into English.

Rodgers, Richard (composer) and **Hart, Lorenz** (lyricist). This famous theatrical team began their collaboration at Columbia University. Their first Broadway production was the *Garrick Gaities,* 1925, and they have since come to be known as the modern Gilbert & Sullivan. Their many collaborations include *Dearest Enemy,* 1925; *Peggy-Ann, Betsy, The Lido Lady, The Girl Friend,* 1926; *One Dam Thing After Another, A Connecticut Yankee, She's My Baby,* 1927; *Present Arms, Chee-Chee,* 1928; *Spring Is Here, Heads Up,* 1929; *Simple Simon, Ever Green,* 1930; *America's Sweetheart,* 1931; *Jumbo,* 1935; *On Your Toes,* 1936; *Babes In Arms, I'd Rather Be Right,* 1937; *I Married An Angel, The Boys From Syracuse,* 1938; *Too Many Girls,* 1939.

Rojas Zorilla, Francisco de (1607-1648). Spanish dramatist. Born in Toledo. From early young manhood he was a successful dramatist. His distinguishing characteristic was that he made the *gracioso* or clown the chief personage in several of his *comedias.* Principal works: *Del rey abajo ninguno* (*No One Lower in Rank Than the King*), also known as *El labrador mas honrado* (*The Most Honorable Pedsant*); and *Garcia del Castanar* (Garcia of the Chestnut Grove); the latter is one of the greatest of all Spanish *comedias* in its portrayal of certain features of the *pundonor* or point of honor. The main dramatic interest is found in the conflict between the pundonor and respect due the king.

Roles, doubling of. The practice of employing a bit-part actor or actress in two or more parts in the same production, or simultaneously in different productions.

Rolland, Romain (1866-   ). French author. Born at Clamecy, Nièvre, he became professor of art history at the École Normale in Paris, and later was appointed to a chair at the Sorbonne, his doctor's thesis on this occasion, *Les Origines du théâtre lyrique moderne,* 1895, being crowned by the French Academy. He wrote a number of plays, psychologically excellent but poor in construction, among which *Danton,* 1901, and *Le 14 Juillet,* 1902, are the best known. His finest work was *Jean Christophe,* 10 vols., 1904-12, for which he received the Nobel prize for literature, 1915. His articles, imbued with philosophic pacifism, published in the *Journal de Genève,* September, October, 1914, made him very unpopular in France, and he went to live in Switzerland. His other works include *Beethoven,* 1903; *Le Théâtre du peuple,* 1904; *Michelangelo,* 1907; *Tolstoi,* 1911; *L'Âme enchantée,* 1922; and *Essai sur la mystique,* 1930.

Rolling. Piece of burlap dipped in paint and rolled over scenery to give the irregular pattern of rough texture.

Romains, Jules (1885-   ). French dramatist and novelist. Born at St. Julien-Chapteuil, he was for a time a teacher of philosophy. His first successful play, *Dr. Knock,* was produced in 1924. Among his other plays are *The Marriage of le Troubadec,* 1925, *The Dictator,* 1926 and *Donogoo,* 1930. Of recent years, M. Romains has devoted most of his energies to his monumental series of novels appearing under the general title, *Men of Good Will.*

Romance of a Poor Young Man, The. Octave Feuillet (French). Drama. 6 Tableaux. Adapted by Lester Wallack and Pierrepont Edwards. 1859.

The arrival of a handsome young man, known as the Marquis de Champcey, causes speculation at a country house. He puts more than one nose out of joint as he succeeds in gaining the interest of the lovely, virtuous and wealthy Marguerite La Rocque. The Marquis turns out to be only a poor young man but with a virtue which wins through at last.

Romantic chronicle. Term devised by Ashley Thorndike to describe a "vast number of narratives that were available for translation into drama but offered no suitability for either the Senecan or the Plautan form." This form combined a medley of incidents, tragic and comic, realistic or impossible, without any critical feeling for what was fit or unfit for stage presentation.

Romantic comedy. A form of drama that was largely Elizabethan and was characterized by adventure, foreign scenes, the idealization of love and of personality, and the fantastic. For this type of comedy, settings were highly imaginative and picturesque. Shakespeare's *Two Gentlemen of Verona, A Midsummer Night's Dream, As You Like It, Twelfth Night, Much Ado About Nothing* are fine examples of the school. (See Ashley H. Thorndike's *English Comedy.*) According to Allardyce Nicoll, this type of comedy is "comedy romantically treated, with characters and scenes viewed through magic casements which transform reality. The settings are imaginative . . . yet all is related to life."

Romantic tragedy. A great love engaged in a struggle that ends disastrously— usually in the death of one or both of the lovers. In the drama, some examples of this type are: Shakespeare's *Romeo and Juliet* and *Troilus and Cressida;* Dumas' *Camille;* Maeterlinck's *Pelleas and Melisande;* and Rostand's *Cyrano de Bergerac.*

Romantic tragi-comedy. A form of drama that made its first appearance with Beaumont and Fletcher's *A King and No King,* 1611. Allardyce Nicoll, in his *British Drama,* says: "Everywhere there is a straining for a more and more impossible romance. Artificiality of sentiment takes the place of truth to character; pruriency that of high moral tone; complication of plot that of due incident and probability of subject-matter. Most of the dramas fail because of the lack of relationship between cause and effect. The *deus ex machina* is everywhere present, and the plays as a consequence lose that unity of purpose, that inevitability, which characterizes the works of Shakespeare." *A King and No King,* for example, a play that was so popular as to continue in public favor until the closing of the theatres in 1642, was marked by a straining for effect, artificial sentiment, a complicated plot, a lack of unity, and a romantic tone that was highly extravagant. The form was further distinguished by frequent fantasy, fancifully poetic language, and the presence of mortal and supernatural beings. Other examples are to be found in Massinger's *The Maid of Honour,* and many of the plays of Ford, Shirley, and Sir William D'Avenant.

Romantic Young Lady, The. Gregorio Martinez Sierra (Spanish). Drama. 1902.

The heroine, bored with life because she cannot seek adventure like her brothers, finds that adventure will seek her when, on a windy night, a straw hat sails in at her casement. The novelist who comes in quest of it writes her a letter of recommendation to be presented in person next day to none other than himself.

Romeo and Juliet. William Shakespeare (English). 5 acts. Tragedy. 1595.

Written about 1595 and published in quarto form in 1597. It is based on a poem by Arthur Brooke which in turn was based on a novel by Bandello. Romeo and Juliet, respectively of the Montague and Capulet families of Verona, fall in love despite the bitter mutual hatred of their houses. They are secretly married. When Romeo kills Juliet's kinsman, Tybalt, in a duel, he is forced to flee to Mantua. Juliet, in order to escape the wedding to Paris which her family desire to force upon her, follows the advice of Friar Laurence and takes a potion causing her to appear dead. Romeo, having missed the friar's news of this device, believes the report that Juliet is actually dead and returns to Verona to kill himself at her tomb. Juliet, on awakening and finding Romeo dead beside her, ends her own life. The double tragedy so shocks the houses of Montague and Capulet that they are led to reconciliation.

Roof, The. John Galsworthy (English). Comedy. 3 acts. 1929.

Trapped by fire, the guests in a small Parisian hotel await rescue on the roof. They include two lovers, three young blades on a spree, a novelists' wife, her two children, and Gustave, the waiter who thinks only of the welfare of his guests. Finally, as the flames reach the roof, the fire trucks and ladders arrive, and the guests are rescued.

Room Service. John Murray and Allen Boretz (American). Farce. 3 acts. 1936.

A producer tries to keep his director, playwright and actors in a hotel room until he can find a backer. Facing eviction he puts the playwright to bed, and has one of the actors pose as a doctor to testify that the patient is far too ill to be moved. The hotel management, having played angel to the company to this point, finally decides to back the play, which turns out to be a hit.

Roppo. The term given to the posture, usually grotesque, taken by an actor in the *danmari* type of *Kabuki* drama at the foot of the *hanamiti* or runway.

Roscius, Quintus (126?-62 B.C.). Roman actor. Born a slave and early adopted the stage for his master's profit. His success was stupendous. It is said that he earned the equivalent of a hundred and seventy-five dollars daily and Pliny estimates his annual profits at fifty thousand sesterces (two million dollars). He was a favorite actor at a period when the Roman passion for the stage was at its height. His success easily enabled him to purchase his freedom and he took the name of Quintus Roscius Gallus, wearing the emblem of equestrian rank. He was able to move the Roman populace and nobles to tears or laughter by his histrionic power, for while he was the outstanding tragedian of the Roman stage, he was also a born comedian. Cicero received instruction from him and spoke of him in terms of affection and admiration. The title "the young Roscius" or "the new Roscius" has been bestowed on actors to denote a mark of supreme distinction. The *British Roscius* was David Garrick; The *Bath Roscius,* John Henderson; The *Young Roscius,* William H. W. Betty; Edwin Forrest was called the *Roscius of the Bowery.*

Rose, Billy (1900-). American impresario. Called Barnum's successor—the king of large scale entertainment. At eighteen world champion shorthand artist and stenographer for the War Industries Board; author of lyrics for *Barney Google* and other song hits; night club proprietor in New York; moving picture script writer. At the beginning of the depression he returned to show business with a tour of *Crazy Quilt;* produced *Sweet and Low* and *The Great Magoo;* opened a circus-type show called *Jumbo* at the Hippodrome in 1935; turned two New York theatres into nightclub restaurants. In 1936 went to Forth Worth and built his original Casa Manana and other attractions at the Frontier Days celebration; in 1937 to Cleveland to stage a water-pageant spectacle at the Great Lakes exposition. In New York he opened his new Casa Manana Cabaret, and planned and prepared the grandest of his projects, the sumptuous Aquacade at the New York World's Fair, starring Eleanor Holm.

Rose Berndt. Gerhart Hauptmann (German). Tragedy. 4 acts. 1903.
Old Berndt, a German peasant boasts of his righteousness, and the fact that his family is considered beyond reproach. His daughter Rose, who has been the household drudge, is seduced by Christopher Flanim, the village magistrate, and later forced to be friendly with Arthur Streckmann, who knows of her relationship with Flanim. Finally when her father learns the truth, Rose becomes defiant and strangles her baby in the woods. As the play ends, she is planning to take her own life.

Rosenpluet, Hans (about 1450). German poet, dramatist. Born in Nurem-berg. With Hans Folz, he was the most important precursor of Hans Sachs as a writer of Shrovetide plays (*Fastnachtspiele*).

Rose Theatre, The. A theatre erected by Philip Henslowe in 1587 on the Bankside, across the Thames from London. The chief occupants of the Rose were Edward Alleyn and the Admiral's Men, principal rivals of Shakespeare, Burbage and the Lord Chamberlain's Men at the neighboring Globe theatre. The Rose was torn down in 1606.

Rosine. Alfred Capus (French). Drama. 5 acts. 1897.

Depicts the struggle for existence of an orphan deserted by her lover, refusing the money he offers, but growing independent as a seamstress and enthralling, in spite of herself, the husband of one of her customers. When a physician proposes to wed her, his father objects, but at length concludes to assist the young couple with the money he had saved for improving his farm.

Rosmer, Ernst (Elsa Bernstein) (1866-   ). German dramatist. Daughter of a Viennese musician, and wife of a Munich author, Max Bernstein. Her *dramen* are *Wir Drei,* 1893; *Daemmerung,* 1894; *Tedeum,* 1896; and *Konigskinder,* 1895, a fairy play for which Humperdinck wrote the music. She has also written several tragedies.

Rosmersholm. Henrik Ibsen (Norwegian). Drama. 3 acts. 1886.

A tragedy of idealism and a study of a strong-minded modern woman.

Rebecca West, a strong willed, individualistic adventurer, comes to Rosmersholm and, falling in love with Rosmer the pastor, causes his wife to destroy herself so that he may be free.

Once the deed is done, however, she finds that she cannot allow herself to marry her loved one. Instead she confesses her actions—also her dubious past. Despite this she claims to love Rosmer deeply.

The pastor will not believe her, unless she is willing to do what she claims his wife has done—efface herself. While demanding this sacrifice of her he expresses willing-ness to join her in that act. They plunge together into the mill-race where his wife had met her death.

The play is notable for its subtle psychological study of the havoc wrought by excessive individualism. Rebecca West is one of Ibsen's most skillfully drawn heroines.

Rostand, Edmond (1868-1918). French dramatist. Born at Marseilles, he achieved his first real acclaim with *Les Romanesques,* 1894. In 1895 he wrote *La Princesse Lointaine,* in which Sarah Bernhardt played the leading part. In 1897 came *Cyrano de Bergerac,* his most famous play and one of the most beloved plays of recent times. *L'Aiglon,* 1900, dealt with the unhappy existence of Napoleon's son at Schon-brunn under the care of Metternich. In 1902, he was elected to the French Academy. He wrote *Chantecler* in 1910. *The Last Night of Don Juan,* published after death, is considered one of his best plays.

Rostrum. Portable platform used for various purposes. It consists of a folding framework and a movable stop; as a stockpiece it is used as a landing place at the end of the stairs, for terraces, etc.

Rouge, dry. A compact powder rouge for coloring cheeks; like rouge compacts for street use.

Rouge, lip. Moist rouge in stick or jar form for coloring lips. Men use darker shades than women.

Rouge, moist. For coloring cheeks and used with grease or powder make-up. Applied after first application of grease paint or cold cream.

Rowe, Nicholas (1674-1718). English dramatist. Augustan playwright, whose tragedies were a combination of domestic and heroic dramas. He influenced audiences toward an appreciation of the bourgeois tragedy. He is perhaps the greatest Augustan dramatist and wrote *The Ambitious Step-Mother,* 1700; *The Fair Penitent,* 1703.

Rowley, William (1585-1642). English dramatist. He wrote many of his plays especially for the King's Company, and was frequently associated in collaboration with Thomas Middleton. Both are primarily important for their purely comic work. Among their joint works are: *A Fair Quarrel; The Spanish Gipsy; The Mayor of Quinborough.*

Among Rowley's best known plays written alone are: *A Shoemaker, a Gentleman* and *The Birth of Merlin.*

Royal Family, The. George S. Kaufman and Edna Ferber (American). Comedy. 3 acts. 1927.

The Royal Family of Broadway: Fanny Cavendish, in her Seventies, and planning to tour; Julie, her daughter, at the height of her career; Given, her granddaughter, a promising ingenue; and Tony, a movie idol. For the second act curtain, Julie delivers a tirade against the theatre, begs her daughter to marry and have babies, denounces the theatre for its cruelty, ruthlessness, and false glamour. Just then her maid enters and warns "It's eight o'clock, Miss Julie"; and Julie, muttering an "Oh, My God," rushes off to the theatre.

Royal license. In the records of a provincial town one can discover the growth in the power and prosperity of the professional companies. At first the rivals of local companies and children, they soon were able to lord it over the local authorities, and their royal patents protected them from interference.

In Norwich, England, 1624-25, traveling companies were given gratuities not to play; but in spite of opposition plays continued until 1640, when the city received an order from the Master of the Revels requiring the Mayor and officers to forbid all plays and giving them power to imprison offenders and take away their licenses.

Royalty. The compensation to authors is generally based on a percentage of receipts. This is called a royalty. Customarily, at the time of signing contracts, an advance is paid against future royalties. All royalties are based upon a percentage of the gross weekly box-office receipts and from all sources whatsoever including any and all sums over and above regular box-office prices of tickets, the percentage increasing as the receipts increase until an agreed limit is reached. Should a play be performed by more than one company, each company is considered as a separate undertaking and royalties are paid accordingly. The author receives royalties on stock, radio and television rights. Amateur, foreign language and motion picture publishing are all taken into account in the payment of royalties. In the standard Dramatists' Guild contract the royalty is 5% on the first $5000, $7\frac{1}{2}$% up to $7500, then 10%.

Royalty who have acted. The Empress Theodora of the Eastern Roman Empire was on the stage before her marriage to Justinian. In 1377 Richard I of England was formally praised for his mummer's disguises. The Valois Henri III frequently played with his courtiers in informal theatricals. The Bourbon Louis XIV and Louis XV appeared in the magnificent ballets at their courts. Charming and thoughtless Marie Antoinette lowered her prestige while queen by acting in court plays. Even so recent a monarch as Edward VIII, now the Duke of Windsor, scandalized his father's subjects, when still Prince of Wales, by appearing in women's clothes in *The Bathroom Door.*

Rube. A stock character on the stage portraying a country man in the city.

Rueda, Lope de (1510?-1565). Spanish dramatist. Native of Seville and, early in life, a gold-beater. More affected by the Italian influences of the *commedia dell' arte* than any other Spanish playwright of his time, he created among the people a liking for dramatic representations, although he had played before Philip II. Aside from the fact that he thus democratized the Spanish drama, his principal contribution to the evolution of the Spanish stage was the *paso* (incident), a one-act little play in prose which was a forerunner of the *paso* of the Golden Age, when *pasos* were introduced during the course of the principal drama although their story was entirely extraneous to the principal plot. His *simple* (simpleton) is an advance over the *bobo* of Juan del Encina. Most of his plays were written in prose and this tendency did not reappear until modern times. His plays contain much more plot than those of Juan del Encina.

El paso de las aceitunas is the best-known *paso* of Lope de Rueda. *Eufemia,* a play of Lope de Rueda, contains the honor point that became famous in many later Spanish plays.

Ruffians and Finette. François Porché (French). Drama. 3 acts. 1917.

A symbolic play. The story of a queen whose generosity is abused by certain ruffians. The Queen is France; the Ruffians are the Germans, who would substitute for culture their *Kultur,* first by peaceful penetration, then by blood and iron.

Ruiz de Alarcón, Juan (1581?-1639). Spanish dramatist. Born in Mexico of noble Spanish stock; studied for a legal career, but his fame rests on his *comedies*. Less prolific than the other great dramatists of the Spanish Golden Age (his plays barely exceed twenty), the distinguishing feature of his works is the production of character.

Best-known of his character plays include: *La verdad sospechosa* (*The Suspecting Truth*), against lying; *Las paredes oyen* (*Walls Have Ears*), against calumny.

Rule a Wife and Have a Wife. John Fletcher (English). Comedy. 1624.

Margarita desires to marry a stupid husband so that she can continue with her love affairs. Leon, the brother of Margarita's companion Altea, assumes this character and marries her. After their marriage, he reveals himself in his true colors and eventually wins Margarita's love.

Run. Length of a stage engagement or the total number of performances.

Runway. A narrow extension of the stage into the audience along one of the aisles of the orchestra, upon which characters or chorus girls can walk; has received wide usage with burlesque shows.

Runyon, Damon (1884-   ). American journalist, dramatist, short-story writer. Born in Manhattan, Kansas; fought in the Spanish-American war; was war correspondent in Mexico 1912, with the Pershing Punitive Expedition, 1916, and in the World War, 1917-18. Has been a sports and feature writer for Universal Features (Hearst) since 1918. Author of two volumes of verse, several of short stories. His literary acclaim began with *Guys and Dolls,* 1932, and led to film successes, of which *Lady for a Day, Little Miss Marker,* and *A Slight Case of Murder* (with Howard Lindsay) are the best known. The play *A Slight Case of Murder* (from which the film was made) was produced in 1935 at the 48th Street Theatre, New York.

R.U.R. Karel Capek (Czechoslovakian). Expressionistic play. 3 acts and epilogue. 1921.

The scene is the central office of Rossum's Universal Robots, a corporation which manufactures mechanical men. As time goes on, the Robots rebel, destroy civilization, and spell the doom of the human race. Finally, however, it is discovered that by some miracle the Robots themselves have become human beings.

Rusiñol y Prats, Santiago (1861-1931). Spanish (Catalan) dramatist, painter, sculptor. His chief contributions to the new-born Catalan drama were in such experimental one-act plays as *L'Alegría que passa,* 1898; the symbolic and poetical *La Nuit de l'amor,* 1905; and the satiric *Les Jocs florals de Conprosa;* as well as highly successful longer plays, which include *i Libertat,* 1901; *La Mare,* 1907; *L'Auca del senyor Esteve,* 1918; and three collaborations with Martinez-Sierra: *Vida y dulzura,* 1907; *Aucelles de pas,* 1908; and *Cors de dona,* 1910. Five years after his death a public library was opened in his name and honor at Sitges, Spain.

Russell, Lillian (real name Helen Louise Leonard) (1861-1922). American actress, singer. First appeared at Tony Pastor's Theatre in 1881. Vivid, flamboyant, beautiful, with a Gibson Girl face and figure, she sang in everything from burlesque to light opera for thirty-seven years. She was the toast of the nation, and was surrounded by a haze of flowers, jewels, money, beautiful clothes and admirers. She was probably the most photographed woman in America in her day, and was nicknamed The American Beauty after her appearance in a burlesque of that name, in which, weighted down with jewels, she sat glorified on an elephant. Her looks, personality and voice were superior to her acting ability. She had four husbands: Henry Braham, Edward Solomon, John Chatterton (Signor Perugi), and Alexander P. Moore.

Russell, Sol Smith (1848-1902). American actor. Born in Brunswick, Missouri, he made his first stage appearance in 1860 at Jacksonville, Illinois. During his career he conducted a company of his own in the Middle States and at different times played with the Berger Family and was a member of Augustin Daly's Company. His first great success was *A Poor Relation* at Columbus, Ohio, in 1888; it was twice revived. Other plays in which he was notable were: *Peaceful Valley; April Weather; A Bachelor's Romance;* and *The Hon. John Grisby.*

Russet Mantle. Lynn Riggs (American). Comedy. 3 acts. 1936.
The scene is a ranch near Sante Fe, New Mexico. The Kincaid family is at a loss to know what to do with an unhappy, headstrong niece, Kay Rowley, until young John Galt stops at the ranch, falls in love with Kay, and finally brings her around to reality. He also helps the other members of the family adjust their disappointed lives.

Rustic comedy (Italian). A style of play contemporaneous with the *commedia erudita.* Popular and dialectical, it was best represented by Angelo Beolco of Padua in his play *Il Ruzzante.*

Rutherford and Son. Githa Sowerby (English). Drama. 3 acts. 1912.
Considered Miss Sowerby's masterpiece. A realistic study of a strong man, the owner of a glass factory, and his relations with the family and the staff. Old Rutherford is proud, lonely, and obstinate; but his children are different. One son becomes a clergyman, the other is a pitiable weakling, and the daughter stoops to marrying a foreman in her father's factory. The real villain of the play is Industrialism, and Rutherford is one of its victims.

Rymer, Thomas (1641-1713). English critic. An English poet, critic, and translator. He was educated at Cambridge. He is best known for his adverse criticisms of Shakespeare. He was also a translator of Cicero and the author of the tragedy *Edgar,* which was a failure. His *Short View of Tragedy* was his main contribution to dramatic theory.

Ryskind, Morrie (1895-   ). American dramatist. Born in New York City and educated at Columbia University. He collaborated with George S. Kaufman on *Strike*

Up the Band; with Russell Crouse and Oscar Hammerstein, II, on *The Gang's All Here;* with Kaufman and George and Ira Gershwin on *Of Thee I Sing,* which won the Pulitzer Prize for 1931, and *Let 'Em Eat Cake.*

Saavedra, Angel de (Duke of Rivas) (1791-1865). Spanish dramatist. Born in Cordova. From 1823 to 1833 he lived in exile, owing to his participation in favor of a liberal constitution. After living a while in England, he went to Malta where John Hookam Frere, at one time British ambassador in Spain and an amateur of Spanish literature, introduced him to the works of Byron, Walter Scott and Shakespeare. After an additional period spent in Paris, Rivas returned home after the death of Fernando VII (1833).

His best-known dramatic work was *Don Alvaro o la fuerza del sino* (*Don Alvaro; or, the Force of Destiny*), 1835. It is the most typical of all Spanish romantic plays, and the sensation that it created confirmed the success of Romanticism in Spain. Verdi made this play the libretto of *La Forza del destino.*

Sabatini, Rafael (1875-   ). English dramatist, novelist. Born of Italian and English parentage at Jesi, Italy, he made his name as a writer of historical fiction with *The Tavern Knight,* 1904, which was followed by a long series of similar tales that enjoyed great popularity both for their faithfulness to their historical periods and personages and for the author's charm of style. His plays include *Bardelys the Magnificent,* 1911; *The Rattlesnake,* 1921 (with J. Harold Terry); *In The Snare,* 1924 (with Leon M. Lyon); *The Tyrant,* 1925; *The Carolinian,* 1925 (with J. Harold Terry); *Scaramouche,* 1927. Sabatini also wrote the biographical works *Life of Cesare Borgia,* 1912, and *Torquemada and the Spanish Inquisition,* 1913.

Sabbatini, Nicolo (1574-1654). Italian author. Commentator upon the theatre of Renaissance Italy, whose *Practica di fabricar Scene e Machine ne' Teatri,* published in Ravenna in 1638, included a study of that theatre. It covers scenery and scene-shifting: as, (1) the *periaktoi;* (2) duplicate paintings of scene-buildings; (3) variously painted canvases detachable from the frames made to carry them; and scenic devices: as, (1) the *periaktoi,* soaked in aqua-vitae, lighted and rapidly turned, could give fire-effect; (2) houses could be made to fall into ruins by constructing frames on connecting iron bars which, when pulled away, would remove necessary support; (3) seas on painted cloths moved by rollers; (4) transformation scenes by means of suddenly raised pieces of scenery to conceal objects on the stage.

Sabine Women, The. Leonid Andreyev (Russian). Burlesque. 3 acts. 1912.

The Romans, exhausted by the weight and the scratching, screaming, and tickling of their Sabine captives, beg a truce, alleging their desire for peaceful domesticity now that Rome is founded. The women are willing, in fact rather intrigued by the idea of having new husbands. Their one disappointment is that their Sabine husbands refuse to come and abduct them from the Romans.

The play makes fun of the Russian situation in 1905 and 1906—the Sabine husbands representing the Constitutional Democratic party; and the Romans, the reactionary administration, not legal but pragmatic.

Sachs, Hans (1494-1576). German dramatist. The author of the finest Shrovetide plays of the early German theatre; a reformer of the German drama; wrote over four thousand songs and two hundred plays, the themes of which were from biblical and classical sources. He is one of the principal characters in Wagner's opera *Die Meistersinger.*

Sacred Flame, The. W. Somerset Maugham (English). Tragedy. 3 acts. 1928.
Maurice, an aviator in the War, has become a hopeless cripple and suffers great physical pain. Without his knowledge, his young wife has become his brother's mistress. Rather than have Maurice discover this and so be submitted to more torture, his mother kills him.

Sacre rappresentazioni. Mystery plays before and during the *commedia dell'arte* period.

Sad Shepherd; or, A Tale of Robin Hood, The. Ben Jonson (English). Pastoral play. Unfinished. Printed 1641.
Robin Hood orders preparation for a great feast. The Sad Shepherd, Eglamour, comes upon the scene. He is distraught over the loss of his love, Erine, reported drowned. The witch, Maudlin, takes the shape of Marian, Robin Hood's love, and abuses his guests. The witch has in the meantime imprisoned Erine in a tree for the pleasure of the witch's son. Robin Hood dispatches his huntsmen to seize the witch, and confronting her in the wood himself, seizes her belt. The witch demands its return, but will not come down from the tree. She finally escapes with the help of Puck.

Sadler's Wells Theatre. This famous London playhouse was first opened April 23, 1753, with a mixed programme. Reopened January 6, 1931, under the direction of Miss Lillian Baylis with *Twelfth Night* and since then has been a favorite playhouse alternating Shakespeare from the Old Vic and opera. Lately it has become a ballet and opera theatre in conjunction with the Old Vic.
See also *Old Vic.*

Sailors of Cattaro. Friedrich Wolf (German). 2 acts. 1934.
An account of the mutiny in the Austrian navy in 1918, when the sailors were weary of the war, and of inferior food and an excess of discipline. The revolt fails, however, and the ringleaders are shot.

Saint-Evremond, Sieur de (Charles de Marguetel de Saint-Denis) (1610-1703). French critic. He was born in the Château de Saint-Denis-le-Guast, near Coutances, of an old and noble family. He was educated in Paris and Caën, specializing in philosophy but intended by his parents for the magistracy. He gave up the study of law after one year and entered the army in 1628, remaining twenty years in the service. A letter criticizing the Treaty of the Pyrenees in 1659 resulted in his exile from France. He spent the remainder of his life in England where he was in especial favor with Charles II and his successors. So pleasant, apparently, was his existence there that he refused the offer of repatriation in 1688. He was an important critic of his time and wrote a number of works on tragedy and comedy, their types and properties. Perhaps his finest contribution to dramatic theory is to be found in his *De la tragédie ancienne et moderne*. He died in London and was buried in Westminster Abbey.

Saint Joan. George Bernard Shaw (English). Drama. 3 acts. 1923.

The play opens in 1429 when Joan, the simple peasant, convinces the Captain in command, Robert de Baudrecourt, to let her lead the French forces against the English to raise the siege of Orleans. Believing that only a miracle can save them, he takes her to the Dauphin. In order to test her they place Gilles de Rois on the throne but she finds Charles behind the courtiers. She is given command, defeats the English and crowns the Dauphin at Rheims. Cauchon the bishop of Beauvais, is convinced that she is a sorceress and a heretic. The English have offered a large reward for her. She is delivered to them and her trial takes place at Rouen. She is charged with heresy, the voices she has heard are called "the voices of her own evil will." It is heresy to take upon one's self the interpretation of God's will. Afraid of burning at the stake and bewildered by all the churchly subtleties, Joan recants. When she hears she is to be imprisoned for life, she tears up the paper she has signed and she is led out to her death. Twenty-five years later, King Charles VII of France rejoices to hear Joan's sentence has been reversed so that he will not continue to rule under the stigma of having been crowned by a witch. The old familiar faces of that time appear to Charles in a dream. Joan appears too in an epilogue that takes place in 1920. A cleric announces her canonization and they all kneel before her. She makes the impassioned plea "Oh, God, when will the world be ready to receive Thy saints."

St. Louis Municipal Outdoor Theatre. Non-profit civic opera enterprise. Amphitheatre seating 10,000, built 1918. First twelve-week season, summer 1919; Laurence Schwab was first production manager. In twenty-one years 231 seven-day productions of 150 separate light and comic operas have been performed. Present production manager, Richard H. Berger, Paul Beisman, the patron saint. Jack Haley, Gertrude Nissen, Tamara, Fritzi Scheff have been among players in such works as *Robin Hood; The Bartered Bride; The Bohemian Girl; The Great Waltz; The Pirates of Penzance; Roberta; The Chocolate Soldier; Of Thee I Sing;* etc.

Sakuntala. Kalidasa (Hindu). Sanskrit drama. c. 700.

King Dushyanta, marries the maiden Sakuntala and gives her a royal ring. One day she loses the ring in a pond and when the king sees her without it he does not recognize her. Heartbroken, she returns to the forest where she givs birth to Bharata, who is destined to be the founder of a glorious race. Meanwhile, a fisherman finds the ring inside of a fish he has caught and takes it to the king. Dushyanta now remembers Sakuntala and goes to find her.

Salaries, Actors'. Actors' salaries are calculated on an arbitrary scale; stars may receive from $1,000 to $1,500 or more per week, or perhaps a split salary and a percentage of the weekly gross receipts, or a star may receive a straight percentage of the gross. Featured players may earn from $200 to $750 per week. Actors in small but important parts may earn between $100 and $150 per week. According to Actors' Equity minimum basic salaries, senior members may not receive less than $40 per week, and junior members not less than $25.

Salle des Machines. This theatre built for Louis XIV in Paris in the 17th century in one of the wings of the Tuileries was the largest theatre in Europe, with a capacity of 7,000. The stage was 32 feet wide, at the proscenium opening, and 132 feet deep. It was famed for its spectacular effects.

Salomé. Oscar Wilde (English). Drama. 1 act. 1892. (Written in French).
The licenser of plays in 1892 refused to sanction its performance. It was translater into English by Wilde's friend, Lord Alfred Douglas, 1894, and afterwards formed the Libretto of an opera by Richard Straus. The original version was produced in 1896. The ban in England was removed in 1931.
Salome, daughter of Herodias and step-daughter of Herod (Tetrarch of Judea), is renowned for her beauty and her dancing. Herod requests her to dance. She refuses. He offers her anything she wishes unto half his kingdom. She dances for him and then requests the head of Iokanaan, the prophet. Herod pleads with her to change her request. She refuses. Finally, he yields and the executioner returns with the head of the prophet. She kisses the mouth of the man that spurned her advance. As Herod leaves the terrace in disgust, he commands his soldiers to kill her.

Salvation Nell. Edward Sheldon (American). Drama. 1908.
The story of a good woman who sacrifices everything for her lover. When he is arrested for murder she faces poverty and disgrace. While her lover is in prison, Nell turns to religion for solace. Upon his release he again takes up his criminal career. Nell goes to desperate measures to restrain him and in one of the most emotional scenes of the play she succeeds in bringing about his regeneration and persuades him to join the religious organizations of which she is a member.

Salvini, Tommaso (1829-1915). Italian actor. Born in Milan, he showed an inclination for the theatre at an early age, and he was taught dramatics by the famous Gustavo Modena. He appeared in *Saul, Wallenstein,* but his reputation was as yet confined to Italy. In 1849 he left the stage to take an active part in the war of Italian independence. On his return to Florence he retired to study the roles of *Othello, Saul, Hamlet* and *Orasmane.* With his troupe he toured the continent, then the United States, South America and received a tremendous ovation everywhere he went. His ability as a great tragedian was recognized not only by the public and critics but his fellow artists were quick to pay him the tributes he deserved.

Salzburg Festival. A summer festival of drama and music in Salzburg, Austria, which reached its greatest glory in the years before the German annexation of Austria. Its theatre was built and developed by Max Reinhardt and became a sensational success. Reinhardt's greatest successes here were with the morality play *Everyman* and Goethe's *Faust*. Toscanini and Bruno Walter were among the music conductors who had a hand in opera productions. These emphasized Mozart, who was born in Salzburg. Lotte Lehmann, the opera and *lieder* singer, has been probably the greatest and most popular single star of the Festivals.

Samson. Henri Bernstein (French). Drama. 5 acts. 1907.

Expresses sympathy for a self-made financier, a Jew, whose Gentile wife, forced into the marriage, despises him and out of resentment gives herself to a lover. Later she comes to admire the husband who, instead of crossing swords with this rival, invites him to dinner and in a smashing climax informs him that by the forced fall of certain shares they both will be ruined. Thereupon the lady refuses to profit by the freedom she is offered, love for her heroic husband having replaced repugnance in her heart.

San Cassiano. The first Italian Opera House, built in Venice in 1637. The wing and border system of scenery was used, moving the wings in grooves in the stage floor. This is supposed to be the first evidence of movable scenery.

Sanniones. Term referring to the two comic characters among the ancient Romans.

Sardoodledum. "Word coined by Bernard Shaw to denote the kind of well-made (or factory designed) play of which the High Priest was Victorien Sardou (1831-1908)"—Harold Downs in *Theatre and Stage*.

Sardou, Victorien (1831-1908). French dramatist. Born in Paris, he first achieved success in 1860 with *Monsieur Garat* and *Les Pres Saint Gervais*. Subsequently he became the most uniformly successful dramatist of his day, his range including comedies of intrigue, such as *Les Pattes de Mouche,* 1860, familiar in English as *A Scrap of Paper;* comedies of manners, such as *La Famille Benoiton,* and *Nos Intimes;* political comedies, such as *Rabagas;* and historical dramas, such as *Patrie, Thermidor,* and *Madame Sans-Gêne.* Many of his later dramas, which included *Fédora* and *La Tosca,* were written for Sarah Bernhardt, and he also wrote two plays, *Robespierre,* 1902, and *Dante,* 1903, for Henry Irving. Sardou's merits were essentially theatrical. His psychology was superficial, but he was a consummate master of technique and stage effect. He was probably best known in England as the author of *Dora,* which under its English title of *Diplomacy* was for many years popular with London audiences.

Saroyan, William (1908-   ). American dramatist and author. Born in Fresno, California, he obtained most of his schooling through reading. He startled the literary world in 1934 with his story, "The Daring Young Man on the Flying Trapeze." Since then he has written 400 short stories, all published in nine volumes. He made his debut as a dramatist in 1939 with his provocative play, *My Heart's in the Highlands.* *The Time of Your Life* opened at the Booth Theatre in 1939, the joint producing venture of the Theatre Guild and Eddie Dowling, the star.

Satire. A form of comedy motivated by sharp derision for an idea or an individual. Its greatest exponents were: first and foremost, Molière, with such plays as *Le Malade Imaginaire* (attacking contemporary medicine), *Le Misanthrope* (attacking duplicity), *L'Avare* (attacking miserliness), etc.; Jonson, particularly with his *Volpone, The Alchemist,* and *Every Man in His Humour.* Perhaps the earliest appearance of satire, though not then given the name, was *The Frogs* by Aristophanes, in which the Greek dramatist pillories contemporary writers. This form of comedy (the goat theory) originated in Greek religious festivals.

Satiromastix. Thomas Dekker (English). Satire. 1602.

This barbed satire is directed at Ben Jonson, who in his *Poetaster* had satirized Dekker and Marston by representing them as Crispinius and Dimetrius while he himself figured as Horace.

Dekker retorts by bringing these same characters on the stage with Horace in the unfortunate position of a poet unable to complete his Rhyme. Horace is made ridiculous by his dress, manners and general appearance and is heaped with profanity by other characters in the play.

Satura. The second form of primitive Roman comedy, supplanting the Fescennine Verses. This was a reaction against the vulgarity of the Fescennine Verses and took form in 364 B.C. during the great national festival known as the *Ludi Romani* when the *ludiones,* or Etruscan actors, performed, with dancing and singing to a flute, several jocular verses with responses which, in quality and form, were superior to the Fescennine Verses. In these verses the dramatic element was more marked than in those that preceded, and, though they had no plot, yet they presented rustic scenes with a genuine dramatic feeling. From its inception the *satura* was marked by greater care in preparation, and genuine skill became evident as a value in itself. By the 2nd century B.C. the *satura* had become an appreciable contribution to literature. This form is considered the herald of true Roman satire.

Saturday's Children. Maxwell Anderson (American). Comedy. 3 acts. 1927.

The Sands, Florrie and Willie, are concerned about Florrie's sister Bobby, yet unmarried. Florrie plans for her to capture the nice Rims O'Neil. The scheme works and Rims cancels a South American job and plans to marry Bobby. The trick haunts the situation, however, until Bobby is convinced Rims really wants her.

A realistic attempt to reveal disillusionment without bitterness. It deals with marriage among young Americans, stressing economic factors. An individuality of characterization distinguishes the play.

Satyr plays. Ancient Greek burlesque drama with a chorus of satyrs, or sylvan deities, or demi-gods, often represented with the tail and ears of a horse, and given to riotous merriment and lasciviousness.

See also *Comedy, Greek, Satyr plays.*

Saunderson, Mary (1647-1710). English actress. She was the first great English actress, and one of the four young women whom D'Avenant engaged when he decided to take actresses into his company, presumably in the Spring of 1661. Thomas Betterton, the actor, was in the same company at the time. He played Solyman, the Magnificent and she Ianthe in *The Siege of Rhodes* when Davenant opened the Duke's Theatre in Lincoln's Inn Fields with that play. At Christmas time, Mary Saunderson and Thomas Betterton were married, and she was afterwards listed in the casts as Mrs. Betterton. She had some thirty years of distinction in her profession, and forty-seven years of happy marriage. Such an account of mutual constancy was most unusual in the playhouses of the era of King Charles II.

She was the first woman to do Juliet, Ophelia, Queen Katharine in *King Henry VIII,* and Lady Macbeth. Colley Cibber considered her an "original master," taking her lights and shades from life.

Savoyard. An actor in the Gilbert and Sullivan operettas. The term comes from the Savoy Theatre in London, the home of many of the original productions. Also a member of the audience who admires extravagantly these productions.

Sawtooth (television). Term pertaining to the shape of waves used to synchronize receiver with transmitter.

Saxe-Meiningen, George II, Duke of (1826-1914). German director. He was one of the great innovators in the theatre. Founder of the Meiningen Theatre, his contribution to the theatre was his insistence on the relations between the design of a setting and the actor's movements within it. His conceptions were realistic. He combined the dual capacities of director and designer.

Scaena ductilis. Sliding panels on the stage of the theatre of Renaissance Italy, drawn to reveal a different scene within.

Scaenicus (fem.: scaenica). Actor in early Roman theatre.

Scaliger, Julius Caesar (1484-1558). Italian critic. An influential theorist on poetry and the drama during the Italian Renaissance. His *Poetics* was an "attempt to reconcile Aristotle's *Poetics* not only with the precepts of Horace and the definitions of the Latin grammarians, but with the whole practice of Latin tragedy, comedy, and epic poetry," according to *European Theories of the Drama* by Barrett H. Clark. It presents the Aristotelian theories as the strictest and narrowest rules.

Scamozzi, Vincenzo (1552-1616). Italian architect. Architect of the theatre of Renaissance Italy; on the death of Palladio in 1580 he took over the building of the Teatro Olimpico, completing it in 1584. Through the influence of Barbaro's interpretation of Vitruvius, he innovated the perspective alleys extending from the arches of Palladio's stage-setting. This innovation became a model for future architects.

Scapino. Stock-character in a *commedia dell'arte;* possibly kin to Brighella; generally a servant. Costume: in early 17th century, loose garments; later, valet's clothing with green and white lace; possibly associated with Mezzetino; in Callot's designs a brigandish type.

See *Mezzetino; Brighella.*

Scaramouche. (a) A famous actor of the *commedia dell'arte;* (b) later the name was applied, generally, to a stock-character in the *commedia dell'arte.*

The Scarecrow. Percy Mackaye (American). 4 acts. 1908. (A tragedy of the ridiculous.)

To work their revenge on Justice Merton, Blacksmith Bess, a witch, and Dickon, a Yankee interpretation of Mephistopheles, construct the figure of a man. The figure has flails for arms, bellows for lungs, etc., into which they breathe the breath of life.

Under the assumed title of Lord Ravensbane, he is sent out to court and win the Justice's daughter.

The plot is foiled when the figure sees himself in the mirror of truth and realizing that his heart is nothing but a red beet, refuses to wreck the girl's life.

Scenario. Word meaning plot outline for a play (Italian) and written in some detail, with entrances and exits noted; not used, as a term, before the beginning of the 19th century. *Soggetto* was the earlier word, or simply *comedia. Scenarii* were divided into two parts: (1) that which concerned non-comic persons; (2) that which concerned comic persons.

The word is now largely confined to the cinema, in which it means a photoplay; a story outlined in terms of the motion picture.

Scene. (a) The setting for action of a play; (b) a division of an act of a play; (c) less precisely, a certain occurrence affecting two or more characters and usually a part of a sequence of occurrences.

Scène à faire. French for a scene which the audience has been led to expect and which, therefore, must be performed. William Archer calls it the "obligatory scene" and bases its necessity on its intrinsic importance to the theme of the play and the play as a whole.

Scène à ne pas faire. French term for a superfluous scene which obliges the audience to sit through an unessential occurrence in the plot of a play.

SCENE DESIGNING

BY NAT KARSON

The term, functional design, is rarely if ever used in reference to scenery and scenic design for the theatre. It has been a much abused term, covering a multitude of decorative sins, and it appears too infrequently in the relatively small vocabulary of the theatre.

Our records of the theatre in its varying forms through the ages show that the earliest form of scenic investiture was purely architectural as in the French theatre. From this form it became imitation architecture as in the Shakespearian theatre and from here went to imitation artificial architecture, as in the Italian and European court theatre. Since then it has had its alternate periods of groping and fumbling for new forms and devices with an occasionally brilliant spark touched off by an Appia or a Craig. However the so called ideal theatre has not as yet been born and the dreams and designs for such a theatre are of necessity relegated to the mental processes which house dreams and illusions of glamour, beauty and excitement.

The present day designer in the Broadway or commercial theatre is faced with the problem of designing for a group of theatres, that almost without exception were built primarily as real estate ventures, and in most instances present a formidable array of nightmarish sightlines, inadequate hanging and technical facilities, lack of stage space and a constant detriment to mechanical working conditions back to the curtain line. In the day of the past, theatres were built primarily for drama and spectacle, and in the present day commercial theatre we are faced with the problem of writing and designing for the inadequate closets that symbolize our Broadway theatres. And so more than ever, the present day designer must of necessity be a functional designer. He is rarely if ever called upon to produce a work of art in the purest aesthetic sense, his function is rather to provide a part of an act of interpretation, an indication in the graphic sense, of the mood, the time, and the place of the play or spectacle to be designed. Whether it be realism or stylization, representation or presentation scenery is of importance only when it is integrally a part of the script, and must as a result confine itself to the frame dictated by the playwright.

However, within that frame, the designer on occasion can find as much scope for expression as the dramatist or actor. While it is true that the majority of plays produced in the commercial theatre call for the proverbial "Living Room of the Jones'," there are and have been occasions when the designer has managed to contribute an important if not major portion of the act of interpretation. Major, in the sense that the contribution has been not only a reflection of the artist's personality, or of value as a physical background, but has also enhanced the literary or poetic value, and added perhaps another "silent character" to the dramatic form.

Unfortunately the realistic dictates of the commercial theatre permit of few designer's holidays since such dreams must inevitably be reduced to preliminary sketches, blue prints, lumber, paint and linen.

We will assume that the designer has been commissioned to design the settings for a production. He is given the manuscript, and from this point the individual methods of approach vary. The majority of designers read the script to get a definite reaction towards establishing a mood. This may lead to a few preliminary sketches, these sketches however are subject to the mechanical dictates of the play, that is the number of settings involved, definite entrances and exits, the facility with which the settings can be manipulated for changes, and the theatre engaged to house the particular play and its physical adaptation to the scheme of production.

The conferences that follow between designer and director have a tremendously important bearing on the marriage of the component aspects of the production, visual and otherwise. It is at the juncture that the delicate boundary line between director and designer is approached. That this boundary line should ever have existed, is one of the mysteries of the theatre, since a complete harmony and co-operation between the director and designer is of prime importance, and therefore there should be no hairline definition as to each other's province. However the net result of these conferences is to establish playing areas, lighting scheme, the placement of important properties and the general feeling of the settings and costumes. The working drawings are then prepared, and color sketches of color notations for the scenic painting studio are completed. The physical production is then entrusted to a scenic builder, and from there it finds its way to the painters' studio.

Once the scenery is in process of being built and painted, the designer is then faced with the problem of finding the correct properties, that is furniture, and incidental trimmings for the production. This may entail a search through the antique shops and the several theatrical property shops or may necessitate another series of drawings for the purpose of having the properties built to specification. This task accomplished, there usually follows a conference with the heads of the carpenter, property and electrical departments as to schedules for hanging settings and lighting the show. The various drawings that are a part and parcel of this conference include the hanging and setting plots and the light plot. The light plot usually includes a plan of the various lighting units, their grouping, their color and a switchboard layout, with the necessary cable lengths and plugging boxes.

The production when completed emerges from the scenic and building studios and is transported to the theatre, where it is set up and the scenic change and light rehearsals start. When the visual aspect of the production is completed the cast then begins to occupy the stage for dress rehearsals, and final coordination of lights, scenery and actors is attempted. Then of course the long awaited opening night, and the designer makes his graceful and perhaps very weary exit, bloody but unbowed waiting for another script to conquer.

Scenery. The subject of stage scenery has two aspects: the mechanical and the aesthetic. Mechanically, a modern designer's first problem is the utilization of space. He must learn what space is available to him on the stage proper, and off stage—areas which vary greatly. He must see to it that he utilizes this allotted space to the best advantage.

His next considerations are the number of scenes in the play, the facilities for shifting them, together with the theatre's supplies which enter importantly into the completed design.

One theatre, for instance, may have a revolving stage where the scenery is set or a turntable, necessitating a particular type of scenery. Another may have a counter-weight system or a rope system for flying the scenery. Then again, the theatre may have a wagon stage, requiring that the scenery be set on low caster-mounted platforms which roll into the proscenium opening. A small stage, with very little off-stage space and no head room (fly space) and no revolving portion demands still another type of scenery.

Sometimes a jacknife set solves scenery problems. For when the sets are flat and covered on both sides with canvas, one set can be folded up to permit another to be opened and revealed.

In any case, the main idea in scenery is to shift it quickly and efficiently, a pro-cedure frequently effected by means of the elevator stage and combinations of other stages mentioned above.

Once having solved space problems, the director must next see to it that his scenery fits into the theatre's shifting plan. If, for instance, the ceiling is to be flown, he must specify that the ceiling plates join the fly lines to the ceiling. He must note also if the ceiling is a book ceiling that folds in the center or a rigid ceiling that flies in one piece. He must know, in all instances, what pieces are to be joined together and specify battens to hold them. Scenery that is to fly cannot have excessive weight. It must be equipped with hanger irons to attach to the fly lines. If the set is to rest on the stage floor, it has to be supported by a stage brace or brace jack and have a brace cleat in the proper place to attach the supporting member.

In other words, size of the stage, equipment and shifting method all determine the type of hardware that must be put into the scenery.

Usually, too, when scenery is shifted, the set is broken into units; that is, a simple interior set may be shifted on three pieces (e.g. 1—Backwall; 2—Right-side wall; 3—Left-side wall). Each unit consists of a series of flats battened together and dutch-manned to cover the cracks where the flats meet. This arrangement makes the wall present an even, unbroken, view from the front.

The designer prepares blue prints of his scenery (front view or designers draw-ings) from which, in turn, the technical or rear view of the scenery is made. These technical blue prints show the method of construction required; the break-up into units, the application of hardware and appliances for shifting. From these blue prints, the scenery is built and then sent to the paint shop. Here again, the designer prepares a scaled elevation, in color; and it is the painter's job to enlarge this elevation to the proportions of the scenery.

In painting the flat scenes, he may hang them on a paint frame which moves up and down in a slot, stand them on a boomerang which is, in itself, a series of levels; or he may use the continental method; that is, the scenery is placed on the floor and is painted with long-handled brushes.

Up till now, scenery has been considered merely from the standpoint of the acting area. The walls of the room are whatever encircles the space in which the action takes place. While the scenic designer is directly responsible for this procedure, he is likewise responsible for the entire visual image; the properties on the stage including furniture and pictures and in the professional theatre the lighting also. The attack of the individual designer is as varied as is the number who practice the art. One designer may approach the problem purely from the standpoint of mood and let his ground plans evolve from this mood. Another may start with the ground plans and work up to his final design. Still another may work with models while his associate uses sketches. But whatever the approach, the responsibility is the same.

Properties and lighting are an integral part of the stage picture. The present trend in the selection of properties is to use real objects. The furniture for a set is carefully chosen with an eye to color and fitness for the scene. Both properties and lighting are an important part of the composition. The lights in particular effect the color of the set. The question of color, as a matter of fact, is becoming more and more important these days. When the number of original ground plans for a drawing room set (the playwright's favorite scene) has been exhausted, variety and interest can be obtained through the use of color. Here his possibilities are endless, permitting many simple sets to stand out with beautiful effect.

While the art of the scenic designer has remained fundamentally the same in the last quarter century, the art of lighting has greatly advanced. Every day new instruments and methods of control are introduced. Lighting equipment that was good ten years ago is today antiquated. As the newest of the arts of the theatre, it is still the least developed. Large bulky spotlights, poor color control, cumbersome switchboards and inefficient light sources are still a troublesome problem.

New methods of control, such as the reactor-type dimmer and placing the switchboard in the front of the auditorium instead of backstage, are all steps in the right direction. In lighting, the goal to the future is clearer than in any other phase of the theatre.

The aesthetic aspects of scene design are discussed in Mr. Karson's article.

See *Staging*.

Scene sketches, author's. An author's outline of a scene or situation, indicating his intentions, scope and manner of treatment, the placing of actors and props on stage, and the directions of exits and entrances.

Schauspielhaus. See *Grosses Schauspielhaus*.

Schembartlaufen. The name given to the procession of players in German Shrovetide drama.

Schildkraut, Joseph (1895-   ). American actor. He studied for the stage in Germany and at the American Academy of Dramatic Arts. While studying in New York he appeared with his father, Rudolf Schildkraut in 1910 at the Irving Place Theatre. Returning to Germany, he made his first professional appearance at the Kammerspielhaus, Berlin, October 23, 1913, under Max Reinhardt, as Jether in *The Prodigal Son*. He played in repertoire in Vienna under Alfred Bernau, 1917-20.

Returning to New York, he appeared at the Princess Theatre, January 4, 1921, as Richard Northcote in *Pagans*. In April, 1921, he began his long association with the name part of *Liliom;* after playing at the Garrick Theatre for the Theatre Guild he toured in it all over the country until 1923. *Peer Gynt*, 1923, and Benvenuto Cellini in *The Firebrand*, 1924, followed. He was manager of the Hollywood Playhouse, Hollywood in 1927, producing *From Hell Came a Lady*, *The Second Year*, *Pomander Walk*, etc. He joined the Civic Repertory Company in October, 1932, and appeared in a revival of *Liliom*, as Armand in a revival of *Camille*, etc. Subsequently he played in *Between Two Worlds*, 1934, and *Tomorrow's a Holiday*, 1935. From 1923 he appeared successfully in the cinema, notably in: *The Song of Love; Orphans of the Storm; The King of Kings; Showboat; The Blue Danube; The Romantic Age; Cleopatra; The Crusades*.

Schiller, Johann Christoph Friedrich von (1759-1805). German author, dramatist, poet. As a dramatist he is considered supreme in his generation. By their mastery of dramatic construction, vitality of character drawing, and the nobility of much of the blank verse, his plays have to a great extent stood the test of time. His optimistic faith, and his propagandizing of current ideas of political liberty were an inspiration to Germans in their struggles of the early 19th century.

Born at Marbach in Wurtemberg, the son of an army surgeon, he was forced in 1873 by Duke Karl Eugen of Wurtemberg to enter his newly established military school. Educated at first as a jurist, he exchanged law for medicine as the lesser of two evils, and in 1780 began practice as an army surgeon in Stuttgart. The publication the following year of his first play, *Die Raeuber*, which had been composed surreptitiously at school, brought him immediate fame, which was enhanced by its production in 1782 at Mannheim. Schiller, determined on a literary career, fled from Stuttgart, and in the following years completed two other prose plays, *Fiesco*, 1783, and *Kabale und Liebe*, 1784.

He moved to the liberally-minded court of Weimar in 1787, and the publication in 1788 of the first volume of a history of the revolt of the Netherlands gained him in 1789, on Goethe's recommendation, a professorship at Jena University. He married Charlotte von Lengefeld in 1790. From 1793 to 1799 Schiller was occupied with historical and philosophical works, but at the end of that time he again turned to the drama. He continued to write poetic drama until his death.

His dramas include *Die Raeuber*, 1782; *Fiesco*, 1783; *Kabale und Liebe*, 1784; *Don Carlos* (first blank verse tragedy), 1787; *Wallenstein*, 1799; *Maria Stuart*, 1800; *Die Jungfrau von Orleans*, 1801; *Die Braut von Messina*, 1803; *Wilhelm Tell*, 1804.

Schlegel, August Wilhelm von (1767-1845). German author, dramatist. Born at Hanover, he became professor of literature and art at Jena, 1798. With his brother, C. W. F. von Schlegel, he was the leading critic in the Romantic school, and after lecturing in Berlin, 1801-04, he became tutor to Madame de Stael's sons. He was secretary to the crown prince of Sweden, 1813-14, and from 1818 until his death, was professor at Bonn. Schlegel was chiefly important for introducing to the new Romantic poets the classics of other countries in masterly translations. He translated the works of Shakespeare, Dante, Calderon, and Cervantes. His lectures on foreign literature and his editions of Sanskrit classics did much to revivify German literature, and most of Mme. de Stael's famous book is based on his ideas. His translations of Shakespeare were done with Tieck, and are known as the Schlegel-Tieck Shakespeare. He is the author of *Dramatic Art and Literature,* 1808. He is also the author of some sixteen plays.

Schnitzler, Arthur (1862-1931). Austrian dramatist. He was born in Vienna in 1862, and graduated from the University in that city in 1885. He afterwards devoted himself to the practice of medicine, and the writing of novels, short stories and plays.

His plays are the epitome of the highly cultivated social life of Vienna. They treat, gracefully and charmingly, of the young well-bred lover and his mistress, in an ever-changing succession. With his quiet cynicism and reminiscent moodiness, he is "content to take as his theme only a few scenes from life, and even in those few scenes he recurs continually to a single passage." His philosophy of life might well be expressed in one of his own lines, "We all play parts, happy he who knows it."

His most important plays are *Anatol* (one-act cycle), 1893; *Light-o'-Love,* 1895; *The Green Cockatoo,* 1899; *Hands Around* (one-act cycle), 1902; *Living Hours,* 1902; *The Lonely Way,* 1904; *Intermezzo,* 1905; *The Hour of Recognition,* 1915; *The Festival of Bacchus,* 1915; *The Sisters,* 1918; *The Comedy of Seduction,* 1924; *The Christening,* 1926; etc.

School. Name given to any group of writers or artists who follow similar principles or technical procedure.

Schoole of Abuse. A treatise by Stephen Gosson, an English dramatist, in 1579. It was "an extravagant and prudish attack on poets and players, interspersed with classical quotations and written in euphemistic style." The result was a bitter controversy, led by Thomas Lodge who wrote *Defence of Plays,* which tried to defend the stage and throw contempt on its ill-wisher. Gosson wrote in defense, *Plays Confuted in True Actions.*

School for Husbands, The. Molière (French). Comedy. 5 acts. 1661.
The story of two old men, brothers, who fall foolishly in love with young girls. The play traces their lives with their brides. One brother pets and pampers his darling and all is well with them. But the other brother, Sganarelle, relys more on the locksmith's theory of kindness to keep his young bride true. How cleverly he is deceived, being made the messenger between his wife and lover, is the amusing plot.

School for Lovers, The. William Whitehead (English). Comedy. 5 acts. 1762.
Written with a grace and refinement of dialogue it stood in marked contrast to contemporary drama. In content the author generously bequeathed the scruple once claimed only by characters portraying princes and princesses, to the characters playing

ordinary ladies and gentlemen. This sentiment found its place later in the ragged but virtuous school. Although based on Fontenelle's *Le Testament,* a closet drama set in ancient Greece, it is adapted to tell a story of English lovers with freshness and delicacy.

School for Scandal, The. Richard Brinsley Sheridan (English). Comedy. 5 acts. 1777.

The greatest of Sheridan's work. Charles and Joseph Surface are brothers. Charles, good-natured and extravagant, is in love with Maria, Sir Peter Teazle's ward; while Joseph, a hypocrite, is courting Maria for her money and at the same time making love to Lady Teazle, Sir Peter's young wife. The scandalmongers, Sir Benjamin Backbite, Lady Sneerwell and Mrs. Candour, provide the background. Sir Oliver Surface, wealthy and old, returns unexpectedly from India and decides to test the characters of his nephews. He finds Charles to his liking. Joseph, attempting to seduce Lady Teazle, is interrupted by the arrival of Sir Peter. The lady hides behind a screen. When Charles arrives, Sir Peter also hides. The conversation between the brothers shows Sir Peter that his suspicion of Charles was unfounded. The screen falls, and Lady Teazle is revealed. Sir Oliver, playing the part of a needy relative, is refused help by Joseph on the plea of the stinginess of his uncle. Joseph is completely exposed, Charles and Maria are united, and Sir Peter is reconciled to the repentant Lady Teazle.

School for Wives, The. Molière (French). Comedy. 5 acts. 1662.

Ridicules the conventions of marriage, satirizes crabbed old age and champions young love. It contains the delightful ingenue, Agnes, who demonstrates that ignorance is not innocence. She has led a sheltered life in the home of her guardian Arnolphe who intends to marry her. Returning from a journey he finds out that Horace, son of his old friend, Orante, has met and fallen in love with Agnes. He tries to separate them but fails. Arnolphe pleads with Agnes to forget Horace and marry him, including in his speech the now famous "Maxims on Marriage." It is disclosed that Horace and Agnes have been betrothed since birth and Arnolphe loses his suit but he remains dramatically the strongest character in the play.

School of Husbands, The (La Scuola Del Marito). Giannino Antona-Traversi (Italian). Drama. 3 acts. 1899.

A study of the complex aspects of the relations between a husband and wife of the idle class whose dissipation portends their ultimate destruction.

Schools of the Theatre. The following lists are of schools which place the principal emphasis on acting—New York: Tamara Daykarhanova's School for the Stage, the Feagin School of Dramatic Art, The American Academy of Dramatic Arts, the New Theatre School, the Alviene School of the Theatre, the Neighborhood Playhouse School of the Theatre, etc. Hollywood: the Max Reinhardt Workshop, Maria Ouspenskaya's Theatre School, etc. Chicago: the Goodman Memorial Theatre School. Cleveland, Ohio: the Playhouse School. Pasadena, California: the Pasadena

Community Playhouse School of the Theatre. Ridgefield, Connecticut: the Chekhov Theatre Studio. Seattle, Washington: The Cornish School. London: the Royal Academy of Dramatic Arts, the Embassy Theatre School of Acting, etc.

For those primarily interested in the technical aspects of the theatre, including the writing of plays, as well as the academic approach to the drama, 600 universities and colleges have special departments. The most noted are located at Yale University, the University of North Carolina, the University of Iowa, Dartmouth College, Leland Stanford University, the University of California, the University of Texas, and Princeton University.

Schreyvogel, Joseph (1768-1832). Austrian manager. Appointed artistic director of the Vienna Burgtheatre in 1817 and made it the first theatre of Europe. Produced Shakespeare, Grillparzer, Schiller and Goethe; brought new and great actors of Germany to the theatre, including Sophie Schroder, the great tragic actress of her time, and Anschuetz, who in turn became one of the pillars of the Vienna Burgtheatre.

Schroeder, Friederich Ludwig (1744-1816). German actor, producer. He was one of the greatest actors in German theatrical history; inspired by and acted with Ekhof but his own art was freer and given more to improvisation; became head of the Hamburg theatre in 1771 beginning a new era in theatrical art; was the first German to act Goethe's *Goetz von Berlichingen;* first to present Shakespeare on the German stage, thus awakening the theatre to a sense of art. *Hamlet* was first performed on the German stage with Schroeder, September 20, 1776; he also produced ballets, light musical comedies; was the first to understand and employ ensemble unity in a play.

Schroeder, Sophia. German actress. She was the greatest actress of the 18th century on the German stage; made her debut with Ekhof in the Schoneman Company in Racine's *Mithridates* in Luneberg Inn, 1740, Mother of Friederich Ludwig Schroder.

Schwartz, Maurice (1890-   ). Yiddish American actor manager. Born in Russia, he came here as a child. Went into a stock company at the age of 15 and toured leading American cities. In 1919 he founded the Yiddish Art Theatre at Irving Place, New York. He has acted in more than 150 plays. Among the more famous are *The Dybbuk, God of Vengeance, Anathema, The Government Inspector,* etc. Toured Europe in 1924. In 1932 he reorganized the art theatre and adapted and presented *Yoshe Kalbe* which was a great success. In 1936 he did *Brothers Ashkenazi* and *Three Cities.* He periodically revives plays by Shalom Aleichem (the Yiddish Mark Twain).

Scoops (television). A type of lighting unit sometimes used in television studios.

The Scornful Lady. Beaumont and Fletcher (British). Comedy. 1615.
Elder Loveless, enamoured of a lady who disdains him, sets out on a voyage, leaving his estate to the younger Loveless. Later when news of the Elder's death

arrives, the younger brother rejoices. After much intrigue, the Elder turns up alive and succeeds in marrying the lady and the rest of the characters marry their respective beloveds.

Scribe, Augustin Eugène (1791-1861). French dramatist and librettist. Born in Paris. Although educated for the law he soon turned to the stage. Began his career at the Théâtre du Gymnase and after writing a dozen plays had his first success in *Une Nuit de la garde nationale*. Produced about four hundred highly popular operas and plays. His works are useful as a source for French social history from 1815 to 1860. He really took vaudeville and developed it into real comedy of intrigue, tragicomedy, or serious drama, but it was not until he aspired to the dignity of the Comédie that we have the best examples of his work. The bourgeois virtues of honest work, economy, and common sense were the bases of his plots. The returns from his productions made him enormously wealthy. He was elected to the French Academy in 1836.

His plays include: *Le Verre d'eau; Camaraderie; L'Ours et le pacha; Bertrand et Raton,* etc. Opera librettos include: *Les Huguenots; Le Prophète; L'Africaine; Fra Diavolo; Robert;* etc.

Script. Contraction of "manuscript"; the typewritten or printed copy of a play used in production. An actor's script may contain only his speeches and cues; a director's, besides the entire play, includes notes on the scenery, lighting, properties, sound effects, etc. Usage also extends to motion picture and radio parlance.

Sculptured stage. A fixed stage setting of the Italian Renaissance theatres which was used for all plays. Serlio and Palladio were the great designers of this stage. The Teatro Olimpico was the outstanding model. Also called "architectural stage."

See also *Formal stage setting*.

Sea Gull, The. Anton Chekhov (Russian). Tragedy. 4 acts. 1896.

Constantin, a young poet and the son of Irina, a somewhat passée actress, is in love with Nina, a young girl with theatrical aspirations. Nina, however, prefers the middle-aged author Trigorin, Irina's lover. Constantin, unhappy at Nina's indifference, tries to kill himself but fails. Two years pass. Trigorin has been attracted by Nina's fresh, youthful beauty, and has taken her with him to Moscow, where she has had a child by him. Now, weary of her, he deserts her for the maturer delights of his old mistress, Irina. Constantin once more tries to win the young girl, but is again rebuffed. Nina goes off with a theatrical troupe, and Constantin commits suicide.

This play, especially in its development of the character of Constantin, reveals the poetic brooding of the Russian mind. It was a brilliant success when performed at the Moscow Art Theatre in 1898. As a reward for his genius Chekhov was made the patron saint of the theatre, and the white wings of the sea gull were taken to adorn its curtain and its printed program.

Sebastiano, Antonio (also known as "Minturno") (?-1574). Italian scholar. He was born at Trajetto. His whole life was spent in the church. He became Bishop of Ugento. His dramatic theories are best expressed in the *Arte poetica.* He died in Crotone, in Calabria.

Sebillet, Thomas (1512-1589). French writer. Little is known of his life but he was born probably in Paris. After studying for the law he became an *avocat* in the Parlement de Paris, but it was not long before he turned to literary occupations. In 1549 he went to Italy and after his return to France he was put in prison for political reasons. Several of his writings and speeches bear testimony to the fact of his having been a reactionary in respect to the political trends of his time. He numbered among his friends some of the most prominent *littérateurs* of the period, among whom were Du Bellay, Pasquier and L'Estoile. His *Art Poétique,* 1548, is his most notable contribution to dramatic theory.

Second lead. The secondary role in a play; the role next to the star's part, in importance.

Second Man, The. S. N. Behrman (American). Comedy. 3 acts. 1927.
A comedy of the dual nature of man. Story of a novelist who realizes that the "second man" in him is an opportunist, and is wise enough to return to his mistress who can supply his luxuries. He prefers to be realistic, rather than heroic.

Second Mrs. Tanqueray, The. Sir Arthur Pinero (English). Drama. 4 acts. 1893.
In this play Pinero achieved real distinction. Many writers date the beginning of contemporary drama from it, since it is one of the earliest realistic problem plays of the English stage, showing the influence of Ibsen. The problem is a woman's struggle with Victorian respectability. A woman with a past marries a man whose grown daughter becomes engaged to an ex-lover of the second wife. Realizing that a woman with a past can have no future, the wife kills herself.

Sedes. Name of a certain scene building, or mansion, of the medieval stage; means, literally, "seat."
See also *Mansions.*

See Naples and Die. Elmer Rice (American). Comedy. 3 acts. 1929.
Nanette Dodge and Charles Carroll quarrel in Paris and Nanette breaks her engagement to Charles and marries Ivan Kosoff, a titled Russian. Charles goes to Sorrento and takes up with Kuny Wandl. Nanette follows him to explain she was forced to marry the Russian to save her sister; she is about to be divorced and she declares she still loves Charles. The latter disbelieves her until a pair of revolutionists shoot Ivan and the situation is resolved.

Seen But Not Heard. Marie Baumer and Martin Berkeley (American). Melodrama. 3 acts. Printed 1936.

A play in which a new twist is given to the murder mystery; the burden of discovery is placed on three children, whose intelligence is brought to bear upon an adult problem. On Christmas Eve, the three children are saddened by the death of their sister Helen, killed in an automobile accident. They are drawn close to John Clyde, Helen's husband, whom they dislike. Tommy has a toy automobile and when he innocently unscrews a wheel, John goes to pieces, his strange terror arousing the suspicion of the children. They communicate this to Bob, the youngest, who accuses John of having killed his wife by loosening a wheel on his car. John admits it, and attacks Bob. Bob in self-defense knocks him down, goes out for water to revive him. Romney, the butler, enters and kills John.

Seldes, Gilbert (1893-   ). American dramatic critic. Since 1937 director of television programmes for the Columbia Broadcasting System. Journalist and war correspondent, who became dramatic critic of the *Dial* and New York newspapers. His books include: *The Seven Lively Arts,* 1924; *The Stammering Century,* 1928; *The Years of the Locust,* 1932; *Your Money and Your Life,* 1937; *The Movies Come from America,* 1937. His play *The Wise-Crackers* was produced in 1925, and in 1930 his adaptation of *Lysistrata.* He has also written fiction, and a historical moving picture, *This is America,* 1933.

Self. Mrs. Sidney F. Bateman (American). Drama. 3 acts. Printed 1856.
The story of Mrs. Apex who attempts to "keep up with the Joneses," and her husband, a merchant, who tries to get his wife to economize. John Unit, a typical, practical Yankee, helps the family out of difficulties.

Self-Portrait of Shakespeare. A document forged by William Ireland.

Selling bargains. An indecent amusement in the Restoration theatre, the point of which lay in inducing one's interlocutor to ask a question and replying to it in the most offensive manner.

Seneca, Lucius Annaeus (3 B.C.-65 A.D.). Roman philosopher. Known as Seneca the Younger, the son of the elder Seneca, he was born at Cordoba, in Spain. After travelling in Greece and Egypt as an advocate, and following a period of exile in Corsica, he was appointed by Agrippina tutor to her son, Nero. His great influence over Nero was undoubtedly for good, for the first years of his reign, when Seneca virtually ruled the empire, were years of good government. Later, he fell into disfavor, and in 65 A.D. was accused of being privy to the conspiracy of Piso, and was compelled to commit suicide.
His extant works are on philosophy, morals and science, the last being of no scientific value. Nine tragedies, including *Medea, Mad Hercules, The Trojan Women,* have also been preserved, which, though quite lacking in dramatic instinct, had great influence upon the drama of the 16th century, being the only extant Latin models of this class of literature. It has been said that Seneca was a moralist whose stoical precepts were better than his hedonistic practice.

Senora Ama. Jacinto Benavente y Martinez (Spanish). Drama. 3 acts. 1908.

Declared by Benavente to be his favorite work, it heralded a new epoch for the playwright. It is a play of the soil. The story has to do with a wife who is proud of her husband's sentimental conquests. She feels complimented when other women seek out her husband and flattered when she realizes that she has him for all times and they but for a short time. Realizing that she is going to have a baby, she resolves to seek his reform. She feels it unfair to the child for her to be so tolerant of his peccadillos. He agrees with her but the feeling of the audience is that it is just a temporary attack of virtue.

Sequence. A series of scenes in which the action is continuous, without any break in time or thought.

Serena Blandish. S. N. Behrman (American). Drama. 3 acts. 1929.

Based upon the English novel. An absorbing study of defeatism. Serena Blandish is unable to marry any of the men in whom she is interested. When a proper proposal comes she cannot accept it, having fallen in love with Edgar, who turns out to be the son of the ambitious butler.

Serlio, Sebastiano (1473-1554). Italian architect, painter, critic. His *Architettura* gave birth to new ideas of the theatre. He studied the ancient Greek and Roman theatres and applied certain of their principles to the theatre of his own time, meanwhile expanding them. He divided the *mise en scène* into 3 types: (1) for Comedy—ordinary houses (*case*) with the house of a courtesan in the foreground; (2) for Tragedy—lofty palaces; (3) for Satyric plays—rustic setting: trees, groves, and cottages. He introduced perspective into the theatre. His characteristic stage setting: two converging rows of solidly, but perspectively, built *case* backed by a curtain on which are other *case* painted flat.

See also *Formal stage setting; Sculptured stage.*

Sertorius; or, The Roman Patriot. David Paul Brown (American). Drama in Verse and Prose. 5 acts. Printed 1830.

Typical of the Philadelphia school of playwrights, illustrative of the notion that sonorous lines meant poetry. Similar to Shakespeare's *Julius Caesar* in plot, particularly in the handling of the conspiracy scene.

Sertorius was the son of Quintus and Rhea, and served under Marius in Gaul. In the wars between Sylla and Marius, he took part with the latter, and upon the overthrow of Marius, Sertorius was banished through the influence of Sylla. He took refuge in Spain where he acquired an almost sovereign control.

Set. A contraction of "setting"; a constructed scene.

Setting. See *Scenery; Scene Designing.*

Seven Against Thebes, The. Aeschylus (Greek). Tragedy. 467 B.C.

A tragedy dealing with the story of Eteocles and Polyneices. Originally part of a tetralogy, it presents the fatal struggle between the sons of Oedipus for the throne of Thebes. After the death of Oedipus, the brothers quarrel over possession of the throne. Eteocles refuses to yield to his brother. Polyneices gathers an army, appointing seven chieftains including himself, to march on the city. Eteocles appoints Seven Thebans to guard the seven gates. Eventually the brothers meet and both are killed in combat and only their two sisters remain.

Seven Keys to Baldpate. George M. Cohan (American). Melodramatic farce. 3 acts. 1913.

An author makes a bet with a friend that if he is given a week-end of absolute quiet, he can write a play. The friend offers him a house on the top of Baldpate Mountain, which unknown to the owner has become a rendezvous for thieves. In spite of becoming involved in their machinations, the author finally wins his bet.

Seven Sisters. F. Herzig (Hungarian). Comedy. 3 acts. Translated by Edith Ellis. Printed 1938.

The plot revolves around the Widow Gyurkovics and her amusing troubles in finding matrimonial "catches" for Katinka, Sari, and Ella, the older of her seven daughters. Her problem is further complicated by the fact that she is bound to the old custom of marrying off her daughters in the order of their ages.

Seventeen. Hugh Stange. Comedy (American). 4 acts. 1917. A dramatization of the book by Booth Tarkington.

This is an amusing comedy of youth, concerning the moods and situations of a seventeen year old boy in his wooing of an amiable flirt.

Shadow and Substance. Paul Vincent Carroll (Irish). Drama. 3 acts. 1937.

This play is concerned with the Catholic Church in Ireland. A young girl who is a steadfast, confirmed believer in the faith, brings back to the fold those who have drifted from the church by her purity and firm beliefs. The roles of the girl and the cynical worldly bishop are created so well that the play is both dramatic and eloquent.

Shadow as an element of scenic design. A theory of Adolphe Appia. According to Lee Simonson in his *The Stage Is Set,* "light that is blocked by an object and casts shadows has a sculpturesque quality that by the vehemence of its definition, by the balance of light and shade, can carve an object before our eyes. It is capable of arousing us emotionally because it can emphasize and accent forms so as to give them force and meaning."

Shadow Fisher, The. Jean Sarment (French). Drama. 3 acts. 1921.

The shadows referred to are a species of trout sought by a harmless madman. He has lost his mental balance on being jilted by his love. His mother, hoping he may be cured, brings the girl home, but the boy's brother, wishing the girl for himself, assures the invalid that she is merely a second person, and the invalid accepts that explanation.

Shadwell, Thomas (1642-1692). English dramatist. Born at Weeting, Norfolk, he studied law in London. He is remembered as the author of some seventeen plays which, though inferior as dramas, show an intimate knowledge of the London underworld of his day. They were chiefly remarkable for their attacks on contemporary morals, and so irritated Dryden that he immortalized Shadwell in *MacFlecknoe; or, A Satire on the True Blue Protestant Poet, T. S.*, 1682, and as Og in *Absalom and Achitophel*. Shadwell succeeded Dryden as poet laureate.

Shairp, Alexander Mordaunt (1887-   ). British playwright. Born in Totnes, South Devon, he was graduated from Oxford. He is a teacher and lecturer in the Universities at Oxford and London. Among his plays are *The Offence*, 1925; *The Crime at Blossoms's*, 1929; *The Green Bay Tree*, 1932.

Shakespeare, William (1564-1616). English dramatist. The known facts of Shakespeare's life are few in comparison with the mass of tradition which has risen concerning him. It is inferred that he was born on April 22 or 23, 1564, in Stratford-on-Avon, Warwickshire, since he was baptized there on April 26 of that year. His father was John Shakespeare, of yeoman stock. John, a glover and butcher, became alderman and city chamberlain of Stratford, but went into a financial and civic decline in 1577. Mary, Shakespeare's mother, was the daughter of Robert Arden, a wealthy farmer of Wilmcote. Nothing is known of Shakespeare's education, although it is supposed that he attended Stratford Grammar School, a good one in its day, and followed the usual course of studies in arithmetic, English, Latin, possibly some Greek and the Bible. He probably was withdrawn from school when his father suffered his reverses, and was taken into the latter's business. In November, 1582, he married Anne Hathaway, eight years his senior. Their first child, Susanna, was born six months later in 1583. Twins, Hammet and Judith, were baptized in 1585. Nothing more is known of Shakespeare until his appearance in London, established in his profession, in 1592. There is no evidence to support the traditions that his marriage was unhappy and that he abandoned his family, that he left Stratford to become a school-teacher, soldier, apothecary, or lawyer, that he joined a company of travelling players in Stratford and went with them to London, or that he was caught stealing deer on the estate of Sir Thomas Lucy and had to leave Stratford to escape the latter's wrath. Equally little is known of his early activities in London, although according to tradition he first served as a holder of horses outside the playhouses and as a call-boy. In 1592 a slur on Shakespeare by Robert Greene and an apology for this remark by Henry Chettle reveals that Shakespeare was already well-known as actor, dramatist and man, and that he had written three parts of Henry VI, a line of which is paraphrased by Greene. Probably he was already at work for Pembroke's or Strange's men. Except for the publication of *Venus and Adonis* in 1593 and *The Rape of Lucrece* in 1594, both with dedications to the Earl of Southampton, little is known of Shakespeare's activities until 1594, although *Richard III, Titus*

Andronicus, and *The Comedy of Errors* were probably written during this interval. Recurrences of the plague during these years kept the theatres for the most part inactive. A contemporary work, *Willobie His Avisa* describes Shakespeare as experiencing an unsuccessful love affair in 1594. 1595 found the dramatist with assured theatrical status as a member of the Lord Chamberlain's Men, and his story from this point forward is one of success and fortune. In 1596 he applied for and received a coat of arms, and in the following year purchased New Place, a fine house in Stratford, where he became a prominent and respected citizen. Apparently he spent little time there, however, as there are several records of his London residences during this period. His fame as a playwright is attested to by Francis Meres, in whose *Palladis Tamia,* 1598, he is "mellifluous and honey-tongued Shakespeare," to be compared with Ovid, Plautus and Seneca. Such praise was based on the Sonnets, *The Taming of the Shrew, Love's Labour's Lost, Romeo and Juliet, Richard II, Midsummer Night's Dream, King John, The Merchant of Venice* and *Henry IV, Parts I and II,* all of which were written before 1598. The poet's income was increased in 1599 when he became a shareholder in the newly-erected Globe Theatre, where his plays were presented by the Lord Chamberlain's Men. There in 1601 his company revived his *Richard II* at a special performance attended by Essex and his followers, who on the following day rebelled against Elizabeth. Among the rebels was Shakespeare's patron, Southampton, but either because of his influence, or because Shakespeare's company was innocent of the purpose of the revival, which was to inspire the projected revolt, no harm came to them or the author. By this time Shakespeare had added *Much Ado About Nothing, Henry V, As You Like It, Julius Caesar, Twelfth Night, Merry Wives of Windsor* and *Hamlet.* According to tradition he was receiving royal attention because of his works, for *Merry Wives of Windsor* is said to have been written at the request of Elizabeth, who wished to see Falstaff in love. As an actor Shakespeare had appeared in Ben Jonson's *Every Man In His Humor* in 1598, in the same author's *Sejanus* in 1603, and, according to tradition, as Adam in his own *As You Like It* and as the ghost in his *Hamlet.* Meantime he became involved in "Poetomachia," siding with Marston and Dekker in their personal and literary quarrel with Jonson. At the death of Elizabeth in 1603 Shakespeare's company passed under the patronage of James and became known as the King's Men. Shakespeare's prestige at court remained undiminished after the change of sovereigns, for several of his older plays were chosen to appear there together with new ones at court performances in 1604. Plays written in this period include the so-called "dark comedies": *Troilus and Cressida, All's Well That Ends Well* and *Measure for Measure.* At this time Shakespeare was residing in London with Christopher Mountjoy, for whose daughter he arranged a wedding with an apprentice. By now Shakespeare had apparently given up acting and was devoting himself solely to writing. The "dark comedies" were a prelude to the series of great tragedies which began about 1604 with *Othello. King Lear* and *Macbeth* followed in 1604 and 1605, and by 1608 *Antony and Cleopatra* and *Coriolanus* had been composed. *Timon of Athens,* probably also in 1608, is so inferior a piece in style and construction that it has been conjectured that the poet suffered a nervous or physical breakdown of some sort at this time. A marked change of spirit pervades the plays which followed, 1608-12; the romantic comedies *Pericles, Cymbeline, Winter's Tale* and *The Tempest*. Their essentially Christian philosophy has been interpreted as lending support to the tradition that Shakespeare "dyed a Papist." In 1610, or shortly after, Shakespeare probably returned to Stratford to make New Place his permanent residence. However, he returned to London occasionally to write for his company. His collaboration with Fletcher on *Henry VIII*, 1613, was probably his last effort of this sort. He was also in London on other business from time to time—in 1612 to make a deposition in Mountjoy's suit against the son-in-law Shakespeare helped him acquire in 1604; in 1613 to design an *impresa* painted by Burbage and carried by the Earl of Rutland in a parade at the Accession day tilt; in the same year to invest in a piece of property in Blackfriars; and in 1614 to discuss business with his cousin, Thomas Greene, and his son-in-law, John Hall. In 1616, according to a story told in 1662 by the Vicar of Stratford, Shakespeare, Ben Jonson and Michael Drayton "had a merry meeting and, it seems, drank too hard, for Shakespeare died of a fever there contracted." The will, signed by Shakespeare in 1616, left various small bequests to the poor, to Shakespeare's fellows in the old Lord Chamberlain's company, and to his children. His wife Anne, well-provided for by legal dower of the Stratford property, received his second-best bed. Shakespeare died on April 23 and was buried in the Chancel of Stratford Church where, thanks to a doggerel curse attributed to him, his remains lie today. A monument, consisting of a bust of the poet and a laudatory inscription, was erected over the grave before 1623.

Dryden says of Shakespeare "He was the man who of all modern, and perhaps ancient poets, had the largest and most comprehensive soul."

Samuel Johnson's attack on Shakespeare, a famous discussion of the unities, is contained in his Preface to Shakespeare, 1765, and states: "He had no regard to distinction of time or place, but gives to one age or nation, without scruple, the customs, institutions and opinions of another, at the expense not only of likelihood, but of possibility."

Shakespeare's Profession of Faith. A document forged by William Ireland to prove Shakespeare a Catholic.

Shancke, John (? -1636). English actor. An actor named in the 1623 Folio list of performers in Shakespeare's plays. He did not become associated with Shakespeare's company until 1616, when they were known as the King's Men. He was best known as a comedian and acted in Ford's *Lover's Melancholy*, Fletcher's *Wildgoose Chase* and other plays.

Sharing system. A scheme first introduced by the Hallams in 1752; actors were partners in a company, receiving salaries on a percentage basis. This system was done away with in 1792 when the theatre began to expand; actors, except for two or three principals, were hired on a straight salary basis.

See also *Commonwealth*.

The Shaughraun. Dion Boucicault (American). Drama. c. 1874.

The action of the play takes place in county Sligo, and is concerned with the Irish political prisoners who had been in English jails for more than ten years, and who, the author felt, had by now paid for the deeds they had committed against the British crown.

Boucicault played the leading role when the play was first presented. The play was instrumental in arousing the interest of a group of liberals who arranged for the release of the Irish political prisoners.

Shaw, George Bernard (1856-   ). British dramatist. He was born in Dublin in 1856. Forced at an early age to earn his own living, he entered a land-agent's office in his native city. But his interest in other things—chiefly music and political science—made him restless, and in 1876 he went to London, where for several years he subsisted on a small allowance from his mother, studying and doing hack literary work. Between 1880 and 1883, he wrote four novels, which were failures from a financial viewpoint. But during this time the young man formed valuable associations in socialistic and literary circles, making friends with William Morris, Sidney Webb, William Archer, Edward Carpenter and others. In the early Nineties he became dramatic critic of the *Saturday Review.* In 1892, his first play *Widowers' Houses* was performed. This was followed by *The Philanderer,* 1893, and *Mrs. Warren's Profession,* which was forbidden by the censor. Meantime he was busy lecturing, propagandizing, writing and participating in the activities of the Fabian Society. Besides, at various times in the Nineties, he was both a music and art critic.

Shaw's contribution to the drama is many-sided: first, his own brilliant plays, satires for the most part on contemporary prejudices; second, his five years' work as dramatic critic; and finally, his ideas as an economist and sociologist. It is rather as a philosopher and popularizer of the philosophies of others than as an artist that his work has penetrated to every corner of Europe and America. Both in theory and practice he has always favored the thesis play, or play of ideas. To him the theatre is a means and not an end.

He is the author of the following plays: *Arms and the Man,* 1894; *Candida,* 1895; *The Devil's Disciple,* 1897; *You Never Can Tell,* 1899; *Caesar and Cleopatra,* 1899; *Captain Brassbound's Conversion,* 1900; *Man and Superman,* 1903; *John Bull's Other Island,* 1904; *Major Barbara,* 1905; *The Doctor's Dilemma,* 1906; *The Dark Lady of the Sonnets,* 1910; *Androcles and the Lion,* 1913; *Pygmalion,* 1913; *Heartbreak House,* 1919; *Back to Methuselah,* 1921; *Saint Joan,* 1923; *The Apple Cart,* 1930; *On the Rocks,* 1933; *The Six of Calais,* 1934; *The Simpleton of the Unexpected Isles,* 1934; *The Millionairess,* 1936; *Geneva,* 1938 (revised September, 1939) ; *In the Days of Good King Charles,* 1939.

Shaw, Irwin (1912-   ). American playwright. Born in Manhattan, he went to Brooklyn College. After writing radio scripts, he was sent to Hollywood where he wrote scenarios. In 1936 he wrote *Bury the Dead* to compete for a prize offered by the New Theatre League. It was produced by the League where it aroused the interest of the drama critics and then was produced professionally, creating a sensation. In 1937, his play, *Siege,* was produced without success. *The Gentle People,* 1939, enjoyed a moderate success.

Sheldon, Edward Brewster (1886-   ). American dramatist. Born in Chicago, he attended Harvard where he studied under George Pierce Baker. In 1907 he wrote his first play, *Salvation Nell*. He followed this with *The Nigger,* one of the first American plays to deal with a social problem. He wrote *The Boss* and *The High Road* and other plays until 1913. When he wrote and produced *Romance* it became an immediate box office success.

Among his plays are: *The Princess Zim-Zim,* 1911; *Egypt,* 1912; *Romance,* 1913; *The Lonely Heart,* 1914; *The Garden of Paradise,* 1914; *Betwitched* (with Sidney Howard), 1924; *Lulu Belle* (with Charles MacArthur), 1926; *Jenny* (with Margaret Ayer Barnes), 1929; *Dishonored Lady* (with Margaret Ayer Barnes), 1930.

Shelley, Percy Bysshe (1792-1822). British poet, dramatist. Born in Sussex, he was educated at Eton and Oxford. He is best known for his poetic works, but is also the author of many plays such as *The Cenci,* 1819; *Prometheus Unbound,* 1820; *Oedipus Tyrannus,* 1820; *Hellas,* 1822.

Shenandoah. Bronson Howard (American). Comedy. 1888.

The success of this play is part of the history of the American stage. Howard first wrote this play as *Drum Taps,* basing it on an incident in the Civil War, but had no success with it. Twenty years later in 1888, he altered the script and changed the title and had it produced again. Once more it was a failure, but in 1889 Charles Frohman became interested in it. He suggested a few more changes, and this time the play was a real hit.

Sheridan, Richard Brinsley (1751-1816). British dramatist. Sheridan was the only man of his or any age to make an equally deep impression as an active politician and as a dramatist.

A member of the famous Sheridan family, he was born in Dublin. His father was Thomas Sheridan, the actor, and his mother, Elizabeth, an actress, wrote plays. He attended Harrow 1762-68, and in 1770 was taken by his parents to Bath where his father taught elocution. He married Elizabeth Linley in 1773, and he and his wife settled in London, where, in 1775, his first comedy *The Rivals* was produced. It attained great popularity immediately, and its author's fame as a dramatist was established. In 1776, with two partners, one his father-in-law, Sheridan purchased the management of the Drury Lane Theatre, with which his name is inseparably associated. His first production at this theatre was the comedy *A Trip to Scarborough,* 1777, which he adapted from Vanbrugh's *Relapse,* and in May of the same year, he produced his greatest comedy, *The School for Scandal*. His dramatic career, which lasted only four years, ended with *The Critic,* a brilliant satirical farce, and the melodramatic tragedy, *Pizarro* (adapted from the German of Kotzebue), both produced in 1799.

In 1780, Sheridan was persuaded to seek election in Parliament, and after one unsuccessful attempt, he entered the Commons as Whig member for Stafford, 1780. He is remembered in the United States for his brilliant speeches in the House, opposing the war with America. As a politician in England, however, he is chiefly thought of in connection with the impeachment of Warren Hastings, a proceeding which lasted from 1787 to 1794. He was also an opponent of union with Ireland and a champion of the liberty of the press. Sheridan's later life is overshadowed by financial embarrassments. He gambled and was extravagant, and in 1813, after rebuilding the Drury Lane Theatre twice, his financial affairs went from bad to worse. In that year he was imprisoned in a sponging-house. Sheridan began to suffer from nervous debility, insomnia and brain-fever. He died with a sheriff's officer beside his bed, and was buried through the generosity of friends, in Westminster Abbey.

As a dramatist Sheridan brought the comedy of manners, witty, satirical and amusing, to its apotheosis. Among his plays are *The Rivals, 1775; St. Patrick's Day, or, The Scheming Lieutenant, 1776; The Duenna, 1776; The School for Scandal, 1777; The Critic, 1799; Pizarro, 1799.*

Sheriff, Robert Cedric (1896-   ). English playwright. Born in Kingston-on-Thames, he was at first on the staff of the Sun Insurance Office. Then he wrote plays for the amateur stage, such as *Profit and Loss,* 1923; *Mr. Bridie's Finger,* 1926. *Journey's End,* 1928, was his first London production and was a tremendous success. Others of his plays are *Windfall,* 1934; *St. Helena,* 1935.

Sherwood, Robert Emmett (1896-   ). American dramatist. Born in New Rochelle, New York. He received his A.B. from Harvard University. Was dramatic editor of *Vanity Fair,* 1919-20; associate editor and film critic for *Life,* 1920-25; editor, 1924; also editor of the New York *Herald* before the consolidation with the *Tribune.* He writes trenchant dialogue; his style swings from mordaunt, occasionally bawdy comedy as in *The Road to Rome* and *Reunion In Vienna* to the simple humor and soul-searching seriousness of *Abe Lincoln In Illinois.* His plays include *The Road To Rome,* 1926; *The Love Nest,* 1927; *The Queen's Husband,* 1928; *Waterloo Bridge, This Is New York,* 1930; *Reunion In Vienna,* 1931; *Acropolis,* 1933; *The Petrified Forest, Tovarich* (adapted from Deval's play), 1935; *Idiot's Delight,* 1936 (Pulitzer Prize winner); *Abe Lincoln In Illinois,* 1938 (Pulitzer Prize winner).

She Stoops to Conquer, or, The Mistakes of a Night. Oliver Goldsmith (English). Comedy. 5 acts. 1773.

Marlow, "one of the most bashful and reserved young fellows in the world," goes with a friend to visit the Hardcastles, as his father, Sir Charles, has proposed a match between Miss Hardcastle and his son. Losing their way at night, they are directed by Tony Lumpkin, Mrs. Hardcastle's son by a previous marriage, to a nearby inn which is really the Hardcastles' house. Marlow takes Hardcastle for the landlord and makes violent love to his daughter, under the impression that she is a servant. This contrasts with his bashful behavior when presented to her in her real character. When Sir

Charles arrives everything is cleared up. The comedy situations are still fresh and new today. It has had many revivals, most of them meeting with great success. The dialogue is bright and the characters amusing.

Shibai. Japanese word for "theatres" and "performances," derives from the performance of certain dances on a grass plot. *Kabuki Shibai* means Kabuki theatre. *Ningyo Shibai* means doll theatre, or puppet theatre.

Shill. A come-on man (slang) ; a false customer who pretends to buy tickets for a tent show or amusement park attraction in order to attract real patrons to the box-office.

Shining Hour, The. Keith Winter (English). Drama. 3 acts. 1934.
David Lindon falls in love with his brother's wife, Mariella. When David's wife, Judy, learns of his love for Mariella, she commits suicide in a burning hay barn. After the tragedy, David, on the verge of insanity, is persuaded to go away with Mariella.

Shoemakers' Holiday; or, A Pleasant Comedy of the Gentle Craft, The. Thomas Dekker (English). Comedy. Printed 1600.
Rowland Lacy, a kinsman of the Earl of Lincoln, loves Rose, daughter of a London Lord Mayor. To prevent the match, the Earl sends him to France in command of a company. Lacy resigns his place to a friend, and disguised as a Dutch shoemaker takes service with Simon Eyre, who supplies the family of the Lord Mayor with shoes. Here he successfully pursues his suit and is pardoned by the King. Simon Eyre, cheery master-shoemaker, becomes **Lord Mayor.**

Shoe-string Production. A production of a play put on with a minimum of financial expenditure; also refers to a poor, shabby or second-rate production.

Shore Acres. James A. Herne (American). Comedy. 4 acts. 1893.
A melodrama of New England farm life, set on the shores of Frenchman's Bay, east of Bar Harbor, Maine, with the well known characters of old Martin, Uncle Nat, and other members of the Berry family.
Meager of plot, the play's importance lies in the fact that it was one of the first to use any form of realism in the theatre. A great deal of critical comment was aroused by the fact that the characters on stage actually ate a real dinner.

Show. General term to cover every type of theatrical entertainment: play, musical, revue, opera, cinema, etc.

Showboat, The (University of Washington). Built with funds from the Federal Government and profits from the University's Penthouse Theatre. Constructed on a 140 by 36 foot barge; has a revolving stage. Built in the summer of 1937.

Show boats. Floating theatres that tie up at various towns along a waterway and give performances. Their beginnings go back to the early years of the American control of the Mississippi Basin. Strolling players, for want of anything better, performed on keel boats and rafts. The first recorded show boat was a rude shelter on a keel boat built in 1817 by N. M. Ludlow, an actor, who plied the Cumberland, the Ohio and the Mississippi. In 1830, William Chapman's passion for fishing led to the building of his Theatre with its little house forward, its small hall with wooden benches and tiny stage with muslin curtains and tallow candles for footlights. It floated from town to town up and down the Ohio and Mississippi Rivers. The company was made up of the entire Chapman family. Acting and fishing were the great interests of their lives and often the two overlapped.

Show business. Popular term used to represent the general affairs of the professional theatre.

Show girl. A girl in a stage production who has no part and is not a member of the chorus, but whose beauty and ability to wear costumes lends glamour to the background or to the production proper; usually used in musical productions.

Show-Off, The. George Kelly (American). Comedy. 3 acts. 1924.
The struggles of Aubrey Piper to satisfy his enormous egotism and at the same time preserve his self-respect in the presence of discouraging obstacles. He is a trial to the family into which he has married and the play presents a satirical view of American life.
Though he has only a humble job at a small salary, Aubrey is one of the world's worst show offs. The basis of the play is his ability to put up a big front in unexpected ways.

Shreveport Little Theatre, Louisiana. This Little Theatre, begun in 1922, now owns a plant estimated to have cost more than $30,000. Adjoining real estate has been acquired so that if continued growth makes further space necessary, it will be available. It uses a wide variety of local players and technical workers. For the past several years it has been headed by John Wray Young.

Shrew. A stock character appearing in English drama from 1350 to 1642 possessing such characteristics as a violent temper, a propensity to scolding, and a domineering temperament. Best historic example appears in Shakespeare's *Taming of the Shrew.*

Shrovetide Plays. The name given to the short, amusing versified plays during the German Middle Ages. They began with a prologue, explaining the subject of the piece, and had a short moral for the finale. They were filthy and coarse in speech. Shrovetide plays were the equivalent of farces.

Shubert, J. J. (1880-   ), **Lee** (1875-   ) and **Sam S.** (1876-1905). American theatrical managers and producers. Born in Syracuse, New York, and educated in the public schools there. Lee and Sam began their theatrical careers managing road companies, with comedies written by Charles H. Hoyt. They organized a stock company for the Bastable Theatre, Syracuse. In 1900 they became managers of the Herald Square Theatre, New York; then the Casino, Princess, Hippodrome, Lyric, and others. The three brothers formed the Shubert Theatrical Company (see *Shubert Theatre Corporation*) which now controls the greater number of theatres in New York, as well as numerous ones in other cities. John Shubert, the son of "J.J.," a Harvard graduate, is also a member of the organization.

Although they are most powerful managers and owners of so many theatres, both Lee and "J.J." are practically unknown to Broadway. Lee is formal, detached and non-talkative; he is fastidious in his dress, and there are legends about how often he shaves. "J.J." occasionally dines at the Stork Club or tarries a moment to talk with a friend. His predilection is musical comedy. Although he despises the sea, he crosses continually in search of new material for his theatres.

Shubert, Milton (1901?-   ). American producer. Nephew of Lee and J. J. Shubert, and head of the Shubert firm from 1935. With Chester Erskin he formed Haymarket, Ltd., to produce musicals and plays. He began directing road companies of *Blossom Time, The Student Prince, My Maryland, Sally, Irene and Mary.* In 1930 he was director of *Show Boat* at the St. Louis Municipal Opera Company, starring W. C. Fields. Important productions have been *No More Ladies,* 1934; *Laburnum Grove,* and *Eden End,* 1935; *Swing Your Lady* and *Green Waters,* 1936; *Bachelor Born,* 1938.

He joined Warner Brothers as associate producer in 1937; in 1938 he produced *Sweepstakes Winner* and *On Trial.*

Shubert Alley. A private thoroughfare, used by the public, between 44th and 45th Street, New York. It lies along the sides of the Sam S. Shubert and Booth Theatres, giving access to their stage doors and the general offices of the Shuberts. It is a favorite spot for actors to congregate.

Shubert Theatre Corporation. Located at 225 West 44th Street, New York City. A corporation organized in 1924 to consolidate the Shubert Consolidated Enterprises, Inc.; Winter Garden Company, Inc.; and affiliated interests established since the beginning of the century by Sam S., Lee and J. J. Shubert. It controls or has interests in about seventy theatres in New York and other principal cities and is the largest operator of legitimate theatres in the United States. It was put in receivership in 1931; the properties were bought in by the Shuberts and others and the old firm was reorganized as the Select Theatre Corporation but it is now known as the Shubert Theatre Corporation.

Shumlin, Herman. American producer. Successively with the New Jersey Metro-Goldwyn-Mayer publicity department, reporter on the now defunct New York *Clipper,* moving picture reviewer for *Billboard,* press agent for Schwab and Mandel, and general manager for Jed Harris during the production of *Love 'Em* *and Leave 'Em,* 1926, *Broadway,* 1926, and *Spread Eagle,* 1927. Besides a dozen other productions his outstanding successes have been *The Last Mile,* 1929; *Grand Hotel,* 1931; *The Children's Hour,* 1934; and *The Little Foxes,* 1939.

Siddons, Sarah Kemble (1755-1831). English actress. Born in the "Shoulder of Mutton," a public house, at Brecon, Wales, the eldest of the twelve children of the actor-manager, Roger Kemble. She married a member of her father's company, William Siddons, in 1773. Stirred by reports of her performance at Cheltenham in 1774 in Otway's *Venice Preserv'd,* Garrick sent a representative to see her play and she was engaged to appear with him at Drury Lane. Her appearance, December 27, 1775, was a failure, she was called awkward, gangling and without power. Broken-hearted, she returned to the provinces for further seasoning. This she got in her celebrated five-year run at Bath and her return to Drury Lane, October 10, 1782, in Garrick's adaptation of Southerne's *The Fatal Marriage,* was a triumph. Her beauty, diction, strength and grace were admired for as long as she chose to grace the British stage. Her Lady Macbeth was her greatest role, perhaps never equalled by another actress. Other parts in which she excelled were Queen Katherine in *King Henry VIII,* with her brother, John Philip Kemble, and Volumnia in *Coriolanus.* She retired June 7, 1812, with a series of farewells that brought gold to the box office, cheers to the playhouse, and tears to the eyes of those who looked for the last time on the acting of the incomparable Mrs. Siddons. She made her final appearance on June 9, 1819, for a benefit of Charles and Mrs. Kemble, as Lady Randolph in Home's *Douglas.* Her beauty was so great that she was painted by the most noted artists of her time, Reynolds, Lawrence and Gainsborough. Her fine mind and sterling worth won the admiration of the great men of this period, including Dr. Johnson and Horace Walpole.

Side. A page of an actor's part.

Side Show. A small show or performance connected with a larger one, as with a circus or a fair.

Sides typed. Half sheets of manuscript paper, neatly bound, holding the actors' parts and cues.

Sidney, Sir Philip (1554-1586). English author. He was born in Penshurst and was educated at Oxford; travelled extensively and had many political affiliations. In 1583 he was knighted. His best known works are *Arcadia, The Lady of May* and *Pastoral Dialogue.* His only treatise on the drama is his *An Apologie for Poesie.*

Sidney Howard Memorial Award. Established after the tragic death (August, 1939) of the dramatist by his friends and associates in the Playwrights Producing Company. Carries with it an annual prize of $1,500 for the best play by an American author produced each season. Its intent is "to create opportunities and provide training for young playwrights, young actors, young directors who will make the 'theatre of tomorrow'."

Siège. Name of a certain scene building, or mansion, of the medieval stage.

Siegfried. Jean Giraudoux (French). Drama. 1922.

A French soldier, rescued from death by a German woman, but suffering from amnesia as the result of a wound, recovers all his powers save memory and develops a German personality. Within seven years, his freshly acquired talents enable him to become minister in the new German state, while his French identity remains unsuspected by others or himself.

Sikake. A gown worn by the courtesan in Japanese *Kabuki* drama, under which a kimono of spectacular and gorgeous fashion is worn. The wig worn by the actor for this part is likewise splendid in decoration and weighs as much as twenty-five pounds.

Silbo. In the Spanish theatre, the whistle of the *mosqueteros* when they were not pleased with acting.

Silver Box, The. John Galsworthy (English). Drama. 3 acts. 1909.

A study in contrasts: The luxurious home of Mr. Barthwick, a member of Parliament, and the home of the charwoman, Mrs. Jones. The rich man's scapegrace of a son, Jack, is brought home drunk by Mr. Jones, who seizes his opportunity for stealing the silver box. Honest Mrs. Jones is charged with the theft. Jack Barthwick has also committed a theft: he has stolen a girl's purse, and she comes to the house to demand its return. The father solves his son's difficulty by means of a cheque; but the Joneses are poor, and the law is set in motion. Jones finally has the decency to take the responsibility for the theft of the silver box.

Silver Cord, The. Sidney Howard (American). Drama. 3 acts. 1926.

Selfish and self centered, Mrs. Phelps contrives to break off wedding plans of one son, Robert, but her interference with the life of another son leads to her own crushing defeat as the latter's wife battles strongly and gets him away, leaving Robert engulfed forever by his mother's side, firmly tied by the Silver Cord.

Simonson, Lee (1888-   ). American scenic designer. Born in New York City. Started with the Washington Square Players and in 1919 became one of the founders and directors of the Theatre Guild. As their stage designer, he has done such famous productions as: *Marco Millions; Liliom; Idiot's Delight; Roar China; Amphitryon 38; The Taming of the Shrew; Madame Bovary; Peer Gynt;* etc.

He was editor of *Creative Art* magazine and wrote *The Stage is Set* in 1932.

Simoon. Henri René Lenormand (French). Drama. 3 acts. 1920.

Reveals the perturbations of a father who is subconsciously in love with his daughter yet unaware of what really troubles him. This incestuous state prompts the father to refuse to give his permission for his daughter, Clotilde, to marry a young Arab. The refusal incites the Arab to retaliate by seizing French messengers sent to the coast in a simoon. Clotilde is slain by her father's mistress, and he is relieved, since he will be free from the torment of his evil love.

Sinjohn, John. See *Galsworthy, John.*

Sinsyuku. A street in Tokyo corresponding to New York's Broadway as an amusement center. Many famous playhouses are to be found on Sinsyuku.

Sir Thomas More, The Play of. A late 16th century play in manuscript containing what is believed to be the only extensive specimen of Shakespearean handwriting. The body of the play, which deals with events in the life of Thomas More, Lord Chancellor of England from 1529 to 1531, is probably by Anthony Munday. Added to the original manuscript are revisions in the hands of several different authors. One of these additions, a whole scene describing More's quelling of a riot, is now generally thought to be by Shakespeare and in his handwriting.

Sister Beatrice. Maurice Maeterlinck (French). Drama. 1900.
The story of a nun who has violated her vows for love. When she finally returns to the convent, she finds that she still is within the realms of sanctity for "who sins for love, sins not."

Sitting on their hands. The unresponsiveness of an audience.

Situation. A term sometimes used synonymously with plot; the relationship of play characters to each other or with external conditions; a play may have, and be built up from, a series of situations. The term "basic situation" refers to that one problem which is central in a play.

Six Characters in Search of an Author. Luigi Pirandello (Italian). Comedy. 3 acts. 1921.
This symbolical play, which has been called the most brilliant of Pirandello's works, asks the questions which always troubled this playwright: What is reality? What is illusion?
It is the story of a play within a play. Six characters created by a playwright insist on acting out a play he does not wish to write. Therefore he abandons them, and they go to a director and ask him to give them artistic life. He does. The drama which they act has as its protagonist a man who twenty years previously allowed his wife to run away with his secretary. The eloping couple later had three children, and eventually the secretary died. The mother's first husband now meets one of the woman's daughters by her second union in a place of ill repute. He takes the girl and the rest of her family home with him. But the man's own children make life difficult for the newcomers. Eventually the girl drowns in a fountain and her brother kills himself.
As the characters finish acting this play within a play, the director shouts that the play is very bad and sends them away. "Bring me *The Bride's Revenge*," he exclaims. "That's what the people want."
Pirandello's play is rather obscure and filled with involved philosophical discussions. It obviously aims to prove two things, however. One is that one's sins will catch

up with one eventually, although retribution may be long in coming. Thus the husband who encouraged his wife to abandon her children and run away with another man has to pay eventually for his error. The other and more important point of the play is that the playwright who creates fictional characters is in the last analysis less important than the beings he brings to life. For the playwright may change or die, whereas the characters are permanent and immutable. Feasible or not, this is a typically Pirandellian paradox.

Skene. Introduced, in 465 B.C., into the classical Athenian theatre: a small wooden shed, designed originally as a dressing-room for the performers but later found to offer many opportunities as scenic background; from this time plays, instead of being set in open country, are presumed to have taken place before a temple or palace.

Sketch. A short and usually simple, single-pointed skit or scene, used in a revue, musical comedy, or vaudeville show; a short outline or rough draft of a play, act, or scene, before actual writing or production.

Skin brushes. Used to remove excess powder make-up.
See *Make-up*.

Skin Game, The. John Galsworthy (English). Drama. 3 acts. Printed 1920.
The play deals with the bitter and costly feud between the Hornblowers, a manufacturing family, and the Hillcrests, landed gentry. The Hornblowers, who have moved to the south of England, plan to build a factory in a location which will greatly decrease the value of the Hillcrest property. The Hillcrests counter attack by threatening to expose a scandal involving the wife of one of the Hornblowers' sons. The town finally joins sides and cuts the Hornblowers. The play ends with both families in deadlock, but with odds for the Hornblowers, who are part of the stream of industrial progress.

Skinner, Otis (1858-   ). American actor, author. Born Cambridge, Massachusetts; educated at Cambridge and Hartford; made his stage debut at the Philadelphia Museum, November, 1877, as Jim in *Woodleigh;* made his first appearance on the New York stage at Niblo's Garden; 1879, as Maclon in *The Enchantment;* supported Booth in 1880; played with Barrett three years; appeared with Augustin Daly's Company, 1884-88; played with Booth-Modjeska Company, 1889-90; played Romeo at the Globe Theatre in London, 1890; played leads with Modjeska, 1890-92; co-starred with Ada Rehan as Charles Surface, Shylock, and Petruchio; appeared in *The Honor of the Family,* 1908; appeared in *Kismet,* 1912-14; appeared as *Mister Antonio,* 1916-18; played Hanaud in *At the Villa Rose,* 1921. His later plays include Falstaff in *King Henry IV* (*Part 1*) and in *The Merry Wives of Windsor* with Mrs. Fiske; Papa Juan in *A Hundred Years Old;* Uncle Tom in the Players' revival of *Uncle Tom's Cabin,* 1933. Author of *Footlights and Spotlights,* 1924; *Mad Folk of the Theatre; The Last Tragedian,* 1939, etc.

Skit. A short scene or sketch, satirical in nature; a brief lampoon.

Sklar, George (1908-). American dramatist. An executive member of Theatre Union, and co-author with Albert Maltz of *Merry-Go-Round*, 1931, and *Peace On Earth*, 1933; with Paul Peters, of *Stevedore*, 1934, and *Parade*, 1935. His own *Life and Death of an American* was produced by the Federal Theatre Project in 1939.
See also *Maltz, Albert*.

Sleeping Clergyman, The. James Bridie (English). Drama. 3 acts. 1933.
Charles Cameron II is a famous physician who abolishes a world plague, while Hope Cameron, his sister, is elected Secretary of the League of Nations.
The play traces their family history, from the grandfather, a debauched and tubercular medical student, to their mother who poisons her lover because he is keeping her from marrying a rich man.

Sly. Giovancchio Forzano (Italian). Drama. 3 acts. 1925.
Derives from the introduction to *The Taming of the Shrew*. However, Forzano makes it more romantic.
A count comes to an inn in quest of a fugitive mistress. He prevails upon her to pose as the wife of a vagabond, who, given a sleeping potion, awakens in a palace and is made to believe himself the count in person, recovering from a long illness.

Slye, William (-1608). English actor. An actor named in the 1623 Folio list of performers in Shakespeare's plays. He was associated with Shakespeare's company, the Lord Chamberlain's Men, from 1594 until his death. In addition to his Shakespearean parts, he played roles in Jonson's *Every Man In His Humor*, *Every Man Out of His Humor*, *Sejanus*, and *Volpone*; and in Marston's *Malcontent*.

Smith, Dodie (Dorothy Gladys Smith) (1896-). English dramatist. Born in Whitefield, Lancashire, and educated in Manchester and at St. Paul's Girls' School, London. After studying at the Royal Academy of Dramatic Art, she made her debut on the stage in musical comedy in 1915. She left the stage and began to write plays. Her first play, *Autumn Crocus*, was produced at the Lyric Theatre in London in 1931, and was an immediate success; and in 1932 a second play *Service* was put on at Wyndham's. Both of these plays have been adapted for the screen. Among her more recent works have been *Call It a Day* and *Dear Octopus*.

Smith, Harry B. (1860-1936). American librettist. Considered with his collaborator, Reginald De Koven, one of the most prolific librettists of this generation. He wrote the book or lyrics for about three hundred stage productions. Some of these were Victor Herbert's light operas. Some of his best known musical comedies were *The Serenade*, *The Wizard of the Nile*, and *Robin Hood*.

Smoke pocket. Metal groove for ends of fire curtain on both sides of proscenium opening.

Snow. Free admissions to the theatre.

Social dramatist. A writer of plays dealing essentially with problems concerning the welfare or organization of society. Such writers include: Shaw, Ibsen, Brieux, Hauptmann, and in the latter day, Odets, Lawson, Wexley, Hellman, Rice and Anderson.

Societé Universelle du Théâtre. An international theatre society founded by Firmin Gemier in Paris in 1927 to promote cultural and artistic relations in the theatre of the world. It is its function to sponsor international theatre congresses. Jules Romains is international president. For the American section, Eugene O'Neill is president and George Freedley, executive secretary.

Sock. (1) Early term for comedy; taken from the light shoe worn by comic actors in Greek and Roman drama. (2) A show successful to the point of standees.

Sock and buskin. Ancient terms for comedy and tragedy.

Soft shoe dancing. A form of dancing or tap dancing performed by dancers wearing noiseless shoes or shoes without cleats or taps.

Soliloquy. A speech representing the thoughts of a character spoken for the audience's ears alone; occasionally overheard, as in *Hamlet*.

Son, The. Walter Hasenclever (German). Drama. 3 acts. 1890.
Deals with the age old conflict between father and son. The boy, having failed his entrance examinations to the University and realizing the uncompromising position his father will take decides to commit suicide. His friend persuades him not to do this. He suggests with the ruthless abandon of an undisciplined youth that the boy shoot his father, and devote his life to pleasure. There will be no restrictions, no censure, all fun. They are anxious to have all sons rebel against their fathers. However, the boy is spared the crime when the father dies of a stroke. The boy feels his father's tyranny has warped his life—he feels all fathers and sons are enemies.

Song-and-dance man. A popular term for a minstrel performer which first came into usage about 1860.

Songs, Shakespearean. Shakespeare's generous use of songs was designed in part to appeal to the Elizabethan love of music. But the poet went further than that and made his songs fulfill a definite dramatic function as well. Thus in the tragedies, where songs are associated with abnormal states of mind and highly emotional situations, they intensify the pathos of the scene, as Ophelia's lyrics in *Hamlet* illustrate. An abundant use of songs in *As You Like It, Twelfth Night* and *The Tempest,* heighten the lyric quality of these plays. Of tunes to which the lyrics were originally sung only two have survived. They are Thomas Morley's settings for "It was a lover and his lass" from *As You Like It* and "O mistress mine" from *Twelfth Night*.

Sophocles (496?-406 B.C.). Greek dramatist. Born at Colonnus, near Athens. He never left Athens except for military service.

Aeschylus, Euripides and Sophocles were the three great masters of Greek tragedy. Sophocles enjoyed more contemporary popularity than the others and he had fifty years on the pinnacle of success in the Greek theatre. He preferred to develop to their highest powers, the old forms. He was not primarily an innovator but he did introduce the third actor and reduced the importance of the chorus. This served to lift speech and action from the orchestra to the stage. Only seven of more than one hundred of Sophocles' plays survive in their entirety: *Ajax, Antigone, Electra, Oedipus Tyrannus* (often called *Oedipus Rex*), *The Women of Trachis, Philoctetes,* and *Oedipus Coloneus.*

See also *Drama, Greek, Ancient.*

Sophonisba. Gian Giorgio Trissino (Italian). Tragedy. 5 acts.

Sophonisba, in Roman legendary history was daughter of Hasdrubal. Affianced to Masinissa, king of the Numidians, her father gave her in marriage to Syphax. Masinissa sent her a bowl of poison, which she drank without hesitation.

Sorcière, La. Victorien Sardou (French). Drama. 5 acts. 1903.

Laid in Granada after its conquest by the Spaniards, the plot concerns that struggle for individual freedom in which truth crushed to earth will rise again. It is the old fight between knowledge and ignorance, religion versus country, etc.

Sothern, Edward Askew (1826-1881). English actor. Father of Edward Hugh Sothern. In 1852 he played in the United States under the name of Douglas Stewart; became a member of Wallack's New York company in 1854; rose to fame as Lord Dundreary in *Our American Cousin,* which part he was playing in Washington on the night of Lincoln's assassination. Also was prominent in *David Garrick* and *Brother Sam.*

Sothern, Edward Hugh (1859-1933). Anglo-American actor, manager. Born in London, he was the elder son of Edward Askew Sothern, the famous English actor, and brother of George Evelyn ("Sam"), a popular London actor. Edward began his stage career as a farcical comedian, but turned to romantic drama in Hauptmann's *The Sunken Bell* and McCarthy's *If I Were King.* He made a great reputation in the United States and was known as the leading American Shakespearean actor. He formed his own company in 1899, playing for the most part Shakespearean dramas. In 1911 he married Julia Marlowe and scored tremendous popularity with her as his leading lady.

Sotie. A medieval (15th century) French comedy of manners coming halfway between the farce and the morality play and performed by a society of *sots,* or fools.

This type was largely satirical and usually treated of typical French persons or events of the period.

Soubrette. Name given to a minor female part in comedies, whose characterization calls for pertness, coyness, coquetry, intrigue, etc.; frequently a showy part.

Sound Effects. Apparatus used during a performance to simulate actual sounds, such as: (1) Thunder—a sheet of tin that is shaken or beaten with a padded mallet; (2) Wind—slatted drum mounted on bearings is rotated toward the free end of a cloth which is fastened to a mounting frame, or strips of bamboo or umbrella ribs are fastened to the shift of a variable speed electric motor; (3) Hoof beats—cocoanut shells are struck together or against a flat surface, in rhythm; (4) Rain—a shallow metal plate containing dried peas or rice is rotated.

Southampton, Henry Wriothesley, 3rd Earl of (1573-1624). Patron of letters. Educated at Cambridge, his main interest was in drama. He was the patron of Shakespeare, as well as of Thomas Nashe and others. He was the friend of Essex and was involved in his political plots.
See also *The Essex Rebellion; Wriothesley, Henry.*

Southerne, Thomas (1659-1746). British dramatist. Born near Dublin. His two best-known plays are *The Fatal Marriage,* 1694 and *Oroonoko,* 1696. Both were the first plays to treat a slave sympathetically.

Southwark Theatre. A playhouse in Philadelphia, constructed by David Douglass in 1766, the lower part of which was of brick and the upper of wood. It was painted red. Plain oil lamps without glasses lighted the stage and large wooden pillars supporting the balcony and roof hid the view. The best actors in the colonies played here. The first performance of *King John* in America was given in this theatre. To gain larger audiences, fireworks were displayed on the stage.

Sowerby, Katherine Ghita. English dramatist, publisher. Her plays include: *Rutherford and Son,* 1912; *Before Breakfast,* 1912; *Jinny,* 1914; *A Man and Some Women,* 1914; *Sheila,* 1917; *The Stepmother,* 1924. She has also written several children's books with her sister but her main interest remains the Drama. *Rutherford and Son* is her most forceful and important play. The play significantly sums up the exacting penalty of ambition and industrial one-mindedness.

Space stage. A method of staging plays with lights focused on actors so that no setting is seen.

Spanish Tragedy, The. Thomas Kyd (English). Tragedy in Blank Verse. 1592.
The background is the victory of Spain over Portugal in 1580. The play adapted Senecan tragedy for the English theatre and gave a powerful impetus to the develop-

ment of Shakespearean tragedy. Bel-imperia is being wooed by Balthazar, captive from Portugal. The King of Spain, and her brother Lorenzo approve of the match largely for political reasons. She however, loves Horatio, son of Hieronimo, marshal of Spain. Balthazar and Lorenzo find them making love and they hang Horatio. Hieronimo finds his son murdered and swear vengeance. He coaxes them to act in a play he has written. In the course of the play Lorenzo and Balthazar are killed, Bel-imperia kills herself and Hieronimo finally takes his own life.

Spectacula. Early Roman theatrical shows.

Spelvin, George (1907-   ). Mythical American actor who first appeared in Winchell Smith's and Frederic Thompson's play, *Brewster's Millions,* in 1907, when a minor actor doubled in the cast, taking one role under his own name and the other as George Spelvin. Since the critics complimented the Spelvin part, and *Brewster's Millions* proved a great success, Winchell Smith had continued to have in his subsequent productions, a George Spelvin for luck. The legend of this versatile actor grows with time, as more and more actors perform under his name and invent exploits for him.

His christening has been latterly attributed to various persons, including William Gillette, William Collier, Sr., and William Seymour.

Harry Selby is another pseudonym used for an actor who doubles in a part; invented by George Haight and H. C. Potter.

Spender, Stephen (1909-   ). English dramatist, poet. Educated at Oxford. He is associated in the general mind with the poets, W. H. Auden and C. Day Lewis and is the author of the verse-play *The Trial of a Judge,* 1938.

Spewack, Bella and Sam (1900-   ). American playwrights. Samuel Spewack was born in Russia and Bella Spewack in Hungary. They both started their careers as journalists. She was press agent for *The Miracle* and *Chauve Souris.* The first play they collaborated on was *The Solitary Man,* 1926. This was followed by *The War Song,* 1928; *Clear All Wires,* 1928; *Spring Song,* 1934. Writing scenarios in Hollywood gave them inspiration for their most successful play, *Boy Meets Girl,* 1935, which created a sensation on Broadway. Since then they have written *Leave It To Me,* 1938; *Miss Swan Expects,* 1939.

Spider, The. Fulton Oursler and Lowell Brentano (American). Melodrama. 3 acts. 1927.

During a magician's performance in a theatre a spectator is shot and suspicion rests upon the performing magician. He is seized by the police, but slips out of the handcuffs. Shots are fired, strange voices are heard, and the house lights go out several times. Finally the magician finds the murderer sitting in the audience.

Spill. Space where scenery fails to connect, permitting natural light to leak through.

Spirit gum. A liquid preparation containing gum arabic and alcohol or ether, used to fasten on crepe hair, whiskers, etc.
See *Make-up*.

Split-stage. A device used in taking dual role pictures or double exposures; also in a play where simultaneous action takes places in two unrelated sections of the stage. Examples are *Gloriana, Dynamo, She Loves Me Not.*

Split-week. A half-week engagement.

Spoken verses. Short conversations in verse between the leader and his fellow performers in the ancient Greek *dithyramb,* said to have been introduced by Arion of Methyma.

Spot. A spotlight used on the stage or in taking films.

Spot (television). The visible point of light caused by the contact of the electron beam with the fluorescent screen in a receiving tube. The smaller the spot, the finer the detail. Also used in reference to the camera tube.

Spotlighting. Stage lighting by a series of spots fixed on a movable stand and fitted with a reflector, used to throw a strong light upon any given place on the stage or on a performer.

Spring Song. Bella and Samuel Spewack (American). Drama. 3 acts. 1934.
Florrie Solomon, because her own young man is away, finds consolation in her sister's fiance, a studious young man named Sidney. He follows where Florrie leads which is to a seduction. Florrie becomes pregnant and cultivates a dislike for Sidney, but Mrs. Solomon insists she marry him. Florrie dies in childbirth.

Springtime for Henry. Benn W. Levy (English). Comedy. 3 acts. 1931.
Henry Dewlip, after long conditioning with many secretaries, is charmed to find that his latest one, Miss Smith, is apparently an innocent. Henry is disillusioned, however, when Miss Smith tells him the story of her life, and he decides to turn her over to his best friend, Mr. Jelliwell. In exchange, Henry receives Mrs. Jelliwell.

Spy, The. Henry Kistemaeckers (Belgian). Drama. 3 acts. 1912.
Treats the case of a patriotic murderer defended by his wife, hitherto his enemy.
A colonel who has sought financial aid from a foreign banker, rejects with scorn the latter's proposal that he hand over plans of a fortification. Then he confides to his wife. Although she had been about to divorce him in order to marry another, his need awakens her protective love.

Squaring the Circle. Valentin Kataev (Russian). Comedy. 3 acts. 1928.
Two Moscow youths, living in a communal lodging, partition their room and get married. The ardent communist finds he has married a home-loving person,

while the quiet youth discovers his wife is a career girl. They solve the problem by exchanging wives.

Squirrel's Cage, The. Tyrone Guthrie (English). Drama. 3 acts. 1931.

The futility of civilized life which runs in circles is expressed by the squirrel's cage, which moves round and round like a treadmill; the sun going round and round the sky; human life consisting of an everlasting daily round. Office life is a series of little circles endlessly repeated. The hero of the play makes one attempt to break away from the squirrel's-cage existence, but he is defeated by parental authority.

S. R. O. Standing room only.

S.S. Glencairn. Eugene O'Neill (American). 1924.

Cycle of four one-act plays of the sea of which O'Neill had first hand experience. The plays are vital and original in pattern. *The Moon of the Caribees* takes place in the West Indies in 1913. From this play emerges the germ of the later *Hairy Ape*. (2) *The Long Voyage Home* is about poor "Swede," all set for home and mother. He takes one last drink, is drugged and shanghaied. It will be a long time if ever before he reaches home.

(3) *In The Zone*—Forecastle of the S.S. Glencairn during the war. The crew, crazed with fear over possible bombing finally finds a suspiciously acting member of the crew, take his black box which he has been hiding furtively and find it contains love letters of a love that is no more.

The fourth is *Bound East for Cardiff*. All four plays have an intermingling of the same characters and were meant to be played on the same program.

S.S. Tenacity. Charles Vildrac (French). Drama. 3 acts. 1920.

Two former soldiers preparing to seek their fortunes in Canada are detained at a French port while their vessel is being repaired. Both fall in love with a pretty waitress at the inn. The more assertive of the two, who has planned the journey, elopes with her because his dreamy friend lacks the decision to carry her off.

Staatsaktion. The name given to 18th century German productions with magnificent scenery; the same as "gala performance."

Stage. The entire floor space behind the proscenium arch in a theatre which represents the area reserved for performances of plays.

See also *Alto del teatro; Apron stage; Bare stage; Jack-knife stage; Picture-frame stage.*

Stage, The (American). Theatrical publication (monthly). Began as a house organ of the Theatre Guild as the *Theatre Guild Bulletin*. Later known as *Theatre Guild Quarterly* and in 1928 became *Theatre Guild Magazine*. Known as *The Stage* since 1932. Ceased publication in 1939.

Stage, The (London). Published weekly in London, 15 York Street, Covent Garden, W.C.2. A theatrical trade paper devoted to the English stage.

Stage, directions. Instructions in the script of a play concerning all movements and arrangements on the acting platform during a performance. It was George Bernard Shaw who fostered the fashion of writing long, detailed, even chatty stage directions for plays in book form. Typical of stage directions were once such hieroglyphics as "R.1E," "R.2E," "RC.," "LU.E.," and "L.C." These letters and numbers represented positions on the stage having to do with the wings and places of entrance. Their use is now, however, outmoded, confined, as William Archer says, *"to French's Acting Edition.* The only rational course is to state the position of your doors in your opening stage directions, and thereafter to say in plain language by which door an entrance or an exit is to be made."

Stage, Elizabethan. The Elizabethan stage was normally composed of three units: the outer stage was the main platform where the action took place; behind it was a smaller recess, the inner stage, where chamber scenes were acted; above the inner stage was the upper stage or gallery, a platform fronted by a balcony. This latter was the "above" in stage directions of Elizabethan plays, the tower of battle scenes, the balcony of comic and romantic scenes. Two heavy columns framed the outer stage and supported a canopy-like roof over the whole.

Stage, floors. Flooring for the stage is commonly accepted as cedar—sometimes Oregon pine—except the apron of maple. One prominent manager used maple successfully to floor his ninety stages.

See *Ideas for Theatre Stages,* by Dariel Fitzkee, technical engineer, in *The Architect and Engineer,* August, 1926, pp. 81-91.

Stage cable. A flexible twin conductor (electric wire) used to connect the various stage lights to the switchboard. The common size for stage use is No. 14 wire which safely carries fifteen amperes or about fifteen hundred watts.

Stage call. A meeting of the cast and director on stage to discuss problems before a performance or rehearsal; also the "call" to actors notifying them of the passage of time before the curtain rises for a performance, usually beginning one-half hour before actual curtain time and given again at fifteen and five minutes.

Stage carpenter. Chief stage hand and responsible for handling scenery on the stage, as well as for all minor repairs.

Stagecraft. Term for general theatrical technique, whether it concerns a dramatist's style of presentation, an artist's scenic effects, an actor's skill in histrionic projection, a director's management of cast or, generally, a producer's handling of his problems.

Stage door. The street (or alley) entrance to the backstage of a theatre.

Stage Door. Edna Ferber and George S. Kaufman (American). Drama. 3 acts. 1936.

The story of Terry Randall who remains loyal to the theatre, enduring a variety of hardships in order to learn her craft, and who finally gets a real part, which will establish her as an actress. Other theatre types at the Footlights Club, where the play is set, include Jean Maitland, who goes to Hollywood before she learns to act and Keith Burgess, the left-wing playwright, who loses his ideology.

Stage door Johnny. Almost obsolete term for admirers of actresses and chorus girls who sent mash notes backstage and then waited at the stage door for a rendezvous or a turndown.

Stage manager. The one person backstage in complete charge of the production and its performances, once the play has opened.

Stage manager's board. Prompter's table used for light cues.

Stage picture (stage grouping). The visual effect of grouping and placing actors on the stage. Directors try to vary stage pictures and groupings by plans or movements and crossings that will result in breaking up old groups and forming new ones for variety and holding the attention of the audience. Certain groupings are used to focus a character whose action is called for in the play script.

Stage Society (London). An organization founded in 1899 for the purpose of presenting plays of unusual literary merit which would not otherwise be likely to be chosen for production. Many of these were later given commercial presentation. The performances, usually on Sunday nights, were private and so circumvented the delicate sensibilities of the official British censor, the Lord Chamberlain. Among dramatists whose plays received first performances under the aegis of the Stage Society were, George Bernard Shaw, Anatole France, Ashley Dukes, Henrik Ibsen, Maurice Maeterlinck, Gerhart Hauptmann, etc.

Stage staff. Consists of: stage carpenter, who plans the rigging and handling of scenery on stage; property master, who secures and is responsible for upkeep, and plans the handling of stage properties; scene technician, who is responsible for the work of mounting the scenery for a production; crew head, who is in charge of direction and supervision of the work of the whole crew; costume and scene designers, who design the wardrobe and scenes of a play. Others include: technical director; business manager; paint crew; wardrobe mistress; electrician and crew; prop master and crew; stage carpenter and crew.

Stage struck. Like gambling, drink and narcotics, the passion to become an actor can take such a hold on an individual that he becomes a wreck and dissipates an entire life trying to prove himself an actor when often he does not have the necessary ability. Usually such a person cannot be convinced of the futility of his aspirations. He continues a hanger-on, clutters up managers' offices, pathetic, older and poorer, incurable.

Stage superstitions. Actors as a whole are extremely superstitious. Many of them have pet superstitions which are peculiar to them alone. Jack Pearl carries a pocketful of coins and good-luck pieces, and should any one touch his ear he would run pathetically after the offender until he had touched his ear in return. Other superstitions include: it is bad luck to whistle in a dressing room; wearing old shoes that were associated with a hit is good luck; before a performance actors never wish each other good luck, but say "I hope you break a leg"; it is bad luck to use an old rabbit's foot for a new make-up; a cat backstage is good luck; on opening nights, telegrams should be read after the performance.

Stage wait. An unexpected delay in the play's action caused by an actor's forgetting his lines, a misplaced property, a late entrance by a member of the company, etc. Usually less than a minute, almost unnoticed by the audience but an eternity to the cast.

Stage whisper. A technical term and a stage convention in which one actor whispers loud enough for the entire audience to hear, but on stage it is heard by only one or by a few intended other actors and is understood not to be overheard by any others, no matter how many people are on stage.

Stagehands. Men employed in any capacity backstage. Their main duty is to set and "strike" (i.e., break up and carry off) scenery and furniture and to operate the curtain. Others are required to work effects and noises offstage.
See also *Stage, carpenter.*

Staging, American, 19th century. Among the more progressive innovators of staging ideas in the American theatre during the 19th century was Charles Fechter, the famous French actor who became manager of the Lyceum Theatre. It was he who abolished the ancient grooves, trapdoors and flats by means of which scenery was raised and lowered while shifting was managed on the mezzanine stage beneath. It was also due to him that ceilings came no longer to be represented by hanging cloths, or walls by open wings, but were both solidly built. All this was after 1870, which was the year when Fechter arrived in America. Steele Mackaye was another manager who introduced new ideas. When he became manager of the Madison Square Theatre in 1879 he inaugurated the double stage, which facilitated the setting of one scene while another was being acted.

Staging, American, 20th century. The 20th century brought the development of a group of native scene designers and directors whose close collaboration and high artistic integrity have raised the level of stage production in this country to compare favorably with that of any of the leading theatres in Europe.
With the coming of the scenic artist, the two-dimensional painted set gave way to the use of plastic pieces. Depth was suggested by planes rather than by painted perspectives. Light had a two-fold purpose; to model the actor and emphasize the

areas in which he moves, as well as to paint the setting, define its form and sustain its mood, and dramatize its meaning. Spotlights of various sizes and projection lanterns became the essential equipment of every theatre. Mechanical devices; the cyclorama, the plaster dome, the revolving stage or small wagon stages came into use in both professional and non-professional theatres.

The American directors have individual styles of direction that add freshness and variety to the native stage. The styles range from the painstaking detail of the late Belasco's direction to the imaginative approach of Hopkins who believes there is a subconscious communication between the actor and the audience. He bases this on the theory that "complete illusion has to do entirely with the unconscious mind. Except in the case of certain intellectual plays the theatre is wholly concerned with the unconscious mind of the audience. The conscious mind should play no part." When Jones designed the setting for Hopkins' production of *Macbeth,* 1921 (starring Lionel Barrymore), he visualized the unconscious force of the witches by placing in the darkness high above the heath huge masks that appeared in vague outline.

McClintic possesses a keen visual sense that causes him to see a play with a painter's eye in terms of color, form and design. For this reason he works in closer association with his designer, usually Mielziner, and often has a clear mental image of the setting he wishes executed.

Kaufman, Abbott and Cohan are the masters of tempo. Each possesses a keen sense of the theatre as well as great industry with detail. The latter is a strong characteristic of Oenslager whom Kaufman chose to design the setting for *You Can't Take It With You, The Fabulous Invalid,* etc.

The two Guild directors, Moeller and Windust, work in close association with Simonson, who believes "the design of a setting depends upon the acting that fills it." Both sensitivity and pace are characteristics of the direction of Jed Harris, who chose to collaborate with Oenslager in the staging of *A Doll's House.*

Margaret Webster brought her collaborator, Ffoulkes, from the Old Vic in London to achieve unusual ensemble effects in her Shakespearean productions. Orson Welles both conceived and staged the streamlined version of *Julius Caesar.* Norman Bel Geddes also believes the art of design and the art of direction are inextricably part of one scenic pattern. In his production of *Hamlet,* in 1931 (starring Raymond Massey), Geddes prepared the promptbook first, then developed the detail of the stage design to suit the action of the play. It was considered somewhat the fault of his theory that an early closing of the production was necessary. In the case, however, of one of his later productions, Kingsley's *Dead End,* his scenery influenced the success of the play to such an extent that it precipitated a discussion as to who was responsible for the immediate hit—the scenic artist or the playwright.

Under any circumstances the interdependence of designer and director, no matter what the procedure or the results, is difficult to approximate.

Lee Simonson, in his *The Stage is Set,* sums up the theory of scenery as follows: "The incentive to design has been primarily the necessity of making the world of the play as real to the audience as it was to the playwright. The scene designer has been enlisted as part of the job of 'putting the play over,' of creating backgrounds that made seeing believing."

Staging, Bulgarian, since the First World War. Massalitinov, also a director and scenic artist as well as teacher of acting, has maintained a flexible style of setting, suitable to all types of play while retaining its fixed psychologically artistic basis. Tsankoff, influenced by Reinhardt, tends more to the side of sharp expressiveness. David, now no longer in Bulgaria, showed a varied talent, ranging from constructivism to farcical fantasy.

Staging, Chinese. In the playhouses, the stage projects into the audience and the performance is seen from three sides. In the West, "the play's the thing," but in China, "the actor's the thing," for the actor, with his magnificent robes and grand gestures, transforms the stage into whatever he wishes it to be. The realistic settings and stage scenery of Western drama leave little to the imagination. In China, painted banners carried over the stage may represent water. Some cloth attached to two bamboos are held up by two men, and the cloth, being divided in the middle, is drawn up to the sides to allow for the passage of the actors.

The nearest approach to the curtain of Western parlance is the flowing sleeve of the principal actor held before his face as he gives a short summary of or prologue to the play that follows. A change of scene or act is indicated by the entire cast moving about the stage. The usual Chinese play has four acts.

The stage has nothing on it but a few tables and chairs which serve for almost anything. The two doors at the back of the stage are called "Spirit Doors"—the entrance is made through the door on the right facing the audience and the exit through the left. As one actor exits another enters. In the center at the back of the stage stands a large mirror which actors often use in changing costumes on stage; they simply turn their backs to the audience and the property men bring them the required garments and take away those they discard. Properties are brought on stage by the property men and handed to the actors or placed about while the action is going on.

Although the scenery is left to the imagination, the costumes of the Chinese drama are essential components of it. The designing of costumes is a highly creative art and the garments are a complete picture gallery in themselves. Most of the costumes used are in the styles of the Han, T'ang, Sung and Ming dynasties. They are created of excellent material and wear so well that a wardrobe may not need replenishing for generations. For actors too poor to own their own wardrobes, establishments exist which rent out costumes by the season. But the costumes must be authentic or exact replicas from the models of the period they serve, down to the last dragon or pheasant symbol, for tradition is the strongest of all rulers.

Chinese theatrical music, loud and cacophanous, is far from the best of China's music, which is soft, sustained, gentle and subtly melodious. Most of the instruments used in modern plays are not of Chinese origin but Mongolian, brought into China during the Yuan dynasty by the Mongols (1280-1368). Thus the Western conception of Chinese music is based on this foreign importation.

Chinese music is almost entirely limited to melody (no true harmony) and conforms largely to a pentatonic scale with five tones and twelve semitones. Rhythm is almost exclusively in duple time. Music for stage purposes is classed under: (1)

Hsi-p'i, rather loud, sharp and shrill music of the Civil and Military plays; (2) *Êrh-huang,* softer and more melodious than *Hsi-p'i* and not pitched in so high a key; (3) *Pang-tzŭ,* cruder and more colloquial than the preceding—excellent time is kept by striking the *pang-tzŭ* (an instrument consisting of two pieces of wood); (4) *K'un-ch'ü,* ancient and scholarly music especially for the recreation of the leisured classes—slow, elegant and plaintive music.

Chinese music is appreciated only intellectually.

See also *Acting, Chinese; Drama, Chinese.*

Staging, English, Elizabethan. There was little or no scenery in Elizabethan public playhouses, but much spectacle, in the form of processions, machines for the ascent and descent of gods, fireworks, sound effects, and the like. There were no women actors; female roles were played by boys. The main action took place on the outer stage which was uncurtained. Locality was seldom indicated; the context of the play itself carried whatever details of setting were necessary. The inner stage was used for restricted localities and properties, for discoveries and tableaux, and to indicate, by a shift from the outer stage, change of scene. The upper stage was employed for tower or balcony scenes. Act and scene divisions were indicated by dumbshows or choruses, but were seldom realized as actual breaks in the movement of the play. During this epoch two types of settings were used, both descendants from the previous medieval tradition: (1) the bare stage backed only by drop; (2) the stage set with "mansions." Accuracy (historically or geographically) of costume and preciseness of locality in a play were of such small consequence to the Elizabethan audiences that conventions were extremely loose. People or objects on the stage could be made "invisible" by a word from the actor. Throughout the period scenery developed from the *décor simultané* through the permanent Serlian type to, about 1633, actual change of set.

Staging, English, Restoration. Settings were prevailingly and increasingly spectacular and elaborate to please the superficial tastes of the Restoration audience; scenery was first used in 1662 by D'Avenant who derived the idea from the French; a "traverse," or a pair of curtains running on a rod, was frequently used in place of a flat for a quickscene; complicated and expensive machinery was used to heighten the realistic effects, such as rain, fire, storms, hail, thunder, scenes of magic, etc. During the afternoon, the customary time for performances, the theatre was not artificially lighted; no footlights existed; the stage was illuminated from above by branches or hoops of candles lowered from the ceiling; the inner stage was equipped with better lighting facilities than the outer, resulting in a minimized importance of the latter.

Staging, English, 18th century. Scenery during this period began to grow in realism—a realism of verisimilitude and detail rather than of idea—called in a later theatre "naturalistic." Augustan settings of palaces, gardens, prisons and temples were the fashion. Foreign scenic designers were largely employed, but the theatre had two outstanding English craftsmen in Harvey and Lambert. Sets originally built for a special production were used many times over for other works. Flats were used to a great extent as well as the usual drops. But box sets of three dimensions came more and more in favor as well as the more complex build-up sets which could be made to collapse onstage. For even more elaborate settings machines were used. Lighting became even more of a problem with the enlarging of the playhouses, which made for "dead spots" in the auditorium where a spectator some-times could neither see nor hear. The stage up to 1750 was lighted in three ways: (1) by footlights, which had appeared as early as 1673; (2) by branches or hoops of candles in front of the proscenium doors; (3) by rings of candles suspended over the stage. In 1765 Garrick introduced side lighting.

Staging, English, 19th-20th centuries. That scenery was the feature of the 19th century theatrical production is evidenced by Charles Kean's use of a printed "Programme of Scenery" describing in detail the sequence of settings. The spectators demanded scenery that duplicated reality. Romantic realism gave way early in the century to a variety which was often represented by solidly built structures rather than flats. Stage effects and offstage sounds were used in abundance.

Toward the close of the 19th century the theory of the plastic stage, in which scenery is made to serve the emotional content of the play, proved of interest to those who questioned the value of the realistic scene design. However Gordon Craig was the only individual who came out in active revolt against the flat and shallow artificiality of the accepted mode of design on the English stage. He experimented with curtains for walls, with folding screens and platforms, then finally with masses of light and shadow, in an attempt to bring simplicity and dignity into scenic design. However, Craig influenced the foreign theatres more than his own and up to the present day the commercial theatre in England has not ventured very far away from realism.

Staging, French (Early). The French *metteur-en-scène* (director) of the medieval drama leaned heavily on realism which held true up to the 16th century. Lee Simonson in his *The Stage Is Set* gives a highly stimulating account of several performances. It was a period of rich costumes and scenery, elaborate stage machinery. Stage lighting was also attempted at Mons, 1501, one of the earliest instances known.

Staging, French, 16th and 17th century. See *Hôtel de Bourgogne.*

Staging, German, medieval. After the Reformation in Germany theatrical performances were withdrawn from the public streets and confined within the walls of a church, convent, or inn yard. Plays were given twice a week. For the first time in the German theatre stage directions were explicit, Hans Sachs indicating them with utmost precision. Actors were tradesmen and artisans who took up the art as a pastime.

Staging, German, 18th century. The scenery of the 1700's was generally mediocre. Three sets—a wood, a hall and a cottage—were considered sufficient for the average production. The Weimar Court Theatre, under Goethe in 1791, had loose wings and back cloths for the representation of rooms or outdoor scenes and used no furniture. Moreover, both costumes and actors were poor. Goethe managed this theatre for twenty-six years, altering it completely as to scenery and scenic effects. Mob scenes, especially, under his tutelage, were greatly heightened and improved. With such progress as these steps connoted, the Weimar Court Theatre eventually became the first theatre in the country. Goethe's influence on staging in general took the form of pictorial illustration, new arrangements of players on the stage and new attention to costuming.

Staging, German, 19th Century. Following Goethe's reign at Weimar, a Romanticist school came into being, although both Goethe and Schiller had balanced Romanticism with their Classicism. Ludwig Tieck, director at Dresden, reformed the style of acting and improved the diction of his actors, teaching them to read lines with proper breaking up and pauses. In contrast he was retrogressive in his stagecraft. Disliking realistic treatment of historic costume, he set down strict rules for dressing a character which were as hidebound as the very realistic approach which he tried to avoid.

Four men are responsible for an awakening of scenic and staging techniques which derive from the play, from the actors appearing in it, as well as from the stage picture. These are Richard Wagner (his contribution is admirably treated in volume five of Dubech's *Histoire Génerale du Théâtre*), George II, Duke of Saxe-Meiningen, Adolphe Wildbrandt and the Swiss Adolphe Appia. Of these Saxe-Meiningen, who was concerned with the dramatic influence of scenery, and Appia, who made the first important use of light as a sculptural quality and a component part of the setting, had the greatest influence on the technique of German staging.

Staging, German, since the First World War and before National Socialism. Settings, through the boldness and enterprise of Reinhardt, showed tremendous progress; the influence of Gordon Craig was powerful; *mise-en-scène* was not simply an imitation of reality but intrinsically a thing of beauty and a value in itself, while serving as a background for dramatic action.

Staging, Greek. See *Drama, Greek; Theatre, Greek.*

Staging, Italian, commedia dell' arte. Used by the *commedia dell' arte* strolling players; the booth or platform stage was backed with curtains which bore rude painted representations of houses with spaces between. These were often drawn with charcoal. When wings came into being, the houses were represented by the front flats with others indicated farther back, which left actors free on the stage center and down front. On outdoor stages all scenery was painted or drawn on curtains behind the acting space.

Staging, Italian, 18th century. *Wings,* now a definite factor in the *mise-en-scène,* once set oblique, soon found their modern position parallel to the stage-front. See also specific architects or scenic artists.

Staging, Italian, 19th and 20th century. A glance into the methods of staging in the 19th century Italian theatre gives evidence of a lack of experimentation, fear of change, and demand of both critics and public to hold to tradition. The century brought no discovery of the need for director-producers. Craig's prophecies, spoken and written from Italy, were not reflected on the stage.

The Italian theatre was under the spell of the great acting of Salvini, Ristori and Duse. No influence from Reinhardt or Copeau could displace the actor-manager system which had, in the hands of second and third-rate actors, brought the physical stage to a deplorable and stagnant state. Performances lacked all unity. Companies became a conglomerate group of individual actors, each interpreting his part in his own fashion. It was a common thing for a company to appear before the public after only one complete rehearsal.

The awakening felt in France, Germany, Russia and England at the close of the century gained sufficient momentum in Italy to bring about the founding of the Roman Art Theatre thirty-five years (1925) after the founding of Antoine's theatre. Even at that date the value of the reforms in staging were questioned by the critic Martini with the warning, "We hope the new resources of staging will not lead the writers of the morrow to desert more humble forms of writing." The critics of the 19th century were even more conservative in holding to traditional methods of staging.

Staging, Hindu. See *Drama, Hindu.*

Staging, Japanese. The *Nō* drama is performed on a wooden stage, eighteen feet square, open on three sides, with a narrow extension in one side for the singers or chorus and another at the back of the stage for musicians and the prompter. The stage is covered with a roof of its own which is shaped like the pointed roof of a Japanese temple. This roof is supported by four pillars, each with its own name and special usage. The First Actor's Pillar (*Shite-bashira*), is used by the *Shite* when he enters from the bridge and stands by it when beginning his performance. The one in front of it is called the Mark Pillar (*Metsuke-bashira*), and is used as a mark for the actor while performing. Diagonally opposite the First Actor's Pillar is the Second Actor's Pillar (*Waki-bashira*), to which the *Waki* withdraws when he finishes his part. The last pillar is called the Flute Player's Pillar (*Fue-bashira*), because the flute player sits by it.

Leading diagonally into the backstage, and used by actors and musicians for exits and entrances, is an open corridor with a railing on both sides called the bridge (*Hashi-gakari*). At the farthest end of the bridge hangs a curtain of five colors lifted by two bamboo sticks by the actor when entering the bridge from the *greenroom* or when exiting after his performance. In front of the bridge, there are three potted pine trees called First, Second and Third pine tree (*Ichi-no-matsu, Ni-no-matsu, San-no-matsu*) ; these symbolize heaven, earth and humanity, and are used as a means of marking position when an actor is playing on the bridge. Behind the curtain of the bridge is a *greenroom* or *mirror-room* (*Kagami-no-ma*). A large mirror for the use of actors hangs in this room, and each actor, musician and member of the Chorus has a space allotted to him.

Performances of the *Nō* drama are part of the theatre and audience because of the structure of the stage which projects into the auditorium; a pebble path separates the stage from the auditors and a staircase descends from the stage. This staircase is never used today.

The box facing the stage is the seat of honor reserved for the use of the Emperor and Empress. Since persons of high rank sit facing south, the stage faces north.

Before a play begins in the *Nō* theatre, three or four musicians enter: a flute player, a shoulder-drum player, a knee-drum player and a flat-drum player. They take their places on the backstage. Shoulder and knee-drum players sit on stools; the flat-drum player and flute player sit on the floor.

On a curtain or wall at the back of the stage is painted a spreading pine tree, a symbol of faithful endurance. On the panel at the farther end of the bridge are painted a few bamboos; at the lower end of this panel is a small side-door called the Hurry-door (*Kiri-do*) or the Coward's door (*Okubyo-guchi*). The Hurry-door is used by actors who have been killed and by Chorus, Prompter and Clown as an exit.

A formal *Nō* play consists of two scenes. The First Actor enters as an ordinary man in the fore scene and in the after scene assumes his true form. Usually the dance (*Mai*) by the First Actor becomes the center of interest and is generally performed in the second scene, with the Chorus singing the important *Kuse* (theme song).

The setting of *Nō* dramas is imaginative except for ornamental properties which are only used when necessary. Change of scene is freely made by changes in the position of the actors.

Symbolism or impressionism is also the keynote of all scenery in the *Kabuki* drama. When a black curtain is used in the background, it symbolizes the darkness of night. When at the right and left two-fold screens made of bamboo are used, they represent a bamboo grove. A sea is symbolized by a board on which waves are painted; sometimes the designer paints a wave pattern extending along the walls around the entire theatre, a device which serves to draw the audience into the heart and spirit of the play.

When a *Kabuki* play is about to begin it is announced by rapping with a wooden hammer. Very often, attendants with long torches illuminate the faces of the actors while they are speaking their parts. The assistant stage manager sits on one side of the stage in full view of the audience; one of his functions is to sound the wooden clappers when attention is to be drawn to the elaborate and artistic posing or *Mie* of an actor.

One of the peculiarities of the *Kabuki* playhouse is the *Hanamichi* or *flower path* which is a projection or runway into the auditorium and used by the actors when representing someone starting or returning from a journey. Sometimes there are two Hanamichi, each projecting from a point near a corner of the stage. The main stage, resting on rollers, can be turned around, actors and all, when a change of scene is desired. This first evidence of the use of a revolving stage (*Mawari-butai*) is attributed to the inventive playwright Syozo Namiki who lived about two hundred years ago. This man is also credited with the invention of the *Serisage,* a device used by actors to ascend from below stage or to disappear from the stage to the sub-stage.

In performances of the *Kabuki* drama, the Western curtain is used. It is called *Maku,* is made of simple-patterned cotton and when used is pulled aside, not up and down. The *Maku* is usually striped with thick bands of green, reddish-brown and black. The *Ki* (wooden clappers) accompany the pulling on and off of the curtain. The *Ki* are used by the assistant stage manager to punctuate the beginning, end and intervals of a play.

Among the more popular musical instruments used in the *Kabuki* theatre are:

Koto—an instrument of four to five and one-half feet long having seven waxed silk strings stretched over a sounding board of hard wood. The *Koto* is placed flat on the ground and played with ivory finger-tips on the right hand while the left attends to the fingering of the strings.

Gekkin—also known as the moon-guitar. It has four strings and resembles a guitar with a circular sounding board and a short neck.

Samisen—three strings. The national instrument of the women, is not unlike a banjo, and played with a large plectrum.

Kokyu—a two-stringed instrument resembling a violin because it is played with a bow, but it is held upright while being played.

At certain Shinto festivals of great sanctity, both string and wind instruments are played in silence. Such a concert should prove very popular with Europeans who have attested frequently to the agonizing sounds produced by Japanese instruments. The combination of discords and ear-piercing tones of singers and musical instruments is enough to drive the foreigner out of the place, and usually does.

See also *Acting, Japanese; Drama, Japanese; Kabuki Drama; Nō Drama; Theatres, Japanese.*

Staging, Korean. See *Drama, Korean.*

Staging, Polish, since the First World War. Scenery was marked by a reaction against merely pictorial painting. Pronaszko, who collaborated with Schiller, was the leader in this reaction. Frycz attacked shoddy pseudo-realism with a subtle accuracy of insight and observation. Drabik was an eclectic master with a flexible imagination and a tendency to all-inclusive monumentalism.

Staging, Roman. Performers in the ancient Roman theatre were customarily gathered, as slaves, into troupes by managers who could flog them or put them to death at will and on the slightest provocation. Acting, as a profession, was consequently despised. It was this popular contempt which contributed, among other factors, to the comparatively speedy decline of the Roman drama. It was an attitude toward the theatre that produced little permanent results for the staging of the future. The water pageant was the principal contribution of the Romans.

See also *Floating stages.*

Staging, Russian, 19th century to Revolution. The opposing production methods of Stanislavsky and Meyerhold were the leading theories of this period and greatly influenced "the new movement" in the modern theatre.

Stanislavsky's staging of Chekhov's *The Three Sisters* (see frontispiece of Bakshy's *Path of the Modern Russian Stage*) is one of the finest examples of the naturalistic method. Here is a setting which seems at first glance not of the theatre but from life itself. The room is broken up into a number of independent parts, with a view of other real rooms seen through the doors. This setting not only gives the complete illusion of reality but affords special advantages for variety in grouping. The furniture and properties are faithful reproductions. Stanislavsky has created the actual environment in which Chekhov's characters lived. His staging of *The Sea Gull* introduces selection into naturalistic staging. That is, he places above detail the emphasis upon the outstanding feature of Chekhov's play. He discovers the tone of the atmosphere is the key to the dialogue and continuity of action through which the flow of movements and words produce on the stage the monody Chekhov wrote into the play.

Meyerhold places in contradistinction to the naturalistic theatre the "theatre of conventions" which achieves variety through deft management of line, symbolism in grouping, and color blending in costumes. This gives the stage, according to Meyerhold, "a thousand times more motion than the naturalistic theatre. The motion on the stage is produced not by motion in the verbal sense of the word, but by a distribution of lines and colors, and by the artistic crossing and vibrating of these lines and colors."

The development of his method is illustrated in his two productions of Sologub's *Victory of Death*. In the 1907 production he used pillars of unpainted cloth and in centre stage, an enormous staircase. In 1914 he used in place of the steps, huge blocks towering over each other on which the actors were grouped as "pictures, both with regard to color and their arrangement in a frame." He uses the term "conventionalism" to indicate a subjective method of representation as opposed to the objectively realistic. He developed this idea into "stylization" by using in his staging, forms that connote the leading sentiment in the play. This meant exaggeration in form, mass, line and color. Finally he carried this to the extreme by developing it on a highly structural and mechanized basis, introducing "constructivism." He stripped the stage of all decoration, leaving only a skeleton structure of stairs or ramps, and platforms. These were held together by plain scaffolding and arranged to permit the running off of the play at its fullest theatrical intensity. This setting represents all of the scenes of the play simplified into one structural background.

The flat-surfaced two-dimensional painted set was awakened to new life by Bakst through his introduction of a kaleidoscopic quality of arrangement. His use of color brought glowing harmony and his fertility of invention fascinated an audience already schooled to exaggeration.

Staging, Russian, Since the Revolution. Stanislavsky's position in the theatre was temporarily overshadowed by political suspicions of his ideology, which disappeared when it was officially recognized that his influence on world theatre was enormous and that Russia benefited by the high regard in which he was held. His methods remained unchanged until his death in 1938. Meyerhold continued as the iconoclast of stage directors, daring brilliantly every Constructivist extreme, eventually arriving at the point beyond which he could not go. He then returned to a style more characteristic of his middle period. His extremes, called by many, fads, caused the official attitude to change towards him. He was deprived of his power and eventually imprisoned; a sad downfall for a brilliant producer, once the Soviet white hope in the theatre.

Tairov continued to function as the leading exponent of Western European and American drama and, to a lesser extent, of foreign producing methods. His integration of music in drama, together with his western predilections, have made his theatre a favorite with foreigners. In contrast, Vakhtangov, distinguished disciple of Stanislavsky, frequently derived from the Orient in his style of production. Though he died in 1922 after his famous production of Gozzi's *Turandot*, his directors and followers have endeavored to maintain his traditions. Zakhava, Simonov and the guest, Akimov, have been responsible for many highly imaginative productions, including *Debâcle, Yegor Bulitchev And Others,* and *Aristocrats*. This last play written by Pogodin was also produced by Okhlopkov, brilliant director of the Realistic Theatre, a staging which derived from both the Chinese and Japanese theatre.

Many other theatres function, encouraged and even financially stimulated by the State. Among them are the Theatre of the Revolution, founded by Meyerhold, with actors from Stanislavsky's company, who eventually declined to follow all of the younger man's innovations, which caused his departure from their ranks. Henriette Pascar, no longer in Russia, and Natalie Satz revolutionized the technique of plays for children by making their audience an integral part of the production.

Staging, Spanish, 16th century. In 16th century Spain planks stretched across trestles were used for a stage, and costumes consisted of shepherds' fleece coats. The orchestra consisted of an ancient guitarist who crooned popular ballads. There was no drop curtain; a momentary clearing of the stage indicated a change of scene, though not infrequently the dialogue indicated a change of scene. A raised partition at the back of the stage served to represent a house, wall, mountain, etc. In this was sunk an alcove, covered by a curtain, which when down represented a tableau. Sheets could be drawn when necessary to divide the stage. Forests were represented by either painted canvas or small trees set on the stage. In all there was little scenery and much appeal to the imagination. Little use of stage machinery was made until toward the middle of the 17th century, when Italian stage carpenters introduced many novelties. Little sense of local color existed, but costumes were exquisite.

Staging, Yugoslav, since the First World War. Futurism, expressionism, the theories of Gordon Craig have all been tried but without conspicuous success. There are, roughly, three groups of producers: (1) those who attempt to adapt modern methods to the romantic Yugoslav character; (2) those who lean to a philosophic fashion; (3) those who seek revolutionary means of expression.

Stallings, Laurence (1894-   ). American journalist, novelist, dramatist. Born in Macon, Georgia, he was educated at Georgetown University. He began writing for the Atlanta *Journal* in 1915, then became editor of a literary column, *The First*

Reader, for the New York *World.* Served as a captain of the 47th company, 3rd battalion, 5th Marines, during the First World War. He wrote *Plumes* (novel), 1924; and plays in collaboration with Maxwell Anderson, *What Price Glory?* 1924; *The Buccaneer,* 1925; *First Flight,* 1925; *Deep River,* 1926. He also wrote the scenarios for the motion pictures of *The Big Parade, Old Ironsides,* and *The First World War.*

Stalls. See *Orchestra.*

Stand-in (motion pictures). One who replaces a star or featured player on the set while the lights are being adjusted, and occasionally in long shots. He must be same height, build and coloring but not necessarily resemble the star in any other way.

Stanislavsky, Constantin (1863-1938). Russian actor, director. One of the greatest directors of the modern drama, the originator of the Stanislavsky method of acting. Basically he used real life as the model for everything, doing away with the artificiality of stage conventions.

Stanislavsky, whose French grandmother had been an actress, was born into the rich manufacturing class of Russia. As a child he went often to the theatre, and he, his brothers, sisters, and cousins were always getting up plays and operettas. After studying for the stage in Paris, he returned to Moscow in 1888, and organized his own group of semi-professional players. By the last decade of the 19th century, he became convinced that the general run of contemporary acting did not present life, but merely a set of cut and dried makeshifts. Accordingly, in partnership with Nemirovitch-Dantchenko, he formed the Moscow Art Theatre, in 1898. Begun as an experiment and a protest it was a great success. With the years, its influence spread far beyond Russia. Its influence in the United States dates from 1923, when Stanislavsky came with the Moscow Art Theatre to America. He remained the director of the theatre, as well as of The Operatic Studio and two other theatres, up to the time of his death.

See also *Moscow Art Theatre; Theatre, Russian, 19th century to the Revolution; Veritism.*

Star. The leading actor or actress of a play whose popularity has won for him, or her, the first, and dominant place of interest in any production, called "top billing," above the title of the play and the name of the dramatist; the star system first genuinely came into being in the days of the great and famous David Garrick about the middle of the 18th century.

Star dressing room. The dressing room reserved for the principal artist in a theatrical company. It often has a star painted on the door, the numeral "1" or some other special means of identification and is usually the dressing room nearest to the stage.

Star entrance. The first appearance of the leading actor in a play, usually following a build-up by the actors and authors by means of an exposition of the character and his importance to the furthering of the plot and co-relative with the element of time in the plot. Stars prefer and are directed at times to make solo stage entrances so that attention will be focused on them immediately. In modern drama such methods are becoming obsolete.

Star system. The custom of selling a play by exploiting a prominent actor whose name is a guarantee for good box-office business. The play is diminished in importance and less care is exercised in selecting and producing it. In production, consideration of the star takes precedence over dramatic considerations. As a system it is an evil, deleterious to the drama.

Star-Wagon, The. Maxwell Anderson (American). Drama. 3 acts. 1937.

Stephen Minch, an inventor, and Hans Wicks, his best friend, get on the Star-Wagon, a time machine, and go back to the past to live their lives over, rectifying all their mistakes, including marrying the right girls and getting on in business. When they find that they haven't made mistakes, and that their lives could have been much worse, they hurry for the time machine, and return to the present.

Stasima (or *chorika*). Part of ancient Greek drama, especially Old Comedy as expounded by Aeschylus; song by the chorus in which conclusions are drawn from the *epeisodia*.

State Theatre. A state endowed organization for the purpose of supplying cultural stimulus in the drama. This producing agency is usually located in a permanent building but may travel frequently to various cities of the country and to foreign countries, as the Duke of Saxe Meiningen's Company. A subsidy is set aside to support the producing schedule and the director is chosen as any other appointive governmental official. The theatre is enabled to give a repertory of the classics as well as experimental modern plays because the ordinary hazards of theatrical producing are removed. Some of the most famous of these state-owned theatres are the *Comédie-Française* and *Odéon* in Paris, the *Burgtheater* in Vienna, the *Staatstheater* in Berlin, the *Moscow Art Theatre* and the *Bolshoi* in Moscow, the *Kingliga Teatern* in Stockholm, the *Nemzeti Szinhaz* in Budapest. Neither England nor the United States possess a national theatre. A foundation, by private subscription, has been set up in London and a site purchased and named the *National Theatre,* but the war has interrupted all plans. Many people refer to the Federal Theatre project as a national theatre, which it was not. It was a relief organization set up on a federated basis with a national director. An act of Congress in 1935 set up the American National Theatre and Academy but no funds were provided to bring about the realization of a dream long held by responsible people in the theatre.

Stationers' Register. A register of Tudor-Stuart publications maintained by the Stationers' Company, an organization of London booksellers and publishers. Entry in the register secured copyright privileges for the publisher. Plays were not always entered, but several of Shakespeare's works were, and the Register is an important source of historical information on the dates and circumstances of publication of these plays.

Steele, Sir Richard (1672-1729). English. Born in Dublin of mixed English and Irish parentage, he was educated at the expense of a maternal uncle at the Charterhouse and at Christ Church and Magdalen College, Oxford. He made the acquaintance of his collaborator, Addison, at school, and the friendship continued during their university days. Steele left Oxford without a degree in 1694, and enlisting in the army, against his uncle's wishes, rose to the rank of captain. His first work, a poem on the death of the queen, made a favorable impression on his colonel, but he was better known for his gaiety than for his literary capabilities among his brother officers. It was to their great astonishment, therefore, that the somewhat dissipated young soldier's next publication was a pious manual, *The Christian Hero,* 1701.

The same year, Steele's first play, a comedy, *The Funeral; or, Grief à la Mode,* 1701, was produced. It was followed by *The Lying Lover,* 1703, and *The Tender Husband,* 1705. The consciously moral tone which characterized these plays was a welcome change after the licence of the Restoration dramatists, and foreshadowed the virtuous humor which was the chief characteristic of *The Tatler* and *Spectator* papers.

The turning point in Steele's life came in 1707, when he was appointed gazetteer to the government. His work in this connection suggested to him the possibility of publishing something on broader and more popular lines than the formal official *Gazette.* The result was *The Tatler,* the first number of which was published by Steele, under the name of Isaac Bickerstaff, April 12, 1709. Addison collaborated after the eighteenth number. In 1711, *The Spectator* was started, and in 1712, *The Guardian,* then *The Englishman* and *The Plebeian,* all short-lived.

In the meantime Steele had received favors such as a commissionership of stamps from the Whigs, and in 1713, he entered active politics as Whig M.P. for Stockbridge, Hampshire. A violent pamphlet issued by him, *The Crisis,* resulted in his expulsion from the House. In 1715, however, he re-entered Parliament, was knighted, and given the supervisorship of the Drury Lane actors. Steele made himself so obnoxious to the government over the Peerage Bill that he was deprived of the latter post, however, and lost the friendship of Addison. He was reinstated in 1721, but his financial difficulties were so acute, in spite of the success of his last and best play, *The Conscious Lovers,* 1722, that he had to retire to the country. He died at Carmarthen. Steele is one of the creators of the sentimental comedy which lived for so long a time in English and in American drama.

Steigerung. A technical term used to describe the growing tension necessary to the development of the second act.

Steinbeck, John Ernest (1901-   ). American novelist, dramatist. He was born in Salinas Valley, California, of German-Irish stock. In 1920 he decided to be a writer, came to New York and got a job as a reporter. He became discouraged and went back to be a watchman in the high Sierras until at last he got leisure to write.

His first three novels were *Cup of Gold, Pictures of Heaven,* and *To a God Unknown.* His fourth novel, *Tortilla Flat,* was his first successful one. That was dramatized by Jack Kirkland and produced in 1937. *In Dubious Battle* came next and *Of Mice and Men* followed and was found to need very little change for the stage; it won the Drama Critics' Circle Award for the best play of 1937-38. His novel, *Grapes of Wrath,* was the outstanding American novel of 1939.

Stendhal (pseudonym of Marie Henri Beyle) (1783-1842). French novelist. He was born at Grenoble; saw service in the Napoleonic Wars; was consul at Trieste and Cività Vecchia, 1830-41. He may be regarded as the creator of the modern novel of psychological analysis which Paul Bourget and Gabriele D'Annunzio did so much to popularize. At the skilful dissection of motives he is unsurpassed, and his style is exceptionally concise and limpid. His chief works are: *Histoire de la peinture en Italie,* 1817; *Racine et Shakespeare,* 1823; *Armance,* 1827; *Le Rouge et le noir,* 1831; *La Chartreuse de Parme,* 1839; and *La Vie de Henri Brulard,* 1890.

Stephen Foster; or, Weep No More My Lady. Earl Hobson Smith (American). Romantic play, with incidental music. 4 acts. 1935.
A story of the romance between Stephen Collins Foster, and Susan Pentland and Jane Denny McDowell. In the course of events, Susan marries, and Stephen falls in love with Jane.

Sternheim, Carl (1878-   ). German dramatist. A follower of Molière, Sternheim is considered the only one of the modern German dramatists who can be characterized as a comic playwright.
He was the son of a Jewish banker in Leipzig, and began to travel when still very young. Wherever he lived, in Berlin, Munich, Brussels, or Switzerland, he regarded the bourgeois world with cynicism and sought to whip it into a painful perception of its shortcomings. Having written tales, novels and an eclectic and erotic play, *Don Juan,* Sternheim found his true field in the drama of social caricature. Of his score of plays one has been translated into English and one adapted.
He is the author of *The Trousers,* 1911; *The Treasure Chest,* 1912; *Burgher Schippel,* 1913; *The Snob,* 1913; *The Candidate,* 1913; *The Needle,* 1915; *Tabula Rasa,* 1916; *Perleberg,* 1917; *Unchained Contemporaries,* 1920; *Berlin; or, Juste Milieu,* 1920; *The Marquise of Arcis,* 1920; *Manon Lescaut,* 1921; *Libussa,* 1922; *The Weakling,* 1922; *The Fossil,* 1923; *Oscar Wilde,* 1924; *The School of Uznach,* 1926.

Stevedore. Paul Peters and George Sklar (American). Drama. 3 acts. 1934.
Deals with racial conflict in the South, and the relation of the economic set-up to the Negro question. It is notable for its presentation of active resistance on the part of the Negroes, supported by the white workers.

Stevens, Ashton (1872-   ). American dramatic critic. Born in San Francisco, California, August 11, 1872, and was educated in the public schools of Oakland; dramatic critic of the *San Francisco News Letter,* 1894-95; the *Morning Call,*

1896; the *San Francisco Examiner,* 1897; editor of the *News Letter* and *Overland Monthly,* 1897. He gave up editorship in 1898 in order to devote his entire time to doing criticisms for the *Examiner,* which he did for ten years. From 1907 to 1910, he was dramatic critic of the *New York Evening Journal;* the *Herald* and *Examiner* in Chicago since 1910 and it has been said of him that he is the dean of active drama critics in the United States. He is the author of a series of interviews with celebrities of the stage and a conductor of "A Column or Less." He wrote *Actor-views* in 1923, and a play with Charles Michelson, *Mary's Way Out,* 1918.

Sticks. The road: rural communities outside the radius of a large city; also called "tank towns."

Stimmung. The name given a motif in German drama during the rise of naturalism in the 19th century which connoted the striving for truth of individual atmosphere and the belief that character is explained to some degree by environment.

Stock. Stock companies were an important part of the American Theatre, 1890-1925. There were stock companies in many cities as well as in neighborhood theatres in large cities.

A stock company usually has a number of productions ready for performance. The same actors have parts in the various productions and one production is given one week and another the next week. In some cases, the productions are changed every night. Because of the many roles each actor has to perform, stock has always been considered excellent training.

The inroads of movies and radio practically ended stock companies but in recent years "summer stock" developed a new vitality. Throughout the country, but chiefly in the East, resort theatres offering well-known plays performed by resident stock companies have been successful. In some cases new plays that later became New York successes were given their first performance by summer stock companies.

STOCK COMPANIES

BY STUART WALKER

Perhaps my idea of the term "stock company" is at variance with the accepted meaning of the term. In my sixteen years as an independent manager—and when I say independent I mean independent to the nth degree—I always had a company of at least fifteen regular members with a small number of jobbers or occasional players, and a large number of apprentices. I had no typing in casting. The lead of this week might be playing a butler the next week or not acting at all. In this way I could keep the spirit of the company fresh, and could expect and get the very best from every individual. At any time I could release an actor on very short notice—at his own request in case he had a chance to play a big part in New York—without crippling any branch of my company. Furthermore I could always find a place for him when he wanted to come back. I think a great measure of my good fortune in the theatre came from the fact that I made no difference in the quality of my company whether we played in New York, Chicago, Cincinnati, Indianapolis, Dayton or Huntington, West Virginia. The actors were of the same standard, they had played together for a long time and liked to play together. Most of them settled quickly and pleasantly into the local life of the city or cities in which they happened to be playing, and like baseball players they always had the feeling that they represented the city. New York was merely one place in which we might play. It was easy to sell New York to New York; but it was not easy to sell the smaller cities to themselves. The local residents could scarcely believe that our productions were usually an assembly of local arts and crafts, yet worthy of any theatre any place.

As an illustration, when we began our local career in Indianapolis—we had already played in New York, Chicago, Boston, and other larger cities—we had great difficulty in selling ourselves to a very estimable lady who was a real leader of local affairs. I think she liked us personally, because she entertained us individually and en masse several times, but we couldn't induce her to come to see our plays. She didn't go to "stock companies," she said. We couldn't even lure her to the world premier of Booth Tarkington's *Seventeen* for which we were charging one dollar. The following autumn she paid two dollars and a half to see us in Chicago in the same *Seventeen*—the same us who had played the same *Seventeen* in Indianapolis but in a larger production. Later, again, she saw us in New York in the usual smaller production and paid three dollars with quite possessive delight. Later still, she saw us do *The Book of Job* in New York. The following summer we played this magnificent drama in Indianapolis during our regular season. Suddenly the lady saw what we were trying to do and did do, and thereafter her loyalty never wavered whether at a dollar or three dollars a seat.

I always encourage the purchase of clothes and properties in every town. *The Gods of the Mountain* was built and produced in New York, but *Seventeen* which ran for a season in New York was built and produced in Indianapolis and cut down for the smaller Broadway stages. *The School for Scandal,* done in the original Sheridan plan, was built in both Indianapolis and Cincinnati; *L'Arlesienne* was built *in Cincinnati.*

It was very amusing to have a well-known New York manager, who came to Cincinnati to negotiate for this last-named production, tell some local newspaper people that he would probably take the play into one of his Broadway theatres but would, of course, enlarge the production. Not one New York legitimate theatre had a stage large enough for the production I had put on in Cincinnati! And I have not often seen dramatic plays in New York or elsewhere with seventy-five supers, much less seventy-five trained singers and dancers.

In a way, I suppose, we carried culture to Cincinnati and Indianapolis and other cities, but I like rather to feel that we did something to co-ordinate their culture. We gave possibly seventy or eighty plays in each place that that particular city might never have seen adequately done, and we felt that we were a sort of show-window for local industries and arts. Rarely did we ever have to go outside a city to find authentic properties and furnishings for such diversified plays as the Scandinavian *The Wild Duck,* the Southern French *L'Arlesienne,* the Spanish *World and His Wife,* the Georgian *School for Scandal,* the Victorian *Peter Ibbetson,* the Oriental *Kismet,* the Medieval *Monna Vanna,* the Pre-Christian *Book of Job.*

In a way we said, "Ladies and Gentlemen, this is your show, made in your town, with your own resources. We want to show you what a versatile place you live in. Keep it individual. Don't let it become a chain-city as mechanical and as standardized as a chain-store. You have to live your life here, don't feel inferior about it." And then we would play *Seventeen* or *The Book of Job* or *The Portmanteau Plays* throughout the country, just to show what could be done from the home town.

Stooge. A tool, a performer who is the butt of the comedian's jokes, or one who heckles the comedian. Frequently planted in a box or in the audience. Phil Baker, Frank Fay, George Jessel and Ted Healy owed much of their success to the manner in which they worked with their stooges.

Stop the show. Applause so prolonged that the performance halts momentarily, "stops the show!"

Storm in a Teacup. Bruno Frank (German). Comedy. 3 acts. Adapted by James Bridie. 1936.

Mrs. Flanagan's dog Patsy becomes a public cause when he is seized because she cannot pay for his license. A journalist attacks the provost for his cruelty and the provost retalitates by condemning Patsy to death. Patsy, however, is finally rescued by the journalist, and the provost loses his election and his wife.

Stormbuehne. A group, or cult calling itself the *Storm,* made up of theatrical artists and operating in Germany, 1910-20. It emphasized the importance of rhythm, harmony, power, etc.

Storming of the Winter Palace, The. A pageant staged in 1920 at the third anniversary of the Russian Revolution with 8,000 persons on the spot where that historic event had actually taken place. It contained rather a somewhat symbolic representation of the struggle between the Reds and Whites, than a more realistic depiction of the actual storming of the palace.

Storm troops (Russian). Travelling companies of actors (called variously shock troops, flying brigades, agit brigades) which sprang up in Russia directly after the Revolution and were designed to carry the Soviet message to the peasants. At first they performed in railroad stations, later in political clubs.

Story of the Forty-Seven Ronins, The. A Japanese *Joruri,* or musical epic, in which the nationally popular tale of *Chiushingura* (The Loyal League) has been amplified and adapted for theatrical presentation. *Harakiri,* or thrusting a knife into one's abdomen, is an ancient and honorable mode of suicide, and at Shinagawa, a suburb of Tokyo, is a celebrated cemetery containing the graves of Forty-Seven Ronins, who dispatched themselves in this heroic manner. The cemetery is a national shrine, and stands as a monument to the memory of Asano, who, in 1701, as Lord of Ako, was entrusted with one of the greatest of state ceremonies—the reception and entertainment of an envoy from the Mikado at Yedo (then the capitol of the Shogunate). Asano, a warrior, was so little versed in such matters that he asked the advice of Kira, another nobleman, whose knowledge of court etiquette was extensive. Kira gave the information grudgingly, the while chiding Asano for being an ignorant country lout. Asano, unable to stand the insults, slashed the insolent wretch across the face with his sword. The palace was soon in an uproar, for, as everyone knew, a private brawl within its sacred environs was only punishable by death. Asano was condemned to perform *harakiri* that very evening; his castle and lands were confiscated, his family declared extinct, and all the members of his clan disbanded, which meant, in Japanese parlance, that they were ronins, "wave-men," wanderers without a lord and home. Asano's senior retainer, Oishi, determined to avenge him, secured the help of forty-six others of the ronins who were willing to undertake the mission and to die in the attempt. For not to take vengeance on an enemy involved social ostracism; to take it involved capital punishment, since such a vendetta was forbidden by law. The *ronins* decided to separate and take up various trades, and thereby managed to gain access to Kira's castle and learn many secrets of its corridors and gardens. Oishi even neglected his wife and children and went to Kyoto, where he plunged into drunkenness and debauchery. Thus, their enemy, to whom reports of these doings were brought by spies, was lulled into complete security. Almost two years after their lord's death, during the night of a violent snowstorm, the band attacked, forcing the castle gates, slaying the guards, and dragging forth the chicken-hearted Kira. Oishi requested Kira to perform harakiri, thus giving him the chance of saving his honor, but Kira was too much of a coward to do so. The ronins slew him and marched with his head to the temple of Sengakuji, amid the rejoicing of the populace. In the temple grounds, they placed Kira's head on their lord's grave. All forty-seven were condemned to commit harakiri, doing so separately in the castles of the various nobles to whose care they had been entrusted for the last days of their lives. They also were buried in the temple grounds. The admiration of a whole people for over two hundred years has been the reward for their observance of an ethical code.

The performance of such an historical drama sometimes lasts several days; it is produced with much pomp of costume. The acting is very realistic, and harakiri is performed almost too violently. *The Story of the Forty-Seven Ronins* is stirring rather than touching in its incidents, and contains much bloodshed. There is a tea-house scene which serves as an excellent example of the Japanese comedy of manners.

There are almost fifty plays on this subject. Perhaps the finest is that by Takeda Izumo who wrote an eleven act version with the help of two collaborators.

Chikamatsu Monzayemon wrote an earlier five act arrangement.

There is a translation of the story by F. V. Dickins: *Chiushingura; or, the Loyal League; a Japanese Romance.*

Straight. A role or performance that is natural, normal and uncolored by eccentricities.

Strand Theatre, London. The home of English burlesque. Opened in 1832 as Rayner's New Subscription Theatre in the Strand by Benjamin Lionel Rayner. Originally built in 1820 as Reinagle and Barker's New Panorama. By 1834 it was called simply the New Strand Theatre. In the course of many successes, and difficulties with the Lord Chamberlain over licensing, the house changed hands several times. In 1858 Miss Swanborough reopened with excellent comedies and burlesque. The house was enlarged in 1865. Mr. Mitchell, Mrs. Waylett, Henry Hall, Charles Young, and the American John S. Clarke, were among those who played in it. Demolished in 1905 to make way for a station for the Underground.

Strange Interlude. Eugene O'Neill (American). Drama. 9 acts. 1928.

This play represents one of O'Neill's most ambitious efforts. It is much longer than the usual drama, and is unconventional in its treatment of dialogue. The characters inform the audience what their true thoughts are, by asides, and then continue with the usual dialogue. Thus O'Neill keeps the spectators aware of what his characters are really thinking and feeling in their inmost hearts and minds, as well as of their superficial and surface reactions. This problem of what Browning calls man's "two soul-sides" is one with which O'Neill has experimented in various of his plays. In *The Great God Brown* masks were used to indicate this duality; in *Days Without End* each character was played by two actors. *Strange Interlude* is the most successful of these attempts to express both the inner and the outer man.

The play is really a case history of Nina Leeds and her search for fulfillment. Nina's fiancé was killed in the war. Regretful that she did not marry him before he left and thus achieve some happy moments, she has grown embittered and neurotic. She becomes a nurse, and goes casually from lover to lover. Finally Dr. Darrel, a noted physician who loves her but will not admit it to himself, advises that she marry Sam Evans. Sam is a simple, honest boy who adores her and believes motherhood would cure her emotional instability. They marry. Nine tells her mother-in-law she is going to have a baby, and Mrs. Evans discloses the fact that there is insanity in Sam's family and urges Nina not to bear Sam's child. She suggests finding another father. Sam, of course, is not to be told of his wife's infidelity.

In this predicament, Nina goes to Dr. Darrel. She becomes his mistress, and eventually has a son, Gordon, by him. Eleven years pass. Sam has grown wealthy. Darrel has continued to be Nina's lover, although his chief devotion has always been to science. Charles Norsden, a novelist who has been a life-long friend, is her other admirer. But since Charles is the victim of a mother complex, his relationship with Nina is a platonic one.

As Gordon grows up, he learns to hate Dr. Darrel. He senses that his mother is unfaithful to her husband, and, turning from her, relies more and more on his father. The boy announces his engagement. Nina, who has become more possessive with the years, wishes to hold him by letting Sam know the boy is not really his. But Sam dies of a stroke before she can tell him the truth, and Gordon goes off with his sweetheart. Darrel has tired of Nina, and decides to devote himself exclusively to his laboratory. To the aging woman there is left only the friendship of the faithful weakling, Charles, whom she marries.

Strasberg, Lee. American director. Acted in *Red Rust* in 1929, in 1931 was co-founder, with Cheryl Crawford and Harold Clurman, of the Group Theatre. Has staged numerous productions for the Group Theatre, including *Success Story, Men In White, Gentlewoman, Case of Clyde Griffiths,* but since 1938 he has not been a member of the Group. Since then he has staged *All the Living* for Cheryl Crawford. He is known as an innovator in staging, and is an editor of *Films*, a quarterly.

The Straw. Eugene O'Neill (American). Drama. 3 acts. 1921.

A young man and a young girl, both patients at a tuberculosis sanatorium, fall in love. When the young man is sent away, cured, the girl despairs, feeling that he is all she cares to live for. At the end he comes back to see her, but she realizes that in the interim he has lost his love for her.

Street Scene. Elmer Rice (American). Drama. 3 acts. 1929.

This play was awarded the Pulitzer Prize in 1929. The emphasis is not so much on plot as it is on characterization. The stage set is the facade of a New York cold water tenement house. Various characters are introduced. The Swedish janitor and his wife, the gossipy busybody, Mrs. Jones. The two children she is always bragging about, her son a bully of a cab driver and her daughter obviously a girl gone wrong. Also the gay Italian musician, the Jewish radical boy in love with Rose Moran, the letter carrier, the social worker and the policeman. Frank Moran, the stagehand, living on the first floor finds his wife in the arms of her lover, the milkman. He shoots them both. He is taken away to await trial. He leaves his daughter Rose to take care of Willie, the younger child. Rose, a simple winning girl is left, bewildered, confused and lost. The tragedy has touched all the tenants indirectly and may yet reach out and touch them personally. The old tenement buzzes like a bee hive.

Streets of New York, The. Dion Boucicault (Irish American). Melodrama. 5 acts. 1857.

"Keep your gold! It would soil my poverty," is Lucy Fairweather's answer to Gideon Bloodgood, who has robbed her father of his fortune, and is trying to trick young Mark Livingstone into marrying his daughter, Alida. Mark loves Lucy, however, and after rescuing "the papers" from a burning tenement, he finally has the money to marry her, and to break the villainous Bloodgood.

Strictly Dishonorable. Preston Sturges (American). Comedy. 3 acts. 1929.

Isabel Parry, from Mississippi, deserted by her fiance at midnight in a New York speakeasy, meets a Judge and an Italian count, who is also an opera singer. The Count takes the girl to his apartment assuring her his intentions are "strictly dishonorable." Isabel gladly takes him at his word, only to have the Count become conscience smitten and later retire to another room. In the morning, however, he is romantic again, and announces his love for Isabel and his intention to marry her.

Strife. John Galsworthy (English). Drama. 3 acts. 1909.

Deals with the antagonism between capital and labor. The character, Robert, holds the view that workmen should have some voice in directing their futures; Anthony, representing the views of labor, believes them too stupid. The first notable treatment of a strike in British drama. It is February and the strike has been going on all winter. The laborers are suffering untold privation but remain loyal to Roberts who tells them to stick to their guns. The directors of the company wish to effect a compromise but Anthony won't yield an inch. Roberts is addressing a meeting of workmen when he is informed that his ailing wife has died. He rushes off and one of the workmen's wives pleads with the men to give in for the sake of their families, who are starving. The men decide to return and desert Roberts. The company forces Anthony to resign. Thus the two individual protagonists find themselves in the same boat. When the terms of the compromise are read Anthony's secretary comments on the fact that it is the identical agreement that the men originally opposed. The union representation replies cynically, seeing the irony of the struggle.

Strike. To clear the stage.

Striking the set. A term meaning to change the setting and remove it from the stage.

Strindberg, August (1849-1912). Swedish dramatist. Born in Stockholm, he entered the University of Upsala at an early age, but was unable to support himself and continue his studies at the same time. He left, though in 1870 he managed to return and to continue his studies. He then began writing plays, and in 1872 *Master Olof* was offered for production. It was, however, refused for six years by the managers. The play, when it finally appeared, is said to have inaugurated Sweden's dramatic renascence. Strindberg turned his hand to many things in his early years. He was schoolmaster, journalist, dramatist, writer of scientific and political treatises and short stories. In 1883 he left Sweden and traveled in Denmark, Germany, France and Italy, at the same time publishing volumes of stories, novels and plays. The production of *The Father* in 1887 established his reputation as one of the most powerful dramatists of Europe. To the period inaugurated by *The Father* Strindberg's characteristically bitter plays belong. As a result of great intellectual strain and the painful proceedings incident to one of his divorces, Strindberg was forced to retire to a private sanitarium for over a year, but in 1897 he returned to his work and published a large number of plays. He also established his Intimate Theatre at Stockholm, where his own plays were produced. In 1897 he returned to Sweden, where he remained until his death. He was married three times, each marriage ending in divorce.

His chief plays are exact, though narrow, analyses of the feminine mind and soul. His own experience was so unfortunate that his bitterness takes the form of a wholesale indictment of the sex.

He is the author of *The Secret of the Guild,* 1880; *Comrades,* 1888; *Miss Julia,* 1888; *Creditors,* 1890; *The Keys of Heaven,* 1892; *Mother-love,* 1893; *The Link,* 1897; *The Dance of Death, I and II,* 1901; *The Bridal Crown,* 1902; *The Pelican,* 1907; *The Black Glove,* 1909; *The Great Highway,* 1909.

Strip tease. An act in burlesque in which a girl disrobes, piece by piece, before the audience.

Strolling Players. Actors who travel in a group from town to town to give performances of a play or of the plays in their repertory. During the middle ages, they were to be found throughout Europe, acting in villages, country crossroads and at fairs. The stage usually consisted of merely a platform with curtains, the players making up for their lack of technical equipment with their zest and originality. Although they have been largely supplanted by other forms of the theatre, strolling players are still to be found in many European countries and in small villages and towns of the United States.

Studio Assistant, The. Jules Lemaitre (French). Drama. 4 acts. 1905.
A middle-aged artist, yearning for lost youth in the person of a charming helper, realizes the depth of his desire for her only when his wife and his son grow jealous. Earlier the wife had objected to the son's making love to the girl, a mere nobody; but now she is won over, not merely by Juliette's graces, but also by the thought that Jacques, in marrying her, will remove a rival.

Sturm und Drang. The name given to the school of writers in 18th century Germany, who in literature and drama threw off the influence of the classic French writers and turned to the freedom inspired by Shakespeare which led them a point further in depicting "liberty, truth and nature" on the stage.
See also *Drama, German, 17-18th centuries.*

Sudermann, Hermann (1857-1932). German dramatist. Germany's most successful representative of the naturalistic school.
Born at Matziken, East Prussia. After attending school at Elbing and Tilsit he was apprenticed to a druggist at the age of fourteen. His university training was received at Koenigsberg and Berlin. Soon after his graduation he began writing. His first important works were novels, one of which *Dame Care* has already taken rank as a modern classic. In 1889 his first play *Honor* was produced by the Free Stage Society under the direction of Otto Brahm. It was very successful, and the young writer was acclaimed as one of the group of rebels which had gathered beneath Brahm's standard. A follower of Ibsen, he adapted during the Nineties a few of the more daring ideas of the day. Since 1900 he has steadily sunk in the estimation of his own countrymen, chiefly because the drama has developed beyond the point to which he helped to bring it. During the First World War Sudermann fell into line with the monarchists and exerted all his influence to plead the Prussian cause.
His most important plays are: *The Destruction of Sodom,* 1891; *Magda,* 1893; *The Battle of the Butterflies,* 1894; *Fritzchen,* 1896; *The Eternal Masculine,* 1896;

The Joy of Living, 1902; *Storm-Brother Socrates,* 1903; *The Faraway Princess,* 1907; *The Beggar of Syracuse,* 1911; *The Woman Friend,* 1916; *The Higher Life,* 1916; *The Raschoffs,* 1919.

Summer theatre. The first summer theatre in New York was opened on July 9, 1800. It was called Mount Vernon Gardens and was on Broadway and Leonard Street.

Elitch's Gardens, at Denver, and the Lakewood Theatre at Skowhegan, Maine, are the two oldest. Since 1926 almost every summer resort in the east has boasted a playhouse, some of them having schools in connection with them.

In addition to the ones already mentioned, the outstanding summer theatres are: The Berkshire Playhouse, Stockbridge, Massachusetts; The Country Playhouse, Westport, Connecticut; The Cape Playhouse, Dennis, Massachusetts; The Wharf Theatre, Provincetown, Massachusetts; The Westchester Playhouse, Mount Kisco, New York; The County Theatre, Suffern, New York; The Bucks County Playhouse, New Hope, Pennsylvania; The Barter Theatre, Abingdon, Virginia.

Summer try-out. A preview of a play, usually to test its potentiality as Broadway material and given in a summer theatre.

Sumner, John Saxton (1876-   ). American moralist. Succeeded Anthony Comstock as Secretary of the New York Society for the Suppression of Vice in 1915; has been a leader in movements and legislation directed against demoralizing influences in publications, the screen, the stage, etc.

Sunday theatre clubs. Private English theatrical ventures which run without interference of the censor on the theory that they are private enterprises. Performances take place in regularly licensed theatres which for the time being cease to function as public playhouses. Performances usually take place on Sundays. Representative clubs of this nature are The Stage Society, the oldest of them all; the Arts Theatre Club; The Gate Theatre; The Players, etc.

See also *Stage Society.*

Sunken Bell, The. Gerhart Hauptmann (German). Symbolic fantasy in blank verse. 4 acts. 1896.

Relates the tragedy of Heinrich, a bell-founder, who sets out to be a superman and suffers failure. Forsaking wife and children in the valley, he ascends to the mountain to attempt to create bells for the worship of the sun, under the inspiration of the elf-maid, Rautendelein. Remorse seizes him as he hears the bell of conscience (the sunken bell) toll, rung by his dead wife. However he still clings to his creative vision.

An exemplification of a philosophy of life. The tragedy of the creative soul and the drama of the creative thinker of the nineteenth century. Places side by side scenes of everyday realism with scenes of fairy romance.

This play served as the libretto for the opera of the same name by Respighi.

Sun-Up. Lula Vollmer (American). Drama. 3 acts. 1923.

The story of a North Carolina mountain woman, Widow Cagle, who has become embittered by successive misfortunes. Her father was killed in the Civil War, her husband shot by revenue officers, and her son, Rufe, killed in the First World War. At the time she learns of her son's death, she also discovers she has been harboring in her house the son of the revenuer who shot her husband. She is about to shoot him and thus be revenged, when the spirit of her dead son whispers to her that the world will never be right until there is more love and less hate in it. She has an immediate and complete change of heart.

Supernumerary. An extra or walk-on in a production; a person who merely appears as in a mob scene or in the background and who has no individual lines of his own to speak.

Suppliants, The (or, The Suppliant Women). Aeschylus (Greek). Tragedy. 490 B.C.

This is the earliest known play by Aeschylus. The Suppliants are the fifty daughters of Danaus. They have been promised in marriage to the fifty sons of their uncle Aegyptus. Determined not to marry them, the fifty girls flee with their father to Argus. They ask protection of the king, Pelasgus, and he, in turn, asks his people what to do. They agree to protect them. The pursuing suitors approach—they demand that the maidens embark on the ships and when they are forcing them to do so, Pelasgus, intervenes and saves the suppliants. Danaus and his daughters show their gratitude by prayer and go off happily to their new abode. The play is rudimentary in plot and character construction and the interest still centers around the chorus.

Support. Actors in the cast with the star; especially the person who plays opposite the star.

Susan and God. Rachel Crothers (American). Comedy. 3 acts. 1937.

Susan Trepel, a selfish and flighty woman, is forced against her will to apply her new found religion to her own family, returning to live with a dipsomaniac husband and a pathetically lonely fifteen-year-old daughter. Her husband and daughter respond to care and the appeal of home life, and Susan, who had planned to stay with them only for a summer, makes it a permanent arrangement.

Swan, The (Hattyu). Ferenc Molnar (Hungarian). Drama. 6 scenes. 1914.

This technically brilliant drama is one of the most successful of Molnar's plays. It deals subtly with a princess and a commoner in love. The princess is named Alexandra. Her mother is anxious to arrange a suitable march for her. With this in mind the queen invites a crown prince to the royal palace. But the prince is only distantly polite to Alexandra, and finally, in desperation, the queen urges her daughter to flirt with her brothers' tutor so as to arouse the jealousy of their guest. The tutor, overwhelmed by such attention, becomees arrogant and insults the prince. Alexandra, living up to her role, steps in and kisses the tutor. By the next day she realizes she loves the commoner. But when the prince finally proposes, she accepts. It will admittedly not be a love match, but there will be compensations.

The title of the play is derived from the fact that the swan is an aristocratic bird, as Alexandra is a woman. When the swan emerges from the water which is its habitat, however, it is nothing but a clumsy and ridiculous figure. And so would Alexandra lose her dignity if she married out of her rank.

Swan Theatre, The (London). A public theatre erected in 1594 or 1595 by Francis Langley on the Bankside, across the Thames from London. The Swan was used only infrequently for plays by the professional companies and had no regular tenants.

Sweet Nell of Old Drury. Paul Kester (American). Comedy. 4 acts. 1900.

Nell Gwynne, former actress and mistress of Charles II, tries to save Sir Roger Fairfax from treason, and nearly loses the King's favor. She saves herself and her friends by finally securing a packet of letters which clear Sir Roger and incriminate none other than Jeffers, the King's Lord Chief Justice.

Swinburne, Algernon Charles (1837-1909). British poet, critic and dramatist. Born in London, and educated at Eton, his fame is primarily due to his poetic works. He is the author, however, of several dramas such as *The Queen Mother*, 1860; *Rosamond,* 1860; *Chastelard*, 1865; *Bothwell,* 1874; *Mary Stuart,* 1881; *Erechtheus,* 1876; *Tristram of Lyonesse,* 1882.

Swing Mikado, The. Swing version of Gilbert and Sullivan's *The Mikado* by Dan Goldberg. Produced by the Federal Theatre Project in Chicago, 1938, and later in New York, 1939. Presented with an all-colored cast and with music played in modern jazz tempo.

Switchboard. A stage electrical circuit consisting of a lamp or lamps, a switch, focuses and a dimmer to control the intensity of the light output, all being connected by the necessary wiring. A number of such circuits form the stage lighting installation, the switches, foci and dimmers being grouped for convenience of control to form the stage switchboard.

Symbolism. Symbolism is designed to convey impressions by suggestion rather than by direct representation. Symbols are almost as old as mankind, but as a literary or dramatic school of thought, symbolism dates its origin to the 19th century revolt against realism and naturalism. France was the leader in this movement which spread to such doctrines as expressionism, imagism, etc. Maeterlinck, Dunsany, Eugene O'Neill made extensive use of symbolism in various plays.

Synge, Edmund John Millington (1871-1909). Irish dramatist. He was born at Newtown Little, near Dublin. Little is recorded of his early life, except that he remained at home until he was nearly twenty, and that he was graduated from Trinity College, Dublin, 1892. Endowed with a natural taste for music and a desire for travel, he wandered through Europe, with his violin, for two or three years. He first went to Germany, intending to study music, but returned to Paris, where he tried to make a living by writing book reviews and essays. But it was not until he was discovered by Yeats, who persuaded him to return to Ireland, 1898, and to study the primitive folk in the unfrequented districts, that he began to turn his thoughts to Irish themes. Yeats induced the young man to write for the new Irish Theatre. In the Aran Islands, in Kerry and Wicklow and Connemara, Synge wandered, and out of a rich fund of folklore, speech and character he created his plays. He died of cancer at Dublin. Synge was by all odds the greatest of the dramatists who wrote for the Irish Theatre. He is the author of the plays *The Shadow of the Glen*, 1903; *Riders to the Sea*, 1904; *The Well of the Saints*, 1905; *The Playboy of the Western World*, 1907; *The Tinker's Wedding*, 1909; *Deirdre of the Sorrows*, 1910.

Syrmata. Long, sweeping robes worn in ancient Roman tragedy corresponding to the Greek *chiton.*

Tableau. A living picture posed by players.

T. A. C. "Theatre Arts Committee," organized to represent the liberal political opinion in the theatre. It also sponsors cabarets, dances, etc., to further its ends. Also, TAC, a monthly periodical published by the organisation.

Tag. Term for the final speech of a scene, act or the entire play, serving as a cue for the curtain and marked by a special flourish for the effective exit of an actor.

Tagore, Sir Rabindranath (1861-   ). Bengali poet, dramatist. Youth spent in Calcutta. Later went to England where he studied until he was 24. In 1901 he founded the internationally famous school of Santiniketan, at Bolpur, now called Visva-Bharati. Awarded Nobel prize for literature in 1913. In 1915, knighted by the King of England. His writings are punctuated by a simple and spirited beauty. Has written about 3000 songs set to music, poetry, drama, novels and essays. His dramatic contributions are refreshing and charming lyrics, unpretentious, fluid, gracious in style, and wise and sane in philosophy. His works include: *The Post Office* (1914), *Red Oleanders* (1924), and *Chitra, Sacrifice,* and *The Cycle of Spring.*

Taille, Jean de la (1540-1608?). French dramatist, theorist. He was born at Bondaroy of noble parentage and was educated first under Muret, later in the law department of the University of Orleans. He became known both as a soldier and a man of letters. His *Art de la tragédie* in *Sauel le furieux* embodies his dramatic theories.

Tairov, Alexander (1885-   ). Russian director. Formerly associated with the Moscow Art Theatre, he seceded to form his own theatre, The Kamerny, in 1914. He headed this with his Swedish actress-wife, Alice Koonen.

It was his idea to bring musical life to the theatre; with this in mind he made lavish use of music in drama. He endeavored to reach the intellectuals among his audience. To do this he has made up his repertoire largely from the plays of Shaw, Chesterton, O'Neill (*The Hairy Ape; Desire Under The Elms; All God's Chillun Got Wings*), Dos Passos, Vsevolod Vishnevsky, etc.

Take a call. To acknowledge the applause of the audience at the close of a play by appearing before the curtain.

Takeda Izumo (1688-1756). Japanese dramatist, impresario. Next to his contemporary, Chikamatsu Monzayemon, he is regarded as having done most for the development of the popular drama in Japan. Wrote for the *Jouri* and *Ayatsuri* stage. His most famous drama is Chiushingura (see *The Story of the Forty-Seven Ronins*), which is even a more masterly rendition of this popular feudal narrative than Chikamatsu's version. Became manager of the renowned *Takemoto-Za* in Osaka when Takemoto Gidayu, the founder of this theatre, retired in 1705.

Takemoto Gidayu (? -1714). Japanese actor, impresario. Gorobei was a farmer living near Osaka who took the name Takemoto Gidayu and began a theatre in Osaka called the Takemoto-Za in 1685. Was skilled in the reading of battle scenes and other violent parts in *Joruri* drama. With Chikamatsu Monzayemon, he developed the *Ayatsuri* puppet drama to its highest position. Retired from the management of his theatre in 1705 and was succeeded by Takeda Izumo.

Tale of Mystery, A. Adapted, 1802, by Thomas Holcroft, from *Coelina; ou, L'Enfant du mystère,* 1800, by Guilbert de Pixésécourt, author of *Le Chien de Montargis* (elsewhere discussed in this book as *Aubry de Montdidier's Dog*) which was the first melodrama in English.

Tall grass. The one-night stands.

Talma, François Joseph (1763-1826). French actor. One of the greatest French actors at the time of the Revolution and First Empire. Both kings and emperors commanded him to perform for them, and the men who were making history by overthrowing existing governments were pleased to call him friend.

Talma was born in Paris and educated in London. He started his career as a dentist, but soon switched to acting. In 1787 he made his début at the Comédie-Française in Voltaire's *Mahomet;* during the next two years Louis XVI was among those who saw him play. Talma himself was against the monarchy, however, and an intimate of such revolutionists as Danton and Desmoulins. In 1789 he performed in Chénier's *Charles IX,* an anti-royalist drama. When he delivered an inflammatory passage prophesying the fall of the Bastille, Mirabeau led the thunderous applause. The performance created a sensation, and led Talma to break with the national theatre. With Danton and Desmoulins acting as his patrons, Talma founded the Théâtre de la République and continued his acting career there.

As he gained experience, Talma's art became more and more perfected. Napoleon was one of his greatest admirers, and took him to Erfurt in 1808 to play in *The Death of Caesar* (La Mort de César) before five crowned heads. In 1813 the emperor took Talma to Dresden to perform. The actor's last appearance before his death was in Delaville's *Charles VI*, 1826.

Talma was an advocate of realism in costumes and scenery. He astounded audiences by being one of the first to play classic tragedies dressed in a toga rather than in the fripperies of the eighteenth century.

Talon, The. Henri Bernstein (French). Drama. 4 acts. 1906.

An adventuress jilts two lovers in order to accept the proposal of a third, thirty years her senior. She then plots against him a she mounts the political ladder to become senator and minister.

Reveals the author as strident a misogynist as August Strindberg.

Tamayo y Baus, Manuel (1829-1898). Spanish dramatist, actor. Born in Madrid. His principal works are *Lopositivo* (*Money*), 1862, an attack on materialism; *Un drama nuevo* (*A New Drama*), 1867, his masterpiece—in it the author imitates Hamlet and places a play within a play.

Tamburlaine. Christopher Marlowe (English). Tragedy. 2 parts, 5 acts each. 1587.

Deals with the rise and fall of an Oriental conqueror. Notable for its use of blank verse and for its Renaissance philosophy of ruthless self-advancement.

Tamburlaine is shown as a peasant lad, who overrides the ordinary moral code of his time, in his attempt to fulfill his ideals.

He plots at murder to take the throne of Persia and tortures the Emperor and Empress of the Turks until they kill themselves.

This is considered one of the greatest works of one of the greatest of the pre-Shakespearean English dramatists.

Taming of A Shrew, The. Anonymous (English). Comedy. 1594.

An anonymous comedy published in 1594 and generally believed to be the source used by Shakespeare for the Induction and main plot of his *Taming of The Shrew*. Recent criticism, however, tends to describe it as a corrupt pirated version of Shakespeare's play. In plot it closely follows the latter, though lacking the Bianca sub-plot.

Taming of the Shrew, The. William Shakespeare (English). Comedy. 5 acts. 1594.

Written about 1594 and published in the Folio of 1623. A play on the same subject, *The Taming of A Shrew*, published in 1594, is believed by some to be the source used by Shakespeare, by others to be a corrupt pirated version of Shakespeare's work. The sub-plot of Bianca's wooing is drawn from Gascoigne's play *The Supposes*, in turn drawn from Ariosto's comedy *Gli Suppositi*. The play, according to the Induction, is presented for the amusement of Christopher Sly, a drunken tinker, who is led to believe, on awakening from a drunken sleep, that he is a wealthy lord. The main action concerns the successful efforts of Petruchio to subdue his temperamental and strong-willed wife, Katherine. His uncouth appearance and behavior at the wedding, his brutality to the servants, his refusal to let Katherine eat or wear respectable clothes soon make her even-tempered and submissive. A sub-plot deals with the wooing and winning of Bianca, Katherine's sister, by Lucentio, in spite of rival suitors and her father's opposition to the match.

Tancred and Sigismunda. James Thomson (English). Tragedy. 5 acts. 1761.
Based on the story inserted in *Gil Blas* in which Tancred, heir to the kingdom of a Sicily, is lured into accepting with the throne a bride whom he does not love, and abandoning Sigismunda, whom he adores.

Tarkington, Newton Booth (1869-   ). American novelist, dramatist. Born in Indianapolis, he was the author of a wide variety of books, among them *Monsieur Beaucaire,* 1900. The dramatic version of this book was a great success. His other novels from which stage and film versions have been produced are: *The Gentleman from Indiana,* 1899; *Penrod,* 1914; *Seventeen,* 1916. He also wrote the novels, *The Magnificent Ambersons,* 1918; *The Midlander,* 1924; *Mary's Neck,* 1932; *Presenting Lily Mars,* 1934. His plays include: *Foreign Exchange,* 1909; *If I Had Money,* 1912; *Beauty And The Jacobin,* 1912; *Mister Antonio,* 1916; *The Country Cousin,* 1916; *Up From Nowhere,* 1919; *Clarence,* 1919; *Poldekin,* 1920 (revised 1939); *The Women,* 1921; *Intimate Strangers,* 1921; *Rose Brier,* 1922; *Bristol Glass,* 1922; *Tweedles,* 1923; *Magnolia,* 1923; *Growing Pains,* 1925; *Hoosiers Abroad,* 1927; *How's Your Health?* 1929; *Colonel Satan,* 1931. Many of these were written in collaboration with Harry Leon Wilson or Julian Street.

Tarlton, Richard (?-1588). English actor. The most popular comedian of the Elizabethan period. His humor was manifest in plays and pamphlets, as well as in acting. He was a favorite of the Queen and is referred to in flattering terms by a host of contemporaries, including such writers as Nashe, Harrington, Dekker, Heywood and Jonson. *Tarlton's News Out of Purgatorie,* c. 1590, and *Tarlton's Jests,* 1611, are collections of anecdotes attributed to him and representative of his comedy.

Tartuffe. Molière (French). Comedy. 5 acts. 1664, 1669.
Orgon, deceived by the hypocritical cant of the beggar Tartuffe, gives him the run of his house, plans to give him his daughter in marriage, and even signs over his estate to him. By the time he is finally convinced of Tartuffe's lechery and dishonesty, Tartuffe reminds him that he now owns the house, and that he has denounced Orgon to the king. In court Tartuffe is recognized as a criminal, Orgon's house and honor are restored and his daughter is free to marry the man she loves.
A satire on religious hypocrisy, its production was delayed for five years by the

Jesuits. The first performance was in May 1664 before Louis XIV at Versailles. Revised and amplified, it finally opened on February 5, 1669, in Paris.

It is interesting to note that although endorsed artistically by the intellectuals, censorship was clamped on the play lest "offense might come to others less capable of discerning good from evil."

Tate, Nahum (1652-1715). Irish writer. Born in county Cavan, he was a prolific adapter of plays, including Shakespeare's *King Lear, Panacea; or, a Poem on Tea,* 1700, is his only notable original poem. His fame rests chiefly on his *New Version of the Psalms,* published in 1696, in collaboration with Nicholas Brady. Tate was appointed Poet Laureate in 1692.

Tatimara. The name given the sword fights in *Kabuki* dramas; conventional and picturesque rather than realistic; when a *Samurai* or noble slays an opponent of low rank, the victim turns a somersault called *tonbo-no-kiru.*

Tayleur, Clifton W. (1831-1887). American actor, dramatist. Served at the Holliday Street Theatre in Baltimore in the capacity of stock dramatist. Here was produced his play, *Horseshoe Robinson,* 1856. This was the year in which Tayleur took his farewell as an actor, but remained connected with the theatre until 1859. He also was at one time a reporter on the Baltimore *Clipper,* and in 1857, became the editor of *Our Opinion.* Tayleur was the author of two original plays, *Won Back* and *The Boy Martyrs of September 12, 1814.*

Taylor, Joseph (1586-1652). English actor. An English actor named in the 1623 Folio list of performers in Shakespeare's plays. In 1619 he joined the King's Men, the company with which Shakespeare had been associated, and remained with them until 1642, succeeding Richard Burbage as their leading actor. In addition to his performances in Shakespeare's plays, he appeared in a large number of others, including Jonson's *Bartholomew Fair, The Alchemist, Volpone, Epicoene,* Massinger's *Believe As You List,* and Fletcher's *The Wild-Goose Chase.* Tradition states that he was instructed in the role of Hamlet by Shakespeare himself; more probably Shakespeare instructed Burbage and the latter instructed Taylor, who came as his successor. Contemporary critics praised Taylor highly for his acting. (It was the recollection of Taylor's performances as Hamlet that enabled Sir William D'Avenant to impart to Betterton the examples and tradition established by the author and which provided a model that has endured to the present day.)

Taylor, Laurette. American actress (1884-   ). Was in vaudeville and then on the Boston legitimate stage. Made her first appearance in New York in *From Rags to Riches,* 1903. Played in stock for a few years. Made a substantial success in *Alias Jimmy Valentine* and in 1912 in *The Bird of Paradise.* In December, 1912, she appeared in *Peg of My Heart.* The play had one of the longest runs in the theatre at that time, over 600 performances. She played the same role in London, for over 500 performances. Later, played Juliet, Portia and Katherine in scenes from Shakespeare.

Some of her other plays were *Humoresque, Sweet Nell of Old Drury, Pierrot, The Progidal, Trelawney of the Wells, In a Garden, Alice Sit By the Fire,* and *The Old Lady Shows Her Medals,* and most recently in the revival of *Outward Bound.*

Tayu. A reciter in *Kabuki* drama who is accompanied by the music of a *samisen* player; the reciter has a playbook before him resting on a small decorative desk called a *kendai* from which he reads in a highly dramatic manner. This pertains only to plays of puppet origin.

Tea parties (Samuel Foote's). A custom thought up in the 18th century by Samuel Foote to evade the licensing laws of the English theatre. These tea parties were held in the morning at the Haymarket Theatre and after the audience, made up of invited "friends and the public," was assembled and tea was being served, Foote would put on an entertainment which, because not technically public performances, escaped subjection to the ruling.

Tear jerker. Slang term descriptive of a play which deliberately works upon the susceptibilities of the audience and makes the tenderhearted weep. Such a one is Dumas' *Camille,* 1853, or Harriet Beecher Stowe's *Uncle Tom's Cabin,* 1853 (notably the death of little Eva scene), or *Way Down East,* 1898.

A player who uses obvious tricks to make the audience cry also is called a tear jerker.

Teaser. (1) A squib in a newspaper or on a billboard worded in such a manner as to pique curiosity without revealing the name of the attraction which it advertises; also (2) the horizontal screen or masking piece, usually the same color as to the tormentor, suspended above and between the arch and the tormentor, to complete the frame.

Teatro alla Scala. A 17th-18th century theatre at Milan distinguished by the horseshoe auditorium; its proscenium arch was single, without façade. It is now one of the most famous opera houses in the world. Its theatrical museum is also notable.

Teatro degli Indipendenti. A modern theatre begun in an underground room of the old Roman baths by Bragaglia and developed later into an experimental studio.

Teatro dei Piccoli. A famous modern puppet theatre created in Rome by Podrecca. One of the outstanding marionette groups of all time.

Teatro di Fano. An Italian theatre of the 17th-18th century distinguished by its straight-sided auditorium; its proscenium arch consisted of pillars at extremities of the stage backed by a false, obliquely receding façade designed to direct the eye to the scenes themselves.

Teatro d'Imola. A 17th-18th century Italian theatre which demonstrates the ovoid auditorium; its proscenium arch had pillars in front complemented by two others set in closer perspective deeper on the stage, all connected by overhead arches, making three altogether.

Teatro di Torino. A 17th-18th century Italian theatre which demonstrates the ovoid auditorium; its proscenium arch was single, without façade.

Teatro Ducale Nuovo. A 17th-18th century theatre built in Mantua by Ferdinando Bibiena, showing a variation of the horseshoe auditorium, in which boxes were built out in projections for the facility of better stage vision.

Teatro Eslava. A modern theatre established in Madrid in 1917. It was directed by the dramatist, Sierra, until 1925.

Teatro Español. A modern theatre in Madrid, occupied from 1894 until 1909 by Maria Guerrero. It has served as a national theatre but has never become entirely a state institution.

Teatro Falcone. A 17th-18th century theatre built in Genoa by G. A. Falcone, showing a variation of the horseshoe auditorium in which boxes were built out in projections for the facility of better stage vision.

Teatro Farnese. A playhouse of Renaissance Italy, at Parma, completed in 1618 or 1619. Its ovoid auditorium was elongated and marked by the traditional semi-circular formation only at the end farthest from the stage. The stage was long and narrow, with instead of the heavily sculptured façade in the rear, the earliest of the modern proscenium arches. The arch consisted of pillars at extremities of the stage backed by a false, obliquely receding façade designed to direct the eye to the scenes themselves; behind this the depth of the stage, designed originally to contain tragic, comic, or satyric settings, but found later, as a masking frame, to hold opportunity for changing scenes such as was denied Serlio's open stage. This theatre was a powerfully important influence on the entire subsequent history of the stage.

Teatro Filharmonico. A 17th-18th century theatre built in Verona by Francesco da Bibiena, showing a variation of the horseshoe auditorium, in which boxes were built out in projections for the facility of better stage vision.

Teatro Olimpico. A theatre of Renaissance Italy, designed by Palladio, completed in Vicenza in 1584; rose from the Olympic Academy of Vicenza; constructed according to the best classical ideas of the time, but with several innovations. Distinguishing features: (1) auditorium in semi-ellipse, not semi-circle; (2) orchestra between the front of the stage and the lowest row of seats; (3) the stage, or *pulpitum*, rectangular, long and narrow as in Roman theatres, with wooden floor painted to resemble marble; (4) behind this proscenium, an ornamented architectural façade similar to those of the theatre at Orange; (5) below this façade four pediments with statues, above it six statues surmounted by six decorative panels and a painted roof; (6) facing the audience a large open arch, the *porta regia* of Vitruvius, flanked on each side by two lesser doors, or *portae minores;* (7) the sides of the stage, or *versurae,* enclosed by walls set at right angles to the proscenium and pierced by doors with boxes above them, these boxes for use both for action of the play and for spectators. Originally, arches were closed by doors or back-drops, but, through the influence of Barbaro's interpretation of Vitruvius, Scamozzi introduced perspective alleys at each of the arches so that every spectator could look down at least one of them.

Teatro Vecchio. A 17th-18th century theatre at Naples, distinguished by the horseshoe auditorium; its proscenium was single, without façade.

Telecast (television). Any television broadcast, whether of live talent, motion pictures or outside news event.

Television. The transmission and reproduction of transient visual images by radio.

TELEVISION (Or The Unknown Art)

BY GILBERT SELDES

As I recall it, the editor of this book asked me to write a short paper on Writing for Television; and I think I replied that television was already slightly overwritten. This of course was a low joke. It referred back to an ancient grudge of mine, namely that the movies, the moment that they began to talk, began to be over-talked; I felt very seriously that no good would come of the microphone in the movie studio, until the camera had re-asserted its pre-eminence. To have a pictorial object which moves, and which therefore can convey certain ideas, emotions and fantasy in the most rapid manner, and then to slow it up by attaching it to an immobilized microphone, seemed to me, about 1930, to be fairly suicidal. The moving picture recovered by doing two things: it began to use the microphone more intelligently, thereby stepping it up to the use made of it in radio; and it reverted to the camera as the prime element in the motion picture.

Nevertheless there is too damned much talk in moving pictures, and although the talk has become more intelligent and more agreeable, in some pictures, since the worst days of whimsery, you still can see a film in which a man and a woman (not his wife, I regret to say) are stranded in the arctic, and talk like slightly undernourished offspring of some of the more wilful characters in the early plays of Philip Barry. If you don't believe this, you may cast your eye back to the conversations between Clark Gable and Loretta Young in *The Call of the Wild.* That is to say, if Clark Gable and Loretta Young were in *The Call of the Wild,* as I believe they were.

This doesn't quite mean that I would prefer to witness a production of Hamlet, Pygmalion, or Hellzapoppin, without the text; it doesn't even mean that I want moving pictures tossed back into the days of the silent film. It simply means that there is a definite and correct way to use the visual image in counterpoint to the spoken word. When that correct way has been found in the movies, you get a great moving picture; unless the correct way of balancing sound and sight is found in television, we will not create an interesting and important art. And the first thing for writers to recognize is that their written words are not necessarily all-important to the world at large. To them it will seem an act of retrogression to prefer the pictured symbol and the animated cartoon, and the moving picture to the sacred word. But the writers who are going to do well, and I am not speaking entirely of financial success, the writers who are going to do well in the next fifty years will be those who will make terms with the new arts of communication—going as far back as photography. The ones who will do best of all will also make terms with the photo-electric cell.

To my great surprise I can actually make a practical suggestion to anyone who is writing with television in mind. I have had printed for myself a large number of the ordinary ruled yellow pads, and about two-thirds of the way over to the right I have had made a solid black line running from top to bottom of the page. That black line is only a reminder that before we can go into production I have to hand to my director a script in which there will be not only a text, but a visual parallel to the text. I do not mean that when a person says "the hat is black" we should have first a picture of a black piece of cloth. By a parallel, I mean only to suggest that there will be something significant or interesting visible on the screen all the time while a program is going on.

Of course as far as dramatic writing goes, the actors in a play will be basically the visual element. Writers for the theatre have always assumed that people would be looking at certain characters while certain words are spoken; and that actions would take place to which the words would be suited. (Consult Hamlet's advice to the players.) Writers for radio have developed an almost uncanny technique for creating visual images by audible means. With television we grant full freedom again to the writer to use the visual and the audible, but with that freedom goes the grave responsibility that his visual channel must be extraordinarily interesting or he will only be boring an audience which has really learned to use its imagination and to enjoy radio without ever feeling a lack of the visual.

It is in the non-dramatic field that I think the writer will have to learn how to use both sides of the black line. I believe that television will offer incalculable opportunities for the development of programs dealing with the news, programs which will be in effect documentaries, programs of exceptional informative value, so brilliantly produced—years from now if not right away that the ancient curse of the *educational* will not rise again. Now if anyone begins to do a television program on the rising birth rate in Sweden compared to the rate of suicides in Vienna—not a subject I recommend for instant treatment, but still a possible subject—every important facet of the subject must be rendered visually. We may have a few feet of a moving picture showing (a) the birth of a baby or (b) the city of Stockholm; we may have a chart, preferably an animated chart; we may have a still picture; we may have an isograph by Neurath or one of Modley's brilliant pictorial statistics; we may have a symbol of some kind. But in any case we will have a smoothly flowing visual program which will precisely correspond to, will illuminate, and will intensify, the spoken text.

I think that what we want to create is a new form of picture writing. The ancient Chinese, according to legend, could express an entire sentence, or a complex philosophical concept, in single pictograph. We have infinitely more materials at our command and we have the great blessing of movement as well. Therefore we should develop a kind of picture writing which will not, of course, live without the spoken word, but which will serve the spoken word completely.

The French writer André Malraux complained some time ago that the writers of the present time have not yet come to terms with the printing press. That, in fact, is where I got the idea which I put forth at the beginning of this piece. I'm not suggesting that anybody knuckle down to any piece of machinery; but I think it's worth while for any man who wants to communicate with his fellow-men, to learn to use the most effective methods of communication.

TELEVISION HISTORY

BY LEIF EID

The story of television begins early in the nineteenth century with the discovery of selenium by a Swedish pharmacist, Berzelius by name. It extends through the discovery of photo-electric effects by Becquerel about 1840. It was, however, the chance discovery of selenium's photo-electric properties by a telegraph operator named May, at the Valentia cable station, in Ireland, that set numerous scientific workers to the task of devising systems for transmitting images by electrical means. May noticed that some selenium resistors he was using became better conductors of electricity when exposed to sunlight. His findings were soon verified and it became apparent that if the element's resistance to the passage of electricity varied with the intensity of the light focused on it, then the lights and shadows that make up a visual image could be transmitted by electrical means.

Numerous schemes were shortly advanced for *seeing by telegraphy*. The one, however, which seemed to hold forth greatest promise of success was that advanced by Dr. Paul Nipkow, whose famous scanning disc clearly dominated television thinking until the later years of the last decade. This was a flat, circular piece of metal near the edge of which was punched a series of holes in spiral form, in such a way that the outermost, when the disc was in motion, gave a view of a strip of the scene. The second afforded a view of the next strip and so on until the whole scene had been dissected in a series of strips. Light reflected from the person or scene through these holes would vary the resistance of a selenium cell, thus transforming the scene from one of lights and shadows into one of electrical impulses of varying intensities. The principle, though not the device, is still used.

It was soon realized, however, that though the ideas might be sound, no apparatus of sufficient sensitivity was available to bring television into being. The next decades, therefore, saw a diminished enthusiasm for television, with, however, an accompanying accumulation of the electrical devices needed. Thomas A. Edison, had in the 70's discovered the "Edison eeffct," that is, the passage of current from a heated filament to a nearby, and positively charged, plate, both inclosed in an evacuated glass tube. This led to the development of the Fleming tube and later, about 1906, to the De Forest *audion,* greatly improved, particularly during radio's rapid development during the World War. This tube is the basis for the essential amplifiers that multiply the intensity of the extremely weak electrical impulses arising in television scanning.

The origin of the modern cathode ray receiving tube can also be traced back into the last century. Sir William Crookes demonstrated cathode rays in 1878; Karl Braun introduced the oscilloscope about the turn of the century. This was a vacuum tube showing visually the variations of an alternating current. It was shown that a magnetic field originating in a coil placed about the neck of the tube improved the sharpness of the fluorescent spot. Obviously, the cathode ray which produced the pot of light at the end of the tube could also be deflected by magnetic means; the ray itself being an electrical current.

The kinescope, and all other cathode ray tubes developed for television, is based on the fact that an electron beam impinging on a fluorescent screen in an evacuated tube produces a spot of light, most of which passes through the screen and is visible from the outside of the tube. The electron beam, originating in an electron gun, is focused to a small point where it touches the screen. It is drawn across this screen in a predetermined pattern in a definite time.

The intensity of the light spot varies with the intensity of the electron beam. The beam, therefore, is modulated by the signal received from the transmitter. Thus the beam reconstitutes the original scene by disposing the image light elements in their proper position so rapidly that the eye perceives only a complete and continuous image.

Boris Rosing patented a system in 1907 in which the Braun tube was used at the receiver and the Nipkow scanning disc at the transmitter. In 1911 A. A. Campbell Swinton outlined a method for television without the aid of a single moving mechanical part. Cathode ray tubes of suitable design would be used at both transmitter and receiver.

Today all important television systems employ cathode ray tubes, in one form or another, in both transmitter and receiver, but Swinton's scheme remained purely theoretical until about 1930.

John Logie Baird, an English experimenter, is generally credited with being the first to transmit true television images. In 1926 he sent, over wire, crude images of 30 scanning lines at the rate of 12½ images a second, in the presence of members of the Royal Institution in London. He used a mechanical system.

American laboratories, however, were already at work on what is now called the *all-electronic* system of television. Dr. Vladimir K. Zworykin, of the Radio Corporation of America, brought out his iconoscope in 1933. This was a large vacuum tube for translating a light image into one of electrical values and for dissecting this electrical *image* into its elements for piecemeal transmission. At the receiver, Zworykin produced a synthetic image by means of his kinescope, a cathode ray tube. Philo T. Farnsworth, another American, is also credited with the development of an all-electronic system. His camera tube is known as the *image dissector*. Projection tubes, casting images on a distant screen, have been developed both in the United States and abroad. Several London motion picture houses are now equipped with such apparatus for the showing of outstanding news events telecast by the British Broadcasting Corporation.

Television broadcasting in the United States, as a regular public service, began on April 30, 1939, when the National Broadcasting Company telecast the opening ceremonies of the New York World's Fair. At the present time NBC offers a minimum weekly service of eleven and one-half hours to its New York audience over Station W2XBS. Eighteen stations in the United States are licensed to telecast experimentally, and it is expected that NBC's service will soon be supplemented in other parts of the country.

Tempest, Marie (née Etherton) (1866-   ). English actress. Made her stage debut in the operetta *Boccaccio* in London 1885. She won great popularity in comic opera and appeared in such notable successes as *Frivoli,* 1886, and *La Béarnaise,* 1887. She made her first appearance in New York City in *The Red Hussar* in 1889. In 1899 she severed her connection with musical plays and turned to comedy and played in such notable successes as *Becky Sharp,* 1901; *The Marriage of Kitty,* 1902; *Caste,* 1902; *Penelope,* 1909; and many other successes both in London and New York. After the war she played in *Hay Fever,* 1925; *Mr. Pim Passes By,* 1928; *The First Mrs. Fraser,* 1929; and other successful comedies. For more than 50 years Marie Tempest has maintained her place on the English speaking stage as one of the most polished and brilliant actresses.

Tempest, The. William Shakespeare (English). Comedy. 5 acts. 1611.

Shakespeare's last complete work, written about 1611 and published in the Folio of 1623. It was probably inspired by the published experience of a group of colonists shipwrecked off the Bermudas in 1609. Alonso, king of Naples, Antonio usurping duke of Milan, Sebastian, brother of the king, and others are shipwrecked on an island where Prospero, rightful duke of Milan, lives with his daughter Miranda, and is served by Ariel, a spirit of the air, and Caliban, a monster of the earth. The king's son, Ferdinand, falls in love with Miranda, and after undergoing trials of hard labor, is accepted by Prospero as a son-in-law. Meantime Sebastian and Antonio plot the death of the king and are prevented by the magic of Prospero, which also frustrates a plot by Caliban and two drunken sailors, Stephano and Trinculo, to seize the island from Prospero. After exhausting both parties with fruitless trips about the island in search of visionary banquets, Prospero forgives them all and is restored to his dukedom.

Tempest, The. Henri Bernstein (French). Drama. 5 acts. 1905.

Hélène, a foolish girl, becomes infatuated with a gambler who embezzles her entire fortune. In a desperate attempt to save the man she loves, she goes to her father for money. She upbraids her father with having forced her to marry a man she does not love, and demands that he pay her now for the wrong he has done her. He refuses, however, and Hélène tries to procure the necessary sum by selling herself to a cousin. The gambler commits suicide, and Hélène realizes that her offer to sacrifice herself has been in vain.

Templeton, Fay (1865-1939). American actress. Appeared as the infant child in *East Lynne* in 1868, when she was three, and was a seasoned performer at ten, having played Puck in *A Midsummer Night's Dream* at the New York Grand Opera House in 1873. She played in New York and Europe until 1900, when she joined Weber and Fields; and in 1905 she played in George M. Cohan's *Forty-five Minutes from Broadway,* in New York and elsewhere, until her retirement from the stage in 1906. She returned, however, in 1911 as Buttercup in *H.M.S. Pinafore* at the Casino, New York; rejoined Weber and Fields in 1912; and entered vaudeville in 1916. She alternately retired and reappeared until 1933, when she played Aunt Minnie in *Roberta* at the New Amsterdam Theatre in New York. At that time Brooks Atkinson, drama critic of the New York *Times,* wrote: "and Fay Templeton, as la bonne Roberta, has a scene that could hardly be excelled for its warmth and sweetness. Theatre-goers are sentimental folk, praise be to God. When the much cherished Fay is disclosed on the stage, doing a little good here and there, it is hard to know whether she or the audience is the more deeply moved."

Ten-twent'-thirt'. Name given to an old form of melodrama built along hackneyed, stereotyped lines played at admission prices of ten, twenty and thirty cents. H. R. Jacobs and F. F. Proctor popularized companies playing successes of the higher-priced organizations. *The Lights of London, Mazeppa* and *The Romany Rye* are typical. Later on these prices became standard for companies playing melodramas in the smaller theatres of America; hence the universal use of the term.

Tennyson, Alfred Tennyson, 1st Baron (1809-1892). English poet, dramatist. Born at Somersby, Lincolnshire. He was educated at the grammar school at Louth and at home, later with his brothers, Charles and Frederick, at Cambridge. His first book, *Poems by Two Brothers,* 1827, was published by Frederick and written by Alfred (mostly) and Charles. His style combined the qualities of his great predecessors, Wordsworth, Coleridge, Byron, Shelley and Keats. He never reached the high point of any of them, but he had the ability to translate their characteristics into a sweet style which was enormously popular in England and America. His lines were eminently quotable. Queen Victoria made him Poet Laureate in 1850. *Locksley Hall, Sixty Years After,* the *Idylls of the King, In Memoriam, The Charge of the Light Brigade,* are perhaps his best remembered poems. His dramas, in which he invariably failed of theatrical success, include *Queen Mary,* 1875 (played by Irving in 1876); *Harold,* 1876 (not staged); *The Falcon* (played by the Kendals), 1879; *The Foresters* (acted in New York with Ada Rehan as Maid Marian), 1892.

Tenor, The. Frank Wedekind (German). Drama. 3 acts. 1899.
A famous singer thinks only of his career and scorns both the old composer and the women who adore him. What matter if one of these women, as he is about to

depart for a performance, should shoot herself because he will not take her along?
He must hasten away to win applause in the role of Tristan, the great lover.

Tentum. Name of a certain scene building, or mansion, of the medieval stage,
meaning, literally, "tent."
See also *Mansions*.

Terence (c. 195-159 B.C.). Roman dramatist. Legend has it that Terence,
whose full name was Publius Terentius Afer, was born in Carthage and brought to
Rome as a slave by the senator Terentius Lucanus. His owner educated and then
liberated him, and he took the senator's name for his own to show his gratitude.
Between 166-160 B.C. six of his plays were produced: *Andria*, 166; *Hecyra*, 165;
Heauton Timorumenos, 163; Eunuchus, 161; *Phorimo*, 161; *Adelphi*, 160. He died
the following year, supposedly of grief at losing his translations of the works of
Menander, on whose plays many of his were based.

Together with Plautus, Terence was the most influential Latin comic dramatist.
Molière and many others have been inspired by him; both his plots and his characterizations are considered outstanding. In his day Terence associated with some
of the most brilliant writers of the period, including Plautus. Both Terence and
Plautus based their plays on the New Comedy of Greece, but Terence's humor is less
broad than that of his contemporary. A stock plot of Terentian comedy concerns
the love of a youth for a girl apparently his inferior in birth, but who is eventually
discovered to be the long-lost daughter of some near friend of his father.

Terror and pity. As indicated by Aristotle in his *Poetics* the two prime emotions which tragedy, by its very nature, is obliged to arouse.

Terry, Dame Ellen Alicia (1848-1928). English actress. A daughter of
Benjamin and Sarah Terry, popular provincial actors; born at Coventry. At the age
of eight she made her first appearance as Mamilius at the Princess' Theatre, London,
in Kean's revival of *The Winter's Tale*. While still a girl she won success as Prince
Arthur in *King John*, and between 1860 and 1863, she acted in stock companies. Her
marriage to the painter, G. F. Watts, in 1864, led to a temporary retirement from
the stage, but after the dissolution of the marriage she began to act again, in 1867,
making in that year her first appearance with Henry Irving, as Katharine in *The
Taming of The Shrew*. A second retirement, 1868-1874, was followed by her reappearance under the management, first of Charles Reade and then, as Portia in *The
Merchant of Venice*, of the Bancrofts. She married E. A. Wardell in 1876. Her
performance as Olivia in *The Vicar of Wakefield* in 1878 set the seal on her reputation, and led to her engagement as leading lady to Irving at the Lyceum Theatre.

During the next twenty years, in a long series of Shakespearean and other roles,
Ellen Terry became the most beloved actress of her own, and probably of any, day.
She was chiefly famous as a Shakespearean actress. Her Beatrice in *Much Ado About
Nothing* proved her genius for light comedy. She toured in America in 1883, and
was extremely popular. Her non-Shakespearean parts included Camma in Tennyson's

The Cup, Rosamund in the same author's *Becket,* Madame Sans-Gêne, and Clarisse in *Robespierre.* She appeared in Barrie's *Alice Sit-by-the-Fire,* 1905, and Shaw's *Captain Brassbound's Conversion,* 1906.

Her partnership with Irving was broken up by his death in 1905. Thenceforth her appearances became more confined to occasional performances in aid of charity. In 1925 she was made a Dame of the Empire.

She was the sister of the actresses Kate, Marion and Florence Terry and of the actor Fred Terry; and the mother of Gordon and Edith Craig.

Thalia. In Greek mythology, the Muse of Comedy and romantic poetry. Thus, a comic actor is sometimes said to have put on the robes of Thalia. Thalia is also one of the three Graces.

Theatre. Word derived from the Greek meaning to see, or view. A general term comprising every department of the stage—acting, producing, directing, play-writing and the playhouse itself. As a form of expression Allardyce Nicoll characterizes it as one of the most traditional, yet an expression subtly symbolic of all literary media and one which consistently meets the needs of a particular age. In its broadest sense theatre means the entire field of amusement; drama, stage, cinema, circus, magic, vaudeville, and the entertainment side of radio and television.

Theatre, The. The first public playhouse in England, erected in 1576 by James Burbage. Accommodating 1,500 people, it cost seven hundred pounds and was situated in Holywell, a district in London beyond the jurisdiction of the city. The Theatre, under Burbage's proprietorship, was used by such groups of professional actors as Warwick's, the Queen's, and the Lord Chamberlain's. The last, for whom Shakespeare wrote, presented here an early version of *Hamlet* in 1596. The Theatre was torn down in 1597 and the salvaged materials were used in constructing the more celebrated Globe theatre across the Thames on the Bankside.

Theatre, American, 17th-18th century. It was in the colleges that early interest in the drama was strongest. In 1690, the early play written by a native American, *Gustavus Vasa* by Benjamin Colman, was produced at Harvard. In 1702 William and Mary College produced a pastoral colloquy. Meanwhile the College of Philadelphia was giving attention to "dialogues" written by students. In colonial times the hour of the curtain was 6 p.m. Ladies sat in boxes, the best of which were reserved for their arrival by their Negro servants. Young gentlemen sat on the stage. The pit was occupied only by men. The noisy and vociferous rabble sat in the gallery. Plays by Farquhar, Fielding, Otway, Jonson and Shakespeare were produced. The theatre was frowned upon in colonial New England and laws were passed banning it there. This was one of the reasons that it was in the southern colonies of Virginia and the Carolinas that the theatre in the New World really began. The arrival of the Hallam Company from England marked the beginning of dignified drama in America. They performed in Charleston. Up to, and during, the Revolutionary War, actors in America were mostly British. Eventually public feeling turned against them because of their allegiance to the mother country. In spite of this audiences continued to grow, more and more theatres were built, the majority by Douglass. In 1774 all public amusements were banned. Four years later a more stringent decree forbade play-acting in any form. The younger among the British officers began giving performances and the theatre thus introduced was run by groups of officers. The law against amusements was repealed in 1789. It was during the season of 1785-86 that Hallam and Henry, managers, first adopted the practice of selling reserved seats. Before this, tickets of admission were sold, the holders of which sent their servants to hold the best seats. Frequently the owners would not show up; and, as servants were not permitted in theatres, the good seats would go unoccupied. Hallam and Henry, to do away with this, innovated the selling of tickets with seat numbers indicated on them. Boston was not permitted to have its first theatre until 1792. Then it was that a group of theatre lovers formed an association and subscribed funds for a building to be a theatre in everything but name. It had a pit, a row of boxes and a gallery, the whole seating about five hundred persons. It was called the New Exhibition Room. On December 5, 1792, the sheriff closed the theatre. In 1793 the law was repealed and a large brick theatre building was erected. This structure was opened to the public on February 3, 1794, as the Boston Theatre. The first appearance of an American Negro on the American stage was that of William Bates in the role of Sambo in J. Murdock's *Triumph of Love* in 1795.

Theatre, American, 19th century. The number of playhouses in America grew rapidly from the early years of the 19th century on, but their structure was not always safe or durable. In 1811 the Richmond, Virginia, theatre was destroyed by a fire in which seventy-one persons perished. This was the first fatal catastrophe of its kind in America and was looked upon as a punishment from heaven. As a result a law was passed forbidding amusements of all kinds for the space of four years. In 1826 the first playhouse to be illuminated by gas, the New York Theatre (the tenth public playhouse in New York) was opened. In Chicago there was no public entertainment of any kind until 1837. In fact this city could not boast a theatre of any consequence until 1847 when John B. Rice erected a frame building on Randolph Street.

The first record of ticket speculation is to be found in the appearance of Jenny Lind at the Castle Garden in 1850. Tickets were in such demand that speculators charged the highest possible rates. The first copyright law was passed in 1856 and was mainly due to the efforts of Dion Boucicault. In the northern states the Sixties was the period of great theatrical progress and success. War profiteering had brought forth a large class of financiers who were willing to contribute to the building of new playhouses. As they were generally enormous in size and thereby more suitable for spectacles than for ordinary plays, the loss to the legitimate drama was great. Between 1861 and 1865 the dramatic fare, as well as the acting companies, was largely British. Before this, in 1860, the travelling company had been developed by Dion Boucicault and was, for the first time, dispatched to what became the road with but a single play. Before this touring companies had a stock repertoire which was frequently run through for the length of a single locality's engagement. The first play thus sent out was Boucicault's *The Colleen Bawn* and was graced by John Drew. It was in 1860 that the combination system first came into effect. This was a blow struck at the already powerful star system and meant the abandonment of resident stock companies and the selection of actors according to type rather than public favoritism.

In 1896 the first theatrical syndicate was formed, and chains of playhouses began to be organized with centralized booking interests. The types of play most popular during the post-Civil-War years were: the fireman drama, with the depiction, generally distorted, of city life; the minstrel show; and the burlesque, which began with the introduction of the leg show in the famous melodrama, *The Black Crook*. Among the best known playhouses of the period, aside from those already mentioned, were the Union Square Theatre, the Madison Square Theatre, and, among the most celebrated of all, Niblo's Gardens.

Theatre, American, 20th century. At the opening of the 20th century American producers were interested in the foreign theatre solely as a source of famous actors to be starred or plays to be adapted. The radical structural and scenic changes being made in the continental theatre had no connection with the shallow box-stage and the naturalistic detail of the stage settings Belasco achieved with painstaking accuracy.

It was not until the second decade of the century, when foreign travel became the vogue, that American artists outside the theatre took up the new movement and brought back to their native theatre the theories and practices of the continental theatre. Robert Edmond Jones served an apprenticeship in Reinhardt's theatre then returned to help found the Provincetown Players in 1916. Sam Hume was a pupil of Craig's then returned to influence the amateur and educational theatre in the West. Maurice Browne, also a pupil of Craig's, assisted in the founding of the Goodman Memorial Theatre in Chicago, a theatre with perfect sight-lines, acoustics, and a stage equipped with a plaster dome. Lee Simonson mastered the aesthetic theories of Appia, studied the methods of Linnebach, another pupil of Appia, and brought back to the Washington Square Players (which later became the Theatre Guild) his method of projecting scenery by means of light on a backdrop or a cyclorama. Joseph Urban and Norman Bel Geddes joined the movement toward new structural theatre designs. Urban and Thomas Lamb designed the elliptical-shaped auditorium of the Ziegfeld Theatre and were successful in creating a façade that reflected the pulse of the present. Geddes has projected a formal platform stage in which the actor is emphasized in space through lighting, and may mingle freely with the audience which practically surrounds him. The greatest experiments in theatre architecture have been made by community and university theatre groups. The Cleveland Play House, for example, has a main auditorium seating five hundred and a smaller stage with an auditorium accommodating two hundred. Both stages are well equipped, the larger with a plastered back wall and removable steps over the orchestra pit. (Small and Rowley, architects.) The Pasadena Playhouse is California Mission style, heavy white stucco loggias and walls, red tile roofs and baroque scrolls. The stage is equipped with a plastered rear wall, elaborate lighting equipment and two wagon stages for scene-shifting. (Elmer Grey, architect.) The Theatre Guild houses in one building the offices and clubrooms of the organization. The building is Italian Renaissance style. (C. Howard Crane, architect.) The cyclorama has become one of the most important pieces of stage equipment in American theatres. Many have revolving stages. The Manhattan Opera House was adapted for large spectacles such as Reinhardt's *The Eternal Road,* by the use of movable equipment, structural stage settings and plastic lighting.

Simonson brought to America Appia's belief that "light is the most important plastic medium on the stage." Designers and directors have come to use colored lights on the stage as a painter uses a brush and paints. Reinhardt's method of spotlighting was one of the first innovations. Today one of our leading directors, McClintic, lights his actors after his own scheme. The designer places the lights as he wishes for the setting. McClintic is concerned with the lighting of mobile form in space, the problem which concerned both Appia and Craig.

The first trip to America of the Moscow Art Players in 1923 acquainted directors and actors with Stanislavsky's theory of acting. In directing the Group Theatre, Clurman uses Stanislavsky's method of character improvisations, and follows the Russian "group feeling" for ensemble effect. Copeau's influence was felt when he directed in New York during the First World War.

The American theatre has developed from this foreign influence a group of designers and a group of directors, each with his own individual approach. It is interesting that a number of director-designer collaborations have resulted in complete harmony and ensemble effect. For example, McClintic's mental picture of a bridge spanning the stage for *Winterset* was worked out to his complete satisfaction by Mielziner. Moeller and Simonson collaborated in the Guild production of *Juarez and Maximilian* by gaining their scenic ends through the combination of the massing of figures and light. There was a similar collaboration by Jones and Hopkins in the expressionistic production of *Macbeth,* in which distortion and statuesque lines were achieved through grouping and scenic design.

American scene designers and directors are checked in their achievement both by outmoded theatre buildings and by native playwrights who hold to prose realism. The plays of O'Neill and Anderson offer challenge after challenge to both director and designer, as do the plays of Shakespeare and other classic writers. But the theatre is still too inflexible to benefit by the experimentation of the last quarter century. Urban and Geddes agree the "new theatre" cannot reach its full maturity until actors can enter naturally from the auditorium as well as from the stage. Every division between the actor and spectator should be eliminated, as in the classic theatre, so that the two are an entity, surrounded by the same walls, thus establishing the spiritual essence of the theatre.

Theatre, architecture. The scope of the drama is governed by the nature of the theatre. The house, and the stage on which the performance is to be given determine, to a great extent, what can be performed. Dramatists must, perforce, write plays in accordance with the possibilities of the theatres available. This is a restriction, and a force that continually shows its influence in the history of the theatre. Spectacle plays will not be written unless there is a theatre for them and conversely a large theatre will stimulate the composition of dramas for it.

Unfortunately the architects of the commercial theatre have lagged behind its other artists. Direction, scenic design, lighting, acoustics, air-conditioning, etc., have made great strides that have not been matched by architecture. Undoubtedly the real estate and economic factors have much to do with this, but whatever the causes, the theatres of today, with but few exceptions like the Radio City Music Hall, do not meet the seating, acoustics, lighting and stage requirements of the Ideal Theatre.

All the arts and modern designers and inventors can be employed to enable a greater and more effective presentation of the drama.

Theatre, auditorium, ovoid. A theatre hall, deriving from the early semi-circular tradition, now elongated into an almost complete oval.

See also *Patte; Teatro di Torino; Teatro d'Imola; Teatro Tor di Nona.*

Theatre, auditorium, straight-sided. A break, in the 17th-18th century Italian theatre, with the semi-circular tradition of the theatrical hall; the galleries extending straight from, at right angles to, the stage front and meeting in the rear in a series of graded angles.

Theatre, Balinese. On his "enchanted isle" the primitive rituals, essentially theatrical in expression, are still observed. The Sword Dance, the *Ranga* (a witch dance) and others are performed. The natives also give plays, including pantomimes performed in masks. The more religious of the ceremonies are not open to the public.

Theatre, box. Portions of the theatre usually to the side of the building (often omitted from modern theatres), railed off from the rest of the house and containing movable chairs. These may be on any level, and in opera houses in Europe and America are usually placed just below the balcony, to form the famous "horseshoe," a characteristic of all court theatres from the end of the 17th to the middle of the 19th centuries.

Theatre, Bulgarian, before the First World War. The theatre in Bulgaria is hardly more than forty years old, due to the fact that the country has been free of Turkish domination only a little over sixty years. But the theatre soon came to be the art most central to the social life of the times. It depended, however, on foreign repertories.

Theatre, Bulgarian, since the First World War. The theatre has grown rapidly since the First World War, with the result that audiences, particularly those in the capital, Sofia, have a high standard of perfection and are among the severest to please in Europe. These audiences are especially critical of repertory as they regard the theatre idealistically as a genuine school of ideas. Reading rooms in the small villages are frequently converted into theatres. The National Theatre in Sofia is a state institution. Some of the actors have been educated in the Moscow Art Theatre in Russia, others in France and Germany. The newer generation of actors was trained by Massalitinov, one of the first artists of the Moscow Art Theatre, who was brought to the National Theatre in Sofia in 1925. No one style of staging has predominated to the exclusion of others that might be useful in a varied repertory that has embraced practically the whole history of the drama: Greek tragedy, the classics, Shakespeare, Goethe, Schiller, Molière, Goldoni, Beaumarchais, Victor Hugo, Dumas *fils,* Ibsen, Hauptmann, Strindberg, Maeterlinck, Oscar Wilde, Bernard Shaw, Galsworthy, Pirandello, and Molnar—these are but a few of a wide range of sources. The National Theatre company toured a few centers of Bulgarian population in the United States, including New York, during the summer of 1937.

Theatre, Chinese. See *Drama, Chinese; Staging, Chinese; Acting, Chinese.*

Theatre, classical Athenian, 5th century, B.C. (1) Religion colored the whole field of drama, and the theatre, not a class affair but essentially popular and dramatic, therefore required adequate housing space. (2) Since the chorus, both in tragedy and comedy, was the very essence of each and remained the central element of the drama, adequate acting space was likewise necessary. In 465 B.C. the *skene* was introduced.

Theatre, closing of (1642-1660). The rise of the Puritans in England led to their closing all public theatres. In 1642 they passed a law suppressing all stage plays. Theatrical productions were not resumed until the Restoration of the Stuarts in 1660, though some private performances were given.

Theatre, Czechoslovak, before the First World War. The National Theatre in Prague has been an institution so close to the people, their interests and problems as to be an object almost of worship, a fact that exemplifies with what ardor the theatre, generally, was cherished by the masses. For example, no other European theatre has given productions of either such quality or quantity of the American dramatist O'Neill. Subert and Kvapil were the leading directors of the Czechoslovak theatre before the World War. Under Kvapil the greatest Czech Shakespearean actor, Eduard Vojan, came into prominence.

Theatre, Czechoslovak, since the First World War. The traditions of the great pre-World War theatre were carried over in Prague under the vigorous tutelage of Hilar, who was an enthusiastic student of Max Reinhardt. Hillar's belief, says Otakar Vacadlo, writing on "The Theatre and Drama of Czechoslovakia" in Dickinson's *The Theatre in a Changing Europe* "was that Czechoslovak theatrical art should combine the spiritual realism of Stanislavsky with the artistic vision of Gordon Craig." Dostal was the most important of his colleagues. There came an era of little theatres, the two most important of which were the Theatre Unbound and *D 36.* Farces and political and social satires began to be performed. Vlasta Burian, the comedian, was the foremost actor, a kind of Czech Chaplin without the underlying feeling of melancholy. The leading stages operated under the repertory system, making, with the constantly overcrowding material, for generally slipshod produc tion. The National Theatre finally became a state institution, thereby ceasing to be a genuine people's theatre.

See also *Theatre Unbound*.

Theatre, Danish. All actors of Denmark must, because theirs is a small country, play a wide variety of roles, ranging in size and prominence from "straight" to "character." They cannot be "typed" as actors in larger countries frequently are, because a single play cannot draw a public longer than a few weeks and the demands for varied repertory are stronger in a theatre unable to support many enterprises. The Neiiendam and Mantzius families have contributed greatly to the Danish stage. The principal playhouse in Copenhagen is the Royal Dramatic Theatre.

Theatre, English, Elizabethan. From the spreading influence of the Italian Renaissance new interest began to spring up in England in the 16th century in the ancient Greek and Roman classics. The works of Plautus were revived and original plays began to be written in the contemporary English vernacular on the early classic models. Professional performers soon took the lead from the purely amateur and scholarly practitioners and organized their own companies, making up a varied repertory ranging from Terence, Plautus, and Seneca to their own national lore, such as the tales of Robin Hood. With increasing popularity these regular acting companies became an integral part of the life of the times, supplanting both the courtly amateurs and the choir boys in their peregrinations among the general populace. They gave their performances not in regular theatres but as strolling players in the yards of inns and taverns, several of which drew such audiences as, virtually or literally to be transformed completely and solely into playhouses. The first permanent public playhouse in London was known as *The Theatre* which was built and opened in 1576. The distinguishing features generally, of the Elizabethan playhouse were: (1) the hall stage—a slightly raised platform with backdrop and utilizing practically no change of scene; (2) the court show—"houses" (mansions) in the style of Serlio, grouped not in the Serlian perspective but in the unorganized style of the French; curtains and backdrops; sometimes the use of the *decor simultane;* (3) the public stage:—an open platform jutting out into a round auditorium; in the rear two doors, and overhead, projecting over at least part of the stage, a roof supported by two pillars; three galleries (in tiers) curving from either side to form the circular hall, one of these galleries continuing onto the back of the stage itself, and used either for spectators or as the scene of further action in the play. After the Theatre came the Curtain, the Rose and others, all built by the groups of players developed from the small touring companies of the earlier years of the century. The Globe Theatre, in Southwark, home of Shakespeare's company, was a major factor in the progress of this genuine people's theatre—also the Hope and the Swan. All of the playhouses suggest much of Palladio's Teatro Olimpico architecturally; but, critically, they were quite different, mainly because of the (implied) change of scene which had become part of its style. Besides the public theatres there were private halls such as the Blackfriars, the winter home of Shakespeare's company. In addition there were the bull and bear baiting pits which existed across the Thames from London proper.

These sporting arenas were circular single story wooden structures small and crude in character, 30 to 35 feet in diameter and 15 feet high. Here greatly simplified multiple scenery, or the *décor simultané,* was used exclusively. In the court masques, performed before James I and Charles I, the enterprising architect and scenic designer, Inigo Jones, designed special ornate proscenium arches to symbolize the moods of their respective pieces. As for the performers themselves, no women were allowed on the stage and all female roles were played by boys, actual companies of boys being formed for the purpose.

See also *Platform theatre; Upper stage.*

Theatre, English, 1642-1660. Rope-dancing exhibitions was the name used to disguise performances of comic scenes and Falstaff scenes first presented by organized bands of players under the leadership of Robert Cox when the theatres were closed and all acting suppressed. These were later published under the name of *Humours and Drolleries* for the use of theatrical booths at fairs. Between 1656 and 1660, D'Avenant made at least two ambitious productions which were overlooked by the law.

See also *Theatre, closing of, 1642-1660.*

Theatre, English, Restoration. (1) Construction: Theatres were built as closable indoor auditoriums; the hexagonal and octagonal arrangements of the outer walls with their arena-like formation were abandoned; externally the theatres began to resemble modern playhouses; internally they were not unlike those of our time, with their galleries and boxes (a modern, doored, balconied proscenium arch was built behind the apron); Dorset Garden and Drury Lane Theatres were the two greatest houses of the time. (2) Conventions: the front boxes, built on the ground floor of the auditorium, were occupied by beauties and toasts of the town, with their escorts behind them; the middle gallery was occupied by the middle classes, frequent partakers in rowdy demonstrations; the upper gallery for the lower classes, the footmen and lackeys—and here the prices were cheap and the demeanor prevailingly ribald and noisy. (3) Dramatic fare: As Charles II was the patron, if not virtual dictator of, the theatre playwrights wrote to please his tastes which derived from his exile associations with the artificial French drama and were correspondingly marked by a distaste for English plays, particularly those of Shakespeare; the King's sole interest appears to have been in amusement; he issued patents to the two major companies, D'Avenant's and Killigrew's, in 1660, the year of his return from exile; the patronage of Charles II continued, with varying vicissitudes, to the end of his reign. The most characteristic form of serious drama was the heroic tragedy, deriving to a great extent from Corneille, best exemplified by Dryden, whose use of the rhymed couplet started a great vogue. The masque, introduced into opera, later incorporated into the ballet and finally passing into pantomime, did not, in itself, achieve great popularity, the King preferring the public playhouse for his entertainment.

Theatre, English, 18th century. Structurally the English theatre of the 18th century carried on the traditions of its predecessor. Audiences were larger, thus encouraging regular stock companies, travelling troupes, and the emergence of private theatricals, or, in the term of our day, little theatres. These little theatres which were so fashionable were results of the disappearance of the intimate theatre, which permitted close association between audience and performers. The rise of the trades- man class had expanded the scope of the theatre from one limited in audience to members of the court.

Theatre, English, 19th and 20th century. Through the 19th and 20th cen- tury the British theatre has been ruled in turn by the structure of the theatre, which was so huge it necessitated theatrical display; by the actor-manager, who submerged all to rhetoric and grandiose passions, and by the playwright, who made the theatre serve his idea. Throughout each phase realism ruled. It first became apparent with the early 19th century craze for historical accuracy in costuming. Scenery was next in line as solid walls replaced shaky flats. Then exact and genuine properties com- pleted the often drab but always accurate picture.

In the Nineties came a discounting of the theory of realism. Craig proposed to displace it through the massing of light and shade, the introduction of various acting planes and the use of the statuesque to achieve symbolic form.

Great changes have been made during the 19th and 20th centuries in the tra- ditional architectural form of the theatre. In the first quarter of the 19th century, the proscenium doors disappeared, the apron was cut away and the modern picture- frame stage was established. Gas lighting was introduced so that for the first time the auditorium could be darkened. New stage effects were achieved and dimming came into constant use. Elaborate mechanical scenic and lighting devices were invented. Then electricity brought untold possibilities for painting the stage with light. The major change in the auditorium was the placing of the stalls in the pit.

Rapid theatre building (nearly twenty new theatres) characterized the years up to 1840. This was followed by a lull that lasted until the Sixties when Robertson's introduction of realism in drama aroused the demand for playhouses of a more intimate variety. In the closing decade theatre building exceeded even the active opening years of the century. Small theatres were also founded by literary groups sponsoring new and important foreign and native playwrights whose works were rejected by commercial producers. The Independent Theatre was founded in 1891, the Stage Society in 1900, the Irish Literary Theatre (later the Abbey Theatre) in 1899.

In the 20th century this literary movement becomes increasingly important. The British Drama League was founded in 1919 and now includes over 2,500 non- professional producing groups. The Stratford-upon-Avon Shakespearean Festival, the Malvern Festival and the open air theatre in Regent's Park have popularized the summer festival. The Old Vic and Sadlers Wells have become classic repertory theatres. Although the majority of the commercial theatres in London are still serv- ing the traditional theatre, the small theatres (Westminster, Gate, Mercury and Arts Theatre Club) offer their stages to new playwrights, directors and actors.

Theatre, Finnish. See *Drama, Finnish.*

Theatre, French, before 1650. Romantic in style its *décor simultané* deriving somewhat from the settings and designs of Serlio, used for the presentation of different localities for each scene of the plays; the *maisons* corresponding to the earlier mansions or *case.*

Theatre, French, 17th century. The late 16th and the 17th centuries were the times of the strolling players. Prominent men of the theatre acted customarily in several capacities, such as dramatist, actor and director. Alexandre Hardy was an early example, later Molière. The most famous playhouse was the Hôtel de Bourgogne. Here was performed an extensive repertory of plays, ranging from moral tragedies, through allegorical or political dramas to farces, *soties,* and even mysteries. Corneille, Molière and Racine formed the distinguished ruling triumvirate of this century. The Comédie-Française was founded in 1680 and became the first theatre of the French classics.

Theatre, French, 18th century. The Comédie-Française was the leading theatre of this time, and it was here that the finest productions and performances were given, notably of the two great works of the century, Beaumarchais' *Le Barbier de Séville* and *Le Mariage de Figaro.* In the meantime the Théâtre de l'Odéon came to the fore as an organization.

Theatre, French, 19th century. In 1812 Napoleon established a new constitution for the Comédie-Française, releasing it from jurisdiction to control by the Minister of Fine Arts. This was a sign of new times, politically and theatrically. In 1829 romantic drama supplanted classical tragedy as the major force in the theatre. Dumas *père* and Alfred de Vigny were the fathers of this form. Rachel was the great actress of the time (from 1838 to 1855) and one not to be approached until the rise of Sarah Bernhardt.

Theatre, French, before the First World War. The outstanding characteristic of the best in the theatre, represented by the Theatre Libre, was the fusion of theatre and literature; the forms of this theatre had wide variety, subtlety and imagination; to it belonged dramatists of the rank of Henri Becque, Brieux, Lemaître, Octave Mirbeau, Paul Bourget, Henri Bernstein, Romain Rolland, Maeterlinck, Jules Romains, Georges Courteline, Sacha Guitry.

Theatre, French, since the First World War. The playhouses, closed during the War, reopened with the question as to what was proper dramatic fare: war themes were impossible in their full, painful reality, and insupportable in any makeshift treatments; love plays were considered selfish and almost anti-social in their individualism; social and psychological plays were constrained to untruth and unreality on behalf of fostering a noble picture of the French character for salutary effects abroad. A reaction to this false theatre came in the smaller, and art, enterprises such as the Vieux Colombier under Copeau, the revived and reorganized Théâtre Libre under Veber, the Grimace under Bastide, L'Oeuvre under Lugné-Poë, and en-heartened by these came such bold directors and producers as Gaston Baty, Louis Jouvet, Pitoeff, etc. Under this collective vanguard, realism was soon suspect, as was old-fashioned romanticism.

Theatre, German, medieval. Performances in the Middle Ages were made up of a series of dialogues divided into acts no one of which had any unity of time or action. Each act was terminated, not by a curtain, but by the exit of the actors on some artificial pretext. All performances were given in the open street.

Theatre, German, 18th century. In the Staatsaktion persons on the stage were divided strictly according to rank. Kings were defined by a series of curving gestures with their scepters. General principals were assembled onstage in a semicircle, one which no secondary character could penetrate from his position in the rear. Stage delivery was slow, beginning as a murmur and rising steadily to a roar. Vowels were deliberately drawn out. Elbows were held tightly against the body or widespread like wings. Hands were never lifted above the head.

Compare with *Acting, Chinese; Acting, Japanese.*

Theatre, German, 19th Century. The century opened with no change because the policies of Goethe and Schiller were still in control for the first thirty years and Goethe's pronouncement *Erst schoen, dann wahr* (Beauty first, then truth) was the ideal of the German stage. The Romantic School in Germany was a feeble imitation of the French, and its chief playwrights were August Wilhelm with *Ion* and Friedrich Schlegel with *Alarcos,* both poor. Grillparzer and Kleist were romantics but neither so termed himself. Both of these men were important dramatists of their period, their plays being as successful in Vienna as in Munich, Dresden or Berlin. At this time an official effort was made to control the Royal Court theatres and to have as directors only persons with ideas acceptable to German officialdom and at the same time to enlarge the importance of the Berlin stage. Count Bruehl was the least offensive of these bureaucrats.

As one result of the Romanticism the French influence was particularly strong at the middle of the century and affected Gustav Freytag, Friedrich Hebbel and Otto Ludwig. Wagner with his music-dramas and the Duke of Saxe-Meiningen with his belief in the development of Naturalism did much to strengthen the German theatre but it was not until the advent of Gerhart Hauptmann and Sudermann that the German dramatists matched the advances in staging brought about by Saxe-Meiningen and Appia. The Meiningen company appeared May 1, 1874 in Berlin and between 1874 and 1890 performed there 385 times as well as 2,206 times on tour.

Dr. Otto Brahm established the *Freie Buehne* and on Sunday, September 29, 1889 produced *Ghosts* to considerable success, though many critics deplored the presentation of a foreign play first, believing native drama should be stimulated. Hauptmann's *Vor Sonnenaufgang* (Before Sunrise) was given next and created an uproar between the adherents of Naturalism (the Youngest Germans) and the Old Guard. A riot broke out in the audience during the second act but the actors continued to play as if perfect quiet reigned. Hauptmann's appearance for a curtain call marked the climax of the disorder.

The *Freie Buehne* continued for two seasons. The naturalistic plays it was founded to produce had entered the repertory of the larger houses; L'Arronge played Hauptmann's *Lonely Lives* at the Deutsches in 1891; Sudermann's *Der Ehre* was produced in one of the larger houses; and in 1894, Otto Brahm assumed the directorship of the Deutsches. Munich and Vienna followed suit in enlarging their repertories to include naturalistic German plays.

Theatre, German, before the First World War. There was no sharp break in tradition at the turn of the century. The forces set loose in the last twenty years of the 19th century continued to develop up to 1918. The *Freie Volksbuehne* (Berlin Free People's Stage), with a membership of 600, opened at the Ostend Theatre, October 19, 1890 with Ibsen's *Pillars of Society*. Season tickets, drawn by lot, were first fifty, then ninety pfennigs. By 1908, the society had a membership of 12,000. The *Neue Freie Volksbuehne* (New Free People's Theatre) was opened with Goethe's *Faust* in November, 1892, under the direction of Bruno Wille, an ardent socialist. This society first staged the great drama, Hauptmann's *The Weavers*. So successful was this organization that by 1914, it had 50,000 members. Other theatres, less successful, were the Schiller-Theatre in Berlin, 1894; the *Freie Volksbuehne* of Hamburg, 1893. Reinhardt's activities in the theatre began in 1894 as an actor of elderly character parts in Salzburg (he was a native of Vienna). Brahm placed him under contract for the Deutsches as an actor. He staged intimate pieces at a little cabaret, *Schall und Rauch,* and at the Kleines theatre between 1902 and 1905 he staged almost fifty productions. In 1905 he went to the Deutsches as director and also produced at the Kammerspiele from 1906 on. His system of repertory was the object of admiration in all Europe. His first large production was *Oedipus Rex* in 1906 in Munich, later performed in Berlin and Vienna. By 1914, in addition, he had already produced Aeschylus' *Orestes,* and Vollmoeller's *The Miracle,* with Humperdinck's music.

Unlike the French and British stage, the German playhouses continued to function night in and night out throughout the First World War. This was due in part to the bureaucratic system of state and municipal theatres, and in part to the fact that Germany was not invaded.

Theatre, German, since the First World War and before National Socialism. This theatre fostered the full flowering of expressionism; it gave to the world dramatists like Gerhart Hauptmann, Wedekind, Werfel, Ernst Toller; director-producers with the creative imagination of Max Reinhardt. A truly democratic, or people's theatre, came into existence with the establishment of the Volksbuehne, a theatrical organization run by directors, actors, and playwrights from the masses which was, nevertheless, opposed to communist and socialist propaganda.

Following the War styles of acting markedly deflected from the stilted, unnatural mannerisms of the past and progressed steadily toward a new naturalism. Such innovations in play styles as expressionism had done much to rob the individual player of his disproportionate importance, for here the whole was the vital feature rather than single, individual performances. In spite of this, however, individual performers were able to find their public. Perhaps the first in point of artistry and technique was Elisabeth Bergner, who held an adoring audience to the day of her flight from National Socialism, with such successes as Shaw's *Saint Joan,* Shakespeare's *Taming of the Shrew,* and Strindberg's *Miss Julie.* Her style was a delicate one of fanciful, childlike imaginativeness and a sure grasp of stage dynamics.

The acme of naturalistic acting was achieved by Oscar Sauer. The Italian Moissi, in spite of his at first imperfect German, attained a great success with his ardent and sensitive playing. Werner Krauss was acclaimed for his powerful plastic interpretations; Fritz Kortner for the poignance of his characterizations and the expressiveness of a unique voice; Emil Jannings for the earthly power made famous throughout the world by the motion picture. Other well-known actors of the time were: Heinrich George, Else Lehmann, Paula Wessely, Eugen Kloepfer, and Max Pallenberg.

Theatre, German, National Socialist. As it has been the principle of nazism, like that of Italian fascism, to glorify the state and correspondingly minimize, deprecate and otherwise discourage individual initiative and distinction, few, if any, plays or dramatists of importance have been produced. Privately owned theatres, following the national Socialist revolution of 1933, fell into ruin, the Volksbuehne and the Buehnenvolksbund were dissolved, although the former continued to exist in name, but quite without its former democratic basis, becoming a state theatre; all Jewish actors and directors were forced to withdraw; all Jewish and socialist-communist authors vanished; a Jewish theatre, known as the Jewish Cultural Society, sprang up for the employment of Jewish actors, playwrights and directors and for the edification and entertainment of the Jewish public prohibited from entering Aryan theatres.

See also *Jewish Cultural Society.*

Theatre, Graeco-Roman, 1st century B.C. Consisted mainly of comedy of ordinary life; saw the development and the elaboration of scenic devices and machines. Structure: (1) the auditorium was the same as earlier forms, extending beyond a semi-circle; (2) the orchestra, encroached on by scene buildings, was still always more than a semi-circle; (3) the lowest row of seats usually abutted on the orchestra; (4) the stage front was made plain, but the background elaborate. This theatre was the product of the meeting of the dying Greek civilization and the rapidly spreading Roman.

Theatre, Greek. Classical Athenian (5th century B.C.); Hellenistic (from 4th century B.C. onward); Graeco-Roman (1st century B.C.).

See also *Theatre, classical, Athenian; Theatre, Hellenistic; Theatre, Graeco-Roman.*

Theatre, Hellenistic. From the 4th century onward; largely in territories outside Greece, but under the impress of Greek, or Hellenic, culture. This form of early theatre included the famous *Phylakes* and saw the beginning of theatrical *machines*. Characteristics of the theatre structure: (1) circular orchestra; (2) auditorium slightly larger than a semi-circle; (3) rectangular *skene* usually divided into various rooms, with from one to three doorways in the front wall of the second story; (4) a series of pillars, with panels set between, from seven to ten feet in front of the *skene*; (5) the stage usually nine feet high, eight to ten feet deep, extending the entire length of the *skene*; (6) the episkenion (or proskenion) was usually pierced by three doors.

Theatre, Hungarian, before the First World War. Naturalism was the predominating fashion in this theatre. Shortly before the beginning of the First World War a general nervousness made itself felt and was best expressed by a growing reaction against the ruling class as well as existent social conditions.

Theatre, Hungarian, since the First World War. The Hungarian theatres are, largely, private organizations, although there is one state theatre, the National, and the Opera is supported by the government.

Theatre, illegitimate. Term for dramatic performances which came into vogue in the early 1800's, so-called because they combined farce, tragedy, opera and anything else that appealed to the author or producer.

Theatre, Italian, Renaissance. With a rebirth of interest, both scholarly and artistic, in the theatre of ancient Greece and Rome, sources of information, such as the works of *Vitruvius,* were discovered and avidly studied, leading to new theories, such as those of *Serlio,* and to new progress for the stage. Setting: simple columns supporting round arches, sometimes in a flat wall, sometimes in a three-sided figure, the spaces between the columns closed by curtains which could be drawn to show tiny rooms with rear windows; the back wall, or proscenium, sometimes flanked by two statuettes, one of Phoebus and the other of Liber; *case* relics of the medieval mansions. Perspective was introduced into this theatre by Serlio. These were *case* to the left and right solid, but those in between, at the rear, painted flat on a back-drop curtain.

Theatre, Italian, 18th century. Auditorium: elongated, but still retaining, partially at least, a somewhat semi-circular or elliptical form. Galleries: sometimes built straight and at right angles to the stage, sometimes ovoid, sometimes in the shape of a horseshoe. Proscenium arch: (1) pillars at extremities of the stage backed by a false, obliquely receding façade designed to direct the eye to the scenes themselves; (2) only the arch, without any façade whatever; (3) pillars in front complemented by two others set in closer perspective deeper on the stage, all connected by overhead arches, making three all together. In certain hands the Roman arch was supplanted by the Gothic; the Egyptian style was also introduced into the service of the theatre; buildings were now Roman, now rococo, now Gothic.

Theatre, Italian, 19th century. The ornament of the Roman stage which surrounded the first picture-frame proscenium (the Farnese theatre at Parma) was still clinging to the proscenia of Italian stages in the 19th century. The stage opening increased in width and the architectural stage gave way to the boxed proscenium stage which is prevalent in Italy today.

The persistence of traditional methods of acting and staging offered no impetus for structural changes evident in theatres of other countries at the close of the century.

The volatile and operatic national temperament placed Italian acting on a grander, more impassioned plane than even the fiery French and English old schools. The greatness of Salvini and Ristori swept scross the native stage then proclaimed the spectacular Italian art of acting through Europe and America. Salvini's electric Othello and lucid Hamlet took London by storm. But his greatest success was in America where audience worship made it possible for him to gain uneclipsed acclaim for acting in his own language with an American speaking cast.

Ristori's Lady Macbeth, Mary Stuart, Medea and Phèdre evidenced her complete mastery of the mechanism of stage. Lewes wrote after her London appearance as Lady Macbeth: "The exquisite grace of her attitudes, the mournful beauty of her voice, the flash of her wrath, and the air of supreme *distinction* which seems native to her, gave a charm to this performance which is unforgettable.

The spirited and compelling acting style of Ristori and Salvini is still evident on the Italian stage, particularly in the acting of Grasso. The two actors who won widest fame after Salvini were Zacconi and Novelli. Novelli first became known for his exuberant and unstudied acting of comedy. Later he acted serious roles, gaining greatest applause in Shylock. Zacconi's interpretations of psychologically abnormal characters aided in the popularity of Ibsen's, Hauptmann's and Turgenev's plays on the Italian stage.

The great gift of Italy to histrionic art was Duse, ennobler of serenity and simplicity. She preferred beauty in truth to romantic elaboration. She brought realism to acting. Stark Young has described it as "a kind of realism of tragic beauty." Without the aid of makeup and other externals, she produced her effects through "dramatic imagination" in Shaw's words, and by putting behind every stroke "a distinctively human idea." Among her greatest roles were Marguerite Gautier, Magda and Francesca.

Theatre, Italian, since the First World War. Under fascist rule, with its principle of glorifying the state and discouraging individual enterprise, little of real distinction has been produced in the field of the drama. In 1931 "someone," according to Silvio d'Amico, writing on the Italian theatre in Dickinson's *The Theatre in a Changing Europe,* said: "Italy has been saved by a dictator; the Italian theatre, also, in order to be saved, needs a dictator. The Italian theatre is overflowing with enterprising authors and excellent actors, with energy, with excitement, and with individual power; its members are talented, but scattered, or disputing among themselves. There is need for one skill to express itself as the head of the others, to co-ordinate them, to harmonize them, to direct them toward an end. In short, the Italian theatre is waiting for its Mussolini." Just then the *Corporazione dello spettacolo* was organized; this controls the two federations uniting all theatrical syndicates, but though it has succeeded financially it has failed artistically. Attempts, supported by

Mussolini, have been made to establish a theatre for the masses, and many outdoor performances have been given with this end in view. In 1935 an Inspectorship of the Theatre, a state institution, was created to undertake in conjunction with the *Corporazione dello spettacolo,* new stage activities and productions.

Theatre, Japanese. The Japanese playhouse is usually a large rectangular building capable of holding four hundred persons or more; floor divided into sections each seating four to six persons; sides lined with boxes sold at a higher price. There is a gallery where, behind a grating, cheap standing room is provided. Theatres used to have tear rooms for those overcome with emotion.

The entrance to the Kabuki playhouse is often adorned with blood-curdling pictures in all the colors of the rainbow and rows of gaudy colored lanterns.

There are eighteen *Nō* theatres in Tokyo; five in China, three in Kyoto, two in Fukui and some in other large cities. The oldest *Nō* theatre is the Nishi-Hongwanjii in Tokyo; built by Hideyoshi at the end of the 16th century, now under government care.

In Osaka exists what is thought to be the oldest marionette theatre in the world.

Kabuki-za Theatre in Tokyo: Finest playhouse in Japan. *Kabuki* plays seen at their best; modern plays and dances also given; seating accommodation about 2,200; prolonged performances lasting from 3 to 11 p.m. are given three times a year in January, April, November.

Meizi-za Theatre in Tokyo; next finest playhouse; seating about 1,700; excellent staging of Kabuki dramas which are given three or four times a year, but only those with small casts; also performances of various kinds.

Daiiti Gekizyo in Tokyo; smaller theatre seating 1,400; training theatre for young actors; Kabuki plays given six or seven times a year.

See also *Acting, Japanese; Drama, Japanese; Staging, Japanese.*

Theatre, jurisprudence. Laws affecting the theatre are many. Some of the most outstanding English laws follow.

(1) Vagabond Law of 1597.—Passed in the thirty-ninth year of Elizabeth's reign, during Shakespeare's heydey, this statute lumped "common players of Interludes and Minstrels" (except those belonging to a Baron or a person of higher rank) with "Schollers . . . Juglers, Tinkers, Pedlars, and Petty Chapmen" and "idle persons using any subtile craft or fayning themselves to have knowledge in Phisiognomye, Palmestry, or other like crafty science," as well as "Fencers and Bearwards." All such were to be "taken adjudged, and deemed Rogues, Vagabonds, and Sturdy Beggars," and were to be stripped naked from the middle upwards, and . . . openly whipped until his or her body be bloodye, and sent to the parish where he was born." This statute was repealed by another in Queen Anne's reign.

(2) Vagrant Act of 1714.—Superceding the Vagabond Law of 1597, this statute, passed in the last year of Queen Anne's reign, included in its application "common players of Interludes" without exception. The penalty for following this and other specified wandering careers was "to be stript naked from the middle, and to be openly whipped until his or her body be bloody, or . . . sent to the House of Correction."

(3) Licensing Act of 1737.—Prohibited, under a penalty of £50, the acting for "hire, gain, or reward" of any play or dramatic performance whatever unless previously sanctioned by letters patent from the Crown, or licenses by the Lord Chamberlain. By further provisions of the bill, copies of all plays had to be submitted to the Lord Chamberlain two weeks before their performance, and all theatres, "not within the verge of the Court, were to be restricted to the city of Westminster and the liberties thereof." It is generally agreed that the Act was passed primarily to put an end to Gay's *Beggars Opera* and Fielding's dramatic lampooning of the Walpole government. See also *Fielding, Henry.*

(4) Vagabond Law of 1743 (or 44).—Passed in the seventeenth year of the reign of George II, this statute implements the Licensing Act of 1737, by providing that unless they are authorized by law, "all common players of Interludes and all persons who shall for Hire, Gain, or Reward, act, represent, or perform any Interlude, Tragedy, Comedy, Opera, Play, Farce, or other Entertainment of the Stage . . . shall be deemed Rogues and Vagabonds . . . (and) . . . publicly whipt" or sent to the House of Correction. This act has been repealed, and the present vagrancy laws of England do not mention actors at all.

(5) Theatres Act of 1843.—Repealing previous laws for regulation of theatres, the Theatres Act of 1843 provides that every place for the performance of stage plays must hold letters patent from the Crown or a license from the Lord Chamberlain, which may be suspended in case of riot or disorder. The Lord Chamberlain must see every play or revision, seven days before announced date of opening, and may disallow all or any part of it. Long sections deal with rules governing exits and entrances, fire hazards and precautions, lighting, heating, structure, seating, ventilation, sanitation, dressing rooms and the like. Boxing matches; profanity, impropriety of language; indecency of dress, dance, or gesture; offensive personalities or representations of living persons, are forbidden on the stage.

See also *Censorship; License commissions; Lord Chamberlain, royal license.*

Theatre, Medieval. In the 12th century, the church revived the dormant theatre in Europe with miracle plays, liturgical dramas representing the sepulchre of Christ. When the drama was brought into the open, the acting place was churchlike in arrangement. There were mansions, in addition, and representations of Heaven and Hell. Other developments were the pageant and the round. The former, chiefly in England, was marked by mansions on wheels drawn around the town. The latter was played in old Roman Amphitheatres with the mansions placed in a circle. The church miracle plays led to the guild mystery plays and the guilds became the dominant force in the drama. The theatre became more secular. Farce was introduced, and often degenerated into Revels, Feasts of Fools, etc.

Theatre, modern. Realism, not only that of the 19th century of presenting real things onstage, but of playing the actually sordid against the romantically beautiful, came into being; Pinero and Jones advanced the theory of realism in the writing of their plays. Ibsen was a champion of the new idea, as was Chekhov; but gradually realism became synonomous with literalness, and dissatisfaction set in. There came a rebirth of theatricalism in the re-discovery that what is real in life is not necessarily real in the theatre merely by being lifted, bodily and unmodified, into it. The revolt against the literalness of excessive scenic realism was led by Gordon Craig. Georg Fuchs in Germany in the early years of the 20th century was also a powerful influence toward the "re-theatricalization of the theatre." Gradually such forms of designing as cubism, futurism, expressionism, impressionism followed, each having its respective effect on the theatre as a whole, both as to production and to writing. Today ours is a heterogeneous theatre, undominated by any one ruling theory and making use of all, including the recently born surrealism.

Theatre, Persian. Akin to the Hindu stage. The theatre was centered upon the throne of the royal auditor or monarch and not upon a stage. The theatre was an informal arrangement of platform, throne and a place for less important members of the audience set in a court or hall.

Theatre, Polish, before the First World War. The theatre, like its country, was enslaved by the foreign usurpers, and the indigenous Polish drama was kept under lock and key. Wyspianski, himself a painter and dramatist, was a leading director-producer, and his theatre was, according to Zawistowski writing in Dickinson's *The Theatre in a Changing Europe,* "a fully matured, brilliantly planned artistic mechanism" which had to wait until the post-War years for full realization.

Theatre, Polish, since the First World War. Playhouses in Warsaw, once under the Russian government and state theatres became, with the evacuation of the Russian troops, municipal, and finally municipal theatres were the rule, excepted only by a few private theatres which have never solidly established themselves. An actors' association grew up which soon dictated to theatrical organizations and by its high standards raised the average level of performances. With the theatrical crisis, certain city governments began in 1931 to devise new management, such as leasing the theatres privately and giving free use of the buildings and equipment, together with a certain small subsidy in return for undertakings of civic and artistic value. Other effects of the crisis were: (1) the establishment, by the state, of a school around the nucleus of the former State Institute of Theatrical Art for the regulating by diplomas, of talent influx, actors and directors; (2) the retention in principle of the actors' association, but with modifications to accommodate different working conditions in different cities; (3) the founding of a Society for the Propagation of Theatrical Culture in Poland which united, as a private social organization under state protection and guidance, five of the principal theatres of Warsaw; (4) the formation of a network of theatres for touring companies designed to fill the cultural requirements of the smaller cities and towns. Repertory ruled the theatres and a run, contrary to that in the American theatre, was a matter only of weeks. State direction, after foreign domination, was inadequate to the presentation of the Polish dramas suddenly released for popular consumption. But by the already formulated principles of Wyspianski stage direction began to improve. Shakespeare's plays aided the theatre in a realization of its own individuality. The Teatr Polski, directed by Arnold Szyfman, brought an application in the Polish theatre of the leading trends in other parts of Europe. Realistic technique was effected by a study of Stanislavsky's theatre in Moscow, the best example of which was shown by the Reduta Theatre in Warsaw. Schiller, the director of the Reduta, re-directed theatrical attention to the common people in his productions of mystery spectacles stemming from popular historical sources. The Boguslawski Theatre, directed by Schiller, established a new, powerful technique of staging which steadied a weak national drama and often served to conceal its deficiencies. Painters of this theatre were: Drabik, with his flexible eclecticism; Frycz, with his subtle realism and taste; Pronaszko, with his attacks on hyper-realistic pictorial painting. Histrionism acting, in the early post-War years, fell heavily under the influence of Moscow naturalism (which directed the actor inward to the point of living the part). Later actors began to turn from excessive untheatricalism to a more evocative style. The two greatest actors were Kaminski and Frenkiel, each representing a type of acting: (1) the "precisionist" type using an economy of means to suggest an inner intensity; (2) the "expansionist" type embodying a freer and more amply extraverted quality.

Theatre, Roman. Theatrical performances were no longer held in a temple or connected with the temple, religious associations having vanished. The first permanent stone theatre was not constructed until 55-52 B.C.; under Pompey this early stone theatre came to be the model on which architects of contemporary as well as later times worked. Distinguishing features: (1) the theatres were built not on hill slopes but on level ground; (2) the *cavea,* or auditorium, was an exact semi-circle; (3) the orchestra was cut in half to a semi-circle, usually for the purpose of added seating capacity, except on special occasions when it was flooded for the presentation of mimic sea fights; (4) the *hyposcenium,* or the stage, was low but deeper than previously; the *frons scaenae,* or the upper- story of the *skene,* the scene building, was gorgeously decorated; (5) the *parodoi,* or entrance ways of the Greek theatre, gave way to the *vomitoria,* or concealed entrances, which were introduced to break down the traditional division line between the auditorium and the stage; (6) there was frequently a roof over the stage; (7) the *auleum,* or curtain, was introduced here for the first time; (8) in general the Roman theatre was more ornate than the Greek theatre, especially in the *frons scaenae* and the *pulpitum,* or friezes.

Theatre, Rumanian, since the First World War. The Rumanian theatre is distinguished by authors with individual initiative and so lacks a fundamental unity or the existence of any formulated school. Fashions of acting have developed out of a conventional classic mold to a more natural and human one. Scenery is more highly developed, usually tasteful, sometimes expensive. Shakespeare, Ibsen and Shaw are great popular favorites; others include Pirandello, Somerset Maugham, Noel Coward, Elmer Rice, Vicki Baum, and, increasingly, O'Neill.

Theatre, Russian, 19th century to the Revolution. The beginning of the 19th century found the theatre well established in Russia. There were two state controlled theatres in St. Petersburg and Moscow, as well as outlying theatres in provincial cities and private stages on large estates. The state-controlled theatres held a monopoly on dramatic presentations and strict censorship determined not only what should be shown on the stages but audience approval as well. Repertories were chosen with this censorship in mind and with an eye to the taste of the merchant class and petty officials who frequented the theatre, rather than that of lovers of the drama. Performances of foreign plays were predominant. In 1839, for instance, there were 345 performances in all the theatres in St. Petersburg, representing 129 new plays of which only sixty-four were in the Russian language.

This situation was deplored by a rapidly rising group of idealists, the Slavophiles, whose theory was to reject Western influences and develop their culture from within on the basis of their own national life. One of the group, the critic Yourev, established the first real peasant theatre, in 1862, in the village of Voskresenskoe. Many other people's theatres were founded in the third quarter of the century. The chief opposition seemed to come from saloon keepers who complained of the competition. In 1895, an exhibition of the Popular Theatre for villages, factories, soldiers, and schools was given in connection with the Congress of Russian Representatives of Technical and Professional Education. From that time on the Popular Theatres became a much discussed part of the Congress of Education, and there was a great deal of disagreement as to the type of play that should be shown on these stages. In 1903, Scheglov published *In Defense of the People's Theatre,* a list of almost 130 articles on the subject written after 1890. This confusion of theoretical speculations of the intellectuals with the actual theatrical activity within the theatres continued until after the Revolution of 1917, when the Popular theatres were organized under a workable plan.

Yourev, the founder of the peasant theatre movement, also pioneered the theory of the "ensemble." His belief that the Russian village commune was based on an inborn sense of communism led him to the theory of the ensemble, and the essential need for it in a truly Russian theatre. In 1868 Tolstoy, in his introduction to *Tsar Fedor Ivanovich,* gave an analysis of the *mise en scène,* mentioning the need of submerging the actor to the ensemble and the importance of a stage director to bring this about.

The professional theatre was emancipated from the monopoly of the state-controlled theatres in 1882. At this same time a nation-wide revival in art and literature was creating new standards of artistic perfection. There was a cry to overthrow outworn traditions. The theatre joined in this revolt. In the same year the monopoly was abolished, Korsh opened a private theatre in Moscow and staged a varied repertoire of new (including Chekhov's first play *Ivanov*) and classic Russian and foreign plays. He introduced Ibsen, Rostand, Björnson and others to the Russian theatre. Eight more private theatres sprang up within the year. Antoine's Théâtre Libre in Paris began to interest these leaders, especially after his production of Tolstoy's *Power of Darkness.* There were predictions of the coming of such an art theatre in Russia.

Nemirovich-Danchenko was a part of this forward movement. This same year his *The Eglantine* was staged at the Maly Theatre. The stage setting showed, at the rise of the curtain, the façade of a two-story brick building whose front was later lifted and the remainder of the action took place in the interior. This was the first indication of naturalistic staging in Moscow. In St. Petersburg, the year before (1881), Vsevolozhski, director of the Imperial theatres, had become an exponent of detail in staging. In 1885 the Meiningen Players visited St. Petersburg and aroused great interest through their carefully executed settings preserving historic truth in all its detail, and through the handling of supernumeraries to make them a vital part of the action. After the visit of the German company Vsevolozhski brought the movement to fuller development.

At this time the critics Youev and Veselovski, were preaching the need of a Russian art theatre, headed by a stage manager. Of particular importance is Youev's fundamental essay on the reform of the theatre, *The Significance of the Theatre,* in which he spoke of the true scenic talent depending upon "artistic synthesis." In 1890, Nemirovich-Danchenko became teacher of dramatic art in the Moscow Philharmonic School. Chekhov and he worked together to form the Society of Russian Dramatic Writers which clarified theories on the future development of scenic art.

In 1897, Nemirovich-Danchenko came to Stanislavsky with a definite plan for a theatre in which plays of Chekhov, Hauptmann and other modern dramatists would be given. After their famous eighteen-hour conference, the Moscow Art Theatre was founded, and the most important phase of scenic and histrionic development in the Russian theatre began. The actors were chosen from graduates of Stanislavsky's and Danchenko's schools, and Moskvin from Korsh's private theatre. They chose Tolstoy's *Tsar Fyodor Ivanovich* for the opening production. No doubt Veselovski influenced them in this by pointing out the importance of a Russian group choosing their own historical plays (rather than a classic, *Julius Caesar* for instance, as the Meiningen Players had done).

Realism reached its zenith in Stanislavsky's productions. From the beginning the Theatre scored success after success with plays permitting elaborate attention to details and clockwork precision of ensemble playing. They included in their repertoire the plays of Shakespeare, Goldoni, Sophocles, Ibsen and other leading realistic and naturalistic writers. Meyerhold, one of the leading members of the group, objected to the excessive literalism of Stanislavsky's productions and wished to replace it with symbolism. In 1902 he, along with ten other actors, withdrew. The Theatre was changed to a stock company of sixteen members, and was financed by Morozov. Meyerhold formed a Society of the New Drama, but three years later returned to the Art theatre. Stanislavsky put him in charge of the Studio where special experimentations were made and where the troupes for the provinces were trained. Immediately, the Studio broke from the naturalism of the organization. Meyerhold was interested in the plays of the symbolists, Maeterlinck, in particular. He experimented with paint on flat surfaces in an effort to present only a stylization of the scenes—"the internal synthesis . . . of their concealed characteristics." This revolt against naturalistic methods in Russia was almost synonomous with the revolt led by Fuchs in Germany.

Meyerhold believed that the stage director must penetrate beyond the external action and mask into the conceptual character of the "inner mask." For this, he advocated a return to the ancient theatre in which there existed "no decorations but three-dimensional space and . . . statuary plasticity."

In 1906 Meyerhold became stage director of Komisarjevskaya's theatre where he developed symbolical stylization with productions of Maeterlinck, Ibsen, Andreyev and Sologub. Komisarjevskaya objected to his reduction of everything to plane and immobility, insisting that by this "the thread between the auditorium and the stage is persistently broken, and meaning is disappearing from our work." She separated from Meyerhold with the words, "The road which leads to the puppet show . . . is not mine."

Evreinov replaced Meyerhold as stage manager for Komisarjevskaya, bringing with him both brilliance and shallowness. He led the theatre of symbols into complete distortion. His theory of monodrama carried his desire to convince the spectator that it is he himself who lives and acts in the world represented on the stage. This meant there must be a new kind of play which develops, not through the actions of a group of characters, but by the actions of the principle character alone. The other characters and the environment change in accordance with his change of sentiment and attitude. This protagonist, or "ego," would conduct the spectator into his own "alter ego." Thus, the illusion of reality would be raised to the highest pitch. To achieve his theory he used every known device in staging, lighting, color, and musical accompaniments.

While these experiments in subjective symbolism were being conducted by Meyerhold and Evreinov, Stanislavsky continued to develop objective representation. He perfected unity of tone in production and established a theory of acting which has influenced the entire world of the theatre. This is particularly true among the outstanding American and English actors because of the clarity of Elizabeth Hapgood's translation of his book *An Actor Prepares*.

See also *Moscow Art Theatre*.

Theatre, Russian, Soviet. Directly after the Revolution plays were censored and regimented to an even greater extent than in the days of the Tsar, and were directed toward the building of the Communist ideal, the collective benefit of the working class. The Moscow Art Theatre has been the great dramatic organ of the Soviets, serving the Revolution while maintaining a strict, high esthetic standard. In October, 1927, a resolution was adopted effecting a greater liberalism of every kind in the theatre, including choice of theme, idea, treatment, style; mechanization prospered with a powerful vogue; "shock troops," counterparts of the old travelling troupes, sprang up, giving performances first in railroad stations, later in political clubs throughout the country; later a course in the theatre (infused, of course, with political propaganda) became a part of the hours of every worker's daily routine. In pre-Revolution Russia there were 250 permanent theatres; today in Russia there are 560. The modern Soviet theatre, in its efforts of production and acting, is immensely superior to its material. Only recently Soviet dramatists were severely criticized for too close adherence to the banal theme of espionage (by counterrevolutionary, bourgeois, terrorist or Trotskyist forces) and triumphant heroism (of the Communist forces). This would seem to show that artistic regimentation, as well as other kinds, is perforce still in existence. Many persons once powerful in the theatre as Meyerhold, Afinogenov (brilliant dramatist, Russia's best after Gorky) are either in prison, or their plays are removed from repertory.

Theatre, Spanish, 15th-17th centuries. With the emerging national theatre, following the long Moorish struggle, the prevailing temper on the stage was rabidly patriotic and devotedly Catholic, a combination which resulted in a brand of mysticism. Here was no slavish imitation of classic models; indeed the medieval state of mind, in spite of the onslaught of the Renaissance, appears to have held sway longer here than elsewhere in Europe, manifesting itself in powerful reminders of the old liturgical dramas, with the addition of vigorous action and romantic colorfulness.

In the structure of the playhouse the stage was set up at one end of the yard. The aristocracy looked down on the stage from the windows of surrounding houses. In front of the stage and to the sides were benches for the audience. At the back of the theatre was a cage (*cazuela,* or stew-pan) into which were crowded the women of the lower classes. In front of the *cazuela* stood the *mosqueteros,* a turbulent element.

Indispensable characters of the theatre of the Golden Age: one or more *galanes* (lovers) ; a *dama* or *damas,* who were the object of the affections of the *galanes;* the gracioso (clown), the confidential servant of his master; the *criada* (woman servant), *moza* (maid) or *graciosa* who is the confidential servant of her mistress and frequently the object of the affections of the *gracioso.*

Characteristics of the theatre of the Spanish Golden Age: a disregard of the unities of time, place and action. A mixture of different meters within the same play. Individual freedom, unhampered by rules. A mixture of prose and poetry within the same play. In sum, liberty of the author and freedom from restrictions. Plot rather than character emphasized by most authors.

It is based mainly on national subjects, and in this respect is a national drama as are those of Greece and England. Thus the Spanish drama appealed to all classes.

Theatre, Spanish, 18th century. See *Drama, Spanish, 18th century.*

Theatre, Spanish, 19th century. See *Drama, Spanish, 19th century.*

Theatre, Spanish, 20th century, before the First World War. Romanticism, under the barrage of such modern influences as Ibsen, Hauptmann and Shaw, gave way to a form closer to realism. The actor Mendoza, coming from a privately owned theatrical company, and the famous actress, Maria Guerrero, together formed a company whose performances were equal to any in Europe. The *zarzuela,* the Spanish musical comedy, and the *sainete,* a play of manners among the lower classes distinguished by vitality rather than form, were among the most popular forms of this theatre.

Theatre, Spanish, 20th century, since the First World War. Barcelona was the first city in Europe to welcome modern art, but its stage, like those of the rest of Spain, remained conservative and unprogressive, in great measure because of the lack of adequate financial means. The writer, Gual, was an advocate of modern staging methods. Repertory, in spite of its requirement of much scenery, has ruled the theatres. The theatres were largely closed during the Civil War, 1936-39, though one or two remained open in Madrid and Barcelona.

Theatre, Swedish, since the First World War. There are two kinds of playhouses in present day Sweden: the state theatre, and the private enterprise. Since 1933 the state has actively supported the theatre, giving to it traditions of academic circumspection and disciplined precision. Per Lindberg is one of the most prominent directors, a student of Reinhardt, a follower of Appia, Craig and Copeau. An extensive repertory of old and new plays has been maintained, ranging from ancient Greek tragedy to contemporary literature. Sweden's greatest modern actor was Gösta Ekman, a man with an aptitude for a wide variety of roles.

Theatre, Yugoslav, before the First World War. With the country largely under Austrian rule, Austrian and German influences necessarily predominated. Travelling companies, grown from the first Serbian theatre, founded in 1861, became schools for young actors. In 1911 opera was introduced in Belgrade. In Croatia the theatre, for long German, finally sought its own individuality and soon reached a higher level, in both drama and opera, than any other pre-war Yugoslav theatre. In Slovenia the theatre was largely German with an occasional Italian *opera buffa*. Here was seen the founding of a Dramatic Society which strove to keep the theatre alive.

Theatre, Yugoslav, since the First World War. The progress of the Yugoslav theatre since the First World War has been rapid. In 1920 it was liberated by the government through nationalization and educational approval, thereby becoming financially independent and an outlet of expression and education for the masses. "Central National Theatres" were formed in Belgrade, Zagreb and Ljubljana, representing all theatrical forms, including drama, opera, operetta, ballet. In smaller towns state theatres were also established. The aims of this national theatre were: (1) to cultivate the best in native drama and opera; (2) to produce to the highest possible standard the classics and the music of the great foreign composers; (3) to acquaint its public with the best modern trends in plays and stagecraft. Works of Ibsen, Gogol, Strindberg, Shakespeare and Molière have been produced. Zagreb has the finest opera house and Ljubljana the finest theatre proper. Smaller permanent regional theatres have been formed in such towns as Sarajevo, Skoplje, Split, Osijek, Novi, Sad, Maribor, all of which are supported by the state.

Théâtre à succès. That brand of French production which deliberately conforms with successful formulas for the attraction of the larger audiences with their well-known favoritism for certain players, subjects and styles.

Theatre Arts. Published monthly by Theatre Arts, Inc., 40 East 49th Street, New York, N. Y. A scholarly magazine devoted to the international theatre in all its phases, handsomely printed and illustrated, and edited by Edith J. R. Isaacs, Rosamond Gilder, Stark Young and Ashley Dukes. Known as *Theatre Arts Monthly* up to November, 1939.

Theatre collections. Collections of books, periodicals, photographs, clippings, programmes, drawings, memorabilia relating to the stage, cinema, radio, circus, magic, drama, etc. Notable are the collections in the New York Public Library, Museum of the City of New York, Columbia University's Brander Matthews Dramatic Museum, The Players, Museum of Modern Art Film Library, Harvard College Library, Folger Shakespeare Library. The Library of Congress, the Huntington Library, etc. The most complete record of this kind is to be found in *Theatre Collections in Libraries and Museums* by Rosamond Gilder and George Freedley.

Theatre Collective, New York. A group within the Theatre of Action (formerly the Workers Laboratory Theatre), organized 1933; devoted to the reflection of social progress; courses in acting, directing, designing, playwriting.

Théâtre de foire. Name given to the stage on which a *commedia dell'arte* was performed. A bare platform backed by a piece of undecorated back cloth, usually located in the market place.

Théâtre de l'Odéon. A classical French national theatre in Paris similar to the Comédie-Française and devoted, like it, to a standard repertory of established French masterpieces—comprising the works of Racine, Corneille, Molière, Dumas *fils*, Rostand—producing only rarely new and untried plays.

Théâtre de l'Oeuvre. A theatre opened in Paris in 1892 by Lugné-Poë and devoted to the production of new plays. The initial piece was Maeterlinck's *Pelléas et Mélisande*. This theatre developed later into a house of experimental works.

Théâtre du Petit Bourbon. Designed by Giacomo Torelli in one of the wings of the Palace at Versailles. It was a small theatre for intimate productions and was used by Molière for his first production.

Théâtre du Vieux Colombier. A theatre founded in Paris in 1913 by Jacques Copeau which became a leader in artful and distinguished productions. Copeau believed in "an orderly décor of which the first purpose was the support of the text, simple draperies, masses of masonry and timbers . . . the purpose of the setting was to interpret the pattern of the play, and to provide the light and shade necessary to create the atmosphere"—*The Theatre in Changing Europe,* by Thomas H. Dickinson. This theatre introduced such new playwrights as Vildrac, Mazaud, Benjamin and de Veyne, and gave new productions to works by Shakespeare, Merimee, Gogol, Ostrovski and Goldoni.

See also *Copeau, Jacques; Garrick Theatre, New York.*

Theatre Guild, The (New York). In 1919, following several years of experimentation as the Washington Square Players, a group of young theatre artists including Philip Moeller, Helen Westley, Lawrence Langner, Josephine A. Meyer, Lee Simonson, Edna Kenton, Helen Freeman and Rollo Peters formed the Theatre Guild. Theresa Helburn, present Executive Director, was Play Representative but not a member of the Board. Through the friendship and financial help of the late Otto H. Kahn, they leased the Garrick Theatre and offered *The Bonds of Interest* on April 14, 1919. This failed but their second effort, St. John Ervine's *John Ferguson,* was extremely successful. Outstanding productions of their first years were *Jane Clegg,* 1920; *Heartbreak House,* 1920; *Liliom,* 1921; *He Who Gets Slapped,* 1922; *Back To Methuselah,* 1922; *R.U.R.,* 1922; *Peer Gynt,* 1923; *The Adding Machine,* 1923; *Saint Joan,* 1923; *The Guardsman,* 1924; and *Processional,* 1925. The Guild floated a bond issue and built the handsome Guild Theatre on West 52nd Street which is now its mother house. Beginning 1927-28, the organization sent out its first company for an extended tour. Since that time subscription lists have been set up in many American cities similar to the one in New York which guarantees five weeks playing time. Boston, Chicago, Philadelphia, Baltimore, Washington, Pittsburgh and St. Louis have a regular season in conjunction with the American Theatre Society (a Shubert-backed enterprise).

The Guild Theatre was opened April 13, 1925 with Helen Hayes and Lionel Atwill in *Caesar And Cleopatra.* Among the most famous Guild productions since this have been: *Goat Song,* 1926; *The Silver Cord,* 1926; *The Brothers Karamazov,* 1927; *Porgy,* 1927; *Marco Millions,* 1928; *Strange Interlude,* 1928; *Wings Over Europe,* 1928; *Hotel Universe,* 1920; *Mourning Becomes Electra,* 1931; *Ah, Wilderness,* 1934; *Idiot's Delight,* 1936; *The Sea Gull,* 1938; *The Time of Your Life,* 1939.

Théâtre Italian, Le. A book of plays, collected by Evaristo Gherardi, written by French authors for the *commedia dell'arte* in France, illustrated.

Theatre League of Philadelphia. Founded in 1933 with an active membership of fifty. It has had five successful years. Housed in an old stable in the heart of the city, it maintains a probation membership of 500 and of this number 200 have been associated for a period of one year or more. It has no star system; the schedule goes from September to June and calls for one production and one revival each month. Plays are given every Saturday night and on one Sunday each month. In 1938 it established a junior workshop for children.

Theatre Library Association. An organization of persons in libraries, and museums, as well as collectors and members of the theatrical profession, who are concerned with the preservation of the treasured records of the drama in public or endowed institutions. This association is affiliated with the American Library Association and had its inception in a meeting in New York in June, 1937, called by H. M. Lydenberg, director of the New York Public Library. Its executive board includes George Freedley, chairman, Sarah Chokla Gross, Barrett H. Clark, Charles E. Rush and Garrison P. Sherwood.

Théâtre Libre. A theatre in Paris founded by André Antoine toward the end of the 19th century. It was a leader in the revitalization and new progressivism of the French theatre before the war. It can be said to be the originator of the modern movement in France. Its outstanding characteristic was a fusion of theatre and literature. After the First World War it was revived under the literary direction of Pierre Veber. It produced several experimental dramas of different kinds.

Theatre of fantasy. Name given by Joseph Gregor in Dickinson's *The Theatre in a Changing Europe* to the style of dramatic presentation represented by Vakhtangov, the Russian director. It means a submerging of the actor in the essential spirit of the play. Expressiveness, relative to the central meaning of a piece, was its keynote. As Vakhtangov showed considerable devotion to Tibetan mysteries, Yoga theories and, generally, the occult themes of the Orient, it made for a certain mysticism. Withal, Vakhtangov's theatre remained true to its preoccupation with the Jewish soul.

Theatre of the Soul, The. Nicolas Evreinov (Russian). Drama. 1912.
Sets its scene in the soul of a professor, where the action is supposed to last for only half a second. The professor is torn between two loves, that for his wife and that for a dancer. After debating his dilemma, he shoots himself.

Théâtre Pigalle. Built at the foot of Montmartre hill in Paris in 1929 by Baron Henri de Rothschild, who turned it over to his son, Phillipe. It has every theatric mechanical device, including four stages on two levels. Its stated policy is to produce intimate comedies and drama, but actually the theatre has housed a variety of entertainments, including operettas and motion pictures. The opening production was Sacha Guitry's *Story of France,* in fifty scenes.

Theatre Unbound (Osvobozené divadlo). A theatre which sprang up in Czechoslovakia shortly after the First World War, first devoted to dilettante dadaistic productions, later becoming a sincere experimental comic theatre.

Theatre Union. American non-profit theatrical company. Formed December, 1932, in New York for the purpose of producing plays of contemporary social significance, on a professional scale yet at the lowest prices in the city, with a section reserved at each performance for the unemployed. The Civic Repertory Theatre on West 14th Street was its playhouse, until in 1937 the Union's last production, *Marching Song* by John Howard Lawson, played at the Nora Bayes Theatre. Sponsors of the Union were Arthur J. Beckhard, Sidney Howard, Walter Hart, John Howard Lawson, Cleon Throckmorton, Blanche Yurka, Sherwood Anderson, Paul Muni, Elmer Rice, Stephen Vincent Benet, Rose McClendon and others. Plays presented by the Union were: *Peace on Earth* and *Stevedore,* 1933-34; *Sailors of Cattaro* and *Black Pit,* 1934-35; *Mother, Let Freedom Ring,* and *Bitter Stream,* 1935-36; and *Marching Song* in 1937. The Union was dispersed in 1937, but it had provided an example, and theatre union groups have been formed in Chicago, Philadelphia, San Francisco and Los Angeles. Its records were placed in the Theatre Collection of the New York Public Library.

Theatrical Burial Places. *Evergreen Cemetery,* New York. (a) *Actor's Plot*— Sadie Martinot, comedienne; Frank Tannahill; Lysander Thompson; Ben Maginley; Augusta Sohlke, dancer; Tom Hengler, song and dance man, once of Delehanty and Hengler. (b) *Elk's Rest*—Ella Wesner, male impersonator; Milt Barlow, old minstrel show man; Charley Worley, impersonator of Negroes; Billy Gray and Mike

Bradley, of *Mulligan Guards* fame; Billy Pastor, brother of Tony Pastor; Frank Girard, long the manager of Tony Pastor; the blackface comedians Frank Goss, Joe Brickley, H. H. Howard, James Tierney.

(c) *Calvary Cemetery,* Queens, N. Y. Cathlic Actors' Guild Plot. Plot given in 1920 by Cardinal Hayes; by 1937, 141 members buried here, including William Elliott, an associate partner of Morris Gest and Ray Comstock; Virginia Earle, Musical comedy favorite of the Nineties; Frank Salor, singing comedian at Tony Pastor's; Barney Fagan, soft shoe dancer; Richard Thornton (he supported Lillian Russell); Lucy McLaughlin, Mary Eagen.

(d) *Woodlawn Cemetery,* New York. Lester Wallack.

(e) *Hollywood: Forest Lawn Memorial Park* (A large mausoleum, tickets of admission necessary to Memorial Terrace). Jean Harlow; Marie Dressler, Irving Thalberg; Alexander Pantages; Will Rogers; Florenz Ziegfeld; Russ Colombo; Charles (Black Crow) Mack; Ernest Torrence; John Gilbert; Wallace Reid; Lon Chaney; Alice Davenport; Harry Pollard; Jack Pickford; Lottie Pickford; Barbara La Marr; Louis Wolheim; William Desmond Taylor.

Westminster Abbey, London: Ben Jonson; Thomas Betterton; Anne Bracegirdle; Anne Oldfield; Spranger Barry, rival of Garrick; Mrs. Barry, known as Miss Crawford; Mrs. Colley Cibber; Samuel Foote; John Henderson; David Garrick.

Père-la-Chaise, Paris: Molière; Talma; Rachel; Sarah Bernhardt; Oscar Wilde and many other people of the theatre.

Stratford-upon-Avon, England: William Shakespeare.

Theatrical clubs. In New York: The Lambs, The Players, Twelfth Night Club, The Friars, The Ziegfeld Club. In Chicago: The Cliff Dwellers, Dill Pickle Club (popular in the Nineties). In London: Garrick, Savage, Green-Room, Old Stagers, The Strollers. In Hollywood: Hollywood Athletic Club.

Theatrical Eating Places. Certain restaurants and clubs have become famous as gathering places for theatrical people. In New York some of the more famous are: the Algonquin, Sardi's, "21," Leon and Eddie's, the Stork Club, Tony's, Lindy's, Dave's Blue Room, Gallagher's, the Astor, Artists and Writers (Bleeck's), etc. In Chicago, the Dill Pickle Club and the Cliff Dwellers. In Hollywood, the Brown Derby, the Beachcomber, Dave Chasen's, Sardi's, Musso and Frank's, Bali, the Tropics, Al Levy's, etc. In London, the Ivy, Romano's, the Savoy, the Savage Club, etc.

Theatricalism. The exploitation of the purely dramatic properties of a play, such as suspence, climax and space. Perhaps the most remarkable example of theatricalism in recent years came in the device (used in O'Neill's *Mourning Becomes Electra*) of the box of poison placed by Lavinia on the chest of her dead father to confront her mother, who has murdered him.

Theatrical Managers, Agents and Treasurer's Union. An A. F. of L. Union composed of house and company managers, press agents, advance men, and

(October, 1939) treasurers. It is expected that the treasurers will form a new union under the sponsorship of the I.A.T.S.E.

Theatrical publications. Present day magazines include *Variety* (New York); *Theatre Arts* (New York); *Cue* (New York); *Cast* (New York); *The Billboard* (Cincinnati); *Drama* (London); *Era* (London); *Stage* (London); *Theatre World* (London); *Play Pictorial* (London); etc.

Famous magazines of the more recent past include *Stage* (New York); *Theatre Workshop* (New York); *One-Act Play Magazine* (New York); *New York Dramatic Mirror* (New York); *New York Clipper* (New York); *Spirit of the Times* (New York); *Theatre Magazine* (New York); *The Mask* (Florence).

Theatricals, private. During the 18th and 19th centuries, many well-to-do and noble families amused themselves on their estates by acting plays purely for their own amusement and that of their guests. A very good account will be found in *"Private Theatricals,"* and *"Private Theatres,"* by James Sandoe, reprinted from the *Colorado-Wyoming Journal of Letters,* February, 1939.

Theatrical Stunts. Thanks to the press agents, many a play has won recognition and lived on, aided by ballyhoo and novelty stunts. Some of the most discussed stunts of recent years included the following: Harry Reichenbach placed a live lion in a downtown hotel room to exploit Tarzan. Will Page captured front page space by announcing the engagement of Delysia to a supposititious nobleman. Howard Dietz astounded Broadway by placing live girls in fleshings on the electric sign for *Hollywood Revue* over the façade of the Astor Theatre. Marc Luescher made an all-time space record by celebrating with elaborate ceremonies a fabricated anniversary of the Palace Theatre. Richard Maney set the town talking with the expression "Nubi, me good girl," the come-on for *The Squall.* Charles Einfeld gained extensive publicity for the Mexican cinema *Juarez* by having Ben Cohen, of his office, engage a taxi driver to take him to Juarez (Pennsylvania). One of the extraordinary theatrical undertakings was that initiated by Edward L. Bernays, who in 1913, as co-editor of the Medical Review of Reviews, produced *Damaged Goods,* at that time regarded as a daring play. He organized the Medical Review of Reviews Sociological Fund and under the auspices of John D. Rockefeller, Jr., Abraham Flexner and others made it possible to overcome the strong existing prejudices of the period. The play memberships were sold under the Medical Review of Reviews Sociological Fund and the play was originally opened only to members.

Theatrical syndicate. A monopoly of theatres in the United States formed by a group of sixteen leading theatrical men in 1896. They centralized booking interests and organized all the houses they controlled in a chain, "time" for which was booked only through Klaw and Erlanger. Many rebelled against this dictatorship to whose whims and terms all attractions and stars had to submit or be barred from first class theatres throughout the country. The syndicate was broken by David Belasco, Sarah Bernhardt, Mrs. Fiske and, later the Shubert brothers who likewise bought a chain of theatres and proclaimed themselves the Independent Movement in 1900.

Theme, Elizabethan. An extemporaneous entertainment which often followed the performance of a play in the Elizabethan theatre. It consisted of improvisations in verse by an actor on a theme or topic supplied by a member of the audience.

Theologeion. The top of the *proskenion,* or first story of the *skene;* also thought to have been a regular piece of theatrical machinery.

There Are Crimes And Crimes. August Strindberg (Swedish). Tragedy. 4 acts. 1899.

Henriette has willed her father's death. She is with her lover who is the father of another woman's child. She wills that child's death. When the child dies, the father is charged with murder and though he is finally cleared, he realizes that he is guilty in thought. The idea of the play is that sins of thought are real sins, but sinning itself is a step towards salvation.

Thesis play. A play, built around an idea for which the dramatist is crusading, the curtain of which is designed to point up and prove the moral. All of Ibsen's plays are thesis plays, carrying forward the torch of social progress. *Ghosts* was a pioneer in the struggle for sexual hygiene and candor and, more deeply and broadly, new social freedom. *A Doll's House* is an example of both a problem play and a thesis play. Most of Shaw's works are thesis plays, the clearest, perhaps being *Mrs. Warren's Profession,* a blow to that body of social "respectables" who made prostitution at once a necessary evil and an enduring stigma to the women their caste system forced into it. Eugène Brieux is one of the best known French writers of their genre, notably *Damaged Goods.*

Thespian. Actor or performer; used as a noun or adjective, and deriving from the early Greek actor-dramatist, Thespis.

Thespis (6th century B.C.). Greek poet. Thespis, a poet of Icaria, in Attica, is supposed to have founded the Greek drama. By profession he was a writer of dithyrambs, or poems composed for the Bacchanalian festivals. Before his day these had been recited in unison by choric groups. Thespis gave one member of the chorus solo responses to make, and thus created the first dialogue. He was also the first poet to write prologues for his dramatic spectacles. In addition, he invented what was really the first stage. This was a raised table on which the leader of the chorus or responder stood so that he might be raised on the altar steps opposite him. This same actor wore a linen mask, a device of Thespis, so that he might convincingly enact more than one role. Fragments of plays supposedly written by Thespis are probably spurious.

From his name is derived the adjective "Thespian," meaning dramatic; and the noun, meaning an actor.

They Knew What They Wanted. Sidney Howard (American). Drama. 3 acts. 1924.

Winner of the Pulitzer Prize for 1924-25.

Amy, waitress in a San Francisco restaurant, marries Tony, a prosperous bootlegger, and goes to live on his small California ranch. Tony's legs are smashed in an accident, and Amy has an affair with Joe, who works on the ranch. When he learns that Amy is carrying Joe's child, Tony is enraged, but he finally forgives her and sends Joe away.

They're handcuffed. An audience that does not applaud.

They Shall Not Die. John Wexley (American). Drama. 3 acts. Printed 1934.
Negro boys and two white girls are taken off a freight train and thrown into jail. The girls are bribed by the sheriff to charge the colored boys with rape, and the boys are beaten into confessing. Later one of the girls admits she has given false testimony, but still the charge remains. In the final courtroom scene, in spite of the excellent brief of the attorney for the defense, there is little hope for any verdict except guilty.
In the play, the locale is called Scottsville, instead of Scotsboro.

Thief, The. Henry Bernstein (French). Drama. 3 acts. 1906.
A beautiful lady is at a chateau with the young son of the host, who, having fallen in love with her, accepts as his own her guilt when certain funds are discovered to be missing. The husband discovers the truth about the situation, but he forgives his wife. The son is sent to Brazil to recover from his infatuation.

Thirteenth Chair, The. Bayard Veiller (American). Melodrama. 3 acts. 1916.
Edward Wales is stabbed to death at a dinner party, the murder occurring during a seance which Wales himself had arranged. Suspicion immediately falls on the medium's daughter who is cleared only when her mother uses psychic power to reveal the real murderer.

Thirty-six Dramatic Situations, The. According to the 18th century Italian dramatist-theorist, Carlo Gozzi, there were only thirty-six types of plot possible to a playwright. "Gozzi maintained that there can be but thirty-six tragic situations. Schiller took great pains to find more, but he was unable to find even so many as Gozzi."—Goethe.
Georges Polti, in his *The Thirty-Six Dramatic Situations,* lists them as follows: (1) supplication; (2) deliverance; (3) crime pursued by vengeance; (4) vengeance taken for kindred upon kindred; (5) pursuit; (6) disaster; (7) falling prey to cruelty or misfortune; (8) revolt; (9) daring enterprise; (10) abduction; (11) the enigma; (12) obtaining; (13) enmity of kinsmen; (14) rivalry of kinsmen; (15) murderous adultery; (16) madness; (17) fatal imprudence; (18) involuntary crimes of love; (19) slaying of a kinsman unrecognized; (20) self-sacrificing for an ideal; (21) self-sacrifice for kindred; (22) all sacrificed for a passion; (23) necessity of sacrificing loved ones; (24) rivalry of superior and inferior; (25) adultery; (26) crimes of love; (27) discovery of the dishonor of a loved one; (28) obstacles to love; (29) an enemy loved; (30) ambition; (31) conflict with a God; (32) mistaken jealousy; (33) erroneous judgment; (34) remorse; (35) recovery of a lost one; (36) loss of loved ones.

Thoma, Ludwig (1867-1921). German dramatist, novelist. Born in Oberammergau. He was noted for the humor and natural Bavarian setting of his comedies. *Moral,* produced at the Kleines Theatre, Berlin, in 1908, is his best known play. It was staged at the Irving Place Theatre, New York, in German in April, 1914. His other plays include *The Medal, Local Train, Magdalene,* etc.

Thomas, A. E. (1872-   ). American dramatist. Born in Chester, Massachusetts. He received his A.B. and M.A. degrees from Brown University, after which he was associated as a journalist with the New York Evening Post, Tribune, Times and Sun. He has written a number of plays, and is known as a skillful dramatic craftsman, particularly in the field of light comedy. The plays which he has written, independently and in collaboration, include *Her Husband's Wife,* 1910; *What the Doctor Ordered,* 1911; *Little Boy Blue,* 1911; *The Rainbow,* 1912; *The Big Idea,* 1914; *Come Out of the Kitchen,* 1916; *The Matinee Hero,* 1919; *Just Suppose,* 1920; *Our Nell,* 1922; *The French Doll,* 1922; *The Jolly Roger,* 1923; *Vermont,* 1928; *Her Friend the King,* 1929; *No More Ladies,* 1934; *Merely Murder,* 1937; etc.

Thomas, Augustus (1859-1934). American dramatist. He started on a journalistic career in St. Louis, Kansas City and New York, and then turned to play-writing. His first play, *Editha's Burglar,* 1887, an adaptation from the novel by Frances Hodgson Burnett, was very successful. This was followed by *Alabama,* 1891, and a series of popular plays which established him as a leading American dramatist of the period. Other of his plays are *In Mizzoura, Colorado, The Witching Hour, Rio Grande, Nemesis, Still Waters.*

Thomas Lord Cromwell. An Elizabethan play published in 1602 with the initials "W. S." on the title page, and included in the Third and Fourth folio editions of Shakespeare's works in 1664 and 1685 respectively. The play deals disconnectedly with events in the life of Thomas Cromwell, a councillor executed by Henry VIII in 1540. Faulty style and construction have led to the general rejection of the play from the canon of Shakespeare's works.

Thompson, Lydia (1841-1908). British actor-manager. Born in London, she made her debut in 1853. Having won a reputation for her beauty and her daring costumes in Europe, she brought her company to New York. Her chorus girls started the craze for the leg show, and initiated the organization of the American burlesque show.

She was distinguished as an actress and a manageress. *Robinson Crusoe* was her best known production.

Thorikos, Theatre of. A tiny, provincial open-air auditorium in Attica. Bieber, in her *History of the Greek and Roman Theatre,* says this theatre "has kept the flat form of the auditorium. It gives us the best idea of the way the Athenian theatre must have appeared in the archaic period, for it has kept the steep slope of the terrace, where a *skene* could never have been erected.

Thorndike, Dame Sybil (1882-). English actress and manageress. Studied for the stage at Ben Greet's Academy 1904. Toured the U. S. with Shakespearean Repertory Co. Appeared on London stage in 1908. Appeared in New York in 1910 with John Drew in *Smith.* Played *Jane Clegg* and many other and varied roles. In 1914 she returned to England and played *Lady Macbeth, Rosalind, Portia* and other Shakespearean roles. She stayed with this company until 1918 not only playing all the main feminine roles but also did *Gabbo* in the *Merchant of Venice, Ferdinand* and *Puck.* Made a great success as Hecuba in *The Trojan Women.* Managed the New Theatre in 1922, appeared as *St. Joan, Major Barbara, Mariners* and many others. More recently she has been in *The Distaff Side* and various films. Honored as Dame Commander of the British Empire in 1931.

Three Daughters of M. Dupont, The. Eugene Brieux (French). Comedy. 4 acts. 1897.

Exposes the evils of the French system of marriage and its bearing upon women. The play deals with three daughters: Caroline, who is religious and fond of children; Angele, who has committed a youthful slip and is banished from home; and Julie, who is the most marriageable. Julie is married off to a man whose selfishness and sensuality does not permit her to have children; Caroline, because of the dowry system, loses her chances of marriage; and Angele is not permitted to return to the family because of her indiscretion.

Three Men on a Horse. John Cecil Holm and George Abbott (American). Comedy. 3 acts. 1935.

Erwin Trowbridge, who has lived all his life in the suburbs writing verses for greeting cards, quarrels with his wife and brother-in-law and instead of going to his office, goes to a bar in New York. There he falls in with two men and a girl who make their livelihood betting on horses. Erwin, whose hobby is doping out races, shows them how he has consistently guessed right, although he himself never bets. The three take his tips. Erwin, still composing his verses, is anxious to return home but they implore him to dope out some more races for them. Since he claims he can only do this on the bus to his home, they accompany him there, then rush him back to the hotel. As time passes, his new-found friends make a fortune and his wife frantically begs his return. At the end Erwin gives up doping the races for the bookies, returns to his verse-writing and his wife.

Three-sheets. Large posters used for show printing.

Three Sisters, The. Anton Chekhov (Russian). Drama. 4 acts. 1900.

The three sisters live a dull life in the Russian provinces and look longingly toward Moscow, where life is gay and where they would like to live. They have faith in their brother and believe he may be able to help them reach the city. However, the brother marries and without their knowledge mortgages the family property. This dashes their last hope of escape. The oldest sister wears out her life as a school-teacher. The middle one, married to a dull teacher, seeks relief in a love affair, only to be forsaken; and the younger seeks happiness in work and loses her affianced when he is killed in a duel. The three sisters and their brother are overcome by circumstances and the weakness of their own characters, since they lack the will to make their aspirations come true.

Three Wise Fools. Austin Strong (American). Comedy. 3 acts. 1918.

A judge, a physician and a financier share a home and live in a masculine paradise of habit until the daughter of a woman all three loved in earlier years comes into their lives and destroys it, first to their annoyance and then to their sentimental delight.

Throckmorton, Cleon (1897-   ). American scenic designer. Formerly a landscape and figure painter but has been engaged in designing and painting for the theatre since 1917. His first New York production was *The Emperor Jones* at the Provincetown Playhouse, November, 1920. Other notable productions have been: *Porgy; All God's Chillun Got Wings; The Old Soak; In Abraham's Bosom; The House of Connelly; Springtime for Henry; The Silver Cord; Alien Corn; Noah; Bitter Oleander.* He has executed settings for many other productions, as well as equipment for many theatres.

Thronus. Name of a certain scene building, or mansion, of the medieval stage, meaning, literally, "throne."

See also *Mansions.*

Throw it away. To give no particular emphasis or expression to a speech in a play.

Throw me the line. An actor's request for cue-ing or prompting.

Thunderstorm. Aleksandr N. Ostrovsky (Russian). Tragedy. 1860.

A bride, Katia, finds that her husband is so dominated by his mother that he neglects her. Deeply depressed and with her husband away she meets a dashing young man and though she has promised her husband fidelity during his absence she falls into the arms of the handsome seducer. After being discovered by her husband and abandoned by her lover to her husband's vengeance Katia commits suicide by jumping into the river.

Thy Blood. Henry Bataille (French). Tragedy. 4 acts. 1899.

The rivalry of brothers enamored of a blind girl comes to a tragic close as the younger, whom she has saved by a blood transfusion, tears the bandages from his arm on learning that she has earlier yielded to the elder.

Thymele. An altar erected, in the center of the orchestra of the ancient Greek theatre, in honor of the god.

Tiao Ch'an (*Sable Cicada*). Chinese *P'i-huang* drama.

Also known as *Têng I T'ing* (Phoenix Ceremonial Pavilion) and *Lu Pu Hsi Tiao Ch'an* (Lu Pu's Dalliance with Sable Cicada).

The plot, based on actual history of about the year 192 (at the end of the Han dynasty), is taken from the *Romance of Three Kingdoms,* but the drama, as played by different companies, is presented with considerable variation.

Tiao Ch'an, a Chinese *femme fatale,* is a sing-song girl in Wang Yun's establishment and the delicate but effective instrument in the plot to kill Tung Cho, a tyrannous and cruel Minister-General who has caused much suffering in the land.

Wang Yun's anxiety over treacherous ministers usurping Imperial power leads him to plot the destruction of Tung Cho with the assistance of Tiao Ch'an. The plan is put into operation at a banquet where, by means of artful coquetry and many sighs, Tiao Ch'an captivates Lu Pu, a young military hero, who is not satisfied until Wang Yun, posing as her father, promises him that the girl shall be his wife. This deception is repeated a few days later at an even more lavish banquet for Tung Cho, the hated Minister-General.

Of course Lu Pu discovers Tiao Ch'an more than once with Tung Cho. She takes him to the Phoenix Pavillion and there tells him that Tung Cho has deliberately tried to alienate her love for him. He, believing her artful tale, is goaded to the verge of insanity and swears he will kill his rival. Tung Cho suddenly arrives on the scene and, at the sight of the lovers in the pavillion, loses his self-control and attacks Lu Pu who takes to his heels. Tung Cho decides to take Tiao Ch'an away to his palace outside the city. By means of a second plan concocted by Wang Yun, Tung Cho is ambushed when next he comes to the city, and killed by Lu Pu.

Tieck, Ludwig (1773-1853). German dramatist, director, critic. Founder of and the only writer of merit of the elder Romantic school in German drama; wrote *Karl von Beweck* at the age of twenty-four; wrote a series of fairy-tale plays—*Topsy-Turvy World, Puss-in-Boots, Bluebeard;* became an important and highly influential critic; was drama adviser for the Dresden Court Theatre in 1824, where he taught actors sound and clear principles of stage diction.

In 1824 he became director of the Dresden Court Theatre, where he returned to primitive forms of stage setting, approximating the Renaissance stage of England.

Tie up. Connection or relation. Usually referred to an association for publicity purposes with a person or event well known or in the public eye.

Till the Day I Die. Clifford Odets (American). Drama. 1 act. 1935.

A study in Nazi terrorism, showing the brutal way in which Communists were treated when Hitler came to power in Germany. Originally produced together with Odets' other famous one-act play, *Waiting for Lefty.*

Tilting (television). A vertical movement of the camera view.

Time Is a Dream. Henri Rene Lenormand (French). Drama. 6 scenes. 1919.

An introspective young man broods over the unreality of time and space. His fiancée tells him that she thinks she has seen a green boat on a pond with a man's face beside it in the water. He confesses having once attempted suicide by hanging but her imagined vision gives him an idea and he drowns himself.

Time of Your Life, The. Wm. Saroyan (American). Drama. 3 acts. 1939.
A group of people, habitués of a San Francisco waterfront saloon, philosophize about life.
The almost startling thing about the play is its scorn for, and lack of, plot. The whole play is in the characters—what they feel and think about life.
The main character is a man named Joe—just Joe—who buys champagne and sends out for toys, because when he was four years a toy stopped his crying. He wants to find out what it is about toys that makes people happy. He drinks because when he doesn't drink he thinks about uninteresting things and then he's just like other people.
A prostitute and various other hangers-on also take the stage. One of them is very anxious to know if one can imagine what it feels like to be in love with a midget just 32 inches high.
A queer but lovable group of characters in a modern morality play.

Times. The dates booked and contracted for the appearance of a traveling company.

Timon of Athens. William Shakespeare (English). Tragedy. 5 acts. 1608.
Written about 1608 and published in the Folio of 1623. The chief source is an incident in Plutarch's life of Anthony. Inconsistency in the action and unevenness in the style suggest that Shakespeare is not responsible for the whole play. Some critics feel that he merely revised an older play, others that a second author completed a work left unfinished by him.
Timon, a wealthy Athenian nobleman, lavishes his fortune on flattering friends who forsake him when his money is gone and when he turns to them for help. Timon becomes a bitter misanthrope, cursing mankind in general. He flees to solitary life in a forest where he finds more gold. Before he dies he gives this to Alcibiades, a faithful friend banished by the Athenian senate, who leads an army against the corrupt Athenian state to avenge Timon's death and the injuries done to himself.

Tinkers Wedding, The. J. M. Synge (Irish). 2 act comedy. 1909.
Sarah Casey and Michael Byrne, two tinkers whose morals and ways of life are highly irregular, appeal to a priest to marry them. At first he refuses, then agrees under their blandishments and the promise of "a bit of gold and a tin can" as a fee.
Old Mary Byrne, however, has exchanged the tin can for some ale, with which to celebrate the ceremony. When the priest finds that his can is gone he refuses to go through with the wedding and all three tinkers set upon him, bind him and threaten him with dire consequences. By use of a Latin malediction he frightens the tinkers away.

Tin Pan Alley. Also known as Racket Row, Songsters' Avenue, Pluggers' Den, and Pluggers' Paradise. A popular name for the region of Broadway and 47th Street, where many New York music publishers have their offices and where composers and musicians foregather. In an abstract sense the term refers to the whole commercialized popular-song-writing world—and in this sense Tin Pan Alley had its origin in Milwaukee in the Nineties when Charles K. Harris put up a sign—"Banjoist and Song Writer—Songs Written to Order." The name came from the title Monroe H. Rosenfeld coined for a newspaper article on the music business in the early 1900's, during an interview in the office of Harry Von Tilzer, the field's dominating figure of that decade.

Tiring house. The combined greenroom and backstage of the Elizabethan theatre. Located in most instances behind the stage with doors opening onto each side of the latter, the tiring house served for rehearsals, prompting, properties, costume changes and other mechanics of the theatre.

'Tis Pity She's a Whore. John Ford (English). Tragedy. 5 acts. Printed 1633.
Annabella and Giovanni, brother and sister, attempt to hide their guilty passion for each other. Marrying one of her suitors, Soranzo, Annabella refuses to name the father of her unborn child. Soranzo, feigning forgiveness, has his servant discover the truth. At a sumptuous feast Soranzo plans to take his vengeance. Giovanni boldly comes, has a last meeting with Annabella, and stabs her, to forestall Soranzo. He then fights with and kills Soranzo, by whose servant he is himself killed.

Title role. The character whose name entitles play as *Marie Antoinette,* generally the most important part, although we have Shakespeare's *Julius Caesar* as a notable exception.

Titus Andronicus. William Shakespeare (English). Tragedy. 5 acts. 1593.
Written about 1593 and published in quarto form in 1594. The revolting plot and crude construction have led many critics to deny that it is Shakespeare's work. A lost play, *Titus and Vespasian,* possibly suggested the theme and treatment, which is not historical. The action concerns the murder of one of Tamora's sons. Aided by Aaron the Moor, her lover, she causes Titus' sons to be murdered and his daughter Lavinia to be maimed and defiled. In return, Titus, feigning madness, kills Tamora's two remaining sons and serves her their heads in a pastry at a banquet. The play ends with a general slaughter of all who are left.

Tobacco Road. Jack Kirkland and Erskine Caldwell (American). Drama. 3 acts. 1933.
The locale of the play is the back country of Georgia. This was once tobacco country, then turned into small cotton plantations which have long since exhausted the soil. Submerged in superstition, ignorance, poverty, the Lester family represents the hopelessness and degeneracy of these farmers who have nothing to look forward to but death.

Jeeter Lester and his wife Ida live in a tumbledown shack with Ellie May and Dude, the two remaining children. The rest have gone off to Augusta, or the cotton mills. Pearl, her mother's favorite, has been married off to a neighbor, Lov, but she refuses to stay with him and runs back to her mother. The family is literally starving and live from day to day on what they can steal. Jeeter just never gets around to planting a crop. Ada's only wishes are to have Pearl happy and have a fancy dress to die in. Ellie May makes up to Pearl's husband, willing to act as a substitute, but he persists in wanting Pearl back. Dude is a heartless wretch of a boy, sixteen, mainly concerned with the ecstatic desire to blow a horn on a car. He gets his wish when Sister Bessie, a self-appointed lady preacher, decides she'll marry him, and buy him a new car. The new car never serves as a source of income as Dude practically demolishes it in two days.

A neighbor brings the news that Cap't John's boy, Tim, is coming back. Cap't John used to own the land and promised they could stay on it. Jeeter is excited, he is sure Tim has some plan for them. But Tim arrives with a banker from Augusta and tells him he has lost the land and Jeeter must get off or pay rent. Jeeter sends Dude and Bessie to a presumably rich son Tom for money. They return empty handed.

In desperation Jeeter grabs Pearl, tells Dude to run and get Lov, who has promised him two dollars a week if she returns. Ada tries to stop them and is run over. As she is dying, she bits Jeeter, he lets go of the girl, and Pearl, seeing her chance runs out through the gate, calling goodbye. Ada laughs triumphantly and dies. Jeeter sends Ellie May to Lov and she leaves eagerly. Jeeter is now alone, he sits with his hat tipped forward, leaning against the house, his hands rubbing the dirt which falls loosely through his fingers.

Although the play got off to a slow start, it soon caught on, and on May 28, 1939 surpassed the record run of *Abie's Irish Rose*.

Toller, Ernest (1893-1939). German dramatist. Born in Smotschin, near Berlin. He was a writer who became involved in the extreme left-wing in politics and eventually embraced Communism. He was imprisoned for his political beliefs and while incarcerated began to write plays, *Man and the Masses* (produced in New York by the Theatre Guild) and *The Machine Wreckers* being the earliest. His other plays include *Hinkemann, Hoppla, The Blind Goddess, Bloody Laughter* (staged in America by Maurice Schwartz), *Draw the Fires, Mary Baker Eddy* (with Herman Kesten) produced in London as *Miracle In America*, and *No More Peace*, staged by the Federal Theatre Project. He left Germany in 1933 and became a British subject, later making several lecture tours in America. In the last two years of his life he was of great use in an advisory capacity to the Dramatists' Guild. He committed suicide in New York in the summer of 1939.

See also *Drama, German, since the First World War and before National Socialism.*

Tolstoy—Leo Nikolayevich (1828-1910). Russian novelist and dramatist. Renowned chiefly as a novelist, his most famous works are *War And Peace*, 1864 and

Anna Karenina, 1875. Late in his career, he turned to drama as a more direct means of propounding his philosophy and ethical doctrines.

The Power of Darkness, one of his most famous plays, deals with susceptibility of the ignorant peasant to evil. The dialogue is distinguished by its literary quality, the characterizations are masterful and direct. Tolstoy constructed his plays naturally and simply. He wrote three comedies, *The Fruits of Enlightenment, The Root of All Evil, The First Distiller.* He also wrote two serious works, *The Living Corpse* and *The Light That Shines in Darkness.* Tolstoy may be considered one of the fore-runners of the naturalistic theatre and though his output of plays was comparatively small, they are constantly being produced.

Tombeau sous l'Arc de Triomphe, Le. Paul Raynal (French). Drama. 3 acts. 1924. Translated as *The Unknown Warrior by Cecil Lewis.*

Up to 1928, one of the finest post-War plays to be written in the classic tradition. Commemorates the First World War. Vehemently criticized, yet staged in all foreign countries. Deals with a few hours in the lives of a front soldier, his father and his fiancée; and the clash between the front and the hinterland. The entire action occurs during the soldier's leave of absence.

Tommers. Actors who play in *Uncle Tom's Cabin.*

Tomorrow and Tomorrow. Philip Barry (American). Drama. 3 acts. 1931.

Gail Redman, afraid of life, has never had a child. When she falls in love with Dr. Hay, she is untrue to her husband, and Dr. Hay's child is born after the doctor has left. Years later the child, through the lack of understanding of his supposed father, becomes seriously ill. Gail summons Dr. Hay, who cures the boy, but she refuses to go away with him because she knows it would ruin her husband's life.

Tom show. A company which plays *Uncle Tom's Cabin.*

Tom Thumb. The famous American dwarf, Charles Sherwood Stratton (1838-1883), exhibited by P. T. Barnum. When first shown he was about two feet high, but grew to be about forty inches in height.

Tom Thumb the Great. Henry Fielding (English). Burletta. Originally in 2 acts, 1730. Later revised to 3 acts, 1731.

Billed as *The Tragedie of Tragedies; or, The Life and Death of Tomb Thumb the Great* this work is typical of the farces that immediately followed the period of sentimental writing in the early 18th century. The play is more or less a burlesque of a tragedy of the time, *Sophonisba,* with broad and farcical emphasis laid on a triangle of Tom Thumb, Grizzle, his rival, and Huncamunca, the woman in the case.

Plays of this kind owe more to the vitality and invention of the author than to his intellect or wit. For that reason they have rarely been revived.

Tonight at 8:30. Noel Coward. A series of 9 one-act plays. 1935.

The plays consist of *Hands Across the Sea, The Astonished Heart* and *Red Peppers* as the first group; *We Were Dancing, Fumed Oak* and *Shadow Play* as the second; with *Ways and Means, Still Life* and *Family Album* making up the final group.

The plays are clever satires on contemporary English life.

Tooley, Nicholas (?-1623). English actor. An actor named in the 1623 Folio list of performers in Shakespeare's plays. He joined Shakespeare's company as an apprentice to Richard Burbage in 1605, when the company was under royal patronage, and remained with it until his death. In addition to Shakespeare's plays he appeared in Johnson's *The Alchemist* and *Catiline,* in Webster's *Duchess of Malfi* and in other plays.

Tooth enamel. Liquid in black color for blocking out teeth.
See *Make-up.*

Too True to be Good. George Bernard Shaw (English). 1932.

Shaw has himself described this play as a "collection of stage sermons by a Fellow of the Royal Society of Literature." His own joking comment well fits the play.

Impossible situations, overlong conversations and a surprising lack of any plot to speak of does not prevent Shaw from reeling off a great deal of clever dialogue and many witty epigrams.

Topaze. Marcel Pagnol (French). Comedy. 3 acts. 1928.

Topaze, a timid school teacher, is convinced by circumstance that honesty does not pay. When he is dismissed for being too uncompromising in his probity, he falls among thieves and becomes their tool and finally, thanks to the mistress of the leader and to a decoration which makes him believe in himself, he blossoms into as thoroughgoing and pleasant a rogue as one could wish for.

Top it. To build, or cause the emotional excitement of a play to mount by gradual increase of vocal intensity and quickening of tempo with rapid pick-up of cues.

Topping cues. Pitching the voice slightly higher and with more volume than that of the player who has just spoken.

To Quito and Back. Ben Hecht (American). Drama. 2 acts. 1937.

Reveals the effect of a South American uprising upon a sophisticated American writer. Unable to solve his own problems, the writer is nevertheless able to stand at the side of the leader, Zamiano, to counsel and enspirit him in adversity, and finally to help him write a song that the people, rising again and again in the future, shall sing as they march into battle.

Torch Bearers, The. George Kelly (American). Comedy. 3 acts. 1922.

Fred Ritter, a hard working and much put upon husband, is embarrassed by his wife's interest in amateur theatricals. He finally rebels and orders her to stop her nonsense and commands her to take care of her home, and she obeys.

Torch Song. Kenyon Nicholson (American). Drama. 3 acts. 1930.

After an unhappy love affair, Ivy Stephens, torch singer, joins the Salvation Army. A year later she meets her old lover and, for a while, forgets salvation. However, she is won back to the faith by a fellow worker who wants to marry her.

Tormentor. Flat or curtain on either side of the proscenium to hide the actors after their exits and to hide the prompter and lighting effects downstage.

Torrent, The. Maurice Donnay (French). Tragedy. 5 acts. 1899.

Tragedy results from the retirement to the country of a Parisian who anticipates leading Arcadian existence as a gentleman farmer. Since the unwonted calm makes him only the more aware of the dullness of his wife, he seeks excitement in the wife of an equally dull neighbor. When the lady discovers that their affair can no longer be concealed, she declines to follow the advice of a priest that she keep silent for the sake of their families. She refuses, also, to permit her husband to accept as his own the child that is coming. Instead, she leaps into a torrent.

Torres Naharro, Bartolmé de (?-1531?). Spanish dramatist. Born near Badajoz. Possibly a soldier in his early life; captive of Algerian pirates; later a priest and dramatist. During his residence in Rome, he received the favor of popes, cardinals, and the banker, Chigi.

La Ymenea, the principal contribution of Torres Naharro to the evolution of the Spanish drama, is the first cape-and-sword play in Spanish literature. It first presents the *pundonor* or point of honor, which was to become very important in various works of the Golden Age. The distinction that he draws between comedy and tragedy in his *prohemio* was the first bit of dramatic criticism ever attempted by a Spanish writer.

Tortesa, the Usurer. Nathaniel P. Willis (American). Drama. 5 acts. 1839.

Four installments of the play were published in the New York *Mirror* in 1838.

The outlines of the story were taken from the Florentine tale of *Genevra d'Amori.* Relates how Isabella, who is supposedly dead, escapes from the tomb, is helped by Tortesa, who is in love with her, to marry his rival, Angelo.

Tosca, La. Victorien Sardou (French). Drama. 5 acts. 1887.

Tosca, an Italian singer, tries to save her lover from execution by giving herself to the chief of police. At the last moment she stabs herself; then finding her lover is really to be killed, leaps from a battlement to her death.

Touch and Go. D. H. Lawrence (English). Drama. 3 acts. 1920.

The scene is a mining center in the English midlands. The play introduces the struggle between capital and labor and concludes that compromise on both sides represents the most satisfactory solution.

Toupee tape. A double-faced adhesive tape to hold wigs and whiskers in place; used for make-up.

Tovarich. Jacques Deval (French). Comedy. 3 acts. 1934. Adapted by Robert E. Sherwood.

Grand Duchess Tatiana and Prince Mikail Alexandrovitch, white Russians, rejoice at securing work as maid and butler in the home of Charles Dupont, in Paris. They lose their jobs when one of the Dupont guests recognizes Tatiana in her maid's uniform and curtsies to her. Monsieur Dupont finally recants, however, and permits them to stay.

As the play ends, they give to Soviet Commissar Corotchenko a fortune entrusted to them by the Czar to be used for the good of Russia.

Towneley Cycle. A series of thirty-two English miracle plays dating from the reign of Henry VI, about the year 1450, and named after a small town where the performances were given. Believed the work of the Augustinian friars, these plays were probably written from 1360 on. They were written in the vernacular and express a more secular character than previous miracles, probably with the purpose of amusing the people rather than serving religion.

Tragedy. A style of drama which originated in a religious ceremony in ancient Greece known as the *dithyramb* and which is characterized by its grave and sorrowful ending. Aristotle's definition, in his *Poetics,* is: "an imitation of a worthy or illustrious and perfect action, possessing magnitude, in pleasing language, using separately the several species of imitation in its parts, by men acting, and not through narration, through pity and fear effecting a purification from such like passions." Marlowe's idea of tragedy approximated to a degree the modern tragedy of ordinary man at the mercy of overwhelming and inexplicable forces. His human heroes fight against powers that are finally too much for them. For the Middle Ages, tragedy was a thing only of the nobility, whereas for Marlowe it dealt with individuals. The union of these two concepts, in Shakespeare, gives us the majesty of *Macbeth* and *King Lear.*

Tragedy, domestic. A form of drama which first appeared in the early 17th century but which had to wait until the 18th and 19th centuries for full fruition: a serious play on contemporary topics, particularly those of family life, concerning every day people and marked by a realism of the commonplace. The first play of this kind was Kyd's *Arden of Feversham,* which appeared early in the 17th century, and which was strongly moralistic, with its characters stopping the dramatic action to preach. *A Yorkshire Tragedy* was printed in 1608 and has been erroneously attributed to Shakespeare. The form represented by these and many other plays constituted one of the most vital and creative forces in the whole of tragic drama. All other forms relied on tradition, with the assumption of repetitious themes, characters and stilted language. Bourgeois tragedy, as it came to be known in the 18th and 19th centuries, was progressive and revolutionary, an issue from the sentimental movement, and a pioneer for new expression of tragic themes. It pitted vitality and strength against the more unreal principles of classicism. It falls into three classes: tragedies such as that of Orpheum; tragedies of Fate; and realistic tragedies such as George Lillo's *The London Merchant,* which is a landmark in dramatic history because of the introduction of an essentially middle class hero. Among the foremost examples of this form must be classed Heywood's *A Woman Killed with Kindness* and *The English Traveller,* and Dekker's *The Honest Whore.* Of the modern period such plays as Ibsen's *A Doll's House* and *Hedda Gabler,* Pinero's *The Second Mrs. Tanqueray,* and Granville-Barker's *Waste* may be mentioned as belonging to the category of domestic tragedy.

Tragedy, horror. A form of drama in the 17th century. Allardyce Nicoll, in his *British Drama,* says of this type of drama: "The chief point in common among all the plays is the presence of a somewhat decadent mood and introduction of physical torture in and for itself." Among the best known plays of this type are Middleton's *The Lover's Melancholy,* Ford's *The Broken Heart,* and Shirley's *The Maid's Revenge.*

Tragedy, pathetic. A form of drama prevalent in England in the 18th century. It appeared to a great extent as a reaction against the pseudo-classic drama and was based predominantly on an appeal to pity. It dealt with domestic scenes as well as pure heroic drama as taken from the Restoration. Nicholas Rowe (*The Ambitious Step-Mother* and *The Fair Penitent*) was the foremost exponent of this school.

Tragedy, pseudo-classic. A form of drama prevalent in England in the 18th century which saw a reinstatement of the criteria of the Ancients: compliance with the laws of the three unities, restriction of the number of characters, and the discipline of propriety and order. The greatest example of this form is, perhaps, Addison's *Cato.* James Thomson also wrote in the pseudo-classic manner in such plays as *The Seasons, Sophonisba, Agamemnon* and *Coriolanus.*

See also *Pseudo-classicism.*

Tragedy of Locrine, The. Author unknown (English). Tragedy. 1595.

A tragic drama on the life of Locrine, a legendary king of the early Britons. It has been attributed to Shakespeare on the basis of the initials W.S. on the title page of the 1595 quarto edition and because it was included in the Third and Fourth Folio editions of the dramatists works in 1664 and 1685. Largely on the evidence of its style, however, the majority of critics have rejected it as non-Shakespearean. The action deals with Locrine's defeat of the invader Humber, his passion for the latter's wife Estrild, his abandoning of his own wife Guendolen, and his death at the hands of Guendolen's aroused kinsmen.

The Tragedy of Nan. John Masefield (English). Tragedy. 3 acts. 1910.

Nan Hardwick, daughter of a man who has been hanged, lives in the house of her uncle. She is a drudge and an outcast because of her father's disgrace. She falls in love with Dick Gurvil, who deserts her. Forsaken, she becomes a tragic figure. Finally, thwarted on all sides, she turns murderess and finds her release in death.

Tragi-comedy. A form of drama, combining elements of both tragedy and comedy, first established by Euripides in his *Alcestis* and first introduced into the French theatre at the Hôtel de Bourgogne. In England its inception came in the year 1611 with *A King and No King.*

Traitor, The. James Shirley (English). Tragedy. 5 acts. 1631.

It has some historical foundation in the assassination of Duke Alessandro de' Medici. Lorenzo plots against his kinsman, the duke of Florence and for this purpose furthers the duke's desire to seduce Amidea, sister of Sciarrha, a Florentine noble. He inflames Sciarrha against the Duke's tyranny, so that Sciarrha determines to kill him. Finally Sciarrha kills Amidea to save her from dishonor and lays her body on the bed, where the duke finds her. In amazement he calls for Lorenzo, who stabs him to death and is in turn killed by Sciarrha. The latter, wounded in the affray, also dies.

Transfiguration (Wandlung). Ernst Toller (German). Expressionistic drama. 3 acts. 1935.

Produced in Berlin while the author was in prison. Largely autobiographical, the play deals in expressionistic style with a young German artist who goes to war full of enthusiasm and finally becomes a revolutionary.

Transvestism. The device of a girl dressed in boy's clothing, or vice versa, had, as in Elizabethan times, several advantages because it created an automatic sanction of indecorous scenes; it served to heighten the pathos of certain scenes; and it supplied considerable novelty in plot. Shakespeare, however, discarded the device as early as 1600.

Traps. The floor of the stage is often cut up by traps which open into the basement to permit the use of sunken stairways, scenery, or actors rising from or sinking into the ground.

Travelling company. In 1860 Boucicault developed the travelling company with one play. Before this, travelling companies had a stock repertory; now they went out with one play, simultaneous with its run in a large city; the first play thus sent out was Boucicault's *The Colleen Bawn* with John Drew. Travelling companies (called "road companies," "No. 2 company," etc.) now tour in a play either at the same time or after the metropolitan production.

Travelling stage. A platform in use in Elizabethan times, moved about from place to place and, with backdrop, serving as a set for theatrical performances.

Treadmill stage. A machine device which is a relic of the *Ben-Hur* chariot scene; consists of belts run on the stage floor, or part of the stage floor is broken into a movable belt running either to the right or left so that scenery or actors can be moved across the stage to give the illusion of the passage of distance. Also used in *Uncle Tom's Cabin* for the scene of Eliza crossing the ice; and, also in numerous horse-race plays.

Treasure, The. David Pinski (Yiddish). Drama. 4 acts. 1906.

A play which combines intense realism of details with broad, imaginative sweep, and the mingling of the realism of every day with the supernatural. Judke, the half witted son of the grave digger of a small Russian city, finds a handful of rubles while burying his dog. His imaginative sister immediately jumps to the conclusion that there is a hidden treasure to be unearthed.

The story immediately gets about that Chone, the grave digger, is immensely wealthy, the master of a buried treasure. Chone denies it, but the townsfolk think he is lying and are so insistent that he is himself convinced that he is a wealthy man.

The efforts of the good neighbors to separate him from the imagined treasure form the basis of the plot.

Treasure Chest, The. Carl Sternheim (German). Drama. 3 acts. 1912.

A middle-aged schoolmaster brings home a young second wife and his elderly aunt casts suspicion upon the virtue of the bride. His daughter marries a photographer who has already made love to the bride and earlier to the servant in the house. The schoolmaster, given his aunt's treasure chest to guard, dreams of the wealth he may inherit even while she is dictating a will leaving everything to the Church.

Tree, Helen Maud, Lady (Helen Maud Holt) (1863-1938). English actress.

Born in London, she made her first appearance on the stage in 1883, marrying Herbert Beerbohm Tree in the same year, and later in the year came into prominence as Hester Gould in *The Millionaire.* She joined her husband at the Haymarket in 1887, and in 1902 assumed the direction of Wyndham's theatre. She remained on the stage after her husband's death, and with the coming of the talking films achieved a minor triumph on the screen in *Wedding Rehearsal* and *The Private Life of Henry VIII.* Lady Tree appeared in a wide variety of parts from Shakespeare to modern comedy and melodrama, her most memorable role being probably that of Lady Teazle in *The School for Scandal.* She became widely known in her later years for her children's programs broadcast by the British Broadcasting Corporation.

Tree, Sir Herbert Beerbohm (Herbert Beerbohm). (1853-1917). English actor-manager. The son of an Anglo-German merchant, Julius Beerbohm, he was born in London, and made his professional debut in that city under the name of Beerbohm Tree, as Lord Ingleborough in *Engineering,* 1878. His first great success was in 1884, as the Rev. Robert Spalding in *The Private Secretary.* Three years later he opened in management at the Comedy Theatre, producing the melodrama *The Red Lamp* in which he played Paul Demetrius. A few months later he moved to the Haymarket and began a long series of successes, which included Shakespearean and Sheridan revivals, as well as the production of new plays such as *A Woman of No Importance,* in which he played Lord Illingworth. He also produced *Trilby,* 1895, in which he played Svengali, considered one of the greatest of his roles. After a tour of the United States, he took over the management of Her Majesty's and there began, with *The Seats of the Mighty,* 1897, the series of successful and luxurious productions with which his name is for the most part associated.

Among Tree's best known parts were: Sir Peter Teazle in *The School for Scandal;* King John, 1899; Bottom, 1900; Herod, 1900; Ulysses, Falstaff, with Ellen Terry and Mrs. Kendal, 1902; Zakkuri in *The Darling of the Gods,* 1903; Isidore Izard in *Business is Business,* 1905; Colonel Newcombe, 1906; Fagin in *Oliver Twist,* 1905; Paragot in *The Beloved Vagabond,* 1908; Shylock, 1908; Wolsey, 1910; Drake, 1914; and Micawber and Peggotty in *David Copperfield,* 1915.

He was knighted in 1909, and on Henry Irving's death became president of the Theatrical Managers' Association. In 1916 he lectured in America; he died shortly after his return to England in 1917.

Tree, Viola (1884-   ). English actress. Born in London, the eldest daughter of Sir Herbert and Lady Tree, she first appeared in London in 1904 as Viola, with her father, in *Twelfth Night.* At the Aldwych Theatre, of which she was manager, she ran the Guitry season, 1920. Among later outstanding roles were Salmon in *Symphony in Two Flats,* 1931; Susan in *Never Come Back,* 1932; *She Shall Have Music,* 1934; *Noah,* 1934; *Lady Precious Stream,* etc.

Trelawny of the "Wells." Sir Arthur Wing Pinero (English). Comedy. 4 acts. 1899.

Rose Trelawny, the actress, leaves her friends at the Wells Theatre to marry the man she loves and live with his family in Cavendish Square. Rose, however, is a born trouper and cannot go to bed at reasonable hours or conform in other ways to life in Cavendish Square. Finally she rebels and returns to the theatre, an actress again. This is a favorite play and has been revived many times by well known actors.

Trial by Jury. W. S. Gilbert. Music by Sir Arthur Sullivan. One act operetta. 1875.

It concerns a breach of promise suit. The judge enters, all bow and hail him. He sings the judge's son explaining how he got where he is. They call Angelina, the swooning bride-to-have-been. The judge is smitten by her. The defendant admits in song that he is as changeable as the weather and that he is very tired of Angelina. The lawyer pleads for her. Finally, the judge sings out "all the legal furies seize you, no arrangement seems to please you, I will marry her myself." And he does so.

Trial of Mary Dugan, The. Bayard Veiller (American). Drama. 3 acts. 1928.

Mary Dugan, Follies girl, accused of murdering Edgar Rice, a prominent financier, is saved from the chair by the intelligence and skill of her young brother James Dugan.

The play is noteworthy because of the manner in which it is written. Mr. Veiller has successfully turned a murder trial into a play. All the action, from beginning to the final curtain, takes place in the courtroom.

Triangle Club. Theatrical organization at Princeton University, founded in 1888 as the Princeton Dramatic Association. Present name adopted in 1893. First musical *The Honorable Julius Caesar* by Booth Tarkington in 1890. Claims distinction for its almost complete student responsibility for production. Limited to musicals. Productions go on tour annually throughout the country.

Triangle play. A piece centering around the eternal triangle; that is, the circumstance of two men in love with one woman, or two women in love with the same man; or variations of the theme as in *The Captive* and *The Green Bay Tree*.

Trilby. Paul M. Potter (American). Drama. 1895. Adapted from the novel by George du Maurier (English).

The action takes place in the bohemian quarter of Paris. Trilby is a laundress and artists' model. Her three friends are Tappy, a big Englishman, Laird, a Scotchman and Billie, an English painter of great talent. Billie and Trilby love each other but his family objects to her. She decides to relinquish him. Svengali, a talented musician, is interested in her after discovering she has a beautiful voice. She finds him repulsive yet fascinating. He exerts hypnotic power over her and she goes with him, becoming a famous concert star. Five years later, Billie and his friends attend a concert and are startled to see Trilby. Svengali dies during one of her performances and she can no longer sing. Billie attains fame as a painter but it is empty without Trilby. The two sweethearts, finding life without savour, languish and eventually die of unhappiness.

Trip to Scarborough, A. Richard Brinsley Sheridan (English). Comedy. 5 acts. 1777.

The plot is that of Sir John Vanbrugh's *The Relapse* with some modifications.

In order to punish Towneley for deserting her in favor of Amanda, Berinthia attempts to entice Loveless with an affair. Finally overcome with shame, Loveless returns to his wife Amanda.

Trissino, Gian Giorgio (1478-1550). Italian dramatist. Important because he was the first writer to choose the new Italian tongue, in preference to Greek or Latin, and for his lifeless tragedies.

Tristan and Isolt. John Masefield. Tragedy in blank verse. 1927.

Tristan, a prince, arrives at Cornwall to find his uncle Marc, the rightful king enslaved by Kolbein, a Scandinavian pirate. Tristan mortally wounds Kolbein who makes Marc promise that he will wed Isolt, daughter of his queen. Tristan goes to Ireland to fetch her, they drink of a magic wine and fall deeply in love. On her wedding night, Isolt makes Brangwen, her maid, drink the love-wine. She does so, but breaks the king's goblet, and falls in love with the king. The king is informed of the trysts of Isolt and Tristan. Tristan is banished and Isolt flees with him. Marc, realizing their love, doesn't follow. He comes upon them in the forest and leaves his glove as a token of forgiveness. Isolt, contrite, returns to Marc who makes her queen. Marc is killed in battle, Tristan goes mad and is dying. Isolt having nothing to live for stabs herself.

Triumph of Death, The. Feodor Sologub (Russian). Tragedy. *Prologue* and 4 acts. Translated by John Cournos. Printed 1916.

Illustrative of the author's theory of the tragic hero as one who struggles to impose upon resistant nature an ideal of beauty.

This conflict is symbolized through a prologue in which the peasant girl, idealized by Don Quixote suggests the poet's mission. The plot of the play within the play is taken from the old legend of the daughter of Flor and Blanchefleur destined to wed King Pepin, who believes her beautiful though she is in reality ugly. When he discovers she is not the beauty he thought her, he still is true to her.

Troilus and Cressida. William Shakespeare (English). Comedy. 5 acts. 1602.

Written about 1602 and published in two quarto editions in 1609. It is based on the medieval legend which Shakespeare could have found in Chaucer, Lydgate, Caxton and other sources. He probably also made some use of Chapman's translation of Homer. The romantic plot deals with the love of Troilus and Cressida, facilitated by Pandarus, Cressida's lecherous uncle. This affair ends in disillusionment when the fickle Cressida, removed to the Greek camp from Troy, transfers her affections to Diomede. The military plot deals with the attempts of Ulysses and other Greek leaders to shame Achilles out of his lethargy by sending Ajax instead of Achilles into private combat with the Trojan Hector. Achilles eventually meets Hector and treacherously kills him. The two plots are never clearly interwoven and neither is brought to a definite conclusion.

Trojan Women, The. Euripides (Greek). Tragedy. c. 415 B.C.

Perhaps the most moving of all pacifist dramas. It deals with the destruction of Troy. After the sacking of the city, the Trojan women are enslaved, Hector's son is cast from the walls, Helen is led off by Menelaus and the women are given into bondage.

Tropus. A dialogue, invented by the Swiss monk Tutilo in the 10th century, which was introduced into the *introitus,* or first part of the mass, and which was among the first steps leading to the dramatization of the church ritual into the liturgical play.

Troubadours. See *Jongleurs.*

Troublesome Reign of King John. An Elizabethan play by an unknown author on the same subject as Shakespeare's *King John.* Shakespeare possibly used the earlier play as a source, keeping the general structure, but completely revamping the style, handling of character and arrangement of episodes for heightened dramatic effect.

Troupe du Roi. The company of actors established by Molière in 1660 at the Palais Royal.

Trouper. A seasoned performer whose motto, at all times, is that "the show must go on!"

Trousers, The. Carl Sternheim (Germany). Comedy. 3 acts.
A burgher's wife loses her *"panties,"* and no one on the stage speaks of anything but that banal event. The ridiculous scenes that follow serve to expose the frailties of a journalist and a barber fired with love by the lady's misadventure.

Truc. French for theatrical machine; generally, a knack or trick.

True Tragedie of Richard Duke of New York. A play dealing with the same subject as Shakespeare's *Henry VI, Part III* and long thought to be the source used by Shakespeare as the basis for his play. It is now fairly well established that the *True Tragedie,* published in 1595, is a pirated corrupt version of Shakespeare's play.

True Tragedy of Richard Third, The. Anonymous (English). Printed 1594.
A play on the same subject as Shakespeare's *Richard III.* If Shakespeare used the earlier play as a basis of his own, he completely revised and reshaped the handling of the subject to suit his own purposes.

Truth, The. Clyde Fitch (American). Comedy. 4 acts. 1906.
Mrs. Warder, a born liar, deceives her husband about a tête-à-tête she has had with Fred Linton. After confessing to this and many other lies, she is finally forgiven and reconciled with her husband.

Truth About Blayds, The. A. A. Milne (English). Drama. 1922.
Oliver Blayds, ninety years old, is venerated by his public and family as the last of the great Victorian poets. He has so dominated his family that his son-in-law, Conway, has changed his name to Blayds-Conway and intends to publish the biography of Blayds. His elder daughter, Marion, the wife of Blayds-Conway, has endorsed this ambition and Isobel, the younger daughter, has devoted her life to caring for the old man. When at 90, Blayds confesses that his entire reputation has been founded on poems he stole from a friend who has died, the family is in turmoil. Isobel insists the world be told of this humbug and she is backed up by Royce, her fiancé, and her niece and nephew who are fed up with all this false glory. But Marion and Conway convince them that no good would come of it and they would lose the Blayd's royalties. Isobel compromises by refusing to touch any of the money and Conway compromises by agreeing to mention the scandal in his memoirs in the interest of truth.

Try it on the dog. To have an out of town try-out for a play.

Tucker, Sophie (Sophie Abuza) (1884-   ). American actress. Born in Boston; first appeared as a singer in her father's cafe in Hartford; appeared in cabaret in New York, then in vaudeville; was engaged for Tony Pastor's and then toured with *The Gay Masqueraders;* after more vaudeville she made her first regular New York appearance at the Jardin de Paris in The Ziegfeld *Follies* of 1909; subsequently she appeared in *Merry Mary* and *Louisiana Lou,* 1911; then returned to vaudeville; toured in *Town Topics,* 1916; with McIntyre and Heath in *Hello, Alexander,* 1919; *Shubert Gaieties* 1919; *Earl Carroll Vanities,* 1924; was a success in London for several years; has appeared in vaudeville and cabarets in New York since 1930; made an outstanding success in *Leave It To Me,* 1938.

Tucson Little Theatre, Arizona. A little theatre founded in the late 1920's. Edward Reveaux is present director. It has a workshop and study groups. The aim of this theatre is to justify the theatre by good productions and to foster creative writing.

Turkey. A show that is a failure; term originated some years ago when bad shows were opened on Thanksgiving Day to clear expenses and make a little money in the two or three holiday performances; now, any badly cast and produced show.

Turlupin. A stock-character in French farce.

Turn to the Right. Winchell Smith and John E. Hazzard (American). Comedy. 4 acts. 1916.
Three convicts, just released from Sing Sing, decide to "turn to the right." Returning home, they become a force for law and order, and rid the community of an unscrupulous deacon. They are also successful in selling home-made jam.

Tutilo. The monk in the Swiss monastery of St. Gall in the 10th century who introduced the *tropus* (or dialogue, and first dramatic element) into the *introitus,* or the first part of the mass.
See also *Drama, Spanish, 15th-17th century; Tropus.*

Twain, Mark (Samuel Langhorne Clemens) (1835-1910). American author, humorist. Journalist, printer, river pilot, soldier of fortune; met Artemus Ward and Bret Harte in the far West; first published a story, *Jim Smiley and the Jumping Frog,* in 1865. Soon afterward, became a humorous lecturer, and from 1870 on wrote the classics that have secured him in the first rank of American authors. Represented in the theatre by dramatizations of *The Gilded Age* (made by himself), *The Prince and the Pauper, Huckleberry Finn, Tom Sawyer, A Connecticut Yankee at King Arthur's Court* and *Puddin' Head Wilson.*

Twelfth Night. William Shakespeare (English). Comedy. 5 acts. 1599.
Written about 1599 and published in the Folio of 1623. It is based ultimately on an Italian play *Gl 'Ingannati* and available to Shakespeare in various forms by

Bandello, Cinthio and Barnabe Riche. It probably received its title from the occasion for which it was written, the festivities of the twelfth night after Christmas. Viola, shipwrecked on the coast of Illyria, disguises herself as a boy and becomes a page to duke Orsino, with whom she falls in love. He, unaware of her feeling, employs her as a messenger to convey his love to the lady Oliva, who takes Viola for a boy and falls in love with her. The complications that result are resolved when Viola's twin brother, Sebastian, arrives on the scene, reveals the true identity and sex of Viola, and takes her place in the affections of Olivia. The duke transfers his love to Viola, and both couples are married. In a sub-plot Olivia's uncle Sir Toby Belch, Maria her maid, and Sir Andrew Aguecheek a companion seek to mortify the haughty and puritannical Malvolio, steward to Olivia. They forge a letter which makes him think that Olivia, deeply in love with him, desires him to dress in outlandish fashion. He does and Olivia promptly imprisons him as a madman.

Twelve-Pound Look, The. J. M. Barrie (English). Comedy. 1 act. 1910.

The wife of a wealthy titled Englishman has grown dreadfully bored with her unproductive life, and restless under the thought that her whole existence depends upon her husband's generosity. She meets another woman, a typist, who it turns out, was her husband's ex-wife but who had left him in order to be independent. The wife realizes that this is exactly what she wants and the curtain comes down when she determines to get the 12 pounds—the cost of a typewriter.

TWENTIETH CENTURY ENGLISH DRAMA

BY RICHARD CORDELL

The past fifty years has been the greatest period in English drama since the age of Elizabeth and Shakespeare, its nearest rival being the Restoration Period at the close of the seventeenth century. Except for the bright comedies of Sheridan and Goldsmith the eighteenth century was almost barren of actable, literate plays, but not so barren as the century between Sheridan and Henry Arthur Jones. Except for the faint glimmers of light in the superficially realistic dramas of Tom Robertson and the brilliant musical plays of Gilbert and Sullivan, it was a century of inspissated gloom. People of intelligence and taste could be drawn into the theatre only by Shakespearean revivals or the less trivial of the countless adaptations from the French. For the most part intelligent people stayed away from the theatre; never was the gap between the theatre and literature so vast and ignominious.

Then appeared two playwrights who rescued the English stage from its triviality and vulgarity, and who led the movement to restore the drama to its once honored position among the arts. One of these pioneers, Arthur Wing Pinero, was influenced by Ibsen and introduced the new naturalism into English drama. His grim character studies of Paula Tanqueray and Iris Bellamy were almost as exciting to the English as Ibsen's Nora and Hedda had been to the Scandinavians and Germans fifteen years earlier. Henry Arthur Jones was a militant crusader for a more adult drama—a lecturer, pamphleteer, and playwright. He revived the popularity of the high comedy with *The Case of Rebellious Susan* and *The Liars* and tried, with no great success, to inject intellectual elements into serious drama. Although the plays of Jones and Pinero are no longer acted, it would be hard to exaggerate the importance of these two pioneers.

Within a few years a score of important playwrights were active in the dramatic renascence. Oscar Wilde between 1892 and 1895 wrote four comedies with a flashing and audacious wit absent from the English stage for two centuries. Haddon Chambers, Hubert Henry Davies, and Somerset Maugham followed Jones in the field of high comedy. But the three giants of English drama in the early years of the twentieth century were Bernard Shaw, John Galsworthy, and Sir James Barrie. Shaw established the vogue of the drama of disquisition, and frankly used (and uses) the theatre as a medium for the propagation of his economic, social, and ethical theories. Fortunately Shaw is also at times a great artist with a shrewd sense of dramatic values, and such plays as *Candida, Pygmalion,* and *Saint Joan* are permanent masterpieces. Barrie is perhaps the greatest genius of the group, though his plays with their touches of the supernatural and the whimsical are not socially significant in the contemporary sense. Galsworthy's plays also are intellectually honest, but somewhat enervated by a super-British restraint that makes them often static and undramatic.

In Ireland about 1900 a native drama and theatre were encouraged as a part of the great national revival. The movement was highly successful, producing such dramatists as Lady Gregory, J. M. Synge, Sean O'Casey, Lord Dunsany, Lennox Robinson, Vincent Carroll, and Denis Johnston, and such world-famous playhouses as the Abbey and the Gate.

The most brilliant disciple of Shaw is Granville-Barker, whose dramas have proved a bit too high-brow for the general audience, but who has had a healthful influence on modern stage production and acting technique. A. A. Milne has proceeded successfully in the Barrie tradition of gentle and whimsical humor. Noel Coward best reflected the post-war confusion and disillusion in his Restoration-like comedies, but some of his plays are already "dated." The popularity of the biographical drama has resulted in a great number of plays about such figures as Napoleon, Elizabeth Barrett, Disraeli, Clive, Parnell, Keats, Queen Victoria, etc. Although regional plays are less numerous than in America, Eden Philpotts has written excellent Devonshire comedies, the whole Manchester school under the leadership of Harold Brighouse and Stanley Houghton has produced a tangy Lancashire drama, and recently have come a number of Welsh plays.

An occasional verse play by T. S. Eliot, Humbert Wolfe, or W. H. Auden may attract some attention, but there are no signs that verse drama will supplant the modern realistic prose drama inaugurated by Ibsen and brought to fine flower in France, England, and the United States. Among modern British realists the plays of John Van Druten, R. C. Sheriff, St. John Ervine, Mordaunt Shairp, R. M. Harwood, Dodie Smith, Rodney Ackland, Merton Hodge, Keith Winter, and Ronald Jeans have achieved the greatest popularity, but none have been unusually significant except Sheriff's fine tragedy, *Journey's End.* The psychological thriller has engaged the talents of Emlyn Williams, Frank Vosper, and Barré Lyndon. The historical dramas of John Drinkwater, Gordon Daviot, and Clifford Bax are less turgid and romantic than those of Phillips, Wills, and Lytton of earlier years. The growth of the intimate and satirical revue has all but crowded out the sentimental "moonlight and roses" musical comedy.

Modern English drama is fortunately not merely a matter of productions in the West-end theatres of London. The increase in the number of municipal and repertory theatres in the provinces has been phenomenal, and the Little Theatre movement has penetrated into every part of the Kingdom. Especially noteworthy are such theatres as those of Manchester, Glasgow, Norwich, Liverpool, and Hull, which operate under their own power independent of touring companies and London successes and failures. Especially valuable are such repertory and stock companies operating in or near London such as the Tavistock, "Q," Richmond, Embassy, and Mercury Theatre players, and such experimental groups as the Gate, Torch, and Stage Society.

Although British drama is in a healthy condition, it is lacking in the robustness and originality of recent American drama. The plays of Eugene O'Neill, Irwin Shaw, Clifford Odets, Maxwell Anderson, Paul Green, Sidney Kingsley, John Steinbeck, Elmer Rice, and Lillian Hellman have a freshness and vitality rarely found in modern English drama. *The Gentle People, Golden Boy, Mourning Becomes Electra,* and *Of Mice and Men* have enjoyed a striking success in London largely perhaps because their audacity and vigor contrast so strongly with the gentle domestic comedies which still dominate the West End stage.

Twenty-four sheet. A large advertising poster for billboards.

Two-a-day, The. Old time term for vaudeville meaning matinée and evening performances as opposed to the regular routine of the theatre.

Two Gentlemen of Verona, The. William Shakespeare (English). Comedy. 5 acts. c. 1594.

Written about 1594 or 1595 and first published in the Folio of 1623. Shakespeare drew on a lost play, *The History of Felix and Philomena,* based in turn on Montemayor's *Diana,* for his plot, adding Valentine, Launce and Speed. Proteus leaves Julia, whom he loves, and joins Valentine on a trip to Milan. Both fall in love with Sylvia. The elopement of Valentine and Sylvia is prevented by Proteus, who causes Valentine to be banished. Julia arrives disguised as a boy and becomes a page to Proteus, in order to re-win his love. Sylvia goes to find Valentine, is pursued and threatened by Proteus and rescued by Valentine. Proteus suddenly repents, Julia reveals her identity and the lovers are restored to each other.

Two in One (La Signora Morli, una e due). Luigi Pirandello (Italian). Comedy. 3 acts. 1922.

Originally entitled, *Mrs. Morli, One and Two.* Evelina, who has two souls, is loved by two different men. One loves the soul of Eva, a mad creatures greedy for life; the other loves the soul of Lina, a wise and good wife. At the parting of the ways, Evelina decides to be the orderly Lina.

Two Mrs. Camerons, The. Winifred and Edith Carter (English). Play. 3 acts. Printed 1937.

Pauline Cameron confined to her bed, a cripple for life, is extremely rebellious. Because of a suspicion that her husband is having an affair with the governess, Pauline leaves her estate to her son and Anna Graham, a servant, and cuts off her husband, when she dies. When Michael, the husband, and the governess marry, they begin to receive incriminating letters from Pauline, but posted long after her death. An investigation reveals that Anna Graham, the servant, has sent them in response to Pauline's command before her death.

Two Mr. Wetherbys, The. St. John Hankin (English). Drama. 3 acts. 1903.

A story about James, whose main desire is for a settled domestic life, and finds it difficult to prevent his wife's escaping him; and Richard, who has run amuck, and finds it equally difficult to escape from a wife eager to return to him.

Two Noble Kinsmen, The. A Jacobean romantic drama published in 1634 as the work of John Fletcher and William Shakespeare, and reprinted, with no mention of Shakespeare, in the second folio edition of plays by Beaumont and Fletcher in 1679. Part of the play is clearly recognized as the work of Fletcher; opinion is still divided as to Shakespeare's authorship of the remainder. The poetry in the latter is brilliant, but many critics feel that the character and morality here is non-Shakespearean. The story is that told by Chaucer in his *Knightes Tale* of Palamon, Arcite and Emilia.

Two Nobilities, The. Henri Lavédan (French). Drama. 3 acts. 1894.

The gay Prince d'Aurec commits suicide after losing at cards, leaving a son who is reared in America. There he learns the gospel of labor and becomes a captain of industry. Then the son of this son, back in France, falls in love with the daughter of a marquis, who objects to him as too low in the social scale. But his identity is revealed by a discharged employee of his father, one who has organized a strike to regain his lost position.

The story serves to point a contrast between the aristocracy of birth and the new aristocracy of service. France is to be saved by those who are not too proud to put their shoulders to the wheel.

2 x 2 = 5. Gustav Wied (Danish). Drama. 3 acts. 1906.

By the title of the play, the author would imply that nothing that is so is so if it interfere with our happiness; we are all inclined to adapt the truth to suit ourselves.

A liberal schoolmaster has shocked his wife and her father by writing a book designed to make people see themselves as they really are. He is persecuted by the government and sent to jail. When he emerges, he finds everything changed; and he is finally forced to accept, at an excellent salary, a job on a newspaper—a job which he had refused before because he disapproved of the policy of the newspaper. Thus the champion of truth and freedom barters his intellectual honesty for a fat salary, falling a victim to the very weakness he had assailed in others.

Two Orphans, The. A. P. D'Ennery and Eugene Cormon (French). 1875.

The story of Louise and her blind sister Henriette who become separated when they arrive in Paris from the country. They fall into the hands of abductors and Louise is made to beg on the streets. Henriette is intended as a plaything for dissolute nobility but is saved from this fate by the Chevelier de Vaudrey who falls in love with her.

Throughout the play they search for each other and often are on the verge of meeting but only in the melodramatic climax are they reunited.

Two Shepherds, The. Gregorio Martinez-Sierra (Spanish). Drama. 3 acts. 1913.

A priest and a doctor who are shepherds of the village folk, are replaced because they cannot pass the examination in theology and science required by the new adminis-tration. While they may not have the formal knowledge required they understand human nature and are capable of giving the townspeople the proper guidance. Never-theless, they are forced to give up their posts.

Tyler, Royall (1757-1826). American dramatist. Author of *The Contrast,* the first play by an American author on an American subject to be produced on the American stage. His success as a playwright is of importance to the American stage, because it brought about a complete change in the attitude of the public toward the theatre. All classes now began to see in the theatre an institution by which national traits and genius could be perpetuated. American plays became the fashion.

Type. (1) Noun: An actor suited by looks and personality to a specific part; (2) verb: to limit an actor to one kind of part.

Udall, Nicholas (1506-1556). English schoolmaster, dramatist. A native of Hampshire, and a friend of John Leland, he was successively headmaster of Eton, vicar of Braintree, prebendary of Windsor, rector of Calbourne, Isle of Wight, play-wright to Queen Mary, and headmaster of Westminster school. His first book, a schoolbook of selections from Terence, 1534, was followed probably by a number of interludes or short plays written for performance at court or by his scholars. He next assisted in the translation of Erasmus' paraphrase of the New Testament and other translations; but he is best known as the author of *Ralph Roister Doister,* the earliest known English comedy. Written in rhymed doggerel, and based on a Latin model, it contains the stock classical comic character of the braggart soldier.

Unchastened Woman, The. Louis K. Anspacher (American). Comedy. 3 acts. 1915.

The leading character is a brilliant woman who poses to herself as the heroine of a belated romance. In her devastating way she decides to play the role of destiny in the life of a struggling young architect. She comes to grips with the young man's wife, and it takes the combined efforts of several people to chasten her unscrupulous intentions.

Uncle Tom's Cabin. George L. Aiken (American). Drama. 6 acts. 1853. From the story by Harriet Beecher Stowe, 1851-2.

The story of Uncle Tom, the faithful slave, his loyalty to the St. Clare family, his great love for little Eva, and his final martyrdom when he tells Simon Legree, "My body belongs to you, but my soul belongs to God."

The story was written to show the evils of slavery in an attempt to arouse public opinion. Its influence was tremendous during the last decade of slavery and its part in the creation of anti-slave sentiment incalculable.

It has become an American classic and is still often played by road companies.

Eliza's escape from the bloodhounds by crossing the ice-filled Ohio is a dramatic high spot, and Little Topsy's statement that she was never born but just growed is one of its humorous moments.

Uncle Vanya. Anton Chekhov (Russian). Drama. 4 acts. 1897.

The theme of the play is the infinite sadness of living and the futility of life. Reveals the futility of people without a purpose, and the corrosive effect of egoism. Originally called *The Wood Demon,* it was a failure until rewritten and produced by the Moscow Art Theatre.

Uncle Vanya is embittered and disillusioned at forty-seven. For years he and his relatives have slaved to support and educate Alexander who turns out to be a shallow professor of literature. Hopelessly in love with Mikhail, who is in love with Sonya, Uncle Vanya tries to kill Alexander and fails. Life settles down again to its distressing mediocrity.

Unconquered, The. Carl Glick (American). Domestic comedy. 3 acts. 1937.

Produced by C.W.A. on Federal Portable Theatres. First original play to be produced under government auspices

The story of small city Mrs. Fixit, who tries to run pretty much everybody and everything and neglects her husband and family for her innumerable "movements" and clubs.

Under the Gaslight. Augustin Daly (American). Melodrama. 5 acts. 1867.

The story of Laura Courtlandt, brought up by a wealthy family, who finds she is the daughter of a criminal. Deserted by her sweetheart, she goes back to a life of poverty. After five acts of suffering and adventure, including Laura's rescue of a one-armed soldier from an on-coming locomotive, she finally finds happiness and love.

Understudy. An actor who must be perfect in a given role, know all the lines and business and who appears only when the person playing that part is taken ill and cannot possibly give a performance.

Underwood, John (? -1624). English actor. An actor named in the 1623 Folio list of performers in Shakespeare's plays. After appearances in Jonson's *Cynthia's Revels* and the *Poetaster* with the Children of the Chapel Royal, a company of child actors, he transferred to Shakespeare's company, now the King's men, in 1610. Among plays besides those of Shakespeare in which he acted the most notable were Jonson's *The Alchemist* and *Catiline* and Webster's *Duchess of Malfi*.

Unfaithful Woman, The. Georges de Porto-Riche (French). Drama. 5 acts. 1890.

The secretary of the Doge, who is the hero of the play, is about to leave the city on a mission. Before leaving he vows fidelity to Vanina, who loves him. Vanina, however, discovers that he has already deceived her and attempts to make him jealous by letting him believe she has another lover.

She dons a male disguise and posing as that lover sings a serenade beneath her own window. She is so successful that her lover, in a jealous frenzy, kills her, thinking he is ridding himself of a rival.

Union Square Theatre, New York (1871-1922). Opened on the south side of Union Square as a variety house, September 11, 1871. In 1872 Sheridan Shook transformed it into a first-class "Home of the Drama," with A. M. Palmer as manager. Among the brilliant performances to its credit were: *Jane Eyre; The Rivals; Camille; A Parisian Romance; Romeo and Juliet;* and *Hamlet;* with such players as Joseph Jefferson, Fanny Davenport, McKee Rankin, Stuart Robson, Clara Morris, Margaret Mather, Modjeska, Richard Mansfield, and Mrs. Sarah Le Moyne. In 1888, destroyed by fire; reopened 1893 by B. F. Keith, who inaugurated continuous vaudeville. During its vaudeville career its name varied. As Kahn's Union Square, it alternated between films and burlesque. Reopened in 1922 as the Acme, a straight picture house. In 1932 proclaimed "The Only American Soviet-Kino." Torn down in 1936.

Unions (theatrical). Among the many theatrical unions in America are: Actors' Equity Association; Chorus Equity Association; Grand Opera Choral Alliance; Hebrew Actors' Union; German White Rats; Hungarian Actors; United Scenic Artists of America, local 829; American Federation of Musicians, local 802; International Alliance of Theatrical Stage Employees and Motion Picture Machine Operators; International Brotherhood of Teamsters and Chauffeurs, local 817; Theatrical Wardrobe Attendants' Union, local 16770; International Alliance of Bill Posters and Billers, local Number 1; National Theatre Ticket Distributors; Theatre Ticket Brokers' Association; Theatrical Costumers' Association; Association of Theatrical Agents and Managers; National Dramatic Stock Association; Variety Managers' Protective Association. Associated Actors and Artistes of America,

Inc.; American Guild of Variety Artists; American Federation of Radio Actors; Screen Actors' Guild; Theatrical Managers, Agents and Treasurers' Union.

Uniti. A famous Italian troupe of the *commedia dell 'arte.*

Unities. The three unities, as postulated by Aristotle in his *Poetics,* contributed to the basic criteria of all classical drama. They were: unity of time, or a limitation of the action of a drama to 24 hours; unity of place, a limitation of the action of a drama to a single locality, though allowing of considerable shifting between places within that locality; and unity of action, a limitation of the intrigue of a drama to a tone and atmosphere predominantly tragic for tragedy and predominantly comic for comedy.

See also *Unity, of form.*

Unity, of form (in the ancient Greek drama). (A) in *Old Comedy:* no specific dividing, although the form contained, generally, 7 parts: (1) the *prologos*—prologue, in which was given the general outline of the plot; (2) the *parados*—entrance-song of the chorus; (3) the *agon*—dramatized debate between the principal characters of the *comedy;* (4) the *parabasis*—in which the chorus came forward to address the audience, followed by a number of (5) *epeisodia*—in which more action (narrated) entered into the play; (6) the *stasima* or *chorika*—in which the chorus, singing, drew conclusions for the audience from the *epeisodia;* (7) the *exodos*—the final song by the chorus, often addressing the audience directly, pointing out the salient features of the play.

(B) *In tragedy:* there existed a tendency toward the presenting of five main portions of histrionic action, separated by four or more choral chants; with the disappearance of the chorus these five parts evolved into the five acts. Advocated to young dramatists by Horace and taken over by the critics in the Renaissance.

University Players. This group of young amateurs soon to be professionals organized in 1927-28 to form a summer theatre at Silver Beach near West Falmouth, Massachusetts. They included Charles Leatherbee, Norris Houghton, Margaret Sullavan, Henry Fonda, Bretaigne Windust among others.

University Wits. A heterogeneous, yet generally unified, group of early Elizabethan writers, so-called because all of them, with the single exception of Kyd, had had a university education. This category also included Greene, Lodge, Lyly, Marlowe, Nashe, Peele. Their works, by their qualities of poetry, passion and academic training, served to prepare the way for Shakespeare and the unparalleled richness of his dramaturgy. Lyly was the creator of a new prose style known as Euphuism, the principal characteristic of which was floridness. Nashe was the first writer of the picaresque novel—an innovation that proved a major factor in establishing the foundations of the English theatre.

Upper Stage. In the Elizabethan theatre, a gallery directly over the inner stage and slightly projecting over the outer stage, with a balcony overlooking the audience. Originally occupied by especially-favored spectators, and often by musicians needed in a performance, it soon became chiefly used as the scene of action on city walls, towers, balconies, and those other localities so frequently designated in Elizabethan stage-directions as "above." It was curtained and hence, like the inner stage below, could be set with properties.

Upstaging. An actor's moving rear stage, thus compelling the remainder of the cast, when addressing him, to turn its back to the audience.

Urbanae cantilenae. Historical canticles or scenes illustrating certain legends of the saints acted by *jongleurs* in the 9th century.

Ur-Hamlet. Literally, "original Hamlet," a hypothetical lost dramatic version of the Hamlet story, sometimes attributed to Thomas Kyd, upon which Shakespeare is supposed to have based his own treatment of the theme. The *Ur-Hamlet.* would stand as a bridge between Shakespeare's *Hamlet* and Belleforest's prose translation of the original narrative in Saxo Grammaticus' *Historia Dannica* (1200 A.D.).

Vajda, Ernest (1887-   ). Hungarian dramatist. A graduate of Budapest University, he early became an important playwright by writing *Rozmarin Neni, The Crown Prince, The Unexpected Guest, Grounds for Divorce, Fata Morgana, The Harem, The Carnival Marriage,* and other plays. When *Fata Morgana* was done in New York by the Theatre Guild in 1924 it met with such high praise that Vajda's success was assured. When this play was followed by *Grounds for Divorce* in 1925 and *The Harem* in 1926 he became one of the outstanding contemporary European playwrights.

He has also written or adapted many plays for the films.

Vakhtangov, Eugene (1883-1922). Russian director, actor. In the estimation of many, he was the most brilliant of Stanislavsky's students. He was thoroughly grounded in the Moscow Art system, which is based on the collection of material and the study of life. To this he added intuitive creation. Influenced by the Tibetan mystery, he directed *The Dybbuk* for the Habima Theatre. He believed that a man must grow artistically and so can reproduce ten years later a production once staged. He was active in the First Studio of the Moscow Art and was founder of the Third Studio, now known as the Vakhtangov. He was influenced by the Chinese in his last production, Gozzi's *Turandot.* In *Moscow Rehearsals,* Norris Houghton says that Vakhtangov believed that "the theatre must tackle the deepest things in the life of the time."

See also *Theatre of fantasy.*

Vakhtangov Theatre. A theatre in Russia founded originally in 1913 as the Third Studio of the Moscow Art Theatre, under the direction of E. B. Vakhtangov.

When Vakhtangov died in 1922 the theatre was named after him. This organization is noted for distinguished productions of new plays as well as of old, such as the works of Shakespeare. Through the influence of Vakhtangov it never, at least while he lived, succumbed to the mediocrity of mere political propaganda such as was gestated by the Revolution. It has produced Schukin, one of the great actors of the present day, who died in October, 1939.

Vale of Content, The. Hermann Sudermann (German). Drama. 3 acts. 1896.
Elizabeth who has recently become the wife of a school principal in a small German town meets Von Roecknitz whom she formerly loved. Von Roecknitz, determined not to lose her again, forces Elizabeth to agree to come away with him. Elizabeth finally tells her husband the truth, and they are reconciled.

Valley Forge. Maxwell Anderson (American). Drama. 3 acts. 1934.
A dramatization of the dark winter of 1778 when Washington was compelled to fight not only the complacent English, but the treachery of his own countrymen who were weary of war, the pettiness of Congress which played politics with Congressional aloofness, and the feeble spirit of impatient merchants, who were lusting for trade.

Vanbrugh, Sir John (1664-1726). English dramatist, architect. Born in London, he studied architecture in France, entered the army, and was arrested as a spy in France and imprisoned in the Bastille. He wrote ten comedies, all grossly indecent by modern standards, but undeniably witty and realistic. He stands below Congreve, since he is lacking in finesse and wit. The humor of his plays is shown through practical devices and not through literary conceit. He also adapted many plays from Molière and other writers. In his later years Vanbrugh rose to fame as an architect. His finest work is Castle Howard, Yorkshire, and his largest and most grandiose mansion is Blenheim Palace. He also designed the Haymarket Theatre, London, 1705, and was its first lessee and manager. Knighted by George I, 1714, he held the appointment of controller of the royal works. His plays include *The Relapse,* 1696; *The Provok'd Wife,* 1697; *The Confederacy* (which introduced humble characters for the first time on the stage during the Restoration period), 1705; *The Mistake,* 1705; *The Country House,* 1702.

Van Druten, John (1901-   ). English playwright. Born in London, he studied law and became a lecturer at the University of Wales.
His first play, produced in 1927, was *Chance Acquaintance,* but it was his study of adolescence, *Young Woodley,* 1928, which brought him fame. Later plays include *After All,* 1929; *London Wall* and *There's Always Juliet,* 1931; *Behold We Live,* 1932; *The Distaff Side,* 1933; *Flowers of the Forest,* 1934, and *Most of the Game,* 1935.

Vane, Sutton (English) (1888-   ). Son of a prolific writer, Vane turned naturally toward the theatre. Invalided home from the war, he wrote *Outward Bound,* 1923. He had written two plays previous to this but neither had the stature of

Outward Bound. Since then he has written several plays. Among them are *Time, Gentlemen, Please* and *Marine Parade,* both in 1935.

Vanka the Butler and Page Jean. Feodor Sologub (Russian). Comedy. 9 scenes. 1909.

This drama is presented in two versions, one as the incidents would occur in France and one as they would occur in Russia.

A wife begs of her husband the promotion of their servant who has caught her eye, and the servant in turn responds by philandering with the lady in her boudoir, while the maids quarrel among themselves to win his favor. He succumbs at length to one, thus piquing the jealousy of another. On being exposed, both he and the lady are punished. It is in the harshness of this punishment that the two versions differ. The French count is unrelenting. The Russian prince is less rigorous; he admonishes his princess and forgives her, while the servant escapes, having induced his captors to substitute a beggar at his supposed execution.

Variety. English term for vaudeville of the present day; an earlier term for all vaudeville.

Variety. Published weekly by Variety, Inc., 154 West 46th Street, New York. A theatrical trade paper devoted to stage, screen, radio, night clubs and popular music.

Variety's Box Score. In 1923-1924 Variety originated a system of judging the critics' efficiency, and automatically pitting him against his confrères, by rating him in accordance with his opinions on plays and the manner in which these opinions are confirmed at the box office.

VARIETY'S SHOW BIZ INFLUENCE

BY ABEL GREEN

Sime Silverman founded variety in 1905 for one express purpose, and with one basic editorial mission—to tell the truth. Through a third of a century, up to its founder-editor's death in 1933, and ever since, that cardinal editorial precept has obtained without deviation.

It's for that reason, presumably, that Variety's influence on the trade it covers has been so vivid. It's for that reason, also, that daily newspapermen and periodical writers, away from the show biz, have recognized in this trade paper a unique barometer of the amusement industry, knowing that Variety's contents hew to an inviolable rule of strict neutrality, impartiality, honesty.

Mirroring the passing show business scene through the decades, Variety has seen the rise and decline of sundry show biz manifestations. It's seen vaudeville at its heights and long predicted its passing, later visualizing anew that the vaudeville (or variety form of entertainment) would find fuller expression in other forms, such as in a post-prohibition nitery medium—the cafes or nite clubs—and, even more extensively, on the radio.

Fighting, and ultimately defeating, the vested vaudeville interests through the years, Sime earned the respect and regard of the rank and file of the theatre as he battled Albee, the Shuberts, Klaw & Erlanger. He was caught in the middle of a factional fight between the White Rats (vaudeville union) and the National Variety Artists, which later became a "company union" for E. F. Albee.

He foresaw the rise of the motion picture as a popular art-industry, and switched the makeup of his paper so that where Vaudeville was the major department, it was constantly pushed further back in favor of Pictures and Radio. Showmen, actors, bookers, writers and managers quickly followed Variety's prophetic recognition of Motion Pictures—and later Radio—as a vaster medium of amusement expression. From the "Broadway Bible" of the Times Square actors, Variety's scope extended so that it's become the "show biz Koran" as others have paraphrased it.

Variety, in reporting the show business scene, does it in the argot of the showmen, and from that Variety enriched the American slanguage. It was thus that the dramatic, motion picture, radio editors and commentators on the dailies picked up so much of the Varietyese that has now percolated into everyday American slanguage. In his compilation of the ten foremost language coiners, H. L. Mencken rated Sime Silverman on top of Ring Lardner, Bugs Baer, Walter Winchell, et al.

Variety's (the late) Jack Conway was one of its prolific slang slingers. Walter Winchell, a protégé of Sime's, in turn capitalized the Variety idiom to fuller and greater glories.

It was this widespread journalistic interest by the nation's newspapermen that directly influenced inclusion of a Literati department in Variety which is retained to this day. As source material for the laymen, the dailies have more or less freely made use of Variety's contents, with or without credit, and while all rights are strictly reserved by copyright, this paper has always permitted newsmen to help themselves as they see fit. It's long been a matter of private-office pride to Variety's editors that the nation's press and its newspaper workers have never abused the privilege and, also have been generous in their acknowledgment of source credits, despite the understanding it's by no means obligatory.

Variety is published for the show biz and not laymen, yet the recent years have so extended Variety's scope that, despite itself, it has a 25% so-called "lay circulation." To this day, on a principle laid down by Sime, Variety keeps itself off the subway stands, as one means of keeping its contents restricted, although otherwise it's on all kiosks, news-stands, railroad, steamship and plane terminals and liners. The theory for this is that Sime felt it would detract from the illusion of the box-office if the laymen knew that Jolson was getting $3,500 and a percentage in a Shubert's musical; or that Marilyn Miller at a $2,500 guarantee in "Sally" from Ziegfeld, against a straight 10% of the gross; or that "Ben Hur" grossed $73,000 at the Broadway Capitol; or that Marcus Loew's contract with

Loew's, Inc., was renewed at $3,000 a week, plus a sliding percentage of the profits. That was in the old days, of course.

Today radio speaks of talent salaries in the tens of thousands, and radio program budgets like the Major Bowes-Chrysler Amateurs, with time and line charges, run to $30,000 for one full hour.

The dailies picked up this information and passed it on to their readers, so through the years, the American amusement-loving public today is one of the most sophisticated, or as we say in the trade, "show-wise."

Thus, it's become a Variety axiom that Broadway, today, is a state of mind— a mythical Great White Way that stretches from Times Square to Fallen Arches, Neb. Those who decry the Boweryesque or Coney Island-like appearance of New York's real-life Broadway—and nostalgically hark back to the Broadway of Ziegfeld, Raymond Hitchcock, Jim Brady, Rector's, Shanley's, Victor Herbert, Lillian Russell, or any other standard they have set up in their mind's eye or memory— seem to be living in the past. Broadway in this theatrical season of 1939-40 is, as it has been the past 10 years, an imaginative rialto that stretches across the nation from border to border, and even beyond its borders into foreign lands.

The explanation of this is simple. Through the media of its two major amusements—the screen and the ether—the cream of the talent programs, productions and artistry are brought to the farmer, sheep-herder, cotton worker or plainsman with the same ready accessibility and facility as to the city dweller. Broadway no longer has a monopoly of the cream of the show biz crop. The two vast mediums, radio and films, percolate simultaneously into all walks of life. In fact, in the case of the cinema art, ofttimes a movie will be premiered or screened in some lesser key cities, ahead of New York's rialto or Chicago's Loop.

Variety's slanguage. The following examples readily convey the idea of this type of the modern American language: *Bliz Boffs Buff,* means that a blizzard is hurting Buffalo's box offices; *Wall Street Lays An Egg,* a *Variety* headline published the day after the crash of 1929, explains itself; *Big Faw-Down,* also means that Wall Street has crashed; *Stix Nix Hix Pix* means that the Middle West turned thumbs down on pictures dealing with farm drama; *"icky"* or *"corny"* means old-fashioned; *"laid an omelet"* means they flopped; *"campbelled on their feet,"* is a free plug for Campbell's Funeral Church; *Snare Prez's Boy to Hypo Texas Air Derby* was simply an announcement that Elliott Roosevelt had been hired to promote the Dallas Centennial Exposition. *So-and-so authored Sam Goldwyn's new spec,* means that So-and-so wrote Sam Goldwyn's new play. *"The mike warbler is a looker who coutourieres herself to best s. a. values, not forgetting a nifty gander at her gams,"* is a radio songstress who knows how to dress so that her charms are well set off, not forgetting a quick look at her legs. *No B. O. Blues* means box office is good. *Gigolo on Horseback* was *Variety's* title for George Raft's picture *Proud Rider; Spatted Whodunit,* likewise *Variety's* title for the picture *Murdered By An Aristocrat; Turk Day Tee-Off O.K.,* means that Thanksgiving Day business is good.

Other examples of the slanguage include: *vaudfilmers, legits, circuses, cornys, niteries, danceries, filmusicals; b.o.,* box office; *torso-tosser* or *fanner,* strip-tease artist;

quickies, travels; *trick terping,* intricate terpsichore or fancy dance steps; *legmania,* dancing *hoofology,* modern dancing, swing or tap; *striped ams,* amateur prison show; *AK,* Antediluvian Knight, or an adaptation from the Yiddish; *starrer,* a starring picture for Mae West; *megger,* director; *tinter,* Technicolor; *talker* (never talkie); *disker* or *waxer,* one who makes recordings; *chowmeinery,* Chinese restaurant; *'in a test tube,'* tryout of a new play; *ozoning burg,* Saranac belt; *'caviar mob',* Park Avenue crowd; *confab* or *powwow,* an executive meeting; *'gander the gams,'* look at the legs; *'play the chill,'* ritz; *'pushover,'* easy make; *Mazda Lane,* Great White Way; *whodunit,* mystery play; *a nocuv joint,* no cover charge cabaret; *TWA'D to the Coast,* flew to Hollywood; *oats opry* or *mustanger,* a Western film; *cliffer* or *cliffhanger,* serial film; *calciums,* spotlights; *trench unionists,* pit orchestra; *nsg,* not so good; *nsh,* not so hot; *mike warbler,* singer using a microphone; *ams,* amateurs; *biz,* business; *click,* success, or to succeed, as either productions or players. *Mugging,* exaggerated facial pantomime; *off the nut,* clear profit; *paper,* passes; *open cold,* opening in New York without an out-of-town tryout; *belly laugh,* solid laughter from audience; *beef,* complain about; *angel,* anyone who finances a show; *the bird,* a vocal raucous sound made with lips and tongue to indicate derision; *the boys,* ticket brokers; *clean house,* sold out audience; *coffee and cake,* small salary; *dead wood,* tickets unsold after a performance; *dry up,* an actor's loss of memory; *folded,* a show closed; *ham,* a bad or conceited actor; *hanging the show,* setting up scenery; *laid an egg,* failure; *lay 'em in the aisles,* to cause audience to roar with laughter, or to go over with a tremendous success; *bring down the house,* to win complete audience approval in a number or scene; *pix,* motion pictures; *crix,* critics; *m.c.,* master of ceremonies; *biz upping at the b.o.,* box-office gross improving.

Vaudeville. Name originated, according to one version, with Oliver Bassel or Olivier Basseliri who sang and composed songs which had many imitations, and which took on the name of the place in which Bassel lived, Val-de-Vire; corrupted during the time of Louis XVI to *vaux-de-vire.* This term was eventually changed to *vaux-de-ville,* as a compliment, it is said, to Bassel's native town, the "x" being automatically dropped after a time. Vaudeville, under the term variety, was introduced into America about the time of the Civil War before male audiences. The form of entertainment became important with the opening of Tony Pastor's Opera House, in 1865, who opened the entertainment for women and children. But still called variety, the entertainment had no standing until sponsored by men like F. F. Proctor and B. F. Keith. In 1885, the "two-a-day" or "continuous vaudeville" was introduced, performances running from eleven o'clock in the morning till eleven o'clock at night. From then on variety exploited now as vaudeville grew in popularity, reaching a climax at the time of the boom, and dying off gradually, except for isolated stage shows as a result of cinema competion. Important showmen connected with vaudeville were F. F. Albee, Oscar Hammerstein, who became a grand opera impresario by way of his famous Victoria, John J. Murdock, Sullivan and Considine, Alexander Pantages, Charles E. Kohl and Marcus Loew, later to become the multi-millionaire head of Loew's Incorporated and an official of Metro-Goldwyn-Mayer.

Vaudeville was at its best at the height of the boom, and the Palace Theatre its stronghold. Here the greatest stars "sold their stuff." At the opening matinees on Mondays, all Broadway turned out to see the new acts and to pass judgment, just as it did at the Sunday night concerts at the Winter Garden. Regularly, too, such famous patrons as Ziegfeld and Dillingham were introduced from the stage and took bows. The bills were lengthy and were characterized by certain vaudeville features that grew obnoxious, forced bows—bows followed by bromidic curtain speeches delivered with simulated modesty.

Vega, Lope de (Lope Felix de Vega Carpio) (1562-1635). Spanish dramatist. Born in Madrid of humble parentage. While he wrote a great amount of non-dramatic prose and poetic works, his fame rests on his enormous production of dramatic works whose number has been estimated as high as 1800. He fixed the course of the *comedia* of his time so that students of the Golden Age point to him. de Vega was singularly precocious, claiming authorship of a four-act play at twelve. He became a page in the service of the Bishop of Carthagena and later was educated in the University at Alcala de Henares. After a position under a Madrid theatre manager and an expedition to the Azores he began to make his reputation as a dramatist. In 1588 he underwent temporary banishment for libel. After his marriage, he embarked in the Armada, then followed a secretaryship with the Duke of Alba, a second marriage, and the entering of a monastery. This marked his career. In spite of these vicissitudes, it is estimated that he wrote a large number of plays on religious and secular themes, comedies, tragedies, and moralities, as well as a mass of verse. His influence on European drama was great.

His works include *autos* or religious plays (usually short), *entremeses* to be performed between acts, *comedias* based on stories from the Old and New Testaments, on mythology, classical history, foreign history, the chronicles and dramatic legends of Spain, pastoral themes, the era of chivalry, oriental themes, Italian *novelle,* historical legend, and the manners of various social classes. Between three and four hundred survive.

In his plays character is subordinated to plot, though he sometimes produces strong characters, especially in women. He advocated mixing comic and tragic elements within the same play, and his work shows complexity of intrigue, metrical variety, and frequently portrays splendidly the *pundonor* or point of honor. So famous was he in his time that the advertisement *"Es de Lope"* ("It is Lope's") was a great drawing-card.

Among his best-known *comedias* are: *El mejar alcalde el rey* (The Best Mayor the King); *Amar sin saber a quien* (Loving without knowing which one); *El alcalde de Zalamea* (The Mayor of Zalamea); *La moza de cantaro* (The Girl of the Water-Pitcher); *Fuente ovejund* (The Sheep-Fountain); *Comedia de capa y espada* (Cape-and-Sword play)—a term (Spanish) applied broadly to those *comedias* that represented the customs or manners of the times.

Vehicle. A play or story suitable for performance or production.

Veiller, Bayard (1871-   ). American dramatist. While acting as a press representative in 1910 he wrote a play which was produced under the title of *William.*

He then went in for play writing seriously. His best known plays are *Within the Law*, 1912; *The Thirteenth Chair*, 1917; *The Trial of Mary Dugan*, 1928.

Velarium. Large awning used to roof over the open Roman theatre.

Velten, Johannes (1640-1695). German producer. Formed the "mother troupe" of a series of acting and travelling companies which is the beginning of German theatrical history; in 1678, he became an independent manager, calling his company *The Electoral Saxon Comedians,* which in 1771 became the company of the great Schroeder.

Venice Preserved; or A Plot Discovered. Thomas Otway (English). Tragedy. 5 acts. 1682.
   The story of Belvidera, daughter of Priuli, a senator in Venice. The part was written for Mrs. Barry, the mistress of Lord Rochester, with whom Otway was hopelessly in love, and whose treatment of him was supposedly responsible for his later life of degrading dissipation and utter destitution.

Veritism. The style of dramatic presentation propounded by Constantin Stanislavsky, the great Russian actor-director; "art into life and life into Art," a breaking down of all artificial theatricalisms.

VERSES AND CHORUSES

BY HOWARD DIETZ

Where the tin pan resounds the publishers draw a line between songs to be sung in shows and those intended for the try-this-over-on-your-piano market. Many a songwriter has gone to a Bernstein or a Bornstein with his number, written to be crooned by a Crosby or swung by a Shaw, and has received, instead of an advance, a critical analysis of the poetic impediment in the words or the too subtle emphasis in the first melodic bars, sometimes described as the "front strain." But, giving the publisher his due, there is a discernible difference between the typical popular song and the production number, even if that difference is most apparent to the sensitized professional ear. The master of all songs, Irving Berlin, has two styles of expression, one for the stage and one for the screen. He knows that broad novelty and the colorful phrase are assets to the pop number, but, like others who work successfully in this organized trade—organized by an organization of writers and publishers called the ASCAP—he sees to it that there is a base of what has been described as the corny element. On this dividends are paid and the boys take their royalties to the bank—doubtless the Corn Exchange.
   Most often the difference between a popular song and a production number is in the lyric. Overt excitements about moons, dreams, shacks, rivers, honeymoon, mother, Dixie, little man, rainbows, rhythm, lagoons, nightingales, isles, good times, etc., are offhand not the vocabulary of the musical comedy. We find less tortured conceptions in the haut monde of Cole Porter, the naïve girl-wants-boy of Ira

Gershwin, the rhymed social criticism of Lorenz Hart, the inquiring nostalgia of Oscar Hammerstein and the wistful weltschmerz of Noel Coward. In particular the singable verses of the currently inactive P. G. Wodehouse (who left the theatre haunted with memories of "Oh Boy," "Oh Lady, Lady," "Very Good Eddie" and "Sitting Pretty") describe with eloquence what goes to make the ideal production number.

It must be realized that every song that is a popular success necessarily has popular quality, but every song that has popular quality is not necessarily a popular success. There is the institution of plugging which pulmotors many an undynamic strain into a temporary radio pest. Songs that have become big successes in shows have often been rejected as popular songs and those who know the business would not even dream of saying "I told you so" to a publisher. The shows in which they appeared provided an occasion for their being plugged by the night clubs. The disease then spreads from band to band. Quite often such numbers become extremely noisy on the air without having a reciprocal echo in sheet music sales. The hit song in a show thus serves an important function in its advertising value, but often it is the incidental number that is most entertaining to an audience. The composer strives for melody and for avoidance of cliche and the writer of lyrics most often writes to fit a particular situation. The result may not readily be isolated for release on the radio, no more so than a line of dialogue that is funny in a play may always be easily quotable apart from the context.

The ASCAP has had a subtly noticeable influence on the modern musical comedy insasmuch as the songwriter's standing in that organization is some measure of his success. The association leases the subsidiary rights of song to radio stations, picture theatre and dance halls, and divides the proceeds among the authors and the copyright owners in accordance with a classification system. A double A member of ASCAP receives about fifteen thousand dollars a year and if he has been an active member for a sufficiently long career with a vital catalogue he may become a member for life and even for future generations. It is an incentive and a thing to bequeath as a background to the three other avenues of revenue open to him, for he receives a standing in ASCAP whether he writes songs for direct sheet music scale, writes for the screen on a salary, or writes scores for the stage in return for royalties from the box-office. Subconsciousness of ASCAP has served to make the lines of the hit show number converge with those of the popular song, and has accelerated the departure in lyrics from the tradition of W. S. Gilbert, whose spirit of whimsy and rhyme still is an influence, but who avoided stress on a title with repetitive value, the earmark of the conventional popular success. P. G. Wodehouse, whose lack of sibilants has been the evolution link between Gilbert and Gershwin, contributed songs without the modern accent on titles, but nevertheless seasoned his work with a bit of anglicized Broadway that resulted in many well-remembered ditties. We did not know the titles of "Till The Clouds Roll By" or "Babes in the Wood" or "The Siren Song" until the very last line of the refrains.

Most lyric writers write the words because they can't write the music. Most all of them have tried and have even had occasional success. They find a relief from their frustration in the collaboration with a composer whose music they enjoy and are of valuable aid in the suggestion of rhythms to which they have already arranged words. Many composers like this method of work and find in a title an inspiration for the completion of a thirty-two bar chorus which is the conventional length of a song. While comedy lyrics are often written and then set to music, the usual procedure is for the tune to be written first. The composer of a musical comedy score finds the situation best fitted to his song and writes a melody that suggests the spirit of the scene which his collaborator must complete. Lyric writers learn the tunes thoroughly and often write the lyrics right off while the composer is playing it over and over again on the piano. Some lyric writers work best in the morning under the shower where they can experiment with words without embarrassment.

A musical comedy usually has about a dozen songs, a revue about eighteen. In addition to the opening number there is often the "ice-breaker" or fast number for the girls, the rhythmic love duet and the ballad, the hot number, the comedy numbers and the business number which is planned to fit stage action. Dwight Wiman describes a musical comedy as something with a bad book, and places the burden of entertainment squarely on his songwriters who then, in order to "cinch" the proper rendition of their material, write their songs as vehicles for the cast. That is why the casting of musical shows is usually done before the score is written.

Informally free-for-all as musical comedies may seem to those out front, there are many song problems that have to be solved by careful planning. The chorus must be used with some significance and not merely as a group of girls who dance after the principal has sung. They must have a group character, so to speak. In revues the ensemble is at its best when it assumes its own character, that of a group of girls in a show who are about to tell you something. Also one must nurse the routines of a principal singer and dancer. It is often impractical for him to play a scene after he has danced a number and is therefore out of breath. It is not always wise to have him "follow himself on" in this way, although one admits that escaping from the conventional exits and entrances is often effective.

There are many problems of the physical stage that affect the writers of verses and choruses fully as much as they do the authors of dialogue. Songs in fact are at their best in the theatre when they belong to the plot as a part of the dialogue and the question of reprises is a most delicate one. One should never allow a song to be sung a second time in a show unless it is presented in a different context, a sort of pun on the first presentation. There is no reason for a song to be sung again in the same way as the first time any more than for a scene to be played over again. Or for this article to be repeated in the next section of this book. Or for this article to be reprinted in the second edition, for that matter.

Versurae. The sides of the stage in the theatre of Renaissance Italy.

Vice, The. Stock comic character of the 15th and 16th century English morality plays. He wore a cap with ass's ears, battled Good Deeds and Virtue, and got his deserts finally by being pitched into the pageant wagon's ever-gaping Hell-Mouth.

Victoria Regina. Laurence Houseman (English). Drama. 3 acts. 1935.

The life of Victoria of England from her ascension to the throne through her old age.

The play concerns Victoria's selection of Albert, her German cousin, as her prince consort, her marriage to him and their loving if not tempestuous life together.

Victoria is portrayed as a very strong, though romantic character, with the strength which has earned her the respect and affection of the world.

The English censor felt that the person of Victoria was too sacred for stage presentation and the right for an English production was denied at first, but under Edward VIII this play was successfully staged.

Video (television). Term referring to the transmission of the visual image.

Vigarani, Gaspare (1586-1663). Italian architect. He worked in the French theatre of his time, succeeding Torelli in 1660. Under him the *Salle des Machines* was built.

Vignola, Giacomo Barocchio (1507-1573). Italian architect. Worked in the Accademia della Virtu which was a classical research organization. He took measurements of all the architectural remains of ancient Rome and wrote *The Five Orders of Architecture* which is used by all modern architects. It was also the basis of Renaissance theatre architects and designers.

Vigny, Alfred Victor, Comte de (1797-1863). French author, dramatist. Born at Loches, March 27, 1797, he spent twelve years in the army, and while still a soldier became known as one of the earliest leaders of Romanticism by the publication of his first poems in 1822. His verse, characterized by weight of thought and nobility of style, ranks with the finest philosophical poetry in modern literature. His prose fiction comprises an historical romance, *Cinq-Mars,* 1826; *Stello,* 1832; and three fine *novelles* collected under the title *Grandeur et Servitude Militaires,* 1835. In the drama he produced, besides translations from Shakespeare and a short comedy, two prose tragedies, *La Maréchale d'Ancre,* 1830, and *Chatterton,* 1835, designed to realize his ideal of a drama the interest of which is purely psychological. Vigny was elected to the Academy in 1845, and died in Paris, September 17, 1863.

Vildrac, Charles (1882-   ). French dramatist, poet. Born Charles Messager, as a poet he has founded a new style of classicism. His dramas are of uneven quality, and he is said to be a better poet than playwright. His first play, *Le Paquebot Tenacity,* was successfully produced in 1922 at the Théâtre du Vieux Colombier. He is also the author of *Michel Auclair,* 1922; *L'Indigent,* 1922; *Madame Béliard,* 1922; *Le Pelerin,* 1936; *L'Heure du Temps,* 1938. His *The Pilgrim* was produced by amateurs at the Little Church Around the Corner in New York in 1936. His cinema, *La Belle Equipe,* was filmed in 1936.

Vinegar Tree, The. Paul Osborn (American). Comedy. 3 acts. 1931.

Laura Merrick, in her fifties and married to an elderly husband, believes Max Lawrence is an old lover she hasn't seen for twenty years, and prepares to resume the romance. Unfortunately, however, Mr. Lawrence turns out to be a stranger.

Violin Maker of Cremona, The. François Coppée (French). Drama. 3 acts. 1876.

The story of an instrument maker, famous for his beautiful musical instruments. Based upon an old Italian legend about a cabinet maker.

Taddeo Farrari, the violin maker, lives in a small Italian village. He and his pupils are known as the finest violin makers in the world.

Farrari's beautiful daughter is offered as a prize to the young man who makes the finest violin.

A young crippled pupil who loves the girl dearly but who knows she loves another plans to lose the contest so that she may be happy.

Vitruvius (1st century B.C.). Roman historian. An historian of the ancient Greek theatre (as well as of general classic architecture). He and Pollux were the only two writers to keep in touch with ancient Greek traditions. Both gave to Renaissance architects almost all that was known in the 16th and 17th centuries of the classical stage. The *De Architectura* of Vitruvius was published in 1486. Here he described the *periacti,* devices by which changes of scene were indicated. He described three scenes as they appeared on the three faces of a turning prism, two as architectural views with buildings, for tragedy and comedy, and the third a pastoral view for satyr-plays. This treatise was probably neither popular nor influential among the ancient Romans, but in more modern times its influence has been unbounded.

Vizards. Masks worn by ladies in the Restoration playhouses, the custom of which was revived in 1663; they hid the entire face; the custom was renounced by the respectable ladies in 1667 because the masks had become associated with harlots; and in 1704 Queen Anne, by an edict, forbade their use entirely.

Voice importance in Greek acting. The chief requisite of an actor in ancient Greece was a musical, powerful and expressive voice. This was due to the fact that a great part of the player's lines had to be sung from behind a mask and in an open-air theatre. It was necessary for him to receive a musical training comparable to a modern professional singer.

Voile du Bonheur, Le. Georges Clemenceau (French). 1 act. 1911.

Tchang-L, a blind Chinese mandarin, is happy in the belief that he is loved by his wife and family and respected by his friends. When his sight is restored through the miraculous content of a phial he discovers that his wife is unfaithful, his family disrespectful, and his friends rob him and sell him out. Disillusioned, he drains the phial and again becomes blind.

Volksbuehne. A people's theatre in Germany, founded in 1889, which, according to Julius Bab in Dickinson's *The Theatre in a Changing Europe,* "offered an opportunity to attend performances independent entirely of higher political forces and springing from the people themselves." This organization is often referred to as the *Volkstheater.*

Volkstueck. The name given a type of late 19th century German drama; the study of a certain locality, a form then almost unknown in France; the Volkstueck in Vienna was among the most famous types, Raimund having made the form more delicate and subtle.

Volpone; or, The Fox. Ben Jonson (English). Comedy. 3 acts. 1606.

Volpone, a rich Venetian, pretends to be dying in order to draw gifts from his would-be heirs. Mosca, his parasite, extracts costly presents from each, including the wife of one. Volpone, to enjoy the disappointment of the heirs, wills his property to Mosca and pretends to be dead. Mosca then blackmails him, until the matter is revealed in the senate, whereupon they all receive their just punishment.

An adaptation by Stefan Zweig was produced by the Theatre Guild, New York, in 1928.

Voltaire (François Marie Arouet) (1694-1778). French author, critic, dramatist. Born in Paris, he was the son of a notary, and was educated by the Jesuits at the Collège Louis-le-Grand. He left the school in 1711, by which time he had become acquainted with several literary circles in Paris. He reluctantly studied law for a while at his father's command, but subsequently lived on an allowance, dabbling in literature and making his way in society by his wit and manners. He was virtually exiled, 1714-1715, for some libellous poems, but on his return joined the circle of the Duchesse du Maine, and for lampoons on the regent was again exiled in 1716. For two libels in 1717, he was imprisoned in the Bastille. He had already begun to make his mark as a dramatist, his *Oedipe,* which he revised while in prison, produced in 1718, having a run of forty-five nights at the Comédie-Française. It was about this time that he adopted the name Voltaire. In 1725 Voltaire's talent for epigram gave dire offense to the Chevalier de Rohan-Chabot, whose lackeys chastised him in their master's presence. In vain he sought redress, and when it became known that he was taking fencing lessons with a view to a duel, he was again confined in the Bastille. On his release he obtained permission to go to England, where he was received with honor and remained from May, 1726, until the early spring of 1729. His acquaintances in England included Pope, Bolingbroke, Gay and Swift. He became an admirer, not only of Newton and Locke, but also of the British constitution, and his subsequent attitude towards the French political system was much influenced by his observation of its working. Soon after his return to France, Voltaire amassed a fortune by lucky speculation. He secured a share in some profitable army contracts, acquired a large interest in a commercial house at Cadiz, and lent much money at a high rate of interest. In 1734, the French government, enraged by the appearance of his letters relating to the English, issued an order for his arrest, but left him unmolested when he took refuge in the country house of Mme. du Chatelet at Cirey. This friendship continued until the death of Mme. du Chatelet in 1749, at which time he was persuaded to take up his residence at the court of Frederick the Great, but this lasted only until 1753, since Voltaire refused to bend to the servile flattery which Frederick demanded of his kept poet and philosopher. After some wanderings in Alsace and Switzerland, Voltaire finally settled at Ferney, on French soil, but close to Geneva. There, with his niece, Mme. Denis, keeping house for him, he resided until nearly the end of his long life. At that time he was the wealthiest, the most celebrated, and the most active man of letters in the world. In 1778 Voltaire was persuaded to revisit Paris. His journey was a triumphal progress, and he was crowned with laurel in the theatre after the performance of his last play, *Irene,* but the strain and excitement were too much for him. He was taken ill, and died May 30, 1778. His remains were transferred to the Panthéon in 1791. Voltaire's works fall into five divisions. The first comprises his plays of which there are some fifty in number. His comedies are not particularly significant, but his tragedies *Zaire* and *Mérope* are in their class magnificent. Second, there are his poems, of which *Henriade* and *La Pucelle* are perhaps the best. The third class of his writings are his prose tales, in which Voltaire excelled. The most famous is the ironic epic, *Candide.* In his mass of historical works Voltaire proved himself an entertaining and lucid narrator, and both his *Siècle de Louis XIV* and *Siècle de Louis XV* are extremely valuable. The most readable of his philosophical works is his *Dictionnaire Philosophique.*

Voltaire's correspondence reveals the man most truly. In his letters he is shown as a man of extraordinary versatility and energy, and with powers of sarcasm and faculty of acute penetration that have seen no equal.

Vomitoria. In the ancient Roman theatre, what originally were *parodoi* of the Greek theatre, now concealed and serving to break down the traditional division-line between the auditorium and the stage, making the two architecturally one.

Vortex, The. Noel Coward (English). Drama. 3 acts. 1925.

A mother, Florence Lancaster, and son, Nicky, are forced to face the truth about themselves. The mother is a vain, selfish woman; the son a drug addict.

During the course of the play the mother's lover is stolen from her by her son's fiancee and the son's admission of his pernicious habit is brought about.

Alarmed at finding out the truth about themselves, they cling to each other in a resolve to struggle once more to find health and balance in a normal life.

Voysey Inheritance, The. Harley Granville-Barker (English). Drama. 4 acts. 1905.

Based upon an ethical problem concerning financial honesty. Mr. Voysey, the father, is a prosperous solicitor living in affluence in a large house in Chislehurst. His son, Edward, entering his father's business, makes the discovery that his father, entrusted with large sums to invest, has speculated with them, lost and made fortunes in wild gambles, and has pocketed the spoils. The father justifies his conduct by saying that he is simply carrying on a method established in turn by his father. Edward, after his father's death, attempts to put the business straight, but without much success.

Vultures, The. Henri Becque (French). Drama. 4 acts. 1881.

A story of the Vignerons, a French family, their ideas and tastes, their physical surroundings, and their background. The scene in which the three "vultures" gather is considered one of the most bitterly ironical in all modern drama.

Becque exposes those fair-weather friends who fawn upon the wealthy. A wealthy man dies in the midst of a celebration of his daughter's betrothal. Immediately his friends turn from their fawning to find ways and means to fleece the helpless widow and orphans and threaten to pluck them bare.

V.Z.S.P.S. The "All Trade Union Theatre" in present-day Russia; its main purposes: (1) interpretation according to working-class principles toward the mobilization of the spectator in the direction of any desired propagandistic end; (2) the criterion of social practice as the dominant principle of all facets of a play; (3) an explicit and immediately recognizable form of expression.

Wagner, Wilhelm Richard (1813-1883). German composer. Wagner created a national music drama, and for many people in the modern world, he has become a cult rather than a great figure in the history of art. His stage innovations at this own theatre in Bayreuth greatly influenced the modern stage. He claimed that the tradition of Greek drama, a combination of poetry, music, and dancing must combine in the service of the writer. He felt that Goethe and Shakespeare best represented this unity in their writings. Wagner, a discerning critic, expounds his theory in his books, *Oper und Drama,* 1851; *Eine Mitteilung an meine Freunde,* 1851; and *Das Kunstwerk der Zukunft,* 1849.

He was born at Leipzig, the son of a police official who died shortly after Wagner was born. His mother married again in 1814 and the family moved to Dresden, where Richard attended *Kreuzschule.* About 1820 he began to teach himself music, and upon the family's return to Leipzig, he studied under Gottlieb Muller. Ten years later he studied at Leipzig University and produced a number of works of no particular merit. For two years he was employed as *kapellmeister* at Riga. For several years after the termination of that employment, he travelled from London, to Boulogne, to Paris, trying to find work. He wrote a number of his greatest works during this time. Liszt rescued him from his desperate poverty, and later when he came to the attention of Ludwig, King of Bavaria, he was granted a generous life pension and established in a home at Bayreuth in 1872. The first Bayreuth Festival was given in 1876 when the *Ring des Nibelungen* was first produced, and the festival became a yearly event. For many years after his death, Wagner's second wife, Cosima, who by her sympathetic understanding of his ideals had done much to make his later life happy, was the active director of the Festival. Wagner died in Venice, February 13, 1883.

Among Wagner's music dramas are *Ring des Nibelungen*, 1876, at Bayreuth; *Rienzi*, 1839; *Das Liebesverbot*, 1834; *Tannhaeuser*, 1843; *Lohengrin*, 1843; *Tristan und Isolde*, 1854; *Die Meistersinger*, 1862; *Parsifal*, 1882; *Das Reingold*, 1854; *Die Valkuere*, 1854; *Der Fliegende Hollaender*, 1843.

Wagon stage. See *Platform theatre.*

Waiting for Lefty. Clifford Odets (American). Drama. 1 act. 1935.

The action takes place at a meeting where the taxi-drivers of New York City are deciding whether to go on strike. In quick flash-backs we see dramatic moments in the lives of the taxi-drivers, revealing their poverty, exploitation and the barrenness of their lives. At the climax comes the news that Lefty, the most active of the drivers, for whom they have been waiting, has been ambushed and killed by the strong-arm men of the company owner. When the men hear this, they decide to strike.

Wajang. The national drama of Java, popular and widespread throughout the island. A type of shadow play employing flat puppets made of leather. The puppets' shadow movements are accompanied by the running commentary of a reciter and the music of a *gamelan* (Javanese orchestra). The stories of the performances are based on Hindu and Javanese legend and folklore.

See *Drama, Javanese.*

Walker, Stuart (1888-   ). American producer, dramatist. Born in Augusta, Kentucky, educated at the University of Cincinnati and the American Academy of Dramatic Arts. Actor and stage manager with David Belasco and director with Jessie Bonstelle; founded the Portmanteau Theatre; directed many repertory companies and has been directing and producing motion pictures since 1931.

The plays he has written include: *Five Flights Up*, 1922; *The King's Great Aunt Sits on the Floor*, 1923; *The Demi-Reds* (with Gladys Unger), 1936.

Walk-on. Term applied to person who plays a bit, or a very small part of a few lines, or a person who merely walks on and off a scene as part of a crowd, or as a supplementary character.

See also *Extra, supernumerary.*

Walk through. The rehearsal in which actors get out of their chairs and walk through their business for the first time.

Wallack, Lester (1820-1888). American actor-manager. A noted actor who upon the death of the older Wallack became manager of "Wallack's," gathered the most brilliant players for his stock company; retired in 1887 after becoming the most conspicuous figure on the American stage; played 291 roles.

Wallack Company. During the 1860's the most brilliant company of actors was assembled under the Wallack banner. This made the Wallack Theatre the most famous in America. It was a company of comedians, and older English comedies from Shakespeare to Holcroft were expertly staged. John Gilbert was the most notable character actor of the group.

The first time "Wallack's" appeared over a theatre was in 1852, and until 1887 that name was one of prime importance to the American stage. Lester Wallack, Rose Coghlan, Edward A. Sothern, Charles Coghlan, Maurice Barrymore, and nearly every great actor of the time played under his banner.

Wallenstein. Friedrich Schiller (German). Drama. 1799.

This is an historical drama in three parts: *Wallenstein's Camp,* a prologue in one scene; *The Piccolomini,* five acts; *Wallenstein's Death,* five acts. It is based on the fall and death of Count Albrecht von Wallenstein, commander of the armies of the German emperor, Ferdinand II. In order to strengthen the empire, he crushed the Protestant states and repelled the invasion of the Swedes. He then opened negotiations with the Swedes to protect himself against the enemies at the emperor's court. When the emperor discovered this, he relieved Wallenstein of his command and arranged his assassination.

Walter, Eugene (1874-   ). American dramatist. Born in Cleveland, Ohio. He was a reporter on a Cleveland newspaper, then joined the New York *Sun,* and later served in the army. For some years he was advance agent for theatrical managers. Since 1918 he has devoted himself exclusively to the writing of plays. His plays have for the most part melodramatic situations, well developed and skilfully constructed. He is journalistic, violent, but nearly always interesting.

He is the author of *Sergeant James,* 1901; *The Undertow,* 1907; *Paid in Full,* 1907; *The Wolf,* 1908; *The Easiest Way,* 1908; *Boots and Saddles,* 1909; *Just a Wife,* 1910; *Fine Feathers,* 1913; *The Knife,* 1917; *The Heritage,* 1918; *Nancy Lee,* 1918; *The Challenge,* 1919; *Jealousy,* 1932; *The Trail of the Lonesome Pine* (dramatization of the novel of the same name); *The Little Shepherd of Kingdom Come* (dramatization of the novel).

Waltz of the Dogs, The. Leonid Andreyev (Russian). Drama. 3 acts. 1922.

Henry Tile, jilted by his fiancée and intrigued against by his younger brother Carl, goes wrong on his own account, taking to drink and dalliance and planning to embezzle funds from the bank where he works.

His ex-fiancée, married to another, has an affair with Carl who now begins planning the murder of his brother.

The gradual disintegration of Henry ends by his committing suicide.

The title is taken from a musical piece by the same name, which Henry explains represents little dogs dancing for sugar at the end of strings.

Wang Pao Ch'uan (Lady Precious Stream). Translated by S. I. Hsiung from various Chinese sources. 4 acts. 8 scenes. 1934.

A naive little fantasy, told with beautiful directness, of the defiant third daughter of Prime Minister Wang, who is a victim of her father's plan to marry her off to a wealthy noble. But Lady Precious Stream—for that is her name—is a girl of spirit, and arranges that the young man who catches the embroidered ball which she tosses to her suitors shall be no unknown eligible but the handsome and poetical gardener, Hsieh Ping-kuei, whom she loves. Cast out by her family, she goes to live with her husband in a cave. Poor Precious Stream starves all by herself for eighteen years—for Hsieh Ping-kuei is off to the wars in the Western Kingdom and her wicked brother-in-law, General Wei, steals her separation allowance. Her gardener husband finally returns as King of the Western Regions and finds that Precious Stream has remained faithful. But not so with Hsieh Ping-kuei, for he has been living these many years with a certain Princess of the Western Regions. He tells his wife that the Princess is his sister, but is not convincing. His story is accepted but not believed, and the Princess' interests are fortunately diverted by a minister of Foreign Affairs, who has had many affairs in foreign lands in his own right and whom she finally marries.

In New York, as played by a cast including Helen Chandler and Bramwell Fletcher, it charmed the critics and theatre public. The music was composed by William Furst. Costumes after designs by Mei Lan-fang.

The first act of *Lady Precious Stream* is apparently based on a short Chinese play called *The Flowery Ball*.

War and the Theatre. What happens to art in times of war? This is a question that always agitates the contemporaneous populace. The answer is largely supplied in this extract from an editorial by Brooks Atkinson, in the New York Times, October 8, 1939:

"Nations can be so exhausted by warfare that they contribute nothing to culture for a long time. Germany was so worn out by the Thirty Years' War in the first half of the seventeenth century that it was a hundred years before plays, books and music became important parts of court life again. But the astonishing thing about Western culture is that, since the times of Shakespeare and Molière, it has developed in the midst of internal and external strife. . . .

"England was living dangerously when Shakespeare was composing his sonnets and writing his plays; the tumult of battle runs through much of his work. For Queen Elizabeth was threatened within and without all her days . . . In the time of Molière, Louis XIV was not only bankrupting his country on his fabulous court, but also, uselessly, on the battlefield. He believed in war for glory; he was aggressive and reckless. Yet Molière, Madame de Sévigné and La Fontaine were laying the foundations for modern style and the modern point of view in his reign, and Racine was carrying on where Corneille had left off in the time of Richelieu. The remarkable culture of the court of the Sun King flourished simultaneously with his costly braggadocio on the battlefield.

"As a matter of fact, men of letters have rarely had the pleasure of practicing their trade in a time of peace, public rest and well-being. While Milton was writing some of the greatest poetry in English, his countrymen were beheading their King and Cromwell's army was fighting a grim civil war . . . Throughout most of the eighteenth century England was at war in India, America and on the Continent. But this was the century when Goldsmith, Dr. Johnson, Fielding, Sterne, Smollett and Gray were giving England some of its best literature and Garrick was raising the prestige of the stage. While Napoleon was ravaging Europe, Beethoven was writing some of his greatest masterpieces and Wordsworth in England was drawing poetry out of his soul."

Wardrobe. Theatrical term for the costumes and all articles of dress of a production.

Wardrobe mistress. The woman, backstage, in charge of costumes and who is responsible for their upkeep and appearance.

Warren, Mrs. Mercy (1728-1814). American dramatist. The first American writer to use drama as a political satire. She wrote *The Adulator, The Group,* and *The Blockheads; or, the Affrighted Officers,* all of which ridiculed the British.

Washington Square Players. (1) A group of amateur repertory players from the dramatic department of New York University and its alumni under the direction of Randolph Somerville. (2) First name for the Theatre Guild.

Wayfarers, The (San Francisco, California). The Wayfarers was organized in 1931 by seven young people. After two years of presenting one-act plays and short plays written by members and local playwrights, they began to give important dramas every month and a half, each drama running nine nights. They then obtained two Federal Housing loans and an ambitious theatre was launched. The organization is self-supporting, relying on dues and subscriptions.

Way of the World, The. William Congreve (English). Comedy. 5 acts. 1700.
Mirabell is in love with Millamant, but Millamant's aunt, Lady Wishfort, who is furious with Mirabell, threatens to deprive Millamant of her inheritance. Ensuing complications change Lady Wishfort's feelings. This play excels in scintillating, audacious conversation, and contains Congreve's most brilliant characterizations. Although it is now considered the most finished of his comedies, it was not well received, and after its production Congreve renounced writing for the stage.
The life of this play, a mirror of its time, is apparently never-ending. The comedy is still performed occasionally by advanced groups and in repertoire.
According to Swinburne: "The unequalled and unapproached masterpiece of English comedy."

The Weaker Sex. Sir Arthur Wing Pinero (English). Comedy. 1888.
Philip Lyster has had a quarrel with the Lady Vivash and has gone to America where he has made a name for himself as Ira Lee. On his return he falls in love with Sylvia, Lady Vivash's daughter, but he soon realizes the futility of the situation and goes away again.

Weavers, The. Gerhart Hauptmann (German). Drama. 5 acts. 1893.

Conditions become unbearable in a German community of weavers. They revolt, pillaging their employer's house. Troops are called out, and one of the first casualties is an old weaver, killed by accident, who has tried to stay out of the fight. The bloodshed maddens the men beyond reason and they destroy all that is before them until the mill owners concede their demands.

Webb, John (1611-1672). British scenic designer, philologist. Nephew, son-in-law, disciple and executor of the scenewright, Inigo Jones. Webb designed the proscenium and five scenes for the first performance of Sir William D'Avenant's *The Siege of Rhodes,* the first English opera, 1656. Wrote several essays on China and the Chinese language, and on archeological subjects.

Webster, John (1580?-1625). English dramatist. Probably the son of a London tailor, he became a freeman of the Merchant Taylors Company. He wrote for the theatre proprietor, Philip Henslowe; collaborated with Munday, Middleton, Dekker, Heywood, and others; and completed Marston's *The Malcontent* for the stage. His independent work includes a romantic comedy, *The Devil's Law Case,* and three tragedies, *Appius and Virginia, The White Devil* (or *Vittoria Corombona*), and *The Duchess of Malfi,* of which the two latter show him to have been not only a conscientious craftsman, but also a master of pathos and the portrayal of gloom, grisly horror, and sardonic humor. He raised melodrama almost to the pitch of tragedy, and touched it with lyric beauty, but he lacked humor as his plots lack unity of action and his characters consistency.

Wedekind, Franz (1864-1918). German dramatist. Born in Hanover, he became a journalist, and later secretary of a circus, before starting to act in and produce his own plays. In Zurich where he had continued his studies, he came into contact with some of the modern writers, among them Hauptmann and Strindberg. In 1888, after the death of his father, Wedekind went to Munich, and later visited London, Paris, and "all the centers of European culture, all the sinks of its perversity and crookedness. He squandered his money and his beliefs recklessly. In 1891 he returned again to Munich." A few years later he was imprisoned for *lèse-majesté;* the harsh satire, eroticism, and symbolism of his plays roused controversy.

He was for a short period on the editorial staff of *Simplicissimus.* He read Ibsen's plays in public; composed and wrote songs which he sang in cabarets, and was a prominent member of the Uberbrettl movement. Later on, he formed a company for the purpose of producing his own plays, himself playing the chief roles; he toured the country, literally imposing his work upon theatregoers. Today he is one of the idols of the latest "New" Germany. His plays are performed throughout Middle Europe.

He was the author of the following plays: *The World of Youth,* 1890; *The Awakening of Spring,* 1891; *Earth Spirit,* 1895; *Pandora's Box,* 1902; *The Dance of Death,* 1906; *Hunted by Every Hound,* 1910; *Samson,* 1914; *Bismarck,* 1915; *Herakles,* 1917; *The Fast Painter,* 1920.

Weimar Court Theatre. Originally known as the *Ducal Amateur Theatre,* the personnel was made up of members of the court, of which Charles Augustus, the reigning duke, was the most famous. In 1775, Goethe became his minister of state, a post which he held for ten years. Physically a poor building, the theatre which was turned over to Goethe in 1791 became the foremost theatre in Germany. Iffland's *Der Jager* was Goethe's first production there.

Weisze, Christian Felix (also Weisse) (1726-1803). German dramatist. Born in Annaberg, he studied under Lessing and first became famous for his dispute with Gottsched, whose authority over the theatre was finally abolished by Weisze after a quarrel over his opera, *Der Teufel ist los.* He performed a great service to German literature also by his translations and adaptations of Shakespeare's tragedies, but is perhaps best known for his operas, *Die Jagd, Der Erntekranz,* and several others, set to music by Hiller. Considered one of the two playwrights of any real merit of 18th century Germany.

Welles, Orson (1915-). American actor, director. Born in Evanston, Illinois. Occasionally as a child he appeared on the stage in Chicago. However, his real initiation was with the Gate company in Dublin, where he worked for two seasons beginning when he was about fifteen. Even then, the Elizabethan theatre had a powerful attraction for him. At seventeen or so, in collaboration with his former schoolmaster, he wrote *Everybody's Shakespeare,* a study of three plays by the dramatist, with the intent to make them alive for school children. One of the plays in the volume was *Julius Caesar,* undoubtedly the germ of Welles' modernized staging of the drama at the Mercury Theatre, New York, 1937. He and John Houseman did a re-working of *Macbeth* for the WPA Federal Theatre, using an entire Negro cast. He was also the chief actor as well as director of the Federal Theatre's highly successful presentation of Marlowe's *The Tragical History of Dr. Faustus.*

He has also been an actor in and director of radio programs. It was on one of these that he unwittingly provoked the "attack from Mars" scare with a radio dramatization of H. G. Wells' *War of the Worlds* in the Fall of 1938. This made his name a household word and as a result he now has a Hollywood contract as director and actor. His Mercury Theatre productions on Broadway have included *Julius Caesar, The Cradle Will Rock, The Shoemakers' Holiday, Heartbreak House* and *Danton's Death.* In all his enterprises, John Houseman has been the supporting partner.

Well of the Saints. J. M. Synge (Irish). Tragedy. 3 acts. 1905.

An old blind beggar and his wife come to a well, the waters of which can make the blind see. Having never seen each other, each believes the other beautiful and they have been happy. The saint who owns the well restores their vision, but when they see each other as they really are, they come to blows and part. They become blind again and after time has passed, meet again. They start talking and become friends when the saint reappears, to offer them vision again. This time they refuse it for blindness with hope is better than sight with bitterness.

Werfel, Franz (1890-   ). Austrian novelist, dramatist. Born in Prague. He first attracted notice in 1912 with his poem *Der Weltfreund*. After the First World War he published several notable novels and dramatic works, which include his powerful symbolic trilogy, *Der Spiegelmensch,* 1920, and his highly successful historical plays, *Juarez and Maximilian,* 1924, and *Paulus unter den Juden,* 1926. Both his stories and plays display a clear development and brilliant characterization. English translations of several of his novels include *Verdi; Death of a Poor Man,* 1920; *The Goat Song,* 1926; *Class Reunion,* 1930; *The Hidden Child* (published in Germany as *Barbara*), 1931; *The Pascarella Family,* 1932, and *The Forty Days of Musa Dagh,* 1934.

A sentence in the preface of his adaptation of *The Trojan Women* gives us an insight into Werfel's philosophy. He says there, "There is an essential tragedy in the world, a break, an original sin, wherein all participate, and from which the understanding soul suffers most."

Werner, Friedrich Ludwig Zacharias (1768-1823). German poet, dramatist. Born in Koenigsberg, he served in Prussian Poland in the Ministry of Justice, finally settling in Warsaw, where he became a freemason and adopted mystical views. He went to Weimar in 1807 and there came under the influence of Goethe. In 1811 Werner went to Rome, where he became a Roman Catholic, and was ordained a priest. From then onwards he was famous for his preaching at Vienna, where he held a ministry. His dramas were practically the only ones produced by the romantic poets to enjoy success on the stage. His *Twenty-fourth of February,* 1809, was the model for the German Drama of Fate. All of his plays are full of religious mysticism.

Among his plays are *Das Kreuz an der Ostsee,* 1806; *Martin Luther,* 1807; *Attila,* 1808; *Kunigunde die Heilige,* 1815; *Die Mutter der Makkabäer,* 1820.

West, Mae (1893-   ). American actress, dramatist. Born in Brooklyn, Mae West occupies a fantastic place in the world of the theatre. She started her career in the *Folies Bergères,* 1911, and went into vaudeville in 1913. She gained an important billing as a vaudevillian, and then dropped out of sight for a time. She returned to Broadway as a playwright and star in plays (*Sex, The Drag, Pleasure Man,* and later *The Constant Sinner*) that won the opprobrium of critics and public and a jail sentence. Nevertheless, one of these plays, *Diamond Lil,* though loosely constructed and hokum melodrama, presented one of the few authentic stage pictures of tenderloin night life with its fashionable slumming parties, singing waiters, and *Frankie and Johnnie* balladists. The play's dialogue contained the double entendre line, "Come up and see me some time," which bridged the way to Mae's fame. Thanks to a sudden reversal of public opinion, Mae became a screen star and writer, and so speedy and sensational was her popularity that those who came to scoff, genuflected. The newspapers flaunted her pictures in 1928-29. *The New Yorker* published her profile. She revived the hour glass figure and precipitated a new interest in the styles of the nineties.

Westchester County Center. White Plains, New York. Civic auditorium which includes a Little Theatre seating 520, the home of the Westchester Drama Association, representing more than a score of Little Theatre groups in the county. A committee of Inter-Group Players holds auditions to cast county productions from membership of the various units. A drama conference brings many stage experts and dramatic critics, who criticize productions by the separate Little Theatre units. In 1925 a Little Theatre Tournament, competing for prizes, was organized by the County Recreation Commission, under the leadership of Miss Genevieve Cheney. Out of this enterprise, in 1928, grew the Drama Association. Original play contests are held, and several high school groups are affiliated.

Westward Ho. John Webster and Thomas Dekker (English). Comedy. 1605.
Three merry ladies and their swains go to Brentford. Their husbands find them there at an inn, but they are able to prove their innocence and all is well. The sub-plot deals with an Italian merchant Justiniano who thinks his wife is unfaithful to him and so leaves her and enjoys London life in disguise. The merchant's wife, who has been having an affair with an earl, soon repents and a reconciliation is effected.

We the People. Elmer Rice (American). Tragedy. 20 scenes. 1933.
A minister, a public school teacher and a Polish-American radical band together to demand better conditions for working people. They are impelled by what the depression is doing to Americans, specifically, the Davis family. The father, a factory foreman, loses his job, his savings, and is finally killed in a strike. The son who was to have gone to college, is jailed for stealing coal for the family. On his release, he becomes a radical, and is later hanged for his supposed guilt in the murder of a policeman.

Wexley, John (1902-   ). American dramatic author and actor. Born in New York City he attended New York University. Appeared with the Civic Repertory Theatre and Yiddish Art Theatre. He is the author of *The Last Mile,* 1930; *Steel,* 1931; and *They Shall Not Die,* 1934. These plays all carry messages of social protest. *The Last Mile* preaches against capital punishment; *Steel* has to do with labor problems and *They Shall Not Die* around the famous Scottsboro Trial.

Wharton, Edith (1862-1937). American novelist. Born in New York of socially prominent parents. Her autobiography, *A Backward Glance,* was published in 1934. Her novel *Ethan Frome,* dramatized by Owen Davis and Donald Davis, played at the National Theatre in New York and other cities in 1936 with Pauline Lord, Ruth Gordon, and Raymond Massey. The Margaret Ayer Barnes stage version of *The Age of Innocence* starred Katharine Cornell at the Empire theatre in New York in 1928. Helen Menken and Judith Anderson played in Zöe Akins' Pulitzer Prize-winning adaptation of *The Old Maid* at the Empire in 1935, and toured the larger cities of the United States.

What Every Woman Knows. Sir James M. Barrie (English). Comedy. 4 acts. 1908.

Maggie Shand has played an important part in the success of her husband, John Shand, and in his rise to Parliament. She is now seeing him through an affair with Lady Sybil Lazenby. By giving Lady Sybil enough rope, Maggie wins John back, and charts a shrewd campaign which guarantees his re-election to Parliament.

What every woman knows is that she must never allow her man to realize that she is helping him, but must allow him to think that it is his own intelligence and ingenuity that are getting him on.

The way in which Maggie keeps herself in the background, though it is she and she alone who is responsible for her husband's success, is amusingly and cleverly portrayed.

What Passion, Ye Marionettes! Piermaria Rosso di San Secondo (Italian). Drama. 3 acts. 1920.

The action is drawn from the chance meeting of three people hitherto unknown to each other. Each brings forth confidences of his unhappy past. Except for the final touches of realism the author has omitted all obvious exposition, limiting his drama to elementary emotional outbreaks of his puppet-heroes.

What Price Glory? Maxwell Anderson and Laurence Stallings (American). Drama. 3 acts. 1924.

The plot revolves around Sergeant Quirt and Captain Flagg, professional soldiers, and their private feud which continues regardless of the wars in which they fighting. This time it is the World War and Charmaine, a pretty French girl, is the prize. Quirt takes her away from Flagg in his absence and on his return Flagg is determined to force his old rival to marry her, but Quirt is having none of it. The war scenes are for background only and the play is important because of its realistic portrayal of the thinking and language of soldiers. In the end, Charmaine forgotten, the friendly enemies return to the front lines, Quirt calling out to the captain, who has gone ahead, "Hey, Flagg, wait for baby!"

What will Mrs. Grundy say? The recurrent question in Morton's comedy, *Speed the Plough,* where a Mrs. Grundy is often mentioned, but not introduced. *Mrs. Grundy* has become part of the English language.

When Ladies Meet. Rachel Crothers (American). Comedy. 3 acts. Printed 1932.

One evening in the country, Mary Howard, a novelist, meets Claire Woodruff, and they become friends. Mary talks about life in general, her latest book, and finally Rogers Woodruff whom she is meeting that night, and whom she plans to take as a lover. Not until Woodruff arrives does Mary know that Claire is his wife. The following morning, Woodruff finds he has lost both women. Claire plans to divorce him; while Mary, disillusioned, no longer trusts him.

When the New Wine Blooms. Björnstjern Björnson (Norwegian). Drama, 4 acts. 1909.

A middle-aged wife neglects her husband, being a new woman absorbed in her own affairs, and she sets her daughters an example of lack of respect for their father. When he turns for comfort to a young girl and is supposed to have eloped with her, his wife in anguish learns a lesson.

Whipple, Sidney B. (1888-   ). American dramatic critic. Born in Lowell, Massachusetts; London and Paris newspaper correspondent, 1910-13; managing editor of the *Syracuse* (New York) *Journal,* 1917-19; staff correspondent of the United Press; has been dramatic critic of the New York *World-Telegram* since 1937.

White-Headed Boy, The. Lennox Robinson (Irish). Comedy. 3 acts. Produced 1921.

The story of the "white-headed boy" Denis, of the Geoghegan's, for whose comfort and educational advancement all the family is sacrificed. The conflict centers around the plottings of the propertied spinster, Aunt Ellen, John Duffy, father of Denis's girl, and the hardworking elder brother George. The latter becomes exasperated by Denis's irresponsibility. All of the family have to dig in to repay Duffy for Denis's trifling with his daughter's affections. As she is already married to Denis, it all turns out happily and the pair get the money from Duffy as a wedding present.

White Madness. Henri René Lenormand (French). Drama. 3 acts. 1906.

Suggests the malign influence of a Swiss mountain which attracts yet punishes with death those who would conquer it. The pair of lovers debate what each would do in case they slipped in the ascent. The girl admits she would cut the rope joining them, while he says he would die rather than cut the cord. They make the ascent during a storm. The lover cuts the rope to save himself, then deliberately plunges to his death.

White Marriage. Jules Lemaitre (French). Drama. 5 acts. 1891.

A libertine of fifty, out of curiosity, resolves to make a consumptive girl his wife; but her jealous half-sister, tired of sacrificing all to the invalid, turns upon her and then, as she lies fainting, captivates the libertine, whereupon the invalid, reviving, sees enough to hasten her death.

Whiteoaks. Mazo de la Roche (Canadian). Drama. 3 acts. 1935. Based on the novel, Whiteoaks of Jalna.

Adelaide Whiteoak, matriarch of an English-Canadian family, is 101 years old. Her chief pleasures in life are eating, backgammon and her long midnight chats with her musical grandson Finch. The main interest of the rest of her family is, who is to receive her money when she dies? Renny her oldest grandson seems to be her favorite, but the others also feel that they have a claim to her favor based upon their priority in age and their need for money. When the old lady dies while playing backgammon it is found that the money has been left to Finch who now faces the bitter animosity of the rest of the family.

White Sister, The. Francis Marion Crawford and Walter Hackett (English). Drama. 3 acts. 1897.

Sister Giovanna (before she became a nun) and the Countess Chiaramonte, were both in love with Captain Giovanni Severi, who was ordered away on duty. Giovanna believes him dead, but the Countess has information to the contrary which she keeps to herself. Through an accident to Giovanni's brother, the White Sister and Giovanni meet face to face. Giovanni claims her but she repulses him. She refuses to sign an application for an annulment of her vows and in a struggle with her, Giovanni is mortally wounded by the accidental firing of his revolver.

White Wings. Philip Barry (American). Comedy. 4 acts. 1927.

The Inch family, who have been White Wings or street cleaners for three generations, put up a losing fight against the "horseless carriage." The father, realizing that automobiles are here to stay, tries to shoot himself, but only succeeds in piercing a hole in his white street cleaner's helmet.

Why Marry? Jessie Lynch Williams (American). Comedy in 3 acts. 1918.

This was the first play to win the Pulitzer Prize. Helen, a career girl, has been working as assistant to Dr. Ernest Hamilton, a sincere and conscientious scientist. She has had many proposals of marriage but rejected them to follow her career. She considers herself emancipated since she has not trapped a man into supporting her. Ernest is going to Paris and Helen announces that she is going with him. The family asks him to consider her reputation. He does, and refuses to take her. After this decision, he finds he loves her and wishes to marry her. Believing that it will interfere with his work, she refuses but admits her love for him. She does not see why they cannot go to Paris anyway. Uncle Everett, a genial, liberal soul, asks them about their convictions and statement of their vows and then pronounces them man and wife. Ernest discovers that she has been transformed from a bad woman to a good woman by this simple expedient.

Widower's Houses. G. B. Shaw (English). 1892.

Shaw attacks the slum tenement problem in this play. He does not make it simply a case of poor tenant vs. rich landlord. He makes the audience realize that the problem is more complicated than that.

His hero, Trench, cannot bear to think that his dowry will come from money squeezed out of poor tenants living in the houses of his fiancée, Blanche Sartorius. Trench is soon faced with the bitter realization that his own money is made in precisely the way that he objects to. His idealism falters, he succumbs to pressure and by the end of the play, he is planning how to make more money from his property. Shaw tries to bring out the point that Society and not isolated individuals is responsible for existing conditions.

Wild Duck, The. Henrik Ibsen (Norwegian). Drama. 5 acts. 1884.

The happiness of the Ekdal family is shattered when Hjalmar Ekdal learns from a neighbor that his wife Gina was formerly another man's mistress.

The neighbor then searches out Hedwig, Hjalmar's young daughter. He talks to her about the joy of sacrifice, and tells her she must kill her cherished pet, a wild duck, in order to prove her love for Hjalmar. Instead, Hedwig, confused and miserable with the gossip about her mother, shoots herself.

The neighbor represents those who desire to foist the popular formulae for conduct and who preach the rule that one must always tell the truth. By his truth telling and suggestions of sacrifice he succeeds in bringing misery and tragedy to a once happy family.

Wilde, Oscar (1856-1900). Irish writer and dramatist. Born in Dublin, 1856. Attended Trinity College and Magdelen College at Oxford. He had a brilliant academic career and became leader of a group of aesthetes renowned for their belief in "Art for Art's Sake." On his arrival in London he created quite a sensation with flamboyant posturing and precious wit. He was the object of ridicule and adulation. In 1882 he completed a lecture tour in the U. S. where he was quite popular. After his novel, *The Picture of Dorian Gray,* 1891, he started to write plays. In this field his brilliance and wit is outstanding. *Lady Windermere's Fan,* 1892; *A Woman of No Importance,* 1893; *An Ideal Husband,* 1894; *The Importance of Being Ernest,* 1895, were all successful and skillful. His play *Salome* was banned in England but was played in France with Sarah Bernhardt in the leading role.

While Wilde's conduct had been criticized, his position as a dramatist had made him acceptable to London society until the Marquess of Queensbury made certain accusations against him. Unfortunately the whole thing came to trial and Wilde was convicted and imprisoned for two years. Here he wrote *The Ballad of Reading Gaol* and an apology for his life, *De Profundis.* He died in poverty and obscurity in Paris.

Wilde, Percival (1887-   ). American author, dramatist. Born in New York City, he was educated at Columbia University. From 1906-1911 he was connected with the banking business, but began writing as book reviewer for the New York *Times* and the New York *Post.* Upon the publication of his first story in 1912, he received so many requests for dramatic rights that he turned to playwriting. He also invented several devices for the airplane compass which have been adopted by the United States Navy. He is the author of the plays *Dawn, and Other One-Act Plays of Life Today,* 1915; *Confessional, and Other American Plays,* 1916; *The Unseen Host,* 1917; *The Woman in Room 13* (in collaboration), 1919; *The Aftermath,* 1921; *Eight Comedies for Little Theatre,* 1922; *The Inn of Discontent,* 1924; *The Reckoning,* 1924; *The Toy-Shop,* 1924; *The Dyspeptic Ogre,* 1925; *Catesby,* 1925; *The Devil's Booth,* 1930. He is said to have had more plays produced in American little theatres than any other author, and his many plays for children are notable.

Wildenbruch, Ernst von (1845-1909). German author, dramatist. Born in Beirut, Syria, a junior member of the Hohenzollern family. He entered the diplomatic service, and became known as a dramatist, novelist, and poet. He took his themes from German history, these historical themes having long been popular with German audiences. Though his earlier plays were radical in tone, his later ones expressed passionate Prussian nationalism. His most popular plays are *Vaeter und Soehne,*

1882; *Der Mennonit,* 1882; *Der neue Herr,* 1891; *Heinrich und Heinrichs Geschlecht,* 1895; *Das neue Gebot,* 1886; *Die Quitzows;* and *Der Generalfeldoberst.*

Wilder, Thornton Niven (1897-   ). American author, dramatist. Born in Madison, Wisconsin, became a schoolmaster, 1921-1928, and in 1926 published his first novel, *The Cabala,* a fine study of the life of a small international circle in Rome. A writer with a quiet but distinguished style, he established an international reputation in 1927 with *The Bridge of San Luis Rey; The Angel that Troubled the Waters,* 1928; *The Woman of Andros,* 1930, a tale of ancient Greece; *Heaven's My Destination,* 1934, a novel of modern America. Wilder also wrote the plays, *The Trumpet Shall Sound,* 1927; an adaptation of Obey's *Lucrèce,* 1932; an adaptation of Ibsen's *A Doll's House,* 1937; *Our Town,* 1938, one of the distinguished successes of the New York season, and winner of the Pulitzer Prize; and an adaptation of Nestroy, called *The Merchant of Yonkers,* 1938.

Wild Girl, The. François de Curel (French). Drama. 3 acts. 1902.
A savage maiden, captured by hunters and confined in a barbarian's seraglio, is brought to Europe by the French councillor of the tribe and is taught the ways of civilization in a convent. Impressed at first by the new religion, she grows skeptical the more she learns, and is embittered when the man who had rescued her rejects her love.

Wilhelm Tell. Johann Christoph von Schiller (German). 5 acts. 1804.
The famous Swiss Archer is ordered by the tyrant Gessler to shoot an apple off his son's head at 80 paces. Tell obeys and succeeds in hitting the apple squarely.
He admits that he failed, his next arrow was meant for Gessler. For this he is imprisoned. He escapes and succeeds in killing Gessler. This acts as a signal for a general revolt which destroyed Austrian tyranny. During the same year the Emperor who had commissioned Gessler was assassinated, and the Swiss became independent.

Williams, Jesse Lynch (1871-1929). American author. Winner of the first Pulitzer award in 1918 with *Why Marry?* In 1922, a companion piece to the above was produced called *Why Not?* This was a play about divorce. Mr. Williams was well known for his Princeton stories. One of his early plays, *The Stolen Story,* was based on one of these.

Willis, Nathaniel Parker (1806-1867). American dramatist. Born in Portland, Maine, he was graduated from Yale in 1827. He travelled much abroad, writing the "views afoot" kind of article for magazines and newspapers. After his return from the Continent in 1836, he turned to playwriting. The result was *Bianca Visconti,* written for Josephine Clifton, New York Park Theatre, 1837; *The Kentucky Heiress,* 1837; *The Betrothal,* 1837; *Imei, the Jew,* 1839; *Tortesa, the Usurer,* 1839. This last play is thought to have been written because of the offer of a prize by James W. Wallack, who sought a play suitable for his acting ability. Willis' plays were inclined to be romantic, talky and static.

Will Shakespeare. Clemence Dane (English). Drama. 6 scenes. 1921.

Deals with Shakespeare's disillusionment over Ann Hathaway, his ill luck with the charmer Mary Fitton, his brawl with Christopher Marlowe and his ultimate rise to greatest fame not without some help from Elizabeth.

Wilson, Joseph Maria (1872-1933). Stage designer, architect and illustrator. His architectural successes include the bridge across the Niva at Leningrad, his decoration work at the Paris Exposition of 1900 and of the decoration of the Austrian Building at the St. Louis Exposition in 1904.

He was also well known as a successful designer of stage settings for both classical and modern productions. He did sets for such varied productions as *Parsifal, Tristan and Isolde, Othello, Ziegfeld Follies* and *The Garden of Paradise.*

He was art consultant for the Chicago Century of Progress and created a panorama for the New York State exhibit at that exposition.

Wilson, Robert (1550-1595?). English dramatist. Thorndyke in *English Comedy* states that the "transition from the moral to a satirical comedy of manners is best exemplified in the work of Robert Wilson." Little is known of Wilson's life. He is the author of *Three Ladies of London,* 1584; *The Pleasant and Stately Morall of the Three Lords and Three Ladies of London* (a sequel), 1590; and *The Cobbler's Prophecy.*

Wiman, Dwight Deere (1895-   ). American producer. Born in Moline, Illinois; came to the stage from the films. With William A. Brady, Jr., he produced *The Road to Rome,* 1926; *Command to Love,* 1927; *The Queen's Husband,* 1928; *The Little Show,* 1929; and other plays; then independently he managed *The Vinegar Tree,* 1930; *She Loves Me Not,* 1933; *The Distaff Side,* 1934; *On Your Toes,* 1936; *Babes in Arms,* 1937; *I Married An Angel,* 1938; *Stars in Your Eyes,* 1939, and numerous other successes.

Winchell, Walter (1897-   ). Dramatic critic, columnist. As a boy of thirteen he went on the vaudeville stage in a juvenile company, and later appeared by himself in vaudeville theatres. His story is brimful of originality, daring and success. By specialization in social exposé and anticipating pregnancy he built up a journalistic Frankenstein influence which created local terrorism for a time but which led to his development as an author and star of stage, screen and radio. He is an occasional national influence and has helped to apprehend noted criminals. His force as a journalist is international.

Winchell's journalistic career began on the *Vaudeville News,* 1922; he was dramatic critic and dramatic editor of the *New York Evening Graphic,* 1924-29, when he took a similar post on the *Daily Mirror;* he broadcasts regularly over the National Broadcasting Company network, and contributes to magazines; is the creator of his own type of slang; a man of extraordinary energy and unlimited originality; one of the most powerful journalists of the era.

Windshield (television). Metal shield sometimes fitted over a microphone to protect it from the drafts arising from the air conditioning system used in television studios.

Windsor Castle theatricals. Queen Victoria was very fond of the theatre but she wished the actors brought to her. The first private command performance was on December 28, 1848 with *The Merchant of Venice;* Charles and Ellen Kean and the Keeleys appeared in it. Because of the Prince Consort's liking for plays these performances continued until his death in December, 1861. Rejecting anything that recalled these pleasures Victoria asked no more for productions for twenty years. After that they were given occasionally during her reign and the reigns of Edward VII and George V.

Winesburg, Ohio. Sherwood Anderson (American). Drama. 9 scenes. Printed 1937.

Life in Winesburg, Ohio, as seen through the eyes of its banker, its doctor, and its loafers.

On the order of an anthology, drab, commonplace people are shown in moments of vivid feeling and high emotions—too often suppressed or misdirected.

Sex, here, seems to be the mainspring which motivates most of the characters.

Wing it. To play a part relying not on memorization but on prompting of lines.

Wings. First introduced in the masques of the Elizabethan theatre; four one-sided, painted flats on either side of the stage.

Wings Over Europe. Robert Nichols and Maurice Browne (English). Drama. 3 acts. 1929.

Young Francis Lightfoot discovers he can control the energy in the atom. He offers this secret to the British Cabinet, convinced it can be used to free mankind. When the Cabinet urges him to destroy the formula, Lightfoot determines to blow up the earth, and he is shot by a cabinet member. A few moments later a Union of scientists announces to all the rulers in the world that they, too, have the secret, and are prepared to use it to rule the world for the good of man.

Winter, William (1836-1917). American dramatic critic. Dramatic critic of N. Y. Tribune from 1865 until he retired in 1909. He was held in great esteem in the world of the theatre and for thirty-five years was considered the foremost dramatic critic in America. He wrote several books unrelated to the drama and some on the theatre. Among the latter are *Henry Irving, Mary Anderson, Edwin Booth, Joseph Jefferson, Richard Mansfield,* and *David Belasco.*

The esteem with which Winter was held is shown by a memorial tendered him in March 1916; as an expression of respect and admiration for the *honored veteran of our literature, the critic, scholar, journalist and poet.* The memorial was signed by President Woodrow Wilson, Theodore Roosevelt, Wm. H. Taft, Gov. Whitman of N. Y., Mayor Mitchel of N. Y. C., Nicholas Murray Butler, and most of the leading contemporary actors and actresses.

Winterset. Maxwell Anderson (American). Drama. 3 acts. 1935.

Mio journeys across the continent to avenge the death of his father who was executed for a murder he did not commit. He finds Garth, the only witness who knew the truth and who was not summoned to testify. He meets the judge, who is going mad from a sense of guilt. At last he faces Trock, the gang leader who decreed his father's death, and he is finally slain by Trock's henchmen. Mio's sweetheart, Miriamne dies with him.

The author obviously was translating the Sacco-Vanzetti case into drama as he did in *Gods of the Lightning*.

Winter's Tale, The. William Shakespeare (English). 5 acts. 1610.

Written about 1610 and published in the Folio of 1623. It is based on the romantic prose novel *Pandosto* by Robert Greene, published in 1589.

Leontes, king of Sicily, wrongly believes his wife, Hermione, faithless to him with his friend Polixenes, king of Bohemia, and orders that she and her infant daughter Perdita be killed. Merciful executioners disobey him, hide Hermione, and set Perdita adrift at sea. She is found "on the sea-coast of Bohemia" by shepherds and is raised by them. Florizell, son of Polixenes, falling in love with her against his father's wishes, in order to avoid Polixene's anger, flees with her to Sicily where Leontes receives them joyfully. He is filled with remorse at Hermione's supposed death. Perdita promises to show him a statue of Hermione. The statue turns out to be Hermione herself, whose reported death was a ruse to save her life. There is general joy and reconciliation. Polixenes is delighted with Florizell's marriage when he learns that Perdita is Leontes' daughter.

The action is graced by scenes of pastoral and rustic entertainment, and is seasoned with the roguish humor of Autolycus, who is Shakespeare's own addition to the story and characterization.

Wisdom Tooth, The. Marc Connelly (American). Fantasy. 3 acts. 1926.

When his sweetheart, Sally Field, turns him down, Bemis, clerk in a mercantile organization, realizes the big city has taken his courage and that he is deteriorating into a small-time "yes man."

In a dream he is visited by his grandparents who give him their courage. He also relives his boyhood when he watered elephants, drove old Dobbin, and licked Pork Porky, a bully.

Waking, charged with new found courage and esprit, Bemis shows off by calling his employer and upbraiding him for discharging a stenographer, only to find himself fired. Sally knows Bemis has been a fool and has much to learn, but she admires and believes in him.

Witchcraft in the drama. The seventeenth century was preeminently the age of English witchcraft. Shakespeare wrote three plays in which witch characters figure: *King Henry VI, Macbeth,* and *The Tempest.* Reference to witches and witchcraft are frequent throughout his dramas. Elizabethan and early Stuart literature deals with theses concerned with practices of witchcraft; the dramatist took advantage of the vogue that witchcraft had, and wrote plays dealing with the subject.

Witching Hour, The. August Thomas (American). 4 acts. 1908.

Jack Brookfield resorts to mental telepathy to save his friend, Clay Whipple from the electric chair. He succeeds, and exposes Hardsmith, the District Attorney who has framed his friend. After the trial the District Attorney meets Brookfield, tries to kill him, but through hypnotic influence is forced to drop the gun.

Within the Gates. Sean O'Casey (Irish). Symbolic drama. 3 acts. 1934.

Cross-section of life in Hyde Park, London. In the crowd are the Bishop, his Sister, a Poet, and a young Whore. The young Whore, frightened and sick, is condemned by the Bishop whose illegitimate daughter she is. The old woman seeks release for her by invoking the religion of her father, but to no purpose. Warned by the richness of physical life, the Young Whore turns to the Poet who makes her few months of life happy and gives her the strength to die bravely. Returning to the Church, she dies in the arms of the Bishop.

Wodehouse, Pelham Grenville (1881-   ). English author and playwright. Born in England. Was once dramatic editor of "Vaniety Fair." He has written many plays mostly in collaboration. Among these are *A Thief for a Night* (with Stapleton), 1913; *Have a Heart,* 1917 (with Guy Bolton); *Sitting Pretty,* 1924; *Oh Kay,* 1926; *The Play's the Thing,* adapted from the Hungarian of Molnar, 1926; *Her Cardboard Lover* (from French), 1927. He wrote the lyrics for *Rosalie* and the *Three Musketeers,* 1928; *Leave It to Psmith,* 1930, and *Anything Goes* (with Bolton), 1934. He is renowned for his humor and gift for farce and for the creation of charming and exceedingly ineffectual heroes. Psmith, Jeeves, the butler and Bertie Wooster are among his most famous creations.

Woffington, Margaret (Peg) (1718-60). English actress. Born in Dublin, she made her stage debut in Covent Garden 1740. Later she appeared as Sir Harry Wildair, the famous role which required her to wear breeches. From 1742-1748, she acted with Garrick and became the idol of the London and Dublin stages. She was equally competent in both comedy and tragedy and held the devotion of her public for many years. She is said to have been one of the handsomest women ever to appear on the stage. Walpole admitted she had vivacity and wit, though he did not like her acting. She was scrupulously loyal to her public, never missing a performance. Her presence was sought by all London and Dublin society and she was courted by men of all ranks. Garrick almost married her but found her a bit too temperamental. She was painted by Hogarth, Mercier and Wilson, and altogether was one of the darlings of her era.

Wolf, The. Ferenc Molnar (Hungarian). Drama. 3 acts. 1912.

Performed in English as *The Phantom Rival.*

Plays with the notion that a wife always preserves in her heart the image of her first lover. The middle scenes show this lover as he appears in the lady's dreams. His actual appearance as an unheroic and fleshly figure brings about her complete disillusionment.

Wolf Club. An English organization founded May 5, 1815. It had something of a notorious reputation as a confounder of the rivals of Edmund Kean. In reality it was a democratic body which refused membership to aristocrats and which made its sole exception in favor of Byron, who was permitted to attend the "goings-on."

Wolff, Pierre (1865-   ). French dramatist. Nephew of the famous art critic Albert Wolff; first play, *Le Cheval d'Aristotle,* in one act, produced in 1885 at the Théâtre Déjazet. There followed at the Théâtre Libre: *Jacques Bouchard,* 1890; *Les Filles,* 1891 (this was also produced at Gymnase and l'Ambigu) ; and *Les Maris de Leurs Filles,* 1892. Other plays include *Celles qu'on Respect,* 1893; *L'Hirondelle,* 1894; *Fidèle,* 1895; *Sacré Léonce,* 1901; *Le Secret de Polichinelle,* 1903; *L'Age d'Aimer,* 1905; *Le Ruisseau,* 1907; *Le Lys,* 1908 (with Gaston Leroux) ; and *Les Marionettes,* 1913. He is also the author of *Amants et Maîtresses,* a suite of dialogues, 1896; and a novel, *Sacré Léonce,* 1894—the source of his play of the same name. He has written for *Figaro, Gaulois, Le Journal,* and other periodicals.

Since 1918 he has been president of the *Société des Auteurs et Compositeurs Dramatiques;* he is a member of the "Jurys de concours" of the Conservatoire.

Wolves, The. Romain Rolland (French). Drama. 3 acts. 1898.

The scene is the headquarters of the General Staff of the French Army on the Rhine in 1796. A story of the French Revolution, which having spent its early fury, is beginning to turn in upon itself, and the great leaders fall one by one to satisfy ambition and petty hatred.

Woman Killed With Kindness, A. Thomas Heyward (English). 5 acts. Melodrama. 1603.

A wife commits adultery with her husband's best friend. When her husband discovers her faithlessness he decides to kill her with kindness.

He sends her to a lovely manor house and heaps her with everything possible for her comfort, but she is forbidden to see him or her children.

The loneliness and remorse breaks her spirit and she dies. At her death bed there is a touching scene of forgiveness.

Woman of No Importance, A. Oscar Wilde (English). 1893.

Gerald Arbuthnot, a book clerk, meets Lord Illingworth and they take a liking to each other. Gerald's mother discovers that Lord Illingworth is really Gerald's father who, years ago, forsook her as a woman of no importance. She refuses to allow Gerald to accept the post of secretary to Illingworth but cannot bring herself to tell her son the reason. Illingworth insults a young girl with whom Gerald is in love and the young man attempts to kill the older one, but is stopped by his mother by her confession of parentage. Illingworth now offers to marry Mrs. Arbuthnot but she dismisses him as a man of no importance.

Women, The. Clare Boothe (American). Comedy. 3 acts. 1936.

Mary Haines, prodded by the gossip of her best friends, divorces her husband, Stephen, that he may marry Crystal Allen, a shop girl. Two years later, when Mary learns that Crystal is deceiving him, she adopts Crystal's jungle technique, and wins Stephen back. The play is a biting attack on the empty vicious lives of most wealthy women. It is unique in that the cast consists entirely of women.

Womp (television). A sudden, and violent, increase in signal strength, resulting in a corresponding flare in the received image.

Woods, Albert Herman (Al) (1870-   ). American producer and theatre proprietor. A born showman, he started his career in 1902 by producing sensational melodrama: *The Crooked Path, Secret Service Sam, The Great Express Robbery*. Then he turned to bedroom farces, such as *The Girl From Rector's*, 1911; *His Bridal Night*, 1916; *Up In Mabel's Room,* with which he had tremendous success. Then he decided to forsake the risque comedy and put on a series of *Potash and Perlmutter* plays. Since then he has produced many successful dramas such as *The Shanghai Gesture; The Green Hat; The Trial of Mary Dugan; A Farewell to Arms;* etc.

Woollcott, Alexander (1887-   ). Dramatic critic, author. Born in Phalanx, New Jersey. He was dramatic critic of the New York *Times,* 1914-1922; New York *Herald,* 1922; New York *World,* 1925-1928. He spent two years as an enlisted man in the A.E.F., including one year in the editorial council of *The Stars and Stripes.* He was also contributor to numerous magazines. He is the author of *Mrs. Fiske, Her Views on Acting, Actors and the Problems of the Stage,* 1917; *The Command is Forward,* 1919; *Shouts and Murmurs; Mr. Dickens Goes to the Play,* 1923; *Enchanted Aisles,* 1924; *The Story of Irving Berlin,* 1925; *Going to Pieces,* 1928; *Two Gentlemen and a Lady,* 1928; *While Rome Burns,* 1934; etc.

He is co-author of the plays *The Channel Road* and *The Dark Tower* and has acted, notably in Behrman's *Brief Moment,* 1931, in the film, *The Scoundrel,* with Noel Coward, 1935, and in the Behrman play, *Wine of Choice,* 1938. He is reputed to be the subject of the Kaufman-Hart play, *The Man Who Came To Dinner,* 1939.

Worcester's Men. A company of professional actors which came into prominence in 1602 as principal rivals of the Lord Chamberlain's Men, Shakespeare's company, and the Admiral's Men. William Kempe, Christopher Beeston and other actors left the Chamberlain's Men to join Worcester's group at this time. Thomas Heywood was secured as principal playwright, and Chettle, Dekker, Day and Webster also wrote for the company. After performing for six months at the Boar's Head Inn the company moved to the Rose theatre under the management of Philip Henslowe.

Wordsworth, William (1770-1850) (English). Poet. A famous poet, his great contribution to English letters is his return to simplicity and naturalism and his influence on his contemporaries. In 1795 he began his tragedy *The Borderers* which he finished in 1796. The plot is not well constructed and the verse is uninspired.

Workhouse Ward, The. Lady Augusta Gregory (Irish). Farce. 1 act. 1908. Supposed to symbolize Irish politics.

Two paupers, Mike and Michael, hurl abuse at each other from adjacent beds. Mrs. Donohue enters with the object of performing a charitable act for Mike. She desires to take him from the workhouse and provide a home for him. Mike inquires if Michael may go with him and on receiving a reply in the negative, finds fault with Mrs. Donohue, and refuses to go. She departs in disgust, and Mike and Michael immediately recommence quarreling.

Working area. The space, outside the acting area, where stagehands customarily operate, scenery and properties are stacked, etc.

Working drawings. Blueprints made from the designer's drawings, showing the rear view of the scenery, all the detailed construction, etc. The scenery is built from these plans.

Working light. The large uncovered lamp suspended above the stage, used during rehearsals.

Working title. A tentative title, not entirely satisfactory to the producer or author, which is used to designate the play or picture while it is in rehearsal or production.

THE WORLD AND THE THEATRE

BY WILLIAM SAROYAN

I have just gotten up and have had no coffee. I want to explain everything in six or seven words, and I know it's absurd. I mean it can't be done. I mean nothing can be said.

However:

The world is *the* theatre. The other theatre—the one which charges admission—is *not* the world.

Therefore, the theatre does not exist. Only the world exists. Therefore, there is no point in going to the theatre.

There is no art in the world, therefore; or in the theatre; or in people; or in nature. Which is ridiculous fantasy, since the living cannot live apart from art, since nature is art. The only trouble is that artists are not human or natural.

It goes along something like that. What you get is feeble. Feeble people doing feeble things. The world is great and immortal. The living are great and immortal.

Art is feeble.

Art should be the greatest mortal greatness. The art of the theatre is closest to the art in the world: because it works with living people.

The American Theatre needs only to look clearly at the American World to become the great theatre it must be: perhaps the greatest the world has ever known.

Two hours later:

There is no sense in talking about the theatre.

The thing to do is to write great plays.

I am doing my best.

World We Live In, The. Karel and Josef Capek (Czechoslovakian). Comedy. Prelude, 3 acts, and an epilogue. Adapted and arranged from the Czech by Owen Davis. 1921.

Intoxicated, a man falls asleep in the forest. Dreaming, he watches the lives of the insect world. He finds their existence, their struggles and wars, their dreams and aspirations, pointedly similar to those of man. The butterflies are gay, effeminate, and make passionate love, while the beetles are misers and live niggardly. Each insect commits some human crime, even the yellow and red ants go to war over trivia as humans do.

Would-be Gentleman, The. See *Bourgeois Gentilhomme, Le.*

Wow. (1) (noun) A tremendous box-office success; (2) (verb) to excite an audience to great acclaim.

Wozzeck. Georg Buchner (German). Drama. 5 acts. 1836?

This is an unfinished tragedy of class oppression written about 1836. It is the story of Franz Wozzeck, soldier, who is stumbling along life's highway, obeying orders when he must and the rest of the time wondering what this world is all about. He murders the mother of his little son, born out of wedlock, and then drowns himself.

This play was recently adapted as a libretto for an opera by Alfred Reginald Allen with the music by Alban Berg.

Wren, Sir Christopher (1632-1723). British mathematician, scientist and architect. This most famous of British architects, who is responsible for St. Paul's Cathedral, Christ Church and so many other famous London landmarks, also made some notable contributions to theatre architecture. Among the theatres which he designed are the Sheldonian Theatre, Oxford, 1664; and the Drury Lane Theatre, London, 1674.

Wriothesley, Henry, Earl of Southampton. The young nobleman to whom Shakespeare dedicated his poems *Venus and Adonis* (1593) and *The Rape of Lucrece* (1594). Of Catholic antecedents, Southampton was prominent in court circles until 1596, when, because of his part in a love intrigue, he was forced to retire. For his participation with Essex in the rebellion of 1601 he was condemned to death, but the sentence was commuted to imprisonment and he was eventually released by King James.

THE WRITER IN HOLLYWOOD

ROBERT GESSNER

Why have we practically no screen classics? The cinema is the Twentieth Century way of telling a story, reaching the greatest audience in history, producing more drama than ever before. But why has the motion picture industry failed to produce a Hollywood Shakespeare?

The answer, in part, lies with the problems a writer faces when he works in Hollywood. The novelist produces an individual product, which is at all times identified by the author's name—a sort of trade-mark. Sausages by Armour; *Grapes of Wrath* by Steinbeck. Mr. Armour has pride in his sausages, Mr. Steinbeck in his novels. But no similar sense of authorship has prevailed in America's third largest industry. Although writers of movies are paid more per word than any other class of scribblers in the history of pen and paper, they are as unknown and unheralded as the Arab campfire authors of the *Arabian Nights*. This phenomenon is more amazing when one realizes that their stories reach the largest audience the world has ever known—in America alone over 80 millions a week. This audience pays over $1,250,000,000 annually for the privilege of being entertained, but hardly a dozen per theatre could name the authors of the entertainment.

On the other hand, if a new playwright "arrives" on Broadway, his star immediately joins the constellation of Big Names, side by side and many times above the names of star actors. Within a short time playgoers eagerly await his latest play.

In Hollywood, where squads of writers have been assigned to single stories, no one writer can take pride in the finished product. *The Lives of a Bengal Lancer,* for instance, was re-written 34 times. In the making of a motion picture the story is filtered through so many personalities, from the writers through the producers and executives in the front office, through the director and actors, that little of the original light is flashed on the screen. Without getting into psychological labyrinths, suffice it to say that authorship is essential to a writer as much as motherhood is to a lady who has been delivered. The extension of the ego is a term psychologists also apply to architects, interior decorators, dress designers, and breeders of fine cattle. When this feeling of creation is blocked or diluted, the writer's creative individuality may find expression by wearing a football sweater with the letters RKO or MGM on it.

All of Hollywood's literary eccentricities, however, can't be blamed on producers or frustrated egos. Many of the successful novelists and playwrights who have been imported by Hollywood have been flops because they did not know how to write for the screen, and often weren't interested in learning how.

Aside from the effect of incompetence and thwarted authorship on a writer's stability, there's the little question of economic insecurity. This may sound a bit far-fetched in the face of $2,000 and $3,000 a week salaries, but actually only a handful of writers remain consistently in the big money. Officially, 1200 accredited writers are on call, like so many chorus girls beside a telephone, while hundreds in all degrees of obscurity appear at agent's offices and studio doors, hopeful of writing a bit role even for Poverty Row, that mythological street which winds through the bankruptcies of Hollywood. Of the 1200 only 300 work at one time, and these from periods ranging from three weeks to six months. It has been a tough battle for the average writer to keep up with the Grover Joneses.

Lately, there have been some curious changes in the writers' colony. There has been less excitement about pranks and more awareness of what's going on in the world.

Is this another fad, or an inevitable revolt? No one can say yet, but from all appearances long pants have at last come to Hollywood. At least, it is certain that these writers have let up on their frenzied individualism.

Perhaps Hollywood isn't as much fun today as it was in the salad days of hectic adolescence, but better pictures are being writen. Miracles do happen without camera tricks. The hacks have been jarred out of their hallucinations; the eccentrics have learned to economize in energy and money; and writers are slowly learning the technique of their craft. In all, there is a new feeling of cooperation between producers and writers. It begins to look as though the bad boys are outgrowing their rompers. A Shakespeare may be weaning at this very moment.

Wycherley, William (1640-1716). English dramatist. Attended Queen's College, Oxford. His first play, *Love in a Wood*, was produced in 1671 and had an immediate success. Accomplished and witty, Wycherley typified the Restoration Gentleman. In 1675, *The Country Wife*, and 1677, *The Plain Dealer*, were two plays which enjoyed great vogue. Congreve does not heitate to admit that he patterned his works and characters after Wycherley. His characterizations were ruthlessly realistic, bawdy and vulgar. They are a true barometer of Restoration Conduct and undoubtedly reflected the age in which he lived. That his plays have universal and lasting appeal is proven by their frequent revivals.

Wynn, Edward (Ed) (1886-   ). American actor. Born in Philadelphia, he ran away from home when he was fifteen to enter vaudeville, and worked in that phase of the theatre from 1901 to 1914. He was with *Ziegfeld's Follies*, 1914-15; appeared at the Winter Garden, New York, 1916-1917; played as a star there in 1918. He wrote the music, lyrics, and libretto of *Ed Wynn's Carnival*, 1919; *The Perfect Fool*, 1921; *Simple Simon; The Laugh Parade*. He was the first to broadcast the entire production of a musical comedy by radio. He became famous over the radio as The Fire Chief. He is one of the outstanding comedians of stage and air.

Wyspianski, Stanislaw (1869-1907). Polish poet, dramatist. Intensely nationalistic and idealistic writer, the influence of whose work extended through the years after his death. His plays may be grouped into those tragedies which portray the November revolution of 1830: *A Warsaw Song, Lelewel* and *November Night;* those in which he enunciates the aspirations of his people: *The Legion, Deliverance,* and *The Acropolis;* those in which he writes of the plight of the hapless peasant: *The Curse* and *The Judge;* and his historical dramas: *Boleslas the Bold, The Church on the Rick,* and *King Casimir.*

X-rays. Name applied to the first border lights, usually hung on the bridge.

Yale University. The Yale University Dramatic Association, long under the direction of Monty Woolley, later under the late Alexander Dean, is the undergraduate drama organization. In 1925, through the generosity of Edward Harkness, a department of Drama in the School of Fine Arts was begun under the chairmanship of George Pierce Baker, whom Mr. Harkness had persuaded to transfer his allegiance from Harvard to Yale to further the interests of the American Theatre. He assembled a faculty which has changed occasionally but has included Alexander Dean, Hubert Osborne, Donald Oenslager, Rose Bogdanoff, Evelyn Cohen, Stanley McCandless, Edward C. Cole, Frank Bevan, Agnes Young, Constance Welch, Philip Barber, Isabel Wilder; since Baker's retirement Allardyce Nicoll (present Chairman) and Walter Pritchard Eaton. Together with the courses in dramatic technique for which the Harvard home of 47 Workshop was famous, he offered the most complete course in theatre science given up to that time in America. Many Yale plays began to appear on Broadway and in the tributary theatres. In addition to dramatists, sufficient artists, educators and technicians were trained to staff many of the six hundred colleges and universities of the United States which have drama departments.

Yard. The central area in the Elizabethan public playhouses where less wealthy patrons stood to watch performances. It was open to the sky. Disparaging remarks made in Elizabethan drama to the groundlings refer to the type of people who usually occupied this area in the theatres.

See also *Pit.*

Yeats, William Butler (1865-1939). Irish author, dramatist. Born at Sandymount, near Dublin, the son of a distinguished Irish artist, he spent his early years mainly in County Sligo, memories of this county tingeing much of his early work, and in particular his first book of poems, *The Wanderings of Oisin,* 1889. As a young man he went to London, where he became a frequent contributor to the *Yellow Book* and a friend of W. E. Henley and William Morris. His first verse play, *The Countess Cathleen,* was published in 1892; his first volume of essays, *The Celtic Twilight,* in 1893; and the one act play, *The Land of Heart's Desire,* in 1894.

He was, with Lady Gregory and others, an inaugurator of the Irish Literary

Theatre, which gave its first performance in 1899, and which thriving in spite of much opposition, established itself in 1904 as the Abbey Theatre, Dublin, of which Yeats became a director. He dreamed of an Irish verse theatre, but his own verse plays, *The Shadowy Water,* 1900; *On Baile's Strand,* 1904; *Deirdre,* 1907; and *The Green Helmet,* 1910, though full of magnificent verse, were not sufficient to stem the tide of realism in the Irish theatre, and he gained more material success with his plays in prose, *Cathleen ni Houlihan,* 1902; *The Pot of Broth,* 1902; *The Hour Glass,* 1903; and *The Player Queen.* In his later years he experimented with fantasy in the theatre, seeking to escape from realistic formulas in such plays as the *Four Plays for Dancers,* 1921; *The Cat and the Moon,* 1924; *The Words Upon the Window-Pane,* 1930; *The Dreaming of the Bones;* and *Calvary,* by basing their format on the unrealistic tendencies of the Japanese *Nō* drama. In 1916, in the Introduction to *Certain Noble Plays of Japan by* Ernest Fenellosa and Ezra Pound, Yeats wrote: "In fact with the help of these plays . . . I have invented a form of drama, distinguished, indirect and symbolic, and having no need of mob or press to pay its way—an aristocratic form. . . . It is an advantage of this noble form that it need absorb no one's life, that its few properties can be packed up in a box, or hung upon the walls where they will be fine ornaments."

He was one of the most potent forces in the Irish literature revival of the early twentieth century, as was recognized when he was made a senator of the Irish Free State, 1922, and by the award of the Nobel prize for literature in 1923. He made for the Abbey Theatre, 1928, translations of Sophocles' *Oedipus the King* and *Oedipus at Colonus.*

Yegor Bulitchev and Others. Maxim Gorki (Russian). Tragedy. 3 acts. 1932.

The play opens at the time of the World War in the home of Bulitchev, a rich merchant. Sick with cancer, he still tries to be a war profiteer, and his family wait for his death, and discuss their possible inheritance. Meanwhile, there has been political upheaval in Russia and the revolution progresses to this mall town. Bulitchev, reluctant to forego his bourgeois possessions rushes to the door, on hearing the revolutionary singing and drops dead.

This is a naturalistic drama of the degeneration in the middle-classes just before the revolution.

Yellow Jack. Sidney Howard and Paul De Kruif (American). Drama. 3 acts. 1934.

A dramatic history of medicine's fight to isolate the typhoid germ—leading to Dr. Reed's discovery in Cuba of the Yellow fever-bearing mosquito.

The play is based on a chapter of "Microbe Hunters," by Paul de Kruif, and successfully translated heroes of science into dramatic terms.

The simple facts of the case are dramatic in themselves but Mr. Howard's treatment, showing the sacrifice of the lives of Drs. Carroll, Lozear and Agramont, bring home the great bravery necessary to true men of science.

Besides the doctors there were the privates in the American army who volunteered their services as guinea pigs, that the Yellow fever scourge might be wiped out.

Yellow Jacket, The. George C. Hazelton and J. H. Benrimo (American). 3 acts. 1913.

The story tells of Wu Hoo Git, elder son and hero of the House of Wu, and his struggle with a younger brother, Daffodil, for the Yellow Jacket, ruling symbol of the House of Wu. Surviving many adventures, and Daffodil's treachery, he finally wins the Yellow Jacket and takes as his bride the beautiful Plum Blossom, daughter of Tai Char Shoong.

Yeomen of the Guard. W. S. Gilbert. Music by Sir Arthur Sullivan. Operetta. 1888.

This opera is more realistic than other Gilbert and Sullivan works and concerns Jack Paint, the jester who must be funny. He is never taken seriously even when he tries to convey his love to Elsie Maynard, the young lady who accompanies him in his wanderings. She treats his passion lightly and marries a nobleman. This nobleman is about to be executed and she has married him simply to collect 100 crowns as his widow. When the nobleman manages to escape his fate, she realizes she is really in love with him and they re-marry. Jack Paint, who has been the heartbroken observer of all this, sings for *the love of a ladye* at her wedding, and falls prostrate at her feet.

Yes, My Darling Daughter. Mark Reed (American). Comedy. 3 acts. Printed 1937.

Twenty-five years after she campaigned for women's rights in Greenwich Village, Ann Whitman Murray finds her daughter, Ellen, leaving for a week-end with Douglas Hall. When Ann forbids it, Ellen produces a book of her mother's poetry which is autobiographical. The problem is solved, however, when, at the conclusion of the week-end, Ellen and the young man are married.

Yiddish Theatre in New York. The Yiddish Art Theatre was founded in 1919 by Maurice Schwartz. Their first performance was Hershbein's *An Abandoned Nook* at the Irving Place Theatre. Many of the players are still with the company, but some have become famous in other fields—as Paul Muni, Jacob Ben Ami and Joseph Buloff. They have their own playhouse now on 59th Street and 7th Avenue. Recent successes there were *The Brothers Ashkenazi* in 1937 and *The Three Cities,* 1939. They toured the globe in 1925 and again recently in *Yoshe Kalb.*

David Kessler's Second Avenue Theatre (12th Street and Second Avenue) is famous chiefly for its musical comedies. Molly Picon is the star. She returned from a tour abroad in 1932 and founded Picon Productions to make motion pictures of their productions in New York.

The Artef Players was founded about 1926 by Benno Schneider. For eight years the group served an apprenticeship and finally produced *Yegor Bulitchev and Others* in 1934 at Daly's 63rd Street Theatre. Their 1939 production was *Clinton Street.*

Jennie Goldstein, called the Eva Le Gallienne of the Jewish stage, has been popular for twenty-six years in the Bronx. About 1932 she became actress-manager in charge of the Prospect Theatre. She made her debut in 1903 (at the age of six) in a child role in Tolstoi's *Anna Karenina*. She has toured the United States, South America, Australia and Europe. A collection of photographs relating to her career are in the New York Public Library.

Boris Thomashefsky's Downtown National Theatre was already well-known in 1913 when Celia Adler, daughter of the actor Jacob Adler, made her debut in *The Eternal Wanderer*. Yiddish versions of plays by Hauptmann, Sudermann, Ibsen and Shakespeare have been given there. Thomashefsky's manuscripts were presented to the New York Public Library by Harry Thomashefsky after his father's death in 1939.

Yoke. Square "U" shaped metal strip for mounting spotlights.

York cycle. A series of forty-eight English miracle plays completed about the middle of the 14th century. These plays closely follow the Scriptures.

Yorkshire Tragedy, A. A Jacobean play assigned to William Shakespeare on the title-page of the 1608 quarto edition and included in the Third and Fourth folio editions of the poet's works in 1664 and 1685 respectively. Lacking the characteristics of Shakespeare's verse, plot technique, and characterization after 1605, the play has been generally rejected from the accepted canon of his works. The play is based on a sensational crime committed in 1605 by Walter Callverly, who was executed after he had murdered his two children and stabbed his wife.

You Can't Take It With You. Moss Hart and George S. Kaufman (American). Comedy. 3 acts. 1936.

The story of the mad, gay, Sycamore family, headed by Grandpa Vanderhoef. The family's philosophy is that wealth does not compare with the joy of human affection and the pleasure of doing what really interests them. In contrast to the Sycamores are the rich Kirbys who despite their wealth are basically unhappy. Handsome young Tony Kirby falls in love with Alice Sycamore, who is his secretary, and brings his parents to Alice's home for dinner to meet the family. The Kirbys arrive on the wrong night, are served a delicatessen supper and in the mad confusion that follows show themselves to be very snobbish. Alice realizes that marriage for her and Tony is impossible and goes away. Tony, however, will not give her up for he feels that his family is wrong. In the end, Mr. Kirby is won over to the Sycamore's philosophy and Tony and Alice marry. It was awarded the Pulitzer Play Prize for 1936-37.

You Never Can Tell. George Bernard Shaw (English). Comedy. 1899.

An impetuous and very poor young dentist, Mr. Valentine, gets himself mixed up with the domestically involved Grampton-Clandon family. He falls deeply in love with Gloria Clandon and she with him.

Before they can accept each other there are high social hurdles which must be disposed of, such as his pennilessness, her lack of a father, who incidentally is discovered to be Mr. Grampton, Valentine's landlord.

The story conveys but little of the theatrical charm of the play which lies in the exposition of many and varying types.

Young, Stark (1881-   ). American author, dramatist, dramatic critic. Born in Como, Mississippi; B.A. University of Mississippi; M.A. Columbia University; instructor of English at University of Mississippi, University of Texas and Amherst College; associate editor, *Theatre Arts;* dramatic critic, New York *Times, 1924-25;* now member of editorial staff of the *New Republic.* His plays include: *Guenevere* (verse), 1906; *The Saint, 1924; The Colonnade;* several plays for children, and a number of one-act plays. He is the author of So Red the Rose and other novels besides several books of criticism.

YOU WANT TO GO ON THE STAGE

BY ANTOINETTE PERRY

You want to go on the Stage. You are at the threshold of your career. What must you do to join the Pageant of the Theatre?

What gifts do you bring?

What lessons must you learn?

First and foremost your desire to act must be such that "many waters cannot quench nor neither can flood drown it." You must be confident of the terms of that desire. Be sure that your desire is not based on boredom, an urge for so-called Freedom, or the necessity of earning a livelihood. If these be your motivations, stop where you are, retreat with dignity and be grateful that you have been warned in time to save yourself wasted years and drab, dull heartaches. Boredom with life is a negative quality which makes disastrous cargo for anyone embarking on theatrical waters. Freedom and the Theatre are incompatible. For the Theatre is a despot, a tyrant to whom you must be willing to pay tribute with every breathing moment of your life. As for earnings, the novitiate is long, the fasting painful and at the end most fortunes in the theatre come from by-products of your art, infrequently from Acting itself.

Therefore: know yourself and your desires truly. Granted there are notable exceptions to all formulas, it cannot harm you to take stock of your equipment before casting off on your voyage.

Talent you must have. That indescribable power to create the illusion that you are someone else. And you must know with assurance that you CAN create an illusion. Beauty, or in its absence, personality; strength of body or its compensation in flexibility and expressiveness; and a voice which is not a monotone but which can be developed and whipped into submission; these are essentials. To these fundamentals add determination. Not stubborn, irritating determination, but a long-range determination that has no possible recognition of defeat, one that ploughs through, around or across every obstacle in its path.

Health is needed. A strong body, a rested body, one that can endure day after day of whirling, rushing activity; one that can withstand hours of static waiting, patient immobility.

The desire to be one of a Group and the stimulation of gregarious accomplishment are natural beneficial herd instincts. Those instincts should not be denied. They are the basis for normal response and reactions between players, for the fluidity of harmonious scenes, for the team-work of long established companies. The ability to work as one of a Group is an estimable quality.

But the courage to close the door, to work alone, away from the bolstering companionship and warmth of Group activity is the test of an artist. In the innermost sanctum you must face yourself and learn, by that communion, the truth and depth of your ambitions. Look into your spiritual and emotional background, into your mental storehouse. Have you consciousness of the spiritual as opposed to the material? Have you sympathy, understanding, patience? Do you respond to the excitement of crises with restrained control? Do you think vaguely, blurring your thought processes with muddled emotion and undisciplined prejudice? Or are your thoughts clear? translucent? Do they progress logically, crystallizing as they unfold into an edifice unclouded by irrationalisms?

Think clearly, feel deeply and know the strength of spiritual understanding.

Bring to the Theatre an education which is as broad as your opportunities. The more you know the more you understand, and the more you understand the clearer is your recognition of the viewpoints of other men and women, and the easier will be your task of interpreting their characters. Read, study, enlarge the horizon of your thought. "Get wisdom, get understanding, forget it not."

Develop the tools of your craft, namely, your voice, your body. Guard both well and train them to instantaneous response.

Make use of sports, of exercises, of dances, but be their master always. They must not master you. Play tennis, learn the freedom of movement, the quickness of eye that tennis gives. Play baseball, learn to jump, to run, to hurl a fast one, but don't, I beg of you, walk like an athlete, shake hands like an athlete or stand like an athlete, unless you are playing the part of an athlete. Learn to dance. Have control of your muscles, whether you dance adagio or swing, but don't swing when you should walk, or waltz when you should run.

Exercise your whole body. Not to create arm-swellings and chest expansions, which in an athlete gain the plaudits of the crowd, but teach your muscles quick, effortless response, so that when you sit down, stand up, walk, run, move about, turn, twist, or hold yourself in a suspended movement, your audience will be totally unconscious of the mechanics of control.

Remember, from the tip of your toes to the top of your head, there are muscles to be trained like soldiers in an army, ready to be called upon for service, to move your body as the body of each portrayed character should be moved: slow or fast, awkward or graceful, crippled or upright, aged or youthful.

Learn to speak, to cry, to whisper, to shout. Walk and breathe, run and laugh. Wake your body and voice into activity and learn through "doing" not "theorizing." Master speech, its rhythm, modulation, volume, dialect. Learn the mumble of illiterates, the stilted artificiality of middle-class snobbery, the gentle, the raucous, the sonorous, the whining. Study, strive and learn, remembering that only "Fools despise Wisdom," therefore to be no fool "Take fast hold of instruction; let her not go."

Bring as your offering your spirit, thought, body, voice, imagination, truthfulness, enthusiasm, sensitivity. In Short: mirror the World and the Stars in your understanding and never cease striving for perfection. And when your offerings are heaped high in your arms then in confidence, bring them to the door and knock—knowing at last you have earned the right to Begin.

Young Woodley. John Van Druten (English). Drama. 3 acts. 1925.

Rather vaguely derived from the theme of Frank Wedekind's play, *The Awakening of Spring*. Deals with the adolescent and English public school life.

The story of a young man who, being attracted to the wife of his master at school, suffers from the notion that he has done something dreadful. Although the episode develops to huge proportions in the boy's mind it fortunately has no lasting effect upon him.

Zangwill, Israel (1864-1926). Anglo-Jewish novelist, dramatist. Born in London, he became an elementary school teacher in Spitalfields, but, having become known for his short stories, soon devoted himself entirely to writing these and to miscellaneous journalism, founding and editing *Ariel, The London Puck*. The foundation of his literary reputation was his series of masterly studies of Jewish life of which a dramatization of his *Children of the Ghetto* was produced in both England and America. He was the founder and first president of the International Jewish Territorial Organization.

Other plays include *Merely Mary Ann,* 1904; *Too Much Money,* 1918; *The Melting Pot* (one of his best-known), 1914; etc.

Zanni. Descendants in the later Italy (of the *commedia dell' arte* period) of the earlier Roman, *sanniones*.

Zarzuela. A type of Spanish musical comedy.

Ziegfeld, Florenz (1867-1932). American producer. Known to his friends and the press as "Ziggy" and "Flo." The most powerful name in the history of American musical comedy and revue. His was an extraordinary personality, lovable, cold, suave, alert, driving, ethical, unethical and permanent, as human affairs go, in its influence. From the beginning of his career, when, as the son of Florenz Ziegfeld, Sr., President of the Chicago Musical College, he undertook to manage the bands of the Chicago World's Fair of 1893, Ziegfeld's aim was always the superlative. Resourcefully too, while managing Sandow the Great, he contrived to link up the strong man with Mrs. Potter Palmer, queen of western society, thereby making a side show performer a social favorite. Coming on to New York, the young Ziegfeld met Charles Dillingham, a former friend who helped him get started on Broadway, and who, with A. L. Erlanger, became eventually one of his partners. Ziegfeld's first important accomplishment was presenting Anna Held, vivacious French musical comedy star, to the American public. From her, it is said, Ziegfeld gained his epicurean taste for foods and his unprecedented sensitivity to luxury as manifested in his productions, his penchant for travelling abroad in royal suites and across country in his own private car. He originated the *Ziegfeld Follies,* a revue that ran through twenty-four editions and that penetrated to Palm Beach, Florida, for a glamorous mid-winter season. An inspired press agent, and an extraordinary judge of beautiful women, Ziegfeld won such a name for himself and his players that even obscure show girls like Olive Thomas, and Marion Davies, leaped from theatrical ranks to film stardom. Before many weeks passed the Ziegfeld girl had sloughed the Gibson girl out of existence. Ziegfeld built up his attraction by means of two slogans, "An American Institution" and "Glorifying the American Girl." Both ideals were realized in the fact that the Follies ran until Ziegfeld's death and then were taken over by the Messrs. Shubert in association with Billie Burke, (Mrs. Ziegfeld and mother of Patricia Ziegfeld,) herself one of the most popular stars of the American stage and now a film celebrity.

Ziegfeld was by instinct thoroughly American in spirit. He fostered Will Rogers when he was a crude cowboy comedian. He used Ring Lardner's sketches. He brought a team of boy horseshoe throwers from the south to take part in what should have been the first thoroughly American revue success, *The Comic Supplement,* by J. P. McEvoy.

Ziegfeld went in for society and the Four Hundred with astonishing success. He is credited with having introduced the colored shirt for men. He gambled prodigiously and lost fatuously. His clothes were faultless, his valet Sydney his constant servitor. He touched with a degree of fame almost everyone associated with him.

Among the composers, actors, singers, dancers and lyricists who took part in his shows were Gene Buck, now president of the American Society of Composers, Authors and Publishers, Grace Van Studdiford, Bert Williams, Eddie Cantor, W. C. Fields, Eddie Dowling, producer and star, Ray Dooley, Ann Pennington, George White, producer of the *Scandals* who grew to be Ziegfeld's rival, Joseph Urban, the painter and scenic artist, Irving Caesar, George Gershwin, Maurice Chevalier, Sigmund Romberg, Victor Herbert, Rudolf Friml, Vivienne Segal, Dennis King, Leon Errol, Elsa Ersi, Norma Terris, Ring Lardner, Will Rogers, Jack Pearl, Lupino Lane, who sprang to second fame through the English production of *Me and My Girl,* Dolores, Mary Eaton, Fred and Adele Astaire, Marilyn Miller, Mary Lewis, who became a star at the Metropolitan Opera House, Ina Claire, Brandon Tynan, first to tour in America in Ibsen repertory, Sammy Lee, Bobby Connolly, Ada May, Evelyn Laye, and scores of other notables.

Ziegfeld's wish to have a theatre of his own was gratified with the completion of the structure known since his death as the Loew's Ziegfeld Theatre.

He left a host of creditors, who banded together in an effort to collect the remnants of his estate. As long as there is a theatre, the *Ziegfeld* name will represent an engaging personal quality, superior achievement, innovation and a goading quest for perfection.

Zolotow's Guide. The informal name for the mimeographed list published weekly containing detailed advance information on proposed productions. Its official title is the *Advance Theatrical Guide* Samuel Zolotow, its editor, does the news of the Rialto for the New York *Times,* which he serves as theatrical reporter. He is generally regarded as the most astute of newspaper men dealing with theatrical news.

Zorilla, Francisco de Rojas (1607-1648). Spanish dramatist. Born in Toledo. From early manhood he was a successful dramatist. His distinguishing characteristic was that he made the *gracioso,* or clown, the chief personage in several of his *comedias.*

Principal works: *Del rey abajoninguno (No One Lower in Rank than the King),* also known as *El labrador mas honrado (The Most Honorable Peasant)* ; and *García del Castanar (Garcia of the Chestnut-Grove)*—one of the greatest of all Spanish *comedias* in its portrayal of certain features of the *pundonor* or point of honor. The main dramatic interest is found in the conflict between the *pundonor* and respect due the King.

Zorillay Moral, José (1817-1893). Spanish dramatist, poet. Born in Valladolid.

Principal work: *Don Juan Tenorio* (1844), a play based on the Don Juan legend which varies from Tirso de Molina's play, *El burlador de Sevilla,* in that Don Juan really falls in love with a girl and his soul is saved through her intercession.

BIBLIOGRAPHY

Compiled by George Freedley

This is a working bibliography. Only outstanding books in English printed in the last twenty-five years are included, except where the standard book is either still in print, or available in many libraries, or no book in English exists. A few books with foreign texts are included because of the introductions in English or because of the illustrations which are of great value to the student. For more extensive bibliographical information see Numbers 107-131.

The detailed contents of a number of anthologies are listed at the end of this bibliography.

Acting

1. BENSON, SIR FRANK: *I Want To Go On The Stage.* Do! Don't! How? London: Ernest Benn, 1931.
   A simplified manual for the acting aspirant.

2. BERNHARDT, SARAH: *The Art Of The Theatre.* Translated by H. J. Stenning. Preface by James Agate: London: Geoffrey Bles, 1924.
   The technique of acting, speech and make-up treated by one of the greatest actresses of all time.

3. BOLESLAVSKY, RICHARD: *Acting;* The First Six Lessons. New York: Theatre Arts, 1937. Fourth printing.
   An expert handbook for the student.

4. BOSWORTH, HALLIAM: *Technique In Dramatic Art.* A Delineation of the Art of Acting by Means of Its Underlying Principles and Scientific Laws, with Technical Instruction in the Art of Play Production and Public Speaking. Foreword by Oliver Hinsdell. New York: Macmillan, 1934. Revised edition. Illustrated.
   A practical textbook for school use.

5. CALVERT, LOUIS: *Problems Of The Actor.* Introduction by Clayton Hamilton. New York: Holt, 1918.
   A practical technical handbook for the apprentice actor.

6. CARROLL, SYDNEY W.: *Acting For The Stage.* Art, Craft, and Practice. Foreword by St. John Ervine. London: Pitman, 1938.
   Acting technique in rehearsal and performance, the relation of actor to audience, business arrangements including reproduction of standard London contracts.

7. CRAWFORD, LANE: *Acting, Its Theory And Practice.* Foreword by H. Chance Newton. London: Constable, 1930.
   Handbook for actors with examples of past and present players.

8. CROCKER, CHARLOTTE, VICTOR A. FIELDS and WILL BROOMALL: *Taking The Stage.* Self-Development Through Dramatic Art. New York: Pitman, 1939. Illustrated.
   This considers the technique of the actor; mono-theatre materials and techniques; dialects. Includes the texts of the following monodramas—*Prodigy; How To Win Friends; Magistrate's Court; Tea Time Tableaux; Canzonet; Gemütlichkeit; Hoot, Mrs. Tavish!; Comedie Italiana; Gaelic Mother-Touch; Rule Britannia.* Useful for radio auditions.

9. D'ANGELO, ARISTIDE: *The Actor Creates.* New York: Samuel French, 1939.
   A consideration of the evolution of character and the preparation of a role.

10. FRANKLIN, MIRIAM A.: *Rehearsal.* The Principles and Practice of Acting for the Stage. New York: Prentice-Hall, 1938. Illustrated.
    A practical manual for the amateur.

11. HARDEN, EDWIN LYLE: *Practice In Dramatics.* Selections for Study of Dramatic Values. Foreword by Jeston Dickey. Boston: Baker, 1936.
    This includes selections for response and reaction; transition; pantomime; characterization, etc.

12. HICKS, SEYMOUR: *Acting.* A Book for Amateurs. London: Cassell, 1931.
    This contains the script, *Scrooge,* with diagrams for its performance.

13. MACKAY, EDWARD J. and ALICE: *Elementary Principles of Acting*. Based on *The Art of Acting* by F. F. Mackay. New York: Samuel French, 1934.
A textbook aid for teachers and students.

14. MAULE, DONOVAN: *The Stage As A Career*. Preface by Franklin Dyall. London: Pitman, 1932.
A practical handbook on modern stagecraft for amateurs and professional aspirants.

15. ROSENSTEIN, SOPHIE, LARRAE A. HAYDON and WILBUR SPARROW: *Modern Acting: A Manual*. Foreword by Glenn Hughes. New York: Samuel French, 1936.
A handbook for the college student or little theatre actor.

16. SELDEN, SAMUEL: *A Player's Handbook*. The Theory and Practice of Acting. New York: Crofts, 1934. Illustrated.
A really practical handbook for the student which covers his training in considerable detail.

17. SPEAIGHT, ROBERT: *Acting:* Its Idea and Tradition. London: Cassell, 1939.
This considers the idea, tradition and technique of acting.

18. STANISLAVSKY, CONSTANTIN: *An Actor Prepares*. Translated by Elizabeth Reynolds Hapgood. New York: Theatre Arts, Inc., 1936.
A clear presentation of the famous Stanislavsky method of acting.
See also Nos. 36, 39, 63, 77, 204, 206, 209, 222, 301, 302, 307, 344, 365, 379, 380, 382.

Amateur Stage

19. CARTER, JEAN and JESS OGDEN: *Everyman's Drama*. New York: American Association for Adult Education, 1938.
A study of the non-commercial theatre in the United States, including full descriptions of the principal little, community and university theatres; a comprehensive treatment of the subject.

20. DEAN, ALEXANDER: *Little Theatre Organization And Management*. For Community, University and School. Including a History Of The Amateur In Drama. Preface by Walter Prichard Eaton. New York: Appleton, 1926.
This is still the outstanding book on the functional aspects of the little theatre.

21. MACGOWAN, KENNETH: *Footlights Across America*. Towards a National Theater. New York: Harcourt, Brace, 1929. Illustrated.
The first comprehensive study of the little theatre movement.

22. McCLEERY, ALBERT and CARL GLICK: *Curtains Going Up*. Foreword by Gilmor Brown. New York: Pitman, 1939. Illustrated.
Borrowing precedent from Macgowan, this history records the non-commercial theatre since the Depression.

23. PERRY, CLARENCE ARTHUR: *The Work Of The Little Theatres.* The Groups They Include, the Plays They Produce, Their Tournaments, and the Handbooks They Use. New York: Russell Sage Foundation, 1933.
An excellent handbook, now somewhat out of date.

24. STRATTON, CLARENCE: *Theatron*. New York: Holt, 1928. Illustrated.
A handbook of little theatre history, the beginnings of summer theatre, well illustrated.
See also Nos. 62, 70, 71, 72, 73, 74, 115, 294.

Anthologies (Full Length)

25. BORGEROFF, JOSEPH L., editor: *Nineteenth Century French Plays*. New York: Century, 1931.
Text is in French but the introductions in English are useful.

26. BRENNER, CLARENCE D. and NOLAN A. GOODYEAR, editors: *Eighteenth-Century French Plays*. New York: Century, 1927.
Text in French, introductions in English.

27. CHURCH, VIRGINIA, editor: *Curtain!* A Book Of Modern Plays. New York: Harper, 1932.

*28. CLARK, BARRETT H., editor: *World Drama*. Ancient Greece, Rome, India, China, Japan, Medieval Europe, and England. New York: Appleton, 1933.
   2 vols. Includes forty-six plays.

*29. COE, KATHRYN and WILLIAM H. CORDELL, editors: *The Pulitzer Prize Plays,* 1918-1934. Introduction by William Lyon Phelps. New York: Random House, 1937. Revised and augmented.
   Includes eighteen plays.

*30. COHEN, HELEN LOUISE, editor: *Longer Plays By Modern Authors* (American). New York: Harcourt, Brace, 1922.
   Contains evaluations of Clyde Fitch, Augustus Thomas, George S. Kaufman and Marc Connelly, and Booth Tarkington; together with four plays.

31. DEBENHAM, A. H., editor: *Seven Sacred Plays*. Introduction by Sir Francis Younghusband. London: Methuen, 1934.
   Includes notes on the producing of religious plays.

32. DE ROHAN, PIERRE, editor: *Federal Theatre Plays*. Introductions by Hallie Flanagan. New York: Random House, 1938. 2 vols.
   Includes six of the most important productions.

*33. DICKINSON, THOMAS H., editor: *Chief Contemporary Dramatists*. First series, Twenty Plays From the Recent Drama of England, Ireland, America, Germany, France, Belgium, Norway, Sweden, and Russia; Second series, Eighteen Plays From the Recent Drama of England, Ireland, America, France, Germany, Austria, Italy, Spain, Russia, and Scandinavia. Boston: Houghton Mifflin, 1915, 1921. 2 vols.

*34. DICKINSON, THOMAS H., editor: *Chief Contemporary Dramatists*. Third series, Twenty Plays From the Recent Drama of the United States, Great Britain, Germany, Austria, France, Italy, Spain, Russia, Hungary, Czechoslovakia, The Yiddish Theatre, and Scandinavia. Boston: Houghton Mifflin, 1930.

*35. DICKINSON, THOMAS H., editor: *Continental Plays*. Boston: Houghton Mifflin, 1935. 2 vols.
   Twenty plays from Russia, Belgium, Germany, Austria, Italy, Spain, Hungary, France, Czechoslovakia, and Sweden.

36. ELIOT, SAMUEL A., adapter and editor: *Little Theater Classics*. Boston: Little, Brown, 1918, 1920, 1921, 1922. 4 vols. Illustrated.
   Vol. 1—*Polyxena,* from the *Hecuba* of Euripides; A Christmas Miracle-Play: *The Pageant of the Shearmen and Tailors in the Coventry Cycle of Miracles; Doctor Faustus,* by Christopher Marlowe; *Ricardo and Viola,* from *The Coxcomb* of Beaumont and Fletcher; *The Scheming Lieutenant,* from the *St. Patrick's Day* of Richard Brinsley Sheridan.
   Vol. 2—*Patelin,* from *Maître Pierre Pathelin* by Guillaume Alécis; *Abraham And Isaac,* from *The Book of Brome* and the *Chester Cycle of Miracles; The Loathed Lover,* from *The Changeling* of Middleton and Rowley; *Sgnarelle, or, Imaginary Horns,* from Molière.
   Vol. 3—*Bushido,* from *Terakoya* or *Matsu* by Takeda Idzumo; *The Old Wife's Tale* by George Peels; *Pericles,* from Shakespeare; *The Duchess Of Pavy,* from *Love's Sacrifice* by John Ford.
   Vol. 4—*Shakuntala,* by Kalidasa; *The Wandering Scholar From Paradise,* by Hans Sachs; *All For Love, or The World Well Lost,* by

John Dryden; *The Martyrdom Of Ali,* from the Persian Miracle Play of Hasan and Husain.
An outstanding anthology with full and practical production notes.

37. *Famous Plays Of 1931, 1932, 1932-33, 1933, 1933-34, 1934, 1934-35, 1935, 1936, 1937, 1938-39.* London: Victor Gollancz, 1931-39. 11 vols.
Anthologies of popular plays, which have been successful in the commercial theatre.

38. *Famous Plays Of To-Day.* London: Victor Gollancz, 1930.
Includes six plays.

39. FRANKENSTEIN, LOUISE M., editor: *Dialect Play-Readings.* New York: Samuel French, 1937.
Valuable for the student or for radio auditions.

*40. GASSNER, JOHN: *Twenty Best Plays of the Modern American Theatre.* New York: Crown, 1939.

*41. HALLINE, ALLAN GATES, editor: *American Plays.* New York: American Book Company, 1935.
Includes eighteen plays, bibliographies, and chronological tables of American and European drama and literature.

42. LE GALLIENNE, EVA, editor: *Eva Le Gallienne's Civic Repertory Plays.* New York: Norton, 1928. Illustrated.
Includes four plays from Norway, Denmark, Italy and Russia.

*43. LEVERTON, GARRETT, editor: *Plays For The College Theater.* New York: Samuel French, 1932.
Includes twenty-eight plays.

*44. MACMILLAN, DOUGALD and HOWARD MUMFORD JONES, editors: *Plays of the Restoration and Eighteenth Century,* as they were acted at the Theatres-Royal by Their Majesties' Servants. New York: Holt, 1931.
This anthology contains twenty-four plays.

*45. MANTLE, BURNS and JOHN GASSNER, editors: *A Treasury Of The Theatre.* An anthology of great plays from Aeschylus to Eugene O'Neill. New York: Simon & Schuster, 1935.

*46. MILLETT, FRED B. and GERALD EADES BENTLEY, editors: *The Play's The Thing.* An Anthology of Dramatic Types. New York: Appleton-Century, 1936.
Includes twenty-one plays of all types.

*47. MOSES, MONTROSE J., editor: *British Plays.* From The Restoration To 1820. Boston: Little, Brown, 1929. 2 vols. Illustrated.
This contains eighteen plays with valuable introductions and bibliographies.

*48. MOSES, MONTROSE J., editor: *Dramas Of Modernism And Their Forerunners.* Boston: Little, Brown, 1931.
Includes sixteen plays.

*49. MOSES, MONTROSE J., editor: *Representative American Dramas.* National And Local. Boston: Little, Brown, 1933. Revised edition.
Includes fifteen plays.

*50. MOSES, MONTROSE J., editor: *Representative British Dramas.* Victorian And Modern. Boston: Little, Brown, 1931. Revised edition.
This includes twenty-three plays with valuable introductions and bibliographies.

*51. NETTLETON, GEORGE H. and ARTHUR E. CASE, editors: *British Dramatists From Dryden To Sheridan.* Boston: Houghton Mifflin, 1939.
An anthology including twenty-four plays and separate introductions for each dramatic type.

*52. PARKS, E. WINFIELD and RICHMOND CROOM BEATTY, editors: *The English Drama.* An Anthology 900-1642. New York: Norton, 1935.
This includes thirty-three plays.

*53. QUINN, ARTHUR HOBSON, editor: *Representative American Plays*. From 1767 to the Present Day. New York: Appleton-Century, 1930. Fifth edition, revised.
Includes twenty-eight plays and bibliographies.

*54. *Theatre Guild Anthology, The*. New York: Random House, 1936.
Includes fourteen plays produced by the Theatre Guild.

*55. THOMAS, RUSSELL, editor: *Plays And The Theater*. Boston: Little, Brown, 1937. Illustrated.
Includes twelve plays.

*56. TUCKER, S. MARION, editor: *Modern Continental Plays*. New York: Harper, 1929.
Includes twenty-two plays.

*57. TUCKER, S. MARION, editor: *Twenty-Five Modern Plays*. New York: Harper, 1931.

*58. WATSON, E. BRADLEE and BENFIELD PRESSEY, editors: *Contemporary Drama, American Plays*. New York: Scribner, 1931, 1938. 2 vols.
Five plays in each volume.

*59. WATSON, E. BRADLEE and BENFIELD PRESSEY, editors: *Contemporary Drama: European Plays*. New York: Scribner, 1931. 3 vols. Five plays in each volume.

Anthologies (One-Act)

60. BOURNE, JOHN, editor: *Twenty-Five Modern One-Act Plays*. London: Victor Gollancz, 1938.

61. CLARK, BARRETT H. and KENYON NICHOLSON, editors: *The American Scene*. New York: Appleton, 1930. Illustrated.
Includes thirty-four American plays.

62. COHEN, HELEN LOUISE, editor: *One-Act Plays*. New York: Harcourt, Brace, 1934. Enlarged edition.
Includes twenty-one plays, together with a brief history of the little theatre movement, etc.

63. COSGROVE, FRANCES, editor: *Scenes For Student Actors*. Dramatic Selections from New Plays. New York: Samuel French, 1934, 1935, 1937, 1939. 4 vols.
Useful for radio and student auditions.

64. DRUMMOND, A. M., editor: *Cornell University Plays*. New York: Samuel French, 1932.
Includes ten plays.

65. EASTMAN, FRED, editor: *Modern Religious Dramas*. New York: Holt, 1928.
Includes thirteen plays together with a bibliography.

66. EASTMAN, FRED, editor: *Ten One-Act Plays*. Chicago: Willett, Clark, 1937.

67. HUGHES, GLENN, editor: *Short Plays for Modern Players*. New York: Appleton, 1931.
Includes twelve plays.

68. ISAACS, EDITH J. R., editor: *Plays Of American Life and Fantasy*. New York: Coward-McCann, 1929.
Includes eighteen one-act plays which have appeared in Theatre Arts.

69. KATZIN, WINIFRED, editor: *Short Plays From Twelve Countries*. London: Harrap, 1937.
Includes the following countries: China, Japan, England, Turkey, Russia, Poland, Rumania, Austria, Germany, France, South Africa, and Canada.

70. KOCH, FREDERICK H., editor: *American Folk Plays*. Introduction "American Folk Drama in the Making" by the editor. Foreword by Archibald Henderson. New York: Appleton-Century, 1939. Illustrated.
Includes twenty plays, together with bibliography and list of productions and tours 1931-38.

71. KOCH, FREDERICK H., editor: *Carolina Folk Comedies*. Foreword by Archibald Henderson. New York: Samuel French, 1931. Illustrated.
   Fourth series of Carolina Folk-Plays, includes eight plays and an introduction.

72. KOCH, FREDERICK H., editor: *Carolina Folk-Plays*. New York: Holt, 1922. Illustrated.
   Includes five plays and an introduction by the editor.

73. KOCH, FREDERICK H., editor: *Carolina Folk-Plays*. New York: Holt, 1926. Second series. Illustrated.
   Includes five plays and an introduction by the editor.

74. KOCH, FREDERICK H., editor: *Carolina Folk-Plays*. Foreword by Paul Green. New York: Holt, 1928. Third series. Illustrated.
   Includes six plays and an introduction by the editor.

75. KOZLENKO, WILLIAM, editor: *The Best Short Plays Of The Social Theatre*. New York: Random House, 1939.
   Includes ten plays of the so-called left-wing dramatists.

76. KOZLENKO, WILLIAM, editor: *Contemporary One-Act Plays*. Radio Plays, Folk Plays, Social Plays. New York: Scribner, 1938.
   Includes ten plays.

77. LOWTHER, JAMES B., editor: *Dramatic Scenes From Athens To Broadway*. New York: Longmans, Green, 1937.

78. MARTIN, CONSTANCE M., editor: *Fifty One-Act Plays*. London: Victor Gollancz, 1934.
   Includes plays from England, Scotland, Ireland, Wales, Australia, Canada, America, and a number of translations.

79. MAYORGA, MARGARET, editor: *The Best One-Act Plays of 1937, 1938*. New York: Dodd, Mead, 1938-1939. 2 vols.
   Twelve titles in each volume, together with bibliographies and lists.

80. MAYORGA, MARGARET, editor: *Representative One-Act Plays By American Authors*. Boston: Little, Brown, 1937. Revised edition.
   Includes twenty-five plays.

81. MAYORGA, MARGARET, editor: *Twenty Short Plays On A Royalty Holiday* (1937 to 1940). New York: Samuel French, 1937. Illustrated.
   Includes twenty plays which are royalty free until January, 1940.

82. *New Plays for Men and Boys*. Thirteen One-Act Plays. New York: Samuel French, 1935.

83. *New Plays for Women and Girls*. Fifteen One-Act Plays. New York: Samuel French, 1932.

84. NICHOLSON, KENYON, editor: *Hollywood Plays*. Twelve One-Act Plays from the repertory of the Writers' Club of Hollywood, California. New York: Samuel French, 1930.

85. O'HARA, FRANK HURBURT, editor: *University of Chicago, Plays, Skits, and Lyrics*. Introductions by Whitford Kane and Beatrice Lillie. Chicago: University of Chicago Press, 1936.

86. *One-Act Play Magazine, 1937-1938 Annual Anthology*. Introduction by Alfred Kreymborg. New York: Contemporary Play Publications, 1938.
   Includes ten plays.

87. *One-Act Plays For Stage And Study*. A Collection of Plays by Well-known Dramatists, American, English, and Irish. New York: Samuel French, 1924-1938. A series of nine volumes with prefaces by different authors.
   Standard one-act texts.

88. RICHARDSON, WILLIS, editor: *Plays And Pageants From The Life Of The Negro*. Washington: Associated Publishers, 1930. Illustrated.
   Includes eight plays and four pageants.

89. RICHARDSON, WILLIS and MAY MILLER, editors: *Negro History In Thirteen Plays*. Introduction by Carter G. Woodson. Washington: Associated Publishers, 1935.

90. SAMS, OSCAR E., Jr., editor: *Tested One-Act Plays*. Introduction by William G. B. Carson. New York: Noble and Noble, 1939.
Non-royalty successes from school and college theatre groups. Including suggestions for playwriting and production. Thirteen plays.

91. SHAY, FRANK, editor: *Contemporary One-Act Plays of 1921* (American). Cincinnati: Stewart Kidd, 1922.
Includes twenty plays.

92. SHAY, FRANK, editor: *Fifty More Contemporary One-Act Plays*. New York: Appleton, 1928.

93. SHAY, FRANK, editor: *Twenty-Five Short Plays*. International. New York: Appleton, 1926.
Includes plays from Australia, Austria, Belgium, Bengal, Bohemia, Burma, Canada, China, Cuba, Denmark, England, France, Holland, Hungary, Ireland, Italy, Japan, Mexico, Norway, Russia, Spain, Sweden, Turkey, United States, and one from the Yiddish.

94. SHAY, FRANK, editor: *A Treasury Of Plays For Men*. Boston: Little, Brown, 1923.
Includes twenty-one plays.

95. SHAY, FRANK and PIERRE LOVING, editors: *Fifty Contemporary One-Act Plays*. Cincinnati: Stewart & Kidd, 1920.
Includes plays from Austria, Belgium, Bolivia, France, Germany, Great Britain, India, Ireland, Holland, Hungary, Italy, Russia, Spain, Sweden, United States, and two from the Yiddish.

96. SNOOK, LEE OWEN, editor: *The Second Yearbook Of Short Plays*. Evanston, Illinois: Row, Peterson, 1934. Illustrated.
Twenty-five new non-royalty plays designed for study and production.

97. SNOOK, LEE OWEN, editor: *The Third Yearbook of Short Plays*. Evanston, Illinois: Row, Peterson, 1936. Illustrated.
Twenty-five new non-royalty plays designed for study and production.

98. SNOOK, LEE OWEN, editor: *The Fourth Yearbook Of Short Plays*. Evanston, Illinois: Row, Peterson, 1938. Illustrated.
Twenty-five new non-royalty plays designed for study and production.

99. WILDE, PERCIVAL, editor: *Contemporary One-Act Plays From Nine Countries*. Boston: Little, Brown, 1936.
Includes plays from the United States, England, Scotland, Ireland, Germany, Austria, Hungary, France, and Russia.

100. WISE, CLAUDE MERTON and LEE OWEN SNOOK, editors: *The Yearbook Of Short Plays*. Evanston, Illinois: Row, Peterson, 1931. First series.
Twenty-five new non-royalty plays designed for study or production.

101. *Yale One-Act Plays*. New York: Samuel French, 1930, 1937. 2 vols. Vol. 1 edited by George Pierce Baker; vol. 2 edited by Walter Prichard Eaton.
Six plays in the first volume and nine in the second.

See also Nos. 8, 206.

Architecture

102. ISAACS, EDITH J. R.: *Architecture For The New Theatre*. New York: Theatre Arts, 1935.
Includes articles by Simonson, Pawley, Lescaze and Geddes.

103. SEXTON, R. W.: *American Theatres Of Today*. Vol. 2. New York: New York Architectural Book Publishing Co., 1930. Illustrated.
Same as following text.

104. SEXTON, R. W. and B. F. BETTS: *American Theatres Of Today*. Vol. 1. Foreword by S. L. Rothafel. New York: New York Architectural Book Publishing Co., 1927. Illustrated.

A well illustrated account of legitimate and motion picture theatres in the United States.

105. SHAND, PHILIP MORTON: *Modern Theatres and Cinemas*. London: Batsford, 1930. Illustrated.

An illustrated account of all modern theatres, legitimate and motion picture.

106. URBAN, JOSEPH: *Theatres*. New York: Theatre Arts, Inc., 1930. Illustrated.

Urban's ideas about theatre architecture and construction are of considerable value to the student.

See also No. 128.

Bibliographies

107. ADAMS, W. DAVENPORT: *A Dictionary Of The Drama*. A Guide to the Plays, Playwrights, Players and Playhouses of the United Kingdom and America, from the Earliest Times to the Present. Philadelphia: Lippincott, 1904. Vol. 1 A-G.

This invaluable work was never finished in print but it is to be found in many libraries and is a standard handbook.

108. BAKER, BLANCH M., compiler: *Dramatic Bibliography*. Introduction by Milton Smith. An Annotated List of Books on the History and Criticism of the Drama and Stage and on the Allied Arts of the Theatre. New York: Wilson, 1933.

This bibliography is particularly useful for the student of production.

109. BAKER, DAVID ERSKINE, ISAAC REED and STEPHEN JONES: *Biographia Dramatica, or, A Companion to the Playhouse*. London: Longman, Hurst, Rees, Orme, and Brown, 1812. Vol. 1, 2 parts.

An alphabetical list of British dramatists with lists of their plays and type of same, whether printed or not. 1764-1811.

110. DAMERON, LOUISE: *Bibliography Of Stage Settings*. To which is attached an Index to Illustrations of Stage Settings. Baltimore: Enoch Pratt Free Library, 1936.

A short bibliography, which is generally useful.

111. DANA, H. W. L.: *A Handbook On Soviet Drama*. New York: The American Russian Institute for Cultural Relations with the Soviet Union, Inc., 1938.

The outstanding bibliography on Soviet theatre, drama and stage.

112. *Dramatic Index, The*. Edited by Frederick Winthrop Faxon. Covering articles and illustrations concerning the stage and its players in the periodicals of America and England; with a record of books on the drama and of texts of plays published during 1909 to date. Boston: Boston Book Company, 1910-1939. 29 vols. The volumes for 1936, 1937 and 1938 were edited by Mary E. Bates.

This should be used to supplement the *Readers' Guide To Periodical Literature*.

113. ELDREDGE, H. J.: *The Stage Cyclopedia*. A bibliography of plays. London: The Stage, 1909.

An alphabetical list of nearly 50,000 plays by title, giving production and publication data; occasionally inaccurate.

114. FIRKINS, INA TEN EYCK, compiler: *Index To Plays,* 1800-1926. New York: Wilson, 1927, 1935. 2 vols. Supplement published in 1935.

Includes plays printed in English. There is an index by title and a few plays are arranged by subject.

115. GAMBLE, WILLIAM BURT: *The Development Of Scenic Art And Stage Machinery*. A List of References in the New York Public Library. New York: The New York Public Library, 1928. Revised with additions.

This is the outstanding bibliography on the subject and is to be found in many libraries.

116. GILDER, ROSAMOND: *A Theatre Library*. A Bibliography of One Hundred Books Relating to the Theatre. New York: Theatre Arts, Inc., 1932.
This is the most useful bibliography of its kind to be published to date. It includes informative notes on a hundred titles, together with additional books on the same subjects.

117. GILDER, ROSAMOND and GEORGE FREEDLEY: *Theatre Collections In Libraries and Museums*. An International Handbook. New York: Theatre Arts, Inc., 1936.
A brief description of collections of dramatic materials in the official depositories of twenty-two countries. There is an introduction by Rosamond Gilder and a chapter on fugitive material, its care and preservation, by George Freedley.

118. HILL, FRANK PIERCE, compiler: *American Plays*. Printed 1714-1830. A Bibliographical Record. Palo Alto, California: Stanford University Press, 1934.
This is of great value to all students of American drama.

119. HYATT, AEOLA L., compiler: *Index To Children's Plays*. Introduction by Cora Mel Patten. Based on *Plays For Children,* an annotated index, by Alice I. Hazeltine. Chicago: American Library Association, 1931.
The standard work on this subject.

120. Library of Congress, Copyright Office: *Dramatic Compositions Copyrighted In The United States,* 1870 to 1916. Washington: Government Printing Office, 1918. 2 vols. Supplement published monthly to date since 1917.
This contains a list of all plays and films copyrighted in the United States.

121. LOGASA, HANNAH and WINIFRED VER NOOY, compilers: *An Index To One-Act Plays*. Boston: Faxon, 1924, 1932. 2 vols. Supplement published in 1932.
The standard work.

122. LOWE, ROBERT W.: A Bibliographical Account of *English Theatrical Literature* from the Earliest Times to the Present Day. London: Nimmo, 1888.
The standard bibliographical work on this subject.

123. MACMILLAN, DOUGALD, compiler: *Catalogue Of The Larpent Plays in the Huntington Library*. San Marino, California: The Huntington Library, 1939.
An extremely valuable bibliography of plays in the handwriting of the authors or of copyists attached to the London theatres of 1737-1823.

124. MANTLE, BURNS, editor: *The Best Plays of 1919-1920, 1920-21, 1921-22, 1922-23, 1923-24*. And the Year Book of the Drama in America. Boston: Small, Maynard, 1920-24. 5 vols. Illustrated.
These volumes contain abbreviated texts of the ten outstanding plays of each season together with casts and production data for all plays produced in New York between June 15, 1919, and June 15, 1924.

125. MANTLE, BURNS, editor: *The Best Plays of 1924-25, 1925-26, 1926-27, 1927-28, 1928-29, 1929-30, 1930-31, 1931-32, 1932-33, 1933-34, 1934-35, 1935-36, 1936-37, 1937-38, 1938-39*. And the Year Book of the Drama in America. Boston: Dodd, Mead, 1925-1939. 15 vols. Illustrated.
These volumes contain abbreviated texts of the ten outstanding plays of each season together with casts and production data for all plays produced in New York between June 15, 1924, and June 15, 1939. The annual volumes are issued in the fall of each year.

126. MANTLE, BURNS and GARRISON P. SHERWOOD, editors: *The Best Plays of 1909-1919*. And the Year Book of the Drama in America. New York: Dodd, Mead, 1933. Illustrated.

This includes abbreviated texts of ten outstanding plays together with casts, and production data for all plays produced in New York between June 15, 1909, and June 15, 1919.

127. Monro, Isabel and Dorothy E. Cook, editors: *Costume Index*. A Subject Index to Plates and to Illustrated Text. New York: Wilson, 1937.
This index is essential for the little or college theatre.

128. Pawley, Frederic: *Theatre Architecture*. A Brief Bibliography. New York: Theatre Arts, Inc., 1932.
This is a handy volume for student use.

129. Shay, Frank, compiler: *A Guide To Longer Plays*. A List Of Fifteen Hundred Plays For Little Theatres, Professional & Stock Companies, Art Theatres, Schools, Amateurs And Readers. New York: Appleton, 1925.
First-rate bibliography.

130. Smith, Milton: *Guide To Play Selection*. A Descriptive Index of Full-Length and Short Plays for Production by Schools, Colleges and Little Theaters. New York: Appleton-Century, 1934. Illustrated.
A useful bibliography for the student and small library.

131. Shay, Frank, compiler: *One Thousand and One Plays for the Little Theatre*. Cincinnati: Stewart Kidd, 1923.
A bibliography of plays.
See also No. 222.

Collected Biographies

132. Brown, T. Allston: *History Of The American Stage*. New York: Dick & Fitzgerald, 1870. Illustrated.
This contains biographical sketches of the profession in America, 1733-1870.

133. Clarke, Asia Booth: *The Unlocked Book*. A Memoir of John Wilkes Booth. Foreword by Eleanor Farjeon. London: Faber and Faber, 1938. Illustrated.
This considers the whole Booth family in its relation to John Wilkes Booth.

134. Collins, Charles W.: *Great Love Stories of the Theatre*. New York: Duffield, 1911. Illustrated.
A readable account of certain famous love affairs of Nell Gwyn, Elizabeth Barry, Anne Bracegirdle, Peg Woffington, David Garrick, Dora Jordan and others.

135. Edwards, H. Sutherland: *Idols Of The French Stage*. London: Remington, 1889. 2 vols.
Vol. 1—Armande Béjart; Adrienne Lecouvreur; Madame Favart; Sophie Arnould; Mademoiselle de Camargo, are considered.
Vol. 2—Madeline Guimard; Madame Dugazon; Mademoiselle Clairon; Mademoiselle Contat; Mademoiselle Raucourt; Madame de Saint-Hubert; Rachel; Sarah Bernhardt, are treated.

136. Gilder, Rosamond: *Enter The Actress, The First Women In The Theatre*. Boston: Houghton Mifflin, 1931. Illustrated.
Concerns itself with the great women of the theatre including Hrotsvitha, Isabella Andreini, Madeleine and Armande Béjart.

137. Lyonnet, Henry: *Dictionnaire des Comédiens Français*. Biographie, Bibliographie, Iconographie. Genève. Bibliothèque de la Revue Universelle Internationale Illustrée, 1911-1912. 2 vols. Illustrated.
This is included because it is the standard dictionary of French actors.

138. Melville, Lewis: *More Stage Favourites Of The Eighteenth Century*. London: Hutchinson, 1929. Illustrated.
Biographies of Frances Abington, Sarah Siddons, Mary Anne Robinson and Dorothy Jordan.

139. MELVILLE, LEWIS: *Stage Favourites Of The Eighteenth Century*. London: Hutchinson, 1928. Illustrated.
Biographies of Anne Oldfield, Lavinia Fenton, Kitty Clive, Peg Woffington and others.

140. MOSES, MONTROSE J.: *Famous Actor-Families In America*. New York: Crowell, 1906. Illustrated.
Excellent account of the great American acting families.

141. NUNGEZER, EDWIN: *A Dictionary of Actors*, and of Other Persons Associated with the Public Representation of Plays in England before 1642. New Haven: Yale University Press, 1929.
A scholarly biographical dictionary.

142. ORMSBEE, HELEN: *Backstage With Actors*. From the Time of Shakespeare To The Present Day. New York: Crowell, 1938. Illustrated.
Highly entertaining and readable biographies of actors together with a critical analysis of the acting style of each.

143. PARKER, JOHN, compiler and editor: *Who's Who In The Theatre*. A Biographical Record Of The Contemporary Stage. London: Pitman, 1912-1936. Eight editions. 8 vols.
This is the standard work.

144. RASI, LUIGI: *I Comici Italiana*. Biografia, Bibliografia, Iconografia. Firenze: Fratelli Bocca, vol. 1, 1897; vol. 2, 1905. 2 vols. Illustrated.
A biographical dictionary of the Italian stage, which is included because of its importance and because of the lack of a large literature on the subject.

145. ST. JOHN, CHRISTOPHER, editor: *Ellen Terry And Bernard Shaw*. A Correspondence. Preface by George Bernard Shaw. New York: Putnam, 1931.
Both of these people are of so much importance to the theatre that their letters are invaluable.

146. SKINNER, OTIS: *Mad Folk Of The Theatre*. Indianapolis: Bobbs-Merrill, 1928. Illustrated.
Critical consideration of ten actors including Kean, Junius Brutus Booth, Dora Jordan, etc.

147. SKOLSKY, SIDNEY: *Times Square Tintypes*. Introduction by Gilbert W. Gabriel. New York: Ives Washburn, 1930. Illustrated.
This includes biographies of Ziegfeld, Belasco, Gershwin, Roxy, George M. Cohan, etc.

148. SMITH, WINIFRED: *Italian Actors Of The Renaissance*. New York: Coward-McCann, 1930. Illustrated.
Contains biographies of the principal players, as well as quotations from contemporary evaluations of their work.

149. WILLIAMS, H. NOEL: *Later Queens Of The French Stage*. New York: Scribner, 1906. Illustrated.
Sophie Arnould; Mademoiselle Guimard; Mademoiselle Raucourt; Madame Dugazon; Mademoiselle Contat; Madame de Saint Hubert, are the subjects of brief biographies.

150. WILLIAMS, H. NOEL: *Queens Of The French Stage*. London: Harper, 1905. Illustrated.
Armande Béjart; Marie de Champmesle; Adrienne Lecouvreur; Mademoiselle de Camargo; Justine Favart; Mademoiselle Clairon, are the subjects of biographies.

See also Nos. 107, 307, 387.

Commedia Dell' Arte

See Nos. 136, 154, 371, 372, 373, 374, 393, 399.

Costume

151. BARTON, LUCY: *Historic Costume For The Stage*. Foreword by B. Iden Payne. Boston: Baker, 1935. Illustrated.
This covers the whole field from 4000 B. C. to 1914 with notes on the execution of costume designs.

152. GREGOR, JOSEPH: *Die Masken Der Erde*. Munich: R. Piper, 1936. Illustrated. Included, though in German, because the illustrative material on masks is excellent.

153. KOHLER, CARL: *A History Of Costume*. Edited and augmented by Emma Von Sichart. Translated by Alexander K. Dallas. London: Harrap, 1929. With sixteen colour plates and about 600 other illustrations and patterns. Full consideration of period costume from the beginning through the 19th century including the prehistoric, Greek and Roman, Middle Ages, German, French, English, Norse, Italian, Spanish and Dutch.

154. KOMISARJEVSKY, THEODORE: *The Costume Of The Theatre*. London: Geoffrey Bles, 1931. Illustrated. Costume of all periods, including the commedia dell' arte, to the present day.

155. MACKAY, CONSTANCE D'ARCY: *Costume and Scenery For Amateurs*. New York: Holt, 1932. Illustrated. A practical working handbook with diagrams.

156. SAUNDERS, DOROTHY LYNNE: *Costuming The Amateur Show*. New York: Samuel French, 1937. Illustrated. A handbook for amateur producers with diagrams and patterns.

157. SHERINGHAM, GEORGE and R. BOYD MORRISON, editors: *Robes Of Thespis*. Costume Designs by Modern Artists. Preface by Rupert Mason. London: Benn, 1928. Illustrated. Costume for stage, opera and ballet, practically portrayed and handsomely illustrated.

See also Nos. 108, 115, 127, 209, 220, 237, 238, 239, 248, 365, 393.

Directing, see Acting; Production

Drama

158. BALMFORTH, RAMSDEN: *The Ethical and Religious Value of the Drama*. London: Allen & Unwin, 1925. A study of the influence of drama.

159. BALMFORTH, RAMSDEN: *The Problem-Play*, and Its influence on Modern Thought and Life. New York: Holt, 1928. The influence of drama set forth in the problem-play.

160. BLOCK, ANITA: *The Changing World in Plays and Theatre*. Boston: Little, Brown, 1939. An outstanding history of the modern drama and its reflection of contemporary life.

161. CARTER, JEAN and JESS OGDEN: *The Play Book*. New York: Harcourt, Brace, 1937. Illustrated. This covers plays, burlesque, harlequinades, comic opera, moving pictures, radio plays, choral reading, together with nine plays and some suggestions for the creative use of plays and playing.

162. CHANDLER, FRANK W.: *Modern Continental Playwrights*. New York: Harper, 1931. Extremely useful history of European drama from Ibsen to Giraudoux.

163. CLARK, BARRETT H.: *European Theories of the Drama*. New York: Appleton, 1929. This is invaluable for the student of the European drama.

164. CLARK, BARRETT H.: *A Study of the Modern Drama*. A Handbook for the Study and Appreciation of Typical plays, European, English and American of the Last Three-quarters of a Century. New York: Appleton-Century, 1938. Revised edition. The most influential dramatists are considered in this valuable history of the modern drama.

165. DREW, ELIZABETH: *Discovering Drama*. New York: Norton, 1937. An enthusiastic account of drama as literature as opposed to theatre, in which all the arts are included.

166. FORT, ALICE and HERBERT S. KATES: *Minute History of the Drama*. From
     Its Earliest Beginnings to the Present Day. New York: Grosset & Dun-
     lap, 1935. Illustrated.
     Popular history for the high school student.

167. GOLDBERG, ISAAC: *The Drama of Transition*. Native and Exotic Playcraft.
     Cincinnati: Stewart Kidd, 1922.
     The History of transition drama in South America, Spain, Italy, France,
     Germany, Russia, United States and in the Yiddish theatre.

168. HAMILTON, CLAYTON: *The Theory of the Theatre,* and Other Principles of
     Dramatic Criticism. Foreword by Burns Mantle. New York: Holt,
     1939.
     A consolidation of four earlier books of the same author covering the history
     and theory of drama and stage.

169. HARDWICKE, SIR CEDRIC: *The Drama Tomorrow*. Cambridge: The University
     Press, 1936.
     An inspiring lecture on the drama by a leading actor.

170. HARVEY, SIR PAUL: *The Oxford Companion to English Literature*. Oxford:
     Clarendon Press, 1932.
     This contains valuable information on the American and English drama.

171. HENDERSON, ARCHIBALD: *European Dramatists*. New York: Appleton, 1926.
     Of considerable interest and coming from the biographer of Shaw, it must
     command respect.

172. KOEPFLE, LEO G., editor: *Copyright Protection throughout the World*. Wash-
     ington: Department of Commerce, Bureau of Foreign and Domestic
     Commerce, May, August, September, October, 1936; January, 1937.
     VII Parts.
     The standard work on this subject.

173. KOZLENKO, WILLIAM, editor: *The One-Act Play Today*. A Discussion of the
     Technique, Scope and History of the Contemporary Short Drama. New
     York: Harcourt, Brace, 1938.
     Among the contributors are Percival Wilde, Walter Prichard Eaton, Barrett
     H. Clark, Glenn Hughes; full bibliography.

174. LITTLEWOOD, S. R.: *Dramatic Criticism*. Foreword by Sir Barry Jackson.
     London: Pitman, 1939.
     A controversial treatment of the subject.

175. NICOLL, ALLARDYCE: *The Theory of Drama*. London: Harrap, 1931. Revised
     edition.
     A consideration of the theory of drama, tragedy and comedy.

176. O'HARA, FRANK HURBURT and MARGUERITE HARMON BRO: *A Handbook
     of Drama*. Chicago: Willett, Clark, 1938.
     A popular handbook considering types and technique of the drama together
     with a brief dictionary of terms.

177. PERRY, HENRY TEN EYCK: *Masters of Dramatic Comedy and Their Social
     Themes*. Cambridge: Harvard University Press, 1939.
     An historical appreciation of comic dramatists from Aristophanes to Shaw.

178. SMITH, WILLARD: *The Nature of Comedy*. Boston: Badger, 1930.
     A history of comedy from its beginnings, together with a consideration of its
     ethical functions.

179. STUART, DONALD CLIVE: *The Development of Dramatic Art*. New York:
     Appleton, 1928.
     A one volume history of the drama which lays its principal emphasis on the
     writers who were responsible for changes in the cause of dramatic develop-
     ment.

180. WELSFORD, ENID: *The Court Masque*. New York: Macmillan, 1928. Illus-
     trated.
     Considers the origin and development of the masque in England, France and
     Italy; it is both colorful and scholarly.

181. WILSON, N. SCARLYN: *European Drama*. London: Nicholson and Watson, 1937.
    A one volume, popular history of European drama from the Middle Ages to the present.

182. YOUNG, KARL: *The Drama of the Medieval Church*. Oxford: The Clarendon Press, 1933. 2 vols. Illustrated.
    The most authoritative treatment of the subject in English.

See also Nos. 31, 65, 107, 108, 112, 113, 114, 116, 117, 119, 120, 121, 122, 123, 124, 125, 126, 129, 130, 131, 201, 263, 276A.

Drama, Regional, see Theatre, Regional

Dramatic Technique

183. ARCHER, WILLIAM: *Play-Making*. A Manual of Craftsmanship. Boston: Small, Maynard, 1923.
    First published in 1912, this is still a standard work.

184. BAKER, GEORGE PIERCE: *Dramatic Technique*. Boston: Houghton Mifflin, 1919.
    The outstanding volume on dramatic technique.

185. HAMILTON, CLAYTON: *"So You're Writing a Play."* Boston: Little, Brown, 1935.
    A popular manual for the embryo dramatist.

186. KROWS, ARTHUR EDWIN: *Playwriting for Profit*. New York: Longmans, Green, 1928. Illustrated.
    First rate book on dramatic technique.

187. LAWSON, JOHN HOWARD: *Theory and Technique of Playwriting*. New York: Putnam, 1936.
    An iconoclastic handbook of dramatic technique written by an outstanding left-wing dramatist.

188. OULD, HERMON: *The Art of The Play*. Foreword by Harcourt Williams. London: Pitman, 1938.
    A handbook of dramatic technique with special emphasis on the well-made play.

189. ROWE, KENNETH THORPE: *Write That Play*. New York: Funk & Wagnalls, 1939.
    A manual on dramatic technique, particularly intended for the American playwright.

Lighting

190. FUCHS, THEODORE: *Stage Lighting*. Boston: Little, Brown, 1929. Illustrated.
    An excellent text.

191. McCANDLESS, STANLEY R.: *A Method of Lighting the Stage*. New York: Theatre Arts, Inc., 1932. Illustrated.
    A short and popular form of his earlier *Syllabus of Stage Lighting*.

192. McCANDLESS, S. R.: *A Syllabus Of Stage Lighting*. New Haven: Whitlock's Book Store, 1931.
    A full treatment of stage lighting from an historical, theoretical and practical viewpoint.

193. RIDGE, C. HAROLD and F. S. ALDRED: *Stage Lighting*. Principles and Practice. London: Pitman, 1935. Illustrated.
    This fully illustrates the outstanding methods of stage lighting in readable form. The diagrams are helpful to the student.

194. SELDEN, SAMUEL and HUNTON D. SELLMAN: *Stage Scenery And Lighting*. New York: Crofts, 1936. Revised edition. Illustrated.
    A handbook for non-professionals.

See also No. 210.

225. BURRIS-MEYER, HAROLD and EDWARD C. COLE: *Scenery for the Theatre*. The organization, processes, materials and techniques used to set the stage. Introduction by Arthur Hopkins. Boston: Little, Brown, 1938. Illustrated.
> The most complete and comprehensive manual on the subject for amateurs.

226. CHENEY, SHELDON: *Stage Decoration*. New York: John Day, 1938. Illustrated.
> A complete study of scenic design from the Greeks to Broadway.

227. COGNIAT, RAYMOND: *Décors de Théâtre*. Paris: Editions des Chroniques Du Jour, 1930. Illustrated.
> Included for its excellent illustrations by leading French and Russian designers.

228. CRAIG, EDWARD GORDON: *On The Art Of The Theatre*. New York: Dodd, Mead, 1925.
> A valuable book for students of scenic design.

229. CRAIG, EDWARD GORDON: *The Theatre Advancing*. Boston: Little, Brown, 1919.
> One of the great innovators of the theatre, second only to Appia, considers design and production.

229A. FUERST, WALTER RENÉ and SAMUEL J. HUME: *XXth Century Stage Decoration*. Introduction by Adolphe Appia. London: Knopf, 1928. 2 vols. Illustrated.
> This is a comprehensive, well-illustrated history of modern scenic design.

230. GREGOR, JOSEPH: *Monumenta Scenica*. Denkmaler des Theaters. Vienna and Munich: National Library and R. Piper & Co., 1925-1930. Illustrated.
> A number of American libraries possess these magnificently illustrated volumes which record scenic art of the 17th-19th centuries.

231. GREGOR, JOSEPH: *Wiener Scenische Kunst*. Vienna: Wiener Drucker, 1924, 1925. 2 vols. Illustrated.
> This is included because of its valuable illustrations of scenic and costume design on the Viennese stage for the last 300 years.

232. HELVENSTON, HAROLD: *Scenery*. A manual of scene design. Foreword by Kenneth Macgowan. Palo Alto, California: Stanford University Press, 1931. Illustrated.
> A popular and useful book for the student.

233. JONES, INIGO: *Designs by Inigo Jones*. For Masques and Plays at Court. Introduction and notes by Percy Simpson and E. F. Bell. Cambridge: Oxford University Press, 1924. Illustrated.
> This is a magnificently illustrated catalogue of Jones' drawings.

234. JONES, ROBERT EDMOND: *Drawings For The Theatre*. Introduction by Arthur Hopkins. New York: Theatre Arts, Inc., 1925.
> Thirty-five half-tone reproductions including Jones's designs for *King Richard III, Hamlet,* etc.

235. JOSSIC, YVONNE FRANÇOISE, compiler: *Stage and Stage Settings*. Twenty plates. Philadelphia: H. C. Perleberg, 1933.
> Without text, these illustrations are intended for the student to stimulate his imagination in the design of settings.

236. MACGOWAN, KENNETH and ROBERT EDMOND JONES: *Continental Stagecraft*. New York: Harcourt, Brace, 1922. Illustrated.
> This book of modern European staging has had a profound influence on American methods and is of a practical as well as historical value.

237. MESSEL, OLIVER: *Stage Designs and Costumes*. Introduction by James Laver. Foreword by Charles B. Cochran. London: John Lane, 1933. Illustrated.
> Messel's designs cover enough ground to make them a useful source book for the student.

238. MOUSSINAC, LEON: *The New Movement in the Theatre*. A Survey of Recent Developments in Europe and America. With an introduction by R. H. Packman and a foreword by Gordon Craig. London: Batsford, 1931. Illustrated.

First rate account of the New Theatre with magnificent illustrations.

239. Museum of Modern Art, The: *International Exhibition Of Theatre Art*. January 16-February 26, 1934. New York: The Museum of Modern Art, 1934. Illustrated.

A catalogue of the famous theatre exhibition displaying scenic art from Inigo Jones through the great Adolphe Appia to the present-day designers.

240. OENSLAGER, DONALD: *Scenery Then and Now*. New York: W. W. Norton, 1936. Illustrated.

An informal history of scene design which is nonetheless authentic for all its delightful style.

241. RICCI, CORRADO: *La Scenografia Italiana*. Milan: Treves, 1930. Illustrated.

The text is in Italian but there are 205 illustrations.

242. ROSE, ENID: *Gordon Craig and the Theatre*. London: Sampson Low, Marston, 1931. Illustrated.

An authoritative consideration of Craig's work in England and abroad.

243. ROSSE, HERMAN: *Designs and Impressions*. Chicago: Ralph Fletcher Seymour, 1920. Illustrated.

A book of Rosse's designs.

244. SHERINGHAM, GEORGE and JAMES LAVER: *Design In The Theatre*. London: The Studio, 1927. Illustrated.

Study of 20th century stage design which includes contributions by Gordon Craig, Charles B. Cochran and Nigel Playfair. Excellent plates.

245. SIMONSON, LEE: *The Stage Is Set*. New York: Harcourt, Brace, 1932. Illustrated.

An expert analysis of staging problems in the Greek, Medieval, 19th century and modern theatre written by an authority in the field.

246. SIMONSON, LEE, editor: *Theatre Art*. New York: Norton, 1934. Illustrated.

This includes articles by Allardyce Nicoll, Paul Alfred Merbach, John Anderson, Oliver M. Sayler, and John Mason Brown.

247. *Theatre Arts Prints*. Introduction by John Mason Brown. New York: John Day, 1929. Illustrated.

144 plates recording scenery and theatres throughout the ages in England, on the Continent and in the Orient.

248. ZINKEISEN, DORIS: *Designing for the Stage*. London: The Studio, 1938. Illustrated.

A well illustrated volume outlining the principles and execution of scenic and costume design.

See also Nos. 110, 115, 155, 194, 209, 219, 220, 312, 324, 332, 344, 360, 361, 362, 365, 393, 398.

Theatre

249. ARCHER, WILLIAM and H. GRANVILLE BARKER: *A National Theatre*. Scheme & Estimates. London: Duckworth, 1907.

The standard work for planning a state theatre.

250. BALL, ROBERT HAMILTON: *The Amazing Career of Sir Giles Overreach*. Princeton: Princeton University Press, 1939. Illustrated.

An excellent treatment of the various stage presentations of *A New Way to Pay Old Debts;* a good example of how to write this kind of a book.

251. BERNHEIM, ALFRED L.: *The Business of the Theatre*. New York: Actors' Equity Association, 1932.

Assisted by Sarah Hading and edited by Alfred Harding, this is the most complete study of the business aspects of the American stage.

252. BROWN, IVOR: *Parties of the Play*. London: Benn, 1928.

An analysis of the component parts of the contemporary theatre.

253. BROWN, JOHN MASON: *The Art of Playgoing.* New York: Norton, 1936.

   The theatre as the author likes it; acting technique, realism, the audience, dramaturgy are among the topics considered.

254. BROWN, JOHN MASON: *Letters from Greenroom Ghosts.* New York: Viking, 1934.

   Admitting his indebtedness to Young's *The Flower in Drama,* Brown uses his dramatic imagination to advise modern day theatre people he admires including Cornell, O'Neill, Coward and R. E. Jones.

255. CHENEY, SHELDON: *The Art Theatre.* New York: Knopf, 1925. Revised edition. Illustrated.

   This new edition gives a valuable account of the art theatres in our own country and in Europe.

256. CHISHOLM, CECIL: *Repertory.* An Outline of the Modern Theatre Movement. London: Peter Davies, 1934. Illustrated.

   Contrary to the title, this is a study of the resident stock company and is not true repertory.

257. *Encyclopaedia Britannica:* "The Theatre and Motion Pictures." A selection of articles from the new 14th edition of the *Encyclopaedia Britannica,* an aid to the fuller appreciation of the theatre, motion pictures, and kindred arts together with descriptions of the technique relating thereto. New York: Encyclopaedia Britannica, Inc., 1933.

   Authoritative and written by E. F. Albee, E. W. Bates, W. T. Benda and others.

258. ERVINE, ST. JOHN: *The Organised Theatre.* A Plea in Civics. London: Allen & Unwin, 1924.

   A consideration of the theatre as a producing agency.

259. FLANAGAN, HALLIE: *Shifting Scenes of the Modern European Theatre.* New York: Coward-McCann, 1928.

   A lively description of the modern theatre in Europe, including Russia.

260. ISAACS, EDITH J. R., editor: *Theatre.* Essays on the Arts of the Theatre. Introduction by Edith J. R. Isaacs. Boston: Little, Brown, 1927. Illustrated.

   All aspects considered by a group of authorities including Simonson, Boleslavsky, Cheney, Pichel, Stark Young, John Mason Brown.

261. MILLER, ANNA IRENE: *The Independent Theatre in Europe,* 1887 to the Present. New York: Long and Smith, 1931.

   This is a useful study of art theatres in France, Germany, Russia, England, etc.

262. MITCHELL, ROY: *Creative Theatre.* New York: John Day, 1929. Illustrated.

   An analysis of the aesthetic principles of good theatre based on a sound historical knowledge.

263. MORLEY, MALCOLM: *The Theatre.* Foreword by George Arliss. London: Pitman, 1935.

   A lucid account of drama and stage in the 20th century theatre.

264. YOUNG, STARK: *Theatre Practice.* New York: Scribner, 1926. Illustrated.

   A consideration of the technique of theatre from a professional viewpoint.
See also Nos. 108, 112, 113, 115, 116, 117, 136, 160, 245.

Theatre, American

265. ANDERSON, JOHN: *The American Theatre,* and RENÉ FÜLÖP-MILLER: *The Motion Picture In America.* New York: The Dial Press, 1938. Illustrated.

   This is particularly valuable for its illustrations.

266. ANDERSON, JOHN: *Box Office.* New York: Jonathan Cape and Harrison Smith. 1929.

   The various problems which beset the commercial producer as the road, labor, censorship are here set down and clearly explained.

267. BROWN, JOHN MASON: *Upstage*. New York: Norton, 1930.
A well-considered history of the modern American stage.

268. BROWN, T. ALLSTON: *A History Of The New York Stage*. From the First
Performance in 1732 to 1901. New York: Dodd, Mead, 1903. 3 vols.
Frequently inaccurate but valuable as a supplement to Odell, though out of
print; found in many libraries.

269. CARSON, WILLIAM G. B.: *The Theatre on the Frontier*. The Early Years of
the St. Louis Stage. Chicago: University of Chicago Press, 1932.
Illustrated.
An excellent history which records the work of Sol Smith, Noah M. Lodlow,
Sam Drake, father and son, and other pioneer theatre people.

270. COAD, ORAL SUMMER and EDWIN MIMS, JR.: *The American Stage*. New
Haven: Yale University Press, 1929. Illustrated. (Vol. XIV of *The
Pageant of America*.)
An excellent one volume history of the American theatre.

271. CRAWFORD, MARY CAROLINE: *The Romance of the American Theatre*. Boston:
Little, Brown, 1925. Illustrated.
This is a readable short account of our stage.

272. DEUTSCH, HELEN and STELLA HANAU: *The Provincetown*. Introduction by
Kenneth Macgowan. New York: Farrar and Rinehart, 1931. Illustrated.
A fully documented history of the theatre which produced O'Neill, Susan
Glaspell and George Cram Cook.

273. DIER, CAROLINE LAWRENCE: *The Lady of the Gardens, Mary Elitch Long*.
Foreword by Burns Mantle. Hollywood: Hollycrofters, 1932.
Illustrated.
This is a study of a famous stock theatre, America's first true summer theatre.

274. DISHER, M. WILLSON, editor: *The Cowells In America*. London: Oxford University Press, 1934. Illustrated.
Aside from its biographical interest this contains an accurate picture of producing in New York, New England, the Middle West and deep South in
1860-61.

275. EATON, WALTER PRICHARD: *The Theatre Guild, the First Ten Years*. New
York: Brentano, 1929. Illustrated.
An objective and critical treatment of an important theatre in its great days.

276. EUSTIS, MORTON: *B'Way, Inc*. New York: Dodd, Mead, 1934.
Show business from the professional angle; includes copies of all theatre contracts for actors, managers, dramatists; a list of theatrical unions, addresses,
fee, affiliations, etc.

276A. FLEXNER, ELEANOR: *American Playwrights*: 1918-1938. The Theatre Re-
treats From Reality. Preface by John Gassner. New York: Simon &
Schuster, 1938.
A first-rate dramatic history brilliantly written from the left-wing point of
view.

277. GOLDBERG, ISAAC: *Tin Pan Alley*. Introduction by George Gershwin. New
York: John Day, 1930. Illustrated.
An account of popular American composers and their music.

278. HORNBLOW, ARTHUR: *A History of the Theatre in America*. Philadelphia:
Lippincott, 1919. 2 vols. Illustrated.
Frequently inaccurate but the anecdotal form makes it a readable and inter-
esting account.

279. KRUTCH, JOSEPH WOOD: *The American Drama since 1918*. An Informal
History. New York: Random House, 1939.
An interesting history of the recent theatre by the dramatic critic of *The
Nation*.

280. LEAVITT, M. B.: *Fifty Years in Theatrical Management*. New York: Broadway Publishing Co., 1912. With more than 500 illustrations.
> This gives a valuable account of the business methods utilized by American producers.

281. MANTLE, BURNS: *Contemporary American Playwrights*. New York: Dodd, Mead, 1938.
> A new writing of his earlier *American Playwrights of Today*, 1929; this covers all dramatists of even minor fame which makes it an essential desk book.

282. MAYORGA, MARGARET G.: *A Short History Of The American Drama*. Commentaries On Plays Prior to 1920. New York: Dodd, Mead, 1932. Illustrated.
> A handy volume which is particularly useful because of its arrangement of plays by type.

283. MODERWELL, HIRAM KELLY: *The Theatre of Today*. Introduction by John Mason Brown. London: John Lane, 1927. Illustrated.
> A description of the new forces which entered into the development of the American theatre, 1917-27.

284. MOSES, MONTROSE J.: *The American Dramatist*. Boston: Little, Brown, 1925. Illustrated.
> A critical and analytical survey of American playwrights from Colonial times to O'Neill; it also contains biographical data.

285. MOSES, MONTROSE J. and JOHN MASON BROWN, editors: *The American Theatre as Seen by Its Critics, 1752-1934*. Introduction by John Mason Brown. New York: Norton, 1934.
> A compendium of American dramatic critics' reviews of outstanding performances together with brief biographies of the critics.

286. NATHAN, GEORGE JEAN: *The House of Satan*. New York: Knopf, 1926.
> Collection of America's most iconoclastic critic's pronouncements on the drama.

287. NATHAN, GEORGE JEAN: *The Morning after the First Night*. New York: Knopf, 1938.
> One of many collections of Nathan's criticisms.

288. ODELL, GEORGE C. D.: *Annals Of The New York Stage*. New York: Columbia University Press, 1927-1939. 11 vols. Illustrated.
> A monumental and magnificent work detailing the history of the New York stage, Professor Odell plans to bring it down to 1900.

289. POLLOCK, THOMAS CLARK: *The Philadelphia Theatre In the Eighteenth Century*. Together with the Day Book of the same period. Foreword by Arthur Hobson Quinn. Philadelphia: University of Pennsylvania Press, 1933.
> A factual treatment of the subject.

290. QUINN, ARTHUR HOBSON: *A History of the American Drama, from the Beginning to the Civil War*. 1 vol.; *From the Civil War to the Present Day*, 2 vols. New York: Harper, 1923, 1927. 3 vols.
> This is a full history of the development of American drama, with invaluable bibliographies.

291. REED, JOSEPH VERNER: *The Curtain Falls*. New York: Harcourt, Brace, 1935. Illustrated.
> A sardonic exposé of the author's first experiences in the New York theatre.

292. RENTON, EDWARD: *The Vaudeville Theatre*. Building, Operation, Management. New York: Gotham Press, 1918.
> How to run a vaudeville theatre; though vaudeville has almost died out the methods of the house manager are still valuable.

293. RYAN, KATE: *Old Boston Museum Days*. Boston: Little, Brown, 1915. Illustrated.
> A gossipy account of the most important 19th century Boston playhouse.

294. SAYLER, OLIVER M.: *Our American Theatre.* New York: Brentano, 1923.
A study of the American drama and stage of the 20th century, which considers the Little Theatre movement and the art theatres as well as the commercial theatre. It also contains a list of the more important productions from 1908 to 1923.

295. SCHICK, JOSEPH S.: *The Early Theatre in Eastern Iowa.* Cultural Beginnings and the Rise of the Theatre in Davenport and Eastern Iowa, 1936-1863. Chicago: The University of Chicago Press, 1939.
Complete, scholarly, of historical value as an example of the treatment of regional theatre.

296. SCOTT, MARIAN: *Chautauqua Caravan.* New York: Appleton-Century, 1939. Illustrated.
An informal account of that part of the theatre the country districts see at the present time.

297. SMITH, SOL: *Theatrical Management,* in the West and South For Thirty Years. New York: Harper, 1868.
Of great value to students of American Theatre in the 1830-60 period.

298. WHITMAN, WILLSON: *Bread and Circuses.* New York: Oxford University Press, 1937.
A highly eulogistic account of the first two years of the late lamented Federal Theatre.

299. WILLIS, EOLA: *The Charleston Stage in the XVIII Century.* With Social Settings of the Time. Columbia, S. C.: The State Company, 1924. Illustrated.
Informal history which endeavors to sustain Charleston's first place in early American theatre.

300. WILSON, ARTHUR HERMAN: A History of the Philadelphia Theatre, 1835 to 1855. Foreword by Arthur Hobson Quinn. Philadelphia: University of Pennsylvania Press, 1935.
A scholarly study.

301. WINTER, WILLIAM: *Other Days.* Being Chronicles and Memories of the Stage. New York: Moffat, Yard, 1908. Illustrated.
Essays on acting and actors including Brougham, Boucicault, E. A. Sothern, McCullough, etc.

302. WINTER, WILLIAM: *Vagrant Memories.* Being Further Recollections of Other Days. New York: George H. Doran, 1915. Illustrated.
Included to point the way to earlier books by a distinguished dramatic critic, this is primarily an analysis of acting on the American stage.

303. WOOLLCOTT, ALEXANDER: *Enchanted Aisles.* New York: Putnam, 1924.
A collection of the author's dramatic critiques.

304. YOUNG, STARK: *The Flower in Drama.* New York: Scribner's, 1923.
One of several books of criticism by the dramatic critic of the *New Republic.*
See also Numbers 30, 53, 70, 71, 72, 73, 74, 103, 104, 118, 120, 124, 125, 126, 132, 133, 140, 142, 143, 146, 147, 170.

Theatre, English

305. ADAMS, J. Q.: *Shakespearean Playhouses.* Boston: Houghton, Mifflin, 1917. Illustrated.
Well illustrated study of this subject by the director of the Folger Shakespeare Library.

306. AGATE, JAMES: *The English Dramatic Critics.* An Anthology, 1660-1932. London: Arthur Barker, 1932.
Quite aside from its value as a record of criticism, it is a compendium of acting as well.

307. ARTHUR, SIR GEORGE: *From Phelps To Gielgud.* Reminiscences of the Stage

through Sixty-Five Years. With an introduction by John Gielgud. London: Chapman & Hall, 1936. Illustrated.

Primarily concerned with actors, among those included are Modjeska, Bernhardt, Terry, Tree.

308. BAKER, GEORGE PIERCE: *The Development Of Shakespeare as a Dramatist.* New York: Macmillan, 1917.

A thorough and painstaking study of Shakespeare's dramatic technique by the man who taught playwriting both at Harvard and Yale.

309. BAKER, H. BARTON: *History of the London Stage,* and Its Famous Players (1576-1903). London: George Routledge, 1904. Illustrated.

With Doran, Baker is included because he is authoritative.

310. BEERBOHM, SIR MAX: *Around Theatres.* New York: Knopf, 1930. 2 vols.

These informal dramatic essays are concerned with the English stage between 1898 and 1910.

311. BISHOP, G. W.: *Barry Jackson and the London Stage.* Foreword by Charles B. Cochran. London: Arthur Barker, 1933. Illustrated.

This covers many of the most important London productions of the last twenty-five years.

312. CAMPBELL, LILY B.: *Scenes and Machines on the English Stage during the Renaissance.* New York: Macmillan, 1923. Illustrated.

Miss Campbell covers not only the English but the Italian stage of the 14th and 15th centuries and is valuable for both.

313. CHAMBERS, E. K.: *The Elizabethan Stage.* New York: Oxford University Press, 1923. 4 vols.

An exhaustive work which carries on from the point at which his Medieval volumes end.

314. CHAMBERS, E. K.: *The Mediaeval Stage.* New York: Oxford University Press, 1903. 2 vols.

Treats minstrelsy, folk and religious plays and the interlude both in England and on the Continent.

315. CHAMBERS, E. K.: *William Shakespeare.* A Study of Facts and Problems. New York: Oxford University Press, 1930. 2 vols.

This is the one essential volume for the Shakespearian student.

316. DICKINSON, THOMAS H.: *The Contemporary Drama Of England.* Boston: Little, Brown, 1931. Revised edition.

Scholarly and readable, an excellent combination for the student.

317. DISHER, M. WILLSON: *Music Hall Parade.* New York: Scribner, 1938. Illustrated.

Beautifully illustrated account of English music halls, including singers, minstrels, comedians.

318. DOBRÉE, BONAMY: *Restoration Tragedy,* 1660-1700. New York: Oxford University Press, 1927.

Companion piece to the same author's *Restoration Comedy* (same publisher, 1924), both of which are useful.

319. DORAN, JOHN: *Annals of The English Stage,* from Thomas Betterton to Edmund Kean. Edited and revised by Robert W. Lowe. London: Nimmo, 1888. 3 vols. Illustrated.

Though old, this is still outstanding in its field and is available in many libraries.

320. ELLIS-FERMOR, U. M.: *The Jacobean Drama.* An Interpretation. London: Methuen, 1936.

A short history which gives valuable data on the principal dramatists as well as on the general dramatic theories of the times.

321. GOLDIE, GRACE WYNDHAM: *The Liverpool Repertory Theatre, 1911-1934.* Liverpool: The University Press, 1935. Illustrated.

A history of a standard resident stock company.

322. HOTSON, LESLIE: *The Commonwealth And Restoration Stage*. Cambridge: Harvard University Press, 1928. Illustrated.
An excellent standard text on this phase of the English theatre.

323. ISAACS, SIDNEY C.: *The Law Relating to Theatres, Music-Halls, and Other Public Entertainments, and to the Performers Therein, Including the Law of Musical and Dramatic Copyright*. Foreword by Henry A. McCardie. London: Stevens and Sons, 1927.
Essential for those concerned with legal aspects of the English stage.

324. LAWRENCE, W. J.: *The Elizabethan Playhouse And Other Studies*. Philadelphia: Lippincott, 1913.
Specialized studies of the stage conventions and physical arrangements of the theatres in Shakespeare's day.

325. LAWRENCE, W. J.: *Old Theatre Days and Ways*. London: Harrap, 1935. Illustrated.
Informal treatment of many minor topics of the English stage, 16th-18th centuries, including prompting, admission systems, the green room, the royal box, etc.

326. LEE, SIR SIDNEY: *Life Of William Shakespeare*. New York: Macmillan, 1929.
This is the best short life of Shakespeare.

327. MACMILLAN, DOUGALD, editor: *Drury Lane Calendar 1747-1776*. Compiled from the Playbills. Introduction by Dougald MacMillan. Oxford: The Clarendon Press, 1938.
Published in co-operation with the Huntington Library, this is a day book of Drury Lane casts and box office receipts.

328. MASON, A. E. W.: *Sir George Alexander And The St. James Theatre*. London: Macmillan, 1935. Illustrated.
Interesting for its picture of Wilde, Pinero, Mrs. Patrick Campbell as well as Alexander.

329. NETTLETON, GEORGE HENRY: *English Drama Of The Restoration and Eighteenth Century*. New York: Macmillan, 1921.
A sound study of the period.

330. NICOLL, ALLARDYCE: *British Drama*. New York: Crowell, 1925. Illustrated.
A convenient general history in one volume; to be used with works of more specific nature.

331. NICOLL, ALLARDYCE: *A History Of The Restoration Drama, 1660-1700; Early Eighteenth Century Drama, 1700-1750; Late Eighteenth Century Drama, 1750-1800; Early Nineteenth Century Drama, 1800-1850*. 2 vols. Cambridge: Cambridge University Press, 1923-1930. 5 vols.
Invaluable books which contain hand lists of English plays of known and unknown authorship.

332. NICOLL, ALLARDYCE: *Stuart Masques and the Renaissance Stage*. London: Harrap, 1937. Illustrated.
A comprehensive treatment of the staging of masques, magnificently illustrated.

333. RODWAY, PHYLLIS PHILIP and LOIS RODWAY SLINGSBY: *Philip Rodway and A Tale of Two Theatres*. Birmingham: Cornish Brothers, 1934. Illustrated.
This life of Rodway is a prerequisite for a study of the Birmingham (England) stage.

334. ROSENFELD, SYBIL: *Strolling Players and Drama in the Provinces, 1660-1765*. Cambridge: Cambridge University Press, 1939.
A useful and well-written commentary on the companies which performed in the smaller cities and country districts of England, with particular emphasis on the theatres of Bath, Bristol, Norwich, Ipswich, York, etc.

335. SHORT, ERNEST and ARTHUR COMPTON-RICKETT: *Ring Up The Curtain*.
Being a Pageant of English Entertainment Covering Half a Century.
London: Herbert Jenkins, 1938. Illustrated.

   A study of comic opera, Gilbert and Sullivan, music halls, and stage revues
   of the last fifty years in England.

336. STEIN, ELIZABETH P.: *David Garrick, Dramatist*. New York: The Modern
Language Association of America, 1938. Illustrated.

   Shows Garrick's place in English drama with treatment in general of pantomimes, burlesque, interludes, Christmas and musical plays, etc.

337. THORNDIKE, ASHLEY: *English Comedy*. New York: Macmillan, 1929.

   A history of comedy in English drama.

338. THORNDIKE, SYBIL and RUSSELL: *Lilian Baylis*. London: Chapman & Hall,
1938.

   This biography discusses the Old Vic, built as the Royal Coburg Theatre, as
   well as the life of the woman who made its reopening possible.

339. WARD, A. W. and A. R. WALTER, editors: *The Cambridge History Of English Literature*. Vols. V and VI. The Drama. New York: Putnam, 1910.

   English drama is fully considered in volumes five and six of this great work.

340. WATSON, ERNEST BRADLEE: *Sheridan to Robertson*. A Study of the Nine-
teenth-Century London Stage. Foreword by George Pierce Baker. Cambridge: Harvard University Press, 1926. Illustrated.

   Readable and authoritative history of the English stage.

341. WELLS, HENRY W.: *Elizabethan and Jacobean Playwrights*. New York:
Columbia University Press, 1939. Illustrated.

   This author takes up each type of drama of the period, showing its use by
   each of the principal dramatists.

342. WILLIAMS, HARCOURT, editor: *Vic-Wells,* The Work of Lilian Baylis. London: Cobden-Sanderson, 1938. Illustrated.

   An account of the recent years of Sadlers Wells and the Old Vic.

343. WILSON, A. E.: *Christmas Pantomime*. The Story of an English Institution.
London: Allen & Unwin, 1934. Illustrated.

   A history of a favorite English type of musical show from its beginnings.

See also Nos. 47, 50, 51, 109, 114, 122, 123, 134, 138, 139, 141, 143, 145, 146,
   170, 180, 223, 261.

Theatre, Far Eastern

344. ARLINGTON, L. C.: *The Chinese Drama*. From the Earliest Times until
To-Day. With a Pien by Mei Lan-fang. Foreword by H. A. Giles.
Shanghai: Kelly and Walsh, 1930. Illustrated.

   This is a panoramic study of the Chinese theatre, tracing its origin and
   describing its actors, costumes, make-up, superstitions, stage slang, etc., together with synopses of thirty Chinese plays.

345. KEITH, A. BERRIEDALE: *The Sanskrit Drama*. New York: Oxford University
Press, 1924.

   This is the outstanding study of the classic Hindu drama.

346. KINCAID, ZOË: *Kabuki, the Popular Stage of Japan*. New York: Macmillan,
1925. Illustrated.

   Drawing on Japanese authorities and including much contemporary observation, this book is of particular value to the student.

347. LOMBARD, FRANK ALANSON: *An Outline History of the Japanese Drama*.
Boston: Houghton Mifflin, 1929.

   This covers the development of the drama.

348. ZUCKER, ADOLPH E.: *The Chinese Theatre*. Boston: Little, Brown, 1925.
Illustrated.

   This combines an estimate of Chinese drama with an account of the development of the conventions of its theatre.

See also No. 396.

Theatre, French

349. CHANDLER, FRANK W.: *The Contemporary Drama of France*. Boston: Little, Brown, 1925.
Of high value to the student of French drama from Sardou to the date of publication.

350. HAWKINS, FREDERICK: *The French Stage in the Eighteenth Century*. 2 vols. London: Chapman and Hall, 1888.
Even now the best and most available study of the French stage of this period.

351. MATTHEWS, BRANDER: *French Dramatists of the Nineteenth Century*. New York: Scribner, 1905.
Somewhat dated but a readable and useful account of an important period in French drama.

352. MATTHEWS, BRANDER: *The Theatres of Paris*. London: Sampson Low, Marston, Searle, and Rivington, 1880. Illustrated.
This is still the outstanding book in English on the Parisian theatre.

353. MOORE, A. P.: *The Genre Poissard and the French Stage of the Eighteenth Century*. New York: The Institute of French Studies, Inc.: Columbia University, 1935. Illustrated.
This shows the influence which plays, dialogues, etc., written in the 17th and 18th centuries in the gutter dialect had on French drama and stage.

354. PALMER, JOHN: *Molière*. New York: Brewer & Warren, 1930.
This is included because there is no satisfactory history of the whole French theatre published in English.

355. PALMER, JOHN: *Studies in the Contemporary Theatre*. Boston: Little, Brown, 1927.
Primarily concerned with the French theatre since the First World War.

356. WAXMAN, S. M.: *Antoine and the Théâtre Libre*. Cambridge: Harvard University Press, 1926.
Included because of Antoine's great influence on the foreign theatre as well as on his own stage.
See also Nos. 26, 135, 137, 149, 150, 180, 227, 261, 357.

Theatre, German

357. BRANDES, GEORG: *Main Currents in Nineteenth Century Literature*. New York: Boni & Liveright. 1924. 6 vols.
The second volume, *The Romantic School in Germany* and the fifth, *The Romantic School in France* are especially helpful to the student of the theatre.

358. BRANDES, GEORG: *Wolfgang Goethe*. Boston: Little, Brown, 1924.
Included because an understanding of Goethe is important and because no general history of the German theatre exists in English.

359. CAMPBELL, T. M., editor: *German Plays of the 19th Century*. New York: Crofts, 1930.
The texts of the plays are in German but the highly informative introductions are in English.

360. *Deutsche Buhnenbild, Das,* 1933-1936. Foreword by Joseph Goebbels. Introduction by Benno Von Arent. Berlin: Leonhard Preiss Verlag, 1938. Illustrated.
No text; this is included because the handsome illustrations afford a picture of scenic art in Germany since 1933.

361. ROTHE, HANS: *Max Reinhardt, 25 Jahre Des Deutsches Theater*. Munich: R. Piper & Co., 1930. Illustrated.
This title is included because of the 267 illustrations of the modern German theatre prior to 1933.

362. SAYLER, OLIVER M., editor: *Max Reinhardt And His Theatre*. Translations from the German by Mariele S. Gudernatsch and others. New York: Brentano's, 1924. Illustrated.

This concerns itself with Reinhardt's productions in Germany and in Austria and is essential to understanding the German theatre prior to 1933.

See also Nos. 230, 231, 261.

Theatre, Greek and Roman

363. BIEBER, MARGARETE: *The History of the Greek and Roman Theatre*. Princeton: Princeton University Press, 1939. Illustrated.

An excellent, well documented study of considerable value to the student.

364. FLICKINGER, ROY C.: *The Greek Theatre and Its Drama*. Chicago: Chicago University Press, 1926. Illustrated.

Flickinger is more general than Haigh and frequently disagrees with his conclusions, but with Bieber these three cover thoroughly the Greek theatre.

365. HAIGH, ARTHUR ELAM: *The Attic Theatre*. Third edition edited by A. W. Pickard-Cambridge. New York: Oxford University Press, 1907. Illustrated.

This goes into great detail concerning the construction and equipment of the Greek theatre together with descriptions of scenery, costume, acting and staging.

366. HAMILTON, EDITH: *The Greek Way*. New York: Norton, 1930.

This is particularly valuable because it places Greek drama and stage in its proper niche in its national life.

Theatre, Irish

367. BYRNE, DAWSON: *The Story Of Ireland's National Theatre*. The Abbey Theatre, Dublin. Dublin: The Talbot Press, 1929. Illustrated.

A history of the Abbey Theatre and its influence together with a list of representative little theatres in America which are said to have sprung from the Abbey.

368. FAY, W. G. and CATHERINE CARSWELL: *The Fays of the Abbey Theatre*. An Autobiographical Record. With a foreword by James Bridie. London: Rich & Cowan, 1935. Illustrated.

A personal study of the Abbey Theatre together with a list of first productions and casts, 1902-1907.

369. MALONE, ANDREW E.: *The Irish Drama, 1896-1928*. New York: Scribner, 1929.

This far from unprejudiced account of a great national drama is entirely comprehensive.

370. STOCKWELL, LA TOURETTE: *Dublin Theatres and Theatre Customs (1637-1820)*. Kingsport, Tennessee: Kingsport Press, 1938. Illustrated.

Both authoritative and readable, the notes and bibliography are particularly valuable.

Theatre, Italian

371. DUCHARTRE, PIERRE: *Italian Comedy*. Translated by Randolph T. Weaver New York: John Day, 1928.

An outstanding study of the *commedia dell' arte*.

372. KENNARD, JOSEPH SPENCER: *The Italian Theatre*. New York: Rudge, 1932 2 vols. Illustrated.

This is the only general history of the Italian theatre in English.

373. KENNARD, JOSEPH SPENCER: *Masks and Marionettes*. New York: Macmillan, 1935. Illustrated.

A useful account of the Italian stage.

374. LEA, K. M.: *Italian Popular Comedy*. A Study in the *Commedia Dell' Arte*, 1560-1620. 2 vols. Oxford: Clarendon Press, 1934. Illustrated.

A well authenticated history which points out the strong influence of the Italian on the English stage.

375. MacClintock, Lander: *The Contemporary Drama of Italy*. Boston: Little, Brown, 1920.
> A study of Italian drama which also considers the leading actors of the modern Italian stage.

376. Vittorini, Domenico: *The Drama of Luigi Pirandello*. With a foreword by Luigi Pirandello. Philadelphia: University of Pennsylvania Press, 1935.
> Included because Pirandello was the outstanding Italian innovator in modern drama.

See also Nos. 144, 148, 180, 230, 241, 312.

Theatre, Russian

377. Carter, Huntley: *The New Spirit in the Russian Theatre, 1917-1928*. London: Brentano, 1929. Illustrated.
> History of the Soviet Theatre.

378. Fülöp-Miller, René and Joseph Gregor: *The Russian Theatre*. Its Character and History, with Especial Reference to the Revolutionary Period. Translated by Paul England. Philadelphia: Lippincott, 1930. Illustrated.
> Excellent text and valuable illustrations.

379. Houghton, Norris: *Moscow Rehearsals*. An Account of Methods of Production in the Soviet Theatre. Introduction by Lee Simonson. New York: Harcourt, Brace, 1936. Illustrated.
> The outstanding one volume history of the Soviet stage; readable and provocative.

379A. Nemirovitch-Dantchenko, Vladimir: *My Life in the Russian Theatre*. Translated by John Cournos. Boston: Little, Brown, 1936.
> This contains valuable data on the Moscow Art Theatre and its Musical Studio.

380. Sayler, Oliver M.: *Inside The Moscow Art Theatre*. New York: Brentano, 1925. Illustrated.
> The history of the theatre which is most noted for its ensemble acting.

381. Sayler, Oliver M.: *The Russian Theatre*. New York: Brentano, 1922. Second edition. Illustrated.
> Together with histories of the Moscow Art, Maly and Kamerny Theatres are those of the Soviet playhouses.

382. Stanislavsky, Constantin: *My Life In Art*. Translated by J. J. Robbins. Boston: Little, Brown, 1924. Illustrated.
> A history of the Moscow Art Theatre, which also contains a list of the productions of the Alexeiev Circle, the Society of Art and Literature and the Moscow Art Theatre.

383. Wiener, Leo: *The Contemporary Drama Of Russia*. Boston: Little, Brown, 1924.
> An interesting study of Russian drama from Ostrovsky, through Chekhov, Gorki, Andreyev and Yevreinov.

See also Nos. 111, 227, 259, 261.

Theatre, Scandinavian

384. Koht, Halvdon: *The Life Of Ibsen*. New York: Norton, 1931. 2 vols.
> This is the most authoritative biography of Ibsen yet to be published and was written by a man who knew him.

385. McGill, V. J.: *August Strindberg, The Bedeviled Viking*. New York: Brentano, 1930.
> Included because the literature in English is so slight on Swedish drama, this is a standard text.

Theatre, Spanish

386. Fitzmaurice-Kelly, James: *A New History Of Spanish Literature*. New York: Oxford University Press, 1926.
> This contains a section on the drama and the bibliography is particularly useful.

387. RENNERT, HUGO ALBERT: *The Spanish Stage in the Time of Lope De Vega.*
New York: The Hispanic Society of America, 1909.
The most authentic history of this period; contains a list of Spanish actors
and actresses 1560-1680.

Theatre, Turkish

388. MARTINOVITCH, NICHOLAS W.: *The Turkish Theatre.* New York: Theatre
Arts, Inc., 1933. Illustrated.
This is a scholarly description together with translations of sections of Turk-
ish dramas.

Theatre History

389. BROWN, JOHN MASON: *The Modern Theatre in Revolt.* New York: Norton,
1929.
Short, readable, informative and provocative account of the theatrical revolutions of the last hundred years.

390. CARTER, HUNTLEY: *The New Spirit in Drama and Art.* New York: Mitchell
Kennerley. 1913. Illustrated.
One of the first books to chronicle the change in artistic standards which the
New Art brought about.

391. CARTER, HUNTLEY: *The New Spirit in the European Theatre, 1914-1924.*
A Comparative Study of the Changes Effected by the War and Revolu-
tion. London: Ernest Benn, 1925. Illustrated.
A well illustrated history of the theatre.

392. CHENEY, SHELDON: *The Theatre.* 3,000 Years of Drama, Acting and Stagecraft. New York: Longmans, Green, 1929. Illustrated.
An excellent and convenient one volume history of the theatre.

393. DUBECH, LUCIEN, J. DE MONTBRIAL and HELÈNE HORN-MONVAL: *Histoire
Générale illustrée.* Paris: Librairie de France, 1931-1934. Illustrated.
Included because it is the most authoritative general history of the theatre
and is profusely illustrated. Five volumes.

394. HUGHES, GLENN: *The Story of the Theatre.* A Short History of Theatrical
Art from Its Beginnings to the Present Day. New York: Samuel French,
1928. Illustrated.
A popular history for the student.

395. MACGOWAN, KENNETH: *The Theatre of Tomorrow.* New York: Boni and
Liveright, 1921.
This considers production methods in Europe and America together with mod-
ern theories of play construction.

396. MANTZIUS, CARL: *A History of Theatrical Art in Ancient and Modern Times.*
London: Duckworth, 1906-21. 6 vols. Illustrated.
This covers the prehistoric theatre and the early theatre in China, Japan and
India as well as the European theatre through the 19th century.

397. McKECHNIE, SAMUEL: *Popular Entertainment Through the Ages.* London:
Sampson Low, Marston & Co., Ltd., 1931. Illustrated.
The people's theatre including mimes, minstrels, fairs, *Punch and Judy,* pan-
tomimes, music halls, circus and cinema.

398. NICOLL, ALLARDYCE: *The Development of the Theatre.* A Study of Theatrical
Art from the Beginnings to the Present Day. London: Harrap, 1937.
Revised edition. Illustrated.
An outstanding one volume history of the theatre, profusely and well illus-
trated.

399. NICOLL, ALLARDYCE: *Masks, Mimes and Miracles.* New York: Harcourt,
Brace, 1931. Illustrated.
The non-literary theatre of Greece, Rome and Italy is clearly presented and
excellently illustrated; the mime, and the *commedia dell' arte* are fully described.

400. ROLLAND, ROMAIN: *The People's Theatre*. Translated by Barrett H. Clark. New York: Henry Holt, 1918.

   A brief history of the workers' theatre movement which is supplemented by the various works on the Russian stage.

401. SKINNER, R. DANA: *Our Changing Theatre*. New York: Dial Press, 1931. Illustrated.

   The American and European theatre of the Nineteen-twenties ably analysed by the former dramatic critic of *The Commonweal*.

402. *Spectacles à travers les ages, Les*. Prefaces by Denys Amiel and Henri Fescourt. Paris: Aux Editions du Cygne, 1931-32. 3 vols. Illustrated.

   This is an expert treatment of popular entertainment including theatre, circus, music hall, cafés-concerts, cabarets, music, dance and cinema.

403. STEVENS, THOMAS WOOD: *The Theatre from Athens to Broadway*. New York: Appleton, 1932. Illustrated.

   A general history of theatre from its beginnings, touching the most important phases including the Medieval, Elizabethan, Restoration, Molière and Garrick periods.

DETECTED CONTENTS